The Oxford Handbook of Group Counseling

OXFORD LIBRARY OF PSYCHOLOGY

OXFORD LIBRARY OF PSYCHOLOGY

Editor-in-Chief PETER E. NATHAN

The Oxford Handbook of Group Counseling

Edited by

Robert K. Conyne

OXFORD
UNIVERSITY PRESS

OXFORD
UNIVERSITY PRESS

Oxford University Press, Inc., publishes works that further Oxford University's
objective of excellence in research, scholarship, and education.

Oxford New York
Auckland   Cape Town   Dar es Salaam   Hong Kong   Karachi
Kuala Lumpur   Madrid   Melbourne   Mexico City   Nairobi
New Delhi   Shanghai   Taipei   Toronto

With offices in
Argentina   Austria   Brazil   Chile   Czech Republic   France   Greece
Guatemala   Hungary   Italy   Japan   Poland   Portugal   Singapore
South Korea   Switzerland   Thailand   Turkey   Ukraine   Vietnam

Copyright © 2010 by Oxford University Press, Inc.

Published by Oxford University Press, Inc.
198 Madison Avenue, New York, New York 10016
www.oup.com

Library of Congress Cataloging-in-Publication Data

The Oxford handbook of group counseling / edited by Robert K. Conyne.
p. cm. – (Oxford library of psychology)
Includes bibliographical references and index.
ISBN 978-0-19-539445-0 (hardcover) 1. Group counseling. 2. Group problem solving. I. Conyne,
Robert K. II. Title: Handbook of group counseling.
BF636.7.G76O94 2011
158'.35–dc22   2010044100

9 8 7 6 5 4 3 2 1

Printed in the United States of America on acid-free paper

CONTENTS

OXFORD LIBRARY OF PSYCHOLOGY

The *Oxford Library of Psychology*, a landmark series of handbooks, is published by Oxford University Press, one of the world's oldest and most highly respected publishers, with a tradition of publishing significant books in psychology. The ambitious goal of the *Oxford Library of Psychology* is nothing less than to span a vibrant, wide-ranging field and, in so doing, to fill a clear market need.

Encompassing a comprehensive set of handbooks, organized hierarchically, the *Library* incorporates volumes at different levels, each designed to meet a distinct need. At one level are a set of handbooks designed broadly to survey the major subfields of psychology; at another are numerous handbooks that cover important current focal research and scholarly areas of psychology in depth and detail. Planned as a reflection of the dynamism of psychology, the *Library* will grow and expand as psychology itself develops, thereby highlighting significant new research that will impact on the field. Adding to its accessibility and ease of use, the *Library* will be published in print and, later on, electronically.

The *Library* surveys psychology's principal subfields with a set of handbooks that capture the current status and future prospects of those major subdisciplines. This initial set includes handbooks of social and personality psychology, clinical psychology, counseling psychology, school psychology, educational psychology, industrial and organizational psychology, cognitive psychology, cognitive neuroscience, methods and measurements, history, neuropsychology, personality assessment, developmental psychology, and more. Each handbook undertakes to review one of psychology's major subdisciplines with breadth, comprehensiveness, and exemplary scholarship. In addition to these broadly conceived volumes, the *Library* includes a large number of handbooks designed to explore in depth more specialized areas of scholarship and research, such as stress, health and coping, anxiety and related disorders, cognitive development, and child and adolescent assessment. In contrast to the broad coverage of the subfield handbooks, each of these latter volumes focuses on an especially productive, more highly focused line of scholarship and research. Whether at the broadest or most specific level, however, all of the *Library* handbooks offer synthetic coverage that reviews and evaluates the relevant past and present research and anticipates research in the future. Each handbook in the *Library* includes introductory and concluding chapters written by its editor to provide a roadmap to the handbook's table of contents and to offer informed anticipations of significant future developments in that field.

An undertaking of this scope calls for handbook editors and chapter authors who are established scholars in the areas about which they write. Many of the nation's and world's most productive and respected psychologists have agreed to edit *Library* handbooks or write authoritative chapters in their areas of expertise.

For whom has the *Oxford Library of Psychology* been written? Because of its breadth, depth, and accessibility, the *Library* serves a diverse audience, including graduate students in psychology and their faculty mentors, scholars, researchers, and practitioners in psychology and related fields. They will find in the *Library* the information they seek on the subfield or focal area of psychology in which they work or are interested.

Befitting its commitment to accessibility, each handbook includes a comprehensive index, as well as extensive references to help guide research. And because the *Library* was designed from its inception as an online as well as a print resource, its structure and contents will be readily and rationally searchable online. Further, once the *Library* is released online, the handbooks will be regularly and thoroughly updated.

In summary, the *Oxford Library of Psychology* will grow organically to provide a thoroughly informed perspective on the field of psychology, one that reflects both psychology's dynamism and its increasing interdisciplinarity. Once published electronically, the *Library* is also destined to become a uniquely valuable interactive tool, with extended search and browsing capabilities. As you begin to consult this handbook, we sincerely hope you will share our enthusiasm for the more than 500-year tradition of Oxford University Press for excellence, innovation, and quality, as exemplified by the *Oxford Library of Psychology*.

Peter E. Nathan
Editor-in-Chief
Oxford Library of Psychology

ABOUT THE EDITOR

Robert K. Conyne

Robert K. Conyne, PhD, professor emeritus at the University of Cincinnati, is a licensed psychologist, clinical counselor, and fellow of the Association for Specialists in Group Work (ASGW) and the American Psychological Association. With over 200 scholarly publications and presentations, including 11 books in his areas of expertise (group work, prevention, and ecological counseling), along with broad international consultation in these areas, Dr. Conyne is recognized as an expert in working with people and systems.

DEDICATION

This volume is dedicated to all those leaders and followers over the decades who have envisioned and applied the ever-evolving theory, research, and practice of group counselling, resulting today in a vital and multifaceted method tailored to effectively advance the functioning of people and systems, with the promise of even more robust contributions in the future.

ACKNOWLEDGMENTS

Thanks first to the Oxford University Press book team who worked so effectively in producing this edition, beginning with then Senior Editor Lori Handelman, with the constant support and guidance of Senior Development Editor Chad Zimmerman, and to Karen Kwak, Smitha Raj, and the production staff. As an outgrowth of *The Oxford Handbook of Counseling Psychology*, I thank Betsy Altmaier and Jo-Ida Hansen for their outstanding editing work of that parent volume. And, of course, the present handbook would be impossible without the superb expert contributions of its authors.

CONTRIBUTORS

Sally H. Barlow
Department of Psychology
Brigham Young University
Provo, UT

Sheri Bauman
Department of Disability and
    Psychoeducational Studies
University of Arizona
Tucson, AZ

Virginia Brabender
Institute for Graduate Clinical Psychology
Widener University
Chester, PA

Nina W. Brown
Department of Counseling
Old Dominion University
Norfolk, VA

Gary M. Burlingame
Department of Psychology
Brigham Young University
Provo, UT

Laura M. Côté
Department of Counseling and
    Educational Psychology
New Mexico State University
Las Cruces, NM

Janice DeLucia-Waack
Department of Counseling, School,
    and Educational Psychology
University at Buffalo, SUNY
Buffalo, NY

Kent D. Drescher
National Center for PTSD:
    Dissemination & Training Division
Menlo Park, CA
The Pathway Home: California
Transition Center for Care of Combat
    Veterans
Yountville, CA

Donelson R. Forsyth
The Jepson School of Leadership
    Studies
University of Richmond
Richmond, VA

David W. Foy
Graduate School of Education &
    Psychology
Pepperdine University
Encino, CA

Samuel T. Gladding
Department of Counseling
Wake Forest University
Winston-Salem, NC

Sally M. Hage
Department of Psychology
University at Albany, SUNY
Albany, NY

Alexa E. Hanus
Department of Psychology
University at Albany, SUNY
Albany, NY

Arthur Horne
Department of Counseling and
    Human Development Services
University of Georgia
Athens, GA

Cynthia R. Kalodner
Department of Psychology
Towson University
Towson, MD

Jeanmarie Keim
Counselor Education Program
University of New Mexico
Albuquerque, NM

Jungeun Kim
Department of Psychology
University at Albany, SUNY
Albany, NY

Dennis M. Kivlighan, Jr.
Department of Counseling
University of Maryland
College Park, MD

George R. Leddick
Private Practice in Organizational
Development Consulting
Dallas, TX

Cheri L. Marmarosh
Professional Psychology
The George Washington University
Washington, DC

Mark Mason
Department of Psychology
University at Albany, SUNY
Albany, NY

Debra Theobald McClendon
Department of Psychology
Brigham Young University
Provo, UT

Benedict T. McWhirter
Department of Counseling
Psychology
University of Oregon
Eugene, OR

Ellen Halley McWhirter
Department of Counseling
Psychology
University of Oregon
Eugene, OR

J. Jeffries McWhirter
Department of Counseling
Arizona State University
Tempe, AZ

Paula T. McWhirter
Department of Educational Psychology
University of Oklahoma
Norman, OK

Joseph R. Miles
Department of Psychology
University of Tennessee
Knoxville, TN

Margaret Schwartz Moravec
Department of Educational Psychology
University of Houston
Houston, TX

D. Keith Morran
Department of Counseling and
Counseling Education
Indiana University-Purdue University
Indianapolis
Indianapolis, IN

Mark D. Newmeyer
Wellspring Counseling
Ashland Theological Seminary and
University
Columbus, OH

Jane E. Atieno Okech
Department of Leadership &
Developmental Sciences
University of Vermont, Burlington, VT

David L. Olguin
Counselor Education Program
University of New Mexico
Albuquerque, NM

Betsy J. Page
Counseling and Human
Development Services
Kent State University
Kent, OH

Jill D. Paquin
Department of Counseling
University of Maryland
College Park, MD

Lynn S. Rapin
Counseling Program
University of Cincinnati
Cincinnati, OH

Kathleen Y. Ritter
Department of Psychology
California State University,
Bakersfield
Bakersfield, CA

Maria T. Riva
Counseling Psychology Program
University of Denver
Denver, CO

Deborah J. Rubel
Department of Counseling
Oregon State University
Corvallis, OR

Jonathan P. Schwartz
Department of Counseling and
Educational Psychology
New Mexico State University
Las Cruces, NM

Jerrold Lee Shapiro
Department of Counseling Psychology
Santa Clara University
Santa Clara, CA

Phyllis R. Silverman
Resident Scholar
Brandeis University
Women Studies Research Center
Waltham, MA

Rex Stockton
Program in Counseling Psychology
Department of Counseling and
Educational Psychology
Indiana University
Bloomington, IN

James P. Trotzer
ETC Professional Services
Hampton, NH

Stacy M. Van Horn
Department of Educational
and Human Sciences
University of Central Florida
Orlando, FL

Michael Waldo
Department of Counseling
and Educational Psychology
New Mexico State University
Las Cruces, NM

Donald E. Ward
Department of Psychology
and Counseling
Pittsburgh State University
Pittsburgh, KS

Patricia Watson
National Center for PTSD
Dartmouth Medical School
Hanover, NH

CONTENTS

PART 1

Introduction

Introduction: Solidifying and Advancing Group Counseling

Robert K. Conyne

Abstract

This introductory chapter provides a general orientation to the handbook. After a description of how each chapter is formatted to promote consistency of approach, each of the ensuing 31 chapters is highlighted, arranged within the handbook's parts of Context, Key Change Processes, Research, Leadership, Applications, and Conclusion. The remainder of this introductory chapter presents a brief context for understanding group counseling, material that is excerpted from the editor's chapter in the forthcoming *Oxford Handbook of Counseling Psychology*, edited by Altmaier and Hansen.

Keywords: introduction, group counseling

General Orientation of the Handbook

This handbook is intended to assist in solidifying and advancing practice, training, and research in the broad intervention of group counseling. An outgrowth of the *Handbook of Counseling Psychology*, the current edited work falls under the board umbrella of the Library of Psychology of Oxford University Press, an ambitious and exciting project meant to capture the entire discipline of psychology.

In a sense, group counseling is like the "magical mystery tour" of the Beatles. After all the decades of wonderful music, group counseling—whose practice continually increases and expands—retains an elusiveness with regard to what makes it work (i.e., its "magic") and somewhat of a "mystery" in terms of what it is, what its effects are, and how it fits into the present and future kaleidoscope of helping methods. This edited volume explores and examines its journey, seeking to clarify where group counseling has been and is and where it is headed in relation to magic, mystery, and related issues.

Format for the Book Chapters

Edited works frequently have been criticized due to excessive variability across chapters. We have

intentionally sought to avoid this problem by asking authors to follow a generally consistent approach. Chapter contents have been structured to (1) reflect a thorough and comprehensive review of the broad and deep group counseling literature base, spanning disciplines (e.g., counseling psychology, counselor education, clinical psychology, social work), journals and other publications of professional associations (e.g., the American Psychological Association's Society of Group Psychology and Group Psychotherapy, the American Counseling Association's Association for Specialists in Group Work, and the American Group Psychotherapy Association), books from differing scholarly perspectives, etc. (i.e., not to be drawn primarily from one disciplinary source); (2) follow the chapter outline, format, and guidelines developed by Oxford University Press; (3) be based on a substantial literature review; and (4) be grounded in, but not limited to, the topics sampler that the editor has developed for each chapter.

This introductory chapter provides synopses of what is to come. Each of the next 30 chapters is briefly highlighted. In the final chapter I identify 50 basic premises of group counseling that are culled from the preceding chapters and conclude by suggesting that group counseling needs to be "mainstreamed" to a broader range of scholars and practitioners and to the public at large.

Contents Addressed across the Chapters

As the table of contents suggests, the contents of this edited work examine group counseling from multiple directions. Chapters are organized within parts titled

Introduction (this chapter)
Context
Key Change Processes
Research
Leadership
Applications
Conclusion

Chapters are written by an all-star compilation of group-counseling experts, who have organized their discussions using the most current information available. Chapter highlights follow.

Part Two: Context

CHAPTER 2. *THE NATURE AND SIGNIFICANCE OF GROUPS*
BY DONELSON R. FORSYTH

What are groups, and how does group counseling fit in? What are the dominant and significant features?

Forsyth's chapter frames group counseling within the broad panorama of "groups." He points out that to understand group counseling it is necessary to grasp what groups themselves are all about, what defines their basic nature and processes. He indicates that the essential elements of a group are found in the relationships connecting members, boundaries, interdependence, structure, cohesion, and entitativity. The contents of this chapter organize the general working context within which group counseling can be understood, practiced, and researched.

CHAPTER 3. *DEFINITION OF GROUP COUNSELING*
BY DONALD E. WARD

What is group counseling?

This chapter defines it, paying attention to, describing, and elaborating relevant perspectives drawn from the whole literature related to this topic. In doing so, Ward points out that because professional group work has such varied origins, agreement upon a single, concise definition of *group counseling* has been difficult to achieve. He provides an abbreviated review of the literature that focuses on the origins of modern group work. Systems defining and describing group work are presented,

emphasizing the Association for Specialists in Group Work's model of four types: work and task groups, psychoeducation groups, counseling groups, and psychotherapy groups (Association for Specialists in Group Work, 2000). A consensus definition is extracted from these sources, and future directions are identified.

CHAPTER 4. *THE HISTORY OF GROUP COUNSELING*
BY GEORGE R. LEDDICK

How has group counseling evolved historically? What are the chief markers and highlights over the decades? Who have been dominating contributors?

Leddick illustrates how the history of group counseling is rooted in antiquity, with modern practice evolving from the 1940s. The history weaves a tapestry of influences including social justice groups, community organizations, quality-management groups, and numerous therapeutic orientations. Pioneer group-counseling practitioners included Joseph Pratt, Jane Addams, and Jesse Davis, with substantial contributions provided by Moreno, Lewin, Rees, Deming, Alinsky, Rogers, Perls, Yalom, Gazda, and others. The roles of several professional organizations in the development of group counseling are addressed, especially attending to their professional journals, standards, and guidelines. Leddick concludes that group counseling has emerged from its infancy and continues to mature as a professional specialty. As a bonus, photos of several shapers of group counseling are included in this chapter.

CHAPTER 5. *ETHICS, BEST PRACTICES, AND LAW IN GROUP COUNSELING*
BY LYNN S. RAPIN

What ethical, legal, and best-practice guidelines are relevant for group counseling?

Practitioners may not be aware of significant similarities and differences among philosophical foundations, professional association documents, and legal terms that guide practice. Rapin identifies similarities and differences among them, highlights essential issues specific to group practice, and suggests future directions. She makes it clear that ethical practice in group therapy is not a linear process. Rather, she suggests, ethical conduct is a matrix relationship involving numerous variables. According to her, the following equation highlights the essential components: ethical behavior in group counseling = (moral and ethical development) + (professional ethics) + (core knowledge and skills) + (specialty/best-practice guidelines) + (legal parameters) x decision making model(s).

CHAPTER 6. *DIVERSITY IN GROUPS*

BY JANICE DELUCIA-WAACK

How does a full range of diversity and multiculturalism relate to group counseling?

Recognition and appreciation of diversity in groups are essential to helping group members understand themselves and work together. DeLucia-Waack gives particular attention in this chapter to the relationship between diversity in group counseling and group-counselor training and practice. Different types of multicultural group work are described, as are key concepts in multicultural counseling, cultural values, and assumptions inherent in group work, as well as the importance of training for group leaders.

CHAPTER 7. *A SOCIAL JUSTICE APPROACH TO GROUP COUNSELING*

BY SALLY M. HAGE, MARK MASON, AND JUNGEUN KIM

How does group counseling connect with a social justice perspective?

Hage, Mason, and Kim describe in this chapter how a social justice approach is emerging as a central aspect of the work of the mental health professional. In addition, they show how group work holds significant potential to further a social justice agenda. This chapter then provides an overview of a social justice approach to group counseling. The meaning of *social justice* is clarified, and the historical origins of a social justice approach to group work are presented. Existing theory and research related to group work and social justice are reviewed, and current trends in research with social justice groups are summarized. Finally, the authors discuss barriers to a social justice approach to group counseling and the implications of this approach, for counseling training, practice, and research.

Part Three: Key Change Processes

CHAPTER 8. *THERAPEUTIC FACTORS IN GROUP COUNSELING: ASKING NEW QUESTIONS*

BY DENNIS M. KIVLIGHAN, JR., JOSEPH R. MILES, AND JILL D. PAQUIN

What are therapeutic factors, and how do they influence group counseling?

Kivlighan, Miles, and Paquin review therapeutic factors, describe methods of assessment, document research findings related to therapeutic factors, and discuss future research needs. They explore why therapeutic factors are considered to be key change processes. They ask how counselors can apply the research in this area to their practice and emphatically suggest that research on therapeutic factors in groups will not advance until theorists and researchers begin to develop and test theories and models that have a *group* perspective.

CHAPTER 9. *COHESION IN COUNSELING AND PSYCHOTHERAPY GROUPS*

BY CHERI L. MARMAROSH AND STACY M. VAN HORN

What are the connections between group cohesiveness and group counseling?

Group cohesion is one of the most studied and theorized factors in group counseling. The relatively large amount of research that has been conducted on group cohesiveness is integrated in this chapter. Marmarosh and Van Horn review the history of group-therapy cohesion and the many challenges to both measuring and studying this frequently elusive group factor. The chapter concludes with recommendations for future research and the implications for clinicians who do group work.

CHAPTER 10. *GROUP CLIMATE: CONSTRUCT IN SEARCH OF CLARITY*

BY DEBRA THEOBALD MCCLENDON AND GARY M. BURLINGAME

How is group counseling dependent on group climate?

McClendon and Burlingame review the research related to group climate in group counseling and examine critical questions. Definitions and key measures associated with group climate are examined that underscore definitional confusion and overlap with other group-process constructs, such as cohesion. Research associated with the Group Climate Questionnaire is reviewed and summarized. Finally, findings from an international collaborative research project conducted over the past decade are summarized to provide an alternative definition of *group climate* that encompasses the relationship variables of cohesion, therapeutic alliance, and empathy. A set of questions that this model directly addresses, as well as questions to be addressed by future research, concludes the chapter.

CHAPTER 11. *GROUP DEVELOPMENT*

BY VIRGINIA BRABENDER

What is group development? Why is attending to it by group counselors a key change process?

Brabender provides a historical description of the major models that show how counseling groups change over time. Particular attention is given to the predominant framework, the progressive stage model. In addition, other models reviewed are the life-cycle model, cyclic model, punctuated equilibrium model, and approaches derived from chaos/complexity theory. This chapter considers the question of whether a group's development affects members' abilities to accomplish their goals. Finally, the chapter addresses the application of developmental thinking in unstructured and structured groups and develops the implications of group developmental theory for leadership activities.

Part Four: Research

CHAPTER 12. *EVIDENCE BASES FOR GROUP PRACTICE*
BY SALLY H. BARLOW

What are process and outcome in group counseling? How do they interrelate?

In this chapter Barlow documents how group treatments represent an efficacious and efficient mental health intervention that rival and at times exceed individual therapy outcomes. It reveals how group psychotherapy capitalizes upon group processes that replicate at the micro level the macro struggle for equal access to life-affirming mental health and how change processes occur as skilled group therapists invoke therapeutic factors within the group climate to promote client change. This chapter demonstrates the importance of mental health professionals keeping current with research process and outcome evidence. Barlow suggests how researchers, practicing clinicians, and future clinicians can benefit from exchanges with each other as evidence bases inform expert intervention for participating group members who seek positive change.

CHAPTER 13. *GENERAL RESEARCH MODELS*
BY REX STOCKTON AND D. KEITH MORRAN

What models exist for group research, and how can they be employed?

The authors focus on how general research models promote academic and practitioner collaboration in group-counseling research, how student/trainee research skills can be developed through well-functioning collaborative research teams, how outcomes add to the storehouse of group knowledge and contribute to real-world application, and how to cross disciplinary lines. Stockton and Morran highlight specific issues related to group-counseling research, including research skills training for graduate students, practical skill-application experiences, use of a research team approach to inquiry, practitioner–researcher collaboration, interdisciplinary research, and programmatic research. Major quantitative and qualitative designs for group research are reviewed.

Suggestions and recommendations for future research in the group field are offered.

CHAPTER 14. *ASSESSING GROUPS*
BY JONATHAN P. SCHWARTZ, MICHAEL WALDO,
AND MARGARET SCHWARTZ MORAVEC

How is group counseling assessed? Assessment is critical to understanding the outcomes and processes inherent in group counseling. However, assessment in groups is often ignored or attempted utilizing measures with poor psychometrics.

In this chapter, Schwartz, Waldo, and Schwartz Moravec explore the various purposes of assessment in group counseling, followed by a summary of different types of assessment that may be used. Strengths and weaknesses of various assessments and research designs also are discussed, along with implications for best practice.

CHAPTER 15. *QUALITATIVE RESEARCH APPROACHES AND GROUP COUNSELING*
BY DEBORAH J. RUBEL AND JANE E. ATIENO OKECH

What is qualitative research? How does it apply to group counseling? Why does qualitative research struggle for acceptance and credibility in counseling and related fields? What are its advantages and disadvantages?

Rubel and Okech describe several qualitative research studies in group counseling, probe how a qualitative approach can be activated by group-counseling researchers, and identify how group-counselor practice can benefit from qualitative research applications. The authors explore the fundamental characteristics of qualitative approaches, their strengths and limitations, and various types of qualitative research. They discuss the challenges and needs of group-counseling research and how qualitative approaches may address these needs. An atheoretical research design process aimed at promoting congruent, effective qualitative designs is presented. Finally, Rubel and Okech provide summaries and evaluations of several qualitative group-counseling studies, present key themes from the chapter discussions, and propose future directions for qualitative research applied to group counseling.

Part Five: Leadership

CHAPTER 16. *PERSONHOOD OF THE LEADER*
BY JAMES P. TROTZER

What is meant by the term *personhood*? Why is the personhood of the group counselor important?

The author summarizes research in this area. Questions include, How can a leader's personhood be enhanced, and why is personhood alone not enough for effective group counseling? Trotzer distinguishes between the group leader (who the leader is) and leadership (what the leader does). He explores the role of personhood in relation to a group-work paradigm including the three elements of person, process, and product. Theory and research are examined using a "prism of personhood" developed by the author to identify and validate the central nature and role of personhood in the practice of group counseling.

CHAPTER 17. *GROUP TECHNIQUES*
BY MARK D. NEWMEYER

What are group techniques, and how might they best be used?

The term *group technique* is not well defined. A variety of other terms (e.g., *structured experiences, exercises*) are often used interchangeably. Given this current state, Newmeyer suggests it is of little surprise that few conceptual models have developed to assist group leaders in properly considering and selecting group techniques. One model attempting to fill this gap, the purposeful group techniques model, is described. The model consolidates various established elements of how groups work and function, with six core ecological concepts (i.e., context, interconnection, collaboration, social system maintenance, meaning making, and sustainability). Research to examine the model, as well as developing other such models, is needed.

CHAPTER 18. *GROUP LEADER STYLE AND FUNCTIONS*
BY SHERI BAUMAN

What group-leader styles and functions have been identified, and how do they work?

Bauman defines both leader style and function in group counseling and discusses and summarizes the research on leader style and function. She explores what research is needed to advance understanding and test hypotheses and indicates how knowledge of leader style and function connects with group-counseling practice and training.

CHAPTER 19. *GROUP-LEADERSHIP TEACHING AND TRAINING: METHODS AND ISSUES*
BY NINA W. BROWN

What group-counseling teaching and training methods exist? What is the status of teaching group counseling across disciplines?

In her review of the literature, Brown discovered that few evidence-based studies have been reported on group-leadership teaching methods. The consensus from professional experts is that group-leadership training encompasses three dimensions: knowledge, leader personal development, and techniques and skills. She observes that much of the attention is given to the use of experiential groups as a teaching/learning strategy and the procedural and ethical concerns that surround its use. Brown presents in this chapter historical and current research on teaching models, methods, and issues and concludes with a set of recommendations.

CHAPTER 20. *SUPERVISION OF GROUP COUNSELING*
BY MARIA T. RIVA

Why is supervision of group counseling necessary and desirable? What is meant by *supervision*? What models exist to perform it? How are they executed? What works?

Riva points out that supervision of group counseling is a topic that has received little attention, yet it is crucial to the professional development of group counselors and overseeing group clients' care. In this chapter she highlights the role of supervision in group counseling, the responsibilities of the supervisor, and the tasks involved in the supervisory relationship. A section also addresses research that has been conducted and the need for and directions of future research.

CHAPTER 21. *CREATIVITY AND SPONTANEITY IN GROUPS*
BY SAMUEL T. GLADDING

What is meant by creativity and spontaneity in group counseling? What is the research about these factors? What is the value of these two factors in group counseling? How can these qualities be developed in group counselors? How can group counselors use creativity and spontaneity?

Gladding considers these questions in this chapter, examining creativity and spontaneity and how they can be used in groups of all types including group counseling. These concepts are first defined, and steps in the creative process are discussed. Then, the importance and benefits of creativity and spontaneity in groups are examined. Research related to their use and value in group settings is explored. Ways of promoting creativity and spontaneity in groups are discussed next, along with barriers to being creative in a group. Finally, questions regarding the future of using creativity and spontaneity in groups are raised, and Web sites related to creativity and spontaneity in groups follow the conclusion.

Part Six: Applications

CHAPTER 22. *GROUPS ACROSS SETTINGS*

BY CYNTHIA R. KALODNER AND ALEXA E. HANUS

What settings are especially suited for group counseling?

Kalodner and Hanus observe in this chapter that group interventions exist in a large diversity of settings. Their goal is to provide readers with a sense of the ubiquitous nature of groups. The variety of settings includes a focus on different kinds of groups for clients of different ages with a diversity of clinical issues. Each section provides examples of groups and research to support these groups in particular settings. Selected for depth of coverage in this chapter are Veterans Administration programs, behavioral health and medical settings, college/university counseling centers, and schools. The chapter concludes with suggestions for the future of groups in these settings and an extensive reference list.

CHAPTER 23. *GROUP COUNSELING ACROSS THE LIFE SPAN: A PSYCHOLOGICAL PERSPECTIVE*

BY JEANMARIE KEIM AND DAVID L. OLGUIN

Can group counseling be applied throughout the life span?

Keim and Olguin discuss group work for individuals across the life span, examining it through a psychosocial development lens. They posit that Erikson's contribution of psychosocial stages to the helping professions remains a valuable tool in conceptualizing development, prevention, and treatment and that group work is an appropriate and effective method to promote positive psychosocial growth and assist members to overcome cognitive, behavioral, and emotional difficulties. The authors suggest that due to the broad range of groups that exists it is important for group counselors to conceptualize prospective members within a developmental context, including which psychosocial tasks each person is facing. This chapter opens with a brief overview of Erikson's psychosocial stages, followed by overviews of group literature for 10 specific age groups, related group leader considerations, and future directions.

CHAPTER 24. *GROUP COUNSELING WITH SEXUAL MINORITIES*

BY KATHLEEN RITTER

What is known about how best to work with sexual minority group members? What do group leaders need to appreciate, know, and be able to do?

Ritter demonstrates that when counselors can appreciate the unique life circumstances that lesbian, gay, bisexual, and transgender clients bring to the group experience and possess the skills to lead the group through its many transitions, it becomes possible for growth to occur for every individual involved. She suggests that understanding the concepts of oppression, minority stress, and cohort and developmental differences provides a context for effective and ethical group facilitation. Ritter briefly reviews the existing literature related to sexual minority group members and examines the relevant guidelines, principles, competencies, and ethical codes of several professional associations. Other concepts discussed include group composition, leader sexual orientation, group management, and sexual minority members and group dynamics.

CHAPTER 25. *PREVENTION GROUPS*

BY MICHAEL WALDO, JONATHAN P. SCHWARTZ, ARTHUR HORNE, AND LAURA CÔTÉ

How can group counseling be used preventively?

The authors focus on the connections between "prevention" and "group." Different perspectives on prevention are described, including methods of classifying preventive interventions, followed by a description of current classifications of prevention group work. Next, the advantages of using group counseling for prevention are outlined. Theory and research explaining how prevention group counseling works are reviewed. Therapeutic factors that frequently occur in group counseling are described, with a focus on how these therapeutic factors can contribute to different forms of prevention. Dynamics that develop in groups are then detailed, including how group leaders may employ group dynamics to foster therapeutic factors. Current examples of primary, secondary, and tertiary prevention groups are provided, including evaluative research on their effectiveness. Waldo, Schwartz, Horne, and Côté conclude the chapter with a summary and examination of future directions for prevention group counseling.

CHAPTER 26. *INTERNATIONAL GROUP COUNSELING*

BY J. JEFFRIES MCWHIRTER, PAULA T. MCWHIRTER, BENEDICT T. MCWHIRTER, AND ELLEN HAWLEY MCWHIRTER

What is the status of group counseling globally?

In this chapter J. Jeffries McWhirter and his colleagues consider the field of group counseling from an international perspective. They suggest that the inclusive definition of group counseling provided by Conyne (in this chapter) is compatible with the broad range of interventions being developed and facilitated internationally. Following a summary of facilitation and training issues, they provide an extensive review of research from a global perspective on a continent-by-continent basis. Next, they describe five group-counseling applications, focusing on international indigenous groups based in diverse regions internationally. Finally, the authors address questions and highlight suggestions for further exploration and consider the growth and impact potentials for group work that cross national and cultural perspectives.

CHAPTER 27. *BRIEF GROUP TREATMENT*
BY JERROLD LEE SHAPIRO
What are brief groups, and how do they work?

In this chapter, Shapiro describes brief groups as being time-limited with a preset termination and a process orientation and being led by a professional. Membership is closed, and members are screened for fit, consistent goals and similar ego strength. A short history of the precursors of brief group treatments is presented. The process stages, or group trajectory, are described and related to the nature and timing of interventions. Extant studies in the area of brief group process and outcome research are explored and recommendations made for more carefully designed studies. Finally, Shapiro offers a combination of prediction and wish list for future research, practice, and training in brief group approaches.

CHAPTER 28. *MUTUAL HELP GROUPS: WHAT ARE THEY AND WHAT MAKES THEM WORK?*
BY PHYLLIS R. SILVERMAN
Why do people find it so helpful to meet others who have similar problems or life-changing experiences? Why does finding others like ourselves give us a sense of hope or of being understood and often a direction to a solution to our problem? Are there other aspects of the experience and the setting in which this kind of encounter takes place that matter?

In this chapter Silverman offers some understanding of how mutual help groups emerge, what they do for those who participate, and the kind of settings in which they occur. Silverman concludes that what seems to matter a good deal in mutual help groups is who controls the program and its resources.

CHAPTER 29. *ONLINE GROUPS*
BY BETSY J. PAGE
What are online groups, and how can counselors and other mental health workers use them appropriately?

Page indicates that online support groups encourage and offer acceptance, support, and virtual companionship to participants. In a sense, she says, they can serve to offset social isolation. Page addresses the full-range of online groups including social networking, describing how they work and giving some key examples. Research is summarized and benefits and deficits of online approaches are highlighted. How group counselors can become involved appropriately is outlined, and future projections are offered.

CHAPTER 30. *GROUPS FOR TRAUMA/DISASTER*
BY DAVID W. FOY, KENT D. DRESCHER, AND PATRICIA J. WATSON
How is group counseling being used in trauma and disaster situations?

Foy, Drescher, and Watson describe in this chapter the evolution of trauma and disaster groups. They discuss how group interventions for survivors of trauma were first used following World War II with combat veterans who were struggling with the psychological consequences of their war experiences. Early groups were conducted months or years after combat, while the ensuing evolution of groups for trauma has diversified so that single-session groups are now often used to provide support for disaster survivors within the first few days or weeks after the event. The authors highlight two emerging forms of trauma and disaster groups, psychological first-aid groups and spiritual and trauma groups, and they provide recommendations for group leaders.

Part Seven: Conclusion
CHAPTER 31: *GROUP COUNSELING: 50 BASIC PREMISES AND THE NEED FOR MAINSTREAMING*
BY ROBERT K. CONYNE
This summative chapter includes two parts. The first results from identifying and briefly describing "basic premises" about group counseling that emerged from a review of the preceding handbook chapters. The second part contains an argument for more assertively ushering group counseling and all its benefits into the "mainstream" of professional and public awareness.

A Brief Context for Understanding Group Counseling
The remainder of this introductory chapter consists of adapted excerpts drawn from my overview chapter on group counseling to be found in the forthcoming *Handbook of Counseling Psychology*

(Altmaier & Hansen, in press). Refer to that chapter for expanded coverage and to the following chapters in this volume, all of which are aimed at solidifying and advancing group counseling. The material below is intended to summarize major components of group counseling and to introduce the informative discussion to come contained in the next chapters.

A Definition of Group Counseling

Group counseling is an important therapeutic and educational method that psychologists, counselors, and other helpers can use to facilitate interpersonal problem-solving processes among members as they learn how to resolve difficult but manageable problems of living and how to apply gains in the future. While being a unique service-delivery method, group counseling also shares much in common with related group-work approaches, including psychoeducation groups and psychotherapy groups. In general, group counseling occupies a broad middle section of the helping goals continuum where prevention, development, and remediation all play important roles, depending on member needs and situational supports and constraints (Conyne, in press).

History

Group counseling has emerged over more than 100 years. This protracted period of time can be arranged into four time periods, as follows:

1. Period 1, the "years of development," 1900–1939: marked by early forays into working with people collectively, group work aimed at changing social conditions and laying a foundation for the progress to come
2. Period 2, the "years of early explosion," 1940–1969: a remarkable two decades beginning with accelerating the spread of group approaches following World War II and noted for innovation and experimentation; for production and organization of theory, techniques, and research; for the formation of group organizations; and for the spread of groups throughout society occurring during the "human potential movement" of the 1960s
3. Period 3, the "years of settling in," 1970–1989: two decades noted for sifting through earlier advancements and documenting what worked through substantial and influential publications, the emergence of group training in universities and elsewhere, and the formation of key group-work organizations

4. Period 4, the "years of standardization and further expansion to the age of ubiquity," 1990–present: a time noted for efforts to define group work and the place of group counseling in relation to it, for products intended to clarify guidelines and standards for group training and practice, for the publication of more sophisticated research into process and outcomes, for the emergence of group handbooks, for the wide expansion of group work to fit differing populations and settings, and for experimentation of group methods using online and other electronic vehicles.

Key Change Processes of Group Counseling
Therapeutic Factors, Group Climate, and Group Development

THERAPEUTIC FACTORS

After considering the large body of literature addressing the importance of therapeutic factors, Kivlighan and Holmes (2004) were led to conclude that little progress has been made in answering an initial basic question raised by Yalom: "How does group therapy help patients?" Complexities of client, therapist, and group variables—and their interaction—continue to vex efforts. Future research into these and other areas raised in this section will help to further clarify how therapeutic factors operate and how group leaders can harness their power. Developing answers to these questions is important to group counseling.

GROUP CLIMATE

Kivlighan and Tarrant (2001) suggest the following:

> Group members will increase their active involvement with the group when group leaders refrain from doing individual therapy in the group and actively set goals and norms while maintaining a warm and supportive environment . . . the group leader's major task is to create a therapeutic group climate . . . unlike individual treatment, where the relationship between the client and therapist is tantamount, in group treatment leaders should probably de-emphasize their relationships with individual group members and focus on creating a therapeutic group climate. (p. 231)

GROUP DEVELOPMENT

Patterns are observable when examining many groups from a distance, although chance and serendipity associated with the unique composition of a group and the often unpredictable interactions occurring among members contribute strongly to any one group's development. Still, group developmental models can be used by group leaders to assist in managing events under way in a group, to help in predicting general future events, and to guide creation of a plan for a new group (Conyne, 1997; Conyne, Crowell, & Newmeyer, 2008; MacKenzie, 1997; Wheelan, 1997, 2005). A number of studies (e.g., Kivlighan, McGovern, & Corazzini, 1984) have shown that a successful group outcome is strongly dependent on the group being able to move positively through developmental levels (Donigian & Malnati, 1997).

Leadership

Group leadership is the ability to draw from best practices and good professional judgment to

> Create a group and, in collaboration with members, build and maintain a positive group climate that serves to nurture here-and-now interaction and its processing by leader and members, aimed at producing lasting growth and change (Conyne, in press).

FUNCTIONS, TASKS, AND ROLES
OF GROUP LEADERS

Yalom (1995) maintains that the group leader's initial goals are to create a therapeutic culture drawing largely from task-oriented behaviors; this is known as the "technical expert role." As the group proceeds, the leader may shift to providing increased relationship behaviors and modeling of positive attitudes and behaviors, consistent with a model-setting participant role as the group evolves. Both of these roles are important in shaping the group climate and its norms.

PREGROUP PREPARATION AND PLANNING
IN CREATING THE GROUP

Pregroup preparation has been shown to be essential to promoting group cohesion, member satisfaction, and comfort with the group (e.g., Bednar & Kaul, 1994; Bowman & DeLucia, 1993; Burlingame, Fuhriman, & Johnson, 2001, 2004; Conyne, Wilson, & Ward, 1997; Riva, Wachtel, & Lasky, 2004). Pregroup preparation enjoys the strongest empirical support of all structuring approaches.

POSITIVE VALENCE OF THE GROUP LEADER

As stated by Yalom, "The basic posture of the [group] therapist to a client must be one of concern, acceptance, genuineness, empathy. *Nothing, no technical consideration, takes precedence over this attitude*" (italics retained; Yalom, 2005, p. 117).

STIMULATING AND FOCUSING
HERE-AND-NOW INTERACTION

As Yalom (2005) stressed, "[this is] perhaps the single most important point I make in this entire book: *the here-and-now focus, to be effective, consists of two symbiotic tiers, neither of which has therapeutic power without the other*" (p. 141, italics retained). These tiers are (1) stimulating here-and-now interaction and (2) illuminating and focusing process.

USING MEANING ATTRIBUTION

The experience of group counseling can be bewildering due to its ongoing dynamic activity. It also can be emotionally overpowering at times, or conversely, it can sap the patience of everyone involved. In any and all cases, the experience of group participation can become more understandable and meaningful, as was mentioned earlier, when group leaders assist members in converting experience to cognition (Conyne, 1999; Lieberman, Yalom, & Miles, 1973).

LEADER CHOICE OF INTERVENTIONS

Interventions need to be chosen with intentionality to more purposefully stimulate here-and-now experience and its evolving meaning (e.g., Cohen & Smith, 1976; Corey & Corey, 2006; Ivey, Pedersen, & Ivey, 2001, 2008; Jacobs, Masson, & Harvill, 2006; Stockton, Morran, & Clark, 2004; Trotzer, 2004). Building on Cohen and Smith's classic critical incident model (1976), Conyne et al. (2008) integrate several additional elements thought to be important in group leadership to create the purposeful group technique model. This five-step model is used intentionally to guide the consideration and selection of group techniques. It is based on viewing a group as an ecological system.

DRAWING FROM STANDARDS, GUIDELINES,
AND PRINCIPLES TO GUIDE GROUP LEADERSHIP

The increased intentionality in group leadership has been marked by the creation and adoption of various standards, guidelines, principles, and codes that are particular to group work. It is important for group leaders to be aware of and guided by existing ethics, best-practice guidelines, legal statutes, and other professional codes that are relevant to their practice (Wilson, Rapin, & Haley-Banez, 2004).

ETHICAL PRACTICE

Sound ethical practice is accomplished through giving appropriate attention to planning, performing, and processing groups (Rapin, 2004). Thorough planning, for example, can help control for committing errors in confidentiality, informed consent, and recruitment and selection of members as well as help to design a group that more closely reflects the needs and culture of the participants. Careful attention to performing, that is, attending to what leaders do within sessions, can enhance the effectiveness and appropriateness of leader interventions. Thoughtful processing can protect against ignoring how ethical and legal principles apply to situations being confronted and can promote regular scrutiny and evaluation of the group being led.

DIVERSITY AND MULTICULTURAL PRACTICE

Group leaders need to become comfortable and competent in providing multicultural group counseling. Specific recommendations have been provided to assist in meeting this charge (DeLucia-Waack & Donigian, 2003): (1) develop awareness of the worldviews of different cultures and how these might impact group-work interventions, (2) develop self-awareness of racial identity and one's own cultural and personal worldviews, and (3) develop a repertoire of group-leader interventions that are culturally appropriate. The Association for Specialists in Group Work (ASGW, 1998) principles for diversity-competent group workers offer specific guidance; three areas of multicultural competence for group leaders and group members alike are emphasized in the principles: group leader attitudes and beliefs, knowledge, and skills.

IMPROVISATION

Nearly always there are apparent discordances and conflicting melodies running through group interaction. At times group interaction may "sound" cacophonous. Different members "play" idiosyncratic tunes on their own separate instruments, just as in a jazz ensemble, seemingly at times at odds with each other. Yet, underneath there often is a "matter of consistency" (Kaul, 1990)—a unison refrain, a groove, if you will— and it is the group leader's role to find it, if no one else can, to bring it home to every member's awareness. And then leaders need to show members how their interactive participation can become harmonious even as they continue to express their individuality. Theory, research, and supervised practice contribute substantively to inform and guide group leadership, indeed; but personal factors, along with spontaneity and intuition, may be just as important.

Expansion of Groups in Contemporary Society: The "Age of Ubiquity"?

There are, of course, professionally led groups, commonly referred to as "counseling and therapy groups." These have garnered the attention of this review chapter. As well, many specifications and adaptations exist of ASGW's four types of groups (task, psychoeducational, counseling, and psychotherapy), including a myriad of support groups and self-help/mutual help groups. Groups are multisplendored, therefore. They are tailored to a wide range of specific populations, addressing a myriad of health and mental health–care issues. Groups are offered across the life span and provided in brief therapy formats supported by managed care (but, alas, much more needs to be done in this arena). There are quality circle groups, community action groups, prevention groups, social justice groups, trauma groups, and the list goes on . . . and on.

Brief Group Therapy

Brief group therapy (BGT) is of considerable interest for a variety of reasons. Research attests to its efficacy and wide applicability (e.g., Spitz, 1996). In addition, BGT may be a treatment of choice for specific client problems, such as complicated grief, adjustment problems, trauma reactions, existential concerns, and more recently medically ill patients and in combinations for those with personality disorders (Piper & Ogrodniczuk, 2004).

Mutual Help Groups

Drawing from a national survey, Kessler, Michelson, and Zhao (1997) reported that approximately 7% (about 11 million) of adults in the United States participated in a mutual (self) help group in the year studied and that 18% of Americans had done so at some time during their lives. Klaw and Humphreys (2004) point out that these kinds of groups are low-cost, participation in them can produce positive health outcomes while often lowering health-care expenditures, and professionally led groups can be improved by integrating with self-help approaches.

Social Justice Groups

After decades where group work targeted person-change areas while minimizing attention to social change, the end of the last century was marked by renewed vigor in addressing change approaches aimed at social justice and community development (e.g., Lee, 2007; Toporek, Gerstein, Fouad,

Roysircar-Sodowsky, & Israel, 2005), including attention to using groups for these purposes. Examples of groups being used for social justice and system change can be found in the area of community-based participatory research and action (Finn & Jacobson, 2003; Jacobson & Rugeley, 2007), expanding learning from the group social microcosm to external system application (Orr et al., 2008), and using empowerment groups in schools (Bemak, 2005). Using groups and group processes for social justice is emerging as an important approach.

Online Groups

Groups always have been conducted face-to-face, and nearly all of the existing research and practice knowledge is premised on that direct format. With the explosion in the creation and availability of computers and online technologies, however, a whole new arena has been opened. Although there remains concern about losing the value of personal, face-to-face groups online formats have flourished in what was termed an "electronic frontier" (Bowman & Bowman, 1998)—an eon ago when counting in technological years.

An increasing range of possibilities exist for online group application. These include, but are not limited to, interactive E-journaling (Haberstroh, Parr, Gee, & Trepal, 2006), Internet support groups (Lieberman, Wizlenberg, Golant, & Minno, 2005), online discussions that are synchronous and asynchronous (Romano & Cikanek, 2003), and videos and computer simulations for training (Smokowski, 2003).

Conclusion

Face-to-face group counseling is effective and efficient at promoting change and growth in members. Its more than 100-year history is marked by expansion, solidification, and continued innovation. Standards, principles, and guidelines have emerged as reference points.

Group counseling and other group forms are conducted across the spectrum of remediation, development, and prevention to address a range of target populations. Groups are located in an array of settings, from private practice to schools, communities, and organizations. They are professionally led, self-help, offered face-to-face and online, and brief or longer-term; and they address trauma and wellness. Mechanisms for positive change have been identified generally, with further refinements

emerging in robust research programs being disseminated through respected scholarly vehicles. We have entered an "age of ubiquity," with a future full of opportunities and challenges.

Future Directions

The future of group counseling is bright. To intensify and expand its glow, the following 10 points are offered, which evolve from the preceding narrative. They are arranged generally into research and practice categories.

Research

1. The group-research agenda needs to deepen, widen, and integrate. The promising lines of research focused on the process engines that drive groups, including cohesion, culture, and therapeutic factors, are revealing important practice applications that invite deepening (e.g., Kivlighan et al., 2000; Riva et al., 2004). A widening of group research will explore multicultural, online, prevention, trauma, and other expansions of group application (Chen, Kakkad, & Balzano, 2008; DeLucia-Waack, Gerrity, Kalodner, & Riva, 2004; Gazda, Ginter, & Horn, 2001).

2. Continued investigation of the evidence basis for group counseling needs to continue and be extended (Burlingame & Beecher, 2008). This focal area is beginning to coalesce around the designation of research-supported group treatment (RSGT) (Johnson, 2008). As well, RSGT efforts need to include cultural and setting differences (Chen et al., 2008) and the whole span of group dynamics (Kivlighan, 2008).

3. Adopting common conceptions of group counseling and other group formats (e.g., the ASGW delineation of group-work types [task, psychoeducation, counseling, and psychotherapy], the multifaceted model of group psychotherapy described by Burlingame, Kapetanovic, & Ross [2005], the group work grid of Conyne [1985]) would assist group research, for example, of therapeutic factors across different types of groups and settings (Kivlighan, 2008; Kivlighan & Holmes, 2004). Such definitions could emerge through coordinated attention by major professional associations in the area of groups, such as the Group Practice and Research Network, which presently includes the American Group Psychotherapy Association, the ASGW, the

Division of Group Psychology and Group Psychotherapy of the American Psychological Association (APA), the Division of Addictions of the APA, and the Group Section of the Division of Psychoanalysis of the APA.

4. The connection among group research, group training, and group practice needs to be bridged more fully (Anderson & Wheelan, 2005). This is a continuing challenge in virtually all areas of counseling psychology, and it certainly exists in the domain of groups. For instance, relevant research findings in social psychology need to find their way more quickly and strategically into group practice.

5. Group research, practice, and training knowledge that is reported through the organs of different professional associations, and sometimes in different disciplines, needs to be interconnected by scholars, with emerging best practices made available to trainers and practitioners (Berdahl & Henry, 2005).

6. Group researchers need to study the various forms of online group systems (Williams, 2002) for efficacy and to determine what modes work best for what situations and which people. As well, tending toward practice, more group counselors need to explore the appropriate use of electronic and online vehicles in their work (McGlothlin, 2003). Ethical guidelines that are specific to these online group systems also await development (Page, 2004). Online offerings would match the daily life practice of millions of teens and adults in contemporary society.

Practice

7. The "age of ubiquity" in group counseling means, in part, that training in counseling psychology must rearrange itself to make obvious room for group work in the curriculum (Conyne et al., 1997; Conyne & Bemak, 2004). Group counseling should not be a postdoctoral specialty only. In addition, it should permeate and support other counseling and psychological interventions and stand on its own as an important method, capable of delivery by a wide range of trained practitioners.

8. Groups are effective (e.g., Payne & Marcus, 2008) and, of course, efficient. Group-counseling advocates must build on these realities to develop concerted strategies to influence the future of health care, particularly managed care, to fully incorporate group-delivery formats as reimbursable

services (Spitz, 1996). Group services must become an integral part of any future renovation of the nation's health-care system.

9. Professionally led group methods—developed largely from group psychotherapy research with a majority of adults in closed groups—need to be intentionally adapted, where needed, to support work with open groups and with groups for children, minorities, and the aged for prevention and social justice (Conyne, 2004).

10. Barriers against group counseling (e.g., ineffective referral processes, cumbersome processes for organizing groups within agencies, or inaccurate myths about group counseling) need to be reduced to allow groups to become more attractive and available to more people (Trotzer, 2006).

References

Altmaier, E. M., & Hansen, J. C. (Eds.) (in press). *The Oxford handbook of counseling psychology*. New York: Oxford University Press.

Anderson, G., & Wheelan, S. (2005). Integrating group research and practice. In S. Wheelan (Ed.), *The handbook of group research and practice* (pp. 545–552). Thousand Oaks, CA: Sage.

Association for Specialists in Group Work (1998). *Principles for diversity-competent group workers.* Retrieved October 30, 2007 from http://www.asgw.org/PDF/Principles_for_Diversity.pdf

Association for Specialists in Group Work (2000). *Professional standards for the training of group workers. Retrieved from http://www.asgw.org*

Bednar, R., & Kaul, T. (1994). Experiential group research: Can the cannon fire? In A. Bergin & S. Garfield (Eds.), *Handbook of psychotherapy and behavior change* (4th ed., pp. 631–663). New York: Wiley.

Bemak, F. (2005). Reflections on multiculturalism, social justice, and empowerment groups for academic success: A critical discourse for contemporary schools. *Professional School Counseling, 8,* 401–406.

Berdahl, J., & Henry, K. B. (2005). Contemporary issues in group research. In S. Wheelan (Ed.), *The handbook of group research and practice* (pp. 19–37). Thousand Oaks, CA: Sage.

Bowman, R., & Bowman, V. (1998). Life on the electronic frontier: The application of technology to group work. *Journal for Specialists in Group Work, 23,* 428–445.

Bowman, V., & DeLucia-Waack, J. (1993). Preparation for group therapy: The effects of preparer and modality on group process and individual functioning. *Journal for Specialists in Group Work, 18,* 67–79.

Burlingame, G., & Beecher, M. (2008). New directions and resources in group psychotherapy: Introduction to the issue. *Journal of Clinical Psychology, 64*(11), 1197–1291.

Burlingame, G., Fuhriman, A., & Johnson, J. (2001). Cohesion in group psychotherapy. *Psychotherapy, 38,* 373–379.

Burlingame, G., Fuhriman, A., & Johnson, J. (2004). Process and outcome in group counseling and psychotherapy: A perspective. In J. DeLucia-Waack, D. Gerrity, C. Kalodner, &

M. Riva (Eds.), *Handbook of group counseling and psychotherapy* (pp. 49–61). Thousand Oaks, CA: Sage.

Burlingame, G., Kapetanovic, S., & Ross, S. (2005). Group psychotherapy. In S. Wheelan (Ed.), *The handbook of group research and practice* (pp. 387–405). Thousand Oaks, CA: Sage.

Chen, E., Kakkad, D., & Balzano, J. (2008). Multicultural competence and evidence-based practice in group psychotherapy. *Journal of Clinical Psychology, 64*, 1261–1278.

Cohen, A., & Smith, R. D. (1976). *The critical incident in growth groups: Theory and technique.* La Jolla, CA: University Associates.

Conyne, R. (Ed.). (1985). *The group worker's handbook: Varieties of group experience.* Springfield, IL: Thomas.

Conyne, R. (1997). Developing framework for processing experiences and events in group work. *Journal for Specialists in Group Work, 22*, 167–174.

Conyne, R. (1999). *Failures in group work: How to learn from our mistakes.* Thousand Oaks, CA: Sage.

Conyne, R. (2004). Prevention groups. In J. DeLucia-Waack, D. Gerrity, C. Kalodner, & M. Riva (Eds.), *Handbook of group counseling and psychotherapy* (pp. 621–629). Thousand Oaks, CA: Sage.

Conyne, R., & Bemak, F. (2004). Teaching group work from an ecological perspective. *Journal for Specialists in Group Work, 29*, 7–148.

Conyne, R., Crowell, J., & Newmeyer, M. (2008). *Purposeful group techniques: How to use them more purposefully.* Upper Saddle River, NJ: Prentice Hall.

Conyne, R., Wilson, F. R., & Ward, D. (1997). *Contemporary group work: What it means & how to teach it.* Alexandria, VA: American Counseling Association.

Corey, M., & Corey, G. (2006). *Groups: Process and practice* (7th ed.). Pacific Grove, CA: Brooks/Cole.

DeLucia-Waack, J., & Donigian, J. (2003). *The practice of multicultural group work: Visions and perspectives from the field.* Monterey, CA: Wadsworth.

DeLucia-Waack, J., Gerrity, D., Kalodner, C., & Riva, M. (Eds.). (2004). *Handbook of group counseling and psychotherapy.* Thousand Oaks, CA: Sage.

Donigian, J., & Malnati, R. (1997). *Systemic group therapy: A triadic model.* Pacific Grove, CA: Brooks/Cole.

Finn, J., & Jacobson, M. (2003). *Just practice: A social justice approach to social work.* Peosta, IA: Eddie Bowers.

Gazda, G., Ginter, E., & Horne, A. (2001). *Group counseling and group psychotherapy: Theory and application.* Boston: Allyn and Bacon.

Haberstroh, S., Parr, G., Gee, R., & Trepal, H. (2006). Interactive E-journaling in group work: Perspectives from counselor trainees. *Journal for Specialists in Group Work, 31*, 327–337.

Ivey, A., Pedersen, P., & Ivey, M. (2001). *Intentional group counseling: A microskills approach.* Pacific Grove, CA: Brooks/Cole.

Ivey, A., Pedersen, P., & Ivey, M. (2008). *Group microskills: Culture-centered group process and strategies.* Hanover, MA: Microtraining Associates and the American Counseling Association.

Jacobs, E., Masson, R., & Harvill, R. (2006). *Group counseling: Strategies and skills* (5th ed.). Pacific Grove, CA: Brooks/Cole.

Jacobson, M., & Rugeley, C. (2007). Community-based participatory research: Group work for social justice and community change. *Social Work with Groups, 30*, 21–39.

Johnson, J. (2008). Using research-supported group treatments. *Journal of Clinical Psychology, 64*, 1206–1225.

Kaul, T. (1990). A matter of consistency: There are just two things. *Counseling Psychologist, 18*, 121–125.

Kessler, R., Michelson, K., & Humphreys, K. (1997). Patterns and correlates of self-help group membership in the United States. *Social Policy, 27*, 27–46.

Kivlighan, D., Jr. (2008). Overcoming our resistance to "doing" evidence-based group practice: A commentary. *Journal of Clinical Psychology, 64*, 1284–1291.

Kivlighan, D., Jr., Coleman, M., & Anderson, D. (2000). Process, outcome and methodology in group counseling research. In S. Brown & R. Lent (Eds.), *Handbook of counseling psychology* (3rd ed., pp. 767–796). New York: Wiley.

Kivlighan, D., Jr., & Holmes, S. (2004). The importance of therapeutic factors. In J. DeLucia-Waack, D. Gerrity, C. Kalodner, & M. Riva (Eds.), *Handbook of group counseling and psychotherapy* (pp. 23–36). Thousand Oaks, CA: Sage.

Kivlighan, D., Jr., McGovern, T., & Corazzini, J. (1984). The effects of the content and timing of structuring interventions on group therapy process and outcome. *Journal of Counseling Psychology, 31*, 363–370.

Kivlighan, D., Jr., & Tarrant, J. (2001). Does group climate mediate the group leadership–group outcome relationship? A test of Yalom's hypotheses about leadership priorities. *Group Dynamics: Theory, Research, and Practice, 5*, 220–234.

Klaw, E., & Humphreys, K. (2004). The role of peer-led mutual help groups in promoting health and well-being. In J. DeLucia-Waack, D. Gerrity, C. Kalodner, & M. Riva (Eds.), *Handbook of group counseling and psychotherapy* (pp. 630–640). Thousand Oaks, CA: Sage.

Lee, C. (2007). *Counseling for social justice* (2nd ed.). Alexandria, VA: American Counseling Association.

Lieberman, M., Wizlenberg, A., Golant, M., & Minno, M. (2005). The impact of group composition on Internet support groups: Homogeneous versus heterogeneous Parkinson's groups. *Group Dynamics: Theory, Research, and Practice, 9*, 239–250.

Lieberman, M., Yalom, I., & Miles, M. (1973). *Encounter groups: First facts.* New York: Basic Books.

MacKenzie, K. R. (1997). Clinical application of group development ideas. *Group Dynamics: Theory, Research, and Practice, 1*, 275–287.

McGlothlin, J. (2003). Response to the mini special issue on technology and group work. *Journal for Specialists in Group Work, 28*, 42–47.

Orr, J., Wolfe, A., & Malley, J. (2008, February 22). *From ripple to wave: Using social microcosms in group to address systemic change.* Paper presented at the national conference of the Association for Specialists in Group Work, St. Pete Beach, FL.

Page, B. (2004). Online group counseling. In J. DeLucia-Waack, D. Gerrity, C. Kalodner, & M. Riva (Eds.), *Handbook of group counseling and psychotherapy* (pp. 609–620). Thousand Oaks, CA: Sage.

Payne, K., & Marcus, D. (2008). The efficacy of group psychotherapy for older adult clients: A meta-analysis. *Group Dynamics: Theory, Research, and Practice, 12*, 268–278.

Piper, W., & Ogrodniczuk, J. (2004). Brief group therapy. In J. DeLucia-Waack, D. Gerrity, C. Kalodner, & M. Riva (Eds.), *Handbook of group counseling and psychotherapy* (pp. 641–660). Thousand Oaks, CA: Sage.

Rapin, L. (2004). Guidelines for ethical and legal practice in counseling and psychotherapy groups. In J. DeLucia-Waack, D. Gerrity, C. Kalodner, & M. Riva (Eds.), *Handbook of* group counseling and psychotherapy (pp. 151–165). Thousand Oaks, CA: Sage.

Riva, M., Wachtel, M., & Lasky, G. (2004). Effective leadership in group counseling and psychotherapy. In J. DeLucia-Waack, D. Gerrity, C. Kalodner, & M. Riva (Eds.), *Handbook of group counseling and psychotherapy* (pp. 37–48). Thousand Oaks, CA: Sage.

Romano, J., & Cikanek, K. (2003). Group work and computer applications: Instructional components for graduate students. *Journal for Specialists in Group Work, 28,* 23–34.

Smokowski, P. (2003). Using technology to enhance modeling and behavioral rehearsal in group work practice. *Journal for Specialists in Group Work, 28,* 9–22.

Spitz, H. (1996). *Group psychotherapy and managed mental health care: A clinical guide for providers.* New York: Brunner/Mazel.

Stockton, R., Morran, D. K., & Clark, M. (2004). An investigation of group leaders' intentions. *Group Dynamics: Theory, Research, and Practice, 8,* 196–206.

Toporek, R., Gerstein, L., Fouad, N., Roysircar-Sodowsky, G., & Israel, T. (Eds.). (2005). *Handbook for social justice in counseling psychology.* Thousand Oaks, CA: Sage.

Trotzer, J. (2004). Conducting a group: Guidelines for choosing and using activities. In J. DeLucia-Waack, D. Gerrity, C. Kalodner, & M. Riva (Eds.), *Handbook of group counseling and psychotherapy* (pp. 76–90). Thousand Oaks, CA: Sage.

Trotzer, J. (2006). *The counselor and the group: Integrating theory, training, and practice* (4th ed.). New York: Routledge.

Wheelan, S. (1997). Group development and the practice of group psychotherapy. *Group Dynamics: Theory, Research, and Practice, 1,* 288–293.

Wheelan, S. (Ed.). (2005). *The handbook of group research and practice.* Thousand Oaks, CA: Sage.

Williams, K. (2002). Groups and the Internet. *Group Dynamics: Theory, Research, and Practice, 6*(1), 3–127.

Wilson, F. R., Rapin, L., & Haley-Banez, L. (2004). How teaching group work can be guided by foundational documents: Best practice guidelines, diversity principles, training standards. *Journal for Specialists in Group Work, 29,* 19–29.

Yalom, I. (1995). *The theory and practice of group psychotherapy* (4th ed.). New York: Basic Books.

Yalom, I. (with Leszcz, M.) (2005). *The theory and practice of group psychotherapy* (5th ed.). New York: Basic Books.

PART 2

Context

The Nature and Significance of Groups

Donelson R. Forsyth

Abstract

An understanding of group counseling requires an understanding of groups themselves, their basic nature and processes. Given that human beings are a social species and spend their lives in groups rather than alone, an individual-level analysis of adjustment, well-being, and treatment, with its focus on internal, psychological processes, should be supplemented by a group-level analysis. The defining features of a group are relationships linking a substantial number of members, boundaries, interdependence, structure, cohesion, and *entitativity* (perceived groupness); and groups with more of these features are more influential than other forms of association, such as social networks. The chapter reviews a number of group-level processes that influence members' adjustment, including loneliness, ostracism, social support, socialization, social identity, and performance, before recommending a synthesis of the individual- and group-level perspectives in a multilevel analysis of human development, adjustment, and potential.

Keywords: individual-level analysis; group-level analysis; cohesion; entitativity; social networks; loneliness, ostracism, social support.

People, no matter what they are doing—working, relaxing, studying, exercising, worshiping, playing, socializing, watching entertainment, or sleeping—are usually in a group rather than alone. Some people seem to keep to themselves, but a preference for solitude is considered unusual by most; sociality is far more typical, for most people live out their lives in groups, around groups, and seeking out new groups. Humans are so group-oriented that at every turn we encounter groups. No one knows for certain how many groups exist at this moment, but given the number of people on the planet and their proclivity to form groups, 30 billion is a conservative estimate.

Groups are ubiquitous, not only in the context of day-to-day living but also in counseling settings. *Group counseling*, by definition, is an intervention that in some way involves groups and group processes. In schools counselors work with small groups of students as they deal with problems of development, adjustment, and achievement. Peers meet to offer each other support and wise counsel as they cope with problems they share in common. Hospital counselors meet with families to help them deal with the consequences of illness, disease, and death. Mental health professionals in a range of settings work with people in groups to set new goals for adjustment and help their clients learn the skills they need to connect with others. In communities social workers and organizers meet with residents to share information and identify solutions to communal issues. Consultants and trainers in organizations teach clients the skills they need to set realistic goals and to identify the steps they must take to reach them. Even when working with single individuals, the influence of groups cannot be ignored, for in many cases individuals' difficulties and satisfactions are intimately linked to groups: those to which they belong, those that they are seeking to join, those that exclude them, and even those that reject and denigrate them.

This chapter is based on a single assumption: To understand group counseling—and, more generally, to understand people—one must understand groups themselves, their basic nature and processes. All too often a group-level explanation of people's thoughts, emotions, and actions is overlooked in the search for an explanation of the causes of dysfunction and adjustment, just as a group approach to treatment is viewed as a second-best choice compared to an individualistic intervention. A truly multilevel approach, however, requires the integration of many levels of analysis in the development of a comprehensive theory of human adjustment and treatment. The chapters in this handbook stress the group rather than the individual not because the group level is viewed as more important than the individual but rather because the individual level has received favorable treatment for so long that an analysis that takes into account group-level processes is overdue.

This chapter examines three related questions. First, what does the analysis of groups and their dynamics contribute to an overall understanding of human behavior? For those who, by tradition, adopt an individual-centered approach to understanding individuals' thoughts, actions, and emotions, what does a multilevel perspective that recognizes that individuals are also members of larger social units offer? Second, what are the unique characteristics of groups that provide the foundation for their psychological and interpersonal significance? From small, problem-focused, and highly structured psychoeducational groups to large and geographically scattered community groups, groups come in a staggering assortment of shapes and sizes. What qualities do these various groups have in common, and what distinguishes them from other social aggregations, such as networks of associations and communities? Third, what is the connection between the individual and the group? If individuals are not isolates but rather more frequently members of groups, in what ways do these groups influence the individual members, and how do the members in turn influence their groups?

The Reality of Groups

Emile Durkheim (1897/1966), at the end of the nineteenth century, presented evidence that suggested that suicide results more from interpersonal causes than intrapsychic ones. People did not take their own lives, he maintained, because of psychological maladjustment or delusion but rather when

the groups that they belonged to no longer provided them with reliable alliances with others or regulative support systems. He maintained that groups provide a buffer against the stresses of daily life events, and as a result, those who were closely associated with traditional integrative groups enjoyed greater happiness and health (Joiner, Brown, & Wingate, 2005; cf. Kushner & Sterk, 2005).

Many scholars of that period agreed with Durkheim's idea that groups profoundly influence their members (e.g., Le Bon, 1895/1960; McDougall, 1908). Others, however, took a different position. Allport (1924), for example, questioned the need to look beyond psychological processes when explaining why people acted as they did. Groups, according to Allport, were not even real; and he felt that the behavior of individuals in groups could be understood by studying the psychology of the group members since "the actions of all are nothing more than the sum of the actions of each taken separately" (p. 5). He is reputed to have said "you can't trip over a group" (Pepitone, 1981).

Vestiges of Allport's skepticism continue to influence theorists' and researchers' willingness to consider group-level concepts when explaining maladaptive and adaptive processes. Although most, in principle, admit that groups are influential, in practice when they search for the causes of behavior and when they make choices about the best way to solve personal and interpersonal problems, they adopt an individual-centered perspective rather than a group-centered one. This section examines the sources and the ramifications of the tendency to think individual first and group second, in theory, research, and practice.

Perceiving Individuals and Groups

The well-known face–vase visual illusion can be construed as depicting either a vase or the faces of two individuals looking at each other. Illustrating the figure–ground Gestalt principle of perception, when people report seeing a vase, the image of the vase becomes the figure and the individuals become the ground. Conversely, when people report seeing two individuals looking at each other, the faces become figure and the vase retreats into the background. The image hides a third image however: a two-person group, whose members are facing one another. Yet, the group is rarely noticed.

In terms of Gestalt principles of perceptions, groups are the ground, whereas individuals are the figure. The most famous painting in the world depicts a single individual. The number of words in languages that can be used to describe individuals and their personality characteristics is substantial— Norman (1963), for example, identified 2,800 trait-descriptive adjectives in his study of personality— but how many words describe qualities that are specific to groups? Groups are not generally described as jolly, brave, playful, assertive, nosey, sensual, cool, reasonable, or stingy; but individuals are. Concepts that are used to describe qualities of individuals, such as personality, needs, intelligence, and self, have made their way easily into everyday language; but concepts that were developed to describe aspects of groups—for example, Cattell's (1948) syntality, Bogardus's (1954) groupality, and Moreno's (1934) sociometry—rarely find popular acceptance. Even though people speak of such concepts as teamwork, leadership, and cliques in their discussions of contemporary issues, they tend to translate these group-level processes into individualistic ones. The key ingredient for teamwork, they suggest, is having a particular type of personality that stresses cooperation and communication. Leadership continues to be viewed as a personality trait, rather than a process that emerges during cooperative interactions. Cliques, and their negative tendencies, are attributed to the motives of the clique members, rather than group-level processes.

Individuals, when considering the causes of their own and others' behavior, are less likely to favor an explanation that stresses group-level causes relative to one that stresses such psychological, individualistic causes as motivations, emotions, intentions, and personality. The well-documented fundamental attribution error occurs because perceivers are more likely to attribute a person's actions to personal, individual qualities rather than external, situational forces (Ross, 1977). Evidence suggests that social perception starts with an assumption of dispositionality; the attributor initially categorizes the behavior as one that reflects a particular trait or quality and then uses this behavioral label to characterize the actor. Only then, and only if he or she has the cognitive resources and motivation to process fully information about the situation, does the perceiver consider group-level causes (Gilbert, 1998). Hence, even when individuals engage in unusual behaviors in response to an extreme degree of group pressure, perceivers believe that actions reflect qualities of the person rather than the group (Nolan, Schultz, Cialdini, Goldstein, & Griskevicius, 2008). Perceivers also expect that individuals will behave similarly in all groups to which they belong; after all, if personal, individualistic qualities are the primary causes of behavior, then group-level process should play only a minor role in determining outcomes (Darley, 1992).

This tendency to see individuals first and groups second may vary from one culture to another. Western countries such as the United States and Great Britain lean toward individualism: the equality of separate individuals and the rights of the individual over the group. Individuals are the center of such societies, and their rights to private property, to express themselves, and to engage in actions for their own personal gain are protected and even encouraged. Many non-Western societies, in contrast, stress collectivism. Individuals in such societies think of themselves as group members first and individuals second and, thus, emphasize the unity of all people in their group rather than each person's individuality. Social existence is centered on group relations, for it is the group that creates social obligations based on respect, trust, and a sense of community (Triandis & Suh, 2002).

Because of these varying priorities, people raised in individualistic cultures differ in many ways from people raised in cultures that are based on collectivism. To speak in general terms (for people vary considerably within any given culture), individuals in Asian, western European, African, and Middle Eastern countries tend to be more loyal to their group and more suspicious of individuals who do not belong to their group. Collectivistic cultures also tend to be more hierarchical in organization, and they stress conformity and obedience to authority. Individuals' self-concepts also differ in individualistic and collectivistic contexts, with greater emphasis on personal identity in the former and greater emphasis on social identity (e.g., roles, membership, relations) in the latter. Triandis and his colleagues illustrated this difference by asking people from various countries to describe themselves. As they expected, these self-descriptions contained more references to social identities—membership in groups, roles in society, ethnicity—when people were from collectivistic countries (e.g., Japan, China). They discovered that some individuals from the People's Republic of China described themselves exclusively in interpersonal terms, whereas some US residents used only personal descriptors: They had no elements of a group-level identity (Triandis, McCusker, & Hui, 1990).

Levels of Analysis
Researchers, theorists, and practitioners, whether they are psychologists, social workers, consultants,

counselors, or clinicians, accept as givens some core assumptions about humans and their basic nature. These guiding assumptions, far from being biases, are instead useful heuristics, for they provide the means of dealing with the countless alternative and correct interpretations of the evidence and issues that they must confront and interpret in their work.

Coan (1968), Rosenberg and Gara (1983), and Watson (1967) present a sampling of the divergent assumptions that have characterized various approaches in psychology since the field's inception. Are unconscious processes influential determinants of behavior, or are actions primarily the result of reinforcement mechanisms? Is behavior caused by forces present in the immediate external environment or historical factors whose force is still felt in the distant future? Can psychological processes be broken down into specific elements, or is a holistic approach that avoids analysis more informative? Watson (1967) suggested that these "prescriptions" serve to orient researchers, theorists, and practitioners when they conceptualize problems and search for solutions.

THE INDIVIDUAL-LEVEL PERSPECTIVE

One of the most enduring prescriptions within the field of psychology is *psychogenicism*: the focus on the internal, psychological determinants of behavior. With behaviorists providing a notable exception, the theorists who provided the foundations for contemporary psychology offered models that included reference to the structure of personality, dynamic intrapsychic mechanisms, and the relationships between the individual's particular qualities and his or her behavior. Adler, Freud, Jung, Horney, Maslow, Murray, and others were generalists; but at the core their theories assumed that personality, needs, motivations, and other psychogenic mechanisms play a pivotal role in adjustment and dysfunction. The psychogenic orientation was summarized by Urban (1983, p. 163), who argued strongly that when psychologists look for causes outside of the individual they "deny and distort the essential quality of human existence. Everything of significance with regard to this entire process occurs within the inner or subjective experience of the individual." Psychogenicism is also compatible with general *endogenism*, in which behaviors are attributed to a host of internal processes such as genetic factors, past events, and biological processes. Psychogenic approaches assume that psychological states mediate the relationship between the external world and the person's reaction to it (Forsyth & Leary, 1991).

THE GROUP-LEVEL PERSPECTIVE

The individual-level approach suggested by psychogenicism contrasts with a group-level approach. This orientation assumes that if one wishes to understand individuals, one must understand groups. As a highly social species, humans are rarely separated from contact and interaction with other humans, and in most cases these connections occur in a group context. In consequence, groups and their processes have a profound impact on individuals; they shape actions, thoughts, and feelings. Although people often consider their cognitive ruminations, including thoughts, decisions, attitudes, and values, to be private and personal, these are shaped by the groups to which they belong. Sherif (1936) and Asch (1957), in early demonstrations of the impact of a group on members' most basic judgments, discovered that people will base their decisions on the statements made by other group members rather the evidence of their own senses. Groups prompt their members to endorse certain ideas and attitudes, and even nonconformists will eventually take on the standards of the groups to which they belong (Newcomb, 1943). People also process information collectively, through discussion and other group communication processes, so such basic cognitive processes as planning, evaluating, judging, decision making, and problem solving are made, not by individuals, but by groups (Kerr & Tindale, 2004).

Groups also influence members' emotions, in both direct and indirect ways. As Schachter and Singer's (1962) classic study of how people label their physiological states indicates, people often rely on cues in the group setting to decide if they are happy, sad, angry, or frightened. Emotions are also sometimes contagious in groups, with the feelings of one individual passing rapidly from one member of the group to the next (Smith, Seger, & Mackie, 2007). Crowds and mobs, for example, often experience waves of strong emotions, to the point that external observers often feel that such groups act as if they possess a shared, or collective, conscious. Even members of more commonplace and highly structured groups, such as work groups and sports teams, become more and more similar in their overall mood the longer they remain together (Kelly, 2004).

Groups also influence members' actions and reactions. As Durkheim concluded, people respond very differently when they are isolated rather than integrated in a group, and this shift has been documented time and again in studies of a wide variety of behaviors in many different situations. Young children imitate the way their playmates dress, talk, and act (Adler, Kless, & Adler, 1992). Older children's actions are guided by their family's influence, until by adolescence the peer group becomes the primary determiner of behaviors (Harris, 1995). Groups can, in some cases, change people's behavior so dramatically that their behavior in a group bears no relationship to their behavior when isolated. The early group psychologists may have exaggerated the apparent madness of people when immersed in large crowds, but contemporary researchers have confirmed the discontinuity effect: In many cases the actions of individuals when in groups cannot be predicted by studying the qualities and actions of each individual group member (Wildschut, Pinter, Vevea, Insko, & Schopler, 2003).

A group-level approach also assumes that information will be lost, or at least overlooked, if the focus is solely on individuals rather than the larger social unit since groups possess characteristics "that cannot be reduced to or described as qualities of its participants" (Sandelands & St. Clair, 1993, p. 443). A group's cohesiveness, for example, is more than the mere attraction of each individual member for one another (Hogg, 1992). Individuals may not like each other on a personal level, yet when they form a group they experience powerful feelings of unity and esprit de corps. As Lewin's (1951) Gestalt orientation argued that a group is greater than the sum of its parts, so it cannot be understood through piecemeal, individual-only, analysis.

THE MULTILEVEL PERSPECTIVE

Theorists, researchers, and practitioners offer a range of solutions to problems of human adjustment and dysfunction. Some highlight aspects of the individual: their personalities, motivation, emotions, and perceptions. Others focus on interpersonal factors, such as relations with friends and relatives and group memberships. Some stress the larger social context by suggesting that the most important factors to consider are cultural ones. These perspectives are often viewed as mutually exclusive views that resist integration. As Sarason (1981, p. 175) explained, "built into psychology, part of its world view, is the polarity man and society. Call it a polarity or a dichotomy or even a distinction, it makes it easy for psychology to focus on one and ignore the other."

A multilevel perspective, in contrast, does not favor a specific level of analysis when examining human behavior, for it argues for examining processes that range along the micro–meso–macro continuum. Asked why an individual acts altruistically, acts in ways that create conflict with others, or engages in aberrant actions, a multilevel approach does not stop at the micro level by considering only the qualities, characteristics, and actions of the individual members. A multilevel approach also considers meso-level group processes, including group influence, cohesion, composition, and structure. The approach also considers macro-level factors, which are the qualities and processes of the larger collectives that enfold the groups, such as communities, organizations, or societies. Groups, then, are nested at the meso level where the bottom–up micro-level variables meet the top–down macro-level variables (Forsyth, 2010).

A multilevel approach has several advantages to a one-level-only analysis of human behavior. An individual-level analysis stresses the causal importance of the individual's past and future and best deals with situational factors by filtering them through individual-level mechanisms. Because personality, experience, attitudes, and values must be represented within the individual, a group-level-only analysis tends to ignore them, choosing instead to focus on contemporaneous causes present in the immediate setting. The result is a model that suggests people are mechanistic, static, and purposeless, whereas they are, in reality, motivated, goal-seeking, and dynamic. A multilevel approach is more theoretically egalitarian, recognizing the causal influence of factors that range along the individual–group–organization continuum.

The Nature of Groups

A group-level analysis argues that groups influence their members' adjustment and mental health, but the magnitude of this impact depends on the nature of the group. Groups, unlike individuals, are not all created equal. Some aggregations of individuals seem, intuitively, to deserve to be called "groups": Families, gangs, support groups, school boards, production teams, and neighborhood associations are examples. Other collections of people—bystanders to a mugging, the audience in a theater, or Internet users arguing with one another via commentaries to a blogger's post—may lack the defining features of a group. But what are those defining features?

Relationships

Definitions of the concept of group abound, but most theorists would agree that a group comes into existence when people become connected by and within social relationships. Both Lewin (1948) and Cartwright and Zander (1968) stressed the importance of relationships among members as the key defining feature of a true group, with Cartwright and Zander (1968, p. 46) concluding a "group is a collection of individuals who have relations to one another that make them interdependent to some significant degree."

Groups create and sustain relationships between individual members, but the relationships that link the members of a group together are not of one type. In families, for example, the relationships are based on kinship, but in the workplace the relationships are based on task-related interdependencies. In some groups members are friends of one another, but in others the members express little mutual attraction, liking, or loving for one another. Nor are the relationships linking members of different types of groups equally strong or enduring. Some relationships, like the links between members of a family or a clique of close friends, are enduring ones, which have developed over time and are based on a long history of mutual influence and exchange. In other cases, however, the ties between members may be relatively weak ones that are so fragile they are easily severed. Nor need all relationships be mutual ones. In a group of friends, for example, some members may be liked by all the group members but these group members may like only a subset of the group members in return. But no matter what the nature of the relations, a group exists when individuals are connected to one another by some type of social tie.

Theoretically, the number of relationships needed to create a completely interconnected group—one where every member is linked to every other member—is given by the equation $n(n-1)/2$, where n is the number of people in group (and if we assume that all relationships are mutual). A relatively small group—for example, a 12-person jury or committee—would require the development and maintenance of 66 relationships if every member was connected to every other member. In consequence, in many cases the number of ties in a group is less than the number of potential relationships. Evolutionary theorist Dunbar (2008) goes so far as to suggest that the need to track connections with others—to remember who can be trusted to share, who will act in helpful ways, or who is owed a favor and who is not—spurred the development of a larger brain in primates. Dunbar's social brain hypothesis assumes that group life is more psychologically demanding than a more isolated, independent one. Moreover, given the number of relationships that must be tracked in larger groups, Dunbar suggests that humans likely evolved to live most comfortably in groups of 150 people or fewer.

In general, the stronger the relationships linking members, the more influence the group has on its members. A young man who is part of a gang, for example, may act in ways that the group requires because the relationships that bind him to the group are so numerous and so strong that the group is too powerful to resist. In contrast, a member of a club may break the group's attendance rules regularly because there are few ties that bind him or her to the group or those ties are relatively weak. As with other relationships, such as friendships and partnerships, the strength of the relationship is determined, in large part, by the rewards the group provides, the costs the relationship incurs, and the member's degree of commitment to the group (Thibaut & Kelly, 1959).

Boundaries

The relationships that sustain a group not only link members to one another but also define who is in the group and who is not. A group is therefore *boundaried*, in a psychological sense, with those who are included in the group recognized as members and those who are not part of the group excluded as non-members. These boundaries set the members apart from other people, and hence, they distinguish a group from another psychologically significant aggregate: the social network. To become part of a *social network*, an individual need only establish a relationship of some sort with a person who is already part of the network. If persons A and B already know each other—they are linked by a social relationship—then person C can join their network by establishing a relationship with either A or B. But a group, unlike a network, is more than a chain of individuals joined in dyadic pairings. Even though A and B are friends and B and C are friends, if these individuals are linked only in these dyadic pair-bonds, then they are part of a social network but not a group. A group exists when members form a relationship with the group as a whole and when it is the group that sustains, at least in part, the relationships among each of the individual members. If A, B, and C are not linked to a supervening aggregate, then they are just sets of friends and not members of a group.

Groups' boundaries vary from the stable and relatively formalized to the unstable and highly permeable. As Ziller's (1965) theory of open and closed groups suggests that group membership can fluctuate for various reasons: members are voted out of the group (e.g., governing committees), members voluntarily come and go (e.g., community service groups), and so on. Regardless of the reasons for group fluctuation, open groups are especially unlikely to reach a state of equilibrium since members recognize that they may lose or relinquish their place within the group at any time. Members of such groups, especially those in which membership is dependent on voting or meeting a particular standard, are more likely to monitor the actions of others. Ziller writes, "In the expanded frame of reference of the open groups in which transfers frequently occur, more accurate and more reliable ratings of the members are possible" (1965, p. 168). In contrast, closed groups are often more cohesive as competition for membership is irrelevant and group members anticipate future collaborations. Thus, in closed groups, individuals are more likely to focus on the collective nature of the group and to identify with the group. Ziller's theory suggests that open groups, by their very nature, are less cohesive.

Interdependence

Groups entwine the fates of their members. As Cartwright and Zander (1968, p. 46) noted, it is not just that the members are related to each other but that these relationships "make them interdependent to some significant degree." Shaw (1981, p. 454), in his definition, concluded that a group is "two or more persons who are interacting with one another in such a manner that each person influences and is influenced by each other person." When individuals are interdependent, their outcomes, actions, thoughts, feelings, and experiences are determined in part by others in the group.

Some groups create only the potential for interdependence among members. The people standing in a queue at the checkout counter in a store, audience members in a darkened theater, or the congregation of a large mega-church are only minimally interdependent; but other groups—such as gangs, families, sports teams, and military squads—create far higher levels of interdependency since members reliably and substantially influence one another's outcomes over a long period of time and in a variety of situations. In such groups the influence of one member on another also tends to be mutual; member A can influence B, but B can also influence A in return. In other groups, in contrast, influence is more unequal and more one-directional. In a business, for example, the boss may determine how employees spend their time, what kind of rewards they experience, and even the duration of their membership in the group. These employees can influence their boss to a degree, but the boss's influence is nearly unilateral.

Interdependence increases the degree of power the group holds over each member, for the greater the members' dependence on the group, the more likely they are to act in ways that will sustain their membership—even if that means engaging in behaviors that they find personally objectionable. As social exchange theory explains, the greater the individual members' commitment to the group—with commitment generally increasing with time spent in the group, the costs already incurred by membership, the level of rewards received from the group, and the lack of alternative group memberships—the greater the group's power.

Structure

Moreno (1934), in his analysis of the nature of groups and their durability, argued that the psychological impact of a group on its members depends in large part on the group's structural integrity. He believed that groups with harmonious attraction and authority relations among members were likely to survive and that the individuals in such groups would be more likely to prosper psychologically.

Groups are structured, rather than unstructured, when roles, norms, and patterned relations organize the actions and activities within them. Sherif and Sherif (1956, p. 144), suggest that these structural features are what differentiate a group from a haphazard assortment of individuals: "A group is a social unit which consists of a number of individuals who stand in (more or less) definite status and role relationships to one another and which possesses a set of values or norms of its own regulating the behavior of individual members."

The more structured the group, the more clearly defined the actions taken by specific members. Many groups are structured by design, for by defining roles, norms, and relations the group and its founders hope to facilitate goal attainment. But even without a deliberate attempt at organizing, the group will probably develop a structure anyway. Initially, members may consider themselves to be just members, basically similar to each other. But over time each group member will tend to perform a specific range of actions and interact with other group members in a particular way. The role of leader emerges in many groups, but other roles arise in groups over time. Benne and Sheats (1948), in one of the earliest analyses of the roles that members take in groups, concluded that a group, to survive, must meet two basic demands: it must accomplish its tasks and the relationships among its members must be maintained. They suggested that the roles that frequently emerge in groups match these two basic needs, with task roles including coordinator, elaborator, energizer, evaluator-critic, information-giver, information-seeker, and opinion-giver and the relational, socioemotional roles including compromiser, encourager, follower, and harmonizer. Benne and Sheats also identified a third set of roles: the individualistic roles occupied by individuals who stress their own needs over the group's needs.

Norms are the consensual and often implicit standard that describe what behaviors should and should not be performed in a given group context and are part of the group's socially shared structure. Although agreement among members is often implicit and taken for granted, only when a degree of consensus emerges regarding a standard does it function as a norm. Sherif's (1936) seminal work confirmed the interpersonal, group-level status of norms by experimentally creating norms in a laboratory setting. The norms his groups generated had a reality independent of the individual members who supported them so that when new members joined the groups they learned, and subsequently passed on, the standards that they themselves had acquired through group interaction.

Roles, norms, and other structural aspects of groups, although unseen and often unnoticed, lie at the heart of their most dynamic processes. Individuals who occupy roles that grant them more status within the group tend to be more influential, even when examining issues that fall outside their areas of expertise. When several members form a subgroup within the larger group, they exert more influence on the rest of the group than they would individually. When people manage to place themselves at the hub of the group's information-exchange patterns, their influence over others increases. As Moreland and Levine (1982) explain in their theory of group socialization, when people join a group, they initially spend much of their time trying to come to terms with the structural requirements of their group. If they cannot meet the group's demands, they might not remain a member for long. As their commitment to the group increases and the group becomes increasingly committed to the individual, individuals transition into the role of full member and tend to fulfill the requirements of their position within the group.

Cohesion

A group is not just the individuals who are members or even the dyadic pair-bonds that link members to one another. A group, viewed holistically, is a unified whole; an entity formed when interpersonal forces bind the members together in a single unit with boundaries that mark who is in the group and who is outside of it. This quality of "groupness," solidarity, or unity is generally termed *cohesion* and is a necessary, if not sufficient, condition for a group to exist. A group without cohesion would disintegrate since forces that keep the group intact are insufficient to counteract the forces that pull the group apart (Dion, 2000).

Durkheim (1897/1966, 1900/1973) discussed how groups vary in terms of cohesiveness; he proposed that groups with greater solidarity had more influence over their members. A more formal analysis of cohesion was supplied by Lewin (1948), who suggested that cohesion involved both individual-level and group-level processes. At the individual level, cohesiveness derives from each member's attraction to other group members, whether this attraction is based on liking, respect, or trust. At the group level, cohesiveness reflects that "we-feeling" that joins people together to form a single unit (Cartwright, 1968; Festinger, 1950). Many factors combine to determine a group's level of cohesiveness, including attraction among members, similarity of members to one another, group size, and structural features such as the absence of subgroups, a flatter status structure, and so on.

Cohesion is a uniquely group-level concept, for cohesion comes about if, and only if, a group exists. Although a group with low levels of cohesiveness may be a durable one, cohesiveness usually signals the health of the group. A cohesive group will be more likely to prosper, over time, since it retains its members and allows them to reach goals that would elude a more incoherent aggregate. The group that lacks cohesion is at risk, for if too many members drift away, the group may not survive. The concept of cohesiveness, too, offers insights into some of the most intriguing questions people ask about groups: Why do some groups fail to retain their members, whereas others grow rapidly in size? Why do some groups stand loyally behind the decisions of their leaders, whereas the members of other groups dissociate themselves from their group at the first sign of conflict? When do members put the needs of their group above their own personal interests? What is the source of the feeling of confidence and unity that arises in some groups and not in others? If one understands the causes and consequences of cohesion, then one is further along in understanding a host of core processes that occur in groups, including productivity, members' satisfaction and turnover, morale, formation, stability, influence, and conflict.

Entitativity (Groupness)

Groups are real not just in a physical sense but also in a perceptual sense. Groups are often construed to be unified Gestalts whose parts mix together to form a single thing by members and nonmembers. Perceivers readily hypostasize groups: They perceive them to be real and assume that their properties are influential ones. Brown (2000, p. 3) considered this aspect of a group—that members define the group as real and see themselves as members of it—to be the sine qua non of a group. He writes: "A group exists when two or more people define themselves as members of it and when its existence is recognized by at least one other." Turner, Hogg, Oakes, Reicher, and Wetherell (1987, pp. 1–2) similarly suggested "a psychological group is defined as one that is psychologically significant for the members, to which they relate themselves subjectively for social comparison and the acquisition of norms and values . . . that they privately accept membership in, and which influences their attitudes and behavior."

Campbell (1958) believed that this aspect of a group was so essential to understanding how people perceive groups that he coined the word *entitativity* to describe a group's perceived unity. Entitativity, as perceived cohesiveness, depends on certain perceptual cues that perceivers rely on intuitively to decide if an aggregation of individuals is a true group or just a collection of people. Many aggregates of individuals occupying the same physical location—commuters waiting for a bus or spectators at a sporting event—may lack entitativity since they seem to be a disorganized mass of individuals who happen to be in the same place at the same time, but if they begin to cheer, express similar emotions, and move together, they may look more like a group to those who are observing them. Entitativity, according to Campbell, is substantially influenced by degree of interdependence (common fate: Do the individuals experience the same or interrelated outcomes?), homogeneity (similarity: Do the individuals perform similar behaviors or resemble one another?), and presence (proximity: How close together are the individuals in the aggregation?).

Calling an aggregation a "group" is not mere labeling. Groups that are high in entitativity tend to be more cohesive (Zyphur & Islam, 2006), and their members also experience enhanced feelings of social well-being (Sani, Bowe, & Herrera, 2008).

When people believe they are part of a highly entitative group, they are more likely to respond to the group's normative pressures (Castano, Yzerbyt, & Bourguignon, 2003); and this tendency is particularly strong when people feel uncertain about themselves and the correctness of their beliefs (Hogg, Sherman, Dierselhuis, Maitner, & Moffitt, 2007). The concept of entitativity also helps to explain the varied reactions people display when they are part of groups that are created using technology, such as conference calls or Internet-mediated connections. Some members do not consider such groups to be very entitative because they lack physical presence, but others report that such groups are as high in entitativity as any face-to-face group to which they belong (Lowry, Roberts, Romano, Cheney, & Hightower, 2006). Entitativity, then, is often in the eye of the beholder. As Zander and his colleagues demonstrated many years ago, simply telling a collection of people they constitute a group is sufficient to trigger intragroup dynamics. When they repeatedly told women working in isolation that they were nonetheless members of a group, the women accepted this label and later rated themselves more negatively after their "group" failed (Zander, Stotland, & Wolfe, 1960).

Entitativity also influences nonmembers' perceptions of the group and its members. Perceivers are more likely to stereotype specific individuals when they are members of a group that is thought to be high in entitativity (Rydell, Hugenberg, Ray, & Mackie, 2007). Observers are more likely to assume the members of such groups are highly similar to one another (Crawford, Sherman, & Hamilton, 2002) but different in significant ways from nonmembers (Pickett, 2001). Their perceptions of such groups also reveal a tendency toward *essentialism*: the belief that the group has deep, relatively unchanging qualities that give rise to their more surface-level characteristics (Haslam, Rothschild, & Ernst, 2002; Yzerbyt, Judd, & Corneille, 2004). When people think that a group is entitative, they assume that the group members act as they do because that is simply the nature of people who are members of that particular group.

The Significance of Groups

Groups are scientifically, practically, and clinically significant. Groups—particularly groups with many, rather than few, of the defining features of groups, including relationships linking a substantial number of members, boundaries, interdependence, structure, cohesion, and entitativity—influence the thoughts, emotions, and actions of their members, so a scientifically informed understanding of people requires understanding groups. Groups, as the final section of this chapter concludes, provide members with the resources they need to meet the demands they encounter in a wide range of environmental contexts across the span of their lives.

Groups and the Need to Belong

Baumeister and Leary's (1995) belongingness hypothesis argues that "human beings have a pervasive drive to form and maintain at least a minimum quantity of lasting, positive, and impactful interpersonal relationships" (p. 497). Although groups with superficial relationships among members do not satisfy this need, members of long term, emotionally intensive groups—therapeutic groups, support groups, combat units, and high-demand religious organizations—display strong bonds between themselves and other group members—to the point of showing withdrawal when someone leaves the "family." A psychodynamic perspective suggests that groups provide a means of regaining the security of the family by creating emotional ties among members by providing a sense of security like that of a nurturing parent and making possible relations with others that are similar in affective tone to sibling bonds (Freud, 1922; Lee & Robbins, 1995).

Loneliness

Studies of people who are socially isolated attest to the distress caused by too few connections to others. Loneliness covaries with depression, anxiety, personality disorders, and interpersonal hostility; and prolonged periods of loneliness have been linked to such physical illnesses as cirrhosis of the liver, hypertension, heart disease, and leukemia (Hojat & Vogel, 1987; Jones & Carver, 1991). Individuals who are extremely lonely display elevated levels of Epstein-Barr virus and reduced levels of B lymphocytes—characteristics that are associated with reductions in immunity and increased vulnerability to mononucleosis (Kiecolt-Glaser, Speicher, Holliday, & Glaser, 1984). Loneliness is also linked to suicidal thoughts and suicide attempts (Van Orden et al., 2010).

Individuals who are members of social groups report less loneliness than individuals with few memberships. Weiss (1973) draws a distinction between social loneliness, which occurs when people lack ties to other people in general, and emotional loneliness—the absence of a meaningful, intimate relationship with another person. Open, transitory groups do little to prevent either social or emotional loneliness; but closed, highly engaging groups are sufficient to prevent social loneliness, and a group with many of the defining characteristics of a group (relationships, boundaries, interdependence, structure, cohesion, groupness) may meet members emotional as well as social needs. People who belong to more groups and organizations report less loneliness than those who keep to themselves, and this effect is stronger for groups with many interconnections among members (Kraus, Davis, Bazzini, Church, & Kirchman, 1993; Stokes, 1985) and highly cohesive ones (Anderson & Martin, 1995; Schmidt & Sermat, 1983).

Isolation and Rejection

Membership in a group promotes a range of positive social and psychological outcomes, but these benefits are not as positive as the effects of exclusion are negative. Voluntary isolation apparently has few negative consequences, but unintended, involuntary isolation is associated with emotional instability, insomnia, memory lapses, depression, fatigue, and general confusion (Suedfeld, 1997). Deliberate social exclusion, or ostracism, has particularly negative consequences, in part since the isolation from groups it produces is intentional rather than accidentally produced. When Williams (2007) asked people who had been ostracized to describe themselves, they used words such as "frustrated," "anxious," "nervous," and "lonely." They evidence physiological signs of stress, including elevated blood pressure and cortisol levels (a stress-related hormone), and brain-imaging research suggests that the pain of exclusion is neurologically similar to pain caused by physical injury (Eisenberger, Lieberman, & Williams, 2003; MacDonald & Leary, 2005).

Leary (1990) suggests that people are satisfied when a group takes them in but a group that actively seeks them out provides maximal inclusion. In contrast, individuals respond negatively when a group ignores or avoids them, but maximal exclusion—the group rejects, ostracizes, abandons, or banishes—is particularly punishing (Williams & Sommer, 1997). He and his colleagues found an association between ostracism and acts of violence, often aimed at those group members who were the rejectors (Leary, Kowalski, Smith, & Phillips, 2003).

Exclusion also influences self-esteem. Leary's sociometer model, for example, suggests that self-esteem is not based on private, personal appraisals of worth. Instead, Leary maintains that "self-esteem is part of a sociometer that monitors people's relational value in other people's eyes" (Leary, 2007, p. 328). Self-esteem drops when exclusion is likely and is designed to motivate individuals to identify the steps they should take to decrease the risk of social exclusion. In consequence, self-esteem rises when people feel included in groups and liked by others or when they think about a time when they were in a group that made them feel they belonged (Srivastava & Beer, 2005).

Groups and Social Support

When people find themselves in stressful, difficult circumstances, they often cope by forming or joining a group (Dooley & Catalano, 1984). In many cases support is drawn from dyadic relationships, such as a single close personal friend or intimate partner, but in other instances the support stems from membership in an informally organized friendship group or some other type of social aggregate. Hays and Oxley (1986), for example, found that college students cope with the stresses of entering college by forming extensive social networks of peers, which evolve into friendship clusters. Stressful life circumstances increase the risk of psychological and physical illness, but groups can serve as protective buffers against these negative consequences (Herbert & Cohen, 1993; Uchino, Cacioppo, & Kiecolt-Glaser, 1996; Wills, 1991). This buffering effect argues that individuals who are part of a group may not be able to avoid stressful life events but they respond more positively when these stressors befall them.

It should be noted, however, that the bulk of the research has focused on the effects of support from friends and loved ones rather than groups per se. Hence, until recently, it has not been possible to distinguish between support drawn from close relationships, such as dyadic relationships or a family member, and support drawn from friendship cliques, networks of acquaintances, or social groups such as clubs, sports teams, church groups, work units, or self-help associations. Overall, however, the evidence suggests that people who belong to groups are healthier than individuals who have few ties to other people (Stroebe, Stroebe, Abakoumkin, & Schut, 1996). Work by Stroebe and Stroebe (1996) and Sugisawa, Liang, and Liu (1994) even suggests that group members have longer lives.

Attitudes and Values

Cooley (1909) drew a broad distinction between two types of groups: primary groups and secondary groups (or complex groups). *Primary groups* are small, close-knit groups, such as families, friendship cliques, or neighbors. *Secondary groups* are larger and more formally organized than primary groups. Such groups—religious congregations, work groups, clubs, neighborhood associations, and the like— tend to be shorter in duration and less emotionally involving. Both of these types of groups provide members with their attitudes, values, and identities. Cooley maintained that groups teach members the skills they need to contribute to the group, provide them with the opportunity to discover and internalize the rules that govern social behavior, and let them practice modifying their behavior in response to social norms and others' requirements. Groups socialize individual members (Parsons, Bales, & Shils, 1953).

In most cases, when conflicts over opinions, choices, and lifestyle occur, they can be traced back to the socializing effects of groups. Norms in gangs encourage members to take aggressive actions against others. Adolescent peer cliques pressure members to take drugs and commit illegal acts. Fraternities insist that members engage in unhealthy practices, such as drinking excessive amounts of alcohol. Work groups develop such high standards for productivity that members experience unrelieved amounts of stress. Sororities may convince members to adopt habits with regard to dieting and exercise that trigger bulimia (Crandall, 1988). Some groups can adopt even more unusual standards, and members may come to accept them. Radical religious groups, for example, may be based on beliefs that nonmembers consider extraordinary but that members accept without question.

These emergent group norms are sustained by a common set of group-level informational, normative, and interpersonal processes (Forsyth, 1990). Informational influence occurs when the group provides members with information that they can use to make decisions and form opinions. People who join a group whose members accept bizarre ideas as true will, in time, explain things in that way as well. Normative influence occurs when individuals tailor their actions to fit the group's norms. Many people take such norms as "Bribery is wrong" and "Contribute your time and resources to the community" for granted, but some societies and some groups have different norms which are equally powerful and widely accepted. Normative influence accounts for the transmission of religious, economic, moral, political, and interpersonal attitudes, beliefs, and values across generations. Interpersonal influence is used in those rare instances when someone violates the group's norms. The individual who publicly violates a group's norm will likely meet with reproach or even be ostracized from the group. These three factors—informational, normative, and interpersonal influence—can be readily observed in groups as diverse as military units, street gangs, college fraternities, and religious denominations.

Identity

The self is often viewed as an aspect of personality—the outgrowth of private personal experiences and self-reflection. But the self is also shaped, in part, by group-level processes. Just as Freud (1922) believed that identification causes children to bond with and imitate their parents, identification with the group prompts members to bond with, and take on the characteristics of, their groups. The psychological experience of group membership is a central premise in social identity theory of groups and intergroup relations. Tajfel and Turner (1986) and their colleagues originally developed social identity theory in their studies of intergroup conflict. In their studies they created what they thought were the most minimal of groups, for their groups were temporary assemblies of completely unrelated people with no history, no future, and no real connection to one another. Yet, they discovered, even in these minimal conditions, that group members began to identify with their groups, even to the point of favoring their group and its members over other groups. The groups became, very quickly, psychologically real for members.

Social identity theory suggests the group becomes represented in each individual member, so their selves share some qualities in common (Turner et al., 1987). Brewer and her colleagues further divide the group-level side of the self into two components: the relational self and the collective self (Brewer, 2007; Brewer & Gardner, 1996; Brewer & Chen, 2007). The *relational self* is defined by ties to other people, particularly dyadic and reciprocal roles such as father–son and leader–follower, whereas the *collective self* is determined by membership in larger groups and categories if individuals consider these groups important and relevant to their self-concept. Individuals may, for example, come to define themselves as employees of the place where they work, as dedicated followers of a particular religious group, or as patriotic citizens of their nation.

People who identify with their groups experience a strong sense of belonging in their groups and take pride in their membership. They are more involved in the group's activities and willingly help the group meet its goals (Abrams, Hogg, Hinkle, & Often, 2005). But with the increased identification with the group comes the tendency to engage in self-stereotyping: the integration of stereotypes pertaining to the group in one's own self-descriptions (Biernat, Vescio, & Green, 1996). Social identity is also connected to feelings of self-worth. People who belong to prestigious groups tend to have higher self-esteem than those who belong to stigmatized groups (Brown & Lohr, 1987). However, as Crocker and Major (1989) noted in their seminal analysis of stigma, even membership in a socially denigrated group can sustain self-esteem. In many cases members of stigmatized groups and minority groups protect their personal appraisals of their groups from unfair negative stereotypes by rejecting the disparaging elements of their group's label. So long as individuals believe the groups they belong to are valuable, they will experience a heightened sense of personal self-esteem.

The identity-sustaining aspects of group memberships have a downside however. Membership in a group or social category may provide a social identity, but it can set in motion the tendency to derogate members of other groups. Group-based identities sow the seeds of conflict by creating a cognitive distinction between "us" and "them." According to Tajfel and Turner (1986, p. 13), the "mere perception of belonging to two distinct groups—that is, social categorization per se—is sufficient to trigger intergroup discrimination favoring the in group." Groups thus sustain individual members' self-esteem but at the cost of creating animosity toward those who belong to other groups.

Goal Attainment

Groups, in addition to yielding substantial psychological benefits for members, are the means by which most of the world's work is accomplished. Although the accomplishments of lone explorers are often highlighted by historians—Columbus, Marco Polo, Sir Edumund Hillary—these individuals were supported in their efforts by groups. Most inventions are not developed by single individuals working in isolation but by teams of collaborators. In some cases even great artists—such as the impressionists and da Vinci—produced their works as members of groups. A hundred years ago single craftspeople created commodities which were then sold to others, but in modern times most things are built by groups. Groups also make nearly all decisions—at least ones dealing with complex or consequential matters.

McGrath (1984) uses two dimensions (generate/negotiate and choose/execute) to generate an eight-category typology of group goals. *Generating groups* concoct strategies to be used to accomplish their goals (*planning tasks*) or to create altogether new ideas and approaches to problems (*creativity tasks*). *Choosing groups* make decisions about issues that have correct solutions (*intellective tasks*) or answer complex questions that defy simple solution (*decision-making tasks*). *Negotiating groups* must resolve differences of opinion among members regarding their goals or decisions (*cognitive conflict tasks*) or resolve competitive disputes among members (*mixed-motive tasks*). *Executing groups* do things, including competing against other groups (*contests/battles/competitive tasks*) or working together to create some product or carry out actions that require coordinated effort (*performances/psychomotor tasks*). McGrath's model thus distinguishes between conceptual-behavioral goals and purely collaborative goals—they require that group members work together to accomplish their goals—versus those that pit individuals and/or groups against each other.

Adopting the Group-level Perspective: Future Directions

Twentieth-century theorists, researchers, and practitioners made great strides in their quest to understand human behavior. They maintained that individuals are psychologically complex, that that their inner mental life can be described and examined systematically, and that issues of psychological adjustment and dysfunction are determined, in large part, by such psychological states and processes as needs, motivations, thoughts, personality, and perceptions. As Baars (1986, p. 412) concluded, "psychodynamic thought, broadly conceived, has probably provided the richest and most humanly relevant vein of psychological theorizing in the century." What is the next step that will be taken in the analysis of the human condition?

What Level of Analysis?

A multilevel approach recommends augmenting the individual-level perspective with other perspectives, including one that focuses squarely on groups and group processes. At the level of the individual, people's actions, thoughts, and emotions cannot be understood without taking into consideration the groups they belong to and the groups that surround them. Culturally, all kinds of societies—hunting/gathering, horticultural, pastoral, industrial, and postindustrial—are defined by the characteristics of the small groups that compose them. On a practical level, much of the world's work is done by groups, so enhanced understanding of their dynamics may mean they can be designed to be efficient. To improve productivity in a factory, problem solving in a boardroom, or learning in the classroom, one must understand groups.

What Discipline Will Take Responsibility for the Study of Groups?

A multilevel approach requires that researchers share the study of groups with researchers in a variety of scientific disciplines and professions. Groups are and will continue to be studied in psychology, sociology, communication studies, business, political science, economics, and anthropology; but in many cases researchers in these fields are not mindful of one another's work. By tradition, researchers tend to publish their findings in their own discipline's journals and to present their findings at conferences with colleagues from their own fields but only rarely explore connections between their work and the work being done in other disciplines. Since no one discipline can claim the study of groups as its rightful domain, future investigators should strive to adopt a multidisciplinary, as well as a multilevel, perspective on groups, and changes in communication across fields should facilitate that process.

Will Groups Continue to Be Influential?

Political scientist Robert Putnam (2000) wrote, in his whimsically titled book *Bowling Alone*, about the declining frequency of traditional groups. His analyses suggested that, since the 1960s, the number of groups and people's involvement in groups have steadily declined. He did not fully consider, however, changes in the nature of groups that have occurred recently. Interest in some types of groups—community groups, fraternal and professional organizations, or even church-based groups—has decreased, but other types of groups—book groups, support groups, teams at work, and so on—have taken their place. In fact, even though Putnam's book title suggests that people are bowling alone rather than in groups, bowling remains a popular social activity, for hardly anyone bowls alone. They now bowl with friends, coworkers, and family members. Given that the desire to join groups is likely woven into humans' genetic makeup, it is likely that groups—in one form or another—will continue to play a central role in human existence.

Will Group-Level Approaches Gain Momentum?

In 1950 Slavson predicted that group therapy would largely replace individual methods of treatment. In 1954 Bogardus predicted that researchers would soon develop extensive measures of group personality and that groupality would become as important a concept in group psychology as personality is in individual psychology. In 1974 Steiner predicted that the 1980s would see groups emerge as the centerpiece of social psychology.

These predictions have not been fully confirmed. Group approaches have proven themselves to be effective, but they are not the preferred mode of treatment for most therapists and clients (Durkin, 1999). Concepts like groupality and syntality have failed to generate theoretical unity or empirical interest. The surge of interest in groups predicted by Steiner did not occur, for groups are understudied relative to such topics as personality, social cognition, attitudes, and relationships (Wittenbaum & Moreland, 2008).

What does the future hold for the group-level approaches to understanding human adjustment and well-being? Although the course of science, because of its stress on discovery and innovation, is difficult to predict, the contents of this volume suggest that group-level approaches are garnering increased interest among theorists, researchers, and practitioners. Past theoretical, empirical, and applied work has built a sturdy foundation for the continued development of the study of groups. Interest in meso- and macro-level processes has increased steadily in recent years, suggesting that a purely individualistic orientation is giving way to a multilevel orientation. Therapeutic applications that utilize a group setting are becoming increasingly common, and empirical studies of their utility have documented their therapeutic effectiveness (Burlingame, MacKenzie, & Strauss, 2004). As theorists, researchers, and practitioners confirm the central importance of groups in people's lives, people will in time begin to think of themselves as group members first and individuals second (Forsyth, 2000).

References

Abrams, D., Hogg, M. A., Hinkle, S., & Often, S. (2005). The social identity perspective on small groups. In M. S. Poole & A. B. Hollingshead (Eds.), *Theories of small groups: Interdisciplinary perspectives* (pp. 99–137). Thousand Oaks, CA: Sage.

Adler, P. A., Kless, S. J., & Adler, P. (1992). Socialization to gender roles: Popularity among elementary school boys and girls. *Sociology of Education, 65*, 169–187.

Allport, F. H. (1924). *Social psychology*. Boston: Houghton Mifflin.

Anderson, C. M., & Martin, M. M. (1995). The effects of communication motives, interaction involvement, and loneliness on satisfaction: A model of small groups. *Small Group Research, 26*, 118–137.

Asch, S. E. (1957). An experimental investigation of group influence. In *Symposium on preventive and social psychiatry*. Washington, DC: US Government Printing Office.

Baars, B. J. (1986). *The cognitive revolution in psychology*. New York: Guilford.

Baumeister, R. F., & Leary, M. R. (1995). The need to belong: Desire for interpersonal attachments as a fundamental human motivation. *Psychological Bulletin, 117*, 497–529.

Benne, K. D., & Sheats, P. (1948). Functional roles of group members. *Journal of Social Issues, 4*, 41–49.

Biernat, M., Vescio, T. K., & Green, M. L. (1996). Selective self-stereotyping. *Journal of Personality and Social Psychology, 71*, 1194–1209.

Bogardus, E. S. (1954). Group behavior and groupality. *Sociology and Social Research, 38*, 401–403.

Brewer, M. B. (2007). The social psychology of intergroup relations: Social categorization, ingroup bias, and outgroup prejudice. In A. W. Kruglanski & E. T. Higgins (Eds.), *Social psychology: Handbook of basic principles* (2nd ed., pp. 695–715). New York: Guilford.

Brewer, M. B., & Chen, Y. (2007). Where (who) are collectives in collectivism? Toward conceptual clarification of individualism and collectivism. *Psychological Review, 114*, 133–151.

Brewer, M. B., & Gardner, W. (1996). Who is this "We"? Levels of collective identity and self representations. *Journal of Personality and Social Psychology, 71*, 83–93.

Brown, B. B., & Lohr, N. (1987). Peer group affiliation and adolescent self-esteem: An integration of ego-identity and symbolic-interaction theories. *Journal of Personality and Social Psychology, 52*, 47–55.

Brown, R. (2000). *Group processes: Dynamics within and between groups (2nd ed.)*. Malden, MA: Blackwell.

Burlingame, G. M., MacKenzie, K. R., & Strauss, B. (2004). Small group treatment: Evidence for effectiveness and mechanisms of change. In M. J. Lambert (Ed.), *Bergin & Garfield's handbook of psychotherapy and behavior change* (5th ed., pp. 647–696). New York: Wiley & Sons.

Campbell, D. T. (1958). Common fate, similarity, and other indices of the status of aggregates of persons as social entities. *Behavioral Science, 3*, 14–25.

Cartwright, D. (1968). The nature of group cohesiveness. In D. Cartwright & A. Zander (Eds.), *Group dynamics: Research and theory* (3rd ed., pp. 91–109). New York: Harper & Row.

Cartwright, D., & Zander, A. (Eds.). (1968). *Group dynamics: Research and theory* (3rd. ed.). New York: Harper & Row.

Castano, E., Yzerbyt, V., & Bourguignon, D. (2003). We are one and I like it: The impact of ingroup entitativity on ingroup identification. *European Journal of Social Psychology, 33*, 735–754.

Cattell, R. B. (1948). Concepts and methods in the measurement of group syntality. *Psychological Review, 55*, 48–63.

Coan, R. W. (1968). Dimensions of psychological theory. *American Psychologist, 23*, 715–722.

Cooley, C. H. (1909). *Social organization*. New York: Scribner.

Crandall, C. S. (1988). Social contagion of binge eating. *Journal of Personality and Social Psychology, 55*, 588–598.

Crawford, M. T., Sherman, S. J., & Hamilton, D. L. (2002). Perceived entitativity, stereotype formation, and the interchangeability of group members. *Journal of Personality and Social Psychology, 83,* 1076–1094.

Crocker, J., & Major, B. (1989). Social stigma and self-esteem: The self-protective properties of stigma. *Psychological Review, 96,* 608–630.

Darley, J. M. (1992). Social organization for the production of evil. *Psychological Inquiry, 3,* 199–218.

Dion, K. L. (2000). Group cohesion: From "field of forces" to multidimensional construct. *Group Dynamics: Theory, Research, and Practice, 4,* 7–26.

Dooley, D., & Catalano, R. (1984). The epidemiology of economic stress. *American Journal of Community Psychology, 12,* 387–409.

Dunbar, R. I. M. (2008). Cognitive constraints on the structure and dynamics of social networks. *Group Dynamics: Theory, Research, and Practice, 12,* 7–16.

Durkheim, É. (1966). *Suicide.* New York: Free Press. (Original work published 1897)

Durkheim, É. (1973). *Emile Durkheim on morality and society.* Chicago: University of Chicago Press. (Original work published 1900)

Durkin, J. N. (1999). Group psychotherapy's big problem, group psychotherapy's little secret. *Group Psychologist, 9*(1), 7–8.

Eisenberger, N. I., Lieberman, M. D., & Williams, K. D. (2003). Does rejection hurt? An fMRI study of social exclusion. *Science, 302,* 290–292.

Festinger, L. (1950). Informal social communication. *Psychological Review, 57,* 271–282.

Forsyth, D. R. (1990). The pecking order. In R. Brown (Ed.), *Human behavior: How groups work* (Vol. 15, pp. 1820–1827). New York: Marshall Cavendish.

Forsyth, D. R. (2000). The social psychology of groups and group psychotherapy: One view of the next century. *Group, 24,* 147–155.

Forsyth, D. R. (2010). *Group dynamics* (5th ed.). Belmont, CA: Cengage.

Forsyth, D. R., & Leary, M. R. (1991). Metatheoretical and epistemological issues. In C. R. Snyder & D. R. Forsyth (Eds.), *Handbook of social and clinical psychology: The health perspective* (pp. 757–773). New York: Pergamon.

Freud, S. (1922). *Group psychology and the analysis of the ego* (J. Strachey, Trans.). London: Hogarth Press and the Institute of Psycho-Analysis.

Gilbert, D. T. (1998). Ordinary personology. In D. T. Gilbert, S. T. Fiske, & G. Lindzey (Eds.), *The handbook of social psychology* (4th ed., Vol. 1, pp. 89–150). New York: McGraw-Hill.

Harris, J. R. (1995). Where is the child's environment? A group socialization theory of development. *Psychological Review, 102,* 458–489.

Haslam, N., Rothschild, L., & Ernst, D. (2002). Are essentialist beliefs associated with prejudice? *British Journal of Social Psychology, 41,* 87–100.

Hays, R. B., & Oxley, D. (1986). Social network development and functioning during a life transition. *Journal of Personality and Social Psychology, 50,* 304–313.

Herbert, T. B., & Cohen, S. (1993). Stress and immunity in humans: A meta-analytic review. *Psychosomatic Medicine, 55,* 364–379.

Hogg, M. A. (1992). *The social psychology of group cohesiveness: From attraction to social identity.* New York: New York University Press.

Hogg, M. A., Sherman, D. K., Dierselhuis, J., Maitner, A. T., & Moffitt, G. (2007). Uncertainty, entitativity, and group identification. *Journal of Experimental Social Psychology, 43,* 135–142.

Hojat, M., & Vogel, W. H. (1987). Socioemotional bonding and neurobiochemistry. *Journal of Social Behavior & Personality, 2,* 135–144.

Joiner, T. E., Jr., Brown, J. S., & Wingate, L. R. (2005). The psychology and neurobiology of suicidal behavior. *Annual Review of Psychology, 56,* 287–314.

Jones, W. H., & Carver, M. D. (1991). Adjustment and coping implications of loneliness. In C. R. Snyder & D. R. Forsyth (Eds.), *Handbook of social and clinical psychology: The health perspective* (pp. 395–415). New York: Pergamon.

Kelly, J. R. (2004). Mood and emotion in groups. In M. B. Brewer & M. Hewstone (Eds.), *Emotion and motivation* (pp. 95–112). Malden, MA: Blackwell.

Kerr, N. L., & Tindale, R. S. (2004). Group performance and decision making. *Annual Review of Psychology, 55,* 623–655.

Kiecolt-Glaser, J. K., Speicher, C. E., Holliday, J. E., & Glaser, R. (1984). Stress and the transformation of lymphocytes by Epstein-Barr virus. *Journal of Behavioral Medicine, 7,* 1–12.

Kraus, L. A., Davis, M. H., Bazzini, D. G., Church, M., & Kirchman, C. M. (1993). Personal and social influences on loneliness: The mediating effect of social provisions. *Social Psychology Quarterly, 56,* 37–53.

Kushner, H. I., & Sterk, C. E. (2005). The limits of social capital: Durkheim, suicide, and social cohesion. *American Journal of Public Health, 95,* 1139–1143.

Leary, M. R. (1990). Responses to social exclusion: Social anxiety, jealousy, loneliness, depression, and low self-esteem. *Journal of Social & Clinical Psychology, 9,* 221–229.

Leary, M. R. (2007). Motivational and emotional aspects of the self. *Annual Review of Psychology, 58,* 317–344.

Leary, M. R., Kowalski, R. M., Smith, L., & Phillips, S. (2003). Teasing, rejection, and violence: Case studies of the school shootings. *Aggressive Behavior, 29,* 202–214.

Le Bon, G. (1960). *The crowd: A study of the popular mind.* New York: Viking Press. (Original work published 1895)

Lee, R. M., & Robbins, S. B. (1995). Measuring belongingness: The social connectedness and the social assurance scales. *Journal of Counseling Psychology, 42,* 232–241.

Lewin, K. (1948). *Resolving social conflicts: Selected papers on group dynamics.* New York: Harper.

Lewin, K. (1951). *Field theory in social science.* New York: Harper.

Lowry, P. B., Roberts, T. L., Romano, N. C., Jr., Cheney, P. D., & Hightower, R. T. (2006). The impact of group size and social presence on small-group communication: Does computer-mediated communication make a difference? *Small Group Research, 37,* 631–661.

MacDonald, G., & Leary, M. R. (2005). Why does social exclusion hurt? The relationship between social and physical pain. *Psychological Bulletin, 131,* 202–223.

McDougall, W. (1908). *An introduction to social psychology.* London: Methuen.

McGrath, J. E. (1984). *Groups: Interaction and performance.* Upper Saddle River, NJ: Prentice Hall.

Moreland, R. L., & Levine, J. M. (1982). Socialization in small groups: Temporal changes in individual–group relations. *Advances in Experimental Social Psychology, 15,* 137–192.

Moreno, J. L. (1934). *Who shall survive? A new approach to the problem of human interrelations.* Washington, DC: Nervous and Mental Disease Publishing.

Newcomb, T. M. (1943). *Personality and social change*. New York: Dryden.

Nolan, J. M., Schultz, P. W., Cialdini, R. B., Goldstein, N. J., & Griskevicius, V. (2008). Normative social influence is underdetected. *Personality and Social Psychology Bulletin, 34*, 913–923.

Norman, W. T. (1963). Toward an adequate taxonomy of personality attributes: Replicated factor structure in peer nomination personality ratings. *Journal of Abnormal and Social Psychology, 66*, 574–583.

Parsons, T., Bales, R. F., & Shils, E. (Eds.). (1953). *Working papers in the theory of action*. New York: Free Press.

Pepitone, A. (1981). Lessons from the history of social psychology. *American Psychologist, 36*, 972–985.

Pickett, C. L. (2001). The effect of entitativity beliefs o n implicit comparisons between group members. *Personality and Social Psychology Bulletin, 27*, 515–525.

Putnam, R. D. (2000). *Bowling alone: The collapse and revival of American community*. New York: Simon & Schuster.

Rosenberg, S., & Gara, M. A. (1983). Contemporary perspectives and future directions of personality and social psychology. *Journal of Personality and Social Psychology, 45*, 57–73.

Ross, L. (1977). The intuitive psychologist and his shortcomings: Distortions in the attribution process. *Advances in Experimental Social Psychology, 10*, 173–220.

Rydell, R. J., Hugenberg, K., Ray, D., & Mackie, D. M. (2007). Implicit theories about groups and stereotyping: The role of group entitativity. *Personality and Social Psychology Bulletin, 33*, 549–558.

Sandelands, L., & St. Clair, L. (1993). Toward an empirical concept of group. *Journal for the Theory of Social Behavior, 23*, 423–458.

Sani, F., Bowe, M., & Herrera, M. (2008). Perceived collective continuity and social well-being: Exploring the connections. *European Journal of Social Psychology, 38*, 365–374.

Sarason, S. B. (1981). An asocial psychology and a misdirected clinical psychology. *American Psychologist, 36*, 827–836.

Schachter, S., & Singer, J. (1962). Cognitive, social, and physiological determinants of emotional state. *Psychological Review, 69*, 379–399.

Schmidt, N., & Sermat, V. (1983). Measuring loneliness in different relationships. *Journal of Personality and Social Psychology, 44*, 1038–1047.

Shaw, M. E. (1981). *Group dynamics: The psychology of small group behavior* (3rd ed.). New York: McGraw-Hill.

Sherif, M. (1936). *The psychology of social norms*. New York: Harper & Row.

Sherif, M., & Sherif, C. W. (1956). *An outline of social psychology* (rev. ed.). New York: Harper & Row.

Slavson, S. R. (1950). Group psychotherapy. *Scientific American, 183*, 42–45.

Smith, E. R., Seger, C. R., & Mackie, D. M. (2007). Can emotions be truly group level? Evidence regarding four conceptual criteria. *Journal of Personality and Social Psychology, 93*, 431–446.

Srivastava, S., & Beer, J. S. (2005). How self-evaluations relate to being liked by others: Integrating sociometer and attachment perspectives. *Journal of Personality and Social Psychology, 89*, 966–977.

Steiner, I. D. (1974). Whatever happened to the group in social psychology? *Journal of Experimental Social Psychology, 10*, 94–108.

Stokes, J. P. (1985). The relation of social network and individual difference variables to loneliness. *Journal of Personality and Social Psychology, 48*, 981–990.

Stroebe, W., & Stroebe, M. (1996). The social psychology of social support. In E. T. Higgins & A. W. Kruglanski (Eds.), *Social psychology: Handbook of basic principles* (pp. 597–621). New York: Guilford Press.

Stroebe, W., Stroebe, M. S., Abakoumkin, G., & Schut, H. (1996). The role of loneliness and social support in adjustment to loss: A test of attachment versus stress theory. *Journal of Personality and Social Psychology, 70*, 1241–1249.

Suedfeld, P. (1997). The social psychology of "invictus": Conceptual and methodological approaches to indomitability. In C. McGarty & S. A. Haslam (Eds.), *The message of social psychology: Perspectives on mind in society* (pp. 329–341). Malden, MA: Blackwell.

Sugisawa, H., Liang, J., & Liu, X. (1994). Social networks, social support, and mortality among older people in Japan. *Journals of Gerontology, 49*, S3–S13.

Tajfel, H., & Turner, J. C. (1986). The social identity theory of intergroup behavior. In S. Worchel & W. G. Austin (Eds.), *Psychology of intergroup relations* (2nd ed., pp. 7–24). Chicago: Nelson-Hall.

Thibaut, J. W., & Kelley, H. H. (1959). *The social psychology of groups*. New York: Wiley.

Triandis, H. C., McCusker, C., & Hui, C. H. (1990). Multimethod probes of individualism and collectivism. *Journal of Personality and Social Psychology, 59*, 1006–1013.

Triandis, H. C., & Suh, E. M. (2002). Cultural influences on personality. *Annual Review of Psychology, 53*, 133–160.

Turner, J. C., Hogg, M. A., Oakes, P. J., Reicher, S. D., & Wetherell, M. S. (1987). *Rediscovering the social group: A self-categorization theory*. Cambridge, MA: Basil Blackwell.

Uchino, B. N., Cacioppo, J. T., & Kiecolt-Glaser, J. K. (1996). The relationship between social support and physiological processes: A review with emphasis on underlying mechanisms and implications for health. *Psychological Bulletin, 119*, 488–531.

Urban, H. B. (1983). Phenomenological humanistic approaches. In M. Hersen, A. E. Kazdin, & A. S. Bellack (Eds.), *The clinical psychology handbook* (pp. 155–175). New York: Pergamon.

Van Orden, K. A., Witte, T. K., Cukrowicz, K. C., Braithwaite, S. R., Selby, E. A., & Joiner, T. E., Jr. (2010). The interpersonal theory of suicide. *Psychological Review, 117*, 575–600.

Watson, R. I. (1967). Psychology: A prescriptive science. *American Psychologist, 22*, 435–443.

Weiss, R. S. (1973). *Loneliness: The experience of emotional and social isolation*. Cambridge, MA: MIT Press.

Wildschut, T., Pinter, B., Vevea, J. L., Insko, C. A., & Schopler, J. (2003). Beyond the group mind: A quantitative review of the interindividual–intergroup discontinuity effect. *Psychological Bulletin, 129*, 698–722.

Williams, K. D. (2007). Ostracism. *Annual Review of Psychology, 58*, 425–452.

Williams, K. D., & Sommer, K. L. (1997). Social ostracism by coworkers: Does rejection lead to loafing or compensation? *Personality and Social Psychology Bulletin, 23*, 693–706.

Wills, T. A. (1991). Social comparison processes in coping and health. In C. R. Snyder & D. R. Forsyth (Eds.), *Handbook of social and clinical psychology: The health perspective* (pp. 376–394). Elmsford, NY: Pergamon.

Wittenbaum, G. M., & Moreland, R. L. (2008). Small group research in social psychology: Topics and trends over time. *Social and Personality Psychology Compass, 2,* 187–203.

Yzerbyt, V., Judd, C. M., & Corneille, O. (Eds.). (2004). *The psychology of group perception: Perceived variability, entitativity, and essentialism.* New York: Psychology Press.

Zander, A., Stotland, E., & Wolfe, D. (1960). Unity of group, identification with group, and self-esteem of members. *Journal of Personality, 28,* 463–478.

Ziller, R. C. (1965). Toward a theory of open and closed groups. *Psychological Bulletin, 64,* 164–182.

Zyphur, M. J., & Islam, G. (2006). *Toward understanding the existence of groups: The relationship between climate strength and entitativity* (IBMEC Working Paper WPE–12–2006). Retrieved December 15, 2008, from http://www.ibmecsp.edu.br/

Definition of Group Counseling

Donald E. Ward

Abstract

Because professional group work has such varied origins, agreement upon a single, concise definition of group counseling has been difficult to achieve. An abbreviated review of the literature highlighting the origins of modern group work is presented. Definitions provided by various professional organizations of group workers are presented. Systems describing group work are presented, emphasizing the Association for Specialists in Group Work's model of four types: work and task groups, psychoeducation groups, counseling groups, and psychotherapy groups. A consensus definition is extracted from these sources, and future directions are identified.

Keywords: group counseling, group work, classification of group work, group types

Introduction

Humans are a social species. We need others, we want to be with them, and our relational connections are a major aspect of who we are. Forsyth clearly expressed the importance of social interaction when he stated that "The tendency to join with others in groups is perhaps the single most important characteristic of humans, and the processes that unfold within these groups leave an indelible imprint on their members and on society" (Forsyth, 2010, p. 1). In fact, one of the most surprising aspects of the technological revolution of the last three decades is that, far from the expected consequence of driving people further and further away from one another into isolated, self-absorbed beings, it sometimes appears that humans find it even more important to be in almost constant contact with others, if not in face-to-face communication, then through electronic means such as cell phone conversations, texting, e-mailing, blogging, and social networking in its myriad and rapidly expanding electronic formats.

The early years of the modern, systematic study of and psychological applications to human functioning were dominated by behavioral paradigms in experimental and academic study and by the powerful influence of the Freudian psychoanalytic perspective in treatment. These major influences emphasized the individual to such an extent that group work in mental health services settings was generally seen as a very weak, palliative method, appropriate only for supportive or minor educational applications to human problems characterized by psychological pain and distress. Although this emphasis upon the individual may have been necessary to begin the systematic investigation and treatment of human beings given the enormous complexity of the task, it impeded efforts to investigate and apply knowledge of the interpersonal nature of human beings in models for helping people increase their understanding of themselves and overcome psychological problems.

Despite these impediments, group counseling has developed and evolved into a major method of working with people to help them to learn and change. Jerry Corey, one of the current major authors in the area of group counseling, states that "Group counseling offers real promise in meeting today's challenges (2008, p. 3)." Considered one of the leading experts on group therapy, Irvin Yalom has stated that "Group therapy methods have proved to be so useful in so many different clinical settings that it is no longer correct to speak of group therapy. Instead, we must refer to "*group therapies*" (Yalom, 2005, p. 475, italics retained). Conyne (2012) suggests that group work is currently in an "age of ubiquity," with rapidly increasing applications in many heretofore unimagined settings. He goes on to say,

> The use of group work approaches, in general, has grown exponentially over the last two decades, finding application in the major settings of society. These settings include education, private practice, religious organizations, social service agencies, planning boards, health care organizations, mental health care agencies, and business and industry. At the same time, successful incorporation within managed care occurs but awaits more progress. (Conyne, 2012, p. 3)

The growing use of group work has led to evidence of the effectiveness of the group medium. In fact, Barlow, Burlingame, and Fuhriman (2000) summarized the evidence in the following manner:

> With few exceptions (cf. Piper & McCallum, 1991), the general conclusion to be drawn from approximately 730 studies that span almost three decades is that the group format consistently produced positive effects with a number of disorders using a variety of treatment models. (p. 122)

Since it has become evident that group work has earned a major position in counseling and mental health, it would seem that the fundamental nature of group counseling ought to be clear and easily definable. However, this is far from the case. Some of the reasons for the complexity and lack of consensus may be inferred from an abbreviated review of the literature highlighting the myriad origins of modern group work theory and practice.

Historical Influences

A number of detailed historical reviews of the development of group work are available, including Andronico (2001); Barlow et al. (2000); Barlow, Fuhriman, and Burlingame (2004, 2005); Bertcher (1985); Burlingame, Fuhriman, and Mosier (2003); Burlingame, Fuhriman, and Johnson (2004a, 2004b); Gazda (1982, 1985); Gazda, Ginter, and Horne (2001); Forester-Miller (1998); Gladding (2002); Hadden (1955); Leddick (2008); and Scheidlinger and Schmess (1992). However, a brief description highlighting major

people and events will demonstrate the multiple origins of various approaches to modern group work. This diversity has both enriched and complicated group work to the extent that defining group counseling is a challenging and, some would suggest, impossible task.

Joseph Pratt's work with patients suffering from tuberculosis in 1905 is generally accepted as the origin of modern group work (Gazda et al., 2001; Hadden, 1955). Two years later Jesse B. Davis held weekly group meetings at a high school to initiate the use of guidance groups in schools (Gazda et al., 2001). Shortly thereafter, Jane Addams introduced deliberate group process work as part of social work programming at Hull House in Chicago. By the second and third decades of the twentieth century, Alfred Adler was using collective counseling and family councils as group applications of his individual psychology and Jacob Moreno had created psychodrama, all innovative approaches to helping people at the time.

Following these seminal efforts to infuse group methods into such diverse settings as psychological support of patients with medical problems, students in schools, and individuals and families needing assistance from social workers, the deliberate lack of attention to the importance of interpersonal relationships that had characterized formal counseling and mental health treatment heretofore began to be reversed during the second quarter of the twentieth century. Trigant Burrow developed group analysis in the late 1920s, a major deviation from the highly introspective and intrapsychic Freudian psychoanalytic model predominant at the time. By 1931, group work in the schools had developed to such an extent that Richard Allen published an article describing a curriculum for group guidance in high schools, referring to this guidance method as "group counseling" (Gazda, 1982). A very influential new group approach was initiated by Bill Wilson and Dr. Bob Smith in 1935 in the form of the first formal self-help group in the United States, Alcoholics Anonymous (AA) (Alcoholics Anonymous, 1981). The American Association for the Study of Group Work was formed in 1936. Samuel Slavson established the American Group Psychotherapy Association (AGPA) in 1943. AGPA's influential journal, the *International Journal of Group Psychotherapy*, was established in 1951.

Lewin's work in the area of social psychology and action research moved specifically into the study of group leadership and other group dynamic factors in the 1930s and 1940s (e.g., Lewin, 1944; Lewin, Lippitt, & White, 1939). His emphasis upon the fundamental social nature of human beings stimulated dramatically increased development and use of group methods over the last half-century to facilitate self-exploration, learning, growth, problem solving, remediation, and improved functioning. In fact, a major impetus to this increased emphasis upon the importance of interpersonal relationships and group interaction patterns was the discovery and development of basic skills training groups, or T-groups, in New Britain, Connecticut, and the establishment of the National Training Laboratories at Bethel, Maine, in 1946 by Lewin, Bradford, and Benne. Following Lewin's unexpected death less than a year later, this method of working in groups of normally functioning people to facilitate self-exploration and personal growth through interpersonal learning grew in many directions and was a major influence, leading to the incorporation of interpersonal and group-level theory and interventions in counseling and mental health applications and, therefore, to the prominent role that group work plays in mental health treatment today. That Lewin's work was so influential in the development of modern group work is especially appropriate since one of his fundamental principles was his "law" of change in groups: "It is usually easier to change individuals formed into a group than to change any one of them." (Lewin, 1951, cited in Forsyth, 2006, p. 525).

The emerging T-group movement in all of its manifestations (i.e., sensitivity training, encounter groups, personal growth groups, etc.) stimulated scholarly inquiry and the publication of a number of articles and books describing aspects of the T-group process. Wilfred Bion identified and applied group-level processes such as group cohesiveness, dependency, and fight–flight mechanisms in working with groups in England at the Tavistock Institute following its establishment in 1946 (Gazda, 1968). Bales (1950) and Benne and Sheats (1948) studied consistent patterns of behavior as members learn to work together in groups and independently published very similar summaries of their finding of common member roles that develop as a group progresses. Cartwright and Zander (1953) and Hare, Borgatta, and Bales (1955) published influential books describing research related to social psychology and groups. Helen Driver then published what is considered to be the first textbook on group work, *Counseling and Learning through Small-Group Discussion*, in 1958.

Further important publications followed throughout the 1960s, and a number of prominent counseling and psychotherapy theorist-practitioners described their incorporation of group methods and interventions into their theoretical models. Leland Bradford, Jack Gibb, and Kenneth Benne wrote *T-Group Theory and Laboratory Method: Innovation in Re-education* in 1964, and Robert Golembiewski and Arthur Blumberg edited *Sensitivity Training and the Laboratory Approach: Reading about Concepts and Applications* in 1970 (see Golembiewski & Blumberg, 1977). William Fawcett Hill and Will Schutz created and published sophisticated models for describing, categorizing, and measuring interpersonal styles and group-level processes in the *HIM: Hill Interaction Matrix* (Hill, 1965) and the Fundamental Interpersonal Relations Orientation-Behavior Scale (FIRO-B), respectively. Hill's book *Learning through Discussion* described his model (1969). Schutz described his model in his book *FIRO: A Three-Dimensional Theory of Interpersonal Behavior* (1958), and he later went on to publish popular books in the human potential movement, especially *Joy: Expanding Human Awareness* (1967). Variations of the T-group gained great popularity in a variety of settings as part of the human potential movement with little regard for the appropriateness of the specific group for specific members. Counselor education training programs began to include a course in group work, often entirely experiential in nature, into their master's degree curricula.

By the 1960s and into the 1970s, a number of prominent counseling and psychotherapy theorists and practitioners had incorporated group work into their work, such as Rogers (1970), Berne (1970), Perls (Corey, 2008), and Ellis (Corey, 2008). Rogers' work with groups was firmly in the T-group and human potential movement tradition in the form of his basic encounter groups and would now be understood to be most suitable for helping humans functioning in the normal range to explore and expand their self-awareness. On the other hand, these other major theorists applied their original theories of counseling and psychotherapy in psychologically oriented treatment groups, incorporating interpersonal and group-level processes to varying extents (see Ward, 1982, for a more complete analysis of these theories and group processes).

From the mid-1960s through the early 1970s, a number of articles and books were published that strongly stimulated theoretical understanding of group dynamics and processes and the application of the knowledge gleaned from the earlier studies to group treatment. Bruce Tuckman conducted a literature review of models of group development (1965) and summarized his findings by identifying four major stages of group development, which he labeled "forming," "storming," "norming," and "performing." His follow-up summary of the literature on group development over the next 12 years (Tuckman and Jensen, 1977) supported the original four stages but added a fifth stage, which he labeled as "mourning or adjourning." Although variations of the five-stage model have been described, most can be reformatted into the five-stage model, and Tuckman's work has been one of the seminal influences in moving group-treatment models to more than simply individual treatment in a group setting. Lieberman, Yalom, and Miles's *Encounter Groups: First Facts* (1973) identified four foundational group-leadership functions, and a number of styles that their empirical investigation had demonstrated were related more directly to outcome than the leaders' self-identified counseling theoretical style. Another seminal set of publications systematically described the conceptualization and application of three levels of potential group activity: the individual or intrapsychic, the interpersonal or relationship, and the group-as-a-whole level (Cohen & Smith, 1976a, 1976b). Their model for application included two other dimensions, the target modality at which a leader intervention is directed, consisting of cognitive, affective, and behavioral elements, and high, medium, or low intensity of the target of leader intervention. The entire model consisted of a 27-cell cube for the conceptualization and choice of interventions aimed at specific aspects of member, member–member, and group-level activity.

In 1970, Yalom published the first of five editions of his influential text *Theory and Practice of Group Psychotherapy* (see Yalom, 1970, 1975, 1985, 1995, 2005). His extensive description of an interpersonally based, process-oriented approach to group therapy has been extremely influential and enduring, influencing group treatment for four decades. Particularly seminal was his list of 11 curative factors, later renamed "therapeutic factors" (Yalom, 2005), most responsible for positive outcome in group therapy, which he identified through his clinical experience, expert consensus, and major research investigations of therapy groups. A number of additional textbooks were published during these years that provided the beginnings of a conceptual foundation to add to the primarily experiential T-group model that had stimulated the rapid growth of group work and the

study of group dynamics for two decades (e.g., Luft, 1963; Gazda, 1968, 1971; Napier & Gershenfeld, 1973: Ohlsen, 1973, 1977; Shaffer & Galinsky, 1974; Hansen, Warner, & Smith, 1976, 1980). Gerald and Marianne Corey published the first of two of their textbooks specifically directed toward group counseling (Corey, 1981; Corey & Corey, 1977) that have proven to be widely used through eight editions. Their books may be viewed as representing the beginnings of the plethora of textbooks that are now available on the topic of group work in its various manifestations (e.g., Berg, Landreth, & Fall, 2006; Bernard & MacKenzie, 1994; Bieling, McCabe, & Antony, 2006; Brabender, 2002; Brabender & Fallon, 2009; Brabender, Fallon, & Smolar 2004; Brown, 2009; Capuzzi, Gross, & Stauffer, 2006; Chen & Rybak, 2004; Conyne, 1989; Conyne, Crowell, & Newmeyer, 2008; Corey, 2008; Corey, Corey, Callanan, & Russell, 2004; Corey, Corey, & Corey, 2010; Day, 2007; DeLucia-Waack, 2006; Drossel, 2008; Gazda, 1982; Gazda et al., 2001; Gladding, 2008; Hulse-Killacky, Killacky, & Donigian, 2001; Ivey, Pedersen, & Ivey, 2001; Jacobs, Massen, & Harvill, 2009; Kline, 2002; Kottler, 2001; Macgowan, 2008; MacKenzie, 1992; Ohlsen, Horne, & Lawe, 1988; Posthuma, 1999; Rutan, Stone, & Shay, 2007; Toseland & Rivas, 2001; Trotzer, 2006; Wheelan, 2005a, 2005b).

The experimentation with various interpretations of group work and group methods provided so much new information that a number of scholars attempted to organize the current knowledge base by joining together to publish useful handbooks and focused literature reviews. Among the most prominent have been those edited by Altmaier and Hansen (2012); Anderson and Wheelan (2005); Barlow et al. (2004, 2005); Bednar and Kaul (1978); Burlingame and Fuhriman (1994); Burlingame et al. (2004a, 2004b), DeLucia-Waack, Gerrity, Kalodner, and Riva (2004); Fuhriman and Burlingame (2004); Kaplan and Sadock (1993); Lubin, Wilson, Petren, and Polk (1996); Moreno (1966); Petrocelli (2002); and Wheelan (2005a, 2005b).

Perhaps most significant over the last 25 years of the twentieth century in the emerging descriptions and definitions of group work in general and group counseling in particular were the founding and subsequent activities of professional organizations devoted to group work, such as the Association for Specialists in Group Work (ASGW), a division of the American Counseling Association (ACA, then known as the American Personnel and Guidance

Association). Its journal was first published as *Together* in 1976, with a name change to the *Journal for Specialists in Group Work* in 1978. In that same year, *Social Work in Groups* was founded. Group Psychology and Group Psychotherapy was founded in 1991 as Division 49 of the American Psychological Association (APA), and its journal was founded as *Group Dynamics: Theory, Research, and Practice* in 1997. Most significantly, the ASGW has produced and revised a number of documents describing various aspects of group work, including ethical guidelines, best-practices guidelines, best practices with diversity guidelines, and, perhaps most important, *Professional Standards for the Training of Group Workers* (see ASGW, 2000). The most recent versions of these standards may be accessed at the ASGW Web site (asgw.org). In the training standards, a model of four types of group work is described: work/task groups, psychoeducation groups, counseling groups, and therapy groups. The rationale for revision of the standards was described by Conyne et al. (1992). These definitions and the knowledge and skills recommended for working with each of the group types have stimulated a good deal of analysis and debate (e.g., Bauman & Waldo, 1998; Betz, 1973; Conyne & Wilson, 1998; Gerrity, 1998; Keel, 1998; MacNair-Semands, 1998; Taub, 1998; Ward, 1998, 2006a, 2006b; Wilbur, Roberts-Wilbur, & Betz, 1981). AGPA has actively advocated for and supported the application of group work in a variety of settings. The organization's Web site (http://www.agpa.org/group/consumersguide2000.html) provides access to an extensive and impressive array of informational documents for professionals and the public. These include a five-page document primarily directed toward the lay public interested in seeking group treatment that describes the AGPA view of group therapy in some detail (American Group Psychotherapy Association, n.d.). The organization has also posted an extensive document entitled *Practical Guidelines for Group Psychotherapy* (2007).

Definitions

It should not be surprising that, with the multiplicity of approaches to group work and resources describing and guiding group practice that are available, defining group counseling clearly in a way that professionals and the lay public find meaningful and useful is difficult and challenging. As long ago as 1980, ASGW president Allan Dye identified the difficulty in defining group work:

A stroll through the ASGW archives wherein are stored the records of the association's activities—meetings, conferences, workshops, journals, and newsletters—would clearly reflect a preoccupation with practical rather than theoretical matters. We are interested in the everyday, moment-to-moment stuff of which group work consists. Specifically, we have directed our energies to methods and techniques and our activities have consisted primarily of description and demonstration. This is as it should be, for there is a clear consensus among us regarding this first priority. Assuming their journals are valid indicators of current thinking and practice, other professional organizations devoted to group work are similarly disposed. By inference, the conclusion is that group work, broadly described, has not yet achieved accurate definition as a form of applied behavioral science. This may be the case for a long time. Further, there seems to be little evidence in the literature of any sense of urgency because of this circumstance. Those who are exhilarated by the experience of traveling spend little time in either selecting destinations or tallying mileage. Nevertheless, great progress has been made and the technology of group work has advanced significantly during the past few years.

The fundamental emphasis on identifying and promulgating methods, techniques, and programs will be retained as the cornerstone of ASGW. (p. 52)

Conyne describes this challenge to a clear, consensual definition in the following way:

Defining group counseling has proven to be an elusive and, some would claim, frustrating task. Perhaps this situation should be expected. After all, group counseling has emerged over decades from a number of different academic disciplines, traditions, professions, and organizations. (Conyne, 2012)

Burlingame, MacKenzie, and Strauss (2004) identified similar challenges when they attempted to define group psychotherapy: "Beginning group therapists face several challenges as they attempt to master the group psychotherapy literature. The first is a definitional conundrum. Extremely divergent models of treatment find their home under the rubric of group psychotherapy" (p. 647).

The task is further exacerbated by the lack of a commonly accepted definition of the term *counseling* itself. Kottler and Shephard (2008) describe the difficulty in defining counseling in the following manner:

Counseling is indeed an ambiguous enterprise. It is done by persons who can't agree on what to call themselves, what credentials are necessary for the practice of counseling, or even what the best way to practice *is*. They debate whether counseling should deal with feelings, thought, or behaviors; whether it should be primarily supportive or confrontational; whether it should focus on the past or the present. Further, the consumers of counseling services often can't exactly articulate what their concerns are, what counseling can and can't do for them or what they want when it's over. (pp. 16–17)

In 1997, the Governing Council of the ACA adopted the following definition of the practice of professional counseling: "The application of mental health, psychological, or human development principles, through cognitive, affective, behavioral or systematic intervention strategies, that address wellness, personal growth, or career development, as well as pathology" (American Counseling Association, 1997). This definition is useful, although somewhat awkward, and Kaplan recently stated that the seven committees of the 20/20: A Vision for the Future of Counseling initiative are currently working to "compose a short definition of counseling that both professionals and the public can remember and use in defining the profession" (Kaplan, personal communication, August 4, 2009). The working definitions developed by the seven committees, which are currently the focus of Delphi polling procedures to extract a single definition, are quite disparate and reflect the challenges and differences in trying to meet the ultimate goal of agreement upon a unified definition of professional counseling.

In light of these challenges and the complexity of the task, an organizational system is needed to present definitions offered by scholars in a meaningful manner. Conyne provided such a system, describing three ways in which group counseling can be conceptualized: as undifferentiated from other types of groups, including group counseling as an independent type within a broader range of group work types, or as a process that overlaps on a continuum with therapeutic and educational goals and processes (Conyne, 2012).

Examples of the way in which group-work scholars have described group counseling and suggestions for summarizing its major elements and clarifying the process will be provided. Their definitions vary among Conyne's three ways of conceptualizing group work in general and group counseling specifically and as it compares to other types of group work.

Undifferentiated or Partially Undifferentiated

Pratt's work with a group of hospitalized individuals in 1905 is generally considered the beginning of deliberate treatment in groups, although he called the group a "class" (Pratt, 1922). In this seminal effort to provide a systematic group-treatment experience, he did not concern himself with differentiating this group from other possible group applications. His description of the group included member–member interpersonal interaction and group support. He described his reasons for establishing the group in the following manner:

I originally brought the patients together as a group with the idea that it would save my time, that of my associates and of the social worker. It was planned as a labor saving device. I did not have the time to instruct or encourage the patients individually. Advice, encouragement or admonition given to one I hoped would be heeded by all. (Pratt, 1922, p. 403).

Gazda et al. (2001, p. 29) quoted Sullivan's early general definition of group work:

The group must be a small stable one which feels itself as an entity and which the individual can feel close identification. Membership . . . is voluntary. There is a group leader, who is consciously making constructive use of the process of personality interaction among the members. The leader utilizes the desire of a normal person to be accepted by his fellows. He establishes the dignity of the individual and teaches acceptance of differences in race, creed, and nationality. Group work stresses programs evolved by the group itself, in consultation with the leader who guides toward socially desirable ends. Creative activities are encouraged to provide legitimate channels of self-expressions and to relieve emotional stress. . . . The atmosphere is friendly, informal, and democratic. (Sullivan, 1952, p. 189)

Group work as an undifferentiated process also seems to characterize some aspects of Corsini's descriptions of group psychotherapy as "a conglomerate of methods and theories having diverse multiple origins in the past, resulting inevitably from social demands, and developed in various forms by many persons" (1957, p. 9) and one that "consists of processes occurring in formally organized, protected groups, and calculated to attain rapid ameliorations in personality and behavior of individuals through specified and controlled group interactions" (1957, p. 5).

An undifferentiated interpretation of counseling and psychotherapy is common. For example, Austad stated that, "Today there is little distinction made between the two . . . the terms *counseling* and *therapy* are used interchangeably—both are activities that help clients or patients (also interchangeable terms) achieve psychological change" (2009, p. 2).

Many authors have recognized various perspectives from which to conceptualize and describe group counseling and other group applications, including an undifferentiated view. For instance, Hansen et al. (1980) also recognized the confusion in differentiating group counseling and group therapy, suggesting that they are overlapping forms that others attempt to differentiate in a variety of ways. Chen and Rybak (2004) observed that *group counseling* and *group therapy* are often used interchangeably but suggest that psychotherapy groups are often more in-depth and longer than counseling groups by design. DeLucia-Waack et al. (2004) used *group counseling* and *psychotherapy* interchangeably in their handbook, although they also recognized the value of the use of typological and continuum models. Wheelan (2005b) stated that "While there is some lingering disagreement concerning the definitions of therapy, counseling, and personal-growth groups, there is considerable consensus that the differences among them are related to the population that each approach is designed to serve" (p. 174).

Jacobs et al. (2009) discussed counseling and therapy groups together, suggesting that some differences may arise depending upon the severity of problems and stating that "Group experts do not agree on how counseling and therapy groups should be conducted" (p. 13). Brown (2009) described both counseling and therapy groups as "clinical groups": "The defining boundary between these groups has become more vague and ambiguous as techniques, strategies, foci, and other group factors are increasingly used for both types" (p. 13). She added, however, that group members are more active participants, emphasizing problem-centered work from a wellness perspective in counseling groups, whereas therapy groups help members overcome deeper, longer-standing character issues by focusing on less than conscious reasons for experience.

Although both Gazda et al. (2001) and Corey (2008) see value in all three perspectives, they also recognize that *group counseling* is often used interchangeably with other terms such as *group therapy* and *psychoeducation*.

The AGPA *Group Works* document posted on its Web site (AGPA, n.d.) is directed toward the lay public and potential clients. Its description of the group therapy process seems to be broad and inclusive of what many would describe as group counseling, especially in regard to the strong emphasis upon an interpersonal, process-oriented approach:

> Group therapy helps people learn about themselves and improve their interpersonal relationships. It addresses feelings of isolation, depression or anxiety. And it helps people make significant changes so they feel better about the quality of their lives. Additionally, group therapists can apply the principles of group to other settings and situations such as businesses, schools and community organizations. (p. 1)

Independent Types

Attempts to create systems of group types have been described at least since Betz's 1973 model. Wilbur et al. (1981) elaborated on this model by describing differences among three types of group work across five variables: functions, objectives, size, leader behavior, and member expectations and roles. They placed group counseling in their "psycho-process cluster" with such other applications as group therapy, marathon, and conjoint family therapy (p. 227).

Ward suggested that "A major motivating factor for the development of the current classification system was the concern that problems had arisen with the rapid proliferation of a wide variety of often experimental groups that came into being during 1960's and 1970's" (1998, p. 186). He continued by saying that typological systems and continua of models of group work were stimulated by the need to find a "valid and practical structure within which to classify types of group work to make decisions regarding appropriate member placement to maximize group effectiveness and member outcome" (1998, pp. 186–187).

It is most likely that the ASGW typology is the best-known and most widely used typology due to its publication and availability in a number of places, the research that has been conducted upon it, and the influence of having been endorsed by the ASGW (ASGW, 1983, 1992, 2000). The 1983 standards "mirrored the conception of the time that whatever counselors did with groups of individuals should properly be referred to as group counseling" (ASGW, 2000, p. 327). Beginning with the 1992 standards and continuing through the latest version (2000), the emphasis changed to a description of recommended knowledge and skill competencies in core group work for all counseling students and "the differentiation among four distinct group work specializations: task and work group facilitation, group psychoeducation, group counseling, and group psychotherapy" (ASGW, 2000, p. 327).

The specialization in group counseling was defined as follows:

> The application of principles of normal human development and functioning through group-based cognitive, affective, behavioral, or systemic intervention strategies applied in the context of here-and-now interaction that address personal and interpersonal problems of living and promote personal and interpersonal growth and development among people who may be experiencing transitory maladjustment, who are at risk for the development of personal or interpersonal problems, or who seek enhancement of personal qualities and abilities. (ASGW, 2000, p. 331)

Group counseling was described as differing from each of the other three types of group work in one or more of the phrases in this definition. For instance, the definition of *psychoeducation groups* emphasized group-based educational and development strategies facilitating interpersonal growth and development for individuals who may be at risk for the development of problems. On the other hand, group psychotherapy included application of knowledge of abnormal human development and functioning, a context of negative emotional arousal, and remediation of distortions or patterns of dysfunctional behavior for those with severe and/or chronic maladjustment (ASGW, 2000).

In 1998, Waldo and Bauman described limitations of the ASGW classification system and published a proposed alternative, entitled the "GAP" (for goals and process) model. They identified three types of group work—guidance, counseling, and therapy—and presented them in a nine-cell matrix with the goals of development, remediation, and adjustment being the potential targets of each of the three process types of groups. In introducing the article and reaction papers, DeLucia-Waack described the complexity of defining group counseling in the following manner:

> To people outside of the counseling profession, I find myself often explaining what I do as group counseling because they understand, or at least have a sense of, what group counseling is. Now, the term *group work* is a different story. Lay persons do not seem to understand what group work is, and when I try to explain, they say "Oh, you mean group

counseling." So I have just shortened my explanation. (1998, p. 117)

A lively set of reactions to the GAP model followed the major article and identified a number of limitations that seemed to render it no better than the ASGW model (Conyne & Wilson, 1998; Gerrity, 1998; Keel, 1998; MacNair-Semands, 1998; Taub, 1998; Ward, 1998) followed by a rejoinder by Bauman and Waldo (1998).

Although Corey (2008) stated that a major difference between group *therapy* and group *counseling* lies in the group's goals, he also suggested that counseling groups focus on growth, development, enhancement, prevention, self-awareness, and releasing blocks to growth, whereas therapy groups focus on issues such as remediation, treatment, and personality reconstruction (p. 8). He went on to say that "Group counseling has preventive as well as remedial aims" (p. 5), and he separately defined each of the four group work types identified in the ASGW typology. His definition of counseling groups is lengthy and consistent with, but expands upon, the ASGW definition:

> The group involves an interpersonal process that stresses conscious thought, feelings, and behavior. Counseling groups are often problem oriented, and the members largely determine their content and aims. These group members don't require extensive personality reconstruction, and their concerns generally relate to the developmental tasks of the life span. Group counseling tends to be growth oriented in that the emphasis is on discovering internal resources of strength. The participants may be facing situational crises and temporary conflicts or they may be trying to change self-defeating behaviors. The group provides the empathy and support necessary to create the atmosphere of trust that leads to sharing and exploring these concerns. Group members are assisted in developing their existing skills in dealing with interpersonal problems so that they will be better able to handle future problems of a similar nature. (Corey, 2008, p. 5)

Gazda et al. (2001) present an often-cited continuum of overlapping types of groups work, but they also recognize that there are some elements of different types of group work that are most characteristic of each specific type by stating the following:

> Although *group counseling* and *group psychotherapy* are frequently used interchangeably, we believe each term has a distinctive quality that can serve a useful

purpose. In other words although there is overlap between group counseling and group psychotherapy, there are qualities possessed by each that allows each to be used independent of the other. (p. 4)

Hansen et al. (1980) provided a clear definition: "Group counseling is an interpersonal process involving a counselor and several members who explore themselves and their situations in an attempt to modify their attitudes and behaviors" (p. 4). They added that "Group counseling may be preventative and/or remedial for the person. Preventive counseling permits an individual to resolve concerns before serious problems develop" (p. 5). They also recognized the confusion in differentiating group counseling and group therapy, using Gazda's conceptual framework of a continuum of overlapping group types (1969) and Ohlsen's suggestion that it is the characteristics of the targeted members, rather than the methods, that change (1977).

Gladding (2008) generally followed the ASGW typology but also cited the Gazda continuum of three overlapping types of group work, therefore defining group counseling as "preventive, growth oriented, and remedial. . . . The focus of counseling groups, which are also referred to as interpersonal problem-solving groups, is on each person's behavior and development or change within the group and through the help of the group" (Gladding, 2008, p. 31). He went on to emphasize that "These groups emphasize group dynamics and interpersonal relationships" (p. 32).

Ivey et al. described the ASGW typology but combined task and psychoeducational as "structured" groups to form a three-type overlapping continuum (2001, pp. 22–23). Capuzzi et al. (2006) essentially used the ASGW typology model and suggested that the differences among psychoeducational, counseling, and therapy groups are primarily in the scope of practice being directed toward members with varying degrees of psychological functioning.

Chen and Rybak (2004) also described the ASGW typology and stated (p. 59) that group counseling is preventative, developmental, and remedial as well as more interpersonally oriented than symptom-oriented. They went on to observe that *group counseling* and *group therapy* are often used interchangeably but suggested that psychotherapy groups are often more in-depth and longer than counseling groups by design. Jacobs et al. (2009) cite the ASGW typology and then cite Ward's suggestion (2006a, p. 95) that activities representing more than one typology often coexist in the same group experience.

Berg et al. (2006) quoted Berg and Johnson's detailed definition of group counseling:

> [A] dynamic, inter- and intrapersonal process whose content is generated out of the feelings and behavior of the individual group members. The leader is a professionally trained counselor who is capable of creating a climate of trust, openness, responsibility, and interdependency through the therapy process of understanding, caring, and conflict management. The group is comprised of persons functioning within the normal ranges of adjustment who are seeking increased awareness of self and others so that they may better deal with developmental situations. (Berg & Johnson, 1971, p. x)

They presented a table showing differences in leader, methodology, and client population among guidance, counseling, and therapy groups, suggesting that practice overlaps across types (Berg et al., 2006, p. 15).

Wheelan (2005b) stated, "While there is some lingering disagreement concerning the definitions of therapy, counseling, and personal-growth groups, there is considerable consensus that the differences among them are related to the population that each approach is designed to serve" (p. 174). She added, "Group therapy attempts to remediate psychological problems that seriously interfere with the ability of individuals to function in work, social, or family roles. Group counseling seeks to help individuals to resolve specific, short-term issues or problems . . ." (p. 175).

Burlingame et al. (2004a) cited Conyne, Wilson, and Ward's (1997) expanded explanation of the ASGW typology of group types at the beginning of their chapter. They use Conyne et al.'s description of the typology to present the four types of group work: psychoeducation, counseling, psychotherapy, and task. Specifically, they summarize Conyne et al.'s definition of the focus of counseling groups as follows: "Counseling groups are traditionally aimed at enhancing members' interpersonal potential and increasing their interpersonal growth" (Burlingame et al., 2004a, p. 651).

Trotzer (2006) presented the ASGW typology and expanded upon the definition of group counseling as

> The development of a face to face interpersonal network or system characterized by trust, acceptance, respect, warmth, communication, and understanding through which a counselor and several members come into contact in order to help each other address the purposes of the groups and discover, understand,

and implement ways of accomplishing the objectives inherent in the group's formation and purpose. (p. 27)

Dye (2008, p. 3) argued that the ASGW should change its name to the International Association for Group Counseling to best represent the current status of group work in which group counselors differentially apply all four types of group work in appropriate situations.

Ward (2006b) stated the following:

It seems to me that, for most of us mere mortals, it is very difficult to deliver all of the elements of all types of groups in a single group experience. Meeting very disparate client needs from the need for simple information through major personality reconstruction seems to be an unwieldy and unrealistic goal unlikely to be accomplished in a single group and more likely to lead to mediocre outcomes or even failure. (p. 93)

He continues as follows:

The use of a common classification system of group types is therefore important to efforts that design and deliver high-quality groups designed to provide maximum gains for members with specific target characteristics and needs. It does seem logical, however, that any set of discrete group types is bound to be only partially reflective of the very real richness and complexity of meaningful group experiences. (p. 94)

Examples of authors who advocate the continuum perspective of group work applications are presented in the next section.

Overlapping Continuum

During the early days of the rapid increase in, and resulting influence of, the use of group work as a training component in counselor education programs, Gazda, Duncan, and Meadows conducted a survey of counselor educators (1967). They summarized the results of this survey by presenting a definition of group counseling best representing the feedback from the counselor educators in this way:

Group counseling is a dynamic interpersonal process focusing on conscious thought and behavior and involving the therapy functions of permissiveness, orientation to reality, catharsis, and mutual trust, caring, understanding, acceptance, and support. The therapy functions are created and nurtured in a small group through the sharing of personal concerns with one's peers and the counselor(s). The group

counselees are basically normal individuals with various concerns which are not debilitating to the extent requiring extensive personality change. The group counselees may utilize the group interaction to increase understanding and acceptance of values and goals and to learn and/or unlearn certain attitudes and behaviors. (p. 305)

It appears that the most common model for understanding various ways in which group work can be applied combines a continuum model with nondiscrete types of group work. The summary definition of Gazda et al. (1967) seems to be consistent with this approach. Ohlsen (1977) and Ohlsen et al. (1988) presented continua. Gazda described a conceptual framework of a continuum of overlapping group types in 1969. The updated model presented in Gazda et al.'s continuum model (2001) is most often cited in the current literature. They described group counseling as falling on a continuum as a mid-range activity, emphasizing preventive, growth, engendering, and remedial intervention overlapping with group guidance, which focuses most upon preventive and growth-engendering intervention, on one side, and group psychotherapy, focusing primarily on remedial interventions, on the other side (Gazda et al., 2001). Thus, in their interpretation, group counseling is the broadest approach. They therefore include T-groups and sensitivity and encounter groups under group counseling and include life-skills training groups across all three dimensions, which can be somewhat confusing and reflects Gazda's lifelong work to develop and advocate for the use of life-skills training groups (Gazda, 1989).

As mentioned earlier, Hansen et al. (1980) recognized the confusion in differentiating group counseling and group therapy. They used Gazda's (1969) conceptual framework of a continuum of overlapping group types and Ohlsen's (1977) suggestion that it is the characteristics of the targeted members, rather than the methods, that change to explain their view and how group counseling fits in the broader group work context.

Conyne described three approaches to conceptualizing the various applications of group counseling: as undifferentiated from other types of groups, including group counseling; as an independent type within a broader range of group work types; and as a process that overlaps on a continuum with therapeutic and educational goals and processes (Conyne, 2012). He then suggested an integrative description of group counseling that is also compatible with the continuum model.

Trotzer (2006, pp. 40–46) also presented a three-type overlapping model of group guidance/psychoeducational, counseling, and psychotherapy groups, with the focus being on prevention and skills learning in psychoeducational groups, being primarily remedial with a problem-solving emphasis in counseling groups, and being remedial with an emphasis on personality reconstruction for members with more pernicious maladjustment in group therapy. The process begins with more emphasis on information and leader structure and less rigorous leader training and emotional involvement necessary in psychoeducational groups to the least emphasis on information and external leader structure and more upon more leader training and emotional involvement of members as the perspective moves through group counseling to group psychotherapy. In fact, he suggested that group counseling and group psychotherapy are very similar in many ways and primarily differ in terms of the severity of problems and degree of personality reconstruction required in group psychotherapy.

Day (2007) presented the ASGW typology and then, in the tradition of Gazda and others, described group counseling as occupying the middle position with more of an emphasis "on the group members themselves" and "their interactions and mutual problem-solving efforts" (p. 8). She described psychotherapy groups as being designed for people with more severe problems and maladjustment needing personality reconstruction. In similar fashion, Ivey et al. (2001, pp. 22–23) described the ASGW typology but then combined task and psychoeducational as "structured" groups to form a three-type overlapping continuum consistent with that described by Gazda and others. Posthuma (1999) stated that all counseling and therapy groups have change as their purpose (p. 4) but differentiated the focus of counseling groups as more exploratory and that of therapy groups as more curative (p. 69).

Other approaches consistent with the continuum model include Corey (2008), who, in addition to describing the ASGW typology, implied the value of a continuum model by stating that "Group counseling has preventive as well as remedial aims" (p. 9). Capuzzi et al. (2006) essentially described the ASGW typology model within a continuum and suggested that the differences among psychoeducational, counseling, and therapy groups are primarily in the scope of practice being directed toward members with varying degrees of psychological functioning. Chen and Rybak (2004) also described the ASGW typology but went on to state (p. 59) that

group counseling is preventative, developmental, and remedial as well as more interpersonally oriented than symptom-oriented. They also observed that *group counseling* and *group therapy* are often used interchangeably but suggested that psychotherapy groups are often more in-depth and longer than counseling groups by design. Gladding (2008) generally followed the ASGW typology as well but also cited the Gazda et al. (2001) continuum of three overlapping types of group work, therefore defining group counseling as "preventive, growth oriented, and remedial. . . . The focus of counseling groups, which are also referred to as interpersonal problem-solving groups, is on each person's behavior and development or change within the group and through the help of the groups" (p. 31). He goes on to emphasize that "These groups emphasize group dynamics and interpersonal relationships" (Gladding, 2008, p. 32). Other authors who described undifferentiated and/or independent-type models also implied the value of a continuum perspective include Wheelan (2005a, 2005b), Brown (2009), and Berg et al. (2006).

Kottler and Shephard (2008) presented Kottler's continuum of group work styles, identifying discussion groups at one end, group therapy at the other, and counseling next to group therapy and defining group counseling as a process in which

> The techniques and strategies are all designed to help resolve interpersonal conflict, promote greater self-awareness and insight and help individual members work to eliminate their self-defeating behaviors. Most often the clientele have few manifestations of psychopathology; they simply wish to work on personal concerns in daily living. In addition, counseling groups are also designed to be rather brief treatments, often focusing on resolving specific problems within a time-limited format. (p. 271)

Is Consensus Possible?

Working in groups to assist people in their personal and interpersonal functioning is an effective and important method for professional counselors and other mental health workers. As Barlow et al. (2004) conclude, "The human group phenomena titled 'group counseling' or 'group psychotherapy' clearly has a set of recognizable factors (skilled leaders or therapists, appropriately referred client or group members, defined goals, etc.) that create positive outcomes" (p. 18). With the complex historical development and varied origins of group work, is it currently possible to extract a clear, concise, consensus definition of group counseling in order to clarify and guide scholars, instructors, practitioners, clients, and the lay public in the study and application of, and participation in, this valuable resource?

This review of the history and current status of the way in which group counseling has been described and defined leads to the conclusion that a working definition is possible, provided it is understood within a more comprehensive context of the broad category of group work. How can this larger context be understood? Cashwell, Kleist, and Scofeld (2009) described a perspective based upon the dialectic between all of the functions performed by professional counselors and the narrower function within this larger array of activities called counseling that may be applied to our understanding of groups: "At the heart of various arguments surrounding identity issues in the Counseling Profession is the failure to distinguish between the tasks of counseling (with a lower-case 'c') and the Counseling Profession (with an upper-case 'C')" (p. 60).

In similar fashion, group work can therefore be understood to be the larger, more comprehensive set of activities described by Gazda three decades ago as:

> Group work refers to the dynamic interaction
> between collections of individuals for prevention or
> remediation of difficulties or for the enhancement of
> personal growth/enrichment through the interaction
> of those who meet together for a commonly
> agreed-on purpose and at prearranged times. (Gazda,
> 1978, p. 260)

In contrast, group counseling is most generally described as emphasizing the activity of a professional leader working through an emphasis upon the facilitation of member–member interpersonal interaction to assist individuals considered to manifest problems that bother themselves and/or others but who do not show symptoms of serious psychopathology to explore and improve their personal and interpersonal functioning. Conyne's integrative definition may suffice as a working description:

> Group counseling is an important therapeutic and
> educational method that psychologists, counselors,
> and other helpers can use to facilitate interpersonal
> problem solving processes among members as they
> learn how to resolve difficult but manageable
> problems of living and how to apply gains in the
> future. While being a unique service delivery
> method, group counseling also shares much in
> common with related group work approaches,

including psychoeducation groups and psychotherapy groups. In general, group counseling occupies a broad middle section of the helping goals continuum where prevention, development, and remediation all play important roles, depending on member needs and situational supports and constraints. (Conyne, 2012)

Therefore, group counseling is a distinctive set of activities which overlap with psychoeducational group methods that emphasize prevention and learning and growth-based methods, on the one hand, and therapeutic applications that stress remediation of serious limitations in personal and interpersonal functioning as well as major change in cognitive, affective, and/or behavioral functioning and personality reconstruction, on the other.

This perspective of group counseling serving as a more specific application within the larger range of group-work applications incorporates elements of all three of the ways of perceiving group counseling identified by Conyne (2012) and reflects the complexity of the issues and common practice in the field at the current time. What then should be the primary variable that determines whether group counseling is being conducted or the method being used is more accurately described as group therapy or group psychoeducation? Most counselors and counselor educators support the ASGW distinction between types of the intensity of the activities and interventions and the level and degree of change targeted for the members. Therefore, as previously emphasized, group counseling focuses upon interpersonal problem solving and learning from focused, facilitative interaction with both the group leader and other members to improve the cognitive, affective, and behavioral functioning of members who are competent and not demonstrating symptoms of serious psychopathology.

It should be noted that, if interpreted narrowly, limiting the definition of group counseling only to the degree of intensity of the work in relation to the level of psychological functioning of the members can lead to groups being considered to be counseling groups that deemphasize the importance of change through interpersonal interaction among members. This emphasis upon the critical importance of interpersonal learning, perhaps best described by Yalom (2005), can, of course, also be applied to group therapy and psychoeducation. In fact, it is the primary model of group psychotherapy espoused in the AGPA practice guidelines (AGPA, 2007). Therefore, it cannot be used to differentiate group counseling from the other types along the continuum. However, although most strongly support the emphasis upon process-oriented, interpersonal learning as characteristic of group counseling (Ward & Litchy, 2004), some mental health scholars and practitioners would disagree, especially those who advocate narrow, evidence-based applications of behavioral and cognitive-behavioral interventions directed solely or primarily at symptom reduction (Raps, 2009). It should be noted that even within the cognitive-behavioral movement major alternative understandings of cognitive-behavioral group work are being identified and described that emphasize the incorporation of a strong interpersonal, process-oriented group foundation within which specific cognitive-behavioral interventions aimed at ameliorating specific client symptoms are systematically applied (e.g., see Bieling et al., 2006).

Conclusions

Group counseling is an effective tool to assist counselors and other mental health professionals in their work to improve the lives of the people to whom they provide services. The origins of group counseling may be found in a variety of efforts, and descriptions have varied widely concerning the nature of the process. However, by understanding group counseling as a process in the middle range of professional group work stressing facilitation by a professional of interpersonal, process-oriented interaction among members who are not in need of remediation of psychopathology and who desire improvement of their personal and interpersonal functioning within a broader continuum of group work applications, a useful, contemporary understanding of group work emerges. This perspective can help to guide efforts to study, explain, and apply group counseling for the improvement of the lives of those we serve.

Future Directions

It is clear that the term *group counseling* continues to have utility to counselors and other mental health professionals as we move into the second decade of the twenty-first century. Four points may be extracted from the presentation that suggest direction for the future of group counseling.

1. Work with people in groups should continue to be understood as consisting of a number of overlapping types, including group counseling. The ASGW model of four overlapping types of group work has become one of the most commonly cited

systems for both differentiating and integrating various emphases in group work. The term *group work* continues to be the most logical title to describe this larger view of the broad field of helping people in groups.

2. Group counseling should continue to be understood and applied from an interpersonal, process-oriented perspective. Although group counseling may include goals that overlap with other types of group work, such as psychoeducational and remedial emphases, the most common target is identifying and increasing the use of strengths and increasing wellness within members. Support for these perspectives is quite strong among scholars.

3. Efforts to increase the empirical evidence for group counseling in specific settings with specific populations and members should be undertaken and supported. Although the complexity of finding meaningful and reliable results in the extremely complex arena of human experience and group interaction remains challenging, acquiring evidence from research that may be integrated with clinical wisdom about best practices in group counseling should become a priority.

4. The practice of requiring substantive training for professional counselors in group work and specifically group counseling should continue in order to insure that counseling and other treatment groups are conducted with knowledge and appropriate differential application of group dynamics and group processes beyond simply conducting individual counseling within a group setting.

References

Alcoholics Anonymous. (1981). *Twelve steps and twelve traditions*. New York: Alcoholics Anonymous World Services.

Altmaier, E., & Hansen, J. C. (Eds.). (in press). *Handbook of counseling psychology*. New York: Oxford University Press.

American Counseling Association. (1997). *Definition of professional counseling*. Retrieved August 8, 2009, from http://www.counseling.org/Counselors

American Group Psychotherapy Association. (n.d.). *Group works! An introduction to group therapy*. Retrieved May 18, 2009, from http://agpa.org/group/consumersguide2000.html

American Group Psychotherapy Association. (2007). *Practical guidelines for group psychotherapy*. Retrieved May 18, 2009, from http://www.agpa.org/guidelines/index.html

Anderson, G., & Wheelan, S. (2005). Integrating group research and practice. In S. Wheelan (Ed.), *The handbook of group research and practice* (pp. 545–552). Thousand Oaks, CA: Sage.

Andronico, M. (2001). A history of Division 49 (Group Psychology and Group Psychotherapy). *Group Psychologist*, June, 10–18.

Association for Specialists in Group Work (ASGW). (1983). *ASGW professional standards for group counseling.* Alexandria, VA: Author.

Association for Specialists in Group Work (ASGW). (1992). Professional standards for the training of group workers. *Journal for Specialists in Group Work, 17,* 12–19.

Association for Specialists in Group Work (ASGW). (2000). Professional standards for the training of group workers. *Journal for Specialists in Group Work, 25,* 327–342.

Austad, C. S. (2009). *Counseling and psychotherapy today: Theory, practice, and research.* New York: McGraw-Hill.

Bales, R. F. (1950). *Interaction process analysis: A method for the study of small groups.* Reading, MA: Addison-Wesley.

Barlow, S., Burlingame, G., & Fuhriman, A. (2000). Therapeutic applications of groups: From Pratt's "thought control classes" to modern group psychotherapy. *Group Dynamics: Theory, Research, and Practice, 4,* 115–134.

Barlow, S., Fuhriman, A., & Burlingame, G. (2004). The history of group counseling and psychotherapy. In J. DeLucia-Waack, D. Gerrity, C. Kalodner, & M. Riva (Eds.), *Handbook of group counseling and psychotherapy* (pp. 3–22). Thousand Oaks, CA: Sage.

Barlow, S., Fuhriman, A., & Burlingame, G. (2005). The history of group practice: A century of knowledge. In S. Wheelan (Ed.), *Handbook of group research and practice* (pp. 39–64). Thousand Oaks, CA: Sage.

Bauman, S., & Waldo, M. (1998). Improving the goals and process (GAP) matrix for groups: Incorporating feedback from the field. *Journal for Specialists in Group Work, 23,* 215–224.

Bednar, R., & Kaul, T. (1978). Experiential group research: Current perspectives. In A. Bergin & S. Garfield (Eds.), *Handbook of psychotherapy and behavior* (4th ed., pp. 631–663). New York: Wiley.

Benne, K. D., & Sheats, P. (1948). Functional roles of group members. *Journal of Social Issues, 1*(2), 41–49.

Berg, R. C., & Johnson, J. A. (1971). *Group counseling: A source book of theory and practice.* Fort Worth, TX: American Continental.

Berg, R. C., Landreth, G. L., & Fall, K. A. (2006). *Group counseling, concepts and procedures* (4th ed.). New York: Routledge.

Bernard, H. S., & Mackenzie, K. R. (1994). *Basics of group psychotherapy.* New York: Guilford Press.

Berne, E. (1970). *Group treatment.* New York: Grove Press.

Bertcher, H. (1985). Social group work: Past, present, and future. *Journal for Specialists in Group Work, 10,* 77–82.

Betz, R. L. (1973). A proposed typology of group processes. *Michigan Personnel and Guidance Journal, 4*(2), 18–24.

Bieling, P. J., McCabe, R. E., & Antony, M. M. (2006). *Cognitive behavioral therapy in groups.* New York: Guilford Press.

Brabender, V. (2002). *Introduction to group therapy* (2nd ed.). New York: John Wiley & Sons.

Brabender, V. A., & Fallon, A. E. (2009). *Group development in practice.* Washington, DC: American Psychological Association.

Brabender, V. A., Fallon, A. E., & Smolar, A. I. (2004). *Essentials of group therapy.* Hoboken, NJ: John Wiley & Sons.

Bradford, L., Gibb, J., & Benne, K. (Eds.). (1964). *T-group theory and laboratory method: Innovation in re-education.* New York: Wiley.

Brown, N. W. (2009). *Becoming a group leader.* Upper Saddle River, NJ: Pearson Education.

Burlingame, G., & Fuhriman, A. (Eds.). (1994). *Handbook of group psychotherapy: An empirical and clinical synthesis* (pp. 559–562). New York: Wiley.

Burlingame, G., Fuhriman, A., & Johnson, J. (2004a). Current status and future directions of group therapy research. In J. DeLucia-Waack, D. Gerrity, C. Kalodner, & M. Riva (Eds.), *Handbook of group counseling and psychotherapy* (pp. 651–660). Thousand Oaks, CA: Sage.

Burlingame, G., Fuhriman, A., & Johnson, J. (2004b). Process and outcome in group counseling and psychotherapy: A perspective. In J. DeLucia-Waack, D. Gerrity, C. Kalodner, & M. Riva (Eds.), *Handbook of group counseling and psychotherapy* (pp. 49–61). Thousand Oaks, CA: Sage.

Burlingame, G., Fuhriman, A., & Mosier, J. (2003). The differential effectiveness of group psychotherapy: A meta-analytic perspective. *Group Dynamics: Theory, Research, and Practice, 7,* 3–12.

Burlingame, G. M., MacKenzie, K. R., & Strauss, B. (2004). Small group treatment: Evidence for effectiveness and mechanisms of change. In M. Lambert (Ed.), *Handbook of psychotherapy and behavior change* (5th ed., pp. 647–696). New York: John Wiley & Sons.

Capuzzi, D., Gross, D. R., & Stauffer, M. D. (2006). *Introduction to group work* (4th ed.). Denver, CO: Love Publishing.

Cartwright, D., & Zander, A. (Eds.). (1953). *Group dynamics.* New York: Harper & Row.

Cashwell, C. S., Kleist, D., & Scofeld, T. (2009, August). A call for professional identity. *Counseling Today,* 60–61.

Chen, M.-W., & Rybank, C. J. (2004). *Group leadership skills: Interpersonal process in group counseling and therapy.* Pacific Grove, CA: Brooks/Cole.

Cohen, A. M., & Smith, R. D. (1976a). *The critical incident in growth groups: A manual for group leaders.* La Jolla, CA: University Associates.

Cohen, A. M., & Smith, R. D. (1976b). *The critical incident in growth groups: Theory and technique.* La Jolla, CA: University Associates.

Conyne, R. K. (1989). *How personal growth and task groups work.* Newbury Park, CA: Sage.

Conyne, R. K. (2012). Group counseling. In E. Altmaier & J. C. Hansen (Eds.). *Handbook of counseling psychology.* New York: Oxford University Press.

Conyne, R. K., Crowell, J. L., & Newmeyer, M. D. (2008). *Group techniques: How to use them more purposefully.* Upper Saddle River, NJ: Pearson Education.

Conyne, R. K., Dye, H. A., Kline, W. B., Morran, D. K., Ward, D. E., & Wilson, F. R. (1992). Context for revising the Association for Specialists in Group Work Training Standards. *Journal for Specialists in Group Work, 17,* 10–11.

Conyne, R. K., & Wilson, F. R. (1998). Towards a standards-based classification of group work offerings. *Journal for Specialists in Group Work, 23,* 177–184.

Conyne, R. K., Wilson, F. R., & Ward, D. E. (1997). *Comprehensive group work: What it means and how to teach it.* Alexandria, VA: American Counseling Association.

Corey, G. (1981). *Theory and practice of group counseling.* Monterey, CA: Brooks/Cole.

Corey, G. (2008). *Theory and practice of group counseling* (7th ed.). Belmont, CA: Thomson Brooks/Cole.

Corey, G., & Corey, M. S. (1977). *Groups: Process and practice.* Monterey, CA: Brooks/Cole.

Corey, G., Corey, M. S., Callanan, P., & Russell, J. M. (2004). *Group techniques* (3rd. ed.). Pacific Grove, CA: Brooks/Cole.

Corey, M. S., Corey, G., & Corey, C. (2010). *Groups: Process and practice* (8th ed.). Belmont, CA: Brooks/Cole.

Corsini, R. J. (1957). *Methods of group psychotherapy*. Chicago: William James Press.

Day, S. X. (2007). *Groups in practice*. Boston, MA: Houghton Mifflin.

DeLucia-Waack, J. L. (1998). *Grouping our groups: What works?* *Journal for Specialists in Group Work, 23,* 117–118.

DeLucia-Waack, J. L. (2006). *Leading psychoeducational groups for children and adolescents*. Thousand Oaks, CA: Sage.

DeLucia-Waack, J. L., Gerrity, D. A., Kalodner, C. R., & Riva, M. T. (Eds.). (2004). *Handbook of group counseling and psychotherapy*. Thousand Oaks, CA: Sage.

Drossel, C. (2008). Group interventions. In W. T. O'Donahue & J. E. Fisher (Eds.), *Cognitive behavior therapy: applying empirically supported techniques in your practice*. New York: John Wiley & Sons.

Driver, H. I. (1958). *Counseling and learning through small-group discussion*. Madison, WI: Monona.

Dye, A. (1980). Message from the president: Semifinal thoughts. *Journal for Specialists in Group Work, 23,* 335–337.

Dye, A. (2008, Spring). Our rightful title. *The Group Worker.* 3.

Forester-Miller, H. (1998). History of the Association for Specialists in Group Work: ASGW Timeline of significant events. *Journal for Specialists in Group Work, 5,* 52–54.

Forsyth, D. R. (2010). *Group dynamics* (5th ed.). Belmont, CA: Wadsworth, Cengage Learning.

Fuhriman, A., & Burlingame, G. M. (Eds.). (2004). *Handbook of group psychotherapy: An empirical and clinical synthesis*. New York: John Wiley & Sons.

Gazda, G. (1968). *Basic approaches to group psychotherapy and group counseling*. Springfield, IL: Charles C. Thomas.

Gazda, G. (1969). *Theories and methods of group counseling*. Springfield, IL: Charles C. Thomas.

Gazda, G. (1971). *Group counseling: A developmental approach*. Boston: Allyn & Bacon.

Gazda, G. M. (1978). *Group counseling: A developmental approach* (2nd ed.). Boston: Allyn & Bacon.

Gazda, G. (1982). *Basic approaches to group psychotherapy and group counseling* (3rd ed.). Springfield, IL: Charles C. Thomas.

Gazda, G. (1985). Group counseling and therapy: A perspective on the future. *Journal for Specialists in Group Work, 10,* 74–76.

Gazda, G. (1989). *Group counseling: A developmental approach* (4th ed.). Needham Heights, MA: Allyn & Bacon.

Gazda, G. M., Duncan, J. A., & Meadows, M. E. (1967). Counseling and group procedures Report of a survey. *Counselor Education and Supervision, 6,* 305–310.

Gazda, G., Ginter, E., & Horne, A. (2001). *Group counseling and group psychotherapy: Theory and application*. Boston: Allyn & Bacon.

Gerrity, D. A. (1998). A classification matrix using goals and process dimensions: Issues for therapy groups. *Journal for Specialists in Group Work, 23,* 202–207.

Gladding, S. (2002). *Group work: A counseling specialty* (4th ed.). Upper Saddle River, NJ: Prentice Hall.

Gladding, S. (2004). *Counseling: A comprehensive profession* (4th ed.). Upper Saddle River, NJ: Prentice Hall.

Gladding, S. T. (2008). *Groups: A counseling specialty* (5th ed). Upper Saddle River, NJ: Pearson Education.

Golembiewski, R. T., & Blumberg, A. (1977). *Sensitivity training and the laboratory approach: Readings about concepts and applications* (3rd ed.). Itasca, IL: F. E. Peacock.

Hadden, S. (1955). Historic background of group psychotherapy. *International Journal of Group Psychotherapy, 5,* 62.

Hansen, J. C., Warner, R. W., & Smith, E. M. (1976). *Group counseling: Theory and process*. Chicago: Rand McNally.

Hansen, J. C., Warner, R. W., & Smith, E. M. (1980). *Group counseling: Theory and process* (2nd ed.). Chicago: Rand McNally.

Hare, A. P., Borgatta, E. F., & Bales, R. F. (Eds.). (1955). *Small groups: Studies in social interaction*. New York: Alfred A. Knopf.

Hill, W. F. (1965). *HIM: Hill interaction matrix*. Los Angeles: University of Southern California Youth Studies Center.

Hill, W. F. (1969). *Learning through discussion*. Beverly Hills, CA: Sage.

Hulse-Killacky, D., Killacky, J., & Donigian, J. (2001). *Making task groups work in the world*. Upper Saddle River, NJ: Prentice Hall.

Ivey, A. E., Pedersen, P. B., & Ivey, M. B. (2001). *Intentional group counseling: A microskills approach*. Belmont, CA: Brooks/Cole.

Jacobs, E. E., Masson, R. L., & Harvill, R. L. (2009). *Group counseling: Strategies and skills* (6th ed.). Belmont, CA: Thomson Brooks/Cole.

Kaplan, H. I., & Sadock, B. J. (Eds.). (1993). *Comprehensive group psychotherapy*. Baltimore: Williams & Wilkins.

Keel, L. P. (1998). A task group practitioner's response to Waldo and Bauman's article on regrouping the categorization of group work. *Journal for Specialists in Group Work, 23,* 192–195.

Kline, W. B. (2002). *Interactive group counseling and therapy*. Upper Saddle River, NJ: Merrill Prentice Hall.

Kottler, J. A. (2001). *Learning group leadership: An experiential approach*. Boston: Allyn & Bacon.

Kottler, J. A., & Shephard, D. S. (2008). *Introduction to counseling* (6th ed.). Belmont, CA: Brooks/Cole.

Leddick, G. (2008, February 22). *Illustrated history of group work*. Paper presented at the national conference of the Association for Specialists in Group Work, St. Pete Beach, FL.

Lewin, K. (1944). The dynamics of group action. *Educational Leadership, 1,* 195–200.

Lewin, K., Lippitt, R., & White, R. (1939). Patterns of aggressive behavior in experimentally created "social climates." *Journal of Social Psychology, 10,* 271–299.

Lieberman, M. A., Yalom, I. D., & Miles, M. (1973). *Encounter groups: First facts*. New York: Basic Books.

Lubin, B., Wilson, C. D., Petren, S., & Polk, A. (1996). *Research on group treatment methods: A selectively annotated bibliography*. Westport, CT: Greenwood.

Luft, J. (1963). *Group processes*. Palo Alto, CA: National Press Books.

Macgowan, M. J. (2008). *A guide to evidence-based group work*. New York: Oxford University Press.

MacKenzie, K. R. (Ed.). (1992). *Classics in group psychotherapy*. New York: Guilford Press.

MacNair-Semands, R. R. (1998). Encompassing the complexity of group work. *Journal for Specialists in Group Work, 23,* 208–214.

Moreno, J. L. (Ed.). (1966). *The international handbook of group psychotherapy*. New York: Philosophical Library.

Napier, R. W., & Gershenfeld, M. K. (1973). *Groups: Theory and experience*. Boston: Houghton Mifflin.

Ohlsen, M. M. (Ed.). (1973). *Counseling children in groups: A forum*. New York: Holt, Rinehart, & Winston.

Ohlsen, M. M. (1977). *Group counseling*. New York: Holt, Rinehart, & Winston.

Ohlsen, M. M., Horne, A. M., & Lawe, C. F. (1988). *Group counseling* (3rd ed.). New York: Holt, Rinehart, & Winston.

Petrocelli, J. V. (2002). Effectiveness of group cognitive-behavioral therapy for general symptomatology: A meta-analysis. *Journal for Specialists in Group Work, 27*, 92–115.

Piper, W., & McCallum, M. (1991). Group interventions for those who have experienced loss. *Group Analysis, 24*, 363–373.

Posthuma, B. W. (1999). *Small groups in counseling and therapy: Process and leadership* (3rd ed.). Boston: Allyn & Bacon.

Pratt, J. H. (1922). The principles of class treatment and their application to various chronic diseases. *Hospital Society Services Quarterly, 6*, 401–411.

Raps, C. S. (2009). When we research "conditions–treatments," is there a misnomer? *American Psychologist, 64*, 275–276.

Rogers, C. R. (1970). *On encounter groups.* New York: Harper & Row.

Rutan, J. S., Stone, W. N., & Shay, J. J. (2007). *Psychodynamic group psychotherapy* (4th ed.). New York: Guilford Press.

Scheidlinger, S., & Schmess, G. (1992). Fifty years of AGPA 1942–1992: An overview. In K. R. MacKenzie (Ed.), *Classics in group psychotherapy* (pp. 1–22). New York: Guilford.

Schutz, W. (1958). *FIRO: A three-dimensional theory of interpersonal behavior.* New York: Rinehart.

Schutz, W. (1967). *Joy: Expanding human awareness.* Baltimore: Penguin.

Shaffer, J. B. P., & Galinsky, M. D. (1974). *Models of group therapy.* Englewood Cliffs, NJ: Prentice Hall.

Sullivan, D. F. (Ed.). (1952). *Readings in group work.* New York: Association Press.

Taub, D. J. (1998). Promoting student development through psychoeducational groups: A perspective on the goals and process matrix. *Journal for Specialists in Group Work, 23*, 196–201.

Toseland, R. W., & Rivas, R. F. (2001). *An introduction to group work practice* (4th ed.). Boston: Allyn & Bacon.

Trotzer, J. P. (2006). *The counselor and the group: Integrating theory, training, and practice* (3rd ed.). New York: Routledge.

Tuckman, B. (1965). Developmental sequence in small groups. *Psychological Bulletin, 63*, 384–389.

Tuckman, B. W., & Jensen, M. A. C. (1977). Stages of small group development revisited. *Group and Organizational Studies, 2*, 419–427.

Waldo, M., & Bauman, S. (1998). Regrouping the categorization of group work: A goals and process (GAP) matrix for groups. *Journal for Specialists in Group Work, 23*, 164–176.

Ward, D. E. (1982). A model for the more effective use of theory in group work. *Journal for Specialists in Group Work, 7*, 224–230.

Ward, D. E. (1998). Regrouping groups: A reaction to Waldo and Bauman. *Journal for Specialists in Group Work, 23*, 185–191.

Ward, D. E. (2006a). Classification of groups. *Journal for Specialists in Group Work, 31*, 93–97.

Ward, D. E. (2006b). Complexity in group work. *Journal for Specialists in Group Work, 31*, 1–3.

Ward, D. E., & Litchy, M. (2004). The effective use of processing in groups. In J. DeLucia-Waack, D. Gerrity, C. Kalodner, & M. Riva (Eds.), *Handbook of group counseling and psychotherapy* (pp. 3–22). Thousand Oaks, CA: Sage.

Wheelan, S. (Ed.). (2005a). *The handbook of group research and practice* (pp. 545–552). Thousand Oaks, CA: Sage.

Wheelan, S. A. (2005b). *Group processes: A developmental perspective.* Boston: Allyn & Bacon.

Wilbur, M. P., Roberts-Wilbur, J., & Betz, R. L. (1981). Leader and member behaviors in three group modalities: A typology. *Journal for Specialists in Group Work, 6*, 224–234.

Yalom, I. (1970). *The theory and practice of group psychotherapy* (1st ed.). New York: Basic Books.

Yalom, I. D. (1975). *The theory and practice of group psychotherapy.* (2nd ed.). New York: Basic Books.

Yalom, I. D. (1985). *The theory and practice of group psychotherapy* (3rd ed.). New York: Basic Books.

Yalom, I. (1995). *The theory and practice of group psychotherapy* (4th ed.). New York: Basic Books.

Yalom, I. D. (with Leszcz, M.). (2005). *The theory and practice of group psychotherapy* (5th ed.). New York: Basic Books.

The History of Group Counseling

George R. Leddick

Abstract

The history of group counseling has its roots in antiquity, but the modern practice evolved as recently as the 1940s. Dimensions of group work include group counseling, group therapy, psychological education, and organizational task groups. The history therefore weaves a tapestry of influences including social justice groups, community organizations, quality-management groups, and numerous therapeutic orientations. Pioneer group-counseling practitioners included Joseph Pratt, Jane Addams, and Jesse Davis. Substantial contributions to the evolution of group counseling were provided by Moreno, Lewin, Rees, Deming, Alinsky, Rogers, Perls, and Yalom. Several professional organizations have provided an international conversation about group counseling, especially through publication of professional journals, standards, and guidelines. Group counseling has emerged from its infancy and continues to mature as a professional specialty.

Keywords: history: group, counseling, psychology, therapy

Introduction

When defining *group psychology* as three or more people meeting for a common conscious purpose, its historical roots travel further than the earliest records of humankind. Chinese legend has it that Lao Tse, although never convening a formal school, attracted a large number of students and disciples for improved self-understanding. Some believe Lao Tse was a contemporary of Confucius and report details of philosophical discussions between the two; others believe Lao Tse was an invented literary figure and point out that the name translates as the honorary title "Old Master" (Turner, 1903). The Greek academy where Socrates posed provocative questions to groups eager to better "know thyself," is similarly an example of gatherings of groups for the purpose of enlightenment (Cornford, 1945).

Thus, the history of group psychology is inextricably bound to the term's definition. For the purposes of this chapter, *group work* encompasses group therapy, group counseling, psychological education, and the facilitation of organizational development. Group work has been shaped by practitioners of many professions, including psychology, social work, counseling, psychiatry, family therapy, and organizational management. Rather than taking a parochial view of group counseling from the limited perspective of a single profession or group modality, this chapter describes a rich tapestry of interwoven influences.

In a time prior to desktop computers, Corsini (1957) sorted through professional journals by hand, seeking discussions of group work. He concluded that the history of group work was divided into three eras: (1) origins (before 1899), (2) pioneer (1900–1930), and (3) modern (after 1930).

Origins

The origins of group work (Corsini, 1957) took root when influential people drew attention to groups or lauded the idea. Sigmund Freud and Alfred Adler each praised the concept of working with groups of clients but never focused their respective practices on group therapy. Psychiatrist Jacob Levy Moreno (1889–1974), creator of psychodrama, proclaimed group work as the third most important revolution in the history of psychiatry. The first two turning points in psychiatry's history were Freud extending help to neurotics as well as psychotics and the public viewing the mentally ill as sick rather than possessed by demons.

For example, a famous institution in fourteenth-century London was St. Mary of Bethlehem Hospital (O'Donoghue, 1915), built to house "distracted people" and "lunatics." Dozens of people who were actively hallucinating, shrieking, and moaning were routinely chained to the wall; and the din was so discomforting that the hospital's name "Bethlehem" entered the language as "bedlam," to capture its pathos and misery. By 1753 the hospital had become a tourist attraction and much of its revenue was generated by the public's two-pence admission fee.

Moreno's "psychodrama" was a form of group therapy that heeded Shakespeare's comment "all the world's a stage" and we are all actors on the stage of life. He encouraged group members to direct and star in enactments of their life struggles and in return serve as actors in the plays of others. Rehearsals emphasized improvisational dialogue during encounters and a protagonist's alternatives. Moreno emphasized acting in the here and now (Buber, 1958) and incorporated theatrical techniques of role play, role reversal, and use of an alter ego.

In the 1930s and 1940s Moreno attracted the attention of notable luminaries, cross-pollinating psychotherapy. Fritz Perls, Eric Berne, Ronald Lippitt, and Karl Menninger attended his workshops (Fox, 1987). In 1937 he founded the journal *Sociometry*; contributors included Margaret Mead, Kurt Lewin, and Rudolf Dreikurs. In 1942 he founded the American Society for Group Psychotherapy and Psychodrama (ASGPP), which became the new field's professional association. In 1947 Moreno initiated the official journal of the ASGPP, *Sociatry, Journal of Group and Inter-Group Therapy*, which later became the *Journal of Group Psychotherapy, Psychodrama, and Sociometry* (Marineau, 1989).

Pioneer Era: Pratt, Addams, and Davis
Physician Joseph Hersey Pratt (1872–1956, Fig. 4.1) worked with patients recovering from tuberculosis in Boston at a time when the primary treatment was isolating infectious patients in sanatoriums. Patients quarantined in sanatoriums for 6 months to a year became discouraged and depressed. Pratt was among the first to write about his experiences working in groups, noting that not only was the method time-effective but also patients provided each other with emotional support (Pinney, 1978). He subsequently described treating patients with psychosomatic illness in a group setting. A long-time medical educator, the Pratt Diagnostic Clinic and Hospital was named in his honor, forming the basis for what eventually became Boston's New England Medical Center.

Jane Addams (1860–1935, Fig. 4.2) was a social worker who organized immigrants at Hull House in Chicago. Neighborhood groups engaged in reading, crafts, and activities to improve social skills, language, hygiene, and nutrition. Addams's groups emphasized the common needs and goals of

Fig. 4.1 Joseph Pratt. Photograph courtesy of the Trustees of Tufts University.

Fig. 4.2 Jane Addams. WHS Image ID 6126, reproduced with permission of Wisconsin Historical Society.

members and rallied a support system to help members identify with a social community larger than one's own family. Addams's work with immigrants at Hull House is considered the beginnings of social group work (Pottick, 1988). In addition to initiating groups to improve support and social skills, she achieved notoriety for organizing social justice groups. She was a founding member of both the National Association for the Advancement of Colored People (1909) and the American Civil Liberties Union (1920) and an ardent supporter of a woman's right to vote. Addams was awarded the Nobel Peace Prize in 1931. In addition to writing provocative articles about social problems in popular magazines of the day, she was the author of seven books, including *Twenty Years at Hull House* (1910) and *The Second Twenty Years at Hull House* (1930).

When Jesse Buttrick Davis (1871–1955, Fig. 4.3) was principal of Michigan's Grand Rapids High School in 1912, he decreed every student would experience one class each week on vocational guidance, using groups to teach career exploration, social skills, and values. Vocational guidance was a new and fascinating contribution to school curricula, and Dr. Davis was among the vanguard. He promoted "group guidance" or psychological education as a means to inform and educate. He joined the faculty of Boston University in 1924 and was named dean of education in 1935. He was a founder and former president of both the National Vocational

Guidance Association and the National Association for Secondary School Principals (see Dr. Jesse Davis, 1955).

Modern Era

Formation of professional societies helped to establish group work as a legitimate specialty. Shortly after Moreno established the ASGPP, Samuel Slavson founded the American Group Psychotherapy Association (AGPA) in 1943. The AGPA's journal, the *International Journal of Group Psychotherapy*, was started in 1949. This journal, in addition to ASGPP's journal *Sociatry*, provided group work with a research base.

Along with the establishment of professional societies and journals, a number of key events and figures significantly affected group work during what Corsini (1957) called the "modern era" and provided a foundation for group work as we know it today.

Treatment of World War II Veterans

Corsini (1957) noticed a tremendous growth in the number of group journal article titles following World War II. He attributed this growth to the high number of veterans suffering from "battle fatigue," now referred to as "posttraumatic stress," and a shortage of professionals trained to help them. Working with veterans in groups rather than individually proved to be time-effective. Equally important,

Fig. 4.3 Jesse B. Davis. Photograph courtesy of the Grand Rapids Community College Archive.

To expand such findings into practical workshops and learning institutes, Lewin and colleague Ronald Lippitt founded the National Training Laboratory in Group Development (now the NTL Institute), dedicated to understanding and investigating group dynamics, interpersonal behavior, and intergroup conflict. A key feature of these meetings was the use of a process observer, who at regular intervals would identify and comment upon the group's process and dynamics most recently apparent (Marrow, 1969). Group leadership training for both basic skills training (T-groups) and organizational task group leadership continues at the NTL Institute to this day. Following Lewin's sudden death at only 57 in 1947, Lippitt moved to the University of Michigan, where he joined the fledgling Institute for Social Research while concomitantly facilitating the further development of NTL.

Tavistock Institute of Human Relations

At about the same time that Lewin established the National Training Laboratory in Group Development, the Tavistock Institute of Human Relations was founded in London with a grant from the Rockefeller Foundation. Originally called the "Tavistock Group" because the founders had met at

group leaders noticed the positive effects of veterans interacting with peers who had experienced the reality of combat. Group interaction provided veterans with an environment in which they could both receive and give support; cope with feelings of isolation, anger, and guilt; and process the trauma.

Kurt Lewin—National Training Laboratory in Group Development

In 1946, Kurt Lewin (Fig. 4.4), a social and Gestalt psychologist and director of the Research Center for Group Dynamics at the Massachusetts Institute of Technology, conducted experiments to investigate human communication and interaction. To escape the summer heat of Boston, he moved his operation to Bethel, Maine, where he was able to rent space in the Gould Academy, which was vacant for the summer. Each evening, Lewin met with his graduate student assistants to discuss the day's experiments on communication (Sherwood, personal communication, October 1979). It quickly became evident that distinct communication patterns existed both in the daily experiments and in the roundtable evening discussions.

Fig. 4.4 Kurt Lewin.

London's Tavistock Clinic, this talented assortment of psychiatrists, psychologists, and anthropologists worked with groups of British Army veterans of World War II. Primarily influenced by Sigmund Freud and his followers, many other well-known therapists participated at Tavistock over the years, including Wilfred Bion, John Bowlby, Melanie Klein, Carl Jung, and R. D. Laing (Faher, 2004). Kurt Lewin was considered an important influence on the work of the Tavistock Group (Neumann, 2005).

After World War II the Tavistock Clinic was incorporated into the newly established British National Health Service, and the Tavistock Institute became a charitable foundation offering training in organizational consultation (Faher, 2004). Founding members of Tavistock influenced world affairs; for example, Ronald Hargreaves became deputy director of the World Health Organization and Brigadier General John Rawlings Rees became the first president of the World Federation for Mental Health. Currently, the Tavistock Institute continues its mission to improve the effectiveness of groups and organizations and apply "social science to contemporary issues and problems" (Tavistock Institute, http://www.tavinstitute.org/).

Fig. 4.5 W. Edwards Deming. Photograph courtesy of the W. Edwards Deming Institute®.

W. Edwards Deming—Total Quality Management

Other seminal postwar influences on group work were the contributions of William Edwards Deming (1900–1993, Fig. 4.5), who pioneered "total quality management" in industrial settings. These organizational task groups focused on quality control in manufacturing, customer satisfaction, and participatory management (Holusha, 1993).

W. Edwards Deming was convinced that more effective quality control was crucial to the long-term success of any company. American enterprises paid the newly minted business school professor little heed, but audiences in Japan were eager to learn how to rebuild their industries following a devastating war. Deming emphasized systemic attention to quality, whereas US companies were focused on short-term quarterly profit. When some suggested that Deming's methods contributed to Japanese automakers overtaking General Motors as the largest producer of automobiles, progress was instead attributed to the benefits of cheap labor. It was not until the Japanese also began surpassing the West in the production of computer memory that companies began to take notice (Holusha, 1993).

Deming served as a consultant, working with industry to form groups for quality management. His "14 points" (Deming, 1982, 2000) were slogans that focused attention on the key parts of an organization's development. He exhorted enterprises to break down boundaries between departments, remove barriers to pride of workmanship, and "drive out fear, so all may work for the company." Deming reasoned that quality should be predictable and satisfying. Another motto focusing on performing correctly the first time was "less rework." Thousands of Japanese managers study Deming's books each year, especially near the time the Deming Prize (an annual industrial award) is presented on national television amid ceremonies akin to the motion picture Academy Awards. In 1960 Deming was bestowed with the Second Order of the Sacred Treasure, Japan's premier imperial honor; and in 1987 he was recognized by President Ronald Reagan with the National Medal of Technology (Holusha, 1993).

Human Potential Movement

In the 1960s, group practice became so popular the *New York Times* designated 1968 as "the year of the group" (Gladding, 2003). That decade's human potential movement proposed that the well-being of individuals took precedence over the desires of institutions and that people are responsible for their lives and for their experiences of living (Stone, 1978).

The movement attempted to increase public awareness and foster social change. Examples of social activism in the 1960s included mounting protest over racial inequality, growth of the women's movement, demonstrations against US involvement in Vietnam, and the hippy movement.

During the second wave of the women's movement that occurred in the 1960s, "consciousness-raising" groups were a core component of grassroots efforts. These gatherings provided women, primarily white middle-class housewives living in social isolation, the opportunity to realize that the discontent and resulting guilt and self-doubt they experienced in their daily lives was not theirs alone. Instead, they were able to begin framing their individual experiences as part of a larger, systemic problem. By so doing, they laid a foundation for social action (Olson, 2001).

Social justice group work and community organizing flourished in this era. In Chicago, Saul Alinsky (1909–1972) focused on improving the living conditions of poor people through active participation in the political process. Notable were his strategies to form coalitions among disparate ethnic groups, labor unions, and church groups. "Any effective means is automatically judged by the opposition as being unethical," he cautioned in his book *Rules for Radicals* (Alinsky, 1971, p. 35). His community organizing strategies were the focus of study for progressive politicians Hillary Clinton and Barack Obama, conservative author William F. Buckley labeled him nearly "an organizational genius," and the *New York Times* (Cohen, 2009) reported that Alinsky's strategy of using a spectacle to make up for reduced numbers was evident in the disruption of town hall meetings attempting to discuss US health-care legislation. As Alinsky's daughter-in-law Joanne Linowes Alinksy pointed out (2009), community organizers are not working toward long-term, meaningful results when they simply grab an Alinsky rule here and an Alinsky tactic there; they are simply trying to craft a disruption or get noticed. What makes Alinsky organizing so successful (Alinsky, 2009) is that there is a process that has focused, intensive, specific, before-during-and-after steps that move an issue from complaints to action. The action results in progress for the group's cause but also makes measurable and enduring change while, in the end, gaining the respect of the decision makers and the community.

Carl Rogers (Fig. 4.6) found himself using his "person-centered counseling" more and more often in groups rather than in individual settings. By the

Fig. 4.6 Carl R. Rogers. Photograph courtesy of Department of Special Collections, University of California, Santa Barbara.

mid-1960s Rogers decided to work exclusively in groups. He coined the term "basic encounter groups" (Rogers, 1970) to describe groups based on person-centered theory, which he later shortened to "encounter groups." During this period, Rogers established a training center near his home in La Jolla, California. Encounter groups quickly grew in popularity.

Fritz Perls conducted numerous Gestalt therapy leadership-training workshops at the Esalen Institute in Big Sur, California. William Schutz also offered encounter group training workshops at Esalen. Schutz introduced a theory of interpersonal relations in which a group member's needs for inclusion, control, and affection explained one's interactions. The FIRO-B was the instrument he created to measure those dimensions (Schutz, 1958), and the test was frequently employed during group work (Leddick, 2009).

Increased Research and Evaluation

The 1970s was marked by the growth of group research (Bednar & Kaul, 1994). This research resulted from the realization among practitioners that improvement of practice was an ethical responsibility. Lieberman, Yalom, and Miles (1973) conducted groundbreaking studies into encounter group processes and outcomes. They provided conceptual entry points for research on groups by employing systematic and insightful observations of actual clients. Inspired by his research into group leader and member characteristics, Irvin Yalom (1975) described 11 curative factors found in group methods (e.g., cohesion, catharsis, self-understanding, interpersonal learning, instillation of hope) (Fig. 4.7).

In 1973, the Association for Specialists in Group Work (ASGW) was founded as a division of the American Personnel and Guidance Association, later renamed the American Counseling Association. At one time reaching nearly 7,000 members, the ASGW became the largest such professional association in the world. The *Journal for Specialists in Group Work* was founded in 1976 (Carroll & Levo, 1985) and is currently published in both print and online versions. In 1991 the American Psychological Association (APA) added Division 49—Group Psychology and Group Psychotherapy. APA Division 49 began publishing its journal, *Group Dynamics: Theory, Research and Practice*, in 1997. George Gazda (Fig. 4.8) was elected the first president of both the ASGW and APA Division 49. The American Group Psychotherapy Association, founded by Slavson in 1943, today includes 2,000 members in several countries. Historically populated by psychoanalytically oriented social workers, it has recently broadened its membership to include counselors, psychologists, and marriage and family therapists (Scheidlinger & Schamess, 1992).

Professional associations help to guide and shape the field. For example, in 1990 the ASGW published *Professional Standards for the Training of Group Workers*, which distinguished between core group competencies and the four group specialty areas: group counseling, group therapy, group guidance, and organizational groups. The ASGW also guided practitioners through ethical dilemmas with their *Professional Standards for Group Counseling* (1983), now called *Best Practices*. One example of the ASGW "Guidelines for Best Practice" (1998) addressing group-specific ethical dilemmas are the guidelines for confidentiality among group members. The ASGW was the first group organization to establish diversity competencies for group leaders (1999). APA Division 49—Group Psychology and Group Psychotherapy publicizes several sets of guidelines relevant to group work that have been formally adopted as APA policy: *Guidelines for Psychological Practice with Girls and Women* (APA, 2007); *Guidelines on Multicultural Education, Training, Research, Practice, and Organizational Change for Psychologists* (APA 2002); *Principles for the Validation and Use of Personnel Selection Procedures* (APA, 2003a); *Guidelines for Psychological Practice with Older Adults* (APA, 2003b); *Guidelines for Education*

Fig. 4.7 Irvin Yalom. Photograph courtesy of Reid Yalom.

Fig. 4.8 George Gazda. Photograph courtesy of Arthur Horne.

2. Even among professions where group counseling is a core requirement, there are no accreditation standards demanding that faculty teaching group courses have minimum levels of previous group coursework or group-specific experience in either publication or supervised practice. What prevents professional accreditation from insisting on quality assurance, especially in clinical competencies such as group?

3. There are few centers offering advanced training to group leaders. Is there a business model to inspire a profit motive for advanced experiential training?

4. Will increased Internet communication facilitate the international growth of group counseling theory and practice? Or will geopolitical and turf issues isolate and fragment the field?

5. What effect have insurance providers had on the practice of group counseling? Is there a difference between the influence of private providers and that of government?

6. What effect will conversion of patient records to a standard electronic format have on group-counseling services when confidentiality and privacy cannot now be guaranteed from other group members?

and Training at the Doctoral and Postdoctoral Level in Consulting—Psychology/Organizational Consulting Psychology (APA, 2005) and *Professional Practice Guidelines for Psychotherapy with Lesbian, Gay and Bisexual Clients* (APA,2000). Professional associations such as the ASGW, AGPA, and APA Division 49 provide common ground for both practitioners and researchers to improve the field of group work.

Conclusion

Originators of therapeutic models gain avid followers during their lifetimes, but eager fans grow less fervid after the founder's death. Once the cult of personality subsides, what remains in our collective imaginations are the effective strategies, helpful conceptual frameworks, and useful techniques. Hopefully, these can be synthesized and configured in innovative combinations by the new generation of original thinkers who can galvanize a following to inspire further improvement. Will the next generation make history? We shall know it only when we see it.

Future Directions

1. What are the obstacles to identifying group counseling as a "specialty" area in the profession of psychology?

References

Addams, J. (1910). *Twenty years at Hull House*. New York: MacMillan.

Addams, J. (1930). *The second twenty years at Hull House*. New York: MacMillan.

Alinksy, J. L. (2009, August 26). Letter: The organizer's organizer. *New York Times*. Retrieved from http://www.nytimes.com

Alinsky, S. (1971) *Rules for radicals: A pragmatic primer for realistic radicals*. New York: Random House.

American Psychological Association. (2000). Professional practice guidelines for Psychotherapy with lesbian, gay and bisexual clients. *American Psychologist, 55*, 1440–1451.

American Psychological Association. (2002). Guidelines on multicultural education, training, research, practice, and organizational change for psychologists. Retrieved from http://www.apa.org/pi/oema/resources/policy/multicultural-guideline.pdf

American Psychological Association. (2003a). *Principles for validation and use of personnel selection procedures* (4th ed). Retrieved from http://www.siop.org/_Principles/principles-default.aspx

American Psychological Association. (2003b). Guidelines for psychological practice with older adults. Retrieved from http://www.apa.org/practice/guidelines/older-adults.pdf

American Psychological Association. (2005). Guidelines for education and training at the doctoral and postdoctoral level in consulting—psychology/organizational consulting psychology. Retrieved from http://www.apa.org/about/governance/council/policy/div-13-guidelines.pdf

American Psychological Association. (2007). *Guidelines for psychological practice with girls and women: A joint task force for APA Divisions 17 and 35.* Retrieved from http://www.apa.org/about/division/girlsandwomen.pdf

Association for Specialists in Group Work. (1983). *ASGW professional standards for group counseling.* Alexandria, VA: Author. Retrieved from: www.asgw.org

Association for Specialists in Group Work. (1990). *Professional standards for the training of group workers.* Alexandria, VA: Author. Retrieved from: www.asgw.org

Association for Specialists in Group Work. (1998). Guidelines for best practice. *Journal for Specialists in Group Work, 23,* 237–244. doi:10.1080/01933929808411397.

Association for Specialists in Group Work. (1999). ASGW principles for diversity-competent group workers. *Journal for Specialists in Group Work, 24,* 7–14. doi:10.1080/0193392990 8411415.

Bednar, R. L., & Kaul, T. J. (1994). Experiential group research: Can the cannon fire? In A. E. Bergin & S. L. Garfield (Eds.), *Handbook of psychotherapy and behavior change* (4th ed., pp. 631–663). New York: John Wiley & Sons.

Buber, M. (1958). *I and thou* (R. G. Smith, Trans.). New York: Scribner. (Original work published 1923)

Carroll, M., & Levo, L. (1985). The Association for Specialists in Group Work. *Journal for Counseling and Development, 63,* 452–454.

Cohen, N. (2009, August 22). Know thine enemy. *New York Times.* Retrieved from http://www.nytimes.com

Cornford, F. M. (1945). *The republic of Plato.* New York: Oxford University Press.

Corsini, R. J. (1957). *Methods of group psychotherapy.* New York: McGraw-Hill.

Deming, W. E. (2000). *Out of the crisis.* Cambridge, MA: MIT Press. (Originally published 1982)

Dr. Jesse Davis, 84, Boston U Ex-Dean [Obituary]. (1955, November 3). *New York Times.* Retrieved from http://select.nytimes.com/mem/archive/pdf?res=F60917FB3D5F117B9 3C1A9178AD95F418585

Faher, A. L. (2004). *A history of group study and psychodynamic organizations.* London: Free Association Books.

Fox, J. (Ed.). (1987). *Moreno: Writings on psychodrama, group method, and spontaneity by J. L. Moreno.* New York: Springer.

Gladding, S. T. (2003). *Group work: A counseling specialty* (5th ed.). Upper Saddle River, NJ: Pearson Education.

Holusha, J. (1993, December 21). W. Edwards Deming, expert on business management, dies at 93 [Obituary]. *New York Times.* Retrieved from http://www.nytimes.com/1993/12/21/obituaries/w-edwards-deming-expert-on-business-management-dies-at-93.html?scp=1&sq=W.%20Edwards%20Deming&st=cse

Leddick, G. R. (2009). Key historical events in group work. In *The ACA encyclopedia of counseling* (pp. 233–235). Alexandria, VA: American Counseling Association.

Lieberman, M. A., Yalom, I. D., & Miles, M. B. (1973). *Encounter groups: First facts.* New York: Basic Books.

Marineau, R. F. (1989). *Jacob Levy Moreno 1889–1974: Father of psychodrama, sociometry, and group psychotherapy.* London: Routledge.

Marrow, A. J. (1969). *The practical theorist: The life and work of Kurt Lewin.* New York: Basic Books.

Neumann, J. E. (2005). Kurt Lewin at the Tavistock Institute. *Educational Action Research, 13,* 119–136. doi:10.1080/09650790500200271.

O'Donoghue, E. G. (1915). *The story of Bethlehem Hospital: From its foundation in 1247.* New York: E. P. Dutton.

Olson, L. (2001). *Freedom's daughters: The unsung heroines of the civil rights movement from 1830 to 1970.* New York: Touchstone.

Pinney, E. L. (1978). The beginning of group psychotherapy: Joseph Henry Pratt, M.D., and the Reverend Dr. Elwood Worcester. *International Journal of Group Psychotherapy, 28*(1), 109–114.

Pottick, K. J. (1988). Jane Addams revisited: Practice theory and social economics. *Social Work With Groups, 11,* 11–26. doi:10.1300/J009v11n04_04.

Rogers, C. R. (1970). *Carl Rogers on encounter groups.* New York: Harper and Row.

Scheidlinger, S., & Schamess, G. (1992). Fifty years of AGPA 1942–1992: An overview. In R. MacKenzie (Ed.), *Classics in group psychotherapy* (pp. 1–22). New York: Guilford Press.

Schutz, W. C. (1958). *FIRO: A three-dimensional theory of interpersonal behavior.* New York: Rinehart.

Stone, D. (1978). The human potential movement. *Society, 15*(4), 66–68. doi:10.1007/BF02694714.

Turner, W. (1903). *History of philosophy.* Boston: Athenaeum Press.

Yalom, I. D. (1975). *The theory and practice of group psychotherapy* (2nd ed.). New York: Basic Books.

Ethics, Best Practices, and Law in Group Counseling

Lynn S. Rapin

Abstract

Group-counseling practitioners may not be aware of significant similarities and differences among philosophical foundations, professional association documents, and legal terms that guide practice. I will identify similarities and differences among them, highlight essential issues specific to group practice, and suggest future directions. In my discussion, it will be clear that ethical practice in group therapy is not a linear process. Rather, ethical conduct is a matrix relationship involving numerous variables. The following equation highlights the essential components: ethical behavior in group counseling = (moral and ethical development + professional ethics + core knowledge and skills + specialty/best-practice guidelines + legal parameters) × decision-making model(s). While the equation seems linear in its representation, it is not necessarily linear in application.

Keywords: ethics, group counseling, best practice in groups, professional ethics codes and standards, legal issues (in counseling, psychology, social work) with groups

Group counselors have multiple training pathways. Professionals in counseling, psychology, and social work, among others, may describe themselves as providing group counseling. Further, each of these identified professions includes subspecialty practitioners in a myriad of settings. Therefore, in considering general rules of the road for ethical and legal practice, group counselors must appreciate the diversity of contexts within which they function and the many information sources that are available to them.

For the purposes of this chapter, I am using Conyne's (in press) integrative definition of group counseling, which lies midway on a continuum of group interventions from task groups to therapy groups. Group counseling focuses on interpersonal problem solving for issues of daily living. Group purposes of prevention, development, and remediation are all represented in group-counseling interventions.

I focus my review on areas pertinent to the ethical practice of group counseling in the United States and

Canada because global cultural values vary widely and therefore significantly shape professional behavior. In a discussion on the development of professional ethics across national boundaries, Pettifor (2004) commented that some international ethics codes exist but they rarely provide guidance when cultural beliefs and codes of ethics are in conflict. Blickle (2004) added to the discussion that there is a lack of shared theoretical background for such an international code for psychologists. Fisher (2004) responded in her commentary that such an international code might take aspirational, educational, enforceable, or combination formats. Fisher concluded that a shared definition of the common good is but a first step in defining an international ethics code for psychologists. Parallel issues within the professions of social work and counseling can be presumed. For those interested in ethical practice in other countries, Gabriel and Casemore (2009), Francis (2009), and the journal *Groupwork: An Interdisciplinary Journal for Working with Groups* serve as excellent sources.

On the surface, it may appear that appropriate ethical practice is a matter of common sense. Group counselors intend to do the right thing. One might assume that group counselors are well educated and supervised, practice within the scope of their training, and have strong moral and ethical foundations and that decisions flow naturally from these sources. Unfortunately, the roles of moral principles and values; codes of ethics; standards of practice; specialty guidelines for practice; training standards; certifications; and laws across key professions influence ethical behavior, sometimes in conflicting fashion. Each of these elements is central to ethical practice but independently insufficient to guide decisions faced by a group counselor.

Equation for Ethical Behavior in Group Counseling

Practitioners may not be aware of significant similarities and differences among philosophical foundations, professional association documents, and legal terms. I will identify similarities and differences among them, highlight essential issues specific to group practice, and suggest future directions. In my discussion, it will be clear that ethical practice in group therapy is not a linear process. Rather, ethical conduct is a matrix relationship involving numerous variables. I will discuss ethical behavior by using the following equation to highlight the essential components: ethical behavior in group counseling (EBGC) = (moral and ethical development (MED) + professional ethics (PE) + core knowledge and skills (CKS) + specialty/best-practice guidelines (SBPG) + legal parameters (LP)) × decision-making model(s) (DM). While the equation seems linear in its representation, it is not necessarily linear in application.

Moral and Ethical Development in Group Counseling

A group counselor could act morally and not ethically, for example, by holding a particular moral belief (e.g., people of a certain ethnic or demographic group have less to contribute to a group) which is inconsistent with accepted professional ethical behavior. Further, a group counselor may very well act ethically while violating legal statutes and, in contrast, may follow legal statutes but not act ethically (e.g., when a state statute and professional code of ethics are in disagreement). A number of conflicting concepts are at the root of such inconsistency. A discussion of key terms and guiding documents will highlight the threads and contradictions.

General Ethics Definitions

Kitchener (1984) pointed out that the terms *moral* and *ethical* are sometimes defined as separate concepts, with *morality* referring to human beliefs and *ethics* referring to the study and evaluation of moral beliefs and behaviors. At other times, the terms encompass both beliefs and actions. The term *values* refers to the central beliefs that guide action. In the *Encarta World English Dictionary* (Encarta, 2009) *values* is defined as accepted principles or standards, and in its companion thesaurus the word *values* is synonymous with *morals, ethics, principles, standards,* and *ideals*. In the following discussion, both the terms *moral* and *ethical* denote individual beliefs and actions taken upon evaluation of beliefs. One might need to be a philosopher or ethicist to understand the nuances of these terms. One can conclude that debate on precise definitions of moral behavior and ethics will continue. Group counselors benefit from considering the moral beliefs that undergird their personal and professional identities and the behaviors they enact in the conduct of work with groups.

In a special section on ethics in counseling psychology, Kitchener (1996) commented that her previous theoretical model of principle ethics has limitations. She stated that knowing the principled thing to do is not in and of itself sufficient to guarantee ethical behavior. Meara, Schmidt, and Day (1996) suggested that principle ethics are insufficient to describe adherence to or violation of principles. They introduced into the dialogue the consideration of an individual's character strengths (or virtue ethics). Examples in the extreme are relatively easy to generate. For example, a group counselor may know (principle) that sex with a group member is inappropriate but that counselor may have a character flaw (virtue flaw) in thinking that the rule need not apply in his or her specific case. Much more challenging are the subtle situations group leaders face in considering the relative merits of one principle in comparison with another, for example, client protection vs. welfare of the group. Therefore, theorists and researchers have begun to explore the execution of both principle ethics and value ethics (Bersoff, 1996).

In his challenging book on the role of virtue in psychology practice, Fowers (2005) devoted 28 pages to the definition of *virtue*, in which he focused "especially on the pursuit of what is good as the heart of virtue, for virtues are the character strengths that make that pursuit possible" (p. 11). Fowers used the singular term *virtue* to encompass the broad collection of individual virtues and the capacity to act on them. He used the words *virtues* and *character strengths* interchangeably in describing a particular positive aspect of behavior, for example, *beneficence*, the doing good for others. Fowers posited that US psychology's historical focus on individualism, for example, in the setting of goals, has led to deficiencies in our view of the world. He stated that "we have blinded ourselves to the depth of our social embeddedness and dependency on others" (p. 84). He argued further that virtue and character develop within a social and cultural context and that those contexts "are indispensable for human flourishing" (p. 92). In his review of the literature, Fowers concluded that individuals who perceive support for their goals from others have more success in reaching their goals and demonstrate more persistence in seeking their goals (p. 102). Certainly, there is direct application to the power of the group, be it a counseling group, social group, or community. Fowers argues, "Virtue ethics highlights the ways in which the social world helps to constitute the individual and provides an ongoing and essential context for the possibility of individual pursuits and flourishing" (p. 103).

Virtue ethics can bridge the gap between the actor (professional group counselor) and the action of sorting through a decision process (through the implementation of principle ethics). Considering the application of virtue ethics to social work training and practice, Adams (2009) suggests that virtue ethics attend to the decision maker's character, culture, history, and life influences as well as to how any one decision affects other decisions (p. 86).

Intellectual and Moral Development

People acquire moral beliefs throughout their lifetimes and refine them in personal, educational, and career paths through social experience. In considering the moral development of group counselors, maturation as an individual and as a professional interacts with ethical choice points. In consideration of virtue or character, some authors (Kitchener, 1992, 1996; Fowers, 2005) have wondered whether developing mental health practitioners can learn to have character strengths/virtue ethics or whether they should be selected into training programs with such strengths already present. Kitchener (1992, p. 194) further recommended the following: "However, because screening interviews sometimes miss characterological problems that appear later, faculty have a responsibility to continue to evaluate a student's personal and professional competence to practice." To date, there is no either/or answer to the question.

Research on intellectual and ethical development suggests an additional dimension. Perry (1970) documented in a longitudinal study of college undergraduates that the forms in which individuals perceive the world have value beyond the specific content of the individual's attitudes and concerns. That is, the "how" of an individual's thinking and view of the world (the process) can be more powerful than the specific content that he or she is encountering. In Perry's nine-step scheme, students move from a dualistic view of the world (there is a specific right way to respond, the world is good or bad, information is known, one can learn the one correct response) through a long phase of multiplicity, where there are initially exceptions to the absolute, then the world is seen as completely relativistic. As maturation continues and experience becomes more complex, individuals move to commitment within a relativistic world. At each developmental step, the learner can regress to a previous form of world perception as he or she learns the new rules of behavior. Perry found that extremely dualistic students were unlikely to pursue advanced study because of the increasing levels of ambiguity present in academic and professional settings. Following Perry's developmental model, ethically mature group counselors would actively engage in ongoing self-exploration of the processes by which they formulate responses to ethical challenges.

Rest (1984) proposed that four components are required for moral behavior to occur and that each component has distinct cognitive and affective interfacings. These include (1) moral sensitivity, or the ability to interpret a situation as a moral one; (2) moral reasoning, or the ability to consider a moral course of action; (3) choosing from among value options the one to enact; and (4) implementing the moral action. Rest's model has unique utility in that it does not depend upon a particular theoretical model but rather on the complex interactions of cognition, affect, and behavior.

Research and Recommendations on Moral and Ethics Education

Research on ethics education and practice has shown inconsistent findings. There are far more examples of ethical principles and models than there are of research on ethical practice. This is true for both general ethics training and training in ethics applications to groups.

Rest (1984) used his four-component model in reviewing a large body of research on moral deveopment and concluded that multifaceted, interdisciplinary efforts are necessary in the moral education of counselors. He stated that moral education programs for mental health professionals should include complements to curriculum including participation from practitioners in the field to provide realism and relevance to training programs in the provision of moral models; theoretical contributions from philosophy, law, and theology for analysis of problems and solutions; and research contributions to assess beginning and advanced competence.

In a special section on ethics education in professional psychology, Welfel (1992) used Rest's model in her review of 35 years of research on moral education. Welfel found that there was a discrepancy between students' understanding of ethical standards and their ability and willingness to apply ethics and standards in practice. In a subsequent study of psychology internship directors, Welfel found that internship directors gave positive reports of interns' ethical understanding of 16 areas of ethics content (including, e.g., dual relationships, confidentiality, right to treatment, therapy with culturally diverse), cited few instances of ethical misconduct, and perceived ethics training to be improving. Unfortunately, Welfel found research "evidence of poor ethical awareness, limited skills in interpreting the Ethical Principles . . . and a good deal of unwillingness to carry out ethical action even when known." Based on her research findings, Welfel suggested that there is little empirical data to support the effectiveness of any particular ethics education format.

Wilson and Ranft (1993) conducted an exploratory study of ethics training for doctoral-level counseling psychology students. The authors reviewed the evolution of ethics training in psychology and identified as a major impetus the American Psychological Association's (APA's) 1979 requirement of teaching ethics and standards in APA doctoral programs. In their review, Wilson and Ranft found little consistency in the methods of ethics training. Their research study concluded that in the early 1990s most of the counseling psychology ethics instruction was in discussion (with 98%), lectures (with 76%), and scenarios (with 58%). Experimental methods, such as decision-making labs, accounted for 20% of instruction. Most of the instruction was on content (e.g., specific codes) rather than on processes of legal and ethical decision making and problem solving (p. 452). One unique finding was that students perceived their preparation for ethical decision making to be greater than their training in content, in spite of the report that training programs spent more time on content.

In a survey of clinical and counseling psychology training directors, Fly, van Bark, Weinman, Kitchener, and Lang (1997) found that the most common ethical errors encountered by graduate students occurred in the areas of confidentiality and dual-role relationships. The authors recommended that more attention be devoted to ethics training of graduate students.

Betan and Stanton (1999) reviewed the literature on ethical compliance and found that "Research repeatedly indicates a discrepancy between what psychologists define as the appropriate ethical decision and their intention to implement the decision toward ethical action" (p. 295). Betan and Stanton conducted a further study of clinical psychology graduate students and found an interaction between students' ability to make ethical decisions and their confidence to act on their decision. They found that while 95% of sampled students indicated the appropriate action of reporting colleague behavior, they were likely to initially opt for a less direct action (talking with a colleague before reporting) when pulled by emotions. Betan and Stanton recommended that training models include (1) attention to the impacts of personal emotions and concerns, (2) active education in how emotions can serve as cues to appropriate or inappropriate action, and (3) the idea that educators can promote the integration of emotions into effective ethical responses. In application, they suggested that a response may be to recognize the feeling, realize how the feeling may affect behavior, and then decide what to do with the knowledge.

Research on General Ethics Practice

Pope, Tabachnick, and Keith-Spiegel (1987) surveyed a national sample of Psychotherapy Division members of the APA on their ethical beliefs. Each psychologist rated 83 behaviors on three variables: relevance, degree of participation, and ethical degree of the behaviors. Participants then rated a list of 14 resources for level of guidance in their practice. Twelve behaviors were difficult to rate as ethical. Results were discussed around seven organizing principles: (1) do no harm, (2) practice with competence, (3) do not exploit, (4) treat people with respect, (5) protect confidentiality, (6) employ informed consent, and (7) promote equity and justice. With regard to helpful resources, the three most endorsed sources were informal colleague network, APA ethical principles, and internship. The three lowest-rated resources were state and federal laws, published research, and local ethics committees.

Pope and Bajt (1988) examined the responses of 100 psychologists with significant experience on state ethics committees, on the APA ethics committee, as authors of ethics texts, and as diplomates. Respondents identified what law or ethical principle they had violated to protect client welfare or other deeper value. More than 50% reported such activity, with the greatest (48%) occurring to protect client confidentiality. In considering assistance with the decision, 50% consulted someone before the action and 68% discussed it afterward. Seventy-three percent said that they would make the same decision again, and about the same percentage reported that psychologists might violate legal or ethical standards. Few respondents (18%) said that their education, training, and supervision were adequate and only 22% reported that such conflicts are adequately addressed in scholarly work. This study is a good example of the inconsistency and potential conflicts arising among the variables that protect the public and guide professional behavior.

Pope and Vetter (1992) conducted a study of 679 APA members (a return rate of 51% of an original sample of 1,319), soliciting incidents of ethical concern that respondents may have experienced in the prior 2 years. Results produced 703 ethically troubling incidents in 23 general categories. The three most frequently identified issues were confidentiality (*n* = 128); blurred, dual, or conflictual relationships (*n* = 116); and issues with payment sources, plans, settings, and methods (*n* = 97). Pope and Vetter noted that in 1990 issues of confidentiality accounted for only 2% of APA ethics complaints. In the current study, 18% of the ethical examples cited were about confidentiality, suggesting that ethics codes revisions reflect major areas of concern for psychologists, as well as complaints.

McMinn, Buchanan, Ellens, and Ryan (1999) conducted a study on psychologists' use of 40 technologies in their independent practices. Their findings demonstrated that advances in technology have outpaced psychologists' comfort, skill, and awareness of the ethical implications of technology use and the development of guidance documents. Technology in group work has received attention in professional publications via special issues of journals (McGothlin, 2003; Page, 2003a, 2003b), general reference texts (American Counseling Association, 2009), and dedicated chapters in group-counseling and group-therapy texts (Meier, 2004; Page, 2004), among others.

Nowell and Spruill (1993) conducted a study of willingness to disclose personal material in three levels of confidentiality: (1) when complete confidentiality was promised, (2) when legal limits were generally defined, and (3) when specific limits were described. The researchers found a significant ($P < 0.05$) increase in willingness to disclose personal material in the full confidential group. Additional detail showed no significant differences. Although this study was conducted on willingness to disclose in general counseling, it has specific application to group situations in which major limits exist in confidentiality.

In a national study of social workers with master's degrees, DiFranks (2008) surveyed relationships between social workers' belief in the National Association of Social Workers Code of Ethics (for the year 2000), their behavior, and resulting disjunctive distress. Items on the behavior scale reflected code values or did not reflect the values. For example, one item states, "Despite all intentions to do otherwise, there have been times when I have had to compromise my professional integrity in my job setting" (p. 173). Items on the disjuncture scale reflected levels of distress with behaviors, for example, "I feel increased stress because, at times, my professional integrity has been compromised by practice realities" (p. 173). Higher disjuncture (stress) occurred when beliefs and behavior were inconsistent. Stress increased with incongruent behavior. The managed care item had the second highest stress score, and social workers employed in managed care had the highest disjuncture scores. A puzzling finding was that the positive relationship between belief and behavior was not significant. DiFranks recommended further study.

Research on Ethics in Groups
As the conceptual and research literature on the ethical behavior of mental health professionals has expanded, complexity has increased. The *Journal for Specialists in Group Work* (Forester-Miller, 1990) devoted a special issue to ethical and legal issues in group work. Subsequently, more attention has been devoted to ethics issues in group work.

Major ethics issues in groups consistently identified in the literature since the 1980s include leader values, member screening and orientation, voluntary and involuntary membership, group facilitator preparation and behaviors, protection of members, confidentiality, dual relationships, and billing (Berg, Landreth, & Fall, 1998; Capuzzi & Muffett, 1980, Corey, Corey, & Callanan, 2003; Glass, 1998; Paradise & Kirby, 1990; Paradise & Siegelwaks, 1982; Pepper, 2007; Posthuma, 2002). More recently, leader cognitions (Stockton, Morran, & Krieger, 2004), diversity and multiculturalism (Corey et al., 2003;

incongruence

Ethical Issues In Group

DeLucia-Waack and Donigian, 2004; Debiak, 2007; Posthuma, 2002), leader values (Corey et al., 2003), the use of modern communication technologies (American Telemedicine Association, 2009; Counseling Psychologist, 2005; Maheu & Gordon, 2000; Page, 2003a, 2003b, 2004), and record keeping (Knauss, 2006) have received more attention.

In a study with members of the Association for Specialists in Group Work (ASGW) on ethical practices and standards for group facilitators, Gumaer and Duncan (1982) found consistency in the degree of agreement on two sets of guidelines, one for facilitators and one on implementation of group activities. Further, those surveyed showed consistency between their beliefs and actions. Study participants with more academic training (those with doctorates) were found to have more variability in surveyed responses. Results may reflect movement from more dualistic responses to more informed, nuanced responses to guidelines expected from moral and ethical development (Perry, 1970; Rest, 1984). Gumaer and Scott (1986) found no significant differences among ASGW members surveyed with ethics vignettes. The researchers suggested that group leaders ask reflective questions when considering ethical situations.

Lakin (1994) did a content analysis of the 1992 APA ethics code in application to group and family therapy. Issues of leader competence, informed consent, mutual assistance, group cohesion, and diversity were discussed, with the general suggestion that the complexities of ethical decisions are magnified in the group setting.

In their contribution to empirically supported group treatments, Burlingame, Fuhriman, and Johnson (2001) identified six leader behaviors that foster relationship building and cohesion: (1) pregroup preparation; (2) clarification of group processes across the life of the group; (3) promotion of relationship building, modeling here-and-now responses, and guiding appropriate feedback; (4) considering timing of feedback; (5) modeling appropriate emotional expression; and (6) facilitating member participation in the process of disclosure and meaning making (cf. Rapin, 2004).

A special issue of the *Journal for Specialists in Group Work* (Conyne & Bemak, 2004a) devoted to teaching group work serves as an excellent resource for ethics education in groups. Conyne and Bemak (2004b) present an ecological perspective in teaching group work. Key ASGW documents are provided as guidance for teaching group skills and competencies (Bemak & Chung, 2004; Wilson,

Rapin, & Haley-Banez, 2004). Core (Gillam, 2004; Guth & McDonnell, 2004; Killacky & Hulse-Killacky, 2004) and advanced (Barlow, 2004) group skills are examined. Special ethical issues in the teaching of group work (Davenport, 2004; Kottler, 2004; O'Halloran & McCartney, 2004; Riva & Korinek, 2004) and applications to work with children (Akos, Goodnough, & Milsom, 2004; Van Velsor, 2004) are discussed.

Lasky and Riva (2006) reviewed the literature on confidentiality in groups and identified several issues, including (1) member and leader understanding of the definition of *confidentiality*, (2) its limits in group counseling and therapy, (3) whether leaders presented information to group members, and (4) violations of confidentiality by group leaders. General results showed poor understanding of the concept and its limits in group counseling and therapy.

Fallon (2006) offered a lengthy review of the literature on informed consent. She identified via the literature potential conflicts among professional values in the provision of informed consent in therapy groups (e.g., between beneficence and nonmaleficence or among member autonomy and beneficence and nonmaleficence). Fallon identified ethical issues in providing informed consent, including leader values, member screening and orientation, voluntary/involuntary membership, group leader preparation, and protection of members. Fallon also identified the risks inherent in group treatment, including the potential for no goal accomplishment or deterioration, mismatches between group and member goals, and potential unintended consequences of information disclosure.

Knauss (2006) reviewed the literature on record keeping in groups and presented via case vignettes common ethical issues. Considered were the advantages of keeping individual records for each group member, demonstrating the potential conflicts between beneficence in comparison with autonomy and nonmaleficence. Also demonstrated were risks to confidentiality without individual records. Knauss recommended that group practitioners be mindful of the legal risks in keeping only group records when situations regarding one group member arise, for example, with a complaint or with a court-ordered information release.

Using a survey with experienced American Group Psychotherapy Association (AGPA) members, Mangione, Forti, & Iacuzzi (2007) explored ethical issues in ending group treatments. Via case vignettes, the researchers identified concerns with difficult or unanticipated endings and the ethics principles that were reflected. Concerns included informed consent; member expectations, including individual versus group goals; time boundaries and their alteration; dual relationships; and confidentiality.

In a two-volume special issue of the *International Journal of Group Psychotherapy* on ethics in group therapy, Roback and Moore (2007, see also *International Journal of Group Psychotherapy*, 2007) challenged the special issue authors and readers to expand their ethical analyses to include not only the most frequently referenced perspective (principle ethics) and the occasionally referenced virtue ethics but also other ethics models. Other models were embraced in a clever case example, with ethical reflection from several additional values perspectives. These included (1) casuistry, in which one does not apply principles to solve ethical dilemmas but rather studies ethical dilemmas to identify principles; (2) a geocultural view of considering moral context within a particular culture; (3) a feminist perspective of care and consideration of all applicable relationships; and (4) radical feminism, in which power relationships are key. They beautifully demonstrate that group counselors have many and often conflicting values choices that can influence ethical decision making. MacNair-Semands (2007) added her commentary from a social justice framework, expanding on the moral principle of justice.

Brabender and Fallon (2009) examined group and individual case vignettes from several ethical perspectives, first using principle ethics guided by beneficence, nonmaleficence, autonomy, fidelity, and justice. They then analyzed the case through three "context-based ethical paradigms" (p. 136). They employed the virtue of prudence to demonstrate how virtue ethics can assist with group decisions. They applied feminist ethics, reflecting inherent asymmetry in counseling relationships, to demonstrate the influence of power and authority in decision making. By questioning whether preservation of life applied to the ethical situation, Brabender and Fallon were implementing casuistry as an ethical model. They concluded that practitioners improve ethics decisions with the integration of multiple perspectives.

Major Professional Ethics Codes and Group Counseling

The professions of counseling, psychology, and social work have unique identities but share ethical foundations with each other and with older professions such as law and medicine. All follow the fundamental ethical principle of the Hippocratic oath of first do no harm. For members of a profession or organization, ethics documents that govern appropriate behavior reflect shared values (Acuff et al., 1999; Fisher, 2004; Kitchener, 1996; Northen, 2004; Rapin, 2004; Rapin & Conyne, 2006). Furthermore, counseling, psychology, and social work are professions governed by licensure and specific state or provincial regulation. (See the section Legal Parameters in this chapter for more discussion.)

Principles in Ethics Documents

Acuff et al. (1999) refer to ethical decisions as those pertaining to overarching moral principles that guide behavior. Adapting medical ethics principles to psychology, Kitchener (1984) postulated that the five moral principles of autonomy, beneficence, nonmaleficence, justice, and fidelity serve as the foundation of ethical guidelines. Welfel & Kitchener (1992) and Kitchener (1992) employed Kitchener's list of five moral principles in a special journal section on ethics education in psychology. Posthuma (2002) concentrated on autonomy, nonmaleficence, and beneficence in her text on small groups in counseling. Meara et al. (1996) added veracity to the core set of principles but cautioned that any such list of core ethical principles is somewhat arbitrary. They argued that "one could present a convincing rationale for adding or subtracting a particular entry" (p. 15). Brabender (2006; 2007and Koocher and Keith-Spiegel (1998, 2008) have made ongoing contributions to the narrative both through definitions of values and in their applications.

In her discussion of counseling, Welfel (2006) enumerated four dimensions of ethics that include having (1) adequate knowledge and skill to employ interventions, (2) respect for human dignity and freedom of clients, (3) demonstration of responsibility, and (4) promotion of public confidence. In the counseling and psychology codes in the United States, the five key ethical principles postulated by Kitchener (1984) permeate and ground most documents. Gazda, Ginter, and Horne (2001) and Koocher and Keith-Spiegel (2008) applied the key five plus an additional four principles. Gazda et al. applied the principles specifically to counseling groups. The four additional principles parallel Welfel's (2006) ethical dimensions and include dignity, professional performance, accountability, and care and compassion. The following five key principles do not presume a priority order.

Autonomy refers to individual freedom of participation. Steere's definition (as cited in

Posthuma, 2002, p. 144) of autonomy is particularly applicable to group counseling: "individuals should be free to act according to their own beliefs and perceptions providing that, in doing so, they do not impede the freedom of others to do the same thing." Inherent in autonomy is the assumption that group members are capable of making good decisions. Posthuma highlighted the potential of group influence to both promote participants' positive change and exert peer-level coercion or pressure for a particular level of disclosure or participation. Cultural differences and variations have great potential impact on autonomy. For example, silence for one participant may indicate respect, while for another member it may indicate resistance. The power of the group is influenced by its contexts.

Nonmaleficence is the oldest of ethical principles, defined as do no harm. Gazda et al. (2001) note that nonmaleficence applies to "acts of omission or commission" (p. 98). Consequences of leader and member action or inaction may have deleterious effects on the members or on the relationships that members have outside of the group. Consideration of stage of group development, in balance with therapeutic choices in each phase, can protect group members and leaders alike.

Beneficence encompasses positive actions for the benefit of others (e.g., the members individually and the group as a whole). It also implies harm prevention. In application to groups, beneficence supports both individual and group goals and the concept of mutual support. Meara et al. (1996) argued that beneficence also applies to serving the common good, for example, in policy construction.

Justice, the concept of fairness, permeates the responsibilities of group-counseling leaders in that it presumes that the leader will treat all members in an even-handed manner. This principle can be especially relevant in groups with high diversity.

Fidelity refers to the leader's obligation to be faithful to the group purposes in working with members. This principle may often be in conflict with other ethical or organizational imperatives. For example, when an agency has long waiting lists, it may assign clients to group treatment with the intent of providing prompt and economical care. Specific client needs may be overridden by agency or staff member concerns about units of service delivered or caseload requirements. Leader knowledge and skill in providing a counseling

group may thus be overridden by organization needs. Additionally, fidelity may be in direct conflict with ethical standards or practice laws regarding reports of certain types of client risk. Threats to self and specific others and child or elder abuse serve as ready examples.

The Canadian Psychological Association (CPA, 2000) uses slightly different language in their identification of four key principles and ranks them in order of consideration from respect for the dignity of persons to responsible caring, integrity in relationships, and responsibility to society. Responsible caring is similar to the APA principle of fidelity. The principle of responsibility to society is specifically identified in the Canadian code as having the least weight when principles conflict. The CPA ethics code preamble (p. 2) states, "the dignity and well-being of a person should not be sacrificed to a vision of the greater good of society, and greater weight must be given to respect and responsible caring for the person."

The Canadian Association of Social Workers (CASW, 2005a) frames its code around six values: value 1, respect for inherent dignity and worth of persons; value 2, pursuit of social justice; value 3, service to humanity; value 4, integrity of professional practice; value 5, confidentiality in professional practice; and value 6, competence in professional practice. Each value is associated with practice principles. The National Association of Social Workers (NASW, 1999) shares all of the values with the CASW except that of confidentiality, which is covered in their accompanying standards.

Social work has a unique distinction from counseling and psychology in that social justice is a core social work value. In its latest revision to the code, the CASW moved social justice from the sixth to the second chapter of their document to reflect the importance of the social justice mission of social work (CASW, 2005b). Psychology and counseling emphasize justice in practice documents, but they do not specify the level of responsibility that counselors or psychologists have to the societal level of justice. However, counseling and psychology have increased their attention to social justice. The American Counseling Association (ACA) has a social justice division. Thirteen APA divisions currently participate in the informal Divisions for Social Justice to increase visibility of social justice issues in governance and programs. For psychologists, there is not a firm commitment to social justice. Pettifor (2004) said, "Psychologists do not agree on whether they have a responsibility to promote social justice and to bring about societal changes" (p. 270).

Core Knowledge and Skills in Group Counseling

As group-counseling practitioners gain more experience and consider numerous sources of guidance in ethical decision making, they encounter increased burdens of ethical responsibility and nuance. For a more experienced group counselor, contextual variables multiply, rather than simplify, potential actions. In discussing an ecological-systems perspective in social work with groups, Tropman (2004) posited, "It is the context, or extragroup influences and resources . . . that form the crux of the ecological perspective" (p. 33). Consideration of scope of practice, group membership, confidentiality, appropriateness of fit to the group, community needs, choice of group activities, consistency with a theoretical model, or unintended consequences may produce many potential choice points and responses about what to do in each session or phase of the group. Reliance on codes of ethics that denote prescribed behaviors or prohibited behaviors would prove insufficient in many situations.

Because membership in professional associations is optional, nonparticipating group counselors may not be obligated to adhere to a particular professional code or standard of practice. For group counselors who do belong to professional associations of counseling, psychology, or social work, major documents guide broad practice. Professional organizations reviewed here include the ACA (2005), American Mental Health Counselors Association (AMHCA, 2010); College Student Educators International (American College Personnel Association, 2006); APA (2002), National Association of Social Workers (2008), CPA (2000), and CASW (2005a, 2005b). Over time, each of the identified professional associations has revised its governing documents to reflect current community standards and advances in delivery systems.

Sections of ethics documents can be aspirational, representing virtue ethics (e.g., APA, 2002, *Ethical Principles*; ACA, 2005, *Code of Ethics* section introductions), and are not enforceable. Other sections, representing principle ethics, specifically prescribe professional conduct (e.g., APA and ACA codes of ethics) and require adjudication. Other professional documents provide guidance and are not associated with the investigation or disposition of ethical complaints (e.g., AMHCA, 2010, *Code of Ethics*).

Group counselors need to be knowledgeable of the distinctions in the documents of their professional associations.

While the ethics documents of the major professional associations of counseling, psychology, and social work cover general practice, there are specific references to group work within them that deserve attention. Group counselors need to be aware of the most current versions of the documents that guide their practice and the unique responsibilities that accompany group work.

Group Counseling in Counseling Ethics Documents

The structure of the latest revision of the ACA *Code of Ethics* (2005) has significantly changed from previous versions in that the code itself defines minimum expected behaviors. The code no longer includes a set of prescriptive standards of practice. Group-counselor responsibilities are delineated in three sections of the code (Counseling Relationship; Confidentiality, Privileged Communication and Privacy; and Supervision, Training and Teaching).

In considering the counseling relationship, group counselors consider their roles regarding multiple clients. Item A7 is, "When a counselor agrees to provide counseling services to two or more persons who have a relationship, the counselor clarifies at the outset which person or persons are clients and the nature of the relationships the counselor will have with each involved person. If it becomes apparent that the counselor may be called upon to perform potentially conflicting roles, the counselor will clarify, adjust, or withdraw from roles appropriately." In item A8a, screening is clarified: "Counselors screen prospective group counseling/therapy participants. To the extent possible, counselors select members whose needs and goals are compatible with goals of the group, who will not impede the group process, and whose well-being will not be jeopardized by the group experience." Item A8b, Protecting Clients, is framed as follows: "In a group setting, counselors take reasonable precautions to protect clients from physical, emotional, or psychological trauma." Item B4a applies to involvement with groups and families: "In group work, counselors clearly explain the importance and parameters of confidentiality for the specific group being entered." Item B4b is more specific to group work with couples and families: "In couples and family counseling, counselors clearly define who is considered 'the client' and discuss expectations and limitations of confidentiality.

Counselors seek agreement and document in writing such agreement among all involved parties having capacity to give consent concerning each individual's right to confidentiality and any obligation to preserve the confidentiality of information known." Item F6e, on peer relationships, is as follows: "Counselor educators make every effort to ensure that the rights of peers are not compromised when students or supervisees lead counseling groups or provide clinical supervision. Counselor educators take steps to ensure that students and supervisees understand they have the same ethical obligations as counselor educators, trainers, and supervisors."

The AMHCA *Code of Ethics* (2010) has four references to group counselor responsibilities. In Counselor–Client Relationship, item IA2l regarding confidentiality, group counselors are advised as follows: "In working with families or groups, the rights to confidentiality of each member should be safeguarded. Mental health counselors must make clear that each member of the group has individual rights to confidentiality . . . within legal limits." Under Counseling Process, group screening is specified in IB3e: "When working in groups, mental health counselors screen prospective group counseling/therapy participants. Every effort is made to select members whose needs and goals are compatible with goals of the group, who will not impede the group process, and whose well-being will not be jeopardized by the group experience." In item IB3f, client protection is specified: "In the group setting, mental health counselors take reasonable precautions to protect clients from physical, emotional, and psychological harm or trauma."

Group-counselor members of the American College Personnel Association (ACPA), College Student Educators International, work within postsecondary educational settings with students from around the world. The one reference to group counseling found in the ACPA *Statement of Ethical Principles and Standards* (2006) appears in Student Learning and Development (2.14): "Assure that required experiences involving self-disclosure are communicated to prospective graduate students. When the preparation program offers experiences that emphasize self-disclosure or other relatively intimate or personal involvement (e.g., group or individual counseling or growth groups), professionals must not have current or anticipated administrative, supervisory, or evaluative authority over participants." Yao (2004) has suggested guidelines for facilitating groups with international college students.

The National Board for Certified Counselors *Code of Ethics* (2005) refers to group counseling in section B: Counseling Relationship, item 1: "In a group setting, the certified counselor is also responsible for taking reasonable precautions to protect individuals from physical and/or psychological trauma resulting from interaction within the group." In item 16, confidentiality in group counseling is further denoted: "In group counseling, counselors clearly define confidentiality and the parameters for the specific group being entered, explain the importance of confidentiality, and discuss the difficulties related to confidentiality involved in group work. The fact that confidentiality cannot be guaranteed is clearly communicated to group members. However, counselors should give assurance about their professional responsibility to keep all group communications confidential."

Group Counseling in Psychology Ethics Documents

The APA's *Ethical Principles of Psychologists and Code of Conduct* (2002) guides the broad practice of psychology and therefore has few references to specific specialties. Three items directly address participation in training groups and defining roles and responsibilities in groups. Ethical standard 7.02, Descriptions of Education and Training Programs, states, "Psychologists responsible for education and training programs take reasonable steps to ensure that there is a current and accurate description of the program content (including participation in required course- or program-related counseling, psychotherapy, experiential groups, consulting projects, or community service), training goals and objectives, stipends and benefits, and requirements that must be met for satisfactory completion of the program. This information must be made readily available to all interested parties." The related standard 7.05, Mandatory Individual or Group Therapy, states, "(a) When individual or group therapy is a program or course requirement, psychologists responsible for that program allow students in undergraduate and graduate programs the option of selecting such therapy from practitioners unaffiliated with the program. (b) Faculty who are or are likely to be responsible for evaluating students' academic performance do not themselves provide that therapy." Ethical standard 10.03 states, "when psychologists provide services to several persons in a group setting, they describe at the outset the roles and responsibilities of all parties and the limits of confidentiality."

The CPA's *Code of Ethics for Psychologists* (2000) defines a client as "an individual, family, or group (including an organization or community) receiving service from a psychologist." In the Principle of Respect for the Dignity of Persons (I.44) on confidentiality, psychologists "Clarify what measures will be taken to protect confidentiality, and what responsibilities family, group, and community members have for the protection of each other's confidentiality, when engaged in services to or research with individuals, families, groups, or communities." In principle II, Responsible Caring, psychologists conduct a risk/benefit analysis, in item II.13, by assessing "the individuals, families, groups, and communities involved in their activities adequately enough to ensure that they will be able to discern what will benefit and not harm the persons involved." To offset or correct harm, item II.38 cautions psychologists to "Refuse to help individuals, families, groups, or communities to carry out or submit to activities that, according to current knowledge, or legal or professional guidelines, would cause serious physical or psychological harm to themselves or others." Further, in item II.43, psychologists are instructed to "Not place an individual, group, family, or community needing service at a serious disadvantage by offering them no service in order to fulfill the conditions of a research design, when a standard service is available." The Principle of Integrity in Relationships cautions groups, in item III.32, to "Not offer rewards sufficient to motivate an individual or group to participate in an activity that has possible or known risks to themselves or others."

Group Counseling in Social Work Ethics Foundations

In the NASW *Code of Ethics* (2008), there are two specific references to confidentiality in groups in ethical standard 1, Responsibility to Clients, Ethical Privacy and Confidentiality, 1.07f : "When social workers provide counseling services to families, couples, or groups, social workers should seek agreement among the parties involved concerning each individual's right to confidentiality and obligation to preserve the confidentiality of information shared by others. Social workers should inform participants in family, couples, or group counseling that social workers cannot guarantee that all participants will honor such agreements." Standard 1.07g further clarifies informed consent and confidentiality: "Social workers should inform clients involved in family, couples, marital, or group counseling of the social worker's, employer's, and agency's policy concerning the social

worker's disclosure of confidential information among the parties involved in the counseling."

In its companion documents *Code of Ethics* and *Guidelines for Ethical Practice*, the CASW (2005a, 2005b) refers to values and principles rather than to ethical duties, obligations, and responsibilities as organizing constructs. The code defines "client" as "A person, family, group of persons, incorporated body, association or community on whose behalf a social worker provides or agrees to provide a service or to whom the social worker is legally obligated to provide a service." Guidelines refer specifically to group work in the Ethical Responsibilities to Clients section, item 1.5.4: "When social workers provide services to families, couples, or groups, social workers seek agreement among the parties involved concerning each individual's right to confidentiality and the obligation to preserve the confidentiality of information shared by others. Social workers inform participants in family, couples, or group counselling that social workers cannot guarantee that all participants will honour such agreements."

Group Counseling Ethics Concurrence across Professions

In reviewing the above documents for professions of counseling, psychology, and social work in the United States and Canada, three areas of specific ethical concern about group counseling appear: the client relationship, confidentiality, and protection of students. Across the professions, group counselors have the duty of defining roles and responsibilities for group members and leaders.

Key to the process is the screening of group members for appropriate fit to the goals of the group and the needs of its members. Professionals are guided by the principle of doing no harm, even if it means that services are withheld from an interested potential participant. Confidentiality and its limits are crucial to the practice of group counseling in that each participating member of the group owns confidentiality. Group counselors must be able to discuss with members the responsibility of keeping information about fellow participants confidential while also defining the limits of confidentiality. Members of counseling groups must be aware of the limits of confidentiality on their personal disclosure. Group counselors must balance the importance of confidentiality with the reality that it cannot be guaranteed. Additionally, professional documents define the responsibility of group counselors to disclose situations in which they might be obligated by agency policy or state/provincial law to violate confidentiality. Confidentiality limits will be discussed in more detail in the Legal Parameters section of this chapter.

The third area in which professional documents refer specifically to group work involves the dual relationships for providers of student preparation, training, and supervision. There is an inherent conflict of interest if a student preparing to be a group counselor must participate in a group led by his or her direct supervisor, professor, or another student in the program. Suggestions for avoiding such conflict include providing alternate participation experiences with people unaffiliated with the evaluation process or with individuals outside of the training program. While these suggestions may work in many environments, they may be challenging to accomplish in communities with limited resources. Sklare, Thomas, Williams, and Powers (1996) and Kottler (2004) have made recommendations about how to incorporate here-and-now and professor-led training groups, respectively, into ethics training.

Group Specialty Association Training Standards and Best-Practice Guidelines

Group specialty associations provide guidance that is more specific to group facilitators who may be counselors, psychologists, social workers, or practitioners in related fields. In every case, parent organizations govern ethical conduct. Each group specialty organization identifies values, knowledge, and skills uniquely pertinent to the practice of group work. Each association publishes a journal to support the science and practice of group work, and some have additional aspirational group-work guidelines and documents. Specialty documents are time-sensitive and revised periodically to reflect the current ethical codes of conduct and standards of practice of their professional associations, laws, advances in technology, and community standards. Comparisons of training standards (Table 5.1) and best-practice guidelines (Table 5.2) are presented for review of several factors.

Group Work in Counseling Training Standards

In its 2009 accreditation standards for counseling programs, the Council for Accreditation of Counseling and Related Educational Programs (CACREP) specified group work as one of eight required common core curricular areas. Included in the group work core are five broad areas critical to beginning-level group practice. CACREP does not mandate a particular number of group courses in the current revision of the standards, although it does require student participation as members of a group. CACREP (2009) defined *group work* as studies that provide both theoretical and experiential understandings of group purpose, development, dynamics, theories, methods, skills, and

Table 5.1 Group training standards comparison

Organization	Audience	Competencies	Group Types	Clock Hours
CACREP	Master's programs	Core		10 in 1 term
ASGW	Master's programs	Core		1 Course + 10 Observation and Participation
				(20 recommended)
	Doctoral/specialty	Advanced	Task, psychoed	30 in specialty
	Programs			(45 recomm.)
	Doctoral/specialty	Advanced	Counseling, therapy	45 in specialty
				(60 recomm.)
AGPA	Terminal degree	Core		12 Course/training
CGP	Postdegree + license	Advanced	Therapy	300 Leading group
				+75 Supervision

CACREP, Council for Accreditation of Counseling and Related Educational Programs; ASGW, Association for Specialists in Group Work; AGPA, American Group Psychotherapy Association; CGP, certified group psychotherapist.

Table 5.2   Group organization best-practice guidelines comparison

	ASGW Best-Practice Guidelines	AASWG Standards for Social Work Practice with Groups	AGPA Clinical Practice Guidelines for Group Psychotherapy
Audience	Master's advanced degree	All	Terminal degree
Required/aspirational	Aspirational	Required	Aspirational
Competency	Core specialty	Core and advanced	
Group Type(s) Specified	Task, psychoed, counseling, therapy	—	Therapy
Presentation	Planning, performing, processing	Pregroup planning, beginning, middle, end	Group issues and stages

other group approaches in a multicultural society, including all of the following:

• *Principles of group dynamics*, including group process components, developmental stage theories, group members' roles and behaviors, and therapeutic factors of group work
• *Group leadership or facilitation styles and approaches*, including characteristics of various types of group leaders and leadership styles
• *Theories of group counseling*, including commonalities, distinguishing characteristics, and pertinent research and literature
• *Group counseling methods*, including group counselor orientations and behaviors, appropriate selection criteria and methods, and methods of evaluation of effectiveness
• *Direct experiences*, in which students participate as group members in a small group activity, approved by the program, for a minimum of 10 clock hours over the course of one academic term.

The Association for Specialists in Group Work (ASGW), a division of the ACA, has three aspirational documents addressing group practice. "Best Practice Guidelines" (1998, 2007) and "Principles for Diversity-Competent Group Workers" (1999) use the organizing categories of planning, performing, and processing in groups. "Professional Standards for the Training of Group Workers" (2000) encompasses four group types (task, psychoeducation, counseling, and therapy) to organize knowledge and skill areas. Each ASGW document provides a wealth of information to the group counselor (Wilson et al., 2004).

The ASGW aspirational training standards correlate with counseling program accreditation via the CACREP recommendations for master's- and doctoral-level programs. The ASGW training standards were written to guide counseling and related programs in their design of coursework and experience components of group training. The training standards are divided into two sections, (1) requirements for any masters'-level training in counseling and (2) specialization guidelines that specify aspirational levels of training for advanced practice in one of four group type specializations. Over time, CACREP has reduced the requirements for group skill training and coursework.

Core group knowledge and skills (for masters'-level training) and advanced group knowledge and skills (for specialization, doctoral work, or postdoctoral training) in each of the four group types are articulated.

Core standards include knowledge and skill objectives in the following areas:

• *Nature and scope of practice*, demonstrating knowledge of and application to a professional disclosure statement and group design
• *Assessment of group members and their social systems*, demonstrating assessment knowledge and understanding of group processes and their direct applications to a group
• *Planning group interventions*, demonstrating knowledge and skill in planning for group work grounded in sensitivity to environmental and diversity contexts and in applying them to planning activities
• *Implementing group interventions*, demonstrating knowledge and skill in group dynamics, leader functions, therapeutic factors, and principles of group formation
• *Leadership and coleadership*, demonstrating knowledge and skill in group leadership styles

and approaches, group work methods, and evaluation

• *Ethical practice, best practice, and diversity-competent practice*, demonstrating knowledge and application of ethical, best practices, and diversity competency through a chosen specialty.

ASGW specialization guidelines are intended to assist programs in the articulation of philosophy and development of training experiences to prepare group counselors for specialization practice. Coursework competencies and training in one or more of the group types, including counseling, are articulated. Advanced knowledge and skill in counseling groups, for example, would be required of the standards identified in core training.

Wilson and Newmeyer (2008) developed an instrument that measures the degrees of importance of, and confidence in, the ASGW core group knowledge and skills enumerated in the training standards document. Wilson (2009) has continued to refine the psychometrics of the ASGW training standards and to apply them to counselor education. Members of the ASGW may be nominated and approved for fellow status by demonstrating unusual contribution to group work and then upon the completion of work review and election by the Committee of Fellows.

Counseling ASGW Best Practice Guidelines

The ASGW's best practice guidelines (1998, 2007) complement the ACA's code of ethics by defining the responsibilities of group workers in the planning, performing, and processing of groups.

Best practice in planning includes nine broad areas of preparation:

• Professional context and regulatory requirements
• Scope of practice and professional framework
• Assessment
• Program development and evaluation
• Resource coordination
• Professional disclosure statement
• Group and member preparation
• Professional development
• Integration of trends and technological changes

Best practice in performing covers eight areas essential in the active stages of group counseling:

• Self-knowledge
• Group competencies knowledge and skill
• Group plan adaptation

• Therapeutic conditions and dynamics
• Meaning
• Collaboration in goal accomplishment
• Evaluation
• Ethical surveillance

Best practice in group processing involves the planning and execution of within-group and between-group processing and evaluation:

• Processing schedule
• Reflective practice
• Evaluation and follow-up
• Consultation and training with other organizations

Social Work Group Practice Standards

The Association for the Advancement of Social Work with Groups (AASWG) is affiliated with the NASW and CASW. Core values, knowledge, and general ethical considerations anchor the *Standards for Social Work Practice with Groups* (2005) in the four phases of pregroup and group work in the beginning phase, in the middle phase, and in the ending phase. Social work values of autonomy, diversity, respect, creation of a socially just society, and serving the poor, disenfranchised, and minorities guide the contents.

In the pregroup phase are included broad tasks, for example, group selection; goal identification; assessment of contextual, environment, and societal impacts; and evaluation planning.

The beginning phase includes active contracting with group members to cultivate cohesion and establish working norms and culture. Theory, group type and technology, and beginning group stage development are included.

The middle phase is the key working phase of the group and includes activities toward individual and group goal accomplishment. Leaders demonstrate skill and knowledge in the application of group dynamics.

The ending phase deals with closure issues and preparation for continued goal accomplishment after the termination of the group. Evaluation of personal and group goals in coordination with organization policies is completed.

Psychology Group Guidelines

The Society for Group Psychology and Group Psychotherapy (Division 49 of the APA) is a psychology organization devoted to the theory of group dynamics and the broad practice of group psychotherapy. Fellow status is available through the demonstration of advanced knowledge or skill in groups and then upon division and APA evaluation and approval. Members are additionally eligible to apply for the diplomate in the Society for Group Psychology (see advanced credentials in the next section).

Interdisciplinary Group Practice Guidelines

The American Group Psychotherapy Association (AGPA) is an interdisciplinary association that has published a number of documents to assist group therapists, including "Clinical Practice Guidelines for Group Psychotherapy" (Bernard et al., 2008) and the AGPA and National Registry of Certified Group Psychotherapists (NRCGP) *Guidelines for Ethics* (2002). The practice guidelines encompass values, knowledge, and skills in each phase of psychodynamic, interactional, and relationally based group psychotherapy. The components are widely applicable to other group types, including group counseling, and are intended to bridge clinical practice with evidence-based practice and research. Leszcz and Kobos (2008) provide a good example of the application of the AGPA guidelines to practice situations. The 2002 document identifies the responsibilities to the client and the responsibility of abiding by professional standards.

The clinical practice guidelines are presented in 10 sections that provide practice and research information:

• Creating successful therapy groups: client referrals and administrative collaboration
• Therapeutic factors and mechanisms: mechanism of action, cohesion, assessment of therapeutic mechanisms
• Selection of clients: member selection, premature terminators, selection instruments, therapy group composition
• Preparation and pregroup training: objectives, methods and procedures, developmental stages
• Group development: models and stages
• Group process: groups as social systems, therapeutic and antitherapeutic work, group as whole, splits and subgroups, member and leader roles
• Therapist interventions: executive function; caring, emotional stimulation; meaning attribution; fostering member self-awareness; establishing group norms; therapist transparency and use of self

• Reducing adverse outcomes: ethics, principles, codes, guidelines, and state regulations; group pressures; record keeping; confidentiality/boundaries and informed consent; monitoring of progress
• Concurrent therapies: group and individual, group and pharmacotherapy, 12-step
• Termination: aspects, rituals, and therapist departures

Group Specialty Association Advanced Credentials

The AGPA certifies individual group therapists through application and evaluation of credentials, group training/coursework, and experience. Members who have received the highest professional credential from one of its participating interdisciplinary fields and who hold the appropriate practice license may seek specific training and recognition as a certified group psychotherapist.

Several specialty boards have informal or formal relationships in psychology group practice. The American Board of Professional Psychology (ABPP) currently manages specialty expertise and postdoctorate diplomate credentialing in 13 psychology areas. The American Board for Group Psychology (ABGP) is the ABPP board that established the guidelines and examination procedures for psychologists who choose to pursue the advanced diplomate credential in group psychology. Extensive application, credential review, work sample, and oral examination comprise the evaluation process. As a joint venture of the APA and ABPP, the Council of Specialties in Professional Psychology facilitates development and functioning of 12 currently recognized specialties in professional psychology, including the 2003 acceptance of Society for Group Psychology. Furthermore, the APA Commission for the Recognition of Specialties and Proficiencies in Professional Psychology (CRSPPP) began in 2008 to regulate specialty areas of psychology through the APA governance structure. In its application for specialty practice within the APA through the CRSPPP, the Society for Group Psychology and Group Psychotherapy has integrated training, organization, and practice recommendations from its fellow professional associations into its petition (Barlow, 2008; in press).

Integration and Applications of Standards and Guidelines

Table 5.1 shows a comparison of the group training standards across the fields of counseling, social work, and psychology. As demonstrated in the table, standards vary in their target audiences, specification of core or advanced knowledge and skills, and curricular requirements. Group counselors who wish to strengthen their specialty group skills can draw from each of these sets of standards.

Group best-practice guideline comparisons are presented in Table 5.2. The guidelines share many components, for example, in articulation of group phases, in core and advanced skills, and in broad areas of preparation, practice, and evaluation. Unique characteristics of each set of guidelines are reported.

There are a number of advantages in becoming familiar with the guiding documents in counseling group practice across key professions. Group counselors are prepared in different traditions and at different education levels but share common values and respect for the nuances of group leadership and participation. Professionals in counseling, social work, and psychology can enhance their understanding of ethical behavior by crossing professional boundaries in continuing education, research, and practice.

GROUP PRACTICE AND RESEARCH NETWORK

The Group Practice and Research Network was established in 2007 at the initiation of the Society for Group Psychology and Group Psychotherapy, with the goal of increasing dialogue and collaboration among major professional group specialty associations. Representatives from the Society for Group Psychology and Group Therapy, Division 49 of the APA; ASGW; AGPA; AASWG; and additional APA divisions have formed a collaborative network and defined general goals and initial activities for collaboration. Each association has completed a survey of needs for conversion to joint initiatives. The network serves as a hopeful model for sharing knowledge, skill, and research bases across traditional professional boundaries.

Legal Parameters

In the earlier discussion of ethics codes and group counseling, specific code references to practice with groups were identified. Legal considerations in group-counseling practice multiply the number of factors to consider. Group counselors encounter some ethical risks and legal consequences that do not affect providers of individual services. Among the most significant are issues regarding screening, multiple client relationships, the limits of confidentiality, the legal concept of privileged communication,

record keeping, scope of practice, agency assignments, impacts of managed care, use of advanced communication technologies, and the structuring of training experiences.

Group counselors have a number of resources to assist them in determining what legal parameters affect their practice. Each of the professions (counseling, psychology, and social work) considered in this chapter is regulated by state or provincial law. However, there is great variety in how state and provincial laws govern the practice of each profession. There is even greater diversity among professions in how they define the scope of practice, in how licensing boards evaluate credentials, in how professionals are required to keep current in their fields, in how each jurisdiction defines levels of practice, and in how the regulatory bodies work with professional associations.

There is no consistency across training programs in the number of required courses in core group knowledge and skills or advanced group knowledge and skills. Unfortunately, the number of required group training experiences has dwindled over time. For example, while all states now have counselor licensing laws (with California passing their law in 2009), states have differing levels of training requirements and licensure. In social work, the range is even larger because social workers can practice at the bachelor-degree level. While psychology generally is licensed at the doctoral level, many states have grandfather clauses that allow licensure for master's-level practitioners whose training predated doctoral requirements. For all practitioners, the rule of thumb is to keep current with the specific laws governing practice. Some states do not mandate any particular continuing education, while others specify a minimum number of hours per license cycle. In many states, continuing education credits are required in the area of ethics. For example, in Ohio psychologists (Ohio Psychological Association, 2010) are required to complete 3 hours of ethics education plus 20 additional hours of general continuing education in every 2-year licensure period. For counselors and social workers, the Ohio requirements are to obtain 30 clock hours of continuing education every 2 years, of which three must be in ethics (Ohio Counselor, Social Worker and Marriage and Family Therapist Board [CSWMFT], 2010).

Professional associations, states, and provincial jurisdictions revise ethics codes and licensing requirements from time to time in response to current issues. Continuing with another state example, the Ohio CSWMFT Board added a new board exam on state laws and rules to be required of all applicants effective January 1, 2010 (J. Rough, personal communication, October 8, 2009). At the national level, the governing Council of Representatives of the APA revised its 2002 *Ethical Principles of Psychologists and Code of Conduct* in 2010 to address potential conflicts in the code. The change in wording of two standards clarifies potential ambiguity in previous language regarding the violation of human rights. Underscored sections have been added. Ethical standard 1.02, Conflicts between ethics and law, regulations, or other governing legal authority, now states, "If psychologists' ethical responsibilities conflict with law, regulations, or other governing legal authority, psychologists *clarify the nature of the conduct*, make known their commitment to the Ethics Code and take *reasonable* steps to resolve the conflict *consistent with the General Principles and Ethical Standards of the Ethics Code. Under* no *circumstances may this standard be used to justify or defend violating human rights.*" Related item 1.03, Conflicts between ethics and organizational demands, now states, "If the demands of an organization with which psychologists are affiliated or for whom they are working *are in* conflict with this Ethics Code, psychologists clarify the nature of the conflict, make known their commitment to the Ethics Code, and *take reasonable steps to resolve the conflict consistent with the General Principles an Ethical Standards of the Ethics Code. Under* no *circumstances may this standard be used to justify or defend violating human rights.*"

Research on Legal Issues

Montgomery, Cupit, and Wimberley (1999) surveyed psychologists on their experiences with malpractice, complaints with state licensing boards, and risk management. They found that people filed more complaints with state licensing boards than lawsuits because of the ease of filing jurisdictional complaints. Montgomery et al. found that threats preceded most reported complaints. Psychologists were advised to carry malpractice insurance and to be informed about reducing risk in professional practice.

Reviewing 27 state regulatory bodies for actions against social workers from 1999 to 2004, Boland-Prom (2009) found that the most frequent violation occurred in the areas of dual relationships, licensing problems, basic-practice elements, criminal actions, and not meeting care standards. While the study did not differentiate individual vs. group services, the trends identified are parallel to research on group practice.

General Considerations Regarding Legal Issues in Group Counseling

Recommendations regarding legal issues in group counseling follow the general guideline of "be prepared." There are a number of excellent resources on legal issues in the helping professions, for example, Anderson (1996); Bennett et al. (2006); Hopkins and Anderson (1990); and Pope and Vasquez (2010). Group counselors, however, must take a preventive stance in addressing such risks.

Bennett and colleagues (2006) recommended an individual preventive approach based on the application of Bloom's education taxonomy to risk management in mental health. In discussing how professionals might respond to ethical/legal issues, Bennett and colleagues identified three lower levels of risk management and three higher levels. The three items in the lower levels of risk management include (1) knowledge of ethics code, for example, having read the code; (2) ability to describe a risk-management situation to a colleague; and (3) application of a risk-prevention principle (e.g., do not disclose information without written consent). The three higher levels of response include (1) analysis of general risk-management principles (e.g., informed consent and documentation) and general applications, (2) synthesis of risk-management principles into daily work, and (3) evaluation of relative benefits of alternatives generated.

In this model, ethical and legal practitioners anticipate issues; prepare for them via education, training, and supervision; and use risk-management strategies to reduce the likelihood of legal problems. Bennett et al. (2006) apply the risk-management principles to the areas of practitioner self-care; competence areas; boundary issues and multiple relationships; privacy, confidentiality, and privileged communication; termination; and special client situations. Group practice was not identified as a special topic of discussion. Sample applications include practice only with professional liability insurance coverage, limit practice to areas of competence or have a specific acquisition plan and supervision for new areas of practice, have redundant systems in place to manage and protect client information, never serve as your own representative during an ethical or legal investigation, and know the rules for practice.

Ethical Decision-Making Models

Abundant ethical decision-making models exist in psychology, counseling, and social work to guide practitioners in identifying ethical dilemmas and in generating resolutions (e.g., CPA, 2000; Fisher, 2004; Hansen and Goldberg, 1999; Kitchener, 1984; Koocher and Keith-Spiegel, 2008; Pope and Vasquez, 2010; Welfel, 2006). Excellent case books are also available to assist in identifying and responding to ethical dilemmas (Corey et al., 2003; Motherwell & Shay, 2005; O'Donohue & Ferguson, 2003; Nagy, 2005). While it is beyond the scope of this chapter to review variations developed over decades (see Cottone and Claus, 2000; Hansen and Goldberg, 1999; Rapin, 2004), elements related to contemporary group-counseling practice are highlighted here. Kitchener's (1984) model reflects the five ethics principles that serve as a foundation to many ethics documents. Hansen and Goldberg (1999) added legal considerations to the process and proposed a matrix model with seven components: (1) moral principles and ethical values; (2) cultural and clinical variables; (3) codes of ethics; (4) agency or employer policies; (5) local, state, and federal law; (6) rules and regulations; and (7) case law. They applied the matrix to two case presentations, one involving group counseling. They emphasized that consideration of one variable may be in conflict with one or more of the additional variables, just as one ethical principle may be in conflict with other principles.

As stated in the ethical decision-making equation at the beginning of this chapter, decision making is inexorably tied to the development of an ethical frame of reference that is relevant to both the individual and the profession. Thus, in the equation EBGC = MED + PE + CKS + SBPG + LP × DM, major elements of ethical behavior are applied *in interaction* with a decision-making model. Without consideration of ethical development and the context in which a dilemma occurs, decision making is likely to be an unsuccessful exercise.

Decision-making models presume careful consideration of the factors most likely to influence actions. My discussion of a group-counseling decision-making model assumes that the elements of the ethical behavior in group counseling equation are present. Pulling from several models (CPA, 2000; Fisher, 2004; Goldberg & Hansen, 1999; Knapp et al . (2007); Koocher & Keith-Spiegel, 2008; Pope & Vasquez, 2010; Welfel, 2006), the following decision steps are suggested for group counseling. In implementing any decision-making process, the group counselor must be aware that no model will cover every ethical situation. Some group-counseling situations may require immediate action. Others may profit from introspection and consultation before taking any action. The process implies a way of thinking about decision points in group counseling.

1. Practice and monitor the elements of the ethical behavior in group counseling equation in daily practice.

2. Identify whether the group situation involves an ethical dilemma.

3. Clarify the facts and cultural contexts that might be in play in the counseling group.

4. Identify individuals or groups who might have a stake in the decision or might be affected by it.

5. Define the key issues in the dilemma.

6. Identify how ethics principles, standards, guidelines, or laws may be involved.

7. Review relevant practice literature for potential options or risk identification applications to the group-counseling situation.

8. Generate potential response options and their intended and unintended consequences.

9. Consult, as appropriate, with colleagues (while protecting confidentiality).

10. Evaluate alternatives and choose the most appropriate.

11. Monitor and evaluate the chosen action.

12. Use reflection and evaluation to alter the group plan as necessary.

Future Considerations

Numerous opportunities are available for professional collaboration in the ethical practice of group counseling. One of the most basic possibilities is for professionals across training fields to collaborate in conversation and research on the fundamental constructs of group counseling. While there are many ideas about how mental health professionals should act by aspiration or mandate, little research is available on how the mechanisms work and how they affect ethical practice in group counseling.

Further research on any component of the equation used as the foundation of this chapter would be welcome. The more that professionals understand the specific ways in which the moral character of individuals, guiding principles, therapeutic models, best practices, and the myriad of choices for therapeutic intervention impact group counseling, the more possibility exists for consistent practice and increased ethical behavior. Deficiencies in these areas may be considered threats to the wide use of group counseling in mental health settings. Group practitioners, group educators, supervisors, and researchers have deep-rooted resources that guide their specialty areas.

More sharing is needed to integrate the research and practice foundations of group counseling.

References

Acuff, C., Bennett, B. E., Bricklin, P. M., Canter, M. B., Knapp, S. J., Moldawsky, S., et al. (1999). Considerations for ethical practice in managed care. *Professional Psychology: Research and Practice, 30,* 563–575.

Adams, P. (2009). Ethics with character: Virtues and the ethical social worker. *Journal of Sociology & Social Welfare, 36,* 83–105.

Akos, P., Goodnough, G. E., & Milsom, A. S. (2004). Preparing school counselors for group work. *Journal for Specialists in Group Work, 29,* 127–136.

American College Personnel Association. (2006). *Statement of ethical principles and standards.* Washington, DC: Author.

American Counseling Association (ACA). (2005). *ACA code of ethics.* Alexandria, VA: Author.

American Counseling Association (ACA). (2009). *The ACA encyclopedia of counseling.* Alexandria, VA: Author.

American Group Psychotherapy Association & National Registry of the Certified Group Psychotherapists. (2002). *AGPA and NRCGP guidelines for ethics.* New York: Author.

American Mental Health Counselors Association. (2010). *Code of ethics of the American Mental Counselors Association: 2010 revision.* Alexandria, VA: Author.

American Psychological Association (APA). (2002). *Ethical principles of psychologists and code of conduct.* Washington, DC: Author.

American Psychological Association (APA) (2010). *Ethical Principles of Psychologists and Code of Conduct: 2010 Amendments.* Washington, DC: Author.

American Telemedicine Association. (2009). *Practice guidelines for videoconferencing-based telemental health.* Washington, DC: Author.

Anderson, B. S. (1996). *The counselor and the law* (4th ed.). Alexandria, VA: American Counseling Association.

Association for the Advancement of Social Work with Groups (AASWG). (2005). *Standards for social work practice with groups* (2nd ed.). Alexandria, VA: Author.

Association for Specialists in Group Work (ASGW). (1998). Association for Specialists in Group Work best practice guidelines. *Journal for Specialists in Group Work, 23,* 237–244.

Association for Specialists in Group Work (ASGW). (1999). Principles for diversity-competent group workers. *Journal for Specialists in Group Work, 24,* 7–14.

Association for Specialists in Group Work (ASGW). (2000). Association for Specialists in Group Work: Professional standards for the training of group workers, 2000 revision. *Journal for Specialists in Group Work, 25,* 327–342.

Association for Specialists in Group Work (ASGW). (2007). Association for Specialists in Group Work best practice guidelines, 2007 revisions. *Journal for Specialists in Group Work, 33,* 111–117.

Barlow, S. H. (2004). A strategic three-year plan to teach beginning, intermediate, and advanced group skills. *Journal for Specialists in Group Work, 29,* 113–126.

Barlow, S. H. (2008). Group psychotherapy specialty practice. *Professional Psychology: Research and Practice, 39,* 240–244.

Barlow, S. H. (in press). *Group specialty practice.* Oxford, U.K.: Oxford University Press.

Bemak, F., & Chung, R. C. (2004). Teaching multicultural group counseling: Perspectives for a new era. *Journal for Specialists in Group Work, 29,* 31–41.

Bennett, B. E., Bricklin, P. M., Harris, E., Knapp, S., VandeCreek, L., & Younggren, J. N. (2006). *Assessing and managing risk in psychological practice: An individual approach.* Rockville, MD: The Trust.

Berg, R. C., Landreth, G. L., & Fall, K. (1998). *Group counseling concepts and procedures* (3rd ed.). Philadelphia: Taylor & Francis.

Bernard, H., Burlingame, G., Flores, P., Greene, L., Joyce, A., & Kobos, J. (2008). Clinical practice guidelines for group psychotherapy. *International Journal of Group Psychotherapy, 58,* 455–542.

Bersoff, D. N. (1996). The virtue of principle ethics. *Counseling Psychologist, 24,* 86–91.

Betan, E. J., & Stanton, A. L. (1999). Fostering ethical willingness: Integrating emotional and contextual awareness with rational analysis. *Professional Psychology: Research and Practice, 30,* 295–301.

Blickle, G. (2004). Professional ethics needs a theoretical background. *European Psychologist, 9,* 273–274.

Boland-Prom, K. W. (2009). Results from a national study of social workers sanctioned by state licensing boards. *Social Work, 54,* 351–360.

Brabender, V. M. (2006).The ethical group psychotherapist. *International Journal of Group Psychotherapy,56,* 395–414.

Brabender, V. M. (2007). The ethical group psychotherapist: A coda. *International Journal of Group Psychotherapy, 57,* 41–47.

Brabender, V. M., & Fallon, A. (2009). Ethical hot spots of combined individual and group therapy: Applying four ethical systems. *International Journal of Group Psychotherapy, 59,* 127–147.

Burlingame, G. M., Fuhriman, A., & Johnson, J. E. (2001). Cohesion in group psychotherapy. *Psychotherapy: Theory/ Research/Practice/Training, 38,* 373–379.

Canadian Association of Social Workers (CASW). (2005a). *Code of ethics.* Ottawa: Author.

Canadian Association of Social Workers (CASW). (2005b). *Guidelines for ethical practice.* Ottawa: Author.

Canadian Psychological Association. (2000). *Canadian code of ethics for psychologists.* Ottawa: Author.

Capuzzi, D., & Muffett, L. (1980). An overview of ethical standards for group facilitators. *Journal for Specialists in Group Work, 5,* 98–106.

Conyne, R. K. (in press). Group counseling. In E. Altamaier & J .C. Hansed (Eds.), *Oxford handbook of counseling psychology.* New York: Oxford University Press.

Conyne, R. K., & Bemak, F. (Eds.). (2004a). Teaching group work [Special issue]. *Journal for Specialists in Group Work, 29*(1).

Conyne, R. K., & Bemak, F. (2004b). Teaching group work from an ecological perspective. *Journal for Specialists in Group Work, 29,* 7–18.

Corey, G., Corey, M. S., & Callanan, P. (2003). *Issues and ethics in the helping professions* (6th ed.). Pacific Grove, CA: Brooks/ Cole.

Cottone, R. R., & Claus, R. E. (2000). Ethical decision-making models: A review of the literature. *Journal of Counseling and Development, 78,* 275–283.

Council for Accreditation of Counseling and Related Educational Programs (CACREP). (2009). *2009 standards.* Alexandria, VA: Author.

Counseling Psychologist. (2005). Online counseling: Challenges for the information era. *Counseling Psychologist, 33*, 761–921.

Davenport, D. S. (2004). Ethical issues in the teaching of group counseling. *Journal for Specialists in Group Work, 29*, 43–49.

Debiak, D. (2007). Attending to diversity in group psychotherapy: An ethical imperative. *International Journal of Group Psychotherapy, 57*, 1–12.

DeLucia-Waack, J. L., & Donigian, J. (2004). *The practice of multicultural group work*. Belmont, CA: Brooks/Cole, Thompson Learning.

DiFranks, N. N. (2008). Social workers and the NASW code of ethics: Belief, behavior, disjuncture. *Social Work, 53*, 167–176.

Encarta. (2009). *Encarta World English Dictionary*. Retrieved from http://encarta.msn.com

Fallon, A. (2006). Informed consent in the practice of group psychotherapy. *International Journal of Group Psychotherapy, 56*, 431–453.

Fisher, C. B. (2004). Challenges in constructing a cross-national ethics code for psychologists. *European Psychologist, 9*, 275–277.

Fly, B. J., van Bark, W. P., Weinman, L., Kitchener, K. S., & Lang, P. R. (1997). Ethical transgressions of psychology graduate students: Critical incidents with implications for training. *Professional Psychology: Research and Practice, 28*, 492–495.

Forester-Miller, H. (Ed.). (1990). Ethical and legal issues in group work [Special issue]. *Journal for Specialists in Group Work*, 15(2).

Fowers, B. J. (2005). *Virtue and psychology: Pursuing excellence in ordinary practices*. Washington, DC: American Psychological Association.

Francis, R. D. (2009). *Ethics for psychologists* (2nd ed.). West Sussex: British Psychological Society and Blackwell Publications.

Gabriel, L., & Casemore, R. (Eds.). (2009). *Relational ethics in practice: Narratives from counselling and psychotherapy*. London: Routledge.

Gazda, G. M., Ginter, E. J., & Horne, A. M. (2001). *Group counseling and group psychotherapy: Theory and application*. Needham Heights, MA: Allyn & Bacon.

Gillam, S. L. (2004). Preplanning considerations in teaching group counseling courses: Applying a general framework for conceptualizing PEDAGOGY. *Journal for Specialists in Group Work, 29*, 75–85.

Glass, T. A. (1998). Ethical issues in group therapy. In R. M. Anderson, T. L. Needels, & H. V. Hall (Eds.), *Avoiding ethical misconduct in psychology specialty areas* (pp. 95–126). Springfield, IL: Charles C. Thomas.

Gumaer, J., & Duncan, J. A. (1982). Group workers' perceptions of their philosophical ethical beliefs and actual ethical practices. *Journal for Specialists in Group Work, 7*, 231–237.

Gumaer, J., & Scott, L. (1986). Group workers' perceptions of ethical and unethical behavior of group leaders. *Journal for Specialists in Group Work, 11*, 139–150.

Guth, L. J., & McDonnell, K. A. (2004). Designing class activities to meet specific core training competencies: A developmental approach. *Journal for Specialists in Group Work, 29*, 97–107.

Hansen, N. D., & Goldberg, S. G. (1999). Navigating the nuances: A matrix of considerations for ethical–legal dilemmas. *Professional Psychology: Research and Practice, 30*, 495–503.

Hopkins, B. R. & Anderson, B. S. (1990). *The counselor and the law*. Alexandria, VA: American Counseling Association.

International Journal of Group Psychotherapy. (2007). The ethical group psychotherapist [Special issue]. *International Journal of Group Psychotherapy, 57*(1).

Killacky, J., & Hulse-Killacky, D. (2004). Group work is not just for the group class anymore: Teaching generic group competency skills across the counselor education curriculum. *Journal for Specialists in Group Work, 29*, 87–96.

Kitchener, K. S. (1984). Intuition, critical evaluation and ethics principles: The foundation for ethical decisions in counseling psychology. *Counseling Psychologist, 12*, 43–55.

Kitchener, K. S. (1992). Psychologist as teacher and mentor: Affirming ethical values throughout the curriculum. *Professional Psychology: Research and Practice, 23*, 190–195.

Kitchener, K. S. (1996). There is more to ethics than principles. *Counseling Psychologist, 24*, 92–97.

Knapp, S., Gottlieb, M., Berman, J. & Handelsman, M. M. (2007). *Professional Psychology: Research and Practice, 38*, 54–59.

Knauss, L. K. (2006). Ethical issues in recordkeeping in group psychotherapy. *International Journal of Group Psychotherapy, 56*, 415–430.

Koocher, G. P., & Keith-Spiegel, P. (1998). *Ethics in psychology: Professional standards and cases* (2nd ed.). New York: Oxford University Press.

Koocher, G. P., & Keith-Spiegel, P. (2008). *Ethics in psychology and the mental health professions: Standards and cases* (3rd ed.). New York: Oxford University Press.

Kottler, J. A. (2004). Realities of teaching group counseling. *Journal for Specialists in Group Work, 29*, 51–53.

Lakin, M. (1994). Morality in group and family therapies: Multiperson therapies and the 1992 ethics code. *Professional Psychology: Research and Practice, 25*, 344–348.

Lasky, G. B., & Riva, M. T. (2006). Confidentiality and privileged communication in group psychotherapy. *International Journal of Group Psychotherapy, 56*, 455–476.

Leszcz, M., & Kobos, J. (2008). Evidence-based group psychotherapy: Using AGPA's practice guidelines to enhance clinical effectiveness. *Journal of Clinical Psychology, 64*, 1238–1260.

Macnair-Semands, R. (2007). Attending to the spirit of social justice as an ethical approach in group therapy. *International Journal of Group Psychotherapy, 57*, 61–66.

Maheu, M. M., & Gordon, B. L. (2000). Counseling and therapy on the Internet. *Professional Psychology: Research and Practice, 31*, 484–489.

Mangione, L., Forti, R., & Iacuzzi, C. M. (2007). Ethics and endings in group psychotherapy: Saying good-bye and saying it well. *International Journal of Group Psychotherapy, 57*, 25–40.

McGlothlin, J. (2003). Response to the mini special issue on technology and group work. *Journal for Specialists in Group Work, 28*, 42–47.

McMinn, M. R., Buchanan, T., Ellens, B. M., & Ryan, M. K. (1999). Technology, professional practice, and ethics: Survey findings and implications. *Professional Psychology: Research and Practice, 30*, 165–172.

Meara, N. M., Schmidt, L. D., & Day, J. D. (1996). Principles and virtues: A foundation for ethical decisions, policies, and character. *Counseling Psychologist, 24*, 4–77.

Meier, A. (2004). Technology-mediated groups. In C. D. Garvin, L. M. Gutierrez, & M. J. Galinsky (Eds.), *Handbook of social work with groups* (pp. 479–503). New York: Guilford Press.

Montgomery, L. M., Cupit, B. E., & Wimberley, T. K. (1999). Complaints, malpractice, and risk management: Professional issues and personal experiences. *Professional Psychology: Research and Practice, 30,* 402–410.

Motherwell, L., & Shay, J. J. (2005). *Complex dilemmas in group therapy: Pathways to resolution.* New York: Bruner-Routledge.

Nagy, T. F. (2005). *Ethics in plain English: An illustrative casebook for psychologists* (2nd ed.). Washington, DC: American Psychological Association.

National Association of Social Workers. (1999). *Code of ethics.* Silver Spring, MD: NASW Press.

National Association of Social Workers (NASW). (2008). *Code of ethics.* Washington, DC: Author.

National Board for Certified Counselors (NBCC). (2005). *Code of ethics.* Greensboro, NC: Author.

Northen, H. (2004). Ethics and values in group work. In C. D. Garvin, L. M. Gutierrez, & M. J. Galinsky (Eds.), *Handbook of social work with groups* (pp. 76–89). New York: Guilford Press.

Nowell, D., & Spruill, J. (1993). If it's not absolutely confidential, will information be disclosed? *Professional Psychology: Research and Practice, 24,* 367–369.

O'Donohue, E., & Ferguson, K. (Eds.). (2003). *Handbook of professional ethics for psychologists: Issues, questions, and controversies.* Thousand Oaks, CA: Sage.

O'Halloran, T. M., & McCartney, T. J. (2004). An evaluation of the use of technology as a tool to meet group training standards. *Journal for Specialists in Group Work, 29,* 65–73.

Ohio Counselor, Social Worker and Marriage and Family Therapist Board. (2010). *Renewal information.* Retrieved April 21, 2010, from www.cswmft.ohio.gov/reqren.stm

Ohio Psychological Association. (2010). *OPA MCE forms and procedures for psychologists.* Retrieved April 21, 2010, from www.ohpsych.org/psychologists.aspx

Page, B. (2003a). Introduction to using technology in group work. *Journal for Specialists in Group Work, 28,* 7–8.

Page, B. (Ed.). (2003b). Technology and group work [Special issue]. *Journal for Specialists in Group Work, 28,* 7–47.

Page, B. (2004). Online group counseling. In J. DeLucia-Waack, D. Gerrity, C. Kalodner, & M. Riva (Eds.), *Handbook of group counseling and psychotherapy* (pp. 609–620). Thousand Oaks, CA: Sage.

Paradise, L. V., & Kirby, P. C. (1990). Some perspectives on the legal liability of group counseling in private practice. *Journal for Specialists in Group Work, 15,* 114–118.

Paradise, L. V., & Siegelwaks, B. J. (1982). Ethical training for group leaders. *Journal for Specialists in Group Work, 7,* 162–166.

Pepper, R. (2007). Too close for comfort: The impact of dual relationships on group therapy and group therapist training. *International Journal of Group Psychotherapy, 57,* 13–23.

Perry, W. G. (1970). *Forms of intellectual and ethical development in the college years: A scheme.* New York: Holt, Rinehart, and Winston.

Pettifor, J. P. (2004). Professional ethics across national boundaries. *European Psychologist, 9,* 264–272.

Pope, K. S., & Bajt, T. R. (1988). When laws and values conflict: A dilemma for psychologists. *American Psychologist, 43,* 828–829.

Pope, K. S., Tabachnick, B. G., & Keith-Spiegel, P. (1987). Ethics of practice: The beliefs and behaviors of psychologists as therapists. *American Psychologist, 42,* 993–1006.

Pope, K. S., & Vetter, V. A. (1992). Ethical dilemmas encountered by members of the American Psychological Association: A national survey. *American Psychologist, 47,* 397–411.

Pope, K. S. & Vasquez, M. J. (2010). *Ethics in psychotherapy and counseling: A practical guide* (4th ed.). Hoboken, NJ: Jossey-Bass/Wiley.

Posthuma, B. W. (2002). *Small groups in counseling and therapy: Process and leadership* (4th ed.). Boston: Allyn & Bacon.

Rapin, L. S. (2004). Guidelines for ethical and legal practice in counseling and psychotherapy groups. In J. DeLucia-Waack, D. Gerrity, C. Kalodner, & M. Riva (Eds.), *Handbook of group counseling and psychotherapy* (pp. 151–165). Thousand Oaks, CA: Sage.

Rapin, L. S., & Conyne, R. K. (2006). Best practices in group work. In J. Trotzer (Ed.), *The counselor and the group: Integrating theory, training, and practice* (4th ed., pp. 291–318). New York: Routledge.

Rest, J. R. (1984). Research on moral development: Implications for training counseling psychologists. *Counseling Psychologist, 12,* 19–29.

Riva, M. T., & Korinek, L. (2004). Teaching group work: Modeling group leader and member behaviors in the classroom to demonstrate group theory. *Journal for Specialists in Group Work, 29,* 55–63.

Roback, H. B., & Moore, R. F. (2007). On the ethical group therapist. *International Journal of Group Psychotherapy, 57,* 49–59.

Sklare, G., Thomas, D. V., Williams, E. C., & Powers, K. A. (1996). Ethics and an experiential "here and now" group: A blend that works. *Journal for Specialists in Group Work, 21,* 263–273.

Stockton, R., Morran, D. K., & Krieger, K. (2004). An overview of current research and best practices for training beginning group leaders. In J. DeLucia-Waack, D. Gerrity, C. Kalodner, & M. Riva (Eds.), *Handbook of group counseling and psychotherapy* (pp. 65–75). Thousand Oaks, CA: Sage.

Tropman, J. E. (2004). An ecological-systems perspective. In C. D. Garvin, L. M. Gutierrez, & M. J. Galinsky (Eds.), *Handbook of social work with groups* (pp. 32–44). New York: Guilford Press.

Van Velsor, P. (2004). Training for successful group work with children: What and how to teach. *Journal for Specialists in Group Work, 29,* 137–146.

Welfel, E. R. (1992). Psychologist as ethics educator: Successes, failures, and unanswered questions. *Professional Psychology: Research and Practice, 23,* 182–189.

Welfel, E. R. (2006). *Ethics in counseling and psychology: Standards, research and emerging issues.* Belmont, CA: Thompson Brooks Cole.

Welfel, E. R., & Kitchener, K. S. (1992). Introduction to the special section: Ethics education an agenda for the 90s. *Professional Psychology: Research and Practice, 23,* 179–181.

Wilson, F. R. (2009). *Content validity of the ASGW training standards: Using psychometrics to advance rigor in counselor education.* Paper presented at the AACE 2009 National Assessment and Research Conference, Norfolk, VA.

Wilson, F. R., & Newmeyer, M. D. (2008). A standards-based inventory for assessing perceived importance and confidence in using ASGW's core group work skills. *Journal for Specialists in Group Work, 33,* 270–289.

Wilson, F. R., Rapin, L. S., & Haley-Banez, L. (2004). How teaching group work can be guided by foundational documents: Best practice guidelines, diversity principles, training standards. *Journal for Specialists in Group Work, 29,* 19–29.

Wilson, L. S., & Ranft, V. A. (1993). The state of ethical training for counseling psychology doctoral students. *Counseling Psychologist, 21,* 445–456.

Yao, T. (2004). Guidelines for facilitating groups with international college students. In J. DeLucia-Waack, D. Gerrity, C. Kalodner, & M. Riva (Eds.), *Handbook of group counseling and psychotherapy* (pp. 253–264). Thousand Oaks, CA: Sage.

Diversity in Groups

Janice DeLucia-Waack

Abstract

Recognition and appreciation of diversity in groups are essential to helping group members understand themselves and work together. This chapter describes the different types of multicultural group work, key concepts in multicultural counseling, cultural values and assumptions inherent in groups work, as well as the importance of training for group leaders.

Keywords: diversity, multicultural counseling, training

Introduction

This chapter will discuss diversity in groups. The types of multicultural group work and basic definitions relevant to these groups will be highlighted. Cultural assumptions inherent in multicultural group work will be discussed. Suggestions for the training of multicultural group leaders and examples of multicultural group work will be provided.

Anderson (2007) defines multicultural group work as follows:

> a helping process that includes screening, assessing, and diagnosing dynamics of group social systems, members, and leadership for the purpose of establishing goals, outcomes, processes, and interventions that are informed by multicultural counseling knowledge, skills, and abilities. It is a process of planning, implementing, and evaluating group work strategies from a socio-cultural context of human variability, group, and individual identity, worldviews, statuses, power, and other salient demographic factors to facilitate human and organizational development. The goal of multicultural group work is to promote human development and to enhance interpersonal relationships, promote task achievement, and prevent or identify and remediate mental, emotional or

behavioral disorders or associated distress that interfere with mental health, and to lessen the risk of distress, disability, or loss of human dignity, autonomy, and freedom. (p. 225–226)

Diversity and multicultural issues are inherent in groups and essential to consider. Interactions, and individual interpretations of such interactions, vary based on ethnicity, culture, religion, gender, sexual orientation, and age. Effective groups help members understand themselves and others as individuals within the context of their culture. Multicultural counseling competencies suggest that group leaders choose interventions and methods of change based on the interplay between individuals and their worldviews. "Given the dramatically changing diversity in the U.S. population, it is critical that group workers are culturally competent" (Bemak & Chung, 2004, p. 33).

Yalom (1995) emphasized the need for heterogeneity in groups. "The social microcosm theory postulates that, since the group is regarded as a miniature social universe in which patients are urged to develop new methods of interpersonal interaction, the group should be heterogeneous in order to maximize learning opportunities" (p. 261). Thus, diversity in groups and the resulting range of experiences, beliefs, worldviews, coping styles, and problem-solving strategies enhance group effectiveness.

Two professional organizations have developed guidelines for effective group work that emphasize multicultural facets, including the Association for Specialists in Group Work (ASGW) and the American Group Psychotherapy Association (AGPA). The AGPA Practice Guidelines for Group Psychotherapy (AGPA, 2007) assert that "many of the principles articulated here are relevant to diverse group therapy approaches which employ a variety of techniques, with various client populations, and in a variety of treatment or service settings" (p. 3). The ASGW Principles for Diversity-Competent Group Workers (1999) state that "issues of diversity affect group process and dynamics, group facilitation, training, and research" (p. 1).

Multicultural group-work skills are essential in the training of psychologists, social workers, and counselors. Constantine, Hage, Kindaichi, and Bryant (2007) proposed that social justice competencies be infused into the training of all group leaders. Diversity-competent group leaders possess "attitudes and beliefs, knowledge and skills to facilitate a group process where diversity and culture are not only acknowledged, understood, and valued but also mobilized for the collaborative productivity of the group and the therapeutic benefits of its members" (Merchant, 2006, p. 323). Arredondo (1999) theorized that multicultural-competence skills development consists of three domains: (1) counselor's awareness of personal beliefs and attitudes, as well as knowledge and skills for effective practice; (2) counselor's understanding of beliefs and attitudes, as well as knowledge he or she holds about the worldview of the client; and (3) counselor's ability to provide ethical and culturally relevant counseling with appropriate interventions and techniques.

Basic Definitions Related to Multicultural Group Work

It is important to understand key definitions and concepts related to multicultural counseling. Several important definitions follow. These concepts help to shape the identities of group members and leaders and influence their views about the helping process, the role of the leader, and norms about communication, conflict, and intimacy.

Culture: Shared beliefs, values, rules, and practices of a group of individuals. Cultural socialization usually occurs in the family, and any individual can be part of multiple cultural groups (Sue & Sue, 2008).

Racial/Ethnic Group: Members of a group from the same geographic place of origin "who live, or once lived, in close proximity to another and, as a consequence, share ways of thinking, feeling, and behaving learned from similar life circumstances shared over generations" (Fouad & Brown, 2000, p. 381).

Social Class/Status: An individual's access to levels and varieties of economic resources and control and influence in society, as well as social valuation (Fouad & Brown, 2000).

Religion: A system of beliefs and practices usually related to acknowledgment of a higher being or power and what is sacred (Pargament, 1997).

Spirituality: One's personal, emotional, unsystematic, and subjective processes of finding and transforming experiences of religious beliefs (Hill & Pargament, 2003).

Sexual Orientation: One's preference for intimate partners who are of the same sex and/or the opposite sex as the individual (Fassinger, 2000).

Ethnic Identity: The magnitude to which an individual appreciates and actively engages in his or her own cultural values, traditions, beliefs, and behaviors (Nesdale, Rooney, & Smith, 1997).

Acculturation: The processes by which ethnic groups adapt to mainstream culture with varying degrees across different social–cultural contexts (Epsin, 1987).

Types of Multicultural Group Work

Group interventions vary in type, goals, and interventions. Merchant (2009) suggested "three types of multicultural groups: 1) *Culture-specific groups* that focus specifically on the needs of a particular cultural group; 2) *Intercultural learning groups* that promote better relations and reduce oppression and bias between diversity groups; and 3) *Other-content focused groups* that address other topics and themes but view diversity issues as an important consideration in the group" (p. 13).

Culture-specific groups help group members from a similar cultural background come together with a common goal, which can range from education to support to counseling and therapy. "The shared cultural context allows a safe space for group members to engage in self exploration and problem resolution, without added pressure to explain or teach others about their culture"

(Merchant, 2009, p. 14). Group goals include support, education, guidance, healing, and/or counseling with group members who share common experiences as a result of their diversity (Merchant, 2006). Table 6.1 includes examples of *culture-specific groups* for specific populations and references.

Intercultural learning groups focus on learning about similarities and differences in cultures "to promote greater understanding across cultural groups to increase cultural knowledge and improve relationships among diverse groups of people. Such work typically addresses personal values, biases, prejudices and forms of oppression such as racism, sexism, homophobia and ageism" (Merchant, 2009, p. 14). Table 6.1 includes examples of *intercultural learning groups* and references.

Other-content-focused groups are typically counseling and therapy groups that recognize the diversity of group members and utilize that diversity to facilitate group process and dynamics. "Although diversity may not be the focus of the group, leaders need to attend to the cultural context of group members and the impact of various forms of diversity on group process" (Merchant, 2009, p. 15). Table 6.1 includes examples of how diversity can be addressed in groups to facilitate effective group work.

Cultural Assumptions Inherent in Group Work

Traditional group work is based on Eurocentric values, beliefs, and assumptions about counseling, specifically individualism, independence, competitiveness, and achievement (Taha, Mahfouz, & Arafa, 2008; Toseland, Jones, & Gellis, 2004). Leong (1992) cautioned "the tendency to use one's framework as if it were universal is not unique to Western groups, but it behooves us to become aware of that tendency" (p. 228). Each culture has its own set of beliefs about healing, loyalty, honor, and family that influence counseling and group work. Table 6–2 highlights areas where cultures may differ in their beliefs and values. Eurocentric assumptions of counseling affect how group work is conceptualized and enacted and may potentially conflict with other cultural values.

For example, traditionally, groups are composed of individuals who do not know each other. The assumption is that individuals who know and interact with each other outside of group will form coalitions and alliances in group based on preestablished roles and patterns of interaction that may negatively affect group cohesiveness. This contradicts the collective nature of many cultures and the emphasis on seeking helping first from family and community. Chen and Mak (2008) reported that

Table 6.1   Types of diversity groups and resources by topic

Group Type	Reference
Culture-specific groups	
International students	Yau (2004)
Gay–lesbian–bisexual–transgendered	Firestein (1999), Horne & Levitt (2004)
Haitian American adolescents	Nicolas et al. (2009)
Latinos	Hernandez et al. (2006); Peeks (1999); Rayle et al. (2006); Torres-Rivera, Wilbur, Roberts-Wilbur, & Phan (1999); Villalba (2003)
Native Hawaiian adolescents	Kim, Omizo, & D'Andrea (1998)
Native Americans	Appleton & Dykeman (1996); Colmant et al. (2005); Colmant & Merta (1999); Garrett (2004)
African Americans	Brown, Lipford-Sanders, & Shaw (1995); Pack-Brown & Fleming (2004); White & Rayle (2007); Williams, Frame, & Green (1999)
Asians	Bentelspacher, DeSilva, Goh, & LaRowe (1996); Chen (1995); Chong (2005); Chung (2004); Devan (2001); Pan (2000); Queener & Kenyon (2001); Shen (2007); Singh & Hays (2008); Suh & Lee (2006); Zaretsky (2009)
Survivors of Asian tsunami	Fernando (2009)

(continued)

Table 6.1 (*continued*)

Group Type	Reference
Students with disabilities	Corrigan, Jones, & McWhirter (2001); Epp (2008); McEachern & Kenny (2007); Milsom, Akos, & Thompson (2004); Mishna & Muskat (2004); Shechtman & Gilat (2005); Seligman & Marshak (2004)
Elderly adults	Campbell (2004); Christensen, Hulse-Killacky, Salgado, Thornton, & Miller (2006); Husaini et al. (2004); Kelly, Schofield, Booth, & Tolson (2005); Payne & Marcus (2008)
Intercultural learning groups	
College students	Bowman (2009)
Diversity training	Karp & Sammour (2000)
Safe-zone training	Diehm & Lazzari (2001)
Diversity in schools	Molina, Brigman, & Rhone (2003); Nikels, Mims, & Mims (2007)
White and Asian students	Smith, Boulton, & Cowie (1993)
JCC/ready intervention: African American and Jewish students	Sweifach (2009)
Arab–Jewish relations in Israel	Bargal (2004)
Other content-focused groups	
Optimal theory	Haley-Banez & Walden (1999)
Culturally responsive interventions for Asians based on racial identity	Chen & Han (2001)
Multicultural counseling training	Rowell & Benshoff (2008)
Dialectic perspective	Anderson (2007)
Minority groups within predominantly white treatment settings	Merchant & Butler (2003)
Tasks and teams	Foldy, Rivard, & Buckley (2009)

students from Hong Kong or mainland China and Chinese-born American students reported being less likely to seek treatment for mental health issues than European American students.

In addition, the therapeutic factors of group counseling are based on the Eurocentric assumption that people need to self-disclose, with verbalization being seen as a sign of group participation, trust, and cohesiveness. This position espouses that (1) a responsible person talks so that something can be accomplished, (2) silence does not accomplish anything, and (3) a person who is quiet either is not very bright or does not have any ideas. Other cultures, however, emphasize the value of silence and listening to gain wisdom. Rose (2001) quoted an old Ethiopian proverb that suggests the wisdom of listening: "If one person talks, everyone can hear; if everyone talks, no one can hear." Chung (2004) noted than many Asians are uncomfortable with direct communication, so the goal of group counseling that emphasizes direct and honest feedback may conflict with their beliefs about not openly expressing feelings and not drawing attention to oneself. Jim and Pistrang (2007) emphasized the concepts of shame and "losing face" as reasons not to seek mental health services. Because of the differences in values and beliefs around self-disclosure and verbalization, it is important as a group leader to understand and look for potential differences and to discuss them in group to come to

Table 6.2   Issues related to diversity and differences in perspective issues

Issue	Possible Perspectives
Relationship structure	Formal – informal
	Collateral – hierarchical
	Same-sex – opposite-sex interactions
	Male – female roles
Focus of treatment	Family – group – individual
	Respect – mistrust
	Inherited – achievement
	Within family – from outside
Time orientation	Clock – quorum time
Temporal focus	Past – present – future
Intrapersonal focus	Thoughts – feelings
Silence	Respectful – resistant
Talking	Attention-seeking – establishing relationship
Locus of control	Internal – external
	Individual – family – community
Nature of humankind	Good – evil
Relationship between people and nature	Mastery – harmony – subjugation
Expressiveness	Behavioral – emotional – verbal
Activity	Being – being-in-becoming – doing
Relational aspects	Lineality – collaterality – individualism
Worldview	Formism – contextualism – mechanism – organism
Communication patterns	Verbal – nonverbal
	Direct – indirect
	I – you statements
Physical contact	Between family – friends – strangers
Self-esteem	Achievement – relationships

a consensus on how group members will interact with each other.

Consequently, cultural norms that prescribe an order or structure of participation mediate, but do not destroy, group process. Such cultural norms must be identified and discussed in order to facilitate accurate perceptions of an individual's behavior in group. The one instance where groups tend to be structured is in starting and ending at a prescribed time to create safety and trust for the group. Other cultures, however, particularly Latino and Native American, view time very differently. "The interpretation of timeliness or lateness may have a profoundly different meaning in diverse cultures" (Bemak & Chung, 2004, p. 36).

It is imperative that group leaders examine their beliefs about how people learn, change, and grow from both a cultural and a theoretical perspective, then begin to think about how people from other cultures may view the group process and interactions differently.

"Group leaders' basic personalities, worldviews, cultural selfhoods, and experiences combine to influence and inform their work. Leaders bring to a group their attitudes, values, and beliefs that shape the way they perceive the world, others, and themselves" (Salazar, 2009b, p. 4). Bolyard and Jensen-Scott (1996) identified cultural assumptions and biases in the traditional models of crisis intervention (help during natural disasters and personal trauma), while Kincade and Evans (1996) discussed several Eurocentric assumptions inherent in different theoretical approaches to counseling. Other recent publications discuss specific cultural groups and how their values help or hinder the process of groups (Gladding, 2008), specifically Native Americans (DeLucia-Waack & Donigian, 2004; Garrett, 2004), African Americans (Pack-Brown & Fleming, 2004), Asians (Chung, 2004), Latinos (Carter, Yeh, & Mazzula, 2008; Torres Rivera, 2004), gay–lesbian–bisexual–transgendered individuals (Horne & Levitt, 2004), Canadian Indians (Shulman, 1999), and Arab Americans (Gladding, 2008).

Training of Multiculturally Competent Group Leaders

The ASGW's *Principles for Diversity-Competent Group Workers* (1999) specifies three competencies: awareness of self, awareness of group members' worldviews, and diversity-appropriate intervention strategies. DeLucia-Waack and Donigian's (2004) model expands on these principles with four steps:

Step 1: Examine your own culture, ethnic values, and racial identity to understand who you are as a person.

Step 2: Examine your beliefs about group work and the inherent assumptions within the Eurocentric view of group work.

Step 3: Learn about other cultures in terms of what they value and how these values may affect group work.

Step 4: Develop your personal plan for group work that emphasizes and utilizes cultural diversity guidelines for leading effective multicultural groups.

Step 1: Examine your Own Culture, Ethnic Values, and Racial Identity to Understand Who You Are as a Person

DeLucia-Waack and Donigian (2009, p. 51) suggested that group members, first by themselves and then as part of group introductions, address the following:

1. Who are you in terms of age, race, any physical disability, sexual orientation, ethnicity and culture, family patterns, gender, socioeconomic status, and intellectual ability (educational background)?

2. How do you see yourself as a unique individual based on your ethnic, cultural, and family background?

3. How does your background contribute to your view of how groups work?

4. What strengths do you bring to this group based on your cultural background and beliefs? What limitations do you bring as well?

Salazar (2009b) suggested that counselors begin this process by interviewing family members about cultural heritage and tradition and creating their own cultural genogram. Hardy and Laszloffy (1995) presented a model of a cultural genogram. They suggested two major steps: (1) getting organized and (2) putting it together. The getting-organized step includes defining one's culture of origin, organizing principles and pride/shame issues, creating symbols to denote all pride/shame issues, selecting colors to represent each group that comprises a person's culture of origin, and identifying intercultural marriages. The putting-it-together step consists of establishing cultural framework charts; constructing a genogram of at least three generations that identifies intercultural marriages, the composition of each person's cultural identity, and the symbols denoting pride/shame issues; and considering questions to identify the various sociological factors that contribute to cultural identity.

Experiential activities and discussions of concepts and interventions are vital to multicultural counseling competence (Bowman, 2009; Rowell & Benshoff, 2008). Williams (2005) compared a workshop-based educational intervention for cultural competence to typical diversity activities for social workers and concluded that greater multicultural awareness (and anticipated changes in therapy practice) resulted from participation in the workshop. Two publications by ASGW, *Group Work Experts Share Their Favorite Activities: A Guide to Choosing, Planning, Conducting, and Processing* (DeLucia-Waack, Bridbord, Kleiner, & Nitza, 2006) and *Group Work Experts Share Their Favorite Multicultural Activities: A Guide to Choosing, Planning, Conducting, and Processing* (Salazar, 2009a), include several activities to explore cultural backgrounds.

Step 2: Examine Your Beliefs about Group Work and the Inherent Assumptions within the Eurocentric View of Group Work

> Group leaders must undergo an in-depth examination of their own racial/ethnic identity, honestly examining personal prejudices, stereotypes, and biases. This calls for assessment of their own socialization and conditioning with regards to other racial or ethnic groups, the prejudice and bias towards that group, as well as, the stereotypes they hold of that group. They must be aware, understand, acknowledge and accept issues of racism, discrimination, and oppression, as well the concept of White privilege. (Roysircar, 2008)

For white group leaders, Salazar (2009a) emphasized the importance of understanding white privilege. She suggested reviewing the list of unearned privileges that McIntosh (1988) ascribed to skin color. Smith and Shin (2008) also provided an overview of privilege within social justice competencies for group leaders. In addition, it is helpful to assess racial identity development and acculturation (Merchant, 2006). DeLucia-Waack and Donigian (2004) summarized several models of racial identity development for white group leaders and group leaders of color.

Gladding (2008, p. 225–226) identified four myths about multicultural groups that group leaders must assess and work through in order to lead effective multicultural groups:

- Discussion of racial or cultural differences will offend group members
- Groups can be truly homogeneous
- Group member differences do not affect the process and outcome of task and psychoeducational groups
- Group-work theory is appropriate for all clients

Step 3: Learn about Other Cultures in terms of What They Value and How These Values May Affect Group Work

The next step in the self-assessment process for group leaders is the understanding of different cultures, specifically how cultural norms and values influence interactional styles, perceptions of problems, and perceptions of interventions and change relevant to group counseling. Group leaders must develop a framework that organizes cultural information but remains flexible enough to recognize when a client's behavior and/or attitudes differ from

cultural norms. Thus, it is important to utilize information about cultures in general as a background upon which to collect data and to generate hypotheses both as a group counselor and as a person living in a multicultural world. As a group counselor, it is important to collect data about different cultures' values related to group counseling on topics such as authority figures, self-disclosure, relationship styles, interactional patterns, and perceptions of mental health and change. The distinction between *emic* and *etic* is important as one learns about similarities and differences between cultures. Draguns (1976) distinguished between the two as follows: *emic* refers to the viewing of data in terms of being indigenous or unique to the culture in question and *etic*, to the viewing of data in light of categories and concepts external to the culture but universal in their applicability (p. 2).

Conyne (1988, 2009) adapted Hanson's (1972) "What to Look for in Groups" "to include and be responsive to multicultural dimensions that are important in group life, and to provide a set of guidelines for using this approach" (Conyne, 1988, p. 23). Group leaders can use group simulations, group videos, or actual groups (with permission, of course) as a stimulus for this activity. They observe the group interactions and then answer a series of questions focused on the following areas: participation, influence, decision-making procedures, task functions, maintenance functions, group atmosphere, membership, feelings, and norms. Questions include the following: How might silence be related to cultural differences? In general, what cultural similarities and differences might be influencing a member's involvement, and how are they affecting the group? Are some members resentful that they have to make a special attempt to understand another member's culture? Do members of different cultural backgrounds overtly disagree or agree with each other? What cultural values may help members to seek group work, and what values might inhibit them from seeking group work or from participating in group sessions? What cultural values may help group members to connect with the group leader or other group members, and what cultural values might inhibit their connection with the group leader or other members? What cultural values support the traditional concept of group work, and what cultural values are in conflict with it? How do these values vary within a culture? How does acculturation affect these values?

D'Andrea (2004) discussed 31 competencies developed by the Association for Multicultural

Counseling and Development, several of which emphasize the importance of being able to accurately identify and respectfully address the unique cultural–racial differences that persons from diverse client populations exhibit in individual and group counseling. These competencies emphasize that counselors not only must be knowledgeable of the between-group differences but also must understand the numerous within-group differences that are routinely manifested among individuals from the same cultural–and/or racial background (D'Andrea & Daniels, 2004).

Chung (2004), in discussing Asian Americans, highlighted the importance of inter- and intragroup differences. First, with regard to intergroup differences, Chung noted that there are potentially 40 groups of persons considered to be Asian American: "each group has its own distinct historical and social-political backgrounds, languages, identity issues, cultures and challenges encountered in mainstream society" (pp. 200–201). As an example, Japanese Americans present very different issues and dynamics as a group compared to Chinese Americans, whose ancestors migrated to the United States to become laborers and never faced internment. Filipino Americans are very different from other Asians because of English being the official language of the Philippines and the predominance of Catholicism as a religion (Tuason, Taylor, Rollings, Harris, & Martin, 2007).

Intragroup differences must also be taken into consideration. Chung (2004) suggested that premigration versus postmigration experiences significantly influence worldview, adjustment problems, and acculturation; for example, the first wave of Southeast Asian refugees experienced fewer adjustment problems in the United States than subsequent waves of refugees due to differences in education, English proficiency, and premigration trauma experiences.

Related to group differences is the issue of intergroup conflict. Chung (2004) described an example of a teacher who, thinking she was displaying cultural sensitivity, placed Chinese and Japanese students together to work on a class project. The teacher was confused when the students refused to work together. Chung noted that "given the sociopolitical and historical background between China and Japan, this was not surprising. The Japanese attacks in China during World War II have intergenerational impacts and may result in tension between Chinese and Japanese students" (p. 201).

To gain cultural knowledge and begin to understand inter- and intragroup group differences,

DeLucia-Waack and Donigian (2004) included a resource section summarizing journals, books, and journal articles related to multicultural group work, in general and with regard to specific groups. Clay and Shulman (1993) developed a video demonstrating group process in culturally diverse groups. Several sources also discuss the issue of inter- and intragroup variability in general and specifically for Asian Americans (Chung, 2004; Costigan, Bardina, Cauce, Kim, & Latendresse, 2006).

Several resources are available that compile information about effective multicultural group work. *Multicultural Groups*, part III of the *Handbook of Group Counseling and Psychotherapy* (DeLucia-Waack, Gerrity, Kalodner, & Riva, 2004), integrates current research and practice of group work with different groups, ethnic and social, as well as the impact of racial identity, language, and natural healing methods on groups. Two special issues of the *Journal for Specialists in Group Work* are now in press, focusing on social justice and multicultural group work. Anderson (2007) provided suggestions for assessment and stage-specific interventions to address diversity within groups. Wilson, Rapin, and Haley-Banez (2004) described how to use ASGW standards as a framework for teaching multicultural group work.

Step 4: Develop Your Personal Plan for Group Work that Emphasizes and Utilizes Cultural Diversity Guidelines for Leading Effective Multicultural Groups

DeLucia-Waack and Donigian (2004) emphasized the importance of group leaders understanding who they are as people and how that affects what they do as a counselor and group leader. They suggested the following:

1. Clarify your personal values.
2. Clarify the values inherent in your theoretical approach to group work.
3. Identify particular situations where your personal and/or theoretical values, beliefs, and assumptions may conflict with the values of a person from another culture or diverse background.
4. Identify particular situations where values inherent in your approach to group work may conflict with the values of a person from another culture or diverse background.
5. Identify particular situations, presenting problems, and specific group members that might lead you, because of conflicts with your personal

values and beliefs, to refer a member to another group or counseling professional.

6. Identify potential situations in group where the values of group members may be in conflict.

7. Identify situations when you will need supervision or to consult with other group leaders to discuss biases in group work.

8. Identify a list of sources to which you can refer for information about different cultures, acculturation, and potential conflicts and issues related to group work. (p. 27–28)

Guidelines for Leading Effective Multicultural Groups

This section is organized based on the three sections in the ASGW (2007) *Best Practice Guidelines*: planning, performing, and processing.

Planning

PARTNER WITH TARGET POPULATION

Gladding (2008) emphasized taking inventory of the needs and issues within a community. It is important to get input from members of the community, perhaps the elders, as to what is needed and what services would be acceptable within the community. Merchant (2009) also suggested asking about the pragmatic issues of potential group members, such as transportation and child care.

DETERMINE TYPE AND GOALS OF THE GROUP

Based on the needs assessment, determine the focus of the group (task, psychoeducational, counseling, or therapy) and which type of diversity group (culture-specific, intercultural learning, or other-content-focused) would be appropriate. Anderson (2007) suggested a multicultural group work treatment design and plan that takes into consideration (1) human problems being addressed, (2) useful theories of counseling and psychotherapy, (3) composition of group, (4) members' mental health status, and (5) members' uniqueness. Bemak and Chung (2004) suggested that "implicit in multicultural group work is the fostering of acceptance, respect, and tolerance for diversity within and between members" (p. 36).

GROUP LEADER PREPARATION

Once type and focus of the group have been established, group leaders need to prepare themselves to lead the group. Once group members have been identified, leaders need to think about potential cultural influences related to authority figures, self-disclosure, relationship styles, interactional patterns,

and perceptions of mental health and change. For example, for an eating disorders–counseling group, how the role of food, perceptions of body size and attractiveness, and expression of feelings may be represented in different cultures must be examined to prepare for how these issues may play out in group and help or hinder the group process.

PAY ATTENTION TO GROUP COMPOSITION IN SELECTION OF GROUP MEMBERS

Selection of group members is vital to effective group work. The two goals of group member selection are to (1) provide information to potential group members about details of the group (goals, topics, typical interventions) so that they are truly giving informed consent when they agree to participate and (2) gather information to decide whether potential group members would benefit from participation in this particular group.

> This is an opportunity for the group worker to discuss the group member's specific needs related to diversity issues and brainstorm ways in which barriers can be minimized and how best to address those issues in group. . . . When making such inquiries the group leader needs to avoid being insensitive and unnecessarily intrusive. By introducing the terms cultural variable, values, and stereotypes by means of providing definitions and examples, the group leader can then inquire as to whether any of the variables are personally relevant. (Merchant, 2006, p. 336)

While Yalom (1995) stressed the importance of heterogeneity of group members, he also cautioned against scapegoating a particular group member by making him or her appear so different that other group members cannot relate. Gender, race, socioeconomic status, and ethnicity of group members should be taken into consideration when trying to prevent scapegoating. One suggestion to prevent scapegoating is that "any one group member should not be so different that they feel isolated or scapegoated by the group. . . . Each group member must have at least one person in the group with whom they can initially connect and one person who will be able to serve as a role model" (DeLucia-Waack, 2006, p. 51). More specifically, Gladding (2008) noted that "including just one member of a culturally distinct group is usually not very productive. That person may have difficulty identifying with others in the group and may be stereotyped by the group" (p. 227). In an attempt to understand the group member within a cultural context, Shulman (1999) suggested people create cultureagram that include(s)" reasons for immigration, length of time in the community, legal or undocumented status, age at time of immigration, language spoken at home and in the community, contact with cultural institutions, health benefits, holidays and specific events, and values about family, education, and work" (pp. 119–120).

Merchant (2006) emphasized the importance of racial identity and acculturation of group members in addition to cultural background. To further support the importance of understanding group leaders' and group members' racial identity development, Helms (1990) adopted her model of relationship types for individual counseling to the relationship between group members and group leaders and suggested the potential impact of these relationships on group interaction, dynamics, and effectiveness. Helms suggested that it is useful to assess the racial identity development of both the group leader and specific group members. She described four types of leader–member relationships.

Parallel relationships are those in which the group leader and a coalition (some, but not all, group members) of the group share the same or analogous stages of racial identity. For example, in all-white groups, parallel relationships between leaders and a coalition of the group occur when both are in the contact or disintegration stage. For an all-black group, parallel relationships occur when leaders and a coalition share the same stage of black identity. For groups that are racially heterogeneous, parallel relationships would include the preencounter/reintegration, internalization/autonomy, and perhaps the encounter/disintegration status (Helms, 1990). The common theme in parallel relationships is inertia because the majority of the participants in the group, including the group leader(s), are all at the same stage and, thus, share similar worldviews, which makes it difficult for them to challenge one another to move beyond their common world. It makes sense that some heterogeneity in racial identity development is useful to group productiveness.

Regressive relationships are characterized by a coalition of members whose stage of racial identity development is more advanced than that of their leader; thus, the major theme of this type of relationship is regression (Helms, 1990). Group leaders' attempts to influence coalitions in their view of racial issues are no longer functional because they are not at the level that is needed.

Crossed relationships occur when the group leaders' stage of identity development is conceptually opposite from that of a coalition of members; thus, relationships tend to be combative.

Progressive relationships, as described by Helms (1990), appear to be the most useful and desirable ones in group work. In this type of relationship, the group leader is at a stage of racial identity that is more developed than those of the coalition of group members. The general theme in progressive relationships is movement and energy, with the leader encouraging the coalition to move beyond its present level of development.

Pack-Brown and Fleming (2004) suggested a series of questions that group counselors might use to compare and contrast their worldviews with those of potential group members:

- What are the racial, ethnic, and cultural situations of each group member?
- What goals for the group does each member have?
- What are possible cross-cultural issues that may be evidenced in group?
- What possible thematic cultural value and belief system differences and similarities might be evidenced in group?
- What is my personal level of racial identity development?
- How will I assess each group member's racial identity development?
- What is my personal theory of effective group work with diverse and multicultural populations? (p. 190)

Performing

PREGROUP PREPARATION

Merchant (2006) advocated the use of pregroup preparation, particularly for culturally diverse group members. There are several reasons for conducting pregroup preparation. First, clients from diverse backgrounds infrequently participate in group counseling (Leong, 1992). Second, if minority clients do begin counseling, they often experience relationship barriers and/or terminate prematurely (Sue & Sue, 1999). Thus, it is important that they have a good sense of what happens in groups, typical interventions, group leader behaviors, and how they might participate in group.

Bowman and DeLucia-Waack (1993) suggested a three-part preparation session where potential group members read about, view, and then participate in activities about typical group goals, topics, and interventions. Ceaser (2009) has developed a DVD to illustrate the group process and group interventions. Bauman and Steen's (2009) DVD of adolescents and Corey, Corey, and Haynes's (1999) video of adults also illustrate group process and discussion of cultural issues. Wood, Chiu, Hwang, Jacobs, and Ifekwunigwe (2008) also suggested an orientation session for families of Mexican American youth to increase family understanding and participation.

ESTABLISH CULTURALLY SENSITIVE GROUP NORMS

Because many of the values and behaviors encouraged in groups are Eurocentric in origin, it is important to discuss from the beginning the goals of the group and how people can work on them in a way that is helpful to them and respectful of their culture. "Cultural variations in communication styles, such as the norms and rules that guide behavior and shape individual communication goals, may lead to different perception of interpersonal behavior. Variations among cultures in their tolerance for the expression of qualities such as support, disagreement, and disapproval may also contribute" (Costigan et al., 2006, p. 711).

To prevent misunderstandings due to different communication styles, group members might be asked to compile a list of ways to show support in group sessions and then share the lists with the group. Members might comment on similarities and differences to promote universality and altruism and to identify possible new behaviors. It is also helpful to discuss ground rules in terms of their purpose and how they best facilitate member growth in the group. For example, beginning and ending on time may be viewed differently by different members, so it is important to explain how it provides safety and ensures each member time to talk.

Other norms may be negotiable based on the type of group and group members. D'Andrea and Daniels (2004) suggested that the traditional guideline of not allowing food (as it is a distraction) may not apply in some cultures. Singh and Hays (2008), in their model of groups for South Asian women, suggested modification of the norms around food and lingering after group sessions to share conversation and food as a way to develop community and cohesion that respects cultural norms. It may also be useful to hold group sessions where people naturally gather, rather than a counselor's office. Out-of-group socializing is another norm that may need to be renegotiated as that contact may be needed to establish trust and/or cannot be avoided in some groups.

Marbley (2004) suggested discussing the topic of racial differences in the initial stage by asking group members to tell the group about their ethnicity, nationality, race, and culture. "The above exercise of letting the group members self-identify sets the tone for discussing the racial differences existing in the group" (p. 254). She also emphasized ground rules that help members "communicate with each other in the least offensive, hurtful, and oppressive manner, such as insisting that the group members' responses first acknowledge and validate the member's feelings and experiences" (Marbley, p. 255). Following from that, Bemak and Chung (2004) advocated for appreciation, respect, acceptance, and tolerance as ground rules, not as implicit norms.

MODEL BEING CULTURALLY SENSITIVE

It is useful for group members to understand how group leaders will interact with them. Discussion of theoretical orientation, assumptions of how groups work, and potential interventions are important to describe beginning in the initial interview. It is also important for group leaders to discuss with group members how their worldview will impact their beliefs about groups and group process. Toporek, Davis, Ahluwali, and Artwohl (2002) reported a significant positive relationship between client perceptions of counselor cultural understanding and satisfaction with counseling.

Group members will typically vary in their communication styles and conflict-resolution strategies, so it is important in initial sessions to discuss differences and misconceptions and how they will respectfully but honestly talk about these issues in the group. It is also helpful for group leaders to discuss how stereotypes will be displayed in any group, how they negatively impact the group process, and how the group will work through such events.

Pandya (2005) stated that "the most common empowering technique used by contemporary group work facilitators is to pointedly discuss when the group members bring their outside lived world to the group for issues relating to power, equality, and justice" (p. 604). Such a technique may result in other group members identifying with the issues and creating a collective consciousness. McCubbin and Coleman (2002) suggested that multicultural counseling competency be defined as three specific skills: context empathy, exploring cultural factors, and recovery from insensitive comments. Such skills suggest that it is important for group leaders to acknowledge group members' thoughts and feelings, to explore cultural values and worldviews in defining the problem, to make suggestions for change, and to model humanness and understanding of the fact that people do make mistakes.

Marbley (2004) identified self-disclosure as a tool to model how to discuss racial issues. She provided an example of how she made a stereotypic assumption about racial identity based on skin color. She acknowledged the error and the group then discussed it. Bemak and Chung (2004) suggested that group leader(s) model taking risks to introduce cultural differences and difficult interpersonal issues into the group process, to establish norms that embrace and facilitate discussion of emotionally charged and difficult issues.

CHOOSE CULTURALLY SENSITIVE INTERVENTIONS AND ACTIVITIES

Group leaders' cultural knowledge should be viewed as a backdrop, not a definitive statement. Within–cultural group variability is as great, if not greater, than between–cultural group variability (Chung, 2004). Jim and Pistrang (2007) stated "a critical skill is knowing when to generalize and when to individualize; that is, the therapist must be able to recognize when and how cultural values or cultural group characteristics may be relevant to the client's problems but also to see the client as an individual" (p. 462).

Early interventions to help diverse group members connect to group are critical as their potential for leaving group prematurely is much higher than for other group members (Leong, 1992). Several authors have suggested that diverse clients, particularly Asian clients, may benefit from concrete gains in the first session, analogous to the act of gift giving in Chinese culture (Jim & Pistrang, 2007; Sue & Zane, 2009). The gift is the immediate benefit from the therapeutic encounter, particularly given the lack of experience with and misgivings about Western therapy. Sweifach (2009) focused early sessions on "nurturing the commonalities among members" (p. 114), to create cohesiveness and universality (Chen, Kakkad, & Balzano, 2008) and help members feel a part of the group. In addition, it is important to establish goals early so that members view the group as potentially helpful to them.

Establishing goals within a cultural context is vital. DeLucia-Waack and Donigian (2004) suggested helping group members conceptualize their goals for the group in a personal and cultural context

so that a plan of action can be formulated that is consistent with the individual's belief system. What is the presenting problem? What are possible interventions? What does the culture(s) say about the problem, cause, and cure?

Anderson (2007) conceptualized diversity in terms of culture, worldview, identities, statuses, and demographics. Jim and Pistrang's (2007) study of Asian clients identified cultural formulation as key to the creation of a therapeutic alliance; the therapist had been able to recognize and make sense of how cultural values played a role in their problems. Sue and Zane (2009) suggested that credibility of the counselor is based on conceptualization of the problem, means for problem resolution, and goals for treatment from within a client's belief system.

Culturally sensitive interventions approach all events and behaviors in the group from a functional perspective. Does it work for that individual? The emphasis in group must be on exploring cultural differences without assuming that one way of behaving is necessarily better than others. Group leaders must help group members make sense of new behaviors, beliefs, and skills within a cultural context. What are the cultural implications for this changed or new behavior? As group members examine their relationships with other group members based on perceived similarities and differences, they gain a better sense of their own identity and their relationships with others. The focus of group counseling is to help group members develop a sense of self and at the same time connect and relate to others.

Bieschke, Gehlert, Wilson, Matthews, and Wade (2003), based on qualitative analyses of training groups, suggested that multicultural issues were clustered by stage of group. In the initial stage, events were focused on observations and awareness of multicultural differences (e.g., I am the oldest person in the group) as well as implications (e.g., finally, we begin to discuss the issue of race and how it affects our group). Throughout group sessions, events related to stereotypes, socialization, and assumptions were noted by group members. During the later sessions, discomfort with multicultural issues was noted: specifically, group and individual avoidance, feeling singled out, discomfort with lack of recognition, discomfort or fear of being misunderstood, and conflict. Group members also noted that incidents related to positive feelings associated with multicultural differences were regarded as multicultural turning points throughout group sessions.

ACKNOWLEDGE AND WORK THROUGH GROUP DIFFERENCES AND CONFLICT

Bemak and Chung (2004) suggested "become comfortable with conflict. Historical differences in multicultural groups may generate conflict and strong emotional responses. It is important that educators are able to examine these strong reactions and historically conflictual relationships interpersonally within the group context" (p. 38). Bargal's (2004) philosophy is "the current reality for people who live in Western pluralistic societies is full of conflict" (p. 292).

It is important from the beginning of a group to discuss similarities and differences between members and how they are useful in group to emphasize that such discussions are part of the group process. Early in the group process, it is important to emphasize similarities of members so that they can connect and learn how to work together. It is also useful to begin to point out how group members have different approaches to events or problems so that the value of diverse opinions, coping styles, and behaviors becomes apparent.

However, excessive conflict occurring too soon may be counterproductive. Jacobs and Schimmel (2009) stated that "a decision has to be made regarding how much conflict is productive in helping members to understand each other. Too much conflict can cause a deterioration of trust" (p. 139). Anderson (2007) suggested that "group work effectiveness can be diminished by misunderstanding or misinterpreting the origin and meaning of human behavior as a result of confusing emic, etic, and dialectic points of view" (p. 228). Leong (1992) stated that "many therapeutic problems are created when value conflicts generated by cultural differences among racial and ethnic minorities in group counseling situations are not recognized and attended to" (p. 222).

INCORPORATE TRADITIONAL AND SPIRITUAL HEALING

The incorporation of traditional methods of healing and wellness into current group-work practices is another way to utilize effective practices and integrate culture. Caldwell (2002) emphasized that "counseling and therapy are not culturally universal concepts; therefore it is necessary to identify and learn from culturally indigenous practices of health and healing" (p. 7). Several authors have provided guidelines for the use of cultural ritual, not only with persons of the same culture but also with diverse groups. Garrett and Crutchfield (1997)

provided guidelines for using Native American principles with children and adolescents to develop self-esteem, self-determination, body awareness, and self-concept. Roberts-Wilbur, Wilbur, Garrett, and Yuhas (2001) suggested the use of a Native American talking circle in a peer education program for college students. Lawrey (2006) described the Native American talking stick as an icebreaker in college classrooms. Pack-Brown (2006) adapted the Afrocentric group-work intervention of drumming. Brinson and Fisher (1999) applied the Ho'oponopono conflict-resolution technique for use in the schools. Garrett, Brubacker, Torres-Rivera, West-Olatunji, and Conwill (2009) provide specific situations about how to use the Native American technique of centering at different stages of the group process.

Rayle, Sand, Brucato, and Ortega (2006) suggested the use of the Latino/Latina value of *compadre*: "For Mexican women, the compadre represents an important figure in their culture; another female that is sister-like and considered a close friend, advisor, and confident p. 7."

PROCESS ACTIVITIES WITH A SPECIFIC FOCUS IN MIND

Effective processing of activities and critical events helps group members to make sense of group events and apply what they have learned outside of group. Processing is important because it allows group members to create meaning through reflection, sharing, connecting, and extrapolating. To help group members make sense of what happens in group within a culturally sensitive framework, Jacobs and Schimmel (2009) suggested multiple foci of processing:

- members' reactions to what other members said and how their culture may be influencing them
- cultural similarities or differences among the members
- interactions in the group that are driven by culture or cultural differences
- interactions in the members' lives that are driven by culture or cultural differences
- how members' experiences of the activity can translate to the world in which they live
- the past—things one may miss about a former country or culture
- the present in group—difficulties being in this group because of cultural differences
- the present—difficulties living in the present country because of cultural differences (p. 37)

Some examples of processing questions that put the event within a cultural framework include the following:

How do you feel different from those in school or at work or in your neighborhood?

What did the exercise make you aware of with regard to how you participate in the group?

How do your cultural upbringing or view(s) influence how you see the issue being discussed? (Jacobs & Schimmel, p. 38)

Processing

SEEK SUPERVISION AND CONSULTATION WHEN APPROPRIATE

Supervision is key to effective group work. Coleaders must meet regularly to plan and process group sessions and to plan interventions for group members to help them meet their goals. Consultation is useful around cultural issues (Gladding, 2008). Other group leaders and elders in the community may be helpful in selecting interventions that are culturally sensitive.

USE CULTURALLY APPROPRIATE EVALUATIONS

Most group-process and outcome measures are validated in English and with white, middle-class group members. Consider translating measures into the first language of group members or using measures that have been validated with persons of color. The Group Therapy Survey (Slocum, 1987) is one of the few measures to be examined with regard to cultural influences. Leong, Wagner, and Kim (1995) found that attitudes toward group counseling were predicted by level of acculturation for Asian American college students. The Critical Incidents Questionnaire (Kivlighan & Goldfine, 1991) asks group members to describe the most important event in a group session and why it is important. Answers can then be coded into therapeutic factors.

What Is Needed in the Future

Culturally appropriate forms of treatment (Sue & Zane, 2009), particularly group interventions, are needed. "Practice principles for culturally competence must be built on an empirical foundation as we gather data from and about diverse ethnic and racial groups" (Garvin, Gutiérrez, & Galinksy, 2004, p. 6). Then, research must systematically evaluate and help tailor culturally sensitive group treatments. "Compared to individual psychotherapy, much less research attention has been devoted to diversity in group therapy" (Chen et al., 2008, p. 1265).

There are a few research studies that have investigated the effectiveness of group treatment for diverse groups, such as those conducted by Colmant, Eason, Winterowd, Jacobs, and Cashel (2005) and Rayle et al. (2006). Huey and Polo (2008) reviewed evidence-based treatment for ethnic minority youth, both individual and group treatments, and were cautiously optimistic. Two studies supported the use of cognitive-behavioral therapy with Latino and African American youth with anxiety disorders (Ginsburg & Drake, 2002; Silverman et al., 1999). Snyder, Kymissis, and Kessler (1999) also indicated that anger-management groups were effective for African American, Latino, and mixed-race youth. Bernal, Jimenéz-Chafey, and Domenech Rodríguez (2009), in their review of evidence-based treatment that considered culture, identified only two group interventions, one for Haitian Americans (Nicolas, Arntz, Hirsch, & Schmiedigen, 2009) and one for Mexican Americans with anxiety disorders (Wood et al., 2008). However, Huey and Polo (2008) noted that "Although many of the treatments included culture-responsive elements, none directly tested for culture-responsive effects and thus say little about the true impact of culture-related modifications on differential treatment outcomes" (p. 286).

Hwang (2009) suggested a community-based model to help develop and evaluate culturally sensitive treatments, the Psychotherapy Adaptation and Modification Framework. This framework contains six domains of cultural adaptations: dynamic issues and cultural complexities; orienting clients to psychotherapy and increasing mental health awareness; understanding cultural beliefs about mental illness, its causes, and appropriate treatment; improving the client–therapist relationship; understanding cultural differences in the expression and communication of distress; and addressing cultural issues specific to the population.

Challenges and Opportunities

Social class is often neglected in discussions of diversity and specifically in group interventions. Ballinger and Wright (2007), based on a qualitative study, suggested that social class is often neglected because it is inextricably linked to education and sometimes race and because of the unique set of values inherent in generational poverty. Only one reference was found for groups for the poor (and the homeless), Carr (2004).

In addition, much of the literature fails to address the cultural background of the group leader. Merchant (2006) raised the issue of whether the group leader needs to be from the same cultural group as the members but does not offer a definitive answer. Sue and Zane (2009) called for more bilingual counselors. However, research has not addressed the issue of the impact of the cultural background of the group leader on group effectiveness.

Conclusion

Group leaders must have a good understanding of the diversity of cultural worldviews and of their potential impact on the relationships, behaviors, and willingness to participate in therapeutic group work. It is not essential to research every potential worldview; it is more important for group leaders to understand that each person approaches participation in a group from his or her own unique perspective. Dyche and Zayas (1995) suggested that

> the major benefit to therapists from the study of other cultures is less to understand their clients than to understand themselves. A thoughtful reading of cross-cultural literature can open therapists to the diversity of answers to life's universal questions, and arouse a curiosity that competes with their native ethnocentrism. In the end, the most important application of cultural theory to practice is self-discipline; never assume with the client; always inquire. (p. 391)

References

American Group Psychotherapy Association. (2007). *Practice guidelines for group psychotherapy.* Retrieved September 22, 2009, from www.agpa.org

Anderson, D. (2007). Multicultural group work: A force for developing and healing. *Journal for Specialists in Group Work, 32,* 224–244.

Appleton, V. E., & Dykeman, C. (1996). Using art in group counseling with Native American youth. *Journal for Specialists in Group Work, 21,* 224–231.

Arredondo, P. (1999). Multicultural counseling competencies as tools to address oppression and racism. *Journal of Counseling and Development, 77,* 102–108.

Association for Specialists in Group Work. (1999). *Association for Specialists in Group Work principles for diversity-competent group workers.* Retrieved September 22, 2009, from www.asgw.org

Association for Specialists in Group Work. (2007). *Association for Specialists in Group Work best practice guidelines (rev).* Retrieved September 22, 2009, from www.asgw.org

Ballinger, L., & Wright, J. (2007). Does class count? Social class and counselling. *Counselling and Psychotherapy, 7,* 157–163.

Bargal, D. (2004). Groups for reducing intergroup conflict. In C. D. Garvin, L. M. Gutierrez, & M. J. Galinsky (Eds.), *Handbook of social work in groups* (pp. 292–306). New York: Guilford Press.

Bauman, S., & Steen, S. (2009). *Celebrating cultural diversity: A group for 5th graders* [DVD]. Alexandria, VA: Association for Specialists in Group Work.

Bemak, F., & Chung, R. C. (2004). Teaching multicultural group counseling: Perspectives for a new era. *Journal for Specialists in Group Work, 29,* 31–42.

Bentelspacher, C. E., DeSilva, E., Goh, T. L. C., & LaRowe, K. D. (1996). A process evaluation of the cultural compatibility of psychoeducational family group treatment with ethnic Asian clients. *Social Work with Groups, 19,* 41–55.

Bernal, G., Jiménez-Chafey, M. I., & Domenech Rodríquez, M. (2009). Cultural adaptation of treatments: A resource for considering culture in evidence-based practice. *Professional Psychology: Research and Practice, 40,* 361–368.

Bieschke, K. J., Gehlert, K. M., Wilson, D., Matthews, C. R., & Wade, J. (2003). Qualitative analysis of multicultural awareness in training groups. *Journal for Specialists in Group Work, 28,* 325–338.

Bolyard, K. L., & Jensen-Scott, R. L. (1996). Worldview and culturally sensitive crisis intervention. In J. L. DeLucia-Waack (Ed.), *Multicultural counseling competencies: Implications for training and practice.* Alexandria, VA: Association for Counselor Education and Supervision.

Bowman, N. A. (2009). College diversity courses and cognitive development among students from privileged and marginalized groups. *Journal of Diversity in Higher Education, 2,* 182–194.

Bowman, V. E., & DeLucia-Waack, J. L. (1993). Preparation for group therapy: The effects of preparer and modality on group process and individual functioning. *Journal for Specialists in Group Work, 18,* 67–79.

Brinson, J., & Fisher, T. A. (1999). The Ho'oponopono group: A conflict resolution model for school counselors. *Journal for Specialists in Group Work, 24,* 369–382.

Brown, S. P., Lipford-Sanders, J., & Shaw, M. (1995). Kujichagulia: Uncovering the secrets of the heart: Group work with African-American women on predominantly white campuses. *Journal for Specialists in Group Work, 20,* 151–158.

Caldwell, L. (2002). *Beyond textbook multicultural competence: Addressing multicultural skill development in training.* Paper presented at the annual conference of the American Psychological Association, Chicago, IL.

Campbell, R. (2004). Groups for older adults. In C. D. Garvin, L. M. Gurierrez, & M. J. Galinsky (Eds.), *Handbook of social work in groups* (pp. 275–291). New York: Guilford Press.

Carr, E. S. (2004). Accessing resources, transforming services: Group work with poor and homeless people. In C. D. Garvin, L. M. Gurierrez, & M. J. Galinsky (Eds.), *Handbook of social work in groups* (pp. 360–383). New York: Guilford Press.

Carter, R. T., Yeh, C. J., & Mazzula, S. L. (2008). Cultural values and racial identity statuses among Latino students. *Hispanic Journal of Behavioral Sciences, 30,* 5–23.

Ceaser, M. A. (2009). *Preparing veterans for group psychotherapy* [DVD]. Houston, TX: Department of Veteran Affairs.

Chen, C. P. (1995). Group counseling in a different cultural context: Several primary issues in dealing with Chinese clients. *Group, 19,* 45–55.

Chen, E. C., Kakkad, D., & Balzano, J. (2008). Multicultural competence and evidence-based practice in group therapy. *Journal of Clinical Psychology, 64,* 1261–1279.

Chen, M., & Han, Y. S. (2001). Cross-cultural group counseling with Asians: A stage-specific interactive approach. *Journal for Specialists in Group Work, 26,* 111–128.

Chen, S. X., & Mak, W. W. S. (2008). Seeking professional help: Etiology beliefs about mental illness across cultures. *Journal of Counseling Psychology, 55,* 442–450.

Chong, W. H. (2005). The role of self-regulation and personal agency beliefs: A psychoeducational approach with Asian high school students in Singapore. *Journal for Specialists in Group Work, 30*, 343–362.

Christensen, T. M., Hulse-Killacky, D., Salgado, R. A., Thornton, M. D., & Miller, J. L. (2006). Facilitating reminiscence groups: Perceptions of group leaders. *Journal for Specialists in Group Work, 31*, 73–88.

Chung, R. Y. (2004). Group counseling with Asians. In J. L. DeLucia-Waack, D. A. Gerrity, C. R. Kalodner, & M. T. Riva (Eds.), *Handbook of group counseling and psychotherapy* (pp. 200–212). Thousand Oaks, CA: Sage.

Clay, C., & Shulman, L. (1993). *Teaching about practice and diversity: Content and process in the classroom and in the field* [Videotape]. Alexandria, VA: Council on Social Work Education.

Colmant, S., Eason, E. A., Winterowd, C. L., Jacobs, S. C., & Cashel, C. (2005). Investigating the effects of sweat therapy on group dynamics and affect. *Journal for Specialists in Group Work, 30*, 329–342.

Colmant, S., & Merta, R. (1999). Using a sweat lodge ceremony as group therapy for special Navajo youth. *Journal for Specialists in Group Work, 24*, 55–73.

Constantine, M. G., Hage, S., Kindaichi, M. M., & Bryant, R. M. (2007). Social justice and multicultural issues: Implications for the practice and training of counselors and counseling psychologists. *Journal of Counseling and Development, 85*, 24–29.

Conyne, R. K. (1988). What to look for in groups: Helping trainees become more sensitive to multicultural training issues. *Journal for Specialists in Group Work, 23*, 22–32.

Conyne, R. K. (2009). What to look for in groups: Using the group multicultural sensitizer activity. In C. Salazar (Ed.), *Group work experts share their favorite multicultural activities: A guide to diversity-competent choosing, planning, conducting, and processing* (pp. 238–241). Alexandria, VA: Association for Specialists in Group Work.

Corey, M. S., Corey, G., & Haynes, R. (1999). *Evolution of a group* [Video]. New York: Wadsworth.

Corrigan, M. J., Jones, C. A., & McWhirter, J. J. (2001). College students with disabilities: An access employment group. *Journal for Specialists in Group Work, 26*, 339–349.

Costigan, C. L., Bardina, P., Cauce, A. M., Kim, G. K., & Latendresse, S. J. (2006). Inter- and intra-group variability in perceptions of behavior among Asian Americans and European Americans. *Cultural Diversity and Ethnic Minority Psychology, 12*, 710–724.

D'Andrea, M. J. (2004). The impact of racial–cultural identity of group leaders and members: Theory and recommendations. In J. L. DeLucia-Waack, D. A. Gerrity, C. R. Kalodner, & M. T. Riva (Eds.), *Handbook of group counseling and psychotherapy* (pp. 265–282). Thousand Oaks, CA: Sage.

D'Andrea, M. J., & Daniels, J. (2004). *Multicultural counseling: Empowering strategies for a diverse society*. Pacific Grove, CA: Brooks/Cole.

DeLucia-Waack, J. L., Bridbord, K. H., Kleiner, J. S., & Nitza, A. (Eds.). (2006). *Group work experts share their favorite activities: A guide to choosing, planning, conducting, and processing* (rev. ed.). Alexandria, VA: Association for Specialists in Group Work.

DeLucia-Waack, J., Gerrity, D., Kalodner, C., & Riva, M. (Eds.) (2004). *Handbook of group counseling and psychotherapy*. Thousand Oaks, CA: Sage.

DeLucia-Waack, J. L., & Donigian, J. (2004). *The practice of multicultural group work: Visions and perspectives from the field*. Pacific Grove, CA: Wadsworth Press.

DeLucia-Waack, J., & Donigian, A. (2009). Cultural autobiography: My identity as a diverse person. In C. Salazar (Ed.), *Group work experts share their favorite multicultural activities: A guide to diversity-competent choosing, planning, conducting, and processing* (pp. 163–165). Alexandria, VA: Association for Specialists in Group Work.

Devan, G. S. (2001). Culture and the practice of group psychotherapy in Singapore. *International Journal of Group Psychotherapy, 51*, 571–577.

Diehm, T. M., & Lazzari, M. M. (2001). The university's role in promoting human rights through nurturing human diversities. *Journal of Gay and Lesbian Social Services, 13*(1/2), 171–189.

Draguns, J. G. (1976). Counseling across cultures: Common themes and distinct approaches. In P. B. Pederson, W. J. Lonner, & J. G. Draguns (Eds.), *Counseling across cultures* (pp. 3–21). Honolulu: University Press.

Dyche, L., & Zayas, L. H. (1995). The value of curiosity and naivete for the cross-cultural psychotherapist. *Family Process, 34*, 389–399.

Epp, K. M. (2008). Outcome-based evaluation of a social skills program using art therapy and group therapy for children on the autism spectrum. *Children & Schools, 30*, 27–36.

Epsin, O. (1987). Psychological impact of migration on Latinas: Implications for psychotherapeutic Practice. *Psychology of Women Quarterly, 11*, 489–503.

Fassinger, R. E. (2000). Gender and sexuality in human development: Implications for prevention and advocacy in counseling psychology. In S. D. Brown & R. W. Lent (Eds.), *Handbook of counseling psychology* (3rd ed., pp. 346–378). New York: John Wiley & Sons.

Fernando, D. M. (2009). Group work with survivors of the 2004 Asian tsunami: Reflections on an American-trained counselor. *Journal for Specialists in Group Work, 34*, 4–23.

Firestein, B. A. (1999). New perspectives on group treatment with women of diverse sexual identities. *Journal for Specialists in Group Work, 24*, 306–315.

Foldy, E., Rivard, P., & Buckley, T. (2009). Power, safety, and learning in racially diverse groups. *Academy of Management, Learning, and Education, 8*, 25–41.

Fouad, N. A., & Brown, M. T. (2000). Role of race and social class in development: Implications for counseling psychology. In S. D. Brown & R. W. Lent (Eds.), *Handbook of counseling psychology* (3rd ed., pp. 379–408). New York: John Wiley & Sons.

Garret, M. T. (2004). Sound of the drum: Group counseling with Native Americans. In J. L. DeLucia-Waack, D. A. Gerrity, C. R. Kalodner, & M. T. Riva (Eds.), *Handbook of group counseling and psychotherapy* (pp. 169–182). Thousand Oaks, CA: Sage.

Garrett, M. T., Brubaker, M., Torres-Rivera, E., West-Olatunji, C., & Conwill, W. (2009). The medicine of coming to center: Use of the Native American centering technique Ayeli to promote wellness and healing in group work. *Journal for Specialists in Group Work, 33*, 179–198.

Garrett, M. T., & Crutchfield, L. B. (1997). Moving full circle: A unity model of group work with children. *Journal for Specialists in Group Work, 22*, 175–188.

Garvin, C. D., Gutiérrez, L. M., & Galinsky, M. J. (2004). *Handbook of social work in groups*. New York: Guilford Press.

Ginsburg, G. S., & Drake, K. L. (2002). School-based treatment for anxious African-American adolescents: A controlled pilot study. *Journal of the American Academy of the Children and Adolescent Psychiatry, 41*, 768–775.

Gladding, S. T. (2008). *Groups: A counseling specialty.* New York: Pearson.

Haley-Banez, L., & Walden, S. L. (1999). Diversity in group work: Using optimal theory to understand group process and dynamics. *Journal for Specialists in Group Work, 24*, 404–422.

Hanna, F. J., Talley, W. B., & Guindon, M. H. (2000). The power of perception: Toward a model of cultural oppression and liberation. *Journal of Counseling and Development, 78*, 430–440.

Hanson, P. (1972). What to look for in groups: An observation guide. In J. Pfeifer & J. Jones (Eds.), *The 1972 annual handbook of group facilitators* (pp. 21–24). San Diego, CA: Pfeiffer.

Hardy, K. V., & Laszloffy, T. A. (1995). The cultural genogram: Key to training culturally competent family therapists. *Journal of Marital and Family Therapy, 21*, 227–237.

Helms, J. E. (1990). *Black and white identity: Theory, research, and practice.* New York: Greenwood Press.

Hernandez, D. V., Skewes, M. C., Resor, M. R., Villanueva, M. R., Hanson, B. S., & Blume, A. W. (2006). A pilot test of an alcohol skills training programme for Mexican-American college students. *International Journal of Drug Policy, 17*, 320–328.

Hill, P. C., & Pargament, K. I. (2003). Advances in the conceptualization and measurement of religion and spirituality. *American Psychologist, 58*, 64–74.

Horne, S. G., & Levitt, H. M. (2004). Psychoeducational and counseling groups with gay, lesbian, bisexual, and transgendered clients. In J. L. DeLucia-Waack, D. A. Gerrity, C. R. Kalodner, & M. T. Riva (Eds.), *Handbook of group counseling and psychotherapy* (pp. 224–239). Thousand Oaks, CA: Sage.

Huey, S. J., & Polo, A. J. (2008). Evidence-based psychosocial treatments for ethnic minority youth. *Journal of Clinical Children and Adolescent Psychology, 37*, 262–301.

Husaini, B. A., Cummings, S., Kilbourne, B., Roback, H., Sherkat, D., Levine, R., et al. (2004). Group therapy for depressed elderly women. *International Journal of Group Psychotherapy, 54*, 295–320.

Hwang, W. (2009). The formative method for adapting psychotherapy (FMAP): A community-based developmental approach to culturally adapting theory. *Professional Psychology: Research and Practice, 40*, 369–377.

Jacobs, E., & Schimmel, C. (2009). Processing activities to facilitate the transfer of learning outside the group. In C. Salazar (Ed.), *Group work experts share their favorite multicultural activities: A guide to diversity-competent choosing, planning, conducting, and processing* (pp. 135–145). Alexandria, VA: Association for Specialists in Group Work.

Jim, J., & Pistrang, N. (2007). Culture and the therapeutic relationship: Perspectives from Chinese clients. *Psychotherapy Research, 17*, 461–473.

Karp, H. B., & Sammour, H. Y. (2000). Workforce diversity: Choices in diversity training programs and dealing with resistance to diversity. *College Student Journal, 34*, 451–458.

Kelly, T. B., Schofield, I., Booth, J., & Tolson, D. (2005). The use of online groups to involve older people in influencing nursing home guidance. *Groupwork, 16*, 69–94.

Kivlighan, D. M. Jr., & Goldfine, D. C. (1991). Endorsement of therapeutic factors as a function of stage of group development and participant interpersonal attitudes. *Journal of Counseling Psychology, 38*, 150–158.

Kim, B. S. K., Omizo, M. M., & D'Andrea, M. J. (1998). The effects of culturally consonant group counseling on the self-esteem and internal locus of control orientation among Native American adolescents. *Journal for Specialists in Group Work, 23*, 145–163.

Kincade, E. A., & Evans, K. M. (1996). Counseling theories, process, and interventions within a multicultural context. In J. DeLucia-Waack (Ed.), *Multicultural counseling competencies: Implications for training and practice* (pp. 89–112), Alexandria, VA: Association for Counselor Education and Supervision.

Lawrey, J. D. (2006). College classroom ice breaker combined with Native-American council process. In J. L. DeLucia-Waack, K. H. Bridbord, J. S. Kleiner, & A. Nitza (Eds.), *Group work experts share their favorite activities: A guide to choosing, planning, conducting, and processing* (rev. ed., pp. 52–53). Alexandria, VA: Association for Specialists in Group Work.

Leong, F. (1992). Guidelines for minimizing premature termination among Asian American clients in group counseling. *Journal for Specialists in Group Work, 17*, 218–228.

Leong, F., Wagner, N. S., & Kim, H. H. (1995). Group counseling expectations among Asian American students: The role of culture-specific factors. *Journal of Counseling Psychology, 42*, 217–222.

Marbley, A. F. (2004). His eye is on the sparrow: A counselor of color's perception of facilitating groups with predominantly white members. *Journal for Specialists in Group Work, 29*, 247–258.

McCubbin, L. D., & Coleman, H. L. K. (2002, August). *Empirical challenge to the distinction between multicultural and general counseling competence.* Paper presented at the annual conference of the American Psychological Association, Chicago, IL.

McEachern, A. G., & Kenney, M. C. (2007). Transition groups for high school students with disabilities. *Journal for Specialists in Group Work, 32*, 165–177.

McIntosh, P. (1988). *White privilege and male privilege: Coming to see correspondences through work in women's studies* (Working Paper 189, Wellesley College Center for Research on Women). Retrieved from ERIC Document Reproduction Service (ED335262).

Merchant, N. (2006). Multicultural and diversity-competent group work. In J. P. Trotzer (Ed.), *The counselor and the group: Integrating theory, training, and practice* (4th ed., pp. 319–350). New York: Routledge.

Merchant, N. (2009). Types of diversity-related groups. In C. Salazar (Ed.), *Group work experts share their favorite multicultural activities: A guide to diversity-competent choosing, planning, conducting, and processing* (pp. 13–24). Alexandria, VA: Association for Specialists in Group Work.

Merchant, N. M., & Butler, M. K. (2003). A psychoeducational group for ethnic minority adolescents in a predominantly white treatment setting. *Journal for Specialists in Group Work, 27*, 314–332.

Milsom, A., Akos, P., & Thompson, M. (2004). A psychoeducational group approach to postsecondary transition planning for students with learning disabilities. *Journal for Specialists in Group Work, 29*, 395–412.

Mishna, F., & Muskat, B. (2004). "I'm not the only one": Group therapy for older children and adolescents who have learning disabilities. *International Journal of Group Psychotherapy, 54,* 455–476.

Molina, B., Brigman, G., & Rhone, A. (2003). Fostering success through group work with children who celebrate diversity. *Journal for Specialists in Group Work, 28,* 166–184.

Nesdale, D., Rooney, R., & Smith, L. (1997). Migrant ethnic identity and psychological distress. *Journal of Cross-Cultural Psychology, 28,* 569–588.

Nicolas, G., Arntz, D. L., Hirsch, B., & Schmiedigen, A. (2009). Cultural adaptation of a group treatment for Haitian American adolescents. *Professional Psychology: Research and Practice, 40,* 378–384.

Nikels, H. J., Mims, G. A., & Mims, M. A. (2007). Allies against hate: A school-based diversity sensitivity training experience. *Journal for Specialists in Group Work, 32,* 126–138.

Pack-Brown, S. P. (2006). Drumming. In J. L. DeLucia-Waack, K. H. Bridbord, J. S. Kleiner, & A. Nitza (Eds.), *Group work experts share their favorite activities: A guide to choosing, planning, conducting, and processing* (rev. ed., pp. 183–186). Alexandria, VA: Association for Specialists in Group Work.

Pack-Brown, S. P., & Fleming, A. (2004). An Afrocentric approach to counseling groups with African-Americans. In J. L. DeLucia-Waack, D. A. Gerrity, C. R. Kalodner, & M. T. Riva (Eds.), *Handbook of group counseling and psychotherapy* (pp. 183–1199). Thousand Oaks, CA: Sage.

Pan, P. J. D. (2000). The effectiveness of structured and semi-structured Satir model groups on family relationships with college students in Taiwan. *Journal for Specialists in Group Work, 25,* 305–318.

Pandya, V. (2005). Contemporary group work practice. In A. Gitterman & L. Shulman (Eds.), *Mutual aid groups: Vulnerable and resilient populations, and the life cycle* (3rd ed., pp. 597–614). New York: Columbia Press.

Pargament, K. I. (1997). The sacred and the search for signifi-cance. In K. I. Pargament (Ed.), *The psychology of religion and coping: Theory, research, and practice* (pp. 21–33). New York: Guilford Press.

Payne, K. T., & Marcus, D. K. (2008). The efficacy of group psychologist for older adult clients. *Group Dynamics, 12,* 268–278.

Peeks, A. L. (1999). Conducting the social skills group of Latino adolescents. *Journal of Child and Adolescent Group Therapy, 9,* 139–153.

Queener, J. E., & Kenyon, C. B. (2001). Providing mental health services to Southeast Asian adolescent girls: Integration of a primary prevention paradigm and group counseling. *Journal for Specialists in Group Work, 26,* 350–367.

Rayle, A. D., Sand, J. K., Brucato, T., & Ortega, J. (2006). The "Comadre" group approach: A wellness-based group model. *Journal for Specialists in Group Work, 31,* 5–24.

Roberts-Wilbur, J., Wilbur, M., Garrett, M. T., & Yuhas, M. (2001). Talking circles: Listen, or your tongue will make you deaf. *Journal for Specialists in Group Work, 26,* 368–384.

Rose, S. R. (2001). Group work to promote the occupational functioning of Ethiopian minority men with disabilities who have immigrated to Israel. *Journal for Specialists in Group Work, 26,* 144–155.

Rowell, P. D., & Benshoff, J. M. (2008). Using personal growth groups in multicultural counseling courses to foster students' ethnic identity development. *Counselor Education and Supervision, 48,* 2–15.

Roysircar, G. (2008). A response to "Social privilege, social jus-tice, and group counseling: An inquiry." Social privilege: Counselors' competence with systematically determined inequalities. *Journal for Specialists in Group Work, 33,* 377–384.

Salazar, C. (Ed.). (2009a). *Group work experts share their favorite multicultural activities: A guide to diversity-competent choosing, planning, conducting, and processing.* Alexandria, VA: Association for Specialists in Group Work.

Salazar, C. (2009b). Diversity-competent group leadership: Self-awareness and cultural empathy as a foundation for effective practice. In C. Salazar (Ed.), *Group work experts share their favorite multicultural activities: A guide to diversity-competent choosing, planning, conducting, and processing* (pp. 3–13). Alexandria, VA: Association for Specialists in Group Work.

Seligman, M., & Marshak, L. (2004). Group approaches for per-sons with disabilities. In J. L. DeLucia-Waack, D. A. Gerrity, C. R. Kalodner, & M. T. Riva (Eds.), *Handbook of group counseling and psychotherapy* (pp. 239–252). Thousand Oaks, CA: Sage.

Shechtman, Z., & Gilat, I. (2005). The effectiveness of counsel-ing groups in reducing stress of parents of children with learning disabilities. *Group Dynamics, 9,* 275–290.

Shen, Y. (2007). Development model using gestalt-play versus cognitive-verbal group with Chinese adolescent: effects on strengths and adjustment enhancement. *Journal for Specialists in Group Work, 32,* 285–305.

Shulman, L. (1999). *The skills of helping individuals, families, groups, and communities* (4th ed.). Itasca, IL: Peacock.

Silverman, W. K., Kurtines, W. M., Ginsburg, G. S., Weems, C. F., Lumpkin, P. W., & Carmichael, D. H. (1999). Treating anxiety disorders in children with group cognitive-behavioral therapy: A randomized clinical trial. *Journal of Consulting and Clinical Psychology, 67,* 995–1003.

Singh, A., A., & Hays, D. (2008). Feminist group counseling with South Asian women who have survived intimate partner violence. *Journal for Specialists in Group Work, 33,* 84–102.

Slocum, Y. S. (1987). A survey of expectations about group ther-apy among clinical and non-clinical populations. *International Journal of Group Psychotherapy, 37,* 39–54.

Smith, L. C., & Shin, R. Q. (2008). Social privilege, social jus-tice, and group counseling: An inquiry. *Journal for Specialists in Group Work, 33,* 351–366.

Smith, P. K., Boulton, M. J., & Cowie, H. (1993). The impact of cooperative group work on ethnic relations in middle school. *School Psychology International, 14,* 21–42.

Snyder, K. V., Kymissis, P., & Kessler, K. (1999). Anger manage-ment for adolescents: Efficacy of brief group therapy. *Journal of the American Academy of Children and Adolescent Psychiatry, 38,* 1409–1416.

Sue, D. W., & Sue, S. (1999). *Counseling the culturally different: Theory and practice.* New York: Wiley.

Sue, D. W., & Sue, D. (2008). The superordinate nature of mul-ticultural counseling and therapy. In D. W. Sue & D. Sue (Eds.), *Counseling the culturally diverse: Theory and practice* (5th ed., pp. 29–52). Hoboken, NJ: John Wiley & Sons.

Sue, S., & Zane, N. (2009). The role of culture and cultural tech-niques in psychotherapy: A critique and reformulation. *Asian American Journal of Psychology, 5,* 3–14.

Suh, S., & Lee, M. (2006). Group work for Korean expatriate women in the U. S. *Journal for Specialists in Group Work, 31,* 353–370.

Sweifach, J. (2009). Cross-cultural group work practice with African-American and Jewish adolescents: JCC/READY. *Social Work with Groups*, *32*, 109–124.

Taha, M., Mahfouz, R., & Arafa, M. (2008). Socio-cultural influence on group psychotherapy leadership style. *Group Analysis*, *41*, 391–406.

Toporek, R. L., Davis, C., Ahluwali, M. K., & Artwohl, R. (2002, August). Effects of perceived counselor cultural understanding on client satisfaction among white clients and clients of color at a university counseling center. Paper presented at the annual conference of the American Psychological Association, Chicago, IL.

Torres Rivera, E. (2004). Psychoeducational and counseling groups with Latinos. In J. L. DeLucia-Waack, D. A. Gerrity, C. R. Kalodner, & M. T. Riva (Eds.), *Handbook of group counseling and psychotherapy* (pp. 213–223). Thousand Oaks, CA: Sage.

Torres Rivera, E., Wilbur, M. P., Roberts-Wilbur, J., & Phan, L. (1999). Group work with Latino clients: A psychoeducational model. *Journal for Specialists in Group Work*, *24*, 383–404.

Toseland, R. W., Jones, L. V., & Gellis, Z. D. (2004). Group dynamics. In C. D. Garvin, L. M. Gurierrez, & M. J. Galinsky (Eds.), *Handbook of social work in groups* (pp. 13–31). New York: Guilford Press.

Tuason, M. T., Taylor, A. R., Rollings, L., Harris, T., & Martin, C. (2007). On both sides of the hyphen: Exploring the Filipino-American identity. *Journal of Counseling Psychology*, *54*, 362–372.

Villalba, J. A. (2003). A psychoeducational group for limited-English proficient Latino/Latina children. *Journal for Specialists in Group Work*, *28*, 261–267.

White, N. J., & Rayle, A. D. (2007). Strong teens: A school-based small group experience for African-American males. *Journal for Specialists in Group Work*, *32*, 178–189.

Williams, C. C. (2005). Training for cultural competence: Individual and group processes. *Journal of Ethnic & Cultural Diversity in Social Work*, *14*, 111–143.

Williams, C. D., Frame, M. W., & Green, E. (1999). Counseling groups for African-American women: A focus on spirituality. *Journal for Specialists in Group Work*, *24*, 260–273.

Wilson, F. R., Rapin, L. S., & Haley-Banez, L. (2004). How teaching group work can be guided by foundational documents: Best practice guidelines, diversity principles, training standards. *Journal for Specialists in Group Work*, *29*, 19–29.

Wood, J. J., Chiu, A. W., Hwang, W., Jacobs, J., & Ifekwunigwe, M. (2008). Adapting cognitive-behavioral therapy for Mexican American students with anxiety disorders: Recommendations for school psychologists. *School Psychology Quarterly*, *23*, 515–532.

Yalom, I. D. (1995). *The theory and practice of group psychotherapy*. New York: Basic Books.

Yau, T. Y. (2004). Guidelines for facilitating groups with international college students. In J. L. DeLucia-Waack, D. A. Gerrity, C. R. Kalodner, & M. T. Riva (Eds.), *Handbook of group counseling and psychotherapy* (pp. 253–264). Thousand Oaks, CA: Sage.

Zaretsky, S. (2009). The conversation group: Using group psychoanalytic techniques to resolve resistances of recently immigrated Chinese students to learning English in a high school setting. *International Journal of Group Psychotherapy*, *59*, 335–356.

A Social Justice Approach to Group Counseling

Sally M. Hage, Mark Mason, *and* Jungeun Kim

Abstract

A social justice approach is emerging as a central aspect of the work of the mental health professional. In addition, group work has significant potential to further a social justice agenda. This chapter provides an overview of a social justice approach to group counseling. The meaning of *social justice* is clarified and the historical origins of a social justice approach to group work are presented. Existing theory and research related to group work and social justice are reviewed, and current trends in research with social justice groups are summarized. Finally, barriers to a social justice approach to group counseling are briefly discussed, and implications of a social justice approach to group counseling for counseling training, practice, and research are presented.

Keywords: group counseling, group work, social justice, multicultural, marginalized populations, prevention, social change

> Counselors have a responsibility, personally and collectively, to pursue justice at the collective level so that wellness may flourish at all levels.
> *Prilleltensky, Dokecki, Frieden, & Wang* (2007, p. 28)

A Social Justice Approach to Group Counseling

Calls for counselors and psychologists to adopt a social justice stance in their work have been increasingly prevalent in the literature (Aldarondo, 2007; Kenny, Horne, Orphinas, & Reese, 2009; Ratts, DeKruyf, & Chen-Hayes, 2008; Toporek, Gerstein, Fouad, Roysircar, & Israel, 2006). Scholars have challenged counseling psychology (e.g., Speight & Vera, 2004; Vera & Speight, 2003; Ivey & Collins, 2003; Palmer, 2004), clinical psychology (e.g., Chen, Kakkad, & Balzano, 2008), social work (e.g., Sullivan, Mesbur, Lang, Goodman, & Mitchell, 2003; Snyder, Peeler, & May, 2008), counseling (e.g., Anderson, 2007; Lee, 2007; Ratts, D'Andrea, & Arredondo, 2004; Toporek, Lewis, & Crethar, 2009; Toporek et al., 2006; Kiselica & Robinson, 2001), school

counseling (e.g., Bemak, 2005; Field & Baker, 2004), and group counseling (e.g., Smith & Shin, 2008) to broaden their roles and responsibilities to incorporate individual and systems advocacy and a critical consciousness of power and privilege among historically oppressed and privileged groups both inside and outside the therapeutic context.

Support for a social justice approach has also emerged as a central part of national organizations such as the American School Counselor Association; American Counseling Association (ACA), most notably within the ACA's association of Counselors for Social Justice; and the Divisions for Social Justice, a coalition of representatives from 10 American Psychological Association's (APA) divisions for social justice. As such, social justice is considered by many scholars to be the "fifth force" of the mental health professions (Ratts, D'Andrea, & Arredondo, 2004). Efforts aimed at furthering social justice and creating social policy change have been identified as the "next frontier" for psychology (Prilleltensky & Nelson, 2002, p. 176).

Group work, perhaps more than any other counseling intervention, has the potential to facilitate social justice. As microcosms of social dynamics, groups contain important mechanisms for addressing issues of power, privilege, and oppression (Morrow, Hawxhurst, Montes de Vegas, Abousleman, & Castañeda, 2006). Furthermore, within collectivistic value cultures, often disproportionately affected by social injustice in our society, a natural linkage exists between group counseling and a worldview rooted in the social networks of family and community, thus facilitating efforts to address issues of oppression (Bemak & Chung, 2004). In addition, the very foundation of counseling groups, built upon trust, safety, and the resulting process of honest interaction among group participants, makes such social transformation at the deepest levels of human experience possible.

Effective group leaders foster social justice through several avenues, including the promotion of intercultural communication and the empowerment of members to engage in social change processes. Facilitators of social justice groups recognize the importance of moving beyond traditional roles to model risk taking, discussion of sensitive issues, and leadership for social change and advocacy (Bemak & Chung, 2004).

The intent of this chapter is to provide an overview of a social justice approach to group counseling. We begin by describing what we mean by *social justice* and connecting this definition to group counseling. Next, we outline the historical origins of a social justice approach to group work, provide an overview of research related to social justice groups, and briefly discuss barriers to this approach. Finally, we discuss the implications of a social justice approach to group counseling for counseling training, practice, and research.

Defining Social Justice

Social justice may be defined as the fair and equitable distribution of power, resources, and obligations in society to all people, regardless of race, gender, ability status, sexual orientation, and religious or spiritual background. Social justice concerns include issues related to the justice of processes and procedures as well as issues related to the justice of outcomes (Van den Bos, 2003). Fundamental principles underlying this definition include values of inclusion, collaboration, cooperation, equal access, and opportunity. Such values are also the foundation of a democratic and egalitarian society (Sue, 2001). Finally, while social justice has not ordinarily been associated with issues of health, our definition includes recognition of the crucial link that exists between social justice and well-being. For individuals, the absence of justice often represents increased physical and emotional suffering as well as greater vulnerability to illness. In addition, social justice issues and access to resources are inexorably tied to the collective well-being (e.g., relationships and political welfare) of families, communities, and society (Prilleltensky & Nelson, 2002).

Group Counseling and Social Justice

The field of group counseling has just begun to integrate the constructs of social justice, collective well-being, and social privilege into group theory, processes, and training (Smith & Shin, 2008). Holcomb-McCoy (2007) argues that counseling professionals "must be willing to redefine traditional counseling models and roles in order to serve diverse groups" (p. 17). This argument, consistent with Lee (2007) and Bemak and Chung (2004), recognizes that broad, systemic injustice exists in society and that such injustices require counselors to take responsible action to eliminate systemic oppression, such as racism, sexism, heterosexism, and classism.

> Social justice–oriented group counseling may be distinguished from the traditional practice of group counseling by its particular emphasis on an empowerment and strength-based counseling model (McWhirter, 1994), an awareness of sociocultural and environmental factors (e.g., poverty, discrimination), and an emphasis on issues of equity and social transformation (Holcomb-McCoy, 2007). Goodman et al. (2004) also assert that a social justice perspective in clinical work entails an ongoing process of examining how one's values, biases, and power influence clients and/or groups and that being aware of the layers of social power inherent in groups is a core task for group therapists.

McWhirter's (1994) definition of *empowerment* is illuminating in further explicating a social justice approach. She defines *empowerment* as a process by which people, organizations, and groups who are powerless and marginalized

> (a) become aware of the power dynamics at work in their life context, (b) develop the skills and capacity for gaining some reasonable control over their lives,

(c) which they exercise, (d) without infringing on the rights of others, and (e) which coincides with actively supporting the empowerment of others in the community. (p. 12)

This definition clarifies that such work begins with awareness, leads to action, and, perhaps most importantly, takes place in the context of relationships with others as part of a community. Hence, groups, led by facilitators attuned to process issues and experiences of marginalization, are particularly suited to support social change processes.

Furthermore, group work is inherently multicultural (DeLucia-Waack, 1996). Social justice–themed groups not only acknowledge, include, and empower all individuals from diverse social identities but also create identity-affirming environments that advocate for the empowerment of historically and currently marginalized populations and communities. Rather than continuing the power and interpersonal dynamics that are influenced by racism, sexism, classism, and heterosexism, social justice groups aim to transform and heal group members (MacNair-Semands, 2007) and refrain from perpetuating prejudice, oppression, and victimization (Anderson, 2007).

Historical Context for a Social Justice Approach to Group Counseling

The process of creating social change and advocacy through counseling has a long-standing tradition in the helping disciplines (Kiselica & Robinson, 2001; Toporek et al., 2009). Indeed, the roots of the social advocacy and social justice movement can be traced to the very beginnings of the helping fields (Hartung & Blustein, 2002). In the late nineteenth century, the field of social work was born, with its unique commitment among mental health professions to creating social equity and supporting charitable giving in the community (Aldarondo, 2007). In addition, in the early 1900s, the pioneer work of Frank Parsons, the father of vocational psychology, included efforts to dismantle injustice and unfairness, providing an early model of socially responsible counseling (Goodman et al., 2004; Hartung & Blustein, 2002). Appalled by the poor living conditions of his neighborhood, Parsons began to advocate for the impoverished and the working class by helping to establish advocacy organizations such as the Boston Vocational Bureau and the Breadwinner Institute. As noted by Hartung and Blustein (2002), "Frank Parsons envisioned a practice of vocational guidance based on rationality

and reason with service, concern for others, cooperation, and social justice among its core values" (p. 41). Following in this tradition, in 1989, Jane Addams and her colleagues cofounded Hull House in Chicago, Illinois, the first settlement house in the United States, and conducted groups aimed at extending services and cultural opportunities to immigrant populations in the neighborhood (Brown, 2000).

Throughout the early years of the field of counseling psychology, access to work was considered vital for achieving social equity (Fouad, Gerstein, & Toporek, 2006). Aligned with this notion, Minnesota counseling psychologists designed a project aimed to help people return to work during the Depression period. Later during the Depression, the rank-and-file movement, without overtly addressing the social injustice of the time, was led by social workers who protested New Deal programs (Gil, 1998). Also, efforts to help students find the best college environments were made by counseling psychologists at the University of Missouri–Columbia and Ohio State University (Fouad et al., 2006).

After World War II, counseling professionals raised their voices in support of social justice in their work with veterans in the 1940s and 1950s and assisted the poor and the homeless during the 1960s (Fouad et al., 2004). Later, during the civil rights movement, along with its subsequent impact on feminism through most of the 1960s and 1970s, the helping professions were challenged to examine their own theories and practices for dominant cultural biases and assumptions. At this time, helping professionals began to examine the impact of the dynamics of race, ethnicity, socioeconomic status, sexual orientation, religion/spirituality, gender, age, and ability on the sociocultural environment and on conditions on mental health.

Hence, since the 1960s and 1970s, much of the critical consciousness-raising group work developed under the framework of feminist principles (Israeli & Santor, 2000; Morrow et al., 2006). Expanding the traditional delineations of social justice topics, feminist scholars have conceptualized issues such as partner violence (e.g., Singh & Hays, 2008; van Wormer, 2009) as manifestations of the existing gender power dynamics in a socially unjust world. Feminist group-counseling approaches have emphasized the core belief that "the personal is political" and have sought to "give voice" to marginalized groups, especially women, within a restorative justice model (van Wormer, 2009) or feminist multicultural group counseling (Morrow et al., 2005).

The experience of oppression and marginalization of women and minority populations has led researchers and clinicians to reclaim and clarify the role of the helping professional as an advocate for social justice (Manis, Brown, & Paylo, 2008). However, in the 1980s, the emergence of managed care affected by global economic competitiveness shifted helping professionals' attention and preference toward a medical model, highlighting remedial and individual treatment (Fouad et al., 2006). It is not surprising that many people in the helping professions paid greater attention to professional identity issues rather than systemic issues existing in society during this period. Indeed, many of the Division 17 presidential speeches in the 1980s and the early 1990s addressed outside influences affecting the field, underlining the importance of positioning mental health professionals for survival when faced with competitive market forces (Fouad, Helledy, & Metz, 2003).

Due to this trend, the staggered movement of social advocacy and justice faced its "identity crisis" in the field. However, some helping professionals continued to expand social justice research regarding gender and multicultural issues. For instance, Derald Sue raised his voice about the necessity to develop the cross-cultural counseling competencies (Sue et al., 1982), and Janet Helms (1986) extended racial identity theory to include the counseling process. Further, in 1997, the Association for Specialists in Group Work (ASGW) endorsed the American Multicultural Counseling and Development Association's multicultural counseling competencies and standards (Arredondo et al., 1996). Two years later, in 1999, the ASGW developed and adopted the "Principles for Diversity-Competent Group Workers" (ASGW, 1999), which was a significant step with a direct relationship to training group counselors. In addition, women's career-inhibiting variables affecting self-efficacy were investigated (Betz & Hackett, 1981).

Thus, these continued efforts facilitated a movement toward rapprochement, with activist helping professionals who had worked at the margins of the profession (Aldarondo, 2007). However, until that time, work had been conducted mainly by individual professionals and there were few systematic entities to strategically advocate social justice work for enhancing the mental health of individuals, groups, and communities (Kagan et al., 1988).

By the late 1990s progressive social change efforts began a renewal as scholars began to share an expanded vision of social justice work among mental health professionals. As Prilleltensky (1999) noted,

Psychological problems do not exist on their own, nor do they come out of thin air; they are connected to people's social support, employment status, housing conditions, history of discrimination, and overall personal and political power. [Therefore,] promoting complete health means promoting social justice for there cannot be health in the absence of justice. (p. 106)

The helping professions began to be more actively oriented to social justice in practice as well as in research. For example, school counselors were encouraged to promote social equity in schools (Worthington & Juntunen, 1997), and psychologists were urged to adopt a prevention agenda (Romano & Hage, 2000) and to engage in antiracism work (Thompson & Neville, 1999). In 2001, social action groups, targeting efforts to dismantle racism, domestic abuse, and community violence, were created at the National Counseling Psychology Conference in Houston and played an important role in expanding social justice movements beyond the conference itself (Fouad et al., 2004). Indeed, after the Houston conference, informal meetings about social advocacy, including roundtable discussions and symposiums, have been held at annual conferences and the need to create a special interest group in the APA on social advocacy was recognized (Fouad et al., 2006).

Moreover, along with the increasing recognition of the need for counselors to become multiculturally competent, the APA's (2003) "Guidelines on Multicultural Education, Training, Research, Practice and Organizational Change for Psychologists" provided the helping professions with the rationale and impetus for becoming agents of social advocacy in education, training, research, and practice. With these efforts, a series of articles were published in the *Counseling Psychologist* focusing on social justice (e.g., Goodman et al., 2004; Ivey & Collins, 2003; Speight & Vera, 2004). Further, group-work approaches aimed at community development and social justice were highlighted (e.g., Toporek et al., 2006), in particular addressing the areas of community-based participatory research and action (Jacobson & Rugeley, 2007) and empowerment groups in school (Bemak, 2005).

It is clear that many more helping professionals have engaged in systemic change efforts in the twenty-first century and have developed various theories, principles, and strategies of social action and social advocacy (e.g., Kenny & Hage, 2009). These efforts highlight the need for helping professionals to pay more attention to power imbalances that characterize the structure of our society and to develop skills and strategies for social change. Within this context of social justice in the helping fields, group processes appear promising to benefit the public and our society and address social injustice.

Research and Social Justice Groups

Research demonstrating the efficacy of group work to effect social change is limited, yet work in this area has been increasing over the past two decades as renewed efforts to advocate for marginalized groups' voices, experiences, development, and social change have begun to emerge (Chen, Kakkad, Balzano, 2008; Portman & Portman, 2002). This section will begin by reviewing the theoretical literature related to group work and social justice. An overview of existing research related to social justice–oriented psychoeducational groups will follow. Finally, current trends in research of social justice groups will be summarized.

Theoretical Foundations for Social Justice Group Work

Scholars and clinicians of social justice–oriented group work have stressed the importance of research aimed at identifying and understanding issues of oppression, privilege, and social inequities within the context of conducting groups (e.g., Anderson, 2007; Smith & Shin, 2008). Arguments for expanding group counseling's traditional intrapsychic and interpersonal focuses have been based on a broad principle of justice (Brabender, 2006), an ethical mandate to engage in social change, and the emphasis on justice in virtue ethics (Fowers & Davidov, 2006; MacNair-Semands, 2007; Vera & Speight, 2003).

In addition, scholars emphasize the importance of addressing negative societal processes that are replicated within group counseling, such as social privilege (Roysircar, 2008; Smith & Shin, 2008), and biases and discrimination of people from different cultural backgrounds (Debiak, 2006). For example, MacNair-Semands (2007) noted that "being aware of the layers of social power inherent in groups is a core task for group therapists" (p. 62) to prevent the reenactment in the group of the existing power dynamics in the society at large. To facilitate systemic changes in the underlying social, political, and economic structures, Smith and Shin (2008) applied the first four competencies of Constantine, Hage, Kindaichi, and Bryant's (2007) social justice competencies to group counseling. Specifically, Smith and Shin recommended that group counselors incorporate an awareness about

individual and institutional injustices according to different marginalized communities (e.g., awareness of heterosexism and homophobia across and within communities and social institutions); examine issues of power, privilege, and oppression in their own lives; continually explore and reexamine potential inadvertent expressions of bias and marginalization in their lives across varied roles (e.g., with clients or in consultation with a community organization); and avoid group therapeutic interventions that may be inappropriate or exploitative while promoting the well-being of marginalized communities (e.g., creating a support group for lesbian, gay, bisexual, and transgendered [LGBT] clients). In sum, Smith and Shin (2008) reiterated the importance of attending to social privilege within the context of group counseling.

Roysircar (2008) emphasized the importance of group counselors' awareness of the unique dynamics of diverse cultural groups and their experiences of marginalization and social alienation. In addition to traditional group dynamics, social justice group work requires attention to issues of social privilege and hierarchical power structures both inside and outside the group experience. Therefore, group counselors are advised to be aware of not only their own values, assumptions, and biases but also clients' worldviews during the educational and therapeutic processes of group work.

The social justice and group literatures have addressed not only group facilitator awareness and expanded roles working with underserved populations but also specific interventions and models. Anderson (2007) expanded on Gladding's (2003) contribution (which indicated specific interventions according to different stages of group work) to create the multicultural group work treatment planning model. The model integrates traditional group-development factors with dialectic group process factors unique to multicultural treatment plans and interventions, such as dominant and subordinate group member inclinations. Within such models, which infuse social justice orientations into group counseling, group counselors must incorporate an awareness and understanding of not only group dynamics but also social injustices and historical and ongoing oppressions.

Psychoeducational Groups and Social Justice

Psychoeducational groups are increasingly relying on social justice frameworks to create social change through self-advocacy and the development of members' critical consciousness. The latter is a concept, originally developed by Freire (1970, 1972), in which individuals break free of the internalization of negative social attitudes. Such psychoeducational group interventions incorporate both psychological and educational components, seeking to foster understandings of the sociopolitical and sociocultural contexts of racism, sexism, heterosexism, classism, and ableism among group members. Indeed, social work scholars have linked these two goals by asserting that personal healing and social change are integrally related (Breton, 1995; Getzel, 2003) and have been a part of social work groups since the 1930s (Henry, 2003). These groups are sometimes described as "barrier-breaking groups" (Mannik, 2003, p. 183) and include consciousness, competency, community, social capital, and citizenship-building aspects. Anecdotal and empirical evidence of the efficacy of these psychoeducational groups is beginning to emerge in the social justice group literature.

To counteract the systemic barriers faced by black adolescents both inside and outside secondary schools, Dowden (2009) created a brief psychoeducational group that taught self-advocacy skills to enhance academic motivation and self-concepts. To combat systemic racism and growing educational gaps between black and white students, the five-session group harnessed the power of the group format to provide members with interpersonal feedback, brainstorm strategies for social change, and practice new skills (e.g., social justice–oriented behaviors). Dowden offered a framework for teaching about "issues of equity and access" (p. 128) in a group format. In addition, follow-up efforts suggested that many of the six participants improved (e.g., fewer behavior and truancy problems, successful advancement).

To build life skills and social justice awareness and advocacy, Portman and Portman (2002) established an eight-session, developmental, psychoeducational group that cultivated students' knowledge, awareness, and advocacy skills. Their model, named empowering students for social justice (ES2J), guided elementary and junior high school students to discuss social justice topics, such as oppression, racism, and prejudice through activities and a social service project. Through their participation, students gained knowledge about different populations' histories and sociopolitical experiences and worked collaboratively to enact social change.

Howard and Solberg (2006) created another school-based, group psychoeducational curriculum for low-income students of color. The group was based on their ecological developmental cognitive framework, Field and Baker's (2004) "empowered frame of reference," and a social justice orientation. The program, called Achieving Success Identity Pathways, challenged all students to perform better academically by incorporating an understanding of how oppression affects disadvantaged youth. Although no control group comparisons were present, program evaluations suggested substantial academic improvement among participants.

Psychoeducational group efforts have also employed nontraditional methods to foster critical consciousness. Ciardiello (2003) applied hip-hop music to therapy groups with adolescents in residential programs in New York City. Although no empirical or demographic data were described, Ciardiello's activity-centered therapy selected songs (based on the development of the group) to facilitate clients' "experiences of survival, strength, and suffering" (p. 115). The social group project sought to incorporate sociorecreational, psychotherapeutic, cognitive-behavioral, and psychoeducational interventions into one framework in order to foster adolescents' willingness to change. Creative interventions like Ciardiello's program that incorporate sociopolitical awareness and consciousness may help group members to explore and understand their life narratives that are often influenced by the effects of oppression. Such narrative approaches to individual therapy (e.g., Monk, Winslade, Crocket, & Epston, 1997; V. E. White, 2002; M. White, 2007) may also apply to social justice–oriented group work by operating from a strengths-based, multicultural, and psychoeducational framework.

Narrative approaches can also help group members tell and understand their stories through a critical consciousness, acknowledging the influences of oppression, discrimination, and cultural identities. Marsiglia (2003) promoted culturally grounded approaches to social justice in group work through a narrative approach that encouraged adolescents to connect with their "cultural roots" (p. 86). Marsiglia created an identity-developmental framework that assisted group members in learning about societal oppression and internalized racism whereby they connected their experiences of marginalization and acculturation statuses with ongoing personal issues. In addition, the predominantly Mexican/Mexican American adolescents were encouraged to share challenges of becoming bicultural and living in "two worlds," listening to and supporting each other in their processes of awareness development.

Morsillo and Prilleltensky (2007) integrated cultural awareness development and social action interventions in working with youth in school and community settings. Advancing the concepts of *psychopolitical validity* (defined according to the way in which research and action consider the power dynamics of oppression, liberation, and wellness at the individual, group, and community levels; Prilleltensky, 2003, 2008) and *transformational psychopolitical validity* (or changing the nature of the power inequalities in society), the authors applied a participatory action research orientation to working with low-income adolescents and same sex–attracted youth in Australia. Through a series of community projects (e.g., drama presentations about homophobia, drug-free dance party, battle of the bands), the interventions enhanced individual, group, and community sociopolitical awareness, group participation and solidarity, and community engagement and problem solving. Qualitative data indicated that individuals gained assertiveness, acceptance, and peer support and developed a heightened sense of community awareness. Both group interventions led to increases in the youths' perspectives of hopefulness and individual and group agency.

Morrow et al. (2006) highlighted the use of music therapy and creative arts interventions in their feminist support group for battered women. The group was transformed from a "therapy group" to a "performance group" (York, 2004) through the power of music and feminist principles. Similarly, Singh and Hays (2008) used a case study method to explore the strengths and limitations of feminist group work with South Asian women who had survived partner violence. Interventions included such techniques as bibliotherapy, gender-role analysis, leaders' self-disclosure for egalitarian relationships, and culturally affirmative practices such as respect for group harmony and cohesion and regular interactions outside the group environment. Group evaluations demonstrated that the most helpful contributors to their healing were meaningful discussions about the roles of South Asian gender and cultural messages on their experiences of abuse.

In sum, feminist and social justice–themed groups expand and develop underserved populations' strengths through empowerment, self-determination, and self-fulfillment (Chen et al., 2008), which are core principles in social work (Breton, 2004), counseling and counseling psychology (Smith, 2006), and prevention work (Hage & Kenny, 2009; Kenny & Hage, 2009). Many scholars have asserted the importance of empowerment within counseling (e.g., McWhirter, 1994, 1998; White, 2002), including the "5 Cs of empowerment," namely, collaboration, competence, context, critical consciousness, and community (McWhirter, 1998).

Bemak (2005), in discussing five key issues within the empowerment groups for academic success (EGAS) approach to working with at-risk and marginalized students, reasserted the importance of authentic empowerment. Emphasizing a self-directive approach, Bemak encouraged counselors to relinquish power and authority by allowing group members to formulate group goals. Thus, social justice groups that incorporate empowerment, critical consciousness raising, and egalitarian power sharing may foster self-determination and prevent the replication of existing social power dynamics within groups.

Such transformational, egalitarian relationships between clinicians and group members offer the potential to integrate social justice practice and research. Jacobson and Rugelely (2007) advocated for a community-based participatory research agenda as a means to engage local communities and empower individuals for social change. Indeed, researchers have increasingly applied a community-based, participatory action research agenda when working with people from oppressed groups (e.g., Morsillo & Prilleltensky, 2007). Combining social justice group work and research may provide opportunities for social change as well as increase group members' critical consciousness. Harris (2009) argued for more frequent application of community-based research while theorizing about the interconnections of counseling practice and community-based research. He noted that this method has been underutilized despite many shared, overarching tenets, such as a focus on relationships, cultural appreciation, deep learning and discovery, and empowerment and collaboration.

An example of a community-based, empowerment model of group work is Vera, Daly, Gonzales, Morgan, and Thakra's (2006) outreach prevention program for mostly Latino urban adolescents. Through classroom-based psychoeducational groups with students (including experiential activities such as role plays and discussion), parent workshops, and consultations with teachers and administrators, the program sought to prevent students' involvement in risky activities (e.g., substance abuse), enhance student retention, and focus on barriers to academic and personal achievement. Such programs address the cultural contexts and highlight the social injustice issues that are ongoing for many communities.

For example, Vera et al. discussed systemic issues (e.g., immigrant families working multiple jobs, social norms about academic performance) that influence youths' and families' psychological well-being and explored the possibility for change through group work.

Juntunen et al. (2006) applied a self-sufficiency and empowerment orientation to their six-session career preparation group, which sought to incorporate social justice into vocational psychology interventions. The program, Honoring Occupational and Personal Empowerment (HOPE), included four stages in a group format, including self-exploration, self-determined goals, skills training for barriers, and work behavioral practice (e.g., resume development or interview skills). Results indicated that the HOPE program led to lower rates of depression (according to Beck Depression Inventory scores), although significant attrition from the sample was reported. Qualitative evaluations and data suggested that self-exploration and the development of job skills were critical aspects of the program. Participants also acknowledged improved communication skills, more awareness about interests and skills, and a change in individual goals.

Watts, Williams, and Jagers (2003) merged empowerment and critical consciousness in their work with African American youths. They advocated for a sociopolitical development theory in community psychology, which incorporates knowledge of liberation and resistance to oppression. Through interviews with African American activists, the authors promoted a paradigm of community psychology that included an awareness of ecological perspectives (e.g., knowledge of unjust social dynamics) and encouraged liberation behaviors (e.g., both process and outcomes of activism and more just communities). Watts et al. (2003) also cited the work of Zimmerman, Ramirez-Valles, and Maton (1999), whose empirical results suggested that higher levels of sociopolitical control were correlated with less negative mental health outcomes.

In addition, psychoeducational groups may be applied to reduce participant biases and resolve intergroup conflicts among privileged and disenfranchised groups, such as through intergroup dialogue groups (Dessel, Rogge, & Garlington, 2006; Kivlighan & Arsenau, 2009). Defined as a "facilitated community experience designed to provide a safe yet communal space to express anger and indignation about injustice" (Dessel et al., 2006, p. 303), intergroup dialogues aid social workers and group counselors who seek to enact social change within the current hierarchical system. Indeed, social work group practitioners have sought to apply the principles of intergroup dialogue to group counseling and public policy change to bridge the apparent gap between the discipline's macro and micro foci and to constructively tackle cultural differences, power relationships, and contested issues (Agbaria & Cohen, 2002; Dessel et al., 2006). Although the processes and goals may be different from those of group therapy, intergroup dialogue groups demonstrate the potential to effect social change at the micro and macro levels (Dessel et al., 2006).

Current Trends in Social Justice Group Work Research

Research and practice efforts to incorporate and study consciousness raising, empowerment, and social justice–infused psychoeducational group work are still in their nascent stage. Much of the current research and practice are applied from individual therapy contexts, without necessarily capturing the power of group dynamics and interpersonal interactions. However, the current trends highlight the potential for individual, community, and social change with social justice–informed group work.

First, much of the social justice group work has been based on existing paradigms of group counseling, modifying interventions to include social justice principles and frameworks. Such work considers contextual and individual factors with social justice orientations for people of color, LGBT populations, individuals with disabilities, older individuals, women, and individuals with low income. For example, Safren, Hollander, Hart, & Heimberg (2001) described a group intervention that seeks not to help LGB individuals adjust to a homophobic environment but rather to empower LGB youths in their coming-out process. New paradigms (e.g., community-based participatory research agendas) are needed to encourage inclusive, egalitarian relationships between practitioners, scholars, and group members.

Second, evidence is emerging that advocacy, activism, and critical consciousness may serve as buffering or protective factors against the effects of oppression. Increasingly conceptualized as life skills, the awareness and ability to navigate and recognize social injustices and enact changes in the sociocultural domain may hold psychological benefits for marginalized communities and individuals as well as result in significant social change.

Third, much psychoeducational social justice group work is informed by feminist and narrative approaches that embrace and validate stories from marginalized communities. Such holistic, inclusive interventions "give voice" to invalidating and disturbing experiences with oppression and discrimination. Indeed, identifying and labeling experiences as "microaggressions" (e.g., Sue et al., 2007) may be therapeutic and result in secondary gains (e.g., higher motivation in school, improvements in academic performance).

Fourth, social justice–informed group work is not limited to specific settings. Social justice and empowering frameworks and interventions may be applied to vocational, school, social work, community, college and university, and traditional group-counseling settings, collaboratively sharing power among group leaders and members to explore and understand the pain associated with discrimination and oppression. For example, intergroup dialogue programs at colleges and universities that directly address intergroup conflicts and encourage difficult conversations highlight the ability of groups to collectively address social injustices.

Obstacles to a Social Justice Approach to Group Work

Before addressing the implications of a social justice approach for group-counseling practice, training, and research, it is important to recognize that group leaders who adopt a social justice approach are likely to encounter some resistance in carrying out this proposed vision of group work. Group work from a social justice perspective calls into question many of the assumptions and structures that support not only our profession but also our social and economic systems. As counselors, we are deeply influenced by the combined "power of tradition, habituation, and the status quo" (Evans, Hanlin, & Prilleltensky, 2007, p. 330). To challenge these powers takes considerable effort and a strong sense of inner conviction as one is likely to encounter negative feedback from others operating from "This-is-the-way-we-have-always-done-it" mode (Prilleltensky et al., 2007).

At the same time, we would argue that the alternative, which is to deny some group members' experiences of marginalization and oppression, is unacceptable because it encourages complicity toward unjust social conditions and thereby, albeit indirectly, focuses counseling on helping clients adjust to the sources of oppression (Prilleltensky & Nelson, 2002). In sum, group counseling cannot be conducted within a "value neutral" paradigm (Lee, 2007). When counseling paradigms "legitimize the social status quo rather than examine it critically,

they become instruments of social oppression and control and by definition contribute to social injustice" (Greene, 2008, p. 500).

A possible resolution to this dilemma of balancing traditional roles with new roles for counselors is to see their work as aimed at creating opportunities for clients to be engaged in groups that promote social justice and community wellness. This work is not intended to replace traditional counseling but is seen as an addition to it. Not every counselor will be able to engage in both individual and social change at every level. However, counselors are encouraged to collaborate with other professionals in making such services available to their clients who need them (Prilleltensky et al. 2007).

Implications of a Social Justice Approach for Group Work
Practice

To begin, the implications of a social justice perspective for group work practice include a commitment by mental health professionals to confront their own participation in systems of privilege and oppression. As suggested by the multicultural guidelines of the APA (2003), when people work through their own conscious and unconscious biases and negative attitudes toward ethnic minority groups as well as other groups (e.g., LGBT and religious minorities), they increase their resolve to eradicate not only racism but all forms of oppression (Helms, 1995; Thompson, Murray, Harris, & Annan, 2003). In sum, leader awareness of justice includes both being responsive to the particular needs of those subjected to oppression and being attentive to one's own socially and culturally based identity issues (MacNair-Semands, 2007).

In addition, a social justice perspective to group practice implies an expanded set of intervention techniques capable of addressing clients' needs at all levels (Prilleltensky et al., 2007). For example, to broaden the base of clients served, group leaders need to identify concrete institutional barriers that prevent clients from marginalized communities from using counseling services and to work with decision-making entities to eliminate or reduce these barriers (Arredondo et al., 1996). Group facilitators might work to broaden the base of clients served by offering a sliding-fee scale or providing transportation vouchers for group members of low income. In addition, to serve linguistically diverse group members, mental health centers and schools can make a strong commitment to hiring bilingual counselors (Ridley, Liddle, Hill, & Li, 2001).

Also, group counselors need to embrace a social justice advocacy perspective and help lead efforts to challenge social and educational inequities such as school achievement gaps stemming from the less than ideal learning environments that are prevalent in many schools (Bemak & Chung, 2004; Cox & Lee, 2007). Social justice advocacy is needed to right injustices, increase access, and improve educational and social outcomes for clients and the larger society. To this end, group leaders can look to the American Counseling Association's advocacy competencies as a framework for engaging in social justice advocacy strategies (Ratts, 2006). The advocacy competencies include three levels: (1) client or student advocacy, (2) school or community advocacy, and (3) public advocacy (Lewis, Arnold, House, & Toporek, 2003). They assist counselors with promoting equity and with becoming a social change agent.

Training

Scholars have emphasized the importance of infusing a social justice perspective into graduate training programs (Baluch, Pieterse, & Bolden, 2004; Prilleltensky & Nelson, 2002; Vera & Speight, 2003). Yet, historically, not much attention has been given to a social justice framework in the training of helping professionals, at least partly due to the fact that the influence of social justice movements in the helping fields has fluctuated over time (Toporek & McNally, 2006). Hence, it is important for the helping professions to search for innovative ways to expand their awareness and competency in addressing social justice issues since these issues surface regularly in groups (MacNair-Semands, 2007).

Palmer and Parish (2008) note that the creation of an appropriate climate to engage in discussion surrounding social injustice is vital for enabling graduate students to expand their knowledge and practice in justice advocacy. Efforts to integrate social justice group work into training have included, but are not limited to, student training (Graham, 2003), faculty training (Toporek & McNally, 2006), service-based learning experiences (Wutzdoff & Giles, 1997), and interdisciplinary training models and projects (e.g., First Year Experience, Goodman et al., 2004; the Graduate Interdisciplinary Training Project [GIT], Kenny, Sparks, & Jackson, 2007).

NARRATIVE APPROACHES

Regarding student training, Graham (2003) noted that the typical goal of a lecture is to facilitate an individual's learning and that group dynamics and process have been neglected among educators, despite the fact that education in the United States is delivered in a group format. Along with more attention to group process issues in the classroom, more focus might be given to constructivism, thus fostering open discussion about student and faculty subjectivity in the classroom and promotion of ethically responsible participation that is consistent with social justice principles (Allen, 1993; Graham, 2003). This method, with a notion that trainers and trainees cobuild knowledge based on genuine uncertainty about the subject, might be a useful framework in a social justice course for training and can provide an opportunity for both faculty and students to explore social justice–related topics through their lived experiences.

Similarly, group-work instructors are encouraged to go beyond traditional roles of educators and utilize active learning methods to facilitate the dynamic learning process, such as sharing personal stories, reading poems, and playing video clips (Graham, 2003). This simultaneous process work may imply that individuals who teach students social justice must be aware of their own inherent assumptions, beliefs, prejudices, and worldviews and must assume greater leadership as social agents of change (Bemak & Chung, 2004).

In addition, similar to graduate students, faculty can have different levels of awareness of social justice research and practice. Suggesting the use of consciousness-raising groups in a course of multicultural and gender issues, Leonard (1996) noted that trainers ought not to set any direction of change in trainees' values in order to avoid eliciting reactance. Rather, it is important to openly share trainers' own values and beliefs so that trainees can do the same. To carry out this goal, ongoing support and mentoring of faculty (e.g., faculty retreats) may be necessary given that personal factors (e.g., ethnicity, perceived discrimination, socioeconomic status) that faculty members bring to the classroom can be very impactful for students and can create climate change in the classroom.

TRAINING MODELS

The helping professions can facilitate the exchange of ideas on social justice issues by offering courses that include service-learning group-work experiences with a focus on skill building in alternative roles (e.g., consultation, prevention). For instance, a multicultural counseling class might provide doctoral students in training with an opportunity to go into immigrants' community houses and run group counseling aimed at awareness of social justice and career planning. A group-counseling course might have students visit a shelter for teenage mothers or a Sunday school for refugee kids to provide them with group counseling as well as to enhance sensitivity to the social and political aspects of real problems. These community-immersion methods of training may be an effective way of integrating social justice, prevention, and outreach into the group work framework. The emphasis on service-learning experiences is consistent with the pragmatic or volitional dimensions of justice (Buckley, 1998), which address expanding students' vision of social justice at multiple levels for communities.

A further example of how graduate programs can instill a commitment to social justice by integrating a social justice perspective into their model of training is illustrated by the Graduate Interdisciplinary Training Project (GIT; Toporek & McNally, 2006). The GIT was designed to establish interprofessional collaboration between graduate students in nursing, social work, and counseling (Kenny et al., 2007). The GIT project created the First Year Experience, which required first-year doctoral students to attend weekly seminars, participate in a prevention program for high-risk urban school students, and actively evaluate the intervention. This collaborative social justice curriculum with community-based groups aims at facilitating students' process of examining an array of complex values simultaneously.

Other universities have implemented the interdisciplinary model into their curriculum and training (Toporek & McNally, 2006). For example, social justice has been infused into every aspect of the Counseling Development Program at George Mason University (Toporek & McNally, 2006). The Counseling Development Program is unique in that it strives to diversify the faculty and student body, implement the notion of social justice to its program mission and statements, and include internship sites that embrace multiculturalism, social advocacy, and change. Students in this program are given an opportunity to design course materials by sharing their ideas with faculty and peer students. These ideas are then included in the course syllabi (Toporek & McNally, 2006), including the group-work courses.

In sum, academic training programs play an important role in educating students to become mental health professionals and social advocates who are professionally responsible. It may be most beneficial to combine personal awareness, group work, and community partnerships to promote

such education. In doing so, the helping professions will be one step closer to propelling training endeavors toward an era of expanding social advocacy in the helping professions.

Research

Group-work research that is oriented toward social justice is guided by an awareness of power dynamics and directed at social change that benefits those who are marginalized (Kirby & McKenna, 1989). The intentional focus on social change addresses existing deficiencies of traditional research (Jacobson & Rugeley, 2007). These limitations include the failure of traditional research approaches

> (1) to generate knowledge that meaningfully addresses locally identified problems and concerns of daily living (Israel et al., 2005; Minkler & Wallerstein, 2003); (2) to account for the oppressive, exploitative legacy of research *done on* indigenous people and the lack of trust of researchers in communities of color today (Christopher, Burhansstipanov, & McCormick, 2005; (3) to come to grips with the health, environmental, and social disparities experienced by people based on race, class, and gender and how they continue to plague communities around the globe (Israel et al., 2005; Minkler & Wallerstein, 2003); and (4) to recognize and value the voices of community residents whose lived experiences make them invaluable contributors to sustainable community and social change (Freire, 1970). (Jacobson & Rugeley, 2007, p. 23)

To prepare mental health professionals to give more emphasis to social justice concerns in their research with groups, they need to be introduced to methods that are particularly oriented toward social change (Prilleltensky & Nelson, 2002). Several methods aimed at social change–oriented research have been identified in the literature (Fine, 1994; Kirby & McKenna, 1989; Prilleltensky & Nelson, 1997).

The first of these methods includes work that researchers must do prior to engaging in group research; that is, they must attend to their own values and cultural context. This point acknowledges the fact that research findings emerge from the interaction of the values and assumptions of the investigator with the unique historical representation of the phenomenon under study (Prilleltensky & Nelson, 2002). Similarly, Fine (1994) encourages us as researchers to acknowledge the realities of "self" and "other" in our work, with whom we are "knottily entangled" (p. 71). What we need to do, writes Fine (1994), is to acknowledge the tension existing at the interface between these two realities and recognize our position as classed, gendered, raced, and sexual subjects who construct our own locations.

In addition, group-work researchers need to give greater emphasis to working collaboratively with members of marginalized communities. The authentic voices and experiences of people who are marginalized in our society (e.g., people in poverty, LGBT people) must be at the heart of our efforts from the earliest phases of the research, to insure that research is of benefit to the participants' communities (Council of National Psychological Associations for the Advancement of Ethnic Minority Interests, 2000). The community is essential in defining a research problem or question (Toporek et al., 2006, p. 534). The goal, as much as possible, is to construct knowledge collaboratively and make ethical and conscious decisions about how much we involve ourselves in social struggles with those who have been exploited (Fine, 1994).

Furthermore, research that examines processes that facilitate or impede social change may not fit neatly into experimental or quasi-experimental designs (Hage, 2005). As a result, social justice scholars have urged researchers to consider the significance of additional methodologies (e.g., qualitative methods) in furthering a social justice agenda, such as a naturalistic case study or qualitative approach (Prilleltensky & Nelson, 1997). A significant advantage of qualitative approaches is that the perceptions and experiences of those frequently left out of traditional scholarship (e.g., racial and ethnic minorities, people in poverty) are highlighted. Qualitative approaches recognize the importance of understanding experience from the participants' point of view and regard participants as potential experts in describing their reality. In sum, the movement toward methodological diversity in group research is consistent with a focus on respect for the personal, subjective experience of participants and multifaceted approaches to knowing (Hage, 2003).

Community-based participatory action research (CBPR) is one type of research that merits further consideration, in the effort to give greater emphasis to social justice concerns (Prilleltensky & Nelson, 2002). The fundamental principles that guide CBPR include involving people who are most affected by community problems as partners from the earliest stages of research to help define the goals, to decide how the project will be carried out, and to provide input in every aspect of the research

process. In addition, CBPR is particularly suited to group approaches as it is at its core a group process through which participants define their social reality and build collective capacity to confront and change that reality (Finn, Jacobson, & Campana, 2004). In sum, the CBPR process is aimed not only at knowledge development but also at education and informed action (Maguire, 1987), recognizing that knowledge is coproduced in collaboration and in action with those whose have traditionally been left out of research and whose lives are most affected by the problem under study.

Conclusion

This chapter has provided an overview of a social justice approach to group counseling. Mental health professionals, as demonstrated, have begun the movement toward implementing such an approach. In order to further this work, counseling professionals need to take a proactive stance to carry out additional steps that are needed to revise training curriculum, research agendas, and practice orientations to include multilevel interventions and a focus on social transformation (Prilleltensky et al., 2007). It is no longer possible to treat mental health problems in isolation from social problems (Nelson & Prilleltensky, 2005). Group work and training must take socioeconomic, political, and demographic trends in modern society into account when devising therapy models and curricula (Bemak & Chung, 2004). In sum, counselors have a responsibility, both personally and as professionals, to join together in the pursuit of social justice so that wellness may flourish at every level (Prilleltensky et al., 2007).

References

Agbaria, F., & Cohen, C. (2002). *Working with groups in conflict: The impact of power relations on the dynamics of the group.* Waltham, MA: Brandeis University, International Center for Ethics, Justice, and Public Life.

Aldarondo, E. (2007). Rekindling the reformist spirit in the mental health professions. In E. Aldarondo (Ed.), *Advancing social justice through clinical practice* (pp. 3–18). Mahwah, NJ: Lawrence Erlbaum.

Allen, J. (1993). The constructivist paradigm: Values and ethics. *Journal of Teaching in Social Work, 8,* 31–55.

American Psychological Association. (2003). Guidelines on multicultural education, training, research, practice and organizational change for psychologists. *American Psychologist, 58,* 377–402.

Anderson, D. (2007). Multicultural group work: A force for developing and healing. *Journal for Specialists in Group Work, 32,* 224–244.

Arredondo, P., Toporek, R., Brown, S. P., Jones, J., Locke, D. C., Sanchez, J., et al. (1996). Operationalization of the multicultural counseling competencies. *Journal of Multicultural Counseling and Development, 24,* 42–78.

Association for Specialists in Group Work. (1999). ASGW principles for diversity-competent group workers. *Journal for Specialists in Group Work, 24,* 7–14.

Baluch, S. P., Pieterse, A. L., & Bolden, M. A. (2004). Counseling psychology and social justice: Houston . . . we have a problem. *Counseling Psychologist, 32,* 89–98.

Bemak, F. (2005). Reflections on multiculturalism, social justice, and empowerment groups for academic success: A critical discourse for contemporary schools. *Professional School Counseling, 8,* 401–406.

Bemak, F., & Chung, R. C. (2004). Teaching multicultural group counseling: Perspectives for a new era. *Journal for Specialists in Group Work, 29,* 31–42.

Betz, N. E., & Hackett, G. (1981). The relationship of career-related self-efficacy expectation to perceived career options in college women and men. *Journal of Counseling Psychology, 28,* 399–410.

Brabender, V. (2006). The ethical group psychotherapist. *International Journal of Group Psychotherapy, 56,* 395–414.

Breton, M. (1995). The potential for social action in groups. *Social Work with Groups, 18,* 5–13.

Breton, M. (2004). An empowerment perspective. In C. D. Garvin, L. Gutierrez, & M. J. Galinsky's *Handbook of Social Work with Groups* (pp. 58–75). New York: Guilford Press.

Brown, V. B. (2000, February). Jane Addams. *American National Biography Online.* Oxford University Press. Retrieved from http://www.anb.org/articles/15/15–00004.html

Buckley, M. J. (1998). *The Catholic university as promise and project: Reflections in a Jesuit idiom.* Washington, DC: Georgetown University Press.

Chen, E. C., Kakkad, D., & Balzano, J. (2008). Multicultural competence and evidence-based practice in group therapy. *Journal of Clinical Psychology, 64,* 1261–1278.

Christopher, S., Burhansstipanov, L., & Knows His Gun McCormick, A. (2005). Using a CBPR approach to develop an interviewer training manual with members of the Apsaalooke nation. In B. Israel, E. Eng, A. Schulz, and E. Parker (Eds.), *Methods in community-based participatory research for health* (pp. 128–145). San Francisco: John Wiley & Sons.

Ciardiello, S. (2003). Meet them in the lab: Using hip-hop music therapy groups with adolescents in residential settings. In N. E. Sullivan, E. S. Mesbur, N. C. Lang, D. Goodman, & L. Mitchell (Eds.), *Social work with groups: Social justice through personal, community and societal change* (pp. 103–117). New York: Haworth Press.

Constantine, M., Hage, S., Kindaichi, M., & Bryant, R. (2007). Social justice and multicultural issues: Implications for the practice and training of counselors and counseling psychologists. *Journal of Counseling and Development, 85,* 24–29.

Council of National Associations for the Advancement of Ethnic Minority Issues. (2000). *Guidelines for research in ethnic minority communities.* Washington, DC: American Psychological Association.

Cox, A. A., & Lee, C. C. (2007). Challenging educational inequities: School counselors as agents of social justice. In C. C. Lee (Ed.), *Counseling for social justice* (2nd ed.). Alexandria, VA: American Counseling Association.

Debiak, D. (2006). Attending to diversity in group psychotherapy: An ethical imperative. *International Journal of Group Psychotherapy, 57,* 1–12.

DeLucia-Waack, J. L. (1996). Multiculturalism is inherent in all group work [Editorial]. *Journal for Specialists in Group Work, 21,* 218–223.

Dessel, A., Rogge, M. E., & Garlington, S. B. (2006). Using group dialogue to promote social justice and change. *Social Work, 51,* 303–315.

Dowden, A. R. (2009). Implementing self-advocacy training within a brief psychoeducational group to improve the academic motivation of black adolescents. *Journal for Specialists in Group Work, 34,* 118–136.

Evans, S. D., Hanlin, C. E., & Prilleltensky, I. (2007). Blending ameliorative and transformative approaches in human service organizations: A case study. *Journal of Community Psychology, 35,* 329–346.

Field, J. E., & Baker, S. (2004). Defining and examining school counselor advocacy. *Professional School Counseling, 8,* 56–63.

Fine, M. Working the hyphens: Reinventing the Self and Other in qualitative research. In N. Denzin and Y. Lincoln. (Eds.) *Handbook of qualitative research.* Newbury Park, CA: Sage, 1994, 70–82.

Finn, J., Jacobson, M., & Campana, J. D. (2004). Participatory research, popular education, and popular theater. In C. Garvin, L. Gutierrez, & M. Galinsky (Eds.), *Handbook of social work with groups* (pp. 326–343). New York: Guilford Press.

Fouad, N. A., Gerstein, L. H., & Toporek, R. L. (2006). Social justice and counseling psychology in context. In R. L. Toporek, L. H. Gerstein, N. A. Fouad, G. Roysircar, & T. Israel (Eds.), *Handbook for social justice in counseling psychology: Leadership, vision, and action* (pp. 1–16). Thousand Oaks, CA: Sage.

Fouad, N. A., Helledy, K. I., & Metz, A. J. (2003). Leadership in Division 17: Lessons from the presidential addresses. *Counseling Psychologist, 31,* 763–788.

Fouad, N. A., McPherson, R. H., Gerstein, L., Blustein, D. L., Elman, N., Helledy, K. I., et al. (2004). Houston, 2001: Context and legacy. *Counseling Psychologist, 32,* 15–77.

Fowers, B. J., & Davidov, B. J. (2006). The virtue of multiculturalism: Personal transformation, character, and openness to the other. *American Psychologist, 61,* 581–594.

Freire, P. (1970). *Pedagogy of the oppressed.* New York: Herder and Herder.

Freire, P. (1972). *Cultural action for freedom.* Harmondsworth, UK: Penguin.

Getzel, G. S. (2003). Group work and social justice: Rhetoric or action? In N. E. Sullivan, E. S. Mesbur, N. C. Lang, D. Goodman, & L. Mitchell (Eds.) *Social work with groups: Social justice through personal, community and societal change* (pp. 53–64). New York: Haworth Press.

Gil, D. G. (1998). *Confronting injustice and oppression.* New York: Columbia University Press.

Gladding, S. T. (2003). *Group work: A counseling specialty* (4th ed.). Upper Saddle River, NJ: Simon & Schuster.

Goodman, L. A., Liang, B., Helms, J. E., Latta, R. E., Sparks, E., & Weintraub, S. R. (2004). Training counseling psychologists as social justice agents: Feminist and multicultural principles in action. *Counseling Psychologist, 32,* 793–837.

Graham, M. A. (2003). Justice in teaching: Teaching as group work. In N. E. Sullivan, E. S. Mesbur, N. C. Lang, D. Goodman, & L. Mitchell (Eds.), *Social work with groups: Social justice through personal, community and societal change* (pp. 213–226). New York: Haworth Press.

Greene, B. (2008). Psychology, diversity, and social justice. In G. C. Gamst, A. Der-Karabetian, & R. H. Dana (Eds.), *Readings in multicultural practice* (pp. 495–504). Thousand Oaks, CA: Sage.

Hage, S. M. (2003). Reaffirming the unique identity of counseling psychology: Opting for the "road less traveled by." *Counseling Psychologist*, *31*, 555–563.

Hage, S. M. (2005). Future considerations for fostering multicultural competence in mental health and educational settings: Social justice implications. In M. G. Constantine & D. W. Sue (Eds.), *Strategies for building multicultural competence in mental health and educational settings*. Hoboken, NJ: John Wiley & Sons.

Hage, S. M., & Kenny, M. E. (2009). Promoting a social justice approach to prevention: Future directions for training, practice and research. *Journal of Primary Prevention*, *30*, 1–10.

Harris, G. E. (2009). Reflections on ideological consistency between community-based research and counselling practice. *Canadian Journal of Counselling*, *43*, 3–17.

Hartung, P. J., & Blustein, D. L. (2002). Reason, intuition, and social justice: Elaborating Parsons' career decision making model. *Journal of Counseling and Development*, *80*, 41–47.

Helms, J. E. (1986). Expanding racial identity theory to cover counseling process. *Journal of Counseling Psychology*, *33*, 62–64.

Helms, J. E. (1995). An update of Helm's white and people of color racial identity models. In J. G. Ponterotto, J. M. Casas, L. A. Suzuki, & A. Charlene (Eds.), *Handbook of multicultural counseling* (2nd ed., pp. 181–198). Thousand Oaks, CA: Sage.

Henry, S. (2003). Social group work, social justice. In N. E. Sullivan, E. S. Mesbur, N. C. Lang, D. Goodman, & L. Mitchell (Eds.), *Social work with groups: Social justice through personal, community and societal change* (pp. 65–77). New York: Haworth Press.

Holcomb-McCoy, C. (2007). *School counseling to close the achievement gap: A social justice framework for success*. Thousand Oaks, CA: Corwin Press.

Howard, K., & Solberg, V. S. (2006). School-based social justice: The Achieving Success Identity Pathways Program. *Professional School Counseling*, *9*, 278–287.

Israel, B., Eng, E., Schulz, A., & Parker, E. (Eds.) (2005). *Methods in community-based participatory research for health*. San Francisco: John Wiley & Sons.

Israeli, A. L., & Santor, D. A. (2000). Reviewing effective components of feminist therapy. *Counselling Psychology Quarterly*, *13*, 233–247.

Ivey, A. E., & Collins, N. M. (2003). Social justice: A long-term challenge for counseling psychology. *Counseling Psychologist*, *31*, 290–298.

Jacobson, M., & Rugeley, C. (2007). Community-based participatory research: Group work for social justice and community change. *Social Work with Groups*, *30*, 21–39.

Juntunen, C. L., Cavett, A. M., Clow, R. B., Rempel, V., Darrow, R. E., & Guilmino, A. (2006). Social justice through self-sufficiency. In R. L. Toporek, L. H. Gerstein, N. A. Fouad, G. Roysircar, & T. Israel (Eds.), *Handbook for social justice in counseling psychology: Leadership, vision and action* (pp. 294–309). Thousand Oaks, CA: Sage.

Kagan, N., Armsworth, M. W., Altmaier, E. M., Dowd, E. T., Hansen, J. C., Mills, D. H., et al. (1988). Professional practice of counseling psychology in various settings. *Counseling Psychologist*, *16*, 347–365.

Kenny, M. E., & Hage, S. M. (2009). The next frontier: Prevention as an instrument of social justice. *Journal of Primary Prevention*, *30*, 1–10.

Kenny, M. E., Sparks, E., & Jackson, J. (2007). Striving for social justice through interprofessional university-school collaboration. In E. Aldarondo (Ed.), *Advancing social justice through clinical practice* (pp. 313–335). Mahwah, NJ: Lawrence Erlbaum.

Kirby, S., & McKenna, K. (1989). *Methods from the margins: Experience, research, social change*. Toronto, Canada: Garmond Press.

Kiselica, M. S., & Robinson, M. (2001). Bringing advocacy counseling to life: The history, issues, and human dramas of social justice work in counseling. *Journal of Counseling and Development*, *79*, 387–397.

Kivlighan, D. M., & Arseneau, J. R. (2009). A typology of critical incidents in intergroup dialogue groups. *Group Dynamics: Theory, Research, and Practice*, *13*, 89–102.

Lee, C. C. (Ed.). (2007). *Counseling for social justice* (2nd ed.). Alexandria, VA: American Counseling Association.

Leonard, P. (1996). Consciousness-raising groups as a multicultural awareness approach: An experience with counselor trainees. *Cultural Diversity and Mental Health*, *2*, 89–98.

Lewis, J., Arnold, M. S., House, R., & Toporek, R. (2003). *Advocacy competencies* [Electronic version]. Retrieved November 20, 2009, from http://www.counseling.org/Publications

MacNair-Semands, R. R. (2007). Attending to the spirit of social justice as an ethical approach in group therapy. *International Journal of Group Psychotherapy*, *57*, 61–66.

Maguire, P. (1987). *Doing participatory research: A feminist approach*. Amherst, MA: Center for International Education, University of Massachusetts.

Manis, A., Brown, S., & Paylo, M. (2008). The helping professional as an advocate. In J. Carlson and C. M. Ellis (Eds.), *Cross cultural awareness and social justice in counseling* (pp. 23–44). New York: Routledge.

Mannik, M. (2003). From fragile to wild: Group work as the transforming element in redressing social inequities for older women. In N. E. Sullivan, E. S. Mesbur, N. C. Lang, D. Goodman, & L. Mitchell (Eds.), *Social work with groups: Social justice through personal, community and societal change* (pp. 181–193). New York: Haworth Press.

Marsiglia, F. F. (2003). Culturally grounded approaches to social justice through social work with groups. In N. E. Sullivan, E. S. Mesbur, N. C. Lang, D. T. Goodman, & L. Mitchell (Eds.), *Social work with groups: Social justice through personal, community and societal change* (pp. 79–90). New York: Haworth Press.

McWhirter, E. H. (1994). *Counseling for empowerment*. Alexandria, VA: American Counseling Association.

McWhirter, E. H. (1998). An empowerment model of counselor training. *Canadian Journal of Counseling*, *32*, 12–26.

Minkler, M., & Wallerstein, N. (Eds.). (2003). *Community-based participatory research for health*. San Francisco: Jossey-Bass.

Monk, G., Winslade, J., Crocket, K., & Epston, D. (1997). *Narrative therapy in practice: The archaeology of hope*. San Francisco: Jossey-Bass.

Morrow, S. L., Hawxhurst, D. M., Montes de Vegas, A. Y., Abousleman, T. M., & Castañeda, C. L. (2005). Toward a radical feminist multicultural therapy: Renewing a commitment to activism. In R. L. Toporek, L. Gerstein, N. Fouad, G. Roysircar, & T. Israel (Eds.), *Handbook for social justice in counseling psychology: Leadership, vision, and action.* Thousand Oaks, CA: Sage.

Morsillo, J., & Prilleltensky, I. (2007). Social action with youth: Interventions, evaluation, and psychopolitical validity. *Journal of Community Psychology, 35,* 725–740.

Nelson, G., & Prilleltensky, I. (Eds.). (2005). *Community psychology: In pursuit of liberation and well being.* New York: Palgrave Macmillan.

Palmer, A., & Parish, J. (2008). Social justice and counselling psychology: Situating the role of graduate student research, education, and training. *Canadian Journal of Counselling, 42,* 278–292.

Portman, T. A., & Portman, G. L. (2002). Empowering students for social justice (ES2J): A structured group approach. *Journal for Specialists in Group Work, 27,* 16–31.

Prilleltensky, I. (1999). Critical psychology foundations for the promotion of mental health. *Annual Review of Critical Psychology, 1,* 100–118.

Prilleltensky, I., Dokecki, P., Frieden, G., & Wang, V. O. (2007). Counseling for wellness and social justice: Foundations and ethical dilemmas. In E. Aldarondo (Ed.), *Advancing social justice through clinical practice* (pp. 19–42). Mahwah, NJ: Lawrence Erlbaum.

Prilleltensky, I., & Nelson, G. (1997). Community psychology: Reclaiming social justice. In D. R. Fox & I. Prilleltensky (Eds.), *Critical psychology: An introduction* (pp. 166–184). Thousand Oaks, CA: Sage.

Prilleltensky, I., & Nelson, G. (2002). *Doing psychology critically: Making a difference in diverse settings.* New York: Palgrave Macmillan.

Ratts, M. (2006). Social justice counseling: A study of social justice counselor training in CACREP-accredited counselor preparation programs (Doctoral dissertation, Oregon State University, 2006). *Dissertation Abstracts International, 67,* 1234.

Ratts, M., D'Andrea, M., & Arredondo, P. (2004). Social justice counseling: A "fifth force" in the field. *Counseling Today, 47,* 28–30.

Ratts, M., DeKruyf, L., & Chen-Hayes, S. F. (2008). The ACA advocacy competencies: A social justice advocacy framework for professional school counselors. *Professional School Counseling, 11,* 90–97.

Ridley, C. R., Liddle, M. C., Hill, C. L., & Li, L. C. (2001). Ethical decision making in multicultural counseling. In J. G. Ponterotto, J. M. Casas, L. A. Suzuki, & A. Charlene (Eds.), *Handbook of multicultural counseling* (2nd ed., pp. 165–188). Thousand Oaks, CA: Sage.

Romano, J. L., & Hage, S. M. (2000). Prevention: A call to action. *Counseling Psychologist, 28,* 854–856.

Roysircar, G. (2008). A response to "Social privilege, social justice, and group counseling: An inquiry": Social privilege: Counselors' competency with systemically determined inequalities. *Journal for Specialists in Group Work, 33,* 377–384.

Safren, S. A., Hollander, G., Hart, T. A., & Heimberg, R. G. (2001). Cognitive-behavioral therapy with lesbian, gay, and bisexual youth. *Cognitive and Behavioral Practice, 8,* 215–223.

Singh, A. A., & Hays, D. G. (2008). Feminist group counseling with South Asian women who have survived intimate partner violence. *Journal for Specialists in Group Work, 33,* 84–102.

Smith, E. (2006). The strength-based counseling model. *Counseling Psychologist, 34,* 13–79.

Smith, L. C., & Shin, R. Q. (2008). Social privilege, social justice and group counseling: An inquiry. *Journal for Specialists in Group Work, 33,* 351–366.

Snyder, C., Peeler, J., & May, J. D. (2008). Combining human diversity and social justice education: A conceptual framework. *Journal of Social Work Education, 44,* 145–162.

Speight, S. L., & Vera, E. M. (2004). Social justice: Ready, or not? [Invited commentary]. *Counseling Psychologist, 32,* 109–118.

Sue, D. W. (2001). Multidimensional facets of cultural competence. *Counseling Psychologist, 29,* 790–821.

Sue, D. W., Bernier, J. B., Durran, M., Feinberg, L., Pedersen, P., Smith, E., & Vasquez-Nuttall, E. (1982). Position paper: Cross-cultural counseling competencies. *Counseling Psychologist, 10,* 45–52.

Sue, D. W., Capodilupo, C. M., Lin, A. I., Torino, G. C., Bucceri, J., Holder, A., et al. (2007). Racial microaggressions in everyday life: Implications for clinical practice. *American Psychologist, 62,* 271–286.

Sullivan, N. E., Mesbur, E., Lang, N., Goodman, D., & Mitchell, L. (Eds.). (2003). *Social work with groups: Justice through personal, community and societal change.* New York: Haworth Press.

Thompson, C. E., Murray, S. L., Harris, D., & Annan, J. R. (2003). Healing inside and out: Promoting social justice and peace in a racially divided U.S. community. *International Journal for the Advancement of Counselling, 25,* 215–223.

Thompson, C. E., & Neville, H. A. (1999). Racism, mental health, and mental health practice. *Counseling Psychologist, 27,* 155–223.

Toporek, R. L., Gerstein, L. H., Fouad, N. A., Roysircar, G., & Israel, T. (2006). *Handbook of social justice in counseling psychology.* Thousand Oaks, CA: Sage.

Toporek, R. L., Lewis, J., & Crethar, H. C. (2009). Promoting systemic change through the advocacy competencies. *Journal of Counseling and Development, 87,* 260–269.

Toporek, R. L., & McNally, C. J. (2006). Social justice training in counseling psychology in context. In R. L. Toporek, L. H. Gerstein, N. A. Fouad, G. Roysircar, & T. Israel (Eds.), *Handbook for social justice in counseling psychology: Leadership, vision, and action* (pp. 37–73). Thousand Oaks, CA: Sage.

Van den Bos, K. (2003). On the subjective quality of social justice: The role of affect as information in the psychology of justice judgments. *Journal of Personality and Social Psychology, 85,* 482–498.

Van Wormer, K. (2009). Restorative justice as social justice for victims of gendered violence: A standpoint feminist perspective. *Social Work, 54,* 107–116.

Vera, E. M., Daly, B., Gonzales, R., Morgan, M., & Thakra, C. (2006). Prevention and outreach with underserved populations: Building multisystemic youth development programs for urban youth. In R. L. Toporek, L. H. Gerstein, N. A. Fouad, G. Roysircar, & T. Israel (Eds.), *Handbook for social justice in counseling psychology: Leadership, vision, and action* (pp. 86–99). Thousand Oaks, CA: Sage.

Vera, E. M., & Speight, S. L. (2003). Multicultural competence, social justice, and counseling psychology: Expanding our roles. *Counseling Psychologist, 31,* 253–272.

Watts, R. J., Williams, N. C., & Jagers, R. J. (2003). Sociopolitical development. *American Journal of Community Psychology, 31,* 185–194.

White, M. (2007). *Maps of narrative practice.* New York: W. W. Norton.

White, V. E. (2002). Developing counseling objectives and empowering clients: A strength-based intervention. *Journal of Mental Health Counseling, 24,* 270–279.

Worthington, R. L., & Juntunen, C. L. (1997). The vocational development of non-college-bound youth: Counseling psychology and the school-to-work transition movement. *Counseling Psychologist, 25,* 323–363.

Wutzdoff, A. J., & Giles, D. E. (1997). Service learning in higher education. In J. Schine (Ed.), *Service learning* (pp. 105–117). Chicago: University of Chicago Press.

York, E. (2004). Finding voice: The music of Utah battered women. Unpublished manuscript.

Zimmerman, M. A., Ramirez-Valles, J., & Maton, K. I. (1999). Resilience among urban African American male adolescents: A study of the protective effects of sociopolitical control on their mental health. *American Journal of Community Psychology, 27,* 733–751.

PART 3

Key Change Processes

Therapeutic Factors in Group-Counseling: Asking New Questions

Dennis M. Kivlighan, Jr., Joseph R. Miles, *and* Jill D. Paquin

Abstract

Since the first appearance of psychotherapy groups in the 1940s, practitioners, theorists, and researchers have asked the following question: How do therapy groups help their participants? Given the "intricate interplay of human experiences" (I. Yalom, & M. Leszcz. *The theory and practice of group psychotherapy* (5th e.). New York: Basic Books, p. 1) occurring within therapy groups, this question is not an easy one to answer. In this chapter, we address how researchers have both asked and attempted to answer this question. Additionally, we provide a critique of this literature and its methodologies and recommend new directions for research in this area.

Keywords: group counseling, therapeutic factors

> I suggest that therapeutic change is an enormously complex process that occurs through an intricate interplay of human experiences, which I will refer to as "therapeutic factors." There is considerable advantage in approaching the complex through the simple, the total phenomenon through its basic component processes.
>
> *Yalom and Leszcz* (2005, p. 1)

Researchers have examined the therapeutic factors described by Yalom and Leszcz (2005) individually and as a whole. In this chapter we focus on studies that have examined these factors as a whole. We use a series of questions to organize our review of this research: Where did research on therapeutic factors begin? What is the best way to measure group members' perceptions of therapeutic factors? Do we really need more studies examining the ranked perception of therapeutic factors in yet another group setting or population? Are there 12 unique therapeutic factors? Is examining perceived helpfulness enough? Are therapeutic factors an individual- or a group-level phenomenon? When should therapeutic factors be measured? Are therapeutic factors related to other group-process variables? Where are we, and where do we need to go?

Where Did Research on Therapeutic Factors Begin?

Early group-therapy research examined large undifferentiated questions, like which approaches to group structure were most effective (e.g., active vs. inactive) with which populations (e.g., inpatient vs. outpatient). By the 1970s and 1980s, however, researchers focused their attention on what *process variables* (termed "curative factors" and later "therapeutic factors") might be linked with client change and outcome (Barlow, Fuhriman, & Burlingame, 2004). Yalom, Tinklenberg, and Gilula (1968) were among the first to develop a method for assessing therapeutic factors. Specifically, they developed a 60-item therapeutic factor Q-sort by writing five items corresponding to each of the 11 factors, as described by Yalom and Leszcz (2005) (see Table 8.1). Twenty group-therapy clients placed the 60 therapeutic factor Q-sort items into categories ranging from "Least helpful to me in group" to "Most helpful to me in group." Using these categories, Yalom et al. (1968) derived a ranking of the relative client-perceived importance of therapeutic factors. Specifically, the clients in Yalom et al.'s study ranked the factors from most to least important as follows: (1) interpersonal learning (input), (2) catharsis, (3) cohesiveness, (4) self-understanding, (5) interpersonal learning (output), (6) existential factors, (7) universality, (8) instillation of hope, (9) altruism, (10) family reenactment, (11) guidance, and (12) identification (in this measure,

interpersonal learning was split into interpersonal learning input and interpersonal learning output categories, thereby creating 12 therapeutic factors).

Yalom et al.'s (1968) compendium of 11 therapeutic factors was intended to capture a basic framework for understanding the most crucial and fundamental components of the change process in group-therapy, amid a myriad of treatment settings, populations, problems, and therapeutic styles. From within this framework, Yalom posited that group practitioners could employ "tactics and strateg[ies]" to enhance the therapeutic nature of groups across settings, people, and problems (Yalom & Leszcz, 2005, p. 1). The work by Yalom and his colleagues built on the writings of other group theorists (for a review of the historical development of research on counseling and psychotherapy groups, see Barlow et al., 2004) and provided a unifying framework for understanding processes of change in group psychotherapy. Additionally, although the Q-sort designed by Yalom et al. (1968) has only occasionally been

Table 8.1 Yalom's (1995) therapeutic factors

Factor	Description
Altruism	Group member offers support, reassurance, suggestions, and insight to other group members.
Catharsis	Group member experiences and expresses strong affect.
Corrective recapitulation of the primary family group	Group member relives early familial conflicts in group in a corrective, more satisfying way.
Development of socializing techniques	Group member develops basic social skills through interactions with other group members.
Existential factors	Group member confronts issues on the ultimate concerns of existence: death, isolation, freedom, and meaninglessness.
Group cohesiveness	Group member feels connection to and solidarity with group leader(s), other group members, and group as a whole.
Imitative behavior	Group member learns to model behaviors from group leader(s) or other group members.
Imparting information	Group member receives didactic instruction or direct advice from group leader(s) or other group members.
Instillation of hope	Keeps group member in the group so that the other therapeutic factors may take effect; group member's faith in treatment itself is therapeutic.
Interpersonal learning	Group member learns about own maladaptive interpersonal patterns through social microcosm of the group; group member has corrective emotional experiences in group and practices new, more adaptive interpersonal behaviors in group.
Universality	Group member learns that she or he is not alone or unique in her or his problems and suffering.

used in subsequent therapeutic factors research, Yalom and his colleagues established an important research paradigm: asking group members' about their experience of therapeutic factors. This paradigm has commonly been used in subsequent group research and has remained central to the study of therapeutic factors in groups. As such, the utility and influence of their work in this area cannot be understated.

Bloch, Reibstein, Crouch, Holroyd, and Themen (1979) created an alternative way to operationalize group members' perceptions of therapeutic factors. They used a "critical incidents" questionnaire to gather qualitative data from group therapy participants regarding moments during group sessions that they perceived as being the most important incidents from that session. Bloch et al. then classified these critical incidents into 10 therapeutic factors (see Table 8.2). Unlike the ranking of a predetermined set of therapeutic factors used by Yalom et al. (1968), this alternative paradigm did not assume the presence of all of the therapeutic factors in each session. Rather, this method inductively allowed researchers to ascertain what factors might be present in a given session and the relative importance of these factors to the group participants.

Expanding on the work of Bloch et al. (1979), Bloch and Crouch (1985) argued that Yalom et al.'s (1968) taxonomy of therapeutic factors was problematic because the concept of therapeutic factors is blurred with conditions of change (i.e., the conditions necessary for therapeutic factors to operate), and techniques (i.e., the devices used to promote the operation of therapeutic factors). Using their definition of therapeutic factors (i.e., "an element of the group process which exerts a beneficial effect on group members" [p. 245]), Bloch et al. and Bloch and Crouch created the revised list of 10 factors shown in Table 8.2.

Despite different definitions and different systems for measuring therapeutic factors, a large literature has developed examining group members' perceptions of therapeutic factors across settings, populations, and group approaches. In an attempt to synthesize this literature on therapeutic factors in group psychotherapy, several previous review chapters have been written (Kivlighan, Coleman, & Anderson, 2000; Kivlighan & Holmes, 2004). In their review of the group therapeutic factors literature, Kivlighan et al. (2000) failed to discern a pattern in the research on the rank ordering of therapeutic factors. Additionally, Kivlighan and Holmes (2004) discussed the diverse and sometimes

Table 8.2 Bloch and Crouch's (1985) therapeutic factors

Factor	Description
Acceptance	Group member feels valued, supported, understood, cared for, and/or a sense of belonging in the group.
Altruism	Group member feels better about him- or herself through helping other group members.
Catharsis	Group member feels relieved through the ventilation of feelings, about life events or other members.
Guidance	Group member receives useful information or advice from others.
Instillation of hope	Group member gains a sense of optimism about his or her progress or potential progress.
Learning from interpersonal actions	Group member attempts to relate constructively and adaptively with other members in the group.
Self-disclosure	Group member reveals personal information to the group.
Self-understanding	Group member learns something important about him- or herself.
Universality	Group member recognizes that his or her problems are shared or similar to those of other group members.
Vicarious learning	Group member experiences something of value for him- or herself through observation of other group members.

conflicting results of rank-order studies. They attributed this to a lack of a theoretical rationale for comparing such divergent types of groups, settings, and populations. Kivlighan and Holmes (2004) also provided a review of the different heuristics that have been used to make sense of these findings. For example, Crouch, Bloch, and Wanlass (1994) suggested that an "inpatient vs. outpatient" distinction might be a useful heuristic for understanding the differential importance of therapeutic factors. The authors suggested that, because of their different needs, outpatients would place more value on self-understanding and learning through interpersonal actions, whereas inpatients would find greater value in acceptance and hope. Unfortunately, these heuristics did not hold up well when various studies were examined.

As part of their review, Kivlighan and Holmes (2004) conducted a meta-analysis of 37 studies on therapeutic factors in groups. Rather than continuing to deductively seek to understand why the relative importance of therapeutic factors was so different across studies post hoc, the authors asked a different question: What were the underlying similarities of the studies on therapeutic factors? Using cluster analysis, the authors found that the 37 studies could be grouped by similarity into four group typologies: affective insight, affective support, cognitive insight, and cognitive support.

Recent Literature on Therapeutic Factors

Despite Kivlighan et al.'s (2000) failure to find any discernable differences in therapeutic factors by setting or population and Kivlighan and Holmes's (2004) call for different research questions, much of the recent research has continued to examine which therapeutic factors are ranked as most important by specific client populations. For example, researchers have examined therapeutic factors in emotional-supportive psychotherapy groups for children (Shechtman, 2007; Shechtman & Gluk, 2005), cognitive-behavioral groups for patients with anxiety and mood disorders (Oei & Brown, 2006), and ongoing therapy groups for men who commit intimate partner violence (Roy, Turcotte, Montminy, & Lindsay, 2005). Most of these studies have continued the trend of asking group participants to identify critical incidents (Shechtman & Gluk, 2005) or to sort therapeutic factors (Roy et al., 2005) based on what they found to be most important in their group experience. The assumption in these studies is that therapeutic factors operate consistently across group members in a given group.

This assumption is problematic, as noted by Shaughnessy and Kivlighan (1995), because differences between groups may not be as salient as differences among clients within groups. The majority these studies do not tie therapeutic factor rankings to group member outcomes.

There are, however, a few studies that examined the relationship between therapeutic factors and outcomes for group members. For example, recent research has examined the relationship between therapeutic factors, mood and anxiety symptoms (Oei & Brown, 2006); depression symptoms (Crowe & Grenyer, 2008); and general symptoms, grief symptoms, and target objectives/life satisfaction (Joyce, Piper, & Ogrodniczuk, 2007). While these studies go a step beyond those asking participants to rank or otherwise indicate which therapeutic factors they feel were most important or helpful by tying the therapeutic factors to objective outcomes, researchers have not begun to examine more complex questions regarding therapeutic factors, such as potential indirect relationships between therapeutic factors and outcomes (Joyce et al., 2007) or whether the same therapeutic factors operate across participants within a group and across sessions.

Since the publication of these review chapters, several researchers have also created new typologies of therapeutic factors in group psychotherapy in response to limitations of the previously articulated taxonomies of therapeutic factors (Johansson & Werbart, 2009; Dierick & Lietaer, 2008). While these typologies may prove useful, additional research is needed on the relationship between these therapeutic factors and objective outcome variables. Further, it is unclear whether these new therapeutic factors operate consistently across group members and across time.

While much of the recent literature on therapeutic factors in groups has continued the trends of past research, several new approaches to therapeutic factors research have emerged. For example, Hornsey, Dwyer, and Oei (2007) suggested that examining social psychology research and theory may offer new insights into therapeutic factors in group psychotherapy. Specifically, they suggested that group identification, homogeneity, and task interdependence may be potentially useful constructs for understanding processes of change in group psychotherapy. Additionally, Fontao and Mergenthaler (2008) used computer-assisted text analysis of transcripts of a single psychotherapy group over time to examine how emotion-abstraction patterns in group psychotherapy related to therapeutic factors and group process. Their research suggests that different therapeutic factors may be operating at different points in a group's development. While this research provides an important way of understanding how the importance of different therapeutic factors changes across time, it does not address the need to examine whether the importance of different therapeutic factors is consistent across group members.

Finally, researchers have begun to examine whether the same therapeutic factors operate across cultures (Shechtman & Halevi, 2006). This is an important area for future research on therapeutic factors in groups because "group psychological approaches have Eurocentric assumptions about the primacy of the individual in treatment and intervention for personal and interpersonal concerns, [so] certain assumptions about what is effective may be problematic for some ethnic minority clients" (Vasquez & Han, 1995, p. 110). While this is an important new research domain, it will be important for researchers to remain cognizant that differences within groups may be greater than differences across groups, in terms of the therapeutic factors that are most important.

In examining the past and current research on therapeutic factors, there are a number of important theoretical and methodological questions that arise. The following sections attempt to delineate several of these questions.

What Is the Best Way to Measure Group Members' Perceptions of Therapeutic Factors?

Yalom et al.'s (1968) focus on identifying clients' perceptions of the relative importance of the therapeutic factors has proven heuristic. Over 50 studies have examined group clients' perceptions of the relative importance of the therapeutic factors described by Yalom and Leszcz (2005). Some of these studies have used the Q-sort method developed by Yalom et al. (1968), other studies have used Likert-type scales developed from the Q-sort items written by Yalom et al., and still others have used Bloch et al.'s (1979) therapeutic factors classification scheme to categorize critical incidents questions completed by group members. It is unfortunate, however, that no studies have compared these different approaches for deriving group clients' perceptions of the therapeutic factors. Therefore, group researchers have no empirical evidence for deciding the "best" methodology for identifying clients' perceptions of the relative importance of the therapeutic factors, nor do we know if the different

methodologies provide divergent or convergent results.

Regardless of methodology, however, group researchers have now amassed a number of studies that identify clients' rankings of therapeutic factors across a number of different settings and patient populations. The implicit goal of these studies is to identify the most and least important therapeutic factors in various forms of group treatment.

Do We Really Need More Studies Examining the Ranked Perception of Therapeutic Factors in yet Another Group Setting or Population?

As noted, over 50 studies have examined clients' perceptions of the relative importance of therapeutic factors in groups with different content/themes or with different client populations. For example, recent studies have examined therapeutic factors in groups for men who commit intimate partner violence (Roy et al., 2005), and adolescent sex offenders' rankings of therapeutic factors in residential treatment groups (Sribney & Reddon, 2008). An important problem for researchers and theorists, then, lies in making sense of the multiple studies that examine group member perceptions of therapeutic factors. It is clear that the rank ordering of the therapeutic factors differs across these studies, but it is not clear what variables explain the different rankings. Yalom and Leszcz (2005) suggested that therapeutic factors are perceived differentially as a function of (1) type of group (outpatient vs. inpatient), (2) stage of group development, and (3) individual differences among group members (Yalom, 1995). As noted, however, research has not provided consistent results to support this assertion. Time spent in a group has proved a useful dimension for understanding how the perception of therapeutic factors changes both across and within studies.

As noted, Kivlighan and Holmes (2004) proposed a unique way to understand the differences in the rank ordering of therapeutic factors across multiple studies. Rather than start with preexisting categories (e.g., type of group) or dimensions (e.g., individual difference characteristics), Kivlighan and Holmes started with the rank orderings of the therapeutic factors and tried to discover natural groupings across the studies. Specifically, they clustered studies that examined therapeutic factors based on the relative ranking of the therapeutic factors found in the study. Based on this cluster analysis, they described four types of groups. The affective insight groups had relatively high levels of the acceptance, catharsis, interpersonal learning, and self-understanding therapeutic factors. The affective support groups had relatively high levels of the acceptance, instillation of hope, and universality therapeutic factors. The cognitive support groups had relatively high levels of the vicarious learning and guidance therapeutic factors and relatively low levels of the self-understanding therapeutic factor. Finally, the cognitive insight groups had relatively high levels of the interpersonal learning, self-understanding, and vicarious learning therapeutic factors and relatively low levels of the guidance therapeutic factor.

We believe that this taxonomy represents an important tool for understanding how therapeutic factors operate across various group dimensions. Researchers can compare the rank ordering of the factors in their studies with the rank ordering of the factors in the affective insight, affective support, cognitive support, and cognitive insight groups. For example, the ranking of therapeutic factors for adolescent sex offenders in the Sribney and Reddon (2008) study correlated significantly with the affective insight groups (Spearman's rank-order correlation = 0.77, p < 0.01) and was uncorrelated with the rankings in the affective support, cognitive support, and cognitive insight groups. This level of correlation suggests that the groups in the Sribney and Reddon (2008) study should be classified as affective insight groups. If the rankings of therapeutic factors in future studies correspond to the affective insight, affective support, cognitive support and cognitive insight groups typology, then the validity of the typology is strengthened. If the rankings of therapeutic factors in future studies do not correspond to one of the four group types, it will indicate that the typology needs to be expanded. In either case, comparing the rankings of therapeutic factors in a study with the four-group typology will let authors connect their study to the larger literature. We recommend that this type of comparison be routinely done in future studies of group members' perceptions of therapeutic factors.

Are There 12 Unique Therapeutic Factors?

As early as the mid-1970s, researchers were examining the construct validity of the Q-sort Yalom et al. (1968) developed to examine therapeutic factors. Rohrbaugh and Bartels (1975) conducted a factor analysis of Q-sort ratings for 72 group members in 13 groups and found 14 factors that they referred to as "revised therapeutic mechanisms." These authors also conducted a second-order factor analysis using group participants' scores on the 14 first-order factors. The second-order factor analysis resulted in seven dimensions. Unfortunately, Rohrbaugh and Bartels did not name these seven factors, nor did they use these second-order factors in their further analyses.

The first authors to describe the underlying factor structure of a therapeutic factors questionnaire were Fuhriman, Drescher, Hanson, Henrie, and Rybicki (1986). They conducted a factor analytic study of a revised curative factor instrument using 161 group members in community mental health, Veterans Administration, university counseling center, and group dynamics class groups. They found three underlying dimensions, which they labeled "catharsis," "cohesion," and "insight," that explained a substantial proportion of the interitem variance. These dimensions are displayed in Table 8.3. Kivlighan, Multon, and Brossart (1996) also used factor analysis to examine therapeutic factor ratings of open-ended responses to a critical incident questionnaire. They found four underlying components for these

Table 8.3 Factor analyses of therapeutic factors inventories

Fuhriman et al. (1986)	Kivlighan et al. (1996)	Dierick and Lietaer (2008)
Cohesion	Relationship–climate	Group cohesion
		Interactional confirmation
Catharsis		Cathartic self-revelation
Insight	Emotional awareness–insight	Self-insight and progress
	Other vs. self-focus	Observational experiences
	Problem identification–change	Getting directives
		Interactional confrontation

therapeutic factors ratings: (1) emotional awareness–insight, a strong affective experience connected with gaining awareness and insight, (2) relationship–climate, the formation and maintenance of relationships among group members; (3) other vs. self-focus, focus outside of her- or himself or inward; and (4) problem identification–change, cognitive identification and understanding of a problem as well as the behavioral change measure. These dimensions are also displayed in Table 8.3.

Dierick and Lietaer (2008) also developed a new measure of clients' perceptions of therapeutic factors in group-therapy. In this large and sophisticated study, 489 members of 78 psychotherapy and growth groups responded to a 150-item therapeutic factors inventory. Cluster and factor analyses were used to determine the latent structure of these 150 items. Dierick and Lietaer found seven scales contained in two higher-order dimensions of relational climate and psychological work. The relational climate dimension encompassed three constructs: (1) group cohesion, containing items concerning acceptance, belonging to a cohesive working group, and empathy and support; (2) interactional confirmation, consisting of items related to the expression of mutual positive feelings, experiencing positive feelings in encountering others, and finding self-confidence in helping others; and (3) cathartic self-revelation, containing items related to authentic self-expression, intimate self-disclosure in a climate of acceptance, and "getting things off one's chest." The psychological work dimension encompassed four constructs: (1) self-insight and progress, consisting of items related to making progress in relating to others, self-understanding, insight into and corrective reexperiencing of problems from primary family relationships, and becoming conscious of existential responsibility; (2) observational experiences, containing items relating to gaining awareness, discovering similarity with other group members, engendering hope by seeing the progress of other group members, and discovering the universality of problems; (3) getting directives, consisting of items related to getting suggestions from other group members, learning a method of problem resolution, and guidance from group therapist; and (4) interactional confrontation, consisting of items related to getting interpersonal feedback and expressing negative feelings toward others. These dimensions are also listed in Table 8.3.

As seen in Tables 8.1, 8.2, and 8.3, there is considerable overlap across the studies examining the construct validity of systems designed to study therapeutic factors. Unfortunately, none of the factor analytically derived systems has enjoyed widespread use. The study of therapeutic factors will probably not advance substantially until there is agreement among theorists and researchers about the underlying structure of the therapeutic factors. The state of affairs in therapeutic factors research is akin to that in personality research before the "Big Five" factors were established.

In addition to the lack of consensus about the dimensions that characterize therapeutic factors, there is an important methodological problem that hampers research in this area. As noted by Kenny, Mannetti, Pierro, Livi, and Kashy (2002), the data from studies of groups are nonindependent. *Nonindependence* means that group members who are in the same group are more similar (or dissimilar) to one another than are group members in different groups. For studies seeking to determine the underlying structure of therapeutic factors, this nonindependence among the scores of group members undermines the statistical assumption made in factor analysis that observations are independent. Unfortunately, even relatively sophisticated studies like Dierick and Lietaer's (2008) have not taken into account nonindependence in their statistical analyses.

Johnson et al. (2006) pointed out a related problem for studies in this area. Specifically, it is not clear if therapeutic factors are group- or individual-level phenomena. Most theorists suggest that therapeutic factors are group-level phenomena; however, therapeutic factors are invariably measured at the individual level, ignoring the nonindependence of data obtained in groups. There are statistical methods for analyzing therapeutic factors simultaneously at the individual and group levels. These statistical models make it possible to compare the group- and individual-level properties of scales measuring therapeutic factors. Unfortunately, these multilevel statistical tools are rarely used in group process research (for an exception, see Johnson, Burlingame, Olsen, Davies, & Gleave, 2005). We encourage researchers to use these new multilevel statistical techniques to examine the structure of therapeutic factors at both the group and individual levels.

Is Examining Perceived Helpfulness Enough?

A *therapeutic factor* has been defined as "an element of group-therapy that contributes to improvement in a patient's condition and is a function of the actions of the group therapist, the other group members, and the patient him or herself" (Bloch & Crouch, 1985, p. 4). This definition highlights the critical link between therapeutic factors and group member outcomes. Unfortunately, this link has received scant attention in the therapeutic factors literature. Finding that group participants' perceptions of certain therapeutic factors are more or less important than other therapeutic factors does not mean that the factors perceived as relatively more important are related to the participants' outcomes or amount of change from the group experience. To examine the important question of how therapeutic factors relate to group member outcomes, a researcher needs to examine the relationship between the level of endorsement of a therapeutic factor as helpful and a measure of group member outcome.

Cheung and Sun (2001) make an important distinction between what they term as "sustaining" and "beneficial" therapeutic factors (p. 295). They labeled the experiences perceived as important by members as "sustaining factors." Cheung and Sun contend that the absence of sustaining factors would be associated with disappointment, hindered group development, and member dropout. The therapeutic factors that are related to client outcomes were labeled as "beneficial factors." According to Cheung and Sun, beneficial factors are necessary for groups to achieve their purpose.

In a classic early study, Lieberman, Yalom, and Miles (1973) compared the therapeutic factors endorsed by the 20 group participants who experienced the most change from a personal growth group experience to the therapeutic factors endorsed by the 20 participants who experienced the least change from this experience. Both the group participants who experienced the most and those who experienced the least change endorsed the same set of sustaining therapeutic factors as most important: interpersonal learning (input), universality, guidance, and self-understanding. However, the beneficial therapeutic factors that distinguished the least and most changed participants were acceptance, advice, and family reenactment, which were all endorsed more frequently by the "high" learners, those group members who experienced the most change. The Lieberman et al. study is important because these authors showed that a high level of endorsement of a therapeutic factor was not necessarily related to the amount of participant change. Therefore, it is important to continue to examine the relationship between the endorsement of the therapeutic factors and group member outcomes. Unfortunately, Lieberman et al. discarded important information about the amount of group member change when they created categories of least and most changed instead of examining the amount of change displayed by all members of their population.

Cheung and Sun (2001) studied therapeutic factors for 120 group participants in a mutual aid organization for persons with emotional disturbance. In their study, the sustaining factors the group members perceived as most helpful were universality, self-disclosure, and instillation of hope. The beneficial therapeutic factors that were most highly correlated with member-rated outcome were support and catharsis. In the Dierick and Lietaer (2008) study, the four therapeutic factors that the clients rated as most helpful were the same factors that had the highest correlations with (1) satisfaction with personal result of sessions, (2) client perception of personal change, and (3) therapist perception of client change. These four factors were group cohesion, interactional confirmation, cathartic self-revelation, and self-insight.

Shechtman (2003) used Kivlighan et al.'s (1996) Group Helpful Impacts Scale (GHIS) to examine therapeutic factors in group-therapy for aggressive boys. The GHIS has four dimensions of therapeutic impact: other vs. self-focus, emotional awareness–insight, problem identification–change, and relationship–climate. For the aggressive boys in these groups, other vs. self-focus was the most frequently mentioned therapeutic factor, followed by problem identification–change. A stepwise regression revealed that both other-vs. self-focus and problem identification–change were related to outcomes in group treatment. Specifically, higher levels of self-focus and problem identification–change contributed positively to the prediction of change in aggressive behavior.

It is interesting that in the Lieberman et al. (1973) and Cheung and Sun (2001) studies, the factors perceived by the group members as most helpful were different from the factors that were correlated with client outcome. In the Shechtman (2003), and Dierick and Lietaer (2008) studies, however, the factors perceived as most helpful were identical to the factors that correlated with group member outcome. The difference in findings between the Lieberman et al. and Cheung and Sun studies, on the one hand, and the Shechtman, and Dierick and Lietaer studies, on the other hand, suggests that the sustaining and beneficial therapeutic factors distinction proposed by Cheung and Sun may need to be reevaluated. Alternatively, for some types of outcomes, perceptions of helpfulness of therapeutic factors may matter and for others they may be irrelevant.

Before the usefulness of this distinction can be evaluated, however, we need more studies that simultaneously examine both perceived importance and relation to outcome. We also need studies that use more sophisticated ways of operationalizing client outcome. Only the Lieberman et al. (1973) and Shechtman (2003) studies operationalized outcome as group member change from prior to the group experience through group completion and follow-up. Both the Cheung and Sun (2001) and Dierick and Lietaer (2008) studies operationalized group member change as one-time ratings of perceived change or satisfaction. This area of therapeutic factors research will not advance unless the experience of therapeutic factors is tied to more sophisticated ways of operationalizing group member outcomes. At a minimum, pre- and posttest designs should be used to assess group member outcomes. It would be helpful, however, if group researchers used more studies that examine change across time and not just pre- to postchange. In addition, it is important for studies examining group member change to account for nesting of group members within groups.

Are Therapeutic Factors an Individual or a Group Level Phenomenon?

In his review of group-therapy process research, Greene (2003) commented on the simplistic and nondynamic nature of most of the research examining therapeutic factors:

Yalom's (1975) original contribution was his brilliant, clinically rich depiction of
curative processes, but for the most part he stopped short of developing theories or models of the
interrelationships among these processes. He himself doubted the capability of research for developing
such models. To a significant degree, then, the research that followed has largely remained at a
descriptive level, failing to advance understanding of dynamic pathways. (p. 132)

It is now well known that a number of important group processes, such as cohesion and group climate, operate and should be investigated at both the level of the individual group member and the level of the group (Moritz & Watson, 1998). This is also true for theory and research concerning therapeutic factors. To date, however, all of the research on therapeutic factors has focused on either the individuals' perceptions of therapeutic factors or the therapeutic factors operating in the group as a whole. As noted,

much of the research on therapeutic factors in groups has examined the rank order of perceived helpfulness either within or between groups. Not a single one of these studies, however, has reported any measure of how consistently or inconsistently the helpfulness of the therapeutic factors was perceived by different group members across the group. For example, if one of the group members reports that self-disclosure was the most important event that happened for her in a group session, would the other group members be more or less likely to report that self-disclosure was also important for them in that session? Therefore, it is impossible to empirically determine how much of the variance in the perception of the therapeutic factors is at the level of the individual group member and how much is at the level of the group. Said another way, it is impossible to determine the consistency of therapeutic factors across the members of a group. Also, it is not clear if this exclusive focus on therapeutic factors as either an individual or a group phenomenon is due to (1) a lack of theory specifying how therapeutic factors operate at both the group and individual levels or (2) group researchers' lack of knowledge of multilevel statistical models that can be used to simultaneously explore therapeutic factors at both the group and individual levels.

Neglecting how therapeutic factors may operate at both the individual and group levels is problematic because research focusing on only a single level of analysis has at least two fundamental problems (Rousseau & House, 1994). First, single-level research can result in overgeneralization. This overgeneralization happens when researchers assume that a therapeutic factor examined at the individual level has the same relationships as a seemingly similar therapeutic factor examined at the group level. Second, single-level research underestimates cross-level effects. That is, studies of individuals' perceptions of therapeutic factors underestimate the effects of how the other group members may influence a group member's perception of the therapeutic factors. For example, does one group member's experience of catharsis in a session increase the likelihood that other group members will experience vicarious learning in that session? Not only does this research miss the interesting group aspects of group-counseling, but failing to account for group-level effects results in serious statistical problems (see Baldwin, Murray, & Shadish, 2005). Additionally, studies of therapeutic factors at only the group level underestimate how individual group members affect their group environment. We believe that expanding theory and research on therapeutic factors to include multilevel conceptualizations will help to develop a more meaningful and clinically useful approach to understanding how therapeutic factors operate in counseling and therapy groups.

To obtain a preliminary understanding of the relationship between individual and group member perceptions of therapeutic factors, we reanalyzed data from Kivlighan and Goldfine (1991). Thirty-six growth-group members, participating in six experiential groups, filled out critical incident forms (asking "What was the most important thing that happened in today's session? Why was it important to you?") that were rated on the 10 therapeutic factors dimensions described by Bloch et al.'s (1979) taxonomy. These therapeutic factor ratings were analyzed using the actor–partner interdependence model applied to groups.

In their paper "The Statistical Analysis of Data from Small Groups," Kenny et al. (2002) describe how Kashy and Kenny's (2000) actor–partner interdependence model can be applied to small-group research. In the actor–partner interdependence model, both the individual group member and the other group members affect the individual group member's outcome. The group effect is not the effect due to the *entire* group because the individual is also a member of the group, but rather it is the effect due to the *other* group members (Kenny et al., 2002). Therefore, the group effect is viewed as the mean score of the other members of the group. In terms of therapeutic factors, we were particularly interested in reciprocal actor and partner effects both within and across therapeutic factors. For instance, what is the relationship between an individual group member's endorsement of a therapeutic factor and the endorsement of therapeutic factors by the other group members?

Table 8.4 displays these reciprocal and cross-factor partial correlations for the therapeutic factors ratings from the Kivlighan and Goldfine (1991) study. All of the correlations are partial because the correlations between any two therapeutic factors (e.g., catharsis and group self-disclosure) have the other eight therapeutic factors partialed out. Therefore, the correlations in Table 8.4 represent the unique variance between the two variables. The coefficients in bold face on the diagonal indicate significant reciprocal relationships. Most of these correlations represent positive reciprocity (e.g., altruism and group altruism). For example, when the critical incident from a group member from a group session had a high level of altruism, the critical incidents

from the other group members from that session also had a high level of altruism. The correlations along the diagonal suggest that learning from interpersonal actions, universality, acceptance, altruism, guidance, and self-understanding were positively reciprocated in the group. Catharsis, however, was negatively reciprocated. When the critical incident from a group member from a group session had a high level of catharsis, the critical incidents from the other group members from that session had a low level of catharsis.

The bolded off-diagonal correlations represent significant cross-factor relationships. For example, when the critical incident from a group member from a group session had a high level of catharsis, the critical incidents from the other group members from that session had a high level of self-understanding (group) and vicarious learning (group). As another example, when the critical incident from a group member from a group session had a high level of self-disclosure, the critical incidents from the other group members from that session had a low level of learning from interpersonal actions (group) and a high level of altruism (group). These few examples illustrate the complex relationships among therapeutic factors. The individual experience of some factors (e.g., acceptance) is related to other group members experiencing the same factor. For other factors, an individual experience of a factor (e.g., catharsis) is related to the other group members experiencing a complementary factor (e.g., vicarious learning). As noted, we need more sophisticated theories that explain how the therapeutic factors operate interactively for individual group members and the group as a whole. In addition, group researchers need to use the sophisticated analytic models that will let them test more complex models of how therapeutic factors interact.

When Should Therapeutic Factors Be Measured?

Yalom et al. (1968) asked group members to complete the therapeutic factors Q-sort retrospectively, following termination of the group. Following the example of the early researchers, much of the research on therapeutic factors has assessed group members' perceptions following completion of their group experience. Yalom (1995), however, suggested that the importance of the different therapeutic factors varies as a function of a group member's time in the group or according to the stage of the group's development. Researchers have examined Yalom's hypothesis with both cross-sectional

Table 8.4 Similarity correlations examining individual group member and group perceptions of therapeutic factors from the Kivlighan and Goldfine (1991) study

	Catharsis	Self-disclosure	LIA	Universality	Acceptance	Altruism	Guidance	Self-understanding	Vicarious learning	Hope
Group catharsis	**-0.09***	0.00	-0.02	0.07	-0.05	0.04	-0.03	**0.08***	**0.16***	-0.03
Group self-disclosure	0.03	-0.01	**-0.11***	0.00	-0.03	0.05	0.00	-0.01	0.01	-0.02
Group LIA	-0.02	**-0.14***	**0.14***	-0.06	**-0.08***	-0.03	0.04	0.02	0.00	-0.01
Group universality	0.04	0.00	-0.04	**0.11***	0.02	-0.01	-0.01	-0.02	0.01	0.07
Group acceptance	-0.03	-0.03	-0.06	-0.00	**0.17***	0.04	-0.01	0.00	0.00	0.05
Group altruism	0.06	**0.08***	-0.04	0.00	0.05	**0.25***	0.05	-0.03	0.03	-0.05
Group guidance	-0.03	-0.01	0.01	-0.00	0.00	0.05	**0.08***	-0.00	0.03	0.02
Group self-understanding	**0.11***	0.04	0.03	-0.03	0.05	-0.02	0.02	**0.09***	0.00	-0.01
Group vicarious learning	**0.17***	0.03	0.02	-0.01	0.01	0.01	0.05	0.01	0.04	0.03
Group hope	-0.01	-0.02	-0.02	0.06	0.01	-0.04	0.03	0.00	0.04	0.02

LIA = learning from interpersonal actions.
*$P < 0.001$.

and longitudinal designs. In an early cross-sectional study, Butler and Fuhriman (1983) examined the endorsement of therapeutic factors as a function of time in group. They divided their group participants into subsamples representing their length of time in group treatment (6 months or less, 7 months to 2 years, and over 2 years). Butler and Fuhriman found that cohesiveness, self-understanding, and interpersonal learning were significantly related to length of time in group treatment.

Kivlighan and Mullison (1988) used a longitudinal design to examine the relationships among the stage of group development and members' endorsement of therapeutic factors in three interpersonal growth groups meeting for 11 weeks. Differences were also found between the early (first six) and late (second six) group sessions. There was an overrepresentation of universality in the early sessions and more of an emphasis on learning through interpersonal actions in the late sessions. Kivlighan and Goldfine (1991) conducted a similar study using the Group Climate Questionnaire (MacKenzie, 1983) to identify engaged, differentiation, and individuation stages of group development. As hypothesized, universality and hope decreased and catharsis increased across the three stages of group development. Contrary to Kivlighan and Mullison (1988),

learning through interpersonal action did not show an increase in importance during the later stages of group development.

All of these studies used unsophisticated models of the effects of time. Dividing the group experience into early and late segments or even using an instrument like the Group Climate Questionnaire to identify stages of group development misses the richness of the longitudinal data that could be captured when therapeutic factors are collected for each group session. There are interesting models that can be used to capture the richness of these longitudinal data. For example, Brossart, Patton, and Wood (1998) illustrated how Tuckerized growth curve analysis could be used to identify patterns of group climate development over time. Tuckerized growth curve analysis is a longitudinal statistical method that is useful for examining growth or change in longitudinal data.

Recently, Gold, Patton, and Kivlighan (2009) used a different statistical technique, multidimensional scaling, to identify profiles (change patterns) for how the endorsement of therapeutic factors varied across 26 group-counseling sessions. In this study, 36 growth-group participants filled out critical incident forms after each group session and these forms were rated along the affective, behavioral, and

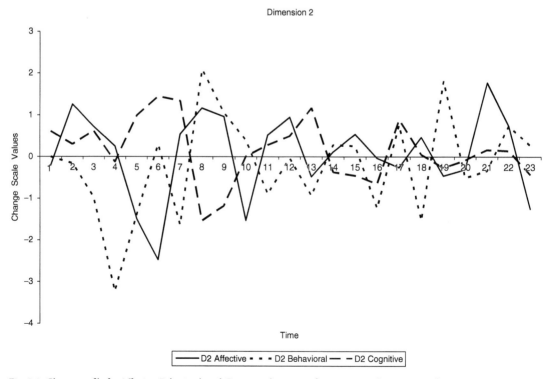

Fig. 8.1 Change profile for Affective, Behavioral, and Cognitive therapeutic factors across 26 group counseling sessions.

cognitive therapeutic factor dimensions described by Bloch et al. (1979). Multidimensional scaling change profile analysis (Ding, Davison, & Peterson, 2005) identified three change profiles for the affective, behavioral, and cognitive therapeutic factors across time. One of these change profiles is depicted in Figure 8–1. Gold et al. labeled this change profile "experiencing and reflecting." As seen in Figure 8–1, group sessions with a greater emphasis on affective factors were followed by sessions with a greater emphasis on cognitive and behavioral factors. This alternating pattern reoccurred across the 26 group sessions. The experiencing and reflecting change profile was the only profile related to a significant pre- to postgroup decrease in group member interpersonal problems.

Kivlighan et al. (2000) encouraged group researchers to pay more attention to how group processes change over time. Researchers examining therapeutic factors have paid some attention to changes over time but have not begun to use sophisticated analytic tools to examine the effects of time. It will also be important for group theorists to develop more sophisticated conceptualizations of how the therapeutic factors interact and change over time.

Are Therapeutic Factors Related to Other Group Process Variables?

For group counselors and therapists, studies examining variables such as group leadership or group climate and their relationship to group members' experiences of the therapeutic factors are among the most informative and practical. Unfortunately, there are few studies that examine these important relationships. MacKenzie (1983) suggests that group climate measures identify aspects of the group environment that "encourage compatible types of interpersonal events" (p. 159). Therefore, there should be a relationship between dimensions of group climate and the therapeutic factors that group members perceive as most helpful. Group climate is a particularly important dimension because theory (Yalom and Leszcz, 2005) and research (Kivlighan & Tarrant, 2001) view it as an important mediator between leader behavior and group helpfulness. Kivlighan et al. (1996) examined the relationship between MacKenzie's engaged, avoiding, and conflict dimensions of group climate and the emotional awareness–insight, relationship–climate, other vs. self-focus, and problem identification–change therapeutic factor dimensions. Only the problem definition–change dimension showed a significant

positive correlation with the engaged dimension of group climate. This suggests that when group members experienced an engaged and work-oriented group climate, they also experienced more problem definition and a greater sense of making changes.

In addition to group climate, group leader behavior also has been found to relate to which therapeutic factors are endorsed by group members. For example, Kivlighan et al. (1996) examined the relationship between Dies's (1983) technical and personal aspects of group leadership and the therapeutic factors endorsed by group members. Technical leadership consisted of group leader dominance, conditionality, and conceptual input, whereas personal leadership consisted of group leader affection, congruence–empathy, openness, and perceptiveness. The technical dimension of group leadership was related to the emotional awareness–insight and the problem definition–change therapeutic factors. The personal dimension of group leadership was related to the relationship and other vs. self-focus therapeutic factors. When group members saw their group leader as more dominant, conditional, and providing more conceptual input, they reported more emotional awareness–insight and greater problem definition–change. When group members saw their group leader as more affectionate, empathic, open, and perceptive, they reported more relationship impacts and self-focus.

The most sophisticated examination of the relationship between group leadership and therapeutic factors is the study by Lieberman and Golant (2002). They hypothesized that therapeutic factors would mediate the relationship between leader behaviors and group member outcomes for cancer patients in professionally directed support groups. Lieberman and Golant examined five dimensions of group leadership: evoke–stimulate (i.e., challenge, confront), meaning attribution (i.e., explain, summarize), support–caring (i.e., support, affection), executive–management (i.e., suggest procedures, norm setting), and use of self (i.e., reveal "here-and-now" experience, participate as a member). The therapeutic factors were support (i.e., belonging to and being accepted by the support group), disclosure (i.e., expressing true feelings), existential factors (i.e., confronting difficult problems and fears), cognitive–information (i.e., getting new understandings or explanations), attitudes and beliefs specific to the philosophy of the support group organization (i.e., discussing ways that I can participate in my fight for recovery), and membership (i.e., modeling myself after other group members). Lieberman and Golant found that meaning attribution and executive–management aspects of leadership were related to lower depression, fewer physical problems, and higher well-being; however, these relationships were fully mediated by the support and disclosure therapeutic factors. When group leaders provided support and empathy and helped members derive meaning from the group experience, these members reported more support and disclosure therapeutic factors, which in turn related to a better outcome from the group experience.

Examining how leadership and climate relate to the experience of therapeutic factors is a critical area for further study. The studies examined here provide some beginning information about how group leaders may influence the members' experience of the therapeutic factors. As with other therapeutic factors research, these studies suffer from data-analytic problems. Neither Kivlighan et al. (1996) nor Lieberman and Golant (2002) took into account the nested nature of their data; therefore, their results and conclusions need to be viewed tentatively.

Where Are We and Where Do We Need to Go?

The therapeutic factors that are the core concepts in Yalom and Leszcz's (2005) interpersonal group therapy approach have generated considerable clinical and empirical interest. As pointed out by Greene (2003), however, Yalom and Leszcz (2005) did not develop theories or models of the interrelationships among the therapeutic factors. In addition, research on therapeutic factors has not envisioned sophisticated models of the interactions among the therapeutic factors or the dynamic pathways connecting therapeutic factors to other group process variables and group member outcomes. With a few notable exceptions, Greene's conclusions about research on therapeutic factors is as valid today as it was in 2003.

It is clear there are a smaller number of fundamental dimensions that underlie the therapeutic factors described by Yalom and Leszcz (2005) and others, but there is not a consensus on the content of these fundamental dimensions. Until a consensus is reached, research on therapeutic factors will be hampered because it is difficult to compare results across studies. It is also clear that group members see some of the therapeutic factors as more important than others, but this ranked importance varies across studies. The affective insight, affective support, cognitive support, and cognitive insight typology described by Kivlighan and Holmes (2004) may prove to be a useful way to understand the differential rankings across the studies; but the validity of this typology can be determined only if future studies compare their results to these categories.

Therapeutic factors focus on group members' subjective perceptions of helpfulness. It is unclear, however, how these perceived helpfulness ratings or rankings are related to measures of outcomes. In some studies the factors with the highest ratings of perceived helpfulness are not the same factors that correlate with pre- to posttest change or are rated as beneficial (i.e., Lieberman et al., 1973). In other studies the therapeutic factors perceived as most helpful and those related to outcome are identical (i.e., Shechtman, 2003). Cheung and Sun's (2001) distinction between sustaining therapeutic factors (i.e., those perceived as most helpful by the group members) and beneficial therapeutic factors (i.e., those related to member outcome) may be a helpful heuristic for understanding this area, but more research is needed in this area. Finally, it is likely that both leader behaviors and group climate are related to group members' perceptions of therapeutic factors. To have confidence in specifying which leader behaviors are related to which therapeutic factors will require further research.

In reviewing the research on therapeutic factors (and at the risk of tragically dating ourselves) we are reminded of the old commercial: "Where's the beef?" In this case, we think the question is, "Where is *the group* in the research on therapeutic factors?" Specifically, the lack of focus on the group takes two forms. First, while researchers are obviously interested in the group, it is usually not examined explicitly. For example, we do not know if group members agree or disagree on their perceptions of the therapeutic factors measured in a group. This is because researchers have not examined measures of consensus or intermember agreement in their studies. In addition, researchers have not used analytic schemes that account for the nesting of group members within groups. Second, and more fundamentally, researchers have not examined important group interactional constructs like mutual influence (Kenny et al., 2002). For example, the research examining the relationship between therapeutic factors and outcomes takes an individual perspective, assuming that a group member's outcome is a function of the therapeutic factors that she or he finds most helpful. A group perspective on this question would examine mutual influence among the group members. A mutual influence perspective assumes (as do most practicing group counselors and therapists) that a group member's outcome is a function of the therapeutic factors that she or he finds most helpful and the therapeutic factors that the other group members find most helpful. We believe that research on therapeutic factors in groups will not advance until theorists and researchers start formulating and testing theories and models that have a group perspective.

References

Baldwin, S. A., Murray, D. M., & Shadish, W. R. (2005). Empirically supported treatments or Type I errors? Problems with the analysis of data from group-administered treatments. *Journal of Consulting and Clinical Psychology, 73,* 924–935.

Barlow, S. H., Fuhriman, A. J., & Burlingame, G. M. (2004). The history of group counseling and psychotherapy. In J. L. Delucia-Waak, D. A. Gerrity, C. R. Kalodner, & M. T. Riva (Eds.), *Handbook of group counseling and psychotherapy* (pp. 3–22). Thousand Oaks, CA: Sage.

Bloch, S., & Crouch, E. (1985). *Therapeutic factors in group psychotherapy.* Oxford: Oxford University Press.

Bloch, S., Reibstein, J., Crouch, E., Holroyd, P., & Themen, J. (1979). A method for the study of therapeutic factors in group psychotherapy. *British Journal of Psychiatry, 134,* 257–263.

Brossart, D. F., Patton, M. J., & Wood, P. K. (1998). Assessing group process: An illustration using Tuckerized growth curves. *Group Dynamics: Theory, Research, and Practice, 2,* 3–17.

Butler, T., & Fuhriman, A. (1983). Level of functioning and length of time in treatment: Variables influencing patients' therapeutic experience in group psychotherapy. *International Journal of Group Psychotherapy, 33,* 489–505.

Cheung, S., & Sun, S. Y. K. (2001). Helping processes in a mutual aid organization for persons with emotional disturbance. *International Journal of Group Psychotherapy, 51,* 295–308.

Crouch, E. C., Bloch, S., & Wanlass, J. (1994). Therapeutic factors: Interpersonal and intrapersonal mechanisms. In A. Fuhriman & G. M. Burlingame (Eds.), *Handbook of group psychotherapy.* New York: John Wiley.

Crowe, T. P., & Grenyer, B. F. S. (2008). Is therapist alliance or whole group cohesion more influential in group psychotherapy outcomes. *Clinical Psychology and Psychotherapy, 15,* 239–246.

Dierick, P., & Lietaer, G. (2008). Client perception of therapeutic factors in group psychotherapy and growth groups: An empirically-based hierarchical model. *International Journal of Group Psychotherapy, 58,* 203–230.

Dies, R. R. (1983). Clinical implications of research on leadership in short-term group psychotherapy. In R. R. Dies & K. R. MacKenzie (Eds.), *Advances in group psychotherapy: Integrating research and practice* (pp. 27–75). Madison, CT: International University Press.

Ding, C. S., Davison, M. L., & Peterson, A. C. (2005). Multidimensional scaling analysis of growth and change. *Journal of Educational Measurement, 42,* 171–192.

Fontao, M. I., & Mergenthaler, E. (2008). Therapeutic factors and language patterns in group therapy application of computer-assisted text analysis to the examination of microprocesses in group therapy: Preliminary findings. *Psychotherapy Research, 18,* 345–354.

Fuhriman, A., Drescher, S., Hanson, E., Henrie, R., & Rybicki, W. (1986). Refining the measurement of curativeness: An empirical approach. *Small Group Behavior, 17,* 186–201.

Gold, P. B., Patton, M. J., & Kivlighan, D. M., Jr. (2009). *The pattern of endorsement of therapeutic factors over time and change in group member interpersonal problems.* Unpublished manuscript. Department of Counseling and Personnel Services, University of Maryland.

Greene, L. R. (2003). The state of group psychotherapy process research. *International Journal of Group Psychotherapy, 53,* 130–134.

Hornsey, M. J., Dwyer, L., & Oei, T. P. S. (2007). Beyond cohesiveness: Reconceptualizing the link between group processes and outcome in group psychotherapy. *Small Group Research, 38,* 567–592.

Johansson, L., & Werbart, A. (2009). Patients' views of therapeutic action in psychoanalytic group psychotherapy. *Group Analysis, 42,* 120–142.

Johnson, J. E., Burlingame, G. M., Olsen, J. A., Davies, D. R., & Gleave, R. L. (2005). Group climate, cohesion, alliance, and empathy in group psychotherapy: Multilevel structural equation models. *Journal of Counseling Psychology, 52,* 310–321.

Johnson, J. E., Pulsipher, D., Ferrin, S. L., Burlingame, G. M., Davies, D. R., & Gleave, R. (2006). Measuring group processes: A comparison of the GCQ and CCI. *Group Dynamics: Theory, Research, and Practice, 10,* 136–145.

Joyce, A. S., Piper, W. E., & Ogrodniczuk, J. S. (2007). Therapeutic alliance and cohesion variables as predictors of outcome in short-term group psychotherapy. *International Journal of Group Psychotherapy, 57,* 269–296.

Kashy, D. A., & Kenny, D. A. (2000). The analysis of data from dyads and groups. In H. Reis & C. M. Judd (Eds.), *Handbook of research methods in social psychology* (pp. 451–477). New York: Cambridge University Press.

Kenny, D. A., Mannetti, L., Pierro, A., Livi, S., & Kashy, D. A. (2002). The statistical analysis of data from small groups. *Journal of Personality and Social Psychology, 83,* 126–137.

Kivlighan, D. M., Jr., & Goldfine, D. C. (1991). Endorsement of therapeutic factors as a function of stage of group development and participant interpersonal attitudes. *Journal of Counseling Psychology, 28,* 150–158.

Kivlighan, D. M., Jr., Coleman, M. N., & Anderson, D. C. (2000). Process, outcome and methodology in group counseling research. In S. D. Brown & R. W. Lent (Eds.), *Handbook of counseling psychology* (3rd ed., pp. 767–796). New York: John Wiley & Sons.

Kivlighan, D. M., Jr., & Holmes, S. E. (2004). The importance of therapeutic factors: A typology of therapeutic factors studies. In J. L. Delucia-Waak, D. A. Gerrity, C. R. Kalodner, & M. T. Riva (Eds.), *Handbook of group counseling and psychotherapy* (pp. 23–48). Thousand Oaks, CA: Sage.

Kivlighan, D., Jr., & Mullison, D. (1988). Participants' perception of therapeutic factors in group counseling: The role of interpersonal style and stage of group development. *Small Group Behavior, 19,* 452–468.

Kivlighan, D. M., Jr., Multon, K. D., & Brossart, D. F. (1996). Helpful impacts in group counseling: Development of a multidimensional rating system. *Journal of Counseling Psychology, 43,* 347–355.

Kivlighan, D. M., Jr., & Tarrant, J. M. (2001). Does group climate mediate the group leadership–group member outcome relationship: A test of Yalom's hypotheses about leadership priorities. *Group Dynamics: Theory, Research and Practice, 5,* 220–234.

Lieberman, M. A., & Golant, M. (2002). Leader behaviors as perceived by cancer patients in professionally directed support groups and outcomes. *Group Dynamics: Theory, Research and Practice, 6,* 267–276.

Lieberman, M. A., Yalom, I. D., & Miles, M. B. (1973). *Encounter groups: First facts.* New York: Basic Books.

MacKenzie, K. R. (1983). The clinical application of a group climate measure. In R. R. Dies & K. R. MacKenzie (Eds.), *Advances in group psychotherapy: Integrating research and practice* (pp. 159–170). Madison, CT: International University Press.

Moritz, S. E., & Watson, C. B. (1998). Levels of analysis issues in group psychology: Using efficacy as an example of a multilevel model. *Group Dynamics: Theory, Research, and Practice, 2,* 285–298.

Oei, T. P. S., & Browne, A. (2006). Components of group processes: Have they contributed to the outcome of mood and anxiety disorder patients in a group cognitive-behaviour therapy program? *American Journal of Psychotherapy, 60,* 53–70.

Rohrbaugh, M., & Bartels, B. D. (1975). Participants' perceptions of curative factors in therapy and growth groups. *Small Group Behavior, 6,* 430–456.

Rousseau, D. M., & House, R. J. (1994). Meso organizational behavior: Avoiding three fundamental biases. In C. L. Cooper & D. M. Rousseau (Eds.), *Trends in Organizational Behavior* (Vol. 1, pp. 13–30). London: John Wiley & Sons.

Roy, V., Turcotte, D., Montminy, L., & Lindsay, J. (2005). Therapeutic factors at the beginning of the intervention process in groups for men who batter. *Small Group Research, 36,* 106–133.

Shaughnessy, P., & Kivlighan, D., Jr. (1995). Using group participants' perceptions of therapeutic factors to form client typologies. *Small Group Research, 26,* 250–268.

Shechtman, Z. (2003). Therapeutic factors and outcomes in group and individual therapy of aggressive boys. *Group Dynamics: Theory, Research, and Practice, 7,* 225–237.

Shechtman, Z. (2007). How does group process research inform leaders of counseling and psychotherapy groups? *Group Dynamics: Theory, Research, and Practice, 11,* 293–304.

Shechtman, Z., & Gluk, O. (2005). An investigation of therapeutic factors in children's groups. *Group Dynamics: Theory, Research, and Practice, 9,* 127–134.

Shechtman, Z., & Halevi, H. (2006). Does ethnicity explain functioning in group counseling? The case of Arab and Jewish counseling trainees in Israel. *Group Dynamics: Theory, Research, and Practice, 10,* 181–193.

Sribney, C. L., & Reddon, J. R. (2008). Adolescent sex offenders' rankings of therapeutic factors using the Yalom Card Sort. *Journal of Offender Rehabilitation, 47,* 24–40.

Vasquez, M. J. T., & Han, A. L. (1995). Group interventions and treatment with ethnic minorities. In J. F. Aponte, R. Y. Rivers, & J. Wohl (Eds.), *Psychological interventions and cultural diversity* (pp. 109–127). Needham Heights, MA: Allyn & Bacon.

Yalom, I. D. (1975). *The theory and practice of group psychotherapy.* New York: Basic Books

Yalom, I. D. (1995). *The theory and practice of group psychotherapy* (4th ed.). New York: Basic Books.

Yalom, I., & Leszcz, M. *The theory and practice of group psychotherapy* (5th ed.). New York: Basic Books.

Yalom, I., Tinklenberg, J., & Gilula, M. (1968). *Curative factors in group therapy.* Unpublished manuscript.

Cohesion in Counseling and Psychotherapy Groups

Cheri L. Marmarosh *and* Stacy M. Van Horn

Abstract

Group cohesion is one of the most studied and theorized factors in group counseling. Despite the literature that describes cohesion, how it relates to group process, its mediating potential, and how it directly predicts change, we are still unsure exactly how cohesion operates in different groups and the best way to measure it. This chapter will review the history of group-therapy cohesion and the many challenges to both measuring and studying this illusive group factor. Research that has focused on how group cohesion relates to group process and outcome is summarized. The chapter concludes with recommendations for future research and the implications for clinicians who do group work.

Keywords: group cohesion, group counseling, group work, therapeutic factors, group climate

Introduction

During a course I was teaching on group psychotherapy, a student raised her hand and asked me to define the word *cohesiveness*. I thought it was a simple question at first and then found myself struggling to find the exact words to express a powerful emotional experience that I could easily recall. Despite comprehending the word and experiencing cohesion in many therapy and nontherapy groups, it was not easy to capture the experience with words alone. Similar to describing *love*, it was difficult to define and more complex than it appeared. I was relieved to find that Yalom and Leszcz (2005) also struggled to define *cohesion* and that it is a common challenge to simplify an experience that is powerfully felt from within. Group theorists who have written about cohesion have described it as feeling connected, a sense of "we-ness," or a feeling of being a part of something bigger than oneself.

Despite its elusiveness, group counselors have long recognized that a sense of cohesion in groups is one of the most important therapeutic factors (Yalom & Leszcz, 2005). According to Yalom and Leszcz (2005), cohesion is not only a necessary condition

for meaningful group work but also a prerequisite to change. Group-therapy researchers suggest that group cohesion not only has a direct relationship to change but also is a mediator of outcome, providing the necessary therapeutic environment that facilitates group work (MacKenzie, 1994; Ogrodniczuk, Piper, & Joyce, 2006; Tschuschke & Dies, 1994). Despite the many papers and studies that have examined the direct and indirect influences of cohesion in group counseling, we are still only beginning to scratch the surface behind this complex therapeutic factor. The current chapter reviews the many theoretical definitions of *cohesion*, describes how cohesion develops and influences group-therapy process, and explores how cohesiveness relates to outcome. In addition, the chapter discusses how cohesion is assessed, future research that is needed to provide a clearer understanding of the role of cohesiveness in group work, and how group counselors can apply this research to practice.

Group-Therapy Cohesion: What Is It?

Borrowing from social psychologists and group dynamic researchers (Festinger, Schachter, & Back,

1950; Hogg, 1992; Lewin, 1947), group therapists originally defined *group cohesion* as a mechanism or force that keeps members connected to the group. Yalom and Leszcz (2005) described group-therapy cohesion as the attractiveness of the group which engenders an emotional experience that is comparable to a sense of "we-ness" or "esprit de corps." Many others have emphasized the bond between group members (Joyce, Piper, & Ogrodniczuk, 2007); the commitment to the group, to the leader, and members (Piper, Marrache, Lacroix, Richardsen, & Jones, 1983); and the attraction to the group as a whole (Frank, 1957). In addition to the force of attraction to the group, many have emphasized how cohesion facilitates commitment to the group. Kottler (1994) described cohesion as "the glue that holds the group together that makes them safe enough environments in which to accomplish therapeutic work" (p. 64). Corey (1995) argued that, "Without a sense of 'groupness' the group remains fragmented, the members become frozen behind their defenses, and their work is of necessity superficial" (p. 111). Some have argued that commitment to the group is most indicative of cohesion when the group is struggling and members continue to sustain themselves in the group during times of stress and conflict (Budman, Soldz, Demby, Davis, & Merry, 1993). It appears that all definitions of *cohesion* emphasize the sense of connection group members have to their groups, which instills a sense of unity and safety even during time of conflict or duress. The definition of *cohesion* has evolved over time and has become more complex and more diffuse as it has incorporated more dimensions.

Over a decade ago, Bednar and Kaul (1994) reviewed the group-therapy literature and revealed disappointment in the lack of progress made with regard to defining and understanding cohesion in group therapy. The frustration has only increased, with recent group theorists wondering if the term *cohesiveness* should be completely replaced with alternatives that are more specific and less vague (Hornsey, Dwyer, Oei, & Dingle, 2009). Despite the controversy, group cohesion has been the focus of an expansive literature and has been emphasized in most group training texts (Yalom & Leszcz, 2005; Corey, 2008; Corey & Corey, 1997; Rutan & Stone, 2001). This chapter will review the history of group cohesion to tease apart how this once simple group factor, "force of attraction," developed into such an amorphous and emotionally charged group process.

Dion (2000) described the evolution of cohesion and the turning point where cohesion shifts from being mainly a unifying "force" to being the sum of different group members' feelings and attitudes about the group. Group cohesion becomes the result of many forces in the group such as the desire to be accepted by the group and members' identification with the group (Bloch & Crouch, 1985). Yalom and Leszcz (2005) described earlier items used to measure cohesion, and they include the sense of belonging in the group, the ability to disclose embarrassing things about the self in the group, and the desire for continued contact with the group. In other words, cohesion transforms from being focused on a unifying force of attraction to one's description of multiple qualities of the group that, when added together, create cohesion. Borrowing from anatomy, cohesion has developed from a single cell concept into a multicellular system.

In addition to the movement toward multiple factors that make up cohesiveness, earlier definitions were unidimensional and focused on the overall group (Cartwright, 1968; Evans & Jarvis, 1986; Yalom & Leszcz, 2005), while more recent definitions are multidimensional in nature and separate the relationship with the leader, group, and members (Piper et al., 1983). In a similar fashion, Bliese and Halverson (1996) discriminated between vertical and horizontal cohesion in work groups. They defined *vertical cohesion* as the relationship between the member and the leader, while *horizontal cohesion* is based on members' relationships with each other. This is an important distinction for group therapists because it raises the issue of the relationship with the therapist/leader and whether or not it is a part of cohesion.

In individual psychotherapy, the working relationship between the client and the therapist is described as the working "alliance" (Bordin, 1979). Marziali, Munroe-Blum, and McCleary (1997) argued that, in group therapy, the therapy alliance is also defined as the relationship between the member and the leader, while cohesion remains focused on the relationship between the member and the group. Burlingame, Fuhriman, and Johnson (2001, 2002) described a complex matrix of relationships within a group that make up cohesion that include how members relate to other group members, how members relate to the group as a whole, how members relate to the leaders, and how the leaders relate to the members and coleaders. In essence, group alliance and cohesion are viewed more as overlapping and less distinct constructs (Budman, Soldz, & Demby, 1989). To summarize, cohesion becomes more complex because it addresses the multiple relationships within the group. It is no longer one multicellular system but an organism with multiple systems functioning simultaneously. The resulting complexity increases the difficulty we face when measuring cohesion and the dilemma we encounter with regard to who rates cohesion and how it is determined, the level of analysis (Dion, 2000). We can measure cohesion from the individual's perspective or step back and assess it from the group's perspective.

Many studies have emphasized perceived cohesion and focus only on the specific members' ratings. Johnson et al. (2006) used multilevel analyses to explore group effects and found that there was little intragroup dependence when members completed the curative climate inventory to assess group cohesion. Simply stated, members' perceptions of how helpful the group was to them were not significantly influenced by the group, and the authors argued that cohesion may only need to be assessed at the individual level. Still others have emphasized the group aspect of cohesion and how it is best determined from an outside rater who is neutral to the group process and can observe the entire group (Budman et al., 1987). They also argue that group cohesion is a group phenomenon that requires a total group rating where individual perceptions need to be combined. Kipnes, Piper, and Joyce (2002) found support for this distinction when they studied group member–perceived group cohesion and outside-rater cohesion and found that there was no significant relationship between the two. They also found that group cohesion was not based on the sum of individual perceptions of cohesion. These authors suggested that there is a hierarchical structure to cohesion and that future researchers should include all perceptions of cohesion when studying group-therapy process and outcome.

In addition to the level of analysis influencing cohesiveness, the developing nature of cohesion is an important characteristic that has been described. Although cohesion has been defined as the sense of unity and force of attraction, Yalom and Leszcz (2005) argued that group-therapy cohesion does not just happen but is the result of resolved conflict and risk taking. They stated that "it would be a mistake to equate cohesiveness with comfort" (p. 63). If this is true, then measuring cohesion at the very beginning of group counseling may be problematic. It also means that there are developmental levels of cohesion: immature cohesion, based on perceived compatibility and similarity alone, and mature cohesion, based on exposing vulnerability, increased

risk taking, and sense of knowing members more intimately. Gladding (1991) described cohesion using Tuckman and Jensen's (1977) stage theory of group development. He argued that cohesion occurs during the norming stages of group development, after forming and storming have already taken place.

A similar distinction was raised by Dion (2000), who addressed the difference between socioemotional cohesion and task cohesion. *Socioemotional cohesion* is derived from interpersonal support and sense of community, while *task cohesion* is derived from productivity and the accomplishment of goals. In counseling groups, socioemotional cohesion is more likely to precede task cohesion, and it is possible that some groups develop cohesion that is solely based on emotional closeness without accomplishing group work. Kivlighan and Lilly (1997) studied cohesion over time and found that it was related to successful outcome when a specific pattern emerged. Similar to the alliance in individual psychotherapy, the pattern that was most related to positive outcome was a high-cohesion/low-cohesion/high-cohesion pattern. These findings support Yalom and Leszcz's (2005) notion that cohesion is not static, that it evolves over time in groups, and that it is strengthened after a period of stress or conflict in the group. It also raises an important issue with regard to the different types of cohesion that develop in groups and how these distinct types relate to group process and outcome.

Looking back on the literature, we see how our understanding of cohesion has evolved; it is no longer solely focused on the force of attraction to the group and is now a more complex group factor about which many theorists and researchers disagree. Although some may conclude that there is little cohesion in the cohesion literature (Bednar & Kaul, 1994; Dion, 2000), a significant number of empirical and theoretical papers have argued that it is a critical aspect of group dynamics and worthy of our continued attention. One of the most frequent recommendations in the literature is the need to clearly define cohesion and distinguish it from other therapeutic group factors (Burlingame et al., 2001, 2002; Johnson, Burlingame, Olsen, Davies, & Gleave, 2005).

Group Cohesion: Relationships to Group Alliance, Climate, Identity, and Universality
Group Cohesion and Alliance
Group cohesion, the sense of attraction of belonging in the group, has often been confused with different

aspects of group therapy that include the therapy alliance, group identity, group climate, and universality. Many theorists and clinicians compare cohesion in group therapy to the concept of the alliance in individual therapy. The therapy *alliance* in individual psychotherapy refers to the "working" relationship with the therapist and has been theoretically described as being the result of three components (Horvath & Greenberg, 1989). The alliance includes how the therapist facilitates the goals of treatment (goals), the perception that the therapist and patient are on the same page (task), and the sense that the therapist genuinely cares about the patient (bond). Marziali et al. (1997) argued that the group therapy alliance is defined as the relationship between the member and the leader, similar to individual therapy, while cohesion remains focused on the relationship between the member and the group. In essence, they see group alliance as being more distinct from cohesion in group treatment. The findings in the Gillaspy, Wright, Campbell, Stokes, and Adinoff (2002) study support this distinction; they found that bonds between members are most indicative of cohesion, while bonds between members and leaders are more indicative of alliance. Burlingame et al. (2001, 2002) endorsed a less differentiated perspective toward the alliance and included how members relate to the leaders and how the leaders relate to the members in their conceptualization of cohesion.

Measures of group alliance parallel the different definitions of alliance. Some studies have included a revised Horvath and Greenberg measure that changes the word *therapist* to *group leaders* to specifically assess the member alliance only to the leaders (Crowe & Grenyer, 2008). Other studies have used measures that assess an overall group alliance (California Psychotherapy Alliance Scales-Group [CALPAS-G], see Gaston & Marmar, 1991, 1993; Penn Group Alliance Scale, see Budman et al., 1989) by exploring both member–leader and member–member relationships in the group. The CALPAS-G has been used to assess cohesion in studies, and there appears to be more confusion between group cohesion and alliance to the group.

Despite the overlap between cohesion and group alliance, the research suggests that, although correlated, they are distinct aspects of group treatment and have different relationships to outcome. Studies have compared the alliance and cohesion in group therapy and have found contradictory findings. Some researchers have found that both alliance and cohesion contributed to outcome (Joyce et al., 2007; Piper, Ogrodniczuk, Lamarche, Hilscher, & Joyce, 2005; Marziali & Munroe-Blum, 1994; Taft, Murphy, King, Musser, & DeDeyn, 2003; vanAndel, Erdman, Karsdorp, Appels, & Trijsburg, 2003), that group alliance alone accounted for outcome (Lorentzen, Sexton, & Hoglend, 2004), that cohesion alone contributed to outcome (Crowe & Grenyer, 2008), and that neither related to outcome (Woody & Adessky, 2002). Although Crowe and Grenyer (2008) found that cohesion alone predicted outcome, they used the CALPAS-G to determine cohesion; and this measure has also been used to measure alliance in other studies (Lindgren, Barber, & Sandahl, 2008). One of the difficulties in sorting out the contradictory findings is the lack of consistent measures used to assess cohesion and alliance, the use of different group populations, and studies that compare different types of group interventions that include different lengths of treatment and different measures of outcome. Despite the different findings, it is safe to say that both cohesion and alliance are important relational factors in group work and are often, but not always, related to group process and outcome.

Cohesion and Group Identity

Yalom and Leszcz (2005) theorized that one way that cohesion facilitates changes in members is via the development of group identity and group-derived self-esteem. A number of clinical studies have supported this notion and have found a relationship between group cohesion and increases in self-esteem (Aviram & Rosenfeld, 2002; Lipman et al., 2007; Marmarosh & Corazzini, 1997). Hornsey, Dwyer, and Oei (2007) encourage group therapists to study the group-therapy identity and apply social identity theory (Tajfel & Turner, 1979) to group therapy. They even believe that this might resolve the many difficulties described with regard to studying cohesion.

Aviram and Rosenfeld (2002) applied social identity theory to group therapy for stigmatized adults. They found that increasing members' attachment to the group with fellow stigmatized members reduced stigma and enhanced self-esteem. Other studies have focused on helping members rely on their group-therapy identity to facilitate change (Marmarosh & Corazzini, 1997; Zabusky & Kymissis, 1983). Only one study was found that applied measures of both cohesion and group identity. Marmarosh, Holtz, and Schottenbauer (2005) tested Yalom (1995) assumption that cohesion facilitates group therapy–derived self-esteem for students in counseling center groups. Using path analyses, they found that cohesion led to collective self-esteem derived from the group identity. They also explored the distinctions between cohesion—the attraction to the group—and collective self-esteem—the concern with how others viewed the member, the perception that the group is a part of one's identity, and the sense that one is an important member in the group. Their findings revealed that group-therapy cohesion and collective self-esteem were highly correlated yet distinct constructs. Regression analyses revealed that cohesion leads to collective self-esteem but does not relate directly to depression. Only group members' perceptions of how others view their therapy group and their internalization of their therapy group accounted for significant variance in the prediction of depression. The path analyses with *cohesion* entered first revealed the best fit and supported Yalom and Leszcz's (2005) and Mullen and Copper's (1994) assumption that cohesion facilitates the development of a group atmosphere where curative factors can develop, such as group-therapy identities. Future research is needed to continue to explore the relationship among cohesion, therapy group identity, and different outcomes in diverse counseling groups.

Cohesion and Group Climate

Yalom and Leszcz (2005) argue that group cohesion facilitates an environment where members can take risks and engage in the therapy process. Cartwright (1968) highlighted the link between trust and cohesion in groups and argued that both provide the incentive to take risks and disclose in group therapy. Given the close relationship between cohesion and the group-therapy environment, distinguishing between cohesion and group climate is a challenge. While *cohesion* is the sense of unity and attachment to the group, *group climate* is described as the overall perception of the group environment. MacKenzie (1983) developed the widely used Group Climate Questionnaire, which includes three subscales—engagement, avoidance, and conflict. Using this measure, the group climate can be described as being open and freely self-disclosing (engagement), as being avoidant of the change process (avoidance), or as being hostile and lacking trust in the group (conflict). Johnson et al. (2005, 2006) compared measures of cohesion and group climate and found that there was a strong positive relationship between cohesion and engagement. Johnson et al. (2005) found a negative relationship between cohesion and avoidance as well as conflict. As expected, the less

the member rated cohesion, the more the member perceived the group as being avoidant, untrustworthy, and hostile. Findings suggest that groups with higher engagement scores also tend to have greater cohesion and better outcomes (Johnson, 2007). Future research is needed to gain a clearer understanding of how cohesion and group climate relate. It is possible that early cohesion facilitates trust in the group and allows for the engaged atmosphere. It is also possible that the leaders facilitate the group atmosphere and that engagement and ability to cope with conflict lead to increased cohesion (Yalom & Leszcz, 2005).

Group Cohesion and Universality

In addition to the importance of the group environment and the alliance, the sense of belonging and not being alone in the world is a significant curative mechanism in group counseling (Yalom & Leszcz, 2005). *Universality* has been defined as a sense of being connected with others who are also suffering and the experience of no longer being "unique in one's wretchedness" (Yalom & Leszcz, 2005, p. 6). According to Corey and Corey (1997), when group members allow themselves to be known in the group, they facilitate cohesion, which then leads to the awareness that one is not alone and that others also struggle with frightening problems, feelings, and thoughts.

Cohesion facilitates the group process that allows members to take risks and creates the space where members can hear about others' emotional experiences. Despite the differences in the content expressed in group, the underlying emotions experienced by members are often more similar than different. Studies have asked group members to rank order the curative factors that they felt most helped them (for review, see Butler & Fuhriman, 1983). When reviewing the literature, Butler and Fuhriman (1983) found that four of seven studies of group members in outpatient treatment rated cohesion as one of the most important factors. Of those four, only one study found that both cohesion and universality were rated as most valued. In other words, cohesion and universality were not always rated highly together by group members in outpatient treatment. The same was true of personal growth groups. One study found members who rated universality but not cohesion and another study found members who rated cohesion but not universality. Interestingly, both cohesion and universality were rated highly by hospitalized patients in group treatment. Future research is necessary to explore how cohesion facilitates universality and how universality relates to group outcome for different types of group members with different needs.

Group Cohesion, Alliance, and Group Climate

Recently, studies have started to explore the complex relationships among the group-process factors in order to identify the most important variables that facilitate treatment. Johnson et al. (2005) administered measures of cohesion, group climate, working alliance, and empathy to 662 group members from 111 counseling center and personal growth groups. As hypothesized, the researchers found a significant degree of overlap between the different aspects of the curative relationship (cohesion, alliance, empathy, and group climate). The authors noted that the correlations they found between these separate factors were as high as correlations found in subscales measuring the same construct. Despite the high correlations they found among the group-process variables, the authors suggested that these factors did not reflect a single group factor. Using exploratory analysis, the authors identified three aspects of group process that were less focused on who the relationship was with (group, member, leader) and more focused on the quality of the relationship. They found that aspects of cohesion, leader empathy, and engagement loaded onto a factor they defined as the "positive bonding relationship." The member to member and member to leader agreement on tasks and goals of therapy loaded onto a factor defined as the "positive working relationship," and member–group conflict and items indicating group member and leader deficiencies in empathy loaded onto a factor defined as the "negative relationship." In essence, they found that cohesion, engagement, and leader empathy were all important aspects of positive bonding in groups and that working aspects of the relationship were distinct (such as tasks and goals of the working alliance). These findings help us to clarify the distinctions between cohesion, group climate, and alliance. They also address the challenges of measuring group-process variables, specifically a group factor like cohesion.

The Measurement of Group-Therapy Cohesion

The multiple definitions of cohesion have led to a wide range of instruments designed to assess cohesion in group psychotherapy. In a review of the group psychotherapy relationship, Burlingame et al. (2002) found 23 different measures used to assess cohesion in 31 studies. We found a wide variety of cohesion measures used and describe them in Table 9.1 so that it will be easier to compare the many studies of cohesion that reveal discrepant findings. The decision to use a group cohesion measure would be overwhelming given the variety of measures available to clinicians. Measures range from member-reported perceptions of attraction to the group to observer ratings of the overall cohesion in the group.

The earlier definitions of cohesion that emphasize the unidimensional force of attraction of members to the group led to measures focused mainly on patient-rated attraction (Lese & MacNair-Semands, 2000; Lieberman, Yalom, & Miles, 1973; Moos, 1986; Schutz, 1966). One of the simplest measures is Lieberman et al.'s (1973) Curative Factors Scale, which assesses the 12 curative factors and includes two items to specifically assess cohesion. This measure is very similar to the Curative Climate Instrument (Fuhriman, Drescher, Hanson, Henrie, & Rybicki, 1986), which is derived from Yalom's (1995) theory and based on catharsis, insight, and cohesion. The cohesion subscale is designed to measure how helpful the group member perceives cohesion to be and includes five items that assess belonging, loneliness, acceptance, and liking of the group. The group cohesion subscale of the Group Environment Scale (Moos, 1986) includes nine true-or-false statements that assess group members' concerns for the group and involvement in the group, while the cohesion subscale of the Therapeutic Factors Inventory (Lese & MacNair-Semands, 2000) includes 12 items to assess cohesion. Evans and Jarvis's (1986) measure, the Group Attitude Scale, includes 20 items to measure members' degree of attraction to the group. All of these measures rely on member self-reporting and do not take into account the multiple relationships within the group. In essence, these measures do not include items or multiple subscales that appear to overlap as much with other group factors such as alliance and group climate.

More complex cohesion measures include subscales to determine the multiple components of cohesion. These measures are based on a definition of cohesion that includes multiple relationships within the group. The Group Atmosphere Scale (Silbergeld, Koeing, Manderscheid, Meeker,

Table 9.1 Commonly used measures of group cohesiveness

Measure of Group Cohesiveness	Complexity
Group Cohesion Questionnaire (Piper et al., 1983): 9-item self-report measure using a 6-point Likert scale to assess stimulation, commitment, and compatibility	Multidimensional
Group Attitude Scale (Evans & Jarvis, 1986): 20 items using a 9-point Likert scale to assess feelings about the group, self-report	One-dimensional
Cohesion Subscale of the Group Environment Scale (Moos, 1986): 9 true-or-false statements to assess involvement in group and concern for members, self-report	One-dimensional
California Psychotherapy Alliance Scales-Group (Gaston & Marmar, 1991, 1993): 24-item group version rated on 7-point Likert scale	Multidimensional
Group Cohesion Scale-Revised (Treadwell et al., 2001): 25-item self-report measure to assess cohesion in terms of communication, member retention, decision making, vulnerability, and goals	Multidimensional
Cohesiveness Questionnaire (Schutz, 1966) modified by Lieberman et al. (1973): 13-item measure assessing the attractiveness of a group and members' perception of belonging in the group	One-dimensional
Harvard Community Health Group Cohesiveness Scale (Budman et al., 1987): 5 scales to assess group-level cohesiveness, rated by outside observer via videotape/audiotape	Multidimensional
Cohesion Subscale of the Therapeutic Factors Inventory (Lese & MacNair-Semands, 2000): 99 items total to assess group members' perception of the factor in their group; 12 items to assess cohesion, self-report; 7-point Likert scale	One-dimensional
Therapeutic Factor Scale (Yalom, 1985): 60-item curative factor inventory, 5 items for each curative factor to determine rank order of factor importance	One-dimensional
Curative Factor Scale (Lieberman et al., 1973): 12 items to assess therapeutic factors, 2 items to assess cohesion	One-dimensional
Curative Climate Instrument (Fuhriman et al. 1986), based on Yalom's 12-factor theory: 14-item self-report, 4 items combined make up cohesion—belonging, acceptance, desire for contact, liking group	One-dimensional
Group Atmosphere Scale (Silbergeld et al., 1975): developed to measure systematically the psychosocial environment of therapy groups; 12 content subscales, each containing 10 true-or-false items, assess the consensual psychosocial environment; several of these serve as indicators of group cohesion and conformity	Multidimensional
Three Factor Group Questionnaire (Stokes, 1983): 3 subscales assess individual attraction, instrumental value, and risk-taking behavior	Multidimensional

& Hornung, 1975), the Three-Factor Group Questionnaire (Stokes, 1983), the Group/Member/Leader Cohesion Questionnaire (GCQ) (Piper et al., 1983), and the Group Cohesion Scale-Revised (GCS-R) (Treadwell, Laverture, Kumar, & Veeraraghavan, 2001) all include subscales to assess multiple components to cohesion. For example, the GCS-R is a 25-item measure designed to assess group interaction, member retention, vulnerability, and consistency between group and member goals. The GCQ developed by Piper and colleagues (1983) includes member-rated scales that rate cohesion to the group, to the leader, and to the other group members. The CALPAS-G (Gaston & Marmar,

1991, 1993) is a measure of group cohesion derived from a measure of psychotherapy alliance. The authors changed the wording of items so that ratings of "therapist" became ratings of "group." The four subscales include group commitment, working capacity, consensus regarding working strategy, and leader involvement and understanding. As one examines the subscales, it becomes clear that the definition of cohesion has started to include a wide range of aspects of group treatment and that the majority of measures continue to focus on the individual perception of group cohesion.

The Harvard Community Health Plan Mental Health Research Program developed an approach to studying group cohesion that emphasized the attraction to the group but did so without relying on member self-report. The Group Cohesiveness Scale (GCS) (Budman et al., 1987) relies on trained observer ratings of 30-minute segments of videotaped group sessions. The measure consists of five subscales that include ratings of withdrawal versus involvement, trust versus mistrust, disruption versus cooperation, abusiveness versus expressions of nurturance, and unfocused versus focused. The trained raters are provided the definitions of the subscales and then asked to rate the group based on the process in the sessions. No other cohesion measure reviewed focused on the overall group cohesion assessed by neutral trained observers. Kipnes et al. (2002) used the GCS in conjunction with the Piper et al. (1984) self-report measure. The authors found that there was no significant relationship between member-perceived cohesion and group-rated cohesion. In addition, members reported a decline in their perceptions of group cohesion as the group went on, while the outside raters perceived increased group cohesiveness. This study reveals the importance of using multitrait–multimethod procedures to assess the different definitions of cohesion in group-therapy research (Dion, 2000).

It also raises the question as to the level of analysis of group cohesion (Dion, 2000) and if it resides within the member, within the group, or both. Even though the majority of studies have relied on individual member perceptions of cohesion, it is possible to analyze the group effects. Using hierarchical linear modeling, it is possible to explore the impact of the group and assess aspects of group cohesion. Studies have recently been using multilevel analyses, and it has facilitated an understanding of the influence of the group individual effects (Joyce et al., 2007).

Group-Therapy Cohesion and Group-Therapy Process: Empirical Findings

The link between group cohesion and group performance has been widely debated and studied by group researchers (Evans & Dion, 1991; Mullen & Copper, 1994). Evans and Dion (1991) performed a meta-analysis of 16 studies to determine the relationship between cohesion and group performance in noncounseling/clinical groups. They concluded that it was safe to assume that there is a positive relationship between members' bond to the group and their performance in the group.

Exploring group performance in group counseling requires identifying important group processes and behaviors that are critical to group-treatment success. Group-therapy theorists argue that attendance, disclosure, and risk taking are important processes that facilitate the therapeutic work across diverse groups (Corey, 2008; Corey & Corey, 1997; Yalom and Leszcz, 2005; Rutan & Stone, 2001).

The relationships between group-therapy cohesion and these factors that influence group treatment have received empirical support. Researchers have found that group cohesion is related to a host of process variables that include group members' attendance (Connelly, Piper, DeCarufel, & Debanne, 1986; Ogrodniczuk et al., 2006), decision to drop out (Hand, Lamontagne, & Marks, 1974), disclosure in group (Tschuschke & Dies, 1994), participation in group (Budman et al. 1993), ability to tolerate conflict (MacKenzie, 1994), and satisfaction with the group (Perrone & Sedlacek, 2000). These studies have found that members who have a greater sense of cohesion tend to be more committed to the group treatment (Burlingame et al., 2001).

Commitment to treatment can be expressed in many ways. One of the hallmarks of commitment is attending group sessions and staying in treatment (Yalom & Leszcz, 2005). Barrett, Thompson, Chua, Crits-Christoph, and Gibbons (2008) reviewed the obstacles to understanding client attrition from individual psychotherapy. They report studies that indicate attrition rates as high as 50% dropout before the third session. Similar to individual treatment, dropping out of group therapy is a frequent problem (MacNair-Semands, 2002) and is extremely disruptive to group process and outcome (MacNair & Corazzini, 1994). Researchers studying cohesion found that it often sets the stage for necessary group processes to emerge such as reduced dropout and increased desire to continue in treatment (Butler & Fuhriman, 1983; Budman et al. 1989;

Connelly et al., 1986). In essence, low cohesion is related to less desire to continue in group therapy and more cohesion is related to increased desire to continue in treatment. It is possible that cohesion is related to satisfaction with treatment and, therefore, less desire to prematurely terminate. Perrone and Sedlacek (2000) found a positive relationship between group members' ratings of cohesion and ratings of satisfaction with the group. Connelly and colleagues (1986) studied differences between members who dropped out of psychodynamic groups (i.e., prematurely terminated) and those who continued to termination. They found that patients who dropped out of the group treatment felt less cohesion with the group compared to patients who completed the treatment. Hand et al. (1974) provided structured interventions to facilitate group-therapy cohesiveness for patients with agoraphobia. They found that groups where cohesiveness was emphasized had fewer dropouts compared to groups that did not have added attention to cohesion and that therapists reported an easier time facilitating these groups. McCallum, Piper, Ogrodniczuk, and Joyce (2002) also studied the differences between patients who dropped out of short-term group treatment for complicated grief and those who remained. These authors found no differences between patient-rated cohesion for members who dropped out and those who continued in treatment; however, they did find a significant difference in therapist-rated cohesion between patients who continued and those who dropped out. They found that therapists rated patients who dropped out as "being less likable, less desirable as friends, and having less significance as group members" compared to patients who continued in treatment (McCallum et al., 2002, p. 251).

Ogrodniczuk et al. (2006) studied how cohesion relates to attendance for patients in group therapy with personality disorders. These authors wondered if group cohesion influenced attendance for patients who may have significant interpersonal difficulties. The authors found that cohesion did mediate the effect of interpersonal stress on attendance for patients in supportive group treatment but not interpretive group treatment. In essence, patients in the supportive therapy groups, who felt less interpersonal distress, also felt less connected to the group and had poorer attendance compared to those who reported interpersonal distress. It appears that self-reported interpersonal distress is important to the development of cohesion in supportive group therapy with patients who have avoidant, dependent, and borderline personality disorders. The authors

wondered if supportive therapy groups, compared to interpretive groups, were less able to stimulate the engagement of group members with personality disorders who reported less interpersonal distress. They suggested that interpretive group treatments for patients who minimize interpersonal distress and meet criteria for a personality disorder may be better at facilitating cohesion and therefore keeping patients in treatment.

Once patients come to group therapy, it is critical to have them share their feelings and thoughts with the group. It has been argued that meaningful disclosure is an integral component of group therapy and facilitates trust, intimacy, and risk taking (Corey, 2008; Yalom & Leszcz, 2005). Budman et al. (1993) developed a study to explore what types of behaviors related to cohesion, and they relied on trained raters and actual transcripts from time-limited psychotherapy groups. They asked trained clinicians to rate the group cohesion and graduate students to rate the interpersonal behaviors of group members and found that ratings of cohesion were related to the overall number of members' statements made during the early and middle phases of therapy. They also found that early disclosure of outside issues was related to more cohesive interaction, while too much focus on the therapist early on in treatment often indicated less cohesion. Tschuschke and Dies (1994) reported similar findings when they studied patients in two long-term psychoanalytic groups and found a positive relationship between group-therapy cohesion and self-disclosure. They found that meaningful disclosure was also related to other group members providing frequent and meaningful feedback to each other and facilitated the group process. They found that cohesion was most important during the first 30 minutes of a therapy session. The authors suggested that even though the two groups developed different climates that facilitated change, cohesion was a critical element in both groups.

When group members disclose, it is critical for the leaders and members to be able to cope with the anxiety, conflict, and emotions that are revealed or surface. Wheelan (1994) described how group cohesion is important in the beginning of the group because it allows members to feel safe enough to challenge one another and progress through conflict. The author suggested that the "we-ness" associated with the experience of cohesion is strengthened by the intimacy that results from resolving conflict and taking risks together. MacKenzie (1994) found empirical support that cohesion facilitates members' abilities to tolerate the emotions that surface during conflict in group therapy. Castonguay, Pincus, Agras, and Hines (1998) studied group members who were participating in cognitive-behavioral treatment for binge-eating disorder. They studied factors related to the most improvement and found that those members who improved the most rated the middle of therapy to be negative and the early phase of group to be supportive. The authors concluded that the cohesive nature of the group early on allowed the group members to endure the conflict and challenges that are important aspects of successful group experiences. Budman, Simeone, Reilly, and Demby (1994) argued that cohesion is required to facilitate the group process and is even more important in short-term therapy groups, where there is less time to foster a sense of safety within the group.

One of the most important aspects of group-therapy cohesion is how it facilitates the other curative factors in group therapy (Yalom & Leszcz, 2005). According to Yalom and Leszcz (2005), cohesion creates the safety and security required to challenge interpersonal maladaptive patterns and to engage in curative factors such as catharsis, recapitulation of the family, and instillation of hope. Although Yalom (1995) argued that cohesion was the primary curative factor, group-therapy researchers have not fully studied if cohesion is truly necessary for other curative factors to evolve in group treatment. Marmarosh et al. (2005) developed one study to explore Yalom's (1995) notion that group-therapy cohesion facilitated group-derived hope and self-esteem. Using path analyses, the authors demonstrated that group cohesiveness was the primary group factor that directly related to group-derived self-esteem and hope for the self but was not directly related to self-reported depression.

Most group therapists will acknowledge that one of the most important aspects of group process involves not only what happens with group members and the group as a whole but also what happens with the leaders. Burlingame et al. (2001, 2002) described how leaders can facilitate group cohesion by modeling behavior, being present and emotionally engaged, and managing their own emotional reactions. They do not address how the group's cohesion influences the leaders' reactions to the group and countertransference. A group that is cohesive is one that can engender positive feelings in the leader. Hand et al. (1974) found that groups that received structured training were not only more cohesive but also rated as more easy to run by therapists. These findings

were similar to McCallum et al.'s (2002) findings that therapists rated members who dropped out as less important to the group and less likable. In essence, the members who were less engaged in the group engendered negative feelings in the leader. One wonders how groups that struggle with cohesion influence the leader over time. It is possible that groups that are detached and disengaged influence the group leaders' commitment to the group, reactions to group members, interventions used, and even relationship with their coleaders.

Although there is much evidence linking cohesion to therapy process, there are studies that have found no significant relationship. Completing outside homework is one task that reflects members' engagement in the treatment but was not found to be related to members' cohesion. Woody and Adessky (2002) studied the relationship between cohesion, alliance, and homework compliance over the course of cognitive-behavioral group therapy for patients with social phobia. They found that there was no significant relationship between member-rated cohesion and therapist-rated homework compliance. They also found that homework compliance had no relationship to treatment outcome. The authors suggested that the bond between group members may not have been emphasized during the cognitive-behavioral interventions (it remained static over the course of treatment) that focus on cognitive restructuring and in vivo exposure within the group to personally relevant social situations. Continued research is needed to fully understand the importance of cohesion in different types of counseling groups and how cohesion relates to a variety of group behaviors that include disclosure, engagement, violating group rules, and completing homework. Not only is it important to study how cohesion influences the group process, but it is also important to explore how it relates to outcome.

Group-Therapy Cohesion and Outcome

According to reviews of the literature, the majority of studies have found that group-therapy cohesion has been positively linked to group-therapy outcome (Bednar & Kaul, 1994; Burlingame et al., 2001). However, a few studies have failed to replicate these findings and do not support the universal link between cohesion and treatment success. Understanding the mixed findings is challenging because many of the studies use different measures of cohesion, compare different types of group interventions with different populations, and rely on diverse outcome measures that range from interpersonal symptoms to measures of diastolic heart rate. Table 9.2 includes many of the studies that have empirically tested the relationship between cohesion and outcome and describes the populations studied, the measures used to assess group cohesion, and the findings. Because the definition of cohesion has remained a matter of debate (Bednar & Kaul, 1994; Kaul & Bednar, 1986; Johnson et al., 2005; Hornsey et al., 2009), studies that focus on similar constructs, such as group climate, alliance, and empathy, but do not include a measure of cohesion are not included in this review.

If group cohesion is related to dropout rate, attendance, affect regulation, and commitment to treatment, it makes sense that it relates to treatment outcome. A variety of studies using different types of group therapy with members struggling with different issues have supported this relationship. The most convincing research has utilized experimental designs to empirically study the impact of cohesion reinforcement on treatment outcome. These studies truly facilitate our understanding of how group leaders' emphasis on cohesion relates to outcome because we can statistically compare those groups

Table 9.2 Outcome studies using validated measures of cohesion

Author(s)	Population Studied	Measure of Group Cohesiveness Used	Group Process	Group Outcome
		Positive Findings		
Liberman (1971)	Patients in group treatment: unclear what type of group therapy	Sociometric questionnaire to assess liking of the group; interaction process analysis (Bales, 1950) score "live" ongoing group behavior to assess cohesion		Cohesion intervention facilitated greater changes in members' MMPI and personality dimensions compared to members in the comparison group
Hand et al. (1974)	Patients with agoraphobia		Some groups structured to increase social cohesion during exposure in vivo; these groups had fewer dropouts; therapists found it easier to run cohesive groups	At term, all groups showed improvement on phobic scale, structured groups showed significantly more improvement at 3–6 months' follow-up on phobia and goal improvement
Etringer et al. (1984)	Smokers who were trying to quit	Hill interaction matrix (Hill, 1965)	Enriched cohesiveness in the intervention for some groups; this increased their level of cohesiveness	Increasing cohesiveness increased the short-term effectiveness of satiation and nicotine fading; it also influenced abstinence
Braaten (1989)		Group Atmosphere Scale (Silbergeld et al., 1975)		The affiliation subscale was correlated to outcome; overall cohesion was not
Tschusche & Dies (1994)	Clients with personality disorders			Cohesion related to long-term outcome
Marziali et al. (1997)	Patients with borderline personality disorder in 30 sessions of group treatment	Group Atmosphere Scale (Silbergeld et al., 1975)		Found a relationship between cohesion and objective measure of outcome

(continued)

Table 9.2   Outcome studies using validated measures of cohesion (*continued*)

Author(s)	Population Studied	Measure of Group Cohesiveness Used	Group Process	Group Outcome
Taft et al. (2003)	Men in treatment for domestic violence	Cohesion subscale of the Group Environment Scale (Moos, 1986)		Cohesiveness at sessions 4 and 12 predicted lower physical and psychological abuse at term and 6-month follow-up
Lindgren et al. (2008)	Patients with depression who are in psychodynamic therapy groups	California Psychotherapy Alliance Scales-Group (Gaston & Marmar, 1991, 1993)		Alliance to the group as a whole at session 3 was not related to outcome; alliance to the group as a whole later in treatment (when focusing on interpersonal problems) was predictive of outcome
Taube-Schiff et al. (2007)	Patients with social phobia in CBT groups	Group Cohesion Scale-Revised (Treadwell et al., 2001)	Using HLM, found that group cohesiveness should be assessed as an individual variable rather than at group level	Changes in cohesion related to changes in outcome—improvements in social anxiety symptoms, general anxiety, depression, and functional impairment
vanAndel et al. (2003)	Cardiac patients in CBT group	Group Cohesion Scale-Revised (Treadwell et al., 2001)		Cohesion contributed to prediction of posttreatment systolic and diastolic blood pressure and quality of life
Lipman et al. (2007)	Low-income, single mothers in 10-week support group	Group Atmosphere Scale (Silbergeld et al., 1975)	Did find differences between groups, some more cohesion than others	Total score related to improved self-esteem but not changes in mood, social support, or parenting
Hilbert et al. (2007)	Patients with binge-eating disorder in CBT and IPT groups	Group Attitude Scale (Evans & Jarvis, 1986)	People with greater interpersonal problems and general psychopathology perceived less cohesiveness	Greater interpersonal problems and cohesiveness were central to determining outcome
Crowe & Grenyer (2008)	Patients with depression in 16 sessions of dynamic group therapy	California Psychotherapy Alliance Scales-Group (Gaston & Marmar, 1991, 1993)		Cohesiveness subscales were related to outcome: PWC was related to changes in BDI, WSC was related to satisfaction & therapy success, MUI was related to therapy success

Table 9.2 (*continued*)

Author(s)	Population Studied	Measure of Group Cohesiveness Used	Group Process	Group Outcome
		Negative Findings		
Roether & Peters (1972)	Patients in group treatment for sex offenses			Cohesion was not related to outcome and those with greater cohesion had greater rates of reoffense
Kipnes et al. (2002)	Patients in short-term dynamic group treatment for complicated grief	Group Cohesion Questionnaire (Piper et al., 1983), Harvard Community Health Group Cohesiveness Scale (Budman et al. 1987)	Group cohesiveness should be assessed using individual- and group-level analyses	Neither related to symptom outcome, either session by session or averaged
Gillaspy et al. (2002)	Residential patients with substance abuse		Cohesiveness was reinforced	Neither alliance nor cohesion was related to outcome
Woody & Adessky (2002)	Patients with social phobia	Group Attitude Scale (Evans & Jarvis, 1986)		Cohesiveness was not related to outcome
Lorentzen et al. (2004)	Patients in long-term analytic group treatment in private practice	Group Cohesion Questionnaire (Piper et al., 1983)	Patients with fewer symptoms rated greater cohesiveness to leader early in treatment, cohesion and alliance were not strongly correlated	Early ratings of cohesion did not predict change in symptoms and interpersonal problems, patient alliance was the better predictor of outcome
Oei & Browne (2006)	Patients in CBT groups for mood disorders	Group Cohesion Questionnaire (Piper et al., 1983)		Cohesion was not related to outcome
Joyce et al. (2007)	Patients with complicated grief in short-term group therapy	Group Cohesion Questionnaire (Piper et al., 1983)	Alliance (rated by therapist and patient) was correlated with patient-rated commitment and compatibility	Overall cohesion was not significantly correlated with outcome, ratings of member's compatibility in the group by fellow members was the only aspect of cohesiveness predictive of outcome

MMPI, Minnesota Multiphasic Personality Inventory; CBT, cognitive-behavioral therapy; IPT, interpersonal psychotherapy; HLM, hierarchical linear modeling; PWC, patient working capacity; BDI, Beck Depression Inventory; WSC, working strategy consensus; MUI, member understanding and involvement.

that receive the intervention to groups that do not. Liberman (1971) studied the impact of a cohesion-reinforcement intervention with patients treated in group therapy. Members in the cohesive group made greater improvements than those in the matched comparison group. Hand et al. (1974) found that members with agoraphobia in cognitive-behavioral therapy (CBT) groups where cohesiveness was emphasized (the group leader used interventions to increase and foster group members' connection to one another) felt more helped by the groups compared to those in groups where cohesion was not emphasized. Interestingly, they found that there was no significant difference in outcome between the cohesion group and the noncohesion group at termination, but a significant difference between these groups was detected months following the end of treatment. Those members who were in the more cohesive groups continued to improve even after treatment ended. More importantly, members in the groups that did not receive the cohesion intervention began to relapse after termination. Teasdale, Walsh, Lancashire, and Mathews (1977) replicated these findings, but they found less significant differences.

Cohesion reinforcement has also been applied to group interventions to treat addictions, specifically smoking addictions (Etringer, Gregory, & Lando, 1984). Etringer et al. (1984) developed two treatments for group members, one that focused on a satiation-based intervention and one based on enriched cohesiveness. The cohesiveness intervention included exercises that increased group interactions, encouraged group disclosure, and included watching videotaped modeling of cohesive interactions. The results revealed that members who received the cohesion intervention in behaviorally oriented groups had better outcomes than members in the satiation group. These members were more abstinent 2 months posttermination.

In addition to fostering cohesion via interventions within the group, Marmarosh and Corazzini (1997) studied the impact of enhancing members' group-therapy identity outside of the therapy session. Group members in the experimental condition were given cards to carry with them that symbolized their group identity and instructed to rely on the group during times of duress—to carry the group in their pockets. The results revealed that group members who received the intervention had increased personal and group-derived self-esteem compared to those who did not receive the intervention.

In addition to studying the impact of cohesion-focused interventions, group therapists have studied the relationship between group cohesion during treatment and group outcome and found a relationship between group cohesion and symptom reduction (Braaten, 1989; Flowers, Booraem, & Hartman, 1981; Marziali et al., 1997). One of the first studies to explore cohesion and outcome relied on external raters of both cohesion and improvement and found a positive correlation between cohesion and change (Flowers et al., 1981). That study found that the more attentive group members were to each other, the more positive changes they made. Although this study demonstrated the relationship between cohesion in group and symptom change, the authors relied on a simple measure of cohesion—the extent to which the members made eye contact while speaking to each other.

Taft et al. (2003) found that member-rated group cohesion, rated early and late in treatment, was related to less physical and emotional abuse after treatment for men who were in group therapy for domestic violence. Crowe and Grenyer (2008) focused on the outcome of brief dynamic group therapy for patients with major depression. They compared group cohesion and therapy alliance as predictors of change in symptoms and found that member-rated "alliance" at the fourth session did not predict changes in symptoms. Aspects of cohesion, as measured by the CALPAS-G (Gaston & Marmar, 1993), were related to subjective reports of therapy success. The authors found that the more the group members perceived being able to work well together to achieve therapeutic goals, the less depressive symptomatology they reported at termination. Similar findings were reported by Lindgren et al. (2008), who examined alliance to the group as a whole using the CALPAS-G to explore the relationship between cohesion and outcome in short-term dynamic group therapy with depressed patients. They found that the level of alliance to the group at the mid-point of treatment was correlated to outcome, but they did not find any support for the growth of alliance being related to outcome or a relationship between third session–rated cohesion and outcome.

In addition to brief dynamic group therapy, studies have found support in extremely different types of group treatments—long-term psychoanalytic treatments, time-limited CBT groups, and support groups. Tschuschke and Dies (1994) found that the level of cohesion in the second half of long-term psychoanalytic group treatment for inpatients was correlated with treatment outcome. They also found that patients who made significant progress in treatment had rated strong group cohesion after the first few sessions. Taube-Schiff, Suvak, Antony, Bieling, & McCabe (2007) studied cohesion at the mid-point and termination of CBT for social phobia. They found that cohesion ratings increased over time and were related to improvements in social anxiety symptoms, in addition to improvements in general anxiety, depression, and overall functioning. In addition to studying CBT for social phobia, researchers have found support for the relationships between cohesion and outcome in CBT and interpersonal group therapy for binge-eating disorder (Hilbert et al., 2007). Using a sophisticated analysis, Hilbert et al. (2007) found that decreased cohesion at the sixth session of therapy predicted long-term nonresponsiveness to treatment. The authors also used several measures of group cohesion in their study—the CALPAS-G, the Group Attitude Scale (Evans & Jarvis, 1986), and the Group Climate Questionnaire (MacKenzie, 1981). With the growing application of group therapy for patients with medical conditions, group-therapy researchers have found relationships between group cohesion and effective outcome for patients who recently underwent coronary angioplasty and were in CBT groups to reduce coronary risk (van Andel et al., 2003). After the fifth and tenth sessions, the Group Cohesion Questionnaire (Piper et al., 1983) was administered, and hierarchical regression revealed that bonding with the group members contributed to the prediction of systolic and diastolic blood pressure and quality of life.

Prevention groups that provide support to at-risk populations have also benefitted from the cohesion gained from belonging to a group (Lipman et al., 2007). Lipman et al.'s study focused on the influence of cohesion for low-income, single mothers participating in 10-week supportive, psychoeducational groups. Unlike some studies that emphasized symptom reduction alone, the researchers also included measures of social support, self-esteem, and parenting skills. The Group Atmosphere Scale (Silbergeld et al., 1975) was used to assess cohesion and was administered only posttreatment. Analyses revealed that the total Group Atmosphere Scale score was significantly related to improved self-esteem, but it was not related to changes in mood, social support, or parenting skills.

Overall, the findings reveal that group cohesion, even when assessed by different measures, is related to outcome in diverse group populations with different types of interventions. Despite the different methodologies and patient populations, the findings indicate that group cohesion measured later in treatment, not at the very early phases, can be predictive of many different measures of group outcome that include improved self-esteem, decreased depression, decreased social phobic symptoms, and even a healthier heart rate. Although these findings lend strong evidence of a positive relationship between cohesion and outcome, several studies have not supported this relationship (Gillaspy et al., 2002; Lorentzen et al., 2004; Oei & Browne, 2006; Woody & Adessky, 2002).

Unlike Taube-Schiff et al.'s (2007) findings that cohesion ratings increased over time and were related to improvements in social anxiety symptoms, Woody and Adessky (2002) found that cohesion was relatively lower compared to comparable studies, did not increase over time, and did not relate to reduced social phobic symptoms. Taube-Schiff et al. (2007) suggested that one of the differences between the studies is the measure of cohesion used. Woody and Adessky used a unidimensional measure of cohesion that assessed only members' attraction to the group (the Group Attitude Scale, see Evans & Jarvis, 1986), while Taube-Schiff et al. (2007) used Treadwell et al.'s (2001) measure that assesses multidimensional aspects of cohesion that may be more relevant to social phobia. There are also many other possible differences between these studies. One possibility is that the leaders in the Woody and Adessky (2002) study did not facilitate group cohesion as effectively. In their study, group members reported lower cohesion than in comparable studies with no increases over time, and they found that patients in the groups decreased compliance with homework over time. In addition, these researchers did not find any relationship between alliance and outcome. It is possible that the leaders did not create the same cohesive environment in these groups and, despite the effectiveness of the cognitive-behavioral strategies to reduce social phobic symptoms, the group relationship components of the treatment were not main contributors.

In addition to these inconsistent findings using groups to treat social phobia, Lorentzen et al. (2004) did not find the relationship between cohesion and outcome in long-term psychoanalytic group treatment that Tschuschke and Dies (1994) found. Lorentzen et al. (2004) studied patients in private practice groups and administered the Group Cohesiveness Questionnaire (Piper et al., 1983) every month of treatment. The authors used the mean of the cohesion ratings for the first 2 months of the treatment, and they found that the members' ratings of cohesion to group and to leader did not predict change in symptoms or interpersonal problems. Although both studies focused on long-term analytic groups, Tschuschke and Dies (1994) studied more severely disturbed patients who were hospitalized. Studies have shown that patients with more severe mental illness rate cohesion as one of the most curative aspects of the group compared to higher-functioning patients (for review, see Butler & Fuhriman, 1983). It is difficult to compare the findings given the different patient populations and methods used to calculate cohesion, but the results may help us tease apart how cohesion relates to outcome in analytic group therapy with higher-and lower-functioning patients.

Two major studies found a relationship between cohesion and symptom reduction in group treatment for members with depression (Crowe & Grenyer, 2008; Lindgren et al., 2008); however, Oei and Browne (2006) did not find a significant relationship between cohesion and outcome in their study. One of the significant differences between these studies was the type of time-limited treatment being used. Oei and Browne studied CBT groups, while the other two studies focused on brief dynamic group treatment. These findings may indicate the different role that cohesion plays in different types of group treatment for the same disorder, in this case depression. Cohesion may be a significant factor in groups where interpersonal process and dynamic issues are the focus compared to groups were cognitive-behavioral strategies and individual change processes are emphasized.

One population studied that has consistently challenged the direct relationship between cohesion and outcome has been patients in time-limited group therapy for complicated grief. Two studies have revealed no significant relationship between member-rated cohesion and outcome. Kipnes et al. (2002) studied 154 adult outpatients who were in 12-session short-term therapy groups for complicated bereavement. The authors administered two measures of cohesion, the member-rated Group Cohesiveness Questionnaire (Piper et al., 1983) and the observer-rated Harvard Community Health Group Cohesiveness Scale (GCS) (Budman et al. 1987). Similar findings were reported by Joyce et al. (2007), who studied patients in both interpretive and supportive group therapy who had endured a loss and who met criteria for pathological mourning. The authors also used the Group Cohesiveness Questionnaire (Piper et al., 1983) at sessions 4, 8, and 12 and found that the relationship between the member-rated cohesion variables and measures of outcome did not reach significance. They did find one significant positive relationship between therapists' ratings of patient compatibility in the group and general symptom improvement. McCallum et al. (2002) also found that therapist-rated cohesion, not patient-rated cohesion, was negatively related to dropout in short-term groups for complicated bereavement.

The authors speculated that the time-limited nature of the groups may have inhibited the development of cohesion that would have functioned as a curative mechanism directly related to outcome, although they described the group as very connected with a high level of disclosure early on. It is possible that, in highly cohesive groups, the therapist is more able to detect subtle differences that relate to group process and outcome compared to the members. This raises an important issue in the literature that has not received much attention, the distinction between rapid immature cohesion found early in group process and the more mature cohesion found later in group treatment after conflict and true intimacy have developed (Robbins, 2003).

It is certainly a possibility that 10 sessions is not sufficient time to develop mature cohesion that relates to outcome; however, Taube-Schiff et al. (2007) found significant findings in 10 sessions of cognitive-behavioral group treatment for social phobia. Other studies also used brief models and found a relationship between cohesion and outcome (Crowe & Grenyer, 2008; Lindgren et al., 2008; Lipman et al. 2007). There may be many factors influencing the relationship between ratings of cohesion and outcome for people specifically struggling with complicated bereavement. It is possible that they require more time in group to develop more mature cohesion because of the intensity of the connectedness found early on in the treatment. The authors also noted that the measure of cohesion they used (GCQ) focused on real-life relationships with group members compared to the therapeutic relationships within the group. Johnson (2007) said it was not surprising that the researchers found alliance to be related to outcome in this study because it was directly related to the therapy treatment, while the measure of cohesion was not.

When reviewing the literature, only one study indicated a negative relationship between cohesion and outcome. Roether and Peters (1972) studied the relationship between cohesion in groups for male sex offenders. They found not only that cohesion was not significantly related to positive outcome but also that sex offenders' ratings of cohesion were related to their tendency to reoffend. The greater the member-rated group cohesion, the greater his rating of tendency to engage in sexual offenses in the future. This study failed to distinguish between immature and mature cohesion, which is an important distinction in the treatment of abusive offenders (Robbins, 2003). Robbins describes the characteristics of group members in court-mandated group treatment and how the personal history of early trauma, the mistrust of leaders who are part of the system, and the personality that tends to externalize influence how quickly cohesion develops but can inhibit change. Although only one group-therapy study revealed the darker side of group cohesion, there has been speculation that group cohesion has the potential to interfere with group process and outcome (Miles, 1957; Frank, 1957; Gladding, 1991; Hartmann, 1981; Hornsey et al., 2009, Pines, 1985).

Nothing Is Perfect: The Dark Side of Group-Therapy Cohesion

Despite the many benefits of group cohesion, group clinicians have raised the potential negative consequences of cohesiveness in groups. Miles (1957) mentioned that cohesion can be a mixed blessing because cohesive groups can foster dependence and reduce the likelihood that members will engage in constructive conflict. The common denominator is that the emphasis on group solidarity overshadows the importance of risk taking, conflict, and true intimacy in the group. Hartmann (1981) not only addressed the negative side effects of cohesion but described pathological cohesion in groups where the pressure to belong within the group causes members to regress. During this regression, members lose their sense of self and are unable to engage in the group process. Fears of group-counseling cohesion are not surprising and parallel the fears of groups documented in social psychology. "Groupthink," social loafing, conformity, and deindividuation are all negative phenomena attributed to groups.

Social psychologists have explored the phenomenon of groupthink (Janis, 1972). They describe how group members can inhibit independent thought and avoid expressing conflicting views. Does cohesion in group counseling lead to groupthink? According to Janis (1972), cohesion is one factor in groupthink, but it is not the only ingredient. Groupthink requires a leader who punishes members for disagreeing and does not support conflict in the group, an environment that is isolated, and pressure within the group to make the right decision. Cohesion is certainly one factor that influences groupthink, but the leadership, environment, and objective of the group all influence the development of this phenomenon. In essence, groupthink is not likely to occur in counseling groups where leaders emphasize diversity of opinions and the disclosure of conflict while minimizing the pressure to agree.

Social loafing (for a review, see Karau & Williams, 1995) has been described as members doing less in groups than they would alone because the group allows for members to hide their individual contributions. Does cohesion increase social loafing in groups? Karau and Hart (1998) studied the impact of cohesiveness on social loafing and found that group cohesion actually eliminated social loafing. They stated that group members who are in cohesive groups and have the opportunity to make positive contributions to group outcomes engage in less social loafing. They even suggest that building cohesion and focusing on common goals can reduce social loafing in groups. These authors focused on groups of college students, not counseling or therapy groups; and future research is needed to explore cohesion and social loafing in group therapy.

If cohesion does not necessarily lead to social loafing or groupthink, then how would cohesion inhibit positive changes for members in groups and even increase the desire to engage in offensive behaviors? Roether and Peters (1972) found that cohesion negatively impacted the treatment of group members who were in treatment for sexual offenses. They found that the more cohesive the group, the more resistant it was to treatment. Robbins (2003) argued that not all cohesion is the same and that there are specific populations where early cohesion may inhibit growth and positive outcome. He argued that certain populations, such as sex offenders, are more likely to be at risk for immature cohesion and have more difficulty moving to mature cohesion. The group situation (i.e., a prison setting) where members are in mandated treatment, have leaders who are part of the system, are concerned about being evaluated, and are already mistrustful of the establishment does not facilitate or encourage honest disclosure. In addition, the history of trauma and abuse that many sex offenders experience leads to externalizing defenses where it is safer to blame others and protect the self than to reflect on personal failures. The crime of sexually offending is often correlated with severe character pathology and inability to empathize with others. The combination of factors can lead to members developing rapid solidarity in their group without encouraging risk taking, painful disclosure, conflict, or true intimacy. It is no wonder that the assessment of cohesion early in treatment in these groups is more indicative of playing it safe and bolstering the self than engaging in therapeutic change. Studies are needed to further understand how different levels of cohesion influence group process and outcome depending on the type of group and population (Dion, 2000).

Group-Therapy Cohesion: Leader and Member Contributions
Leader Factors that Encourage Cohesion

Burlingame et al. (2001, 2002) emphasize group leader behaviors that engender cohesive groups. These behaviors are captured in six (2001, seven principles in 2002) empirically based principles that focus on group leader factors that contribute and foster group cohesion (see Table 9.3). These principles address how the leader can foster cohesion via planning, verbal interactions, and facilitation of emotional intimacy in the group. The first principle they describe focuses on pregroup preparation. Principle I states that leaders should conduct "pre-group preparation that sets treatment expectations, defines group rules, and instructs members in appropriate roles and skills needed for effective group participation and group cohesion" (Burlingame et al., 2001, p. 375). Sufficiently preparing patients entering group psychotherapy is significant because it sets the tone and environment for group cohesion to develop (Bednar & Kaul, 1994; Lindgren et al., 2008; Yalom & Leszcz, 2005). Burlingame et al. (2001, 2002), among others, emphasize how pregroup preparations that include reviewing client expectations, establishing group procedures, and providing information about group boundaries and confidentiality are critical when establishing a therapeutic environment. Group leaders can prepare patients by conducting individual or group interviews prior to the start of group and reviewing clinical procedures, such as fee arrangement, time and length of sessions, and termination procedures. Professional school counselors who do group work in the schools may need to coordinate student schedules, consult with teachers, determine room availability, and screen potential group members in order to set the stage for a healthy group climate (Erford, 2010). Similarly, Burlingame et al. (2002) expressed a need for group leaders to seek balance within the group by determining those clients who are not suited for group (e.g., due to deficient cognitive and interpersonal abilities, resistance to policy) and those who are well suited for group (e.g., motivated, adequate skills to provide feedback and show empathy).

Leaders can enhance group homogeneity among members by ensuring an even gender distribution; being sensitive to members' race, culture, and sexual orientation; and including members within the same age range (Yalom & Leszcz, 2005). Research conducted by Perrone & Sedlacek (2000) explored both homogenous and heterogenous groups, where members shared similar or different presenting issues. They found that homogenous groups had greater satisfaction than heterogenous process groups. The leaders' active emphasis on cohesion is even more important in time-limited groups where there is less time to develop cohesion

Table 9.3 Burlingame et al.'s (2001) six empirically supported principles for group leaders that facilitate the group relationship

Principle I: Conduct pregroup preparation that sets treatment expectations, defines group rules, and instructs members in appropriate roles and skills needed for effective group participation and group cohesion.

Principle II: The group leader should establish clarity regarding group processes in early sessions since higher levels of structure probably lead to higher levels of disclosure and cohesion.

Principle III: Leader modeling real-time observations, guiding effective interpersonal feedback, and maintaining a moderate level of control and affiliation may positively impact cohesion.

Principle IV: The timing and delivery of feedback should be pivotal considerations for leaders as they facilitate this relationship-building process.

Principle V: The group leader's presence affects the relationship with not only individual members but all group members as they vicariously experience the leader's manner of relating; thus, the therapist's managing of his or her own emotional presence in the service of others is important.

Principle VI: A primary focus of the group leader should be on facilitating group members' emotional expression, the responsiveness of others to that expression, and the shared meaning derived from such expression.

Adapted with permission of APA.

(Budman et al., 1994). Leaders should consider the length of the group and who would be appropriate for the group before the group begins.

Corey (2008) pointed out the significance of a leader who can establish group structure in the initial stages by providing a general direction for goals and procedures, while still encouraging positive communication among members. This notion is represented in the second principle addressed by Burlingame et al. (2001, 2002). Principle II states that "the group leader should establish clarity regarding group processes in early sessions since higher levels of structure probably lead to higher levels of disclosure and cohesion" (Burlingame et al., 2001, p. 375). In productive groups there are many positive factors that leaders display to influence cohesion. Leaders can actively engage members and provide the necessary structure to foster a sense of safety in the group. This is especially true in groups that have cultural norms that do not value open disclosure of emotions (Debiak, 2007). Wong, Chau, Kwok, and Kwan (2007) studied CBT for people with chronic illness who live in Hong Kong. The authors developed a culturally sensitive protocol that emphasized a structured format to facilitate the expression of emotions and opinions in the group based on the leaders' awareness that structure would facilitate cohesion and outcome for Chinese group members. Group leaders who are sensitive to the diverse needs of members are more likely to facilitate cohesion in their groups.

The third principle highlights the importance of the leader modeling here-and-now interventions, offering positive feedback to members, and having the ability to moderate control early on in the group process. Principle III states that leaders should model "real-time observations, guide effective interpersonal feedback, and maintain a moderate level of control and affiliation in order to positively impact cohesion" (Burlingame et al., 2001, p. 375). It is always difficult to balance group members' disclosure of outside experiences with ingroup process. Group leaders who ensure that the here-and-now interactions are emphasized, and not avoided, facilitate cohesion because they encourage within-group disclosure that leads to healthy conflict and intimacy (Burlingame et al., 2001, 2002; Tschuschke & Dies, 1994; Yalom, 1985). This approach allows members to disclose how they are feeling and experiencing others within the group, as opposed to sharing stories and feelings about people outside the group (Corey, 1995; Yalom & Leszcz, 2005).

When group leaders encourage ingroup process, Burlingame et al. (2001, 2002) suggest that leaders use a verbal style that encourages sharing among all members, model self-disclosure focused on responsibility, and provide feedback free of judgment. It is also necessary for leaders to gauge the emotional climate of the group and create surroundings of support while also facilitating healthy conflict. Group therapists describe how the resolution of conflict facilitates trust, intimacy, and cohesion (Corey, 2008; Corey & Corey, 1997; Yalom & Leszcz, 2005); and group researchers have supported the increase of cohesion after periods of conflict (Castongauy et al., 1998; Kivlighan & Lilly, 1997).

When group leaders facilitate members' risk taking, it is important that they pay attention to the developmental needs of the group and the ability of members to use feedback effectively. Principle IV states that "the timing and delivery of feedback should be pivotal considerations for leaders as they facilitate this relationship-building process" (Burlingame et al., 2001, p. 375). Modeling corrective feedback and warmth, maintaining appropriate eye contact, valuing openness, and encouraging member-to-member relationships can facilitate closeness within the group (Burlingame et al., 2002). Corey (1995, 2008) points out how group leaders can provide a greater connection and belonging between members by actively encouraging interaction among members by exploring common themes and linking members' experiences. This in turn increases self-disclosure and security within the group setting. Group leaders are crucial in establishing this trust between members within the early stages of the group's development. Kottler (1994) described leader techniques that facilitate cohesion such as encouraging group norms, warm and caring facial expressions, eye contact, and humor. Martineau (1972) pointed out that humor between group members creates solidarity, cuts status lines, and emphasizes commonality. Flowers et al. (1981) found that eye contact with group members was a factor in determining level of cohesiveness and that groups with more cohesion disclosed more about their problems. Attending-to-the-speaker skills are critical because the more engaged members become in the group, the more problems are disclosed and the higher the level of cohesion.

Not only is the group leader's ability to provide structure and positive feedback and to encourage risks important to the development of cohesion; it is also important for the leader to maintain the emotional climate of the group via the leader's own personal behaviors in the group and the leader's ability to foster that capacity in group members. The following two principles focus on the leader's own ability to be present in the group and his or her ability to facilitate empathy and engagement in group members. Principle V states that "the group leader's presence not only affects the relationship with individual members, but all group members as they vicariously experience the leader's manner of relating; thus the therapist's managing of his or her own emotional presence in the service of others is important" (Burlingame et al., 2001, p. 375). Many, if not all, group-counseling texts recommend that the group leader be open, genuine, and empathic in order to facilitate cohesion (Corey, 2008; Corey & Corey, 1997; Yalom & Leszcz, 2005). Johnson et al. (2005) studied the relationship between empathy, group alliance, and cohesion and found that empathy and cohesion were both correlated and loaded onto a common factor described as the positive bonding relationship in groups. In essence, perceived empathy from the leader and members was related to perceived cohesion and contributed to a positive group environment. Shapiro and Gans (2008) described how the group leader's courage can foster hope in group members and help to neutralize negative emotions. They say that the leader's confrontation and ownership of mistakes, ability to face his or her own and the group's anger, and immediate acknowledgment of unexpected moments facilitates the group process.

According to Burlingame et al. (2001), it is not enough for the leader to be empathic within the group; it is also important for the leader to help group members be empathic with one another. They describe principle VI, which states that "a primary focus of the group leader should be on facilitating group members' emotional expression, the responsiveness of others to that expression, and the shared meaning derived from such expression" (Burlingame et al., 2001, p. 375). Group member empathy, support, and encouragement are all important to the development of a cohesive group (Braaten, 1990).

Leader Factors that Inhibit Cohesion

Group cohesion is hindered when leaders do not allow members to freely express negative feelings toward other members, the group, and their leaders (Corey, 1995; Yalom & Leszcz, 2005). In addition, a group facilitated by a leader with limited training, expertise, and knowledge might be unable to model appropriate self-disclosure, feedback, and communication skills to members. Group members who

lack these skills might not be able to connect or interact with other members in a positive way, and this will negatively affect the level of trust and closeness within the group. Leaders who are unable to express genuine feelings of warmth and fail to encourage interactions among group members will likely experience a lack of cohesion within their groups.

Competition with coleaders, judgmental attitudes, allowing scapegoats, and accepting subgroups without exploration are ways leaders inhibit group cohesion. It is important for leaders to pay attention when anger is directed at only one member who becomes the scapegoat. Moreno (2007) addressed scapegoating and how the targeting and attacking of a single group member can often prevent conflict within the group, lead to premature termination, and hinder cohesion. A leader who is able to explore the underlying motivation for the scapegoating can protect the group from this toxic phenomenon and foster a more intimate group environment (Yalom & Leszcz, 2005). Failure to screen patients who are unable to succeed in group and failure to address clients' missed sessions and tardy behavior will also negatively affect the development of cohesion within a group (Corey, 2008; Yalom & Leszcz, 2005).

In order to promote trust and self-disclosure from group members, the leader has to be accepting of negative and positive feelings so that members feel secure and safe in sharing. When leaders demonstrate avoidance of genuine interaction, members do not feel safe to expose themselves to the group (Corey, 2008). One factor that may influence a leader's ability to remain engaged in the group and tolerate intimacy is his or her personal attachment style. Marmarosh et al. (2006) found that therapists' attachment styles influenced their perceptions of their patients' attitudes about group counseling. The more anxious the therapist felt about being a member in a group, the more he or she feared that patients would be overwhelmed or fearful of group therapy. This fearfulness can lead to avoidance of emotionally charged topics in group. Despite a large literature exploring how therapist attachment styles influence individual psychotherapy and factors such as alliance (for review, see Daniels, 2006; Shaver & Norman, 1995), we could not find one empirical study that explored the impact of leader attachment on group-therapy cohesion.

Social psychologists have studied how leader attachment relates to group functioning (Rom & Mikulincer, 2003; Berson, Dan, & Yammarino, 2006) and found that leader's attachment is related to group cohesion. Specifically, one study found that the greater the level of leader avoidance, the less the members rated the cohesion in the group. The greater the leader's anxiety, the more the members rated the leader as being self-focused (Davidovitz, Mikulincer, Shaver, Izsak, & Popper, 2007). These findings encourage group therapists to explore how leaders' attachment styles influence the development of cohesion in counseling groups.

Member Factors that Influence Cohesion

The level of acceptance that group members have for one another influences the therapeutic group environment (Yalom, 1985). Burlingame et al. (2002) described how specific member behaviors can increase the likelihood of higher cohesion within a group. For instance, members who take turns sharing within group, avoid judgmental and evaluative emotional responses, and support and encourage members in expressing feelings are more likely to have stronger alliances. Bostwick (1987) emphasized the importance of being accepted by one's group members and how member acceptance was equal in importance to therapist acceptance. Tschuschke and Dies (1994) conducted research that connected self-disclosures to the level of cohesion within the group. A member who was able to share more meaningful self-disclosures facilitated a higher level of cohesion and influenced the act of sharing and receiving feedback from group members.

Relationship histories often influence members' ability to provide useful feedback and engage in helpful group disclosure. Kivlighan, Marsh-Angelone, and Angelone (1994) suggested that group members' interpersonal style, problems, and transference dynamics influence the degree of affiliation that individual group members experience within the group. Recent studies have applied attachment theory to understand the impact of past relational experiences on group members' behaviors (Chen & Mallinckrodt, 2002; Lindgren et al., 2008; Shechtman & Dvir, 2006; Shechtman & Rybko, 2004). Shechtman and Dvir (2006) found that once group therapy starts, adolescents with avoidant attachments, who prefer to rely on themselves to manage stress, avoided self-disclosure and were less appreciative of such disclosures by others in the group. Chen and Mallinckrodt (2002) studied graduate students participating in an interpersonal group as part of a course requirement and found that members high in attachment anxiety displayed problematic interpersonal behaviors in the group,

such as nonassertiveness, vindictiveness, and intrusiveness. They also found that attachment avoidance was negatively correlated with group attraction, a measure of the working alliance in group treatment. In addition, they found that attachment anxiety and avoidance were associated with inaccurate perceptions of themselves and others in the group. Anxiously attached members perceived excessive friendliness in others while avoidantly attached group members overestimated hostility. Lindgren et al. (2008) were the only researchers to include a measure of attachment when exploring the alliance to the group as a whole using actual therapy groups. These authors found that anxiously attached members focused more on being accepted in the group, and they rated the alliance to the group higher compared to other group members. The more avoidantly attached group members rated the alliance to the group as a whole significantly less initially, but attachment avoidance was related to increases in alliance over time. The authors argue that a rapid attachment to the group may not always be indicative of true cohesion and a lower rating of alliance initially may not indicate an inability to develop cohesion over time. In essence, cohesion at the beginning of therapy may be more related to a member's personality and way of coping in a group than about the characteristics of the group. These findings illuminate how group members' relationship histories influence the group process and highlight the need for future research.

In addition to attachment styles, group members' diagnoses and presenting problems often influence cohesion in groups. Woody and Adessky (2002) maintain that certain members have disorders that present challenges to group cohesion. Members with personality disorders, disorders that come with long-standing interpersonal difficulties, often struggle to build alliances and closeness in group therapy. These members often engage in inappropriate behaviors, where they may act out due to an abusive past, clinical depression, suicidal thoughts, or an inability to cope with emotions (Yalom & Leszcz, 2005). These unique group members struggle with closeness and intimacy and often avoid personal relationships, become overwhelmed in relationships, or have difficulty with self-expression. Hilbert et al. (2007) found empirical support in their study when members with greater interpersonal problems and general psychopathology perceived less cohesion in groups compared to healthier group members. Lorentzen et al. (2004) also found that members with less severe symptoms rated greater cohesion to the leader early in treatment compared to members with more severe symptoms. One interesting study asked patients with borderline personality disorder who dropped out of group therapy why they decided to leave the group (Hummelen, Wilberg, & Karterud, 2007). The most frequent response was that the emotions stirred in the group were too overwhelming and they could not cope with their feelings. Interestingly, research also found that more severely ill patients who are hospitalized rated cohesion as one of the most curative components of the group compared to members who were higher-functioning (Butler & Fuhriman, 1983).

In addition to personality factors, group member education and race/ethnicity can influence cohesion (DeLucia-Waack & Donigian, 2004). The amount of education group members have can play a role in how much they share about themselves and their problems within the group setting. Reimer and Mathieu (2006) reported that the more education members had in the group, the more likely they were to engage in self-disclosing activities. This may be due to a host of variables related to education that include socioeconomic status, comfort with the language and verbal communication, overall functioning, and cultural background that encourages or discourages disclosure in groups. White (1994) and Salvendy (1999) described the impact of race and ethnicity in groups and how group counseling has the potential to stir up prejudice, racism, and discrimination intensely compared to other forms of counseling. Despite the extensive literature describing how race and ethnicity relate to the alliance and treatment outcome in individual therapy, we could not find any empirical studies that explore specifically how the race and ethnicity of group members influence the development of cohesion in group counseling. Many group clinicians describe the ways that the avoidance or denial of diversity can be destructive to the group process and outcome (Debiak, 2007; DeLucia-Waack & Donigian, 2004), and future research is needed to explore the relationship between leader multicultural competency, group diversity, and cohesion.

Summary of Findings and Future Implications
Recommendations for Future Research
Although the empirical literature has revealed contradictory findings and there are more measures of cohesion than we know what to do with, cohesion remains an important aspect of group counseling. Some have responded to the challenges of studying

cohesion with the attitude that it is time to let go of cohesion (Hornsey et al., 2007, 2009). Hornsey et al. (2009) made a strong argument for the replacement of cohesion in group-counseling research because it is too ambiguous. We argue that too many studies and theories have supported its importance for us to abandon it now. Johnson et al. (2005, 2006) found that cohesion is an important contributor to positive bonding in groups, and many studies have found that it contributes to the process and outcome of group therapy. The main challenges that lie before us appear to be the same ones that all psychotherapy researchers face. Baldwin, Wampold, and Imel (2007) described the same difficulty sorting out the alliance research in individual psychotherapy. It is extremely difficult to study all therapy and counseling processes, including group, family, and individual, because there are multiple factors that influence very complex relational processes (Wampold, 2001). The diverse interventions, contradictory perspectives on change, individual and therapist factors, and ambiguous constructs contribute to a literature that is often difficult to interpret; yet when we step back from the multiple factors, the therapeutic relationship is often at the heart of successful treatments (Wampold, 2001). In group therapy, cohesion, alliance, and group climate are the relationship factors that provide the foundation for successful treatment.

In order to facilitate a deeper understanding of cohesion and make sense of the contradictory literature, we have several recommendations for future research. It is clear that in order to facilitate a richer understanding of cohesion, we must continue to build on past research findings. We need to implement future studies that (1) explore the direct and indirect ways cohesion relates to process and outcome, (2) consistently define cohesion and utilize validated measures of cohesion from different perspectives in the same studies, (3) consider the development of the group and measure cohesion at different points in time over the course of counseling, (4) continue to replicate studies using similar group populations in order to understand inconsistent findings, (5) continue to study cohesion in diverse groups that utilize different interventions, (6) explore the impact that leader and group member individual differences bring to the development and usefulness of cohesion, and (7) continue to explore the overlapping relationships between cohesion and other curative mechanisms.

Specifically, researchers need to be sensitive to the timing of cohesion and the difference between measuring cohesion at the beginning of treatment, in the middle, and at termination. In many studies, measuring cohesion in the middle of treatment is more significant to outcome than measuring it early in the process. In other studies, measuring cohesion at the beginning relates to dropping out of treatment. Many researchers who found no relationship between cohesion and outcome studied cohesion only in very brief group treatments, 10 sessions. Their termination session would be in the mid-phase of many other group treatments. Future studies that compare brief and longer-term groups with the same population (i.e., grief groups) would help us to understand if and how the length of treatment influences cohesion and change.

In order to truly understand how cohesion relates to outcome, researchers need to expand their assessment of change. When studying outcome, it is critical to measure at termination, at 6 months' follow-up, and at 12 months' follow-up. We have seen findings where cohesion does not appear to be a predictor at termination but then is a significant predictor when predicting posttreatment follow-up months after termination (Hand et al., 1974).

It is important to collect leader and group member perceptions of cohesion. Some researchers have found a significant relationship between member-rated cohesion and outcome, while others have found that only therapist-rated cohesion was related to outcome. Future studies are needed to explore the differences between member and leader ratings and how these relate to outcome in different types of groups. In addition to exploring member and leader ratings, researchers can use advanced statistical analyses (i.e., hierarchical linear modeling) to explore the influence of the group on individual perceptions of cohesion (Johnson et al., 2006).

Future research is needed to explore the mediational nature of cohesion (Dion, 2000; Hornsey et al., 2007). Ogrodniczuk et al. (2006) found that cohesion did mediate the relationship between distress and attendance in supportive groups. This study explored not only how cohesion was related to outcome but also how cohesion would relate to specific populations of members (those with personality disorders) in different types of groups (interpretive and supportive). Similar future studies are needed that explore the mediating nature of cohesion for different populations of patients using different types of group counseling.

Research is desperately needed to explore the impacts that member qualities have on the development of cohesion in groups. We found only one study that explored how the attachment styles of group members influenced the development of cohesion in group counseling (Lindgren et al., 2008), but this study did not explore how the attachment styles of all the members in the group influence group cohesion. We could not find one empirical study that explored the impact of the group leader's attachment style on cohesion in counseling groups. It does not take much to imagine how having too many avoidant group members or a leader with a dismissive style would impact the group atmosphere. In addition to attachment style, the race, ethnicity, and sexual orientation of group members and leaders are likely to influence the development of group cohesion (Johnson et al., 2005). We could not find any empirical study that explored leader multicultural competency and cohesion in group counseling with diverse group members. We also could not find any empirical study that explored the impact of racism, discrimination, or prejudice on the development of group cohesion in counseling groups.

Lastly, the finding that cohesion may predict poor outcome is extremely important to the understanding of cohesion. Roether and Peters's (1972) finding that sex offenders' ratings of cohesion were related to their tendency to reoffend is an important contribution to the literature. This study raises an important distinction between different types of cohesion in group counseling. Future research is needed to distinguish between cohesion that facilitates positive changes and cohesion that may prevent growth and even defend against individual insight. This is especially true in different populations in group counseling. Robbins (2003) described this phenomenon with sex offenders, and it may certainly apply to other group populations.

Although we have made many suggestions for future research, empirical findings are useless if they do not benefit the leaders and members in counseling groups. After reviewing the literature, we summarized the major findings that we believe to be helpful to group counselors.

Cohesion: What Group Counselors May Want to Know

1. Group counselors can best instill group cohesion when they plan ahead for their groups. They can foster cohesion even before the group begins by screening out members who may not be ready to participate in the group, preparing members about the group process, discussing

boundaries and explaining how they will be valuable members, and providing appropriate information about group structure and goals.

2. Group counselors can research the specific population of patients they are working with to prepare for specific challenges that may promote or inhibit cohesion in their groups. More severely ill patients may benefit most from cohesion but also struggle more to establish it. It is important for group leaders to consider the specific issues their members struggle with and how that will influence emotion regulation, externalizing defenses, and ability to cope with group process. Group counselors need to consider the makeup of their group and ensure that one minority members is not the only representative minorities in a group. It is important to ensure enough diversity that members do not feel they are the token minority member.

3. Group counselors and therapists can encourage the development of mature cohesion and be sensitive to their own anxieties that may inhibit healthy conflict in groups. Cohesion that is based on a false sense of unity without the ability to tolerate healthy disagreement and honesty may inhibit individual growth in different groups.

4. Group counselors can educate themselves as to the impact of race, ethnicity, and culture and explore how this may influence group members' needs in the group and the group's sense of cohesion. Group counselors should also explore their own bias and prejudice that will often impact the group.

5. Group counselors need to address behaviors that discourage group cohesion—avoidance, lateness, missed sessions, dropouts, lack of disclosure and risk taking, and leadership difficulties that inhibit trust and safety in groups.

6. Group counselors can facilitate better outcome when they are sensitive to the importance of relationship factors in group, regardless of whether the group intervention mainly emphasizes didactic material or behavioral interventions. The relationship is always influencing the group and can hinder or facilitate group processes.

7. Group counselors can emphasize empathy, cohesion, and a safe environment to foster positive bonding early in the group. The decrease in cohesion during the middle phase of treatment is a normal process in group counseling and is often indicative of a healthy pattern of group development. Leaders need to be cautious about a false sense of cohesion that prevents growth.

8. McCullough and Soldz (2000) described the importance of bridging research and clinical practice. They also described the critical role clinicians provide when developing and implementing clinically based studies. Group counselors are the best qualified to empirically study the groups they run and contribute to the field's knowledge and understanding of cohesion. The more studies we have that explore cohesion in group counseling, the more we will understand how it influences different groups, at different times, and for different reasons.

References

Aviram, R. B., & Rosenfeld, S. (2002). Application of social identity theory in group therapy for stigmatized adults. *International Journal of Group Psychotherapy, 52,* 121–130.

Baldwin, S., Wampold, B., & Imel, Z. (2007). Untangling the alliance–outcome correlation: Exploring the relative importance of therapist and patient variability in the alliance. *Journal of Consulting and Clinical Psychology, 75,* 842–852.

Bales, R. F. (1950). *Interaction process analysis.* Cambridge, MA: Addison-Wesley.

Barrett, M. S., Thompson, D., Chua, W., Crits-Christoph, P., & Gibbons, M. B. (2008). Early withdrawal from mental health treatment: Implications for psychotherapy practice. *Psychotherapy Theory, Research, Practice, Training, 45,* 247–267.

Bednar, R. L., & Kaul, T. J. (1994). Experiential group research: Can the canon fire? In A. E. Bergin & S. L. Garfield (Eds.), *Handbook of psychotherapy and behavior change* (4th ed., pp. 631–663). New York: John Wiley & Sons.

Berson, Y., Dan, O., & Yammarino, F. J. (2006). Attachment style and individual differences in leadership perceptions and emergence. *Journal of Social Psychology, 146,* 165–182.

Bliese, P. D., & Halverson, R. R. (1996). Individual and nomothetic models of job stress: An examination of work hours, cohesion, and well-being. *Journal of Applied Social Psychology, 26,* 1171–1189.

Bloch, S., & Crouch, E. (1985). *Therapeutic factors in group psychotherapy.* New York: Oxford University Press.

Bordin, E. S. (1979). The generalizability of the psychoanalytic concept of the working alliance. *Psychotherapy: Theory, Research, and Practice, 16,* 252–260.

Bostwick, G. (1987). "Where's Mary?" A review of the group treatment drop out literature. *Social Work with Groups, 10,* 117–132.

Braaten, L. J. (1989). Predicting positive goal attainment and symptom reduction from early group climate dimensions. *International Journal of Group Psychotherapy, 39,* 377–387.

Braaten, L. J. (1990). The different patterns of group climate critical incidents in high and low cohesion sessions of group psychotherapy. *International Journal of Group Psychotherapy, 40,* 477–493.

Budman, S. H., Demby, A., Feldstein, M., Redondo, J., Scherz, B., Bennett, M. J., et al. (1987). Preliminary findings on a new instrument to measure cohesion in group psychotherapy. *International Journal of Group Psychotherapy, 37,* 75–94.

Budman, S. H., Simeone, P. G., Reilly, R., & Demby, R. A. (1994). Progress in short-term and time-limited group psychotherapy: Evidence and implications. In A. Fuhriman & G. M. Burlingame (Eds.), *Handbook of group psychotherapy: An empirical and clinical synthesis* (pp. 319–339). New York: John Wiley & Sons.

Budman, S. H., Soldz, S., & Demby, A. (1989). Cohesion, alliance, and outcome in group psychotherapy. *Journal for the Study of Interpersonal Processes, 52*, 339–350.

Budman, S. H., Soldz, S., Demby, A., Davis, M., & Merry, J. (1993). What is cohesiveness? An empirical examination. *Small Group Research, 24*, 199–216.

Budman, S. H., Soldz, S., Demby, A., Feldstein, M., Springer, T., & Davis, M. S. (1989). Cohesion, alliance and outcome in group psychotherapy. *Psychiatry, 52*, 339–350.

Burlingame, G. M., Fuhriman, A., & Johnson, J. (2001). Cohesion in group psychotherapy. *Psychotherapy, 38*, 373–379.

Burlingame, G. M., Fuhriman, A., & Johnson, J. (2002). Cohesion in group psychotherapy. In J. C. Norcross (Ed.), *Psychotherapy relationships that work: Therapist contributions and responsiveness to patients* (pp. 71–88). New York: Oxford University Press.

Butler, T., & Fuhriman, A. (1983). Curative factors in group therapy: A review of recent literature. *Small Group Behavior, 14*, 131–142.

Cartwright, D. (1968). The nature of group cohesiveness. In D. Cartwright & A. Zander (Eds.), *Group dynamics: Research and theory*. London: Tavistock.

Castongauy, L. G., Pincus, A. L., Agras, W. S., & Hines, C. E. (1998). The role of emotion in group cognitive-behavioral therapy for binge-eating disorder: When things have to feel worse before they get better. *Psychotherapy Research, 8*, 225–238.

Chen, E., & Mallinckrodt, B. (2002). Attachment, group attraction, and self-other agreement in interpersonal circumplex problems and perceptions of group members. *Group Dynamics: Theory, Research, and Practice, 6*(4), 311–324.

Connelly, J. L., Piper, W. E., DeCarufel, F. L., & Debanne, E. G. (1986). Premature termination in group psychotherapy: Pretherapy and early therapy predictors. *International Journal of Group Psychotherapy, 36*, 145–152.

Corey, G. (1995). *Theory and practice of group counseling* (4th ed.). Pacific Grove, CA: Brooks/Cole.

Corey, G. (2008). *Theory and practice of group counseling* (7th ed.). Pacific Grove, CA: Brooks/Cole.

Corey, M. S., & Corey, G. (1997). *Group process and practice* (5th ed.). Pacific Grove, CA: Brooks/Cole.

Crowe, T. P., & Grenyer, B. F. (2008). Is therapist alliance or whole group cohesion more influential in group psychotherapy outcomes? *Clinical Psychology and Psychotherapy, 15*, 239–246.

Daniels, S. (2006). Adult attachment patterns and individual psychotherapy: A review. *Clinical Psychology Review, 26*, 968–984.

Davidovitz, R., Mikulincer, M., Shaver, P., Izsak, R., & Popper, M. (2007). Leaders as attachment figures: Leaders' attachment orientations predict leadership-related mental representations and followers' performance and mental health. *Journal of Personality and Social Psychology, 93*, 632–650.

Debiak, D. (2007). Attending to diversity in group psychotherapy: An ethical imperative, *International Journal of Group Psychotherapy, 57*, 1–12.

DeLucia-Waack, J. L., & Donigian, J. (2004). *The practice of multicultural group work*. Belmont, CA: Brooks/Cole, Thompson Learning.

Dion, K. L. (2000). Group cohesion: From "field of forces" to multidimensional construct. *Group Dynamics: Theory, Research, and Practice, 4*, 7–26.

Erford, B. (2010). *Group work in the schools*. Boston: Pearson Education.

Etringer, B. D., Gregory, V. R., & Lando, H. A. (1984). Influence of group cohesion on the behavioral treatment of smoking. *Journal of Consulting and Clinical Psychology, 52*, 1080–1086.

Evans, C. R., & Dion, K. L. (1991). Group cohesion and performance: A meta-analysis. *Small Group Research, 22*, 175–186.

Evans, N. J., & Jarvis, P. A. (1986). The group attitude scale: A measure of attraction to group. *Small Group Behavior, 17*, 203–216.

Festinger, L., Schachter, S., & Back, K. (1950). *Social pressures in informal groups*. New York: Hayes.

Flowers, V. J., Booream, C. D., & Hartman, K. A. (1981). Client improvement on higher and lower intensity problems as a function of group cohesiveness. *Psychotherapy: Theory, Research, & Practice, 18*, 246–251.

Frank, J. D. (1957). Some determinants, manifestations, and effects of cohesiveness in therapy groups. *International Journal of Group Psychotherapy, 7*, 53–63.

Fuhriman, A., Drescher, S., Hanson, E., Henrie, R., & Rybicki, W. (1986). Refining the measurement of curativeness: An empirical approach. *Small Group Behavior, 17*, 186–201.

Gaston, L., & Marmar, C. R. (1991). *Manual for the California Psychotherapy Alliance Scales- Patient Version*. Unpublished manuscript. McGill University, Montreal.

Gaston, L., & Marmar, C. R. (1993). *Manual of Private California Psychotherapy Alliance Scales*. McGill University, Montreal, and University of California, San Francisco.

Gillaspy, J. A., Jr., Wright, A. R., Campbell, C., Stokes, S., & Adinoff, B. (2002). Group alliance and cohesion as predictors of drug and alcohol abuse treatment outcomes. *Psychotherapy Research, 12*, 213–229.

Gladding, S. T. (1991). *Group work: A counseling specialty* (4th ed). New York: Merrill.

Hand, I., Lamontagne, Y., & Marks, I. M. (1974). Group exposure (flooding) in vivo for agoraphobics. *British Journal of Psychiatry, 124*, 588–602.

Hartmann, J. (1981). Group cohesion and the regulation of self-esteem. In H. Kellerman (Ed.), *Group cohesion: Theoretical and clinical perspectives* (pp. 255–267). New York: Grune and Stratton.

Hilbert, A., Saelans, B. E., Stein, R. I., Mockus, D. S., Welch, R. R., Matt, G. E., et al. (2007). Pretreatment and process predictors of outcome in interpersonal and cognitive behavioral psychotherapy for binge eating disorders. *Journal of Consulting and Clinical Psychology, 75*, 645–651.

Hill, W. F. (1965). *The Hill interaction matrix method of studying interaction in psychotherapy groups*. Los Angeles: Youth Study Center, University of Southern California.

Hogg, M. A. (1992). *The social psychology of group cohesiveness: From attraction to social identity*. New York: New York University Press.

Hornsey, M. J., Dwyer, L., & Oei, T. P. S. (2007). Beyond cohesiveness: Reconceptualizing the link between group processes and outcomes in group psychotherapy. *Small Group Research, 38*, 567–592.

Hornsey, M. J., Dwyer, L., Oei, T. P. S., & Dingle, G. A. (2009). Group processes and outcomes in group psychotherapy: Is it time to let go of cohesiveness? *International Journal of Group Psychotherapy, 59*, 267–278.

Horvath, A. O., & Greenberg, L. S. (1989). Development and validation of the Working Alliance Inventory. *Journal of Counseling Psychology, 36*, 223–233.

Hummelen, B., Wilberg, T., & Karterud, S. (2007). Interviews of female patients with borderline personality disorder who dropped out of group psychotherapy. *International Journal of Group Psychotherapy, 57*, 67–91.

Janis, I. L. (1972). *Victims of groupthink*. Boston: Houghton Mifflin.

Johnson, J. E. (2007). Cohesion, alliance, and outcome in group psychotherapy: Comments on Joyce, Piper & Ogrodniczuk (2007). *International Journal of Group Psychotherapy, 54*, 537–543.

Johnson, J. E., Burlingame, G. M., Olsen, J. A., Davies, D. R., & Gleave, R. L. (2005). Group climate, cohesion, alliance, and empathy in group psychotherapy: Multilevel structural equation models. *Journal of Counseling Psychology, 52*, 310–321.

Johnson, J. E., Pulsipher, D., Ferrin, S. L., Burlingame, G., Davies, D. R., & Gleave, R. (2006). Measuring group processes: A comparison of the GCQ and CCI. *Group Dynamics: Theory, Research, and Practice, 10*, 136–145.

Joyce, A. S., Piper, W. E., & Ogrodniczuk, J. S. (2007). Therapeutic alliance and cohesion variables as predictors of outcome in short-term group psychotherapy. *International Journal of Group Psychotherapy, 57*, 269–296.

Karau, S. J., & Hart, J. W. (1998). Group cohesiveness and social loafing: Effects of a social interaction manipulation on individual motivation within group. *Group Dynamics: Theory, Research, and Practice, 2*, 185–191.

Karau, S. J., & Williams, K. D. (1995). Social loafing: Research findings, implications, and future directions. *Current Directions in Psychological Science, 4*, 134–140.

Kaul, T., & Bednar, R. (1986). Research on group and related therapies. In S. Garfield and A. Bergin (Eds.), *Handbook of psychotherapy and behavior change* (3rd ed., pp. 671–714). New York: John Wiley & Sons.

Kipnes, D. R., Piper, W. E., & Joyce, A. S. (2002). Cohesion and outcome in short-term psychodynamic groups for complicated grief. *International Journal of Group Psychotherapy, 52*, 483–509.

Kivlighan, D. M., & Lilly, R. L. (1997). Developmental changes in group climate as they relate to therapeutic gain. *Group Dynamics: Theory, Research, and Practice, 1*, 208–221.

Kivlighan, D. M., Jr., Marsh-Angelone, M., & Angelone, E. O. (1994). Projection in group counseling: The relationship between members' interpersonal problems and their perception of the group leader. *Journal of Counseling Psychology, 41*, 99–104.

Kottler, J. A. (1994). *Advanced group leadership*. Pacific Grove, CA: Brooks/Cole.

Lese, K. P., & MacNair-Semands, R. (2000). The Therapeutic Factors Inventory: Development of a scale. *Group, 24*(4), 303–317.

Lewin, K. (1947). Frontiers in group dynamics: Concept, method, and reality in social science, social equilibria and social changes. *Human Relations, 1*, 5–41.

Liberman, R. (1971). Reinforcement of cohesiveness in group therapy. *Archives of General Psychiatry, 25*, 168–177.

Lieberman, M., Yalom, I., & Miles, M. (1973). *Encounter groups: First facts*. New York: Basic Books.

Lindgren, A., Barber, J. P., & Sandahl, C. (2008). Alliance to the group-as-a-whole as a predictor of outcome in psychodynamic group therapy. *International Journal of Group Psychotherapy, 58*, 163–184.

Lipman, E. L., Waymouth, M., Gammon, T., Carter, P., Secord, M., Leung, O., et al. (2007). Influence of group cohesion on maternal well-being among participants in a support/education group program for single mothers. *American Journal of Orthopsychiatry, 77*, 543–549.

Lorentzen, S., Sexton, H. C., & Hoglend, P. (2004). Therapeutic alliance, cohesion and outcome in long-term analytic group: A preliminary study. *Nordic Journal of Psychiatry, 58*, 33–40.

MacKenzie, K. R. (1983). The clinical application of group measures. In R. R. Dies & K. R. MacKenzie (Eds.), *Advances in group psychotherapy: Integrating research and practice* (pp. 159–170). New York: International Universities Press.

MacKenzie, K. R. (1994). Group development. In A. Fuhriman & G. M. Burlingame (Eds.), *Handbook of group psychotherapy: An empirical and clinical synthesis* (pp. 223–268). New York: Wiley.

MacNair, R. R., & Corazzini, J. G. (1994). Client factors influencing group therapy dropout. *Psychotherapy, 2*, 352–362.

MacNair-Semands, R. R. (2002). Predicting attendance and expectations for group therapy. *Group Dynamics, 6*, 219–228.

Marmarosh, C., & Corazzini, J. (1997). Putting the group in your pocket: Using the collective identity to enhance personal and collective self-esteem. *Group Dynamics: Theory, Research, and Practice, 1*, 65–74.

Marmarosh, C. L., Holtz, A., & Schottenbauer, M. (2005). Group derived collective-self-esteem, group derived hope, and the well-being of group therapy members. *Group Dynamics: Theory, Research, and Practice, 9*, 32–44.

Marmarosh, C., Franz, V. A., Koloi, M., Majors, R., Rahimi, A., Ronquillo, J., et al. (2006). Therapists' group attachments and their expectations of patients' attitudes about group therapy. *International Journal of Group Psychotherapy, 56*, 325–388.

Martineau, W. H. (1972). A model of social functions of humor. In J. H. Goldstein & P. E. McGhee (Eds.), *The psychology of humor*. New York: Academic Press.

Marziali, E., & Munroe-Blum, H. (1994). *Interpersonal group psychotherapy for borderline personality disorder*. New York: Basic Books.

Marziali, E., Munroe-Blum, H., & McCleary, L. (1997). The contribution of group cohesion and group alliance to the outcome of group psychotherapy. *International Journal of Group Psychotherapy, 47*, 475–497.

McCallum, M., Piper, W. E., Ogrodniczuk, J. S., & Joyce, A. S. (2002). Early process and dropping out from short-term therapy for complicated grief. *Group Dynamics, 6*, 243–254.

McCullough, L., & Soldz, S. (2000). Research and practice: Where are we? In S. Soldz & L. McCullough (Eds.), *Reconciling empirical knowledge and clinical experience: The art and science of psychotherapy*. Washington, DC: American Psychological Association Books.

Miles, M. (1957). Human relations training: How a group grows. *Teachers College Record, 55*, 90–96.

Moos, R. H. (1986). *Group environment scale manual* (2nd ed.) Palo Alto, CA: Consulting Psychologists Press.

Moreno, J. K. (2007). Scapegoating in group psychotherapy. *International Journal of Group Psychotherapy, 57*, 93–104.

Mullen, B., & Copper, C. (1994). The relation between group cohesiveness and performance: An integration. *Psychological Bulletin, 155*, 210–227.

Oei, T. P. S., & Browne, A. (2006). Components of group processes: Have they contributed to the outcome of mood and anxiety disorder patients in a group cognitive behavior therapy program? *American Journal of Psychotherapy, 60,* 53–70.

Ogrodniczuk, J. S., Piper, W. E., & Joyce, A. S. (2006). Treatment compliance among patients with personality disorders receiving group psychotherapy: What are the roles of interpersonal distress and cohesions? *Psychiatry: Interpersonal and Biological Processes, 69,* 249–261.

Perrone, K. M., & Sedlacek, W. E. (2000). A comparison of group cohesiveness and client satisfaction in homogenous and heterogenous groups. *Journal of Specialists in Group Work, 25,* 243–251.

Pines, M. (1985). Psychic development and the group analytic situation. *Group, 9,* 24–37.

Piper, W. E., Marrache, M., Lacroix, R., Richardsen, A. M., & Jones, B. D. (1983). Cohesion as a basic bond in groups. *Human Relations, 36,* 93–108.

Piper, W. E., Ogrodniczuk, J. S., Lamarche, C., Hilscher, T., & Joyce, A. S. (2005). Level of alliance, pattern of alliance, and outcome in short-term group therapy. *International Journal of Group Psychotherapy, 55,* 527–550.

Reimer, W., & Mathieu, T. (2006). Therapeutic factors in group treatment as perceived by sex offenders: A "consumers' report." *Journal of Offender Rehabilitation, 42,* 59–73.

Robbins, R. N. (2003). Developing cohesion in court-mandated group treatment of male spouse abusers. *International Journal of Group Psychotherapy, 53,* 26–284.

Roether, H. A., & Peters, J. J. (1972). Cohesiveness and hostility in group psychotherapy. *American Journal of Psychiatry, 128,* 1014–1017.

Rom, E., & Mikulincer, M. (2003). Attachment theory and group processes: The association between attachment style and group-related representations, goals, memories, and functioning. *Journal of Personality and Social Psychology, 84,* 1220–1235.

Rutan, J. S., & Stone, W. N. (2001). *Psychodynamic group psychotherapy* (3rd ed). New York: Guilford Press.

Salvendy, J. (1999). Ethnocultural considerations in group psychotherapy. *International Journal of Group Psychotherapy, 49,* 429–464.

Schutz, W. (1966). *The interpersonal underworld.* Palo Alto, CA: Science and Behavior Books.

Shapiro, E. L., & Gans, J. S. (2008). The courage of the group therapist. *International Journal of Group Psychotherapy, 58,* 345–361.

Shaver, P. R., & Norman, A. J. (1995). Attachment theory and counseling psychology: A commentary. *Counseling Psychologist, 23,* 491–500.

Shechtman, Z., & Dvir, V. (2006). Attachment style as a predictor of behavior in group counseling with preadolescents. *Group Dynamics: Theory, Research, and Practice, 10*(1), 29–42.

Shechtman, Z., & Rybko, J. (2004). Attachment style and observed initial self-disclosure as explanatory variables of group functioning. *Group Dynamics: Theory, Research, and Practice, 8*(3), 207–220.

Silbergeld, S., Koenig, G. R., Manderscheid, R. W., Meeker, B. F., & Hornung, C. A. (1975). Assessment of environment-therapy systems: The Group Atmosphere Scale. *Journal of Consulting and Clinical Psychology, 43*(4), 460–468.

Stokes, J. P. (1983). Components of group cohesion: Intermember attraction, instrumental value, and risk taking. *Small Group Behavior, 14,* 163–173.

Taft, C., Murphy, C., King, D., Musser, P., & DeDeyn, J. (2003). Process and treatment adherence factors in group cognitive-behavioral therapy for partner violent men. *Journal of Consulting and Clinical Psychology, 71,* 812–820.

Tajfel, H., & Turner, J. C. (1979). An integrative theory of inter-group conflict. In W. G. Austin & S. Worchel (Eds.), *The social psychology of intergroup relations* (pp. 33–47). Monterey, CA: Brooks-Cole.

Taube-Schiff, M., Suvak, M. K., Antony, M. M., Bieling, P. J., & McCabe, R. R. (2007). Group cohesion in cognitive-behavioral group therapy for social phobia. *Behavior Research and Therapy, 45,* 687–698.

Teasdale, D., Walsh, P. A., Lancashire, M., & Mathews, A. M. (1977). Group exposure of agoraphobics: A replication study. *British Journal of Psychiatry, 130,* 186–193.

Treadwell, T., Laverture, N., Kumar, V. K., & Veeraraghavan, V. (2001). The group cohesion scale-revised: Reliability and validity. *International Journal of Action Methods: Psychodrama, Skill Training, and Role Playing, 54,* 3–12.

Tschuschke, V., & Dies, R. R. (1994). Intensive analysis of therapeutic factors and outcome in long–term inpatient groups. *International Journal of Group Psychotherapy, 44,* 185–208.

Tuckman, B. W., & Jensen, M. A. (1977). Stages of small group development revisited. *Group and Organizational Studies, 2,* 419–427.

van Andel, P., Erdman, R. A., Karsdorp, P. A., Appels, A., & Trijsburg, R. W. (2003). Group cohesion and working alliance: Prediction of treatment outcome in cardiac patients receiving cognitive behavioral group psychotherapy. *Psychotherapy and Psychosomatics, 72,* 141–149.

Wampold, B. (2001). *The great psychotherapy debate: Models, methods, and findings.* Mahwah, NJ: Lawrence Erlbaum.

Wheelan, S. A. (1994). *Group processes: A developmental perspective.* Boston: Allyn & Bacon.

White, J. C. (1994). The impact of race and ethnicity on transference and countertransference in combined individual/group psychotherapy. *Group, 18,* 89–94.

Wong, D. F. K., Chau, P., Kwok, A., & Kwan, J. (2007). Cognitive-behavioral treatment groups for people with chronic physical illness in Hong Kong: Reflections on a culturally attuned model. *International Journal of Group Psychotherapy, 57,* 367–385.

Woody, S. R., & Adessky, R. A. (2002). Therapeutic alliance, group cohesion, and homework compliance during cognitive behavioral group treatment of social phobia. *Behavior Therapy, 33,* 5–27.

Yalom, I. (1985). *The theory and practice of group psychotherapy* (3rd ed.). New York: Basic Books.

Yalom, I. (1995). *The theory and practice of group psychotherapy* (4th ed.). New York: Basic Books.

Yalom, I., & Leszcz, M. (2005). *The theory and practice of group psychotherapy* (5th ed.). New York: Basic Books.

Zabusky, G. S., & Kymissis, P. (1983). Identity group therapy: A transitional group for hospitalized adolescents. *International Journal of Group Psychotherapy, 33,* 99–109.

Group Climate: Construct in Search of Clarity

Debra Theobald McClendon *and* Gary M. Burlingame

Abstract

The definitions and key measures associated with group climate that underscore definitional confusion and overlap with other group process constructs (e.g., cohesion) are reviewed. Next, research associated with the Group Climate Questionnaire (GCQ), which has become the default definition of climate in the literature, is reviewed. More specifically, 83 studies examining the GCQ relationship with outcome, group development, and other process variables are summarized. Finally, findings from an international collaborative research project over the past decade are summarized to provide an alternative definition of group climate that encompasses other relationship variables (e.g., cohesion, therapeutic alliance, and empathy). We end with a set of questions that this model directly addresses as well as questions to be addressed by future research.

Keywords: group climate, group psychotherapy, group outcomes, group process, three-factor model of therapeutic relationships in group

In preparing for this chapter we examined individual studies as well as summative reviews relevant to the construct of group climate in therapeutic groups. We define *therapeutic groups* as group interventions that have a symptom remediation and/or personal growth focus (e.g., group therapy, group counseling), which can be contrasted with task or work groups. As we read, we were reminded that previous reviewers have described the group psychotherapy literature as "conglomerate, complex, confabulatory, and conflictual" (Anthony, 1971, p. 5). Twenty-five years later we added three *b*'s to the mix, noting that the group psychotherapy literature often seems to have "begged, borrowed, and bilked" from the individual literature (Fuhriman & Burlingame, 1994, p. 6). These *c*'s and *b*'s characterize our reading of parts of the group climate literature, leading to a past conclusion that at times the group climate literature seems to be caught in a conceptual quagmire.

We initially thought to carefully detail the conceptual quagmire so that readers could fully grasp its "squishy" nature. We refrained when we realized that this would have been an experiential exercise in confusion and entanglement—our process at times. We have opted to limit that experience for the reader and, instead, use the opportunity to more fully present the forward momentum of the field as it currently seeks conceptual and empirical maturity.

We begin the chapter with a dip into the depths of this quagmire by reviewing how group climate is discussed in the literature, to illustrate both the diversity and similarity of definitions. We also review key group climate measures. This brief exposure sets the historical context for the rest of the chapter, where we review what has become the gold standard in the group climate literature, the Group Climate Questionnaire-Short Form (GCQ-S) (MacKenzie, 1983). We provide a summary of the GCQ-S literature, examining its relationship with outcome, its potential as a mediator of outcome, its relationship to other group processes, as well evidence for its ability to track group development. We end the chapter by extending the group climate discussion beyond the GCQ-S to follow a line of research that involves teams from three countries (Germany, Norway, and the United States) that have produced a model that may clarify our understanding of group climate. This model embraces the complexity of group relationships by incorporating both content and structural definitions. We end by considering how this model might help our conceptual, empirical, and clinical understanding of group climate.

Group Climate Conceptually Defined

Group climate is like many constructs in the group literature; it suffers from a variety of definitions, clouding our clinical and empirical understanding. We identified three facets of the group climate literature that make it difficult to understand: definitional challenges, overlap with other key group relationship constructs, and diversity of content domains assessed by current measures of group climate. We will discuss each in turn.

Definitional Challenges

The definition of group climate in the extant literature creates a puzzling landscape for readers desiring a crisp and concise understanding. In an attempt to clarify, we reviewed available definitions from both empirical studies and reviews that spanned the last four decades, taking note of terms authors used to describe group climate. Illustrative examples in Table 10.1 evidence the wide variety of descriptors. Some authors used more than one term, while others adopted past definitions (e.g., Beech & Hamilton-Giachritsis, 2005). As we waded through the squishy empirical studies, we even noted definitional evolution in our own work (Burlingame, Fuhriman, & Johnson, 2002; Burlingame & McClendon, 2008; Hoag, Primus, Taylor, & Burlingame, 1996; Johnson, Burlingame, Olsen, Davies, & Gleave, 2005; Johnson, Burlingame, Strauss, & Bormann, 2008). The difficulty of describing the taste of salt comes to mind when we consider group climate definitions. We all know how salt tastes, but how do we describe it? Might this be what's happening with group climate?

The definitions in Table 10.1 have been grouped into three types: general, factors, and specific construct. The predominant definition of group

climate is the general emotional atmosphere of the group. Examples include those who view group climate as the consensually perceived psychosocial environment that members work within as well as the socioemotional/feeling tone of the group. A second theme describes how two or more relationship dynamics interact with one another to create group climate. Stated differently, group climate is the product of interacting forces in a group. For example, some writers holding this perspective view group climate as the dynamic created by the interaction of two or more opposing forces (harmony–anger, engaged–avoidant, close–withdrawn). Others employ complementary processes so that group climate emerges as the interactional product of interpersonal and group forces (relationship dynamics and group cohesion, respectively). More complicated formulations describe climate as the product of similar (resistance and friction) and complementary (cohesion) forces. Finally, a third perspective is that group climate is synonymous with a single construct, cohesion.

Overlap with Other Group Constructs

A second difficulty is the conceptual overlap with other group-relationship constructs. For example, cohesion plays a significant role in many of the conceptualizations of group climate across all three definitional perspectives (Table 10.1). MacKenzie (1981) indicated that engagement is "equivalent to the concept of cohesion as it is commonly but loosely used" (p. 290). Given this, we return to a commonly accepted and cited definition of cohesion: "the condition of members feeling warmth and comfort in the group, feeling they belong, valuing the group and feeling, in turn, that they are valued and unconditionally accepted and supported by the other members" (Yalom, 1995, p. 48). This definition appears similar to the general atmosphere definitions of group climate in Table 10.1. This socioemotional definition has a distinct "psychotherapy" feel and is in contrast to how task cohesion is defined in work groups and sports teams (i.e., a measure of group productivity) (Johnson, 2007).

Cohesion in treatment groups is undoubtedly related to group climate. Some authors suggest that cohesion contributes to group climate (Braaten, 1989; Burlingame et al., 2002; Kivlighan & Lilly, 1997; Kivlighan & Tarrant, 2001; MacKenzie, 1997). For example, Kivlighan and Lilly (1997) stated, "Most authors agree that cohesion is but one facet of the broader, multidimensional construct of

Table 10.1   Group climate defined

Reference	Definition/Term(s) Used	Type	New Model[a]
Bolman, 1971	Group tension, group withdrawal	Factors	−r
Hawkins et al., 1973	Group culture	General	+w
Hawkins et al., 1973	Cohesion	Single construct	+b
Lieberman et al., 1973	Intensity, harmony	Factors	+w/b
Silbergeld et al., 1975	Consensual psychosocial environment	General	+b, −r
Silbergeld et al., 1977	Perceived psychosocial environment	General	+b, −r
MacKenzie, 1979	Environmental press, group culture	General	+w
Braaten, 1989	Cohesion, relationship	Factors	+b
MacKenzie, 1983	Engaged, avoiding, conflict	Factors	+b, −r
Yalom, 1995	Group culture	General	+w
Kivlighan et al., 1996	Socioemotional climate, perception of the group atmosphere	General	+b/w
Hoag et al., 1996	Therapeutic milieu, curative climate	General	+w/b
MacKenzie, 1997	Group environment, interactional atmosphere, group culture	General	+w
Brossart et al., 1998	General group atmosphere	General	+w
Burlingame et al., 2002	Emotional climate	General	+b
McCallum et al., 2002	Cohesion, resistance, friction	Factors	+b/w
Riva, Wachtel, & Lasky, 2004	Cohesion	Single construct	+b
Johnson et al., 2005	Constructive interpersonal investigation	General	+w
Shechtman & Gluk, 2005	Cohesion	Single construct	+b
Burlingame et al., 2006	Tone of factors: closeness, withdrawal, conflict	Factors	+b, −r
Burlingame & McClendon, 2008	Feeling tone	General	+b, −r
Johnson et al., 2008	Enduring themes of behavior and atmosphere	General	+w

[a]Notation corresponds to new model proposed later in the chapter: +b, positive bond; +w, positive work; −r, negative relationship.

group structure or group atmosphere" (p. 208). Our most recent view (Johnson et al., 2008) is that "Cohesion and other positive features of group treatment occur so often together in groups that it is difficult to determine what is the cause and what is the effect" (p. 66). Until dominant measures of both group climate and cohesion are simultaneously measured and empirically tested for common latent factor structure, we believe the literature is "stuck" in definitional mud.

Overlap has also been documented with relationship constructs such as culture, group development, norms, and working alliance. The following are illustrative of this overlap. The term group culture is used synonymously with group climate (Hawkins, Norton, Eisdorfer, & Gianturco, 1973; MacKenzie, 1979). Johnson et al. (2005) found that measures of group climate, cohesion, alliance, and empathy were as highly correlated with each other as scales that measure the same construct.

MacKenzie (1997) discussed how constructs such as cohesion and group climate "interweave" (p. 280) with group development and indicated that each of these constructs contribute to the understanding of the "nature of groupness" (p. 280).

Researchers have expressed concern about the overlap of these relationship constructs (Ogrodniczuk & Piper, 2003; Johnson et al., 2005; Sexton, 1993). For instance, Johnson and colleagues (2005) noted that conceptual ambiguity may be traced to identical or closely related constructs being defined from different theoretical orientations; that is, the construct is the same, but the language used to describe it is different. They concluded that differences in definitions have "provided the field conceptual richness, [but] they have also contributed to empirical inefficiency" (p. 319).

Group Climate Measures

In an effort to clarify how group climate was being used in the extant literature, we examined definitions from existing group climate measures. A PsycINFO search revealed several group climate measures (Table 10.2). While our list is not comprehensive, it includes the most frequently used face valid measures of group climate. Close examination by item and subscale reveals surface similarities as well as an assortment of divergent items.

Early measurement attempts were foundational for the field of group psychotherapy as it expanded

Table 10.2 Group-climate measures

Measure	Description of Scales	Frequency
Group Environment Scale (Moos & Humphrey, 1974; Moos, 1986, 1994, 2004)	*Relationship* examines cohesion, leader support, and the amount of freedom of action and expression of feelings encouraged in the group. *Personal Growth* examines independent action and expression among members, the degree of the group's task orientation, the group's encouragement of discussion of personal problems, and anger and disagreement. *System Maintenance and Change* measures the degree of organization, structure, and rules in the group; the role of the leader in making decisions and enforcing rules; and how much the group promotes diversity and change in its own process.	22
Group Atmosphere Scale (Silbergeld et al., 1975, 1977)	*Group Cohesion* includes autonomy, affiliation, involvement, insight, spontaneity, support, and clarity. *Submission* examines group conformity. *Aggression, Order, Practicality,* and *Variety* contribute to other aspects of perceived environment. The authors did not define these scales. Validity: There are *Halo* ("exaggerated feelings toward the group, and to reveal inconsistency by willingness to accept both extremely positive and negative statements," Silbergeld et al., 1975, p. 461) and *Inconsistency* subscales.	10
Group Climate Questionnaire-Short Form (MacKenzie, 1983)	*Engaged* measures the degree of self-disclosure, cohesion, and work orientation in the group. *Avoiding* examines the degree to which individuals rely on the other group members or leaders, avoiding responsibility for their own change process. *Conflict* measures interpersonal conflict and distrust.	83
Curative Climate Instrument (Fuhriman et al., 1986)	*Cohesion* involves attractiveness of the group to the members. *Catharsis* involves the release of intense emotional material previously controlled or restricted. *Insight* includes finding meaning and understanding from one's thoughts, feelings, and actions.	7
Group Counseling Helpful Impacts Scale (Kivlighan et al., 1996)	*Emotional Awareness–Insight* examines strong emotional experiences and insight. *Relationship–Climate* examines the formation and maintenance of group relationships. *Other Versus Self-Focus* examines learning from others. *Problem Definition–Change* examines solving problems and change in behavior.	5

its empirical inquiry in the 1970s. Some psychoanalytic models were shifting focus from individuals to group dynamics, and models originally developed for the individual format were being adapted to group (Burlingame & Baldwin, 2010). Thus, early group climate measures were pioneers in capturing the complexity of group relationships. For example, Lieberman, Yalom, and Miles (1973) presented a primer for climate in their examination and measurement of group norms and process in their classic study of encounter groups. Hawkins et al. (1973) used a descriptive observer questionnaire to assess feelings and interaction in the group. Historical efforts aside, it is clear from Table 10.2 that later measurement efforts (1980s) were still struggling to define group climate; that is, there was no manifest consensus.

Authors have pointed out limitations with each measure found in Table 10.2. For example, MacKenzie (1981) noted concern about the sensitivity of the Group Environment Scale (GES) (Moos & Humphrey, 1974) with its dichotomous true–false question format. The GES, now in its third edition (Moos, 2004), is used mainly in the area of social psychology and nonclinical groups. The Group Atmosphere Scale (GAS) (Silbergeld, Koenig, Manderscheid, Meeker, & Hornung, 1975; Silbergeld, Manderscheid, & Koenig, 1977) contains group climate items but also assesses group cohesion and conformity. MacKenzie (1981) viewed the GAS as a group climate measure, but we have argued that it can also be viewed as a measure of cohesion (Johnson et al., 2008).

Fuhriman, Drescher, Hanson, Henrie, and Rybicki (1986) developed the Curative Climate Instrument (CCI) to psychometrically refine Yalom's (1975) original measure of the therapeutic factors. The CCI is not a group climate measure per se but rather a refined measure of a member's perceived sense of how helpful Yalom's therapeutic factors have been in his or her group experience. The factor analysis conducted by these authors of Yalom's 12 therapeutic factors identified three distinct latent factors (cohesion, catharsis, and insight). Unfortunately, the authors use the term climate when naming their measure. We are quite familiar with the CCI, having used it in our own studies (Hoag et al., 1996; Johnson et al., 2006) and having recommended its use for others (Burlingame, MacKenzie, & Strauss, 2004). However, for the novice reader trying to understand the construct of group climate, we can see how group climate might be confused with therapeutic factors assessed by the CCI.

If our discussion of the difficulties with the group climate definition and measures has made you dizzy, we have successfully shared our bewildering experience as we tried to make sense of the extant literature. Definitional challenges, conceptual and statistical overlap with other group relationship constructs, and wide variability in the content assessed by measures indicate that climate is a theoretically loose construct with "a rather vague quality" (Hawkins et al., 1973, p. 917). The one bright spot in the group climate literature is the development and widespread use of the GCQ-S.

Group Climate Questionnaire (GCQ-S)

We tabulated the number of studies that have used each measure found in Table 10.2 using both PsycINFO and Google Scholar searches. The GCQ-S dominates the group climate literature with 83 studies located, which agrees with our prior assessment that it remains one of the most widely used self-report group process instruments in the group literature (Burlingame et al., 2004). The GCQ-S is a revision of MacKenzie's (1981) Group Climate Questionnaire-Long Form (GCQ-L). The QCQ-L had 32 items and eight scales, including Engagement, Disclosure, Support, Conflict, Challenge, Practicality, Cognition, and Control. MacKenzie (1983) felt the GCQ-L was too long and developed the short form to be more clinically practical; the long form is now obsolete.

The GCQ-S purports to measure individual group members' perceptions of the therapeutic environment, made up of three interacting dimensions: engagement, avoidance, and conflict. The GCQ-S has 12 items rated on a 7-point Likert scale (0 = "not at all" to 6 = "extremely"), ranking a group member's level of agreement with the item statement (Table 10.3). It takes less than 5 minutes to complete and is scored by summing the items for each scale and calculating the mean. MacKenzie does not recommend summing all GCQ-S items into a total score but encourages users to examine the three scale scores across the entire group as well as to look for individual member deviation from a group pattern. MacKenzie (1983) recommended gathering repeated measures, giving the GCQ-S after every group session since there are significant shifts in group climate dimensions from session to session. Indeed, Brossart, Patton, and Wood (1998) indicated that the GCQ-S can be conceptualized as a session impact measure.

Engaged, Avoiding, and Conflict scales were derived from MacKenzie's (1983) study, which

Table 10.3   MacKenzie's (1983) group climate questionnaire-short form (GCQ-S) with summary of evidence

		Outcome	Process	Development
1. The members liked and cared about each other.	Engaged	Strong	Strong	Moderate
2. The members tried to understand why they do things they do, tried to reason it out.				
4. The members felt what was happening was important and there was a sense of participation.				
8. The members challenged and confronted each other in their efforts to sort things out.				
11. The members revealed sensitive personal information or feelings.				
6. There was friction and anger between the members.	Conflict	Moderate	Strong–moderate	Moderate
10. The members rejected and distrusted each other.				
12. The members appeared tense and anxious.				
3. The members avoided looking at important issues going on between themselves.	Avoiding	Moderate–weak	Weak	Weak
5. The members depended upon the group leader(s) for direction.				
7. The members were distant and withdrawn from each other.				
9. The members appeared to do things the way they thought would be acceptable to the group.				

utilized a large group of clinical outpatients. In considering the GCQ-S scale descriptions (Table 10.2), it is important to note that the Conflict scale measures hostility, such as anger, distrust, and rejection, rather than confrontation (Johnson et al., 2008). This factor structure has been replicated in several studies. For example, MacKenzie, Dies, Coché, Rutan, & Stone (1987) identified three factors in their study of American Group Psychotherapy Association (AGPA) institute groups composed of graduate students and residents, advanced therapists, and instructors. To provide greater context for understanding the GCQ-S, Table 10.3 provides each of the specific measure items organized under its corresponding scales as reported by the AGPA (Burlingame et al., 2006). It should be noted that Johnson et al. (2006) grouped item number seven with Conflict rather than Avoiding as an item measuring distancing.

Table 10.3 also provides a summary of the extant literature relative to the strength of evidence we located. Study findings were reviewed and noted relative to the strength of association for the various GCQ-S scales. A "strong" rating reflects consistent findings, a "moderate" rating reflects mixed results, and a "weak" rating reflects that few studies could be

found that endorse significant results. The Engaged scale had a strong relationship to outcome and the greatest number of studies. Indeed, the engagement–outcome relationship is one of the strongest we observed in the group climate literature. The Engaged scale also had a strong relationship with other group processes and some support for studies trying to capture patterns associated with group development. The Conflict scale has moderate levels of evidence across all types of studies, and the Avoiding scale had moderate to weak evidence for outcome and weak evidence for process and group development.

The validity of the GCQ-S has been well established, with studies supporting its ability to distinguish different types of group therapy (Joyce, Azim, & Morrin, 1988), duration (Kanas, Stewart, Deri, Ketter, & Haney, 1989), and clinical populations (Daroff, 1996; Tasca, Flynn, & Bissada, 2002). In the midst of the aforementioned conceptual quagmire, researchers have advanced empirical understanding of group climate by its use. As a result, most of what we know about group climate in recent years comes from research using the GCQ-S, referred to as GCQ for the remainder of the chapter.

Group Climate Research

There are four themes that are consistently tested in GCQ studies. The first and most frequent theme is the GCQ's relationship with treatment outcome. The obvious implication from this research is the possibility of providing group clinicians with a process assessment that might be a harbinger of patient improvement. Indeed, this was one of MacKenzie's original goals in creating the GCQ. The second, less studied theme is the use of the GCQ as a mediator of group treatment outcomes. While certainly related, this theme invokes a higher scientific standard because it entails specialized assessment and analytic techniques. The third theme is the use of the GCQ to examine process variables; these studies are less frequent than outcome studies. Finally, when the GCQ was introduced, it was tied to a specific theory of group development. MacKenzie proposed specific temporal patterns for each of the three GCQ scales that have been submitted to independent study. Given the difficulty of supporting the myriad of theories regarding group development, the advent of a measure tied to a concise theory of group development was viewed with considerable interest, leading to a number of empirical studies testing such. A summary of each theme follows.

Group Climate and Outcome

We (Johnson et al., 2008) recently reviewed 14 studies (1987–2007) published in the English and German literature that tested the relationship between the GCQ and treatment outcome. Twelve used data examined at the individual level (correlations between individual member scales and their own outcomes), while two used group-level data (GCQ data were aggregated at the group level). It has been argued that group-level data are theoretically closer to assessing "group" relationship constructs, so the findings of these studies were given greater weight. The two studies that used group-level data reported positive findings relative to outcome. The first (MacKenzie et al., 1987) found that groups with better outcomes had higher levels of engagement and that engagement increased over time, while levels of conflict decreased over time. The second found higher levels of engagement for successful groups (Phipps & Zastowny, 1988).

Interestingly, studies that analyzed their data at the individual level produced mixed findings regarding the relationship between the GCQ scales and outcome. The most reliable finding was the relationship between the Engaged scale and outcome. Group members who reported higher engagement

scores on the GCQ tended to have improved outcomes over those who did not (Beutel et al., 2006; Braaten, 1989; Hurley, 1989; Mattke & Schreiber-Willnow, 2004; Ogrodniczuk & Piper, 2003; Tschuschke & Greene, 2002). Exceptions to this were studies that used the GCQ with psychodynamic and psychoanalytic groups. In these exceptions, engagement was not related to outcome (Grabhorn, Kaufhold, Burkhardt, Kerkhof, & Overbeck, 2000; Hilbert et al., 2007; MacKenzie & Tschuschke, 1993; McCallum, Piper, Ogrodniczuk, & Joyce, 2002). Indeed, in a few studies lower levels of engagement were related to better outcome (Strauss & Burgmeier-Lohse, 1994) or produced differential relationships depending on group type (i.e., engagement was related to a better outcome for eating disorder groups but not obsessive compulsive disorder, anxiety, and depression) (Sehring & Engel, 1998).

Outcome has also been related to the Conflict and Avoiding scales. The two group-level studies found conflict to be negatively related to outcome. MacKenzie et al. (1987) found that conflict in groups led to poorer outcomes. Phipps and Zastowny (1988) found higher levels of conflict for poorly functioning groups. However, individual-level studies of psychodynamic groups found that conflict was associated with better outcomes (Grabhorn et al., 2000; Strauss & Burgmeier-Lohse, 1994; Tschuschke & Greene, 2002), while other studies found negative or mixed results (Hurley, 1989; Ogrodniczuk & Piper, 2003; Sehring & Engel, 1998). Johnson and colleagues (2008) found that the Avoiding scale was not related to outcome in the group-level studies and that the findings in the individual-level studies were mixed and often contradictory. Thus, it is unclear how avoidance scores are related to outcome.

The study by Ogrodniczuk and Piper (2003) may be instructive relative to the Conflict and Avoiding scales. These authors found that the Conflict and Avoiding scales of the GCQ were not significantly related to outcome using early ratings, averaged ratings, or change in ratings. When group members perceived high levels of conflict in the group, less avoidance within the group was related to worse outcome on measures of grief and general symptoms. On the other hand, when members perceived conflict to be at low levels, avoidance had little relation to outcome. These authors also found a significant interaction between engagement and conflict after the early stages of therapy. When group members perceived conflict in the group, higher levels of engagement were related to poorer outcome in relation to grief symptoms. Yet, higher levels of engagement were related to more improved outcome for grief symptoms when levels of perceived conflict were low.

Recently, Ryum, Hagen, Nordahl, Vogel, and Stiles (2009) conducted a randomized controlled trial examining the use of the GCQ factors as predictors of long-term (1 year) follow-up in a manualized, structured, time-limited, cognitive-behavioral group therapy for those with comorbid psychiatric disorders. Higher levels of engagement were associated with positive outcome on four of five outcome measures at follow-up (anxiety symptoms being the exception). Higher levels of avoidance were associated with lower anxiety symptoms at follow-up. The GCQ Conflict scale was unrelated to all follow-up scores.

In summary, the scales of the GCQ vary in their relationship to outcome based on a number of variables including the theoretical orientation of the group being offered and the manner in which the data are analyzed (group vs. individual). Furthermore, interactions among scales suggest a more complex, rather than a simple, linear understanding of how engagement, conflict, and avoidance relate to treatment outcome.

Group Climate as a Mediator of Outcome

MacKenzie (1981) stated that "the group climate is seen as a mediating variable through which the leader exerts influence on the members" (p. 294). Researchers have found partial support for his claim (Bolman, 1971; Phipps & Zastowny, 1988). For example, Phipps and Zastowny used the GCQ to study outpatient groups. A positive leadership style predicted greater levels of engagement, and a more engaged group climate predicated improved group member outcomes. Yet, these early studies had a monomethod bias, with group members providing all ratings of leader, group climate, and outcome.

Kivlighan and Tarrant (2001) sought to improve on earlier studies and examined whether group climate mediated the group leadership–group member outcome relationship with adolescent groups. Group therapists rated their intentions in the group sessions; intentions were defined as the rationale for why leaders intervened as they did in session. These were rated along four dimensions: therapeutic work, safe environment, interpersonal focus, and group structure. Group members completed the GCQ and an outcome measure. Kivlighan and Tarrant found that leader intentions of therapeutic work

were negatively related to group climate and intentions toward a safe environment were positively related; a group climate that decreased in conflict and distance predicted a more positive relationship with the group leader, and an engaged and active climate predicted more positive outcomes. Thus, they confirmed and expanded upon earlier studies relative to group climate as a mediator of the relationship between group leader activity and group member outcome.

Group Climate and Process

Several process variables have been examined relative to their relationship with group climate. Leadership style is a common process variable explored in the literature. It contributes to the ability of a therapist to create a group atmosphere which is helpful to facilitating member change (MacKenzie, 1979) by "developing a climate of constructive emotional dialogue" (Leszcz & Kobos, 2008, p. 1252). A principle supported repeatedly throughout the literature serves as an overall guide to navigating group climate and process: Use a positive leadership style to build a therapeutic group climate (Dies, 1983, 1994; Hurley & Rosenberg, 1990; McBride, 1995; Morran, Stockton, & Whittingham, 2004). GCQ studies have enhanced our understanding of this principle, showing that positive leadership style predicts higher levels of engagement (Kivlighan & Tarrant, 2001; Phipps & Zastowny, 1988).

Few group-process studies have taken into account individual member contributions. Those that have frequently do not test member variables as moderators. For example, might a member's interpersonal style or presenting problem be related to his or her perception of group climate? Kivlighan and Angelone (1992) studied the relationship between group members' interpersonal problems and their perception of the group climate, administering a problem inventory and the GCQ. They found that perception of the group climate was related to the types of interpersonal problems the group members experienced. For example, group members who perceived themselves as too dominant experienced the group climate as more avoidant and conflictual. Members who saw themselves as too cold saw the group as less engaged, having less conflict and less anxiety. Those who were too nurturant and too nonassertive saw the group as engaged but also conflictual and anxious. The authors noted that because their participants were students, rather than help-seeking clients, they had less severe interpersonal problems than would generally be found in clinical groups; they suggested that studies utilizing a clinical population would find yet a stronger relationship between interpersonal problems and perceptions of group climate.

A similar pattern of results appeared in two German inpatient studies that assessed cohesion, not climate. Schauenburg, Sammet, Rabung, and Strack (2001) conducted a pilot study and found that a member's interpersonal style moderated the relationship between cohesion and outcome. Specifically, patients with interpersonal problems described as too friendly seemed to improve more when their experience of cohesion decreased during therapy, whereas patients with cold or hostile interpersonal problems improved most when their experience of cohesion increased during the group. In an attempt to replicate their first study, Dinger and Schauenburg (2010) studied a much larger sample of 327 inpatients participating in group therapy in a German psychiatric hospital. Results from this study showed that higher levels of cohesion as well as an increase in cohesion over the life of the group were associated with greater symptom improvement, replicating the strong engagement–outcome relationship found in previously described studies. Of particular importance was that patient interpersonal style also predicted treatment outcome. Specifically, patients who described themselves as too cold and who reported increased cohesion posted the greatest improvement. The opposite pattern was found for those who described themselves as too friendly at the beginning of treatment. These studies from the climate and cohesion literature both introduce the important consideration of patient variables moderating the relationship between climate and outcome.

Other process studies have explored similar variables. Kivlighan and Jauquet (1990) studied the relationship between group member session agendas and group climate. Session agendas were rated on their specificity (abstract to realistic), the focus on group members and events (there-and-then to here-and-now focus), as well as relationships among the group members (intrapersonal to interpersonal focus). Realistic agendas were related to early levels of engagement. Both here-and-now and interpersonal dimensions of agendas were related to greater levels of perceived engagement and lower levels of avoiding during the middle and late sessions. Finally, the here-and-now focus was related to conflict in the middle of therapy.

Stockton, Rohde, and Haughey (1992) examined the effect of structured exercises on the GCQ scales. They found a main effect for Conflict, suggesting that structured exercises immediately reduced conflict. They also found a structure-by-time interaction for Engaged and Avoiding, illustrated by steady and gradual increases in engagement and decreases in avoidance over the course of the group. Although process studies make up a smaller literature base than do outcome studies, these illustrative examples demonstrate the ability of the GCQ to highlight important group dynamics. These processes contribute to a therapeutic group climate that may influence member perceptions of their group experience.

Group Climate's Interaction with Group Development

It has been proposed that psychotherapy groups undergo a natural developmental process, with different emotional tones characterizing the group climate of different stages. The most influential theory is by MacKenzie and Livesley (1983), revised by MacKenzie (1997) with three stages becoming prominent in clinical practice. The first stage is *engagement*, in which interaction and cohesion increase and tasks such as member commitment and participation are negotiated. Self-disclosure, interpersonal challenge, and introspective challenge are present within the group at this stage at superficial levels, with low levels of conflict and avoidance of member-to-member interactional issues. The second stage, *differentiation*, is when conflict between group members becomes manifest. In this stage, members are either resisting or simply not enjoying the therapeutic work, so the therapist becomes an important sustaining figure. The *interpersonal work* stage is characterized by an increase in engagement and a decrease in conflict. The evidence of psychological work of the members is prominent with an increase in self-disclosure, cognitive mastery, and interpersonal challenge.

Kivlighan and Goldfine (1991) studied changes in the GCQ as a function of stage development with students in personal growth groups. They found group climate changes that supported MacKenzie's theory. In the early stage of group, the GCQ Engaged and Conflict scales were relatively low, while the Avoiding scale was high. In the middle stage of group treatment, Engaged and Avoiding scale scores were moderate, while Conflict was high. In the latter part of group, the Engaged scale was relatively high, and the Avoiding and Conflict scales were low.

Later, Kivlighan and Lilly (1997) studied outcome and developmental changes in group climate, using the term *group climate development*, which they defined as "the structure of growth in the group climate construct" (p. 210). Scores on the GCQ and an outcome measure were used to study the relationship between developmental changes in group climate and therapeutic outcome for undergraduate and graduate students attending interpersonal process groups for a class on group theories. Over the course of treatment, they found a high-low-high pattern on the Engaged scale, a low-high-low pattern on the Conflict scale, and a cubic pattern (i.e., low–high–low–high) on the Avoiding scale to be related to improved outcomes for group members.

Early group development is particularly important relative to the level of engagement that group members experience. Several studies have illustrated that early engagement is related to improved outcome (Braaten, 1989; Davies, Burlingame, Johnson, Gleave, & Barlow, 2008; MacKenzie et al., 1987; Ogrodniczuk & Piper, 2003). For example, Ogrodniczuk and Piper (2003) found that levels of engagement after the fourth session of group and average levels of engagement over the entire group were directly related with improvement. MacKenzie et al. (1987) found that engagement levels predicted the outcomes of an AGPA 2-day group training session when the GCQ was given at the end of the first 3.5-hour session. Kivlighan and Angelone (1992) and Kivlighan and Lilly (1997) found that low levels of conflict early in the therapy process allow for the development of cohesion and other therapeutic factors. Crowe and Grenyer (2008) found that higher levels of perceived conflict at session 6 predicted poorer outcome at the end of a 16-session treatment.

In summary, there are a sizable number of GCQ studies that support the developmental predictions made by MacKenzie. Thus, development may be one way to predict a group's climate at a given point in time. Specifically, early levels of group engagement seem to be particularly critical to good client outcomes, with high levels of engagement and low levels of conflict predicting improvement. Findings for the Avoiding scale are mixed.

GCQ Limitations

The GCQ has become the bedrock of our current understanding of climate in therapeutic groups. However, there are at least two notable limitations. The first and perhaps most notable involves the Avoiding scale. Johnson et al. (2005) found that it had "unacceptably low internal consistency (0.36) and consistently failed to load well with other subscales" (p. 319). The factor structure often does not support this scale (Hurley & Brooks, 1987, 1988; Johnson et al., 2005, 2006), with at least two of our studies finding a two-factor structure that omitted the Avoiding scale. This has led to our recommendation that *the Avoiding scale should not be scored or interpreted for clinical use* (Burlingame et al., 2006).

A second limitation also relates to the three-factor structure. We found a single study that involved adolescents which also produced a two-factor structure of group climate: active engagement and conflict–distance (Tarrant & Kivlighan, 2000). This factor structure was used by Kivlighan and Tarrant (2001) in their study of the mediational role of group climate, yet it has not been replicated by other studies. Thus, more research is necessary before generalizing reported GCQ findings to adolescent populations.

Establishing Group Climate within a Larger Framework of Group Relationships

Group climate falls under the more encompassing rubric of therapeutic relationships in group. A common framework in describing therapeutic relationship in group is structure. Specifically, the three most common structural elements are member-member, member-leader, and member-group relationships (Burlingame et al., 2002). These structural considerations can be considered independently of the content assessed in the aforementioned relationship constructs of group climate, cohesion, and the like (Burlingame et al., 2002; Johnson et al., 2005, 2008). As noted, group climate has several conceptual and definitional challenges that have not remitted over the past few decades with the exception of the GCQ literature. Indeed, Sexton (1993) noted that many of the process constructs studied in group-therapy literature are highly interconnected and probably characterize a small number of fundamentals. Within the past half-decade we have begun to see progress in identifying this small number of fundamentals. What follows is a brief summary.

For years, reviewers have bemoaned the methodological challenges of group research and occasionally, almost parenthetically, suggested that a cooperative partnership between multisite group research teams might overcome these methodological, definitional, and generalizability obstacles (Fuhriman & Burlingame, 1994). The belief underlying a cooperative partnership is as follows:

If identical measures were used by multiple teams studying diverse leaders guided by varying theoretical orientations treating different patient populations, the generalizability of findings would be significantly increased compared to extant studies in the group literature. Moreover, we would have a better chance of determining if there were indeed fundamental properties that could be measured reliably and validly across the vast array of settings where the group format is used.

Burlingame (2010) recently summarized the creation and work products of a cooperative partnership between several research teams in Germany, Norway, and the United States. This cooperative was initially cosponsored by a task force formed by the AGPA and a grant from the TransCoop program in Germany. The stated goal of the AGPA/TransCoop cooperative was a revision of the AGPA battery of selection, process, and outcome instruments for group clinicians. Strauss, Burlingame, and Bormann (2008) described the clinical success of this battery, while Burlingame (2010) summarized the scientific success of this work group. What follows is a summary of his analysis.

One of the first studies emanating from the AGPA/TransCoop cooperative was a North American study conducted by Johnson and colleagues (2005). The cooperative had suggested several small group-process measures to be added to the CORE battery, each of which tapped the group relationship (cohesion, group climate, therapist empathy, and working alliance). Unfortunately, these measures had never been studied simultaneously to examine conceptual and empirical overlap. To determine this, the researchers asked 662 group members from 111 different groups drawn from 15 clinical (primarily U.S. counseling centers) and 2-day personal growth groups conducted at the AGPA's annual conference to complete a copy of each measure. Using multilevel modeling, they developed a three-factor latent variable structure (positive bond, positive work, and negative relationship) that fit both nonclinical and clinical groups and explained a sizable proportion of variance from the four measures (59% and 66% of the variance, respectively). Their results were promising enough that the AGPA/TransCoop cooperative reframed the CORE-R group process section using Johnson et al.'s three-factor model. However, what is perhaps more important is that the Johnson et al. study became a "muse" for four other studies. The common goal of the five studies (Table 10.4) was to clarify

the multitude of relationship constructs used in the group literature (empathy, cohesion, climate, and alliance).

Bormann and Strauss (2007) represented the German branch of the AGPA/TransCoop cooperative and conducted the next study. They collected data from 67 groups drawn from 15 hospitals in Germany and Switzerland using the same four measures. While Johnson et al.'s model was not completely replicated (a few items varied), the same three factors emerged: positive bond, positive work, and negative relationship (Table 10.4). Moreover, they found support for the three structural components of the therapeutic relationship (member-member, member-leader, and member-group).

Coherent findings from nearly 200 groups and three countries were sufficiently attractive to entice a third research team from Norway to participate. Lorentzen and colleagues used the same four group process measures in a randomized trial of short- and long-term (20 vs. 80 sessions) psychodynamic group therapy in outpatient settings throughout Norway (Bakali, Baldwin, & Lorentzen, 2009; Lorentzen, Hoglend, Ruud, 2008). They reported a very similar three-factor model. However, findings varied on one of the factors by stage of treatment (Table 10.4). Data from early sessions suggested the importance of the member-leader alliance, while later sessions (10–11 and 17–18 sessions) produced a factor structure that included positive bonds with other members and the group. Lorentzen and colleagues (2009) noted that one explanation for this difference is that the group leader met with each member for up to five sessions prior to the group, placing the leader in a more important initial role. A second difference is length of treatment (2 years) and theoretical orientation. Nonetheless, the remarkable impact of this study was the replication of the three-factor model in a fourth country with a very diverse setting and theoretical orientation.

The three preceding studies provided sufficient promise to engage the North American branch to conduct an item-reduction process to eliminate items with redundant information or poor fit. In other words, they wanted to determine if the same robust three-factor model could be supported with fewer items, thereby increasing the clinical utility of a common group-therapy relationship measure. Using archival data from Johnson et al.'s original study, a 40-item instrument called the Group Questionnaire (GQ) was developed from the four original measures (Krogel, 2009; Krogel, Beecher, Presnell, Burlingame, & Simonsen, 2009). More

Table 10.4 Summary of five international studies examining AGPA/transcoop measures of cohesion, empathy, alliance, and climate

Research Team	Clinical Setting	Members/Groups	Primary findings
Johnson et al., 2005	14 US counseling centers US nonclinical process groups	326/81 336/30	Positive bond, positive work, and negative relationship factors produced best fit; little interfactor correlation
Bormann & Strauss, 2007	15 psychiatric hospitals in Germany & Switzerland	453/67	Differences at item level with Johnson model but 3-factor model best fit - positive bond, positive work, and negative relationship - correlated errors required for model fit
Bakali et al., 2009	20-session psychodynamic groups 80-session psychodynamic groups	145/18	3-factor model best fit—very similar to preceding studies Differences × time and relationship structure: - relationship with therapist important in early sessions - relationship with member/leader emerges in later sessions - member–leader alliance, positive bond, and negative relationship best fit model
Krogel, 2009—30-item GQ[a]	2 US counseling centers US nonclinical process groups Inpatient state hospital groups	207/na 160/na 118/na	3-factor model produced best fit using 30-item differences × structure found - evidence for member–leader, member-group, and member–member structure distinction - factors correlated with one another - model held with 3 distinct populations
Bormann & Strauss, 2009—30-item GQ	9 psychiatric hospitals in Germany	424/63	Model fit with Krogel, 2009 - GQ criterion validity established with Group Experience Scale, Stuttgart Questionnaire, Helping Alliance Questionnaire, and Bonn Questionnaire for Therapy & Counseling
Totals	16 US counseling centers 30+ US nonclinical process groups 1 inpatient state hospital 24 hospitals Germany/Switzerland 18 Norwegian psychodynamic groups	2,169/259+	3-factor structure held across multiple settings and patient populations Items on factor structure change by group development in one study

[a]Group Questionnaire.

specifically, Krogel's team examined each scale (positive bond, positive work, and negative relationship) and, guided equally by clinical and empirical criteria, arrived at a consensual definition. The empirical criteria for item selection included eliminating redundant items and factorial fit, and the clinical criteria were items that tapped actionable clinical material to assist group leaders.

Krogel replicated Johnson et al.'s original study using the same two group populations (counseling centers and nonclinical AGPA process groups) and adding a third population—seriously mentally ill (SMI) inpatients participating in groups at a state psychiatric hospital. SMI populations are often treated with group formats (Burlingame et al., 2004) but unfortunately receive virtually no attention in the group-therapy process literature. Using a sample of 485 group members across three populations, Krogel (2009) found the same three-factor structure (Table 10.4). The model adequately explained variance at extreme ends of the clinical spectrum (SMI inpatients and university students at a counseling center) as well as with nonclinical process groups. Like Bakali and colleagues (2009), Krogel found evidence for the importance of structure in the relationship (member-member, member-leader, and member-group). More importantly, this team recommended a shortened 30-item measure that provided nearly identical information.

Finally, Bormann and Strauss (2009) took the 30-item GQ and tested its factor structure and criterion validity with 424 new group members from nine psychiatric hospitals in Germany (Table 10.4). These authors once again found support for the same three-factor model and reported that the three factors correlated highly with four frequently used measures of small-group process (including a group climate measure), thereby supporting the criterion validity of the GQ.

Thus, what has emerged from over 2,000 group members being treated in four countries with a wide variety of theoretical orientations is a common conceptual and empirical model to describe the therapeutic relationship. The importance of this accomplishment cannot be understated and in our view is a harbinger of conceptual clarity for the group climate literature.

A New Framework

Might this model allow us to more clearly define—conceptually and empirically—the group climate construct? Positive bond, positive work, and negative relationship factors are clearly a robust and parsimonious framework for describing therapeutic relationships in group. Support for the model across four languages and countries and five distinct clinical and nonclinical populations (SMI inpatients, personal growth groups, counseling center groups, Norwegian outpatients, and German/Swiss inpatients) add to its appeal. Furthermore, the general support for the importance of considering relationship structures (member- member, member-leader, and member-group) adds a second dimension for potentially clarifying past research.

Do the findings from this international cooperative research program make group climate obsolete? One could certainly make this argument. On the other hand, we would like to consider how these findings might clarify our understanding of group climate. Our proposal relies upon the three latent and three structural factors produced by the five aforementioned studies. Table 10.5 presents a 3×3 matrix produced by the crossing of the two sets factors. We have outlined three cells that we believe correspond to past definitions and that also capture scales from the GCQ. We review the member-group structural column and then each cell in turn.

The most common definitions of group climate (Table 10.1) identify the "group" as the unit of analysis. For example, Silbergeld and colleagues (1977) defined climate as "perceived psychosocial environment," while Kivlighan, Multon, and Brossart (1996) define it as the "perception of the group atmosphere." Thus, we believe group climate is structurally a member-group phenomenon, and there appears to be agreement on this aspect as we considered past definitions. Having proffered this definition, we hasten to add that it may have more conceptual than empirical value. For example, Krogel (2009) found very high correlations between all three structural units on the positive bond items.

Positive Bond

We return to the last column of Table 10.1 to support the potential clarifying value of the new model of group climate proposed in Table 10.5. Reviewing past definitions, we note that at least 14 authors have used terms to capture the positive affective bond found between and among members. For instance, words such as *harmony, cohesion, socioemotional culture, emotional climate, closeness,* and *feeling tone* have all appeared in past definitions of group climate noted in Table 10.1. Given the large empirical overlap found in the feeling tone measures (cohesion, engagement, alliance, empathy) assessed

Table 10.5 Proposed framework for conceptualizing group in three-factor model of therapeutic relationship in group therapy

		Relationship Structure		
		Member-to-member	Member-to-therapist	Member-to-group
Relationship Content	Positive bonding relationship			Group climate
	Positive working relationship			
	Negative relationship			

by the five international studies, we propose that we no longer use these terms separately but consider the higher-order latent factor of positive bond as a more precise construct. Indeed, past studies have found nearly perfect correlations from member perspectives when they are asked to rate these feeling tones in a group.

Positive Work

We also believe that the positive work factor can be found in up to 10 definitions of *group climate* noted in Table 10.1. For instance, authors discuss the intensity and environmental press of the group atmosphere, the curative climate of the group, and even climate as an atmosphere for interpersonal investigation. When we review actual items loading on these scales, it appears that the underlying construct that authors may be tapping into is the working atmosphere of the group. This is clearly indicated by the positive work dimension.

Negative Relationship

Finally, several authors also specifically tap into aspects of the negative affect that can occur in the group, using terms such as *group tension and withdrawal*, *avoiding*, and *conflict*. Others introduce emotional terms that do not have a positive or negative valence. Examples include *feeling tone* and *emotional climate* of the group. In the absence of a specific valence, we can see an argument for both positive (i.e., positive bond) and negative (i.e., negative relationship) valence items, supporting the three-factor model we are proposing. We went back and recoded the definitions in Table 10.1 using this three-factor model to show how it might be used to clarify past definitions of group climate in the last column.

In summary, we see the potential to "locate" past definitions of group climate in the latent factors that have emerged over the past 5 years from an international cooperative. Because these studies used a single yet dominant measure of group climate (GCQ), it is unclear to us if the 3×3 matrix in Table 10.5 will explain an equal amount of variance for other measures of group climate noted in Table 10.2. However, we are hopeful and invite future empirical and conceptual inquiry into this new model of therapeutic relationships in group.

Conclusion

Hopefully, our serpentine journey through the group climate literature has led you to an optimistic perspective. It is clear that there are significant challenges in conceptualizing group climate, separating it from other therapeutic processes and facing the empirical overlap that it has with other group relationship constructs, such as cohesion. However, the research on the GCQ is robust and provides clinically relevant, theory-grounded, actionable information for the group clinician spanning over two decades with application to diverse clinical populations and used across different theoretical orientations. In some groups, engagement has a direct and important relationship with treatment outcomes for group members. In other groups, it may interact with the type of group being offered and/or the dominant interpersonal style of group members. Nonetheless, there is sufficient depth and breadth to our knowledge that we can feel confident that group climate can be viewed as an empirically supported process to consider by evidence-based group clinicians (see Burlingame, Strauss, Bormann, & Johnson, 2008). Indeed, recent group-psychotherapy practice guidelines ratified by the AGPA support consideration of group climate (Bernard et al., 2007).

We have also introduced a new empirically grounded model that might provide some clarification on where group climate fits when considering the larger rubric of therapeutic relationships in group. The model comes from one of the largest collaborative group research projects that we know of, making it noteworthy in our literature. Furthermore, its apparent "fit" with past definitions gives us hope for its heuristic value in coming years from both a theoretical and an empirical perspective. Like MacKenzie (1983), we believe that the ultimate value of group climate is the provision of actionable information for the group leader. In our opinion, if group climate is to survive and flourish as a construct in group treatments, it must yield to this mold.

Future Directions

Future directions for the group climate literature, difficult problems to be addressed, and topics that remain unaddressed have, to some extent, been addressed throughout our chapter. What follows is a high-level summary:.

1. Group climate has been found to be related to outcome and to mediate outcome, yet additional research examining mediators and moderators is warranted, particularly relative to member contributions. Recent work in Germany examining the dominant interpersonal style and problems of group members is highly promising, and we encourage future work in this direction.

2. Two of the three scales of the GCQ have proven to be moderately to highly predictive of group outcome and other important processes. We continue to endorse our earlier recommendation of the GCQ application to the changing array of group treatments being offered in today's evidence-based world. While we expect it to continue to show robust findings, this hope must be founded upon good empirical work.

3. Drawing upon a new model to describe therapeutic relationships in group, we have proposed how group climate "fits" this model based upon research with the GCQ. While this measure has four times more research than any other group climate measure, we encourage future research into whether this seemingly parsimonious model explains variance in the other measures of group climate listed in Table 10.2.

4. MacKenzie and the AGPA/Transcoop cooperation both endorse the importance of actionable information to empirically guide group leaders. Both have made recommendations regarding their respective measures (GCQ and GQ). We encourage authors of existing and future group climate measures to adopt the same perspective so that research results have a direct impact on the clinical practice of group treatment.

5. There is another acid test of the proposed three-factor model. It is clear that this model is robust in "clearing up" some definitional overlap in frequently invoked therapeutic relationship constructs. However, what remains is its use to explain past empirical findings by perhaps using it in future meta-analytic studies as well as testing its predictive power in summarizing ongoing findings of new research. We have seen preliminary work (Chapman, 2010) supporting the clinical relevance of using the three factors in providing real-time feedback to group leaders and await future studies.

References

Anthony, E. J. (1971). The history of group psychotherapy. In H. I. Kaplan & B. J. Sadock (Eds.), *Comprehensive group psychotherapy* (1st ed., pp. 4–31). Baltimore, MD: Williams & Wilkins.

Bakali, J., Baldwin, S., & Lorentzen, S. (2009). Modeling group process constructs at three stages of group psychotherapy. *Psychotherapy Research*, 19(3), 332–343.

Beech, A. R., & Hamilton-Giachritsis, C. E. (2005). Relationship between therapeutic climate and treatment outcome in group-based sexual offender treatment programs. *Sexual Abuse: Journal of Research and Treatment*, 17, 127–140.

Bernard, H., Burlingame, G., Flores, P., Greene, L., Joyce, A., Kobos, J., et al. (2007). *Practice guidelines for group psychotherapy*. New York: American Group Psychotherapy Association.

Beutel, M. E., Knickenberg, R. J., Krug, B., Mund, S., Schattenburg, L., & Zwerenz, R. (2006). Psychodynamic focal group treatment for psychosomatic inpatients: With an emphasis on work-related conflicts. *International Journal of Group Psychotherapy*, 56, 285–305.

Bolman, L. (1971). Some effects of trainers on their T groups. *Journal of Applied Behavioral Science*, 7, 309–325.

Bormann, B., & Strauss, B. (2007). Gruppenklima, Kohäsion, Allianz und Empathie als Komponenten der therapeutischen Beziehung in Gruppenpsychotherapien—Überprüfung eines Mehrebenen-Modells. [Group climate, cohesion, alliance, and empathy as components of the therapeutic relationship within group psychotherapy—Test of a multilevel model]. *Gruppenpsychotherapie und Gruppendynamik*, 43, 1–20.

Bormann, B., & Strauss, B. (2009, June). *The German Group Questionnaire: A multi-site validation study*. Paper presented at the annual meeting of the Society for Psychotherapy Research, Santiago, Chile.

Braaten, L. J. (1989). Predicting positive goal attainment and symptom reduction from early group climate dimensions. *International Journal of Group Psychotherapy*, 39, 377–387.

Brossart, D. F., Patton, M. J., & Wood, P. K. (1998). Assessing group process: An illustration using Tuckerized growth curves. *Group Dynamics: Theory, Research, and Practice*, 2, 3–17.

Burlingame, G. (2010). Small group treatments: Introduction to special section. *Psychotherapy Research*, 20(1), 1–7.

Burlingame, G. & Baldwin, S. (2011). Group Therapy. In Norcross, J., VandenBos, G & Freedheim, D. (Eds.), *History of Psychotherapy: Continuity and Change* (2nd Ed.) (pp. 505–515). Washington DC: American Psychological Association.

Burlingame, G. M., Fuhriman, A., & Johnson, J. E. (2002). Cohesion in group psychotherapy. In J. Norcross (Ed.), *Psychotherapy relationships that work: Therapist contributions and responsiveness to patients* (pp. 71–88). New York: Oxford University Press.

Burlingame, G. M., MacKenzie, K. R., & Strauss, B. (2004). Small group treatment: evidence for effectiveness and mechanisms of change. In M. Lambert (Ed.), *Bergin and Garfield's handbook of psychotherapy and behavior change* (5th ed., pp. 647–696). New York: John Wiley & Sons.

Burlingame, G. M., & McClendon, D. T. (2008). Group psychotherapy. In J. Lebow (Ed.), *Twenty-first century psychotherapies: Contemporary approaches to theory and practice* (pp. 347–388). Hoboken, NJ: John Wiley & Sons.

Burlingame, G., Strauss, B., Borman, B., & Johnson, J. (2008). Gibt es allgemeine Veränderungsmechanismen in Gruppenpsychotherapien? Ein Einführung in ein konzeptuelles Modell. [Are there common change mechanisms for all small group treatments? A conceptual model for change mechanisms inherent in small groups.] *Gruppenpsychotherapie und Gruppendynamik, 44*, 177–241.

Burlingame, G. M., Strauss, B., Joyce, A., MacNair-Semands, R., MacKenzie, K.R., Ogrodniczuk, J., et al. (2006). *CORE Battery-Revised: An assessment tool kit for promoting optimal group selection, process, and outcome.* New York: American Group Psychotherapy Association.

Chapman, C. (2010). *Clinical judgment and prediction in group psychotherapy: Do assessments of group process, member outcome and therapeutic interventions provide useful feedback?* Unpublished dissertation, Brigham Young University, Provo, UT.

Crowe, T. P., & Grenyer, B. F. S. (2008). Is therapist alliance or whole group cohesion more influential in group psychotherapy outcomes? *Clinical Psychology and Psychotherapy, 15*, 239–246.

Daroff, R. B. (1996). Group climate in an open-ended cancer support group. *Group, 20*, 313–322.

Davies, D. R., Burlingame, G. M., Johnson, J. E., Gleave, R. L., & Barlow, S. H. (2008). The effects of a feedback intervention on group process and outcome. *Group Dynamics: Theory, Research, and Practice, 12*, 141–154.

Dies, R. R. (1983). Clinical implications of research on leadership in short-term group psychotherapy. In R. R. Dies & K. R. MacKenzie (Eds.), *Advances in group psychotherapy: Integrating research and practice* (pp. 27–78). New York: International Universities Press.

Dies, R. R. (1994). Therapist variables in group psychotherapy research. In A. Fuhriman & G. M. Burlingame (Eds.), *Handbook of group psychotherapy* (pp. 114–154). New York: John Wiley & Sons.

Dinger, U., & Schauenburg, H. (2010). Effects of individual cohesion and patient interpersonal style on outcome in psychodynamically oriented inpatient group psychotherapy. *Psychotherapy Research, 20*(1), 7–14.

Fuhriman, A., & Burlingame, G. M. (1994). Group psychotherapy: Research and practice. In A. Fuhriman & G. M. Burlingame (Eds.), *Handbook of group psychotherapy* (pp. 3–40). New York: John Wiley & Sons.

Fuhriman, A., Drescher, S., Hanson, E., Henrie, R., & Rybicki, W. (1986). Refining the measurement of curativeness: An empirical approach. *Small Group Behavior, 17*, 186–201.

Grabhorn, R., Kaufhold, J., Burkhardt, M., Kerkhof, K., & Overbeck, G. (2000). Die Bedeutung differentiellen Gruppenerlebens während einer stationären Psychotherapie. [Differential treatment experience in group therapy.] *Gruppenpsychotherapie und Gruppendynamik, 36*, 317–332.

Hawkins, D. B., Norton, C. B., Eisdorfer, C., & Gianturco, D. (1973). Group process research: A factor analytical study. *American Journal of Psychiatry, 130*, 916–919.

Hilbert, A., Saelens, B. E., Stein, R. I., Mockus, D. S., Welch, R. R., Matt, G. E., et al. (2007). Pretreatment and process predictors of outcome in interpersonal and cognitive behavioral psychotherapy for binge eating disorder. *Journal of Consulting and Clinical Psychology, 75*, 645–651.

Hoag, M., Primus, E., Taylor, N., & Burlingame, G. (1996). Pretraining with adolescents in group therapy: A special case of therapist iatrogenic effects. *Journal of Child and Adolescent Group Psychotherapy, 6*(3), 119–133.

Hurley, J. R. (1989). Affiliativeness and outcome in interpersonal groups: Member and leader perceptions. *Psychotherapy: Theory, Research, Practice, Training, 26*, 520–523.

Hurley, J. R., & Brooks, L. J. (1987). Brief reports group climate's principal dimension: Affiliation. *International Journal of Group Psychotherapy, 37*, 441–448.

Hurley, J. R., & Brooks, L. A. (1988). Primacy of affiliativeness in ratings of group climate. *Psychological Reports, 62*, 123–133.

Hurley, J. R., & Rosenberg, D. B. (1990). Group members' gains in acceptance of self and others associated with leader's behavior. *Genetic, Social, and General Psychology Monographs, 116*, 413–434.

Johnson, J. (2007). Cohesion, alliance, and outcome in group psychotherapy: Comments on Joyce, Piper, & Ogrodniczuk (2007). *International Journal of Group Psychotherapy, 57*, 533–540.

Johnson, J. E., Burlingame, G. M., Olsen, J. A., Davies, D. R., & Gleave, R. L. (2005). Group climate, cohesion, alliance, and empathy in group psychotherapy: Multilevel structural equation models. *Journal of Counseling Psychology, 52*, 310–321.

Johnson, J. E., Burlingame, G. M., Strauss, B., & Bormann, B. (2008). Die therapeutischen Beziehungen in der Gruppenpsychotherapie [Therapeutic relationships in group psychotherapy]. *Gruppenpsychotherapie und Gruppendynamik, 44*, 52–89.

Johnson, J. E., Pulsipher, D., Ferrin, S. L., Burlingame, G. M., Davies, D. R., & Gleave, R. (2006). Measuring group processes: A comparison of the GCQ and CCI. *Group Dynamics: Theory, Research, and Practice, 10*, 136–145.

Joyce, A. S., Azim, H. F. A., & Morin, H. (1988). Brief crisis group psychotherapy versus the initial sessions of long-term group psychotherapy: An exploratory comparison. *Group, 12*, 3–19.

Kanas, N., Stewart, P., Deri, J., Ketter, T., & Haney, K. (1989). Group process in short-term outpatient therapy groups for schizophrenics. *Group, 13*, 67–73.

Kivlighan, D. M., Jr., & Angelone, E. O. (1992). Interpersonal problems: Variables influencing participants' perception of group climate. *Journal of Counseling Psychology, 39*, 468–472.

Kivlighan, D. M., Jr., & Goldfine, D. C. (1991). Endorsement of therapeutic factors as a function of stage of group development and participant interpersonal attitudes. *Journal of Counseling Psychology, 38*, 150–158.

Kivlighan, D. M., Jr., & Jauquet, C. A. (1990). Quality of group member agendas and group session climate. *Small Group Research, 21*, 205–219.

Kivlighan, D. M., Jr., & Lilly, R. L. (1997). Developmental changes in group climate as they relate to therapeutic gain. *Group Dynamics, 1*, 208–221.

Kivlighan, D. M., Jr., Multon, K. D., & Brossart, D. F. (1996). Helpful impacts in group counseling: Development of a multidimensional rating system. *Journal of Counseling Psychology, 43*, 347–355.

Kivlighan, D. M., Jr., & Tarrant, J. M. (2001). Does group climate mediate the group leadership–group member outcome relationship?: A test of Yalom's hypotheses about leadership priorities. *Group Dynamics, 5*, 220–234.

Krogel, J. (2009). The Group Questionnaire: A new measure of the group relationship. Unpublished Dissertation, Brigham Young University, Provo, UT.

Krogel, J., Beecher, M., Presnell, J., Burlingame, G., & Simonsen, C. (2009). The Group Selection Questionnaire: A qualitative analysis of potential group members. *International Journal Of Group Psychotherapy, 59*, 529–542.

Leszcz, M., & Kobos, J. C. (2008). Evidence-based group psychotherapy: Using AGPA's practice guidelines to enhance clinical effectiveness. *Journal of Clinical Psychology: In Session, 64*, 1238–1260.

Lieberman, M., Yalom, I. D., & Miles, M. B. (1973). *Encounter groups: First facts.* New York: Basic Books.

Lorentzen, S., Hoglend, P., & Ruud, T. (2008, June). *The efficacy of short- and long-term psychodynamic group psychotherapy: A Norwegian multi-center study.* Panel presentation at the annual meeting of the Society for Psychotherapy Research, Barcelona, Spain.

MacKenzie, K. R. (1979). Group norms: Importance and measurement. *International Journal of Group Psychotherapy, 29*, 471–480.

MacKenzie, K. R. (1981). Measurement of group climate. *International Journal of Group Psychotherapy, 31*, 287–295.

MacKenzie, K. R. (1983). The clinical application of a group climate measure. In R. R. Dies & K. R. MacKenzie (Eds.), *Advances in group psychotherapy: Integrating research and practice* (pp. 159–170). New York: International Universities Press.

MacKenzie, K. R. (1997). Clinical applications of group development ideas. *Group Dynamics: Theory, Research and Practice, 1*, 275–287.

MacKenzie, K. R., Dies, R. R., Coché, E., Rutan, J. S., & Stone, W. N. (1987). An analysis of AGPA institute groups. *International Journal of Group Psychotherapy, 37*, 55–74.

MacKenzie, K. R., & Livesley, W. J. (1983). A developmental model for brief group therapy. In R. R. Dies & K. R. MacKenzie (Eds.), *Advances in group psychotherapy: Integrating research and practice* (pp. 101–116). New York: International Universities Press.

MacKenzie, K. R., & Tschuschke, V. (1993). Relatedness, group work, and outcome in long-term inpatient psychotherapy groups. *Journal of Psychotherapy Practice and Research, 2*, 147–156.

Mattke, D., & Schreiber-Willnow, K. (2004). Das Gruppenklima in geschlossenen Kurzzeitgruppen in der stationären Psychotherapie. [The group climate in closed, short-term inpatient psychotherapy groups.] *Gruppenpsychotherapie und Gruppendynamik, 40*, 360–378.

McBride, L. C. (1995). Toward group process understanding: Leadership and group climate. *Dissertation Abstracts International, 55*, 5571.

McCallum, M., Piper, W. E., Ogrodniczuk, J. S., & Joyce, A. S. (2002). Early process and dropping out from short-term group therapy for complicated grief. *Group Dynamics, 6*, 243–254.

Moos, R. H. (1986). *Group environment scale manual* (2nd ed.). Palo Alto, CA: Consulting Psychologists Press.

Moos, R. H. (1994). *Group environment scale manual* (3rd ed.). Palo Alto, CA: Consulting Psychologists Press.

Moos, R. H. (2004). *Group environment scale manual* (4th ed.). Menlo Park, CA: MindGarden.

Moos, R. H., & Humphrey, B. (1974). *Group environment scale.* Palo Alto, CA: Consulting Psychologists Press.

Morran, D. K., Stockton, R., & Whittingham, M. H. (2004). Effective leader interventions for counseling and psychotherapy groups. In J. L. DeLucia-Waack, D. A. Gerrity, C. R. Kalodner, & M. T. Riva (Eds.), *Handbook of group counseling and psychotherapy* (pp. 91–103). Thousand Oaks, CA: Sage.

Ogrodniczuk, J., & Piper, W. (2003). The effect of group climate on outcome in two forms of short-term group therapy. *Group Dynamics: Theory, Research, and Practice, 7*, 64–76.

Phipps, L. B., & Zastowny, T. R. (1988). Leadership behavior, group climate and outcome in group psychotherapy: A study of outpatient psychotherapy groups. *Group, 12*, 157–171.

Riva, M., Wachtel, M., & Lasky, G. (2004). Effective leadership in group counseling and psychotherapy. In J. DeLucia-Waack, D. Gerrity, C. Kalodner, & M. Riva (Eds.), *Handbook of group counseling and psychotherapy* (pp. 37–48). Thousand Oaks, CA: Sage.

Ryum, T., Hagen, R., Nordahl, H. M., Vogel, P. A., & Stiles, T. C. (2009). Perceived group climate as a predictor of long-term outcome in a randomized controlled trial of cognitive-behavioural group therapy for patients with comorbid psychiatric disorders. *Behavioural and Cognitive Psychotherapy, 11*, 1–14.

Schauenburg, H., Sammet, I., Rabung, S., & Strack, M. (2001). Zur differentiellen Bedeutung des Gruppenerlebens in der stationären Psychotherapie depressiver Patienten [On the differential importance of group experience in inpatient psychotherapy of depressive patients]. *Gruppenpsychotherapie und Gruppendynamik, 37*, 349–364.

Sehring, H., & Engel, K. (1998). Selbstwahrnehmung und Gruppenerleben in stationärer Gruppenpsychotherapie. *Gruppenpsychotherapie und Gruppendynamik, 34*, 337–354.

Sexton, H. (1993). Exploring a psychotherapeutic change sequence: Relating process to intersessional and posttreatment outcome. *Journal of Consulting and Clinical Psychology, 61*, 128–136.

Shechtman, Z., & Gluk, O. (2005). An investigation of therapeutic factors in children's groups. *Group Dynamics: Theory, Research, and Practice, 9*, 127–134.

Silbergeld, S., Koenig, G. R., Manderscheid, R. W., Meeker, B. F., & Hornung, C. A. (1975). Assessment of environment-therapy systems: The Group Atmosphere Scale. *Journal of Consulting and Clinical Psychology, 43*, 460–469.

Silbergeld, S., Manderscheid, R. W., & Koenig, G. R. (1977). The psychosocial environment in group therapy evaluation. *International Journal of Group Psychotherapy, 27*, 152–163.

Strauss, B., & Burgmeier-Lohse, M. (1994). Prozess-Ergebnis-Zusammenhänge in der analytisch orientierten Gruppenpsychotherapie: eine Erkundungsstudie im stationären Rahmen. [Process-outcome relationships in an analytically oriented inpatient group treatment.] *Psychotherapeut, 39*, 239–250.

Strauss, B., Burlingame, G. M., & Bormann, B. (2008). Using the CORE-R battery in group psychotherapy. *Journal of Clinical Psychology: In Session, 64,* 1225–1237.

Stockton, R., Rohde, R. I., & Haughey, J. (1992). The effects of structured group exercises on cohesion, engagement, avoidance, and conflict. *Small Group Research, 23,* 155–168.

Tarrant, J. M., & Kivlighan, D. M., Jr. (2000). *An evaluation of the Choices group program.* Unpublished manuscript, University of Missouri–Columbia.

Tasca, G. A., Flynn, C. Y., & Bissada, H. (2002). Comparison of group climate in an eating disorders partial hospital group and a psychiatric partial hospital group. *International Journal of Group Psychotherapy, 52,* 409–417.

Tschuschke, V., & Greene, L. R. (2002). Group therapists' training: What predicts learning? *International Journal of Group Psychotherapy, 52,* 463–482.

Yalom, I. (1975). *The theory and practice of group psychotherapy* (2nd ed.). New York: Basic Books.

Yalom, I. (1995). *The theory and practice of group psychotherapy* (4th ed.). New York: Basic Books.

Group Development

Virginia Brabender

Abstract

This chapter provides a description of the major models of how counseling groups change over time. Particular attention is given to the predominant framework, the progressive stage model. However, other models reviewed are the life-cycle model, cyclic model, punctuated equilibrium model, and approaches derived from chaos/complexity theory. This chapter considers the question of whether a group's development affects members' abilities to accomplish their goals. Finally, it addresses the application of developmental thinking in unstructured and structured groups and develops the implications of group developmental theory for leadership activities.

Keywords: group development, progressive stage model, leadership

Group development is one of the core concepts by which groups are understood. Models of how change occurs within a group vary. Yet, they all contain the notion that how groups change over time is systematic rather than random and that from group to group some common features can be discerned. These patterned changes include the group atmosphere; the ways in which members relate to one another and the therapist; the affects, impulses, and fantasies stimulated; and the themes of the sessions. Group development as a key topic has been recognized in the practice guidelines of the American Group Psychotherapy Association (Bernard et al., 2008) and the *Professional Standards for the Training of Group Workers* of the Association for Specialists in Group Work (ASGW, 2000). This topic has great importance to group counselors because if developmental phenomena occur, they can be a force, positive or negative, in determining the extent to which a group, and the members therein, meet the group's goals. Hence, the group counselor cannot afford to ignore group developmental phenomena but rather should include them as a component of the group design—the plan for conducting the

group. This chapter will provide the fundamentals for incorporating a developmental focus regardless of the theoretical model the therapist employs.

The notion of group development rests upon the assumption that the group is a distinct entity. To see the group as having the capacity to develop, one must first affirm the existence of the group, a unit with its own properties, processes, and potentials. The many models of group development that have been constructed in the last seven decades all rest upon earlier scholarly work on the character of the group itself.

The Study of the Group as a Distinct Entity

Gustav LeBon (1895/1960) was the first significant writer to attempt to characterize the life of the group. He grappled with the fact that individuals will engage in actions when in a large group that they would never commit individually, actions that violate their own moral strictures and good judgment. Giving the French Revolution as an example, LeBon talked about the group process of *contagion*, wherein the group member will give him- or herself over to the will of another. To explain this phenomenon (for example, why, when the command was given to "Storm the Bastille," most peasants did so without a moment's hesitation), he posited the existence of a *group mind*. When the group mind is activated, the behavior of the group resembles that of a child in that it is oriented to what will bring immediate pleasure ("I want it now!") and allows for the fullest expression of impulse and affect. Much like the very young child, LeBon held, the group mind does not pause to consider the consequences of deeds.

McDougall (1920) affirmed LeBon's view of the group as an irrational, affectively driven entity. At the same time, he explored the conundrum that groups, despite having enormous regressive potential, also have the potential to make great achievements. McDougall posited certain features that would allow the group to mature rather than regress. One feature he emphasized was the capacity for group members to be together over time, a temporal feature critical for group development.

Sigmund Freud (1921/1955) admired Le Bon's and McDougall's work and extended their thinking further by examining the properties of smaller, more stable groups. Freud claimed that the features observed by Le Bon are for the most part unconsciously driven. Because members are unaware of what conflicts drive their behavior, the conflicts remain irresolvable (McClure, 1990). Yet, Freud addressed a question regarding groups that has primacy over all others: How does a collection of individuals become a group? In answering it, he highlighted the process of identification wherein members feel connected with one another by virtue of their shared relationship with the group leader, a figure perceived as a parental surrogate.

The problem identified by LeBon (1895/1960), that groups can behave differently and more destructively than the members populating them could individually, was embraced in a thoroughgoing way during and after the two world wars, each of which wrought destruction that was tremendous and unprecedented. These developments spawned a renewed interest in understanding the workings of groups, with particular attention to group-level phenomena. Although a variety of group scholars made notable contributions, none was as significant as those of Wilfred Bion (1961), who was a military psychiatrist and ultimately a group counselor. Based on his observations of groups that he ran in a military hospital in London, Bion identified various behavioral patterns exhibited by them and the conscious and unconscious elements that underlie these patterns.

Groups configure themselves, according to Bion (1962), into two forms: the work group and the basic assumption group. The *work group* is what we might think of as a mature, productive group in which the behaviors of members are consistently geared toward the goals of the group. For example, staff members on an inpatient unit who participate in a case conference and exert themselves with consistency and effectiveness to develop treatment plans for the inpatients function as a work group. In a work group, rationality reigns. Leaders are picked by their skills to move the group toward its goals. In the work group, members tolerate both frustration and new ideas that may catapult a group's work (Grinberg, Sor, & Bianchedi, 1977). Contrasting greatly with work groups are the *basic assumption groups*, which are characterized by the dominance of primitive modes of psychological functioning and relating. Each of the three basic assumption groups has at its core an unconscious fantasy that members construct, a fantasy to ameliorate a basic anxiety stimulated by group membership. In the *basic assumption dependency group*, the fantasy that members are helplessly awaiting rescue by an omnipotent figure who can care for all of their needs predominates and organizes members' interactions. As Cohen, Ettin, and Fidler (1998) described it, "members behave as though their reason for coming together is to make contact with a healer whose extraordinary capability, in effect, absolves them of responsibility for their own health and competence" (p. 120). In the *basic assumption fight-or-flight group*, members fantasize that their survival is being imperiled and they require a powerful leader who will rally them to fight or flee. In the *basic assumption pairing group*, members are guided by the unconscious fantasy that a group messiah will emerge from the union of two or more members, a figure who will rescue members from their difficulties.

Bion saw group life as characterized by a constant and inherent tension between the work group and the basic assumption groups. The dominance of any particular organizing principle was temporary and the eventual pull of another form, irresistible. For example, our case conference group mentioned earlier, if observed closely, could be seen to enter periods in which little true work was accomplished. At such times, the group members may be unrealistically preoccupied by an external threat and, by so doing, betray their movement into a fight-or-flight group. Also, they may enter into a dependent basic assumption mode by becoming consumed with a sense of the utter futility of their efforts and their need for a leader who will enable them to be successful. Regardless of which basic assumption group dominates at the moment, what is common to all of them is the collective opposition to the group's development; the function of the basic assumption group is to interfere with the group's growth. Bion's ideas were enormously influential for later observers of group life, most likely because they had resonance for these observers. The descriptions of the basic assumption groups and work groups made coherent many pieces of group life that otherwise seemed fragmentary and chaotic.

A few other writers during this time had specific influences on later group developmental thinking. Robert Bales (1950), like Bion, characterized different states through which a group can proceed over time. Based on his research with work groups, groups convened in an employment context, Bales identified two different sets of processes that groups use in the context of problem solving. The first, the *task function*, involves a pronounced focus on the end goal and the steps that would lead to its fulfillment. The second, the *socioemotional function*, involves attention to members' emotional status. Bales posited that when a group emphasizes one function over another, it moves into a state of disequilibrium. Tension builds and pressure increases for the alternate function to take hold of the group and thereby restore equilibrium. Both Bales and Bion saw different psychological states as cyclical. The group moves through one or another without any real progression.

Kurt Lewin (1948, 1951) was a social scientist whose theoretical conceptions of the group strongly affected group developmental approaches. Lewin viewed the group as a social field that is embedded within a larger environment but also distinct from that environment. For the individual group members, the group constitutes their environment. The individual members, the group, and the group's environment all comprehend a set of forces that may have a facilitative (or driving) or inhibiting (restraining) influence on the likelihood of any given member, set of members, or group as a whole's engagement in a behavior.

For example, what is the likelihood that members of a counseling group will respond to distress by running out of the room in which the group is held? Whether the broader unit would sanction a member's precipitous departure from the session might be a factor. Whether the therapist had disallowed such behavior by establishing a rule against it would be another. Whether in the history of the group distressed members had remained and had a positive outcome (for example, relief from the distress) would be still another. Lewin termed the whole array of forces that drive or restrain a given behavior a "field of force." This force-field analysis of the interrelationships of the individual group member to the broader group and the surrounding environment was important because it set the stage for understanding the extent to which the conditions for development in the group existed at any point in the group's life.

The Construction of Developmental Models

The next major step was taken when theoreticians began to consider the possibility that the various patterns had a potential growth or building aspect. A major question arose as to how these states related to one another and the mechanics of this building process. Group scholars have proposed, and continue to propose, different types of models as solutions to this problem. No model has as yet explained comprehensively all of the phenomena witnessed by the group counselors; some combination of models described in the sections that follow may be needed to do justice to the complexity of group developmental phenomena.

Progressive Stage Models

The type of model group scholars most commonly posit to describe the development of a psychotherapy group is a progressive stage depiction of group life. Within this framework, the group is seen as consisting of a set of stages much like the stages that have been observed in the development of an individual. As in individual development-stage theory, the order of stages is invariant, the achievements of one stage are based upon the accomplishments of the prior stage, the transition from one stage to another is generally gradual, and fixation and regression are other alternatives to growth.

BENNIS AND SHEPARD MODEL

The scholarly work done in the first half of the twentieth century provided the rudiments for understanding how groups change over time, but the shift toward a truly developmental perspective came with the work of Bennis and Shepard (1956). These investigators studied experiential groups of graduate students over a 5-year period. Based on these observations, they posited that Bion's basic assumption groups emerge in a pattern over the course of a group's life. That is, certain basic assumption states seem to appear before other states because the former set a foundation for the latter. Each basic assumption state is characterized by a conflict that must be resolved before the group can advance. In contrast to Bales (1950) and Bion (1962), Bennis and Shepard's approach was a *progressive stage model* in that later group work built upon earlier accomplishments. They address conflicts unique to each period of group life, which constitute phases, akin to the phases identified in individual development by Piaget (1928) and others. In setting forth this progressive stage model, Bennis and Shepard were establishing what has been the dominant perspective on group change over time. Although the number of developmental models has been legion, most share with the Bennis and Shepard model the notions that the order of stages is invariant, each stage builds upon the work of prior stages, and as the group matures, it becomes more effective at performing tasks.

In consonance with Freud's (1921/1955) views, Bennis and Shepard (1956) held that the inevitable, universal conflicts that group members have with authority figures (parental surrogates) must be satisfactorily addressed before the group can take up conflicts pertaining to peer relationships. The first period, the *dependence phase*, entails the group's focus on its relationship with authority figures. This phase comprises three subphases: dependence–flight; counterdependence–fight, and resolution–catharsis.

In the *dependence–flight subphase*, the uncertainties of group life evoke a sense of utter helplessness in members, a response that leads the group to turn to the leader for comfort and protection. Members act as though they can neither think nor act on their own behalves. Their behavior continually communicates to the leader their expectancy that he or she will provide direction. Yet, even if direction is forthcoming, members regard it as unsatisfactory: The primitiveness of their longings precludes their satisfaction.

As frustration grows, members move into the *counterdependence–fight subphase*, in which members form subgroups. *Subgrouping*, a concept that figures very prominently in theorizing on group development, entails a subset of members sharing a common position in relation to a conflict. One subgroup will attempt to provide that structure which the therapist has been apparently unwilling to offer. For example, one member may suggest that members pursue a go-around and other members of the dependent subgroup will support this idea. However, in another subgroup, the counterdependent subgroup, members will aim to circumvent whatever direction the dependent subgroup establishes. For example, counterdependent subgroup members may mock the notion of a go-around as juvenile and refuse to participate. The warfare between the dependent and counterdependent subgroups may appear heated, yet it is a camouflage for reactions of disappointment in the leader, a figure who is too forbidding to confront directly.

Were it not for the presence of individuals who are in neither the dependent nor the counterdependent subgroup, the group could become stalemated in its position of active conflict. However, groups will invariably have some members for whom dependency issues are not intensely conflictual. These individuals can stand apart and appreciate the position of each subgroup and mediate between them. These independent members are willing to approach the feelings that lie underneath the members' internecine warfare—their dissatisfaction with the leader. Through their activity, they enable the group to do the work of the *resolution–catharsis subphase*. The counterdependent members can see that their wish to attack the dependent subgroup is derivative of their impulse to challenge the leader. The dependent subgroup can recognize that their longing for structure is based on their frustration with the leader's not providing structure. The mediating activity of the independents and the burgeoning awareness of both subgroups of the actual object of their discontent consummate in a direct, unified expression of dissatisfaction with the leader, a symbolic act termed a *barometric event*. By making a direct challenge upon the leader's authority, members manifest their willingness both to abandon their dependent posture vis-à-vis the leader and to look to their own resources to accomplish the group's goals. Following this expression is a celebratory mood, a festive state that incorporates affective elements of relief, pride, and joy, all of which are elicited by members' perceptions of having liberated themselves from an oppressive force.

The consummation of the barometric event ushers in the second major era or phase of group life, *interdependence and personal relations*. Members show a drastically diminished preoccupation with authority issues and a much keener interest in one another. They reveal, through their explorations with one another, that they recognize that the capacity of the group to address their needs lies in their own efforts and their interactions with one another. The initial subphase of the event, *enchantment–flight*, is one in which members take delight in the camaraderie that the group has achieved. Basking in the glow of their recent triumph, they see in themselves and others only that which is lovable and pleasurable. Members flee from those aspects of self and other that are associated with negative affects and appraisals.

Yet, not all members can enter into the spirit of this subphase equally. A subgroup of members will be aware that only those reactions on one side of the emotional/cognitive ledger are being expressed. Despite this awareness, they will also feel inhibited in expressing sentiments that seem at odds with the group culture. Within a relatively short period, their reluctance will diminish; it will appear to them that the atmosphere is more inviting of their potential contributions. These members, the *counterpersonals*, will be instrumental in ushering in the next subphase, *disenchantment–flight*, which is characterized by mistrust and disharmony. The *overpersonals*, the active members in the prior subphase, respond enthusiastically to the promises of intimate involvement with one another. They value intimacy not only in its own right but also as a shield from the recognition of separateness and the burdens it brings. In contrast, the counterpersonals see intimacy as fraught with danger. For them, closeness challenges the self as an autonomous entity, a challenge that seems all the more vivid and immediate given the evident longing of the overpersonals to blur or ignore all differences among members.

The overpersonals and counterpersonals represent two sides of a conflict related to establishing intimate ties with others. Each subgroup demonstrates that the conflict for them is a highly active one in that they are not able to recognize within themselves the inclinations associated with the unexpressed side of the conflict. That is, one side of the conflict is too threatening to own. Leading the group into the third subphase, *consensual validation*, are independent members, individuals who have achieved a resolution to intimacy issues prior to the group's entrance into this subphase. They are in a unique position to help each subgroup tolerate the psychological position of the opposite subgroup. In so doing, they assist members in accepting as forces within themselves each side of the conflict. This activity enables them to move toward the integration of the conflictual elements within them. For Bennis and Shepard (1956), the vehicle by which this integration occurs is the evaluation of the group experience, precipitated by the group's coming to an end. Members, in taking stock of their relationships with each other, have an opportunity to acknowledge

both similarities and differences, positive and negative elements, that require bringing to the fore both sides of the intimacy-based conflict. Independents often function as leaders in this activity, offering themselves up as pioneer candidates in the group's evaluation efforts.

The Bennis and Shepard (1956) model incorporated many elements seen in later developmental theory. First, each phase clearly rested upon the accomplishments of the prior phase. This concept is known as a *progressive stage model*, and it is to be distinguished from earlier models of change in which groups moved from one psychological state to another without any real aspect of the group's building upon the work of the prior period. Second, they recognized that progress in a group is never assured but dependent upon a constellation of factors such as group composition, freedom from disruption, and leader competence.

TUCKMAN MODEL

Following the publication of the Bennis and Shepard (1956) model, a great array of stage models appeared over the next 40 years; and to varying extents, these models were inspired by this 1956 model. Many of these models, generated in a variety of clinical and nonclinical contexts, were presented with supporting evidence, some experimental and some anecdotal. In 1965, a seminal development was the publication of a review article by Bruce Tuckman that examined the models and the 50 extant group-development studies that provided confirmatory or disconfirmatory evidence for the model. In this article, he proposed a four-stage model that captured the commonalities among many models described in the literature and thereby lent a measure of order to prior fragmented efforts. Each stage, he believed, had a task element and an emotional/interpersonal element. Tuckman also differentiated among three types of groups—clinical, training, and experiential—and examined empirical findings to assess whether the type of group affects how development proceeds. He emphasized that in less structured groups that have as a goal understanding the self, group dynamics, or both, the emotional/interpersonal element is evident. In highly structured groups with extremely concrete goals, the task element will be most obvious.

In Tuckman's initial model, the following four stages were presented:

- *Stage 1—Forming*: The significance of this name is that the members transform themselves from a mere collectivity to a group that feels as such to its members. The members establish their norms (spoken and unspoken rules) and processes. Tuckman, like Bennis and Shepard (1956), noted that members see their own abilities to produce the change they desire as nil and the therapist's, as great; without the therapist's efforts, members would be unable to move toward their goals.

• *Stage 2—Storming*: In this stage, members struggle with their own differing views of how members will manage to accomplish their goals in the group. Differing stances toward the role of the leader create tension among members, and this tension leads to expressions of hostility toward one another. As members give expression to their reactions and recognize their own responsibility in producing the changes they seek, the group moves into those stages most critical for their realization of their goals.

• *Stage 3—Norming*: At this time, members have a shared recognition that if any positive changes are to be obtained within the group, they will occur through the members' own efforts and their collaboration with one another. With this awareness of their own role in moving the group, members manifest a new sense of purpose and care in embracing those norms that will operate in the service of group goals.

• *Stage 4—Performing*: Tuckman saw the group as arriving at this stage with a structure enabling it to do the essential work for which it was convened. Members have a substantial investment both in the task and in their relationship with one another. Members are more flexible in their ways of working as well as in the roles they assume so that personal and group goals can be met.

Subsequently, Tuckman and Jensen (1977) added a fifth stage, *adjourning*, in which members have an opportunity to grapple with feelings associated with endings and separation. The Tuckman model had a great influence on both group developmental scholars and group counselors because it had a summative character—that is, to a large extent, it synopsized extant research on developmental stages. The names of the stages—forming, storming, norming, performing, and adjourning—have a memorable ring, enhancing their accessibility and utility. The Tuckman model continues to be used. For example, Ford, Cabrales, and Williams (1997) describe AmeriCorps programs in which team leaders are trained on how to intervene at each stage of development (electronic communication, November 13, 2009, www.nationalserviceresources.org).

CONTEXT-DEPENDENT MODELS

Since the publication of the Tuckman model, the number of progressive stage models has exploded. The vast majority of these models are consistent with the Tuckman model in terms of both the number and content of the stages. The differences among the models are attributable to the fact that they were developed in different clinical venues for specific patient populations and the group phenomena observed derive some of their character from these local factors. Most often, the authors describing these models were not interested in proposing a universal model but simply wished to describe the process they observed in their groups. In fact, often they were interested in highlighting the contribution of the contextual factors to the particular complexion of the developmental stages. Some of the variables that have driven the creation of particular models are diagnosis, setting, and age.

Diagnosis

Specific models have been proposed for diagnostic groups, such as groups for individuals with post-traumatic stress syndrome (Robertson, Rushton, Bartrum, & Bus, 2004), bulimia (MacKenzie, Livesley, Coleman, Harper, & Park, 1986), schizophrenia (Kanas, Stewart, Deri, Ketter, & Haney, 1989), and personality disorders (Cooley, Demby, Koppenal, Koslof, & Powers, 1996). Writers have noted that the dynamics associated with the symptom patterns will give the stages their particular character. For example, Robertson et al. (2004) made the point that in the stage in which members grapple with differences among them and reactions to authority figures (Tuckman's storming stage), they exhibit exaggerated fight-or-flight responses associated with reactions to trauma. In the termination stage, they are prone to reaction to loss with intrusive trauma-related symptoms such as nightmares. In some cases, the dynamics pertain not so much to the diagnosis but to the homogeneity of diagnosis. MacKenzie et al. (1986) noted that in their group of bulimic individuals members' sharing of symptoms facilitated the forging of an intense bond but hindered their acknowledging of differences.

Settings

Models have been developed for different settings and particular structural characteristics such as Beeber's (1988) model for open-ended inpatient groups, Brabender's (1988) model for close-ended inpatient groups, and Jackson's (1999) forward groups—groups of staff and patients that take place on a daily basis. Both Beeber and Jackson write about how, in open-ended inpatient groups, not only do members change but therapists frequently change as well. Beeber argues that rather than positing a beginning stage, it should be conceptualized as a "rebeginning" because the latter term captures the regressive aspect of the phenomena exhibited. Brabender (1988) writes about the potential to see a more dramatic manifestation of stage 2 authority issues because the inpatient group's expression of discontent can be a condensation of its frustration with of all of the hospital authority figures with whom the members must contend.

Age Groups
Models have been developed for particular age groups, such as Spinner's (1992) description of the evolution of culture in a group of ego-impaired children and Malekoff's (1997) for adolescents. Although Spinner and Malekoff argue for a fairly traditional stage sequence such as that suggested by Tuckman (1965), they point out that in the working phase the surfacing of intense dependency needs will create a much stronger vulnerability on the part of individuals in the group and the group as a whole, to regression and fragmentation. Shechtman's (2007) empirical investigations of children's groups have yielded a model that contrasts considerably with models of adult development. According to Shechtman, a sequence of two stages best describes children's groups. In the first stage, members engage in a high level of self-disclosure (greater than that typically observed in adults at the initial stage) and appear to show a strong interest in working. In the second stage, members become more defiant and aggressive and engage in disruptive behaviors which undermine the maintenance of a work culture. As this second stage progresses, the aggressive behaviors diminish.

MAJOR CONTEMPORARY PROGRESSIVE STAGE MODELS
Besides the explicitly contextual stage models, a number of models have been constructed that, unlike the models cited in the prior section, offer a universal account of group development. They focus less on contextual variations and more on the developmental properties that groups share across contexts. Although the number of models in this category are many, within the literature, certain models have achieved particular importance: the Beck (1974) model, the MacKenzie and Livesley (1983) model, and the systems-centered (Agazarian, 1997) model. Each will be mentioned briefly here, although the reader is encouraged to consult primary texts for a full exposition of each model.

Beck Model
Ariadne Beck and colleagues' (Beck, 1974; Dugo & Beck, 1984) model sees group development as involving a dialectical interaction of psychological forces across a set of nine phases. Serving as voices for, or expressions of, these forces are members who take on leadership roles and, by doing so, enable the development of the group. These leaders are emergent; that is, their leadership activity is not preordained (as in the case of the therapist) but emerges over the course of the group by virtue of their relative suitability for a given role. In this context, a leader is regarded as "a person who has a great deal of influence in determining the group's direction, timing, or content during its life, and usually in a manner that can be characterized as having a particular pattern or a style" (Beck, 1974, p. 427).

The role of the *task leader* is to facilitate members in engaging in those actions that move the group toward its goals. For example, early in the group's development, a task leader might remind the group members of the importance of participating if they wish to derive something from the group. The *emotional leader* works to maintain connection among members (Dugo & Beck, 1984) and comfort within the group. For example, if tension becomes unbearably high, the emotional leader may make a joke. If a member is disconnected from others, the emotional leader may identify a commonality between that member and others. The *defiant leader* helps the group to recognize threats whether they occur within the group or outside. For example, the defiant leader will assist the group in recognizing dissatisfaction with the designated leader of the group, the therapist. The *scapegoat leader* serves as a container for members' unwanted affects and impulses until such time as the group is ready to own them. The group-level issues from phase to phase vary and, accordingly, so does the type of leader who is active and conspicuous in the stage.

This section will not review each of the nine stages but, rather, will focus on a single phase or stage, phase 1, in order to give the reader a flavor of this model. In this phase, the task and emotional leaders emerge with particular prominence. At the group level, the task is for members to bond with one another as a group. At the member level, the task is to answer the following questions: How do I feel about this group of members? and Do I see myself as someone capable of working within this particular group? Typically, the therapist occupies the role of task leader and has established a relationship with each member before entering the group. This prior connection provides a grounding wherein members can begin to bond with others besides the task leader. The task leader must, on the one hand, show a willingness to serve as an emotional anchor for members and, on the other, refrain from interfering as members establish new bonds with others.

Yet, the task leader does not lead alone. This phase sees the emergence of the emotional leader, whose importance to the group throughout its development is inestimable and who will begin the development of an intensely close and warm relationship with the task leader. The emotional leader will assist the group in completing a task, the sharing of highly personal material, which is essential to the completion of this stage. Beck (1974) noted that in one group this process commenced when a member asked the others if anyone had ever awoken in terror in the middle of the night only to have the realization that there was no one with whom to share this frightening experience. Other members then resonated with the horror of that abject sense of aloneness. The emotional leader may be the one to make the initial self-disclosure or, if not, to assist the members of the group in connecting to it. This sharing of an emotionally sensitive experience results in the formation of a beginning contract to work together. With it, members are ready to move onto phase 2.

Each one of the nine phases provides members the opportunity to restructure their experience via the processes of differentiation and integration. By engaging in these processes in relation to a sequence of issues, members achieve a clearer sense of personal identity and the unique identity of others, as well as a greater capacity to achieve a sense of cohesion with others.

Significant research support has been obtained for Beck's model of group development. A central premise of the Beck model is that different leadership roles emerge across the nine phases. In fact, a series of studies (Beck & Peters, 1981; Beck et al., 1983; Brusa, Stone, Beck, Dugo, & Peters, 1994; Peters & Beck, 1982) involving sociometric observations supported the four types of leaders identified by Beck and their emergence at particular points in the life of the group.

MacKenzie and Livesley's Model

Roy MacKenzie and W. John Livesley have been active contributors to the literature on group counseling for many years and have written critical reviews on the topic (MacKenzie & Livesley, 1983; MacKenzie, 1994, 1997). They have proposed a four-stage model that is descriptive of a wide variety of group types, including those that meet on a short-term basis (3–6 months). It is also distinguished by its simplicity. MacKenzie (1997) notes that more complex models with a greater number of stages most likely present periods of group life that would, within his model, be seen as substages of his four stages. The four stages are engagement, differentiation and conflict, interpersonal work, and termination. Each stage is defined by a task or set of tasks that the group must complete before moving on to the next stage; Mackenzie (1997) also specifies leader interventions that assist the members in performing this sequence of tasks.

In stage 1, *engagement*, the group's task is for each member to achieve a sense of belonging to, and being involved in, the group. This task is achieved by members' fledgling efforts to talk about themselves, efforts which deepen over the course of this stage and eventually constitute significant self-disclosures. MacKenzie sees it as critical that each member of the group shares personal material, and hence, one of the requirements upon the leader is to monitor interactions to facilitate less active members in sharing material about themselves. Members' disclosures typically precipitate a heightened sense of well-being stimulated by the perception that other members accept and understand one another. Furthermore, other members' ability to identify with shared experiences leads members to enjoy the relief of a diminished sense of aloneness. These positive feelings strengthen members' commitment to the group, an important accomplishment needed for the more challenging tasks of stage 2.

In order for members to pull together as a group, they must focus on what unites them, their similarities to one another. Yet, members are different from one another; they have diverse beliefs, positions on issues, personality features, life situations, and so on. Eventually, members must grapple with these differences; and it is in stage 2, *differentiation*, that they do so. The recognition of disagreements precipitates tension and often hostility. The negative emotions characteristic of this stage also extend to the leader. After all, in relation to the members, the leader is in a different position—one of authority. The developmental task of the group is to acquire the capability of constructively managing conflicts in the group. Part of this process involves a revisiting of the norms of the group, set by those member behaviors that are perceived to be regarded favorably by therapist and members. Though initially, members see the norms as therapist-determined, their questioning of these norms enables them to develop norms that are truly their own. In this way, members come to take responsibility for the group and its progress.

MacKenzie (1997) notes that the work that members do in these first two stages, often taking no more than 2–4 weeks, brings considerable symptom relief and an elevation in self-esteem relative to members' entering the group. The work of these two formative periods provides for interpersonal and intrapsychic change. In stage 3, *interpersonal work*, members shift from a group focus to a more individual focus. At this time, members explore highly personal concerns related to intimacy, dependency, and the maintenance of individuality in the context of closeness. The group task is for members to learn to balance the opposing pulls of individuation and intimacy. The therapist must develop the skill to recognize when an intervention is most productively directed at the individual level or the dyadic level. When the therapist focuses on the individual, it is often useful to draw out the way in which that individual is expressing some psychological content for the group as a whole (MacKenzie, 1997).

In stage 4, *termination*, members have an opportunity to deal with the range of reactions that loss evokes. Among these reactions are dealing with disappointment, functioning independently, and facing grief, including that in relation to earlier losses. The task of the group is to explore these reactions rather than denying them, a task whose performance the therapist can abet by dealing constructively with his or her own reactions to the group's ending. For example, the therapist might have some disappointment in relation to goals left unaccomplished by the group; to the extent that the therapist acknowledges this reaction, the group members will be able to approach their own painful realizations (MacKenzie, 1994).

Systems-Centered Group Therapy
One of the most significant developmental models to appear on the group-counseling landscape is the systems-centered therapy model of Agazarian and colleagues (Agazarian, 1997; Agazarian & Gantt, 2005). Serving as a foundation for this model is

Agazarian's theory of living human systems, which provides a unified set of principles to describe the interrelationships between and among systems and their subsystems and thereby averts the problem of having separate nomenclature for describing the dynamics of the individual and group dynamics.

The theory of living human systems adopts the notion derived from General Systems Theory that any given system exists within a hierarchy of systems (Miller, 1978; Von Bertalanffy, 1968). A system is embedded in a set of progressively larger systems, and rooted in it are a set of progressively smaller systems. A counseling group is a system, which may be embedded in a residential treatment center, a suprasystem of a unit of a still larger system. Nested in the group are the individual members, who themselves are composed of various systems (for example, mental, physical, spiritual). The theory of living human systems incorporates the general systems theory notion that isomorphies exist within the systems and subsystems of any given hierarchy (Von Bertalanffy, 1968). An *isomorphy* is a structural or functional feature that is shared by a set of nested systems. For example, in an inpatient counseling group, members may show a disregard for time boundaries, that is, the starting and ending times of the group sessions. This disregard may reflect staff and patients' attitude toward time on the unit in which the group is held. The unit may parallel a laxity on the part of the hospital about punctuality. Isomorphies create the potential for changing a system by influencing a subsystem or vice versa. Isomorphies also exist across systems in different hierarchies so that by learning about a system within one hierarchy or context, knowledge can be obtained about systems in other contexts.

One isomorphic feature across systems is their continual pursuit of the goals of survival, development, and transformation. To ascertain whether a system such as a counseling group will move toward or away from a goal or in a state of stasis (or fixation), the theory of living human systems employs and advances Lewin's (1951) force-field analysis. When a system establishes a goal, the extent to which that system will move toward it depends upon the relative weight of the driving and restraining forces that are externally and internally present. Suppose a group member joins the group with the goal of improving his or her relationships. Driving forces toward that goal might be the individual's desire to have an intimate relationship, wish to please the referring professional, and eagerness to relate to the other members who seem to have similar problems.

The restraining forces might be anxiety about being rejected by other members, shame about exposing vulnerabilities, and, on perhaps a less conscious level, apprehension that improving peer relationships may mean lessening dependent ties on parental figures. The extent to which this group member will organize his or her energy to pursue the goal of transformation will depend upon the extent to which the driving forces outweigh the restraining forces.

According to the theory of living human systems, phases of group development are another isomorphic feature of systems; that is, they are universal across systems in different contexts and within all of the systems and subsystems in a hierarchy. Agazarian largely adopts the Bennis and Shepard (1956) description of phases and subphases but reframes it and the general concept of group development within a theory of living human systems. According to this scheme, each of the developmental phases has its own goals and accompanying driving and restraining forces. The restraining forces consist of a set of progressively more complex, phase-specific defenses that must be modified in order for driving forces to move the group toward the goal of each phase. However, the restraining forces are not mere obstacles but, rather, energies directed toward an unacknowledged goal that exists in conflict with the group's developmental goal (Agazarian & Gantt, 2003). Hence, each phase is characterized by a conflict between two opposing goals, the resolution of which earns the group passage to the next phase.

Systems-centered therapy provides a methodology for defense modification. For example, in the earliest phase of development, "members introduce themselves by name with a low probability that the names will be remembered, report their outside lives with a probability that a hierarchy will be established on status rather than on resources useful to work, and give opinions rather than facts" (Agazarian & Gantt, 2003, p. 243). The restraining forces in the group operate to reproduce the stereotypes with which members are familiar in their lives outside the group. If these forces hold sway, members will subgroup according to stereotype (for example, high-status people connecting with each other more than they do with low-status people). The implicit or unconscious goal is to avoid work and maintain the status quo, an aim clearly at odds with the goal of becoming a group that will be an instrument of transformation and development.

To lessen the effect of the restraining forces, the therapist uses functional subgrouping before

stereotypic subgrouping can take hold. *Functional subgrouping* organizes members into subgroups based upon their similar positions in regard to basic group conflicts rather than a stereotypic classification. For example, in the initial stage in the life of the group, members will functionally subgroup according to different stances on dependency—those who openly accept dependency longings and those who disavow them. Functional subgrouping affords each member freedom from isolation in the group and, with it, greater security in exploring and expressing aspects of the experience. As members of a given subgroup do so, inevitably, they will begin to differentiate their positions from one another. For example, members of a dependency-avowing subgroup will see that whereas one member wants to depend totally on authority, another member feels only some authority figures deserve such trust. This process, in turn, will enable these subgroup members to have an increased identification with the positions of members of the dependency-disavowing subgroup. Members' ability to discriminate among members whose positions they share and identify and members whose positions they previously opposed enables them to integrate various aspects of their own person. These processes of discrimination and integration catapult the group to the next developmental phase.

Comparison among the Stage Models
These three models share a number of features. They all assert the position that development is organized into a series of stages or phases that are universal and invariant across social systems. They all allow for the possibility not only of progression but also of regression and fixation. They share a perspective that diversity among members in interpersonal styles constitutes a resource to the group in that members who are deviant on any given dimension give voice to elements that other members cannot express but share and perform functions that other members cannot contribute as easily. All models see the processes of differentiation and integration as critical change mechanisms.

The differences among these models reflect the variations that are present generally in progressive stage approaches to group life. We see that models are variable in terms of the number of stages. This difference may be more apparent than real in that MacKenzie may be combining into a single stage, two or more of the stages in other models. Even so, the number of stages is an important consideration because it organizes the therapist's thinking and interventions. A system may be so nuanced that, though accurately capturing the changing patterns of interaction, it encumbers the therapist. Conversely, a system that fails to make critical differentiations will not offer the therapist sufficient information to help him or her recognize what interventions are most useful within a given segment of group life. The models also differ in the unit of analysis on which the group focuses. For example, all of the models attend to the individual and group levels, but the systems-centered model distinguishes itself for its use of subgroup phenomena. Finally, the models vary in terms of the extent to which they have a task versus a conflict emphasis. A task focus sees each stage consummating in an achievement, whereas a conflict focus regards the resolution of a conflict as being the pinnacle event enabling passage to the ensuing stage.

Each of these models makes a valuable contribution to understanding the developmental characteristics of groups. The Beck model helps the group counselor to identify the different resources that the group requires in order to advance and how the necessary resources vary from one period of group life to another. The MacKenzie and Livesley (1983) model is probably the most user-friendly framework, provided the practitioner already has a solid background in conducting psychotherapy groups. Unlike, for example, the systems-centered model, it does not offer a high level of specificity concerning the interventions of the therapist. A strength of this model is that it is amenable to application within a short-term time frame. The systems-centered model provides the most sophisticated picture of the relationship of the individual member to the group and of the group to the broader environment. This model offers the therapist the most technically rich approach; it provides an extremely detailed blueprint for how the therapist intervenes at each stage of development. Yet, it is the most conceptually demanding model and is most beneficially used by practitioners with a very substantial knowledge of psychodynamic theory. However, systems-centered therapy offers the therapist a plenitude of educational resources to pursue an organized training program in this approach.

Life-Cycle Models

Although progressive stage models dominate the literature and practice, a range of other models exist. The first type is the class of life-cycle models, which shares many features of the progressive stage models; and indeed, some writers (e.g., Smith, 2001) see

this category as a variant of the progressive stage model. Like the progressive stage models, life-cycle models see the group as proceeding through a set of invariant stages, with later stages being affected by earlier ones. The notion that the group becomes progressively more effective is either absent or downplayed, and the last stage of the group is characterized by a decline in group functioning and regression of members to earlier modes of functioning (Mann, 1966). For example, Mann writes about the group's return to an avoidant mode of functioning seen in the earliest stages. Progressive stage models sometimes also see regression as a possibility in this stage. However, these models also hold that members can potentially understand regression as a defense against the affects and impulses stimulated by termination. In such a circumstance, the regression supports the group's maturation.

Cyclical Approaches to Group Development

Although both Bales (1950) and Bion (1961) saw the group repetitively moving through different stages, they did not see the group as advancing as it did so. Such models, strictly speaking, are not developmental. Yet, some cyclical models do have a growth aspect. For example, Schutz (1958) posited a model in which the psychotherapy group recurrently grapples with issues pertaining to inclusion, control, and affection. However, each time the group does so, its work is more effective and a greater number of members become actively engaged in the group's work.

In some cases, the structural features of a group may make a cyclical model most serviceable for a particular type of group. When the membership turnover is extremely rapid, the group may never achieve the stability to advance to the later stages of development. For all practical purposes, these later stages might be regarded as nonexistent. Instead, the group is best depicted as cycling back and forth between stages 1 and 2, making only an occasional foray into stage 3.

Cyclical models also have importance in that they can describe the fluctuation of processes within a given stage. Although Kurt Lewin (1951) did not propose a theory of group development per se, he did hold that living systems may mature according to a set of stages and that, within those stages, the system may cycle between or among different states. Years later, MacKenzie (1997) noted the potential compatibility between progressive stage models and cycle models. For example, groups may cycle within each stage between Bales's task and emotional domains. Beck (1974) wrote about how groups cycle from differentiation to integration or cohesion within stages.

Contemporary Models

Within the last 20 years, new models have emerged that are primarily being applied in organizational settings. Yet, particularly because they do have some empirical backing and account for group phenomena that have not been explained previously, they are being given closer scrutiny by group counselors for their descriptive and explanatory value regarding the developmental aspects of a group.

COMPLEXITY THEORY

Two additional models have emerged more recently, and both run counter to the description of group life as separate from the broader environment in which the group resides. The first, the complexity/chaos class of models, while emerging from the physical sciences, provided an account of change that had resonance for group counselors because of its compatibility with another influential conceptual framework, general systems theory (Von Bertalanffy, 1968), which studied those features and patterns common to all systems. General systems theory considered the implications of the fact that the group is a system in a hierarchy of systems. The group is embedded in a larger system, and individual members are embedded in the group and are subsystems of the group. Every system has boundaries with the larger system in which it is embedded, but these boundaries are porous, allowing for an influx and efflux of information. These exchanges of information enable systems and subsystems to influence and adapt to one another. A change in the system of the group has reverberations within the subsystem of each member (Durkin, 1982). Complexity theory shares with general systems theory a view of living systems as possessing properties that enable them to grow and adapt to the environments in which they reside.

Within complexity theory, four features have particular importance (Brabender, 1997; Masterpasqua & Perna, 1997). The property of *irreversibility* entails that the group's current status is a consummation of all events that preceded the present moment. In the psychotherapy group, then, the past cannot be taken back; the totality of the group's history will shape the present. Moreover, whatever impulses, affects, and fantasies enter the group are never obliterated; rather, they may merely take their place within a progressively more complex system. If in a group session Jeff insults Susan, he can never, strictly speaking, take back the insult. However, he can give Susan additional information to enable her to experience the insult differently from the way she did originally.

The property of *nonlinearity* refers to the phenomenon wherein a stimulus may evoke a response incommensurate with that stimulus. Consistent with this property is the phenomenon of *sensitivity to initial conditions* (or butterfly effect) wherein a seemingly minor or incidental event can have profound ramifications for a system, particularly early in its life. For example, an event early in the life of the group that seems trivial may have a role in shaping the character of the group. As is true with other living systems, the events of the group may appear random or chaotic because their tie to early events in the life of the group may not be evident (Brabender, 1997). This sensitivity to initial conditions may, in part, account for a property of all groups (Conyne, in press): uniqueness. Groups differ because the initial conditions that inform them differ in subtle or nonsubtle ways.

The property of *dissipativeness* pertains to the constant exchange of information between a system and its broader environment and between a system and its subsystems. This dissipative feature provides for system vitality and adaptive change: The information the psychotherapy group derives from the broader environment enables it to know how it must adapt to that environment. Finally, the feature of *self-organization* enables a system to move from chaos to order through use of its own internal resources. Consequently, the counseling group can proceed through a period of turbulence to one of coherence without the imposition of order by an external agent (McClure, 1998).

Within complexity theory, each developmental era of group life can be understood as the reorganization of the group from a period of chaos (McClure, 1998). What is interesting about the interface between complexity theory and group developmental theory is that it has been interpreted in different ways. It has been seen as compatible with a progressive stage model (Brabender, 1997), at odds with a progressive stage model and consistent with the notion of change particular to that group based on local conditions (Stacey, 2005), and compatible with a stage model contrasting in significant ways with the traditionally posited stages (McClure, 1998). Part of the reason for this variability is that complexity theory is a mathematical model, but it has been used primarily in a metaphorical way, which affords writers consider leeway in application. Some researchers (e.g., Wheelan, 1996) have begun to test the mathematical predictions made by complexity theory, and this research holds promise for demonstrating its degree of compatibility with progressive stage concepts.

Punctuated Equilibrium Model
This model of change (Eldridge & Gould, 1972) is derived from evolutionary theory and is based on the observation that for extended periods a system can remain in stasis, a state in which its fundamental properties (or deep structure) do not change. Rather than occurring incrementally and cumulatively, change punctuates the equilibrium. That is, it occurs in bursts that have a transforming effect upon those fundamental properties. This model shares with complexity theory the notion that groups may proceed through a period of relative disequilibrium until order is restored through a process of internal restructuring.

Gersick (1988) has applied the punctuated equilibrium model to different types of groups, including psychotherapy groups. According to Gersick, key to group development is a process of pacing. Early in a group's history certain patterns of interaction develop that take hold for a protracted period and any adjustments that members make are minor, that is, within the framework of the existing communication patterns. For example, if the group were assigned to develop a creative solution to a problem, it would quickly establish a mode of working on the problem and persist in that mode until it becomes aware that it is reaching the mid-point of its life. The perception of the mid-point promotes a process of taking stock (members ask privately or publicly, "What are we accomplishing? What can we achieve in our remaining time?"). It thereby provides a stimulus for members' achievement of greater openness toward one another, a collective openness that transforms the group. The change that occurs at this time is revolutionary, discontinuous, and inclusive of multiple aspects of the system. For example, an abrupt shift in members' communication patterns, behavioral norms, emotional tone, and thematic emphases may be observed.

The punctuated equilibrium model was posed as an alternative to the progressive stage model. Supportive evidence for this model has been garnered in work settings in which the group was given a highly concrete task such as the creation of a 60-second commercial within a 1-hour time span (Gersick, 1989). However, work is needed to address

the counseling group (both long-term and short-term groups) specifically to see if this model provides a better description of group development than competing models.

Empirical Evidence Concerning Group Development and Its Importance
This chapter rests upon two premises: (1) group development occurs and (2) it is relevant to members' achievement of their treatment goals. Considerable research has been done to address the first question and a smaller set of studies, the second.

The Reality of Group Development
How do we know if group development is a phenomenon that characterizes groups, in general, and counseling groups, specifically? Three lines of evidence exist that support group development: (1) research on therapeutic factors, (2) studies on group climate, and (3) theme-based analysis of verbalization.

THERAPEUTIC FACTORS
First, studies examining patterns in members' endorsement of therapeutic factors and group climate have obtained results that are largely, although not entirely, consistent with a progressive stage model. The therapeutic factors are elements within the therapy that may contribute to favorable outcomes. Various classification schemes of therapeutic factors, most notably that described in Yalom (2005), derive from Corsini and Rosenberg's (1955) original list. Progressive stage models predict that factors pertaining to morale would figure prominently early in the sessions, while those pertaining to psychological work would increase. These models, particularly Beck's (1974) model, predicted that self-revelation would be very high at the beginning of the group, would drop as the group began to address differences, and would increase following the resolution of their conflictual stance toward authority. MacKenzie (1987), using a longitudinal design with four outpatient groups, found that this pattern is obtained. Therapeutic factors associated with morale (acceptance, instillation of hope, and universality) decreased over time, factors associated with work (self-understanding, learning from interpersonal actions, and vicarious learning) increased, and factors associated with self-revelation (catharsis and self-disclosure) decreased and then increased in the advanced sessions. Studying the last 11 sessions of student groups, Kivlighan and Mullison (1988) found that, consistent with developmental predictions, universality was

perceived as highly important early in the life of the group and interpersonal learning, later in the group's life. Kivlighan and Goldfine (1991), examining six process groups in a group-counseling course, also found that universality declined in importance, as did hope. However, contrary to predictions of the progressive stage model, interpersonal learning, self-understanding, and vicarious learning did not change across the life of the group. The authors hypothesized that perhaps the group over its relatively short life simply did not develop sufficiently.

GROUP CLIMATE

Second, progressive stage models predict that over time systematic changes occur in the atmosphere of the group, and studies have examined these changes (see Chapter 10 for more information on group climate). A major tool that has been used in these studies is the Group Climate Questionnaire-Short Form (GCQ-S) (MacKenzie & Livesley, 1983), which consists of 12 items, each descriptive of a facet of the group climate. The group member endorses each item on a 1–7 Likert scale. A factor analysis of the responses yielded three dimensions—engaged, avoiding, and conflict.

In a study mentioned earlier, Kivlighan and Goldfine (1991) administered the GCQ-S after every session of 13-week student growth groups. The investigators found that engagement increased and avoidance decreased as the session number increased. Conflict increased and then decreased. These results were interpreted to be consistent with a progressive stage model. Brossart, Patton, and Wood (1998), using a Tuckerized growth curve methodology (Tucker, 1966), assessed the consistency between changes in their group participants' GCQ-S scores over 28 sessions based on the MacKenzie and Livesley (1983) model. Their analysis, which focused on the Conflict scale, revealed a decrease in score across the sessions. Although an eventual decrease is expected as participants accept differences with each other" and authority, a prior trend clearly predicted by most progressive stage models is an increase in conflict. Hence, these results provide definite support for systematic changes in groups over time but only partial support for a traditional stage model. The authors hypothesized that the fact that the group leaders were relatively inexperienced may have made a difference in the unfolding processes of the groups.

THEME-BASED ANALYSIS

Third, Wheelan (2005) developed a scale, the Group Developmental Observation System (GDOS), to permit a thematic analysis of group members' verbalizations. The themes were organized according to the types of issues that a traditional progressive stage model would predict members would explore. Every statement of group members is placed into a thematic category. Wheelan, Davidson, and Tilin (2003) used this system with ongoing for-profit and not-for-profit organizational groups that met in their natural settings. They found that groups that met for longer durations were more likely to be making statements that observers perceived to be associated with the later stages of development. Likewise, in groups that had been meeting relatively briefly, members made statements that were thematically consistent with a developmentally early stage of development.

The Significance of Group Development

Existing research suggests that group development is more than an interesting set of phenomena; whether or not a group develops and the extent to which it develops appear to influence what members can derive from their participation in group counseling (Conyne, in press). Evidence for an association between the developmental status of the group and outcomes has been found with different populations, settings, and group formats. For example, Tschuschke and MacKenzie (1994) studied two weekly psychoanalytic outpatient groups composed of German members. They found that groups in which members proceeded to the stage in which they recognized differences had more favorable outcomes than less developed groups. Castonguay, Pincus, Agras, and Hines (1998) studied a structured cognitive-behavioral group composed of binge-eating members. They found that those members who showed a pattern that would be typical of a stage progression with high positive affectivity in the beginning and negative affectivity in the middle had more favorable outcomes than members who did not show this pattern of perceptions. This study is interesting in that it suggests that some members may not participate in the group's development and thereby may not reap its benefits.

The literature on process and training groups more substantially addresses process and outcome relationships. In one large-scale study of 53 training and process groups, MacKenzie, Dies, Coche, Rutan, and Stone (1987) measured the level of success of groups as a function of scores on the GCQ-S. The investigators observed patterns of GCQ-S scores consistent with group development. Moreover, they found that groups that made greater progress through the developmental stages had more favorable outcomes. Wheelan and Lisk (2000) found that undergraduate students in groups operating at a more mature level had higher grade point averages. Wheelan, Burchill, and Tilin (2003) found that the staff of an intensive care unit operating in the advanced stages of development had lower mortality rates. Wheelan and Kesselring (2005) found that students taught by faculty groups who reach more advanced stages of development had higher scores on standardized tests.

How the Group Counselor Can Use Group Developmental Phenomena

All group counselors can and should take group development into account as they acquire an understanding of their group and plan interventions. Two broad approaches exist for using developmental concepts. The first is to embrace a developmental model as the primary framework for conducting the group. When a developmental model is the dominant motif, the therapist's efforts are directed toward helping the group to develop as fully as possible and assisting individual members in participating as fully as possible in the group's development. The second approach is to use another framework as the key model, for example, cognitive-behavioral therapy, and to consider developmental phenomena as either obstructing or facilitating the goals of that key model.

Group Development as a Primary Model

When group development is the centerpiece of the therapist's conceptualization of, and intervention in, the group, it informs all of the therapist's activities such as the creation of a group design, the selection of members, and the ongoing manner in which the therapist intervenes within the group. In creating a group design, the therapist establishes structural features that are consonant with the group goals. If the group goal is its progression through the developmental stages, then in the group design the therapist will identify those structural features that are conducive to group development.

What type of environment promotes group development, specifically within the context of the dominant model in the field—a progressive stage model? Although many features may bear upon the group's development, three factors are especially important. First, groups that are stable have greater developmental potential than groups that are constantly in flux. Constancy of such features as time and place make the group a more palpable entity,

worthy of members' investment. Especially important is a stable membership. Group scholars (for example, Wheelan, 2005) agree that a change in group membership promotes regression as members must undergo the kind of group-formation process that occurs at the earliest stage of the group. With inpatient groups in which membership changes on a near-daily basis, the group is prone to recycling through the earliest stages of development and failing to move beyond these. Nonetheless, consistent with certain developmental models (e.g., Agazarian, 1997) is the idea that groups that regress to an earlier stage carry with them the gains of prior work. Within such a scheme, groups that have retreated to earlier stages have greater potential to work through the conflicts of those stages than groups that are making their fledgling passage through them.

Stability of membership means that members not only remain in the group but also attend the sessions on a regular basis. Assessment tools have been developed to assist in the task of identifying members who have a high potential of establishing a good attendance pattern. The Group Selection Questionnaire (MacNair-Semands, 2002) is a self-report instrument that can be administered as part of the member-selection process. MacNair-Semands found that the features of extreme hostility and social inhibition are associated with poor attendance patterns. By selecting members who have the potential of making a very serious commitment to the group, the therapist goes a long way to ensuring that the group will have the capacity to develop.

Second, group formats that allow for the spontaneous expression of thoughts and feelings facilitate development. Although evidence suggests that group development can take place with varying levels of structure (Schopler & Galinsky, 1990), a session in which members' contributions are highly orchestrated is probably less conducive to development than one in which members are given greater leeway. When group process is highly prescribed, members have little freedom to express and explore the thoughts, impulses, and feelings characteristic of a given developmental stage, activities that enable members to complete developmental tasks and resolve developmental conflicts. Although a fully structured session may not facilitate development, certain structural elements may. For example, in the preparation for the group, the therapist can provide members with instruction in the processes that will move members toward their goals. If the group is short-term, it is important that these goals be developed prior to participation with a high level of specificity.

The third factor concerns the leadership of the group. The leader, as we have seen, plays an important role in organizing a group that has the capacity to thrive. Beyond this factor, the therapist's ability to intervene with sensitivity at each stage of development will be instrumental in ensuring the group's successful passage through the stages. In the section that follows, the developmental stages will be described and illustrated with particular focus on the therapist's interventions.

The model (Brabender & Fallon, 2009) presented in this section has considerable overlap with models previously described in this chapter, especially the Bennis and Shepard (1956) model, the MacKenzie (1997) model, aspects of the systems-centered model (Agazarian, 1997), and the initial stages of Beck's (1974) model.

STAGE 1: FORMATION AND ENGAGEMENT STAGE

In this stage, the goal is for members to transform themselves from a collection to a true group. That is, members must achieve a modicum of cohesion, or esprit de corps. Cohesion is important in that higher levels tend to be associated with more favorable outcomes (Tschuschke & Dies, 1994) but also because its presence is necessary for members to move on to later stages.

As Agazarian (1997) notes, the goal of becoming a group will be reached depending upon the relative strength of driving versus restraining forces. Although psychotherapy group members are naturally propelled to become a group to receive assistance in addressing their difficulties, restraining forces exist as well. A major restraining force is members' set of fears about what could happen if the collection of people becomes a group. Members are afraid of being criticized, rejected, or attacked. The therapist responds to member concerns by establishing consistent boundaries in terms of time, place, and membership that foster a sense of safety in the group. The therapist assists members in talking directly about their fears, and by doing so, members come to understand that their apprehensions are shared. They learn that others have an investment in creating a safe environment, a reassurance that lessens the strength of the restraining force of fear.

The therapist should also support members in building positive connections with one another. Consider the following exchange:

George: I have felt very isolated since I have come to this day treatment program.

Jill: For Chrissake, there are people all around you.

George (shakes head wearily): I know . . . I know . . . I just . . . [fades off]

Therapist: It's true. A lot of people are around all of us, but sometimes loneliness can occur anyway. And I'm reminded, Jill, of how you talked about a kind of loneliness when Nancy and Carol were talking about their difficulties with their boyfriends and how you long to have a boyfriend. I think you felt lonely right here in the session.

Jill: Yeah, it's true, I did feel that way . . . and when I'm around others and I see what they have that I don't, then, I feel much more isolated than when I was just by myself. Probably, George, I just didn't want to think about that right now.

Here, the therapist is engaging in activity that is critical for stage 1—fostering identifications among members. Although inevitably some members will be present who need no assistance, invariably others will require help. The therapist should strive for every member to make a significant connection with at least one other member. Members failing to do so are at risk for leaving the group prematurely or, if they remain, exhibiting poorer outcomes than more engaged members (Tschuschke & Dies, 1994).

Some members will make very significant self-disclosures at this stage. Typically, the self-disclosures concern their lives outside the group. Therapists trained in process group methodology might be tempted to move the group from a then-and-there to a here-and-now focus. Although this type of intervention will be very important at various junctures of the group, at this point it is not developmentally optimal to reroute the group. The significance of the self-disclosure is not in its content but in the fact that sensitive material is being shared. These disclosures, which convey trust, will nurture the trust of more hesitant participants. On the other hand, the therapist plays an important role in titrating self-disclosures so that disclosing members do not feel unduly exposed or nondisclosing members coerced into making their own disclosures. Once members have shared personal material, the therapist can foster a here-and-now focus by having members reflect on how those disclosures altered their feelings about one another.

Finally, helping members to acknowledge their trepidations about group involvement can be useful in two ways. Some members will deny any apprehensions and move headlong into the group process.

Evidence (Hoffmann, Gleave, Burlingame, & Jackson, 2009) suggests that these members will tend to show deteriorated functioning over the course of the group. Helping them to overcome their denial of their worries allows them to "test the waters" in the group before they venture a total immersion. Those members with exaggerated worries can test them against the likely consequences of their involvement, a process that assists them in modulating fear sufficiently to become involved with the other members. *& talk abt fears*

STAGE 2: CONFLICT AND REBELLION

Up until the present, members have had an expectation that the therapist would eventually step in and eradicate their difficulties. During stage 1, they patiently wait for the therapist to begin the critical work. At the dawning of stage 2, following the establishment of a rudimentary sense of cohesion, members' restiveness increases. They begin to question whether the therapist is going to satisfy their expectations. At the same time, they increasingly become aware of their differences with one another, and these differences are irritating to members because they are seen as an impediment to, rather than a resource in, group work. Whereas the affective climate of late stage 1 is extremely positive, in stage 2 members become tense and fretful.

A particularly predictable but fascinating dynamic that emerges during this period of group life is that a member whose vulnerability is especially palpable will be identified as the patient of the group and another member will serve as the therapist. The identified patient will represent the enormity of psychological need for all members, and the therapist will represent the model of that figure for whom the group members yearn. Yet, the dyad is doomed to failure. The patient is not helped, the therapist is not effective, and the animosity felt for the actual therapist is displaced onto the person serving this role.

The function of the identified patient–therapist dyad is to help the dissatisfaction members have about their group experience to crystallize in a way that enables them to identify it, label it, and ultimately express it to its rightful target—the therapist. Often, members will engage in a unified action that symbolically expresses not only their fury at the therapist for his or her failures but also their readiness to liberate themselves from the therapist. As noted earlier, Bennis and Shepard (1956) saw this occurrence as a barometric event—an event that at once reveals the extent of atmospheric pressure and simultaneously relieves that pressure.

Probably more than any other, this stage tests the fortitude of the counselor. The task is to support members' eventual expression of dissatisfaction with his or her leadership (Bernard et al., 2008). How natural it is for the counselor (especially the beginning group counselor) to recoil at the thought of having not only one member angry at him or her but the entire group is another matter altogether (Bemak & Epp, 2001) Brabender (2002). Yet, for development to proceed, this step is necessary. Just as the therapist may be a reluctant recipient of members' hostilities, so too are group members hesitant to communicate such feelings. One shield against communication is awareness. Typically, one subgroup of members will deny to themselves the presence of negative reactions toward the leader. These negative reactions, having been barred from conscious manifestation, will reveal themselves in derivative or symbolic form. Group members will express disappointment with various other caretakers in their lives, and the therapist can point out possible parallels between complaints members have toward external figures and those characterizing their group experiences.

Another technique is to prevent any one member from being seen as the sole repository of anger in the group. If one member expresses a negative sentiment toward the therapist, it is helpful for the therapist to broaden that expression:

> Tariq (to the therapist): I just am not getting my money's worth from this group. You talk but offer no real solutions and I'm really getting irritated.
>
> Benita: She's just very professional.
>
> Amaya: Yes, I've heard that's how therapists are. You never get solutions.
>
> Therapist: And whether it's because I'm being professional or just withholding information, it's annoying to the group when I don't provide what you want and need.

In this circumstance, Tariq was at risk of being regarded as the sole possessor of negative feeling toward the therapist. If fully realized, this defensive maneuver would deprive members of recognizing in themselves the same feeling, would potentially lead Tariq to be the object of other members' hostility, and would hinder the group from advancing. For these reasons, the therapist delivered an interpretation that conveys acceptance of the affect, normalizes it, and identifies it as belonging to the group as a whole. Such a framing can then allow other members to feel some safety in identifying with Tariq.

Must encourage expression of feelings abt therapist

Probably more important than any particular technique used in this stage, though, is the therapist's openness to the group's affects toward him or her. When therapists are unaware of their own worries about being the focus of the group's fury, many maneuvers can be used to quash that fury (Brabender, 1987). For example, the therapist may respond in a silently withholding way or a solicitous way as members make their first forays in communicating dissatisfaction. Members will perceive these fledgling attempts as highly risky and will monitor the therapist's reaction closely. Even subtle negative responses on the part of the therapist will lead them to retreat, the cost of which is a failure to progress to the next stage.

STAGE 3: INTIMACY AND UNITY

In this stage, members feel a triumph over having challenged the therapist and survived and closeness to one another in relation to the success of their collaboration. During this stage, members will forge stronger ties with one another that are necessary for their pursuing the difficult interpersonal work that lies ahead in stage 4. The therapist must assist the group in nurturing these ties in several ways.

First, the therapist must be aware of the acting out potential of this stage and discourage members from its engagement. The closeness members experience evokes a wish to eradicate all boundaries. Commonplace temptations include sexual liaisons outside of the group session and bringing refreshments to the sessions. The therapist must catch glimmerings of these behaviors and remind members of the group rules. If evidence of violations presents itself, the therapist must encourage the group to talk about the transgressions and understand their consequences for members' ability to use the group therapeutically (Brabender & Fallon, 2009).

Second, the therapist must encourage members' self-disclosures. In this stage, members achieve greater intimacy by sharing increasingly private information about themselves. These communications also intensify members' commitment to the group because of the relief they effect. However, some members may deny themselves the opportunity to both deepen their connection with other members and obtain release. As in stage 1, the therapist plays a role in helping members to identify with one another so that more reluctant members can draw connections between their own reactions and those of more easily forthcoming members.

Third, the therapist must help members to begin to use the feedback process. The conclusion that positive feedback is easier for individuals to accept is both commonsensical and empirically based (Brabender, 2006). In this stage, because of the affective climate, members are disposed to offer positive feedback. The therapist should take advantage of this bias so that when members are prepared to offer more constructive feedback, they are inured to the feedback process. The therapist can also help members to learn how to deliver feedback so that it is maximally helpful. For example, the therapist can assist members in fine-tuning their feedback so that it is concrete and directed toward their immediate experience (Brabender, 2006).

STAGE 4. INTEGRATION AND WORK

The group moves from stage 3 to stage 4 as members become increasingly concerned with the denial of differences that attends members' efforts to achieve a greater sense of unity with one another. Early in this stage, fractiousness dominates members' interactions as some try to assert their uniqueness from other members and others attempt to quash this effort. However, increasingly, members come to recognize that the focus on differences—the fine points of each member's interpersonal style—and how they affect others is precisely what they came into the group to address.

Work

However, providing and receiving feedback, especially negative or constructive feedback, is a formidable task. Often, members will feel a great reluctance to dispense information that they see as critical. The therapist's role in helping members to identify their fears about offering feedback and to test these fears is crucial. Additionally, members continue to need assistance in refining feedback so that it is sufficiently concrete to be useful to the recipient:

Milieck: You say you are frustrated because I am not connecting with you, but I don't know what you mean.

Frank: It's just an impression I get. You seem so remote.

Therapist: It can be difficult to pinpoint what others do to make us feel a certain way. But knowing that it may be incomplete, can you just identify one aspect of Milieck's behavior that makes you see him as remote?

Frank: When he talks to me, he looks away. I'm not even sure if he's talking to me or to someone else.

Milieck: I never realized that.

Tanisha: Are you kidding? You do it all the time!

As part of members' evolving skill in securing the information they need to make constructive changes in themselves, members must learn to take a global impression and convert it to a description of a pattern of behavior. Flowers and Booraem (1990) found that in both psychodynamic and cognitive-behavioral groups the mere description of a behavioral pattern had a more positive effect on outcome than any of a number of other types of interventions.

In this stage, too, the leader must recognize that members' newfound ability to approach differences qualifies them for a maturity of decision making that was heretofore unavailable. Members can identify and process elaborately different positions on an issue. They can tolerate the tension of having an issue suspended into its various facets as it is fully explored. This ability enables the members to be given greater responsibility for their group (Bernard et al., 2008). Consider the following:

> Adrienne: I saw Victor a block away from the group walking in the pouring rain. I wanted to offer him a ride, but I thought I might be violating the of not socializing outside the group rule.
>
> Fiona: That seems a little too strict to me. Picking Victor up in that rainstorm would be a humanitarian gesture.
>
> Therapist: Let's think about this now. Let's look at the pros and cons of offering or not offering a member a ride and make a group decision about how whether the no socializing outside of group rule has applicability to such an instance.

When rules are established, invariably gray areas will emerge in which the correct application of the rule is uncertain. Early in the group, typically, were the therapist to give the members latitude to make a decision, little processing of the different sides of the issue would occur. At this stage, members do have the ability to conduct an in-depth examination, and their having an opportunity to do so enables them to acquire practice in the kind of mature decision making that will enhance their lives outside of group.

STAGE 5. TERMINATION

In the last stage of development, the therapist's interventions are directed toward two goals. The first is to help members to unpack the feelings and thoughts that attend the loss of the group. Facing the ending of the group is somewhat akin to stage 2's addressing dissatisfaction with the therapist—both are experiences that members might be eager to ward off. In both cases, members will respond to their developing reactions with defenses; the group counselor's job is to assist members in recognizing these means of denying themselves a full experience of the event at hand.

Members often summon the defenses of idealization and devaluation in relation to the group's ending. Rather than seeing the group as an involvement having both good and bad aspects, members will attempt to make their reactions more manageable by simplifying their experience. Often, a subgroup of members will emerge who will see the group in all-good terms, ignoring any disappointments with the group. For example, rarely will members' difficulties be completely eradicated by the end of the group, yet, upon entering the group, this will be most members' hope. Another typical subgroup is one that minimizes the connection among members, seeing the loss aspect of the group as minimal. Whatever the defense, the basic challenge is holding on to the diverse feelings—the disappointment, the gratitude, the sorrow, the pride—together. When the therapist helps members to see their defensiveness in relation to the group's ending, he or she enables the members to have the kind of full experience of loss that creates openness to new relational possibilities in the future.

The second goal is to aid members in consolidating learning and planning for the future (Bernard et al., 2008). Members benefit from a final appraisal in which they consider their goals upon entrance into the group and their progress in relation to these goals. For some types of groups (for example, Smullens's [2010] short-term model for victims of emotional abuse), a written component may be useful to deepen reflection. This evaluation is not merely introspective but interpersonal. At this time, many group members will offer appraisals of members' transformations over time ("When you first came in here, I couldn't believe how you interrupted everyone but now . . .") that are fresh and often heartening. From this process, three benefits typically accrue. First, members are bolstered by learning about their positive changes. Second, the identification of continuing areas of growth enables members to make plans for the future. Third, the final wrap-up cements the feedback process and encourages members to be data-driven in their changing thoughts about themselves and others. For the therapist's part, this process requires encouraging members to take a long-term perspective, if members do not do so spontane-ously, and ensuring that each member obtains this kind of thoroughgoing attention.

APPLICATIONS USING AN ALTERNATE MODEL AS THE PRIMARY THEORETICAL MODEL

In the preceding discussion, an assumption was made that the group counselor was using group developmental thinking as the primary theoretical framework informing his or her interventions in the group. However, the group developmental approach can be used secondarily to another model, including models that require a highly structured session such as cognitive-behavioral groups (Beck, 1995), inter-personal problem-solving groups (Spivack, Platt, & Shure, 1976), and psychoeducational groups (Brown, 2005). Research demonstrates that even within the context of structured sessions, develop-ment can occur over the life of the group (Castonguay et al., 1998). Given that the ability of a group to accomplish its goals is related to its developmental maturity, a counselor operating within a structured format should intervene in such a way as to maximize the group's development. Doing so requires that the therapist's interventions be stage-specific.

For example, in stage 1, formation and engage-ment, just as in less structured approaches, the ther-apist using a more structured session can emphasize members' identification of commonalities and ensure that all members find at least one other member with whom to connect. The therapist should not occupy so much time in delivering didac-tic material that members do not have an opportu-nity to affiliate with one another and develop cohesion (Brabender, 2002). In stage 2, conflict and rebellion, the group is likely to show a lessened com-mitment to tasks outside of the group that are part of the treatment. Members may also show a dimin-ished participation in the session, greater tardiness, and more frequent absences. By ignoring these man-ifestations, the therapist may contribute to their prolongation. By acknowledging the thoughts and feelings, the therapist can take advantage of an opportunity. How the therapist does so depends upon the particular treatment model employed. For example, within a cognitive-behavioral model, the therapist can examine the underlying thoughts con-nected to members' feelings of annoyance and rebel-lion and possibly the dysfunctional schema that concern authority figures and caretakers.

In general, within the structured approaches, the therapist should look for the themes associated with the developmental stages and see how they can be addressed in a manner consistent with the model. The therapist may also use the developmental stages to know when to introduce certain tasks. For example, if the model requires the delivery of highly individual positive and negative feedback, this task is likely to be accomplished most effectively once the group has reached stage 4.

Future Directions

Significant progress has been made over the past five decades in describing the changes that occur in a psychotherapy or counseling group over time. Yet, a contemplation of the questions that remain reveals that the work of group scholars and researchers remains at an early stage.

How might different models of change be com-bined to create a more complete description and understanding of group development? Currently, within the group-counseling literature, the progres-sive stage model reigns. Yet, for the most part, research has not been conducted in which different change models have been pitted against one another in an experimental context (Brabender & Fallon, 2009). Although research suggests that the progres-sive stage model has descriptive power, whether it more adequately accounts for changes than other models has not been determined. Moreover, might the different models account for different aspects of change phenomena, thereby requiring that a multi-plicity of models be employed? MacKenzie (1994) points out that within a single stage, a cyclic model may be most descriptive, whereas progressive stage models may capture change phenomena over longer intervals. Although some studies (for example, Arrow, 1997) have tested the relative predictive accuracy of different models, these studies have been preliminary with nontherapeutic groups.

How should the leader intervene in each stage of development? In this chapter, although suggestions were offered for how the therapist might intervene in each stage of development, these recommendations were based on the literature and the author's own experiences. What is missing is research on develop-mentally linked interventions (an absence reflective of a general lack of empirical evidence concerning leadership interventions [Kivlighan, 2008]). Yet, the literature contains the basis for such investigations. For example, MacKenzie (1997) urges the therapist to adopt a somewhat more confrontational manner in stage 2. A research study might compare degrees of confrontational activity on the part of the thera-pist as this variability is associated with short-term and long-term outcomes. For example, does variation in use of confrontations affect the number of sessions it requires to complete stage 2 (short-term outcome or proximal goal) or the members' achievement of their goals at the end of therapy and beyond (long-term outcome or distal goal)? Additionally, if certain interventions make a difference, it would be important to understand the mechanism of action. An intervention may mediate change (e.g., confrontations mediate favorable outcomes) or may affect a mediator (e.g., confrontations affect the group atmosphere, which affect outcomes). Also, modulating variables might be identified. Confrontations at stage 2 may be effective, harmful, or neutral depending on the member population.

How should group developmental thinking be applied within a structured model? The suggestions on the application of developmental thinking are tentative and await empirical confirmation. For example, the suggestion that acknowledging members' resistance in stage 2 is helpful could be tested in a cognitive-behavioral group by seeing if this intervention is followed by more consistent completion of homework assignments. See Brabender and Fallon (2009) for additional suggestions of how developmental theory could be applied within a cognitive-behavioral model.

What structural conditions facilitate group development? Very little is known about how such factors as leadership structure, session length, size of the group, and composition affect group development, particularly in counseling groups. Although the therapist does not have control over all of these variables—for example, in a hospital setting, composition may be determined by external factors—to the extent that the therapist does, he or she can make decisions with group development in mind. Also, what preparation for group counseling affects how the group members approach developmental tasks? Wheelan (2005) argues that participants who train in the developmental stage theory prior to entering the group are more likely to negotiate the stages successfully. Certainly, what has been learned from the study of groups with mental health professionals is that their knowledge of the stages does not hinder the groups in which they participate from having a developmental life.

Conclusions

The counseling group is absorbing to its members and its leaders in part because of its perpetually changing character. Yet, amid the flux is stability; therapy groups change in ways that are orderly, systematic, and potentially progressive. That is,

groups can not only change but grow. Whether or not the group grows is a matter of importance to the members; their ability to accomplish their purposes for being in the group is affected by whether the group progresses, languishes, or retreats. Therefore, group development is of importance to the counselor as well. He or she is entrusted with the task of safeguarding the group's development and ensuring that all members participate. Although group development has been studied for many years, the topic of how systematic progressive change is facilitated by its leader has just begun.

References

Agazarian, Y. M. (1997). *Systems-centered therapy for groups*. New York: Guilford Press.

Agazarian, Y., & Gantt, S. (2003). Phases of group development: Systems-centered hypotheses and their implications for research and practice. *Group Dynamics: Theory, Research, and Practice, 7*, 238–252.

Agazarian, Y., & Gantt, S. (2005). The systems-centered approach to the group-as-a-whole. *Group, 29*, 163–185.

Arrow, H. (1997). Stability, bistability and instability in small group influence patterns. *Journal of Personality and Social Psychology, 72*, 75–85.

Association for Specialists in Group Work. (2000). *Professional standards for the training of group workers*. Retrieved December 17, 2000, from www.asgw.org/PDF/Best_Practices.pdf

Bales, R. F. (1950). *Interaction process analysis: A method for the study of small groups*. Cambridge, MA: Addison-Wesley.

Beck, A. P. (1974). Phases in the development of structure in therapy and encounter groups. In D. Wexsler & L. N. Rice (Eds.), *Innovations in client centered therapy* (pp. 421–462). New York: Wiley InterScience.

Beck, J. S. (1995). *Cognitive therapy: Basics and beyond*. New York: Guilford Press.

Beck, A. P., & Peters, L. (1981). The research evidence for distributed leadership in therapy groups. *International Journal of Group Psychotherapy, 31*, 43–71.

Beck, A. P., Dugo, J. M., Eng, A. M., Lewis, C. M., & Peters, L. N. (1983). The participation of leaders in the structural development of therapy groups. In R. Dies & K. R. MacKenzie (Eds.). Advances in group psychotherapy: Integrating research and practice (pp. 137–158). New York: International Universities Press.

Beeber, A. R. (1988). A systems model of short-term, open-ended group therapy. *Hospital and Community Psychiatry, 39*(5), 537–542.

Bemak, F., & Epp, L. (2001). Countertransference in the development of graduate student group counselors: Recommendations for training. *Journal for Specialists in Group Work, 26*(4), 305–318.

Bennis, W. G., & Shepard, H. A. (1956). A theory of group development. *Human Relations, 9*, 415–438.

Bernard, H., Burlingame, G., Flores, P., Greene, L., Joyce, A., Kobos, J. C., et al. (2008). Clinical practice guidelines for group psychotherapy. *International Journal of Group Psychotherapy, 58*(4), 455–542.

Bion, W. R. (1961). *Experience in groups* (2nd ed.). New York: Basic Books.

Bion, W. R. (1962). *Learning from experiences in groups*. New York: Basic Books.

Brabender, V. (1987). Vicissitudes of countertransference in inpatient group psychotherapy. *International Journal of Group Psychotherapy, 37*(4), 549–567.

Brabender, V. (1988). A closed model of short-term inpatient group psychotherapy. *Hospital & Community Psychiatry, 39*, 542–545.

Brabender, V. (1997). Chaos and order in the psychotherapy group. In F. Masterpasqua & P. A. Perna (Eds.), *The psychological meaning of chaos: Translating theory into practice* (pp. 225–252). Washington, DC: American Psychological Association.

Brabender, V. (2002). *Introduction to group therapy*. New York: John Wiley & Sons.

Brabender, V. (2006). On the mechanisms and effects of feedback in group psychotherapy. *Journal of Contemporary Psychotherapy, 36*(3), 121–128.

Brabender, V., & Fallon, A. (2009). *Group development in practice: Guidance for clinicians and researchers on stages and dynamics of change*. Washington, DC: American Psychological Association.

Brossart, D. F., Patton, M. J., & Wood, P. K. (1998). Assessing group process: An illustration using Tuckerized growth curves. *Group Dynamics: Theory, Research, and Practice, 2*(1), 3–17.

Brown, N. W. (2005). Psychoeducational groups. In S. Wheelan (Ed.), *The handbook of group research and practice* (pp. 511–529). Thousand Oaks, CA: Sage.

Brusa, J., Stone, M. H., Beck, A. P., Dugo, J. M., & Peters, L. N. (1994). A sociometric test to identify emergent leader and member roles: Phase I. *International Journal of Group Psychotherapy, 44*, 79–100.

Castonguay, L. G., Pincus, A. L., Agras, W. S., & Hines, C. E. (1998). The role of emotion in group cognitive-behavioral therapy for binge eating disorder: When things have to feel worse before they get better. *Psychotherapy Research, 8*, 225–238.

Cohen, B. D., Ettin, M. F., & Fidler, J. W. (1998). Conceptions of leadership: The "analytic stance" of the group psychotherapist. *Group Dynamics: Theory, Research, and Practice, 2*(2), 118–131.

Conyne, R. (in press). Group counseling. In J. C. Hansen & E. Altmaier (Eds.), *Handbook of counseling psychology*. New York: Oxford University Press.

Cooley, S. H., Demby, A., Koppenal, G., Koslof, J., & Powers, T. (1996). A mode of time-effective group psychotherapy for patients with personality disorders: The clinical model. *International Journal of Group Psychotherapy, 46*(3), 329–355.

Corsini, R., & Rosenberg, B. (1955). Mechanisms of group psychotherapy. *Journal of Abnormal and Social Psychology, 51*, 406–411.

Dugo, J. M., & Beck, A. P. (1984). A therapist's guide to issues of intimacy and hostility viewed as group-level phenomena. *International Journal of Group Psychotherapy, 34*(1), 25–45.

Durkin, H. E. (1982). Change in group psychotherapy: Therapy and practice: A systems perspective. *International Journal of Group Psychotherapy, 32*(4), 431–439.

Eldridge, N., & Gould, S. J. (1972). Punctuated equilibria: An alternative to phyletic gradualism. In T. J. Schopf (Ed.), *Models of paleobiology* (pp. 82–115). San Francisco: Freeman, Cooper.

Flowers, J. V., & Booraem, C. D. (1990). The frequency and effect on outcome of different types of interpretation in psychodynamic and cognitive-behavioral group psychotherapy. *International Journal of Group Psychotherapy, 40*(2), 203–214.

Ford, C., Cabrales, D., & Williams, E. N. (1997, Summer). Stages of group development for AmeriCorps and other national service programs. Retrieved November 13, 2009, from http://www.nationalservicesources.org/stages-group

Freud, S. (1955). Group psychology and the analysis of the ego. In J. Strachey (Ed. & Trans.), *The standard edition of the complete psychological works of Freud* (Vol. 14, pp. 243–258). London: Hogarth Press. (Original work published 1921)

Gersick, C. J. G. (1988). Time and transition in work teams: Toward a new model of group development. *Academy of Management Journal, 31*, 9–41.

Gersick, C. J. G. (1989). Marking time: Predictable transitions in task groups. *Academy of Management Journal, 32*, 274–309.

Grinberg, L., Sor, D., & Bianchedi, E. T. (1977). *Introduction to the work of Bion*. New York: Jason Aronson.

Hoffman, L. L., Gleave, R. L., Burlingame, G. M., & Jackson, A. P. (2009). Exploring interactions of improvers and deteriorators in the group therapy process: A qualitative analysis. *International Journal of Group Psychotherapy, 59*(2), 179–197.

Jackson, D. A. (1999). The team meeting on a rapid turnover psychiatric ward: Clinical illustration of a model for stages of group development. *International Journal of Group Psychotherapy, 49*(1), 41–59.

Kanas, N., Stewart, P., Deri, J., Ketter, T., & Haney, K. (1989). Group process in short-term outpatient therapy groups for schizophrenics. *Group, 13*, 67–73.

Kivlighan, D. (2008). Overcoming our resistances to "doing" evidence-based group practice: A commentary. *International Journal of Group Psychotherapy, 64*(11), 1284–1291.

Kivlighan, D., & Goldfine, D. C. (1991). Endorsement of therapeutic factors as a function of stage of group development and participant interpersonal attitudes. *Journal of Counseling Psychology, 38*(2), 150–158.

Kivlighan, D., & Mullison, D. (1988). Participants' perception of therapeutic factors in group counseling: The role of interpersonal style and stage of group development. *Small Group Behavior, 19*, 452–468.

LeBon, G. (1960). *The crowd*. New York: Viking. (Original work published 1895)

Lewin, K. (1948). *Resolving social conflicts: Selected papers on group dynamics*. New York: Harper & Row.

Lewin, K. (1951). *Field theory in social science: Selected theoretical papers* (D. Cartwright, Ed.). New York: Harper & Row.

MacKenzie, K. R. (1987). Therapeutic factors in group psychotherapy: A contemporary view. *Group, 11*, 26–34.

MacKenzie, K. R. (1994). Group development. In A. Fuhriman & G. M. Burlingame (Eds.), *Handbook of group psychotherapy: An empirical and clinical synthesis* (pp. 223–268). New York: John Wiley & Sons.

MacKenzie, K. R. (1997). Clinical application of group development ideas. *Group Dynamics: Theory, Research, and Practice, 1*, 275–287.

MacKenzie, K. R., Dies, R. R., Coche, E., Rutan, S. J., & Stone, W. N. (1987). An analysis of AGPA Institute groups. *International Journal of Group Psychotherapy, 37*, 55–74.

MacKenzie, K. R., & Livesley, W. J. (1983). A developmental model for brief group therapy. In R. R. Dies & K. R. MacKenzie (Eds.), *Advances in group psychotherapy: Integrating theory and research* (pp. 101–135). Madison, CT: International Universities Press.

MacKenzie, K. R., Livesley, W. J., Coleman, M., Harper, H., & Park, J. (1986). Short-term therapy for bulimia nervosa. *Psychiatric Annals*, *16*, 699–708.

MacNair-Semands, R. R. (2002). Predicting attendance and expectations for group therapy. *Group Dynamics: Theory, Research, and Practice*, *6*(3), 219–228.

Malekoff, A. (1997). *Group work with adolescents: Principles and practice*. New York: Guilford Press.

Mann, R. D. (1966). The development of the member–trainer relationship in self-analytic groups. *Human Relations*, *19*, 84–117.

Masterpasqua, F., & Perna, P. A. (Eds.) (1997). Introduction: The history, meaning, and implications of chaos and complexity. In *The psychological meaning of chaos: Translating theory into practice* (pp. 1–22). Washington, DC: American Psychological Association.

McClure, B. A. (1990). The group mind: Generative and regressive groups. *Journal for Specialists in Group Work*, *15*(3), 159–170.

McClure, B. A. (1998). *Putting a new spin on groups: The science of chaos*. Mahwah, NJ: Lawrence Erlbaum.

McDougall, W. (1920). *The group mind: A sketch of the principles of collective with some attempt to apply them to the interpretation of national life and character*. New York: Putnam.

Miller, J. G. (1978). *Living systems*. New York: McGraw-Hill.

Peters, L. N., & Beck, A. P. (1982). Identifying emergent leaders in psychotherapy groups. *Group*, *6*, 35–40.

Piaget, J. (1928). *The child's conception of the world*. London: Routledge and Kegan Paul.

Robertson, M., Rushton, P. J., Bartrum, D., & Bus, R. R. B. (2004). Group based interpersonal psychotherapy for post-traumatic stress disorder: Theoretical and clinical aspects. *International Journal of Group Psychotherapy*, *54*(2), 145–175.

Schopler, J. H., & Galinsky, M. J. (1990). Can open-ended groups move beyond beginnings? *Small Group Research*, *21*, 435–449.

Schutz, W. C. (1958). *FIRO: A three-dimensional theory of interpersonal behavior*. New York: Holt, Rinehart, & Winston.

Shechtman, Z. (2007). *Group counseling and psychotherapy with children and adolescents*. Mahwah, NJ: Lawrence Erlbaum.

Smith, G. (2001). Group development: A review of the literature and a commentary on future research directions. *Group Facilitation: A Research and Applications Journal*, *3*, 14–46.

Smullens, S. (2010). The codification and treatment of emotional abuse in structured group psychotherapy. *International Journal of Group Psychotherapy*, *60*(1), 111–130.

Spinner, D. A. (1992). The evolution of culture and cohesion in the group treatment of ego impaired children. *International Journal of Group Psychotherapy*, *42*(3), 369–381.

Spivack, G., Platt, J. J., & Shure, M. B. (1976). *The problem-solving approach to adjustment*. San Francisco: Jossey-Bass.

Stacey, R. (2005). Social selves and the notion of the group-as-a-whole. *Group*, *29*, 187–209.

Tucker, L. R. (1966). Learning theory and multivariate experiment: Illustration by determination of generalized learning curves. In R. B. Cattell (Ed.), *Handbook of multivariate experimental psychology* (pp. 476–501). New York: Rand McNally.

Tuckman, B. W. (1965). Developmental sequence in small groups. *Psychological Bulletin*, *63*, 384–399.

Tuckman, B. W., & Jensen, M. A. C. (1977). Stages of small-group development revisited. *Group and Organizational Studies*, *2*, 419–427.

Tschuschke, V., & Dies, R. R. (1994). Intensive analysis of therapeutic factors and outcome in long term inpatient groups. *International of Group Psychotherapy*, *44*, 185–208.

Tschuschke, V., & MacKenzie, K. R. (1994). Empirical analysis of group development: A methodological report. *Small Group Behavior*, *20*, 419–426.

Von Bertalanffy, L. (1968). *General systems theory*. New York: Braziller.

Wheelan, S. A. (1996). An initial exploration of the relevance of complexity theory to group research and practice. *Systems Practice*, *9*, 49–70.

Wheelan, S. A. (2005). *Group processes: A developmental perspective* (2nd ed.). Boston: Allyn & Bacon.

Wheelan, S., Burchill, C., & Tilin, F. (2003). The link between teamwork and patient outcomes in intensive care units. *American Journal of Critical Care*, *12*, 527–534.

Wheelan, S. A., Davidson, B., & Tilin, F. (2003). Group development across time: Reality or illusion? *Small Group Research*, *34*, 223–245.

Wheelan, S. A., & Kesselring, J. (2005). Link between faculty group development and elementary student performance on standardized tests. *Journal of Educational Research*, *98*, 323–330.

Wheelan, S., & Lisk, A. (2000). Cohort effectiveness and the educational achievement of adult undergraduate students. *Small Group Research*, *31*, 724–738.

Yalom, I. (with Leszcz, M.) (2005). *The theory and practice of group psychotherapy (5th ed.)*. New York: Basic Books.

PART 4

Research

Evidence Bases for Group Practice

Sally H. Barlow

Abstract

Group treatments represent an efficacious and efficient mental health intervention that rivals and at times exceeds individual therapy outcomes. Group psychotherapy capitalizes upon group processes that replicate at the micro level the macro struggle for equal access to life-affirming mental health. Change processes occur as skilled group therapists invoke therapeutic factors within the group climate to promote client change. Because group members approach groups with equal parts hope and dread, it is important that mental health professionals keep current with research process and outcome evidence, which has been aided by filtered databases such as the Cochrane Library. One hundred years of research on group psychology and group psychotherapy have yielded helpful reviews, relevant themes, and meta-analyses on group vs. individual outcomes, although a few methodological problems remain given the highly complex nature of groups. Researchers, practicing clinicians, and future clinicians will benefit from exchanges with each other as evidence bases inform expert intervention for participating group members who seek positive change.

Keywords: group psychotherapy, evidence-based medicine, evidence-based psychology, group research

Introduction

American physician John Pratt published his study of treating tuberculosis patients in a group setting in 1905 as "thought-control classes," which gave the written history of group psychotherapy research its most likely start (Barlow, Fuhriman, & Burlingame, 2000; see also Chapter 4, in this volume for details). A little over 50 years later, Archie Cochrane, a Scottish physician treating patients with tuberculosis, realized he could not in good faith intervene with one treatment rather than another (after all, deliberately collapsing a lung was no small thing) without more hard evidence. He pioneered what later became known as the Cochrane Library, a huge electronic database of empirical evidence staffed by volunteers and accessed daily by thousands of clinicians (Cochrane & Blythe, 1989).[1] Tuberculosis was the common disease tying these two physicians together across the startlingly productive scientific decades of the twentieth century. It had high mortality and morbidity rates at the turn of the century when Pratt was practicing, although a vaccine and improved health-care standards helped rates recede when Cochrane was at work. Still, tuberculosis represented a significant threat to public health then as now, especially with the current increase in antibiotic-resistant strains. Mental health disorders such as major depression and schizophrenia represent a significant public health threat as well, with equally high morbidity and mortality rates. Like Cochrane, mental health professionals worldwide are seeking reliable and valid interventions.

Efficient and efficacious group psychotherapy might be one of those valid interventions as both group-process and outcome studies suggest that appropriate matching between patients and treatment models yields reliable change. What is "process" in group therapy? What exactly is "outcome?"

How do they interrelate? More fundamentally, what is group counseling, group psychotherapy? Differing definitions exist (Conyne, 2011, Chapter 1), as well as important contexts such as history, practice, training, and ethics (see Chapters 2–7) that shape the complex discourse of what it means to conscientiously assemble humans together in a group for therapy. Dominant research continues to reveal and at times further conceal this very complex domain. How can researchers and clinicians—often portrayed as coming from the illusory separate domains of the "ivory tower" and "the trenches"—contribute to the accumulating evidence bases that comprise group research and in their combined professional efforts help reduce mental disorders, which seriously impair large numbers of the public? For instance, depression alone is considered to be the leading cause of the disease burden combining quality-adjusted life years (QALYs) and disability-adjusted life years (DALYs)—an index that examines morbidity and mortality rates in North America that is expected to increase worldwide. As we consider other mental disorders as well, it becomes clear that many people need assistance now.

The eminent Harvard political philosopher John Rawls reminds us that we have a contract with each other for social justice; that because we are humans living with other humans, we coexist in formal and informal economic, political, and social networks or groups (personal communication with Claudia Card, one of Rawls's graduate students, September 12, 2010; see also Card, 2002, her work which moves the social justice research of her mentor Rawls further into the philosophical discussion of evil itself). It is upon this very foundation that group psychotherapy establishes itself. How we capitalize upon these group processes, which replicate at the micro level the macro struggle for equal access to life-affirming good mental health, is one of the reasons group therapy is powerful. Agreement from the members of the group about whether or not their contract with each other and the leader is being met as they pursue social well-being, interpersonal skills, and more meaningful lives has direct relevance for key factors in group psychotherapy: consensus, interpersonal learning, issues of diversity, and ethics (see Chapters 2–7 for further discussion).

Samuel Slavson, one of group's early practitioners, suggested that, since we are often harmed by the group (e.g., family of origin), it is by the group (e.g., group therapy) we can be helped. Most likely these change processes occur as leaders invoke therapeutic factors, particularly cohesion, and other aspects of group climate when focusing interventions toward individual members' target complaints as well as group-level processes, while also paying careful attention to group stages of development (see Chapters 8–11). Group interventions can come in the form of education (psychoeducation groups), human growth (T-groups or sensitivity groups), or mental health treatment (therapy groups). Regardless of the group's particular focus, many potential members approach groups with equal parts hope and dread since help or harm could result. Therefore, it matters that mental health professionals receive sufficient training in group skills and rely on continuing evidence to guide them (dealt with in more detail in Chapters 16–21).

This chapter deals with research and group psychotherapy, which has been underutilized (Piper, 2008) given that it is an efficient and effective treatment intervention with some caveats (Burlingame, MacKenzie, & Strauss, 2004), by examining the evidence-based movement in group psychotherapy as it has been developing over the past century. This chapter examines historical background, group review articles, group vs. individual meta-analyses, group psychotherapy, and group psychology themes; substantive themes by clinical populations and how these topics address, thus far, the six-factor model (Burlingame et al., 2004) of formal change theory, small-group processes, leader, member/patient, group structure, and group-treatment outcomes.

The Scientific Method and Evidence-Based Medicine and Psychology

The classic steps of the scientific method form the background for the evidence-gathering efforts of evidence-based medicine (EBM) and evidence-based practice of psychology (EBPP). For example, below are the 5 A's of EBM according to Sackett, Straus, Richardson, Rosenberg, & Haynes (2000):

Ask or formulate the question
Acquire evidence, search for answers
Appraise evidence for quality and relevance
Apply results, findings
Assess outcomes

These five steps are very similar to the twentieth century's hypotheticodeductive model for the scientific method found in basic science textbooks. The *Encyclopaedia Britannica* of our age, the Internet's Wikipedia presents a similar paradigm when one enters the descriptors "scientific method" paraphrased here: use experience—try to make sense of the problem with your senses; present a conjecture—state an explanation; deduce a prediction from that explanation—if your explanation is true, what are the consequences; and finally, test—look for the opposite of each consequence in order to disprove your conjecture. Many of us remember these traditional steps from our early science classes. Such steps are integrated into primary studies as well as systematic reviews, which add detail to the scientific method for the purposes of mental health research.

If I were considering referring a client for possible group treatment, I would *ask* myself, "Are Robert's presenting complaints—trouble with spouse, trouble at work—treatable in a group? And if so, would he thrive better in a structured relationship skill-building, time-limited group or a longer-term, unstructured process group?" Let us say I believed Robert's lower psychological mindedness might be better served in a structured skills group. Once referred and attending, I would check with, or *acquire* information from, the group leader, having obtained written permission, for appropriate updates so that I could address relevant issues in our individual sessions, mindful that his particular style of dismissal might make him a candidate for early dropout. (Group researchers consistently lament that dropouts routinely reach 43% in the majority of group studies [Burlingame et al., 2004]). I would suggest that we *appraise* together his experience at mid-point, being careful to encourage his fledgling ability to assert; perhaps go over his Outcome Questionnaire (OQ)[2] scores, which let us say increased over the last 4 weeks. Such an increase in symptoms would necessitate an explanation. I would hope that the two of us might develop the hypothesis that because his only way of being in the world has been through strict control of himself and attempts at control of others, which has resulted in the problems in his marriage and at work, it makes sense that his discomfort would increase in the new interpersonal setting of group therapy, where he is trying to be less controlling. We could *apply* that as a working hypothesis and strengthen his resolve to finish the group, especially since the last four sessions were to be spent on conflict resolution and communication skills—skills he desperately needs. At the end of the 8-week group, we would *assess* the outcome. Was it a success given our mutual goal setting at the beginning that focused on his skills of communication, conflict resolution, and assertiveness? I would also hope that his OQ scores would be much lower as he gained genuine skills that he might have seen pay off at home and at work. Group

measures[3] might inform me about his ability to negotiate the complex climate of the group, perhaps strengthening his ability to relate to others. Further, it would be great if he *asked* to be considered for the upcoming process group once he realized he had learned a great deal from the first more structured group and was ready to try another one with less structure and perhaps more interpersonal risk.

Most clinicians do this every day. They listen to their clients' distress, they formulate a plan to help, and they check to see if it is working. At every step of this hypothetical example, research can aid our clinical expertise given our particular client or patient's needs. For instance, at step 1, asking the right question—"Will a group help Robert, and what kind of group ought that to be?"—I am informed by the studies by Piper (2006) and Piper, Joyce, McCallum, Azim, and Ogrodniczuk (2002), where lower psychological mindedness predicted early dropout. Additionally, they found that those with lower psychological mindedness did better in supportive, rather than interpretive, groups. If I want Robert to succeed in his first ever therapy group, I will need to match him to the appropriate model of treatment. Pregroup training, appropriate referral, guarding against dropout, combining the appropriate kinds of treatment—in this case, individual and group—and assessing progress or lack of it help to increase the odds of a good outcome for Robert by making science matter in psychology (Beutler, 2009).

What might be missing from the average clinician's tool kit are weekly assessments of improvement or deterioration and a formal measure of change at the end of therapy. Individual and group therapists are not always reliable observers of their individual clients (Lambert, Harmon, Slade, Whipple, & Hawkins, 2005) and group members (Chapman, 2009). Much as we would like to think this is not an accurate assessment given the years we spent in graduate school and the efforts we put into everyday interactions with the clients we hope to help in therapy, it is nevertheless true (see Meehl, 1954, for a compelling argument about statistical vs. clinical prediction).

The convergence of several factors makes clinical research easier to undertake. Measures that allow us to assess group member experiences are often easily obtainable. Clients coming to college counseling centers and community mental health agencies appear more amenable to the idea of group treatment (Carter, Mitchell, & Krautheim, 2001), and many counseling centers are gathering research

(Davies, Burlingame, Johnson, Barlow, & Gleave, 2007). Single group case studies are becoming more acceptable as a legitimate source of information about therapy process and outcome (Kazdin, 2008; Yalom, 2005). The number of clinicians who are conducting larger experiments—comparing several groups, utilizing formal measures and a multimethod approach—is growing every year. We might call this the "up side" of data.

The accumulation of 100 years of past research and the current researchers who continue to apply such methods in order to study relevant variables in group psychotherapy results in a huge database. What such efforts, excellent as they are, yield is literally tons of articles (printed material in the form of chapters, books, and refereed journal articles) as well as the more recent electronically available databases, equally as vast, if not as heavy, that require some kind of synthesis. This is perhaps what might be called the "down side" of data. Surely, this is one of the more salient reasons that many of us do not keep as current in the literature as we might otherwise: It is, at the outset, a Herculean endeavor, as Archie Cochrane realized in the 1950s. His efforts at aggregating scientific data helped organize the evidence-based movement.

EBM, defined as the "integration of best research evidence with clinical expertise and patient values" (Sackett et al., 2000, p. 147; Steinberg & Luce, 2005), is the forerunner of EBPP, in which the three-pronged approach—research, clinical expertise, and patient values– is utilized to provide the best available knowledge for patient care. Empirically validated treatments (EVTs), referred to also as empirically supported treatments (ESTs) in the late 1990s, are efforts within psychology, focusing more narrowly on specific treatments, which ask whether such treatments work for certain disorders in certain circumstances. In their watershed article, Chambless and Ollendick (2001) suggest that ESTs are important to consider, although a healthy debate has ensued (Cochrane, 1972; Smith, 2009; Stewart & Chambless, 2007; Chambless et al., 2006).

By comparison, EBPP starts with the client or patient and asks, "Which research (including relevant results from randomized controlled treatments [RCTs]) will assist the psychologist to achieve the best outcome" (Levant, 2005, p. 6). Thus, EBPP is a broader-based decision-making process that integrates intersecting lines of inquiry such as psychological assessment and the therapy relationship. These research efforts provide an important backdrop for interventions in group psychotherapy.

Both EBM and EBPP clearly and, in some instances, emphatically represent the status quo as well as the future. These relatively new acronyms represent a concerted effort for both researchers and clinicians to (1) gather scientific evidence about interventions that work, in our case, group psychotherapy; (2) agree on core measures—available at www.agpa.org—(Strauss, Burlingame, & Borman, 2008) to be used when gathering such evidence that would result in a marked improvement to the validity and reliability of group studies; and (3) move this empirical evidence from the refereed journals to the broader clinical domain such as the Science-to-Practice Taskforce of the American Psychological Association. EBM and EBPP represent noble scientific efforts. Still, many clinicians do not rush to read the latest journal on psychotherapy research. Is it that they experience the arguments against ESTs as viable? For example, (1) ESTs should be ignored as they are the work of a small, biased work group out of APA Division 12; (2) quantitative research is an inappropriate paradigm for psychotherapy as qualitative case reports serve clinicians better; (3) ESTs are based only on manual-driven treatment that will lead to decrements in the quality of therapy; (4) ESTs are unnecessary as there is no difference between differing therapies; and (5) ESTs do not/will not generalize to actual practice given that they are based on strict research protocols. Do they fear an encroaching kind of *scientism* (Burtt, 2003/1924; Heath, 2002) that seeks to overshadow the therapeutic relationship per se, which is based upon a strong positive alliance with the patient, client, or group member as the sine qua non of treatment?

Clinicians might be reluctant regarding the entire evidence-gathering movement, which clearly has momentum, because it appears that anything other than the status quo will garner less attention in the (1) scientific (research), (2) clinical (practice), and (3) insurance (reimbursement) domains. This has a significant monetary impact ranging from which researchers may receive government grants to which clinicians are readily referred to and which third-party payments will be approved. Any reality that reflects other than the status quo may be in danger of disappearing as a viable alternative to the received view. These represent serious implications, to be sure.

An example of an alternate view is humorously represented by British physicians Isaacs and Fitzgerald (1999) and Smith (1996). They suggest that there are alternatives to EBM whose markers are represented by, for example, RCTs, meta-analyses, and odds ratios—also referred to as "likelihood ratios" as the unit of measurement. Isaacs and Fitzgerald recommend, tongue in cheek, that we should use such markers as "eminence-based medicine," which uses the whiteness of one's hair as a marker, or "providence-based medicine," which uses piety as the relevant unit of measurement. Criticism of both EBM and EBPP is more seriously represented by others (see Eddy, 2005; Hoagwood, Hibbs, Brent & Jensen, 1995; Hunsley, 2007; Westen & Morrison, 2001) who highlight such issues as lack of generalizability, publication bias, and cost.

A specialized language has resulted from RCTs; for instance, the *area under the receiver operating characteristic curve*, which reflects the relationship between the sensitivity and specificity of a particular test. Graduate students routinely learn about *sensitivity* (does the test include true positives accurately?) and *specificity* (does the test exclude true negatives accurately?). Two other arcane but nevertheless much used terms are *number needed to treat* (NNT) and *number needed to harm* (NNH), which reflect the effectiveness and safety of interventions. EBM routinely utilizes such terms and includes large-scale drug studies that yield such statistics more readily than psychological studies do. Interested readers can access details in Sackett, Rosenberg, Gray, Haynes, and Richardson (1996) and Sackett et al. (2000). Whether or not psychological research should have followed the medical model by invoking the language, methods, and statistics of drug studies may be a cause for concern that we may need to address in the near future.

The American Psychological Association's past president Alan Kazdin (2008) states in his article, whose title covers the issues, "Evidence-Based Treatment and Practice: New Opportunities to Bridge Clinical Research and Practice, Enhance the Knowledge Base, and Improve Patient Care," that we are perhaps on a path toward rapprochement (inferring that the divide still exists between clinicians and researchers). Researchers in the mental health fields of social work, psychiatry, psychiatric nursing, and marriage and family therapy echo these sentiments (Carr, 2000; Drake et al., 2001; McNeece & Thyer, 2004; Stuart, 2001). Bray (2009) reminds us finally that all interventions must be found within the umbrella of the biopsychosociol perspective.

At issue here is exactly how research finds its way into practice for all of these mental health domains. Stanley Messer calls this nothing short of "EBP culture wars" (2004). Barber (2009) suggests an earnest "working through" (invoking a classic psychodynamic term) of these differences. With Smith (2009, p. 34) stating, "The EST program assumes a model of therapy as technology or applied science that poorly fits the reality of psychotherapeutic practice" and others (Perepletchikova, Hilt, Chereji, & Kazdin, 2009; Perepletchikova, Treat, & Kazdin, 2009) proposing that outcome researchers themselves need to adhere to treatment integrity procedures, where are clinicians to turn?

Kazdin proposes a reasonable path by reviewing some history of ESTs. He uses the term *empirically supported treatments* to refer to controlled trials that have produced therapeutic change. In contrast, he uses the term *evidence-based treatment* to refer more broadly to "clinical practice that is informed by evidence about interventions, clinical expertise, and patient needs, values and preferences and their integration in decision making about individual care. EBP is not what researchers have studied." He continues, "From the standpoint of research, one might say that there is evidence for specific interventions in the highly controlled contexts in which they are studied but not yet much evidence for EBP in the clinical contexts where judgments and decisions are made by individual clinicians informed by evidence, expertise, and patient considerations" (2008, p. 147). How might we rectify this situation? Given how Kazdin portrays the issue, it might be depicted as two unequal circles with some overlap headed in the same direction (Fig. 12.1). A vortex may be a particularly relevant kind of container given that it represents the zeitgeist of the current, complex health-care context as viewed by many. The narrowing suggests that much is at stake. Norcross, Hogan, and Koocher (2008, p. 8) state, "While unanimity exists on the purposes of EBP, the path to that goal is crammed with contention."

Compromises exist. Johnson suggests that one way to address research concerns for clinicians would be to adopt a research-supported group-treatment strategy, where "treatments that have been found to be efficacious for specific disorders in randomized clinical trials" be accessed via reliable summaries of relevant RCTs (2008, p. 1206)—a point that Kazdin and others have made. Sackett and colleagues (1996, 2000) have worked diligently to include clinical experience and patient values with the best research available, strongly asserting that important values-based medicine must be included (e.g., the value of patient uniqueness), as do others (see Brown, Brown, & Sharma, 2005; Dickenson &

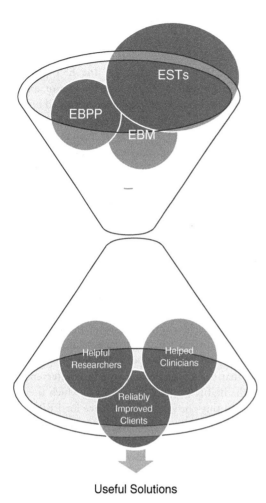

Useful Solutions

Fig. 12.1 Vortex containing clinician fears (empirically supported treatments [ESTs] will squeeze out evidence-based practice of psychology [EBPP], evidence-based medicine [EBM]) but, once through the tight spot, hoped-for solutions.

encourages us to be proud of an accumulating database, which has moved from mere tally research to sophisticated multimethod analyses. Fourth, we need to tackle several problematic methodological concerns. Fifth, and finally, we need a synthesizing method to sift through the enormous amount of material available.

Examining the themes, effectiveness, history, and method problems in group psychotherapy research, however, requires that we first define *process* and *outcome*. An early definition of *process* illustrates the powerful tool Lewin and others wrote about initially, later described by Bradford et al, 1964 : "Process analysis [is] shared examination of the [group members'] relationship in all respects relevant to their interdependence." What happens during the group between all members, including the leader(s), is subjected to equal and shared analysis that often requires an unlearning of norms and procedures that might interfere with such analysis as "it is a good thing to know what you are doing, whether you are an individual, a group, or a society" (Bradford, Gibb, & Benne, 1964, p. 379). Moving the definition from group dynamics to group psychotherapy, Beck and Lewis review a number of group process–analysis systems in order to more clearly understand the relevant components of process, which "has as its primary task positive individual change" (2000, p. 5), based on suggested directions by Fuhriman and Barlow (1994). Earlier definitions of *group process* research argue that too narrow a distinction between process and outcome will limit the researcher and clinician (Greenberg &

Fulford, 2000; Hunnik et al., 2001) who all attend to critical issues of the EBM/EBPP movement as it intersects with decision theory, health economics, public policy, and clinical ethics within and between the mental health treatment domains. Figure 12.2 depicts the hoped-for interrelationships between the three key variables of the approach of EBPP.

What Does the Extant Group Research Tell Us?

Over 100 years of group research informs us at many levels. First, if we examine recent themes represented by dimensions and categories, we see that current journal articles follow what clinicians and researchers are concerned about. Second, upon closer inspection we can learn specific details about differential effectiveness. Third, historical perspective

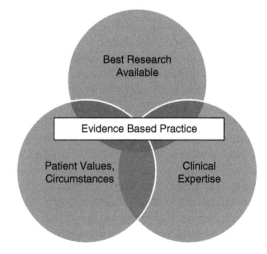

Fig. 12.2 The evidence-based practice model. Interrelationship between research evidence, clinical expertise, and patient values representing balanced overlap.

Pinsoff, 1986; Kiesler, 1973). *Outcome research* refers to the results that accrue from examining such interacting systems (therapist, client, stages of therapy, etc.). The role of moderators (those variables such as age or gender that interact with an independent variable to influence outcomes on the dependent variable) and mediators (specific causal agents that lead to change in the dependent variable) has become critical in process and outcome research as explanatory models of change are being applied to group psychotherapy.

Relevant Themes

In a recent article, Kivlighan and Miles (2007) identified major themes by rank of articles published in the group journal he edited, using latent semantic analysis of journals 1–5 of *Group Dynamics: Theory, Research, and Practice*. Utilizing multidimensional scaling, Kivlighan found three dimensions of the nearly 100 articles: applied vs. theoretical, individual vs. the group as a whole, macro vs. micro level. Additional cluster analysis revealed categories of articles in order of frequency: first, cohesion and group identification; second, attributions and perceptions of groups; third, leadership and performance in groups; fourth, power and relationships among group members; fifth, group psychotherapy. Were such analyses to be conducted on the other group journals (e.g., *International Journal of Group Psychotherapy*) similar categories would likely appear as these are fairly representative. The Kivlighan dimensions and categories reflect the general concern of most group leaders, a zeitgeist of sorts. The initial three dimensions address leaders' concerns about the interaction between the social psychology of groups and group psychotherapy, individual identity in the group and the group as a whole, and societal/cultural macro groups vs. the micro groups represented by group psychotherapy. Group therapists often think about how to deal with inclusion, stereotyping, and other domains researched by the social psychologists with a specialty in group dynamics. They think about how individual members negotiate the multiple roles of individual identity and group membership, and they constantly have to maneuver through the minefield of "outsiders" in the group—family, church, community, and other loyalties that often represent an antitherapy stance, which can fight against the individual's struggle for autonomy. The categories reflect the multiple "alliances" of groups. The bulky term *cohesion*, which some suggest we ought to do away with (Hornsey, et al 2009) while others disagree (Burlingame,

Fuhriman, & Johnson, 2001), at present covers the relationships between and among members and between members and leaders (Fuhriman & Barlow, 1983). Overall, given the multitude of topics addressed, it is fair to state that the group journals represent fertile ground.

Differential Effectiveness

Once we drill down to detailed content in the articles, not just overarching themes, especially the evidence-based interventions of process and outcome, many facts come to light. Burlingame et al. (2004) examined 107 studies and 14 meta-analyses across six disorders—mood, anxiety, eating, substance abuse, personality, and psychotic—as well as several patient populations. Using a modified version of the Periodic Health Examination classification system for rating quality of evidence obtained, they tackled the oftentimes divergent literature (group as primary intervention, group as augment, group for severely mentally ill, and individual vs. group formats) to determine differential effectiveness. Group treatments for social phobias and eating disorders fare better than group treatments for mood disorders, for instance. Useful figures illustrate the complex interplay of forces that govern the boundaries of group treatment (p. 667) and the forces that govern the therapeutic outcomes of group psychology (p. 648). These latter forces are particularly important to attend to group treatment outcomes, formal change theory, small group processes, group structure, leaders, and members.

Historical Perspective

Another vista of the group literature that might be helpful is a longitudinal view across the last 100 years of group review articles, group vs. individual meta-analyses, group psychotherapy and group psychology themes, and substantive themes by clinical populations (Tables 12.1 through 12.5). From 1962 to 2010, a period of almost 50 years, a number of reviews of group treatments were conducted, with varying results. Filtered and unfiltered databases examined included EBSO, ERIC, PubMed Medline, CINAHL, CogNet, Psychnet, and Cochrane. Careful scrutiny of Table 12.1 reveals first and foremost that the researchers' initial questions often reflected what they found. For instance, appraisals of effectiveness and efficiency were posed "in comparison to what?" and the method each researcher used appears to have affected the answer. Although not exhaustive, the list of studies is representative of reviews in group psychotherapy.

Table 12.1 Group psychotherapy review articles

Author	Treatment Orientation	Number of Studies	Comparison* WLC, OT, I, COM	Sample	Conclusions
Rickard (1962)	Nondirective, psychoanalytic, psychodrama	22	X X X X	Mixed inpatient and outpatient	Too much variability among patients, therapists, and measures for comparison to be more than tentative. Efficacy of group remains to be empirically validated.
Pattison (1965)	Psychodrama, milieu, analytic	U		Inpatient, prison, addict, delinquent	Group activity is therapeutic using behavioral criteria, disappointing with psychometric criteria, and promising with construct criteria. Notes that the research on individual psychotherapy and small-group research has yet to be effectively incorporated into group psychotherapy research.
Stotsky & Zolik (1965)	Psychodrama, round table, and heterogeneous group	U	X X X X	Psychotics	The results of controlled experimental studies do not offer clear support for using group therapy as an independent modality, but they do support group as an adjunctive or helpful intervention when combined with other treatments (drugs, individual, etc.).
Mann (1966)	Psychodrama, nondirective	41	X X X	Mixed diagnosis, adult and children, most institutionalized	Group therapy produces change in behavior, attitude, and personality regardless of orientation, method of comparison, or instruments.
Anderson (1968)	Counseling groups	6	X X X	Elementary students	Group counseling associated with higher grade point average and personality change when compared with control. No difference when compared with other treatment combined.
Meltzoff & Kornreich (1970)	Heterogeneous, expressive, nondirective, systematic, desensitization, behavior, analytic	6	X X X	Hospitalized adults, adult outpatients, children	80% of adequately controlled studies reviewed showed primarily positive results with both individual and group therapy. Six studies that made direct comparisons between group and individual therapy found equivalent outcomes, with a slight tendency for individual to be more effective.
Bednar & Lawlis (1971)	Heterogeneous, group psychotherapy, self-help, activity, milieu, work, insight	38	X X X X X	Mixed inpatient, seven outpatients, delinquents, alcoholics, sex offenders, students	Group therapy is valuable in treating neurotics, psychotics, and character disorders. It is a two-edged sword that can facilitate client deterioration.

Study	Type of groups	N		Population	Findings/conclusions
Luborsky, Singer, & Luborsky (1975)	Heterogeneous	12	X X X	Unspecific	Majority of comparisons showed no significant differences between group and individual treatments. There was a tie in nine comparisons: group was better in two comparisons, and individual was better in two comparisons.
Grunebaum (1975)	Unspecified	U	X	Heterogeneous	Only meager data exist comparing group and individual therapies, and the evidence suggests that they are equally effective in most instances. Some findings suggest that benefits may be disorder-specific: for example, individual therapy is better for phobias, and group is more effective for schizophrenic outpatients.
Emrick (1975)	Heterogeneous	384	X X X	Alcoholics	Found a general trend for both individual and group to be effective in treating alcoholism.
Lieberman (1976)	Heterogeneous, psychotherapy, and personal growth groups	47	X X	College students, adults	Group consistently produced favorable outcome over controls. Reported no outcome differences in studies that compared group with individual formats. Noted that the indices used to measure outcome are relatively insensitive to the potentialities of different treatment contexts such as group and individual psychotherapy.
Parloff & Dies (1977)	Heterogeneous, psychotherapy groups	39	X X X X	Psychoneurotics, schizophrenics, addicts, legal offenders	Group has no unique advantage over other treatments with schizophrenic patients, no firm conclusions can be drawn with psychoneurosis, and limited support for effectiveness with addicts.
Bednar & Kaul (1978)	Heterogeneous, behavioral, transactional analysis, unspecific group therapy, and encounter groups	21	X X X	College students, delinquents, prisoners, psychiatric patients	Group treatments have been more effective than no treatment, placebo, and other recognized psychological treatments.
Solomon (1983)	Psychodynamic, aversion	2	X X X	Alcoholics	Combined individual and group therapy is related to poorest outcome, while individual and group as independent treatments showed equivalent outcomes.
Kanas (1986)	Heterogeneous	32	X X	Outpatient and inpatient schizophrenics	Group therapy proved to be superior to controls in 67% of inpatients and 80% of outpatients studied, with long-term therapy being the best.
Kaul & Bednar (1986)	Experimental psychotherapy groups	17	X X	Primarily adult mixed diagnosis	Mixed but favorable outcomes for the efficacy of group psychotherapy.

(continued)

Table 12.1 (Continued)

Author	Treatment Orientation	Number of Studies	Comparison* WLC, OT, I, COM	Sample	Conclusions
Toseland & Siporin (1986)	Heterogeneous	32	X X	Heterogeneous	Results of this new review indicated that group treatment was as effective as individual treatment in 75% of the studies included and was more effective in 25%. In the 32 studies reviewed, there was no case in which individual treatment was found to be more effective than group treatment.
Bostwick (1987)	Unspecified	13	X X	Unspecified	Individual treatment had less premature termination than group, while combined individual and group treatment proved superior at reducing dropouts over either modality.
Oesterheld, McKenna, & Gould (1987)	Heterogeneous (e.g., behavioral, insight, cognitive behavioral, dynamic)	18	X X X	Bulimia	Group seems to be helpful, but methodological limitations preclude robust conclusions.
Zimpfer (1987)	Heterogeneous (e.g., group counseling, multimodal, growth, insight)	19	X X	Elderly	Group seems to be helpful, but methodological limitations preclude robust conclusions.
Freeman & Munro (1988)	Cognitive behavioral, eclectic, supportive, didactic	13	X X X X	Bulimics	Neither drug nor group therapy was as effective as individual, but all are more effective than placebo. Group is most cost-effective, and combined group and individual is most effective of all treatments.
Cox & Merkel (1989)	Heterogeneous	32	X X X	Bulimics	In a review of 15 group and 17 individual studies (only one study provided a comparison between the two modalities, the rest were inferential), it was concluded that there was no support for the two treatments having any differential effectiveness.
Zimpfer (1990)	Cognitive behavioral, psychoeducational behavior	31	X X	Bulimics	Regardless of treatment type and outcome criteria, group was shown to be an effective treatment.
Piper & McCallum (1991)	Self-help, consciousness, cognitive restructuring, behavioral skills, dynamic	5	X X X X	Grief	Group treatment has not been adequately tested to determine its efficacy.

Authors (year)	Approach	k		Population	Findings
Vandervoort & Fuhriman (1991)	Cognitive behavioral, psychodynamic, cognitive	12	X X	Outpatients, depression	Group is efficacious in treating depression with little evidence for differences between individual and group.
Piper & Joyce (1996)	Behavior 30%, cognitive behavioral 26%, interpersonal/psychodynamic 14%, didactic 1%	86	X X X X	Lifestyle problems, medical conditions, mixed psychiatric disorders, mostly adults	A variety of patient problems treated in interactive therapy groups for 6 months or less were examined for evidence of efficacy, applicability, and efficiency of time-limited, short-term group therapy (TSGT). Strong evidence for all three factors was found. Of 50 studies that had TSGT versus control comparison, 48 provided evidence of benefit of group treatment. A difference in benefit was found for the 6 studies that used TSGT versus individual.
Hoag & Burlingame (1997a)	60% behavioral or cognitive behavioral	56	X X X X	Male and female children and adolescents (4–18), primarily problems of disruptive behavior, self-esteem	Review of studies from 1974 to 1997 of group interventions for children and adolescents (including preventative, psychotherapy, guidance) revealed that treatments occurred mostly in school setting and groups were beneficial.
Marotta & Asner (1999)	Psychoanalytic, cognitive behavioral, self-help, psycho-educational	21	X X X X	Adult females	Review of studies from 1978 to 1995 of group interventions for women with incest histories (using a wide array of treatment models)—categorized by six criteria: design, sample, inclusion criteria, replicability, analysis, and outcome. 14 were descriptive or case studies. Some support for group treatment was provided. Minimal adequacy of research design.
Harney & Harney (1999)	Cognitive behavioral, interpersonal transaction (Yalom), information processing, psychodynamic	5	X X X	Male and female adults	Review of studies of trauma survivors assessed important variables along eight domains: authority over memory, integration of memory with affect, affect tolerance, symptom mastery, self-esteem/self-care, self-cohesion, safe attachment, meaning-making. Multidimensional, stage-oriented approaches worked best.
Shechtman (2002)	Educational, counseling, psychotherapy (multitheoretical and cognitive behavioral)	U	X X X X	Male and female children and adolescents	Review of studies of group interventions for children found that all three types of groups were effective as long as suitable goals were set. Findings regarding process in children's groups showed that very little research exists.
Pinquart, Duberstein, & Lyness (2007)	CBT, dynamic, reminiscence, exercise, psychoeducation	57	X X X X	Clinically depressed older adults	Significant findings for CBT, reminiscence therapy. Almost 20% dropout in group, higher than individual. Authors did not directly compare individual and group.

(continued)

Table 12.1 (Continued.)

Author	Treatment Orientation	Number of Studies	Comparison* WLC, OT, I, COM	Sample	Conclusions
Himelhock, Medoff, & Oyeniyi (2007)	CBT and supportive therapy	8	X X	665 depressed mostly males HIV-infected	CBT groups and supportive therapy groups had pooled ES of 0.37, 0.58. "Of note, women were nearly absent from this study."
Jonsson & Hougaard (2008)	CBT, exposure and response prevention, ERP	13	X X	828 male and female adults with OCD	CBT combined with ERP is effective, better results than drug therapy. Authors suggest next step is to compare group with individual
Brunwasser, Gilham, & Kim (2009)	Penn Resiliency Program (PRP)—a group CBT intervention	17	X X X X	2,498 depressed youth	Participants reported fewer symptoms at 1-year follow-up. Works best when group leaders are research team members and community providers. Authors wonder if CBT mediates PRP.

*WLC, wait list controls or comparable control group; OT, other group-treatment comparison including pharmocotherapy; I, individual therapy comparison groups; COM, combination; CBT, cognitive-behavioral therapy; OCD, obsessive–compulsive disorder ES, effect size; U, Unknown.

Source: Fuhriman & Burlingame (1994), adapted with permission. List of references available from the authors.

Prior to the 1960s, limited studies essentially catalogued and tallied different group phenomena (e.g., Burchard, Michaels, & Kotkov, 1948; Thomas, 1943). But as group researchers moved into the 1960s, 1970s, and forward, their work turned to discovering possible interactions. Table 12.1 highlights treatment orientation, number of studies of each review, what group was compared with in order to determine effectiveness, as well as population and outcome. From the 1960s and beyond studies included basic comparisons: wait list control or comparable control group, other group treatment comparison including pharmacotherapy, individual therapy comparison groups, and combined treatment group (e.g., group plus individual, group plus ward treatment). Clearly, the most prominent feature of the 1960s (five total) review studies was institutionalization. These studies of mostly captive participants did not indicate clear support of one method of group psychotherapy over another. The sheer numbers of studies, measures, and comparison groups make the outcomes suspect. Studies in the 1970s (eight total) demonstrated superior results when compared to controls and represent improving results. Reviews in the 1980s (nine total) reflect further refinements in group studies, including the growing awareness that methodological limitations may preclude more robust findings (Oesterheld et al., 1987). A robust finding was that combined individual and group treatment results in superior outcomes. By the 1990s reviewers were carefully considering significant differential and general improvement. But it was becoming increasingly clear that there were so many variables to study that programmatic research covering many years was the most reasonable way to go about collecting information. For example, initial efforts did not determine effectiveness of grief groups, although Piper et al, were able to demonstrate effectiveness in their programmatic research (1992, 2002, 2006, 2007).

Table 12.2 highlights group vs. individual treatment meta-analyses where direct comparisons were made by the researchers between some kind of group therapy and some kind of individual therapy. Treatment orientation, group characteristics, and participants are reported. In the now classic Smith and Glass (1980) study, group and individual treatments fared almost exactly the same. Almost 30 years later Piper (2008) pointed out not only that this finding was interesting because both treatment modes had equal effect sizes but that he had to search assiduously in the appendices before he discovered that fact. The 12 studies over almost

30 years of studies of adults, adolescents, and children indicated that individual and group treatments were better than the no-treatment groups, individual was slightly more effective than group, and the particular cognitive-behavioral treatment model was gaining ground. Still, it is important to list caveats when making such bold bottom-line statements. First, several of these meta-analyses were comprised of studies that did not capitalize on the unique properties of groups but appeared instead to use groups only as a convenient and cost-effective strategy. Second, a number of the meta-analyses utilized studies that did not directly compare individual and group treatments in the same study. Those meta-analytic studies that corrected for these caveats demonstrated equivalence between individual and group treatments.

By categorizing according to topics, studies from group psychology and group psychotherapy yield helpful information (Tables 12.3 and 12.4). Table 12.3 indicates that group psychologists' interest grew over the decades regarding models and approaches, problem solving and decision making, group structure, group climate, and leadership. By 1970 group psychologists were interested in all of them. This parallels the intense theory building that was going on in social psychologists' circles as they struggled to assemble forces that made up group dynamics.

During the same time period, group psychotherapy studies (Table 12.4) were addressing similar topics (models/formats/theories, structure, leaders/therapists, interpersonal influence/interaction analysis) as well as topics particularly relevant to group psychotherapists such as patient populations. By 2010 it had become clear that all of these forces are critical. Combining the efforts of group dynamics specialists and group psychotherapists will likely allow us to uncover the necessary and sufficient conditions that make groups helpful.

Table 12.5 reviews substantive themes by clinical populations. As can be seen, a number of models and approaches, therapeutic factors, therapist variables, structure, and interaction cover a wide variety of clinical populations such as the elderly, eating disorders, and depression to create an informative matrix.

Methodological Concerns
Meta-analysis, the main methodological tool used to compare individual with group treatments (Table 12.2), for instance, has been heralded as a helpful statistical tool that often allows us to compare apples

Table 12.2 Group versus individual meta-analysis

Author	Treatment Orientation	Group Characteristics	Sample	Conclusions
Smith, Glass, & Miller (1980)	Heterogeneous	Variable	Heterogeneous	The mode in which therapy was delivered made no difference in its effectiveness. Indeed, the average effects for group and individual therapy are remarkably similar. The average ES was 0.87 for individual therapy and 0.83 for group therapy. Of the studies, 43% were individual and 49% were group.
Shapiro & Shapiro (1982)	Heterogeneous	Average time spent in therapy was 7 hours	Heterogeneous	This is a refined meta-analysis of the one conducted by Smith & Glass (1980), who reported that although individual therapy appeared the most effective mode (M = 1.12), it was closely followed by the predominant group mode (M = 0.89), and the only striking treatment mode finding was for couple/family therapy (M = 0.21).
Miller & Berman (1983)	CBT	Duration of treatment relatively short	Adolescents and adults, student/community volunteers and outpatients, anxious and/or depressed	This meta-analysis of 48 studies reported that CBT was equally effective in group and individual formats when compared with a nontreatment group (individual = 0.93, group = 0.79) and when compared with other treatment controls (individual = 0.31, group = 0.18); it should be noted that none of the studies in the review directly compared individual with group treatment within a single study.
Dush, Hirt, & Schroeder (1983)	CBT self-statement modification	Mean weeks of treatment were 5.9 with a range of 1–26	About one-fourth of studies used outpatients, one-fourth used community volunteers, and half used undergraduate depressed and anxious volunteers	Treatment modality was highly influential, with the mean effect for individual therapy nearly double that of group therapy across all comparisons. When compared with no-treatment controls, ES was 0.93 for individual and 0.58 for group; when compared with placebo controls, it was 0.71 for individual and 0.36 for group.
Nietzel, Russel, Hemmings, & Gretter (1987)	CBT and other	Mean number of hours in treatment was 16.3, with a range of 3–69 (distribution between group and individual hours not made)	Individuals with unipolar depression, adults	Reports a reliable difference between individual and group treatments, with group treatment being less effective. Clients treated with group (M = 12.47) reported more depressive symptoms than clients receiving individual treatment (M = 0.06).

Study	Included treatments		Population	Findings
Robinson, Berman, & Neimeyer (1990)	Included treatments with a prominent verbal component (i.e., cognitive, cognitive-behavioral, behavioral, and general verbal therapy)	Number of clients per group ranged from 3 to 12 (M = 7)	Depressed individuals	Analysis indicated that both group and individual therapy produced more improvement than no treatment and that the effects of the two approaches were comparable. The 16 studies that compared individual and group therapy with a wait-list control and the 15 studies that compared group with a wait-list control produced nearly equal ESs (0.83 and 0.84, respectively).
Tillitski & Siporin (1990)	Therapy, counseling, psychoeducational	Heterogeneous	Adults, adolescents, children diagnostically heterogeneous	In this reexamination of a subset of the studies looked at by Toseland and Siporin (1986), Tillistski reports finding the same average effect size for both group and individual treatments (1.35) and states that this effect was consistently greater than that of controls (0.18). Also, group counseling was found to be almost twice as effective as either therapy or psychoeducation. Recent studies produced larger ESs, and group tended to be better for adolescents, whereas individual tended to be better for children.
Hoag & Burlingame (1997a, 1997b)	60% behavioral or cognitive-behavioral	79% took place in school groups (focused primarily on disruptive behavior, social skills, self-esteem), average group size was 5–9, average treatment length: 14 sessions	Male and female children and adolescents (4–18)	56 outcome studies from 1974 to 1997 of group interventions (including preventative, psychotherapy, and guidance) revealed an ES of 0.61 for group treatments over wait list and placebo controls.
McRoberts, Burlingame, & Hoag (1998)	Cognitive, behavioral, dynamic, supportive, eclectic	Average groups of 26 sessions, lasting 90 minutes each, 44% had cotherapists	Adult outpatients with heterogeneous diagnoses	In this meta-analysis of group versus individual therapy, the general finding was overall equivalence (0.01), although under certain circumstances, individual therapy fared better (depression, CBT approach, 0.16); in other circumstances, group fared better (with circumscribed problems, researcher's allegiance to format, attendance of member).

(continued)

Table 12.2 (Continued)

Author	Treatment Orientation	Group Characteristics	Sample	Conclusions
McDermut, Miller, & Brown (2001)	95% behavioral or cognitive-behavioral; 5% interpersonal, psychodynamic, or nondirective	Highly diverse clinical settings, typical group lasted 12 sessions, once a week, and variety of therapists	Male (30%) and female (70%) outpatient adults with diagnosis of depression (mean age 44)	48 studies from 1970 to 1998 examined group therapy for depression. Patients showed clinically meaningful improvement compared with untreated controls, although their scores on Beck Depression Inventory were still higher than normals. Of studies that compared group with individual therapy, slightly more reported individual to be superior.
Burlingame, Fuhriman, & Mosier (2003)	Cognitive, behavioral, dynamic, supportive, eclectic	University, correctional, and outpatient mental health settings	Adult outpatients with heterogeneous diagnoses	Examining 20 years of studies, the report found that patient diagnosis resulted in differential effects, homogeneous groups outperformed those in groups with mixed symptoms, and behavioral fared better than eclectic orientation. Homogeneous topic-centered outperformed.
Aderka (2008)	Cognitive-behavioral	Outpatient	511 adult participants with social phobia	Adults with social phobia were individual and group treatments. Giving video feedback was not a mediator of treatment efficacy, but treatment format was. Larger ES in individual and lower attrition than group.
Payne & Marcus (2008)	Cognitive-behavioral, reminiscence	Outpatient, inpatient medical setting, hospital	Male and female older adults (55 and over)	Groups benefit older adults. Those receiving CBT benefited more than those receiving reminiscence therapies. The older the average age of group members, the less they benefited. Number and length of sessions, living situation were not significant moderators. Overall ES matched adult and child samples.
Waldron & Turner (2008)	Cognitive-behavioral, some motivational interviewing	Outpatient, schools, community, groups averaged 7–12 sessions	Adolescent male (75%) and female substance abusers	Meta-analysis on 17 studies of individual, group and family CBT; inactive control group. 2,307 adolescents total. Group and family therapies emerged as best model, although authors state all active treatments were significantly better than inactive control. ES = 0.62, 0.58, respectively.
Liber et al. (2008)	Cognitive-behavioral	Routine care settings	Male and female children (8–12 years old) with anxiety	227 randomly assigned children. No significant difference between individual and group CBT (group and individual treatments compared using chi-squared, regression, not meta-analysis.)

Source. Fuhriman & Burlingame (1994), adapted with permission.

Table 12.3 Group psychotherapy and group psychology themes

	1900–1910	1911–1920	1921–1930	1931–1940	1941–1950	1951–1960	1961–1670	1971–1980	1981–1990	1991–2000	2001–2010
Models/approaches						X	X	X		X	X
Interpersonal influence	X				X	X	X	X	X	X	X
Problem solving, decision making	X		X	X	X			X	X	X	X
Group structure				X	X			X	X	X	X
Group climate				X	X	X	X	X	X	X	X
Leadership						X	X	X	X	X	X

The last two columns show that research reflects the Burlingame et al. (2004) six-component model: FCT, formal change theory; SGP, small-group processes; L, leader; P, patient; GS, group structure; GTO, group treatment outcomes.
Source: Fuhriman & Burlingame (1994), adapted with permission.

Table 12.4 Group psychotherapy topics by decade

	1900–1910	1911–1920	1921–1930	1931–1940	1941–1950	1951–1960	1961–1670	1971–1980	1981–1990	1991–2000	2001–2010
Formats/theories/models	X	X	X	X	X	X	X	X	X	X	X
Patient/client populations	X	X	X	X	X	X	X	X	X	X	X
Therapeutic relationship			X	X	X	X	X	X	X	X	X
Therapist variables							X	X	X	X	X
Therapeutic factors	X	X	X	X	X	X	X	X	X	X	X
Structure							X	X	X	X	X
Interaction analysis							X	X	X	X	X
Client outcomes						X	X	X	X	X	X
Ecosystem	X	X	X		X		X	X	X	X	X

Source: Fuhriman & Burlingame (1994), adapted with permission.

and oranges; nevertheless, it does have its detractors. As Howard et al. (2009) state, "Meta-analysis is now the accepted procedure for summarizing research literatures in areas of applied psychology. Because of the bias for publishing statistically significant findings, while usually rejecting non-significant results, our research literatures yield misleading answers to important quantitative questions (e.g., How much better is the average psychotherapy patient relative to a comparable group of untreated controls?" (p. 146). Staines and Cleland (2007) echo this claim in their article "Bias in Meta-Analytic Estimates of the Absolute Efficacy of Psychotherapy." They point out that these various biases—including nonsystematic, underestimation, overestimation—all exist, which influences the effect size estimate. Hsu (2003) adds that pretreatment nonequivalence leads to the Simpson paradox, where the successes of groups seem reversed when the groups are combined. Mullen and Ramirez (2006) weigh in from a public health perspective, suggesting that meta-analyses and systematic reviews offer a false sense of rigor.

Another concern regarding group research has to do with the nonindependence of observations

Table 12.5 Substantive themes by clinical populations

Models/approaches	Child/Adolescent	Medical	Depressed	Eating Disorder	Substance Abuse	Criminal	Inpatient	Family/Marital	Elderly	Outpatient	Schizophrenic	Sexual Abuse	Personality Disorder	Not Specified	Other
Cognitive-behavioral	X	X	X	X	X	X	X	X	X	X	X	X	X	X	X
Short-term	X	X	X		X		X	X	X	X	X	X	X	X	
Rogerian										X					X
Gestalt											X			X	
Personal growth						X								X	
Psychodrama	X					X	X								
Therapist variables	X	X	X	X	X	X	X	X	X	X	X		X	X	X
Directiveness			X									X		X	
Interpretation												X		X	
Therapeutic factors	X	X	X	X	X	X	X	X	X	X	X	X	X	X	X
Structure	X	X	X	X	X	X	X	X	X	X		X	X	X	
Development						X				X				X	
Pregroup training								X		X				X	
Interaction		X	X	X	X	X	X	X	X	X	X	X	X	X	X

Source. Fuhriman & Burlingame (1994), adapted with permission.

(Baldwin, Murray, & Shadish, 2005, Baldwin, Stice, & Rohde, 2008; Baldwin, Berkeljon, Atkins, Olsen, & Nielsen, 2009). "Because of the shared environment, the scores of members within the same group may become correlated, which violates the assumption of independence of observations common to many statistical techniques" (Imel, Baldwin, Bonus, & MacCoon, 2008, p. 735). This statement refers to the intraclass correlations (ICCs) that provide an effect size for the group effect. Such ICCs can be interpreted as the "proportion of variance in the outcome associated with group membership" (Imel et al., 2008, p. 739). In other words, group members who share the same group environment can become like each other as a result of the group.

A number of researchers treat nonindependence, in part, as a statistical nuisance (Barcikowski, 1981; Kenny & Judd, 1986). Glass and Stanley (1970) suggest that treatments administered individually yield observations that are independent. In contrast, treatments that are administered in groups (where there are interactions among group members) might influence each other and are, thus, nonindependent. This violates a fundamental statistical rule for analysis of variance that we all learned in our basic statistics courses. Stevens asks, "What should be done with correlated observations. . . . Test at a more stringent level of significance, use the group mean as the unit of analysis?" (1992, p. 243). He further suggests that perhaps these ICCs are not necessarily an artifact. Other concerned researchers suggest that we need to be interested in nonindependence as a "substantive focus in itself [reflecting] how individual behavior is modified by group contexts" (Kenny & Judd, 1986, p. 431; Scariano & Davenport, 1987); in other words, the nonindependence of observations is *not merely a statistical nuisance* but may be a fundamental issue in psychological research. The following research designs handle this problem differently—both recent, both highly complex in their attempts to uncover mediator variables, both representing state-of-the-art group psychotherapy research, and both illustrating that the jury is still out regarding how best to handle this tricky statistical problem in group research.

The first study is an examination of long-term vs. short-term psychodynamic outpatient groups in an effort to understand interrelationships between group members, members and leader, and stages of group development (Bakali, Baldwin, & Lorentzen, 2009), which revealed, among other things, that later-stage leader–member bonding was no longer relevant to member–group cohesion, "indicating

that cohesion and alliance and the member–leader versus member–group bonding represent different processes" (p. 332). In the second study, Kirchmann et al. (2009) examined patient attachment styles again in psychodynamic group psychotherapy but this time with inpatients. This was a large, multisite study. Patient perception of group climate was found to be a primary predictor of outcome, and attachment related to that perception. Given the current focus on the explanatory power of attachment (Benjamin, 2003; Bowlby, 1988; Fonagy et al., 1996), this study is particularly timely. The researchers proposed that individually identified patient attachment styles (ambivalent, avoidant, secure) would predict outcome via certain mediator variables (e.g., group climate, helpful therapist, social learning). They found that it is indeed a complex relationship. For instance, avoidant inpatients did rely heavily on the helpful therapist variable, in fact perhaps too heavily. Overall, however, inconsistent findings between patient attachment style and outcome resulted.

These studies bear careful scrutiny as they seek critical knowledge in the pursuit of group psychotherapy effectiveness that may lead the way to clearer delineation of mediator and moderator variables, their relationship to such variables as group cohesion (akin to alliance in individual therapy), and outcome. Each study dealt with the controversial statistical issue of nonindependence in different ways, suggesting that statistical uniformity has yet to be determined regarding this methodological dilemma in group research.

Valuable Synthesizing Tools

Norcross et al. (2008) have written a helpful guide to EBP. Hopefully, more such guides are on their way. This particular text covers all the relevant information any clinician would need to understand EBP—how to utilize it, how to replicate it, how to teach it. They remind readers that enlisting the tools of this heuristic will help them identify what does work and what does not work (they label this the "dark side"). Discredited, detrimental practices are easy to uncover when they are in the distant past, say trephining or bloodletting. What might be the equivalent today? According to Dryden and Norcross (1990), 480 registered therapies—covering individuals, families, and groups—existed by 1990, which have certainly proliferated since that time. It could be difficult to ferret out the bad ones among that array. This is why it is a good thing to rely on the foundational and functional skills expected of solid mental health training programs, as well as continued education in those specialties we wish to demonstrate expertise. Group specialty practice refers not simply to conducting therapy with an audience. Specialized skills such as group psychotherapy represent the acquisition of layered skills that require some "unlearning" (Barlow, 2004) as well as new learning drawing upon EBPP.

The unfiltered available research electronic databases include Medline, CINAHL, PsycINFO, Google Scholar, and CENTRAL (from Cochrane Libraries). University libraries routinely access these and other databases. Less often university libraries will access Cochrane Databases of Systematic Reviews, Campbell Collaboration Reviews of Interventions and Policy Evaluations, National Institute for Health and Clinical Excellence, as well as British Medical Journal Clinical Evidence and other evidence-based journals. However, individual users can access these databases through any generic search engine. Many of these databases are essentially clearinghouses that can be depicted as a pyramid: The large base of the pyramid is made up of the actual studies; the filtering that occurs from there to the narrow tip of the pyramid includes such processes as sorting studies into RCTs, evaluating for internal and external validity threats, comparing to already existing databases; and a final filtering that involves grading the particular review from A–E letter grade or 1–5 number system. These are

generally very helpful, although Campbell and Cochrane are heavily medical, less psychological. Such reliable and valid synthesizing and evaluation can greatly aid the clinician. Many mental health groups in nursing, psychiatry, psychology, and social work have Web sites that offer clinician-friendly, up-to-date information about recent findings. Examples include www.psychologicaltreatment.org and www.nationalregistry.samhsa.gov.

Another helpful tool involves those professional journals that reserve comment by the "opposite" point of view. For instance, *Group Dynamics* journal makes a concerted effort to balance content between the pertinent social psychological aspects of group dynamics as well as group practice or the application found in group psychotherapy. This is an important balance to maintain as group psychology is the foundation for group psychotherapy. Additionally, several group journals invite group therapists to comment on social psychological articles and group psychologists to comment on psychotherapy articles. This makes for a rich exchange (see Moreland & McMinn, 1999, for an excellent example of this kind of exchange).

Valuable Compromising Tools

Table 12.6 lists potential controversies and dilemmas of what has been called the EBP culture wars (Messer, 2004) and possible solutions. For instance, researchers and clinicians have been arguing about whether

Table 12.6 Current controversies and possible compromises

	Current Controversies	Possible Compromises
Barber (2009)	Alliance vs. technique =outcome Therapist vs. patient = outcome RCTs valuable vs. RCTs worthless	Technique ensures alliance Interactions need to be studied RCTs must be supplemented
Kazdin (2008)	RCTs are specific interventions from highly controlled contexts less relevant to clinicians	Study mechanisms of change Translate moderators to practice Do qualitative research
Yalom (2005)	Why are we not offering the best group experience to our patients? Current therapy scene is driven by economics. Longer term heterogeneous groups are more ambitious, demand more from client and therapist but yield more	Do not mistake appearance of efficiency for true effectiveness Do not expect from psychotherapy what it cannot deliver: Quick character change Do not expect from research what it cannot deliver: Rapid major change to practice
Piper (2008)	Groups are underutilized given the evidence that supports efficacy, applicability and efficiency	Overcome patient/therapist bias re groups Find solutions to research problems (a) Meta-analyses obscure potentially potent elements (b) Can be comprised of methodologically weak studies

technique was more important than alliance. Barber (2009) suggests that alliance and technique, therapists and patients are important. Further, he states that RCTs are useful as long as they can also be supplemented with qualitative studies. Kazdin (2008) concurs. Yalom (2005), focusing specifically on group therapy, suggests treatment driven by economic concerns will shortchange consumers and adds that the appearance of efficiency should not be confused with true effectiveness. Finally, Piper (2008) recommends that therapists and clients overcome their biases about group treatment in order to take part in client-effective and professionally rewarding experiences.

Conclusions, Recommendations, and Practice

During the past half-century, somewhere between Eysenck's claim that therapy does not work (1952) and the subsequent flurry of handbooks on psychotherapy and behavior change from 1973-2004 that proved otherwise and somewhere between the "unconscionable embarrassment" touted by Baker, McFall, and Shoham (2008) and Mischel (2009) of the current training programs in psychology and the work by Kivlighan and Kivlighan (2009) and others that strongly suggests that careful teaching lays critical foundations for psychologists today, we might

find middle ground. Subsumed within this important search for the middle ground of this "great psychotherapy debate," as Wampold calls it in his eponymous book, would be the compromises we must pursue between ESTs and EBPP for the good of our patients, our profession, both research and practice. Table 12.7 depicts the debate from Eysenck to Bergin, through individual therapy to group issues and on to special methodological problems in group research, ending with the critical issues of group psychotherapy training. While simplistic in form, it represents the complex function of almost 60 years of mental health issues, which require our thoughtful attention.

Finally, bottom-line findings are important to reiterate. Earlier reviews of group psychotherapy (Bednar & Kaul, 1994) concluded that group treatment was more effective than no treatment, placebo attention, and nonspecific treatment comparisons. The latest review (Burlingame et al., 2004) states that although we have indeed accumulated good evidence about groups, it is becoming increasingly clear that certain treatment models for particular patient populations work best. This continuing search for more precise key mechanisms will lead to even more important connections. In order for this to happen more quickly, it will help if researchers include relevant facts about the study, choose a

Table 12.7 The great psychotherapy debate

	The Great Psychotherapy Debate		
General Therapy	Psychotherapy doesn't work Eysenck (1952)	Vs.	Psychotherapy works Bergin & Garfield series (1978, 1986, 1994 etc); Lambert (2004)
Specific kind of therapy: Group	Individual better than group Dush et al (1983) Nietzel et al, (1987)	Vs.	Group outcomes equivalent to individual outcomes Burlingame, MacKenzie & Strauss (2004)
General Research Issues in Individual Therapy	ESTs based on RCTs Chambless & Ollendick, (2001)	Vs.	EBPP – patient values, clinical expertise, best research available Kazdin, (2008) Sackett, et al, (1996, 2000)
Special Methods Problem in Group Research	CCIs, non independence in group research is fatal Baldwin et al (2005) Imel et al (2008)	Vs.	Non-independence may be more than a statistical nuisance Stevens, (1992)
Educational and Training Issues	Training of psychologists is an "unconscionable" embarrassment Baker et al (2009) Mischel (2009)	Vs.	Training can be carefully constructed, evaluated to teach expert skills Kivlighan & Kivlighan (2009) Wampold (2001)

state-of-the-art research design, study already determined efficacy and effectiveness models of group treatment at the individual level for interaction effects, include follow-up assessments as well as report attrition rates, focus on process–outcome links, transfer usable individual change theories to group formats, revisit key aspects of leadership, utilize core group measures, and increase focus on understudied groups such as the severely and persistently mentally ill (Burlingame, MacKenzie & Strauss, 2004, pp. 683–684). Although this research review did not include qualitative studies, it is clear from Kazdin (2008), Barber (2009), and others that these are needed.

A desideratum, or essential desire, of all practitioners requires a "constant and continuing faith in the pursuit of knowledge while acknowledging human contextuality" (Villemaire, 2002, 237). I use the term *practitioner* to mean those who strive for mastery by practicing, as one might when attempting to master a musical instrument or a complex sport: gaining incremental skills through effort that eventually leads to expertise whether practicing interventions with patients, practicing process and outcome research with data, or practicing professors who teach the next generation.

Notes

1. www.thecochranelibrary.com. Also, see history of Cochrane reviews, library, DARE, etc. at http://www.update-software.com/history/clibhist.htm.

2. The OQ (Lambert et al., 1996) is a 45-item assessment easily taken and scored that yields three subscales: Interpersonal Functioning, Work, Symptoms.

3. The Group Questionnaire is currently under development (Burlingame & Thayer, 2010). It is a 30-item self-report measure of the quality of therapeutic interactions (i.e., positive bonding, positive working, and negative relationships) across three structural parameters of the group therapeutic relationship (i.e., member–member, member–group, and member–leader relationships).

References

Bakali, J., Baldwin, S., & Lorentzen, S. (2009). Modeling group process constructs at three stages in group psychotherapy. *Psychotherapy Research*, *19*(3), 332–343.

Baker, T., McFall, R., & Shoham, V. (2008). Current status and future prospects of clinical psychology: Toward a scientifically principled approach to mental and behavioral health care. *Psychological Science in the Public Interest*, *9*(2), 67–103.

Baldwin, S., Berkeljon, A., Atkins, D., Olsen, A., & Nielsen, L. (2009). Rates of change in naturalistic psychotherapy: Contrasting dose-effect and good-enough level models of change. *Journal of Consulting and Clinical Psychology*, *77*(2), 203–211.

Baldwin, S. A., Murray, D. M., & Shadish, W. R. (2005). Empirically supported treatments or type I errors? Problems with analysis of data from group-administered treatments. *Journal of Consulting and Clinical Psychology*, *73*, 924–935.

Baldwin, S. A., Stice, E., & Rohde, P. (2008). Statistical analysis of group-administered intervention data: Reanalysis of two randomized trials. *Psychotherapy Research*, *18*, 365–376.

Barber, J. (2009). Toward a working through of some core conflicts in psychotherapy research. *Psychotherapy Research*, *19*(1), 1–12.

Barcikowski, R. S. (1981). Statistical power with group mean as the unit of analysis. *Journal of Educational Statistics*, *6*, 267–285.

Barlow, S. (2004). A strategic three-year plan to teach group competencies. *Journal of the Specialists in Group Work*, *29*(1), 113–126.

Barlow, S., Fuhriman, A., & Burlingame, G. (2000). The therapeutic application of groups: From Pratt's "thought control classes" to modern group psychotherapy. *Journal of Group Dynamics*, *4*(1), 115–134.

Beck, A., & Lewis, C. (2000). *The process of group psychotherapy: Systems for analyzing change*. Washington, DC: American Psychological Association Press.

Bednar, R. & Kaul, T. (1994). Experiential group research: Can the canon fire? In S. Garfield & A. Bergin (Eds.), *Handbook of psychotherapy and behavior change: An empirical analysis* (4th ed., pp. 631–663). New York: Wiley.

Benjamin, L. S. (2003). *Interpersonal diagnosis and treatment of personality disorders* (2nd ed.). New York: Guildford Press.

Benjamin, L., & Critchfield, K. (2010). An interpersonal perspective on therapy alliances and techniques. In J. C. Muran & J. P. Barber (Eds.), *The therapeutic alliance: An evidence-based guide to practice*. New York: Guilford Press, 123–149.

Beutler, L. E. (2009). Making science matter in clinical practice: Redefining psychotherapy. *Clinical Psychology: Science and Practice*, *16*, 301–317.

Bowlby, J. (1988). *A secure base*. London: Basic Books.

Bray, J. (2009). Federally funded treatment effectiveness research should include behavioral and psychosocial interventions, says APA president. Press release March 20, 2009. Retrieved from http://www.apa.org/releases/bray-testimony.html

Brown, M., Brown, G., & Sharma, S. (2005). *Evidence-based to value-based medicine*. Chicago: Medical Association Press.

Burchard, E. M. L., Michaels, J. J., & Kotkov, B. (1948). Criteria for the evaluation of group therapy. *Psychosomatic Medicine*, *10* (13), 257–274.

Burlingame, G., Fuhriman, A., & Johnson, J. (2001). Cohesion in group psychotherapy. *Psychotherapy: Theory, Research, Practice, Training*, *38*(4), 373–379.

Burlingame, G., Fuhriman, A., & Mosier, J. (2003). The differential effectiveness of group psychotherapy: A meta-analytic perspective. *Group Dynamics: Theory, Research, and Practice*, *7*(1), 3–11.

Burlingame, G., MacKenzie, R., & Strauss, B. (2004). Small group treatment: Evidence for effectiveness and mechanism of change. In M. Lambert (Ed.), *The handbook of psychotherapy and behavior change*. New York: John Wiley & Sons.

Burlingame, B., & Thayer, S. (2010, June). The Group Questionnaire: Clinically useful normative values for diverse clinical populations. Paper presented to the Society for Psychotherapy Research, Asilomar, CA.

Burtt, E. A. (2003/1924). *The metaphysical foundations of modern science*. Mineola, New York: Dover Publications.

Card, C. (2002). *The atrocity paradigm: A theory of evil*. Oxford: Oxford University Press.

Carr, A. (2000). Evidence-based practice in family therapy and systemic consultation. *Journal of Family Therapy, 22*, 29–60.

Carter, E., Mitchell, S., & Krautheim, M. (2001). Understanding and addressing clients' resistance to group counseling. *Journal for Specialists in Group Work, 26*(1), 66–80.

Chambless, D., Crits-Cristoph, P., Wampold, B., Norcross, J., Lambert, M., Bohart, A., et al. (2006). What should be validated? In J. Norcross, L. Beutler, & R. Levant (Eds.), *Evidence-based practices in mental health: Debate and dialogue on the fundamental questions* (pp. 191–256). Washington, DC: American Psychological Association.

Chambless, D., & Ollendick, T. (2001). Empirically supported psychological interventions: Controversies and evidence. *Annual Review of Psychology, 52*, 686–716.

Chapman, C. (2009, October 23). Clinical prediction in group psychotherapy. Paper presented to the Society for Psychotherapy Research, North American Chapter, Orem, UT.

Cochrane, A. (1972). Effectiveness and efficiency: Random reflections on health services. Retrieved from www.Cochrane.org

Cochrane, A. L., & Blythe, M. (1989). *One man's medicine: An autobiography of Professor Archie Cochrane*. London: British Medical Journal.

Davies, D. R., Burlingame, G. M., Johnson, J. E., Barlow, S. H., & Gleave, R. L. (2008). The effects of a feedback intervention on group process and outcome. *Group Dynamics: Theory, Research, and Practice, 12* (2), 141–154.

Dickenson, D., & Fulford, K. (2000). *In two minds: a casebook of psychiatric ethics*. Oxford: Oxford University Press.

Drake, R. E., Goldman, H., Leff, H. S., Lehman, A. F., Dixon, L., Mueser, K. T., et al. (2001). Implementing evidence-based practices in routine mental health service settings. *Psychiatric Services, 52*(2), 179–182.

Dryden, W., & Norcross, J. (1990). *Eclecticism and integration in counseling and psychotherapy*. Loughton, UK: Gale Centre Publishing.

Eddy, D. (2005). Evidence based medicine: a unified approach. *Health Affiliation, 24*(1), 9–17.

Eysenck, H. J. (1952). The effects of psychotherapy: An evaluation. *Journal of Consulting Psychology, 16*, 319–324.

Fonagy, P., Leigh, T., Steele, M., Steele, H., Kennedy, R., Mattoon, G., et al. (1996). The relation of attachment status, psychiatric classification, and response to psychotherapy. *Journal of Consulting and Clinical Psychology, 64*, 22–31.

Fuhriman, A., & Barlow, S. (1983). Cohesion: Relationship in group therapy. In M. Lambert (Ed.), *Psychotherapy and patient relationships* (pp. 263–289). Homewood, IL: Dorsey Press.

Fuhriman, A., & Burlingame, G. (1994). *The handbook of group psychotherapy: An empirical and clinical synthesis*. New York: John Wiley & Sons.

Glass, G., & Stanley, J. (1970). *Statistical methods in education and psychology*. Englewood Cliffs, NJ: Prentice Hall.

Greenberg, L., & Pinsoff, W. (1986). *The Psychotherapeutic Process: A Research Handbook*. New York: Guilford Press.

Heath, G. (2002). Does a theory of mind matter? The myth of totalitarian scientism. *International Journal of Psychotherapy, 7*(3), 1–37.

Hoagwood, K., Hibbs, E., Brent, D., & Jensen, P. (1995). Efficacy and effectiveness in studies of child and adolescent psychotherapy. *Journal of Consulting and Clinical Psychology, 63*, 683–687.

Hornsey, M., Dwyer, L., Oei, T., & Dingle, G. (2009). Group processes and outcomes in group psychotherapy: Is it time to let go of "cohesiveness"? *International Journal of Group Psychotherapy, 59* (2), 267–278.

Howard, G., Hill, T., Maxwell, S., Baptista, T., Farias, M., Coelho, C., et al. (2009). What's wrong with research literatures and how to make them right. *Review of Psychology, 13*(2), 144–166.

Hsu, L. (2003). Random sampling, randomization, and equivalence of contrasted groups in psychotherapy outcome research. In A. Kazdin (Ed.), *Methodological issues and strategies in clinical research* (3rd ed., pp. 147–161). Washington, DC: American Psychological Association Press.

Hunink, M., Glasziou, P., Siegel, J., Weeks, J., Pliskin, J., Elstein, A., et al. (2001). *Decision-making in health and medicine: Integrating evidence and values*. Cambridge: Cambridge University Press.

Hunsley, J. (2007). Addressing key challenges in evidence-based practices in psychology. *Professional Psychology: Research and Practice, 38*, 113–121.

Imel, Z., Baldwin, S., Bonus, K., & MacCoon, D. (2008). Beyond the individual: Group effects in mindfulness based stress reduction. *Psychotherapy Research, 18*(6), 735–742.

Isaacs, D., & Fitzgerald, D. (1999). Seven alternatives to evidence based medicine. *British Journal of Medicine, 319*(7225), 1618.

Johnson, J. (2008). Using research-supported group treatments. *Journal of Clinical Psychology: In Session, 64*, 1206–1224.

Kazdin, A. E. (2008). Evidence-based treatment and practice: New opportunities to bridge clinical research and practice, enhance the knowledge base, and improve patient care. *American Psychologist, 63*(3), 146–159.

Kenny, D., & Judd, C. (1986). Consequences of violating the independent assumption in analysis of variance. *Psychological Bulletin, 99*, 422–431.

Kiesler, D. (1973). *The Process of Psychotherapy: Empirical foundations and systems analysis*. Chicago: Aldine.

Kirchmann, H., Mestel, R., Schreiber-Willnow, K., Mattke, D., Seidler, K., Daudert, E., et al. (2009). Associations among attachment characteristics, patients' assessment of therapeutic factors, and treatment outcome following inpatient psychodynamic group psychotherapy. *Psychotherapy Research, 19*(2), 234–248.

Kivlighan, D., & Kivlighan, M. (2009). Training related change in the ways that group trainees structure their knowledge of group counseling leader interventions. *Journal of Group Dynamics: Theory, Research, and Practice, 13*(3), 190–204.

Kivlighan, D., & Miles, J. (2007). Content themes in Group Dynamics: Theory, Research, and Practice, 1997–2002. *Group Dynamics: Theory, Research, and Practice, 11*(3), 129–139.

Lambert, M. J., Burlingame, G. M., Umphress, V., Hansen, N., Vermeersch, D. A., Clouse, G., et al. (1996). The reliability and validity of the Outcome Questionnaire. *Clinical Psychology and Psychotherapy, 3*, 249–258.

Lambert, M. J., Harmon, C., Slade, K., Whipple, J. L., & Hawkins, E. J. (2005). Providing feedback to psychotherapists on their patients' progress: Clinical results and practice suggestions. *Journal of Clinical Psychology, 61*(2), 165–174.

Levant, R. (2005). *Report of the 2005 Presidential Task Force on Evidence-Based Practice*. American Psychological Association. Retrieved from http://www.apa.org/practice/ebpreport.pdf

Lewin, K. (1951). *Field theory in social psychology*. New York: Harper.

McNeece, C., & Thyer, B. (2004). Evidence-based practice and social work. *Journal of Evidence-Based Social Work*, *1*(1), 7–25.

Meehl, P. (1954). *Clinical vs. statistical prediction*. Minneapolis: University of Minnesota Press.

Messer, S. (2004). Evidence based practice: Beyond empirically supported treatments. *Professional Psychology: Research and Practice*, *36*, 580–588.

Mischel, W. (2009). Connecting clinical practice to scientific progress. *Association for Psychological Science*, *9* (2), i–ii.

Moreland, R., & McMinn, J. (1999). Views from a distant shore: A social psychological perspective on group psychotherapy. *Group Dynamics: Theory, Research, and Practice*, *3*(1), 15–19.

Mullen, P., & Ramirez, G. (2006). The promise and pitfalls of systematic reviews. *Annual Review of Public Health*, *27*, 81–102.

Norcross, J., Hogan, T., & Koocher, G. (2008). *Clinician's guide to evidence-based practices: Mental health and addictions*. Oxford: Oxford University Press.

Oesterheld, A., McKenna, M., & Gould, N. (1987). Group psychotherapy of bulimia: A critical review. *International Journal of Group Psychotherapy*, *37*(2), 163–184.

Perepletchikova, F., Hilt, L., Chereji, C., & Kazdin, A. (2009). Barriers to implementing treatment integrity procedures: Survey of treatment outcome researchers. *Journal of Consulting and Clinical Psychology*, *77*(2), 212–218.

Perepletchikova, F., Treat, T., & Kazdin, A. (2009). Treatment integrity in psychotherapy research: Analysis of the studies and examination of the associated factors. *Journal of Consulting and Clinical Psychology*, *75*(6), 829–841.

Piper, W. (2006). Short-term group therapy for complicated grief. *Directions in Psychiatry*, *26*, 69–78.

Piper, W. (2008). Underutilization of short-term group therapy: Enigmatic or understandable? *Psychotherapy Research*, *18*(2), 127–138.

Piper, W., Joyce, A., McCallum, M., Azim, H. F., & Ogrodniczuk, J. S. (2002). Interpretive and supportive psychotherapies: Matching therapy and patient personality. Washington, DC: American Psychological Association.

Piper, W., McCallum, M., & Azim, H. (1992). *Adaptation to loss through short-term group psychotherapy*. New York: Guilford Press.

Sackett, D., Rosenberg, W., Gray, J., Haynes, R., & Richardson, W. (1996). Evidence-based medicine: What it is and what it isn't. *British Medical Journal*, *312*(7032), 71–72.

Sackett, D., Straus, S., Richardson, W., Rosenberg, W., & Haynes, R. (2000). *Evidence-based medicine: How to practice and teach EBM* (2nd ed.). Edinburgh: Churchill Livingstone.

Scariano, S. M., & Davenport, J. M. (1987). The effects of violations of independence in the oneway ANOVA. *American Statistician*, *41*(2), 123–129.

Smith, A. (1996). Mad cows and ecstasy: Chance and choice in evidence-based society. *Journal of the Royal Statistical Association, Series A*, *159*, 367–383.

Smith, K. (2009). Psychotherapy as applied science or moral praxis: The limitations of empirically supported treatment. *Journal of Theoretical and Philosophical Psychology*, *29*(1), 34–46.

Smith, M., Glass, G., & Miller, T. (1980). *The benefits of psychotherapy*. Baltimore, MD: John Hopkins University Press.

Staines, G., & Cleland, C. (2007). Bias in meta-analytic estimates of the absolute efficacy of psychotherapy. *Review of General Psychology*, *11*(4), 329–347.

Steinberg, E., & Luce, B. (2005). Evidence based? Caveat emptor! *Health Affiliation*, *24*, 80–92.

Stevens, J. (1992). *Applied multivariate statistics for the social sciences* (2nd ed.). Mahwah, NJ: Lawrence Erlbaum.

Stewart, R., & Chambless, D. (2007). Does psychotherapy research inform treatment decisions in private practice? *Journal of Clinical Psychology*, *63*(3), 267–281.

Strauss, B., Burlingame, G., & Borman, B. (2008). Using CORE-R Battery in group psychotherapy. *Journal of Clinical Psychology: In Session*, *64*(11), 1225–1237.

Stuart, G. (2001). Evidence-based psychiatric nursing: Rhetoric or reality? *Journal of the American Psychiatric Nurses Association*, *7*(4), 103–114.

Thomas, G. (1943). Group psychotherapy: A review of recent literature. *Psychosomatic Medicine*, *5*, 166–180.

Villemaire, D. (2002). *E.A. Burtt, historian and philosopher: A study of the author of the metaphysical foundations of modern physical science*. Dordrecht, The Netherlands: Kluwer Academic.

Wampold, B. E. (2001). *The great psychotherapy debate: Model, methods, and findings*. Mahwah, NJ: Erlbaum.

Westen, D., & Morrison, K. (2001). A multidimensional meta-analysis of treatments for depression, panic, and generalized anxiety disorder: An empirical examination of the status of empirically supported treatments. *Journal of Consulting and Clinical Psychology*, *69*, 875–889.

Yalom, I. (2005). *The theory and practice of group psychotherapy* (5th ed.). New York: Basic Books.

Rex Stockton *and* D. Keith Morran

Abstract

Selected issues related to group counseling research are addressed in this chapter. The topics include research-skills training for graduate students including practical skill-application experiences, using a research-team approach to inquiry, practitioner–researcher collaboration, interdisciplinary research, and programmatic research. Major quantitative and qualitative designs for group research are reviewed. Suggestions and recommendations for future research in the group field are offered.

Keywords: collaborative research, group counseling, group research, group work, programmatic research, research designs, research training

Introduction

The practical realities of conducting group research often seem daunting due to the many logistical problems encountered, problems such as recruiting sufficient numbers of group participants and leaders, having the flexibility to randomly assign leaders and members to various treatment and control groups, adhering to a research protocol while simultaneously gearing the group experience to member needs, and selecting the appropriate research design and analysis methods. Many of these logistical and methodological problems are common to all types of inquiry but particularly challenging in group research, where large numbers of participants may be needed in order to provide sufficient numbers of groups for meaningful generalization of findings and where the interactive nature of the group experience does not always allow for tight control of treatment protocols.

Despite the many obstacles researchers encounter, continued inquiry into group processes and outcomes will be essential if the group counseling field is to grow and move forward in meaningful directions during the coming decades. In order for group research to be maximally informative, however,

certain problems and current limitations must be addressed. In reviewing group research methodology, Fuhriman and Burlingame (1994) concluded that the most serious threats to the soundness of the research base involve construct validity issues. Although studies often report positive outcomes as a result of group therapy, few studies describe in detail the characteristics of the therapy, the group members, or the therapist. Given such limited information, it is difficult to determine what actually occurred in the group to produce the positive results. Another frequently cited limitation to the group research base is that many studies are isolated, one-time investigations with no long-term outcome follow-up and without systematic attempts to replicate significant findings. This has led to a call for more programmatic research efforts where group phenomena can be studied over an extended period of time in an increasingly systematic and in-depth manner (e.g., Burlingame, Fuhriman, & Johnson, 2004; Kivlighan, Coleman, & Anderson, 2000; Stockton, Toth, & Morran, 2006).

Although methodological obstacles will always exist in the field of group research, there is evidence that researchers have begun to address some of the key problems in recent years. Group research has become increasingly rigorous and meaningful over the past decade, employing more sophisticated designs and statistical models; and this has served to enhance theory, clinical practice, and training while also pointing out avenues for new inquiry. Additionally, systematically planned programmatic research efforts are gradually becoming more prominent in the group counseling literature (Burlingame et al., 2004).

At this point in time it has been well established that group counseling is at least equal in effectiveness to individual counseling across a variety of group formats and client populations, while providing other advantages in terms of time and cost economy (e.g., Bednar & Kaul, 1994; Burlingame et al., 2004; Horne & Rosenthal, 1997; Kosters, Burlingame, Nachtigall, & Strauss, 2006; McRoberts, Burlingame, & Hoag, 1998). The good news is that, as Barlow, Fuhriman, and Burlingame (2004) conclude in their review of the history of group counseling and psychotherapy, "the efficacy of group psychotherapy has been undeniably established in the research literature" (p. 5).

In this chapter we will focus on selected aspects of the group research enterprise that, based on our experiences, are important elements of successful inquiry. The topics will address such areas as graduate student research training with an emphasis on applied practice and working with research teams, which may involve students, practitioners, and other research colleagues. We will also address such topics as practitioner–researcher collaboration, the need for interdisciplinary research, and the importance of long-term programmatic research efforts. Additionally, we will present an overview of the major quantitative and qualitative research designs that are most relevant to group counseling and therapy research. We conclude the chapter with recommendations and suggestions for future research directions.

Research Training

Research knowledge and skill can be acquired at any point in one's training or career; however, most group-work professionals will receive their first systematic training in research basics at the master's-degree level. As Gelso (1993) has noted, it is in graduate school training that students' attitudes toward research, as well as their motivation to persevere and make sense of research, are first formed. At the master's level, students generally will complete courses that introduce them to basic statistics, quantitative and qualitative designs, and psychological measurement principles. As is the case with more advanced work, these courses are generally taught independently of the real-world, real-life experiences of students. Thus, these courses may sometimes be viewed as hurdles to be overcome rather than as opportunities to actually participate in research. Even at the doctoral level, students are often stressed at the prospect of taking research courses and want to learn just enough to get them through the dissertation.

Ideally, graduate programs should seek to provide all master's-level students with a firm understanding of research basics (both quantitative and qualitative approaches) supplemented by applied practice such as having students design and implement their own small-scale studies, participate in simulated research projects, and/or participate as a member of a research team. These types of applied practice can be very useful in terms of increasing students' skill, confidence, and enthusiasm for the research process. Students who wish to become researchers can then continue on to more advanced research courses and experiences, and students who become practitioners will have developed a solid research background to effectively collaborate on research projects and to be knowledgeable consumers of the research literature.

The field of group counseling is indebted to Gelso (1993) for his systematic attention to and recommendations regarding research training. He emphasized that environmental factors in the various graduate programs have a significant influence on the development of students who are both knowledgeable and interested in research. Gelso's research training environment considers all the "forces in graduate training . . . that reflect attitudes toward research and science" (p. 475). Later, Gelso, Mallinckrodt, and Judge (1996) provided very useful suggestions that can be helpful in developing a positive research environment. These include (1) positively reinforcing student research activities; (2) encouraging students' early involvement in research activities that maximize successes and minimize threats to self-esteem; (3) emphasizing the flawed and restricted nature of all research; (4) embracing different, and even competing, research strategies; and (5) integrating science and practice. Having positive role models is another very important element in the training of beginning researchers. As Stockton and Hulse (1983) have emphasized, "unless students have active contact with role models whose efforts exemplify research as a dynamic process subject to revisions, false starts, and intuitive hunches, it will be difficult for them to view it as the extremely pleasurable process it can be" (p. 304).

In our work with graduate students we have found that certain stumbling blocks are common for beginners. Consequently, we have found it useful to emphasize the following tips for our research team members: (1) whenever possible, join or form a group of others who are interested in your research project, to insure that multiple perspectives can be considered as you plan and conduct your study; (2) begin with a careful review of the existing literature to find out what is and is not already known in relation to your intended topic; (3) formulate and clearly state the research questions or hypotheses that have emerged from your literature review; (4) identify process and outcomes measures (multiple measures whenever possible) that are directly related to the questions or hypotheses of the study; (5) consult with others to choose research design and data-analysis procedures that can validly address your particular questions or hypotheses; (6) carefully consider the support resources you have available (e.g., financial resources, available groups and leaders, access to computer support) to ensure that you have the means to complete the study; and (7) be realistic and keep the project manageable (e.g., it may be reasonable to administer a questionnaire to 200 participants but unrealistic to interview 200 participants unless you have access to a large staff of assistants) (Stockton et al., 2006).

Gelso et al. (1996) help us understand that a research environment can be created so long as a critical mass of individuals and resources is available and that there are a variety of ways to enhance research. The use of research teams, collaboration between practitioners and researchers, and interdisciplinary collaboration are closely related means of pooling resources and creating such a critical mass and are discussed below.

A Team Approach to Research

In addition to formal classroom instruction, one mechanism to facilitate the development of research sophistication is the use of research teams. Research teams can certainly provide the intellectual resources if the other ingredients (e.g., facilitated environment, willing participants, material resources, time) are available. We have worked for many years with research teams that included graduate students as well as group practitioners who were interested in being involved in inquiry. This has enabled us to do programmatic research that others (e.g., Kivlighan & Luiza, 2005; Ward, 2005) have cited as having

made a contribution to the field, while also providing a meaningful learning experience for students.

In addition to assisting in the production of a programmatic series of research studies, graduate students have learned a great deal about how to do research from both a methodological and a logistical perspective. Our series of studies relating to interpersonal feedback, for example, could not have been conducted without the assistance of graduate student research team members who, in some cases, went on to become researchers in their own right. In each case they developed sophistication and knowledge that enabled them to understand and appreciate research in a more applied and sophisticated manner. They also learned the "real-world" difficulties that sometimes can occur when one is doing research.

Beginner-Level Team Members

In the model that we have evolved over the years, students with little or no experience join the research team at the beginner level. If they have not taken a graduate research course, we encourage them to do so as soon as their class schedule permits. Even at this beginning level, students are able to contribute to the overall project while learning logistical skills. The experience of working in a real-life situation can be very valuable to those who otherwise would understand research only as a textbook recipe. Students also begin to understand the necessity of good planning and cooperative efforts. They are initially assigned various logistical tasks such as collecting, coding, and entering data. They also begin to work on reviews of the research literature that inform planned or ongoing studies. As apprentices, students at this level assist more senior team members (including those doing dissertation studies) whose studies are ongoing.

During this time, in addition to working on logistical tasks, team members attend weekly research meetings where various projects, whether ongoing or in the planning stage, are discussed (team meetings typically include 8–10 students plus two faculty members). A great deal of brainstorming and feedback exchange occur in these weekly meetings, often followed up with e-mail messages and other communications throughout the week. During the weekly meetings beginning student team members are able to observe discussions focused on research design, the choice of measurement instruments, logistical problems, and related issues and are encouraged to ask any questions and share any ideas they might have. As they familiarize themselves with the material, they are able to knowledgeably participate in discussions. These discussions also can serve as motivators for novice research team members to begin to explore research ideas on their own outside of the team meetings. A former team member who later became a well-known researcher commented on his beginning team experience, "One of the first lessons I learned was that some of the most important tasks in successful research investigations are among the least glamorous." (F. Robison, personal communication, September 2005).

It is particularly important that beginning researchers develop a sense of confidence and a feeling of success in their initial research endeavors as these will enhance their willingness to engage in research throughout their careers. This can usually be accomplished by involving beginners in projects closely related to their own interests, by initially assigning them to tasks that are nonthreatening and require only basic knowledge and skill, and by closely supervising their experiences and providing ongoing encouragement. It is equally important to establish research team norms whereby all team members, including beginners, feel free to share ideas without fear of embarrassment.

Advanced-Level Team Members

After experience in the first level of research, students who want to gain more knowledge and to actively conduct research from conceptualization to completion of actual projects (varying from pilot studies to dissertations) enter the second level. At this level they are encouraged to present their own ideas regarding proposed research in the team meetings, where they receive feedback from their peers and mentors. We have found it useful to have team members present their ideas in the form of written proposals even if those proposals are initially only in rough outline form. In some cases a student may begin with only a research question and will refine and expand the proposal as input from the rest of the team is incorporated. As the research study progresses, students continue to receive technical assistance as well as encouragement from team members. It is at this level that they are able to prepare and present conference papers and coauthor journal articles.

During this time (second-level) students are also taking more advanced coursework that allows them to further understand the analytical issues faced by researchers. We recommend advanced coursework on such topics as research design, univariate

and multivariate analyses, qualitative inquiry, psychometric theory, research proposal writing, and computer analysis of data. Eventually, they progress to the point of dissertation topics, which are also discussed in team meetings. By this time students are able to do independent research as well as to contribute to the team projects. As students develop sophistication and are of substantial value in a research project, they are included in the reporting process—presenting research papers at conferences or contributing to publications. Some of them have gone on to be researchers in their own right, and all of them have a better appreciation for research. If in their career they are focusing more on practice, they leave the research-team experience prepared to draw upon their experience and be knowledgeable research collaborators.

Practitioner–Researcher Collaboration

The need for continued development of the research base for group counseling has been well documented and frequently includes the call for a closer linkage between research and clinical practice (e.g., Burlingame et al., 2004; Coché & Dies, 1981; Morran & Stockton, 1985; Riva & Kalodner, 1997). One way of promoting closer linkage is through practitioner–researcher collaboration. By working in concert, practitioners and researchers can arrange a division of labor that emphasizes the specialized knowledge of each and can result in research findings that are both valid and relevant to the practice setting. Researchers may benefit from such an arrangement by establishing relationships that may enhance access to a variety of real-world groups for study. Practitioners may benefit from research findings by gaining valuable information concerning the efficacy of the groups conducted within their agencies, an important benefit given the increasing need to document accountability. Practitioners and researchers, of course, can both benefit from the sharing of knowledge, skills, and ideas that naturally occurs while working together.

In the preceding section of this chapter, emphasis was given to providing a real-world experience for graduate students in order for them to get a sense of research from the beginning to completion, including logistics, research review, research design, measurement, and report writing. In this manner, students (including future practitioners) come to understand the interrelated components of the research process and the trade-offs and compromises that often must be made. When these students have completed their clinical training and academic preparation, including the level of research sophistication appropriate to their degree, they frequently enter clinical practice settings rather than settings emphasizing research. Here, they get a reality-based understanding of the gap between research and practice. In the practice-based reality they become acquainted with the nature of clinical practice in today's managed care environment. As Trotzer (2006) has noted, the research perspective, which is an integral part of graduate training, is not likely to be the priority in clinical settings. He further notes that this can result in a choice to focus on practice at the expense of research. As Trotzer makes clear, the choice between research and practice does not have to be polarized by choosing one to the exclusion of the other.

From the beginning of what we think of as professional counseling today, one of the field's characteristics has been how much it is dependent on the socioeconomic and political context (Stockton, Garbleman, Kaladow, Clawson, & Smith, 2002). Perhaps the biggest single phenomenon we are facing in mental health work today is the managed care environment, which affects the provision of all health-care services. Managed care has emerged as a major cost-containment strategy for rapidly rising health-care costs since the Health Maintenance Organization Act of 1973. This phenomenon has grown into wide-scale practice. Along with this development has come an emphasis on clinical practice guidelines, empirically supported treatments, and treatment manuals. Counselors must be knowledgeable about and able to implement clinical practice guidelines and empirically supported treatments. This approach has meant that agencies and their counseling staffs have greatly increased paperwork and must demonstrate accountability. While this certainly has its negative side, at least it does encourage counselors to utilize outcome-assessment and consumer-satisfaction measures. Thus, even though managed care and other societal events have changed mental health service practices and, among other things, made the paperwork burden on counselors much heavier, it is still possible for researchers to work with practitioners and develop collaborative research projects that can be beneficial to both parties.

The collaboration of practitioners and researchers would appear to be a natural winning combination. Practitioners often have many years of experience in the clinical setting and may have insightful ideas and hypotheses based on their direct observations. However, practitioners often do not have the time, resources, and research experience to conduct their own independent studies. Group researchers may have the time, resources, and experience to conduct investigations but may lack experience with groups in the applied setting and may not typically have ready access to such groups. Through collaboration there is the potential for practitioners and researchers to pool their experience and talents to produce rigorous and meaningful studies (Riva & Kalodner, 1997).

Since collaborative group research is likely to be conducted outside the laboratory, it is especially important that practitioners and researchers are comfortable in a collaborative effort. Well-designed field studies utilizing proper procedures may fail due to misunderstandings or lack of close communication between practitioners and researchers. When collaborating, we have found it useful to work with practitioners using a research team approach and to involve practitioners in all aspects of the study from initial planning through data analysis and reporting. Additionally, we have found it useful to include an agency administrator as part of the research team whenever feasible. When administrators are fully involved in the research, they can be of great assistance in recruiting group members and leaders and in monitoring adherence to the research protocol at the agency site.

Practitioners do not have to be skilled in the most sophisticated research methodology and design; however, they do need to understand the basics of research in order to critically evaluate findings and adapt new concepts to their own practice setting. Also, they are much better able to participate in a collaborative study if they understand the basics of research. A research-team approach allows practitioners an opportunity to refresh their basic research skills while also contributing their clinical knowledge to the research project.

An example of practitioner–researcher collaboration may help to illustrate some of these points. Currently, we are involved in a transnational research project which can illuminate both the value of graduate student research teams and collaboration with practitioners. Our research team has been collaborating with an institution, the Institute for Development Management (IDM), in Botswana, Africa. In the United States, IDM would be considered a junior college. In Botswana, IDM has been training paraprofessional counselors to work with HIV/AIDS clients and provides graduates with a certificate of training. IDM is a three-country cooperative institution with branches in Botswana,

Lesotho, and Swaziland. It has a very broad mission, of which the training of HIV/AIDS counselors is but one part. However, because of the seriousness of the HIV/AIDS problem in the country, it is an important component of the public health part of their activities. Our project is working with the IDM in Botswana and is countrywide; it is anticipated that we will be able to work with the Swaziland and Lesotho branches at a later date. Our overall goal for this project is to work with IDM to enhance the clinical skills and identify the resource, in-service training and supervision, and other needs of HIV/AIDS paraprofessional counselors. Although our training efforts in Botswana have focused primarily on the development of group-counseling skills, both our training and research efforts have also encompassed individual, couples, crisis, prevention, and other forms of counseling.

Although we have conducted training seminars in Botswana for several years, IDM staff members are the ones who best understand the history and culture of the country. Both IDM and our project have much to gain by collaboration. The IDM trainers want to know more about the effectiveness of counselor-training programs and the impact counselors are having on HIV/AIDS client welfare, and as counselor educators, we too have a vested interest in this knowledge. We have entered into an agreement to provide research expertise, including instrument development and data analysis, for a survey that is designed to assess the perceptions of HIV/AIDS counselors in relation to such dimensions as quality of training and in-service supervision, dealing with social stigma issues, personal and emotional reactions to working with HIV/AIDS clients, barriers or obstacles to effective HIV/AIDS counseling in Botswana, and self-perceived therapeutic effectiveness.

Our Botswana colleagues (including an IDM administrator) participated in overall project planning and, essentially, became long-distance members of our research team. The entire team, including our Botswana colleagues, collaborated on all aspects of the survey research, including the brainstorming of items for the survey and the planning for data collection and analysis. After the data have been analyzed, team members will also participate in the report writing and any publications which may result from the study. This team approach to practitioner–researcher collaboration has enabled all of our team members to gain knowledge and experience concerning the basics of survey research and, it is anticipated, will result in more meaningful

findings than we and our students or our Botswana colleagues could have achieved independently.

This particular project is currently in the data-analysis phase and is expected to be completed in the near future. Collaborating at such a distance and across cultures has been a challenge that we have met with a combination of face-to-face meetings and numerous e-mails and other electronic communications. As an example of issues that may arise when collaborating across cultures, we learned early on that our Botswana colleagues were eager to participate with us, and each time we sent them survey drafts to review, they responded with lots of feedback—all positive. Only after firm assurances from us that we really did value their input and that their corrective feedback was essential to success did they begin to suggest substantive changes to our instrument drafts. Once this issue was dealt with, we began to receive excellent and detailed feedback; and it is clear that the quality and relevance of the research have been greatly enhanced through collaboration with our Botswana colleagues. Obstacles such as this are to be expected in collaborative efforts but, in our experience, can usually be overcome through honest and straightforward communication between collaborators.

Our collaboration has been made much easier through technology. Africa is two continents and several time zones away from the Midwest. After establishing personal relationships and a basis for trust through face-to-face contact in various meetings, workshops, and other experiences, we were able to communicate through various forms of technology. We are fortunate to live in a world that is technology-intensive. This allows us to speed up the spread of information. It has been possible for quite some time to communicate with colleagues in various locations worldwide through e-mail; however, in today's world there are many more options. The recent phenomenon of social networks is just one example of the possibilities for furthering practitioner–researcher contact. While not as new, the ability to videoconference has also opened up significant opportunities. For example, after providing a workshop for counselors in Botswana, it was possible to provide a videoconference follow-up for more advanced training with participants, who gathered at the University of Botswana where the appropriate technology was available. The improvements in technology make it possible to see the participants in life size, almost as if they were in the same room. Since they already are familiar with the trainer, there is an ease of communication similar to being on site in Botswana.

It is anticipated that the results from this study will be published as the information should give us a better understanding of the work of paraprofessional counselors. Very little emphasis has been placed on the social–emotional needs of HIV/AIDS clients and the impact of counseling, much less on the effects of the counseling on the counselors themselves. In addition to the standard journals, the authors will have the option of online journals, which is another way that technology has shortened the time between the actual analysis of data and reporting it to the field. This is widely being done in the physical and life sciences and is beginning to be adopted by those of us in the social sciences as well.

Some of these publication outlets are readily adopted by applied fields such as counseling and provide relevant and immediately applicable information for practitioners. The publication *VISTAS Online* would be a good example of this. In the case of this journal, not only is it providing information in a more timely fashion but the articles are designed to be practitioner-friendly. While these technologies are routinely being utilized by new professionals entering the field, it is also possible for those already in the field—and even those in their 70s, such as the senior author (Stockton)—to take advantage of electronically assisted collaborative opportunities such as Facebook and Wiki and to find publication outlets for their activities.

Interdisciplinary Research

Group counseling is utilized by virtually all disciplines concerned with human behavior. In addition to counseling, group work has been influenced by many areas including the theoretical and research activities of psychiatrists, psychologists, organizational development theorists, and social workers. For example, Kurt Lewin is regarded as the father of the organizational development movement, which makes heavy use of group process. The results of the research in this area are typically published in journals read by those interested in how to improve organizational problem solving. These research findings are often relevant in other group settings but are easily overlooked by those in other disciplines. The same is true in social work, where groups play an important part in social work practice. The influential *Handbook of Social Work with Groups* (Garvin, Gutierrez, & Galinsky, 2004) provides insight into the number of ways that group work is utilized in a variety of settings and includes a chapter on research issues. This and other social work group-work books

and journals are not typically read by those outside the social work discipline. However, the results of the studies are very relevant to any group counseling researcher or practitioner. The same is true of social psychology. Whittenbaum and Moreland (2008) noted that research on small groups in social psychology has a long history. Each disciplinary area has contributed importantly to our knowledge base. Thus, it is important for those in the field to be in close communication with those in related group work areas rather than remaining in disciplinary "silos" in order that progress can be made as new knowledge becomes available.

The utilization of interdisciplinary (or multidisciplinary) teams to address research questions has the potential to promote valuable cross-fertilization between disciplines and may lead to a more complete and integrated understanding of the group processes and outcomes being studied. At present, interdisciplinary team approaches to group inquiry are rare, partly due to institutional, funding, and related obstacles to working across disciplines. However, the payoffs from such collaboration are potentially great and can justify the extra time and effort to deal with these realities.

At present, there appear to be few specific or firm guidelines for the successful operation of interdisciplinary research teams. However, Kapila and Moher (1995) present some general guidelines that may prove useful. They recommend that the research team be composed of individuals from disciplines that reflect the key facets of the complexity involved in the research issues being studied. A key first step is to carefully form clear and concise research questions and to keep the focus on these issues and not on the disciplinary perspectives involved or on the methodology. All team members should make clear the assumptions they bring to the project concerning the research problem/question, the research goal, and the key terms. Once the problem has been jointly defined, it is possible to articulate clear objectives that are agreed upon by all of the team members and other stakeholders involved in the process. Kapila and Moher also stress the importance of continuous recognition of a common goal; regular communication, consultation, and exchange of data; and the ongoing discussion of provisional conclusions among the team members. They also note the importance of having a team leader who can negotiate with a wide variety of stakeholders and work effectively across discipline boundaries while also having the capacity to mobilize the team. Disagreements may sometimes arise among team members, and these should be discussed openly when they first arise. Finally, there needs to be ongoing synthesis and integration of the different perspectives of team members so that the final conclusions and written report represent an integration of inputs from all of the various disciplines involved in the project.

A Brief Review of Major Research Designs

Beginner-level members of our research team often start with little or no knowledge of research design beyond what they have learned in a basic statistics course. For those interested in more advanced research design skills, we encourage taking coursework that focuses on a variety of quantitative and qualitative methodologies. We also attempt, as opportunities permit, to directly involve our advanced-level team members in research projects that will expose them to a variety of inquiry approaches that will provide hands-on experience. As team members gain in their knowledge of research design, this enables the speaking of a common research language and facilitates members full participation in brainstorming and decision-making activities. In this section we will briefly review the major categories of research designs that we believe are important for group researchers.

Inquiry in the group work field can be broadly classified as quantitative, qualitative, or a mixture of quantitative and qualitative methodologies. Currently, the vast majority of group-research studies employ quantitative methodologies; however, qualitative methodologies are gradually becoming more common, as are mixed methodologies. Quantitative research is characterized by the collection and analysis of numerical data (e.g., behavior counts, ratings, scale scores) to determine relationships among variables of the study (Hittleman & Simon, 1997). This type of research uses statistical methods to address predetermined questions or to test predetermined hypotheses concerning the relationships among the variables under study. Qualitative research, by contrast, relies primarily (though not exclusively) on the collection and analysis of nonnumerical data (e.g., observations, interviews, responses to open-ended questions) to identify patterns, themes, and holistic features of the phenomena being studied. This type of research often emphasizes a process of discovery whereby new hypotheses and theory are generated from the data (Hittleman & Simon, 1997).

The appropriate choice of either a quantitative or a qualitative methodology for group research is dependent on a number of factors, such as the objectives of the study, the degree of control the investigator has over the conditions being studied, and the expected regularity or predictability of the behaviors being examined. Quantitative methodologies, for example, may be most appropriate when the purpose is to address predetermined questions or hypotheses or to test theory, when extraneous variables can be adequately controlled or statistically accounted for, and when the behavior to be studied can be objectively measured and is expected to be relatively predictable across individuals or groups. Qualitative methodologies may be most appropriate when the purpose is to generate new ideas, hypotheses, or theories; when the intent is to study behaviors within the dynamic context of the natural environment; and when the focus is on the subjective experiences or perceptions of individuals.

Quantitative and qualitative approaches both have their particular advantages and disadvantages. Quantitative research, for example, under certain conditions, has the potential to produce findings that are generalizable beyond the groups or individuals studied; however, the nature of such inquiry tends to be reductionist by focusing on narrow and specific aspects of the group experience in order to exercise more rigorous control of extraneous variables. Qualitative research leads to findings that are specific to the groups or individuals studied and are, thus, less generalizable but allow for deeper and richer descriptions of subjective experiences. Both approaches are capable of adding valuable information to the knowledge base of group counseling when appropriately matched with the purposes of the research and when appropriately applied. A comprehensive explanation of quantitative and qualitative approaches is beyond the scope of this chapter; however, the major types of quantitative and qualitative methods are briefly outlined in the following sections and may serve as a refresher for those with a background in research basics and as a starting point for those wishing to learn more about these research approaches.

Quantitative Research Approaches

Quantitative research is designed to describe, compare, and/or attribute causality through the use of statistical analysis (Hittleman & Simon, 1997). This approach is guided by predetermined questions or hypotheses and is based on the assumption that behaviors or characteristics of interest can be objectively measured and numerically represented through the use of valid data-collection instruments or procedures. Some of the major quantitative approaches that may be most applicable to group-counseling research are described below.

TRUE EXPERIMENTAL DESIGNS

True experimental designs are considered to be the gold standard when seeking to determine cause-and-effect relationships among variables. The hallmarks of true experimental design include active manipulation of independent variables (control and treatment groups), common measured outcomes, and random assignment of participants (Ingersoll, 1998; Sprinthall, Schumutte, & Sirois, 1991). The researcher (we will use the term "researcher" throughout this section, though "research team" would be equally appropriate) attempts to test a hypothesis by experimentally manipulating one variable (the independent variable) to measure its effects on another variable (the dependent variable). For example, the researcher may wish to determine the effect on a measure of group climate when some groups in a study receive pregroup training while other groups receive no pregroup training. In this case, random assignment of members and leaders across multiple groups would help to ensure that the experimental and control groups were initially equivalent and that observed differences in the group-climate measure were not the result of preexisting or extraneous factors but were due to the experimental manipulation. Some examples of true experimental designs include the posttest-only, equivalent-groups design; the pretest–posttest, equivalent-groups design; and the Solomon four-group design (Best & Kahn, 1986).

SINGLE-SUBJECT DESIGNS

Single-subject research is another type of experimental design used to identify causal relationships between independent and dependent variables (Horner et al., 2005; Martella, Nelson, & Marchand-Martella, 1999). Single-subject designs may involve only one participant (or group) but, contrary to the name, typically involve multiple participants who serve as their own experimental control. This approach is characterized by repeated measurements of the dependent variable(s) across time while actively and systematically implementing (or implementing and withdrawing) the independent (treatment) condition. By comparing the participant's performance in the absence of treatment (baseline) and during and after treatment, causal inferences can be made (Horner et al., 2005). There are several variations of single-subject designs that employ the basic concept of implementing and withdrawing treatment conditions in order to observe the effect on the dependent variable(s); examples include A–B–A–B designs, multiple baseline designs, and alternating treatment designs. These types of designs offer the advantage of requiring a small number of participants (or groups); however, due to such small numbers, external validity must be established through replication across multiple participants, settings, etc. (Martella et al., 1999).

QUASI-EXPERIMENTAL DESIGNS

Quasi-experimental designs are similar to true experimental designs in that they involve active manipulation of independent variables (e.g., treatment and control groups) but without random assignment of participants to create equivalent groups (Sprinthall et al., 1991). In some cases random assignment may not be possible, practical, or ethical; and this precludes the use of a true experimental design. For example, a researcher may wish to investigate the impact of high versus low leader protecting behaviors on member ratings of group cohesion by studying therapy groups in an agency setting. However, random assignment of group leaders and members to the treatment and control groups may not be possible due to such factors as participant schedules or agency protocols; thus, the groups may not be equivalent before the experimental intervention and any differences on the dependent measure (cohesion in this example) cannot be attributed to the experimental manipulation with great confidence. In such cases where random assignment is not an option, quasi-experimental designs are often used and represent an alternative, or compromise, to the true experiment (Sprinthall et al., 1991). Quasi-experimental designs are commonly used in the social sciences due to the difficulties with meeting the strict requirements for true experiments; however, such studies are limited in that they can make only tentative conclusions regarding the cause-and-effect relationships among variables. Some of the commonly used quasi-experimental designs include the nonequivalent-groups, posttest-only design; the nonequivalent-groups, pretest–posttest design; and time series designs (Best & Kahn, 1986).

EX POST FACTO DESIGNS

Ex post facto or causal-comparative designs are used when the researcher cannot actively manipulate the independent variable(s) of the study but must assign participants to conditions based on preexisting characteristics (e.g., gender, age, interpersonal style) (Sprinthall et al., 1991). For example, the researcher may want to compare whether males and females (the independent variable) benefit differentially from a structured group format on a goal-attainment outcome measure (the dependent variable). Since the researcher cannot manipulate the gender of the participants, randomization has not occurred and the two groups may also differ on other variables that could influence outcome (e.g., there may be a tendency for males and females to have very different types of goals). A variety of techniques can be used to deal with the problem of nonequivalent groups in ex post facto research, techniques such as matching participants of the treatment and control groups so that they are similar in terms of confounding variables that may influence outcome or using statistical procedures such as analysis of covariance to adjust for initial group differences. However, in the absence of rigorous control over such confounding variables, ex post facto designs do not allow for cause-and-effect inferences, though they may help to establish better-than-chance predictions (Sprinthall et al., 1991).

CORRELATIONAL RESEARCH

Correlational research is designed to assess the degree of relationship between two or more quantitative variables (e.g., the relationship of self-disclosure frequency to ratings of satisfaction with the group experience). The relationship between variables is expressed as a coefficient between +1.00 and −1.00 and may depict either a positive (e.g., higher self-disclosure associated with higher satisfaction) or negative (e.g., higher self-disclosure associated with lower satisfaction) relationship between the variables. This type of research is valuable in that it can identify relationships among key variables but does not allow for cause-and-effect inferences to be made. However, as in ex post facto research, correlational studies may identify better-than-chance predictions concerning variable relationships, and findings can potentially be subjected to subsequent experimental studies to determine if a cause-and-effect relationship exists (Sprinthall et al., 1991).

DESCRIPTIVE RESEARCH

Descriptive research is designed to collect data in order to answer questions or test hypotheses concerning what is currently happening within a group. In essence, the objective is to describe selected processes or outcomes as they occur (Sprinthall et al., 1991). These types of studies typically seek to measure variables of interest across multiple participants and present aggregate statistics such as frequencies, means, standard deviations, percentages, or statistical trends. Data are often collected in the form of behavior counts, survey responses, self-ratings, or scale scores. Descriptive approaches can be very useful in presenting a picture of what actually occurred in a group (e.g., how members rated the cohesion of the group) but do not attempt to assess the causes of what was found (e.g., what caused cohesion to be high, moderate, or low).

Qualitative Research Approaches

Qualitative research includes a broad range of strategies to study the subjective perceptions of subjects within a given context. Brantlinger, Jimenez, Klinger, Pugach & Richardson (2005) describe qualitative research as "a systematic approach to understanding qualities, or the essential nature, of a phenomenon within a particular setting" (p. 195). These approaches typically collect verbal rather than numerical data, using methods such as interviews, observation, participant observation, open-ended questions, document analysis, and field notes. Qualitative studies typically involve relatively small numbers of subjects who are purposely rather than randomly selected; thus, findings are not readily generalizable to other subjects or settings. Instead of aiming for generalizable knowledge, qualitative studies emphasize the value of examining the breadth and depth of a given phenomenon to provide rich and in-depth descriptions, to identify themes and patterns, and/or to generate hypotheses and theories to explain what was observed. Some of the major qualitative approaches that may be most useful in group research will now be outlined.

CASE STUDY

Case studies are often characterized as a qualitative methodology, though they may be qualitative, quantitative, or a mixture of both depending on the types of data collected. The case study is designed to provide a detailed analysis of a particular individual (or group), usually within the natural setting. Rather than focusing on what is common to the whole population, this approach focuses on the factors considered relevant to the individual or group under study and attempts to describe the phenomenon in all its complexities (Merriam, 1998; Stake, 1994). Researchers may also conduct multiple case studies in order to explore similarities and differences across cases. Qualitative case studies typically rely on data collected through observation, participant observation, interviews, and the examination of documents or artifacts when available. For example, a researcher might conduct an interview with an individual (or a limited number of individuals) who has dropped out of a group experience in order to better understand that person's reasons for leaving the group. Although the findings of such a study would not necessarily reveal why others drop out of a group experience, they would suggest at least some factors that can potentially lead to dropping out (hypothesis development).

GROUNDED THEORY

Grounded theory is an emergent methodology (no predetermined hypotheses are tested) that begins with data collection (e.g., observations, interviews) and seeks to develop a theory to explain trends and patterns in the data (Glaser, 1978, 1998: Glaser & Strauss, 1967; Strauss & Corbin, 1990). Through a process of constant comparison, data from each new case are compared to data from previous cases using purposive sampling to increase the diversity of the sample. The constant comparison methodology allows the researcher to identify patterns in the data and to derive a tentative theory that explains and is "grounded in" the data. For example, a researcher might observe adolescent counseling groups and collect data to formulate a theory of the factors that enhanced or hindered the observed groups' progress toward the working stage of development.

ETHNOGRAPHY

Ethnography is an approach used to study a culture from the "insider" perspective of individuals who are part of that culture (Cherry, 2000). The focus of ethnographic studies may be on large ethnic groups or other communities or may focus on smaller units such as families or therapy groups. Ethnography is rooted in cultural anthropology and is designed to describe the shared values, norms, beliefs, perceptions, etc. of the group being studied (Spradley, 1979). Close observation or participant observation and in-depth interviewing (and reinterviewing) are key techniques used by the researcher to learn about the meanings individuals attach to their experiences within the culture. For example, an ethnographic approach might be used to explore the interactions of members in a grief group and how individuals perceived the dynamics that occurred within the group experience.

Choosing a Research Design

The designs described here represent only a few of the many possible approaches that may be used in research studies. The appropriate choice of a particular approach will depend on factors such as the purpose of the proposed study, the type of data that can be collected, the availability of subjects, and the degree of control the researcher has over extraneous variables.

When making design decisions, the researcher will necessarily face trade-offs such as whether to focus on the discovery of generalizable knowledge or on the subjective perceptions of participants, whether to guide the research with predetermined hypotheses or to generate hypotheses from the emerging data, or whether findings will be more meaningful if the study is conducted in a controlled or a natural environment. Polkinghorne (1988) makes the point that good research is not a matter of simply following a recipe that unerringly guides one to the correct research approach; rather, it is "the creative search to understand better, and it uses whatever approaches are responsive to the particular questions and subject matters addressed" (p. 3). The fact that research is a creative process involving inevitable trade-offs highlights the potential value of collaboration and team work where multiple perspectives can be shared and considered. This allows the researcher to benefit from the expertise and perceptions of others and, often times, to avoid the many potential pitfalls that sometimes appear in even the most simple and straightforward research projects.

Programmatic Research

Reviewers of the group-research literature have consistently noted the limitations of one-shot studies and have called for more programmatic lines of inquiry (e.g., Burlingame et al., 2004; Kivlighan et al., 2000; Stockton et al., 2006). Burlingame et al. (2004) strongly encourage group research that is both programmatic and complex. They define research programs as complex when "they test relationships among pretherapy characteristics of the patients (i.e., moderator variables), group process patterns believed to moderate change, formal change theories (e.g., psychodynamic or interpretive models), and multivariate outcomes" (p. 654).

A carefully planned and well-conducted single research study has the potential to add to the knowledge base of group counseling. However, studies that are part of an ongoing programmatic series of related studies are likely to be more valuable than isolated, single-shot studies. Programmatic studies allow for more in-depth and long-term investigation of research questions. In essence, a carefully conducted programmatic approach enables a given line of research to evolve so that it develops and matures over time and can become increasingly detailed, rigorous, and meaningful as each study informs and provides direction for the next study.

Programmatic lines of inquiry also allow researchers to systematically replicate earlier studies that have produced interesting findings. The scientific method assumes that knowledge is never final but is always subject to revision as new findings emerge. Therefore, inquiry cannot provide absolute and final answers to research questions but, depending on the research evidence, may provide tentative answers that can be viewed with varying degrees of confidence. Findings from a single isolated study, for example, would need to be viewed as highly tentative, while we might have much greater confidence in findings that have been consistent after many carefully planned replication studies across various settings and types of groups or clients. Replication would seem to be particularly important in the group counseling field where the relationships among various process and outcome variables are likely to be quite complex due to the unique dynamics that result from group member interactions.

Conclusion

Research in the group counseling field has become increasingly sophisticated during the past few decades, and the effectiveness of group counseling has been well established across a wide variety of settings and types of groups. Continued progress is likely to be enhanced as more long-term programmatic inquiry efforts are undertaken to investigate the complex interactions among member characteristics, group dynamics, therapist characteristics, types of groups, and outcomes. Progress may also be enhanced as a greater variety of research approaches are employed, including quantitative, qualitative, and mixed research designs.

Given the need for more long-term and complex inquiry efforts in group counseling, it would seem important to emphasize the value of teamwork. The formation of ongoing research teams allows researchers to pool their knowledge, experience, and resources productively. Additionally, a research team model provides an excellent training environment for graduate students and novice researchers, while also providing a natural format for practitioner–researcher

collaboration, interdisciplinary collaboration, and programmatic lines of inquiry.

Future Directions

As we noted earlier in this chapter, the research base for group counseling has been developed and refined over time and recent decades have seen the emergence of increasingly sophisticated, complex, and meaningful studies. Despite these positive developments, there is still much work to be done and we offer the following suggestions and recommendations:

1. Future researchers need to seek further understanding of the complex interactive, connected, and holistic processes of group phenomena and to link these with long-term outcomes across the wide variety of group types (e.g., Burlingame et al., 2004; McRoberts et al., 1998). Due to such complexities, meaningful research is most likely to be accomplished through the work of research teams involved in programmatic efforts. Additionally, group approaches are increasingly utilized across multiple disciplines; thus, it may be advantageous to recruit research team members representing the various disciplines involved in the groups under study.

2. As group counseling approaches continue to grow and expand to new settings and clientele, researchers need to address these new applications by studying the processes and outcomes of increasingly specific group protocols for increasingly specific client populations (e.g., educational settings, health-care settings, business and industry settings, social services settings).

3. While laboratory studies of group phenomena often serve a valuable purpose, there is a need for more practice-based research on groups conducted in clinical settings. Such studies can add ecologically valid and meaningful data to the group-research knowledge base and may do much to help close the often lamented gap between practice and research.

4. Yalom's (1995) seminal work on group therapeutic factors has had a major influence on the direction of group research. As noted by Kivlighan and Holmes (2004), however, "much of the research on therapeutic factors in group therapy has stayed at a simplistic and atheoretical level" (p. 32). Continued research will be needed to better understand the complexities of which group therapeutic factors are most important at various group stages for which types of groups (e.g., Kivlighan et al., 2000).

5. Closely related to the previous item, more research addressing the connection between leader interventions and group therapeutic factors is needed to better understand how the group leader can intentionally influence the development of key therapeutic forces within the group.

6. Although progress has been made over the past few decades, much work remains to be done in the area of group leader training (e.g., Riva, Wachtel, & Lasky, 2004; Stockton, Morran, & Krieger, 2004). Future research is needed to establish the best approaches to helping novice group leaders acquire knowledge competencies, basic and advanced skill competencies, clinical experience competencies, coleader competencies, and multicultural competencies.

References

Barlow, S.H., Fuhriman A. J., & Burlingame G. M. (2004). The history of group counseling and psychotherapy. In J. L. DeLucia-Waack, D. A. Gerrity, C.R. Kalodner, & M. T. Riva (Eds.), *Handbook of Group Counseling and Psychotherapy*. (pp. 3–22). Thousand Oaks, CA: Sage.

Bednar, R., & Kaul, T. (1994). Experiential group research: Can the cannon fire? In A. Bergin & S. Garfield (Eds.), *Handbook of psychotherapy and behavior change* (4th ed., pp. 631–663). New York: John Wiley & Sons.

Best, J. W., & Kahn, J. V. (1986). *Research in education*. Englewood Cliffs, NJ: Prentice Hall.

Brantlinger, E., Jimenez, R., Klinger, J., Pugach, M., & Richardson, V. (2005). Qualitative studies in special education. *Exceptional Children, 71*, 195–207.

Burlingame, G. M., Fuhriman, A. J., & Johnson, J. (2004). Current status and future directions of group therapy research. In J. L. DeLucia-Waack, D. A. Gerrity, C. R. Kalodner, & M. T. Riva (Eds.), *Handbook of group counseling and psychotherapy* (pp. 651–660). Thousand Oaks, CA: Sage.

Cherry, A. L., Jr. (2000). *A research primer for the helping professions: Methods, statistics, and writing*. Belmont, CA: Brooks/Cole.

Coché, E., & Dies, R. R. (1981). Integrating research findings into the practice of group psychotherapy. *Psychotherapy: Theory, Research & Practice, 18*(4), 410–416.

Fuhriman, A., & Burlingame, G. M. (Eds.). (1994). *Handbook of group psychotherapy: An empirical and clinical synthesis*. New York: John Wiley & Sons.

Garvin, C. D., Gutierrez, L. M., & Galinsky, M. J. (2004). *Handbook of social work with groups*. New York: Guilford Press.

Gelso, C. J. (1993). On the making of a scientist-practitioner: A theory of research training in professional psychology. *Professional Psychology: Research and Practice, 24*, 368–476.

Gelso, C. J., Mallinckrodt, B., & Judge, A. B. (1996). Research training environment, attitudes toward research, and research self-efficacy: The revised research training environment scale. *Counseling Psychologist, 24*, 304–322.

Glaser, B. G. (1978). *Theoretical sensitivity: Advances in the methodology of grounded theory*. Mill Valley, CA: Sociology Press.

Glaser, B. G. (1998). *Doing grounded theory: Issues and discussions*. Mill Valley, CA: Sociology Press.

Glaser, B. G., & Strauss, A. L. (1967). *The discovery of grounded theory: Strategies for qualitative research*. Chicago: Aldine.

Hittleman, D. R., & Simon, A. J. (1997). *Interpreting educational research: An introduction for consumers of research*. Upper Saddle River, NJ: Prentice Hall.

Horne, A., & Rosenthal, R. (1997). Research in group work: How did we get where we are? *Journal for Specialists in Group Work, 22*, 228–240.

Horner, R. H., Carr, E. G., Halle, J., McGee, G., Odom, S., & Wolery, M. (2005). The use of single-subject research to identify evidence-based practice in special education. *Council for Exceptional Children, 71*(2), 165–179.

Ingersoll, G. M. (1998). Applying experimental methods to diabetes education research and evaluation. *Diabetes Educator, 24*(6), 751–759.

Kapila, S., & Moher, R. (1995, January). *Across disciplines: Principles for interdisciplinary research*. Ottawa, Canada: International Development Research Centre, Policy and Planning Group.

Kivlighan, D. M., Jr., Coleman, M. N., & Anderson, D. C. (2000). Process, outcome and methodology in group counseling research. In S. D. Brown & R. W. Lenf (Eds.), *Handbook of counseling psychology* (3rd ed., pp. 767–796). New York: John Wiley & Sons.

Kivlighan, D. M., & Holmes, S. E. (2004). The importance of therapeutic factors: A typology of therapeutic factors studies. In J. L. DeLucia-Waack, D. A. Gerrity, C. R. Kalodner, & M. T. Riva (Eds.), *Handbook of group counseling and psychotherapy* (pp. 23–36). Thousand Oaks, CA: Sage.

Kivlighan, D. M., Jr., & Luiza, J., (2005). Examining the credibility gap and the mum effect: Rex Stockton's contributions to research on feedback in counseling groups. *The Journal for Specialists in Group Work, 30*, 253–269.

Kosters, M., Burlingame, G., Nachtigall, C., & Strauss, B. (2006). A meta-analytic review of the effectiveness of inpatient group psychotherapy. *Group Dynamics: Theory, Research, and Practice, 10*, 146–163.

Martella, R., Nelson, J. R., & Marchand-Martella, N. (1999). *Research methods: Learning to become a critical consumer*. Boston: Allyn & Bacon.

McRoberts, C., Burlingame, G., & Hoag, M. (1998). Comparative efficacy of individual and group psychotherapy: A meta-analytic perspective. *Group Dynamics: Theory, Research, and Practice, 2*, 101–117.

Merriam, S. (1998). *Case study research in education: A qualitative approach*. San Francisco: Jossey-Bass.

Morran, D. K., & Stockton, R. (1985). Perspectives on group research programs. *The Journal for Specialists in Group Work, 10*(4), 186–191.

Polkinghorne, D. E. (1988). *Narrative knowing and the human sciences*. Albany, NY: SUNY Press.

Riva, M. T., & Kalodner, C., (1997). Group research: Encouraging a collaboration between practitioners and researchers. *Journal for Specialists in Group Work, 22*(4), 226–227.

Riva, M. T., Wachtel, M., & Lasky, G. B. (2004). Effective leadership in group counseling and psychotherapy. In J. L. DeLucia-Waack, D. A. Gerrity, C. R. Kalodner, & M. T. Riva (Eds.), *Handbook of group counseling and psychotherapy* F. Robison, personal communication, September 2005. (pp. 37–48). Thousand Oaks, CA: Sage.

Spradley, J. P. (1979). *The ethnographic interview*. New York: Harcourt Brace Jovanovich College Publishers.

Sprinthall, R. C., Schumutte, G. T., & Sirois, L. (1991). *Understanding educational research*. Englewood Cliffs, NJ: Prentice Hall.

Stake, R. E. (1994). Case studies. In N. K. Denzin & Y. S. Lincoln (Eds.), *Handbook of qualitative research* (pp. 236–247). Thousand Oaks, CA: Sage.

Stockton, R., Garbleman, J., Kaladow, J., Clawson, T., & Smith, C. (2002). Mental health practitioners and trainees. In *Mental Health, United States* (pp. 357–361). Washington, DC: Center for Mental Health Services, Department of Health and Human Services.

Stockton, R., & Hulse, D. (1983). The use of research teams to enhance competence in counseling research. *Counselor Education and Supervision, 22*, 303–310.

Stockton, R., Morran, D. K., & Krieger, K. M. (2004). An overview of current research and best practices for training beginning group leaders. In J. L. DeLucia-Waack, D. A. Gerrity, C. R. Kalodner, & M. T. Riva (Eds.), *Handbook of group counseling and psychotherapy* (pp. 65–75). Thousand Oaks, CA: Sage.

Stockton, R., Toth, P. L., & Morran, D. K. (2006). The case for group research. In J. P. Trotzer *The counselor and the group* (4th ed.). New York: Routledge.

Strauss, A. L., & Corbin, J. (1990). *Basics of qualitative research: Grounded theory procedures and techniques*. Newbury Park, CA: Sage.

Trotzer, J. P. (2006). *The counselor and the group* (4th ed.). New York: Routledge.

Ward, D. E. (2005). Introducing a special issue on the contributions of Rex Stockton. *The Journal for Specialists in Group Work, 30*(3), 197–198.

Whittenbaum, G. M., & Moreland, R. L. (2008). Small groups research in social psychology: Topics and trends over time. *Social & Personality Psychology Compass, 2*(1), 187–203.

Yalom, I. D. (1995). *The theory and practice of group psychotherapy* (4th ed.). New York: Basic Books.

Assessing Groups

Jonathan P. Schwartz, Michael Waldo, *and* Margaret Schwartz Moravec

Abstract

Assessment is critical to understanding the outcomes and processes inherent in group counseling. However, assessment in groups is often ignored or attempted utilizing measures with poor psychometrics. The purpose of this chapter is to explore the various purposes of assessment in group counseling, followed by a summary of different types of assessment that may be used. Strengths and weaknesses of various assessments and research designs will also be discussed, along with implications for best practice.

Keywords: group, assessment, dynamics, counseling, process

The often-posed question "If a tree falls in the forest and there is no one there to hear it, does it make a sound?" has relevance to group work. One answer is "Yes, it probably makes a sound, but if no one perceives it, it doesn't matter." Perception may not be reality, but it is the reality that is perceived that matters. This is certainly true in group work. While many practitioners undoubtedly believe that they lead successful psychotherapy groups, if the group outcomes and processes are not measured, perception of change may be impossible. However, group processes and outcomes are sufficiently nebulous to intimidate even the most optimistic of scientists and practitioners. To observe and understand these phenomena, it is essential to have verifiable methods of categorizing and quantifying group events (Bednar & Kaul, 1986, 1994; Stockton & Hulse, 1981). Furthermore, these methods will be most helpful if they are tied to relevant theory, demonstrate reliability, and show valid relationships to each other. Unfortunately, when group assessment does occur, it has historically lacked reliable and valid instruments, often utilizing measures constructed by the researchers for the purpose of the study (Riva & Smith, 1997).

Challenges of Assessment in Groups

There are challenges inherent in all forms of psychological assessment; for example, one challenge is that it is difficult to measure fleetingly observed (or often not even directly observed) aspects of human experience (Goodwin, 1998). The systemic nature of group interaction makes assessment geometrically more complex in groups. All incidents in groups can be seen as interdependent because they are influenced by the interpersonal context in which they occur (Yalom, 2005). Any one member's experience can be seen as dependent on other members' behaviors, reducing the relevance of ideographic measurement. Additional systemic influences include the maturation of the group over time, external influences on the group, and the context in which the group occurs. For example, as the group matures, unique dynamics will occur within the group as a whole (e.g., group cohesion) that will impact each member in similar and somewhat unique ways (Kivlighan & Lilly, 1997; Schwartz & Waldo, 1999). Further, the setting in which the group occurs (e.g., inpatient, outpatient) and local and national events (e.g., economic outlook) will also have a systemic impact on the group.

Another critical aspect of assessment in groups is defined by a continuum. At one end of the continuum, assessment can focus on the entire group (i.e., stages of group). At the other end of the continuum, assessment can focus on individual members (i.e., symptom reduction). Furthermore, all levels of this continuum interact with each other. That is, whole-group dynamics impact individual behavior and individual behavior impacts whole-group dynamics (Yalom, 2005). Recognizing this interaction is critical to assessment in groups.

Interdependence of Measures in Groups

Interaction and interdependence are thought to make groups a powerful approach to counseling. Unfortunately, the fact that the group is impactful because of the interaction of the group and the fact that each member makes unique progress also complicate the use of inferential statistics to analyze measures from group members (Anderson & Ager, 1978; Kenny & Judd, 1996; Kenny & LaVoie, 1985; Sadler & Judd, 2001; Zaccaro, Cracraft, & Marks, 2006). Inferential statistics assume that measures are independent. It is argued that the assumption of independence is not met when analyzing measures of different members of the same group because the members affect each other (Kenny, Mannetti, Oierro, Livi, & Kashy, 2002; Kenny & Judd, 1996; Kenny, Kashy, & Bolger, 1998). This problem is most obvious with process measures. For example, if a group achieves a cohesive atmosphere, it is likely that a number of members will report experiencing higher levels of cohesion. Each member's experience is related to the experience of the others. An argument can also be made that individual members' outcomes from group counseling are not independent of each other. For example, is it fair to believe that one member's development of assertiveness skills in a counseling group that is focused on assertion is independent of other members' learning and using those skills? It seems likely that part of why successful assertiveness groups are successful is the modeling and reinforcement that occur between group members. For these reasons, some authors believe statistical analysis of assessments of group members must assume interdependence between assessments (Bednar & Kaul, 1978; Kenny & Judd, 1996; Kenny & LaVoie, 1985; Zaccaro et al., 2006).

As a result, they suggest that the appropriate statistical procedures for group-assessment data assume that each group (as opposed to each group member) is the unit of analysis. This is an impactful suggestion because it means that the number of groups, rather than the number of group members, will be used for computing parametric statistics. Large numbers of groups/group data are needed (typically $n = 30$ or greater) to find statistically significant results through parametric statistics. The implication is that for parametric statistics research needs to be done on 30 groups, as opposed to 30 group members. Because it often is not practical to conduct research on that many groups, it has been suggested that nonparametric statistics be used to analyze data from groups. Nonparametric statistics can be conducted on fewer measures. However, nonparametric statistics typically are not as sensitive for detecting significant results. For this reason, many authors conducting group-counseling research ignore concerns about interdependence of data and analyze data from individual group members using parametric statistics (Brooks, Guerney, & Mazza, 2002; Kingsep, Nathan, & Castle, 2003; Martin & Thienemann, 2005).

Needs Assessment: Determining Group Goals and Process

One important function of assessment in group work is determining what goals will be met by the group. Careful attention to the needs of the population that will be served by the group shows respect for their concerns and allows counselors to target the group's goals to directly address those concerns (Trotzer, 2000). For example, adolescents who are at risk of gang involvement might identify lack of opportunities, isolation, and boredom as persistent irritants in their lives. Group work focused on helping participants recognize their potential, connect with each other, and engage in compelling activities could address these needs and reduce the potential for gang involvement. A needs assessment can also guide group process (Schlosser, 1993).

Understanding the participants' perceptions of their needs allows group leaders to choose formats and to foster interactions that are relevant to those needs (Trotzer, 2004). For example, adolescents are at a developmental stage that makes establishing identity and involvement with peers particularly compelling (Erikson, 1968). Group processes in line with these needs could include engaging participants in interviewing each other and exchanging feedback about strengths and areas for growth.

Three common methods of needs assessment are (1) accessing previously existing data about the target population, (2) interviewing key informants, and (3) collecting data directly from the population.

Each will be described and illustrated using the example of adolescents at risk of gang involvement.

USING EXISTING DATA AND OBSERVATIONS

Typically, there is abundant information available on any target population. One source for existing data is published literature. Primary in this category are scientific reports in professional journals and books. Sources on adolescents include the *Journal of Adolescent Research, Journal of Youth and Adolescence*, and *Youth at Risk: A Prevention Resource for Counselors, Teachers, and Parents* (Capuzzi & Gross, 2005). Journalism may also be a helpful source of relevant information. Newspaper and magazine articles can provide information about a target population that is both timely and local. For example, a newspaper article describing teens' involvement in a skateboarding contest could provide information on local activities that adolescents have found compelling. Another source for existing data resides in the institutions that interact with the target population. For adolescents, such institutions might include schools (e.g., graduation rates, involvement in extracurricular activities, truancy and disciplinary actions), social services (e.g., welfare, food stamps), and police (e.g., arrest records). There are a number of advantages to using existing data. A central advantage is that accessing the data does not require contact with and cooperation from the target population, avoiding inconveniencing them and the time and effort it may take to reach them. Many at-risk adolescents are reluctant to provide professionals with information about their experience, increasing the value of accessing existing data. Existing data are also typically available from a continuum of levels (e.g., global, national, regional, local) and time periods (e.g., distant past, recent past, present, future projections) and can be compared to identify locations with accented need and/or trends in needs (Hatry, 1994; Nardi, 2003; Zaitzow & Fields, 2006).

INTERVIEWING KEY INFORMANTS

A disadvantage of using existing data to assess needs is that the questions that can be asked are limited by the nature of the data that have already been collected (Hulley, Cummings, Browner, Grady, & Newman, 2007; Nardi, 2003). This limitation is overcome in the second major approach to needs assessment, interviewing key informants. This method involves identifying people who have knowledge about the needs of a target population and are willing to share that knowledge (Marshall, 1996; Tremblay, 1957). Key informants can include people who work with or serve the target population. Continuing with the example of adolescents at risk for gang involvement, key informants could be teachers, coaches, counselors, police, and physicians. Key informants can also be family members and friends of the target population as well as other members of the population. Leaders and other well-networked members of the population make particularly useful key informants because they can speak about both their own experience and their knowledge of others' experience. Interviewing allows the asking of questions that are directly relevant to group counseling. Open-ended questions like, "In what ways do you think adolescents could benefit from group counseling?" are often the most productive because they allow the interviewees to provide any information they think is relevant. Interviewing also allows follow-up questions that emerge from the initial information the interviewee provides. For example, if the interviewee indicated that adolescents might develop positive peer relationships in a group, the interviewer might ask, "What kind of peer relationships would be most beneficial for adolescents?" A third advantage to interviewing key informants is that the process of interviewing can develop relationships that are helpful in establishing and maintaining groups. Key informants can assist in identifying resources for groups, recruiting group members, and supporting group member involvement.

COLLECTING DATA DIRECTLY FROM THE POPULATION

While existing data and interviewing can provide valuable insights into group participants' needs, they do not directly measure the target population. Potential group participants' needs can be assessed efficiently through questionnaires and standardized measures. Standardized measures have the advantage of allowing comparisons between potential group members' responses and those of norm groups (Gehart, 2009). Examples of standardized measures related to adolescents include the Adolescent Adjustment Screening Inventory (Reynolds, 2001) and the Gang Membership Inventory (Pillen & Hoewing-Roberson, 1992). When these instruments are given to potential group members, they can be used as screening tools. In addition to quantifying needs, questionnaires and standardized measures have the advantage of potentially serving as outcome measures. If participants take the measures prior to and at the termination of the group, their pre-and postgroup scores can be compared to determine if there have been gains.

Assessment for Preparation and Screening of Group Members

From a professional ethics perspective, perhaps the most important function of assessment in group work is related to screening potential members (Gladding, 2008; Rapin, 2004). One of the characteristics that distinguishes group from individual counseling is the reduced ability of the counselor to modify the group in response to the emerging needs of an individual member. Once a group is running, leaders need to attend to the needs of all members. Dramatically altering the membership, goals, or process of the group to meet one member's needs could detract from other members' experience. Also, group leaders are not able to fully control the behavior of other members, making it uncertain whether leaders can modify the group in a sufficiently flexible and timely fashion to accommodate the needs of one member (Yalom, 2005). For these reasons, it is important that there be a good match between potential members' needs and the goals and process of the group *before* members join the group. And the stakes are high. Extensive research indicates that members who are inappropriately placed in a group are likely to have a negative experience that detracts from their adjustment and development (Gladding, 2008; Corey, 2008; Rapin, 2004; Yalom, 2005).

In addition, research suggests that inappropriately placed members detract from the experience of other members (Yalom, 2005). Often, inappropriately placed members end up withdrawing from groups, or they are asked to leave. Unplanned termination of group members has also been shown to detract from the member's well-being and the group's functioning (Rapin, 2004).

Clearly, appropriate placement of members in groups is an essential component of competent group practice. An important first step in assessment and a key source of information is from the referral source (Klein, 1983). Assessment plays a critical role in determining if members are appropriate for groups. Pregroup assessment of members includes measuring their needs and/or symptoms that are related to the group's goals, their motivation for involvement, and their capacity to engage in the group's process. Assessment related to each of these areas will be described (Table 14.1).

Needs and Symptoms

Research suggests that group members will value and benefit from groups that address their concerns (American Counseling Association, 2005; Brabender, Smolar, & Fallon, 2004; Corey, 2008). The previous section on needs assessment presented measures that can be used to assess group members' needs. Examining how members' needs, as determined by these assessments, fit with a group's goals

Table 14.1 Group assessments guide

Purpose	Type	Sample Measure
Preparation and screening		
	Needs/symptoms	Symptom Checklist-90
	Motivation for treatment	Group-specific questions
	Capacity to engage in process	Beck Anxiety Inventory
	Interpersonal skills	Interpersonal Reactivity Index
	Interpersonal styles	Fundamental Interpersonal Relations Orientation–Behavior
Postgroup assessment/ outcomes		
	Group outcome	Group Therapy Questionnaire
Group process		
	Therapeutic factors	Critical Incident Questionnaire
	Leadership	Leadership Effectiveness and Adaptability Descriptor

is a valid way of determining group membership. For example, potential members' scores on the Symptom Checklist-90 Revised (Derogatis, 1994) could be used to guide their referral to groups. Potential members who scored high on the Depression scale could be referred to a group offering cognitive-behavioral treatment of mood disorders, while potential group members who scored high on the Interpersonal Sensitivity scale could be referred to a group focusing on improving interpersonal relations. In contrast, a potential participant who scored high on the Psychoticism scale is unlikely to be appropriate for either of these groups.

Other measures that can be used to assess potential members' needs and symptoms include examples such as the Minnesota Multiphasic Personality Inventory-2 (Butcher et al., 2001), the Millon Clinical Multiaxial Inventory (Millon, Davis, & Millon, 1997), and the California Psychological Inventory (Gough, 1987). A number of experts have suggested individual structured interviews to assess potential members, which provide a more interactional assessment while protecting confidentiality (Couch, 1995; Jacobs, Masson, & Harvill, 2009).

Motivation

There is abundant evidence suggesting that the most important variable in determining if members will remain engaged and have a positive group experience is their belief that the group can help them and their motivation to participate (Seligman, 1995). Motivated participants consistently attend groups, follow through on suggestions that arise from the group, and put up with minor frustrations (like sharing time with other members) when their needs are not being met by the group.

Because motivation to participate in a group may be best measured in response to a particular group's goals and process, the best ways to assess motivation may be group-specific. One assessment procedure that has been successfully employed is to present an orientation to a group and then ask potential members to respond verbally and/or in writing to the following questions:

1. *What do you understand to be the goals and process of this group?* If potential members are not able to answer this question accurately, it suggests the possibility that they are not fully informed about the group and are not in a position to benefit from it.

2. *In what ways do you think this group will help you achieve the goals you plan on pursuing by*

participating? Potential members' answers to this question can offer a clear picture of how the group's goals fit the goals of the potential members.

3. *In what ways do you think you will enjoy participating in this group? What aspects of group participation do you think you will not enjoy?* Answers to these questions can point to process expectations that can either motivate potential participants or make them disinclined to fully commit themselves to group participation.

Evidence that potential members are not motivated to be in a group or that their motivation is based on a mistaken understanding of the group's goals or process can be used to screen out members who are unlikely to benefit from the group. This information can also be used as a basis for efforts to correct misunderstanding among potential members and educate them about the benefits they might receive through group participation. Often, efforts to correct problems with motivation that are identified through assessment before the group begins are successful at preparing members for beneficial participation.

Capacity to Engage in Group Process

Successful group counseling typically requires members to engage in specific interpersonal behaviors (Joyce, McCallum, Piper, & Ogrodniczuk, 2000; Martin, Garske, & Davis, 2000; Sotsky et al., 1991). These behaviors include nonverbal attending, self-disclosure, expressing emotions, empathic listening, and giving and receiving feedback. Members need to be able to focus on their own issues and share their experience, as well as focus on other members' issues and experience. Group members who are significantly less able to engage in these activities than the majority of other members are likely both to have a negative experience themselves and to detract from other members' experience (Yalom, 2005).

Several measurement procedures have been found to be helpful in assessing potential group members' ability to engage in the group-counseling process. Measures of interpersonal anxiety are useful in determining if potential group members will struggle with self-disclosure and dialog. Measures of interpersonal anxiety include the Beck Anxiety Inventory (Beck & Steer, 1990), the Endler Multidimensional Anxiety Scales (Endler, Edwards, & Vitelli, 1991), and the State-Trait Anxiety Inventory (Spielberger, Gorsuch, & Lushene, 1970).

Interpersonal Skills

A second area of assessment that is relevant to group process is level of interpersonal skills. In particular, measures of assertiveness and empathy can offer indices of how well potential members will be able to express themselves and relate to others during group interaction. Examples of measures of assertiveness include the Adult Self-Expression Scale (Gay, Hollandsworth, & Galassi, 1975), the Rathus Assertiveness Schedule (Rathus, 1973), and the Wolpe-Lazarus Assertiveness Scale (Wolpe & Lazarus, 1966). Measures of empathic ability include the Interpersonal Reactivity Index (Davis, 1980), the Empathy Quotient (Baron-Cohen & Wheelwright, 2004); the Basic Empathy Scale (Jolliffe & Farrington, 2006), and the Davis Empathy Scale (Davis, 1994).

Interpersonal Styles

Potential members' interpersonal styles are a third area of assessment that is relevant to group process. Members may be predominantly passive, aggressive, expressive, withdrawn, dependent, or collaborative. Assessment of all potential members' interpersonal styles can allow group leaders to speculate about how the members will interact with each other. For example, a member who has a passive style may consistently defer to a member who has a more aggressive style. Assessing how members' interpersonal styles will fit with other members of the group can inform decisions about group membership. One measure of interpersonal style is the Fundamental Interpersonal Relations Orientation–Behavior (Schutz, 1992), which measures aspects of interpersonal relations and has demonstrated the ability to predict task and work group effectiveness (Armstrong & Priola, 2001). The Hill Interaction Matrix-B (HIM-B) (Hill, 1965) was designed to classify interaction styles of prospective group members. The HIM-B was found to predict prospective group members' willingness to engage in therapeutic work (Stockton, Robison, & Morran, 1983). The Group Psychotherapy Evaluation Scale (Kew, 1975) was created to measure whether potential group members have the interpersonal skills to be successful in group.

Another approach to assessing potential members' ability to engage in group process is to provide them an opportunity to experience and respond to processes that are likely to occur in the group. This can occur by having potential members read an example of a group interaction, review a recording of the group, engage in a role-play of group interaction, and/or attend group on a trial basis (Gladding, 2008). In each situation, the potential members can be asked how they would respond. Potential problematic responses can be identified and addressed prior to inclusion of the member in the group.

Typically, there are no absolute values of needs/ symptoms, motivation, or capacity to engage in group process that can be used to determine if a potential member should be included. Instead, these assessments inform group leaders' clinical judgment about membership. One method for exercising clinical judgment is to compare assessment of a potential member to the average values on the same assessment for other group members. Research suggests that members who are distinctly different from other members on important variables are more likely to have a negative experience in the group (Yalom, 2005). They are also more likely to detract from other members' experience. However, identification of members whose assessment results suggest that they may not fit with the group need not result in their being excluded. Instead, steps can be taken to address the mismatch so that it presents less of a problem and may even become a source of benefit, both for the potential group member and for the group as a whole. For example, a potential member who lacks assertion skills could be made aware of this deficit and offered help in using the group as a place to practice assertiveness. Or a potential member of an interpersonal skills group who is suffering from depression could be encouraged to explore how developing more positive interpersonal relations could help with depression. In these ways, pregroup assessment can contribute as much to group member preparation as to screening.

Use of Assessments as Part of Group Process

In addition to the aforementioned functions, pregroup assessment can be employed to deepen group process. When members are made aware of their scores on relevant variables, as well as the scores of other members, they can use that information to establish goals, focus feedback, and assess progress. For example, a group focused on fostering development and interpersonal relations employed pregroup measures of participants' development, attachment style, and communication skills (Schwartz, Waldo, & Halperin, 1999). Scores on these measures were interpreted to participants as part of the group process. Limitations of the measures were stressed during interpretation, and members were asked to judge for themselves if the measures depicted them accurately. Members were then offered opportunities to share their scores and their thoughts about their scores with each other. Members were encouraged to decline to share scores if they were uncomfortable doing so. Members chose to share their scores, and the leaders felt the information had a profoundly positive effect on the group process. During this task one member said a measure of personal development suggested that he has had difficulty establishing his identity. He said he was not sure if that was true and asked for feedback from other members about whether he seemed to lack identity. Another member said the same measure suggested she is facing challenges in developing intimate relationships. She said that she agreed and that she would like to work on relating well with other members in the group. A third member said a measure of communication style suggested she could benefit from increasing her assertiveness skills and expressed that she would like to practice being more assertive in the group. In these ways, shared awareness of their group development issues enhanced participants' use of the group interaction to promote their growth in their individual developmental areas. Similar use could be made of any of the assessments described.

Postgroup Assessment

There are advantages to assessing clients at the end of their participation in groups. Postgroup assessment provides information about how clients are functioning at termination. Postgroup assessment using the same instruments that were administered at the beginning of group allows clients to assess their progress by comparing how they were functioning prior to counseling with their functioning when they end. Information from this kind of assessment can help clients recognize and consolidate the gains they have made. It may help them commit to the changes they have made that enabled those gains and motivate them to continue to generalize what they have learned in group to other situations in their life outside of group. It may also increase their appreciation for the group and the likelihood that they will recommend the group to others and/or return to it in the future if they feel the need. When assessment indicates that there is room for further improvement, postgroup assessment can be used to motivate clients to seek further services and guide what services they will receive. Postgroup measures also can be used to evaluate the overall effectiveness of the group when they are used for outcomes assessment.

Group Outcomes Assessment

The call for accountability in counseling has become ubiquitous (Astramovich & Coker, 2007; Bleuer, 1983; Norcross, Beutler, & Levant, 2006; Vacc, Rhyne-Winkler, & Poidevant, 1993). Efforts to demonstrate that counseling is effective began in the middle of the twentieth century and have expanded in response to the rising costs of health care. However, counseling efficacy is more than just an economic concern; ethical standards regarding beneficence and nonmaleficence dictate that counselors employ effective approaches that cause no harm. Outcomes assessment is central to ensuring ethical counseling practice and may be even more important in group work than in individual counseling. Group counseling as an intervention strategy is approximately half the age of individual counseling and is less well accepted by professionals and the general public. Also, group counseling has a checkered record. Imprudent use of group techniques in the 1960s and 1970s resulted in group counseling developing a reputation as a procedure that was frivolous at best and dangerous at worst. In fact, research on the problems emerging from those groups served as the impetus for development of best-practice ethical standards for group work. Fortunately, since that time a tremendous amount of outcome research has demonstrated that group counseling is both safe and effective (Bednar & Kaul, 1978, 1994; Bruce, Getch, & Ziomek-Daigle, 2009; Burlingame, Fuhriman, & Mosier, 2003; Cox & Merkel, 1989; Lieberman, Yalom, & Miles, 1973; Nelson, Dykeman, Powell, & Petty, 1996; Page & Chandler, 1994; Riva & Haub, 2004; Wen, Zhang, & Li, 2006; Yalom, 2005). However, the continuously changing populations served and concerns addressed through group counseling, contexts in which groups are offered, and leadership techniques that are employed dictate that group-counseling outcome research be an ongoing effort.

The previous sections in this chapter offer examples of variables that are relevant to outcomes assessment. Measures of group participants' needs prior to engaging in counseling can be compared to their needs after group involvement to assess the impact of the group. Similarly, measures that are used in pregroup preparation and screening of members can be used as posttests to assess the gains members have made. Measures used to evaluate group-counseling outcomes typically can be categorized into one or more of the following domains: measures that assess clients' subjective experience of well-being, measures that compare clients to recognized "objective" models of healthy functioning and/or development, and measures of how clients' status and/or behavior are viewed by society. Examples of measures employed to evaluate group-counseling outcomes within each domain will be described.

CLIENTS' SUBJECTIVE EXPERIENCE OF WELL-BEING

These instruments ask clients to report how they feel they are doing in relation to any of a wide variety of criteria. Examples include the Symptom Checklist-90 Revised (Derogatis, 1994), which asks clients to rate their experience of symptoms, and the Tennessee Self-Concept Scale (Roid & Fitts, 1991), which asks clients to rate their level of self-esteem. The advantages of these kinds of measures include their flexibility in assessing a variety of variables, their ease of administration, and that they relate directly to clients' experience, making them easy for clients to understand and value. When clients report a reduction in symptoms or an increase in self-esteem following participation in group counseling, those changes are readily recognized as beneficial. Criticisms of these measures include the potential that clients can misrepresent their experience and that how clients feel may not be of central importance. Other examples of instruments to assess clients' subjective experience include the Beck Depression Inventory (Beck, Ward, Mendelson, Mock, & Erbaugh, 1961), the Millon Clinical Multiaxial Inventory (Millon et al., 1997), and the Rosenberg Self-Esteem Scale (Rosenberg, 1965).

MEASURES THAT ATTEMPT TO OBJECTIVELY ASSESS CLIENTS IN RELATION TO MODELS OF HEALTH AND DEVELOPMENT

These instruments compare how clients are functioning in relation to recognized models of health and/or development. Examples include assertiveness scales that look at clients' interpersonal skills and differentiation scales that assess levels of differentiation in interpersonal relations. An advantage of these instruments is that they go beyond clients' subjective report and assess clients in relation to what is considered an objective standard. When group participants show positive changes on these instruments, it is possible to say the group has promoted health and/or development. However, reliable and valid instruments that objectively assess health and development are hard to develop and, as a result, are relatively uncommon. Also, questions arise about what characteristics of client functioning can be objectively determined as

healthy. Differences in how health is defined in different cultures show that universal, objective definitions are hard to come by.

MEASURES OF HOW CLIENTS' STATUS AND/OR BEHAVIOR ARE VIEWED BY SOCIETY

These measures are considered by some to be the most concrete and objective because they assess societal definitions of clients' status or functioning, rather than relying on clients' self-reports. Examples include criminal convictions and employment status. When men who participate in an anger-management counseling group show a lower rate of recidivism for domestic violence than similar men who did not participate in a group, the result suggests that the group is effective. In addition to being perceived as highly objective, this form of assessment has the advantages of not requiring clients to complete instruments and of often being directly related to institutional and/or economic objectives. For example, if group counseling results in more students graduating from high school and getting jobs, there typically are few questions about the meaning or value of the result. Disadvantages of this form of measurement include difficulty in accessing relevant data (often these data are buried in institutional records and/or confidential), that many variables might impact the outcomes that have no relation to group involvement (like a downturn in the economy), and that participants may not have the same values as society or institutions. For example, adolescents' abstinence from involvement with sex or drugs is highly valued by high schools but often not seen as a goal by adolescents.

These differences in strengths and potential problems with the subjective, objective, and societal perspectives on outcomes assessments argue for using all three in conjunction. Assessing clients' subjective experiences allows flexible measurement of an array of variables that are likely to be immediately affected by groups. Assessing improvements in clients' functioning in relation to an accepted measure of health or development offers evidence that clients have achieved real and lasting benefits from group participation. Assessing changes in clients' status in society potentially demonstrates the long-term impact of the group. And assessment in all three areas allows demonstration of how they are related. For example, group career counseling might result in participants feeling more confident about their career choices, those choices being aligned with their interests and abilities, and their subsequent career success. Of course, assessment in all three areas requires more time and effort on the part of group leaders and members. One way to overcome this problem is to find a measure in one of the areas that has been shown to have a significant relationship to measures in other areas. For example, self-esteem has been shown to relate to students' emotional adjustment and success in school, suggesting that groups that raise self-esteem also impact emotional adjustment and academic progress. Examples of group outcome measures that have shown solid relationships with other indices of well-being include the Group Therapy Questionnaire (Krogel, Burlingame, & Gleave, 2006) and the NEO-Five Factor Inventory (Ogrodniczuk, Piper, Joyce, McCallum, & Rosie, 2003).

Use of assessment in determining group outcome requires a variety of research designs. Similar to the differing methods of assessment, each research design has its respective strengths and limitations. However, a thorough review of research designs for evaluating group outcome is beyond the scope of this chapter. A few common designs will be offered as examples, including their advantages and disadvantages.

POSTTEST-ONLY DESIGN

This is perhaps the simplest design and has the advantage of being easy to implement (Campbell, Stanley, & Gage, 1963). Assessment instruments are given when members complete their participation in a group. If the participants have positive scores on these instruments, it suggests the group was helpful. For example, after participating in a counseling group focused on assertion, members could be given an instrument assessing assertiveness. If they score high on assertiveness, it would seem that the group was successful. However, a distinct disadvantage of this design is that there is no way of knowing if the participants might have received the same scores on the instruments whether they had participated in the group or not. A second disadvantage is that if there are no norms on the measures, it is hard to be sure what scores should be considered positive.

PRETEST, POSTTEST DESIGN

This design is also very simple and relatively easy to implement in group-counseling practice. In this design, participants complete instruments relevant to the group's goals prior to and at the conclusion of the group. The pregroup administration of the measure can be part of the member preparation and screening process, and the postgroup administration

can be used for outcomes assessment and to assist in making decisions about referral for other services. Comparing pre- and posttest scores for all group members offers evidence regarding the average amount of change participants achieve. If pre and post measures are available on enough participants, statistical tests can be employed to assess if the changes achieved by participants are statistically significant. Lack of positive change is compelling evidence that counseling groups are not effective, suggesting that modification in the group goals and/or procedures is warranted. Positive changes in participants' scores offer some evidence that counseling groups are effective. However, there are problems with the pretest, posttest design that limit confidence in positive findings (Campbell et al., 1963). First, it is possible that something besides the group caused the improvements in clients. Often, people who experience problems grow out of them naturally or find ways to overcome them without formal help. Group members may have improved with or without group participation. Also, with regard to statistical significance, there is potentially a difference between statistically significant change and clinically significant change. For example, if enough people are tested, an average 3-point change on a 100-point assertiveness scale will be statistically significant, even though a 3-point change may make no clinically discernable difference in how any one group member relates to others.

EXTENDED BASELINE DESIGN

Including an extended baseline is a modification of the pretest, posttest design for group outcome assessment that also fits well with counseling practice, while offering some evidence to suggest that clients would not have changed without participating in the group. In this design, potential participants are given measures when they first indicate interest in joining a group, again at the beginning of the first meeting of the group, and again when they complete their participation. Because it usually takes at least a week or two (often quite a bit longer) to arrange for a group to begin and to get members started, comparing the first assessment to the assessment at the first meeting provides information on whether members are changing without participating in the group. Comparing changes that occur before they are in the group to changes that occur when they are in the group offers reasonably good evidence of the impact of the group. A disadvantage of this approach is that members have to take the same instruments at least three times. Additionally, it is still possible that members would have changed without group participation but that change would not have occurred until around the time they started participating in the group.

RANDOM ASSIGNMENT WAIT LIST CONTROL GROUP DESIGN

This group outcomes–assessment design addresses many of the problems of the designs already mentioned, while still fitting reasonably well with typical counseling practice. This design works when there are potentially more people available to participate in groups than there are groups available to serve them, as is common in many situations. Typically, what happens in group-counseling practice is that the extra people are placed on a wait list to receive service as soon as an opening in a group becomes available. If all people interested in participating in a group (those who can immediately be served and those who have to wait for service) are assessed prior to any one joining a group and again after those who were able to enter groups complete their involvement, then the people on the wait list can serve as a control group. If people who receive immediate service show gains in comparison to the people on the wait list, then this suggests the group, as opposed to natural development or other sources of help, is responsible for the change. Evidence that it is the group that causes the change is particularly compelling if potential participants are randomly assigned to the immediate group or the wait list. Random assignment makes it unlikely that some other factor (like how badly a member wanted to get in a group) caused the difference in how group participants and wait list control group members progressed. Statistically and clinically significant positive changes for randomly assigned group participants in comparison to those randomly assigned to a wait list offer compelling evidence that a counseling group is effective. Random assignment of potential clients to a wait list seems fair and ethically defendable if all potential clients cannot be served. Problems arise with this outcomes assessment design if one or both of these assumptions are not true. In many situations there are barely enough potential group members available to make up a viable group. And often, when there are more clients seeking group services than there are groups, decisions regarding who is served first are based on how extensive and pressing the individual clients' needs are, rather than random assignment.

Assessing Group Process

Understanding the underlying dynamics that make group successful is one of the key facets of group assessment. This is particularly challenging since the dynamics that occur in group are difficult to measure directly. In this section, the following aspects of group process will be reviewed: therapeutic factors, group leadership, and group dynamics and stages.

Therapeutic Factors

In addressing assessment in group work, a seminal question is what actually causes or is the mechanism of change for those participating in group. There has been extensive research on the therapeutic factors that are responsible for the change that occurs through group. There are currently 11 accepted therapeutic factors that create change in group counseling (Yalom, 2005). These factors are instillation of hope, universality, imparting information, altruism, the corrective recapitulation of the primary family group, development of socializing techniques, imitative behavior, interpersonal learning, group cohesiveness, catharsis, and existential learning. The therapeutic factor of group cohesiveness has received the most attention in the literature as the best measure of the relationship factor in group counseling (American Group Psychotherapy Association, 2007; Burlingame, Fuhriman, & Johnson, 2002; Yalom, 2005). Theory and research suggest that some factors are more prevalent at the beginning of the group (e.g., universality), while other factors may take longer to develop (e.g., cohesion) (Waldo, 1985; Kivlighan & Lilly, 1997; Schwartz & Waldo, 1999).

Assessing therapeutic factors in group work has typically consisted of two different methods, direct and indirect (Bloch & Crouch, 1985). The "critical incident" analysis is an example of the indirect approach. Participants are asked to describe the most significant incident that happened in group, and then experts use a qualitative rating scale to identify the primary therapeutic factor that is evident in the description (MacKenzie, 1987). This approach has been criticized for the lack of standardized and validated methods for rating the factors (Kivlighan, Multon, & Brossard, 1996). The Q-sort protocol is an example of the direct approach to measuring therapeutic factors (Yalom, 1970, 1995). The Q-sort consists of 60 statements that assess 12 therapeutic factors. Unfortunately, there is a lack of psychometric data on the reliability and validity of the Q-sort (MacNair-Semands & Lese, 2000), and it should be used with caution.

Group Leadership

One critical group-counseling process variable that has received considerable assessment attention is group leadership. Group leaders' impact on group process and outcome is considered to be both pervasive and profound (Gladding, 2008; Riva, Wachtel, & Lasky, 2004). Measuring differences in leadership styles and functions offers the potential for identifying the relationships between specific leadership behaviors and counseling group effectiveness. This information could guide leaders' responses to specific group situations and eventually guide how leaders are selected and trained.

Initial conceptualizations of group counselor leadership organized counselors' styles along a continuum related to authoritarianism. At one end of the continuum, leaders who exercise very little control over their groups were typified as laissez-faire (Capuzzi & Gross, 2002; Gladding, 2008; Hansen, Warner, & Smith, 1986; Lewin, 1939). These leaders offer minimal direction to the group and may not even be very actively involved in the group's activities. At the other end of the continuum are authoritarian leaders (Capuzzi & Gross, 2002; Gladding, 2008; Hansen et al., 1986; Lewin, 1939). These leaders are highly involved in directing the group and may allow few opportunities for members to take responsibility for the group's activities. The leadership style at the center of this continuum was described as "democratic." Democratic leaders provide facilitative direction to groups, while inviting members to take initiative and responsibility for the group's activities. An example of a scale that has been employed to measure leaders along this continuum is the Multifactor Leader Questionnaire (Bass & Avolio, 1990).

Subsequent approaches to assessing group leadership have criticized the single-continuum perspective as too limited. One popular revision of the single-continuum assessment model, the Leadership Effectiveness and Adaptability Descriptor (LEAD), employs two interacting continuums (Hersey & Blanchard, 1973). One continuum assesses the extent to which leaders are involved in the tasks associated with the groups. A second continuum assesses the extent to which leaders are involved in relationships with and between group members. The two continuums form a matrix that describes four different descriptions of leaders, as follows: high-task/low-relationship leaders, who are invested and direct the task while being minimally involved in relationships; high-task/high-relationship leaders, who are actively involved in both moving the task forward and relating closely with members; low-task/high-relationship leaders, who leave pursuit of the task more in the hands of group members but remain very involved in group member relations; and low-task/low-relationship leaders, who are minimally involved in group tasks or relations.

An addition in this popular leadership-assessment approach is the recognition that leadership styles can and probably should vary depending on the needs of the group (Gladding, 2008; Jacobs et al., 2009). Termed "situational leadership," this assessment approach measures leaders' propensity to adapt their leadership style in relation to the group's level of maturity. New groups and/or immature groups are thought to function more effectively with high-task/low-relationship leaders. As groups begin to mature, they benefit from leaders who become increasingly involved with relationships in the group, while remaining invested in the task. As the group continues to mature, leaders can support members as they take increasing levels of responsibility for the group's tasks. When groups have fully matured, leaders can reduce their involvement, allowing members to take responsibility for both the group's tasks and relationships. In addition to assessing leaders' primary and secondary leadership styles, the LEAD assesses leaders' ability to flexibly respond in a style that is appropriate to the needs of the group (Hersey & Blanchard, 1976).

Group Dynamics and Stages

There is significant evidence that groups develop and mature over time in a somewhat reliable and predictable fashion. A number of group models have theorized how groups develop in a systematized way through phases or stages (Beck, 1974; Bion, 1961; LeBon, 1910; MacKenzie, 1994). The accepted group models view group development as epigenetic, with each stage building on the successful completion of the prior stage (Schwartz & Waldo, 1999). There is general agreement that groups develop based on the following summarized stage model (Tuckman, 1965; Wheelan, Davidson, & Tilin, 2003). The initial stage of group, or "forming," involves the members' tentative involvement, dependence on the group leader, and focus on finding their place in or out of group. Once the group is established, it will enter the "storming stage," characterized by the emergence of competition and conflict, challenge to the group leader, and a focus on power and the hierarchal order of the group. It is theorized that successful storming is needed to create trust within the "norming stage," in which groups become cohesive with a focus on positive feedback. After cohesion, groups are able to move to a "performing stage," where feedback is constructive and the focus is on the task of the group. Finally, the "adjourning stage" is characterized by activities associated with termination. Research has generally supported these stages of group (Kivlighan, McGovern, & Corrazini, 1984; Wheelan & Hochberger, 1996), although the order may vary, particularly from individual to individual (Brabender, 1997). Additionally, variables such as group format (e.g., open vs. closed), composition (e.g., sex, ethnicity), and leadership style will all impact group development (Schiller, 1995; Verdi & Wheelan, 1992).

Although there is research support for the development of group dynamics over time, at this time there is not a clear method to measure stages of group. There is a need for a psychometrically sound method to measure the dynamics that underlie stages of group.

Integration of Research and Group Practice

Overall, group research suggests that assessment of the group format as a whole demonstrates that it is efficacious, on par with individual counseling (Bednar & Kaul, 1994; Burlingame, MacKenzie, & Strauss, 2004; Forsyth, 2006; McRoberts, Burlingame, & Hoag, 1998; Yalom, 2005). A number of authors have suggested that understanding whole-group dynamics can guide interventions to foster more effective group interaction (Gladding, 2008; Lewin, 1948; Yalom, 2005). However, there is limited empirical evidence validating this concept as the complex interactions of whole-group dynamics with individual participant dynamics are not well understood. In these ways, group dynamics and leadership may be thought of as a young science. The importance and abundance of group work (i.e., tasks, guidance, counseling, therapy) point to the critical need for empirically supported group practice. The need for empirical research mandates pursuit of effective and accurate measurement. The American Group Psychotherapy Association's practice guidelines (2007) offer principles for clinicians with regard to the provision of evidence-based best practice. There has been a stated need for greater guidance on the utilization of empirically supported practice in group therapy (Lambert & Ogles, 2004), and we believe that more widespread use of assessment in group counseling and research is the first step toward establishing better standards for group practice.

References

American Counseling Association. (2005). *American Counseling Association code of ethics*. Alexandria, VA: Author.

American Group Psychotherapy Association. (2007). *Practice guidelines for group psychotherapy*. New York: Author.

Anderson, L. R., & Ager, J. W. (1978). Analysis of variance in small group research. *Personality and Social Psychology Bulletin, 4*, 341–345.

Armstrong, S. J., & Priola, V. (2001). Individual differences in cognitive style and their effects on task and social-orientation of self-managed work teams. *Small Group Research, 32*, 283–312.

Astramovich, R. L., & Coker, J. K. (2007). Program evaluation: The accountability bridge model for counselors. *Journal of Counseling & Development, 85*(2), 162–172.

Baron-Cohen, S., & Wheelwright, S. (2004). The Empathy Quotient (EQ). An investigation of adults with Asperger syndrome or high functioning autism, and normal sex differences. *Journal of Autism and Developmental Disorders, 34*, 163–175.

Bass, B. M., & Avolio, B. J. (1990). *Multifactor leadership questionnaire*. Palo Alto, CA: Consulting Psychologist Press.

Beck, A. T. (1974). Phases in the development of structure in therapy and encounter groups. In D. A. Wexler & L. N. Rice (Eds.), *Innovations in client-centered therapy* (pp. 421–463). New York: John Wiley & Sons.

Beck, A. T., & Steer, R. A. (1990). *Manual for the Beck Anxiety Inventory*. San Antonio, TX: Psychological Corporation.

Beck, A. T., Ward, C. H., Mendelson, M., Mock, J., & Erbaugh, J. (1961). An inventory for measuring depression. *Archives of General Psychiatry, 4*(6), 561–571.

Bednar, R. L., & Kaul, T. J. (1978). Experimental group research: Current perspectives. In S. L. Garfield & A. E. Bergin (Eds.), *Handbook of psychotherapy and behavior change* (2nd ed., pp. 769–816). New York: John Wiley & Sons.

Bednar, R. L., & Kaul, T. J. (1986). Experimental group research: Results, questions, and suggestions. In S. L. Garfield & A. E. Bergin (Eds.), *Handbook of psychotherapy and behavior change* (3rd ed., pp. 631–663). New York: John Wiley & Sons.

Bednar, R. L., & Kaul, T. J. (1994). Experimental group research: Can the cannon fire? In S. L. Garfield & A. E. Bergin (Eds.), *Handbook of psychotherapy and behavior change* (4th ed., pp. 631–663). New York: John Wiley & Sons.

Bion, W. (1961). *Experiences in groups*. New York: Basic Books.

Bleuer, J. (1983). *Accountability in counseling. Highlights: An ERIC/CAPS fact sheet*. Ann Arbor: ERIC/CAPS Clearinghouse, University of Michigan.

Bloch, S., & Crouch, E. (1985). *Therapeutic factors in group psychotherapy*. Oxford: Oxford University Press.

Brabender, V. (1997). Chaos and order in the psychotherapy group. In F. Masterpasqua & P. Perna (Eds.), *The psychological meaning of chaos* (pp. 225–253). Washington, DC: American Psychological Association Press.

Brabender, V., Smolar, A. I., & Fallon, A. E. (2004). *Essentials of group therapy*. Hoboken, NJ: John Wiley & Sons.

Brooks, L. W., Guerney, B., Jr., & Mazza, N. (2002). Relationship enhancement couples group therapy. *Journal of Family Social Work, 6*(2), 25–42.

Bruce, A., Getch, Y. Q., & Ziomek-Daigle, J. (2009). Closing the gap: A group counseling approach to improve test performance of African American students. *Professional School Counseling, 12*(6), 450–457.

Burlingame, G. M., Fuhriman, A., & Johnson, J. E. (2002). Cohesion in group psychotherapy. In J. C. Norcross (Ed.),

Psychotherapy relationships that work: Therapist contributions and responsiveness to patients (pp. 71–88). New York: Oxford University Press.

Burlingame, G. M., Fuhriman, A., & Mosier, J. (2003). The differential effectiveness of group psychotherapy: A meta-analytic perspective. *Group Dynamics, 7,* 3–12.

Burlingame, G. M., MacKenzie, D., & Strauss, B. (2004). Small group treatment: Evidence for effectiveness and mechanisms of change. In S. L. Garfield & A. E. Bergin (Eds.), *Handbook of psychotherapy and behavior change* (5th ed., pp. 647–696). New York: John Wiley & Sons.

Butcher, J. N., Graham, J. R., Ben-Porath, Y. S., Tellegen, Y. S., Dahlstrom, W. G., & Kaemmer, B. (2001). *Minnesota Multiphasic Personality Inventory-2: Manual for administration and scoring* (rev. ed.). Minneapolis: University of Minnesota Press.

Campbell, D. T., Stanley, J. C., & Gage, N. L. (1963). *Experimental and quasi-experimental designs for research.* Boston: Houghton Mifflin.

Capuzzi, D., & Gross, D. R. (2002). *Introduction to group counseling* (3rd ed.). Denver, CO: Love Publishing.

Capuzzi, D. E., & Gross, D. R. (2005). *Youth at risk: A prevention resource for counselors, teachers, and parents* (4th ed.). Alexandria, VA: American Counseling Association.

Corey, G. (2008). *Theory and practice of group counseling* (7th ed.). Pacific Grove, CA: Brooks/Cole.

Couch, R. D. (1995). Four steps for conducting a pregroup screening interview. *Journal for Specialists in Group Work, 20,* 18–25.

Cox, G. L., & Merkel, W. T. (1989). A qualitative review of psychosocial treatments for bulimia. *Journal of Nervous and Mental Disease, 177,* 77–84.

Davis, M. H. (1980). A multidimensional approach to individual differences in empathy. *JSAS Catalog of Selected Documents in Psychology, 10,* 85.

Davis, M. H. (1994). *Empathy: A social psychological approach.* Boulder, CO: Westview Press.

Derogatis, L. (1994). *SCL90R administration, scoring, & procedures manual III.* Minneapolis, MN: NCS Pearson.

Endler, N. S., Edwards, J. M., & Vitelli, R. (1991). *Endler Multidimensional Anxiety Scales (EMAS): Manual.* Los Angeles: Western Psychological Services.

Erikson, E. H. (1968). *Identity, youth and crisis.* New York: Norton.

Forsyth, D. R. (2006). *Group dynamics.* Belmont, CA: Wadsworth.

Gay, M. L., Hollandsworth, J. G., Jr., & Galassi, J. P. (1975). An assertiveness inventory for adults. *Journal of Counseling Psychology, 22,* 340–344.

Gehart, D. (2009). *Mastering competencies in family therapy: A practical approach to theories and clinical case documentation.* Belmont, CA: Brooks/Cole.

Gladding, S. T. (2008). *Group work: A counseling specialty* (5th ed.). Upper Saddle River, NJ: Prentice Hall.

Goodwin, J. C. (1998). *Research in psychology: Methods and design* (2nd ed.). New York: John Wiley & Sons.

Gough, H. G. (1987). *California Psychological Inventory administrator's guide.* Palo Alto, CA: Consulting Psychologists Press.

Hansen, J. C., Warner, R. W., & Smith, E. J. (1986). *Group counseling: Theory and process* (2nd ed.). Boston: Houghton Mifflin.

Hatry, H. P. (1994). Collecting data from agency records. In J. S. Wholey, H. P. Hatry, & K. E. Newcomer (Eds.), *Handbook of practical program evaluation* (pp. 374–385). San Francisco: Jossey-Bass.

Hersey, P., & Blanchard, K. H. (1973). The importance of communication patterns in implementing change strategies. *Journal of Development in Education, 6*(4), 66–75.

Hersey, P., & Blanchard, K. H. (1976). *Leader effectiveness and adaptability description.* La Jolla, CA: University Associates Press.

Hill, W. F. (1965). *Hill interaction matrix.* Los Angeles: University of Southern California.

Hulley, S., Cummings, S. R., Browner, W. S., Grady, D. G., & Newman, T. B. (2007). *Designing clinical research* (3rd ed.). Philadelphia: Lippincott, Williams, & Wilkins.

Jacobs, E., Masson, R., & Harvill, R. (2009). *Group counseling: Strategies and skills* (6th ed.). Pacific Grove, CA: Brooks/Cole.

Jolliffe, D., & Farrington, D. P. (2006). The development and validation of the basic empathy scale. *Journal of Adolescence, 29,* 589–611.

Joyce, A. S., McCallum, M., Piper, W. E., & Ogrodniczuk, J. S. (2000). Role behavior expectancies and alliance change in short-term individual psychotherapy. *Journal of Psychotherapy Practice & Research, 9,* 213–225.

Kenny, D. A., & Judd, C. M. (1996). A general procedure for the estimation of interdependence. *Psychological Bulletin, 119*(1), 138–148.

Kenny, D. A., Kashy, D. A., & Bolger, N. (1998). Data analysis in social psychology. In D. Gilbert, S. Fiske, & G. Lindzey (Eds.), *The handbook of social psychology* (4th ed., Vol. 1, pp. 233–265). Boston: McGraw-Hill.

Kenny, D. A., & LaVoie, L. (1985). Separating individual group effects. *Journal of Personality and Social Psychology, 4,* 339–348.

Kenny, D. A., Mannetti, L., Pierro, A., Livi, S., & Kashy, D. A. (2002). The statistical analysis of data from small groups. *Journal of Personality and Social Psychology, 83*(1), 126–137.

Kew, C. E. (1975). *A pilot study of an evaluation scale for group-psychotherapy patients. ETC Test Collection* (set A). Princeton, NJ: Educational Testing Services.

Kingsep, P., Nathan, P., & Castle, D. (2003). Cognitive behavioural group treatment for social anxiety in schizophrenia. *Schizophrenia Research, 63*(2), 121–129.

Kivlighan, D. M., & Lilly, R. L. (1997). Developmental changes in group climate as they relate to therapeutic gain. *Group Dynamics: Theory, Research, and Practice, 1,* 208–221.

Kivlighan, D. M., McGovern, T. V., & Corrazini, J. G. (1984). Effects of content and timing of structuring interventions on group therapy process and outcome. *Journal of Counseling Psychology, 31,* 363–370.

Kivlighan, D. M., Multon, K. D., & Brossard, D. F. (1996). Helpful impacts of group counseling: Development of multidimensional rating system. *Journal of Counseling Psychology, 43,* 347–355.

Klein, R. H. (1983). Some problems of patient referral for outpatient group therapy. *International Journal of Group Therapy, 33*(2), 229–241.

Krogel, J., Burlingame, G., & Gleave, R. (2006). *The group questionnaire: A new measure of the group relationship.* Paper presented to the American Psychological Association, New Orleans, LA.

Lambert, M. J., & Ogles, B. M. (2004). The efficacy and effectiveness of psychotherapy. In M. J. Lambert (Ed.), *Bergin and Garfield's handbook of psychotherapy and behavior change* (5th ed., pp. 137–194). New York: John Wiley & Sons.

LeBon, G. (1910). *The crowd: A study of the popular mind.* London: George Allen & Unwin.

Lewin, K. (1939). Field theory and experiment in social psychology: Concepts and methods. *American Journal of Sociology, 44*(6), 868–897.

Lewin, K. (1948). *Resolving social conflicts.* New York: Harper and Brothers.

Lieberman, M. A., Yalom, I. D., & Miles, M. B. (1973). *Encounter groups: First facts.* New York: Basic Books.

MacKenzie, K. R. (1987). Therapeutic factors in group psychotherapy: A contemporary view. *Group, 11,* 26–34.

MacKenzie, K. R. (1994). Group development. In A. Fuhriman & G. Burlingame (Eds.), *Handbook of group psychotherapy* (pp. 223–268). New York: John Wiley & Sons.

MacNair-Semands, R. R., & Lese, K. P. (2000). Interpersonal problems and the perception of therapeutic factors in group therapy. *Small Group Research, 31*(2), 158–174.

Marshall, M. N. (1996). The key informant technique. *Family Practice, 13*(1), 92–97.

Martin, D., Garske, J., & Davis, M. (2000). Relation of the therapeutic alliance with outcome and other variables: A meta-analytic review. *Journal of Consulting and Clinical Psychology, 68,* 438–450.

Martin, J. L., & Thienemann, M. (2005). Group cognitive-behavior therapy with family involvement for middle-school-age children with obsessive–compulsive disorder: a pilot study. *Child Psychiatry and Human Development, 36*(1), 113–127.

McRoberts, C., Burlingame, G., & Hoag, M. (1998). Comparative efficacy of individual and group psychotherapy: A meta-analytic perspective. *Group Dynamics: Theory, Research and Practice, 2,* 101–117.

Millon, T. R., Davis, R., & Millon, C. (1997). *Millon Clinical Multiaxial Inventory–III manual (MCMI–III)* (2nd ed.). Minneapolis, MN: Pearson Assessments.

Nardi, D. A. (2003). Introduction to health and wellness needs assessment. In D. A. Nardi & J. Petr (Eds.), *Community health and wellness needs assessment: a step-by-step guide* (pp. 1–22). Clifton Park, NY: Thompson/Delmar Learning.

Nelson, J. R., Dykeman, C., Powell, S., & Petty, D. (1996). The effects of a group counseling intervention on students with behavioral adjustment problems. *Elementary School Guidance and Counseling, 31*(1), 21–33.

Norcross, J. C., Beutler, L. E., & Levant, R. F. (2006). *Evidence-based practices in mental health: Debate and dialogue on the fundamental questions.* Washington, DC: American Psychological Association.

Ogrodniczuk, J. S., Piper, W. E., Joyce, A., McCallum, M., & Rosie, J. S. (2003). NEO-five factor personality traits as predictors of response to two forms of group psychotherapy. *International Journal of Group Psychotherapy, 53,* 417–443.

Page, R. C., & Chandler, J. (1994). Effects of group counseling on ninth-grade at-risk students. *Journal of Mental Health Counseling, 16*(3), 340–351.

Pillen, M. B., & Hoewing-Roberson, R. C. (1992). *Determining youth gang membership: development of a self-report instrument.* Bloomington, IL: Chestnut Health Systems.

Rapin, L. S. (2004). Guidelines for ethical and legal practice in counseling and psychotherapy groups. In J. L. DeLucia-Waack, D. A. Gerrity, C. R. Kalodner, & M. T. Riva (Eds.), *Handbook of group counseling and psychotherapy* (pp. 151–165). Thousand Oaks, CA: Sage.

Rathus, S. A. (1973). A 30-item schedule for assessing assertive behavior. *Behavior Therapy, 4,* 398–406.

Reynolds, W. M. (2001). *Reynolds Adolescent Adjustment Screening Inventory.* Odessa, FL: Psychological Assessment Resources.

Riva, M. T., & Haub, A. (2004). Group counseling in the schools. In J. DeLucia-Waack, D. Gerrity, C. Kalodner, & M. T. Riva (Eds.), *Handbook of group counseling and psychotherapy* (pp. 309–321). Thousand Oaks, CA: Sage.

Riva, M. T., & Smith, R. D. (1997). Looking into the future of group research: Where do we go from here? *Journal of Specialists in Group Work, 22,* 266–267.

Riva, M. T., Wachtel, M., & Lasky, G. (2004). Effective group leadership: Research and practice. In J. DeLucia-Waack, D. Gerrity, C. Kalodner, & M. T. Riva (Eds.), *Handbook of group counseling and psychotherapy* (pp. 37–48). Thousand Oaks, CA: Sage.

Roid, G., & Fitts, W. (1991). *Tennessee Self Concept Scale.* Los Angeles: Western Psychological Services.

Rosenberg, M. (1965). *Society and the adolescent self-image.* Princeton, NJ: Princeton University Press.

Sadler, M. S., & Judd, C. M. (2001). Overcoming dependent data: A guide to group data analysis. In M. A. Hogg & R. S. Tindale (Eds.), *Blackwell handbook of social psychology: Group processes* (Vol. 3, pp. 497–523). Oxford: Blackwell.

Schiller, L. (1995). Stages of development in women's groups: A relational model. In R. Kurland & R. Salmon (Eds.), *Group work practice in a troubled society* (pp. 117–138). New York: Haworth Press.

Schlosser, B. (1993). A group therapy needs assessment survey. In L. VandeCreek, S. Knapp, & T. L. Jackson (Eds.), *Innovations in clinical practice: A source book* (Vol. 12, pp. 383–385). Sarasota, FL: Professional Resource Press/Professional Resource Exchange.

Schutz, W. C. (1992). Beyond FIRO-B—Three new theory driven measures—Element B: Behavior, Element F: Feelings, Element S: Self. *Psychological Reports, 70,* 915–937.

Schwartz, J. P., & Waldo, M. (1999). Therapeutic factors in Duluth model spouse abuser group treatment. *Journal for Specialists in Group Work, 24,* 197–207.

Schwartz, J. P., Waldo, M., & Halperin, D. M. (1999). Fostering the development of identity and intimacy among college students through group counseling examining attachment styles. In *Prevention as social action: Counseling psychology interventions promoting public welfare.* Symposium conducted at the 117th annual convention of the American Psychological Association, Boston, MA.

Seligman, M. E. P. (1995). The effectiveness of psychotherapy: The *Consumer Reports* study. *American Psychologist, 50,* 965–974.

Sotsky, S. M., Glass, D. R., Shea, M. T., Pilkonis, P. A., Collins, J. F., Elkin, I., et al. (1991). Patient predictors of response to psychotherapy and pharmacotherapy: Findings in the NIMH Treatment of Depression Collaborative Research Program. *American Journal of Psychiatry, 148*(8), 997–1008.

Spielberger, C. D., Gorsuch, R. L., & Lushene, R. E. (1970). *Manual for the State-Trait Anxiety Inventory.* Palo Alto, CA: Consulting Psychologists Press.

Stockton, R., & Hulse, D. (1981). Developing cohesion in small groups: Theory and research. *Journal for Specialists in Group Work, 6,* 188–194.

Stockton, R., Robison, F. F., & Morran, D. K. (1983). A comparison of the HIM-B with the Hill interaction matrix model of group interaction styles: A factor analytic study. *Journal of Group Psychotherapy, Psychodrama & Sociometry, 36,* 102–113.

Tremblay, M. A. (1957). The key informant technique: a non-ethnographic application. *American Anthropologist, 59*(4), 688–701.

Trotzer, J. P. (2000). Group work practice ideas: Problem solving procedures in group work. *Group Worker, 29,* 9–12.

Trotzer, J. P. (2004). Conducting a group: Guidelines for choosing and using activities. In J. L. DeLucia-Waack, D. A. Gerrity, C. R. Kalodner, & M. T. Riva (Eds.), *Handbook of group counseling and psychotherapy* (pp. 76–90). Thousand Oaks, CA: Sage.

Tuckman, B. W. (1965). Development sequence in small groups. *Psychological Bulletin, 63,* 384–399.

Vacc, N. A., Rhyne-Winkler, M. C., & Poidevant, J. M. (1993). Evaluation and accountability of counseling services: Possible implications for a midsize district. *School Counselor, 40*(4), 260–266.

Verdi, A. F., & Wheelan, S. A. (1992). Developmental patterns in same-sex and mixed-sex groups. *Small Group Research, 23,* 356–378.

Waldo, M. (1985). A curative factor framework for conceptualizing group counseling. *Journal of Counseling and Development, 65,* 52–58.

Wen, B., Zhang, Q., & Li, W. (2006). Effects of group counseling on depression and anxiety of patients with schizophrenia in rehabilitation. *Chinese Mental Health Journal, 20*(11), 762–764.

Wheelan, S. A., Davidson, B., & Tilin, F. (2003). Group development across time: Reality or illusion? *Small Group Research, 34,* 223–245.

Wheelan, S. A., & Hochberger, J. M. (1996). Validation studies of the group development questionnaire. *Small Group Research, 27,* 143–170.

Wolpe, J., & Lazarus, A. A. (1966). *Behaviour therapy techniques: A guide to the treatment of neuroses.* New York: Pergamon Press.

Yalom, I. D. (1970). *The theory and practice of group psychotherapy.* New York: Basic Books.

Yalom, I. D. (1995). *The theory and practice of group psychotherapy* (4th ed.). New York: Basic Books.

Yalom, I. D. (with Leszcz, M.) (2005). *The theory and practice of group psychotherapy* (5th ed.). New York: Basic Books.

Zaccaro, S. J., Cracraft, M., & Marks, M. (2006). Collecting data in groups. In F. T. L. Leong & J. T. Austin (Eds.), *The psychology research handbook* (2nd ed., pp. 227–237). Thousand Oaks, CA: Sage.

Zaitzow, B. H., & Fields, C. B. (2006). Archival data sets: Revisiting issues and considerations. In F. T. L. Leong & J. T. Austin (Eds.), *The psychology research handbook* (2nd ed., pp. 251–261). Thousand Oaks, CA: Sage.

Qualitative Research Approaches and Group Counseling

Deborah J. Rubel *and* Jane E. Atieno Okech

Abstract

Qualitative research approaches have gained wide acceptance in many social sciences. However, they struggle to gain acceptance and credibility in fields related to counseling and are little used in group-counseling research. This may have limited the development of group-counseling research as the strengths of qualitative research approaches have a unique synergy with the challenges and needs of group-counseling research. This chapter explores the fundamental characteristics of qualitative approaches, their strengths and limitations, and various types of qualitative research. It continues with a discussion of the challenges and needs of group-counseling research and how qualitative approaches may address these needs. The chapter also introduces the issue of quality in qualitative research and describes an atheoretical research-design process aimed at promoting congruent, effective qualitative designs. Finally, this chapter provides summaries and evaluations of several qualitative group-counseling studies, presents key themes from the chapter discussions, and proposes future directions for qualitative research applied to group counseling.

Keywords: qualitative research, group counseling, research methods, qualitative methods, research design

Introduction

The purpose of this chapter is to explore recent and potential use of qualitative research approaches in group-counseling research. This chapter explores the philosophical basis of qualitative approaches, discusses the strengths and limitations of these approaches, and describes the major qualitative methods. The exploration continues with identification of group-counseling research challenges and needs and discussion of how qualitative approaches might be used to respond to these challenges. In addition, this chapter outlines a qualitative research-design process and describes and critiques several recent qualitative studies related to group counseling.

Qualitative Research

Describing the diversity and utility of qualitative research approaches is a daunting task. Denzin and Lincoln (2005) describe qualitative research as a unique field of inquiry marked by widely varied conceptualizations and terms, which are often at odds. This can be confusing to beginning and more experienced researchers alike as they explore applying qualitative methods to group-counseling questions. Denzin and Lincoln further define the practice as follows:

> Qualitative research is a situated activity that locates the observer in the world. It consists of a set of interpretive, material practices that make the world visible. These practices transform the world. They turn the world into a series of representations, including field notes, interviews, conversations, photographs, recording, and memos to the self. At this level, qualitative researchers study things in their natural settings, attempting to make sense of, or interpret, phenomena in terms of the meanings people bring to them. (p. 3)

An emerging understanding of what qualitative research offers the field of group counseling begins with uncovering the assumptions that support qualitative research and includes examining its general strengths and limitations as well as common forms. In particular, understanding the underlying assumptions of qualitative approaches enables the process of identifying appropriate problems and questions. This understanding also informs the process of designing, implementing, and completing qualitative studies that will most benefit group-counseling stakeholders. This section uncovers these assumptions, also known as "paradigms" and "worldviews," and describes how they distinguish qualitative research approaches from other approaches. This section also defines the strengths and limitations of qualitative approaches and outlines several commonly used methodologies. This foundation will later serve to clarify the synergies between group-counseling research challenges and qualitative approaches.

Paradigms and Worldviews that Influence Qualitative Research

Qualitative and quantitative research approaches are grounded in different systems of ideas, known as "paradigms" (Lincoln & Guba, 1985). Lincoln and Guba indicate that research paradigms define the nature of reality, the relationship of the knower to the known, the possibility of generalization, the possibility of causal linkages, and the role of values in research. These differences result in different definitions of researchable problems, research question structures, research purposes, research design and methods, form and presentation of results, and standards by which the research is to be judged (Morrow, 2005; Ponterotto, 2005). Creswell (2007) characterizes the identification of these assumptions as critical to sound research practice.

Ponterotto (2005) describes the field of counseling psychology as "dominated by positivist and postpositivist research paradigms and associated quantitative methods" (p. 126). Lincoln and Guba (1985) indicate that positivism privileges conceptions of reality as "single, tangible, and fragmentable" (p. 37). They associate positivism with dualistic relationships between knower and known, generalizations that are both time-free and context-free, linear causality, and the notion of value-free inquiry. Critiques of positivism are largely related to its inadequacy to address the complexity, interdependence, and deeply personal, or *emic*, meanings inherent in human interaction (Guba & Lincoln, 2005).

Frustration with these limitations, particularly in the social sciences, resulted in the emergence of the *postpositivist* research paradigm.

Guba and Lincoln (2005) describe postpositivism as an imperfect derivative of positivism. Postpositivism maintains assumptions of an extant reality though imperfectly understandable, dualism between knower and known, generalizability, cause-and-effect connections, and the notion of value-free inquiry. Postpositivism shares with positivism a goal of understanding that leads to prediction and control (Ponterotto, 2005). In attempts to make qualitative research accessible to positivist researchers, much qualitative research is influenced by postpositivism. But this uneasy blend results in studies with strong elements of reductionism, empirical data collection, cause-and-effect orientation, and the influence of a priori theories (Creswell, 2007; Ponterotto, 2005). These elements are inconsistent with research purposes that strive for understanding of unique, rather than general, experiences (idiographic understanding) and understanding from an internal (research participant), rather than an external (researcher), perspective (emic understanding). The *constructivist* research paradigm emerged and gained prominence in response to this incongruence.

In early writing, Lincoln and Guba (1985) describe postpositivism as a drastic divergence from positivism and equate it with qualitative research and constructivism. In later works (Guba & Lincoln, 2005), they clearly distinguish between postpositivism and constructivism. They define the constructivist research paradigm as including assumptions that realities are constructed, relative, and multiple; that knower and known are intricately and intimately connected; and that what can be known is bound by time and context. Further, from a constructivist viewpoint causality is mutual, complex, and difficult to assess, with values inexorably shaping the research. The constructivist and related interpretivist perspectives focus on research in the natural setting, humans as instruments of interpretation, purposive sampling rather than random sampling, inductive data analysis, and emergent design (Charmaz, 2006). Ponterotto (2005) indicates that the constructivist–interpretivist paradigm provides the foundation for most qualitative research.

Beyond constructivist perspective, another research worldview becomes important given the recent focus on the role of qualitative research in advancing social justice through counseling and group counseling (Denzin & Lincoln, 2005; Rubel & Pepperell, 2010; Vera & Speight, 2003).

This paradigm has been characterized variously as critical-ideological and advocacy-participatory research (Creswell, 2007; Ponterotto, 2005). This worldview is influenced by feminism, critical theory, and queer theory, among others (Creswell, 2007; Ponterotto, 2005). Research from this perspective contains the underlying assumption that inequality and oppression shape the world, including the form and result of traditional research methods. Thus, this type of research, through a purposeful focus on injustice and inequality, is intended to transform oppressive societal structures. This paradigm truly challenges traditional views of research as "value-free," yet its utility and importance are clear (Denzin & Lincoln, 2005; Ponterotto, 2005). Table 15.1 provides a comparison of the research assumptions associated with positivism, postpositivism, constructivism, and advocacy-participatory and critical research paradigms.

Strengths and Limitations of Qualitative Research Approaches

Because of their largely postpositivist, constructivist, or advocacy-participatory basis, the methods of qualitative research privilege particular types of data, analysis, and end products (Morrow, 2005). Use of these types of data, analysis, and end products renders qualitative approaches ideally suited for some group-counseling problems and questions. However, their use may also present challenges related to the implementation and acceptance of such studies. The world continues to be largely defined by traditional notions of science, where qualitative research methods, processes, and findings are likely to be criticized (Denzin & Lincoln, 2005; Hoyt & Bahti, 2007). Unfortunately, this has pragmatic implications for those interested in doing qualitative research related to group counseling.

The strengths and limitations of qualitative research approaches are related to (1) their nonpositivist basic assumptions (e.g., values inextricably shape the research; attribution of causality is mutual, complex, and difficult to assess; realities are constructed, relative, and multiple; knower and known are intricately and intimately connected in research), (2) the methods by which they are undertaken (e.g., interviews, focus group discussions, researcher and participant conversations, interpretive analysis), and (3) their lower status within the research world. The general strengths and limitations of qualitative approaches will be discussed here in terms of research purposes, as well as practical and personal purposes.

Maxwell (1996) describes the *research purpose* of a study as what one wishes to understand. He indicates that the strengths of qualitative research–related purposes are (1) the potential to understand the meaning that study participants give to significant issues, (2) the potential to understand the context that surrounds the experience of the participants, (3) the ability to discover unanticipated information and patterns associated with the participants' experiences, (4) the opportunity to understand process

Table 15.1 Research paradigms: comparison of research assumptions

Research Paradigm	Assumptions about Nature of Truth and Reality	Assumptions about Research Relationship	Assumptions about the Role of Values in Research
Positivism	Single, tangible, universal truth	Objectivity or distance between researcher and subject is possible and desirable	Value-free inquiry is desirable and possible
Postpositivism	Single, universal truth but not fully comprehensible	Objectivity or distance between researcher and subject is possible and desirable	Value-free inquiry is desirable and, ideally, attainable
Constructivism	Multiple truths that are time- and context-bound	Researcher and participant are connected and mutually influential	Values are inseparable from the inquiry and should be acknowledged
Advocacy/ participatory/critical	Multiple truths that are time- and context-bound, certain truths are privileged and others marginalized	Researcher and participant are mutually influential, and the relationship should create positive change	Values should influence inquiry such that positive social change results

Sources: Creswell (2007), Denzin & Lincoln (2005), Guba & Lincoln (2005), Lincoln & Guba (1985), Ponterotto (2005).

rather than snapshots of information, and (5) the ability to develop causal explanations. The major disadvantages associated with qualitative approaches and research purposes are that they are not as applicable to understanding large and broadly varied populations where generalization becomes necessary to derive predictive power and control (Ponterotto, 2005).

Maxwell (1996) further describes advantages related to what he calls "practical purposes," or those purposes related to accomplishing something. These advantages include (1) the potential to generate results or theories to which participants and audiences such as practitioners can relate and understand (Charmaz, 2006; Maxwell, 1996), (2) the ability to conduct formative evaluations that can influence actions (Patton, 1990), and (3) the potential to collaborate intimately with practitioners and participants. However, disadvantages related to practical purposes have been described by other authors (Denzin & Lincoln, 2005). These disadvantages are related to the relatively low "power" of qualitative research compared to quantitative studies in terms of acquiring funding, influencing larger decisions, and gaining venues for dissemination (Hoyt & Bhati, 2007). This lack of power has been attributed to either bias of such systems toward positivism (Denzin & Lincoln, 2005), lack of understanding of qualitative approaches (Hoyt & Bhati, 2007; Ponterotto, 2005), and the tendency for some to undertake qualitative research because they are uncomfortable using statistics and quantitative designs (Schneider, 2009). Additionally, others have written about the paucity of literature regarding interpreting qualitative studies into useable interventions or change in practices (Goering, Boydell, & Pignatiello, 2008; Morse, Penrod, & Hupcey, 2000).

Maxwell (1996) also describes "personal purposes" that motivate researchers to undertake research. While he does not explicate the strengths of qualitative research in terms of personal purposes, other authors have touched upon this topic (Frey, 1994; Reisetter et al., 2004). In terms of personal advantages, Reisetter et al. indicate that their counselor-participants desired congruence between personal, professional, and research worldviews. The participants achieved this congruence through engaging in qualitative research. Personal disadvantages may include lack of support, mentoring, resources, and material rewards for beginning researchers and experienced researchers alike (Okech, Astramovich, Johnson, Hoskins, & Rubel, 2006).

Additionally, Dickson-Swift, James, Kippen, and Liamputtong (2007) researched challenges facing qualitative researchers and documented such reactions as feelings of guilt and vulnerability, difficulties and emotions regarding ending research relationships, and fatigue related to the energy expenditure required for qualitative research. Table 15.2 provides a summary of the strengths and limitations of qualitative research approaches categorized by research, personal, and practical purposes.

Compatibility of Qualitative Research and Group Counseling

In light of the general strengths and limitations of qualitative approaches, a key question is, What does qualitative research specifically offer to group-counseling researchers? Qualitative research methods, particularly applied in the field, may be a promising way to address various group-counseling research–related challenges and issues (Burlingame, Fuhriman, & Johnson, 2004; Frey, 1994; Riva & Smith, 1997). The group-counseling research literature reveals several interrelated areas in which qualitative research methods may be of benefit to group-counseling researchers. Qualitative approaches may contribute uniquely to (1) addressing methodological challenges that have complicated the study of group counseling; (2) meeting specific gaps in group-counseling research related to process and efficacy; (3) giving voice to group members, particularly those who are culturally different or marginalized; and (4) increasing the motivation of group-counseling researchers by offering methods congruent with their values and experiences.

ADDRESSING METHODOLOGICAL CHALLENGES TO STUDYING GROUP COUNSELING

The group and group-counseling literature contains numerous discussions related to research methods that will increase the predictive potential of research in this area (e.g., Kivlighan, Coleman, & Anderson, 2000; Morgan-Lopez & Fals-Stewart, 2006). This literature presents methodological and statistical challenges inherent to the study of groups. These challenges include the multilayered or nested nature of group-work data, monitoring and evaluating the mutual influences and dependencies inherent in group counseling, understanding group counseling in terms of dynamic and longitudinal processes rather than static measurements, and implementing research designs related to group counseling that have a sufficient sample to provide significant or useful results.

Table 15.2 Qualitative research approaches: strengths and limitations related to purpose

Research Motivation (Maxwell, 1996)	Strengths	Limitations
Research purposes or motivations related to gaining understanding	The ability to: • understand participants' meaning • understand the context of participants' experiences • discover unanticipated information about participants' experiences • understand process • develop causal explanations (Maxwell, 1996)	Not easily applicable when generalization, predictive power, and control are necessary (Ponterotto, 2005)
Personal purposes or personal motivations for conducting the research	High potential for congruence between personal, professional, and research worldviews for counselors and group counselors (Frey, 1994; Reisetter et al., 2004)	• Lack of emotional, material, and training resources for researchers (Okech et al., 2006) • Reactions such as guilt, vulnerability, difficult emotions, and fatigue (Dickson-Swift et al., 2007)
Practical purposes or external motivations for conducting research	The potential to: • generate results that participants and practitioners can understand and appreciate (Charmaz, 2006; Maxwell, 1996) • influence actions through formative evaluation (Patton, 1990) • collaborate intimately with practitioners and participants (Maxwell, 1996)	• Low "power" to acquire funding, influence larger decisions, and be disseminated (Hoyt & Bhati, 2007). • Lack of understanding among editorial boards (Hoyt & Bhati, 2007; Ponterotto, 2005) • Lack of literature that aids interpretation of qualitative studies into real-world practice (Goering et al., 2008; Morse et al., 2000)

While the purpose of qualitative research is not typically to predict or control, the outlined challenges illuminate some of the unique potential that qualitative approaches offer to group counseling. Authors such as Maxwell (1996) have emphasized the relative strength of qualitative methods for understanding the contexts of experiences and developing descriptions of causality. In particular, Frey (1994) contended that qualitative methods were a suitable way to study the complex social interactions and contexts of groups. Methods such as embedded case study design (Yin, 2009), which is described later in this chapter, may be used to understand relationships between individual group members and the group as a whole. Additionally, qualitative methods such as grounded theory, a method which is sensitized to process and involves the collection of data over time (Charmaz, 2006; Corbin & Strauss, 2008), have the potential to develop understanding related to longitudinal processes of group counseling. Finally, with its focus on illuminating unique, rather than general, experiences (idiographic understanding), qualitative research has the potential to offer group-counseling researchers useful understanding through study of small, purposeful samples (Creswell, 2007).

Despite the potential qualitative approaches may have in achieving greater understanding in these areas, methods alone do not guarantee useful results. A focus on careful design and rigorous implementation is necessary to achieve these ends (Maxwell, 1996).

MEETING SPECIFIC GROUP-COUNSELING
RESEARCH NEEDS

Recent group-counseling research literature tends to focus on determining group efficacy with specific patient populations (Burlingame et al., 2004). This approach frequently is accomplished by tracking interactions between treatment protocols and features of group process that occur across long-term longitudinal studies. Increasingly, these studies use sophisticated research designs, statistics, and measures (Burlingame et al., 2004).

A review of these studies has also identified specific research foci that may be uniquely addressed through the use of qualitative methods. These research foci include developing a better understanding of change processes in group as well as understanding the contributions of members, leaders, techniques, and the training process to change (Burlingame et al., 2004; Riva & Smith, 1997). These research foci are supported by the psychotherapy literature, which implies that the benefits of outcome research are limited due to the lack of information about the process of treatment. This literature also prioritizes three types of process questions related to course of change, moderators of change, and mediators of change (Laurenceau, Hayes, & Feldman, 2007; Pachankis & Goldfried, 2007). This highlights the need for research that can identify process variables that are beneficial to group goals and individual change during group counseling.

Burlingame et al. (2004) comment on the utility of qualitative approaches in addressing these concerns: "The intricacies of process and response and the vital linkages occurring during change may more effectively be disclosed through additional in-depth interviewing and on-site observation" (p. 49–62). This is consistent with Maxwell's (1996) descriptions of the general strengths of qualitative research. In particular, methods such as case study and grounded theory may be effective at describing the course of change and moderators of change in groups (what change look likes, who changes, and what conditions are associated with change). Methods focused on deep personal meaning, such as phenomenology, may also help identify mediators of change during group counseling, which is *why* change is occurring.

GIVING VOICE TO AND UNDERSTANDING MARGINALIZED PERSPECTIVES

Much has been written about the importance of understanding the unique experiences of the socially and culturally different client and how these differences affect therapeutic processes (Sue & Sue, 2008). This has also been emphasized in group counseling and group work (Association for Specialists in Group Work, 1999; Riva & Smith, 1997). Additionally, Frey (1994) states, "Researchers simply have neglected the voices of the group members themselves, and we must find a way to give room to their voices in our research reports" (p. 558). According to some authors, qualitative research has the potential to help group-counseling researchers better understand how to serve these populations due to its sensitivity to unique experiences and participant experiences (Merchant & Dupuy, 1996). Similarly, other authors have put forth qualitative methods as a way to promote social justice values at a time when social justice perspectives have increasingly gained focus in the counseling and group-work arenas (Padgett, 2009; Rubel & Pepperell, 2010; Vera & Speight, 2003).

Merchant and Dupuy (1996) argue that research based on positivist assumptions represents and promotes Eurocentric beliefs and practices. Therefore, traditional research methods may be less effective or potentially damaging when used to understand culturally different or marginalized people's experiences. They indicate that the research assumptions of qualitative approaches may offer congruence with (1) the values and worldview of the population being investigated, (2) the nonoppressive or empowering purpose of the study, and (3) the need for studies to be responsive to worldviews different from those of the researchers and traditional positivistic worldviews. Additionally, they characterize the benefits of qualitative research for understanding culturally different or marginalized populations as (1) acceptance of nonlinear causality and interrelatedness; (2) accepted practice of making social and cultural contexts explicit in the research preparation, implementation, and reporting; and (3) inherent valuing of relationships and subjective experience. These benefits may also be useful to group-counseling researchers as they strive to better understand and serve underserved clients.

REVITALIZING GROUP-COUNSELING RESEARCH

The literature at times depicts counselors and group counselors as reluctant to take part in research and attributes the reluctance to several causes. Reisetter et al. (2004) posit that this disengagement is linked to training insufficiencies, counselors' primary identification as practitioners, and perceptions that research does not relate to practice. Okech et al. (2006) indicate that lack of training and mentorship may cause this reluctance, which also translates into quality issues. In discussing group research, Frey (1994) implies that interest is inordinately low due to a lack of a vital connection between real-life problems and group research. Frey hypothesized that the predominant ways of viewing groups and of researching groups are responsible for this disconnection. Additionally, Morgan-Lopez and Fals-Stewart (2006) implicate the challenges of conducting group-work research in this avoidance.

Alongside strengths related to types of understanding that can be gained through qualitative research, the practical strengths of qualitative approaches outlined by Maxwell (1996) seem particularly pertinent to revitalizing group-counseling research. These include relative ease in collaborating with practitioners and participants when using qualitative methods, results that group counselors can relate to and use, and the ability to inform evolving group-counseling practices through formative evaluation (Charmaz, 2006; Maxwell, 1996; Patton, 1990). In terms of increasing motivation to undertake research and the development of a strong research identity, the congruence between the worldviews represented by group counselors and qualitative research offers hope (Reisetter et al., 2004). In summary, Frey states the following:

> Although the dominant paradigm has generated much information about small groups, there is a richness about groups that is missing from this literature, a richness that potentially can be rediscovered by employing an alternative paradigm and its practices. This richness in return, will hopefully renew our sense of purpose and urgency about small group research. (p. 552)

Major Qualitative Research Approaches

The purpose of this section is to summarize several common qualitative research approaches and discuss how each could potentially contribute to a better understanding of group counseling. The approaches that will be covered include phenomenological, ethnographic, case study, and grounded theory methods. Admittedly, these approaches do not represent the entirety of qualitative approaches, and the descriptions represent summarizations of larger bodies of literature which may not capture the variation within each approach.

PHENOMENOLOGICAL RESEARCH

The originator of *phenomenology* is commonly identified as the philosopher Edmund Husserl, whose main concerns were the nature of human consciousness and its relationship to experience (Wertz, 2005). These concerns led to the emergence of the phenomenological movement of philosophy, which influenced the research approaches that share its name. Creswell (2007) summarizes the commonalities of the various phenomenological approaches as a focus on the lived experiences of humans, a commitment to the belief that these lived experiences are conscious and therefore intentional, and a purpose of developing deep descriptions of the essence of the experiences. Thus, research questions focused on process, influence, or cause and effect are not appropriately answered using phenomenological methods (Wertz, 2005).

Two common types of phenomenology are *hermeneutic phenomenology*, which is more focused on the experiencing of the researcher as he or she gains understanding of the phenomena (Van Manen, 1990), and *transcendental, empirical phenomenology*, which is more focused on the participants' experience of the phenomena while setting aside research assumptions (Moustakas, 1994). A third, more recent variation is interpretive phenomenological analysis, which was developed specifically to make phenomenology more easily accessible to psychologists (Smith, Flowers, & Larkin, 2009). Traditional phenomenological methods are undertaken using several similar steps, identified by Creswell (2007):

1. Phenomenology is determined to be the best approach for the research problem.
2. A phenomenon central to the problem is identified and clarified.
3. The researcher orients him- or herself to phenomenology and relates this to the research problem, phenomenon in question, and the process that will be used.
4. The researcher identifies individuals who have experienced the phenomenon and decides how to collect data about their experiences, usually through in-depth interviews with a limited number of broad, open-ended questions.
5. Data analysis generally progresses for each participant from identifying statements significant to the experience to creating clusters of meaning to creating a description of what participants experienced to creating a description of influences upon these experiences.
6. Finally, individual descriptions are used to construct a composite description and essence.

Phenomenology can be applied to group-counseling research to more deeply understand the experiences of group leaders, group members, and potential group members as they engage in the process of group counseling, struggle, and change. For instance, the group-counseling literature emphasizes the importance of members experiencing acceptance. However, this is juxtaposed with how acceptance may or may not be experienced by culturally different group members. To address this tension, researchers could conduct a phenomenological study of how cultural minority group members experience acceptance in culturally heterogeneous counseling groups. A study such as this could inform how group counselors work with such groups.

To accomplish this, the researchers would carefully define the phenomenon related to the problem that they wish to study. For instance, the phenomenon might be *searching for acceptance* in a culturally heterogeneous group or, conversely, *receiving acceptance* in the same group. Once the phenomenon is defined, they should locate participants who have experienced it. Then, data may be collected via in-depth, unstructured interviews with a very few prescribed questions, such as (for searching for acceptance) "What was it like to search for acceptance during your group experience?" or "Can you describe your experience of searching for acceptance in the group?" The researcher might also make decisions about including other types of data such as artwork or poems created or provided by participants that captures the experience.

Interviews would be recorded and transcribed; then, the researcher would sift through the data using one of the well-defined analysis schema related to phenomenology, such as the modification of the Van Kaam method of analysis of phenomenological data (Moustakas, 1994). During analysis the researcher may decide that the data are "thin" or insufficient to capture the experience and may interview participants further or add participants or questions. In the end, the researcher may develop a composite description or essence of participant experiences of searching for acceptance in a culturally heterogeneous group that richly describes the experience and may give insight into their emotional experiences, cognitive structures, and important contextual factors such as helpful or hurtful leader and member interactions.

ETHNOGRAPHIC RESEARCH

Ethnographic research is influenced by varying philosophical, psychological, and sociological schools of thought. However, all types of ethnography are focused on gaining understanding of culture-sharing groups' values, beliefs, behavior patterns, and language (Creswell, 2007). Part of the research process is immersion of the researcher in the culture to observe, interact, interview, and experience. LeCompte and Schensul (1999) characterize ethnographies as being undertaken in the natural setting of the participants and relying upon intensive, in-person engagement with participants and multiple data sources to present an as accurate as possible illustration of the participants' actions and perspectives. Ethnographies utilize data-collection and -analysis strategies that are inductive and interdependent and use culture as the central organizing principle for interpretation to create theories.

Due to the various interpretive lenses used for ethnography, its forms vary in level of interpretation. On one end are realist ethnographies, which focus on reporting the actions and words of the participants

as objectively as possible. On the other end are critical ethnographies, which strive to uncover oppression and enact positive social change. Creswell (2007) summarizes the ethnography process as follows:

1. Ethnography is identified as the most suitable approach for a research problem associated with better understanding of a culture-sharing group.

2. A culture-sharing group is located.

3. Beginning analysis determines on which aspects of the culture to focus.

4. These aspects of the culture direct decision making about what type of ethnography is most suited to the study.

5. Information is collected in the field in the form of interviews, observations, assessments, surveys, and other data.

6. Information is analyzed around key events or over time to form detailed descriptions of the culture-sharing group and eventually themes related to their beliefs and actions.

7. A final product is created in the form of descriptions of the culture from the perspective of the participants and the researcher and based upon patterns or rules identified during analysis.

Very few ethnographies related to group counseling are published, and the approach has untapped potential for group-counseling research. Ethnography may be useful to understand the contexts, such as professional or organizational cultures, within which group counseling does or does not thrive. For instance, manualized group treatments are becoming increasingly important, and research is needed regarding their use (Galinsky, Terzian, & Fraser, 2007). Researchers could use ethnography to document and interpret the culture and practices of agencies that have low levels of success using manualized group treatment. A study such as this could inform such disparate practices as agency hiring, group-work training and supervision, and client preparation for groups.

To accomplish this, the researchers might locate and gain access to an agency that has documented low levels of success using manualized group treatment. Access might include observation of day-to-day practices, reading agency policies and training materials, interviewing staff and clients, interviewing referring agencies, and participating as a group leader or member. Early analysis may uncover themes that could shape the type of ethnography used. For instance, early observations and interviews might indicate that misuses of power and lack of cultural awareness at the administrative level appear to affect both the staff and clients in the groups negatively. This may indicate that including elements of critical ethnography may be appropriate due to its ability to reveal oppressive practices.

The choice of critical ethnography would shape further data collection and analysis, focusing attention on oppressive policies, practices, and even interactions in groups. Data and analysis could center on key events that typify the unsuccessful groups at the site, such as incidences of high attrition in groups. Data would be collected and analyzed until a rich description of the people of the agency and their beliefs, values, language, and interactions was created. This description would likely include the social and political context surrounding the agency. A description of the agency "culture" such as this might provide understanding of how and why the agency's manualized group treatments failed and inform decisions by other programs.

CASE STUDY RESEARCH

Case study research is the approach least associated with a cohesive theoretical framework (Creswell, 2007). Case study research is also considered to be more pragmatic than many other approaches. Indeed, some authors debate whether case study approaches constitute a comprehensive research methodology or simply a way to describe the focus of research undertaken using other methods (Creswell, 2007). However, due to efforts by authors such as Yin (2009) to offer more systematic descriptions of its procedures, case study research is gaining credibility. The purpose of case study research is to understand an issue or problem through study of one or more cases that are defined by *contextual boundaries* (Creswell, 2007; Yin, 2009). Researchers using case study approaches investigate a carefully defined case or cases over time, using multiple, in-depth sources of information. This ideally results in a thorough case description and identification of themes that answer the research question(s). According to Yin, the more the problems and questions seek to explain some present circumstance, the more appropriate case study research might be.

Case studies may vary in how the cases are bounded or defined (Yin, 2009). For instance, a case may be a person and his or her experience, a group of people, or an organization. Cases may also be bound by time and involve interactions between individuals, groups, and organizations (Yin, 2009).

Case studies are also categorized according to intent. Instrumental case studies seek to illustrate a problem or issue through deep study of a single case. Multiple or collective case studies seek similar illustration through exploration of multiple cases. Intrinsic case studies, on the other hand, seek to understand a unique person, group, or circumstance in a more open way. A benefit of case study research, as described by Baxter and Jack (2008), is its reliance upon multiple data sources, which can reveal multiple aspects of the phenomenon. Creswell (2007) and Baxter and Jack summarized case study design and implementation for inexperienced researchers and included the following steps:

1. Deciding if a case study approach will best address the research problem or question.
2. Determining the unit of analysis or case by defining the boundaries of what is to be studied.
3. Making decisions about the type of case study best suited to the purpose of the study.
4. Identifying propositions or tentative hypotheses that will help shape the boundaries, structure, and analysis of the study but will not determine them.
5. Collecting data, which for case study research should include multiple sources such as documents, interviews, observations, participant observations, and physical artifacts. Case studies may also include quantitative assessments if appropriate for the question.
6. Analyzing data through identification of themes and/or cross-case themes.
7. Reporting interpretations or meanings related to the case.

Case study research may be useful to group-counseling researchers in several ways. Like ethnography, case study research may be helpful to group-counseling researchers who want to better understand a focused area of group-counseling practice. In terms of process research, intrinsic case study designs may be appropriate for studying group-counseling programs or individual groups that seem to be unusually effective or ineffective. This would offer insight into the contexts and processes that contribute to their effectiveness or lack thereof. Conversely, instrumental case study designs may be appropriate for group-counseling questions related to specific issues rather than specific groups. For instance, an instrumental, multiple case study design might be used to explore what factors affect development of cohesion in middle school counseling groups.

To undertake this last purpose, researchers would begin by spending considerable effort to clearly define the case. They would need to make decisions about group types and focus, as well as the logistics of the groups they want to include. For instance, they may decide to focus on typical, rather than unusual, middle school counseling groups. The researchers will also need to decide if their purpose is better served by including a variety of group types (for instance, grief, friendship, academic motivation) and compositions (for instance, homogeneous or heterogeneous for such variables as gender, ethnicity, and level of functioning) rather than a more homogeneous selection of type and composition. Bounding the case also requires that researchers to define how much of the context of the group should be included. For instance, will their purpose be better served by defining the case as the group and group leader or by defining it in a broader way that includes information about and from supervisors, administrators, and parents?

After defining the case, the researchers would locate several different groups that fit the case description. Yin (2009) recommends no more than five such cases for a multiple case study. After locating groups, researchers would begin to collect data, which might include interviews with group members, interviews with group leaders, assessments of group cohesion or cohesion-related variables, in-depth descriptions of the contexts of the groups, and observations of the groups. The data gathered for each case would be analyzed for patterns, potentially using an a priori theory, such as group-development theory, as a starting place. Then, researchers would analyze across cases to identify commonalities in factors that appear to affect cohesion. The cross-case analysis and resultant themes could inform group planning and leadership practices of middle school counselors and administrators.

GROUNDED THEORY RESEARCH

Grounded theory originated with the work of Glaser and Strauss (1967). Grounded theory approaches to research are meant to identify elements and processes of an experience over time. These approaches result in dynamic theories grounded in the experiences of the participants. The process of grounded theory involves the systematic and progressive gathering and analysis of qualitative data (Creswell, 2007). Grounded theory approaches are influenced by the sociological school of symbolic interactionism. *Symbolic interactionists* posit that people act toward things on the basis of their meanings and that these meanings are influenced by personal interpretation and interactions with other people and society (Fassinger, 2005).

While grounded theory approaches are praised for their systematic guidelines, they have also been criticized for being rigid and postpositivistic (Charmaz, 2006). More recent iterations of grounded theory, such as those described by Corbin and Strauss (2008) and Charmaz, are more firmly based in constructivism. This results in freer-flowing, more holistic, and less reductionist results. Fassinger (2005) also comments that grounded theory methods are sufficiently flexible to allow integration of feminist or other ideological perspectives. The following represents a summary and synthesis of the steps of grounded theory (Charmaz, 2006; Corbin & Strauss, 2008; Creswell, 2007):

1. Determining if grounded theory is the most appropriate approach for the research problem or question. This is more likely if the question is process-oriented or if explaining variation is part of the research goal.

2. Collecting of data, usually through a series of interviews. Questions are sufficiently general to allow expression of divergent experiences and are focused on the participants' experience of the process. Questions for later interviews are designed to flesh out emerging theory.

3. Analyzing initial data. Data analysis proceeds cyclically as more data are collected. Analysis includes open coding, axial coding, selective coding, use of a conditional matrix, and final theory elucidation.

4. Data collection and analysis continue until saturation is achieved. *Saturation* is the point in the study where no new ideas or dimensions emerge and existing constructs are well described.

5. The result of this process is a theory that has a firm basis in the experience of the participants and is potentially useful and meaningful.

Grounded theory may be useful to group-counseling researchers in several ways. Many of the important constructs of group-counseling theory are not based in systematic observations and inquiry. Thus, their substantiation and development may be enhanced through use of grounded theory procedures. In addition, many such theories have been shown to be applicable to majority populations but not in other populations of concern. And there is still much to understand about the change process from the perspective of group members. Training and development processes of group counselors are also critical and not well understood. Each of these areas represents an opportunity to explore and create substantive theory using grounded theory approaches.

For example, grounded theory might be used to develop or augment group-development theory for adolescent counseling groups. A grounded theory approach would be a good fit for this purpose since group development is a process that occurs over time. Most group-development theory is based upon observations of adult counseling groups, and very little has been written or researched with regard to how adolescent groups develop. Researchers could focus a grounded theory study on how adolescent counseling groups change over time.

Researchers could proceed by accessing several adolescent counseling groups. Data would be collected over the length of the counseling groups, with data sources including interviews with group members and group leaders. Data could also include observations of the group interactions throughout the course of the groups. Data would be analyzed using open coding to identify key concepts related to the groups' development. Axial coding would be used to increase the depth of description of key concepts or categories as well as begin to relate concepts to one another. Selective coding would be used to identify a central organizing concept and bring a sense of flow or process to the emerging theory. Throughout this process more data would be gathered to flesh out "thin" areas of the theory, and more groups could be added to the participant pool if insufficient description was resulting from existing participants. When key concepts and processes are richly described, researchers should be able to describe a theory of adolescent group development over time. This theory might inform group selection and leadership practices for adolescents. Table 15.3 provides a comparison of the typical research foci and problems, processes, and end products of the above qualitative approaches along with their potential application to group counseling.

Applying Qualitative Methods to Group-Counseling Research

The purpose of this section is to explore the effective application of qualitative research approaches to important group-counseling problems and questions. While maintaining a focus on the current priorities of group-counseling research, this section will explore the notion of "good" qualitative research, outline the process of designing a qualitative study, and discuss rigorous implementation.

What Is Good Qualitative Research?

Most descriptions of qualitative research approaches (for example, Lincoln & Guba, 1985; Charmaz, 2006; Creswell, 2007) discuss the issue of promoting and evaluating the quality of studies. Authors have also explored this topic in fields related to group counseling, such as counseling, counseling psychology, social work, and rehabilitation counseling (Choudhuri, Glauser, & Peregoy, 2004; Hanley-Maxwell, Al Hano, & Skivington, 2007; Hoyt & Bhati, 2007; Kline, 2003, 2008; Morrow, 2005; Padgett, 2009). The issue has also been explored with respect to group counseling (Rubel & Villalba, 2009). In this literature a common theme is the difficulty of defining and applying a uniform set of criteria to qualitative research. This difficulty is attributed to the diversity in research assumptions, design, and implementation in qualitative research (Creswell, 2007; Kline, 2003; Morrow, 2005). It is also attributed to the tendency to create evaluation systems that are based on quantitative assumptions, which are inconsistent with the philosophical basis of qualitative research (Forshaw, 2007; Padgett, 2009; Smith & Hodkinson, 2005). While some argue to dispense with evaluation entirely (Forshaw, 2007), others indicate that such criteria are necessary to legitimize the practice of qualitative research and communicate in a positivist and postpositivist world (Morrow, 2005).

According to Morrow (2005), criteria for research quality should be highly dependent upon the assumptions chosen by researchers. Thus, evaluation of qualitative research conducted from a postpositivistic perspective will generally reflect traditional scientific research criteria such as validity, reliability, and objectivity in the form of parallel criteria (Lincoln & Guba, 1985; Morrow, 2005). Evaluation of constructivist and interpretivist qualitative research will diverge further from tradition and include criteria that embrace subjectivity and emphasize understanding, rather than control, and valuing of mutual construction (Morrow, 2005). Such criteria are also applicable to postmodern, ideological, or critical perspectives in qualitative research. Additionally, in these types of studies the potential for positive social impact becomes important. Social impact criteria become increasingly important as the fields of qualitative research, counseling, and group counseling move toward more uniform valuing of social justice and advocacy (Denzin & Lincoln, 2005).

Table 15.3   Major qualitative approaches: comparison of typical foci and problems, processes, end products, and application to group counseling

Approach	Research Foci and Problems	Typical Process	Typical End Product	Potential Application to Group Counseling
Phenomenology (Creswell, 2007; Moustakas, 1994; Wertz, 2005)	Best suited for problems where deep understanding of a lived experience or phenomenon will provide useful information	Use of in-depth interviews to illuminate common experiences of a phenomenon: analysis involves identification of meaning units; creation of textural, structural, and composite descriptions; and final description of essential elements of the phenomenon	Description of the essence of a phenomenon under exploration, typically also contains much information about the context in which the phenomenon occurs	May be useful to more deeply understand the experiences of group leaders, group members, and potential group members as they engage in the process of group counseling and experience phenomena critical to group counseling
Case study (Baxter & Jack, 2008; Creswell, 2007; Yin, 2009)	Best suited for problems where understanding of a case or cases (individuals, sites, or circumstances) will provide useful information	Use of multiple sources of data, potentially quantitative, to richly describe well-bounded cases: analysis involves identifying themes and, for multiple case studies, cross-case themes; may include use of an a priori theory	An in-depth analysis of the case, identifying key factors, patterns, and relationships	May be useful to better understand a focused area of group-counseling practice, particularly where the cases exemplify common group-counseling problems or solutions to problems
Ethnography (Creswell, 2007; LeCompte & Schensul, 1999)	Best suited for problems where understanding of a culture-sharing group will provide useful information	Data collected from multiple sources made possible by immersion in a culture: analysis is variable, dependent upon emergent issues, and influenced by concepts associated with the study of culture	In-depth description of a culture-sharing group, their beliefs, experience, and actions	May be useful to understand how local, professional, or organizational culture affects the implementation of group counseling
Grounded theory (Charmaz, 2006; Creswell, 2007; Corbin & Strauss, 2008)	Best suited for problems where understanding of a psychosocial process will provide useful information	Data collected through progressive theoretical sampling, often multiple rounds of interviews: analysis progressively identifies categories, properties, dimensions, and process through open, axial, and selective coding	Theory or model describing a psychosocial process	May be useful to understand processes of group counseling or that support group counseling, may also be useful in grounding purely theoretical group-counseling concepts in participant experiences

Morrow (2005) also contends that while many criteria for evaluation are specific to the research assumptions chosen and reported by the researchers, there are also several criteria that apply to most qualitative research. This chapter will leave specific description of quality criteria to texts dealing with individual qualitative methods. Rather, this section will focus on the concept of trustworthiness as described by Lincoln and Guba (1985), the three transparadigmatic quality issues identified by Morrow, and the emerging criteria related to methodological congruence (Kline, 2008; Richards & Morse, 2007).

TRUSTWORTHINESS

Lincoln and Guba (1985) authored one of the most utilized sets of criteria for evaluating qualitative research. These criteria are based on the concept of trustworthiness. They discuss the general issue of trustworthiness:

> How can an inquirer persuade his or her audiences (including self) that the findings of an inquiry are worth paying attention to, worth taking account of? What arguments can be mounted, what criteria invoked, what questions asked, that would be persuasive on this issue? (p. 290)

Lincoln and Guba describe the properties of trustworthiness as credibility, transferability, dependability, and confirmability. Respectively, these properties relate to the constructs of internal and external validity, reliability, and objectivity commonly used in quantitative research. While these criteria have gained popularity, they are also criticized by many writers for their reliance upon positivistic constructs to gain legitimacy (Hoyt & Bhati, 2007; Morrow, 2005). Despite this criticism, trustworthiness has become an accepted and useful concept that can bridge the gap between qualitative researchers and often positivist or postpositivist arbiters of research quality.

Strategies suggested by Lincoln and Guba (1985) to promote credibility (analogous to internal validity) are prolonged engagement, peer debriefing, negative case analysis, and member checks. For transferability (analogous to external validity), they suggested thick description or sufficient context to allow readers to make decisions about the applicability of the study to their own circumstances. For dependability (analogous to reliability) and confirmability (analogous to objectivity), they suggest a single technique, a thorough audit trail including data, analysis products, and all other research-related materials.

TRANSPARADIGMATIC QUALITY ISSUES

Morrow (2005) categorizes the common issues concerning qualitative research quality into the domains of how to address subjectivity and reflexivity, how to determine if data are adequate, and how to determine if interpretation is adequate. Each issue will be addressed here, although it is beyond the scope of this chapter to discuss each of these thoroughly. Thus, readers who undertake qualitative studies should carefully consider each domain as they engage in the process of reading the qualitative methodology literature and designing their studies.

Acceptance of subjectivity distinguishes the practice of qualitative research from quantitative approaches, which typically aspire to objectivity (Denzin & Lincoln, 2005). Subjectivity is inherent in the types of data and analysis endemic to qualitative research (Morrow, 2005). Depending up on the qualitative researchers' assumptions, subjectivity may be controlled or embraced (Morrow, 2005). Regardless of which stance is chosen, the question then becomes how to make subjectivity palpable and understandable to the researcher and eventual readers. Controlling strategies, which are most often applied by postpositivists, include use of external auditors and assessment of code frequencies to counteract bias (Morrow, 2005). However, the most common strategies to address subjectivity encourage researchers to reflect upon, become increasingly aware of, and clearly communicate their assumptions about the research phenomena (Merrick, 1999). The characteristic of intentional self-awareness during the research process is called *reflexivity*. Researchers demonstrate reflexivity by documenting their thoughts during the process and by consulting with others to discuss and challenge assumptions (Merrick, 1999; Morrow, 2005). This reflection and transparency serve various purposes, from "bracketing" out the assumptions (Moustakas, 1994) to making biases and agendas transparent to readers. This process may be reflected in a brief statement early in the research report or may take the more extensive form of memos throughout the research process and products.

Another transparadigmatic issue in evaluating qualitative research is data adequacy (Morrow, 2005). Since the purpose of most qualitative research is to describe the inner and unique perspectives of participants, it follows that the results are only as good as the data upon which they are based (Creswell, 2007). Factors such as the appropriateness of sampling procedures, depth and focus of interviews and observations, and variety of evidence all impact judgments of data adequacy (Morrow, 2005).

In terms of sampling, selection of participants or information-rich cases that can best answer the research question, or *purposeful sampling*, is essential for gathering quality data (Creswell, 2007; Patton, 1990). Further sampling strategies used to address more specific needs or purposes of the study involve questions of who specifically should be used and how to access them. Miles and Huberman (1994) and Patton (1990) provide useful descriptions of sampling schema for qualitative research.

The quality of the data-collection procedures is also critical. Researchers who are counselors and group counselors should immediately realize that the way they engage with research participants, or research relationship, can profoundly impact the quality of the data (Maxwell, 1996). More specifically, issues such as flexibility of interviewer, time, setting, openness of questions, and responses of the interviewer all influence the quality of the data gathered (Polkinghorne, 2005). Morrow (2005) cautions against the use of overly specific questions during initial interviews and recommends the use of multiple interviews.

Although quality of data is prioritized over quantity of data, the issue of quantity must be addressed (Morrow, 2005). The issue is often viewed through the concept of data redundancy. Data redundancy is a concept often applied when assessing adequacy of data, though it is also connected to adequacy of interpretation. *Redundancy* is achieved when no new concepts arise from additional data. Finally, the quality of the interpretation will be supported if researchers include multiple forms of data in the study such as interviews, journal entries, focus groups, observations, and artifacts (Creswell, 2007).

The final transparadigmatic quality issue is adequacy of interpretation, which refers to the quality of the translation of participant experiences into concepts, theory, and manuscripts (Morrow, 2005). Adequacy of interpretation extends over three phases of the research process, including data analysis, interpretation, and presentation. Immersion of the researcher(s) during the data-analysis process is critical. Immersion begins during data collection as the researcher(s) becomes familiar with the data and is ultimately marked by the researcher's deep understanding of the whole of the data (Corbin & Strauss, 2008; Creswell, 2007; Morrow, 2005). Though immersion is critical, it is not sufficient for adequate interpretation. Analysis should proceed using an analytic framework or set of procedures that is clearly associated with the qualitative approach selected by the researcher (Kline, 2008).

The issue of adequacy of interpretation also overlaps with the issue of subjectivity. Specifically, the taking of reflexive notes by the researcher, or *memoing*, is a procedure that is associated with addressing subjectivity and with analyzing data. Memoing serves as a method for the researcher to more fully immerse in the data, as well as a means to evaluate and crystallize understandings as they arise. These understandings, carefully considered, coalesce into final interpretations.

Additionally, presentation of the interpretations should reflect a synergy between research understandings and participant quotes that contributes to the overall understanding of the problem (Morrow, 2005; Ponterotto & Grieger, 2007). Qualitative research results should be compelling in both content and presentation and reflect a fresh perspective on the problem (Charmaz, 2006; Corbin & Strauss; 2008; Ponterotto & Grieger, 2007). When considering if one has achieved this in a qualitative group-work study, the following questions should be considered: Do the results provide something unique to group members, group workers, or trainers? Do the results reflect the spirit and depth of the experiences related by participants? Do the results make sense or have that "aha" impact?

METHODOLOGICAL CONGRUENCE

Demonstration of logical correspondence between theoretical framework purpose, questions, methods, and results is emerging as a means for evaluating the quality of qualitative research (Kline, 2008; Maxwell, 1996; Richards & Morse, 2007). Kline (2008) and Maxwell (1996) emphasize the importance of coherence in design and contend that it assists in researchers developing coherent and convincing proposals, implementing quality studies, and developing compelling and useful results. Additionally, Richards and Morse (2007) characterize methodological congruence as critical to the integrity of qualitative research, indicating that part of researchers' responsibility is to make sense of complex experiences. They assert that this becomes a difficult or impossible task when the design and methods are chaotic, arbitrary, or incongruent. Pragmatically, several authors (Creswell, 2007; Padgett, 2009) suggest that, especially for those new to qualitative research, adhering to one well-established qualitative approach is a way to facilitate not only a high-quality end product but also learning. Regardless, methodological coherence or congruence can be demonstrated only when the basic research assumptions and their connection to research design and implementation are clearly understood and reported (Kline, 2008).

Qualitative Research Design Process

Many authors have described the nonlinear trajectory of qualitative research design (Charmaz, 2006; Creswell, 2007; Corbin & Strauss, 2008; Maxwell, 1996). Designing a qualitative study continues past initial implementation of the study through sampling and analysis. Further, qualitative researchers bear a larger responsibility than quantitative researchers for presenting well-reasoned and clear rationales for their research choices, as well as detailed descriptions of their research contexts and processes (Padgett, 2009). This is due to the variety of qualitative traditions, inherent flexibility in design, interpretive nature of analysis, and creativity involved in qualitative research.

In an effort to clarify this ambiguous process, Maxwell (1996) provides a useful model of qualitative research design that is comprised of five components—purposes, conceptual contexts, research questions, methods, and validity. Maxwell emphasizes that all of these components are interdependent and inform each other as the research and design progress. Next, each design phase is described more fully and illustrated with a group counseling–related research project conducted by the authors.

DEVELOPING A RESEARCH PURPOSE

Maxwell (1996) describes the purpose of a qualitative study as the "motives, desires, and goals—anything that leads you to do the study or that you hope to accomplish by doing it" (p. 14). He further illustrates the purpose through these questions, "What are the ultimate goals of this study? What issues is it intended to illuminate, and what practices will it influence? Why do you want to conduct it, and why should we care about the results? Why is the study worth doing?" (p. 4). Research purposes can be personal (researcher's motivation), practical (meeting a need or changing a situation), and research-oriented (understanding something). Maxwell cautions that while all of these purposes have a place in research design, personal motivations must be carefully assessed for how they influence design choices. He further indicates that practical purposes, such as needs to evaluate programs, need to be kept distinct from the research question, to avoid less than optimal data.

Researchers should also consider the purposes that are particularly suitable for qualitative research (Maxwell, 1996). These include understanding participants' meanings, understanding contexts, uncovering unforeseen experiences and influences, understanding processes, and in some cases, forming causal connections. Charmaz (2006) also includes the researcher's personal experiences and observations as a source of research purpose. Creswell (2007) agrees but also indicates that the strongest rationales for a research purpose include a thorough grounding in the scholarly and practice literature.

When starting our recent qualitative study related to group work (Okech & Rubel, 2009; Rubel & Okech, 2009), we noted from our experiences and observations a lack of research-based information about supervision specific to group work. The literature indicated that while supervision is considered important to effective group work and group-work training, systematic exploration of the process was sparse and provided little guidance. Additionally, we had our own writing requirements as assistant professors, curiosity and needs as group-work supervisors, and sense of obligation to the field. Thus, our purpose in engaging in the research was not only to understand the process of group-work supervision better but to provide ideas about how to think and what to do while supervising group workers. Due to the process-oriented nature of the issue and the lack of general information, qualitative research was a natural choice.

DEVELOPING A CONCEPTUAL CONTEXT

Maxwell (1996) indicates that the *contextual context* of a study is comprised of the assumptions the researcher has about what is going on. This serves as a theoretical framework that influences, but does not dictate, the overall study design. The conceptual context may be comprised of the researcher's experiences, existing theory and research, pilot study results, and thought experiments. Maxwell is careful to distinguish between the literature review and the conceptual context. He describes the role of the literature review in constructing a conceptual context. In contrast, he describes the more traditional role of demonstrating a familiarity with the field literature reviews in proposals and reports. Within the qualitative methodology literature, exhaustive a priori literature reviews are sometimes viewed as threats to true exploration (Creswell, 2007).

The construction of a conceptual context represents a thorough exploration and purposeful illumination of underlying assumptions garnered from disparate influences. These assumptions are purposefully streamlined into a framework that focuses the proposed study, yet they are sensitive to new information and concepts (Maxwell, 1996). A common example of how existing theory is incorporated into the conceptual context for a study is the use of feminist or critical race theories in research, which sensitizes researchers during all phases of design and implementation to issues of inequities, socialization, and power (Ponterotto, 2005). Further, Maxwell suggests using a technique called "concept mapping" as a way to visually explore and refine the researcher's conceptual context. With purposes and conceptual context somewhat developed, the research moves on to developing research questions.

For our study (Okech & Rubel, 2009; Rubel & Okech, 2009), the conceptual context was formed by the literature, our own experiences, discussions with others, and prior writing and theorizing we had done on the subject (Okech & Rubel, 2007; Rubel & Okech, 2006). By exploring our assumptions, we clarified what we already knew and how this knowledge might affect how we approached our research both positively and negatively. We had already published a theoretical model of group-work supervision and became aware that we did not want our purpose to be validation of our own model. Thus, we needed to explore the assumptions behind our model closely and to be vigilant about how these ideas could inform, but not dictate, how we moved forward.

DEVELOPING RESEARCH QUESTIONS

Research questions are the center of the qualitative research design process (Creswell, 2007; Maxwell, 1996). However, Maxwell criticizes design schema that place research questions at the start of the design process. He indicates that the process of creating good questions relies heavily upon the interaction of purposes and conceptual context and must remain sensitive to all other parts of the design. Research questions direct the study in a more focused way than the purpose and conceptual context. They do this by specifically describing what the researcher wants to understand and what is not understood. Identification of research questions can be challenging in several ways. Questions can be overly broad and not effectively narrow the focus of data collection and analysis into comprehensible products. They can also be overly narrow, thereby bypassing important data and interpretations later in the process. Finally, research questions can also represent conscious or unconscious efforts to "smuggle" in agendas, practical purposes, or biases (Maxwell, 1996).

Maxwell (1996) emphasizes that qualitative approaches to research are best suited to questions that have a particularizing rather than generalizing purpose, a realist rather than instrumentalist perspective, and a process rather than variance focus. He summarizes these strengths by stating that qualitative researchers tend to focus on "questions about the meaning of events and activities to the people involved in these, and questions about the influence of the physical and social context on these events and activities" (p. 59). Further, Maxwell indicates that the types of understanding most congruent with qualitative research are descriptive, interpretive, and theoretical understanding. This leads to the idea that the type of understanding desired from the study should direct the type of question that should be proposed. In addition to identifying what the study specifically seeks to understand, research questions guide the selection of methods and validation techniques (Creswell, 2007; Maxwell, 1996).

Our own research question related to group-work supervision was shaped by our purposes and our conceptual context (Okech & Rubel, 2009; Rubel & Okech, 2009). As we explored our purpose, experiences, assumptions, and relevant literature, we were drawn toward questions related to existing practice by expert group-work supervisors. This was guided by the purpose of providing useful descriptions that might provide guidance to others. As we further explored literature about group-work supervision, expertise, and in particular expertise in clinical practice, we found some precedent for informing practice through the exploration of expert or master practitioners. Thus, after several iterations, our research question became, What do expert group-work supervisors experiences as they supervise group workers? We were careful to keep the question general and open, to control the influence of our prior assumptions. The general nature of the question placed the focus on what the supervisors experienced, perceived, and did while supervising.

CHOOSING METHODS

Methods constitute the means by which the purposes of the study will be met and the research questions will be answered (Maxwell, 1996). Definition of the research relationship, site and sampling choices, specification of data type and collection techniques, and analysis strategies constitute the methods

(Maxwell, 1996; Patton, 1990). A key issue that Maxwell identifies is the degree of "prestructuring" that occurs. He contends that structuring may be seen as a threat to the flexibility that allows qualitative researchers to fully describe phenomena. He reframes this threat as a trade-off: More prestructuring structure may allow for greater comparability and ability to address variability, while less prestructuring may allow for greater ability to understand single phenomena fully and deeply. Thus, decisions about the degree of prestructuring studies should be linked to the nature of the research problem, purpose, and questions. Regardless, he cautions that studies with little or no prestructuring can be confusing and counterproductive for beginning researchers.

Methods should be consistent or coherent with the overall purpose or specific question(s) of the study (Kline, 2008; Maxwell, 1996; Richards & Morse, 2007). Sampling, data collection, and analysis should all reflect the underlying philosophical assumptions of the study. Intentionality is particularly relevant when selecting methods since the choice of method will inform more concrete implementation decisions (Richards & Morse, 2007). Providing useful illustrations, Creswell (2007) compares and contrasts the design process for several qualitative methods. For instance, phenomenology is used to uncover the essence or meaning of a significant phenomenon experienced by participants; utilizes methods such as in-depth, highly flexible, and personal interviews to gather data; and results in an evocative description of the meaning of that phenomenon. A phenomenology should not result in a mechanistic or impersonal description of behavior.

An initial and ongoing methodological choice is *defining the research relationship* (Denzin & Lincoln, 2005; Maxwell, 1996). Maxwell indicates that defining the research relationship solely in terms of entry and rapport, which is common, minimizes the impact that the research relationship has on other components of the study design. The researchers' experiences, perspectives, and biases influence research assumptions and, in turn, influence focus, questions, analysis, and presentation of the results. Each is reflected in the type of relationship the researcher chooses to have with the participants (Denzin & Lincoln, 2005). Maxwell recommends that the nature of these relationships be thoroughly explored during the design process.

The process of choosing methods also includes choices about sampling. Most qualitative studies

use *purposeful sampling*. This is the practice of sampling the places, people, events, and processes that are best suited to provide useful data for the purposes and questions of the study (Patton, 1990). To gain useful qualitative data, Maxwell (1996) suggests four different strategies that correspond to different types of research questions. Researchers can sample populations to find typical cases, heterogeneity in cases, or extreme cases or to foster comparison. Subsequent sampling choices may not become clear until the study progresses and the researcher gains deeper understanding of the phenomena in question. Sampling choices should take into account the purpose of the research, the desired and extant nature of research relationships, data-collection issues, and, of course, potential ethical issues.

In discussing the process of choosing data types and collection techniques, Maxwell (1996) focuses on two issues, the relationship between research questions and data collection, which may include interview questions, and the use of triangulation. Maxwell cautions against confusing research questions and interview questions and iterates that interview questions and other data-collection techniques should reflect the best means to gather data that will answer the question. Rather than focusing on direct correspondence between research questions and interview questions, which he attributes to positivistic influences, Maxwell suggests anticipating how interview questions will work during data collection and encourages researchers to pilot questions with people similar to eventual participants. He also suggests triangulation of data type (for instance, including observations, journals, and documents along with interview data) to counteract potential data-collection biases, a method also suggested by Morrow (2005) and Creswell (2007).

While much of the qualitative data–analysis literature focuses on specific strategies (e.g., Corbin & Strauss, 2008; Smith et al., 2009), Maxwell (1996) discusses data-analysis choices by comparing two types of analytic strategies and linking them to the purposes and questions of the qualitative study. He describes *categorizing strategies* as a process of parsing data into codes, concepts, themes, and issues either emic or etic in nature. He describes *contextualizing strategies* as strategies that allow researchers to "connect statements and events within a context into a coherent whole" (p. 79). He cautions that if study purposes are to explore linkages between context and process or outcomes, then categorizing analysis strategies will be insufficient. Conversely, he warns that contextualizing strategies alone will not allow researchers to address questions about similarities or differences between individuals or settings. He posits that using both types of strategies is essential to gaining a full picture of a phenomenon through qualitative research. He adds that the use of either or both should be linked to study purposes.

We chose grounded theory methods for our study due to their suitability for analyzing the complex multilayered aspects of group work and their fit with this study's exploratory and process-related purpose (Frey, 1994; Okech & Rubel, 2009; Rubel & Okech, 2009; Corbin & Strauss, 2008). We also found the constructivist foundations of grounded theory to be consistent with our personal views and the purposes of the study. We chose to prestructure the study to a moderately high level for several reasons, including the human subject requirements, our experience level, the relatively narrow phenomena we were exploring, and the pragmatic purposes of the study. We very intentionally chose our methods (data collection and analysis) to be as consistent with a constructivist grounded theory approach as possible.

Our sampling procedures were purposeful. Since the purpose and questions of the study required access to expert group-work supervisors, we used a chain sampling procedure (Patton, 1990) that originated with e-mail contact with a group-work association to identify participants who met our criteria. These contacts led to further contacts and so on. From the qualified pool we sampled further to ensure heterogeneity in theoretical perspective, professional orientation, gender, and supervision context. We attempted to sample for heterogeneity in ethnicity/culture but were unable to find much variety.

In terms of the decisions we made about data type and collection methods, pragmatic issues became paramount. While we felt observations, face-to-face interviews, and use of other types of data would have been beneficial, resource constraints and the fact that our participants were spread out over the country made multiple phone interviews the most practical choice. Interview questions were very general since, while we wanted the participants to focus on what they experienced while supervising group workers, we also wanted them to feel comfortable expressing themselves as freely as possible about those experiences. All of the sampling and data-collection choices reflected and impacted the research relationship we desired. The constructivist position we took meant that we desired a collaborative relationship with participants, with their feedback influencing our findings. Our research question necessitated a sample of experts in group-work supervision, which removed some of the potential vulnerability and power differential between researchers and researched.

Choices about data analysis were informed by our desire to remain congruent with a constructivist grounded theory approach. Consistent with Maxwell's contention that both categorizing and contextualizing strategies be used to get a full picture of the phenomenon, we used open coding as a categorizing strategy and axial and selective coding as a contextualizing strategy. The combination of categorizing and contextualizing strategies enabled us to reflect both the content and process of our expert group-work supervisor participants.

CHOOSING STRATEGIES TO ADDRESS VALIDITY (CREDIBILITY)

Finally, interwoven with all other methodological choices is the issue of validity. Many qualitative researchers reject traditional conceptualizations of validity and embrace other benchmarks such as trustworthiness, goodness, or rigor (Kline, 2008). Maxwell (1996) uses the term *validity* to describe, in general, the credibility of a research-related account. He states that, "Validity is a goal rather than a product; it is never something that can be proven or taken for granted. Validity is also relative: it has to be assessed in relationship to the purposes and circumstances of the research, rather than being a context-independent property of methods or conclusions" (p. 86), and emphasizes that in qualitative research validity is not guaranteed by use of methods and that methods are meant only to collect evidence to counteract threats to validity.

Maxwell (1996) focuses primarily on two major threats to validity in qualitative research, researcher bias and reactivity. These correspond to how much the researcher brings unexamined assumptions to the study and how much the research and researcher affect the setting and participants during the process. He suggests that, in addition to traditional strategies to control bias and reactivity, the most critical strategy is for the researcher to carefully consider, attempt to understand, and describe how bias and reactivity might occur or are occurring in the study. This is strongly connected with the concept of reflexivity (Merrick, 1999; Morrow, 2005). With careful attempts at understanding and identifying specific instances of these anticipated threats to validity, Maxwell suggests that researchers then sift through the multitudes of strategies presented in the literature to identify ones that may best produce evidence to counteract the specific threats.

Our choices to counteract reactivity, researcher bias, and other threats to validity were consistent with Lincoln and Guba's (1985) concept of trust-worthiness: credibility, transferability, dependability, and confirmability (Okech & Rubel, 2009; Rubel & Okech, 2009). To build credibility, we employed prolonged engagement and triangulation (Creswell, 1994; Lincoln & Guba, 1985). Prolonged engagement entailed interviewing the participants multiple times over a period of 8 months. The researchers also conducted member checks with all participants and compared the study findings with the current literature in the field. To address transferability, dependability, and confirmability, we again followed Lincoln and Guba by maintaining detailed descriptions of the context of the study and the study procedures.

Qualitative Studies Related to Group Counseling

This section provides several examples of qualitative studies related to group counseling published in scholarly journals between 2000 and 2009. A search focused on qualitative group counseling–related research indicates that over that last 10 years (2000–2009) a number of journals have published accounts of qualitative research related to group counseling (e.g., *Journal for Specialists in Group Work, Group Analysis, Early Child Development and Care, International Journal of Group Psychotherapy, Journal for Nervous and Mental Disease, Nursing Research*, and *Journal of Psychiatric and Mental Health Nursing*). Despite the variety of journals encountered, the authors found it difficult to find identifiable examples of specific qualitative methods.

Examples were selected to represent a diversity of reported methods, a variety of group-counseling questions, and a diversity of fields in which group counseling might occur. This section will provide a brief description of each study and discuss each in terms of group-counseling research needs, trustworthiness, accounting for subjectivity, accounting for data adequacy, accounting for interpretative adequacy, and methodological congruence. Readers should consider that the editorial practices of the journals which contain these reports may profoundly affect presentation of the research and the amount of context supplied for design decisions (Morrow, 2005).

A Phenomenology Exploring Group Members' Experiences

A recent example of a phenomenological study of group counseling–related issues is Barros, Kitson, and Midgley (2008). The focus of the research is the functioning of a series of Anna Freud parent–toddler groups located at one treatment center. The researchers provide a thorough theoretical and research literature review and identify a problem of insufficient research regarding psychoanalytically informed parent–toddler groups. The purpose is tacitly stated as not a measure of outcome but "an opportunity to learn more about parents' perceptions of their experience of attending these parent–toddler groups to help us understand in greater detail what characterizes such a service, from the parent's own perspective" (p. 276). Citing the exploratory nature of the study, the researchers chose a design based upon interpretive phenomenological analysis (IPA). Throughout the methods section, the authors detail context, sampling, data collection, analysis, and issues of reliability and validity, often referring to methodological literature related to IPA. Results are reported as three plausible superordinate themes related to the parents' experience of the groups (setting of the group, what it was like to be a parent in the group, and perceptions of toddlers' experience of the group), which were supplemented with narrative descriptions of subordinate themes in line with the IPA method. Most themes were described with germane participant quotes.

In terms of the relationship of the problem and question to specific group-counseling research needs, the focus on the parents' perspective of the group experience meets a need for more focus on members' perspectives. Though disappointingly little is said about the basic research assumptions and research questions, IPA and other phenomenological methods seem appropriate for the purposes of the study. The researchers briefly discuss the role of subjectivity and interpretation in their report, but they do not present their own experiences, assumptions, or process in a way that helps the reader trust the interpretations or understand more fully the researchers' intent to address subjectivity. Additionally, little information is given that would indicate data adequacy. For instance, though the authors state that they developed a semistructured interview, the general nature of the questions is not described and no sample questions are provided. Interview lengths and amount of data are not reported. The use of one type of data and reliance upon one interview per participant does not inspire confidence that the researchers achieved prolonged engagement or gathered sufficiently rich data.

The authors attempt to establish interpretive adequacy through use of member checks; however, these were completed with only two participants out of five. The authors do discuss the relevance of their findings, which is roughly equivalent to Lincoln and Guba's (1985) concept of transferability. They indicate that their descriptions of the settings, participants, and procedures are adequate for others to make decisions about the usefulness of the results. Additionally, using IPA, they appropriately limited their analysis to categorizing strategies, which was also reflected in their results, which had a thematic rather than a process structure. Despite limitations, the presentation of the results is impactful and meaningful, providing a small but fresh look at what it is like to be a parent attending a parent–toddler group such as this. In terms of methodological congruence, although the researchers adhere to a fairly systematized version of phenomenology, they do not overtly comment on their understanding of the foundational research assumptions of the method and their connection to design. Thus, it is difficult to determine methodological congruence in this case.

A Case Study of Group Members' and Leader Perceptions

A recent example of case study research related to group counseling is Wanlass, Moreno, and Thomson (2005). The focus of this study is the functioning of a series of outpatient, aftercare eating-disorder groups. These researchers provide a thorough theoretical and research literature review and tacitly identify a problem of insufficient research linking process to outcome in eating disorder–treatment groups. The purpose is explicitly stated as being to provide "an exploratory investigation of therapist and client process and outcome perspectives on group psychotherapy for eating disorders" (p. 49). No rationale for selecting case study design is articulated, and no methodological literature related to case study research is cited. The methods section provides an extensive description of the groups and participants and a brief description of data-collection procedures without relating procedures to the methodological literature, though inclusion of multiple types of qualitative data and a small amount of qualitative data is consistent with case study methods

(Yin, 2009). Data-analysis and -interpretation techniques are only briefly referred to, citing the categorization strategies of grounded theory methods described by Glaser and Strauss (1967). The authors report results in terms of categories of importance, benefits, problems, and critical incidents, describing the origins of these categories as the questionnaire used to gather data. These categories are reported separately for clients and for the therapist. Client themes are not richly described but do include quotes, while the therapist descriptions are extensive but do not contain quotes.

In terms of the relationship of the problem and questions of this study to specific needs in group-counseling literature, this study's focus on both process elements and outcome, including both leader and member experiences, for a specific group type fits with needs outlined in the group-counseling research literature. The purpose of the study, however, is not connected in the report to a rationale for selecting case study methods, and no specific cast study design is identified. Additionally, no efforts are made to define the unit of analysis for this case study. Strategies to increase trustworthiness or validity are not detailed by the authors in the methods section, though limitations related to these are included in the discussion section. Although one of the researchers also served as the source of therapist data/perspective, the issue of subjectivity is not addressed. The research report includes no description of a theoretical position on subjectivity, strategies to control or make transparent subjectivity, or description of the researchers' experiences, assumptions, or biases. While the literature review, results, and discussion all point to Yalom's (1995) therapeutic factors as an a priori theory, they are not explicitly discussed as such. Case study designs are more amenable to use of a priori theory (Creswell, 2007); however, Yalom's (1995) theoretical framework is not overtly incorporated in the design. In terms of data adequacy, group member data were collected via mailed questionnaires using a series of demographic, quantitative, and open-ended qualitative questions. Little indication of the nature or focus of the question is given. Therapist data were collected as written observations after the therapist reread group case notes. The retrospective nature of the data as well as the limited engagement during data collection indicate that the data could have been richer given more immediate and extended engagement. Interpretive adequacy is also suspect in this study, with only fleeting reference to analysis strategies and little discussion of research assumptions. Perhaps due to the influence of a priori theory and emphasis on the therapist's voice, the results feel familiar and confirmatory rather than unique in perspective. In terms of methodological congruence, assessment is difficult given the lack of overtly stated research assumptions and clearly stated methods.

A Microethnography of Group Member Experiences

A recent example of an ethnographic study related to group counseling is Pandya and Gingerich (2002). The study focuses on a single group of male batterers receiving group treatment. The authors present a theoretical and research literature review and identify a problem related to insufficient understanding of batterers' change processes during treatment, which is largely group-based for this population. Several research questions are identified related to this problem. The rationale for choosing a microethnographic study design is related to the focus on one time-limited group to the desire to better understand "the complex meaning systems abusers use to organize their behavior, to understand themselves and others, and to make sense out of the world in which they live" (p. 48) and how this related to their choices to change. The methods section provides a description of the treatment content (group session activities) but not the group process. It also provides descriptions of the context of treatment, cultural influences, data collection, and analyses that are related to two methodological references related to ethnography, Spradley (1979, 1980). Results are reported in the form of one thorough biography to give an example of the depth of description, five abbreviated biographies to save space but still provide context, and finally a theme analysis that describes the change process of those who successfully completed the group.

In terms of the relationship of this study's problem and questions to specific needs in group-counseling literature, the focus on clients' experience of change during group process and identification of contextual factors associated with the change are consistent with needs outlined in the group-work literature. However, the researchers provide little focus on the group's process or interactions but instead prefer data and results related to individual change in the context of the group content (treatment modules). The researchers do not provide any information about the foundational research assumptions behind the design and fall short of being explicit in their description of how the study purpose fits with the strengths of microethnography. For instance, they do not identify the group and members as a distinct cultural group whose values, beliefs, and behaviors need to be better understood. Despite this, microethnography seems like a plausible choice of methodology for the purpose.

The researchers also do not explicitly discuss the concept of, or means to increase, validity. They do not discuss their position on subjectivity or the means used to address it. In terms of data adequacy, the researchers built several different data sources into their design, including extensive observations of the group, clinical file information, homework assignments completed by the group members, and discussions with the therapist. They did not interview the group members or conduct member checks. Data from groups were recorded via notes, not audio- or videotaping, which limits their descriptive adequacy. In terms of interpretive adequacy, the authors describe a plausible framework for data analysis in microethnography utilizing both categorizing and contextualizing strategies, in keeping with the study's change process focus. However, they do not account for their own perspectives and biases, thus putting their interpretations in a less credible light. Presentation of the results is mixed in that the men's stories are compelling but are presented with few quotes. Thus, the themes seem thin rather than rich and well described. In terms of methodological congruence, lack of an explicit discussion of theoretical framework and research assumptions precludes assessment of congruence.

A Grounded Theory Exploring Group Leaders' Experiences

Christensen, Hulse-Killacky, Salgado, Thornton, and Miller (2006) provide a recent example of a ground theory study of group-counseling issues. The focus of the study is a set of doctoral student group leaders who were all engaged in leading reminiscence groups for people who were elderly. These researchers provide a thorough theoretical and research literature review and identify a problem of insufficient research regarding leaders' experiences of leading reminiscence groups for elderly people. The purpose is explicitly stated as being to explore "the perceptions of group leaders who facilitated reminiscence group for elderly persons in a long-term care facility" (p. 73). While no rationale for selecting this design is articulated, description of the methods focuses on grounded theory's strengths related to "interactive and systematic processes of data collection and analysis" (p. 75) and potential sensitivity to multicultural and diverse perspectives. Throughout the methods section, the authors carefully detail context, sampling, data collection, analysis, and issues of quality, often referring to methodological literature related to grounded theory (Strauss & Corbin, 1998). Their results are reported as two categories, but only the central category, group culture, is described, which is common due to journal space limitations. Description of this category is very thorough and includes three interrelated concepts of content, process, and leadership functions. The researchers provide in-depth descriptions of the participants' poignant experiences of encountering and leading groups with elderly people in a long-term care facility and illustrate these descriptions with convincing and engaging participant quotes.

The study's focus on leadership process and groups that serve marginalized populations, in this case elderly people, fits with needs outlined in the group-counseling research literature. Additionally, the authors specifically mention that interview questions addressed contextual factors such as education about the population and institutional culture, which indicates sensitivity to culture and societal power dynamics. The authors do not explicitly discuss trustworthiness or subjectivity but do reject positivistic notions of validity and express an intent to "explore and maintain some sense of analytic objectivity, while also preserving the detailed narratives and depth that emerged from the findings of this investigation" (p. 75). They describe careful data analysis in conjunction with consultation with an outside auditor as a mean by which they bracketed their biases. However, there is no discussion or identification of these biases in the report, nor a clear statement of their position on subjectivity, although their methods suggest a more postpositivist bent (Morrow, 2005).

In terms of data adequacy, the researchers used a variety of types of data and data-collection methods including direct observation of groups, direct observation of supervision of participants, participant interviews, and focus groups. The richness of quotes also speaks to data adequacy. In terms of interpretive adequacy, the authors provide a thorough description of data-analysis procedures, including member checking, and a convincing and compelling

blend of participant quotes and interpretation. Additionally, the results add a fresh perspective on leadership with a marginalized population as group members. In terms of methodological congruence, the authors claim adherence to a cohesive methodology, grounded theory, citing consistent methodological references. They describe methods that are consistent with this approach and their purposes throughout the study. This indicates a relatively high level of methodological congruence, though clearer statements of research assumptions and perspective early in the report would make such determinations more meaningful.

Conclusions

This chapter has reintroduced and further explored the idea, first presented by Frey (1994), that qualitative approaches may have unique applicability to group counseling–related research. Despite essential differences between the purposes of quantitative and qualitative approaches to research, many of the challenges facing quantitative group-counseling researchers are also relevant to qualitative researchers. These challenges include accounting for the complex nature of groups, identifying and linking process elements to the outcomes of group counseling, more closely linking research to group counseling in the field, and the need to better understand the experiences of diverse group members. Revitalizing interest in group-counseling research is also a challenge that must be considered. Each of these challenges can be met, in part, through the use of qualitative approaches.

Certain qualitative approaches may be uniquely suited to exploring specific group-counseling issues and research needs. For instance, case study methods and ethnography may work well to gain understanding of the contexts and process of uniquely successful or unsuccessful counseling groups or group-counseling programs. Phenomenology may be well suited to gaining in-depth understanding of how group members, particularly underrepresented group members, experience what are assumed to be critical aspects of groups, such as cohesion and interpersonal feedback. Additionally, grounded theory methods may be useful for developing an understanding of leadership, development, and change processes in counseling groups.

However, qualitative approaches are not a panacea for the challenges facing group-counseling researchers. Without careful planning and implementation, qualitative group-counseling studies will not meet these challenges and will not have the credibility to impact practice. For example, the group counseling–related qualitative studies discussed in this chapter all began with important problems and questions. However, they met those purposes with varying degrees of success. In all cases, the studies exhibited less than ideal levels of transparency and reflexivity. This lack of information about researcher biases and foundational research assumptions made determinations of quality difficult. Additionally, all of the included studies gave little time to discussion of issues of trustworthiness and goodness. With the exception of Christensen et al. (2006), they mentioned little about intentional strategies to promote trustworthiness. These deficits echo calls in the literature for researchers and editors to become more knowledgeable about qualitative methods and their philosophical foundations. For the critical research needs of the group-counseling field to be met, researchers must carefully consider these needs and challenges and design studies that are intentional and well informed by the qualitative inquiry literature.

Researchers who are considering qualitative approaches for group counseling–related research should be mindful of several factors. First, they should be very clear about the problem they wish to address. This demands an examination of their real-world observations and experiences with groups and the research, publication, and policy that form its context. Researchers who wish to truly add to the body of knowledge about group counseling should be mindful of the challenges and issues on which many authors have commented (Burlingame et al., 2004; Frey, 1994; Riva & Smith, 1997). Consideration of these factors can move studies from superficial to relevant and useful. Concurrent with this examination, researchers should carefully explore their own assumptions about the group-counseling problem they wish to study as well as foundational assumptions about the research process. While this level of personal examination is useful and necessary for both quantitative and qualitative researchers, it is especially essential to qualitative researchers as they attempt to focus more narrowly on research questions and select qualitative methods that are congruent with their own perspectives and the problem they wish to address. Finally, as exploration and intentional choosing move qualitative researchers toward a particular method and design and into implementation, they need to be cognizant that the qualitative research process is not linear or superficial. It is only through deep engagement with the methodological literature, themselves, participants, and the data that meaningful results will be achieved. Understanding of participants' experiences, themselves as researchers, and qualitative methods is a spiraling process of immersion, reflection, reexamination, and collaboration.

References

Association for Specialists in Group Work (ASGW). (1999). ASGW principles for diversity-competent group workers. *Journal for Specialists in Group Work, 24*, 7–14.

Barros, M., Kitson, A., & Midgley, N. (2008). A qualitative study of the experience of parents attending a psychoanalytically informed parent–toddler group. *Early Child Development and Care, 178*, 3, 273–288.

Baxter, P., & Jack, S. (2008). Qualitative case study methodology: Study design and implementation for novice researchers. *Qualitative Report, 13*, 544–559.

Burlingame, G. M., Fuhriman, A., & Johnson, J. E. (2004). Process and outcome in group counseling and psychotherapy: A perspective. In J. L. DeLucia-Waack, D. A. Gerrity, C. R. Kalodner, & M. T. Riva (Eds.), *Handbook of group counseling and psychotherapy* (pp. 49–62). Thousand Oaks, CA: Sage.

Charmaz, K. (2006). *Constructing grounded theory: A practical guide through qualitative analysis.* Thousand Oaks, CA: Sage.

Choudhuri, D., Glauser, A., & Peregoy, J. (2004). Guidelines for writing a qualitative manuscript for the journal of counseling & development. *Journal of Counseling & Development, 82*, 443–446.

Christensen, T. M., Hulse-Killacky, D., Salgado, R. A., Jr., Thornton, M. D., & Miller, J. L. (2006). Facilitating reminiscence groups: Perceptions of group leaders. *Journal for Specialists in Group Work, 31*, 73–88.

Corbin, J., & Strauss, A. (2008). *Basics of qualitative research* (3rd ed.). Thousand Oaks, CA: Sage.

Creswell, J. W. (1994). *Research design: Qualitative and quantitative approaches.* Thousand Oaks, CA: Sage.

Creswell, J. W. (2007). *Qualitative inquiry and research design: Choosing among five approaches* (2nd ed.). Thousand Oaks, CA: Sage.

Denzin, N. K., & Lincoln, Y. S. (2005). Introduction: The discipline and practice of qualitative research. In N. K. Denzin & Y. S. Lincoln (Eds.), *Handbook of qualitative research* (pp. 1–18). Thousand Oaks, CA: Sage.

Dickson-Swift, V., James, E. L., Kippen, S., & Liamputtong, P. (2007). Doing sensitive research: What challenges do qualitative researchers face? *Qualitative Research, 7*, 327–353.

Fassinger, R. E. (2005). Paradigms, praxis, problems, and promise: Grounded theory in counseling psychology research. *Journal of Counseling Psychology, 52*, 156–166.

Forshaw, M. J. (2007). Free qualitative research from the shackles of method. *Psychologist, 20*, 478–479.

Frey, L. R. (1994). The naturalistic paradigm: Studying small groups in the postmodern era. *Small Group Research, 25*, 551–577.

Galinsky, M. J., Terzian, M. A., & Fraser, M. W. (2007). The art of groupwork practice with manualized curricula. *Groupwork, 17*, 74–92.

Glaser, B., & Strauss, A. (1967). *The discovery of grounded theory.* Chicago: Aldine.

Goering, P., Boydell, K. M., & Pignatiello, A. (2008). The relevance of qualitative research for clinical programs in psychiatry. *Canadian Journal of Psychiatry, 53*, 145–151.

Guba, E. G., & Lincoln, Y. S. (2005). Paradigmatic controversies, contradictions, and emerging confluences. In N. K. Denzin and Y. S. Lincoln (Eds.), *Handbook of qualitative research* (3rd ed., pp. 191–216). Thousand Oaks, CA: Sage.

Hanley-Maxwell, C., Al Hano, I., & Skivington, M. (2007). Qualitative research in rehabilitation counseling. *Rehabilitation Counseling Bulletin, 50*, 99–110.

Hoyt, T. W., & Bhati, S. K. (2007). Principles and practices: An empirical examination of qualitative research in the *Journal of Counseling Psychology. Journal of Counseling Psychology, 54*, 2, 201–210.

Kivlighan, D. M., Jr., Coleman, M. N., & Anderson, D. C. (2000). Process, outcome, and methodology in group counseling research. In S. D. Brown & R. W. Lent (Eds.), *Handbook of counseling psychology* (3rd ed., pp. 767–764). Hoboken, NJ: John Wiley & Sons.

Kline, W. B. (2003). The evolving research tradition in *Counselor Education and Supervision. Counselor Education and Supervision, 43*, 82–85.

Kline, W. B. (2008). Developing and submitting credible qualitative manuscripts. *Counselor Education and Supervision, 47*, 210–217.

Laurenceau, J., Hayes, A. M., & Feldman, G. C. (2007). Some methodological and statistical issues in the study of change processes in psychotherapy. *Clinical Psychology Review, 27*, 682–695.

LeCompte, M. D., & Schensul, J. J. (1999). *Designing and conducting ethnographic research.* Walnut Creek, CA: Altamira Press.

Lincoln, Y. S., & Guba, E. G. (1985). *Naturalistic inquiry.* Newbury Park, CA: Sage.

Maxwell, J. A. (1996). *Qualitative research design: An interactive approach.* Thousand Oaks, CA: Sage.

Merchant, N., & Dupuy, P. (1996). Multicultural counseling and qualitative research: Shared worldview and skills. *Journal of Counseling and Development, 74*, 532–541.

Merrick, E. (1999). An exploration of quality in qualitative research: Are reliability and validity relevant? In M. Kopala & L. Suzuki (Eds.), *Using qualitative methods in psychology* (pp. 25–39). Thousand Oaks, CA: Sage.

Miles, M. B., & Huberman, M. (2004). *Qualitative data analysis: An expanded sourcebook* (2nd ed.). Thousand Oaks, CA: Sage.

Morgan-Lopez, A. A., & Fals-Stewart, W. (2006). Analytic complexities associated with group therapy in substance abuse treatment research: Problems, recommendations, and future directions. *Experimental and Clinical Psychopharmacology, 14*, 265–273.

Morrow, S. (2005). Quality and trustworthiness in qualitative research in counseling psychology. *Journal of Counseling Psychology, 52*, 250–260.

Morse, J. M., Penrod, J., & Hupcey, J. E. (2000). Qualitative outcome analysis: Evaluating nursing interventions for complex clinical phenomena. *Journal of Nursing Scholarship, 32*, 125–130.

Moustakas, C. (1994). *Phenomenological research methods.* Thousand Oaks, CA: Sage.

Okech, J. E. A., Astramovich, R., Johnson, M., Hoskins, W., & Rubel, D. (2006). Doctoral research training of counselor education faculty. *Counselor Education & Supervision, 46*(2), 131–145.

Okech, J. E. A., & Rubel, D. (2009). The experiences of expert group work supervisors: An exploratory study. *Journal for Specialists in Group Work, 34*, 68–89.

Okech, J. E. A., & Rubel, D. (2007). Diversity competent group work supervision: An application of the supervision of group work model (SGW). *Journal for Specialists in Group Work, 32*, 245–266.

Pachankis, J. E., & Goldfried, M. R. (2007). On the next generation of process research. *Clinical Psychology Review, 27*, 760–768.

Padgett, D. K. (2009). Qualitative and mixed methods in social work knowledge development. *Social Work, 54*, 101–105.

Pandya, V., & Gingerich, W. J. (2002). Group therapy intervention for male batterers: A microethnographic study. *Health & Social Work, 27*, 47–55.

Patton, M. Q. (1990). *Qualitative evaluation and research methods* (2nd ed.). Newbury Park, CA: Sage.

Polkinghorne, D. E. (2005). Language and meaning: Data collection in qualitative research. *Journal of Counseling Psychology, 52*, 137–145.

Ponterotto, J. G. (2005). Qualitative research in counseling psychology: A primer on research paradigms and philosophy of science. *Journal of Counseling Psychology, 52*, 126–136.

Ponterotto, J. G., & Grieger, I. (2007). Effectively communicating qualitative research. *Counseling Psychologist, 35*, 404–430.

Reisetter, M., Korcuska, J. S., Yexley, M., Bonds, D., Nikels, H., & McHenry, W. (2004). Counselor educators and qualitative research: Affirming a research identity. *Counselor Education and Supervision, 44*, 2–16.

Richards, L., & Morse, J. M. (2007). *User's guide to qualitative methods* (2nd ed.). Thousand Oaks, CA: Sage.

Riva, M. T., & Smith, R. D. (1997). Looking into the future of group research: Where do we go from here? *Journal for Specialists in Group Work, 22*, 266–276.

Rubel, D., & Okech, J. E. A. (2009). The expert group work supervision process: Apperception, actions, and interactions. *Journal for Specialists in Group Work, 34*, 227–250.

Rubel, D., & Okech, J. E. A. (2006). The supervision of group work model: An application of the discrimination model to supervision of group workers. *The Journal for Specialists in Group Work, 31*, 113–134.

Rubel, D., & Pepperell, J. (2010). Applying the ACA advocacy competencies to group work. In M. J. Ratts, J. A. Lewis, & R. L. Toporek (Eds.), *The ACA Advocacy Competencies: An Advocacy Framework for Counselors* (pp. 195–207). Alexandria, VA: American Counseling Association.

Rubel, D., & Villalba, J. A. (2009). How to publish qualitative research in *JSGW*: A couple more voices in the conversation. *Journal for Specialists in Group Work, 34*, 1–12.

Schneider, M. K. (2009). An ounce of prevention: An associate editor's view. *Journal of Mental Health Counseling, 31*, 1–8.

Smith, J. K., & Hodkinson, P. (2005). Relativism, criteria, and politics. In N. K. Denzin and Y. S. Lincoln (Eds.), *Handbook of qualitative research* (3rd ed., pp. 913–932). Thousand Oaks, CA: Sage.

Smith, J. A., Flowers, P., & Larkin, M. (2009). *Interpretive phenomenological analysis.* Thousand Oaks, CA: Sage.

Spradley, J. P. (1979). *The ethnographic interview.* New York: Harcourt Brace Jovanovich.

Spradley, J. P. (1980). *Participant observation*. New York: Harcourt Brace Jovanovich.

Strauss, A. & Corbin, J. (1998). *Basics of qualitative research: Techniques and procedures for developing grounded theory* (2nd ed.). Thousand Oaks, CA: Sage Publications.

Sue, D. W., & Sue, D. (2008). *Counseling the culturally diverse: Theory and practice 5th ed*. New York, NY: John Wiley and Sons.

Van Manen, M. (1990). *Researching lived experience: Human science for an action sensitive pedagogy*. London, Canada: University of Western Ontario.

Vera, E. M., & Speight, S. L. (2003). Multicultural competence, social justice, and counseling psychology: Expanding our roles. *Counseling Psychologist, 31*, 253–272.

Wanlass, J., Moreno, J., & Thomson, H. (2005). Group therapy for eating disorders: A retrospective case study. *Journal for Specialists in Group Work, 30*, 47–66.

Wertz, F. J. (2005). Phenomenological research methods for counseling psychology. *Journal of Counseling Psychology, 52*, 167–177.

Yalom, I. D. (1995). *The theory and practice of group psychotherapy* (4th ed.). New York: Basic Books.

Yin, R. K. (2009). *Case study research: Design and method* (4th ed.). Thousand Oaks, CA: Sage.

PART 5

Leadership

Personhood of the Leader

James P. Trotzer

Abstract

The personhood of the group leader is explicated. *Leader* (who the leader is) is distinguished from *leadership* (what the leader does), and the role of personhood is explored in the context of the person, process, product paradigm of group work, and the relationship of leader character and competence. Theory and research are examined using the "prism of personhood" to identify and validate the central nature and role of personhood in the practice of group counseling.

Keywords: personhood, group counseling, group psychotherapy, group leadership, group leader, leader traits, functions, roles, styles, development, personality

Introduction

Of what importance is the personhood of the group leader? Let us assume two equally trained, equally educated, and equally experienced group leaders: What could explain differences in the qualitative experience of group members (process) and the differentiated result of its impact (outcome)? Each group leader undertakes the task of group leadership with a set of inescapable and non-negotiable characteristics including, but not limited to, gender, age, race, ethnicity, and body style. Yet, there is another factor that seems to affect the quality of the group, an entity that transcends these non-negotiable characteristics. That factor is the personhood of the group leader.

After an extensive multidisciplinary review of literature, Conyne (2011) concludes that the field of group work has entered the "age of ubiquity." He notes that professionally led groups are everywhere and are becoming an ever expanding part of professional and personal life. In addition, one of the primary observations made in the chapter is that group work has become characterized by such a high level of intentionality that the role of the group leader can be scrutinized with a scientific functionality that was heretofore unavailable in and uncharacteristic of the field of group work. This research-informed intentionality has produced improved outcomes in clinical practice and professional training. The resulting emergence of standards-based best practices in both areas is producing more qualified leaders who are enhancing the impact of group work, expanding its application, and increasing the number of recipients who are benefactors of the group process.

However, embedded in the mass of evidence supporting group work's inevitable thrust toward objectifying the validity and viability of the purposes, practices, and process of group work is an astute assertion. Conyne (2011) states that "Theory, research and supervised practice contribute substantively to inform and guide group leadership indeed; *but* personal factors and intuition may be just as important" (in press). In other words, for all the research-informed group practice with its ever increasing intentionality relative to leadership, the importance of "personal factors" must not be overlooked or disregarded. In fact, these personal factors may be more important given the reality that the process in group work is fundamentally interpersonal and human rather than formulaic and technical.

Consequently, an emphasis on the personhood of the group leader commands a central place in this current volume on group counseling.

The purpose of this chapter is to explore the personhood of the group leader as the fundamental resource from which leadership in its various forms and styles emerges. The chapter will create a context for viewing personhood, examine the formative forces that create that personhood, and describe personality characteristics typically associated with group leadership. A distinction between *leader* and *leadership* is made as a springboard to discussing the dynamics of personhood relative to leadership roles, styles, and functions. The chapter will discuss the parameters that constitute personhood and use the "prism of personhood" (a metaphor for delineating the components of personhood) to differentiate and define personhood factors that are embedded in group dynamics, theory, and research relative to leadership. The role of professional development related to personhood will be reviewed, and the chapter will conclude with an integrated learning summary emphasizing personhood as the central component in group leadership, process, and practice.

The Importance of Personhood

The personhood of the group leader contains the natural resources from which the group leader is developed and supplies the material from which leadership style and function emerge to guide the group process.

Perhaps a metaphor is appropriate to explicate the concepts implicated in that statement (Gladding, 1984; McClure, 1989). *Personhood* is the raw material containing the elements that are mined and refined into leaders who provide leadership in small groups. Long before iron ore is mined, formative forces create its essence. So it is with personhood. Many developmental forces and dynamics mold and meld its nature. Once discovered and accessed through the mining process, the raw material must be transformed into a usable product. This represents the training and experiences that transform the person into a professional leader. Just as the smelting process transforms iron ore into a finished product, so training transforms a person into a leader and personality traits into a leadership style. In other words, personhood without refinement is insufficient to provide and sustain professional leadership, but with application of the smelting process (i.e., training and supervised practice), the potential that is inherent in the ore of personhood is

concretized into the form of a leader and realized in the product of leadership.

To add a qualitative perspective, personhood is also like the proverbial "diamond in the rough" that must be professionally cut to bring out its character and brilliance. That cutting occurs in the context of training and practice. And just like a diamond has many facets and features depending on the angle of perception, light, presentation, and setting, so there are innumerable qualities that emerge from personhood to create the variegated abundance of professional leaders, each of whom is unique and different, on the one hand, but cut from the same substance, on the other. The intent here is to illuminate the importance and nature of that transformation process.

Personhood in Context

Figure 16–1 presents a schema delineating how personhood fits into the nature, dynamics, and development of group leaders, leadership, and group work. The broad strokes of the diagram involve personal development, professional development, and professional practice. *Personal development* emerges from the formative factors that produce the personhood or the personal self of the group leader that is introduced to, immersed in, and transformed by the process of professional development. *Professional development* consists of three formative factors (training, supervised practice, and professional experience) that combine to create a leader persona or professional self. That persona is then manifested and further developed in the context of professional practice. *Professional practice* consists of activities across the broad spectrum of group work in a wide range of settings and constitutes those groups the leader forms and leads in the course of a career as a helping professional.

These three developmental categories are not mutually exclusive or strictly sequential in nature. Rather, they often have a reciprocal impact that recycles the formative dynamics over the course of a group leader's career. In other words, professional training may become a formative factor in personhood as well as a transforming dynamic of personhood.

Personal Development: Formative Factors

The formative factors of personhood are numerous, and a full examination of them is beyond the scope of this chapter. However, four dynamic influences will be reviewed: the psychological (psychosocial dynamics) domain, the systemic (family dynamics) domain, the cultural (diversity dynamics) domain,

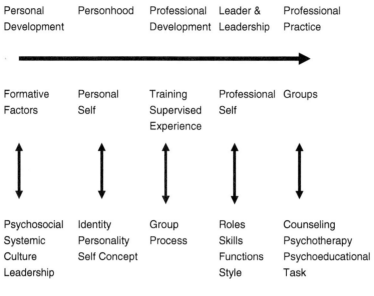

| Personal Development | Personhood | Professional Development | Leader & Leadership | Professional Practice |

| Formative Factors | Personal Self | Training Supervised Experience | Professional Self | Groups |

| Psychosocial Systemic Culture Leadership | Identity Personality Self Concept | Group Process | Roles Skills Functions Style | Counseling Psychotherapy Psychoeducational Task |

Who the Leader is!   What the Leader Does!

Fig. 16.1 Personhood of the group leader in context.

and the behavioral (imitative learning dynamics) domain.

Psychological Factors (Psychosocial Dynamics)

Every theory of human development and personality (Miller, 2002) posits an explanation of personhood and how it develops. The basic assumptions and theoretical tenets of each theory combine to present a conceptual portrait of the person and supply hypotheses that can then be tested via research for purposes of validating the particular point of view of the theory. From a psychosocial perspective, the end product of each theoretical foray is an entity that we refer to as "personhood," which minimally consists of an identity, a personality, and a self concept. Consequently, the importance of the person is critical to the discussion of group leaders and to the process of group work because that process essentially involves persons (members and leaders) interacting together in a social milieu that is organized for a purpose.

In most cases, the explanation of personhood development emphasizes psychological and social factors that combine to form the person. For example, Maslow (1962) postulates that human beings have needs that prompt them to behave in ways that meet those needs. The way each person learns to meet his or her needs over time in the context of relationships (Luft, 1984) produces a pattern of personhood that is manifested in the personality

(Trotzer, 2006). The relational dimension of this process, referred to as the "socialization process," lays the groundwork for interpersonal relating, thereby providing a sustaining connection to the social world in which the person lives.

Generically, personhood is comprised of elements that might be described using the acronym ABCSs (Trotzer, 2006). *A* represents affect, referring to emotions encompassing what or how the person feels; *B* represents behavior, referring to actions reflecting what the person does; *C* represents cognition, referring to thoughts including how the person perceives and mentally processes experience and information; *S* relates to the spiritual or philosophical dimension of personhood that involves faith or belief in a force or entity outside of one's human nature or some explanation of existence that credits a higher power (e.g., God) as an operational influence in human life; and *s* represents the human spirit or the inherent quality within human beings that prompts the best (altruism) and worst (malevolence) of human nature to manifest itself. With this conceptualization in mind, the personhood of the leader can be construed as consisting of an identity (cognitive structure: who I am), a personality (behavioral structure: how I manifest who I am to others), and a self concept (affective structure: how I feel about myself) overlaid or undergirded with personalized characteristics that relate to the human spirit (*s*) and spirituality (*S*). Each of these personhood elements is identifiable and becomes an inherent component in the development and performance of the leader.

Systemic Factors (Family Dynamics)

The impact of family dynamics in the formation of personhood is well documented. Teyber (1997) states unequivocally that "we become who we are in our families of origin" (p. 10). Yalom (1985) states emphatically that "without exception patients enter group therapy with a history of highly unsatisfactory experience in their first and most important group – their primary family" (p. 15). The searing implication of this statement is that family system dynamics leave indelible imprints on their members that they carry with them into life beyond the family for good and ill. This reality is affirmed by Satir (1972), who states simply that "troubled families make troubled people" (p. 18). Donigian and Hulse-Killacky (1999) assert that "the family is the first group in which individuals learn to interact" (p. 124), and Trotzer (in Donigian & Hulse-Killacky, 1999) elaborates that assertion: "The impact of family dynamics is manifested in the predisposition (group) members bring with them in the form of group expectations and their views of themselves as persons and participants" (p. 124).

Like all human beings, the personhood of the group leader is forged in the same dynamic cauldron or family crucible (Napier & Whitaker, 1978). Each of us experiences family dynamics and influences that form our personhood, providing us with powerful blueprints that we carry into the world as we grow up and become our adult selves. These blueprints relate to perceptions of ourselves, our relationships, and the world we live in. They reflect a myriad of factors that impact our worldview. Our gender, view of intimacy, marriage, and family; and a multitude of cultural factors (addressed separately in the next section) are affected by the family's formative mandate to prepare its members to both assimilate and differentiate as individuals in the world outside the family (Trotzer & Trotzer, 1986). The existence of these blueprints is validated by the effort we make to replicate, repudiate, or modify them as we work out our own lives and relationships beyond and apart from our family of origin. Consequently, each person's inherent family blueprints will affect him or her in terms of both the transformative process of human development and the practice of group leadership.

Numerous systems' constructs relate to whether individuals are attracted to or antagonistic to small group dynamics and process. If one grew up in a family that emphasized connectedness and belongingness (Minuchin, 1974), there might be a natural affinity toward process dynamics that form a social milieu stressing cohesion. On the other hand, if emphasis was more on differentiation (Bowen, 1966), independence, and autonomy, one might still be drawn to group work but more because of the product or purpose of the group than its process. Similarly, the type of group leadership a person is drawn to or emulates may be influenced by the nature and style of leadership experienced in the family. If authoritative leadership was modeled by parents with positive resonation of members, potential leaders may be drawn to leadership styles that emphasize structure. On the other hand, if such dynamics were more authoritarian and experienced as onerous or intrusive, a leadership style that is more facilitative or collaborative might be preferred.

Another systemic construct that may impact personhood relative to leadership is "ordinal position in the family constellation" (Bowen, 1966). This construct stipulates that as each child enters the family system (a group with a history) as a member of the sibling subsystem, she or he is faced with a set of parameters that she or he must work with to find her or his place in the family and form an individual identity, personality, and self concept. For example, a first child (oldest) may be subject to higher parental expectations and have to live with more rigorous standards than later children. If the child resonates to these expectations, he or she may become a high achiever and set behavioral benchmarks that later children may have to deal with in their developmental process. If a first child does not buy in to these expectations, he or she may become a rebel or find ways to shed the expectations rather than live up to them. These kinds of differences may then impact the nature and style of leadership a person may choose to utilize in counseling and other groups (groups that create a history). Family system dynamics are formidable with manifold implications related to personhood and leadership. In fact, the impact of family of origin is immutable: "You can't leave home without it!"

Cultural Factors (Diversity Dynamics)

While the formative influence of culture has been long recognized, its role and implications relative to multicultural dynamics and diversity in groups has only recently been raised to a level of consciousness that impacts training and practice (DeLucia-Waack & Donigian, 2003). Confucius observed that "Human beings draw close to one another by their common nature, but habits and customs keep them apart" (Hirokawa, Cathart, Samovar, & Henman, 2003, p. 215). His erudite observation might well be a harbinger of wisdom that group work has finally addressed. Traditionally, group counseling has focused on the "drawing close" dynamics of group process more than the "keeping apart" dynamics. However, "culture is ubiquitous, multi-dimensional, complex and all-pervasive" (Hirokawa et al., 2003, p. 215). Therefore, its influence on the personhood of every individual is unquestioned. From a developmental perspective this means that inherent in every person are cultural factors and forces that will come into play in interpersonal relating and in groups. *Culture* has been defined as "the sum total of beliefs, values, attitudes, meanings, perceptions, customs, practices, language, and other artifacts of social life that are learned, shared and passed on by a group of people" (Hirokawa et al., 2003, p. 215). Culture delineates dynamic forces into factors of race, ethnicity, nationality, gender, sexual orientation, class, education, religion, spirituality, mental and physical abilities, and other sociocultural factors including history, politics, and geography (Merchant, 2006). The impact of these factors relative to small group communication is also well established (Oetzel, Mears, & Fukumoto, 2003; Porter & Samovar, 2003; Reich & Woods, 2003).

Counseling in general and group counseling specifically have made great strides in the cause of training diversity-competent counselors and group leaders by formulating principles (Association for Multicultural Counseling and Development, 1996; Association for Specialists in Group Work [ASGW], 1998b) that inform training and practice (see Chapters 8–11 in DeLucia-Waack, Gerrity, Kalodner, & Riva, 2004) and encouraging research that assesses and explicates the impact of multicultural competence in groups. In each case the personhood of the group leader is fundamental. For example, D'Andrea (2004) begins his treatise on the impact of racial-cultural identity of group leaders and members by stating, "Group counselors need to transcend their own ethnocentric thinking about the content and process of group counseling and psychotherapy to respectfully and ethically address the needs and perspectives of persons who come from multi-racial backgrounds that are different from their own" (p. 265). Relative to personhood, the key words are "need to transcend their own ethnocentric thinking." In other words, it is taken for granted that each leader has inherent traits that were forged in the cauldron of his or her culture that will affect his or her role and function as a leader. Therefore, the first step toward multicultural competency is self-awareness (i.e., knowing and understanding your own cultural identity) (DeLucia-Waack & Donigian, 2003; Merchant, 2006). This is no small task because this self awareness involves not only who you are relative to culture and diversity but also awareness of the impact of those characteristics in the context of and interaction with members who have similar and different characteristics when leading a group. This means that group leaders must have the capacity to transform their cultural identity into an explicit awareness of their attitudes and beliefs, acquire a substantial knowledge of their own and others' cultures, and develop the skills to use these resources in practice (the three domains of multicultural competency) (ASGW, 1998b; Thomas & Pender, 2008). Doing so will help to insure that intentional interventions in group counseling and therapy by group leaders will be culturally and ethically competent (MacNair-Semands, 2007).

An example of the importance, impact, and complexity of culture in personhood and group work is appropriate here. D'Andrea (2004) asserts "members of the dominant racial–cultural group in the United States (white, English-speaking persons from western European descent) continue to disproportionately benefit from a host of social, educational, economic and personal privileges and advantages that individuals from racially disempowered minority groups do not" (p. 267). Take a moment to assess your visceral and cognitive reaction to that statement relative to its embedded acclamation of "privilege" and "oppression." As a straight, white, protestant Christian, educated, middle class male with a western European, German heritage, my response (awareness) may be different from yours, particularly if you are female and have different cultural characteristics racially, ethnically, religiously, and socioeconomically. Depending on your level of cultural awareness, sensitivity, and competence, your reaction may vary from confusion to anger emotionally, denial to affirmative action behaviorally, and agreement to disagreement cognitively. Such is the cultural complexity that emerges from personhood in the context of group interaction.

Behavioral Factors (Modeling Dynamics)

The final formative factor relates to former influential leaders in our lives. Past experience with leaders affects not only our personhood but also our view of who a leader is and what a leader does. The old adage that you teach the way you have been taught has a corollary in the leadership domain: You lead the way you have been led. This imitative learning reality manifests itself in how the leadership role is viewed and implemented. It also relates to successful, positive, and constructive leadership experiences and unsuccessful, negative, and hurtful experiences. In the same way we replicate or repudiate blueprints from our family of origin, we tend to emulate leaders whom we admire and value or from whom we have benefited and refrain from using the practices of those we have not.

The merit of experience with leaders in our lives has been addressed in research investigating how and why leaders emerge in small groups. Geier (1967) studied the emergence of leaders in small, task oriented groups and found that would-be leaders were eliminated from contention on the basis of negative traits. Leaders who were uninformed about the group's task, nonparticipative, extremely rigid, and too authoritarian or who expressed offensive verbalizations were rejected as leaders. Interestingly, the counterpart to this observation proved inconclusive; that is, positive traits that distinguished leaders from nonleaders were not so clear. This finding left the impression that effective leaders emerged somewhat by default as those with negative traits were eliminated, leaving those with other traits to become the leaders, a situation that prompted Hirokawa et al. (2003) to conclude that it is difficult to identify "a set of traits that universally distinguish leaders from non-leaders" (p. 170). Dies (1994,) took a somewhat different tack on this leadership phenomenon, stating that "group members favor and seem to benefit from a positive style of intervention, and that as leaders become more actively negative, they increase the possibility that participants will not only be dissatisfied, but also potentially harmed by the group experience" (p. 139). In any case, the impact of leaders who have modeled and/or mentored us in leadership is unequivocal (Tichy, 1997).

Many other formative factors could be discussed as crucial to the development of personhood of the group leader, but space limits further considerations. However, the impact and influence of psychosocial dynamics, family dynamics, cultural dynamics, and imitative learning dynamics will be evident in the topics addressed in the rest of this chapter.

Personhood of the Leader

A focused perusal of seminal group-counseling texts (e.g., Corey & Corey, 2006; Gladding, 2002; Jacobs, Masson, & Harvill, 2006; Trotzer, 2006; Yalom, 2005) will provide a wealth of personhood traits that are purportedly associated with leaders and leadership. Personality traits are foundational to the discussion of who leaders are, how they function, and how effective they are. The fact that these traits are identified and elaborated upon in every group text so substantially supports their professional merit in terms of concurrent validity and consensual veracity that the subjective nature of the actual terms or concepts is almost overlooked. Yet, just as every theory of counseling, personality, or human development contains assumptions that are taken for granted so that its theoretical essence can be framed, so personhood traits must be identified so that group theory can formulate the nature of group process and differentiate the roles of leaders and the functions of leadership. Once traits and patterns of personhood are identified, research, training, and clinical practice can engage in the process of identifying which traits when associated with what practices and for what purposes are most effective.

Portraits of Personhood
Bates, Johnson, and Blaker (1982) frame the importance of personhood by stating "a group draws definition from its leader. It will be only as good as the leader, as good as his or her skills, and as good as *the leader's own being*" (italics added, p. 73). Mahler (1969) supported this notion, stating "of first importance are the counselor's values – what he [she] stands for and what he [she] believes in" (p. 169). Ohlsen, Horne, and Lawe (1988) relate this conceptualization of personhood to one of the issues of leadership. "*Counselor's needs, values,* clinical experience and professional preparation all influence the degree to which he [she] knowingly or unknowingly elicits transference" (italics added, p. 181). Conyne (2011) refers to the "positive valence" embedded in the personhood and professionalism of the group leader that directly influences the group process. A positive valence contributes to the creation and maintenance of an affirming therapeutic climate, group cohesion, and progress toward members' goals. This aligns with Yalom's assertion that "the basic posture of the (group) therapist to a client must be one of concern, acceptance, genuineness and empathy. Nothing, no technical consideration takes precedence over this attitude" (Yalom, 2005, p. 117), a statement that has clear connotations relative to the personhood of

the group leader. Such allusions to personal qualities are rampant in most treatises on leadership, but many have gone further in delineating syndromes of traits that paint personhood portraits of effective professional leaders.

As early as 1962, Slavson (cited in Hansen, Warner, & Smith, 1980) listed the following traits as essential in group leaders:

> poise, judgment, maturity, ego-strength, freedom from excessive anxiety, perceptiveness, intuition, empathy, imaginativeness, ability to avoid self preoccupation, desire to help people and tolerance of frustration (p. 397).

The comprehensiveness of such a recipe for personhood is mind boggling and begs the question of whether such a person exists (before training, of course). Such thoughts, however, have not deterred respected group counselor educators from embellishing and promoting such pictures.

Corey and Corey (2006) reflect on the personhood of the group leader as follows:

> As a group leader, you bring your personal qualities, values, and life experiences to every group. The person you are acts as a catalyst for bringing about change in the groups you lead. To promote growth in member's lives you need to be committed to reflection and growth in your own life (p. 27).

They then go on to cite 15 personal characteristics that describe effective leaders: (1) courage; (2) willingness to model; (3) presence; (4) goodwill, genuineness, and caring; (5) belief in group process; (6) openness; (7) non-defensiveness in coping with criticism; (8) becoming aware of your culture; (9) willingness to seek new experiences; (10) personal power; (11) stamina; (12) self-awareness; (13) sense of humor; (14) inventiveness; and (15) personal dedication and commitment (pp. 29–33). The breadth and depth of this list encompass characteristics, qualities, attitudes, perceptions, skills, practices, beliefs, values, and professional perspectives all rolled up into their portrait of leader personhood.

Trotzer (2006) adds a capsule summary of personal traits that reflect personhood, incorporating qualities that relate directly to the group process. Effective group leaders are persons who manifest extensive self awareness, communicate an attitude of openness and flexibility, and have a sincere appreciation of diversity. They are able to tolerate ambiguity, convey a positive attitude, and emulate human qualities including the social interest traits of being warm, caring, and genuinely interested in others. Traits such as human objectivity, maturity, and integration or congruence round out the portrait. Trotzer cautions, however, that such traits, though vital and essential, are in and of themselves insufficient to assure leadership effectiveness and professionalism. Training, supervised clinical practice, and professional experience as a group leader are necessary to transform these personal characteristics into professional resources. This position is supported by Gillam's (2004) model for teaching group work and training group leaders, which emphasizes the personhood of group counselor educators who model effective group leadership and mentor emerging leaders. "Effective group counselor educators must have a solid sense of who they are professionally and personally" (p. 83) if they are to be resources to their trainees in transforming their personal assets into professional resources.

Yalom (1995) noted that "given enough time, group members will create in the group the same interpersonal universe they have always inhabited" (p. 28). The same could be said of group leaders; that is, given enough time, they will create the same social milieu in the group that they inhabit outside the group. If such is the case, then self awareness relative to personhood is critical to understanding how that process can happen, and training is crucial to eliciting that awareness and utilizing it in the conduct of groups and in the creation of a therapeutic milieu.

In order to balance the perspective of personhood as a fundamental resource of group leaders in the leadership role, consider the words of Lao-Tze, a sixth-century BCE group guru:

> A Leader is best
> When people barely know he exists,
> Not so good when people obey and acclaim him,
> Worse when they despise him.
> "Fail to honor people," they fail to honor you:
> But a good leader who talks little
> When his work is done, his aim fulfilled,
> They will say, "We did it ourselves." (cited in Cohen & Smith, 1976, p. iii)

The implicit message relative to personhood is that when elements of the above portraits are integrated into the leader's persona and integral to his or her role, the result will be influential in the process of the group but not necessarily credited in the final product.

Dynamics of Personhood

Personhood of the leader is dynamic in both a formative and a summative sense. It emerges out of the qualities, assets, traits, perceptions, beliefs, and values that the leader brings to leadership, creating the valence (positive or negative) of the leader as a person and as a position in the group (Hirokawa et al., 2003). Hulse-Killacky, Killacky, and Donigian (2001) pose a series of process questions that reveal the dynamics of personhood in groups. The first question is *"Who am I?"* This question brings the identity of the leader into focus and delineates what the leader brings to the leadership role as a person. The second question is *"Who am I with you?"* This question surfaces the co-construction dynamics of the interactive impact of personhood as the leader engages with each person in the group and with the group as a whole. It is based on the premise that each interchange between a leader and a member reveals a different facet of the leader's (and member's) personhood. The group aspect of this co-construction process is even more critical because it reveals the dynamics of personhood in relation to the milieu that is developing in the group. The third question is *"Who are we together?"* This is the group identity question that relates personhood to process and reveals the therapeutic nature of the group, which in turn relates personhood to group outcomes.

Kurt Lewin once observed that "it is usually easier to change individuals formed into a group than to change any of them separately" (Forsyth, 2006, p. 525). In contrast, Yalom (2005) noted that "therapeutic change in group is an enormously complex process that occurs through an intricate interplay of human experiences" (p. 1). A central component of those intricacies is the personhood of the leader. In fact, that personhood may well be the determinant not only of whether and what change occurs but also of how much change occurs as a result of group process. Napier and Whitaker (1978) noted this phenomenon in family therapy in that changes in families seem to be contingent on the willingness and ability of the therapist to grow with the family. This same dynamic is at work in groups where the leader's personal elasticity may determine the extent to which the therapeutic conditions needed for members to engage in the change process are generated in the group.

Personal Traits of Group Leaders – The Research Perspective

While our discussion of leader personhood traits is pertinent and provides a form of professional face validity, the objectivity of a research-oriented perspective is also crucial. In order to ferret out the importance and nature of personhood in group process, practice, and productivity, researchers from a variety of professional disciplines grappled with definitions and parameters that affect the perception of personhood and effect an operational definition. Group work researchers basically agree that the first step toward understanding leadership requires separating the entities of "leader" and "leadership" (Conyne, 2011; Hirokawa et al., 2003; Zacarro, 2007). Generally, *leadership* refers to the process of influencing group activities toward goal achievement (Hirokawa et al., 2003, p. 169). Forsyth (2006) extends this conception into the ability to lead others by guiding them in pursuits often by organizing, directing, coordinating, supporting, and motivating their efforts. Conyne (2011)) synthesizes these elements into the following definition:

> Group leadership is the ability to draw from best practices and good professional judgment to create a group, and in collaboration with members build and maintain a positive group climate that serves to nurture here and now interaction and its processing by leader and members aimed at producing lasting growth and change (in press).

The leader is the person who does this. As such, the term *leader* refers to who the leader is as a person and his or her position in a group, and *leadership* refers to how the leader acts or functions in the group (i.e., what he or she does). This distinction must be maintained if sense is to be made of the multiplicity of factors that have been studied in the pursuit of knowledge regarding personhood of the group leader (Hirokawa et al., 2003).[1]

Another parameter that undergirds group research relative to personhood as a foundational factor in group work is the person, process, product paradigm. Research has focused not only on each of these variables separately but more recently on the relationship among them. In other words, how do who the leader is (person and position) and what the leader does (roles and functions) relate to process (what happens in the group), and how in turn does that process affect results (productivity and change)?

Research performed in the context of these parameters contributes to the fundamental knowledge and understanding of the group work field and provides heuristic grist for the research mill, but a more robust schema is needed with regard to the personhood of the group leader. Conyne (2011) elucidated this necessity by posing a series of rhetorical questions relative to group leadership:

Is leadership related to power, to fidelity and honor? Does it involve great people doing heroic things? Is it all about motivating others? Are leaders made or born? Is it a function emerging from structure and processes of a particular organization or environment? Is it shared by everyone in the system? Does it emerge from the wisdom of the leader? Or all of them? (in press).

Certainly, personhood is related to each of those questions. Does the leader as a person have the capacity to be or do all that is implied in them? Group counseling research has made significant strides in formulating a strategy and a framework for answering these questions and deriving insights into the person, process, product relationship in therapeutic groups.

Finding Personhood in Process and Product Research

The purpose of this section is to apply the prism of personhood to research that examines the relationship between leaders and leadership in therapeutic groups and the connection between process variables and outcomes in order to identify personhood factors that are relevant to the quintessential question, How does group therapy help patients? (Yalom, 2005). Despite Kivlighan and Holmes's (2004) assertion that little progress has been made in answering that initial question, the proverbial "where there's smoke, there's fire" pertains. So much research has been generated relative to the use of groups in a helping capacity that it is almost incomprehensible that such answers have not been forthcoming (see DeLucia-Waack et al., 2004). Consider the following rhetorical observation with regard to personhood of the group leader: "If we still don't know *how* group therapy works to effect therapeutic change, then the question of *who* can frame and form the *how* remains even more elusive." My position, however, is that more is known than we think we know, and my intention is to spell out the personhood implications of research related to what makes therapeutic groups effective.

While many different routes may be taken to get to the origin of group therapy from a theoretical, practical, and research perspective, most, if not all, will end with Yalom's (2005) 11 "curative factors." Conyne (2011) states that "one would be hard-put to find any text on the topic of group counseling and group psychotherapy that did not assign a prominent place for a discussion of those therapeutic factors" (in press) The curative factors combined with the 26 group leader characteristics (Lieberman, Yalom, & Miles, 1973) that were reconfigured into eight fundamental factors by Tinsley, Roth, and Lease (1989) provide a heuristic research base that has spawned a vast array of studies designed to support, elucidate, and dispute their essence, impact, and merit. However, while great progress has been made in identifying, defining, and discovering the relevance of these factors to therapeutic process and group outcomes (Burlingame, Fuhriman, & Johnson, 2004; Kivlighan & Holmes, 2004; Riva et al., 2004), little effort has been made to identify personal traits of group leaders that are associated with the creation of these therapeutic factors or to study the impact of such findings on group process and outcomes.

The Formative Factors

Given the premise that personhood is embedded in the leader of a therapeutic group and manifested in the leadership style of said professional and the fact that the curative factors have been found to both characterize the process and produce positive outcomes, the fact of personhood is substantiated and its character identified. For example, when Tinsley et al. (1989) replicated Lieberman et al.'s (1973) study using leaders instead of members, they found that eight factors were significantly related to leadership. Of these eight factors, four were related to leader behavior or style (cognitive direction, affective direction, verbal stimulation, and nonverbal exercises), two were related to leader focus or objectives (group functioning and individual functioning), and two were related to the value of the leader to the group and his or her personal qualities (nurturant attractiveness and charismatic expertness). The complementary nature of these last two factors provides evidence of personhood and infers a conceptually integrated perception of personhood traits that links curative factors (process traits) and therapeutic outcomes (Zacarro, 2007).

Nurturant attractiveness embodies the traits of warmth and caring that are emphasized in every portrait of personhood reviewed so far. In addition, the quality of personal attractiveness relates to McWhirter and Frey's (1987) finding that leader personality was significant in affecting members' evaluations of group leaders in the forming stages of the group. They found that leader personality characteristics were related to members' positive perceptions as the group was forming but faded in influence after the group was formed and functioning in the later phases of the process. This personal attractiveness factor was also noted as influential by Felfe and Schyns (2006) in their study of transformational leadership.

Concurrent validation of the construct of nurturant attractiveness was found by MacLennan (1975), who studied the impact of the leader's life experience on ability to run counseling, growth, and therapy groups. Besides reinforcing the formative factors already noted as crucial to a leader's personhood, MacLennan found four factors that were related to effective leadership: (1) importance of having a similar background to members of the group; (2) expression of honesty and feelings (ability to and willingness); (3) the qualities of perceptiveness, warmth, understanding, empathy, and self awareness; and (4) capacity to be accepted as a leader. Elements of each of these factors relate to the nurturant attractiveness factor.

Morran, Stockton, and Whittingham (2004) support this supposition, stating that "group dynamics and outcomes are influenced by general factors such as leader's interaction style, personal characteristics and attitudes" and that "warm, caring leaders who set and reinforce clear norms are more likely to have cohesive groups" (p. 91). Cohesiveness is a group climate trait that in turn is linked to positive group outcomes. They then identify and describe interventions (skills) that are conducive to developing cohesiveness in groups, thereby linking leader personality (personhood) and skills (training) as critical to generating a therapeutic climate that produces positive outcomes. This idea is supported by Pan and Lin (2004), who found that members' perceptions of leader behaviors were predictors of therapeutic factors in groups, thereby reinforcing the centrality of the leader's personhood in generating the group climate.

Similar personhood commodities are embedded in the *charismatic expertness* factor. Charisma, or the aura of personhood including a visionary element, is integral to the transformational portrait of leadership (Gouran, 2003; Johns & Moser, 1989; Tichy & Devanna, 1986; Zacarro, 2007). Relative to personhood, charisma, like warmth, is more of an affective quality, which makes measurement elusive because it is more felt (experienced affectively) than observed (seen behaviorally) and therefore may have more credence as a catalytic factor of personality than as a causative entity in its own right. Leaders whose personality exudes warmth, attractiveness, and charisma may be more effective at creating alliances with members and forming the therapeutic milieu. The key to assessment of such qualities is not self awareness on the leader's part but rather emanates from perceptions on the members' part. The presence of warmth or charisma is authenticated only if experienced, observed, and reported by group members (McWhirter & Frey, 1987).

The expertness dimension calls to mind the differentiating criteria of personhood that distinguish between the leader's personal and professional selves. The personal self is what the prospective leader brings to training, and the professional self is what the leader develops through training and practice. The encouraging aspect of this element is that it reaffirms the formative influence of professional preparation and the maturing impact of supervision and clinical practice in the ongoing development of leader personhood. The embedded personhood factor here is related to experience (MacLennan, 1975; Riva et al., 2004). Experienced leaders possess more and use more resources and perspectives than inexperienced leaders. Seasoned leaders tend to put more into and get more out of the group process than novices. Put another way, experienced leaders tend to trust the group process while novices are still testing the process. However, this differentiating dynamic brings us back to training, supervised leadership experience, and clinical practice. As novice leaders accrue experience, they evolve from being testers of the process to being trusters of the process. Novices test the process to see if it works, which transforms them into trusters, while experienced leaders depend on and use the process as a resource. Thus, the expertness component of the charismatic expertness factor relates to elements of training, professional experience, and diversity competencies. In each case, the growth dimension is critical, embracing MacLennan's (1975) assertion that ongoing training and experience should enhance the leader's range of understanding of a wide variety of human situations and conditions, thereby enabling him or her to listen and respond effectively to an ever-increasing diversity of individual perspectives (DeLucia-Waack & Donigian, 2003; Merchant, 2006).

In regard to formulating therapeutic factors in a group, Yalom (2005) stipulated that the three primary tasks or functions of the group therapist are (1) to create and maintain the group, (2) to build a group culture, and (3) to activate and illuminate the here and now. The skills needed to do so include self disclosure, feedback, appropriate use of structure, catharsis, and acquisition of social skills. This capsule job description pinpoints the kind of person needed to do the job and raises the question of how personhood morphs from the personal self to the professional self in group leader development.

The Functional Factors

Riva et al. (2004) reviewed the research literature with regard to effective leadership in group counseling and psychotherapy with particular attention to the vital role of the leader in generating process dynamics and positive outcomes in group members. They found six components of leadership that were related to group effectiveness. Each of these components constitutes a leadership function (what the leader does) that is performed by a leader (who the leader is). Therefore, another set of data is provided to which we can apply the prism of personhood in order to see how personhood is embedded in each function, thereby adding to the growing essence of personhood. The six components are: (1) selection of group members, (2) pregroup preparation, (3) positive member-leader relationship, (4) leader's use of structure, (5) group cohesion, and (6) leader communication and feedback.

GROUP MEMBER SELECTION

While the importance of group member selection or pregroup screening is clinically and ethically established as a critical first step in the formation of therapeutic groups, the fact remains that the process is highly subjective (Corey & Corey, 2006), and little direction as to specifics is provided in the group literature (Piper & McCallum, 1994). Typically group member selection depends on the clinical judgment of the leader more than any other factor. Since leader intuition is a pervading dynamic, the personhood of the leader becomes critical. Self awareness, other awareness, and the chemistry between the two are often the fundamental factors that generate the dynamics that drive the member selection process. Because of propensities to prejudge, perceptions emanating from cultural diversity, and transference/countertransference phenomena, the selection process is fraught with vagaries relating to intrapersonal and interpersonal dynamics. For that reason some leaders prefer to conduct screening as a function of the group process (i.e., using group selection and orientation meetings) rather than in the context of dyadic interviews. However implemented, personhood is an operational factor in the performance of the group member selection process.

PREGROUP PREPARATION

While the importance of pregroup preparation and its relationship to positive group process, member satisfaction (Piper & Perrault, 1989; Santasiero, Baker, & McGee, 1995; Trotzer, 2006), and constructive results (Bednar & Kaul, 1994; Burlingame et al., 2004) are consensually validated and frameworks and guidelines for pregroup preparation are prominent (Corey & Corey, 2006; Couch, 1995), the personhood factor involved here relates to the personal diligence and professional meticulousness of the group leader. Conducting effective pregroup preparation takes time and effort, commodities that some leaders may not be aware of when it comes to working in groups and others may not have due to complexities related to other aspects of their lives. Conyne (2011) has pointed out two pragmatic characteristics of group work that may well serve to differentiate persons who will be effective group leaders from those who will not. The factors involve the willingness to make the investment in getting professional group leadership training in both the general and specialized senses and then making a commitment to operate according to best practices and standards of the group work field (Thomas & Pender, 2008).

POSITIVE LEADER - MEMBER RELATIONSHIP

"It is not surprising that group leaders who are warm, supportive and genuinely interested in individual group members, as well as the group as a whole, have group members who make more positive gains" (Riva et al., 2004, p. 39). This assertion, based on substantive research (Dies, 1994), reaffirms the personhood qualities of the group leader. Not only do positive personal qualities generate favorable member perceptions of leaders, resulting in constructive member progress (Antonuccio, Davis, Lewinson, & Breckenridge, 1987), but just as tellingly negative personal traits impede member progress. Smokowski, Rose, and Bacallao (2001) found that group casualties were related to leader behaviors that were overly confrontational and exerted premature pressure on members to self disclose (cited in Riva et al., 2004, p. 40). Thus, once again personal qualities play a vital role in leadership success in a double-edged sword manner. Positive qualities are associated with favorable leader perceptions and constructive results and negative qualities are associated with unfavorable impressions and subsequently less effective results. Conversely, a leader's "personal feelings about individual members may play a significant role in the type of experience members have and the nature of results" (Riva et al., 2004, p. 40), thus adding another dimension to the importance of personhood.

USE OF STRUCTURE BY THE LEADER

The focus on structure has long been a concern in group counseling (Trotzer, 1979), and the role of the leader with regard to structure has been extensively addressed in the literature (Burlingame & Fuhriman, 1994; Kivlighan, McGovern, & Corazzini, 1984). It is generally conceded that structure plays a vital role in the formative phases of the group (Bednar, Melnick, & Kaul, 1974; Donigian & Malnati, 1997; Stockton, Rohde, & Haughey, 1994) and that leaders who use more structure fare better than those who use less with regard to eliciting therapeutic elements such as self disclosure, cohesion, and risk taking in groups (Gazda, Ginter, & Horne, 2001).

Self confidence and self efficacy (Page & Hulse-Killacky, 1999; Page, Pietrzak, & Lewis, 2001) are personal traits that are intrinsic in the structure decisions of group leaders. Relative to self confidence, leaders who lack confidence may use structure to shore up their comfort level in the leadership role until such time as they become comfortable in their role as leader and in their trust of the group process. Just as structure is helpful in the formative stages of groups, so it is helpful in the formative phases of a group leader's professional development. In that sense structure is a resource rather than a prosthesis for shoring up confidence. As personal confidence grows, the choices relative to structure become part of the flexibility and viability of the leader's style rather than a source of dependence. Self efficacy or confidence in the ability to be a leader and perform the leadership role and functions is the bridge between the personal self and professional self of the group leader. Over time these elements merge and meld, providing greater fortitude and versatility to the leader's performance. Consequently, when structure becomes a strategic component of the leader's style, the likelihood of success in leadership is enhanced.

GROUP COHESION

The relationship between group cohesion and positive outcomes is well substantiated (Kivlighan & Tarrant, 2001; Marziali, Munroe-Blum, & McCleary, 1997; Tschuschke & Dies, 1994). Riva et al. (2004) state that "an essential leader behavior is to foster a group climate that is safe, positive and supportive, yet strong enough to, at times, withstand highly charged emotions, challenges, and interactions between members" (p. 41). The inherent personhood element in performing such a function is resiliency. The capacity to moderate the powerful dynamics related to cohesion unleashed in the group process while maintaining and assuring personal and interpersonal elasticity in that process requires a person who has a resilient nature. This characteristic enables the leader to stand up and stand out when necessary to deter the excesses of the process and fade out of focus when the group is performing effectively without losing his or her sense of place or personhood. As such, resiliency becomes another of those catalytic agents (like warmth and charisma) that form the personhood of the effective group leader. An apt analogy to this observation is epoxy glue, which requires two tubes of ingredients to be mixed together for a bonding agent to be formed. In this case the two agents are person (of the group leader) and process (of the group). When the personal qualities of the leader mix with the dynamics of the process, a therapeutic bond is formed that is cohesive and elastic, thus creating a milieu in which constructive change can occur in individual members. After all, it was Yalom (2005) who suggested that cohesion was the "glue" that keeps the group connected until the process can take over.

The implications of this analogy can be construed in two ways. One relates therapeutic factors to the personhood of the leader and the other, to the group process. In the first case therapeutic (curative) factors are like the brushes in the hand of an artist (the group leader), who uses them to create the picture (the group process). In the second, therapeutic factors are like the healing capacity of the human body in that once the milieu has been formed, the curative factors emerge and operate to produce the healing (change).

LEADER COMMUNICATION AND FEEDBACK

The interpersonal skills of the group leader (Beebe, Beebe, & Redmond, 2008) provide the core of this leadership function. The two channels by which information is exchanged in therapeutic groups are self disclosure and giving feedback (Trotzer, 2006). A leader must create an atmosphere that is safe enough and conducive enough for members to disclose their needs, wants, and problems in order for the helping process to be elicited through the mechanism of giving feedback (Morran, Stockton, Cline, & Teed, 1998). The leader's role in that process is vital. The leader must be a person who is comfortable with and values self disclosure and giving feedback so that she or he can model and encourage these behaviors in the group. And, because research and clinical practice have noted that members' self disclosure, group processing, and giving feedback enhance therapeutic effect (Morran et al., 1998; Santasiero et al., 1995; Ward & Litchy, 2004), it is also important for the leader to be other oriented (Beebe et al., 2008) in facilitating group processing and giving feedback. Thus, we get a glimpse of Lao-Tze's wisdom, referred to earlier with regard to effective leadership.

The Foundational Factors

Group climate, the final focus of consideration using the prism of personhood, incorporates many of the personhood ingredients elicited from the formative and functional arenas of group work. Conyne (2011) defines *group climate* as the "atmosphere, culture, or the general personality of the group" (in press) and construes it as the entity that is most critical to the production of therapeutic group outcomes. It is the social structure fabricated by the group leader that houses the therapeutic factors and best explicates the various dynamic reconfigurations of those factors that have been derived from research and implemented in clinical practice. Many different models have been formulated based on research results that validate group climate as the all encompassing variable that has the most potential for explaining the causality dynamics of therapeutic groups.

The American Group Psychotherapy Association (AGPA) has developed the Core Battery-R, a set of instruments designed to track and assess group climates and measure group outcomes (AGPA, 2007; Joyce, 2005; MacNair-Semands, 2006). These instruments measure three group factors: (1) positive relational bond, (2) positive working relationship, and (3) negative factors that interfere with the bond or work (Conyne, 2011). Central to the use of these instruments is the member's perception of the group leader and leadership as well as the member's relationship to the group, all of which reflect on the personhood of the leader.

Kivlighan & Holmes (2004) used a cluster analysis process to configure therapeutic factors into four categories designating types of groups or group climates: cluster 1, affective insight groups (e.g., including therapeutic factor of catharsis); cluster 2, affective support groups (e.g., including therapeutic factor of instillation of hope); cluster 3, cognitive support groups (e.g., including therapeutic factor of universality); and cluster 4, cognitive insight groups (e.g., including therapeutic factor of interpersonal learning). The personhood of the leader is a differentiating factor in each of these group climates.

Johnson, Burlingame, Olsen, Davies, and Gleave (2005) explored the relationship constructs of group climate, cohesion, alliance, and empathy and noted three relationship patterns that operated in therapeutic groups that were associated with therapeutic outcomes: (1) positive relational bonds, referring to the emotional connection or attachment to other members, the leader, and the group as a whole; (2) positive working relationships in the group, or collaborative engagement aimed toward goal attainment; and (3) negative relationship factors, including aspects of process that may unfavorably impact attachments or slow therapeutic progress. Note the congruence between the Core Battery-R instruments noted previously and the patterns noted in this study.

My clinical experience affirms a developmental process that connects group climate and these relational factors. Leaders who are able to facilitate connectedness between themselves and members as well as between the members realize the process benefit of cohesion that leads to the product benefit of cooperation. As connectedness solidifies into an elastic, therapeutic, social milieu, cohesion deepens and cooperation transforms into collaboration. Relative to the problem solving process, groups that are bonded at a level that prompts cooperation tend to use compromise as a problem solving tool, while groups that have bonded at a collaborative level are more likely to use confrontation as a working strategy. These two tools are applied to interpersonal or group process issues related to group functionality and to individual or personal issues related to group purpose. The leader's own comfort level relative to group connectedness and personal problem solving strategies also plays a role in this process.

Wilson (personal communication, 2009) and colleagues are currently engaged in research exploring leadership styles differentiated on the basis of experience. They are using the following role descriptions derived from Lieberman et al.'s (1973) landmark study of group leadership styles and the extensive research related to them. This effort epitomizes Zacarro's (2007) observation that a "defining core of leader trait patterns reflects a stable tendency to lead in different ways across disparate organizational processes" (p. 1) or types of groups. In other words, a conceptually integrated pattern of leader traits (vs. an additive pattern or single traits) not only reliably and consistently differentiates leaders from nonleaders but also serves as a basis for assessment, selection, training, and development of group leaders, providing a link to effectiveness as well (p. 5). As you read each of the descriptions, use the prism of personhood to decipher the personality implications of each leadership portrait and its relationship to the formative, functional, and foundational personhood factors described previously. (Descriptions are formatted in the manner they are being used in the ongoing research project at the University of Cincinnati.)

CARING

Group leaders who are (rated) high on caring emphasize "warmth, acceptance, genuineness, and a real concern for other human beings in the group." Leaders establish "specific, definable, personal relationships to particular group members who the leader works with in a caring manner." Leaders who emphasize caring are perceived as being "giving, genuine, sympathetic, warm, open and kind" (quoted material excerpted from Lieberman et al., 1973, p. 238).

EMOTIONAL STIMULATION

Group leaders who are (rated) high on emotional stimulation emphasize "the release of emotions by demonstration." The leader is a risk-taker who encourages expression of anger, warmth, or love by showing how it is done. The leader evidences a very personal and immediate form of leadership: "the leader is at the center of the group's universe." "It is through the leader's personal powers and force of personality that the group moves ahead and that people in it have specific experiences." The leader engages in frequent dialogues with individual members in the group and challenges their values, attitudes, beliefs, and assumptions about themselves. "Shaking-up or unsettling may be considered a primary learning condition." The leader uses "intrusive modeling" and encourages members "to be like [him or her] in style, values, behavior, and beliefs." Leaders who emphasize emotional stimulation "are perceived as charismatic, inspiring, imposing, stimulating, believing in themselves, and possessing a vision or a sense of mission (quoted material excerpted from Lieberman et al., 1973, pp. 235–238).

EXECUTIVE FUNCTION

Group leaders who are (rated) high on executive function emphasize "the expression or release of emotions through suggestions rather than . . . through demonstration." In many ways they are like "movie directors, stopping the flow of the group to focus the group's attention on specific individual or group phenomena." Unlike the leaders who emphasize meaning attribution, they are more likely to "ask the group to reflect on some action" than they are to "provide the answers for them." Leaders

(rated) high on executive function may use structured group exercises to provide common experience and then process the experience to encourage the members to extract their own meaning from the experience. "Executive function represents behavior primarily directed toward management of the group as a social system, and makes heavy use of structured material as a mechanism for goal achievement" (quoted material excerpted from Lieberman et al., 1973, p. 239).

MEANING ATTRIBUTION

Group leaders who are (rated) high on meaning attribution provide support for meaning making. These leaders are perceived as "interpreters of reality" who facilitate the creation of meaning from personal and group experience by offering explanations of intrapersonal dynamics and interpersonal interactions. The leader "gives (suggests) meaning to the experiences members undergo." "Empathy, understanding the surface and deeper experiencing of members, observing the unique and repeating patterns of group interactions, the emergence of group norms, are all of value to group leaders (who rate) high on *meaning attribution* as is knowledge of the theory of intrapsychic phenomena and interpersonal relations." In addition two styles of leadership have been observed among these leaders: (1) *group focus* leaders who concentrate on recognition of group climate, how the group is working, repeating patterns of interpersonal interaction, and emergence of group norms, and (2) *individual focus* leaders who concentrate on the intrapsychic and interpersonal behavior of individual members (quoted material excerpted from Lieberman et al., 1973, pp. 238–239).

A careful scrutiny of each of these leadership patterns or styles reveals a commonality of factors that pervade each one as well as certain unique qualities that differentiate one from another. In many ways leadership style is a lot like baking bread. All loaves (leadership styles) use the same basic ingredients, but the recipes differ in terms of emphasis, quantity, and quality of those ingredients and what additional ingredients are added to make the final product. Both the common ingredients and the unique or differentiating ones are embedded in the personhood the leader brings to the process, and training provides the recipes for how those ingredients are developed and integrated into the leadership loaf. Do not forget that in baking bread there is a mixing process (training?) and a baking process (supervised practice?). In addition, for some breads, there is a rising process where the ingredients, after being mixed, are left alone to percolate and form before being baked, a process that relates to emergent leadership in the context of group development.

CALL FOR MULTIDISCIPLINARY CONVERGENCE IN LEADER PERSONHOOD RESEARCH

Researchers, scholars, and clinicians in a variety of disciplines related to small group dynamics have addressed the question of who leaders are and what makes them emerge and be effective in relation to process and outcomes in groups (Conyne, 2011; Conyne, Wilson, & Ward, 1997; Garvin, Gutierrez & Galinsky, 2004; Getterman & Salmon, 2008; Hirokawa et al., 2003; Kivlighan & Holmes, 2004; Stockton, Morran, & Krieger, 2004; Stockton, Toth, & Morran, 2006; Wilson, Rapin, & Haley-Banez, 2004; Zacarro, 2007). In doing so they have produced vital information to the field of group work and contributed at least indirectly to the personhood discussion. Though different group languages are spoken in these studies, translation and comparative analysis reveal a commonality that is quite astounding.

As collaborative efforts have attempted to differentiate between core group competencies and specialized competencies and investigated the relationship between leaders (who the leader is) and leadership (how the leader acts) in regard to process (therapeutic factors and group climate) and product (group outcomes), the importance of the personhood factor has been well authenticated. Researchers would now do well to bring together their findings and work conjointly on the personhood construct for the benefit of group work within and across all disciplines. As a group-work clinician and group counselor educator who values the informed impact of group research, I advocate and support such a synergistic dialogue (see also Conyne, 2011).

Professional Development: Impact on Personhood

One final consideration that is vital to the personhood discussion is professional training. Elsewhere I have elaborated on the nature of group work using the aphorism "group work is a bowl of p's" (Trotzer, 2000, 2006) and the analogy that doing group work is a matter of "making p soup." The basis for the p's analogy emanates from the preponderance of constructs and concepts related to group work that begin with the letter p. Briefly, three tiers of p's designate the content and structure of training: basic p's, professional p's, and advanced group practice p's. Basic p's are associated with the beginning stage of training, professional p's with the intermediate stage, and advanced group practice p's with the advanced stage (see Barlow, 2004, for a description of a 3-year strategic plan for teaching beginning, intermediate, and advanced group skills).

The Basic p's (Person, Process, and Purpose)

The basic p's refer to the components of person, process, and purpose that combine to create the psychological rationale for group work. Since groups are composed of *persons* who engage interpersonally with the help of a leader to create a social milieu (group climate), a psychology of persons is needed that explains the nature of human beings and emphasizes their social nature, thereby affirming the relevance of the small group process to meeting the needs of group members and addressing their problems. Personhood of the members and the group leader is the material from which the essence of group process is formed. *Process* refers to the stages/phases counseling and therapy groups move through in the course of developing a therapeutic milieu that is commensurate with the purposes for which the group was formed and the needs of the group members. *Purpose* relates to the reason for the group's existence and the corresponding objectives and dynamics that produce outcomes. The ASGW's four group types designate generic purposes for counseling groups (i.e., personal problem solving), psychotherapy groups (i.e., personality change), psychoeducation groups (i.e., acquiring personally relevant skills and information), and task groups (i.e., task completion). The general objective with regard to helping groups is to dissolve the group by resolving the problems, issues, or tasks that prompted its formation. Every group leader needs a solid foundation of training relative to the basic p's. The dynamic relationship between the basic p entities is depicted in the following formula:

Individual Needs (person component) +
Relationship Development (process component) +
Group Purpose (purpose component) = Group
Work (practice)

The Professional p's (Planning, Performing, and Processing)

The professional p's emanate from the standards-based best practices of training diversity competent, multiculturally effective group leaders (ASGW, 1998a, 1998b, 2000; Thomas & Pender, 2008). The p's involved here relate to the acquisition of perspectives and procedures that organize, implement, and evaluate the conduct of professional group work.

Planning refers to the pregroup agenda for organizing groups including recruiting, selecting, and orienting group members and the preparation required for each group meeting across the course of the group's existence. *Performing* refers to the actual behavior and action of the leader, including leadership strategy, functions, roles, and skills. Acquiring and refining this aspect of leadership is a career-long process that transcends graduate training and embeds itself in the ongoing practice of the professional group leader. *Processing* relates to the assessment, evaluation, and critical analysis that attend to the conduct of groups and the leader's performance with respect to effectiveness, ethics, and expertise. Two types of processing are involved. One relates to the ongoing development of each group the leader leads and involves pre- and postgroup processing in peer or professional supervision. This processing should be a standard part of group work practice for every leader and uses the resource of reflective learning to improve the experience of the ongoing group as well as enhance the effectiveness of the leader. The second form of processing, called "deep processing" (Conyne, 1999; Rapin & Conyne, 2006), is designed to develop leadership expertise over time and, across all group experiences and is usually done in the context of formal supervision.

Advanced Group Practice p's (Procedures, Paradigms, and Protocols)

The advance group practice *p*'s are associated with the ongoing professional development process that is initiated in graduate training and then continues over the career of the professional group leader. They involve the pragmatic work of honing and extending the leader's capabilities and impact first as a practitioner, then as a trainer/educator, theoretician, or researcher. *Procedures* refer to the unending process of implementing and refining techniques and methods based on experiences with different groups, settings, and client populations. This activity begins with the very first group leadership experience and continues for the duration of the leadership career. A second element is the acquisition of an ever-expanding repertoire of tools and techniques to be used in groups, a process that turns the leadership tool kit into a veritable treasure chest of resources for use in leading groups (Trotzer, 2004). *Paradigms* are the cognitive tools that one uses and develops to guide one's practice as a group leader. They are the building blocks of practice protocols. Paradigms are the practitioner's contribution to theory development and the foundation for applied research. Paradigm-making involves using theoretical constructs to inform practice. It keeps practice conceptually sound, deters leaders from being overly rigid, reactive, or compulsive, and provides a heuristic basis for leadership creativity. Finally, *protocols* are the theory-based process and practice frameworks that inform practice generally (i.e., stages of group development) and supply therapeutic models for treating designated problems, diagnoses, or client populations. When one has developed paradigms and protocols to explain and guide a practice, one is in the position of passing them on to others, thus enhancing one's contribution to the group work field and setting oneself up as a trainer and researcher.

Personhood of the Group Leader

Personhood is the thread that connects and weaves together personal development and professional development into the fabric of professional practice. Personal development emerges from psychosocial (psychodynamic), systemic, cultural, and behavioral formative factors that produce the personal self of the prospective group leader. The personal self is subjected to professional training that transforms it into a professional self, which performs the role and functions of leadership in the various types of groups that constitute a career as a professional group leader.

Professional training is informed by the theoretical underpinnings of a wide range of academic disciplines that paint a large number of varied portraits of what professional leaders look like. These portraits are further defined and explicated by research that has examined who leaders are and what they do from the perspectives of traits (i.e., who the leader is), functions (i.e., what the leader does), style (i.e., how the leader does it), and situations (i.e., where and why the leader does it). These efforts have produced a plethora of traits and syndromes related to the personal qualities that constitute the personhood of the group leader. That personhood is an embedded factor in the process, practice, and productivity of group work, and as such, the prism of personhood was applied to delineate its component parts. Personhood ties the process of the group to its outcomes and manifests itself in the formative, functional, and foundational factors that prove its existence and merit as a vital entity in the conduct of group work. A case is made that personhood is the key to, the core of, and the catalyst in effective group work.

From a formative perspective, personhood is related to the curative factors that are identified as the core of the group process and associated with therapeutic change. "Nurturant attractiveness," referring to how the leader treats group members and how the leader is perceived by members, is considered a key personhood trait, as is "charismatic expertness." This trait represents how the leader influences group members and group process. The complementarity of these terms combines personal characteristics and leader competencies to affirm the centrality of group leader personhood in the conduct of group work.

The functional factors of leader personhood are those traits manifested in the performance of the group leader. Personhood makes it possible to function in a leadership role from a pragmatic perspective. Leader skills and competencies honed by training and practice portray attitudes, values, and beliefs, which in turn drive the process. The combination of character and competence is key to the leader's ability to generate, facilitate, and create group cohesion, a vital component of group climate. As such, leader personhood rises to the fore as a dynamic factor in leading and leadership.

The foundational factors of personhood are all about the ability to perform as a leader in a group. Substantial theoretical, clinical, and research evidence points to group climate as the single most influential factor in therapeutic process and progress. The exigencies of personhood are linked to that fact. A general conclusion regarding leadership traits and style is that in some cases many roads lead to the same destination, and in other cases, the same roads lead to different places. The explication of this apparent paradox is quite revealing. First, there does not appear to be one trait, several traits, or even a single combination of traits that insures emergence of leadership or effectiveness in leadership. Rather, many different traits and syndromes do so, attesting to the viability of diversity in personal characteristics that can be mobilized to produce leaders and leadership. To paraphrase the words of higher education expert Parker Palmer (1998), "Community and connectedness (group climate) is the principle behind good teaching (group counseling), but different teachers (leaders) with different gifts create community in surprisingly diverse ways using widely divergent methods" (p. 115). Second, the purposes, settings, or situations of groups always affect leadership as much as leadership affects them. As such, successful leadership requires a personhood that can effect therapeutic process with regard to specified group purposes and adapt processes when situational variables call for such modifications.

Personhood not only is the core of process and practice but needs to assume a greater role in the realm of research. The challenge to group research is to make personhood of equivalent importance in the person, process, product paradigm and to accord it equal status as one of the superpowers in the group research world. The key to doing so requires drawing upon the emerging knowledge, insights, and practices of all disciplines related to group work, thereby creating a "global" (multidisciplinary) group-work enterprise where the benefits are realized in each domain-specific area of practice. Much groundwork has been laid for this challenging endeavor, but each discipline must take up the cause and officially sound the clarion call, "Let the collaboration begin!"

Concluding Comments

In the final analysis, personhood is the drawstring of the group work garment. It is the thread that pulls all the elements of process and practice together. It ties together personal development and professional development; connects person, process, and product; melds character and competence; unites training/teaching, practice, and research; and serves as the key, core, and catalyst for all we have come to know about and associate with group work as a practice and discipline. The centrality of personhood is unquestioned, and its essence is the lifeblood of the group process. It drives the leader (who the leader is) and inspires leadership (what the leader does). With it, group work thrives; and without it, group work disintegrates. To paraphrase and adapt another aphorism of Parker Palmer (1998) in closing, "good teachers (group leaders) join self (personhood) and subject (group work) and students (group members) in the fabric of life" (p. 11). Personhood supplies the essence of that self that prompts the process that produces the change that enhances the growth and mental health of group members. After all, in the helping professions, that impact is the bottom line.

Note

1. The reader is referred to Hirokawa et al. (2003, pp. 169–211) for a detailed discussion of the four conceptual paradigms that have been utilized in the study of small-group leaders and leadership: (1) trait approach, (2) style approach, (3) situational approach, and (4) functional approach. Each perspective reflects a different perception of the leader's personhood.

References

American Group Psychotherapy Association. (2007). *Practical guidelines for group psychotherapy*. Retrieved from http://www.agpa.org/guidelines/index.html

Antonuccio, D. O., Davis, C., Lewinson, P. M., & Breckenridge, J. S. (1987). Therapist variables related to cohesiveness in a group treatment for depression. *Small Group Behavior*, 18, 557–564.

Association for Multicultural Counseling and Development. (1996). *Multicultural competencies*. Alexandria, VA: Author.

Association for Specialists in Group Work. (1998a). ASGW best practice guidelines. *Journal for Specialists in Group Work*, 23, 237–244.

Association for Specialists in Group Work. (1998b). *ASGW principles for diversity competent group workers*. Alexandria, VA: Author.

Association for Specialists in Group Work. (2000). ASGW professional standards for the training of group workers. *Journal for Specialists in Group Work*, 25, 327–342.

Barlow, S. (2004). A strategic three-year plan to teach beginning, intermediate, and advanced group skills. *Journal for Specialists in Group Work*, 29(1), 113–126. Retrieved August 22, 2009, doi:10.1080/01933920490275600.

Bates, M., Johnson, C. D., & Blaker, K. E. (1982). *Group leadership: A manual for group counseling leaders* (2nd ed.). Denver, CO: Love.

Bednar, R., & Kaul, T. (1994). Experiential group research: Can the cannon fire? In A. Bergin & S. Garfield (Eds.), *Handbook of psychotherapy and behavior change* (4th ed., pp. 631–663). New York: John Wiley & Sons.

Bednar, R., Melnick, J., & Kaul, T. (1974). Risk, responsibility and structure. *Journal of Counseling Psychology*, 21(1), 31–37.

Beebe, S. A., Beebe, S. J., & Redmond, M. V. (2008). *Interpersonal communication: Relating to others* (5th ed.). Boston: Allyn & Bacon.

Bowen, M. (1966). The use of family theory in clinical practice. *Comprehensive Psychiatry*, 7, 345–374.

Burlingame, G., & Fuhriman, A. (Eds.). (1994). *Handbook of group psychotherapy: An empirical and clinical synthesis* (pp. 559–562). New York: John Wiley & Sons.

Burlingame, G. M., Fuhriman, A. J., & Johnson, J. (2004). Process and outcome in group counseling and psychotherapy. In J. L. DeLucia-Waack, D. A. Gerrity, C. R. Kalodner, & M. T. Riva (Eds.), *Handbook of group counseling and psychotherapy* (pp. 49–61). Thousand Oaks, CA: Sage.

Cohen, A. M., & Smith, R. D. (1976). *The critical incident in growth groups: Theory and technique*. La Jolla, CA: University Associates.

Conyne, R. K. (1999). *Failures in group work: How we can learn from our mistakes*. Thousand Oaks, CA: Sage.

Conyne, R. K. (2011). Group counseling. In E. Altmaier & J. Hansen (Eds.), *Oxford handbook of counseling psychology*. New York: Oxford University Press.

Conyne, R. K., Wilson, F. R., & Ward, D. (1997). *Comprehensive group work: What it means & how to teach it*. Alexandria, VA: American Counseling Association.

Corey, M. S., & Corey, G. (2006). *Groups: Process and practice* (7th ed.). Monterey, CA: Brooks/Cole.

Couch, R. D. (1995). Four steps for conducting a pre-group screening interview. *Journal for Specialists in Group Work*, 20, 18–25.

D'Andrea, M. (2004). The impact of racial–cultural identity of group leaders and members: Theory and recommendations. In J. DeLucia-Waack, D. Gerrity, C. Kalodner, & M. Riva (Eds.), *Handbook of group counseling and psychotherapy* (pp. 265–282). Thousand Oaks, CA: Sage.

DeLucia-Waack, J., & Donigian, J. (2003). *The practice of multicultural group work: Visions and perspectives from the field*. Monterey, CA: Wadsworth.

DeLucia-Waack, J., Gerrity, D., Kalodner, C., & Riva, M. (Eds.). (2004). *Handbook of group counseling and psychotherapy*. Thousand Oaks, CA: Sage.

Dies, R. R. (1994). Therapist variables in group psychotherapy research. In A. Fuhriman & G. M. Burlingame (Eds.). *Handbook of group psychotherapy: An empirical and clinical synthesis* (pp. 114–154). New York: John Wiley & Sons.

Donigian, J., & Hulse-Killacky, D. (1999). *Critical incidents in group work* (2nd ed.). Pacific Grove, CA: Brooks/Cole.

Donigian, J., & Malnati, R. (1997). *Systemic group therapy: A triadic model*. Pacific Grove, CA: Brooks/Cole.

Felfe, J., & Schyns, B. (2006). Personality and the perception of transformational leadership: The impact of extraversion, neuroticism, personal need for structure, and occupational self-efficacy. *Journal of Applied Social Psychology*, 36(1), 708–739. Retrieved August 22, 2009, doi:10.1111/j.0021–9029.2006.00026.x.

Forsyth, D. (2006). *Group dynamics*. Belmont, CA: Thomson Wadsworth.

Garvin, C. D., Gutierrez, L. M., & Galinsky, M. J. (2004). *Handbook of social work with groups*. New York: Guilford Press.

Gazda, G., Ginter, E., & Horne, A. (2001). *Group counseling and group psychotherapy: Theory and application*. Boston: Allyn & Bacon.

Geier, J. G. (1967). A trait approach to the study of leadership in small groups. *Journal of Communication*. 17, 316–323.

Getterman, A., & Salmon, R. (Eds.). (2008). *Encyclopedia of social work with groups*. New York: Routledge, Taylor & Francis.

Gillam, S. (2004). Preplanning considerations in teaching group counseling courses: Applying a general framework for conceptualizing pedagogy. *Journal for Specialists in Group Work*, 29(1), 75–85. Retrieved August 22, 2009, doi:10.1080/01933920490275475.

Gladding, S. T. (1984). The metaphor as a counseling tool in group work. *Journal for Specialists in Group Work*, 9(3), 151–156.

Gladding, S. (2002). *Group work: A counseling specialty* (4th ed.). Upper Saddle River, NJ: Prentice Hall.

Gouran, D. S. (2003). Leadership as the art of counteractive influence in decision-making and problem-solving groups. In R. Y. Hirokawa, R. S. Cathart, L. A. Samovar, & L. D. Henman (Eds.), *Small group communication: Theory & practice An anthology* (8th ed. pp. 172–183). Los Angeles: Roxbury.

Hansen, J. C., Warner, R. W., & Smith, E. J. (1980). *Group counseling: Theory and process*. Chicago: Rand McNally College.

Hirokawa, R. Y., Cathart, R. S., Samovar, L. A., & Henman, L. D. (2003). *Small group communication: Theory & Practice— An anthology* (8th ed.). Los Angeles: Roxbury.

Hulse-Killacky, D., Killacky, J., & Donigian, J. (2001). *Making task groups work in your world*. Upper Saddle River, NJ: Prentice Hall.

Jacobs, E., Masson, R., & Harvill, R. (2006). *Group counseling: Strategies and skills* (5th ed.). Pacific Grove, CA: Brooks/Cole.

Johns, H., & Moser, H. (1989). From trait to transformation: The evolution of leadership theories. *Education*, 110(1), 115.

Joyce, J. (2005). The revised CORE battery: Assessment of group therapy process. *Group Circle*, (Spring), 5–6.

Johnson, J., Burlingame, G., Olsen, J., Davies, D. R., & Gleave, R. (2005). Group climate, cohesion, alliance, and empathy in group psychotherapy: Multilevel structural equation models. *Journal of Counseling Psychology, 52,* 310–321.

Kivlighan, D., Jr., & Holmes, S. (2004). The importance of therapeutic factors. In J. DeLucia-Waack, D. Gerrity, C. Kalodner, & M. Riva (Eds.), *Handbook of group counseling and psychotherapy* (pp. 23–36). Thousand Oaks, CA: Sage.

Kivlighan, D., Jr., McGovern, T., & Corazzini, J. (1984). The effects of content and timing of structuring interventions on group therapy process and outcome. *Journal of Counseling Psychology, 31,* 363–370.

Kivlighan, D., Jr., & Tarrant, J. (2001). Does group climate mediate the group leadership–group outcome relationship? A test of Yalom's hypotheses about leadership priorities. *Group Dynamics: Theory, Research, and Practice, 5,* 220–234.

Lieberman, M., Yalom, I., & Miles, M. (1973). *Encounter groups: First facts.* New York: Basic Books.

Luft, J. (1984). *Group process: An introduction to group dynamics* (3rd ed.). Palo Alto, CA: Mayfield.

MacLennan, B. (1975). The personalities of group leaders: Implications for selection and training. *International Journal of Group Psychotherapy, 25*(2), 177–183.

MacNair-Semands, R. (2006). CORE-R battery: Group selection and pre-group preparation. *Group Circle* (Winter), 3–4.

MacNair-Semands, R. (2007). Attending to the spirit of social justice as an ethical approach in group therapy. *International Journal of Group Psychotherapy, 57*(1), 61–66.

Mahler, C. A. (1969). *Group counseling in the schools.* Boston: Houghton Mifflin.

Marziali, E., Munroe-Blum, L., & McCleary, L. (1997). Contribution of group cohesion and group alliance to the outcome of group psychotherapy. *International Journal of Group Psychotherapy, 47,* 475–497.

Maslow, A. H. (1962). *Toward a psychology of being.* Princeton, NJ: Van Nostrand.

McClure, B. A. (1989). What's a meta-phor? *Journal for Specialists in Group Work, 14*(4), 239–242.

McWhirter, J., & Frey, R. (1987). Group leader and member characteristics and attraction to initial and final group sessions and to the group and group leader. *Small Group Behavior, 18*(4), 533–547.

Merchant, N. (2006). Multicultural and diversity-competent group work. In J. P. Trotzer (Ed.), *The counselor and the group: Integrating theory, training, and practice* (4th ed., pp. 319–349). New York: Routledge.

Miller, P. H. (2002). *Theories of developmental psychology* (4th ed.). New York: Worth.

Minuchin, S. (1974). *Families and family therapy.* Cambridge, MA: Harvard University Press.

Morran, D. K., Stockton, R., Cline, R., & Teed, C. (1998). Facilitating feedback exchange in groups: Leader interventions. *Journal for Specialists in Group Work, 23,* 257–268.

Morran, D. K., Stockton, R., & Whittingham, M. (2004). Effective leader interventions for counseling and psychotherapy groups. In J. DeLucia-Waack, D. Gerrity, C. Kalodner, & M. Riva (Eds.), *Handbook of group counseling and psychotherapy* (pp. 91–103). Thousand Oaks, CA: Sage.

Napier, A. Y., & Whitaker, C. (1978). *The family crucible: The intense experience of family therapy.* New York: Quill, HarperCollins.

Oetzel, J. G., Meares, M., & Fukumoto, A. (2003). Cross-cultural and intercultural work group communication. In R. Y. Hirokawa, R. S. Cathart, L. A. Samovar, & L. D. Henman (Eds.), *Small group communication: Theory & practice An anthology* (8th ed., pp. 172–183). Los Angeles: Roxbury.

Ohlsen, M. M., Horne, A. M., & Lawe, C. F. (1988). *Group counseling* (3rd ed.). New York: Holt, Rinehart and Winston.

Page, B. J., & Hulse-Killacky, D. (1999). Development and validation of the corrective feedback self-efficacy instrument. *Journal for Specialists in Group Work, 24,* 37–54.

Page, B., Pietrzak, D., & Lewis, T. (2001). Development of the group leader self-efficacy instrument. *Journal for Specialists in Group Work, 26,* 168–184.

Palmer, P. J. (1998). *The courage to teach: Exploring the inner landscape of a teacher's life.* San Francisco, CA: Jossey-Bass.

Pan, P., & Lin, C. (2004). Members' perceptions of leader behaviors, group experiences, and therapeutic factors in group counseling. *Small Group Research, 35,* 174–194. Retrieved August 22, 2009, doi:10.1177/1046496403260557.

Piper, W. E., & McCallum, M. (1994). Selection of patients for group interventions. In H. S. Bernard & K. R. MacKenzie (Eds.), *Basics of group psychotherapy* (pp. 1–34). New York: Guilford Press.

Piper, W. E., & Perrault, E.L. (1989). Pre-therapy preparation for group members. *International Journal of Group Psychotherapy, 39,* 17–34.

Porter, R. E., & Samovar, L. A. (2003). Communication in the multicultural group. In R. Y. Hirokawa, R. S. Cathart, L. A. Samovar, & L. D. Henman (Eds.), *Small group communication: Theory & practice—An anthology* (8th ed., pp. 172–183). Los Angeles: Roxbury.

Rapin, L., & Conyne, R. (2006). Best practices in group work. In J. P. Trotzer (Ed.), *The counselor and the group: Integrating theory, training, and practice* (4th ed., pp. 291–318). New York: Routledge.

Reich, N. M., & Woods, J. T. (2003). Sex, gender, and communication in small groups. In R. Y. Hirokawa, R. S. Cathart, L. A. Samovar, & L. D. Henman (Eds.), *Small group communication: Theory & practice—An anthology* (8th ed., pp. 218–229). Los Angeles: Roxbury.

Riva, M., Wachtel, M., & Lasky, G. (2004). Effective leadership in group counseling and psychotherapy. In J. DeLucia-Waack, D. Gerrity, C. Kalodner, & M. Riva (Eds.), *Handbook of group counseling and psychotherapy* (pp. 37–48). Thousand Oaks, CA: Sage.

Santarsiero, L. J., Baker, R. C., & McGee, T. F. (1995). The effects of cognitive pre-training on cohesion and self disclosure in small groups. *Journal of Clinical Psychology, 51,* 403–409.

Satir, V. (1972). *Peoplemaking.* Palo Alto, CA: Science and Behavior Books.

Slavson, S.R. (1952). The dynamics of group work. In D.F. Sullivan (Ed.), *Readings in group work.* New York: Associated Press.

Smokowski, P. R., Rose, S. D., & Bacallao, M. L. (2001). Damaging experiences in therapeutic groups: How vulnerable consumers become group casualties. *Small Group Research, 32,* 223–251.

Stockton, R., Morran, D.K., & Krieger, K. (2004). An overview of current research and best practices for training beginning group leaders. In J. DeLucia-Waack, D.Gerrity, C. Kalodner, & M. Riva (Eds.), *Handbook of group counseling and psychotherapy* (pp. 65–75). Thousand Oaks, CA: Sage.

Stockton, R., Rohde, R. I., & Haughey, J. (1994). The effects of structured group exercises on cohesion, engagement, avoidance and conflict. *Small Group Research, 23,* 155–168.

Stockton, R., Toth, P.L., & Morran, D.K. (2006). The case for group research. In J. Trotzer (Ed.), *The counselor and the group: Integrating theory, training and practice* (4th ed., pp.529–547). New York: Routledge.

Thomas, R., & Pender, D. (2008). Association for Specialists in Group Work: Best practice guidelines 2007 revisions. *Journal for Specialists in Group Work*, 33, 111–117. Retrieved August 22, 2009, doi:10.1080/01933920801971184.

Teyber, E. (1997). *Interpersonal process in psychotherapy: A relational approach* (3rd ed.). Pacific Grove, CA: Brooks/Cole.

Tichy, N. M. (with Cohen, E.) (1997). *The leadership engine: How winning companies build leaders at every level.* New York: HarperCollins.

Tichy, N. M., & Devanna, M. A. (1986). *The transformational leader.* New York: John Wiley & Sons.

Tinsley, H., Roth, J., & Lease, S. (1989). Dimensions of leadership and leadership style among group intervention specialists. *Journal of Counseling Psychology*, 36, 48–53. Retrieved August 22, 2009, doi:10.1037/0022–0167.36.1.48.

Trotzer, J. P. (1979). Group counseling and the dynamic of structure [Special issue]. *Journal for Specialists In Group Work*, 4(4).

Trotzer, J. P. (2000). Group work practice ideas: Problem solving procedures in group work. *The Group Worker*, 29, 9–12.

Trotzer, J. P. (2004). Conducting a group: Guidelines for choosing and using activities. In J. DeLucia-Waack, D. Gerrity, C. Kalodner, & M. Riva (Eds.), *Handbook of group counseling and psychotherapy* (pp. 76–90). Thousand Oaks, CA: Sage.

Trotzer, J. P. (2006). *The counselor and the group: Integrating theory, training, and practice* (4th ed.). New York: Routledge.

Trotzer, J. P., & Trotzer, T. B. (1986). *Marriage and family: Better ready than not.* Muncie, IN: Accelerated Development.

Tschuschke, V., & Dies, R. R. (1994). Intensive analysis of therapeutic factors and outcomes in long-term inpatient groups. *International Journal of Group Psychotherapy*, 44, 185–208.

Ward, D. E., & Litchy, M. (2004). The effective use of processing in groups. In J. DeLucia-Waack, D. Gerrity, C. Kalodner, & M. Riva (Eds.), *Handbook of group counseling and psychotherapy* (pp. 104–119). Thousand Oaks, CA: Sage.

Wilson, F.R., Rapin, L., & Haley-Banez, L. (2004). How teaching group work can be guided by foundational documents: Best practice guidelines, diversity principles, training standards. Special issue (R. Conyne & F. Bemak, Eds.), Teaching group work, *Journal for Specialists in Group Work*, 29, 19–29.

Yalom, I. D. (1985). *The theory and practice of group psychotherapy* (3rd ed.). New York: Basic Books.

Yalom, I. (with Leszcz, M.) (2005). *The theory and practice of group psychotherapy* (5th ed.). New York: Basic Books.

Zaccaro, S. (2007). Trait-based perspectives of leadership. *American Psychologist*, 62(1), 6–16.

Mark D. Newmeyer

Abstract

The term *group technique* is not well defined. A variety of other terms (e.g., structured experiences, exercises) are often used interchangeably. Given this current state, it is of little surprise that few conceptual models have been developed to assist group leaders in properly considering and selecting group techniques. One model attempting to fill this gap, the Purposeful Group Techniques Model is described. The model consolidates various established elements of how groups work and function with six core ecological concepts (i.e., context, interconnections, collaboration, social system maintenance, meaning making, and sustainability). Research to examine the model, as well as to develop other such models, is needed.

Keywords: group techniques, intervention applications, leader interventions, exercises, structured experiences, ecological concepts, purposeful group techniques model, best practices, group development

Introduction

The proper use of group techniques is vital to successful group counseling. That is to say, group leaders must possess, and be ready to implement, action steps that assist a group and its members in reaching goals. Yet, somewhat surprisingly, there is a limited body of scholarly literature that attempts to operationally define or provide a theoretical framework by which to select, implement, and evaluate group techniques.

Categorizing group techniques has contributed to advancing group work and group counseling by assisting group leaders' considerations in selecting and implementing group techniques. For example, Pfeiffer and Jones (1976) classify group structured experiences according to the following categories: ice breakers, interpersonal communication, group problem solving, awareness expansion, personal feedback, competition, intergroup communication, dyads, leadership, group process, and organization development (p. 6). Corey, Corey, Callanan, and

Russell (2004) categorize techniques according to stages of group development: initial stage, transition stage, working stage, and final stage (pp. xii–xiii, 69–182). Davis (1996) details how group leaders working in religious environments might organize techniques according to spiritual disciplines (e.g., fellowship, serving, prayer). Capuzzi (2003) organizes strategies and exercises mainly across the life span (i.e., children, adolescents, and adults). Kraus (2003) also orders exercises according to the life-span continuum. DeLucia-Waack, Bridbord, Kleiner, and Nitza (2006) edited a compilation of group activities, using a group development model (i.e., orientation, transition, working, and termination), to categorize over 50 activities.

As well, there are numerous strategies and approaches being used by group leaders that are rooted in a specific psychological orientation, such as Gestalt or Adlerian. Kraus (2003) examines how exercises for leading groups are informed by various perspectives (i.e., psychoanalytic and transactional,

⤷techniques

person-centered and existential, Adlerian and reality, Gestalt and psychodrama, and rational-emotive and behavioral). However, this author contends that these schemas mostly derive from a Western or highly individualistic orientation, which in some regards is divergent from the efforts of a group counseling focus that prizes interpersonal relationships. Such a bold assertion is not to suggest that approaches grounded in an individual-oriented psychology are not beneficial in guiding group leaders. As in the case with a Gestalt orientation, asking an individual in a one-on-one counseling session or in group counseling to use "I" statements is likely extremely beneficial.

What is still lacking is a clear conceptual approach that is flexible, adaptable and arises from what have been clearly identified as core tenants and processes of groups (e.g., interdependence, group dynamics, social climate, group development, experiential here-and-now processes, feedback, participant observation) and grounded in group best practice guidelines (Association for Specialists in Group Work [ASGW], 1998). Attending to the selection and use of group techniques will likely translate into effective practice.

Defining Group Techniques

An examination of the monographic literature that substantively contributes to our understanding of group counseling (Beck & Lewis, 2000; Conyne, 1985; Conyne, Crowell, & Newmeyer, 2008; Corey, & Corey, 2006; DeLucia-Waack, Gerrity, Kalodner, & Riva, 2004; Garvin, Gutierrez, & Galinsky, 2004; Gladding, 2008; Hansen, Warner, & Smith, 1980; Jacobs, Masson, & Harvill, 2009; Johnson & Johnson, 2009; Lieberman, Yalom, & Miles, 1973; Napier & Gershenfeld, 2004; Schmuck & Schmuck, 2001; Trotzer, 2006; Yalom, 2005) demonstrates that little attention has been given to operationally defining the term *group technique*. In fact, only three of the 15 texts use the phrase and then attempt to provide definitions:

> intervention applications ("tools of the trade") that are used by group leaders—and sometimes by group members—to focus group processes, try out behavior, accentuate thoughts and feelings, and provide opportunities for learning. (Conyne et al., 2008, p. 8)

> Are leaders' interventions aimed at facilitating movement within a group? Virtually anything a leader does could be viewed as a technique, including being silent, suggesting a new behavior, inviting

members to deal with conflict, offering feedback to members, presenting interpretations, and suggesting homework assignments to be done between group sessions. (Corey, & Corey, 2006, p. 5)

> Group techniques or exercises are structured ways of getting members to interact with one another. They can have a powerful impact on group members and positively affect how people work together or change. (Gladding, 2008, p. 207)

That said, a review of several academic databases confirms *group techniques* as the master term. Yet, its function appears to be as a broad umbrella term—regularly used by authors with little to no operational definition. For example, in examining the PsycINFO database, using "group counseling" as a thesaurus term, "techniques" and/or "group techniques" as key words, and limiting articles from 2000 to 2009, 193 hits were identified. In reviewing the relevant contributions, "techniques" or "group techniques" was in no way operationally defined. Nonetheless, there appears to be an implicit understanding of the term.

A factor limiting the term *group technique(s)* from being more prominent in general usage and being precisely defined appears to correspond to the presence of more specific key words (e.g., exercises, structured experiences, interventions, activities). This is substantiated by observing the synonyms found in the three definitions provided (i.e., "interventions applications," "leader interventions," "exercises," and "structured ways") and in examining these similar terms by means of the PsycINFO database. Results from this effort show significant common characteristics of group "technique(s)," "exercise(s)," "structured experience(s)," "intervention(s)," and "activity(ies)," with minimal new hits beyond the 193 articles already identified; the Google Scholar search engine produced parallel findings. Thus, the current state of group-counseling scholarly literature does support *group techniques* as an overarching term, but clearly a set of interchangeable terms exists that describe similar leader tasks. They all provide the reader with terms to describe action steps that group leaders use to promote the group's work in reaching very general to specific goals, including this expanded terminology of exercises, structured experiences, interventions, and activities.

Because of this current state, it is helpful to think of group techniques in an encompassing sense. While terms like *structured experience* and *exercise* might imply a level of specificity, it is likely more useful to think of *group techniques* as a generic term, much like the term *fruit* is inclusive of apples, oranges, and grapes. Thus, group techniques cover a vast range of intervention applications. In *Group Techniques: How to Use Them More Purposefully*, the following concise definition is offered: "actions group leaders take to move the group and its members forward" (Conyne et al., 2008, p. 208).

Using this viewpoint, a group technique might be something as specific as a leader asking group members to arrange the seating in a circle to more adequately see each other or as ambiguous as asking the group open-ended questions, such as "Would anyone care to share their feelings about what has just happened?" Further, group techniques may be planned or arise suddenly, based upon the group's interactions (Conyne et al., 2008; Corey et al., 2004; Durkin, 1981; Fuhriman & Barlow, 1994; Jacobs et al., 2009; Pfeiffer & Jones, 1980). That is to say, group leaders may plan to implement specific techniques but frequently find the need to improvise or adapt techniques in real time.

Whether they are general or specific, planned or spontaneous, group techniques must be used with intention in a way that appreciates and values the ongoing dynamics and needs of the group. Effective leaders have been known to err by using an otherwise wonderful technique for the wrong reasons because they were excited to try out a newly learned exercise or even felt compelled to fill a silence. To be used properly, and for the best effect, any technique a leader chooses must be purposeful.

This purposeful selection, implementation, and evaluation of group techniques has received little serious attention. While a variety of articles and books have been published that describe and somewhat categorize group techniques or particular occasions when a group technique would be beneficial for leaders to employ, there is a great need to continue such efforts and integrate the core aspects of what has been learned about groups into cohesive models that leaders can bring into play.

Effectively leading counseling groups requires far more than memorizing a collection of techniques. To help members and the group as a whole reach their goals, it is important to have an organizing structure for these techniques, as many have already observed (e.g., Corey et al., 2004; Jacobs et al., 2009). Using a metaphor, it might be helpful to think of techniques as the tools of the trade for group leaders just as hammers and saws are the tools of the carpenter. In that respect, leading a group and working with wood are not that different. Both are a blend of craft and art, forcing one often to improvise; both require a toolbox; and like the carpenter's tools, each group technique has a specific purpose and risk if used inappropriately. Thus, utilizing a method in selecting techniques provides a guiding process and a resulting safe zone for these techniques to be put to work.

Guiding Approaches in Using Group Techniques

Pfeiffer and Jones (1972) assembled a handbook for group facilitators that compiled structured experiences, a groundbreaking effort in 1969–1971. Annual editions since then have identified over 800 group techniques. Initially, guidance concerning the appropriate selection and implementation of any given structured experience was limited, the emphasis being not so much on the structured experience but rather on the processing that immediately follows. By 1973, the handbook included a new series of structured experiences but also 11 specific questions that a group leader must consider in using a structured experience:

Considerations in Using Structured Experiences

1. What are the goals of this group? Why was it formed?
2. At what stage is the group in its development?
3. What is my contract with the group?
4. Why is it important that I intervene?
5. Why does this particular intervention appeal to me?
6. How ready are these participants to take risks, to experiment?
7. What content modifications can I make to have an effective, appealing design?
8. What advanced preparations need to be made?
9. How rigid are the time constraints for the session?
10. How am I going to set up the processing?
11. How am I going to evaluate the effectiveness of the design? (Pfeiffer & Jones, 1973, pp. 4–5)

By 1974, Pfeiffer and Jones's handbook included 10 structured experience categories: ice-breakers, communication, leadership, task group and organization development, dyads, individual feedback, group feedback, awareness expansion, group problem-solving, and competition. As well, communication was split into interpersonal communication and intergroup communication (Pfeiffer & Jones, 1974, p. 5). Compared to Table 17.1, which reflects the categories and subcategories from the 2003 edition, one can see the evolution of techniques in the past 30 years.

Emphasizing an approach that puts the focus on group development when selecting techniques, Corey et al. (2004) categorize group techniques as fitting into the following:

- *Initial Stage*: During the critical first sessions, leaders are working to help members reduce anxiety, get acquainted, and create trust, as well as on other key aspects pivotal to a vital group. Techniques that might fit into this stage include attending to the physical setting (e.g., size of room, lighting, seating) and helping members get acquainted with each other. An example of an initial-stage technique would be to ask the group, "Could we each give our name, followed by what you expect this group to be like for you? What do you hope it will be like for you? What do you fear it will be like?"

- *Transition Stage*: Typically characterized by a period of conflict, leaders during these sessions often find members have built an initial level of trust and begin to test the waters by challenging other members and the leader(s). Techniques in this stage will often emphasis members'

self-appraisal of their participation and function within the group. An example of a transition technique is asking, "John, please state what you were feeling just prior to saying that you felt bored."

- *Working Stage*: Sessions during this stage are typically characterized by a here-and-now emphasis as the group addresses the primary goals that have brought them together and members become ready to take responsibility for them. Group techniques then help the group advance this work. "Jose, you say you just can't talk to your parents, and I've noticed you approach me [the group leader] in a similar manner. Would you be willing to do a role-play and say to me what you would really like to say to your parents?"

- *Final Stage*: Group leaders find themselves guiding the group as it comes to terms with the ending of the group and all this entails—finished business as well as unfinished business, carrying forward with learning and personal growth, evaluation of how things have gone, etc. Techniques during this stage often have a summarizing component and ask members to consider how the future will be altered because of the work accomplished throughout the life of

Table 17.1   Experiential learning activity categories

Individual Development	Teams
Sensory awareness	How groups work
Self-disclosure	Roles
Sex roles	Problem solving/decision making
Diversity	Feedback
Life/career planning	Conflict and intergroup issues
Communication	**Consulting & Facilitating**
Awareness	Consulting: awareness
Building trust	Consulting: diagnosing skills
Conflict	Facilitating: opening
Feedback	Facilitating: blocks to learning
Listening	Facilitating: skills
Styles	Facilitating: closing
Technology	**Leadership**
Problem Solving	Ethics
Generating alternatives	Interviewing/appraisal
Information sharing	Motivation
Consensus/synergy	Diversity/stereotyping
Action planning	Styles
Groups	**Organizations**
How groups work	Communication
Competition/collaboration	Vision, mission, values, strategy
Negotiating/bargaining	Change management

the group. An example of a final-stage technique is asking the group, "What has it been like for you to be a member of this group?"

In addition to selecting group techniques according to the group development stage, Corey et al. (2004) insist that group leaders be guided by ethical considerations. These include providing information about the group to all members, leaders' awareness of motivations guiding their work, working from a theoretical rationale, and limitations in expertise.

DeLucia-Waack et al. (2006) have also found it beneficial to order group techniques according to stage of development. Using the categories orientation stage, transition stage, working stage, termination stage, and activities for all stages, they describe over 50 techniques. Another benefit of this work is the attention given to classifying techniques according to the type of group for which they are best suited. To accomplish this, the ASGW group type classification was adopted:

- *Task Groups*: This group type is used to resolve or to enhance performance and production goals within a work group, through attention to team building, collaborative problem solving, and system-change strategies.
- *Psychoeducation Groups*: This group type is used to educate members and develop their skills, and it often is geared to prevention of future problems. Leaders impart information and train in skills within an interpersonal milieu.
- *Counseling Groups*: This group type is used to help members improve their coping with problems of living by focusing on interpersonal problem solving, feedback, and support within a here-and-now framework.
- *Psychotherapy Groups*: This group type is used to help members to reduce psychological and/or emotional dysfunction by focusing on bringing past history to the present and incorporating diagnosis and assessment within an interpersonal orientation (ASGW, 2000; Conyne, 1999).

Additionally, in this approach the techniques are classified according to population (e.g., adolescents or adults), estimated duration, and materials required. The following is a partial example of a termination-stage activity:

WHAT HAVE WE LEARNED ABOUT OURSELVES?
Goals: The goals of this activity are to help group members: 1) Identify what they have learned about

themselves as a result of participation in the group, 2) verbalize what they have learned in the group . . .
Potential Stage/Session(s): During termination stage.
Type of Groups:
    ____ Task/Work
    __X__ Psychoeducational
    __X__ Counseling
    __X__ Therapy
Populations: Children to Adults
Materials: A copy of Figure for each group member, and pens.
Estimated Time Length: 45 minutes to an hour.
Directions: Today is the last session of the group and one of the things we need to do is to review what we've done as a group. . . . To help us with this task I would like you to write a letter to the group members who may participate in this kind of group at a later date to give them some information (p. 152)

Capuzzi (2003) conceptualizes group techniques organized by the individual member's age; specific group approaches may be more suited for particular age groups. This work, which describes 23 techniques and the intended outcomes, is somewhat different—the goals being accomplished are typically described as occurring over multiple sessions. Kraus (2003) approaches techniques similarly across the life span of the member, while also giving attention to the group's stage of development and theoretical perspective (e.g., psychoanalytic, person-centered, Gestalt, behavioral).

So, how to keep all these options in mind while leading a group? The purposeful group techniques model (PGTM) is a comprehensive way of bringing together key aspects, such as group development and group type, of other approaches.

At the core of the PGTM is an ecological approach to guide leaders' thinking in selecting group techniques. An ecological orientation posits that an essential ingredient in accurately viewing persons requires incorporating contextual factors and influences. Thus, an appreciation of the reciprocal interactions between people and environments is pivotal in promoting growth and change (Conyne & Cook, 2004). Ecological concepts that are of importance for leaders of counseling groups to attend to are context, interconnections, collaboration, social system maintenance, meaning making, and sustainability (Conyne et al., 2008). Because group counseling is both interpersonal and contextualized (Bemak & Conyne, 2004: Conyne & Bemak, 2004; Conyne & Mazza, 2007), leaders will best assist counseling groups by attending to the interaction of all related factors.

The model is comprised of five steps: (1) identify the group type, the relevant best practice area, and the developmental stage; (2) analyze the presenting group situation by applying ecological concepts of context, interconnection, collaboration, social system, meaning making, and sustainability; (3) review possible group techniques; (4) select a "best-fit" technique; and (5) implement and evaluate how well the technique worked. Figure 17.1 illustrates the key aspects of the model.

As already stated, the PGTM assists group leaders in purposefully selecting and applying group techniques by providing an organizing structure. As such, this structure has translated into the development of a techniques "toolbox" that allows group leaders to visually scan group techniques in a variety of ways. A sample of this toolbox is contained at the conclusion of this chapter.

PGTM Step One: Identify

Step one requires a group leader to understand and be aware of fundamental characteristics about the group. In Chapter 1 of this handbook, Dr. Robert K. Conyne grappled with several ways in which *group counseling* has been defined. For this model, Conyne et al. (2008) adopted the ASGW's group type classification and asked group leaders to identify if the group is best described as a task group, psychoeducation group, counseling group, or psychotherapy group.

Generally speaking, techniques are often appropriate for all types of groups (e.g., an ice-breaker at the beginning of a newly formed group). However, subtle distinctions concerning the type of group may dictate which techniques better fit its functions. For example, using a considerable amount of a group's allotted time to provide specific information may match better with psychoeducation

groups, with consideration of therapeutic factors more in keeping with counseling, psychotherapy, and, to a lesser extent, psychoeducation groups. Keeping this in mind, from this point forward this chapter emphasizes counseling groups. A more comprehensive understanding of how the type of group might impact technique selection is undertaken in Conyne et al. (2008), in which a series of carefully crafted critical incidents shed light on the interplay of group type and technique selection.

Zeroing In on Best Practices

Through anecdotal evidence, most group leaders this author has encountered are not aware that best practice procedures exist to aid the effective and ethical delivery of group leadership. In developing best practice guidelines, the ASGW delineated three best practice areas—planning, performing, and processing—informally referred to as the "three *p*'s" (ASGW, 1998). Though often discussed as discrete and separate parts, the three *p*'s are interconnected and should be viewed as such.

• *Planning* as a best practice area addresses all the work a group leader must accomplish prior to carrying out the first session. For example, the group leader will need to consider the overall purpose of the group being offered, a plan or curriculum, contextual factors that could serve to promote or hinder the group's work, optimal size of the group, member inclusion/exclusion criteria, available resources, duration of the group, and a leader model (e.g., solo leader or coleader).

• *Performing*, the actual leading of the group, is where the rubber meets the road. It involves group leaders applying what has been described as the core competencies of group work (ASGW, 2000) and, when needed, modifying plans in real time as the group is happening. Performing requires group leaders to be aware of group development, assist members in identifying goals, create and help maintain therapeutic conditions, correctly observe group processes, value diversity, act in an ethical manner, evaluate the group, and many other critical functions.

• As a best practice area, *processing* focuses on examining and attributing meaning from group events and experiences. Processing is occasionally referred to as the *how* of a group. Processing requires leaders to reflect and work with group members in noticing how events in the life of the group have or are unfolding, how decisions are being made, and how members (individually or

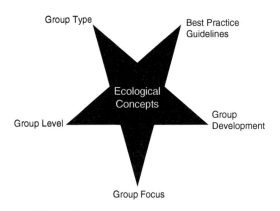

Fig. 17.1 PGTM key aspects.

collectively) are making sense out of the group. Processing take places within sessions, which in some regards makes it a subset of the performing phase. Processing also occurs between group sessions when leaders appraise and evaluate themselves and the group. The processing phase of group leadership is significant! Readers are encouraged to see Ward and Litchy (2004) for a more thorough treatment of the subject.

As part of step one, group techniques can be classified according to the best practice areas. For example, it is easy to identify meeting with an agency director about the need for a coleader in a future group as an example of a planning technique, asking group members to introduce themselves is an example of a performing technique, and asking members "What sense are you making out of what has just happened?" might be an example of processing.

A last element of step one of the PGTM requires group leaders to appreciate group development. Many insightful models examining group development exist. For brevity's sake, conceptualizing groups as having a beginning, middle, and end is adequate to help leaders recognize that a group is subject to different forces and that members' behavior differs in each stage. Thus, when leaders attend to the developmental stage of the group, they gain helpful information concerning the selection of group techniques.

In the beginning stage, members work toward getting acquainted, building trust or commitment, and transitioning toward functioning at a higher level (Johnson & Johnson, 2009; Trotzer, 2006). At this point, the group is typically reliant on the leader and unsure concerning goals, procedures, and rules. The latter emerge as members explore where they fit in the group, gradually internalize the group expectations, and commit to the group as a worthwhile investment. As they engage in this multifaceted process and become more assured of their role in the group, members are willing to take more risks and participate more actively. While this heightened sense of assurance leads to members claiming more ownership in group process and direction, the group is also quite likely to experience varying degrees of stress and conflict. This time of disequilibrium, however, represents a necessary stage in the group's journey to productive work together.

The middle stage of a group is frequently described by productivity and working together. As members connect and demonstrate an openness to pool the energy of the group, there is a sense in which the group is no longer a collection of individuals but more aptly characterized by interpersonal dynamics. An advantage to this stage is that the group leader is able to step back as members take responsibility for the group and assume some of the tasks that chiefly were the responsibility of the leader in the beginning stage.

The end stage of a group is marked by a transition toward much more than a final session. Group leaders must help members forecast their future past the group's last meeting and reflect on their advancements. Sometimes referenced as the "termination phase," leaders also help members' explore not merely their gains and newfound understanding but also difficulties that may emerge with separating and disbanding an interpersonal/cohesive system.

During step one it is crucial that the leader(s) is aware of the type of group being led, its purposes, and its current developmental stage. All this dictates the techniques that will best fit the group's needs.

EXAMPLE OF SANDRA, THE GROUP LEADER

Sandra is leading a 12-session counseling group at the community mental health center. The members are all individuals who have recently being diagnosed with HIV. Typically, Sandra provides a 10–20 minute check-in time, followed by a structured activity that helps members build cohesion and identify issues that might need addressed. The last hour of each session is then utilized for group discussion and process in which all members are asked to participate.

Identify Group Purpose, Best Practice Area, and Developmental Stage

The counseling group is at a beginning stage of development. The second session has just ended, and Sandra is wondering how to proceed in the next session (between-session processing). Monty has monopolized the group's discussion time in both sessions by talking for extended periods that appear to be related to the theme of the group but not allowing other members an opportunity to meaningfully participate. Sandra is wondering how she could develop/select a structured activity that might help the group explore the repercussions when one member monopolizes the discussion time. As well, Sandra is keenly aware that the group is in the beginning stages of development with members who have powerful issues to address. That is to say, members may feel uncomfortable about one member monopolizing the discussion time, yet they may be unsure of how to respond and begin to leave the group altogether. As Sandra continues to process and reflect on this situation, she is doing so to help guide her in selecting a possible technique that will benefit the group.

We will continue with Sandra as we move through the steps.

PGTM Step Two: Analyze

Step two of the PGTM asks group leaders to analyze what is going on in the group by considering six ecological concepts that would guide the selection of techniques. Techniques must always be deliberately chosen to be consistent with the group's ongoing and evolving context.

A group is not an isolated entity. Each group functions based upon a set of ongoing internal and external contexts. That is to say, an ecological orientation fits very well with group counseling because it rests on the premise that "contextualized help-giving is dependent on the meaning clients derive from their environmental interactions, thus yielding an improved ecological concordance" (Conyne & Cook, 2004, p. 6). To put it another way, group counseling stands in contradistinction to individually based services. Though group counseling certainly benefits group members at an individual level of analysis, these benefits occur as a result of transactions rooted in interpersonal dynamics. Ecologically oriented group counseling pushes the envelope by requiring the group to attend to all related contextual factors (Bemak & Conyne, 2004; Conyne & Bemak, 2004; Conyne & Mazza, 2007). To illustrate, consider a counseling group offered by a school counselor in a local public high school. An ecological approach requires the group leader, in this case a school counselor, to appreciate and attend to the high school's policies and procedures (written and unwritten), politics, as well as its physical setting. External factors, such as current events in the news and the cultural mores and political values of the community, have a certain "press" on the counseling group. Internal contexts also have significant impact, such as a group comprised of students from varying backgrounds. Group leaders must keep these contexts in mind when selecting techniques. Remember, "context is everything."

Key examples of contextual factors group leaders must pay attention to include the group's size, composition, demographics, life status of members, number of leaders, leader qualifications and experience, group goals, member goals, degree of group structure, number of sessions, conceptual foundation of the group, its developmental stage, past and immediate history, physical setting, and seating pattern of members.

Interconnection

According to Yalom (2005), cohesion is a key therapeutic factor in groups, without which group productivity and interpersonal learning are limited. To promote cohesion, group leaders must attend to and assist the group to establish and strengthen interconnections among members. Practically put, a group consists of interconnections among its members; without interconnections, the group is perhaps better described as a collection of separate individuals occupying the same space and time. Consider the following example to illustrate this point: Jonathan has decided that he needs to act on his New Year's resolution of "getting in shape." To move forward with this goal, he buys a membership to the local fitness center. Three mornings a week, Jonathan makes his way to the fitness center and begins a routine of stretching, running, and a variety of exercises. Initially, he knows no one, but over the next several weeks he realizes that a handful of other morning people, also new to the fitness center, have a similar zeal to improve their overall health. Conversations about staying motivated, exercise strategies, and dieting tips take place. Eventually, members of this new group engage in rather personal conversations about family and employment and start supporting and encouraging each other in a variety of ways. Jonathan and others even start to call the collection the "early-birds" and take it upon themselves to call or e-mail individuals who miss a workout. Individuals who at one point just shared a space did not constitute a group, but because of a common goal, interconnections evolved and a group formed. An interpersonal style, or "working-together" set of characteristics, now best describes Jonathan and his exercise friends.

Successful group counseling requires forging and maintaining interconnections among the members. Thus, group techniques must take into account how members relate to, work with, and learn from one another and promote the creation, maintenance, and strengthening of interconnections among members:

> Group leaders need to help members to make connections among themselves. One way to think of these interconnections is to imagine a network or a web. The denser the webbing among members, as evidenced by their nonverbal and verbal interactions, the more interconnected they can be—and the more potentially valuable the group experience can become. The strategy, "Forge interconnections among members," emerges from this concept (Conyne et al., 2008, p.17).

How might a group leader observe interconnections among a group? The leader could examine the social distance of group members, eye gaze (inclusive or exclusive), patterns of group member attendance, and physical and verbal members' posture (e.g., moving toward others or away).

Collaboration

Leading a counseling group requires collaboration, or "working with," members. This approach is particularly essential when selecting and implementing group techniques. While the group leader may have valuable training and experience, it is equally true that members are the experts of their lives. Thus, leaders often find success by introducing new techniques cautiously and attending to members' responses.

In their seminal research, Lieberman et al. (1973) documented that successful leaders are not overly controlling but neither do leaders relinquish complete control to the group. Collaboration is an approach that helps leaders strike a balance as they attempt to provide structure (executive function), challenge (emotional stimulation), and support (caring) to help members move toward their goals.

A very simple example of collaboration—and one often seen in first sessions—concerns the issue of breaking to stretch or to use the restroom. A leader could simply inform the members what will be the rule, but typically that approach is not as effective as briefly discussing the issue with the group and coming to a consensus.

> Collaboration means working on important matters together whenever possible, and while it may take longer for decision making than does a leader-based decision, the outcomes can be substantially better. The strategy "Do with, rather than do to" emerges from this concept (Conyne et al., 2008, p. 17).

Ways that leaders might observe collaboration require examining group content and processes to discern mode of decision making (e.g., together or apart), each group member's level of participation in decision-making (i.e., inclusive or exclusive), the degree to which other members solicit ideas and feedback from each other, how differing input is accepted and used, and leader self-examination in promoting or discouraging collaboration.

Social System Maintenance

In group-counseling settings, a leader is attempting to build and promote a unique group culture that can be described by interconnections among all members and where rules and expectations are clearly understood and equitable.

An interesting metaphor is to envision group leaders as hosts or hostesses of a one-of-a-kind social unit. Imagine a dinner party at someone's home. Typically, the hosts are proactive in a variety of ways, such as where the bathroom is located and coasters for drinks. Group leaders, along with the members, forge clear expectations, goals, rules, and patterns of behavior.

In training group-counseling leaders it is beneficial to stress the importance of attending to social system maintenance. One approach this author has found beneficial in promoting positive development of a social system occurs when leaders develop a habit of highlighting to the group that they are

> a unique gathering of people sharing one place in time and history; this opportunity (and experience) will never again be possible. Together, they have the opportunity to create and sustain a novel and personally-significant social system for accomplishing group and personal goals. Members learn to "cherish the moment" by appreciating their experience as they live it and recognizing their role in shaping that experience (Conyne et al., 2008, p. 18).

Some simple ways that group leaders might work to build, maintain, and/or observe these conditions require attending to the existence of clear rules and norms and their effects, flexibility of group functioning, the degree that the social system helps or hinders achievement of member and group goals and/or tasks, quality of the group climate, and how the leaders themselves promote or hinder social system maintenance.

Meaning Making

Group members must learn from their experiences. In attempting to observe and explain this group artifact, Lieberman et al. (1973) coined the term *meaning attribution*. *Meaning making*, though similar, differs by emphasis. Based upon the work of ecological counseling theory, constructivism, and existential psychology, meaning making becomes a key goal of the therapeutic compact (Conyne & Cook, 2004). Consequently, group leaders are tasked with helping group members connect experience with knowing.

Group leaders might consider observing meaning making within the group by attending to the degree of confusion/clarity about group events and personal events, expressions offered of understanding, expressions offered of personal value, opportunities provided for processing, and nonverbal behavior expressed—positive, negative, and how leader(s) promotes or discourages meaning making.

Sustainability

As a general rule, people opt to participate in counseling groups because they want or need to learn or change. Thus, a critical element for group members is to apply and to sustain their efforts beyond the confines of the counseling group. As the group runs its course, leaders and members must make sure that gains are sustainable once the group terminates.

Attempting to attend to the need to sustain members' growth, booster sessions have demonstrated efficacy. For example, Fristad, Gavazzi, and Soldano (1998) in facilitating psychoeducation family support groups found that efficacy of the 12 sessions significantly waned 6 months after the last session. However, asking group members to return for a one-session booster group every 3 months maintained gains.

Likewise, when a leader purposefully encourages members in planning and practicing how to put new skills to work beyond the boundaries of the group, the skills are able to be applied and growth/learning is generalized to other settings. Thus, sustainability increases.

The strategy "Attend to changes lasting over time" emerges from this concept.

The process of attending to sustainable changes is a simple continuum for group leaders: discuss application to outside world, practice application to the outside world, encourage members to articulate when they understand how to use gains and when these changes occur and are replicated in group, and encourage members to report outside application when they can successfully use gains outside.

Returning to Sandra, the Counseling Group Leader

In analyzing the presenting situation by applying ecological concepts, leaders will quickly discover that often several ecological issues are evident in any group situation. The task is to establish which is most relevant at the time. In this case, Sandra determines that Monty's monopolizing behavior disallows interconnections to develop among members. Sandra surmises that the group members need to become more interdependent in order for progress to emerge.

PGTM Step Three: Review

Thus far, the PGTM has asked leaders of counseling groups to

Step one—Identify the purpose of the group, relevant best practice area, and developmental stage.

Step two—Analyze the presenting situation in the counseling group by applying ecological concepts.

Step three, adapted from Cohen and Smith's (1976) seminal contribution, asks leaders to build on this work and consider two key dimensions in considering possible group techniques—focus and level. *Focus* requires the leader to reflect on the benefits of selecting a technique that would primarily be cognitive, affective, behavioral, and/or structural. For example,

- *Cognitive focus*: Ask group members to consider the pros and cons of continuing a discussion.
- *Affective focus*: "Bradley, I'm wondering if you could talk more about feeling sad about your divorce."
- *Behavioral focus*: Arrange seating to encourage optimal participation of all group members.
- *Structural focus*: "Can we go back to an earlier point in our discussion?" This level examines the value in aiming a technique at the individual, interpersonal, or group. For example,
- *Individual level*: "Could you share how *you* are doing with . . ."
- *Interpersonal level*: "Shawn, Sarah seems to be saying the same thing as you. I'm wondering if you would care to respond or add to her thoughts?
- *Group level*: "How are we doing today?" the leader asks the entire group.

This model of technique selection allows for 12 variations of techniques to be put into action (four possible levels of technique focus at one of three technique levels equals 12 types of techniques) (see Fig. 17.2).

Returning to Sandra, the Counseling Group Leader

A variety of potential group techniques usually evidence promise in addressing any particular ecological issue. Sandra identified four possible techniques that she might consider to promote interconnections: (1) she might ask Monty if he is interested in receiving feedback from others in the group (cognitive focus, individual/interpersonal

Level → Focus ↓	Individual	Interpersonal	Group
Cognitive	Cognitive-Individual	Cognitive-Interpersonal	Cognitive-Group
Affective	Affective-Individual	Affective-Interpersonal	Affective-Group
Behavioral	Behavioral-Individual	Behavioral-Interpersonal	Behavioral-Group
Structural	Structural-Individual	Structural-Interpersonal	Structural-Group

Fig. 17.2 Two dimensions in considering group techniques.

level), (2) she might pay closer attention to the nonverbal behavior of other group members the next time Monty launches into a long "monologue" to see if she might determine some clues about their feelings (behavioral focus, individual level), (3) she might carefully design a series of structured activities that would "block" Monty from taking center stage (structural focus, interpersonal level), or (4) she might interrupt Monty and ask if he could describe how he is feeling as he talks, in an effort to help his contributions become more therapeutic (affective focus, individual level).

PGTM Step Four: Select "Best Fit" Technique

Based upon steps one, two, and three, the leader may have in mind implementing a technique or perhaps is unsure as she or he considers several techniques. Step four requires group leaders to evaluate techniques and decide which might be the best fit to promote the goals of the group. To assist in this task, leaders will gain insight when considering the following five questions:

• Is the technique under consideration *appropriate*, taking into account the culture of the group and its members?
• Is the technique under consideration *adequate* for the desired effect—strong enough without being too strong?
• Is the technique under consideration *effective* at achieving the goal?
• Is the technique under consideration *efficient* in its resource allocation?
• What *side effect* exists concerning the technique under consideration? That is, which would minimize negative side effects while

maximizing the positive side effects? (Conyne et al., 2008, p. 212).

Back to Sandra, the Counseling Group Leader

For Sandra and the group, the stakes are high. Selecting a best-fit technique is critical. In considering the evaluative criteria of appropriateness, adequacy, effectiveness, efficiency, and side effects, Sandra selected what she thought was the least intrusive group technique that would have the fewest side effects. Thus, Sandra decided that observation of nonverbal behaviors of group members during the monopolizing behavior of Monty made sense and allowed her to further evaluate the group for additional techniques that would likely need to follow.

PGTM Step Five: Implement and Evaluate

At all the major junctures of the counseling group it is of critical importance for the leader to reflect and learn. This is especially true concerning group techniques that were effective as well as learning about techniques that did not have the intended impact the leader anticipated.

Returning to Sandra, the Counseling Group Leader

When Sandra observed the nonverbal behaviors of group members in the next session during Monty's monopolizing behavior, she was astonished. For instance, Sandra noticed eye rolling by Isabella, shifting in her seat by Harriet, and an occasional sighing by R. J. At this point, she realized that the other group members were indeed communicating dissatisfaction with the current state of the group, and the task was to help the nonverbal become verbal in ways that helped the group move forward with the work they were all there to accomplish. At the next pause in Monty's monologue Sandra decided to ask Monty if he might be interested in hearing from others in the group about their thoughts and feelings during the last few minutes when he was speaking. He seemed somehow relieved by this, saying that this is why he was in the group in the first place, really. So, the group was now moving in a different direction that now afforded the opportunity for increasing interconnected verbal interaction.

A last feature of the PGTM is that it provides group leaders with a way of visually organizing group techniques that assists in the selection process. Conyne et al. (2008) refer to this classification system as the group-techniques toolbox because the metaphor makes sense. Just as having a series of drill bits all aligned and in their place helps the skilled carpenter as well as amateur correctly identify the best size for the job, so too having techniques in an ordered manner can help the group leader. In the Appendix at the end of this chapter are 40 group techniques that have been arranged. Following is a brief prototype group technique for each of the best practice toolboxes.

The toolbox provides a single place to evaluate various techniques. This may be extremely helpful to a beginning leader in building and expanding a repertoire of techniques. Reviewing techniques in this way may also aid the intermediate and advanced leader, by confirming a specific choice or expanding current thinking. Tables 17.2, 17.3, 17.4, and 17.5 provide examples of how techniques can be identified and described in a way that captures the key elements of the PGTM (i.e., best practice area, group development stage, relevant ecological concepts, focus, and level).

The technique described in Table 17.2 is most useful in launching a group. Holding a preliminary group session provides a context for potential members and creates a model for a functioning social system. While demonstrating the intention to be collaborative with members, the leader is also beginning to address many ecological issues.

Group members are required to pay attention as they take turns passing an object, which functions as the "right to speak." This technique especially develops expectations and rules that are part of the social system. It is a structural intervention that also is focused on behavioral skill development at the individual, interpersonal, and group levels. It is also especially effective at slowing down the pace of conversation, developing active listening, and reducing cross-talk.

The within-session processing prototype is an example of processing that can take place during the middle to late stages of any group. Though there is an affective aspect to self-disclosure, the technique also is cognitively focused as the leader may be asking for a type of check-in. Meaning making is an ecological concept that often goes hand in hand with processing practices because leaders are usually intent on challenging members' thinking or behaviors in the group setting while supporting them within the process.

This between-session processing technique is drawn from the deep processing model (Conyne, 1999) and is particularly useful for leader processing between sessions, either independently or with a coleader, supervisor, or colleague. Though simplified greatly in this toolbox, the technique affords a group leader the opportunity to reflect and consider potential courses of action. Deep processing is intended to improve meaning making and the sustainability of leader skills.

Implications for Training, Research, and Practice

In general, there is a significant need to empirically examine the training of group leaders (Wilson & Newmeyer, 2008). Likewise, little is known about the efficacy of any of the technique-selection approaches described in this chapter. Scholarly studies are needed to examine a variety of issues, such as efficacy in training and practice, comprehensiveness, utility, and adaptability.

A strength of the PGTM is that it is intended to be flexible and easily adapted to a variety of group

Table 17.2 Planning technique prototype

Best Practice Planning	Stage	Ecological Concepts	Focus	Level
Hold a preliminary group session to orient potential members.	Beginning	Context, Collaboration, Social system	Cognitive	Interpersonal, Group

Table 17.3 Performing technique prototype

Best Practice Performing	Stage	Ecological Concepts	Focus	Level
Using any object, have the member who is speaking hold that object while all others are silent. She or he gives it to the next speaker, who must address the very last thing said (careful listening skills).	Beginning	Social system	Behavioral, Structural	Individual, Interpersonal, Group

Table 17.4 Processing technique prototype: within-session processing

Best Practice Processing Within Session	Stage	Ecological Concepts	Focus	Level
"Imagine yourself as you are now—silent—and it is the last session. What have you gotten from the group? How do you feel about your level of participation? Share this with the group."	Middle, Late	Meaning making, Sustainability	Cognitive, Affective	Individual

Table 17.5 Processing technique prototype: between-session processing

Best Practice Processing Between Sessions	Stage	Ecological Concepts	Focus	Level
Deep processing model (1) Transpose the group meeting by recording objective observations. (2) Reflect on your subjective awareness of the meeting. (3) Discover meaning through integration of objective and subjective awareness. (4) Apply increased awareness through action plan derived from evaluation. (5) Evolve as the plan grows with integration of best practices into an action plan.	Beginning, Middle, Late	Meaning making, Sustainability	Cognitive, Affective	Group

settings. Because it relies on many core tenants already well established in the group-counseling literature, such as best practices and group development, using the model to train future group leaders is likely beneficial. Conyne et al. (2008) developed the PGTM with training in mind, utilizing a critical incident format to help fledging group leaders to learn and develop a variety of requisite skills and competencies.

The PGTM is not aimed merely at training but also at practice. Because techniques can be visually scanned for key information, such as focus or best practice area, practitioners can examine numerous techniques quickly and with abundantly more information when compared to lists of techniques arranged only according to one dimension or category. This has implications in helping leaders in planning, engaged in between-group processing, or perhaps even working in real time.

Aspects of the model that could be examined include further operationalizing its ecological concepts in measurable and observable ways. As well, the relationships between the ecological concepts and already established therapeutic factors are not well understood, but there would appear to be some overlap. Little is understood concerning the impact of modifying the model such as using a particular approach to group development (e.g., T-group development of dependence and independence). Nonetheless, the PGTM represents a watershed

moment in moving beyond elementary categorizations of group techniques toward a robust model that can aid a leader in attending to various core concepts of the group.

Conclusion

In sum, there is an existing body of literature regarding group techniques, though a variety of other terms (e.g., *structured experiences*) are often used. Useful models to guide leaders in the selection techniques are not readily available, but the time has arrived to develop useful approaches that derive principally from what is known to be axiomatic about groups. The work of several group experts has been described in this chapter. Significant attention was given to the purposeful group techniques model as it is an effort to build on the work of others and offer a comprehensive approach in selecting group techniques. This model brings together key aspects of groups in a way that aids the group leader in "sizing-up" ongoing events and purposefully selecting techniques that will advance the group's goals. While the model consolidates various established elements of how groups work and function, there is a need to further evaluate it through scholarly inquiry. As well, ample room exists for other such models to be developed that can function to guide group leaders' decision making in selecting, implementing, and evaluating group techniques.

References

Association for Specialists in Group Work. (1998). *Association for Specialists in Group Work best practice guidelines.* Retrieved from http://www.asgw.org

Association for Specialists in Group Work. (2000). *Professional standards for the training of group work.* Retrieved from http://www.asgw.org

Beck, A., & Lewis, C. (Eds.). (2000). *The process of group psychotherapy: Systems for analyzing change.* Washington, D.C.: American Psychological Association.

Bemak, F., & Conyne, R. (2004). Ecological group work. In R. Conyne & E. Cook (Eds.), *Ecological counseling: An innovative approach to conceptualizing person–environment interaction* (pp. 195–217). Alexandria, VA: American Counseling Association.

Capuzzi, D. (2003). *Approaches to group work: A handbook for practitioners.* Upper Saddle River, NJ: Merrill-Prentice Hall.

Cohen, A., & Smith, R. (1976). *The critical incident in growth groups.* La Jolla, CA: University Associates.

Conyne, R. K. (ed.). (1985). *The group workers' handbook: Varieties of group experiences.* Springfield, IL: Thomas.

Conyne, R. K. (1999). *Failures in group work: How we can learn from our mistakes.* Thousand Oaks, CA: Sage.

Conyne, R., & Bemak, F. (2004). Teaching group work from an ecological perspective. *Journal for Specialists in Group Work, 29,* 7–18.

Conyne, R. K., & Cook, E. (Eds.). (2004). *Ecological counseling: An innovative approach to conceptualizing person–environment interactions.* Alexandria, VA: American Counseling Association.

Conyne, R. K., Crowell, J. L., & Newmeyer, M. D. (2008). *Group technique: How to use them more purposefully.* Upper Saddle River, NJ: Pearson Merrill Prentice Hall.

Conyne, R., & Mazza, J. (2007). Ecological group work applied to schools. *Journal for Specialists in Group Work, 32,* 19–29.

Corey, M., & Corey, G. (2006). *Groups: process and practice* (7th ed.). Belmont, CA: Thomson Brooks/Cole.

Corey, G., Corey, M., Callanan, P., & Russell, J. (2004). *Group techniques* (3rd ed.). Pacific Grove, CA: Brooks/Cole.

Davis, D. (1996). *Discipleship journal's 101 best small-group ideas.* Colorado Springs, CO: Navpress.

DeLucia-Waack, J., Bridbord, K., Kleiner, J., & Nitza, A. (Eds.). (2006). *Group work experts share their favorite activities: A guide to choosing, planning, conducting, and processing.* Alexandria, VA: Association for Specialists in Group Work.

DeLucia-Waack, J., Gerrity, D., Kalodner, C., & Riva, M. (Eds.). (2004). *Handbook of group counseling and psychotherapy.* Thousand Oaks, CA: Sage.

Durkin, H. (1981). The group therapies and general systems theory as an integrative structure. In J. Durkin (Ed.), *Living groups: Group psychotherapy and general systems theory.* New York: Brunner/Mazel.

Fristad, M., Gavazzi, S., & Soldano, K. (1998). Multi-family psychoeducation groups for childhood mood disorders: A program description and preliminary efficacy data. *Contemporary Family Therapy, 20*(3), 385–402.

Fuhriman, A., & Barlow, S. (1994). Interaction analysis: Instrumentation and issues. In A. Fuhriman & G. Burlingame (Eds.), *Handbook of group psychotherapy: An empirical and clinical synthesis.* New York: John Wiley & Sons.

Garvin, C. D., Gutierrez, L. M., & Galinsky, M. J. (2004). *Handbook of social work with groups.* New York: Guilford Press.

Gladding, S. (2008). *Group work: A counseling specialty.* Upper Saddle River, NJ: Pearson Merrill Prentice Hall.

Hansen, J., Warner, R., & Smith, E. (1980). *Group counseling: Theory and practice* (2nd ed.). Chicago: Rand McNally.

Jacobs, E., Mason, R., & Harvill, R (2009). *Group counseling: Strategies and skills* (6th ed.). Belmont, CA: Brooks/Cole.

Johnson, D., & Johnson, F. (2009). *Joining together: Group theory and group skills* (10th ed.). Upper Saddle, NJ: Pearson.

Kraus, K. (2003). *Exercises in group work.* Upper Saddle River, NJ: Merrill-Prentice Hall.

Lieberman, M., Yalom, I., & Miles, M. (1973). *Encounter groups: First facts.* New York: Basic Books.

Napier, R., & Gershenfeld, M. (2004). *Groups: Theory and experience* (7th ed.). Boston: Houghton Mifflin.

Pfeiffer, J., & Jones, J. (Eds.). (1972). *The 1972 annual handbook for group facilitators.* La Jolla, CA: University Associates.

Pfeiffer, J., & Jones, J. (Eds.). (1973). *The 1973 annual handbook for group facilitators.* La Jolla, CA: University Associates.

Pfeiffer, J., & Jones, J. (Eds.). (1974). *The 1974 annual handbook for group facilitators.* La Jolla, CA: University Associates.

Pfeiffer, J., & Jones, J. (Eds.). (1976). *The 1976 annual handbook for group facilitators.* La Jolla, CA: University Associates.

Pfeiffer, J., & Jones, J. (Eds.). (1980). *The 1980 annual handbook for group facilitators.* La Jolla, CA: University Associates.

Schmuck, R., & Schmuck, P. (2001). *Group processes in the classroom* (8th ed.). New York: McGraw-Hill.

Trotzer, J. (2006). *The counselor and the group: Integrating theory, training, and practice* (4th ed.). Philadelphia: Taylor & Francis.

Ward, D. E., & Litchy, M. (2004). The effective use of processing in groups. In J. L. DeLucia-Waack, D. A. Gerrity, C. R. Kalodner, & M. T. Riva (Eds.), *Handbook of group counseling and psychotherapy.* Thousand Oaks, CA: Sage.

Wilson, F. R., & Newmeyer, M. D. (2008). A standards-based inventory for assessing perceived importance of and confidence in using ASGW's core group work skills. *Journal for Specialists in Group Work, 33,* 270–289.

Yalom, I. (with Leszcz, M.) (2005). *The theory and practice of group psychotherapy.* New York: Basic Books.

Appendix 17.1

Best Practice: Performing Techniques	Stage	Ecological Concepts	Focus	Level
1. *M & M Breaker*: As members enter the room, they take an M & M. When they introduce themselves, what they share is dependent on the color of their M & M. For example, red should explain what they hope to get out of the session; blue shares a significant accomplishment or success.	Beginning	Interconnection, Social system, Meaning making	Affective, Behavioral	Individual
2. *Collective Knowledge*: In subgroups, have members introduce themselves, then as a group name five ground rules for the larger group. Have subgroups report, sharing only what they have that is different from the previous group reports. Reach consensus as a large group regarding the adoption of the ground rules.	Beginning	Interconnection, Collaboration, Social system, Meaning making	Cognitive	Interpersonal, Group
3. *Trust fall*: Member 1 closes his or her eyes and member 2 stands behind. Member 1 falls back into member 2, learning to trust that someone will be there.	Beginning	Interconnection	Behavioral, Structural	Interpersonal
4. *Using "I" terms*: Leader instructs the members to use "I" terms. (Often needed when people make generalizations.)	Beginning	Social system	Behavioral	Individual
5. *Delphi Technique*: A decision-making process that uses opinions of members with the guidance of a facilitator to reach consensus by rank-order process.	Beginning, Middle	Collaboration	Cognitive	Individual, Group
6. *Subgrouping*: Members create subgroups and then are assigned a number. The leader can call a number from each subgroup to have that member respond for the group (to ensure equal participation).	Beginning, Middle	Interconnection, Collaboration, Meaning making	Cognitive, Behavioral, Structural	Individual, Group
7. *Goal Setting*: Have the group set goals for one session.	Beginning, Middle	Context, Interconnection, Collaboration, Social system	Cognitive, Structural	Group
8. *Sociograms*: Have members do individual sociograms to indicate relationships in their lives. Share.	Beginning, Middle	Interconnection	Cognitive	Individual
9. *Say It For Real*: Leaders can have resistant members verbalize attitudes or behaviors such as "I won't say anything." And asking "How are you going to do this? How will you keep things to yourself?"	Beginning, Middle	Interconnection, Social system	Cognitive, Affective	Individual, Interpersonal
10. *Time Tokens*: Pass out the same number of "time tokens" to all members. Each time they want to speak they must use a time token (to ensure wider participation).	Beginning, Middle	Social system, Meaning making	Cognitive, Behavioral	Individual, Interpersonal, Group

(Continued)

Appendix 17.1   (Continued)

Best Practice: Performing Techniques	Stage	Ecological Concepts	Focus	Level
11. *Self-Check*: Leader asks, "Can you take more responsibility?"	Beginning, Middle	Social system	Behavioral	Individual, Group
12. *Permission*: Leader asks, "Would that be OK?"	Beginning, Middle, End	Collaboration	Cognitive	Individual, Interpersonal
13. *Go-arounds*: Have each member check in with a "go-around" at some point in the session.	Beginning, Middle, End	Context, Interconnection, Social system	Cognitive, Affective, Behavioral	Individual
14. *Seating*: Arrange seating to accommodate the most communication among group members.	Beginning, Middle, End	Interconnection, Social system	Structural	Interpersonal, Group
15. *Nominal Group Technique (NGT)*: Up to six steps to initiate ideas, but unlike brainstorming, NGT does not require members' open exposure.	Beginning, Middle, End	Interconnection, Collaboration, Meaning making	Cognitive	Group
16. *Outer Circle*: When a forced client doesn't want to participate, have him or her create an outer circle where participation is not required.	Beginning, Middle, End	Interconnection, Social system, Meaning making	Cognitive, Affective, Structural	Individual, Interpersonal, Group
17. *Direct Feedback*: Leader offers feedback about a troublesome behavior (e.g., always answering with questions) in order to model respectful feedback.	Beginning, Middle, End	Collaboration, Social system	Cognitive, Affective	Individual, Interpersonal, Group
18. *Sentence Completions*: Use sentence-completion statements to explore feelings, thoughts, and ideas. Elicit sharing of the experience.	Beginning, Middle, eEnd	Interconnection, Meaning making	Cognitive, Affective	Individual, Interpersonal, Group
19. *Fish Bowl*: Construct a "fish-bowl" arrangement where a subgroup sits in a circle outside an inner circle. Have members observe process. Switch.	Beginning, Middle, End	Interconnection, Collaboration, Meaning making	Cognitive, Affective, Behavioral, Structural	Interpersonal, Group
20. *Brainstorm*: Members generate ideas in a nonjudgmental manner.	Beginning, Middle, End	Interconnection	Cognitive, Affective, Behavioral	Group

Technique	Stage	Process	Orientation	Level
21. *Toys in Concert*: Give members Tinker Toys™ or Legos™ and ask them to build a representation of what group cohesion looks like (could be done in pairs or triads).	Beginning, Middle, End	Interconnection, Meaning making	Cognitive, Behavioral	Individual, Interpersonal
22. *Summaries*: Have the next speaker in the group summarize what the previous speaker just said (increase understanding and listening skills).	Beginning, Middle, End	Interconnection, Social system	Cognitive	Individual, Group
23. *Out with the Trash*: Have all members sit in a tight circle around the garbage can. Have them all talk to the can at once about what is most on their minds. Leader calls "Stop" at some point. (Often helps people, e.g., lively youngsters, calm down.)	Beginning, Middle, End	Collaboration, Social system	Cognitive, Behavioral	Group
24. *Genograms*: Have members draw genograms to understand family dynamics.	Beginning, Middle, End	Interconnection, Social system, Meaning making	Cognitive, Affective, Behavioral	Individual
25. *Family Sculpting*: Members use the other members to "sculpt" their own family by positioning others with body positions to represent their feelings and understanding about the family and family roles.	Beginning, Middle, End	Interconnection	Cognitive, Affective, Behavioral, Structural	Individual, Group
26. *Special Visitors*: Invite spouse, parents, and/or children of group members to a session.	Beginning, Middle, End	Context, Interconnection, Collaboration, Social system, Meaning making	Cognitive, Affective, Structural	Individual, Interpersonal, Group
27. *Secret pooling*: Members anonymously write a "secret" about themselves that they have not shared in group and place the paper in middle of group. Members draw a secret (not their own) and empathize about what it might feel like.	Beginning, End	Interconnection	Structural	Interpersonal
28. *Exaggerations*: Have a member exaggerate his or her behavior to see it clearly, to tire of it, or to gain insight into its sources.	Middle	Meaning making	Cognitive, Affective, Behavioral	Individual
29. *Physiogram*: Members physically place themselves in relation to the center of the room and in relation to each other.	Middle	Social system, Meaning making	Cognitive	Group
30. *Boxed In*: To help identify ideal approaches to an issue, it will also help identify obstacles as it acts to solve the issue and mobilizes the group as a resource. Pass out sheets of paper with a diamond box; in the center write the ideal solution, and on each of the four sides write a reason or obstacle that keeps you from it. Share.	Middle	Collaboration, Meaning making	Cognitive	Individual

(Continued)

Appendix 17.1 (Continued)

Best Practice: Performing Techniques	Stage	Ecological Concepts	Focus	Level
31. *Role Reversal:* Have members switch roles with other members or with the leader.	Middle	Interconnection, Collaboration, Social system, Meaning making	Cognitive, Affective, Behavioral, Structural	Individual, Interpersonal, Group
32. *Inner Circle:* For multiple silent members, have them form an inner circle and talk about what it is like to be silent. For the active members, form an inner circle and talk about what it is like not hearing from others and not knowing what they are thinking.	Middle	Interconnection, Social system, Meaning making	Cognitive, affective, behavioral, structural	Interpersonal, Group
33. *Strength Bombardment:* Members present to each other what they see as the others' strengths.	Middle	Collaboration, Meaning making	Structural	Interpersonal, Individual
34. *Johari Window:* Have members do a Johari window. Share in the group.	Middle, End	Interconnection	Cognitive, Affective	Individual
35. *Follow-up Session:* Hold a follow-up session weeks or months later and review what was gained in the initial experience.	End	Interconnection, Social system, Meaning making	Cognitive, Affective	Group
36. *Revisit Group Rules and Expectations:* Rechecking what was decided can be helpful and necessary through exploring members' recall.	Beginning, Middle, End	Context	Cognitive	Individual, Group
37. *How Did it Go?:* Simple and direct questions, such as this one, asked at appropriate times during a session can promote reflective participation.	Middle, End	Meaning Making	Cognitive	Individual
38. *Systems-Centered Subgrouping:* Members are encouraged to identify subgroups within the group as a way of exploring interconnections and meaning.	Beginning, Middle	Interconnection, Meaning making	Cognitive, Affective	Interpersonal, Group
39. *String Activity:* Members use string to connect to each other all the possible relationships existing within the group.	Beginning, Middle	Context, Interconnection, Social system	Behavioral, Cognitive, Structural	Group
40. *Thank You. I'm Wondering if We Could Hear from Others:* A simple question intended to open up discussion to involve others.	Beginning, Middle, End	Collaboration	Cognitive	Group
Add your own here.				
Add your own here.				

Group Leader Style and Functions

Sheri Bauman

Abstract

Previous chapters in this section have examined essential aspects of counseling group leadership: the person of the leader as well as techniques and theoretical foundations. In this chapter, I turn our attention to the functions and styles of leaders of counseling groups. Following a review of conceptualizations of group leader functions and style, I will examine the research that has investigated these constructs to determine the level of empirical support for them and consider needs for future research. Finally, I will consider the implications of this material for training group workers.

Keywords: group counseling, leadership, training

Leadership should be born out of the understanding of the needs of those who would be affected by it.
Marian Anderson (1897–1993, American singer)

The task of leadership is not to put greatness into people, but to elicit it, for the greatness is there already.
John Buchan (1875–1940, Scottish politician)

A good leader inspires people to have confidence in the leader; a great leader inspires people to have confidence in themselves
Eleanor Roosevelt (1884–1962)

A prime function of a leader is to keep hope alive.
John W. Gardner (1912–2002, secretary of Health, Education and Welfare, 1965–1968)

Group Leader Functions

Functions refer to the purposes or roles of the leader or to the tasks a leader must perform for the group to meet its goals. Trotzer (1977) defined *functions* as "the means by which the leader helps the group process develop in accord with the need of the members and the goals of the group" (p. 85). Many experts have described the functions of group leaders but not always in the same terms. I will first review the various typologies and then seek commonalities among them. Since the group-work field's development and conceptualization of group leader functions has been an iterative process, with later work building upon earlier descriptions, a chronological approach is taken here, to present the evolution of thinking on this topic.

In Cartwright and Zander's (1960) work on group dynamics, they pointed out that interest in group functions, in contrast to a focus on the characteristics of effective group leaders, increased because research on the latter had not been fruitful. That is, it had not been possible to identify good leaders by compiling a list of traits that effective leaders possess. Rather, the interest shifted to the functions of leadership, which can be more readily identified. In fact, the functions can be even further separated from the person so that leadership functions might be performed by the leader—or members.

Bales and Slater

Bales and Slater (1955) described the two essential functions of group leaders of experimental and small groups: productivity and support of group members. Bales (1958) referred to these as "task" functions and group support and "maintenance" functions. Although there are earlier classifications of leadership functions, those describe functions of leaders in industrial, organizational, and political contexts and do not apply to counseling group leadership (Bass, 1981).

Cartwright and Zander

Cartwright and Zander (1960) considered leadership functions to be tasks that "contribute to such things as goal achievement, viability of the group, satisfactory human relations, satisfaction of members, and minimum cost to members—in short, to group performance" (p. 493). The various functions are enacted in different degrees, in different groups, and at different stages of development. It is also germane to this perspective that any member may take actions that contribute to group performance (leadership functions); it is also the case that a variety of actions may be undertaken to execute any particular functions. Furthermore, each goal or type of group will require different functions.

Cartwright and Zander (1960) refer to two large classes of leader functions—those that are directed toward attainment of the group's goal (including behaviors such as initiating action, keeping attention focused on the goal, and providing access to information) and those that focus on the relationships among members (providing encouragement, etc.). These have become known as *task* and *maintenance* functions (see Bales, 1958; Bales & Slater, 1955), with the former referring to actions necessary to accomplish the goal and the latter referring to attending to relationships among members. These two functions are not exclusive. The most effective leaders perform both functions. In fact, it is the

appropriate balance of these two functions that generates the most favorable outcomes.

Fiedler (1971) applied this classification to his theory of leadership effectiveness, known as the *contingency model*. The theory postulates that group performance is based on the interaction of the leadership style and the "situational favorableness" of the group" (p. 128). He operationalized leadership style using a technique called the least preferred coworker (LPC) measure. Leaders complete the measure by thinking of the coworker they least preferred to work with, ever. Then they rate that individual on 16–24 adjectives, each on an 8-point scale. The higher the score, the more favorable the description. The theory proposes that the relationships between the LPC and group performance (task completion) are moderated by the "situational favorableness" dimension, composed of leader–member relations (is leader accepted and respected by members?), task structure (is the group's task or goal well-defined and highly structured?), and power (what types of power are inherent in the position?). Examining data from a number of early studies, Fiedler found that the groups of low LPC leaders (task-oriented) performed best when situational favorableness was either very low or very high and high LPC leaders' (relationship-oriented) groups had the best outcomes in intermediate levels of situational favorableness. A review of 15 studies led to the conclusion that there is support for the position that group performance varies with leadership style and situational favorableness.

Schutz

Schutz was a well-known proponent of encounter groups (human relations groups, T-groups) and is credited with introducing extensive use of nonverbal techniques into group work (Shapiro, 1978). Much of his research on groups focused on the importance of compatibility of members, which he believed was the most important ingredient for successful groups. He demonstrated that compatible groups (where members were similar on intelligence, dependence on authority, personalness, and assertiveness) were most productive and developed a measure of interpersonal style (Fundamental Interpersonal Relations Orientation–Behavior [FIRO-B]) that he used to assess the interpersonal style variables of inclusion, control, and affection. Schutz (1961) identified four basic functions of group leaders: (1) establishing and acknowledging a priority ranking of group goals and values, (2) considering and negotiating the range of cognitive styles among group members, (3) bringing out the abilities and skills of members, and (4) helping members resolve problems, including those that stem from external demands and those that arise from interpersonal needs. Schutz also stressed the importance of contextual variables, such as cultural factors and the setting in which the group is held.

Dinkmeyer and Muro

In their 1971 work, Dinkmeyer and Muro describe the functions of the leader, first noting that these are predicated upon the existence of a helping relationship between the leader and the members of the group. Although many of these functions could be enhanced or even performed by group member actions, the leader bears the responsibility for carrying them out; it is part of the "job description." In other words, the members may assume some of these functions in a group, but the leader must ensure that the functions are enacted, whether by a member or by the leader.

PROMOTING COHESIVENESS

A sense of "groupness," or being connected to the members and the leader, is not an automatic development. It is the leader's job to actively promote the cohesion of the group. Dinkmeyer and Muro (1971) believe this does not happen if the leader remains aloof and sets her- or himself above or apart from the members. They say that in order to foster cohesiveness, the leader should share immediate reactions and feelings in the group, which shows a willingness to be vulnerable along with the members. The fine line here for the leader is to accomplish this while not becoming the focus of the group or using the group to meet personal needs but to interact on a genuine and immediate level with the members. The leader's acknowledgment of experiencing some anxiety at an initial session is an example of the kind of communication these experts believe is important to building cohesive relationships. Promoting cohesiveness also means that the leader must be alert to existing or potential subgroupings and work to promote interaction among those members who do not naturally gravitate toward one another.

Dinkmeyer and Muro (1971) offer a guiding principle related to cohesiveness: The greater the frequency of interaction, the quicker the development of cohesion. Linking members, and inviting their exchanges, is one way to increase interaction. Frequency of meetings also builds cohesion, so the more often a group meets, the more cohesive it is likely to become. In the interest of cohesion, groups that are closed, rather than open, are more apt to become cohesive. The authors speculate that working with "involuntary" clients in a group is an obstacle to the development of a cohesive group and suggest that counselors should attempt to work with voluntary clients.

SUMMARIZING

Summarizing is more often described as a specific counseling skill than a function, but Dinkmeyer and Muro (1971) see it as a way of making meaning from the events in a session. During the course of a group session, a number of themes or topics may occupy the members; and the role of the leader is to extract (or help the members extract) the essential learning about the theme. The leader summarizes not only content but process. These experts suggest that when summarizing a discussion on which there were opposing viewpoints or perspectives, the leader must be careful to present the summary in a balanced fashion so that no side appears to have more influence and the leader does not seem to be biased toward one or the other.

PROMOTING INTERACTION

Promoting interaction is particularly important early in the life of a group, say Dinkmeyer and Muro (1971). In early meetings, members may be uncertain of the way interaction occurs in a group and anxiety may be high about the new situation. Comments are often directed toward the leader, with much less interaction among members. It is important that the leader assist members in directing these communications to other members or to the group as a whole, rather than to the leader. These experts suggest that establishing a norm of interaction is so important that structured activities and exercises are often the best way to accomplish this. The leader should be particularly attentive to what is being communicated nonverbally and invite members to verbalize what they are thinking and feeling. The physical arrangement of the group setting should be designed to promote interaction—hence, the ubiquitous circle. Other arrangements present barriers to communication and can lead to subgrouping and to an emphasis on interactions with the counselor rather than among members. Dinkmeyer and Muro note that by videotaping group sessions and plotting the interactions, it was easy to see the improvement when a circular seating arrangement was used.

RESOLVING CONFLICTS

Conflicts are best resolved by promoting cohesion so that unnecessary conflicts are minimized. When conflict does occur, these authors believe the leader is obliged to ensure that they are handled carefully so that group process is not harmed. They advocate for using the technique of role playing (role reversal), having the opposing parties switch roles and take the opposing position for a short period, as one means to ensure a positive outcome and an increase in empathy. They also suggest the leader actively intervene, using skills to include all members in the process.

GUIDING

Guiding is the term for a group of tasks that group leaders undertake to maximize the advantages of the group approach. Associated tasks are listed here; they appear to be more usually referred to as "skills," rather than functions, but taken together, and used to support the goals of the group, the commonality among them is that they all "guide" the group.

1. Tone setting
2. Structuring and limit setting
3. Blocking
4. Linking
5. Providing support
6. Reflection
7. Protecting
8. Questions
9. Regulating

PROGRAMMING VERSUS FREE DISCUSSION

Dinkmeyer and Muro (1971) list as a final function of the leader programming versus free discussion. In the time they were writing, many groups would fall under the broad description of "nondirective," given the influence of Rogerian and humanistic approaches. Nevertheless, there were voices in favor of structured activities, particularly in the early stages of group development. While Dinkmeyer and Muro avoid making a strong statement on one side of the debate, they do imply that the use of structured activities early in the group can reduce anxiety and build cohesion, particularly in groups with children and adolescents. This decision is listed as a function of the leader because it is the leader who will introduce and select the activities or exercises if they are used and who will have different tasks to enact if the group is to be completely nondirective.

It is interesting to note that in the second edition of their book (Dinkmeyer & Muro, 1979) the discussion of leader functions is considerably truncated. The authors appear to have abandoned their original schema in favor of the one proposed by Yalom (1975), which they describe in some detail. I will review Yalom's consideration of group functions below.

Lieberman, Yalom, and Miles

Although Dinkmeyer and Muro (1971) drew from their considerable clinical experience in their description of leader functions, the next approach to a delineation of the functions of a leader was based on empirical data. In their seminal work on groups, Lieberman, Yalom and Miles (1973) used data collected from observations of 16 leaders of "encounter groups" to describe a typology of leader functions. Although the focus of the present chapter is counseling groups, Lieberman et al. state that their taxonomies apply to leaders of all groups whose goal is "personal change," including personal growth groups. This is one of the few typologies that are derived from empirical research and that, coupled with the wide influence of this study and the book that described their extensive findings, merits more detailed coverage.

Encounter groups are intensive, high-contact, small-group experiences in which honesty, emotional expression, self-disclosure, and interpersonal confrontation are characteristic. The goals vary but in general involve some type of personal growth or change. This type of group was popular in the 1970s and, as a result, was available to Lieberman et al. (1973) for their research. The members of the groups were volunteer students at Stanford University, two-thirds of whom were male, who responded to advertisements and publications inviting participation. Participants received the equivalent credit for one academic course. Half of the participants had previous experience in an encounter group. There were 210 student participants who were assigned to 18 groups led by 16 leaders (no information on gender) with well-established professional reputations as group leaders. Two of the groups had no leader but were given audiotaped instructions. All groups met for 30 hours, but the distribution of those hours varied. Only leaders who were selected to conduct marathon sessions could do so; the rest scheduled sessions as they saw fit. All sessions were tape-recorded and observed by two trained observers.

There were 29 observers including pre- and postdoctoral interns, graduate students, psychiatric residents, and clinicians. All had either participated in or led encounter groups and underwent 15 hours of training for this role. Two observers attended each session and made notes. Following the session, the observers reviewed their notes and completed rating forms that called for 174 judgments. After the observers completed their individual ratings, they met to resolve any differences and produced a third rating that reflected their joint agreement. The ratings involved ratings of the leader's behavior and general characteristics of the groups. No ratings of members were made.

A control group of 69 students completed all the measures but did not participate in the groups. A battery of measures was used to assess outcomes, interpersonal relationships, and leader and group characteristics. Interested readers can find these measures in the appendix to Lieberman et al. (1973). There was a vast amount of data and analyses of these data (the report is a nearly 500-page book rather than an article), but I will focus here only on aspects of leader functions.

The ratings of leader behavior were analyzed to develop a typology of leader functions. Therefore, the interrater reliability of the ratings is important. For leader behavior checklist items, correlation coefficients ranged from 0.32 to 0.94. The mean interrater correlations were as follows: Evocative Behavior function, 0.63 (seven items); Meaning Attribution, 0.66 (six items); Support, 0.76 (three items); Management, 0.77 (eight items); and Use of Self, 0.79 (four items). The interpretation of a correlation coefficient is that the square of the correlation indicates the percent of agreement, so for Evocative Behavior the two raters agreed on the rating just under 40% of the time.

The research team (Lieberman et al., 1973) used factor analysis of the behavioral observation data to identify underlying functions of group leaders. These functions are Emotional Stimulation, Caring, Meaning Attribution, and Executive Function. Although this procedure provided empirical support for the existence of these functions, the reader should be aware that these groupings were created from a list of 28 leader behaviors identified a priori. These four functions are described next.

EMOTIONAL STIMULATION

Emotional stimulation is a function of leadership that is concerned with encouraging the expression and discharge of affect. According to Lieberman et al. (1973), the leader behaviors that serve this function include "revealing feelings, challenging, confrontation, revelation of personal values, attitudes, beliefs, frequent participation as a member of the group, exhortation, and drawing attention to self" (p. 235). Essentially, the leader encourages emotional expression by modeling those behaviors.

The leader not only expresses warmth and concern but also challenges and confronts members about their assumptions, particularly those about the self. In order to exercise this function, the leader's personality must be charismatic to a degree so that members are inspired to take emotional risks in the group. The leader is the center of the group who encourages emotional expression by exhibiting it.

CARING

Caring involves demonstrations of warmth, acceptance of others, openness, and genuine concern for group members. This function involves encouraging members to seek feedback, while also providing support and praise. The leader is seen by members as kind and loving.

MEANING ATTRIBUTION

Meaning attribution involves helping members understand events in the group and calls for cognitive skills of "explaining, clarifying, interpreting, and providing frameworks for how to change" (Lieberman et al., 1973, p. 240). The leader may make interpretations or invite interpretations from members that apply to the group as a whole (climate in the group, level of functioning of the group, etc.) or to individual members. They may translate contributions of members into more concise or precise terms, or they may give a name to something a member describes. There is an element of teaching, and unlike emotional stimulation, this involves less participation in the group as a member.

EXECUTIVE FUNCTION

Executive function is the last of the four functions. This is the function in which organizational and managerial tasks are performed. In this role, the leader suggests rules or norms, goals, and direction of the group. The leader also manages interactions by blocking, inviting participation, asking questions, interrupting when necessary, managing time, setting limits, and establishing sequences of activities or procedures. With this function, the leader takes charge and gives direction and instructions to members.

Yalom

In Yalom's (1975) influential book on group work, *Theory and Practice of Group Psychotherapy* (currently in a fifth edition), he proposed three fundamental functions of the leader. Those were creating and maintaining the group, culture building, and activation and illumination of the here and now

(1985, p. 113). Yalom points out that the therapist is the person who creates the group, determines logistics (time, place, frequency, duration of meetings, etc.), and selects and prepares members—a critical task. Once the group has formed, under the umbrella of creating and maintaining the group, the leader's focus must shift to preventing attrition of members. When members leave the group (even if it is in the best interest of that individual), the stability of the group is compromised, which threatens the group. In open groups, the leader then has the task of filling the spot with a new person and managing the process of incorporating new members into an existing group. In all of these tasks, the group's needs supersede those of any individual member, so taking time to help a new member integrate the group takes precedence over the needs of a member with a pressing personal issue. The integration of the new member is not simply a service to help that member to be comfortable; it is necessary for the cohesion of the group.

Within the creating and maintaining function, the leader actively works to reduce or eliminate threats to the integrity of the group as a whole. This includes addressing absence or tardiness, subgrouping, and other behaviors that impede the development of a cohesive group. In addition, the leader must help members get to know one another and reduce the centrality of the leader in the group constellation. While the leader is generally the hub of all communication at the beginning of the group, that pattern must be disrupted early on in the service of unity and cohesion, essential to an effective group.

The second main function of the leader, to build culture, is necessary because it is the group that is the therapeutic force and the "therapeutic social system" (Yalom, 1985, p. 115) is essential for that force to be unleashed. Thus, the leader must orchestrate the elements to create the appropriate cultural climate. Yalom points out that the norms in therapy (and counseling groups, I would add) are different from those of social or other groups in which members participate. In counseling and therapy groups, members report their immediate feelings in the group, share their reactions to other members, and engage in self-disclosure at a very personal level. In social groups, these behaviors are often unacceptable, so the leader has to foster the creation of norms (both stated and implied) that promote the growth of members.

Yalom observes that norms of a counseling or therapy group (most groups, in fact) are established early and become very difficult to change. His point is that norms will develop naturally regardless of whether the leader consciously directs the process, and the leader must ensure that the norms that emerge allow the therapeutic factors of groups (instillation of hope, universality, imparting of information, altruism, corrective recapitulation of the primary family group, development of socializing techniques, imitative behavior, interpersonal learning, group cohesiveness, catharsis, and existential factors) to occur. Whether by intention or by default, the leader, by virtue of the position, will influence the norms that become established in the group. The leader shapes norms in two ways: by being the "technical expert" and by modeling. In the expert role, the leader begins to shape norms even prior to the first meeting, by preparing clients and describing the norms to prospective members. In early group sessions, the leader can use his or her natural position as the "expert" to instruct members to share their responses to others or to an issue by directing interactions away from the leader in the direction of other members, using exercises that illustrate the importance of the norms, and nonverbal signals to let the group members know both what is expected and when it is happening. The leader's approval of conduct that is consistent with the norms (by smiling, looking, etc.) will reinforce norm-consistent behavior. If the leader is judicious about making comments or giving instructions, then when those are forthcoming members are likely to take notice.

Modeling is well established as a mechanism by which humans learn new behaviors, and the leader's behavior in the group is modeling the norms for members. The leader then needs to be deliberate and intentional about the behaviors he or she exhibits. By being mindful of what is being modeled, the leader does not have to relinquish the spontaneity that is important in a group; rather, the leader also models responsible behavior by choosing when and what to contribute. Among the most valuable behaviors the leader exhibits, which hopefully will become norms, are openness to feedback and recognizing one's errors. If the leader takes a defensive posture, hiding behind the authority of the position, and avoids accepting useful feedback from a member, it is likely that this will become a norm rather than the receptivity and thoughtful reflection that will promote growth and positive change.

The third function posited by Yalom (1985) is activation and illumination of the here and now. This role involves two elements: experiencing the here and now and illuminating the process. Although material in a group often involves historical or current challenges of members, the "common denominator" (p. 143) of all interpersonal groups is the focus on here-and-now group process. *Here-and-now focus* refers to the feelings and reactions members have toward each other, the leader, and the group as a whole, which are the fodder for group interactions. Yalom proposes that the group leader functions to direct the group's attention to the here and now and to illuminate the process. After an exchange in a group, even one that appears to capture the energy of members, process illumination is necessary for members to have some kind of cognitive structure to organize the experience so that it can be available to them in other situations, both in and outside of the group.

This leader function involves an understanding of the process/content distinction. *Content* refers to the words used, the statements made, whereas *process* refers to the interpersonal relationships of those involved in the communication. In a counseling or therapy group, it is the leader's job to bring the process to the attention of the group members so that they can reflect and have the necessary cognitive structure to utilize their experience. This function is difficult for many reasons, perhaps the most obvious of which is that there are often multiple layers to the processes and the leader must make a decision about which of those is most relevant to the group at the time. Sometimes it will be beneficial to make process observations about a single statement, while in other cases it is a complex interchange that needs illumination. Not only must the leader decide on which of several processes to bring out, but there are often many possible observations or interpretations of a given interaction (or sequence of interactions) and the leader will have to determine which is the most useful to the group. This is not an easy task; the leader must quickly sort through information about the group, the individuals in the group, the stage of the group, and the varied perspectives on the given content and then decide which of these to share with the group. Fortunately, the accuracy of an illumination is not the potent feature, according to Yalom. The effectiveness of the illumination is related to the degree to which it brings the focus of the group to the group itself—to the here and now. He also points out that at times an important process illumination might appear to be an intrusion, an unwanted interruption. He advises the leader to acknowledge that in making the observation and indicating to the members that the process seems to

be critical and important enough to merit the disturbance.

What exactly is process illumination? First, the leader must recognize the process, must be able to see the interpersonal implications that are present in an interaction. Those implications can be related to the timing of a communication, the nature of the communication, the recipient, etc. It requires listening and observing on two levels at once: the content and the process. Leaders can begin to accumulate process data by observing from the first moments of a group's life. Where do members choose to sit? How do members address each other (do they look at each other, at the leader, over the heads of all?), and what do their body posture and facial expression say about their involvement in the group? What is conspicuously absent from interactions? What kinds of question are not being asked? How do absences affect the group? How congruent are verbal and nonverbal behaviors? Another method the leader employs to illuminate process is to invite members to share their observations. The leader may ask members their impression of the meeting at a certain point in the session or what they have observed about the energy in the group. The leader also must help members to accept and reflect on process comments that relate to their interactions. Yalom notes that the leader can model and help members see the importance of delivering process comments in a supportive way, using specific, rather than global, statements and avoiding labels.

Yalom (1985) points out that although group members may also recognize process, the leader's position allows for more objectivity than members can maintain, so it falls upon the leader to illuminate process for the group. The leader is also expected to retain a historical memory of the group's life. Is the current event part of a pattern that has been repeated in the group? Does it represent a new and courageous direction? Peterson and Nisenholz (1998) observed that leaders who exhibited high levels of caring and meaning attribution combined with moderate levels of emotional stimulation and executive function were the most successful, as judged by member outcomes.

Trotzer

Trotzer (1977) identified the functions of group leadership using slightly different terminology. *Promoting interaction* is an essential function that is accomplished by encouraging members to assist one another and by avoiding behaviors that close down member involvement. The leader who uses the role as a platform to promote ideas or dictate agendas will stifle member interactions. In service of this function, the leader uses a variety of techniques, such as linking members and engaging in appropriate self-disclosure that models openness and genuine relating. The physical setting of the group meetings should also be designed to promote interaction. The use of the circle allows all members to see one another, which supports interaction. Trotzer describes this function as one in which the conditions are created for optimal interaction.

While the function of promoting interaction is to stimulate interaction, Trotzer's (1977) list of leader functions includes several other interaction-related tasks. *Facilitating interaction* is a "responsive function" (p. 86) in which the leader enhances interaction that is already occurring. When an interaction occurs, the leader facilitates interaction by providing illumination that makes exchanges more meaningful and effective. To structure the interaction patterns of the group, the leader function of *initiating interaction* is employed so that the topics and direction of interactions are orchestrated. This function is particularly helpful early in the life of a group, when the absence of structure tends to increase the anxiety of members. The final interaction function is *guiding interaction*. When performing this task, the leader keeps the group moving toward its goals, preventing tangential material from diverting the group from its intended direction. In this role, the leader also manages the rate and depth of disclosure. It can be alarming to the group if a member discloses intimate personal information too soon in the life of the group, and it is part of this function for the leader to gently move the group toward deeper levels at an appropriate pace.

In service of protecting group members, Trotzer (1977) lists *intervening* as one of the functions of the leader. The leader at times will need to block interactions that are destructive or damaging to an individual member or to the group as a whole. The leader needs to anticipate the consequence of an interaction almost before it occurs, to contain the potential harm. Particular situations when this is essential include when a member is scapegoated, when groups exert excessive pressure for a particular view or behavior, when anger is displaced, when the group makes unwarranted conclusions, and when groups become complacent and abandon meaningful work.

The *consolidating* function is the one in which the leader brings together various threads and contributions in a way that makes a coherent and meaningful statement that the group as a whole can digest. In this way, the leader ensures that all members have the same understanding of what has occurred in the group. Members may disagree with the consolidating statement, but the leader's job is to bring all the interactions together in a way that keeps all members aware of what has occurred.

Rules-keeping is an executive function that refers to seeing that the norms are guiding the group. In this role, the leader is the authority whose job it is to make sure that the norms that were created to keep the group safe and productive are followed.

Enhancing communication is different from the interaction functions in that the task involves the accurate expression of empathy for members in the service of helping members to be clearer in their communication. The leader observes the reactions of other members when a member communicates and helps the member to express her- or himself more effectively. Leaders undertaking this task will encourage members to speak directly to one another, to speak in the first person, and to acknowledge their feelings.

Trotzer (1977) adds *resolving conflicts* to the list of leader functions. The term is somewhat of a misnomer in that the leader is not going to resolve the conflict but must make sure that it is resolved in a way that allows the group to move forward. Conflicts are an inevitable aspect of most groups and, when dealt with positively, can promote growth. It is when conflicts remain unresolved or when they are resolved in an ineffective manner that they are harmful to the group, so the leader must be prepared to recognize the source of a conflict in order to oversee the resolution.

The final function in Trotzer's (1977) schema is that of *mobilizing group resources*. When exercising this function, the leader attempts to reduce her or his role in helping members and to draw upon the unique experiences and strengths of members so that the group members are empowered to help each other. The function really maximizes the value of the group milieu. If group members always look to the leader, the powerful force that groups possess cannot emerge. The leader must be very skillful in helping the group recognize the value of each member and the collective.

Bates, Johnson, and Blaker

A slightly different perspective on group leader functions includes four basic roles: traffic director, modeler of appropriate behavior, interactional catalyst, and communications facilitator (Bates,

Johnson, & Blaker, 1982). As *traffic director*, the leader promotes behaviors that facilitate communication and inhibits behaviors that block communication. The leader exercises this function by helping members understand how these behaviors encourage or discourage open communication. When the leader functions as *modeler of appropriate behavior*, the behaviors are sometimes directly demonstrated or taught and at other times modeled. Being aware that the leader's behaviors provide models for members means that leaders must be deliberate about what they do and say in the group. The *interactional catalyst* function refers to actions by the leader to encourage communication among members. This function is a subtle one in that the leader may invite or wonder about unspoken thoughts rather than directing members to speak to one another. The *communication facilitator function* is one of illumination: Using reflection of feelings and content, the leader teaches members active listening techniques and effective ways to communicate (e.g., "I" messages).

Scheidlinger

Scheidlinger (1980) observed that much of the theoretical work on leadership comes from fields other than group psychology. He made a distinction between group psychology (academic, theoretical) and group therapy (clinical, applied) and was interested in looking at leadership in a way that would be useful to group therapists. He went so far as to say that he has reservations about the term *leader* to describe the group therapist since it implies that there are also followers. He offered eight functions of group therapists:

1. Deciding the logistics of the group, such as time, place, location, cost.
2. Structuring sessions (or establishing norms). Scheidlinger uses the phrase "structuring the way sessions will be conducted," but the description refers to what would generally be described as "setting norms." It is of interest that he sees this function as the leader's, rather than as a collaborative effort of the leader and members.
3. Having empathic acceptance, or caring for each member and believing in each member's capacity for change.
4. Encouraging expression.
5. Fostering a tolerant and accepting climate, along with a focus on increasing awareness of interpersonal relationships.
6. Controlling the "drive-expression, tension, and anxiety level" (p. 18) of individual members.

7. Maintaining positive group morale.
8. Using verbal interventions, ranging from observations to psychoanalytic interpretations.

Anderson and Robertson

Anderson and Robertson (1985) borrow from the existing models to present their conceptualization of the functions of the group facilitator (leader). They list selection and preparation, establishment of facilitative norms, development of a cohesive group climate, creation of an independent interactional network, and the examination of group processes as the major functions of the leader. The first function echoes Yalom's (1985) creation and maintenance of the group function, while the second mirrors the build culture function in Yalom's schema. The development of a cohesive group climate is implicit in Yalom's first two categories, but Anderson and Robertson emphasize the importance of this task by listing it as a separate function. The cohesive climate allows members to feel psychologically safe and thus encourages risk taking (and growth) in the group. The examination of group process echoes the illumination function described by Yalom (1985).

Krieg

Writing about counseling groups in the school setting, Krieg (1988) proposed that the most important function of the leader is to provide structure. He believes that an absence of structure is the single most common reason for poor outcomes. With this in mind, the functions of the leader are to "construct the group, maintain control and provide protection, facilitate processing of thoughts and feelings, and provide insight into problem behavior" (p. 35). These functions are in order of importance; insight is the least important because it is more effective when it comes from members rather than the leader. It may be that the age group and setting (children and adolescents in schools) account for the differences between this typology and those discussed previously.

I have reviewed a variety of classifications and characterizations of the functions of the leader. Table 18.1 presents these typologies. I now turn to leader styles, or the characteristic ways in which the leader performs the functions.

Leadership Styles

The discussion of leadership functions and styles assumes that leaders can, by inclination, situation, or training, vary those styles (Napier & Gershenfeld, 2004). Thus, leadership styles can be considered to

Table 18.1 Functions of the group leader

Cartwright & Zander (1960)	Dinkmeyer & Muro (1971)	Lieberman et al. (1973)	Yalom (1975)	Trotzer (1977)	Scheidlinger (1980)	Bates et al. (1982)	Anderson & Robertson (1985)	Krieg (1988)
• Task • Maintenance (relationships)	• Promoting cohesiveness • Summarizing • Promoting interaction • Resolving conflicts • Guiding • Programming vs. free discussion	• Emotional stimulation • Caring • Meaning attribution • Executive function	• Creating and maintaining the group • Culture building • Activation and illumination of the here-and-now	• Promoting interaction • Initiating interaction • Guiding interaction • Intervening • Consolidating • Rules-keeping • Enhancing communication • Resolving conflicts • Mobilizing group resources	• Structuring logistics structuring sessions • Demonstrating acceptance, caring, and belief in potential • Encouraging expression • Fostering conducive climate • Controlling emotional levels of members • Maintaining group morale • Using verbal interventions	• Traffic director • Modeler of appropriate behavior • Interactional catalyst • Communications facilitator	• Selection and preparation • Establishment of facilitative norms • Development of a cohesive group climate • Creation of an independent interactional network • Examination of group process	• Construct the group • Maintain control and provide protection • Facilitate processing of thoughts & feelings • Provide insight into problem behavior

be separate from the personality of the leader, although it is undoubtedly the case that some leaders are drawn to particular styles because of intrapersonal characteristics.

The discussion of leadership style must begin with the classic series of studies by Lewin, Lippitt, and White (1939/1946). The experimental design involved after-school activity groups with 10-year-olds, rather than counseling groups; but the findings have been applied to many types of groups in a variety of settings. Readers should keep in mind that all the leaders in these experiments were male and that the type of group (and age of members) necessitated different behaviors from what would be seen in a typical counseling group. Nevertheless, the categorization of leader styles that came from this work has been the template for almost all models that followed.

The leadership styles that were the focus of this work were authoritarian, democratic, and laissez-faire. A helpful comparison of the three styles was provided by Kemp (1970). The authoritarian leader engages in planning, directing, and informing members. He or she controls the group by reward and praise or by punishment and fear of punishment. The *authoritarian* leader considers decisions to be the sole province of the leader and demands a high level of conforming behavior from members. This leadership style tends to engender dependence on the leader. In contrast, the *democratic* leader involves the group in cooperative planning, shares control and direction of the group with members, and promotes freedom of expression. This style is more likely to promote self-reliance and responsibility among members. Gladding (2003) suggests that a more accurate label for leaders using this style is "facilitators," given their humanistic orientation and belief in the potential of members. The *laissez-faire* style is intended to allow the potential of the group to emerge and to allow the group to develop independently, taking responsibility for itself. The climate is nonthreatening and accepting, much as in nondirective counseling. Free communication and participation among members are generated by this style.

Coming from the field of organizational management, McGregor (1960) referred to authoritarian leaders as "theory X" leaders and to democratic leaders as "theory Y" leaders. Leaders who exhibit extreme laissez-faire styles were called "theory Z" leaders by Ouchi (1981). Theory Z leaders believe the group will manage itself.

In the initial experiment by Lewin et al. (1939/1946), two groups (after-school clubs) of 10-year-olds were led by the same leader, who used an authoritarian style on one group and a democratic style in another. The groups were observed by four observers. In the authoritarian group, overt hostility was exhibited 40 times more often in the authoritarian group than in the democratic group and aggression was eight times as common. In the next, more elaborate experiment, the laissez-faire leadership style was added.

Four clubs of five 10-year-old boys were led by four different adults. Observers collected data to confirm that the leaders' behaviors and interactions were consistent with the style they were using for that period. Information on the boys was obtained so that the groups were equivalent on a variety of characteristics represented; the experimenters attempted to control the setting and the activities undertaken in the groups. The experiment continued for 5 months, with group leaders changing every 6 weeks so that each group experienced three different leaders using three different styles during the life of the group. The experimenters were interested in how the different social climates, responding to the different leadership styles, affected the amount of aggressive behavior exhibited by the boys. Considerable data in addition to the observations (interviews, Rorschach tests, parental interviews) were gathered and showed that the groups led by the authoritarian leaders produced the largest quantity of work. The number of aggressive actions per meeting was highest in the laissez-faire condition, followed by the authoritarian condition, with the democratic condition showing the lowest rates of aggressive activity. Groups led in an authoritarian style were characterized by apathetic, nonaggressive behavior in several cases. Although the analyses in the early papers focused on aggression, these studies are frequently cited as evidence of the differences among the three group styles.

In a later publication, White and Lippitt (1960) considered the leader behaviors in the three social climates. They examined the frequency of leader behaviors in the three style conditions and found several statistically significant differences. Giving orders accounted for 45% of verbal behavior among authoritarian leaders, compared to 3% among democratic leaders and 4% among the laissez-faire. Disrupting commands (orders that interrupt what members are doing or wanting to do) were also more common from authoritarian leaders (11%) than the other two styles (<1%). What White and Lippitt call "nonobjective criticism and praise" accounted for 5% in authoritarian leaders and 1% in the other styles. This behavior includes criticism of the person rather than the behavior and was not coupled with suggestions for improvement. The praising component of this style was also based on the leader's evaluation rather than any objective criteria. In contrast to the giving of orders used by authoritarian leaders, democratic and laissez-faire leaders used guiding suggestions, a way of helping members accomplish their own tasks, often guiding by example in addition to verbal suggestions. Guiding suggestions were used in 24% of democratic leaders' utterances and in 14% of laissez-faire and 6% of authoritarian statements. Giving information constituted 49% of laissez-faire leaders', 27% of democratic leaders', and 15% of authoritarian leaders' verbal behaviors. The laissez-faire leaders' information was technical (how to do this, where to find something) in response to member inquiries. Stimulating self-direction was used least by authoritarian leaders (1.2%) and somewhat more by laissez-faire leaders (13%) and democratic leaders (16%). The difference between the last two styles is not simply one of frequency; the laissez-faire leaders tended to remind individual members of their ability to make decisions, whereas the democratic leaders reminded the group as a whole. The only social aspect of behavior included in the analysis was "jovial and confiding behavior," found in 8% of democratic leader behaviors and <1% in the other styles. Democratic criticism and praise was not quantified, but White and Lippitt noted it was used differently by democratic and authoritarian leaders, with democratic leaders using criticism and praise to help members learn how to evaluate their own goals and actions. Finally, egalitarian behavior was observed in the democratic style and was exhibited by indications of unconcern about status and dignity. Given the historical period, the examples included taking off their suit coats and sitting instead of standing.

These three styles are often discussed in the literature. Posthuma (1996) noted that leader style impacts member behavior. In groups with authoritarian leaders, members tend to be compliant but unenthusiastic and rarely take initiative. In democratically led groups, members tend to be enthusiastic, collaborative, and willing to take initiative. Members of groups led with a laissez-faire style are often frustrated with that lack of direction and uncertain about the purpose of the group.

Although other descriptions of leadership styles have been proposed, Gladding (2003) noted that most of these have been modifications of these three styles. The notable exception is that of Lieberman et al. (1973), who derived a typology of six leadership styles (called "types") using several different strategies to cluster their leader behavior data by relative evidence of the functions already described. The six types were energizers, providers, social engineers, impersonals, laissez-faires, and managers. Each of the 16 leaders (who subscribed to a variety of theoretical perspectives) in their study was assigned to one of the styles based on the data. Lieberman et al.'s descriptions are based on the leaders who exhibited the style, which for some types means one or two leaders. *Energizers* were characterized by intensity of emotional stimulation. They also had relatively high ratings on executive function and caring. Leaders whose style was consistent with this type were also considered to be charismatic and strongly associated with a particular philosophy or set of beliefs. *Providers* had high ratings on caring and meaning attribution and moderate ratings on executive function and emotional stimulation. Their style was described as "enlightened paternalism" (p. 243). The group-focused leaders who used group-focused meaning attribution were classified as social engineers. Unlike the providers, they did not have a personal focus but did show a moderate degree of caring while being low on emotional stimulation. These leaders focused on the group as a unit rather than on individual members and were seen by members as not being charismatic. *Impersonals* were described as distant and aggressive in their stimulation (they were moderately high on emotional stimulation but low on caring and executive functions). *Laissez-faire* leaders were low on emotional stimulation, caring, and executive function but moderate to high on meaning attribution. They were seen as technicians by members of their groups; the meaning attribution occurred in isolation. The final style, *managers*, describes leaders who were extremely high on executive function. This type used many structured exercises and exerted a high deal of control over intermember communication.

In additional analyses, these six styles were compared by the degree of change shown by members of their groups. Lieberman et al. (1973) created a complex index of change on 78 measures that were administered to participants and controls pregroup, postgroup, and at a 6-month follow-up. At the conclusion of the encounter group experience, the participants in the groups led by providers demonstrated the highest "weighted impact average" (p. 245, the measure of change), with other positive impact factors shown by members of groups led by energizers and social engineers.

Impersonal leaders' participants were found to be neutral on the outcome measures, while laissez-faire leaders' and managers' members had negative impact scores.

Stogdill

In a review of studies on leadership style, Stogdill (1974) summarized the themes:

1. Person-oriented styles are not always associated with productivity.

2. Of task-oriented styles, structured styles in which the roles of leader and member are clearly defined and expectations well articulated, group productivity tends to be high.

3. Group cohesiveness is associated with styles that include members in decision making and show concerns for members.

4. Task-oriented styles in which member expectations are structured are associated with group cohesiveness.

5. Member satisfaction is found with all person-oriented leadership styles.

6. For work-oriented styles, member satisfaction is positively associated with structuring of member expectations.

Additional Styles

Capuzzi, Gross, and Stauffer (2006) mentioned two other classifications of leadership style: leader-directed vs. group-directed (Jacobs, Masson, & Harvill, 2002) and interpersonal vs. intrapersonal styles, as proposed by Shapiro (1978). It seems that the authoritarian, democratic, and laissez-faire approaches include the degrees to which the leader and members direct the group. However, the interpersonal vs. intrapersonal styles do not appear to be captured in the Lewin et al. (1939/1946) schema and are germane to the nature of counseling groups, rather than organizational contexts. Leaders who exhibit an *interpersonal* style focus on here-and-now interactions among members and emphasize processing of those interactions. Leaders who have an *intrapersonal* style emphasize the concerns of individual members and have been described as conducting individual therapy with an audience. The classic Perls hot-seat approach to groups fits this model.

Though not a separate model of leadership styles, Johnson and Johnson (1994) stated that "initiating structure by clearly defining one's role as a leader and what one expects from other members of the group is the single style of leadership that contributes to group productivity, cohesiveness, and satisfaction" (p. 179). These authors suggested that initiating structure combined with caring and respect for group members is likely to be the most effective style.

Discussions about which style is preferable have been essentially replaced in favor of a situational leadership model (Hersey, 1984; Hersey & Blanchard, 1972, 1977). This theory generates questions about which style is most effective for which group at which developmental stage. Their theory is based on the distinction between task behaviors (one-way communication from the leader to members) and relationship behaviors (two-way communication). They observed that leaders can exhibit one to the exclusion of the other, both, or neither. They proposed that any of those four combinations could be effective in some groups at some times in some situations. They also emphasized the maturity of members as a determinant of which behaviors are most appropriate. Hersey and Blanchard defined *maturity* as group members' achievement motivation for a particular task along with their willingness to accept responsibility. Maturity also reflects the education and experiences of group members. The task-specific nature of maturity is important.

The *situational leadership* theory posits that when group members have low maturity, the leader should be high on task and low on relationship behaviors. This style is called *telling* because it involves one-way communication from the leader to the group, in which the leader tells members how to do tasks. If members are moderately mature, the best style is high task and high relationship at first (known as *selling*, to get the members to invest in decisions necessary to accomplish the task); and then high relationship and low task behaviors are suitable. This style is called *participating* because of shared communication and support. When groups are highly mature for a task, then low task and low maintenance behaviors are called for. This style is called *delegating* because group members have efficacy for the task.

These models discussed are summarized in Table 18.2.

As these schemas were developed primarily from clinical experience (with the exception of the Lieberman et al. study), I now turn to the research to find out whether any of them has been tested, both to determine the validity of the models and to discover whether there are practical applications and implications of these theories.

Table 18.2 Group leader styles

Lewin et al. (1939/1946)	McGregor (1960), Ouchi (1981)	Shapiro (1978)	Lieberman et al. (1973)	Hersey & Blanchard (1977)
Authoritarian	Theory X	Interpersonal	Energizers	Situational leadership
Democratic	Theory Y	Intrapersonal	Providers	Telling
Laissez-faire	Theory Z		Social Engineers	Selling
			Impersonals	Participating
			Laissez-faires	Delegating
			Managers	

Research on Leader Functions and Styles

The Lewin et al. (1939/1946; see also White & Lippitt, 1960) and Lieberman et al. (1973) schemas of leader styles and functions were derived from their own empirical data. I shall now turn to studies by other researchers that tested these approaches. Most of the research has been conducted in settings other than counseling or therapy groups, but findings shed light on the way these styles and functions affect the operations and outcomes of groups.

An interesting line of inquiry was undertaken by Robert D. Meade (1970), who was interested in the cross-cultural implications of these models. He reported that cultures differ in the presence of these leadership styles and that individuals adapt to usual cultural practices. Chinese and Chinese American (first-generation) college students tend to score higher on measures of authoritarianism than their American counterparts. In these cultures, males had higher status than females. Meade (1970) conducted a study with 144 Chinese students at a university in Hong Kong and 144 Chinese American students at a university in Hawaii. At each university, a list of nine current issues of importance to all students was developed via discussion with students and student leaders. The lists were specific to that university.

Two male and two female leaders from each culture were trained in leading small discussion groups in the three "social climates" (leadership styles) described by Lippitt and White (1939). Each leader led six groups, two using each of the three leadership styles. Groups of six students (three males and three females) received lists of the issues and were instructed to rank the issues in order of importance to the university. After individual rankings, the members were instructed to reach consensus on the rankings. After the discussion concluded, democratic leaders called for a vote on the ranking, while in the other two conditions, the leaders wrote what they determined was the consensus and then wrote that on the board. Then, participants completed individual rankings again. Correlations between the group data (with results by gender pooled) and the final individual rankings were calculated. Higher correlation coefficients were considered to be evidence of the group discussion influencing individual rankings. For the Hong Kong group, the highest correlation was found in the authoritarian conditions for male leaders and in the laissez-faire condition for female leaders. Regarding the finding that the greatest cohesion for female leaders was found in the laissez-faire condition, Meade (1970) noted that in two of the four laissez-faire groups a male leader emerged from among the members. Also of interest was the result that there was no significant difference in cohesion among the three leadership styles for female leaders, while for males the authoritarian leaders' groups had the highest levels of cohesion and the laissez-faire, the least. Analysis of variance demonstrated a significant style-by-gender interaction.

For the Hawaii group, the highest correlation was found for the democratic condition for male leaders, with the authoritarian style being almost as high. For female leaders, the democratic leadership showed the strongest correlation. Again, the analysis of variance showed a style-by-gender interaction. However, there were no significant differences by leadership style for either gender. Male democratic leadership was more effective with Chinese American participants than Chinese. Male authoritarian leaders were equally effective with Chinese American participants.

This study highlighted that different styles may be more effective in different cultures. Other studies have examined the relationship between leadership style and the developmental stage of the group. Kivlighan (1997) studied 372 participants in 72 groups held in association with a university class. The groups met for 26 sessions. The first five were considered early sessions, and the last five were considered late sessions. Each group was led by a psychology graduate student enrolled in a group therapy practicum; they received both individual and group supervision by a doctoral-level psychologist. The measures included the Congruence/Empathy (relational orientation) and the Conditionality Scales (task orientation) of the TBS, a measure of leader behavior completed after each session, and the TCS, which asks participants to list and rate problem areas they want to address in the group so that high scores indicate higher levels of stress associated with the problem, completed pre- and postgroup experience. The unit of analysis was the leader, not the individual members. Results indicated that when leaders were more relationship-oriented during later sessions, group members were less distressed at the end of the group and that when group leaders were more task-oriented during early sessions, they also had lower levels of distress at the end of the group. This study illustrated the need for different leadership styles at different developmental stages. At the beginning of the group, members often have anxiety about the process, so clear explanations of the goals of the group, use of more structure, development of norms, etc. help members feel more willing to engage in the group. Close to the end of the group, when self-disclosure and meaningful work have occurred, the relationships increase in importance as the need for task-oriented leadership decreases.

Tinsley, Roth, and Lease (1989) tested the findings reported by Lieberman et al. (1973) in which four leadership functions were identified using factor analysis. Although Tinsley et al. were unable to find evidence of the four-factor structure using confirmatory factor analysis (they do not report the statistics obtained and the method used), there were several major differences in the methodology that make the comparison difficult. First, Tinsley et al. used self-report ratings by 204 participants (group leaders) rather than the observer ratings used by Lieberman et al. They also created a self-report rating scale that asked users about their own behavior in general, rather than in a specific group setting. Different groups with different members may elicit different behaviors in leaders. In addition, there may be influences of social desirability in reporting, as well as inaccurate perceptions of one's own behavior. Finally, in the Tinsley et al. study there was one rating per leader, while in the Lieberman et al. study several observers rated each leader. There were different numbers of observations for each leader in the Lieberman et al. study, and a weighing procedure was used to adjust for that.

Even if the Tinsley et al. (1989) study could not be expected to replicate the Lieberman et al. (1973) findings, it is of interest to examine the factors derived from their analysis. The first factor was *cognitive direction* and reflected leaders who were directive and who emphasized cognitive understanding of group processes. Factor 2, *affective direction*, described leaders who focused the group's attention on feelings and behaviors exhibited in the group. *Nurturant attractiveness* was the label attached to factor 3, which emphasized leader attractiveness and nurturance. Factor 4 was called *group functioning* and included behaviors involved with group building and functioning. Factor 5, *verbal stimulation*, referred to a pattern of leader relationships with members characterized by warmth, personal modeling by the leader, and a component of encouraging members to be like the leader. The final three scales identified using exploratory factor analysis were Charismatic Expertness, Individual Functioning, and Nonverbal Exercises. These factors seem to include leader functions, styles, and personal qualities; it does not appear to be a replacement for Lieberman et al.'s (1973) four functions.

A more recent study used the Lieberman et al. model of leader functions (with *use of self* added as a fifth function) to investigate the effect of these functions on outcomes in 269 cancer patients who participated in support groups led by professionals (Lieberman & Golant, 2002). The participants in the study were recruited from a national organization with 21 centers that offer free weekly support groups to adult cancer patients with a variety of cancer types and life circumstances. Each center distributed the questionnaires to members of one group composed of new members and two groups composed of participants who had been attending for at least 6 months. In the sample, 41% of participants had been group members for less than 6 months. Slightly more than half of participants utilized other professional help in addition to the support groups to deal with the diagnosis. The groups were facilitated by licensed psychotherapists who had received training in the organization's approach. The primary goal of the program is to empower patients to make choices about their own treatment and to reduce aloneness, loss of control, and hopelessness. The researchers used the Leadership Behaviors Questionnaire and Helpful Group Experiences Questionnaire (from Lieberman et al., 1973), the Functional Assessment of Cancer Therapy–General Questionnaire, and the Center for Epidemiological Study Depression Scale. A multivariate analysis of variance found that participants who had longer duration of participation had lower scores on the depression scale and less severe physical symptoms, as well as other positive outcomes. Meaning attribution, executive management, and caring together made up 80% of leader behaviors.

These researchers conducted further analyses to investigate the relationships among leader behaviors and outcomes. The outcome variables were reduced to two factors. The article omits the label of factor 1, which addresses mental and physical problems as well as overall functioning and well-being. Factor 2 included good social and doctor relations. Leaders judged to be high on meaning attribution and managerial behaviors were associated with changes in factor 1, including reductions in depression and physical problems, high well-being, and improvement in functioning. Next, the researchers analyzed the relationship between helpful group experiences (support, attitudes of the organization, existential, cognitive, disclosure, and member role) and outcomes and found that helpful group experiences were significant predictors of positive outcomes, with support and disclosure having the highest beta weights. When leader behaviors were added in the next equation, their added effect was not significant. Finally, leader behaviors were predictive of the helpful group experience elements "support" and "disclosure," with the highest beta for executive function behaviors and a moderate beta for meaning attribution behaviors.

Lieberman and Golant's (2002) study was the stimulus for a study of group leader functions and process and outcome variables in student groups in Israel (Shechtman & Toren, 2009). The researchers hypothesized that leader functions would affect process variables, which would then influence outcomes. Participants in the study were 205 students in master's-level programs to prepare mental health professionals. Counseling group participation was mandatory for students in the program, although participation in the research component was voluntary. The groups were led by two experienced leaders; 11 groups were led by one and three, by the other. The groups met for 13 sessions, were described as "expressive supportive," and could be classified as "affective insight" groups (p. 222). The researchers examined the five leader functions (evoke-stimulate, meaning attribution, support-caring, executive management, and use of self). Process variables were participant self-disclosure, resistance, bonding with the group, and impression of the process. Outcome variables were interpersonal relationships, self-esteem,

and risk taking. Two methods of assessing leader behaviors were used: the Leadership Behaviors Questionnaire and analysis of session transcripts. Other measures were the Risk Intimacy Inventory, Inventory of Interpersonal Problems, Session Impact Scale, Working Alliance Inventory, Client Resistance Scale, and Self-Disclosure Questionnaire.

The data were analyzed using hierarchical models with three levels: time, the individual, and the group. Group-level variables included the size of the group (which ranged from 11 to 22 members) and leader behavior transcripts. Outcome variables were assessed on two occasions, pre- and posttreatment, while process variables were assess after the third, seventh, and thirteenth sessions. Preliminary analyses found that group size had an effect on self-disclosure but only when the data from transcripts were used; no difference was detected on the outcome measures. The researchers included group size as a covariate in all subsequent analyses. All analyses were done separately with the transcript data and the questionnaire data; the results are quite complex, and the details of the analyses are beyond the scope of this chapter. I will, however, summarize the main findings. The results of the analysis of the transcript data indicated that four of the five functions affected some of the process variables. However, using questionnaire data, support affected four of the process variables: resistance, bonding with members, bonding with leader, and impression of therapy. Meaning attribution increased self-disclosure and decreased resistance. Of the process variables, self-disclosure was the best predictor of outcomes. Of the leader functions, management was associated with reduced risk taking, and use of self was found to reduce gains in self-esteem. However, use of self had a positive effect on interpersonal relationships, as did stimulating.

Interestingly, Shechtman and Toren (2009) also found that management had negative effects on both process and outcomes. The conclusion was that meaning attribution and support are the most important leader functions for groups of graduate student trainees. It is difficult to compare findings across these studies because of differences in the populations studied, measures, and other unique aspects of each group.

Rose (2006) used questionnaires to survey 108 members of 36 treatment groups in Israel using three "clusters" of leadership styles. The first cluster included the authoritarian, democratic, and laissez-faire styles; the second included task-oriented vs. social-emotional styles (which I have listed under functions) and used the term *maintenance* to refer to the social-emotional style; the third cluster contained participatory and supervisory styles. Rose was interested in the relationship between leader style and member satisfaction with therapy groups. He noted that several contextual variables may affect this relationship: member expectations regarding leader style, congruence of leader and member personality, interactions among members, and situational or cultural factors. Questionnaires were administered by trained research assistants during a middle session of the groups. Unfortunately, the survey was not included in the report. Information about the training of leaders and the number of different leaders was also absent, as were psychometric properties of the measure. There were 21 variables related to leadership style and 21 variables related to satisfaction. Members perceived authoritarian, laissez-faire, and supervisory styles much less often than they did the other styles. Although this study has methodological limitations, it is unique in asking members to indicate whether they perceived certain leadership styles used in the group. Rose reported that there

was considerable agreement among members about whether a particular style was used in their groups, and in general, members were satisfied with the degree to which the style was used. Perhaps the use of member ratings would add to our understanding of how leadership styles are related to outcomes. This would require a reliable and valid measure, and I do not know whether the questionnaire used in this study is one that meets those criteria.

Table 18.3 summarizes these studies.

Implications for Research, Training, and Practice

I have looked at a variety of models of group leader functions, and several models of group leader styles. The important notion is that these descriptions are all based on observed leader behaviors; they are independent of leader personality and the leader's theoretical perspective. Different techniques can be employed in several styles and functions. In this section, I will review the implications of what we know about leader function and styles for future research, training group leaders, and practice.

Table 18.3 Research on leader function and style

Researchers	Sample	Method	Findings
Meade (1970)	288 university students: 144 Chinese in Hong Kong, 144 Chinese American in Hawaii	Leadership styles used: authoritarian, democratic, laissez-faire; members completed consensus task, higher correlations among members evidence of group discussion influencing individual rankings	In HK group, highest correlation in authoritarian groups for male leaders and laissez-faire for female leaders. No difference in correlations across styles for female leaders; authoritarian had highest for males and laissez-faire the least. In Hawaii group, highest correlation found for democratic condition with male leaders. Authoritarian leaders also had high correlation. For females, democratic style had highest correlation. Male democratic style more effective with Chinese American than Chinese participants. Male authoritarian leaders were equally effective in both cultural groups.
Kivlighan (1997)	372 members of 72 groups associated with university class	Members completed measures of task/relational orientation after each session; also listed problem areas and levels of stress associated with problem pre- and post group.	When leaders were more relationship-oriented in late (last 5) sessions, members had lower stress levels on problems at termination. When leaders were more talk-oriented during early sessions, members reported lower stress at termination.
Tinsley et al. (1989)	204 group leaders recruited from ASGW membership	Participants completed a questionnaire in which they reported on their use of 26 leader behaviors from the Lieberman et al. (1973) study	The four-factor structure was not confirmed. Instead, they identified eight factors: cognitive direction, affective direction, nurturant attractiveness, group functioning, verbal stimulation, charismatic expertness, and individual functioning.

(Continued)

Table 18.3   (Continued)

Researchers	Sample	Method	Findings
Lieberman & Golant (2002)	269 cancer patients	Self-report questionnaires: Leader Behavior Questionnaire, Helpful Group Experiences Questionnaire, Functional Assessment of Cancer Therapy–General Questionnaire, CES-D	Participants who had longer duration of participation were less depressed and had less severe physical symptoms than those who attended fewer sessions. Meaning attribution, executive management, and caring accounted for 80% of leader behaviors. Leaders high on meaning attribution and executive functions were associated with positive outcomes on depression, physical problems, well-being. Helpful group behaviors were most predictive of positive outcomes. Support and disclosure had highest beta weights. Although leader behaviors did not predict outcomes, they did predict helpful group behaviors.
Shechtman & Toren (2009)	205 students in master's-level program in mental health field	Five leader functions were assessed: evoke-stimulate, meaning attribution, support-caring, executive-management, and use of self using questionnaire and session transcripts; process variables were self-disclosure, resistance, bonding with group, and impression of the process. Outcome measures were Risk Intimacy Inventory, Inventory of Interpersonal Problems, Session Impact Scale, Working Alliance Inventory, Client Resistance Scale, and Self-Disclosure Questionnaire	Results differed for the questionnaire and transcript analyses. Based on transcript data, 4 of 5 functions affected some process variables. With questionnaire data, support affected resistance, bonding with members, bonding with leader, and impression of therapy. Meaning attribution increase self-disclosure and increased resistance. Self-disclosure was the best predictor of outcomes. Meaning attribution increased self-disclosure. Management function was associated with reduced risk taking. Use of self reduced gains in self-esteem. Use of self and simulating had positive effects of interpersonal relationships.
Rose (2006)	108 group members from 36 clinical treatment groups in Israel	Questionnaire with 21 leadership style variables and 21 satisfaction variables	Authoritarian, laissez-faire, and supervisory styles not observed by members. Members agreed on whether style was used in the group. Members generally satisfied with leader style.

First, it is notable (and lamentable) that many of the studies used university student participants (Kivlighan, 1997; Lieberman et al., 1973; Meade, 1970; Shechtman & Toren, 2009). As has been the case with psychology research for many decades, students are readily accessible for participation in research (and, in fact, may receive credit for participating); but they may not be representative of the population at large. They are certainly not representative in terms of age. Thus, I would be very cautious in accepting as "truth" models constructed from small, nonrepresentative samples. The two most influential approaches, the Lewin et al. (1939/1946) model of leader styles and the Lieberman et al. (1973) categories of group leader functions, were based on research with a rather restricted population of both leaders and members, yet these are widely cited and used.

In addition, much of the research (and theory) on leader style and function was conducted from the perspective of industrial and organizational leadership contexts. The role of leaders (supervisors, managers) in those settings is clearly different from that of counseling group facilitators. Again, I need to be cautious about incorporating research outcomes and theoretical models that are developed on very different types of groups with differently trained leaders.

Given the long history of the concepts of leader functions and styles, the paucity of research studies is surprising. What has inhibited research productivity on these topics? There are a number of possible explanations that might provide some direction for future research endeavors. First, I want to consider whether further understanding of leader functions and styles would advance the field of group counseling. Perhaps one reason the studies have not been conducted is that the interest in and applicability of this area of group work are low. There is no way to know whether this is the case, but I know that considerable energy in group work research has been directed toward demonstrating the effectiveness of group work (Bednar & Kaul, 1994). It may well be that the focus on effectiveness research has deflected interest in leader functions and styles. Bednar and Kaul pointed out in 1994 that there was already a large body of work that supported effectiveness in group work and that it was necessary for researchers to extend that research by addressing the questions of what variables influence outcomes and how they do so. Although their exhortation was published in 1994, it does not appear to have been heeded. The three leadership styles (authoritarian, democratic, and laissez-faire) are perhaps the best-known and most-researched construct, but most of the research using that model has come from organizational studies. The study most often cited (Lewin et al., 1939/1946) was based on a group whose purpose was dissimilar to most counseling and therapy situations. The boys were making crafts (an appropriate activity for 10-year-olds), and goal attainment could be assessed by the quantity and quality of the productions. In counseling groups, the goals are generally interpersonal and intrapersonal—far less tangible. In their later analysis, Lippitt and White (1960) determined that giving orders accounted for the majority of utterances in the authoritarian group. It is hard to imagine many situations in which a group-counseling leader would give orders. Is this concept of leadership style relevant to the group-counseling arena? Would further studies improve training or assist practitioners?

Perhaps the obstacles for researchers relate to the lack of precision in definition of constructs and the absence of well-defined methods and measures (Bednar & Kaul, 1994). If the definitions of the constructs are precise, we should find high interrater reliability for coding behaviors under the appropriate function. Yet, several of the studies demonstrate that interrater reliability is not consistently high (e.g., Lieberman et al., 1973). In Shechtman and Toren (2009), results differed when the researchers used transcript data and questionnaire data. This suggests that we do not yet have clear, operationalized, precise definitions of leader functions and styles. It follows that if constructs are not clearly delineated, measures will not be able to measure them accurately. Methodologically, the question of the best way to understand leader functions and styles is unclear. Are observer ratings the most accurate? Participant ratings? Leader self-report? (Dies, 1983). Are there more appropriate methodologies than could be appropriated to this line of inquiry?

Future Research

Before high-quality research can be conducted on leader functions and styles, precise definitions need to be put forward. As in any good science, those conceptualizations should be testable, so the next step would be to test, in a variety of group types with a variety of populations, whether these models provide comprehensive explanations of these concepts.

Lieberman et al. (1973) developed their categories of functions based on data that involved judgments of 28 leader behaviors. Is this an exhaustive list of leader behaviors? Does the list include redundancies? The number of behaviors that loaded onto the four functions varied considerably. Could it be that more indicators for all functions would increase reliability? Perhaps reconsidering the leader behaviors that should be coded, using more sophisticated qualitative analyses, would result in a more complete and precise list of behaviors from which the functions could be derived.

Technological advances may allow more innovative methods for research on functions and styles. For example, unobtrusive videotaping (with member consent) allows for more clues to the nature of a given leader behavior. Reading a transcript, for example, may obscure nonverbal or tonal information that adds to or even changes the meaning of an utterance. If rater coding of behavior was based on these data, would there be higher interrater reliability?

Finally, it behooves group-work researchers and practitioners to generate a list of research questions, in priority order. What is it that we need to know about leader functions and styles that would improve training and practice? Is client outcome the best measure of the utility of various functions? How can we take into account all the situational variables (which vary from group to group and from moment to moment in a group) that determine what leader function or style is appropriate? When we can answer these questions with a high degree of confidence, our understanding and application of leader function and style will be able to move forward.

Training Implications

The leadership functions can be viewed as a list of tasks that trainees will need to perform as future group leaders. Training might benefit from a focus on a clear description of the functions, followed by a discussion of various techniques and strategies that can be employed to accomplish these tasks. In this way, training would begin with *what* the leader needs to do, not how to *be* or even *how* to do these tasks. This approach ensures that trainees develop an understanding of what their role entails, and their individual theoretical orientations and knowledge of techniques can inform the methods they select to enact their roles and functions.

When we teach prospective group leaders about stages of group development, they are more able to understand the processes and events that occur in their groups. When they learn various essential techniques, they accumulate a repertoire of interventions they might choose in certain situations or with particular members. If we also teach them the *functions* they must perform as a group counselor, they are much better to understand the purpose of what they will do. When they learn about leadership styles, they can make decisions about which styles are most appropriate for the groups they will lead. This kind of training provides a scaffold upon which future group leaders can conceptualize the rest of the learning.

Practice Implications

When we have more robust research on the relationships between how well leaders perform the necessary functions and member outcomes, leaders can self-monitor and reflect on whether and how carefully they have used this information to guide their practice. This, of course, means that we bridge the gap between research and practice that has been observed repeatedly in the literature. Practitioners are professionals who want to do the best job for clients and members, and if the findings are robust across situations and clientele, they will be receptive. Some practitioners may want to incorporate some assessment of their enactment of functions into their own groups to gain another perspective on their behavior. Others may be highly motivated and arrange to videotape their own sessions, or a sample of them, and evaluate their own performance. This implies that we develop good rating forms that would be useful not just to researchers but to conscientious practitioners.

Conclusion

Leader functions and styles have been the subject of theoretical writings and some research for more than half a century. Several classic studies have been widely influential, and although the studies themselves were innovative and thorough, each has limitations that should give us pause before uncritical adoption of their findings. New research, perhaps utilizing new technological methods, is sorely needed to expand our knowledge of these two essential features of group counseling that could have such important implications for training and practice.

Understanding the essential functions of group leaders, who provide a template for designing training experiences, could help to inform practitioners about how they might best approach their groups. I am not the first to call for more, and more rigorous, research on these topics. I hope the group-work field, with all the new tools available, will finally heed the call.

References

Anderson, L. F., & Robertson, S. E. (1985). Group facilitation: Functions and skills. *Small Group Behavior, 16*, 139–156.

Bales, R. F. (1958). Task roles and social roles in problem-solving groups. In E. E. Maccoby, T. M. Newcomb, & E. L. Hartley (Eds.), *Reading in social psychology*. New York: Holt, Rinehart, & Winston.

Bales, R. F., & Slater, P. E. (1955). Role differentiation in small decision-making groups. In T. Parsons & R. F. Bales (Eds.), *Family, socialization, and interaction processes*. New York: Free Press.

Bass, B. E. (1981). *Stogdill's handbook of leadership: A survey of theory and research*. New York: Free Press.

Bates, M., Johnson, C. D., & Blaker, K. E. (1982). *Group leadership: A manual for group counseling leaders*. Denver, CO: Love Publishing.

Bednar, R. L., & Kaul, T. J. (1994). Experiential group research: Can the canon fire? In A. E. Bergin & S. L. Garfield (Eds.), *Handbook of psychotherapy and behavior change* (4th ed., pp. 631–663). New York: John Wiley & Sons.

Capuzzi, D., Gross, D. R., & Stauffer, M. D. (2006). *Introduction to group work* (4th ed.). Denver, CO: Love Publishing.

Cartwright, D., & Zander, A. (1960). *Group dynamics: Research and theory* (2nd ed.). New York: Harper & Row.

Dies, R. R. (1983). Clinical implications of research on leadership in short-term group psychotherapy. In R. R. Dies & K. R. MacKenzie (Eds.), *Advances in group psychotherapy: Integrating research and practice* (pp. 27–75). Madison, CT: International Universities Press.

Dinkmeyer, D. C., & Muro, J. C. (1971). *Group counseling: Theory and practice*. Itasca, IL: F. E. Peacock.

Dinkmeyer, D. C., & Muro, J. C. (1979). *Group counseling: Theory and practice* (2nd ed.). Itasca, IL: F. E. Peacock.

Fiedler, F. E. (1971). Validation and extension of the contingency model of leadership effectiveness: A review of empirical findings. *Psychological Bulletin, 76*, 128–148.

Gladding, S. T. (2003). *Group work: A counseling specialty*. Upper Saddle River, NJ: Merrill-Prentice Hall.

Hersey, P. (1984). *The situational leader*. New York: Warner.

Hersey, P., & Blanchard, K. (1972). *Management of organizational behavior: Utilizing human resources* (2nd ed.). Englewood Cliffs, NJ: Prentice Hall.

Hersey, P., & Blanchard, K. (1977). *Management of organizational behavior: Utilizing human resources* (3rd ed.). Englewood Cliffs, NJ: Prentice Hall.

Jacobs, E. E., Harvill, R. L., & Masson, R. L. (2002). *Group counseling: Strategies and skills* (5th ed.). Pacific Grove, CA: Brooks/Cole.

Johnson, D. W., & Johnson, F. P. (1994). *Joining together: Group theory and group skills*. Boston: Allyn & Bacon.

Kemp, C. G. (1970). *Perspectives on the group process* (2nd ed.). New York: Houghton Mifflin.

Kivlighan, D. (1997). Leader behavior and therapeutic gain: An application of situational leadership theory. *Group Dynamics: Theory, Research, and Practice, 1*, 32–38.

Krieg, F. J. (1988). *Group leadership, training, and supervision manual*. Muncie, IN: Accelerataed Development, Inc.

Lewin, K., Lippitt, R., & White, L. K. (1946). Patterns of aggressive behavior in experimentally created "social climates." In P. L. Harriman (Ed.), *Twentieth century psychology: Recent developments in psychology* (pp. 200–230). New York: Arno Press. (Original work published 1939)

Lieberman, M. A., & Golant, M. (2002). Leader behaviors as perceived by cancer patients in professionally directed support groups and outcomes. *Group Dynamics: Theory, Research, and Practice, 6*, 267–276.

Lieberman, M. A., Yalom, I. D., & Miles, M. B. (1973). *Encounter groups: First facts*. New York: Basic Books.

Meade, R. D. (1970). Leadership studies of Chinese and Chinese-Americans. *Journal of Cross-Cultural Psychology, 1*, 325–332.

McGregor, D. (1960). *The human side of enterprise*. New York: McGraw-Hill.

Napier, R. W., & Gershenfeld, M. K. (2004). *Groups: Theory and experience* (7th ed.). Boston: Houghton Mifflin.

Ouchi, W. (1981). *Theory Z*. Reading, MA: Addison-Wesley.

Peterson, J. V., & Nisenholz, B. (1998). *Orientation to counseling* (4th ed.). New York: Allyn & Bacon.

Posthuma, B. W. (1996). *Small groups in counseling and therapy*. Boston: Allyn & Bacon.

Rose, S. R. (2006, August 11). *Leadership style and member satisfaction in treatment groups*. Paper presented at the annual meeting of the American Sociological Association, Montreal, Quebec, Canada. Retrieved from http://www.allacademic.com/meta/p102966_index.html

Scheidlinger, S. (1980). The psychology of leadership revisited: An overview. *Group, 4*, 5–17.

Schutz, W. C. (1961). On group composition. *Journal of Abnormal and Social Psychology, 62*, 275–281.

Shapiro, J. L. (1978). *Methods of group psychotherapy and encounter: A tradition of innovation*. Itasca, IL: F. E. Peacock.

Shechtman, Z., & Toren, Z. (2009). The effect of leader behavior on processes and outcomes in group counseling. *Group Dynamics: Theory, Research, and Practice, 13*, 218–223.

Stogdill, R. M. (1974). *Handbook of leadership*. New York: Free Press.

Tinsley, H. E. A., Roth, J. A., & Lease, S. H. (1989). Dimensions of leadership and leadership style among group intervention specialists. *Journal of Counseling Psychology, 36*, 48–53.

Trotzer, J. P. (1977). *The counselor and the group: Integrating theory, training, and practice*. Monterrey, CA: Brooks/Cole.

White, R., & Lippitt, R. (1960). Leader behavior and member reaction in three "social climates." In D. Cartwright & A. Zander (Eds.), *Group dynamics: Research and theory* (2nd ed., pp. 527–553). New York: Harper & Row.

Yalom, I. (1975). *Theory and practice of group psychotherapy* (2nd ed.). New York: Basic Books.

Yalom, I. (1985). *Theory and practice of group psychotherapy* (3rd ed.). New York: Basic Books.

Group Leadership Teaching and Training: Methods and Issues

Nina W. Brown

Abstract

Literature searches produced few evidence based studies on group leadership teaching methods. The consensus from professional experts is that group leadership training encompasses three dimensions: knowledge, leader personal development, and techniques and skills. Much of the attention is given to the use of experiential groups as a teaching learning strategy and the procedural and ethical concerns that surround its use. This chapter presents historical and current research on teaching models, professional mental health organizations' training standards, experiential groups, cultural and diversity concerns, ethics, teaching and training methods, major training issues, and recommendations.

Keywords: groupleadership training, leadershipteaching models, experiential group training, groupleader training standards

Introduction

The basic questions that guide group leadership training for mental health professionals are as follows:

- What do effective group leaders need to know?
- What personal qualities and personal inner development do effective group leaders need to have?
- What techniques and strategies do effective group leaders use?
- What training methods and processes are most effective?

This presentation focuses on research that addresses these questions, and highlights evidence, findings, and major issues and concerns. The methods and issues around supervision and supervised practice are addressed in another chapter and are not a part of this presentation. The designation of "mental health professional" is intended to include all professions, such as psychologists, counselors, social workers, and psychiatrists.

Beginning the discussion is a current definition for *group leadership* and an overview of some major theories and models. The training standards for group leaders provided by some professional mental health organizations have received some attention in the literature, and these studies are reviewed. Mental health professionals work in a variety of settings, with varied clientele; and there is a need for training programs to prepare them to lead various types of groups. This section describes the categories for differing types of groups, their commonalties, and their varying leadership needs. Following this presentation is a description of different teaching models retrieved from the literature, and these are presented in five categories based on the model's emphasis: didactic, simulation and role-play, process and therapy groups, observation, and skills training.

Most of the studies in the past 10–15 years have focused on experiential groups as a group leadership training modality, with particular emphasis on both the learning potential and outcomes and the ethical concerns. This section begins with a presentation of the principles of experiential learning as the foundation for using training experiential groups. However, there can be some confusion about what is being done or meant as some studies use the concept of personal growth groups as being the same as training experiential groups. The intent and boundaries become blurred in this instance, and serious ethical concerns emerge. These concerns, as identified from the literature, center on protection of trainees, the instructor's role, and confidentiality.

Important parts of any training for group leadership are teaching culture and diversity sensitivity and awareness, and ethics. This discussion about culture and diversity emphasizes the importance of these factors, summarizes multicultural competency models, and presents some basic attributes and communication skills for group leaders that facilitate multicultural and diversity sensitivity.

Most of the ethical concerns raised in the literature are about the use of training experiential groups, and these are presented and discussed. A current emphasis is on how to make experiential learning ethically sound and responsible. The next section describes teaching strategies that are categorized as listening, experiential, writing, and practicing. Examples for each are provided, as are the advantages and disadvantages. The final section presents some training needs as developed from this review of the literature and makes recommendations for training needs.

Definition, Theories, and Models of Group Leadership
Definition

Group leadership can be defined and described in numerous ways, but current definitions seem to emphasize the collaborative aspects between the leader and group members. This is an important point when teaching group leadership as trainees can begin their studies with a misunderstanding and misperception of the tasks and functions for group leaders. A definition that captures modern perceptions of group leadership is, "A reciprocal, transactional, and sometimes transformational process in which cooperating individuals are permitted to influence and motivate others to promote the attainment of group and individual goals" (Forsyth, 1999, p. 343).

Expanding the definition includes the following points (Forsyth, 1999):

1. There is mutuality and reciprocity among the leader, group members, and the group as a whole.

2. Both the leader and group members can profit from the process. This is known as a *social exchange process*.

3. The group can be a transformational process, affecting members' motivation, confidence, and satisfaction through the leader's attention to group cohesion strategies that bring members together and an interpersonal feedback loop to encourage change in beliefs, attitudes, and behavior. (Bass, 1985a, 1985b, 1997; Bass, Avolio, & Goldheim, 1987).

4. Motivation and encouragement for productivity and constructive change outcomes are achieved through cooperation and collaboration and not through the use of force, power, control, or coercion.

5. The leader provides and fosters a group climate and process that emphasize goal(s) attainment.

Having a clear understanding of what group leadership is or can be provides both trainees and instructors with a blueprint for strategies to develop group leadership as an art and as a science. Trainees become more aware of the positive contributions members make, the limits of leader responsibility and power, the reciprocal nature of group leadership understanding, and competencies.

Theories and Models

Also helpful in the instruction are models of group leadership. It is interesting to note that many trainees begin their study with little or no understanding of what group leaders are or do, and what they do understand is based on their limited past experiences as group members if they had any, although many have not had such experiences. Many tend to perceive the leader as a teacher with lessons to be taught to group members, as a social director who should keep members entertained and feeling comfortable and pleasant, and even as someone in a power position who tells members how to learn and who can "fix" conditions and/or solve problems. These are misperceptions of the leader's role and function that must be addressed in the preparation of group leaders.

Understanding that there are diverse models of group leadership could be helpful, especially when preparing leaders for a variety of types of groups. Examples for group leadership models include styles (Lewin, Lippitt, & White, 1939; Lieberman, Yalom, & Miles, 1973), situational (Hersey & Blanchard, 1976), contingency (Fiedler, 1978), transformational

(Bass, 1997), and leadership exchange (Johnson & Johnson 2008).

The *style* model of group leadership refers to the preferred mode for leading groups: autocratic, democratic, or laissez-faire. Autocratic leaders assume that the power and control are invested in the leader and conduct the group accordingly. Democratic leaders assume that power and control are shared by the leader and group members. Laissez-faire leaders permit the group to have the power and control and can assume a hands-off perspective.

Situational leadership is contingent on the maturity of group members and has two factors: relationship and task. The leader assumes a different role depending on the maturity of group members uses varied strategies to accommodate members' needs and moves through the phases of telling, selling, participatory, to delegating.

The *contingency* model proposes that leadership effectiveness relies on both the personal characteristics of the leader and the nature of the group situation. Leadership is flexible, moving back and forth between task orientation and maintenance orientation to better adjust to the group's needs at different times.

The model for *transformational* leadership proposes that leaders must exert influence on group members if they are to change or transform. Leaders are active and goal oriented, should have idealized influence, provide inspirational motivation and intellectual stimulation, and attend to individualized considerations.

Evidence-Based Research

Stogdill (1974) bemoaned the lack of positive outcomes for studies of techniques to train group leaders at that time. The evidence for effective training techniques is still under development at this time. The varying needs for leadership strategies in different types of groups that could provide a foundation for preparing group leaders require more empirical validation. However, the work being conducted on the Group Psychotherapy Intervention Scale shows considerable promise for providing some evidence-based research to guide the education and training of group leaders. What follows summarizes some of the research done to date.

Burlingame, MacKenzie, and Strauss (2004) provide a model that summarizes and categorizes group therapeutic benefits that are drawn from empirical studies on group interventions with diverse populations. The categories that seem to have evidence of effectiveness for group members

are as follows: formal change theory that guides the leader's choice of intervention; small-group process that emphasizes the mechanisms of change, such as the various therapeutic factors; client and leader characteristics, relating attributes, and communication; and group structural factors. This model can be used as a general guide for course content and has research evidence that the particular knowledge and skills have been shown to produce positive results for group members. The Association for Specialists in Group Work's (ASGW) training standards, the American Group Psychotherapy Association's (AGPA) core standards, and other such guidelines provide additional clarification for specific content for each category.

A research based system for understanding effective group leader techniques and interventions is seen in the studies on the Group Psychotherapy Intervention Rating Scale (GPIRS) (Burlingame, Fuhriman, & Johnson, 2002; Chapman, Baker, Porter, Thayer, & Burlingame, 2010; Snijders, Trijsburg, & de Groot, 2006). The scale is used to rate the extent to which a group leader uses specific basic skills such as the following:

• Structuring sessions (Burlingame et al. 2004; Kaul & Bednar, 1986; Rohde & Stockton, 1994)
• Group norms (DeLucia-Waack & Fauth, 2004)
• Modeling, feedback, and self-disclosure (DeLucia-Waack & Fauth, 2004; Fuhriman & Burlingame, 2001; Kivlighan & Lilly, 1997)
• Fostering the emergence of group therapeutic factors such as cohesion (Burlingame et al., 2002)
• The importance of the group leader's therapeutic and relating factors (Burlingame et al., 2002)
• Maintaining an emotional presence (Burlingame et al., 2002; Chapman et al., 2010)

The GPIRS has three empirically derived domains, and each domain has specific group leader behaviors and tasks. These behaviors and tasks are valuable as guides to teaching and developing group leaders as these are specific and researched based as having a positive and effective impact on the group and its members. The domains, tasks, and examples are as follows (Baker, 2006):

Domain 1–Group Structuring: Set treatment expectations (rationale, goals, address fears, and anxieties), establish group procedures (participation, rules, confidentiality), role preparation (member responsibilities)

Domain 2–Verbal Interactions: Verbal style and interaction, modeling here and now interactions, relevant and appropriate self-disclosure, feedback that is positive and corrective, and teaching constructive confrontation.

Domain 3–Creating and Maintaining a Therapeutic Emotional Climate: The leader's relating attributes–(warmth, caring, concern, nondefensiveness, and so on); developing an accepting and encouraging group climate where feelings, thoughts, and ideas can be expressed and interpersonal learning occurs; and the group leader's emotional presence.

Cross-cultural validation of the GPIRS continues, with the most recent study conducted at the Utah State Hospital where 60 groups were evaluated to determine if the quality of leader intervention would be enhanced by teaching the leaders the basic group skills as delineated by the scale. Group leaders were hospital staff in disciplines such as social work, nursing, occupational therapy, recreational therapy, and psychiatric technicians. Preliminary analyses show increases in behaviors and tasks across all domains after training for each discipline, with psychiatric technicians having the greatest increases. Group leaders were able to more frequently focus on here and now interactions, use verbal modeling, foster member self-disclosure, appropriately give and receive feedback, refrain from hostility, and prevent problem interactions (Chapman et al., 2010).

Hilsenroth, Ackerman, Clemence, Strarsle, and Handler (2002) investigated the effects of structured clinical training for therapists and found that the most positive effects on both clients' and therapists' perceptions of therapeutic alliance were enhanced when therapists were specifically trained in some skills. The structured clinical program focused on the skills to build rapport, developing collaboration and setting collaborative treatment goals, empathic responding, responsiveness to the client's needs, preparing the client for psychotherapy, exploring the client's relationships and related problems, and attending to the client–therapist interaction.

Training Standards

The ASGW's (2000) *Professional Standards for the Training of Group Workers* further clarified the 1994 standards that set basic training needs for group workers and provided guidelines for specialization training. The guidelines for specialization have general standards and four group specialization–specific standards: task groups, psychoeducational groups, group counseling, and group psychotherapy.

General training standards include a minimum of content (a 3-hour graduate course of formal instruction) and experiential (10 clock hours minimum). Expected knowledge and skill requirements are delineated for nature and scope of practice, assessment, planning, interventions, leadership and coleadership, and ethical and diversity-competent practice. Fundamental specialization recommendations are formal coursework to cover knowledge and skills about the specialty, and a minimum of 30–45 clock hours of supervised practice in the specialty area.

Implementation guidelines propose that the basic standards can be provided in a single course that covers all of the Council for Accreditation of Counseling and Related Educational Programs (CACREP) accreditation standards and could also include the minimum 10 hours of clinical instruction. Also proposed and recommended is additional coursework for each desired specialty area, clinical instruction, and supervised clinical experience. The standards recommend that 25% of all required supervised clinical experiences, such as practica and internships, be focused on group work.

The international Association for the Advancement of Social Work in Groups (AASWG) published standards for social work practice with group in 2005. The purpose for the standards was to provide a guide for social work practice with group, and these can also guide training as a group leader. The standards have six sections: I, values and types of knowledge for group work practice; II, tasks and expectations for the pregroup phase, such as planning, required knowledge, and new group formation tasks and skills; III, tasks and skills for the beginning phase; IV, tasks and skills for the middle phase; V, tasks and skills for the ending phase; and VI, ethical considerations.

Refer to Chapter 5 for more extensive discussion of group work training standards across professional disciplines.

Studies on Training Guidelines

The research literature on training standards and guidelines for potential group leaders is diverse. For example, Huhn, Zimpfer, Waltman, and Williamson (1985); Merta, Wolfgang, and McNeil (1993), and Wilson, Conyne, and Ward (1994) surveyed master's-level counseling programs; and Fuhriman and Burlingame (2001) surveyed predoctoral psychology programs, master's-level social work programs, and postdoctoral psychiatry programs to determine compliance with training standards. Dies (1980) noted that "the literature (on training and supervision) is often confusing and contradictory" (p. 169), and the same can be said today.

Huhn et al. (1985) analyzed data from 76 institutions of higher education with one or more faculty who were members of the American Association for Counseling and Development (now known as the American Counseling Association) and members of either the Association for Counselor Education and Supervision or the ASGW. A 45% response rate was received. Their findings reported that programs did not clearly distinguish the goals for group leader preparation as either providing basic skills in group work or preparing them to become group work specialists. It should be noted that the CACREP accreditation standards have addressed most of these concerns.

Merta et al. (1993) surveyed 504 academic units identified as counselor preparation programs by Hollis and Wantz (1990), with a 54% response rate. This survey was focused on the use of experiential training groups as part of a course and extracted five models as descriptive of their use. The models included no experiential training group (12%), no feedback experiential group where the group is led by an outside leader and the instructor for the course receives no feedback (8%), a feedback experiential group where the instructor for the course does receive feedback (19%), an instructor observed experiential group where the instructor for the course observes and someone outside the class leads the group (22%), and the instructor for the course leads the experiential group (39%).

Wilson et al. (1994) surveyed 86 master's level, CACREP accredited counseloreducation programs with a 79% response rate. The purpose was to determine the extent to which the ASGW knowledge and skills core standards and specializations were met and the extent to which mastery was attained for these. The majority of programs providing self-assessments reported over 90% of competencies met for both knowledge and skills for the core standards. Most programs also had specialty areas and reported high levels for both knowledge and skills for group psychotherapy, psychoeducational group work, and task and work groups.

Fuhriman and Burlingame (2001) surveyed nationally accredited mental health training programs for the American Psychiatric Association ($n = 199$), the American Psychological Association ($n = 301$), and the National Association of Social Workers ($n = 130$). The response rate was 51%. The results varied significantly among the three disciplines, and they concluded that there was an important need for consensual validity about values and knowledge for group leadership training and an integration of science, training, and practice.

Following on the work of Fuhriman and Burlingame (2001), Markus and King (2003) surveyed predoctoral internships on the extent of training provided in group psychotherapy. Their conclusions were that, overall, graduate programs and predoctoral internship programs do not provide the necessary training.

All studies found a greater coverage of knowledge base material than for experiential, practicing group leadership, and supervised group leadership practice.

Types of Groups

Academic and other training programs present material that will prepare group leaders to facilitate different types of groups, and each type can call for differing sets of leadership knowledge, level of personal development, and techniques and skills. There are numerous ways to categorize types of groups, and this presentation will use the following categories: cognitively focused, problem-centered focus, blended cognitive and affective, and distance.

Cognitively focused groups have a main emphasis on cognitive material and dissemination of information, although affective components are still present for these groups. Included in this category are educational groups, such as parenting education; task groups, such as team development; and skills training, such as social skills and study skills groups.

Counseling and therapy/psychotherapy groups are more problem-centered and incorporate emotional expression, exploration, and intensity as part of the group. Counseling groups are defined here as groups having a wellness perspective while, at the same time, being problem-centered. Examples of counseling groups include grief and loss with an absence of complicated mourning, relationship building, and other life transitions. Therapy/psychotherapy groups usually have character change as a goal where assisting and guiding members to overcome deep-seated and longstanding behaviors and attitudes that negatively affect their lives and well-being. Examples for therapy/psychotherapy groups are addictions treatment, psychiatric and emotional disturbances, and deep seated medical illnesses that have a mental health component such as eating disorders.

Blended groups have a balance of cognitive and affective components where both components are important and play major roles. Groups categorized as blended are psychoeducational groups, mental health professionals' training groups, prevention groups, and support/self-help groups.

Training groups for mental health professionals generally have two goals, personal growth and understanding of group and leadership functions, thus placing them in the category for blended instead of skills training. Variations include process groups and T-groups. *Process groups* focus on providing members with opportunities to explore their inner worlds, unresolved issues, unfinished business, and interpersonal relationships. Process groups use a wellness perspective and the here and now interactions and relationships in the group for exploration. *T-groups* emphasize group members' study of the group's process after a session.

Support groups are organized around a specific issue, concern, or condition and focus on education, coping mechanisms, and mutual encouragement and support among members.

Self-help groups are also organized around a specific issue, problem, or condition and are designed for members to provide mutual assistance and support. These groups are usually not dependent on the leader for organization and facilitation.

Distance facilitated groups require a differing perspective for leadership and for training leaders about groups. The lack of face to face time and interaction decreases the impact of understanding some of the concepts and practices. Emotional intensity can be lost when distance is involved. Distance facilitated groups are also termed *cybergroups*, *e-therapy*, *virtual groups*, and *electronically linked groups*. They use the resources of television, the Internet, and other such communication devices to deliver group experiences, such as education team development and therapy at a distance where some, or all, of the members and/ or the leader are not physically present. Businesses and corporations make more extensive use of these resources, but providers of mental health services are increasing their use for this mode of delivery.

Advantages of e-groups include more effective use of time, reduced travel, participants' feelings of safety, and ease of recording of sessions. Limitations include a lack of security, and confidentiality and privacy issues (unless communications are encrypted). In addition, group leaders have less information about members and the group since they cannot see or sense the group as a whole, screening for inclusion in the group may be severely limited, the possibilities of technical failure of equipment exists, and the legalities of practicing across state lines are still murky.

Table 19.1 presents an overview of group leader facilitating tasks and functions relative to the type of group. While almost all tasks and functions are needed for all types of groups, the level and extent of these can differ.

Training Needs Commonalities

Regardless of the type of group, there appear to be some commonalities for training needs that can be used to guide instruction. These are presented in the following three dimensions: knowledge, personal factors, and techniques and skills.

The knowledge dimension includes planning sequence, structural and executive functions; stages of group development; group dynamics; facilitative/ therapeutic group factors; leadership tasks; the roles and impact of intangibles such as resistance,

Table 19.1 Types of groups and need for leader facilitating tasks/functions

Type of Group	Safety & Trust	Interactions	Communication	Feeling Problem Expression	Conflict Solving	Process Resolution	Commentary
Educational	L	L	M	L	M	L	NA
Skills training	M	M	M	L	L	L	NA
Teams/task	M	M	H	L	H	H	L
Psychoeducational	H	H	H	M	H	H	M
Self-help	M	M	M	H	M	L	L
Support	M	M	M	M	M	M	L
Counseling	H	H	H	H	M	M	H
Psychotherapy	H	H	H	H	M	H	H

L, low need; M, moderate need; H, high need; NA, not applicable.

defenses, transference, and countertransference; the contributions and influences of cultural and diversity concerns; and ethics.

The personal factors dimension refers to the extent of inner development for the leader to provide resources for relationship building attributes of warmth, caring, tolerance, respect, and positive regard; the courage to risk; faith in group process; an ability to maintain an emotional presence in the group; extensive, stable/healthy adult narcissism; expertise in managing and containing personal emotions; the ability to tune into and identify group process; awareness of personal issues that have the potential to impact and affect the group, such as unresolved familyoforigin issues and unfinished business from past experiences; and the capacity to be empathic.

The techniques and skills dimension includes an ability to make group level interventions, such as blocking, linking, and making process commentary; communication skills, such as paraphrasing and active listening; modeling interpersonal relating and communication; competency in confrontation and conflict resolution; understanding how to observe, identify, and use group dynamics; promotion of interpersonal relating, communication, and constructive feedback among group members; facilitating the emergence of therapeutic factors; and the ability to teach members group-membership skills, social interpersonal skills, problem-solving and decision-making skills.

Teaching Models

Berman (1975) described the questions whose answers guide training programs as follows: What defines the beginning for training, What methods should be used? How much training is sufficient for entry level group leaders, and How should the training be sequenced? Scant research evidence was available at that time to support the efficacy of the decisions or answers for the questions, and somewhat more evidence is available today. Presented first are five categories or models with a summary of the research for each: didactic, simulation seminar or role-playing, process and therapy groups, observation, and skills training. These were categorized by the focus and emphasis, together with the positive and negative aspects of each.

Didactic Models

Didactic models emphasize cognitive learning about group leadership and use teaching methods of lectures, readings, and discussion. Trainees are introduced to concepts and practices, theories, and, in some instances, research on major group topics. Trainees are able to learn definitions, stay detached, and have a body of knowledge. Fidler (1973) summed up the major negative outcome for this model in noting that the trainees do not experience what they trying to learn. For example, the concept of the importance of establishing trust and safety in the group can be easily explained and learned. However, the experience of either having feelings of safety and trust or the lack of these provides a higher level of understanding of their importance. Facts and other information are important but do not convey the deeper understanding of the impact on the group and on the members that adding the experiencing would do.

Many models and group therapists favor use of didactic approaches as the introduction for learning group leadership (Berger, 1969; Boenheim, 1963; Stockton & Toth, 1996; Jacobs, Masson, & Harvill, 2009) and do so even when they also have other focal elements, such as role-play. Indeed, Stockton and Toth (1996) present an integrated model where didactic instruction is only the first step. Most models include some didactic instruction, and it would be ideal to have a course of didactic information as preparation for other groupleadership components, such as supervised groupleader experiences and an experiential or therapy group. However, few training programs can have a separate course for this as many training programs can be limited to just one semester-long class.

However, the experts do agree that there is a body of knowledge that is important for group leaders to learn and the specificity of this information is seen in the training standards of the ASGW, the AGPA's certified group therapist standards, and the counseling profession's accreditation standards of CACREP and other training programs. The strategies used in the didactic model may be the most efficient to teach the volume of cognitive material in spite of the negative aspects of the didactic model.

Simulation Models

Simulation seminar or *role-play models* allow trainees to experience some aspects of group membership and group leadership without self-disclosure (Berman, 1975). Kaczkowski and Fenton (1985) and Romano (1998) propose simulation as a teaching model and point out how these can produce positive learning experiences by promoting observational learning. The simulation model uses parts of Bandura's (1977) theory of learning, which proposes that observational learning helps organize ideas and behaviors and can facilitate understanding of varied ways to know, understand, and act.

Kaczkowski and Fenton's (1985) simulation model has four steps. The beginning simulation exercise is designed to present types of leader interventions and stages of group development. The second exercise presents events likely to occur in a particular stage of group development. A predesigned scenario is developed to encompass and illustrate events for a particular stage. The third exercise is based on SCRIPT (structured counseling role, interpersonal phased interaction) (Kaczkowski & Fenton, 1985). This one-page outline presents the characteristics of a Cohen & Smith (1976) developmental stage, personality descriptors, personal attributes, and personal concerns for group members.

The group goal is described, and the simulations are performed. The fourth exercise has a group focused simulation and role-play based on a diagnostic category from the *Diagnostic and Statistical Manual*. This model relies heavily on preparation for the simulations that use Cohen and Smith's 30 scenes of critical incidents, the intervention guide developed from Lieberman et al.'s (1973) leadership behaviors, and class discussions of this material.

Romano (1998) presents a simulated group counseling model as an additional experience to didactic coursework. The model has the following components: formation and group roles, co-facilitation, observing, group discussion, assignments, and the instructor's role. These are described in Table 19.2.

These two examples highlight some positive aspects of simulation and role-play; they can be used

Table 19.2 Simulated group counseling model

Instructor

1. Prepare students for role-play and co-facilitation

2. Organize and supervise observers

3. Review assignments

4. Circulate among groups and supervise

5. Meet with observers and group for the discussion

6. Meet with observers after the discussion (#5)

Student Group Co-facilitators

1. Co-facilitate two or more group sessions

2. Meet with instructor prior to group session(s) to plan

3. Meet with instructor between sessions

4. Meet with instructor after completing co-facilitation duties

5. Meet with observers for discussion sessions after group

6. Write a paper on the leadership experience

Observers (Graduate Students Who Complete the Simulated Group-Counseling Experience)

1. Meet with instructor to receive instruction and orientation

2. Record reactions and observations on a specific form to be given to the group members and co-facilitators

3. Facilitate a 30-minute discussion with group members and co-facilitators immediately following the group session

4. Attend a training and supervision session conducted by the instructor immediately following the discussion (#3)

Class Assignments

1. Keep a journal focused on group process for sessions as experienced by the role-play character

2. Participate as a co-facilitator, as a role-play group member, and in the after-group discussion

3. Write an integrative summary paper about the simulation group experience

Source: Reprinted from Romano (1998) with permission of Taylor & Francis.

when other methods for "reallife" experiences are not available, convey a feeling component, and are perceived as safer for the trainees. Negative aspects include the potential for producing competition and acting out among the participants, and role-playing reduces authenticity and does not demonstrate how to use genuine experiencing when leading a group.

Process and Therapy Group Models

Process and therapy groups as teaching models are really separate as the literature is very unified and clear that training groups are not therapy groups. Therapy groups will be presented here as a suggested adjunct to other formal academic and training experiences. This discussion will focus on the positive and negative aspects of using process groups for teaching and learning. A separate section, Experiential Learning and Experiential Groups, also addresses process groups, with attention given to the methodological and ethical dimensions.

Yalom (1995) promotes the dual roles of observer and participant for more intensive and expansive learning, Woody (1971) the use of sensitivity group training, Grothjahn (1970) and Horowitz (1968) the use of unstructured analytic groups, and Tschuschke and Greene (2002) the use of intensive 2-day process groups. Lewin (1944) was the first to introduce and specify a procedure for the group to study its own process as a means for learning group leadership, and that model has been adopted and modified through the years. A process group model where members are both observers and participants seems to produce intensified personal and personalized learning that is unique. Among the many positive aspects and outcomes are the following:

- Experiencing the impact and influence of the group as a social system
- Observing how anxieties and resistances are triggered by the group
- Increasing awareness of personal relating and communicating behaviors and skills

- Gaining a deeper understanding of the leader's role through personal identifications and dependency and increased awareness of unrealistic expectations for the leader's power and knowledge
- Experiencing the member role with both effective and counterproductive behaviors and attitudes
- Obtaining a different and broader perception about the impact of inclusion and exclusion
- Learning to appropriately self-disclose and understanding how difficult this can be
- Understanding and applying the group contract
- Experiencing group development stages, the emergence of some or all group therapeutic factors, the interpersonal feedback loop, and the power of here and now interactions

Although there are differences in definitions of *process* among experts (Brown, 2003), all of the descriptions of process groups in training seem to have the following components: an emphasis and focus on here and now experiencing; examination of relationships and communication among group members; group as a whole examination, observations, and commentary; empowerment of members to be in charge of their participation and self-disclosure; and experiencing of and relationships with the leader are explored.

Although out of group concerns, unresolved family of origin issues, and unfinished business from past experiences are not the focus for process groups, especially process training groups, these factors can and do emerge in process groups. However, they are not explored as they would be in therapy groups, and the primary focus remains on the current and immediate relationships among group members and between group members and the leader.

Table 19.3 presents the typical problems that can occur in process training groups. Additional information and studies are presented in the Experiential Learning and Experiential Groups section.

Table 19.3 Process training group issues and concerns

Increased competition among group members	Some members remain silent
Becomes a forum for expressing discontent with the training program and administrators	Low participation for some members
with the training program and administrators	Some members are passive
Heightened awareness and focus on future peer peer relationships that truncate participation	Intellectualized communication

Source: Reprinted from Berman (1975) with permission of Sage.

The Observation Model

Observation of groups in action is considered by many to be a desired method of teaching and learning (Berman, 1975; Stockton, Morran, & Kreiger, 2004; Yalom, 1995, 2005). Berman describes modes of observation as one-way mirrors, audio- or videotaping, and with an observer sitting with the group. Other modes are the fishbowl experience (Kane, 1995), observers entering the group to provide interventions (Kivlighan, Markin, Stahl, & Salahuddin, 2007), and demonstration groups (Furr & Barret, 2000). The usual intents and purposes for observation are reduction of uncertainty and ambiguity about how groups and leaders function; modeling of leadership behaviors; providing some distance and detachment so that group complex processes can be identified; and identifying effective and ineffective interventions.

There are considerably more negative than positive aspects for observation, with the majority of these impacting the group members being observed regardless of the mode. Table 19.4 presents the negative aspects divided into observer acts and attitudes, impact and reactions of group members, and the leader.

The leader can also be negatively affected with resentment for being observed; experiencing a conflict between observation and commitment to training and therapy; being exposed to criticism, some of which may be unfounded; can feel an increased need to respond on the basis of their exhibitionistic tendencies; concern and/or anxiety about making the "right" intervention; and a desire to protect the group members from intrusions. Although experts seem to favor observation as a teaching tool, there are so many negative effects and outcomes that it should be more carefully examined before implementation in a training program, even those that attend assiduously to ethical consideration.

Skills Based Models

Skills based models emphasize learning specific leadership skills. These skills are separated from process, identified individually, and are described,

Table 19.4   Observer's negative acts and attitudes and their impact

Observer's Acts	
Direct or indirect comments that attack the leader's techniques	
A tendency to identify with one or more group members	
Failure to monitor possible countertransference	
Focus on nonessentials	
Potential role confusion	
Become bored or zone out	
Make negative evaluations and/or judgments about group members	
Noise or other disruptions	
Impact on Group Members	
Fear of being negatively evaluated	Increased defensiveness
Reduced participation	Unannounced absences
Increased tardiness/absences	Increased anxiety and fear
Hidden or disguised resentment toward the leader	Reduced self-disclosure
Reduced willingness to engage in self-exploration	
Impact on the Group Leader	
Resentment for being observed	Feeling exposed to criticism
Conflict between observation and commitment to training	Feeling a need to "perform"
Concern about making the "right" intervention	Desire to protect the group

defined, and practiced with feedback similar to the approach used for teaching individual counseling skills. Teaching models that use a skills based approach include Baker, Daniels, and Greenley (1990), Bruce-Sanford (1998), Conyne and Cook (2004), Harvill, Masson, & Jacobs (1983), Ivey, Pedersen, and Ivey (2001), Smaby, Maddus, Torres-Rivera, & Zimmick (1999), and Toth, Stockton, and Erwin (1998).

Advantages for a skills based teaching approach include providing trainees with a specific behavior or set of behaviors for a focus at any one time; the ambiguity and complexity of the group is reduced, thus reducing some trainee anxiety; instruction is provided for what to do and say; trainees receive practice with immediate feedback; and the use of learning theory as a foundation. There are also disadvantages and drawbacks for this focus, such as the following:

- Many group leadership skills defined in the literature are more complex than those defined for individual counseling
- Isolating needed skills from the context in which they occur changes their form and function
- It is more difficult to identify and recognize needed interventions during group actions; thus, isolation of skills is not done in "real time"
- There can be an overreliance on a set of specific skills
- Skills that are taught can be inadequate for more complex group situations
- Application of skills can become rote, thus not meeting the needs of the group
- This approach does not capitalize on the dynamics and process of the group
- The "feeling" component of group leadership is deemphasized

Isolating and teaching specific skills provides trainees with answers for some of their typical concerns, such as "What am I supposed to do?" and/or "Am I doing it right?" However, the answers to these questions and concerns depend on many complexities of group that cannot be anticipated. While some skills can be taught and learned apart from the group process, many vital and important ones are more dependent on other factors, such as the individual needs of group members, the extent of personal development of the group leader, and the group dynamics and group as a whole concerns.

There are teaching models that integrate skill development as a component but not as the primary focus, for example, the model proposed by Stockton and Toth (1996). This model provides examples of integration where the primary focus is not just skill acquisition but provides for other variables to incorporate the complexity of group leadership.

Teaching the Art and the Science of Group Leadership

Berman (1975) captured the essence for most teaching models, and these approaches are still in use today. There are some additions and variations that have evolved, such as a greater use and debate about process groups for training; but most changes are refinements of what was being done over 30 years ago. Yet, Berman also noted then, "that the student cannot possibly experience the depth and breadth of the group psychotherapy field within the span of his predoctoral education" (p. 342). But few training programs and standards have adjusted to this reality, the components for needed group leadership competencies remain poorly defined and delineated, and effective teaching models cannot be developed until more clarity is achieved and evidence of efficacy found (Fuhriman & Burlingame, 2001; Merta et al., 1993) The importance of both the art and the science of group leadership needs to be respected in teaching models. Brown (2009) describes the art and the science as incorporating basic knowledge, the leader's needed inner development, and the skills and techniques needed for facilitation. The science component emphasizes knowledge, leader tasks, and skills. The art component focuses on the leader's personal qualities, attitudes, and inner experiencing as guides for understanding the group and its members, as a part of the decision-making process for interventions, and as an awareness of potential forces that could have negative impact. Both components interact in complex ways and are important and necessary for becoming an effective group leader.

Knowledge factors are critical to structuring the group and facilitating the emergence of constructive group processes. These factors provide the frame for defining the group and its work, contributing to the development of trust and safety in the group, highlighting the leader's competence for understanding and intervening and for keeping the group focused. Knowledge factors include creating a group, group dynamics, shaping group norms and the group climate, cultural and diversity issues and concerns, group therapeutic factors, ethics, and stages of group development.

Art factors focus primarily on the self of the group leader. The *self* refers to the importance of the group leader's personal development and how the self of the leader can significantly impact the group's functioning, progress, and cohesiveness as well as individual members' growth and development. These self factors are described as core attributes of genuineness, caring, and the like; tolerance of ambiguity and uncertainty; reduction of self-absorption and increase of self-reflection; awareness of potential countertransference and other intangible forces that can negatively impact the group and its members; the capacity to be empathic and to repair empathic failures; understanding what difficult behavior for the group and for individuals is intended to communicate; the ability to be emotionally present in the group; and identifying and facilitating the emergence of therapeutic factors.

Techniques and skills associated with group leadership can be learned, are a blend of art and science factors, and are mostly held in common for all theoretical approaches. For example, the importance of establishing a therapeutic relationship is significant for all kinds of groups, regardless of theoretical perspective. Some techniques and skills can be specific to a particular theoretical perspective, such as the Gestalt exercises. Examples of commonalities for techniques and skills include grouplevel intervention skills that are designed to support and encourage the whole group, such as linking and blocking, exercises and role-play, conflict resolution, encouraging and fostering interactions among group members, facilitating members' emotional expressiveness, and establishing trust and safety.

Experiential Learning and Experiential Groups

Major premises for experiential groups are based on the principles for experiential learning. These are the principles that underlie the groups for human relations training, T-groups, and other such training groups. These are also the principles for cooperative learning that has been successful in various academic courses at all levels. This discussion begins with a definition of *experiential learning* and its principles. It then moves to a review of studies about experiential groups for training group leaders in counseling and other mental health professions.

Definition

Johnson and Johnson (2008) define *experiential learning* as reflection about personal experiences that influences the action theory that guides the individual effectiveness of actions. It is individualistic, uses intentional reflection, and takes place in a

conscious state; and the intent is to learn how to be more effective. Contrasted to experiential learning is procedural learning, where one learns a skill, understands when and how it should be used, and practices to eliminate errors to attain an automated level of mastery.

Kurt Lewin (1944) highlighted the importance of active participation in groups as a means for learning new skills, modifying and developing new attitudes, and acquiring new knowledge. He proposed that learning is most effective and productive when group members interact, followed by reflection on this mutual experience. This perspective is the foundation for the human relations training movement and the work from the National Training Laboratories.

Experiential Groups

Experiential groups can assume many different forms, and this can be confusing when sorting through the literature as designations for training groups and personal growth groups in their many different formats can be used interchangeably. The 2000 ASGW standards and the 2009 CACREP standards mandate 10 clock hours of observation and participation as a group member or leader. When viewed as a program requirement rather than a course requirement, this opens the door for alternative ways to meet the standard. The change is from perceiving the requirement as part of a course which then reduces some of the ethical concerns that can be present for such a course requirement. However, the merging of experiential groups for training with personal growth groups blurs the boundaries and promotes numerous ethical concerns and problems.

Given the differences between the goals and purpose for training groups and personal growth groups, it is especially important that experiential groups used for training purposes have clearly stated goals and purpose and that these not be combined, merged, or confused with the goals and purpose for a personal growth group. While it is certainly possible to obtain some personal growth in the experiential training group experience, that is an additional positive outcome but is not to be expected, planned for, or mandated in any way.

Training groups and personal growth groups can be organized and conducted in a variety of ways. In the interest of clarity, each will be discussed separately. Training groups will be defined as experiential groups based on the principles of experiential learning as presented earlier, whose purpose is to teach elements of group leadership. Personal growth groups are defined as experiential groups whose purposes are to promote growth and development, increase awareness of unresolved issues and concerns that have the potential for countertransference when one becomes a group leader, and to increase relating attributes and communication skills. Each will be discussed separately.

Experiential Training Groups

Examples from the literature that illustrate the variations for these training groups include the following:

- AGPA 2-day institutes (Tschuschke & Greene, 2000)
- Fishbowl (Kane, 1995)
- Simulated (Bruce-Sanford, 1998; Romano, 1998)
- Structured groups workshops (Eicher, 1987)
- Using actors (Fall & Levitov, 2002)
- Group process (Gauron, Proctor, & Schroder, 1979; Horowitz, 1968; Lieberman et al., 1973; Semrad, 1969; Yalom, 1995)
- Skilled group training model (Smaby et al. 1999)
- Integrative (Stockton & Toth, 1996)
- Immersion (Brown, 1992)

Central to the concept of experiential groups as a means to prepare group leaders is the role of the observer-participant. That is, the idea that being both an observer of process and a participant in producing process permits an immersion experience similar to that experienced by group leaders without the responsibilities of leadership. Thus, the observer-participant can learn just how difficult it is to simultaneously tune into group dynamics, group as a-whole concerns, awareness and attendance to personal reactions and feelings and to also have to stay aware of other group members.

One defining characteristic for many of these cited groups is the efforts put forward in their design to address ethical concerns, such as dual relationships and protection of privacy. Most use the process group format described under Teaching Models, where group participants use the here and now immediate experiencing as material where disclosures about family of origin experiences, unfinished business from the past, and revealing secrets are not expected. These can and do emerge in some groups, but they are not expected or sought.

When the goal for the experiential training group is to assist in the integration of the cognitive and affective understanding about groups and how they function and to teach group leadership skills, the following positive outcomes for trainees can result:

- Learn to observe and identify group dynamics as they unfold
- Experience, with awareness, the movement of the group through some or all group development stages
- Identify therapeutic factors and how they emerge and manifest themselves during sessions
- Learn how to observe and participate at the same time
- Increase awareness of personal reactions to ambiguity, conflict, and intense emotions
- Identify resistance, defenses, transference, projections, and projective identification and experience the impact of these on the group
- Become more aware and sensitive to cultural and diversity differences and their impact
- Become aware of the complexity of groups, their dynamics and functions, and the necessary leadership responsibilities
- Understand the importance of the therapeutic relationship/alliance and the difficulties with establishing this for every group member
- Learn group level factors, such as themes, metaphors, and process
- Increase emotional presence
- Learn to give and receive constructive feedback

The literature also presents some major concerns about using these training experiential groups:

1. Trainees may experience role confusion between being a member and being a leader.
2. The boundary between therapy, or personal growth, and training can become blurred.
3. Trainees may not be developmentally ready but do not have an option of choosing when to be in the group.
4. The training group is mandatory in most academic training programs.
5. Ethical concerns in the literature list dual relationships, invasion of privacy, the potential for abuse of power, and lack of informed consent. (These ethical concerns are addressed in the section on Ethics.)
6. The class instructor may have two roles; facilitator and evaluator.

There seems to be considerable agreement among experts that a training experiential group is a significant and important component in the training for group leaders. The task then becomes one of structuring the experience to provide optimal learning opportunities and to responsibly address ethical concerns. Recommendations from the study by Merta and Sission (1991) include experiential training groups should be mandatory, the leader of these groups should not be the instructor or any faculty member in the department or program, no alternative to the training group should be provided or acceptable, the course instructor should be indirectly involved in the evaluation of the trainees, informed consent should be obtained prior to the trainee's enrollment in the program. A discussion about these and other recommendations for professional and responsible implementation of a training experiential group is presented in the final section.

Personal Growth Groups

Opportunities for trainees to experience a group focused on personal growth are recommended by many in the literature (Berman, 1975; Yalom, 2005) and by CACREP and AGPA's professional standards. ASGW's standards specify that trainees should have a minimum of 10 clock hours "observation of and participation in a group experience and/or as a group leader" (p. 5) (ASGW, 2000). Neither the NASW nor the APA accreditation standards specify a personal growth group experience as a part of group leadership training.

Personal growth groups and/or therapy groups can be opportunities to address unresolved family of origin and unfinished business from past experiences and to learn to increase interpersonal effectiveness. Other positive outcomes for these experiences that relate to becoming a group leader are to practice relating and communicating behaviors, increase awareness of personal resistance, foster appropriate emotional expression, and to identify characteristic behavior in conflict situations. The group would provide opportunities for the interpersonal feedback loop, where constructive feedback from other group members and the leader contributes to self-knowledge, self-understanding, and other forms of growth.

Many ethical concerns are taken care of when the groups are not a part of a course, the faculty in the program do not lead these, or they are stand-alone experiences. Fears and anxieties for trainees are reduced, allowing freer exploration of personal issues. However, one concern could be the extent to which the requirement or suggestion is beneficial to the participant who did not choose to take the group but either has that as a program requirement or was presented so strongly stated as to seem a requirement that freedom to choose did not appear to be an option.

An additional concern is that the literature does not specify the goals and objectives for a personal growth group experience, which does not allow participants to know in advance what is supposed to be accomplished. The literature lists some possible outcomes, but even a generalized agreed-upon goal would be helpful for both the leaders of these groups and the participants as the requirement/suggestion is a part of a training/degree program. It really appears from the literature that many are using the same term and concept but have different understandings and meanings for personal growth.

Culture and Diversity

The importance of cultural and diversity factors in groups cannot be overlooked or minimized when preparing group leaders. These factors play significant roles for self-identity of the leader and group members; how the person is perceived and responded to by others; conscious and unconscious stereotyping, prejudice, and bias for leaders and for members; and how these impact diagnosis and treatment planning, identification, and understanding of symptoms and the group leader's judgment (Neighbors, Jackson, Campbell, & Williams, 1989; Pavkov, Lewis, & Lyons, 1989; Salvendy, 1999; Strakowski et al., 1997; Whaley & Geller, 2007).

The ASGW published "Principles for diversity-competent group workers" in 1999. These principles seek to describe and define the areas where group leaders grow in knowledge and understanding of self and others in a sociopolitical and cultural context. Recognizing and respecting differences among people; how culture, privilege, social forces, and disabilities influence attitudes, beliefs, and perceptions for both group members and group leaders; and increasing one's awareness of personal biases, stereotypes, and the like and how these can impact the group and its members are cornerstones for these principles. Presented here are knowledge and skills expected for culture and diversity competent group leaders in three categories: awareness of self, awareness of group members' worldviews, and appropriate intervention strategies.

Definitions

Culture in this presentation is defined as a social group containing and transmitting memories and values from one generation to the next, including knowledge, beliefs, art, morals, law, behavioral patterns, customs, and habits (Sue, Akutsu &

Highski, 1987). *Diversity* includes the visible and invisible personal characteristics that are a function of time, genetics, life circumstance, and/or personal choice and that impact the perceptions of self and of others, including age, gender, sexual orientation, religion, and disability. Both factors can have considerable influences on roles assumed and expected, gender and sexual identity, class and status, race and ethnic identity, and so on. Thus, group leaders also have a responsibility to be sensitive to these factors for several group members, as well as attending to the individuality and separate needs of each member. This complexity is compounded by the impossibility of learning and understanding all the relevant aspects and nuances of culture and diversity factors for the varied group members.

Multicultural Competency Models

There are numerous multicultural competency models available from the literature, and most seem to follow the structure of focusing on awareness, knowledge, and skills (Arrendono et al. 1996; Fowers & Davidov, 2007). However, there is scant research evidence on the efficacy of these methods or even a base level to define competency. Further, some models seem to promote tendencies to generalize and categorize. Generalizing from a summary description of a culture to all who identify with that culture can lead to many misunderstandings, insults, and offenses that would make it difficult for the group leader to repair. Categorizing people or group members on the basis of visible characteristics can also lead to the same negative outcomes.

One underemphasized area that deserves attention is the role of multiple identities as having these defies categorization and makes generalization even more problematic. *Multiple identities* refers to individuals who have several cultural and/or diversity characteristics, all of which can be significant but usually one (or more) is more important for that particular individual. For example, a gay, Black, disabled male who is a member of a Jewish Temple cannot be easily categorized, and assuming which characteristic is most important to him as an identity is likely to be wrong, thus retarding the development of a meaningful therapeutic alliance.

These complexities make it difficult to sort out what and how to teach so that group leaders are able to constructively use culture and diversity factors and increase their contributions to the richness of the group. Because it is impossible to present sufficient information on multicultural competency in this chapter, readers are encouraged to seek out more information on this topic. What is presented is a summary of basic awareness, knowledge, and skills that are intended to promote group leaders' multicultural expertise.

Sue et al. (2007) propose that the following *awarenesses* are of importance for developing multicultural sensitivity: self-awareness of personal racial/cultural identity; increased awareness of personal assumptions, biases, prejudices, and stereotypes; and awareness of the cultural differences and how these impact group members. Brown (2009) adds the following: awareness of the limitation of personal knowledge and understanding of the cultural and diversity factors present for group members; the need for increased awareness of, and attention to the leader's personal verbal and nonverbal communication and how these impact group members; sensitivity to the impact of cultural differences; and possible cultural and diversity related verbal and nonverbal communication among group members.

Knowledge refers to having information about one's own cultural and diversity influences and how these shaped growth and development. It also refers to learning and understanding aspects of other cultures and diversity factors, issues, and concerns, particularly gaining information about cultural taboos, sensitivities, and related customs. The failure to know and understand cultural taboos and sensitivities can lead to unintentional offense and insults; for example, showing the sole of the shoe or foot can be offensive and insulting to people from some cultures. Culturally derived customs include greetings, use of time, formalities that convey respect, and nonverbal communications.

The literature is less clear in specifying multicultural competency skills. *Skills*, as described in standards such as the ASGW's Multicultural Competency Standards, do not seem to substantially differ from those proposed as effective with all clients and seem to be more related to relationship attributes than they are to specific techniques and skills. In addition, there is little or no evidence of the efficacy of proposed multicultural skills. In the face of these two constraints, preparing group counselors to be culturally and diversity sensitive and competent becomes difficult. Conveying this multicultural sensitivity and awareness to culturally and/or diversity different group members is a challenge for group leaders.

Developing and Communicating Multicultural Competency

Brown (2009) provides the following list for what group leaders can develop and communicate.

• Refrain from generalizations about group members concerning their ethnicity/race as there is likely to be considerable variation among those who have the same ethnic/racial identity.

• Learn what communicates respect and acceptance for culturally and/ or diversity different group members.

• Build trust, safety, and respect among group members before using any intervention around cultural and diversity factors.

• Enhance credibility by conceptualizing issues, concerns, and problems congruent with the particular member's culture after ascertaining how that member perceives his or her culture.

• Make personal cultural and diversity sensitivity, knowledge, and awareness a part of continual learning.

Ethical Considerations

The principal ethical concern for teaching and for practice is to do no harm. Dimidjian & Hollon (2010) present a clarification for what harm means in terms of treatment. *Harm* is defined as being caused by the treatment and not an inherent part of the problem. The seven kinds of harm are decelerated rate of client improvement, the cost of unhelpful treatment, distress from interacting with an unhelpful therapist, the therapist's failure to provide helpful treatment, harmful interventions, making the target problem worse, and treatment that causes domains other than the target problem to become worse. All of these are related to the therapist's interventions, and it would be helpful to include an understanding of these in teaching and training programs.

Lilienfeld (2007) published a list of 61 empirically based potentially harmful treatments, referred to in the literature as PHTs. Castonguay, Boswell, Constantino, Goldfred, and Hill (2010) used this list to propose training guidelines to prevent these them and/or to repair them if they should occur. The following list summarizes the guidelines, and each has a sample study as empirical evidence:

1. Skills to enhance the therapeutic relationship (Horvath & Bedi, 2002; Martin, Garske, & Davis, 2000)

2. An understanding of the therapist's impact and contributions to negative interactions, therapeutic alliance ruptures, and influences on improving the therapeutic outcomes (Binder & Strupp, 1997; Castonguay et al. 2004)

3. Monitoring and managing countertransference reactions (Gelso, Latts, Gomez, & Fassinger, 2002)

4. Flexibility about the importance of thoughts and emotions in cognitive therapy (Castonguay, Goldfred, Wiser, Rave, & Hayes, 1996)

5. Attend to transference, but to just note it and do not analyze it with the client (Crits-Christoph & Gibbons, 2002)

6. Use interpretations cautiously and judiciously when treating personality disorders (Schut et al., 2005)

7. Concrete interventions are associated with positive outcomes in cognitive therapy (Feeley, DeRubeis, & Gelfand, 1999)

8. Depth of experiencing is associated with positive outcomes in client-centered therapy (Elliott, Greenberg, & Lietaer, 2004)

9. The effects of the developed self of the therapist can be more predictive of outcomes than the therapeutic alliance (Wampold, 2006)

Castonguay et al. (2010) also lists six clinical theoretical training practices that lack supporting empirical evidence: conducting a comprehensive psychological assessment; the use of interpretations in psychodynamic treatment; avoiding interpretations in experiential therapy; strategies to help avoid errors with clients who are culturally different; assuming that low cognitive development in clients precludes their obtaining insight; the therapist's vulnerabilities, such as need for liking and approval, that may reduce effectiveness and/or harm the client. General recommendations for training are the following:

• Present strategies to enhance the therapeutic relationship

• Learn empirically supported techniques and how to apply them skillfully

• Attend to both process and technical variables to prevent and repair relationship difficulties between the therapist and client, and use flexibility in applying techniques

• Use the client's needs as the deciding factor when choosing treatments and interventions

• Increase awareness of self issues and concerns, such as attachment style, self-perceptions, and countertransference issues rooted in the family of origin as these can negatively impact the client

Most ethical concerns raised in the literature seem to be primarily concerned with the instructor's role and participation in experiential groups, and these are certainly valid. There are also equally valid ethical and professional concerns that receive scant attention in the literature, such as protection of the general public, informed consent, freedom to exit, and confidentiality. Since the focus in the literature seems to be on the experiential group, this discussion will address the expressed concerns.

Instructors who plan the teaching and learning process for leading and facilitating groups have a responsibility to design instruction and other training experiences around the *protection of the general public*, who will be the future group members in groups conducted by the present trainees. Preparing competent future group leaders must be the overriding emphasis, regardless of the type of group, target audiences, or setting where groups are conducted. Thus, even what basic material should be covered becomes of extreme ethical importance. This is the external ethical and professional principle to guide the teaching learning process.

Ethical Concerns and the Experiential Training Group

The focus and emphasis for expressed ethical concerns appear to relate to the protection of student trainees in experiential groups, especially protection from the instructor's knowledge of their personal issues and concerns and the possible misuse of this information to the detriment of the student (Feiner, 1998; Furr & Barret, 2000; Merta & Sission, 1991). Nowhere in the literature is there a single case where misuse of student personal information gathered from a training experiential group has occurred. However, the concern is valid as the potential for misuse is certainly present, as it is in any dual relationship; but it can be argued that other courses also carry this concern, and there is little in the literature that suggests constraining instructors for these courses as for instructors of group courses.

It may be that the discussion needs to be around how dual relationships and multiple roles differ and consensus obtained as to the differences and how or if potential for harm also differs. For example, a group instructor's role can include the following:

• Modeling and demonstrating expectations, concepts, and skills of group leadership
• Providing constructive feedback and correcting mistakes, misperceptions, and misinformation
• Illustrating complex concepts, practices, and the like

• Challenging, and encouraging experimentation with learning new behaviors and attitudes

In spite of the many positive attributes and skills the instructor can bring to the teaching–learning process, the fear that the instructor will misuse and abuse the power differential seems to be overwhelming, to the point that instructors do not have access to the other roles that can be used to enhance and expand learning about groups and group leadership. These restrictions can make it more difficult for instructors of future group leaders to adequately prepare them.

A variety of methods are used to try and provide responsible and ethical training: skills based, use of actors, structured group workshops, doctoral students and other professionals as group leaders, leaderless groups, simulations, and outside the class groups. *Skillsbased training* (Toth et al., 1998; Smaby et al., 1999) addresses the ethical concern of dual relationships by isolating specific skills and techniques. The *use of actors* (Fall & Levitov, 2002) tries to reduce the potential for invasion of privacy, misuse of information, and dual relationships. *Structured group workshops* (Eicher, 1987) organize and direct the learning experience to eliminate personal disclosure. The use of *doctoral students or outside the program professionals* as experiential group facilitators seeks to eliminate the dual relationship (Furr & Barret, 2000). *Leaderless groups* are designed to eliminate dual relationships and to reduce inappropriate self-disclosure (Elderidge, 1982; Green, Stone, & Grace, 1983; Brown, 1992). *Simulations* and *groups outside the class* are used to eliminate dual relationships (Bruce-Sanford, 1998; Furr & Barrett, 2000; Romano, 1998; Stockton et al., 2004). The wide variety of these methods attests to the great amount of thought and effort expended on the safety of trainees, and this is certainly a worthwhile effort.

Ethical Needs in Training

In spite of their fears and anxieties, students seem to value the experiential group learning experience (Anderson & Price, 2001; Merta et al. 1993). Therefore, it is essential for mental health professions to devise strategies that successfully address the ethical concerns so that this major learning opportunity is not diluted, truncated, or lost. For example, the following items need discussion and consensus:

• A uniform definition for training experiential groups for three levels: entry, practice, and advanced

- A clear set of learning goals and objectives
- How to create, structure, and monitor these groups to obtain learning goals and to protect trainees
- Who should lead the training group experience
- How should learning outcomes be assessed for the individual and for the group

Practices that would help address ethical concerns about trainees' safety include those proposed by Forest-Miller and Duncan (1990) and Pierce and Baldwin (1990) to use informed consent, pregroup preparation, and training in appropriate self-disclosure. Another possibility is proposed by Elderidge (1982), Green et al. (1983), and Brown (1992). They propose the use of leaderless self-directed experiential training groups and/or rotating peer member leader groups. Pierce and Baldwin (1990) and Brown (1992) would address the concern about inappropriate self-disclosure and exploration of personal issues, such as family of origin issues, by having these groups limit disclosure to the here and now, such as what is done in interpersonal process groups.

A question that does not seem to be addressed in the literature is about trainees' suitability for experiential training groups. Related to the question are concerns that trainees' readiness for participation is not assessed in the decision about allowing them to be in the training group and that trainees are not being prescreened for group membership, although both are recommended for participation in many other types of groups. Constraints for assessment and pregroup screening bring up legal issues about the validity and reliability of assessment procedures, prescreening and denial of participation based on the individual's performance on these, subjective judgment, and so on. The lack of valid and reliable instruments, of professional consensus, and of uniform procedures are probably reasons why these questions have not been researched or answered.

Balancing learning group leadership needs and ethical concerns is an ongoing endeavor. More research is needed to evaluate the extent to which the fears about potential harm are realized to better manage the risk, what safeguards are most effective while still producing the necessary learning, and what experiential group procedures fulfill the needed balance.

Ethical Concerns and Observation

There can also be some ethical concerns about observation, to include the instructor's role, peer trainees as observers, and the group being observed. Observation can assume many forms: two-way window, observer sitting in or with the group, video- or audiotaping, fishbowl, and demonstration groups. A major consideration is informed consent for the people being observed, and care should be taken to ensure that it is obtained free from coercion and/or negative consequences for refusal, especially for participants in experiential training groups. Professionally responsible and ethical behavior mandate that groups are not observed with members and the leader's knowledge and consent.

Observation is intrusive, no matter how unobtrusive the observer tries to remain in the background, thus affecting the group's dynamics and the members' and leader's participation. Confidentiality, difficult to ensure with groups under the best of circumstances, becomes even more problematic.

Some of the concerns about observation can be reduced or eliminated when the purpose, goals, use of outcomes, procedures, and process are known in advance to both the observers and those being observed. It can also be helpful to provide feedback about what was observed. Fishbowl, role-play, simulations, and demonstration groups provide the most open and direct means for observation, provided that the observers give feedback after the group or demonstration is completed. The use of two-way windows and an observer in the group are also means for observation but are prone to arousing fears and anxiety for the members and for the leader, especially in the absence of sufficient information about potential uses for information gained from the observations.

It could help allay some fears and anxieties to have the observers focus on group dynamics and group processes rather than on content or individual group members and to make these observations a part of the feedback that is provided (Brown, 1992). The ethical issue of confidentiality must also be addressed with an explicit statement about the observers' responsibility to preserve confidentiality. Maintaining confidentiality can impact supervision if the supervisor for some observers is other than the group class instructor. An explicit statement about confidentiality of observed material can be part of informed consent for allowing the observation.

Confidentiality

One major concern expressed in the literature is instructors' potential misuse of personal information revealed during the mandated class group sessions. Also noted is the quandary the group class instructor faces when students in the program are reviewed by faculty. The group instructors may have information relating to one or more students' suitability for the program and/or for the profession. These are competing ethical and professional standards, and it is difficult to reach a definite conclusion about which should prevail: confidentiality or the professional or accreditation standards. This issue is not explored here but is raised as one of the difficulties for instructors of group courses.

Another issue around confidentiality is when, or if, personal material revealed by trainees in group sessions falls under preservation of confidentiality and when it does not. It can be argued that confidentiality should be strictly maintained, but that may, in rare cases, subject the instructor to violating local, state, or federal laws; and/or the profession's ethical code; and/or the state's licensing standards; and/or the university's or agency's policy. If it becomes necessary to report personal material revealed by a trainee and confidentiality cannot be maintained for professional or legal reasons, the trainees should have been notified of this possibility in advance as part of informed consent for enrolling in the course and repeated as part of the preparation for the group. When such a situation arises, the instructor should speak to the student about the need to report before reporting any confidential material. A statement such as the following could be put on the syllabus:

> Confidentiality is expected for all aspect of this class, including for the instructor. The only rationale for breaking confidentiality is when there is mandated reporting by local, state, or federal laws, ethical and licensure requirements, and/or when university policy is violated. In every case, the student will be notified prior to any reporting.

The literature is silent on the confidentiality issues surrounding other class activities, such as discussions, demonstrations, journals and the like. However, it may be prudent to extend confidentiality to all facets of the class as it is reasonable to expect that some personal material could be revealed by students through these other venues. Further, preserving confidentiality needs to be emphasized to and practiced by the trainees and can be an expectation for the course.

Teaching Strategies

The ecological concepts proposed by Conyne & Cook (Eds.) (2004) for group leadership can be adapted for teaching and selection of strategies. The authors provide exercises and other activities designed to teach ecological concepts. The concepts are as follows:

- Context—internal and external factors impacting the group and its members
- Interconnection—relationships between and among members
- Collaboration—working together to set and attain goals
- Social system maintenance—creating and maintaining the group's culture
- Meaning making—learning from the group experience
- Sustainability—transfer of learning and change to real life outside the group

Other general and common teaching strategies include listening, experiential activities, writing, and practicing. A description and examples for each are provided as illustrations, and the advantages and disadvantages for each.

Listening strategies include lecture; video and other media, such as computer-assisted instruction; observation without participation; and discussion. Advantages for this category include efficient dissemination of information, the ability to isolate and illustrate aspects of groups and leadership, and listening tends to not be anxiety provoking for learners. Disadvantages are that learners are passive and detached from the material, their attention may not be sustained (McKeachie & Svinicki, 2006), and that the complexity of the group and leadership functions are minimized.

Experiential strategies were presented in a separate section and are defined as active participation by learners. Examples of such strategies include exercises and other such activities, participation in demonstration groups and fishbowl, immersion as a member of a group (such as an interpersonal process group), and a group project, such as planning a group and presenting a session. Advantages are that learners are active, are becoming aware of the complexities for groups and for leaders, can learn the importance of awareness of their personal reactions, and can increase their understanding of both cognitive and affective aspects of groups. Disadvantages include possible increased anxiety, perceived invasion of privacy, inappropriate self-disclosure by participants, and emergence of other possible psychological distress.

Writing has not received much attention in the literature, although it usually has a significant role in the classroom. Two studies provide some support for this strategy as a learning tool. Aveline (1986), in a study on training group psychotherapists, provided weekly summaries for their closed group experience as a part of the course. He found that these summaries promoted active learning, helped trainees integrate theory and practice, helped them to anticipate problems in the group, and allowed the session to remain focused on the here and now as analyses were conducted outside of the session. Beck and Bosman-Clark (1989) reported that written summaries increased co-leaders' learning by providing a structure for processing group events, a focus for interventions, and an increase in accountability. Brown (1992) proposed that journals focused on identifying group dynamics during sessions in an experiential group are an effective strategy for learning to observe dynamics in their complexity in real time. Writing activities include: journals that can either be members' personal experiencing and/or focused on group specifics such as group dynamics, research papers on aspects of groups, personal development papers, assigned readings and critiques, and summary papers at the end of a course to integrate learning. Advantages can include personalization and individualized learning for trainees, a check for misunderstandings and gaps in knowledge, and a means for focusing on essentials for learners amid the volume and complexity of material. Disadvantages include the amount of time needed to write and to review.

While the bulk of practicing occurs in supervised practicum, internship, and posttraining, some practicing can also be done in classes, where strategies include skills training, simulation, role-play, and rotating peer leaders in experiential groups. Advantages can be reduced learner anxiety, specific focus on an aspect of group and/or group leadership that isolates it from the complexity, and experiencing the tasks and responsibilities of group leadership. Disadvantages are that learners do not experience group aspects in context and complexity or use of personal experiencing as a means for understanding group process and that the richness of learning through attention to the art factors of group leadership is lost or minimized.

Training Needs
Relatively few studies have been conducted on teaching group leadership, components and models for group leadership and its training, or the end products or outcomes of training. There is not a unified vision for training across mental health professional organizations that defines desired outcomes for training, such as what knowledge, personal qualities and development, and techniques characterize a competent group leader. Little empirical or research evidence is available from the literature to support proposed models, and most studies are narrowly focused on particular and specific skills and techniques, current practices and deficits in academic preparation programs, and trainees' perceptions. However, there is a preponderance of expert opinion about group leader preparation, and that also carries significant weight.

Professional and accreditation organizations, such as ASGW (a division of the American Counseling Association), American Psychological Association (APA), AGPA, National Association of Social Workers (NASW), AASWG, and CACREP, have specified minimal criteria for group leadership training, some for the entry level and others for the advanced level, although this may not be specifically delineated in some standards. A review of these standards did not reveal any empirical or research evidence for required components.

The newly formed organization Group Practice Research Network brings together different mental health professions who have an interest in furthering the understanding of groups and group leadership needs and establishing empirical evidence to support best practices. The groups that belong at this time are APA's Divisions 49 and 39, ASGW, AASWG, and AGPA. Other groups have expressed interest in the mission of this network. Their focus on research could also be useful to suggest teaching principles and strategies that have research backing.

Although there are constraints on what evidence is available about effective teaching and preparation for group leaders, there is still some evidence about these topics. The following list of recommendations for training was developed from the present evidence and professional expert opinions, and the items suggest that there is a need for additional research.

Recommendations
The following list identifies nine training needs.

1. Research to establish training goals, define objectives, and support strategies that can be specified and assessed. These should include goals, objectives, and strategies for the three main areas: knowledge domain, personal factors, and techniques.

2. Evidence based teaching strategies that would accomplish the goals and objectives. Lacking are

controlled studies that define and support desired outcomes for teaching strategies.

3. Professional expert designations for a phased learning developmental sequence that addresses competencies for each level. Suggested is consideration of a three level phase sequence: entry, supervised practice, and advanced.

4. Professional input and agreement for adequacy of entry level preparation. The current state of only one course to teach all of the dimensions of groups and group leadership does not meet the entry level needs for knowledge and skill as group leaders. The supervised practice phase is not adequate in many instances because the course is not dedicated to group leadership and/or because there is a lack of groups available for practice. There are professional organizational guidelines for adequate practice, but it is not known to what extent these are met in academic preparation programs, especially for various types of groups. Ideally, trainees should have opportunities to practice leading different types of groups, but the reality is that trainees are lucky if they have an opportunity to lead one group during the supervised practicum.

5. The teaching strategy that uses training experiential groups seems to be an essential learning strategy for future group leaders according to the literature. There are several primary constraints: no standards exist for how these should be formed and conducted; learning outcomes have not been established or are poorly defined in most cases; safeguards to protect trainees and to adhere to professional ethical standards are an essential concern, but these are not established or specified; the instructor's role lacks an agreed on definition; and guidelines for trainee participation are not established. However, in spite of these constraints, experts in the field support the use of this teaching strategy.

6. There is not a clear boundary in the definition and use of training experiential groups and personal growth groups, and the lack of clarity leads to confusion, especially in terms of the goals for each. Their purposes and goals differ, and clarifying their differences could be of immense help to instructors and to trainees.

7. Specific and clear components for informed consent are needed, and these should be disseminated prior to trainees enrolling in a course and/or training program. This can be facilitated when agreed on goals and objectives are established for every learning dimension: knowledge, personal factors and development, and techniques and skills.

8. Professional organizations' training guidelines should be clearly supported by evidence based research wherever possible, and competencies that can be objectively assessed created. The complexity of many group leadership skills, various theoretical perspectives and applications, and the role of intangibles such as level of the group leader's personal development will most likely prevent evidence based support for some desired competencies; and this is recognized. However, a review of the training standards for five professional organizations did not reveal a clear connection that any standard was developed from research evidence. Even a national survey, such as a job analysis, of group leaders in the field could provide some evidence basis for establishing and mandating some of the standards.

9. Preparation for group leadership training could be standardized, such as requiring knowledge of theory, prior training for counseling individuals, and participation as a member of a group similar to what is defined as a personal growth group before enrolling in a group counseling course. Trainees then would have some relating and communicating skills that can be built on and enhanced for leading groups, an introduction to group procedures and process, and perhaps some reduction of anxiety.

The volume and complexity of available material on groups and group leadership are more than can be reasonably taught and learned in a single course, not to mention the time and opportunities for supervised practice. Thus, instructors are left to make individual decisions about what to present and emphasize from the three domains, leading to inconsistent preparation. Dies (1980) and Feiner (1998) have made convincing arguments that training for group leaders should be a continuous and interactive sequential process, but this remains to be established so that training across disciplines and within disciplines can be consistent as to the basics for group leadership.

References

Anderson, R., & Price, G. (2001). Experiential groups in counselor education: Student attitudes and instructor participation. *Counselor Education and Supervision*, *41*(2), 111–119.

ASGW (1999) ASGW Principles for diversity competent group workers. *Journal for Specialists in Group Work*, 24, 7–14.

Association for Specialists in Group Work. (2000). *Professional standards for the training of group counselors*. Alexandria, VA: Author.

Arrendono, P., Toporek, R., Brown, S., Jones, J., Locke, D., Sanchez, J., et al. (1996). Operationalization of multicultural counseling competencies. *Journal of Counseling and Development, 24*, 42–78.

Aveline, M. (1986). The use of written reports in brief group psychotherapy training. *International Journal of Group Psychotherapy, 36*(3), 477–482.

Baker, E. (2006). *The Group Psychotherapy Intervention Rating Scale training manual for assessing therapist interventions in group psychotherapy.* Unpublished manuscript.

Baker, S., Daniels, T., & Greenley, A. (1990). Systematic training of graduate-level counselors: Narrative and meta-analytic reviews of three major programs. *Counseling Psychologist, 18*(3), 355–421.

Bandura, A. (1977). *Social learning theory.* Englewood Cliffs, NJ: Prentice Hall.

Bass, B. (1985a). Good, better, best. *Organizational Dynamics, 13*, 26–40.

Bass, B. (1985b). *Leadership and performance beyond expectations.* New York: Free Press.

Bass, B. (1997). Does the transactional–transformational leadership paradigm transcend organizational and national boundaries. *American Psychologist, 52*, 130–139.

Bass, B., Avolio, B., & Goldheim, L. (1987). Biography and the assessment of transformational leadership at the world-class level. *Journal of Management, 13*, 17–19.

Beck, R., & Bosman-Clark, J. (1989). The written summary in group psychotherapy revisited. *Group, 13*(2), 102–111.

Berger, M. (1969). Experiential and didactic aspects of training in therapeutic group approaches. *American Journal of Psychiatry, 1126*, 845–850.

Berman, A. (1975). Group psychotherapy training: Issues and models. *Small Group Research, 6*(3), 325–344.

Binder, J., & Strupp, H. (1997). "Negative process": a recurrently discovered and under-estimated facet of therapeutic process and outcome in individual psychotherapy of adults. *Clinical Psychology: Science and Practice, 4*, 121–139.

Boenheim, C. (1963). Dynamic doctor groups as a training method for group psychotherapy. *Mental Hygiene, 47*, 84–88.

Brown, N. (1992). *Teaching group dynamics.* Westport, CT: Praeger.

Brown, N. (2003). *Psychoeducational groups.* New York: Routledge.

Brown, N. (2009). *Becoming a group leader.* Upper Saddle River, NJ: Pearson Education.

Bruce-Sanford, G. (1998). A simulation model for training in group process. *International Journal of Group Psychotherapy, 48*, 393–400.

Burlingame, G., Fuhriman, A., & Johnson, J. (2002). Cohesion in group psychotherapy. In J. C. Norcross (Ed.), *Psychotherapy relationships that work: Therapist contributions and responsiveness to patients* (pp. 71–88). New York: Oxford University Press.

Burlingame, G., MacKenzie, K., & Strauss, B. (2004). Small group treatment: Evidence for effectiveness and mechanisms of change. In M. J. Lambert (Ed.), *Handbook of psychotherapy and behavior changes* (5th ed., pp. 647–696). New York: John Wiley & Son.

Castonguay, L., Boswell, J., Constantino, M., Goldfred, M., & Hill, C. (2010). Training implications of harmful effects of psychological treatment. *American Psychologist, 65*(1), 34–49.

Castonguay, L., Goldfred, M., Wiser, S., Rave, P., & Hayes, A. (1996). Predicting the effects of cognitive therapy for depression: A study of unique and common factors. *Journal of Consulting and Clinical Psychology, 64*, 497–504.

Castonguay, L., Schut, A., Aikens, D., Constantino, M., Laurenceau, J., Bologh, L., et al. (2004). Integrative cognitive therapy for depression: A preliminary investigation. *Journal of Psychotherapy Integration, 14*, 4–20.

Chapman, C., Baker, E., Porter, G., Thayer, S., & Burlingame, G. (2010). *Rating group therapists intervention: The validation of the Group Psychotherapy Intervention Rating Scale.* Unpublished manuscript.

Cohen, A., & Smith, R. (1976). *The critical incident in growth groups* (Vols. 1, 2). San Diego: University Associates.

Conyne, R., & Cook, E. (Eds.). (2004). *Ecological counseling: An innovative approach to conceptualizing person–environment interactions.* Alexandria, VA: American Counseling Association.

Conyne, R., Wilson, F., & Ward, D. (1997). *Comprehensive group work: What it means and how to teach it.* Alexandria, VA: American Counseling Association.

Crits-Christoph, P., & Gibbons, M. (2002). Relational interpretations. In J. C. Norcross (Ed.), *Psychotherapy relationships that work: Therapist contributions and responsiveness to patients* (pp. 285–300). New York: Oxford University Press.

DeLucia-Waack, J., & Fauth, J. (2004). Measures of group process, dynamics, climate, leadership behavior and therapeutic factors: A review. In J. DeLucia-Waack, D. Gerrity, C. Kalodner, & M. Riva (Eds.), *Handbook of group counseling and psychotherapy.* Thousand Oaks, CA: Sage.

Dies, R. (1980). Current practice in the training of group psychotherapists. *International Journal of Group Psychotherapy, 30*, 169–187.

Dimidjian, W., & Hollon, S. (2010). How would we know if psychotherapy were harmful? *American Psychologist, 65*(1), 21–33.

Eicher, M. (1987). Using structured group workshops to teach group process. *Teaching of Psychology, 14*(1), 42–44.

Elderidge, W. (1982). The coordination of experiential and didactic training in teaching social work in groups. *College Student Journal, 16*(1), 18–21.

Elliott, R., Greenberg, L., & Lietaer, G. (2004). Research on experiential therapies. In M. J. Lambert (Ed.), *Bergin and Garfield's handbook of psychotherapy and behavior change* (5th ed., pp. 493–539). New York: John Wiley & Sons.

Fall, K. A., & Levitov, J. E. (2002). Using actors in experiential group leadership training. *Journal for Specialists in Group Work, 27*(2), 122–135.

Feeley, M., DeRubeis, R., & Gelfand, L. (1999). The temporal relation of adherence and alliance to symptom change in cognitive therapy for depression. *Journal of Consulting and Clinical Psychology, 67*, 578–582.

Feiner, S. (1998). Course design: an integration of didactic and experiential approaches to graduate training. *International Journal of Group Psychotherapy, 48*, 439–460.

Fidler, J. (1973). Education for group psychotherapy. In L. Wolberg & E. Swartz (Eds.), *Group therapy 1973: An overview.* New York: Intercontinental Medical Book.

Fiedler, R. (1978). The contingency model and the dynamics of the leadership process. *Advances in Experimental Social Psychology, 12*, 59–112.

Forest-Miller, H., & Duncan, J. (1990). The ethics of dual relationships in the training of group counselors. *Journal for Specialists in Group Work, 15*, 88–93.

Forsyth, D. (1999). *Group dynamics.* Pacific Grove, CA: Brooks/Cole.

Fowers, B., & Davidov, B. (2006). The virtue of multiculturalism: Personal transformation, character, and openness to the other. *American Psychologist, 61*(6), 581–594.

Fuhriman, A., & Burlingame, G. (2001). Group psychotherapy training and effectiveness. *International Journal of Group Psychotherapy, 51*(3), 399–416.

Furr, S. R., & Barret, B. (2000). Teaching group counseling skills: Problems and solutions. *Counselor Education and Supervision, 40*(2), 94–104.

Gauron, E., Proctor, S., & Schroder, P. (1970). Group therapy training: A multidisciplinary approach. *Perspectives in Psychiatric Care, 8*, 262–267.

Gelso, C., Latts, M., Gomez, M., & Fassinger, R. (2002). Countertransference management and therapy outcome: An initial evaluation. *Journal of Clinical Psychology, 58*, 861–867.

Green, B., Stone, W., & Grace, M. (1983). Learning during group dynamics training: The effects of silent versus traditional teaching formats. *Psychiatry, 46*, 130–138.

Grothjahn, M. (1970). The analytic group experiences in the training of therapists. *Voices: Art and Science of Psychotherapy, 5*, 108–109.

Harvill, R., Masson, R., & Jacobs, E. (1983). Systematic group leader training: A skills developmental approach. *Journal for Specialists in Group Work, 8*, 226–232.

Hersey, P., & Blanchard, K. (1976). *Management of organizational behavior: Utilizing human resources* (3rd ed.). Englewood Cliffs, NJ: Prentice Hall.

Hilsenroth, M. J., Ackerman, S. J., Clemence, A. J., Strarsle, C., & Handler, L. (2002). Effects of structured clinical training on patients and therapist perspectives of alliance in psychotherapy. *Psychotherapy: Theory, Research, Practice, Training, 39*, 309–323.

Hollis, J., & Wantz, R. (1990). *Counselor preparation 1990–1991: Programs, personnel, trends* (7th ed.). Muncie, IN: Accelerated Development.

Horowitz, L. (1968). Group psychotherapy training for psychiatric residents. In J. H. Masserman (Ed.), *Current psychiatric therapies*. New York: Grune & Stratton.

Horvath, A., & Bedi, R. (2002). The alliance. In J. C. Norcross (Ed.), *Psychotherapy relationships that work: Therapist contributions and responsiveness to patients* (pp. 37–69). New York: Oxford University Press.

Huhn, R. P., Zimpfer, D. G., Waltman, D. E., & Williamson, S. K. (1985). A survey of programs of professional preparation for group counseling. *Journal for Specialists in Group Work, 10*(3), 124–133.

Ivey, A., Pedersen, P., & Ivey, M. (2001). *Intentional group counseling*. Pacific Grove, CA: Brooks/Cole.

Jacobs, E., Masson, R., & Harvill, R. (2006). *Group counseling strategies and skills* (6th ed.). Belmont, CA: Thompson Brooks/Cole.

Johnson, D., & Johnson, F. (2008). *Joining together* (10th ed.). Upper Saddle River, NJ: Prentice Hall.

Kaczkowski, H., & Fenton, M. (1985). Simulation as a medium for training group leaders. *Small Group Research, 16*, 534.

Kane, C. M. (1995). Fishbowl training in group process. *Journal for Specialists in Group Work, 20*(3), 183–188.

Kaul, T., & Bednar, R. (1986). Experimental group research: Results, questions, & suggestions. In S. Garfield & A. Bergin (Eds.), *Handbook of psychotherapy and behavior change*. New York: John Wiley & Sons.

Kivlighan, D. M., & Lilly, R. (1997). Developmental changes in group climate as they relate to therapeutic gain. *Group Dynamics: Theory, Research and Practice, 1*, 208–221.

Kivlighan, D., Markin, R., Stahl, J., & Salahuddin, N. (2007). Changes in the ways that group trainees structure their knowledge of group members with training. *Group Dynamics, 11*(3), 176–186.

Lewin, K. (1944). Dynamics of group action. *Educational Leadership, 1*, 195–200.

Lewin, K., Lippitt, R., & White, R. (1939). Patterns of aggressive behavior in experimentally created "social climates." *Journal of Social Psychology, 10*, 271–299.

Lieberman, M., Yalom, I., & Miles, M. (1973). *Encounter groups: First facts*. New York: Basic Books.

Lilienfeld, S. O. (2007). Psychological treatments that cause harm. *Perspectives on Psychological Science, 2*, 53–70.

Markus, H., & King, E. (2003). A survey of group psychotherapy training during predoctoral psychology internship. *Professional Psychology: Research & Practice, 34*(2), 203–209.

Martin, D., Gaske, J., & Davis, M. (2000). Relation of the therapeutic alliance with outcome and other variables: a meta-analytic review. *Journal of Consulting and Clinical Psychology, 68*, 438–450.

McKeachie, W., & Svinicki, M. (2006). *Teaching tips*. Boston: Houghton Mifflin.

Merta, R., & Sission, J. (1991). The experiential group: An ethical and professional dilemma. *Journal for Specialists in Group Work, 16*(4), 236–245.

Merta, R., Wolfgang, L., & McNeil, K. (1993). Five models of using the experiential group in the preparation of group counselors. *Journal for Specialists in Group Work, 18*(4), 200–207.

Neighbors, H., Jackson, J., Campbell, L., & Williams, D. (1989). The influence of racial factors on psychiatric diagnosis: A review and suggestions for research. *Community Health Journal, 25*, 301–309.

Pavkov, T., Lewis, D., & Lyons, J. (1989). Psychiatric diagnoses and racial biases: an empirical investigation. *Professional Psychology: Research and Practice, 6*, 364–368.

Pierce, K., & Baldwin, C. (1990). Participation vs. privacy in the training of group counselors. *Journal for Specialists in Group Work, 15*(3), 149–158.

Rohde, R., & Stockton, R. (1994). Group structure: A review. *Journal of Group Psychotherapy, Psychodrama, and Sociometry, 46*, 151–158.

Romano, J. (1998). Simulated group counseling: an experiential training model for group work. *Journal for Specialists in Group Work, 23*(2), 119–132.

Salvendy, J. (1999). Ethnocultural considerations in group psychotherapy. *International Journal of Group Psychotherapy, 49*(4), 429–464.

Schut, A., Castonguay, L., Flanagan, K., Yamasaki, A., Barber, J., Bedics, J., et al. (2005). Therapist interpretation, patient–therapist interpersonal process, and outcome in psychodynamic psychotherapy for avoidant personality disorder. *Psychotherapy: Theory, Research, Practice, Training, 42*, 494–511.

Semrad, E. (1969). Use of group processes in teaching group dynamics. *Group Analysis, 1*, 167–173.

Smaby, M., Maddus, C., Torres-Rivera, E., & Zimmick, R. (1999). A study of the effects of a skills-based versus a conventional group counseling training program. *Journal for Specialists in Group Work, 24*, 152–163.

Snijders, Trijsburg, & de Groot (2006). *Group cohesion, working alliance and therapeutic interventions as variables predicting outcomes in group psychotherapy for personality disorders*. Paper presented at the Society for Psychotherapy Research international meeting.

Stockton, R., & Toth, P. (1996). Teaching group counselors: Recommendations for maximizing preservice instruction. *Journal for Specialists in Group Work, 21*(4), 274–282.

Stockton, R., Morran, D., & Kreiger, K. (2004). An overview of current research and best practices for training beginning group leaders. In J. DeLucia-Waack, D. Gerrity, C. Kalodner, & M. Riva (Eds.), *Handbook of group counseling and psychotherapy.* Thousand Oaks, CA: Sage.

Stogdill, P. (1974). *Handbook of leadership.* New York: Free Press.

Strakowski, S., Hawkins, J., Keck, P., Jr., McElory, S., West, S., Bourne, M., et al. (1997). The effects of race and information variance on disagreement between psychiatric emergency service and research diagnosis in first-episode psychosis. *Journal of Clinical Psychiatry, 58,* 457–463.

Sue, D., Capodilupo, C., Torino, G., Bucceri, J., Holder, A., Nadal, K., et al. (2007). Racial microaggressions in everyday life: Implications for clinical practice. *American Psychologist, 62*(4), 271–286.

Sue, S., Akutsu, P., & Higashi, C. (1987). Training issues in conducting therapy with ethnic minority-group clients. In P. Pederson (Ed.), *Handbook of cross-cultural concerns and therapy* (pp. 275–280). New York: Praeger.

Toth, P., Stockton, R., & Erwin, W. (1998). Application of a skill-based training model for group counselors. *Journal for Specialists in Group Work, 21*(4), 274–282.

Tschuschke, V., & Greene, L. (2002). Group therapists' training: What predicts learning. *International Journal of Group Psychotherapy, 52*(4), 463–482.

Wampold, B. E. (2006). The psychotherapist. In J. C. Norcress, I. Beutler, & R. F. Levant (Eds.), *Evidence-based practices in mental health: Debate and dialogues on fundamental questions* (pp. 200–208). Washington, D.C.: American Psychological Association.

Whaley, A., & Geller, P. (2007). Toward a cognitive process model of ethnic/racial biases in clinical judgment. *Review of General Psychology, 11*(1), 75–96.

Wilson, F., Conyne, R., & Ward, D. (1994). The general status of group work training in accredited counseling programs. *Journal for Specialists in Group Work, 19*(3), 140–154.

Woody, R. (1971). Self-understanding seminars: The effects of group psychotherapy in counselor training. *Psychotherapy: Theory, Research and Training, 10,* 112–119.

Yalom, I. (1995). *Theory and practice of group psychotherapy* (4th ed). New York: Basic Books.

Yalom, I. (with Leszcz, M.) (2005). *Theory and practice of group psychotherapy* (5th ed.). New York: Basic Books.

Supervision of Group Counseling

Maria T. Riva

Abstract

Supervision of group counseling is a topic that has received little attention, yet it is crucial to the professional development of group counselors and overseeing group clients' care. This chapter highlights the role of supervision, the responsibilities of the supervisor, and the tasks involved in the supervisory relationship. A section also addresses research that has been conducted and the need for and directions for future research.

Keywords: supervision of group counseling, group counseling supervision, group supervision of group counseling, supervision, group counseling, group therapy, group psychotherapy

Yalom (2005) stated that "a supervised clinical experience is a sine qua non in the education of the group therapist" (p. 548). Although its importance is not disputed, it is startling how little recognition the supervision of group leadership has received. In fact, it is the author's experience that most group leaders receive little supervision on their group-counseling facilitation. It is also typical that if supervision of groups is provided, the primary focus is on problematic clients and not on the group dynamics. Similarly, if the counseling group has coleaders, minimal time is spent during the supervision session on the coleader relationship.

Research on this topic is seriously lacking (DeLucia-Waack & Fauth, 2004; Rubel & Okech, 2009) in amount and in scope. For example, there has been little attention to the development of the supervisory relationship for group leaders across sessions or the differences in the emphasis of supervision depending on the skill level of the supervisee (or the skill level of the supervisor for that matter), areas that have been studied in the general supervision literature for individual therapists. Although it is certainly intuitive that "the stage of the group and the experience level of group

leader(s) dictates the focus of supervision, ranging from skill development and decreasing anxiety to awareness of group process and dynamics to discussion of countertranference" (DeLucia-Waack & Fauth, 2004, p. 138), these areas have not as yet been investigated for supervision of groups.

Added to these limitations is that the little research that does exist focuses on the supervision of group counseling trainees, with little research (or theory or best practices) centered on supervision with more experienced group leaders. Although the overall inattention to supervision of group counseling might sound rather bleak, it is the opportune time to explore the process and outcome of group-counseling supervision.

Consistently, research on group counseling has proven it to be effective (Fuhriman & Burlingame, 2001). Moreover, the practice of group counseling has greatly expanded to include "many different types of settings, with different populations, and for people who represent the entire continuum of age and a large variety of problems" (DeLucia-Waack, Gerrity, Kalodner, & Riva, 2004, p. x). The popularity and increased growth of group counseling require competent and ethical group leaders.

Many group facilitators have limited training in group leadership, and with the large number of new mental health professionals entering the field who will very likely be asked or required to conduct counseling groups, competent and ethical supervisors of groups are also necessary. "Clearly, the supervision of group leaders is of paramount importance to the field of group leadership" (DeLucia-Waack & Fauth, 2004, p. 136).

Although the supervision of counseling groups has been largely overlooked, the literature on supervision of individual counseling does offer some guidance in informing several areas that are also critical in the supervision of group counseling, such as the role of supervision and the responsibilities and ethical considerations of supervisors. This chapter, then, begins with a brief overview of the supervision literature that speaks directly to individual therapists. Given that supervision of group counseling is much more complex than its individual counterpart, the rest of the chapter almost exclusively focuses on supervision of leaders of counseling groups. A section provides a review of the literature on supervision of groups. Most of the current literature outlines theories and case studies that provide some direction as to group counseling supervision. Also, there have been suggested models of supervision that offer some frameworks for supervision of counseling groups. Therefore, these models and best practices are discussed. The next section discusses the scant research on group counseling supervision. The major focus of this section advocates for more attention to the research on supervision for group facilitators and outlines recommendations for the types of topics and questions that need to be addressed in the next phase of research in this area.

Supervision of Individual Counseling

Bernard and Goodyear (2009) describe the centrality of supervision to the mental health professions. They see supervision as pivotal to the regulatory functions of state boards, credentialing bodies, and training-program accreditations. They state that "It provides a means to impart necessary skills, to socialize novices into the particular profession's values and ethics, to protect clients, and finally to monitor supervisees' readiness to be admitted into the profession" (p. 3). Clinical supervision is recognized as one of the most important mechanisms in training individual therapists and is an essential ingredient in their development of competencies (Falender et al., 2004). Also, it is one of the most frequently endorsed activities by mental health

professionals in both practice and academic settings (Bernard & Goodyear, 2009; Welfel, 2006). Yet, what is supervision? Douce (1989) stated that "supervision is a separate skill similar to teaching— but different; similar to counseling but different; and similar to consulting—but different" (p. 5). In a widely used definition of *supervision*, Bernard and Goodyear define it as

> An intervention provided by a more senior member of a profession to a more junior member of that same profession. This relationship is evaluative and hierarchical, extends over time, and has the simultaneous purposes of enhancing the professional functioning of the more junior person(s); monitoring the quality of professional services offered to the clients that she, he, or they see, and serving as a gatekeeper for those who are to enter the particular profession (p. 7).

Supervision requires necessary preparation and training. There has been a sizable emphasis in the literature on the supervisory process, resulting in concordance that supervision is a complex and multilayered process and that being a competent therapist is a necessary, but not sufficient, ingredient to being a good supervisor. Besides preparation and training, experience is also needed. Supervision has gained more respect within the past 15 years as credentialing bodies have begun to require course work in supervision in doctoral training programs (e.g., American Association of Marriage and Family Therapy [AAMFT] and Council of Accredited Counseling Relation Education Programs [CACREP]), identifying supervision as a core competency (e.g., American Psychological Association, Association of Psychology Postdoctoral and Internship Centers), and stipulating the number of hours of training in supervision that is required to supervise others (e.g., Association for Specialists in Group Work [ASGW], AAMFT, CACREP).

Positive Supervisory Alliance

There is a rich body of literature on the benefits of a positive alliance between the supervisor and supervisee for therapists of individual counseling and psychotherapy. It is important to consider what the purpose of supervision actually is. Returning to the definition of supervision by Bernard and Goodyear (2009), there are two underscored areas: (1) to foster the professional development of the supervisee and (2) to ensure the welfare of the clients. Of course, these two prongs are indisputably integrated. All of the literature on supervision points to the need for a strong supervisory alliance, and its development is the chief task of early supervision sessions (e.g., Nelson, Gray, Friedlander, Ladany, & Walker, 2001). Without a positive supervisor–supervisee relationship, little "supervision" will occur. One of the core aspects of supervision is that it is evaluative. Often, sensitive feedback will need to be given by the supervisor about the roadblocks occurring between the supervisee and the client, additional supervisee skills necessary for client progress, and the supervisee's personality characteristics that may prevent counseling interventions from succeeding. For supervisees to be able to flexibly hear corrective feedback, they need to be able to trust their supervisor and to have a supervisor who is willing to address difficult material. Hoffman, Hill, Holmes, and Freitas (2005) found that corrective feedback was difficult for supervisors to impart to supervisees. Bernard and Goodyear (2009) agreed that *formative feedback* (what a supervisee may need to add to his or her counseling skills) was much easier to deliver than *summative feedback* (which provides an evaluation of how a supervisee is doing), particularly if the supervisee has some real weaknesses.

Cognitive Complexity of the Supervisee

Another important ingredient of effective supervision appears to be related to the cognitive complexity of the supervisee. Current research suggests that there seems to be a relationship between supervisees' level of cognitive complexity, the supervisory alliance, and satisfaction with supervision. In other words, supervisees who have higher levels of cognitive complexity are more satisfied with supervision and have stronger working alliances with their supervisors (Ramos-Sanchez et al., 2002). This is a critical area for supervision as it is clear that for novice counselors, high cognitive complexity signals increased ability in some essential counseling interactions such as empathy and a deeper understanding of client characteristics (Borders, 1989; Stoppard & Miller, 1985). Applying Bloom's *Taxonomy of Educational Objectives* (Bloom, Engelhart, Furst, Hill, & Krathwohl, 1956), Granello and Underfer-Babalis (2004) described a model for supervision of group counselors that encourages the increase of cognitive complexity. Their model matches the characteristics of the taxonomy (i.e., knowledge, comprehension, application, analysis, synthesis, and evaluation) with the developmental stage of the group counselor in order to increase cognitive complexity. With regard to group counseling trainees, Kivlighan and Kivlighan (2009) found that early group trainees' knowledge structures were linear and simplistic compared to those of experienced group leaders. The next steps for future research in the area of cognitive complexity will be to tease out those mechanisms in supervision that help to increase supervisees' cognitive complexity.

Client Outcomes

Only recently has supervision research begun to investigate its effects on client outcomes. Freitas (2002) reviewed two decades (1981–1997) of research on whether clinical supervision improves client outcomes. He reviewed only 10 studies during this time period, all with many methodological problems such as small samples, lack of psychometrically sound measures, and failure to control for Type I and Type II errors. Yet, Freitas stated that "there is reason to be hopeful about the current trend in supervision research" (p. 364). Research is increasing, and some of the methodological problems are easily correctable. Recently, Callahan, Almstom, Swift, Borja, and Heath (2009) found that supervision was moderately positively related to client outcomes. In this study using archival data from 76 discharged clients, 16% of the variability in the outcome was accounted for by the supervision even beyond that accounted for by the clients' initial severity and the therapists' characteristics. Connecting supervision to client progress is the foremost area for future research given the responsibility of supervision to help monitor the quality of services provided to the client(s) by the supervisee.

A case that will be made in the next section is that supervision of counseling groups is many times more intricate than supervision of individual counseling. Yet, it is essential to underscore the complexity of individual supervision as well. Not only does supervision include the supervisor, the supervisee, and the client(s), but there are always other systems that interact in the client's life, such as social relationships, extended family, and work and school environments. Supervision for individual counseling is a multifaceted enterprise that involves systems within and external to the counselor/client and supervisor/supervisee relationships.

Group Counseling Supervision

There are many unique aspects of supervision for group counseling. Supervisors need to attend to countless group components that are not applicable to individual therapy such as group member composition, stages of group counseling, group dynamics, group cohesion, and dealing with difficult clients such as those who monopolize sessions and influence the direction and work of the groups, to name just a few. These unique characteristics do not work in a vacuum but rather interact to affect the functioning of the group and its members. Similar to supervisors of individual therapy, group-counseling supervisors also need to juggle various supervisory roles such as teacher, mentor, and evaluator. Many authors have written about the essential nature of supervision. Moss (2008) painted a clear picture of the many competing pressures that are faced by group therapists and are areas for supervisory intervention when he stated,

> They have to constantly scan their groups for all kinds of verbal and nonverbal phenomena. They must pay attention to boundaries and tendencies to act out. They must look for manifestations of resistances, projections, projective identifications, and transferences. They must observe who is talking and who is silent and speculate as to why. They must constantly ponder when to remain silent and when to speak, what to say, and whom to say it to. All this while they try to monitor their own countertransference, which is aroused not just by one patient, as in individual therapy, but by six to eight. No wonder supervision is essential! (p. 199)

Appreciating the importance of the vital role of education and training for group facilitation, the ASGW outlined in its *Professional Standards for the Training of Group Workers* (2000) specific requirements for the education, training, and supervision of group leaders. These standards relate to the assessment of group leader skills and interventions, the development of the group within and across sessions, and the improvement of individual group members. Other than the ASGW professional standards, no professional organization has developed guidelines to delineate the roles and responsibilities of group counseling supervisors. What is absolutely clear is that there are two essential knowledge areas needed for supervision of groups: supervisors need to be competent in supervision methods and in the complexities of group counseling.

Group Type

The intricacies of group counseling make fundamental the need for supervisors to be well versed in its content, format, and dynamics. Supervisors need to appreciate the different types of groups led by their supervisees such as those endorsed by the ASGW and described by Conyne, Wilson, and Ward (1997). The ASGW outlined four general types of groups: task, psychoeducational, counseling, and psychotherapy groups. For the purposes of the chapter, three of these (i.e., psychoeducational, counseling, and psychotherapy) are relevant to the supervision of group counseling. These types of groups generally differ in the amount of structure used, attention to the group process, and the severity of the problem areas of focus.

Psychoeducational groups typically are skill-based and more highly structured. Counseling groups are less structured and aim to increase the interpersonal relationships and intrapersonal growth of the members. Psychotherapy groups generally address more substantive problems that require behavior change and rely on more group process and less structure. Along with the knowledge and skill of group leaders that generalize to all types of groups, each of these group types benefits from different group leader behaviors. For example, psychoeducational groups typically are brief (e.g., six sessions) and closed to new members after the first session. Leaders need to develop effective time-management skills, the ability to redirect group members when they are off-task, and the ability to articulate clear and specific goals for the group and the members during the first session. Counseling and psychotherapy groups require group leaders who use the dynamics of the group as learning opportunities for the members and who can deal with conflict that occurs more often in these types of less structured groups.

Group Theme

The vast array of groups for special populations also increases the labyrinth of potential knowledge arenas for supervisors. Besides the general considerations of supervision for group counseling, supervision may differ depending on the theme or purpose of the group being facilitated. In these cases, supervisors need to have competence in the specific theme and of the group members' characteristics. Supervision methods have been outlined for numerous counseling groups. A few examples include supervision of child sexual abuse survivor groups (Maidenberg, 2003), eating-disorders groups (DeLucia-Waack, 1999), and a group-analytic approach for psychotic patients (Urlic & Britvic, 2007). Although supervisors of individual counselors also need to have a broad knowledge of clients and their problems, the multitude of interactions that occur within groups result in attention to relationships and interactions with individual group members, with subgroups, between members and leader, and in the group as a whole (DeLucia-Waack & Fauth, 2004). These added layers of intricacies occur for all groups and, therefore, are grist for the supervisory mill.

Supervisor Support

Consistent with the literature on supervision for individual therapists, the role of the supervisor is vital for group counselors. Both supervisees and supervisors have addressed the importance of support expressed by the supervisor, particularly for trainees. For example, supervisees who were satisfied with their supervisory relationship were found to feel supported and saw their supervisors as empathetic. Dissatisfaction resulted in supervisees feeling unheard, criticized, and unhelpful (Leszcz & Murphy, 1994). In a qualitative study of supervisors of trainees conducting counseling groups, supervisors "stressed the role of support during supervision in assisting supervisees to progress as group workers" (Okech, 2009, p. 77).

Diversity Competence

Another area of extreme importance is the multicultural and other diversity competencies of the supervisees who lead groups and of their supervisors. Supervision is thought to play a key role in the development of diversity-competent group leaders (Okech & Rubel, 2007). Seeing the need for group leaders who were competent in addressing the diversity of group members, the ASGW (1998) provided the *Principles for Diversity–Competent Group Workers*, a guiding document that states the following:

> Issues of diversity affect all aspects of group work. This includes but is not limited to: training diversity-competent group workers; conducting research that will add to the literature on group work with diverse populations; understanding how diversity affects group process and dynamics; and assisting group facilitators in various setting to increase their awareness, knowledge, and skill as they relate to facilitating groups with diverse memberships. (p. 7)

This document makes clear the expectation that group leaders need to be competent in responding to diverse group members and calls for supervisors or other persons to oversee that group leaders are aware, sensitive, knowledgeable, and skillful at encouraging and addressing diversity broadly defined.

Supervisee Anxiety

In a review of supervision of group leaders, DeLucia-Waack and Fauth (2004) identified three themes to be addressed by the supervisor. One relates to the anxiety level of the supervisees. Group counseling trainees are often described as having high levels of anxiety. Leszcz and Murphy (1994) described group counselors as being fearful of losing control, looking incompetent, and being overwhelmed by the voluminous amount of material that occurs within group counseling. It is no surprise that research has shown that group counseling trainees often have feelings of apprehension and negative emotional reactions at the beginning of their group therapy leadership experiences (Murphy, Leszcz, Collings, & Salvendy, 1996). Being a group leader for the first time can be a very intimidating undertaking for trainees (Stockton, Morran, & Krieger, 2004). It is important that supervisors acknowledge that anxiety is normal for group leaders-in-training and provide them an opportunity to discuss their feelings and apprehensions in a safe atmosphere.

Parallel Process

A second theme outlined by DeLucia-Waack and Fauth (2004) is parallel process. Friedlander, Siegel, and Brenock (1989) saw the phenomenon of parallel process unfolding when "supervisees unconsciously present themselves to their supervisors as their clients have presented to them" (p. 149). Although parallel process has its roots in psychodynamic supervision, it is a common focus for supervision in general. Etgar (1996) suggested that parallel processes are likely to surface in times of stress and conflict in counseling treatment. With the help of the supervisor, group leaders can examine and work through the parallel process that has been channeled from the counseling group into the supervisory relationship. For example, the author has seen many examples of supervisees leading counseling groups with a highly anxious group member. In supervision, the supervisee presents a description of the case with an urgency expressed by rapid talking, fidgeting, and pleading for a quick solution from the supervisor. This behavior parallels that of the group client, and if processed effectively in supervision, the group facilitator will be able to respond more effectively to the group member's anxiety.

Countertransference

Countertransference often is defined as the group leader's irrational reaction toward the client that emerges from the counselor's unresolved personal issues, often from childhood (Corey & Corey, 2002; Yalom, 2005). Countertransference reactions are likely sparked by responses to authority, conflict, anger, need for control, family relationships, cultural/gender values, and other early learning experiences (e.g., DeLucia-Waack & Fauth, 2004; Halpern, 1989). This third focus area addressed by DeLucia-Waack and Fauth (2004), dealing with the countertransference of group leaders in supervision, requires a solid supervisor–supervisee relationship and sensitivity and skill by the supervisor. Group facilitators may respond to their countertransference by unhelpful methods such as denial or by more productive avenues such as noticing it and discussing it in supervision. Several authors have postulated that identifying and exploring countertransference in a caring supervision environment is the best method for managing this phenomenon with group leaders (Kleinberg, 1999; Murphy et al., 1996).

In the supervisory relationship, countertransference also can relate to the supervisor's responses to the supervisee. Ladany, Constantine, Miller, Erickson, and Muse-Burke (2000) stated that it is "a complex and inevitable process that involves unconscious and exaggerated reactions stemming from a supervisory interaction customarily related to the supervisor's unresolved personal issues or internal conflicts" (p. 102). When supervising group leaders, supervisors need to be cognizant of the countertransference that can occur between supervisees and their group clients as well as their own responses to their supervisees.

Models of Supervision

Theories or models of supervision help to organize large amounts of information and provide guidance on how to conceptualize the supervision and the supervisory relationship. Models of supervision have received considerable interest, as well as debate, along with an increasing amount of research. Bernard and Goodyear (2009) categorized these models into three broad areas: theories of psychotherapy, developmental models, and social role models. The developmental and the social role models were specifically developed for supervision, although much has also been written about supervision using a psychoanalytic lens. None of the models addresses the more intricate features of supervising group counselors, individually or in a group. Yet, these models of supervision are commonly incorporated into all types of supervision.

Psychotherapy Models

Major concepts that are now standard in supervision such as parallel process, countertransference, and the therapeutic alliance were originally derived from psychoanalytic theory. Several psychoanalytic or psychodynamic authors have contributed to the literature on supervision (e.g., Frawley-O'Dea & Sarnat, 2001; Moss, 2008). There also are journals grounded in psychodynamic/analytic theories that regularly include articles on supervision (e.g., *Group Analysis, International Journal of Group Psychotherapy*). From a psychodynamic perspective, the supervisor–supervisee and the supervisee–client relationships are explored and often interpreted. Supervision of group leaders, for example, would likely include a focus on parallel process, being a holding/containing environment for supervisees' anxiety and other feelings, and the countertransference that emerges for group facilitators toward a member or members of their counseling group.

Other psychotherapy theories also have influenced the practice of supervision. From person-centered theory comes the importance of relationship attitudes such as genuineness and positive regard that directly relate to the supervisory alliance (Bernard & Goodyear, 2009) and the relationship between the group leaders and group members. These attitudes are recognized as essential across almost all supervisory models. Cognitive-behavior therapy (CBT) has emphasized the skill-based approach to supervision with the supervisor's responsibilities to teach and help implement these skills. Rosenbaum and Ronen (1998) stated that "the goal of CBT supervision is to help therapists adopt the philosophy of CBT as the basic approach for changing clients' cognitions, emotions, and behaviors. A secondary goal is to teach therapists specific techniques" (p. 220).

Systems theories also have been influential in how supervision is conducted. Although there are many different systems approaches, some of the family systems methods have been incorporated into supervision practiced more broadly. This is particularly true for supervisors who include a family-of-origin emphasis. Live supervision and reflecting teams are strategies that are used in many training programs and training clinics. Systems approaches are very relevant for supervision of group counseling since, similar to counseling groups, family therapy addresses interactions between groups of people. Likewise, many group leaders see family-of-origin behavior that is acted out in the group. For example, a group member may respond to the group leader as if he or she was a parent and, parallel to this, supervisees may respond similarly to supervisors. This is rich material to explore in supervision.

Developmental Models

There are many development approaches to supervision, some published over 40 years ago (e.g., Hogan, 1964). Developmental models became more popular in the 1980s with the publications of Stoltenberg's (1981) counselor-complexity model and later the integrated developmental model (Stoltenberg, McNeil, & Delworth, 1998); Loganbill, Hardy, and Delworth's (1982) conceptual model of supervision; and Ronnestad and Skovholt's (1993) life-span developmental model, the only model that describes stages of development up to the senior professional level. In the ensuing 20 years, there was considerable research and interest in developmental models of supervision. Although these models are different, they all propose that supervisees develop qualitatively across the life of the supervision and that supervisors need to address the stage or phase that a supervisee is in, potentially needing to use distinct supervisory methods that match the particular developmental stage. Although the developmental model is specific to a supervisor and his or her supervisee and for supervisees who conduct individual therapy, the idea that group leader supervisees develop personally and professionally in supervision is just as relevant. Extending these models to group leaders, it makes logical sense that supervisees could be in different developmental stages depending on whether they are leading a counseling group or providing individual psychotherapy.

Social Role Models

Bernard and Goodyear (2009) stated that the "tendency of supervisors to draw on what they already know is complemented by the fact that it is possible to consider supervision a higher order role that encompasses other professional roles" (p. 101). Several authors have talked about the various roles of supervisors, including teacher (Bernard, 1979; Carroll, 1996; Ekstein; 1964; Hess, 1980; Williams, 1995), counselor (Bernard, 1979; Ekstein, 1964; Hess, 1980), consultant (Bernard, 1979; Hess, 1980; Williams, 1995), and evaluator (Williams, 1995). Rather than describing the position taken by a supervisor, Holloway (1995) outlined the functions of the supervisor in her 5 × 5 matrix of functions and tasks. Like other social role models, Holloway demonstrated the elaborate and dynamic process that is embedded in the title "supervisor." When the supervisee is a facilitator of a group with several group members, the tasks and functions of the supervisor multiply.

Methods Specific to Supervision of Groups

There is some literature on methods of supervision that speaks directly to group counseling. Although some of methods of supervision for group counseling have similarities with those already described for individual counseling, they also are unique in several ways. In general, little attention has been paid to the supervision of group leaders (Kleinberg, 1999) and none of the methods that have been proposed has been studied rigorously enough to determine whether it is more effective than any another. This section outlines four frequently used methods of supervising group counselors. For one model, the supervisor meets with the group leader. When the counseling group is being co-led, another option is for the supervisor to meet with the coleaders together. A third widely practiced model is what Leszcz and Murphy (1994) define as *dyadic supervision*, where the supervisor and supervisee colead a counseling group. The fourth possibility is for the supervisor to meet with a group of group leaders, called "group supervision of group leaders."

SUPERVISION WITH THE GROUP LEADER OR COLEADERS

As with all aspects of supervision of group counseling, little energy has been devoted to discussing or investigating supervision with the facilitator(s) of a counseling group. Inferring from the individual supervision literature, Bowman and Delucia (1993) suggested that there are three areas of concentration in supervision: case conceptualization, skill development, and the attention to and resolution of personal reactions that interfere with successfully leading a group. Typically, case conceptualization includes the content of the group material, the dynamics of the group, and the specific clients in the counseling group that is led by the supervisee. The supervisor needs to help the supervisee develop the necessary skills to facilitate the group, including norm setting, goals, providing support, and feedback to group members. The third component addresses the multitude of reactions that can interfere with group facilitation such as countertransference, high anxiety, and parallel process.

When there are coleaders of the group counseling, another layer is added to supervision whether or not the coleaders are supervised together or individually. For supervision that includes the coleaders, Leszcz and Murphy (1994) pointed out that the "cotherapy team is subject to its own process and dynamics, and supervision needs to address issues that invariably arise, including issues of competence, dependency, and rivalry" (p. 112). Several authors have theorized that the development of the coleaders is directly related to the development of the counseling group (Dugo & Beck, 1997; DeLucia, Bowman, & Bowman, 1989; Wheelan, 1997). Although it has not as yet been investigated, it is an intriguing hypothesis. For example, will coleaders who are unable to address their disagreements with each other about how their group is led have a group that is unwilling or unable to disagree with each other or the leader? Yalom (2005) stated that

> it is important that co-therapists feel comfortable and open with each other. They must learn to capitalize on each other's strengths: one leader may be more able to nurture and support and the other more able to confront and to tolerate anger. If the co-therapists are competitive, however, and pursue their own star interpretations rather than support a line of inquiry the other has begun, the group will be distracted and unsettled. (p. 446)

The supervisor will want to encourage the coleaders to not only talk about the group members and group process but also help the coleaders talk directly to each other about their relationship.

SUPERVISOR/SUPERVISEE LEADING A GROUP TOGETHER

Leszcz and Murphy (1994) defined *dyadic supervision* as the "apprenticeship model in which a more experienced group leader co-leads with an inexperienced trainee" (p. 99). In the mental health field, this method enjoys widespread practice as a way of training novice group leaders. It has both advantages and disadvantages. An advantage of this trainee/supervisee coleadership team is that supervisees can observe directly the leadership of a group by an experienced person (Leszcz & Murphy, 1994). Assuming that the supervisory relationship is strong and positive, the group leader supervisor can encourage the supervisee to participate and intervene and not just be an observer. Unfortunately, the author has talked to many supervisees who have co-led a group with their supervisor and unless their supervisor strongly encouraged them to interact and participate, the supervisee sat and watched, feeling like a "substitute leader." Many group leaders who have led a group with their supervisor also revealed that they did not feel like a "real leader" until the supervisor missed a group because of illness and the trainee had to lead the group independently. This model of supervision can work well with a supportive supervisor who discusses the expectations of coleadership with the supervisee, who expects the supervisee to engage with the group, and encourages the supervisee to take on specific functions or tasks in the group. The supervisor will also help the supervisee to manage anxiety that undoubtedly goes with leading a group with one's supervisor. One additional caveat of this supervision style is whether it results in a dual-relationship. If the interactions between a supervisor and supervisee within the coleadership relationship are not supportive or positive and if the senior coleader has supervisory responsibilities of the supervisee coleader outside of the coleadership dyad, a negative working relationship could generalize to other parts of the supervisee's training experience.

GROUP SUPERVISION OF GROUP LEADERS

A commonly discussed model in the literature is providing group supervision with group leaders. In this model, the supervisor meets in a group format with group leaders to discuss group counseling. For many, and especially for those who are psychodynamic, this type of supervision parallels an actual group. This form of supervision is complex but has some advantages over supervision with one group leader supervisee. From a psychodynamic viewpoint, Moss (2008) stated that "being in a supervision group offers opportunities to learn more about group dynamics *in vivo*. Therapists can observe, experience, and explore resistances, splits, transferences, projections, and projective identifications amongst themselves and with the supervisor; thereby increasing their sensitivity to these phenomena in the groups they lead" (p. 188). Newman and Lovell (1993) stated that this format is an "excellent forum for obtaining feedback, encouraging healthy leadership relationships, enhancing group facilitation skills, and fostering counselor-in-training self-awareness" (p. 22). Besides providing unique advantages that demonstrate the group process, it also is seen as an efficient supervision model given that several group leaders can be supervised at the same time. Most of the research on group supervision with groups uses anecdotal interviews with leaders or members or descriptions of the implementation of one supervision group (e.g., Christensen & Kline, 2001; Linton, 2003, Werstlein & Borders, 1997). Obviously, much more research is needed on this important supervision style.

A somewhat complementary body of literature exists on group supervision of individual therapy, which has some of the same dynamics of group supervision of groups. Both models of supervision include group dynamics that occur within the group of supervisees, and these dynamics are often processed and used as learning opportunities by the supervisor. There is some interesting research on group supervision with individual therapy that can provide some parallels to group supervision for group leaders. Similar to group supervision of groups, some of the positive benefits of group supervision of individual therapists include vicarious learning, multiple perspectives, feedback from peers, fostering more cohesion, and exposure to a greater number of clinical cases (Riva & Cornish, 1995, 2008).

One recent study pointed to themes that are related to group leader competence. Bogo, Globerman, and Sussman (2004) conducted qualitative interviews with 18 master's-level social work students who participated in group supervision as part of their field training. Emerging from the interviews were six themes. First, supervision groups were described as positive when the supervisor was available and supportive. Group supervision also was seen as beneficial when there was a clear purpose presented that was educational rather than time-efficient. Most participants stated that they had not received any reason for their participation in the group format, and without a rationale, most group members assumed it was strictly for convenience. A third important component was the need for a leadership style that provided safety and adequate structure and that addressed both content and process. Group supervision was highly valued when group members had time to share information and learn from each other. Another desirable theme was the ability of group leaders to balance personal and public information, as well as individual and group needs. The sixth component spoke to the need for supervisors to adeptly process the dynamics that occur within the supervision group.

Along with any positive group supervision characteristics, there are negative and potentially damaging counterparts to this approach. Enyedy, Arcinue, Puri, Carter, Goodyear, and Getzelman (2003) identified events that could hinder learning in group supervision. Five clusters emerged that ranged from problems between members, with supervisor, supervisee anxiety and other negative effects, logistical restraints, and poor time management. In interviews with four participants of different supervision groups, Linton (2003) found eight themes, similar to those of Bogo et al. (2004) and Enyedy et al. (2003). Components seen as constructive were positive feedback from supervisees and

supervisors, information dissemination, vicarious learning, and acceptance. Prior relationships between group members and with the supervisor were seen as potentially positive or negative based on the type of relationship that existed earlier. Themes that hindered movement in supervision were the lack of constructive feedback, observation by group members of the supervisor's negative response to a supervisee, and poor time management. In a recent study that focused specifically on group processes within group supervision, Linton and Hedstrom (2006) interviewed eight master's students in counseling, outlining five group-process components (i.e., cohesion, conflict, observation, guidance, and feedback from both peers and supervisor). Similar to other studies, they found themes unrelated to group processes such as time considerations, benefits of supervisees with different personal and professions backgrounds, small group size, and educational stressors external to the group supervision.

Another recent study looked at the types of helpful and hindering multicultural events in group supervision (Kaduvettoor et al., 2009). They found that "increased multicultural learning and extra-group multicultural events positively related to supervisees' multicultural competence whereas multicultural conflicts with supervisor, misapplication of multicultural theory, and the absence of multicultural events negatively related to supervisee multicultural competence" (p. 786). This study clearly underscores the importance of multicultural competence for the leader so that he or she can assist group members in increasing their own multicultural competence.

Studies that point to helpful and hindering factors that can occur in group supervision and those that suggest specific types of learning that can take place in this format can be used to guide the practice of group supervision of group counseling as well. Group supervision of group counselors adds one more layer of complexity on top of group supervision of individual psychotherapy. These recent studies also point to positive and negative events that are equally relevant for group counselors who are participating in group supervision (e.g., positive feedback, support, time management, ability to facilitate the group process). An interesting question to consider is whether these same critical events that occur in the group meetings with supervisees also can be extrapolated to those taking place in the counseling groups that these supervisees facilitate, expanding the notion of parallel process.

Future Research Directions
Group Member Outcomes
There are many directions for future research on supervision of group counseling. One critical direction is whether supervision of group leaders improves the outcomes for the group members. It is certainly an expectation in the field that supervision increases the expertise of group leaders, who then are able to transfer this skill to the benefit of their group clients. This area of inquiry is in its infancy. In addressing the scant research on client outcomes in the general supervision literature, Callahan et al. (2009) stated that "cross-tabulation of supervisors by client outcome categories (i.e., recovered, reliably improved, no reliable change, deteriorated) indicated that supervisors are significantly related to client outcomes, generating a moderate effect" (p. 72). They encouraged training programs to consistently track client outcomes as a measure of supervisor quality. It would be wise for those programs that train group leaders to do the same.

Coleadership
Research is also needed on coleadership. Recognizing the limited research on the topic and describing the potential strengths of coleadership, Yalom (2005) stated that

> co-therapists complement and support each other. Together, they have greater cognitive and observational range, and with their dual points of view they may generate more hunches and more strategies. When one therapist, for example, is intensively involved with one member, the co-therapist may be far more aware of the remaining members' responses to the interchange and hence may be in a better position to broaden the range of interaction and exploration. (p. 443)

Many of the advantages espoused for conducting groups with coleadership come from clinical wisdom. Research can begin to tease out whether coleadership really does generate more strategies, actually provides modeling for group members (a commonly stated strength of co-facilitation), or provides more viewpoints for the counseling group. Equally important are studies that investigate positive and negative characteristics of group coleadership teams and effective methods of training and supervising coleadership.

Encouraging and Processing Group Dynamics
Some studies have pinpointed differences between novice and expert group leaders. For example,

Hines, Stockton, and Morran (1995) found that three cognitive categories were positively correlated with group leader experience level: interpretation of group process, internal questions regarding a member, and interpretation of a group member's behavior. Interpretation of the group process (e.g., group leader thinks, "group members just changed the topic to avoid dealing with their anxiety around this discussion") was the most important category to predict experience level. More experienced group facilitators interpreted group process, asked internal questions about the members, and interpreted the behavior of group members more often than less experienced group leaders. Similar differentiations were found by Kivlighan and Quigley (1991). The importance of group leaders attending to group process is well-articulated in the literature, and a small amount of research supports that this variable distinguishes leaders' level of experience. Research now needs to begin to identify training and supervisory methods that effectively increase novice group leaders' awareness, promotion, and facilitation of group process. Related to client outcomes, it will also be essential for researchers to tie the adroitness of group leaders' responses to group process with group members' improvement.

Supervision and Skill Development
Throughout this chapter, there has been a call for more research specifically on supervision of group counseling. Beneficial studies will address effective methods of skill development in supervision and whether these particular skills translate to the supervisee's role of group counselor. The author has an urge to say that, given the lack of research on supervision of group counseling, almost any reasonable question is worth studying. Yet, it is important that this research agenda begins to define what supervisory methods work to increase the skill level of the supervisees, how supervision methods are related to client outcomes, and how supervision can increase cognitive complexity and other valued characteristics seen in expert group leaders.

Ethical Considerations in Supervision of Group Leaders
There are many potential dilemmas in group counseling that are not common in individual therapy. Much of the information on ethical clinical practice surrounds individual therapy. Recently, there has been more discussion of ethical considerations specifically related to group counseling (ASGW, 2000; Lasky & Riva, 2006; Rapin, 2004), although

little has been written about the ethical dilemmas related to supervision of groups. Future research on ethics in the supervision of group leaders needs to address two broad areas. First, studies need to consider ethical dilemmas in group counseling and how familiar supervisors are with the ethical guidelines of their state and national organizations to competently aid group leaders in appreciating and dealing with these potential dilemmas. Group counseling poses many sticky considerations concerning the limits to confidentiality (Lasky & Riva, 2006), informed consent, voluntary participation of group members, working with minors in a group, and multiple relationships for group members and with the leader, etc.

The second area for inquiry relates to the ethical considerations that are involved in the supervisory relationship. There are guiding documents such as those articulated by the Association for Counselor Education and Supervision in their *Ethical Guidelines for Counseling Supervisors* (Supervision Interest Network, 1993). This document discusses what the supervisor should incorporate in supervision, such as informed consent, expectations for participation, and due process as well as the appeal process. Although there are national surveys on ethical and legal considerations for supervision in general, supervision of group counseling is dissimilar enough to supervision of individual psychotherapy that research is needed in a multitude of areas that can inform practice. Some questions are related to how supervisors are practicing supervision with group leaders, what methods are they using to teach ethical decision making, are they up to date with the ethical and legal guidelines for their state, what are effective methods in responding to a supervisee who has inadequate skill development, how do personality difficulties interfere with client care, and supervisor characteristics that are most related to supervisee's positive skill development.

Conclusion

Supervision of group counseling is a vital component in the training of group leaders. The field desperately needs competent and ethical group leaders, especially with the burgeoning of counseling groups across all mental health settings. Supervision research is beginning to show its effect on increasing skill development, and recent studies on the relationship between supervision of individual therapists and client outcomes have been promising. Much more research is needed on supervision of group counseling, specifically given that it is much more intricate than other types of supervision. It is an exciting time to focus on supervision of group counseling. Group counseling has gained increased attention and respect, and there needs to be a commitment to the education, training, and supervision of developing group leaders.

References

Association for Specialist in Group Work (ASGW). (1999). Association for Specialists in Group Work principles for diversity-competent group workers. Retrieved on February 25, 2011 from www.asgw.org.

Association for Specialist in Group Work (ASGW). (2000). Association for Specialists in Group Work professional standards for the training of group workers. *Journal for Specialists in Group Work, 25*, 327–342.

Bernard, J.M. (1979). Supervisor training: A discrimination model. *Counselor Education and Supervision, 19*, 60–68.

Bernard, J. M., & Goodyear, R. K. (2009). *Fundamentals of clinical supervision* (4th ed.). Boston: Allyn & Bacon.

Bloom, B. S., Engelhart, M.D., Furst, F.J., Hill, W.H., & Krathwohl, D.R. (1956). *Taxonomy of educational objectives: Cognitive domain*. New York: McKay.

Bobo, M., Globeman, J., & Sussman, T. (2004). Field instructor competence in group supervision: Student views. *Journal of Teaching in Social Work, 24*, 199–216.

Borders, L. D. (1989). A pragmatic agenda for developmental supervision research. *Counselor Education and Supervision, 29*, 16–24.

Bowman, V. E., & Delucia, J. L. (1993). Preparation for counseling revisited: New applications to meet the goals of brief counseling. *Crisis Intervention & Time-Limited Treatment, 2*, 255–266.

Callahan, J. L., Almstom, C. M., Swift, J. K., Borja, S. E., & Heath, C. J. (2009). Exploring the contributions of supervisors to intervention outcomes. *Training and Education in Professional Psychology, 3*, 72–77.

Carroll, M. (1996). *Counseling supervision: Theory, skills, and practice*. London: Cassell.

Christensen, T. M., & Kline, W. B. (2001). A qualitative investigation of the process of group supervision with group counselors. *Journal for Specialists in Group Work, 25*, 376–393.

Conyne, R. K., Wilson, F. R., & Ward, D. E. (1997). *Comprehensive group work: What it means and how to teacher it*. Alexandria, VA: American Counseling Association.

Corey, M. S., & Corey, G. (2002). *Groups: Process and practice* (6th ed.). Monterey, CA: Brooks/Cole.

DeLucia, J. L., Bowman, V. E., & Bowman, R. L. (1989). The use of parallel process in supervision and group counseling to facilitate counselor and client growth. *Journal for Specialists in Group Work, 14*, 232–238.

DeLucia-Waack, J. L. (1999). Supervision for counselors working with eating disorders groups. Countertransference issues related to body image, food, and weight. *Journal of Counseling & Development, 77*, 379–388.

DeLucia-Waack, J. L., & Fauth, J. (2004). Effective supervision of group leaders: Current theory, research, and implication for practice. In J. L. Delucia-Waack, D. D. Gerrity, C. R. Kalodner, & M. T. Riva (Eds.), *Handbook of group counseling and psychotherapy* (pp. 136–150). Thousand Oaks, CA: Sage.

DeLucia-Waack, J. L., Gerrity, D. D., Kalodner, C. R., & Riva, M. T. (Eds.) (2004). *Handbook of group counseling and psychotherapy*. Thousand Oaks, CA: Sage.

Douce, L. (1989, August). *Classroom and experiential training in supervision*. Paper presented at the annual meeting of the American Psychological Association, New Orleans.

Dugo, J. M., & Beck, A. P. (1997). Significance and complexity of early phases in the development of the co-therapy relationship. *Group Dynamics: Theory, Research, & Practice, 1,* 294–305.

Ekstein, R. (1964). Supervision of psychotherapy: Is it teaching? Is it administration? Or is it therapy? *Psychotherapy, Research, and Practice, 1,* 137–138

Enyedy, K.C., Arcinue, F., Puri, N.N., Carter, J.W., Goodyear, R.K., & Getzelman, M.A. (2003). Hindering phenomena in group supervision: Implication for practice. *Professional Psychology: Research and Practice, 34,* 312–317.

Etgar, T. (1996). Parallel processes in a training and supervision group for counselors working with adolescent sex offenders. *Social Work with Groups, 19,* 57–69.

Falender, C. A., Cornish, J. A. E., Goodyear, R., Hatcher, R., Kaslow, N. J., Leventhal, G., et al. (2004). Defining competencies in psychology supervision: A consensus statement. *Journal of Clinical Psychology, 60,* 771–785.

Frawley-O'Dea, M.G., & Sarnat, J.E. (2001). *The supervisory relationship. A contemporary psychodynamic approach*. New York: Guilford Press.

Freitas, F.J. (2002). The impact of psychotherapy supervision on client outcome: A critical examination of 2 decades of research. *Psychotherapy: Theory, Research, Practice, and Training, 39,* 354–367.

Friedlander, M. L., Siegel, S. M., & Brenock, K. (1989). Parallel process in counseling and supervision. A case study. *Journal of Counseling Psychology, 36,* 149–157.

Fuhriman, A., & Burlingame, G. (2001). Group psychotherapy: training and effectiveness. *International Journal of Group Psychotherapy, 51,* 399–416.

Granello, D. H., & Underfer-Babalis, J. (2004). Supervision of group work: A model to increase supervisee cognitive complexity. *Journal for Specialists in Group Work, 29,* 159–173.

Halpern, D. A. (1989). Countertransference and group psychotherapy: The role of supervision. In D. A. Halperin (Ed.), *Group psychodynamics: New paradigms and new perspectives* (pp. 62–75). Chicago: Year Book Medical Publishers.

Hess, A. K. (1980). Training models and the nature of psychotherapy supervision. In A. D. Hess (Ed.), *Psychotherapy supervision: Theory, research, and practice* (pp. 15–28). New York: John Wiley & Sons.

Hines, P. L., Stockton, R., & Morran, D. K. (1995). Self-talk of group therapists. *Journal of Counseling Psychology, 42,* 242–248.

Hoffman, M. A., Hill, C. E., Holmes, S. E., & Freitas, G. F. (2005). Supervisor perspective on the process and outcome of giving easy difficult, or no feedback to supervisees. *Journal of Counseling Psychology, 52,* 3–13.

Hogan, R. (1964). Issues and approaches in supervision. *Psychotherapy: Theory, Research, and Practice, 1,* 139–141.

Holloway, E. L. (1995). *Clinical supervision: A systems approach*. Thousand Oaks, CA: Sage.

Kaduvettoor, A., O'Shaughnessy, T., Mori, Y., Beverly, C., Weatherford, R.D., & Ladany, N. (2009). Helpful and Hindering Multicultural Events in Group Supervision: Climate and Multicultural Competence. *The Counseling Psychologist, 37,* 786–820.

Kivlighan, D. M., Jr., & Kivlighan, D. M., III. (2009). Training related changes in the ways that group trainees structure their knowledge of group counseling leader interventions. *Group Dynamics: Theory, Research, and Practice, 13,* 190–204.

Kivlighan, D. M., & Quigley, S. T. (1991). Dimensions used by experienced and novice group therapists to conceptualize group process. *Journal of Counseling Psychology, 38,* 415–423.

Kleinbeg, J. L. (1999). The supervisory alliance and the training of psychodynamic group psychotherapists. *International Journal of Group Psychotherapy, 49,* 159–179.

Ladany, N., Constantine, M. G., Miller, K., Erickson, C. D., & Muse-Burke, J. L. (2000). Supervisor countertransference: A qualitative investigation into its identification and description. *Journal of Counseling Psychology, 47,* 103–115.

Lasky, G. B., & Riva, M. T. (2006). Confidentiality and privileged communication in group psychotherapy. *International Journal of Group Psychotherapy, 73,* 284–292.

Leszcz, M., & Murphy, L. (1994). Supervision of group psychotherapy. In S. S. Greben & R. Ruskin (Eds.), *Clinical perspectives on psychotherapy supervision* (pp. 99–120). Washington, DC: American Psychiatric Press.

Linton, (2003). A preliminary qualitative investigation of group processes in group supervision: Perspective of master's level practicum students. *Journal for Specialists in Group Work, 28,* 215–226.

Linton, J.M., & Hedstrom, S.M. (2006). An exploratory qualitative investigation of group processes in group supervision: Perceptions of Master-level practicum students. *Journal for Specialists in Group Work, 31,* 51–72.

Loganbill, C., Hardy, E., & Delworth, U. (1982). Supervision: A conceptual model. *Counseling Psychologist, 10,* 3–42.

Maidenberg, M. P. (2003). Considerations in supervision: Conducting child sexual abuse survivor groups. *Clinical Supervisor, 22,* 81–97.

Moss, E. (2008). The holding/containing function in supervision groups for group therapists. *International Journal of Group Psychotherapy, 58,* 185–201.

Murphy, L., Leszcz, M., Collings, A. K., & Salvendy, J. (1996). Some observations on the subjective experiences of neophyte group therapy trainees. *International Journal of Group Psychotherapy, 46,* 543–552.

Nelson, M. L., Gray, L. A., Friedlander, M. L., Ladany, N., & Walker, J. A. (2001). Toward relationship-centered supervision: Reply to Veach (2001) and Ellis (2001). *Journal of Counseling Psychology, 48,* 407–409.

Newman, J. A., & Lovell, M. (1993). Supervision: A description of a supervisory group for group counselors. *Counselor Education & Supervision, 33,* 22–31.

Okech, J. E. A. (2009). The experiences of expert group work supervisors: An exploratory study. *Journal for Specialists in Group Work, 34,* 68–89.

Okech, J. E. A., & Rubel, D. (2007). Diversity competent group work supervision: an application of the supervisor of group work model (SGW). *Journal for Specialists in Group Work, 32,* 245–266.

Ramos-Sanchez, L., Esnil, E., Goodwin, A., Riggs, S., Touster, L. O., Wright, L. K., et al. (2002). Negative supervisory events: Effects on supervision and supervisory alliance. *Professional Psychology: Research and Practice, 33,* 197–202.

Rapin, L. S. (2004). Guidelines for ethical and legal practice in group counseling and psychotherapy groups. In J. L. Delucia-Waack, D. A. Gerrity, C. R. Kalodner, & M. T. Riva (Eds.),

Handbook of group counseling and psychotherapy (pp. 151–165). Thousand Oaks, CA: Sage.

Riva, M. T., & Cornish, J. A. E. (1995). Group supervision practices at psychology predoctoral internship programs: A national survey. *Professional Psychology: Research and Practice, 26,* 523–525.

Riva, M. T., & Cornish, J. A. E. (2008). Group supervision practices at psychology predoctoral internship programs: 15 years later. *Training and Education in Professional Psychology, 2,* 18–25.

Ronnestad, M. H., and Skovholt, T. M. (1993). Supervision of beginning and advanced graduate students of counseling and psychotherapy. *Journal of Counseling and Development, 71,* 396–405.

Rosenbaum, M., & Ronen, T. (1998). Clinical supervision from the standpoint of cognitive-behavioral therapy. *Psychotherapy: Theory, Research, Practice, Training, 35,* 220–230.

Rubel, D., & Okech, J. E. A. (2009). The expert group work supervision process: Apperception, actions, and interactions. *Journal for Specialists in Group Work, 34,* 227–250.

Stockton, R., Morran, D. K., & Krieger, K. M. (2004). An overview of current research and best practices for training beginning group leaders. In J. L. Delucia-Waack, D. A. Gerrity, C. R. Kalodner, & M. T. Riva (Eds.), *Handbook of group counseling and psychotherapy* (pp. 65–75). Thousand Oaks, CA: Sage.

Stoltenberg, C. (1981). Approaching supervision from a developmental perspective: The counselor complexity model. *Journal of Counseling Psychology, 28,* 59–65.

Stoltenberg, C. D., McNeil, B. W., & Delworth, U. (1998). *IDM: An integrated developmental model for supervising counselors and therapists.* San Francisco: Jossey-Bass.

Stoppard, J. M., & Miller, A. (1985). Conceptual level matching in therapy: A review. *Current Psychological Research and Reviews, 4,* 47–68.

Supervision Interest Network Association for Counselor Education and Supervision (1993, Summer). ACES ethical guidelines for counseling supervisors. *ACES Spectrum, 53* (4), 5–8.

Urlic, I., & Britvic, D. (2007). Group supervision of group psychotherapy with psychotic patients: A group-analytic approach. *Group Analysis, 40,* 269–284.

Welfel, E. R. (2006). *Ethics in counseling and psychotherapy: Standards, research, and emerging issues* (3rd ed.). Belmont, CA: Brooks/Cole.

Werstlein, P.O., & Borders, L.D. (1997). Group process variables in group supervision. *Journal for Specialists in Group Work, 22,* 120–136.

Wheelan, S. A. (1997). Co-therapists and the creation of a functional psychotherapy group: A group dynamics perspective. *Group Dynamics: Theory, Research, and Practice, 1,* 306–310.

Williams, A. (1995). *Visual and active supervision: roles, focus, technique.* New York: W.W. Norton.

Yalom, I. D. (with Leszcz, M.) (2005). *The theory and practice of group psychotherapy* (5th ed.). New York: Basic Books.

Creativity and Spontaneity in Groups

Samuel T. Gladding

Abstract

This chapter examines creativity and spontaneity and how they can be used in groups of all types including group counseling. These concepts are first defined and steps in the creative process are discussed. Then, the importance and benefits of creativity and spontaneity in groups are examined. Research related to their use and value in group settings is explored. Ways of promoting creativity and spontaneity in groups are discussed next, along with barriers to being creative in a group. Finally, questions regarding the future of using creativity and spontaneity in groups are raised, and Web sites related to creativity and spontaneity in groups follow the conclusion.

Keywords: groups, group counseling, creativity, spontaneity, creative groups

Introduction

When the Whiffenpoofs, a Yale a cappella singing group, came on stage, my heart did not skip a beat; but I felt it speed up a bit as I sensed the energy from the group and the creativity that was in the air. I knew the words they were going to sing, "Bright College Years," the Yale alma mater. What I did not know was how they would perform it. To say their rendition of the song was different from how I had heard it performed by the Yale Glee Club many years previously would be an understatement. However, the difference was both enjoyable and stimulating. The songsters produced a delightful, melodious sound with a range of notes and an emphasis on words that I had never heard before. There was a spontaneous, interactive spirit to the group as well. Some of the men put their hands over their hearts or their arms over the shoulders of those who sang beside them. Before me was an exemplary demonstration of group creativity and spontaneity. The group had interacted to produce a variation on a melody and a unique cadence. The familiar had changed. The old had been transformed into something new and wonderful. The results brought a standing ovation as creativity and

spontaneity in the personhood of young college men exited the stage. While the event is now history, the memory of the power of the time still lingers in my mind. That is what creativity and spontaneity can do.

I open this chapter with the Whiffenpoofs story as a representative example of what can transpire in a group when leaders and members allow themselves the freedom and latitude creative processes and spontaneous interactions provide. Whether the task is work, education, counseling, or therapy, creativity and spontaneity are qualities that can make a group more productive, more exciting, and more positive if they are harnessed constructively and effectively.

What Are Creativity and Spontaneity?

Before examining the impact of creativity and spontaneity in groups, it is necessary to define them. That task is more difficult than it would first appear because creativity and spontaneity are elusive concepts to define and measure.

Creativity

There are over 200 definitions of *creativity* (Kaufman & Sternberg, 1996; Sternberg, 1999). In essence, creativity is like the weather in that everyone talks about it and attempts to understand it. However, some attempts are more accurate than others. A widely accepted definition of *creativity* has been given by Sternberg and Lubart (1996), who define it as "the ability to produce work that is both novel (i.e., original or unexpected) and appropriate (i.e., useful or meets task constraints)" (p. 677–678). Thus, a behavior can be new but non-productive, like group members standing on their heads or mooing like cows. Such action is anything but creative because it is useless. Likewise, an action can be suitable for a situation, such as doing an ice-breaker exercise at the beginning of a group. Yet, as functional as this activity may be, it is not considered creative because it is not novel and may be even hackneyed.

Most early definitions, and even some contemporary ones, describe creativity as an innate talent unevenly distributed in society, with some individuals possessing it and others not (Wilson, 2009). These definitions usually attribute original breakthroughs to the genius of one person with extraordinary ability. But such a conceptualization is inaccurate (John-Steiner, 2000).

Creativity is both a social and an individual process (Leonard & Swap, 1999; Montuori & Purser, 1999; Sawyer, 2008). It is a needed condition to build community. It involves communicating with and interacting with others to develop alternative ideas. Bowman and Boone (1998) discuss and define creativity in terms of four words starting with the letter *P*: person(s), press (i.e., environment), process, and product. These factors are embraced by international scholars as well (Kaufman & Sternberg, 1996). Therefore, "creativity does not happen inside people's heads, but in the interaction between a person's thoughts and a sociocultural context" (Csikszentmihalyi, 1996, p. 23). The outcome may be tangible or not, but the process is almost always interesting and sometimes the result is life-changing (Pink, 2006). Take, for example, the discovery of the double-helix structure of the DNA molecule, which is credited to James D. Watson and Francis Crick in 1953. The two men exchanged ideas with one another, but they also interacted with a woman named Rosalind Franklin, who served as a catalyst to Watson's thinking by showing him unpublished X-ray diffraction pictures of DNA. It was only through the dynamic combined work of this group of three that the final ideas about the structure of DNA were formed.

Indeed, creativity is a course of action that is almost always generated in a group regardless of how it is ultimately carried out (Paulus, 2000, 2008; Paulus & Nijstad, 2003; Paulus, Larey, & Dzindolet, 2000). The proof of the power of groups in creativity is verified by citation of historical and contemporary examples of the ways groups foster the creative process. For example, it is generally agreed that Florence was initially the leading city of the Renaissance. Why Florence? The reason is that a culture of creativity grew up among the group of merchants, craftsmen, bankers, and elected officials who controlled the city (Csikszentmihalyi, 1996). This group expected and promoted creativity in order to advance the status of this landlocked city-state. The citizens of Florence, following this leadership, encouraged creativity, especially in the arts. Thus, from this group movement the painters Michelangelo and Botticelli and the architect Brunelleschi, among others, were supported and flourished. However, creativity in groups is not confined to the arts (Leonard & Swap, 1999). In twentieth-century North America, California's Silicon Valley has become synonymous with innovation. A culture of creativity has been fostered in this area by computer makers and information technology leaders (Kaplan, 2000). As a group they have expected and promoted mores where people are free, even expected, to take risks, to be innovative, to make mistakes, and to succeed.

Besides the fact that creativity is fostered in groups is the fact that it is not static or monolithic (Kersting, 2003). Creativity helps people not only establish a bond between themselves and the world but also enlarge their worlds in enriching and expansive ways (Arieti, 1976). There are at least two forms of creativity in a group. In *inventive creativity*, group members offer unique solutions to a problem. For example, how can people in cities be encouraged to recycle more? Some possible solutions include paying them to recycle, having neighborhood contests that reward groups that recycle, and hiring a "recycle cop" to inspect trash for recyclable goods and fine people who throw away recyclable materials. Likewise, in *innovative creativity*, group members examine an issue from alternative viewpoints. For instance, why should society promote the formation of think tanks? Alternative solutions might include keeping deep thinkers employed to prevent a brain drain to other countries and making use of those who have more brains than brawn.

Regardless of how creativity is fostered, it is always evolving. Creativity is a worldwide phenomenon that knows no bounds in regard to ethnicity, culture, gender, age, or other real or imagined barriers that separate people from each other (Kaufman & Sternberg, 1996). In addition, creativity can be both preventative as well as remedial. Like all strengths, creativity exists on a continuum. Basically, there are two types of creativity: "little *c*" creativity and "big *C*" creativity (Csikszentmihalyi, 1996). Big *C* creativity is reserved for once-in-a-lifetime creative acts. Einstein, da Vinci, and Edison are examples of individuals with this type of creativity. They formulated, painted, and invented in such a way that society was transformed and people were given new knowledge and perspectives. In contrast, little *c* creativity refers to day-to-day creativity. "Being creative with a capital C is largely beyond our control. Living a creative personal life is not" (p. 147). It is little *c* creativity that is most often found in creative groups. This type of creativity is often expressed through positive affect (e.g., humor), play, fantasy, divergent thinking, and the use of metaphors, with the results manifesting themselves in increased flexibility, adaptability to change, effective problem solving, resilience, and the accepting of new perspectives (Morgan & Wampler, 2003).

Hard work, deep knowledge, and time are always prerequisites for creativity, whatever its form. Inventors, scientists, teachers, artists, technicians, therapists, engineers, and writers spend years mastering their respective domains before making a valued creative contribution. Group leaders who become skilled in working with a variety of groups do the same. "Creativity is rarely the product of a single moment; perhaps more often it is the result of a lifetime" (Csikszentmihalyi, 1996, p. 192). Cohen (2001) has shown that even in advanced age individuals who have been creative or who have prepared themselves to be creative make significant contributions to their fields.

In examining the creative process, it should also be emphasized that group creativity includes selecting the right mix of people to spark an imagination course of action. For instance, Taggar (2001) found in studying 94 intact autonomous work groups that group creativity increased exponentially with the number of highly creative group members composing the group. Furthermore, creativity is generated or inhibited by taking the necessary time to consider choices (Leonard & Swap, 1999). Groups are much less creative when they are under time pressure, when they are being scrutinized and judged by others, or when external circumstances limit the range of options available.

Spontaneity

Spontaneity is different from creativity, but creativity and spontaneity appear to be linked (Maslow, 1971). Jacob Moreno (1953), the founder of psychodrama, "hypothesized that spontaneity leads to creativity, which, in turn, results in cultural conserves. Once created, cultural conserves encourage further spontaneity through the warm-up process, and the cycle repeats itself" (Kipper, 2006, p. 119). "The first character of the creative act is its spontaneity" according to Moreno (1964, p. 35).

While Moreno's description of the linkage between spontaneity and creativity may not be as strong as he originally thought, Kipper (2006) reports that a factor analysis reveals that creativity is one of five factors that comprise the Spontaneity Assessment Inventory, albeit the smallest one (responsible for 8.85% of the explained variance). He states that although spontaneity and creativity are separate states of mind, they share some characteristics.

Accordingly, the classic definition, as cited by Kipper (2006), has become that "Spontaneity is a state of mind, or a state of readiness to act creatively. It is a form of an intrinsic motivation (i.e., energy) that precedes the process of acting" (p. 119). Other definitions are complementary but propose that spontaneity is uncontainable energy expended in an all-or-nothing, one-time manner (Kipper, 2000). While spontaneity may be such behavior on occasions, these definitions that include phrases such as "uncontrollable" and "all-or-nothing" actually confuse many people about what spontaneity is for as Egan (1976) has noted spontaneity does not mean to be impulsive but rather to have the ability to respond assertively in a variety of ways. Thus, Kipper's (2006) definition is preferred.

Spontaneous expression is particularly helpful in some specific situations. For instance, it "is most useful when an individual is undergoing a significant life event such as an emotional crisis, physical illness, or the process of dying" (Malchiodi, 2003a, p. 47). In such a venue, Bonhote, Romano-Egan, and Cornwell (1999) report how a group member's spontaneous act of bringing in a lover's quotation book to an elderly group on Valentine's Day enabled group members to connect with each other on a much deeper emotional level with the readings, shared experiences, and feeling states. When used in other situations, such as art therapy groups, spontaneous expressions "are containers of repressed emotions as well as sources of transformation" (Malchiodi, 2003a, p. 47).

Overall, spontaneity is seen as observable, teachable, and in many cases therapeutic. For example, spontaneity may be a part of drama therapy. As such, it has been found to be part of a rehabilitation effort in residential treatment centers by groups of women dealing with addiction or incarceration (Stahler, 2006). Spontaneity correlates positively with well-being, self-discipline, and the positive interpersonal connection that can occur in natural settings. For instance, Tucker (2001) found that experiential activities, such as a nature walk, can result in spontaneous learning and positive interactions. Conversely, as would be expected, spontaneity deficits correlate positively with measures of anxiety, obsessive–compulsive behavior, repetition, dull form of living, and an orientation toward the past. As with creativity, "spontaneity is a 'trainable' trait. It may increase with age and practice (Bratton, Ceballos, & Ferebee, 2009). Some individuals (Olson & Thomas, 1999) even advocate management by spontaneity, although no one has tried this style yet and there is no evidence that it would work.

The Creative Process

Creativity does not just happen. It is a process that takes time and effort. The way it occurs is important to understand for it has a bearing on how creativity can be encouraged or discouraged and how it emerges. Like creativity in general, group creativity is a nonsequential experience that involves six steps:

The first step is *preparation*, which is the phase of gathering enough data and background information to make a new response. As Gladwell (2009) so well points out, individuals who have not invested 10,000 or more hours in a domain do not have the background or the skills necessary to make breakthrough contributions to the field. Likewise, groups need time to prepare. They may not require the same amount of time an individual needs because of the collected experience of the group. Nevertheless, a group, especially a counseling group, must work through the stages of forming, storming, and norming before it gets to performing in a productive way (Tuckman, 1965).

The second step is *incubation*, where the mind is allowed to wander away from a task or problem. Just as people do not live by bread alone, a group that becomes creative does so by not constantly and unrelentingly focusing exclusively on a predicament. The importance of incubation to resolving a task or problem can be seen most

graphically in the individual anecdote of Archimedes and his struggle to determine if a gold crown was composed of pure gold. As the story goes, Archimedes figured out the solution to the problem, one of displacement, while taking a bath and noting how the water level changed. He is then purported to have run through the streets naked shouting "Eureka!" because of his excitement. While modern-day groups may not show the drama of an Archimedes, the essential concept of incubation as a major ingredient in group creativity has been experimentally confirmed by Paulus and Yang (2000) in a reflective sharing session among groups that generated ideas together and alone. Groups that shared ideas as they were generated were able in a subsequent session to recall more of these ideas and even expand on them.

The third step in the creative process is *ideation*, in which ideas are generated but not judged (i.e., divergent thinking). "Divergent thinking in groups is reflected in ideational fluency" (Paulus, 2003, p. 237). The more ideas that are generated, the more likely a group will find an idea that is eventually considered useful and, as a result, group creativity will flourish. Simple, straightforward techniques for generating ideas in groups include such activities as "idea garden" (Ricchiuto, 1996). The idea garden is a progressive step procedure like tending a garden. Initially, people are asked to generate broad ideas that do not have to have any details—the kind of ideas that emerge in traditional brainstorming. As thoughts sprout up, more detailed ideas are asked for and mind-mapping styles of recording may be put in place to make sure everything gets recorded. Details that emerge usually stimulate the natural emergence of practical questions and concerns. The group then invents alternative solutions (i.e., variations), to take care of as many of these considerations as possible. There is always compost—ideas that do not work. However, the idea garden usually produces a rich harvest. The tone throughout is consistently positive, conveying that problems are solvable if the group stays provocative, open-minded, practical, and inventive enough together.

Illumination, where there is a breakthrough in thinking, a kind of enlightenment, is the fourth step in the creative process. A classic example of illumination is the invention of the sewing machine by Elias Howe in 1845. After trying to invent the machine with needles that were pointed at both ends with a hole in the middle, Howe had a dream where he was taken prisoner by a group of natives whose spears each had a hole near their tip. This illumination from the group he dreamed of gave him the solution to the problem he faced, with an effective needle for the machine. He made the machine with a needle that had a hole near its tip.

The fifth step in group creativity is *evaluation*, where convergent and critical thinking occur along with fine-tuning and refining thoughts or behaviors. An example of evaluation can be seen in the Manhattan Project of World War II, where a group of Allied scientists, under the direction of Robert Oppenheimer, worked to produce the first atomic bomb. This project initially resulted in the creation of multiple ideas. However, through a coordinated effort, data were evaluated and a process was put in place to pursue only the most promising proposals.

Finally, there is *verification/production*, during which an original idea becomes a new or refined product or action. In this last step of the creative process, a group's life changes, for it is impossible to see or be in the world again as it was before the novel idea or product came into existence. For example, when Margaret Mitchell's epic *Gone with the Wind* was transformed from words in a book to action on a movie screen, the group that produced the film gave viewers a different perspective on the characters in the drama and the original ideas from Mitchell's pen were transformed. How authentic the characters were to their descriptions in the book was verified in a painstaking manner by Mitchell and the producers. Audiences loved the finished product and verified what the film crew did in bringing the book to life.

The Importance and Benefits of Creativity and Spontaneity in Groups

"There is no question that the human species could not survive . . . if creativity were to run dry" (Csikszentmihalyi, 1996, p. 317). That is because life requires flexibility and those who cannot adjust to immediate situations by being spontaneous and flexible are in danger. In fact, historically, groups of human who have not been creative have perished. Likewise, spontaneity plays a significant role in the survival of individuals and groups. Whether in the form of individual expressions of feelings, such as a shout or a whisper, or unplanned group interactions, such as an exchange of hugs or handshakes, spontaneity stirs excitement within a group and is often a catalyst in helping a group bond and build trust.

Successful groups incorporate both innovation and routine in their interactions (Sawyer, 2003; Tubbs, 2008). Constant change leads to lack of direction, confusion, frustration, and reduced productivity. However, too much stability leads to inflexibility, an inability to adapt, and a tendency to follow rules without questioning them. Thus, in counseling groups there needs to be a balance between creativity and standard procedure so that originality is not stifled and yet usual channels for productivity are kept open.

Group creativity involves teamwork and collaboration since individual group members' creative and spontaneous endeavors do not necessarily help the group achieve its goals (Jarboe, 1999). This cooperative process may occur in the interaction of formal and informal groups. Formal groups occur on multiple levels from business and government to college and recreational environments. In these groups, people are brought together in a structured way to think, feel, act, and put together products or processes that are unique and sometimes universal. Assembling a group of engineers to build a bridge is an example of a formal group. Informal groups are much more diverse and less structured. Like formal groups, they often solve or resolve difficulties and make new things. However, an event or a wish is more likely to bring them together. Thus, they may take the form of a neighborhood watch, a spontaneous drive to help an injured friend, an improvisation comedy troupe, or even a jazz band (Sawyer, 2003, 2008). These groups may last for only a brief time, and once they have accomplished their goals or gigs, they may disband. Regardless, both types of groups may produce effective and long-lasting results. The teamwork and interactive collaboration found within these groups are the foundations of their creativity.

Research on Creativity and Spontaneity in Groups

Group work is crucial in different mental health, social, business, and spiritual establishments. However, research on the outcomes of groups has had an uneven history. That is especially true for research on creativity and spontaneity in groups since such processes cannot usually be reduced to techniques because they naturally emerge (Bowman & Boone, 1998). Thus, quantitative research on these two factors in groups is not as prevalent as qualitative studies. However, both forms of research show how creativity and spontaneity influence the outcome of a group's experience, especially in counseling groups and task/work groups.

In counseling groups, for instance, Malchiodi (2003b) and Waller (2003) extol the power of using art as a creative medium for promoting the group process. Specifically, Malchiodi (2003b) employed a wellness model to lead an art therapy group, which she described as a "creativity and wellness group," for women with breast cancer. The focus of the group, which was conducted for 10 weekly sessions of one and a half hours in length, was on identifying and capturing group members' capacity for creativity and art making. Group activities included scribble drawings (to encourage playfulness), body image sketches (to explore body image), the keeping of a visual journal, the drawing of mandalas, and the making of images. The group allowed this patient population to communicate "the 'unspoken aspects' of illness," to enhance their ability to reduce stress and to facilitate a search for meaning (p. 360). Participants were able to focus on who they were and what they could do rather than the disabling aspects of their maladies.

In addition to doing art therapy work in groups by itself, Wald (2003) found that combining creative writing with art can be powerful in a group setting. She used "once-upon-a-time" stories as a way of helping older adults express emotions such as fear, hope, and worry in story booklets. In this way, she worked through these feelings with her participants in a group setting. Wald's idea took the concept of "therapeutic fairy tales," as originated by Hoskins (1985), from the individual level to the group level. The therapeutic effects of creative writing, especially on stressful matters, has been well researched and documented by James Pennebaker (1997, 2002) and utilized in group settings by Wenz and McWhirter (1990).

Pennebaker's extensive research involving expressive writing groups for people of all ages is particularly relevant for utilizing writing as a tool in group counseling. Pennebaker started his work with college students by asking them to write about something that was traumatic. They wrote about something they had never told anybody for 20 minutes a day on four different days of the week. They did so for a couple of months. They focused on their deepest thoughts and feelings, while a control group wrote about something more neutral, like their shoes. Although the expressive writing group was initially more depressed, its members were significantly happier 3 months later when compared to the control group. Furthermore, 6 weeks into this group research, the expressive writing group showed evidence of a stronger immune response on measures of T-cell function compared to the control group and had made fewer visits to student health services. Students who disclosed more from beginning to follow-up also showed greater drops in systolic blood pressure and heart rate than did those who disclosed less.

A model that has also used art and writing as creativity-based intervention strategies to promote increased self-awareness, understanding, and even spontaneity is one originated by Hage and Nasanow (2000) for young adults from divorced families. In these groups, members shared stories and experiences. The leaders used several activities including having participants draw pictures of their families and write letters to their parents that were never sent. In the process they found that the structured and unstructured times where participants could share facilitated greater connections among group members. These clinicians believed that group leaders should model and promote spontaneity in group counseling. Their sentiment is in line with Kottler (1994): "Creative group leaders [should] leave every session bathed in sweat, having exhausted themselves to find new ways of energizing, motivating, and facilitating client growth" (p. 93).

In a group for adults who had recently separated or divorced from their spouses, Lee and Hett (1990) used an eight-session format with some creative interventions such as guided imagery and relaxation exercises. They compared the results to a wait-list control group. They found that adults in the experiential group reaped many benefits. From participating in this type of group counseling environment participants reported feeling more of a sense of belonging and more vicarious learning than those in the control group. At the end of the group, participants improved scores on a spontaneity scale, which the researchers reported reflected that they had gained a greater ability to be themselves and were less restricted in the presentation of themselves to the world.

Groups that incorporate spontaneity and creativity within them have a way of opening individuals up in multiple ways, such as learning cognitive information. In a classic experiment that helped change the teaching of foreign languages, Wade (1981) found that dividing students into small groups of three to five with a student leader improved their abilities to be spontaneous and comfortable speaking French. The small-group format gave students a chance to be active and participate and to learn through their successes and mistakes. It was less threatening for them and, thus, increased their self-confidence as well as their abilities.

The composition of a group, as well as its focus, can make a difference too in how creative it is. In a seminal study, Baer, Oldham, Jacobsohn, and Hollingshead (2008) examined the possibility that teams composed primarily of individuals with personality characteristics conducive to team creativity (e.g., high extraversion, high openness to experience, low conscientiousness vs. high neuroticism, low agreeableness) would show synergistic increases in creativity when they experienced high levels of "team creative confidence" and a shared understanding that the team is more creative than each member individually. Their hypotheses were tested using a sample of 145 three-student teams that worked on a set of idea-generation tasks during a specific time. A second set of idea-generation tasks were given to the teams 2 weeks after their initial meeting. Results indicated that when team creative confidence was high after the first meeting, team creativity at the second meeting increased significantly as the number of members who scored high on extraversion, high on openness, or low on conscientiousness increased. Interestingly, the number of individuals composing a team who scored high on neuroticism or low on agreeableness had no relation to team creativity under conditions of high or low team creative confidence.

Time is also a factor in a group's ability to be creative and spontaneous. For instance, Chirumbolo, Livi, Mannetti, Pierro, and Kruglanski (2004) found that constraints to closure, such as time pressure and pressure to conform, were related to decreases in creative discussion and creative brainstorming in groups. They noted that prior research had found that individuals with a need for cognitive closure (i.e., a desire for a quick firm answer) were less creative than those without that high need. The reason was that cognitive closure tended to limit the generation of new ideas, information processing, and the fluidity in thought processes of individuals and groups. With increased time pressure, consensus was reached prematurely and consideration was not given to thoughts or procedures that would be more helpful.

Overall, group creativity and spontaneity are influenced by the varied characteristics of individual members, as well as group dynamics, and the interactive traits of the organization or team. Research points toward interaction among members in groups as an important factor in the development of spontaneity, creative ideas, and solutions. Group interaction promotes the sharing of ideas (cognitive stimulation), which increases creativity and productivity (Paulus, 2003).

Ways of Promoting Creativity and Spontaneity in Groups

Since creativity can be taught, there are a number of ways to promote creativity, especially in a group. The most powerful expression of the creative process in a group is known as "distributed creativity." It refers to "situations where collaborating groups of individuals collectively generate a shared creative process" (Sawyer & DeZutter, 2009, p. 82). In such a situation, individuals in the group are not credited with or responsible for creativity because it is the collective process or product of the group as a whole. Often, improvising or finessing in an unplanned but purposeful way is at the heart of this process.

There are many ways to involve or engage group members in activities that lead to distributed creativity. Some involve spontaneous means, while others entail creative ways. For instance, in regard to spontaneity, if group members reach an impasse in a discussion or interchange, a group leader "might think 'Perhaps a role-play could be effective;' act on this idea spontaneously and suggest how the members can get involved" (Posthuma, 2002, p. 121). On the other hand, a structured creative process might come from group members in subgroups making the sounds of feelings, such as sad, mad, glad, and anxious, and then sharing the result with the group as a whole (Gladding, 2011).

As a rule, groups become more creative and spontaneous when they develop norms that are supportive of these processes. These are at least four ways groups can be encouraged to develop such standards of conduct.

The first is to seek out, listen to, and incorporate diverse opinions. Group members should encourage each other to own and voice their perspectives on matters that may be different from others. By hearing, considering, and sometimes incorporating different points of view, ideas are generated, mindsets are expanded, and growth occurs within group members and the group as a whole (Kaufman & Sternberg, 1999).

The second is to build a supportive and collaborative group climate. A supportive and collaborative group climate is one where group members are cared for and empathized with and where cooperation, as opposed to competition, is fostered (Gladding, 2012).

A third ingredient that encourages creativity in a group is to expect it and celebrate it when it happens (Csikszentimalyi, 1996). Anticipating new and useful ideas from group members makes a difference. When they are generated, time should be taken to acknowledge them as well as what the group is doing as a result and how that is helpful. Approaching creativity in this systematic way encourages group members to identify the purpose of their creative endeavors and provides discussion time dedicated to creativity.

Finally, group creativity is enhanced when expressive media are used (Malchiodi, 2003a, 2003b). Stimuli that connect to people's senses (tactile, kinesthetic, visual, and auditory) may help them in accessing feelings and thoughts that are not in their immediate awareness. Examples include drawing, collages, painting, puppetry, writing, improvisation, sand play, and movement. These stimuli provide ways to explore and change perceptions of themselves and others as well as to try out new roles or ways of interacting (Bratton et al., 2009). Literature, poetry, music, and art also

> are able to convey experiential insights into profound existential truths. In group [counseling and] psychotherapy, the use of experiential communications can be especially helpful in providing access to potentials that are ordinarily sealed off. This type of communication serves to enhance awareness of inauthentic attitudes, to facilitate acceptance of seemingly paradoxical aspects of human existence, and to provide a deeper sense of life's meaningfulness. (Bonhote et al., 1999, pp. 613–614)

However, there are formulas for creativity that may foster spontaneity but do not depend on it initially. One of the best and most straightforward is the SCAMPER model. This model was formulated by Robert F. Eberle (1971), an educational administrator in Edwardsville, Illinois. His intent in devising this acronym was to give individuals a list of useful letters, representing action words, which could be applied to situations to help leaders think about steps they could take in different circumstances. He hoped the word "scamper" would be seen as playful, inviting, and easily remembered and that it would remind people of what they could do to generate original and pragmatic ideas. The model has been applied to business (Michalko, 1998), family therapy (Gladding & Henderson, 2000), and group counseling (Gladding, 1997).

In SCAMPER "what if," "so that," and "in order to" types of questions and statements are made and potential answers imagined. Each letter in SCAMPER stands for a specific action that can be taken to promote creativity. The letters and corresponding words of SCAMPER are defined in the following.

The letter S stands for "substitute." This process involves inserting or replacing components, people, or materials. Questions to be asked are as follows: What can be used instead? Who else instead? What other ingredients or materials? What other process, person, power, place, or approach? While mundane examples of substituting include vegetarian hamburgers and disposable diapers, in group counseling think "Instead of me or a particular group member doing . . . I (she or he) can . . . in order to. . . ." For example, if communication breakdowns occur, group members can be instructed to replace the word "but" after "Yes" with the word "and", that is, "Yes and . . ." instead of "Yes but. . . ." Such a substitution promotes dialogue and a positive atmosphere as in the following group member exchange.

> Group Member 1: I want to become more outgoing outside of the group.
> Group Member 2 (using "Yes but"): Yes but you are an introvert and you need to face the fact that you will always be more inwardly than outwardly focused.
> Group Member 2 (using "Yes and"): Yes and tell me what are some ways you think you can put in place to help you overcome your natural tendency to be shy.

The letter C stands for "combine." To combine involves mixing or merging people, procedures, and products with others or integrating actions. Questions to be asked are as follows: What can be combined or brought together? How can things be blended or sorted differently? What ideas or behaviors can be united? Examples of substituting in everyday life include musical greeting cards and triathlons. In group counseling think "I or group members might bring together . . . and . . . in order to. . . ." The exercise 1–2–3 (1 minute to write two problem-solving ideas in a group of three) illustrates the power of combining. Such a group experience might occur when a group is stuck in storming or performing and does not seem to be able to work through its immobility.

The A stands for "adapt" or "alter." The process involves acclimating, adjusting, changing, or modifying. Questions to be asked are as follows: What can be adapted for use to bring about a solution? What else is like this? What other idea does this suggest? What could be copied or emulated? Examples of adapting or altering in daily life include snow tires, children's beds that look like racecars, and playing sports in various weather conditions. In group counseling think "I or group members might adapt . . . in this way . . . in order to . . ." or "I or group members might alter what we do in this way . . . in order to. . . ." Thus, a group that usually does a "go round" to start its session, beginning with the leader and going to the left, might alter this procedure to let whomever wishes to speak first, second, or third do so spontaneously in order to promote more genuine interaction among group members and empower members more by freeing them from a structure that is rigid.

The *M* stands for "modify," which means group members may magnify or minimize something about themselves or their actions or behaviors that occurs within the group. The process involves increasing or reducing in scale, changing a shape, or modifying attributes. Questions to be asked are as follows: Can an interaction be changed in some way, such as its meaning, motion, sound, smell, form, shape? Examples of modifying in situations most individuals encounter in daily life include such items as scented crayons and aluminum baseball bats.

If something is being modified by being magnified the question becomes, What can be added, such as more time, greater frequency, extra value, or ingredients, or what can be exaggerated? Examples of magnifying outside of a group include extra-strength medicines, supersized meals, and oversized equipment such as huge televisions. Within a group-counseling venue, magnification can take place when individuals within the group are given more time to interchange ideas or when the group as a whole decides to meet more often or to spend longer on processing what is happening in group sessions.

If something is being modified through minimizing it, questions that arise include the following: What can be removed, made smaller, condensed, lowered, shortened, lightened, or understated? Examples of minimizing in everyday life include bite-size candies and wrist-band televisions. In group counseling think "What might I or group members minimize . . . in this way . . . in order to. . . ." Structuring the group so there is less talking is one way a group might be minimized. In such a situation, group members become more aware of words and careful to use them most effectively. They also find other ways to communicate such as using body language, like head nods, to show agreement. In both magnifying and minimizing, group members come to notice

that when one thing changes within the group everything changes, including perceptions and abilities.

The *P* represents "put to other uses." The process involves using something in a way which it was never intended for. Questions to be asked in this process are as follows: How can something be put to different or other uses? Examples of things being put to other uses in society include using old tires for fences or swings and the development of snowboards. In group counseling think "How can I or the group use or reuse . . . in this way . . . by. . . ." For instance, an outburst or an angry exchange may be used to show that there are a lot of feelings in a group member or in group members who may have appeared quiet at first. The outburst or angry exchange was not meant this way. However, by using it as such and discussing the incident(s), the group may come to realize that what initially appeared as a staid and stale group is really one with a lot of energy. Below the outer calm, there is considerable passion.

The *E* stands for "eliminate." The process of elimination may seem passive, but it involves removing, simplifying, or reducing something to its core functionality. Questions to be asked in this process are as follows: What can be eliminated, removed, understated or reduced in time, effort, or cost? Examples of elimination in society include sodium-free and fat-free foods as well as cords for telephones. In group counseling think "What if I or a group member eliminate . . . by . . . and get . . . as a result." For example, words can be eliminated and group members can be asked to draw out their feelings in a line-of -feeling exercise (Gladding, 2005, 2007).

The last letter in SCAMPER, *R*, can stand for one of two actions: "rearrange" or "reverse." Questions to ask in this process are as follows: What can be gained by reshuffling people or items, or what is the benefit of revisiting previous thoughts or behaviors? Rearranging involves exploring other layouts and other sequencing in order to see new and different patterns, for example, rearranging the furniture in a room. Reversing means restoring something to where it was before or turning around, for example, going back to putting a room full of furniture that was rearranged to its original configuration. Reversing may also involve coming back to ideas that were initially rejected and considering them again. Both of these of these actions are carried out in society. In group counseling think What if we began the group now with the warm-up we tried a few weeks ago that did not seem to work too well? or What if we change the seating in the group so that people who have not been in close proximity to one another now are?

Overall, using the SCAMPER model can be an effective tool within a group-counseling context just as it can be helpful to people in individual, family, or organizational context. At the very least this mnemonic device gives individuals, including group leaders, an idea of what they want to or need to explore in helping a counseling group do something creative and even productively spontaneous for the group as a whole.

Barriers to Group Creativity

Cultures are conservative; otherwise, they would be chaotic (Csikszentmihalyi, 1996). With that being the case, there are a number of roadblocks besides the conservative nature of society for people not being more creative individually, for example, exhaustion, distractibility, lack of discipline, and inability to know what to do (Csikszentmihalyi, 1996).

In groups creativity is suppressed by at least four other elements: conformity, competitiveness, criticism, and communication (Corey, Corey, & Corey, 2010; Gladding, 2012; Jacobs, Masson, & Harvill, 2009). Each can be addressed and resolved.

The first barrier to group creativity is pressure to conform to group norms. In such a situation unanimity or conformity is prized. No one in the groups feels comfortable being different or an outlier. Asch's (1956) "vision test" group exercise, where students were asked to judge the length of a line when compared to three others, is a prime example of the pressure to conform to a group. In this experiment all but one of the group participants were confederates who gave a uniform answer before the control participant did. When the majority answered one way, the student in the experiment often reacted by agreeing with the confederates' answer, even though he or she knew it to be wrong. Laying out group ground rules that invite and encourage differences of opinion is one way to counter conformity. Brainstorming ideas is another.

A second factor that suppresses group creativity is individual competitiveness within groups. Competition among group members results in a zero-sum game where some person wins and others lose. Group members keep information and creative ideas to themselves rather than share because the focus is on being the best individual. Competition also encourages group members to focus on themselves and their own agendas rather than the goals of the group. A popular television show, *Survivor*, is a prime example of competitiveness not only between groups but within groups. To counter competitiveness, a group leader might give a group a problem that depends on the cooperation of the group for a solution (Bordessa, 2005). In such a way, everyone wins. This type of approach is taken in a number of situations where a reward is given only after the slowest, weakest, or least able person in a group completes a task.

A third factor in suppressing creativity in a group is criticism. While criticism may be the catalyst for social movements, critical evaluations are a major characteristic of a defensive and noncreative group (Hornsey, 2006). A steady dose of such feedback makes people more careful about what they say than anything else. Therefore, groups work best when they follow what Frederikson (2009) has described as the "broaden and build" theory of positive emotion. Frederikson suggests that positive emotions are evolutionarily adaptive because they trigger a broadening of our mental states including spontaneity and creativity. Spontaneous actions and creativity are much more likely to occur when people are open to new ideas and new experiences compared to when they are afraid of being criticized for thinking or planning such. Frederikson's research into positive emotions has also found that participants in a happy mood outperformed participants in a negative or neutral mood on tasks requiring a creative solution (Isen, Daubman, & Nowicki, 1998).

Differences in communication styles may also be a barrier to creativity in a group (Adams & Galanes, 2008; Kaufman & Sternberg, 1996). Some group members are more outspoken, extroverted, and vocal in their opinions, while other group members are more reserved, introverted, and hesitant to state their views. More vocal members often dominate group meetings, so only those members' ideas are heard. Ways of resolving such difficulties include having the group leader call on someone in the group for a response, asking those in the group who have not spoken up to give voice to their thoughts, and involving quiet members in either starting a group or summing up what they have heard.

Future Directions

Creativity and spontaneity have always been a part of group work, especially group counseling and task/work groups. By their very nature, these factors add to the vitality of groups and make them richer as well as more interesting and productive. It is hard to imagine a group thriving without these elements being a central part of it. In recent years, research has documented how spontaneity and creativity add to the richness of groups.

However, there are still questions that need to be addressed and answered if groups are going to be more productive in these areas in the future. Some of the essential questions that need to be explored further are as follows.

1. How can group workers identify creative group members prior to selecting individuals for a group experience? In other words, is there a reliable instrument or process that can facilitate this procedure so that the best group members possible can be selected?

2. How can group leaders become more sophisticated in working with creative groups so that the potential of these groups is maximized? How can group spontaneity and creativity be managed in productive ways?

3. Since spontaneity often generates creativity in groups, how can this phenomenon be promoted most effectively to enhance interpersonal interaction and ignite creative movement? In other words, since spontaneity is the spark that lights the fire of creativity and groups are in constant need of this spark, how can spontaneity be encouraged?

4. Are groups with greater spontaneity and creativity more innovative in how they envision those problems or concerns? It appears to be that way, but how do we know for sure?

5. Might creative groups produce ideas for the betterment of society as well as for the group itself? In other words, what are the larger benefits of helping counseling and work/task groups be more creative and spontaneous?

6. While many individuals are aware of the cartoon *Dilbert*, is there a flip side to the bungling and inept characters that appear in this strip? If so, what actions are associated with healthy and well-meaning creative and spontaneous individuals who work in groups for the greater good?

7. How or can spontaneity and creativity be programmed into groups in such a way that most leaders who wish to work with such groups actually have an opportunity to do so? Are there some guidelines for helping group leaders and members be more spontaneous and creative?

Conclusion

Pink (2006) has predicted that the future will belong to right-brainers, that is, those who are creative. His analysis of the world to be merits a lot of consideration. If Pink is correct, then groups that foster creativity and spontaneity will be the backbone of the future. Therefore, it is important to study how groups work and how they create.

As this chapter has indicated, groups vary in their productivity. Part of the reason is the composition of group members and the comfort of group members and leaders in being spontaneous and creative. When groups can be set up so that internal processes are in place to promote creative thought and spontaneous action, the energy generated from the group and the outcome of the group are both enhanced.

This chapter has focused on understanding the following:

- the essential elements of what creativity and spontaneity are
- what the creative process is like
- ways creativity and spontaneity are manifest in groups
- research on creativity and spontaneity in group settings
- methods of promoting creativity and spontaneity in groups
- barriers to group creativity
- future directions

Becoming creative in a group involves preparation, incubation, ideation, illumination, evaluation, and verification. There is no such thing as an instantly creative or spontaneous group. Such a process takes time as well as a concentration of talented and dedicated individuals. It is not easy. Barriers to creativity include personal fear and insecurity, environmental restraints, being too cognitive, lack of a challenge, and lack of reinforcement.

Advantages of being creative in group-counseling situations are as follows. Creativity is playful yet purposeful, and it results in processes and products that are useful. In addition, creativity promotes collegiality, facilitates communication, enables group members to see multiple aspects of themselves and the world, and encourages nonverbal and emotional participation. It promotes interactions that might not occur otherwise.

Drawbacks to using creativity in groups are that members may become too introspective, passive, or overcritical of themselves or situations. They may also be too concrete or stubborn to work in a group where creativity and spontaneity are valued.

Regardless, the research suggests that creativity and spontaneity are valuable elements in conducting a group of almost any kind, including a counseling group. Spontaneity helps facilitate action, and creativity brings forth new and useful results. Not every group can be like the Whiffenpoofs in their spontaneity and creativity. Nevertheless, when creative and spontaneous factors are expected, ways to engender them are utilized and ways to maximize their impact come into play; the result is like that of a harmony that lingers long after the moment in which it was born has faded into the sunset (see Box 21–1).

References

Adams, K., & Galanes, G. (2008). *Communicating in groups: Applications and skills* (7th ed.). New York: McGraw-Hill.

Arieti, S. (1976). *Creativity: The magic synthesis*. New York: Basic Books.

Asch, S. (1956). Studies of independence and conformity: I. A minority of one against a unanimous majority. *Psychological Monographs, 70*(9), 416.

Baer, M., Oldham, G. R., Jacobsohn, G. D. C., & Hollingshead, A. B. (2008). The personality composition of teams and creativity: The moderating role of team creative confidence. *Journal of Creative Behavior, 42*, 255–282.

Bonhote, K., Romano-Egan, J., & Cornwell, C. (1999). Altruism and creative expression in a long-term older adult psychotherapeutic group. *Issues in Mental Health Nursing, 20*, 603–617.

Bordessa, K. (2005). *Team challenges: 170+ group activities to build cooperation, communication, and creativity*. Chicago: Zephyr Press.

Bowman, V. E., & Boone, R. K. (1998). Enhancing the experiences of community: Creativity in group work. *Journal for Specialists in Group Work, 23*, 388–410.

Bratton, S. C., Ceballos, P. L., & Ferebee, K. W. (2009). Integration of structured expressive activities within a humanistic group play therapy format for preadolescents. *Journal for Specialists in Group Work, 34*(3), 251–275.

Chirumbolo, A., Livi, S., Mannetti, L., Pierro, A., & Kruglanski, A. W. (2004). Effects of need for closure on creativity in small group interactions. *European Journal of Personality, 18*, 265–278.

Cohen, G. (2001). *The creative age: Awakening human potential in the second half of life*. New York: Harper.

Corey, M. S., Corey, G., & Corey, C. (2010). *Groups: Process and practice*. Belmont, CA: Brooks Cole/Cengage.

Csikszentmihalyi, M. (1996). *Creativity: Flow and the psychology of discovery and invention*. New York: HarperCollins.

Eberle, R. (1971). *Scamper games for imagination development*. Bel Air, CA: DOK.

Egan, G. (1976). *Interpersonal living*. Pacific Grove, CA: Brooks/Cole.

Frederikson, B. L. (2009). *Positivity*. New York: Random House.

Gladding, S. T. (1997). The creative arts in groups. In H. Forester-Miller and J. A. Kottler (Eds.), *Issues and challenges for group practitioners* (pp. 81–99). Denver, CO: Love Publishing.

Gladding, S. T. (2011). *Counseling as an art: The creative arts in counseling* (4th ed.). Alexandria, VA: American Counseling Association.

Gladding, S. T. (2007). *Becoming creative as a counselor: The SCAMPER model* [DVD]. Framingham, MA: Microtraining Associates.

Gladding, S. T. (2012). *Groups: A counseling specialty* (6th ed.). Upper Saddle River, NJ: Prentice Hall.

Gladding, S. T., & Henderson, D. (2000). Creativity and family counseling: The SCAMPER model as a template for promoting creative processes. *Family Journal, 8*, 245–249.

Gladwell, M. (2009). *Outliers: The story of success.* New York: Little, Brown.

Hage, S. M., & Nasanow, M. (2000). Becoming stronger at broken places: A model for group work with young adults from divorced families. *Journal for Specialists in Group Work, 25*, 50–66.

Hornsey, M. J. (2006). Ingroup critics and their influence on a group. In T. Postmes & J. Jetten (Eds.), *Individuality and the group: Advances in social identity* (pp. 74–92). Thousand Oaks, CA: Sage.

Hoskins, M. (1985, April). *Therapeutic fairy tales.* Paper presented at the annual meeting of the National Association of Poetry Therapy, Chicago, IL.

Isen, A. M., Daubman, K. A., & Nowicki, G. P. (1998). Positive affect facilitates creative problem solving. In J. M. Jenkins, K. Oatley, & N. L. Stein (Eds.), *Human emotions: A reader* (pp. 288–297). Maiden, MA: Blackwell.

Jacobs, E. E., Masson, R. L. L., & Harvill, R. L. (2009). *Group counseling: Strategies and skills* (6th ed.). Belmont, CA: Thomson Brooks Cole.

Jarboe, S. (1999). Group communication and creativity processes. In L. Frey, D. Gouran, & M. Poole (Eds.), *The handbook of group communication & research* (pp. 335–368). Thousand Oaks, CA: Sage.

John-Steiner, V. (2000). *Creative collaboration.* New York: Oxford University Press.

Kaplan, D. (2000). *The silicon boys: And their valley of dreams.* New York: Harper.

Kaufman, J. C., & Sternberg, R. J. (Eds.). (1996). *The international handbook of creativity.* New York: Cambridge University Press.

Kersting, K. (2003, November). What exactly is creativity? *American Psychologist, 43*, 10.

Kipper, D. A. (2000). Spontaneity: Does the experience match the theory? *International Journal of Action Methods: Psychodrama, Skill Training, and Role Playing, 53*, 33–47.

Kipper, D. A. (2006). The canon of spontaneity—creativity revisited: The effect of empirical findings. *Journal of Group Psychotherapy, Psychodrama & Sociometry, 59*(3), 117–125.

Kottler, J. A. (1994). *Advanced group leadership.* Pacific Grove, CA: Brooks/Cole.

Lee, J. M., & Hett, G. G. (1990). Post-divorce adjustment: An assessment of a group intervention. *Canadian Journal of Counselling, 24*(3), 199–208.

Leonard, D., & Swap, W. (1999). *When sparks fly.* Cambridge, MA: Harvard University Press.

Malchiodi, C. A. (2003a). Psychoanalytic, analytic, and object relations approaches. In C. Malchiodi (Ed.), *Handbook of art therapy* (pp. 41–57). New York: Guilford Press.

Malchiodi, C. A. (2003b). Using art therapy with medical support groups. In C. Malchiodi (Ed.), *Handbook of art therapy* (pp. 351–361). New York: Guilford Press.

Maslow, A. (1971). *The farther reaches of human nature.* New York: Penguin.

Michalko, M. (1998). *Cracking creativity: The secrets of creative genius.* Berkeley, CA: Ten Speed Press.

Montuori, A., & Purser, R. (Eds.). (1999). *Social creativity* (Vol. 1). Cresskill, NJ: Hampton Press.

Moreno, J. L. (1953). *Who shall survive?* Beacon, NY: Beacon.

Moreno, J. L. (1964). *Psychodrama* (Vol. 1). Beacon, NY: Beacon.

Morgan, M. L., & Wampler, K. S. (2003). Fostering client creativity in family therapy: A process research study. *Contemporary Family Therapy, 25*, 207–228.

Olson, R. M., & Thomas, M. D. (1999). Management by spontaneity. *School Administrator, 56*, 41–45.

Paulus, P. B. (2000). Groups, teams and creativity: The creative potential of idea generating groups. *Applied Psychology: An International Review, 49*, 237–262.

Paulus, P. B. (2003). Groups, teams, and creativity: The creative potential of idea-generating groups. *Applied Psychology: An International Review, 49*(2), 237–262.

Paulus, P. B. (2008). Fostering creativity in groups and teams. In J. Zhou & C. Shalley (Eds.), *Handbook of organizational creativity* (pp. 165–188). New York: Taylor & Francis.

Paulus, P. B., Larey, T. S., & Dzindolet, M. T. (2000). Creativity in groups and teams. In M. Turner (Ed.), *Groups at work: Advances in theory and research* (pp. 319–338). Hillsdale, NJ: Lawrence Erlbaum.

Paulus, P. B., & Nijstad, B. A. (Eds.). (2003). *Group creativity: Innovation through collaboration.* New York: Oxford University Press.

Paulus, P. B., & Yang, H. C. (2000). Idea generation in groups: A basis for creativity in organizations. *Organizational Behavior and Human Decision Processes, 82*, 76–87.

Pennebaker, J. W. (1997). *Opening up: The healing power of expressing emotions.* New York: Guilford Press.

Pennebaker, J. W. (2002). *Emotion, disclosure, and health.* Washington, DC: American Psychological Association.

Pink, D. (2006). *A whole new mind: Why right brainers will rule the future.* New York: Riverhead.

Posthuma, B. W. (2002). *Small groups in counseling and therapy* (4th ed.). Boston: Allyn & Bacon.

Ricchiuto, J. (1996). *Collaborative creativity: Unleashing the power of shared thinking.* Oak Hill, OH: Oak Hill Press.

Sawyer, K. (2003). *Group creativity: Music, theater, collaboration.* Lawrence Erlbaum.

Sawyer, K. (2008). *Creative genius: The creative power of collaboration.* New York: Basic Books.

Sawyer, R. K., & DeZutter, S. (2009). Distributed creativity: How collective creations emerge from collaboration. *Psychology of Aesthetics, Creativity, and the Arts, 3*, 81–92.

Stahler, W. (2006). Prayerformance: A drama therapy approach with female prisoners recovering from addiction. *Journal of Creativity in Mental Health, 2*, 3–12.

Sternberg, R. (1999). *The handbook of creativity.* New York: Oxford University Press.

Sternberg, R. J., & Lubart, T. I. (1996). Investing in creativity. *American Psychologist, 51*, 677–688.

Taggar, S. (2001). Group composition, creative synergy, and group performance. *Journal of Creative Behavior, 35*(4), 261–286.

Tubbs, S. L. (2008). *A systems approach to small group interaction* (10th ed.). New York: McGraw-Hill.

Tucker, B. (2001). Well planned spontaneity: Some tips for conducting guided walks. *Ontario Journal of Outdoor Education, 13*, 27–30.

Tuckman, B. (1965). Developmental sequence in small groups. *Psychological Bulletin, 6*, 384–399.

Wade, G. G. (1981). Structure and spontaneity: Group dynamics in the college-level French class. *French Review, 54*(3), 401–404.

Wald, J. (2003). Clinical art therapy with older adults. In C. A. Malchiodi (Ed.), *Handbook of art therapy* (pp. 294–307). New York: Guilford Press.

Waller, D. (2003). Group art therapy: An interactive approach. In C. A. Malchiodi (Ed.), *Handbook of art therapy* (pp. 313–324). New York: Guilford Press.

Wenz, K., & McWhirter, J. J. (1990). Enhancing the group experience: Creative writing exercises. *Journal for Specialists in Group Work, 15*, 37–42.

Wilson, O. *On defining creativity*. Retrieved September 27, 2009, from http://www.uwsp.edu/Education/lwilson/creativ/define.htm

PART 6

Applications

Groups across Settings

Cynthia R. Kalodner *and* Alexa E. Hanus

Abstract

Group interventions exist in a large diversity of settings. This chapter focuses on the variety of settings in which groups can be found. The goal is to provide readers with a sense of the ubiquitous nature of groups. The variety of settings includes a focus on different kinds of groups for clients of different ages with a diversity of clinical issues. Each section provides examples of groups and research to support these groups in particular settings; selected for depth of coverage in this chapter are Veterans Administration programs, behavioral health and medical settings, college/university counseling centers, and schools. The chapter concludes with suggestions for the future of groups in these settings and an extensive reference list.

Keywords: setting, Veterans Administration, schools, behavioral medicine, counseling center

Introduction

This chapter provides examples of groups, counseling and psychoeducational in focus, that occur in a large variety of settings. Group approaches exist within the Veterans Administration system, behavioral health and medical facilities, health maintenance organizations, schools, and counseling centers on college campuses, as well as with offenders and mandated clients in correctional environments, inpatients in psychiatric facilities, and outpatients in private practices, community mental health agencies, and the workplace. Indeed, entire chapters have been written on each of these topics (see DeLucia-Waack, Gerrity, Kalodner, & Riva, 2004). In this chapter we focus on several of these settings and provide resources for those interested in learning more about groups in settings that we could not include. Group treatments are heavily used in many of these settings; though the groups vary in focus and format, it is clear that the use of group approaches to therapeutic work is ubiquitous. Conyne (this volume) refers to the "age of ubiquity" in group counseling. In this chapter, we use this concept to highlight the fact that group work is, in fact, everywhere.

Veterans Administration Setting

While each setting in this chapter is an important platform for group therapy, the Veterans Administration (VA) is perhaps the most historically noteworthy as group therapy itself may have begun as a treatment modality within the Department of Veterans Affairs (Grotjahn, 1947; Hadden, 1947; Schwartz, 1945). Large numbers of soldiers returning from World War II with mental health issues placed an impossible demand on therapists in terms of individual treatment. To meet this sudden influx in demand, efforts to treat multiple soldiers at a time began; and ideas regarding symptom treatment and adjustment to civilian life in a group setting were heavily documented in the early literature (Grotjahn, 1947; Hadden, 1947; Schwartz, 1945). Greene and colleagues (2004) point out that these preliminary ideas and methods for group therapy within the VA were not limited to treating war trauma. Their review of the early literature in the area revealed an intent to develop and legitimize group therapy for a wider variety of issues, including medical diseases and alcoholism among veterans (Greene et al., 2004). Powdermaker and Frank (1948, 1953) explained how group therapy, using a model called "situation analysis," could be used to treat more severe psychopathology including schizophrenia.

The National Center for Veterans Analysis and Statistics reports that there are approximately 23.4 million veterans in the United States, with 8.5 million seeking services through the VA in 2008 alone. Service within the VA is comprehensive in nature, with professionals in the Veterans Health Administration coming from nursing, social work, psychology, and medical backgrounds, typically working together to meet the needs of veterans seeking services. Needs continue to be great: "of 289328 Iraq and Afghanistan veterans, 106726 (36.9%) received mental health diagnoses; 62929 (21.8%) were diagnosed with posttraumatic stress disorder (PTSD) and 50432 (17.4%) with depression" (Seal et al., 2009, p. 1651).

Currently, group therapy continues to serve as a main treatment modality utilized by the VA in addressing veterans' mental health issues, including PTSD (Ford & Stewart, 1999) and substance abuse (Greene et al., 2004) as well as PTSD with substance abuse, two disorders that are highly comorbid in this population. Importantly, up to 75% of veterans with PTSD seeking treatment through the VA also struggle with substance-use disorders (Keane, Gerardi, Lyons, & Wolfe, 1988; Meisler, 1999). Accordingly, this section will focus on group-therapy approaches in the treatment of PTSD and substance abuse in the VA setting, but the reader should be aware that professionals in the VA address a wide range of other psychological issues using groups.

While soldiers returning from World War II sparked the beginning of group therapy, Greene and colleagues (2004) point out that the aftermath of Vietnam and the continuing demand for mental health services arguably pushed the VA to develop a more formalized and systematic approach for group therapy in treating PTSD. Indeed, the National Center for PTSD reports that the VA has established a network of over 200 specialized treatment programs and trauma centers nationwide and has served more than 50,000 veterans with PTSD (Fontana, Rosenheck, Spencer, & Gray, 2001).

There are many benefits for utilizing group therapy in treating veterans experiencing PTSD. First, group treatment is the most efficient and cost-effective method to treat clients, reflecting the beginnings of group therapy and the continuing demand for mental health service. Second, the idea of universality (Yalom, 1995) is achieved in a group setting; veterans experiencing the frightening and alienating symptoms of PTSD often find it therapeutic to know that others experience similar distress and that they are not alone in their struggles. Additionally, PTSD can entail socially avoidant behaviors; group therapy pushes for increased social interaction and the improvement of interpersonal skills in a safe environment (Greene et al., 2004).

It is important to note that group treatment for PTSD within the VA does not entail one specific method but rather includes many different approaches for addressing war trauma including prolonged exposure therapy, cognitive-behavioral approaches, dual-diagnosis treatment, expressive art therapies, and support groups. Many VA facilities use a combination of these methods for PTSD treatment, often in group formats.

Supportive group therapy ("rap groups") were used in the 1980s to provide veterans with a place to talk about their experiences (Sipprelle, 1992). These groups may not have been professionally led. In the current VA system, trauma-focused group therapy is led by trained mental health professionals, often as part of a research study. For example, prolonged-exposure therapy is a behavioral approach largely based on conditioning principles. This method typically involves four stages and begins with basic education about trauma and PTSD, as well as learning coping skills such as breathing and relaxation techniques to aid in dealing with common hyperarousal symptoms. In moving to the exposure stages, clients are presented with situations that may be related to the trauma they experienced but have been avoided out of fear. These initial exposure activities can vary depending on the specific therapy modality utilized but can include real-world or mental exposure. Mental exposure can be achieved through repeated telling of memories of the traumatic event. Overall, the exposure stages address the traumatic event itself as well as reminders or cues of the event in a repeated and systematic way. The goals of exposure therapy include desensitizing the client to cues of their traumatic event and teaching and enhancing adaptive coping skills for maintaining control over PTSD-related symptoms with the support of group leaders and other members. While some research has found this approach to be effective for combat-related PTSD (Keane, Fairbank, Caddell, & Zimering, 1989), a more comprehensive examination of a prolonged-exposure group therapy approach within the VA system raises some questions (Schnurr et al., 2003). This study, conducted by the Department of Veterans Affairs and including 10 VA sites, examined 360 male Vietnam veterans who were randomly assigned to a trauma-focused therapy group (TFTG) or a present-centered treatment comparison group. Results showed that posttreatment measures of PTSD severity improved from baseline in both treatment groups with no significant differences between treatment groups (Schnurr et al., 2003). Other variations of this approach that utilize differing amounts of exposure have been found to produce clinically significant and lasting reductions in combat-related PTSD (Ready et al., 2008).

Cognitive-behavioral therapy (CBT) is a common underlying component to many VA treatment programs for PTSD (Greene et al., 2004). This approach often begins with the trauma memory and focuses on the feelings, beliefs, and maladaptive thought patterns related to that experience. The group leader aids the client in understanding his or her reasoning processes and beliefs, and with the support of the leader and other members, clients can adjust maladaptive or harmful cognitions and restructure them into more positive and realistic thoughts. This approach also addresses common areas of problem thinking related to PTSD, including safety, trust, control, self-esteem, and intimacy. An additional and important component in CBT involves the development of self-management skills, including anger-management and relaxation training. As PTSD includes symptoms of hyperarousal, including increased irritability or anger outbursts, as well as sleep difficulties and feelings of "jumpiness," these self-management skills become a necessary and important piece in PTSD treatment. Greene and colleagues (2004) also point out the utility of more nontraditional or alternative approaches in teaching these self-management skills, such as meditation, yoga, and tai chi.

Dual-diagnosis treatment is a necessity within the VA as substance-use disorders often accompany a PTSD diagnosis among veterans seeking treatment (Keane et al., 1988; Meisler, 1999; Seal et al., 2009). In efforts to provide more comprehensive treatment that addresses the whole patient, rather than approaching comorbid diagnoses with separate treatment modalities, the VA system has developed substance-use PTSD teams. Group therapy is the core modality of treatment in these teams, with a trifold focus on psychiatric symptom treatment and management, substance abstinence and reduction,

and relapse prevention for both PTSD and substance use (Greene et al., 2004). The treatment focus on these three components is largely due to the fact that substance use among those who suffer from PTSD is often an attempt to self-medicate the distressing symptoms of PTSD (Meisler, 1999). In this way, the treatment and management of psychiatric symptoms provide patients with skills other than substance use to alleviate or control triggering PTSD symptoms. Likewise, substance reduction and abstinence help to minimize or alleviate the negative biopsychosocial consequences involved with substance use (Marlatt, Larimer, Baer, & Quigley, 1993), and relapse prevention addressing both substance abuse and PTSD provides patients with real-world skills to employ outside the group-therapy setting. Finally, psychoeducation regarding the interplay between substance abuse and PTSD symptoms, including the self-medication phenomenon, becomes critically important for successful treatment and provides patients with an understanding of the treatment paradigm.

It is clear that group treatment is a mainstay within the VA for veterans suffering with PTSD and that the many different approaches described reflect attempts to address the issue in a holistic manner. It is also the case, however, that relatively few studies examining group-therapy approaches for PTSD within the VA system exist (Makler, Sigal, Gelkopf, Kochba, & Horeb, 1990; Ready et al., 2008; Schnurr et al., 2003). Those studies that have been completed highlight the need for further examination, including a focus on specific factors regarding exposure (Ready et al., 2008; Schnurr et al., 2003) in order to ensure the delivery of evidence-based services. Race-related factors (Jones, Brazel, Peskind, Morelli, & Raskind, 2000) may play an underacknowledged role in group approaches to treatment in the VA setting.

Recent research demonstrates that approximately 10% of veterans seeking services through the VA fit the criteria for substance-use disorder (Curran, Kirchner, Allee, & Booth, 2003; Seal et al., 2009). Moreover, this leads to a myriad of further struggles, including unemployment and homelessness (Cooney, Pilkey, Cooney, & Kranzler, 2000). In order to address this issue, the VA relies heavily on an integrated and intensive group-treatment approach, substance-abuse day-treatment programs (SADPs). This is a short-term approach designed to recognize and treat the multiple issues involved with substance use including comorbid disorders, nonsupportive environments, limited social supports, and development of leisure activity skills (Greene et al., 2004). The backbone of SADP treatment consists of group CBT and psychoeduational groups.

The cognitive-behavioral core of SADP treatment usually consists of intensive group therapy for 5 days per week in 45-minute sessions, with a main goal of complete substance abstinence (Greene et al., 2004). During these sessions, veterans are encouraged to identify internal and external high-risk situations or situations in which they are most likely to abuse substances. Once these situations have been identified, focus moves to learning and practicing coping skills to deal with exposure to them, such as assertiveness training for refusing substances, coping with cravings, and anger- or stress-management training.

While the awareness and skills gained in CBT groups are centered around substance use, psychoeducational groups build on those skills and extend treatment by seeking to improve veterans' life skills outside of substance-use activities. These groups tend to be theme-focused and highly structured, with primary goals of creating supportive social environments and social skills, as well as engaging in time-structured activities such as work or volunteering. In this way, psychoeducational groups provide vets with the skills to create a new environment for themselves without substance use.

To create supportive social environments, a common type of psychoeducational group known as a "speakers' group" has been established. During these sessions, SADP graduates who have achieved at least 6 months of sobriety are invited to speak about their experiences in treatment and what strategies they utilize to stay abstinent (Greene et al., 2004). These speakers provide other group members with a sense of hope that substance abstinence is possible and facilitate further social contact with someone who has achieved this abstinence.

To foster the willingness to engage in time-structured activities, many psychoeducational groups include topics on leisure skills and recreation. This is important as patients' recreation activities and skills are limited to substance abuse or to obtaining substances (Greene et al., 2004). In this way, the act of abstaining can leave group members with open time and limited knowledge of what to do with that time. Recreation or life-skills groups encourage members to develop new hobbies or return to abandoned activities in a supportive group environment.

Finally, SADPs also consist of more comprehensive daily group sessions in which members come together in a large-group format and discuss their progress through the program, including any highlights and struggles they experience. The twofold purpose or benefit to this larger format is the fostering of group cohesion and the continued emphasis on abstinence as the larger-group norm. In these group sessions, commonly called "community meetings," members and treatment staff provide open feedback and confrontation when necessary in order to push members toward change and to foster accountability (Greene et al., 2004).

While group work within the VA system serves as a main treatment modality for mental illnesses including PTSD and substance use, this setting presents unique challenges within the context of group work. Specifically, professionals in this field point out that increased dependency, veteran identification, and the impact of gender roles can be particularly challenging within the VA system with regard to group therapy (Deering & Gannon, 2005; Green et al., 2004; Wakefield, 1988; Yakushko, Davidson, & Williams, 2009). Regarding increased dependency, it is the case that the VA provides veterans with other entitlement services including financial, health, and insurance benefits. In this way, the VA represents an institution of total care that can create dependency and counterdependency dynamics (Greene et al., 2004). Further, veterans are often socialized within a hierarchical context in which their specific designation has a clear rank relative to other members of the military, such that veterans often receive and carry out orders from authority figures. The provision of entitlement services from staff and professionals, including mental health services, can represent a continuation of this hierarchical understanding (Greene et al., 2004). In this way, it is important for group leaders to consider and acknowledge this mentality and to address veterans' conceptions of authority and dependence, as appropriate. Ways to address this potential dependence can include encouraging members to give and receive feedback with one another, as well as allowing members to make their own decisions regarding the topic of the group. These methods will place responsibility on members in a more explicit manner to keep the group productive, rather than members looking to the group leader for direction.

Regarding veteran identification, it is the case that every member in group therapy shares the identification of "veteran." Moreover, this identification may be highly salient and can impact therapeutic relationships and processes with other members, as well as the group leaders (Yakushko et al., 2009).

While a major goal of group therapy is the cohesion of its members, because there is an initial sense of cohesion among the members due to shared identification as veterans, the group work serves to, in a sense, "double" or intensify this cohesion (Greene et al., 2004). While this has clear benefits for the functioning of the group, particularly with regard to trust issues, it can present a hurdle regarding individual accountability and moving forward to achieve tasks. Specifically, there can be an increased sense of group mentality, potentially stifling the willingness to explore individual differences.

A third challenge raised by professionals in the field is the unique impact of gender roles (Deering & Gannon, 2005; Green et al., 2004; Wakefield, 1988). Indeed, many male veterans identify with more traditional male gender roles, often including the endorsement and adherence to cultural expectations of masculine characteristics (Deering & Gannon, 2005). Most patients in the VA system are male, while the staff and professionals working with male veterans are predominantly female (Green et al., 2004). This gender stratification is thought to present both struggles and benefits. Regarding the struggles and challenges, common themes that may arise in psychotherapy groups led by a female therapist can include transference and countertransference issues as well as resistance. Indeed, Wakefield (1988) describes themes such as dismissal of women, and the fusion of sexual and aggressive drives in their work with Vietnam veterans. While it is important to acknowledge that gender socialization is ever-evolving and that there are undoubtedly significant within-group differences among male veterans with respect to identification with traditional male gender roles, group leaders should be aware of this potential dynamic as it may impede the overall trust and progress of the group if not addressed and handled appropriately. Professionals working with this population also point to the benefits of this gender dynamic by stressing that these themes and issues may not be uncovered with a male therapist and, thus, cannot be addressed and worked through (Deering & Gannon, 2005; Wakefield, 1988).

Professionals continue to call for more rigorous exploration of different group methods in order to ensure the deliverance of evidenced-based practices with this important population (Jones et al., 2000; Ready et al., 2008; Schnurr et al., 2003). In considering the current and continued demand of mental health services from veterans returning from Iraq and Afghanistan (Seal et al., 2009), comprehensive evaluation and improvement in mental health service delivery within the VA are imperative.

Behavioral Health, Medical Settings, and Managed Health Care

Behavioral health is a vital and increasingly important component within the overall health-care system, and it is a setting in which groups play a major role. In considering that the most prominent contributors to premature death are tobacco use, diet and activity patterns, alcohol abuse, microbial and toxic agents, firearms, sexual behavior, motor vehicles, and illicit drug use (McGinnis & Foege, 1993) and the fact that individual behavior plays a major role in 86% of these deaths (McGinnis & Foege, 1993), efforts to address and improve behavior as it relates to health are vital. Further, increasing behavioral health efforts may be the best way of increasing cost-effectiveness within the health-care system at a time when spiraling costs are of great concern (Blount et al., 2007). Behavioral health group approaches are a valuable treatment option because they are time- and cost-efficient and because they can address a wide range of concerns related to the various medical issues experienced by patients needing care. Group-counseling advocates must build on these realities to develop concerted strategies to influence the future of health care, particularly managed care, to fully incorporate group delivery formats as reimbursable services (Spitz, 1996). Group services must become an integral part of any future renovation of the nation's health-care system. Groups may exist in settings including mental health centers, departments of psychiatry, hospitals, day-treatment programs, and family service agencies (Clifford, 2004).

Group approaches can provide many therapeutic benefits that meet the needs of patients in a variety of ways. Elliot, Rivera, and Tucker (2004) provide a comprehensive overview of these benefits. First, a group format allows for a systematic and controlled way to provide important information to many people at once. After patients are diagnosed with a medical condition or illness, they often seek information about their condition from professionals or other people with a similar diagnosis (Elliot et al., 2004). By providing group counseling, professionals can attend to multiple people at once and ensure that the information they receive about their condition is accurate. Group work also provides a venue for members to learn not only about specific symptoms related to their diagnosis but also about ways to cope with these symptoms in the presence and support of other members. Another therapeutic factor involved in providing group treatment is the idea that members can share any unexpected difficulties they experience related to their condition. In this way, other members can learn of or anticipate any impending difficulties or uncontrollable aspects related to their condition of which they may not have been aware (Elliot et al., 2004). A second step to this process includes members sharing and discussing what coping skills they used to deal with these difficulties. Observing and interacting with others who have coped with a diagnosis in a positive manner instills hope and a positive outlook for other members (Yalom, 1995) and allows a chance for those who have successfully coped with a diagnosis to take an active helping and guiding role (Elliot et al., 2004). Overall, these therapeutic benefits are provided to patients through numerous group formats, including support groups, educational groups, psychoeducational groups, and counseling groups, with each format designed to meet patient needs in different ways.

Support groups are perhaps the best-known and most offered type of group work for people dealing with a medical condition or illness. These groups focus on emotional expression and the building of social supports and encourage members to express concerns and problems, as well as the personal coping skills they currently utilize (Edelman, Craig, & Kidman, 2000). These groups are consumer-oriented and community-based and can be led by trained facilitators or peers with relevant information. They are offered for low fees or free and at various times of day in order to accommodate work schedules. Further, support groups can occur in many different settings, including churches, schools, health-care centers, or even private homes, making the accessibility of these groups very high. Additionally, national organizations such as the American Cancer Society and the Alzheimer's Association offer meeting times through localized chapters across the nation.

The support groups offered to people who seek help in dealing with a medical diagnosis take a less formal approach, with the overall goals of providing information and education related to a range of topics and encouraging problem solving and coping skills in a supportive environment where members can relate to one another and share their experiences. Yalom (1995) describes the therapeutic benefits of support groups as instilling hope in members, exchanging important information and advice, and providing a sense of universality in members. An additional benefit of support groups is that they are voluntary; those who feel they need the support group and are getting something from it will attend and those who do not need it do not attend. Often, members present in a support group have a vested interest in being there and display high motivation (Elliot et al., 2004). It is no surprise, then, that support groups have a high degree of consumer satisfaction. Indeed, women in breast cancer support groups show improved quality of life (Kissane et al., 2007) and report high satisfaction levels with the amount of medical information provided as well as the sense of community fostered within the group (Stevens & Duttlinger, 1998). While this is the case, empirical evidence shows mixed results for support group effects on members' psychological well-being. Despite studies that reveal positive psychological outcomes as a result of participating in support groups (Kissane et al., 2007; Stevens & Duttlinger, 1998), some literature also reveals insignificant changes in psychological outcome (Forester, Kornfeld, Fleiss, & Thompson, 1993; Jacobs, Ross, Walker, & Stockdale, 1983). Researchers point out other factors that may impact well-being, including members' existing social support outside the group as well as the importance of the group leader's training and experience (Helgeson, Cohen, Schulz, & Yasko, 2001; Kelly et al., 1993).

Educational groups in a medical setting provide focused and specific information to members in a direct manner. They are helpful for disseminating medical information to several patients sharing a similar condition at once. Leaders of educational groups are often medical professionals with knowledge or specialties related to the specific condition or diagnosis of focus (Spira, 1997). Further, because the focus is on the exchange of information, self-disclosure is not necessary or required (Elliot et al., 2004). In this way, educational groups can be more appropriate than counseling in cases where the patient needs to gather information in a more specific and direct manner. While these groups are usually open to allow new members at any time, when the information is cumulative or the topic is sensitive, educational groups may be closed in order to limit participant numbers. Examples of closed educational groups include child-birthing classes and HIV support groups (Elliot et al., 2004). The information provided in child-birthing classes is often cumulative; in this way, if a new member were to join halfway through the group, that person will have missed information provided toward the beginning that may be important for understanding and applying the current information being covered. Educational groups providing support for people diagnosed with HIV are closed, to provide members a safe, trusting environment. Since HIV is a sensitive topic, confidentiality is increasingly important. These factors are increased and fostered through a closed, rather than open, group.

Educational groups can be focused on a specific medical condition and provide information to patients who have already been diagnosed, or they can be preventative in nature by providing health and well-being information before medical conditions are an issue (Spira, 1997). They are usually offered as part of an overall treatment program and may include professionals from different fields, including nurses, pharmacists, nutritionists, occupational therapists, or counselors (Burckhardt, Mannerkorpi, Hedenberg, & Bjelle, 1994; Johansson, Dahl, Jannert, Melin, & Andersson, 1998). In this way, patients can receive information that is interdisciplinary in nature. Additionally, some educational groups are open for family members to attend. This allows them to gain additional information and helps to increase their caretaking skills. Finally, while educational groups are primarily focused on disseminating important information regarding a condition, they may also provide members with coping skills to deal with their medical condition through basic cognitive-behavioral ideas (Bucher, Houts, Nezu, & Nezu, 1999). Overall, the literature supports the use of educational groups in a medical setting by showing reductions in negative consequences of medical issues, including personal distress and fear (Helgeson et al., 1999; Vlaeyen et al., 1996), and improvements in coping skills and sense of self-control (Hart & Foster, 1997; Vlaeyen et al., 1996).

Psychoeducational groups are similar to educational groups in that there is still an emphasis on providing educational information, but they go an extra step by specifically addressing psychological content and emphasizing skill building. These groups still focus on a specific theme or topic but also include therapeutic exercises related to the topic, including imagery, role-plays, and thought logs (Keel, Bodoky, Gerhard, & Muller, 1998). Members in psychoeducational groups are encouraged to self-disclose in ways that are relevant to the discussion. Because of the additional focus on psychological content, including increased self-disclosure, these groups are often led by counselors or other mental health professionals, while being cofacilitated by medical professionals who may handle the more specific information regarding the medical topic. An example of a group that incorporates trained facilitators as well as medical professionals who are knowledgeable about a specific medical condition is a group for people diagnosed with type 1 diabetes. While many people with this diagnosis have the knowledge necessary to carry out healthy lifestyles, they often do not make the required adjustments (Glasgow et al., 1999). This highlights the necessity for providing psychoeducational groups to provide information and examine and adjust the psychological and behavioral components. In order to address both components, these groups are often led by trained counselors with nurses or diabetes educators (Snoek, van der Ven, & Lubach, 1999).

Research on psychoeducational groups shows consistent increases in psychological well-being and quality of life, including improved self-efficacy, assertiveness, social skills, and coping skills (Dunn, Van Horn, & Herman, 1981; Glueckauf & Quittner, 1992; Meneses et al., 2007; Telch & Telch, 1986), as well as decreases in the negative consequences of the medical diagnosis, including depression, anxiety, stress, and severity of problems encountered (Keefe et al., 1990; King & Kennedy, 1999). Further, the importance of training group members in coping skills relevant to their specific health condition is shown to provide increased benefits to members when compared to support groups. In a review of the literature, Edelman et al. (2000) examined the relative efficacy of psychoeducational and support groups for patients with cancer. Their results indicate that patients who attend psychoeducational groups experience greater psychological outcome benefits than those who attend purely supportive groups.

Counseling groups emphasize the psychological components of a medical condition or diagnosis even more than psychoeducational groups. In fact, the main focus of these groups is on the psychological and social issues that can affect how well a person adjusts to an illness or condition, and specific educational content is rarely included (Elliot et al., 2004). In this way, counseling groups are more problem-focused and require that members be screened to determine commitment, motivation, and appropriateness for the group. Counseling groups are more interpersonally oriented and require the facilitator to be skilled in assessment and counseling.

The overall structure of counseling groups can vary depending on the facilitator's theoretical orientation and typically follow an interpersonal or cognitive-behavioral paradigm. Groups that are more interpersonally oriented often include members with more psychological resources, such as stable social supports and coping skills, and a shared diagnosis with other members in order to increase group cohesion (Elliot et al., 2004). These groups focus largely on emotional reactions to the condition, as well as personality issues between group members. In this way, members are able to explore their own perspective as it relates to others, with the goal of obtaining a more objective awareness of themselves and their abilities.

Cognitive-behavioral counseling groups are commonly used in the medical field due to the ease with which these groups can be manualized. In this way, cognitive-behavioral groups can be empirically examined for outcome results, leading to the implementation of more evidence-based practices. Further, this standardized platform can be consistently implemented by leaders in a more controlled and systematic way. These groups tend to be more focused and direct in terms of themes and goals to work toward, with a focus on exploring cognitively based explanations for behavior and encouraging behavioral change. Accordingly, these groups often target specific behavioral styles that are associated with a medical diagnosis and the ways in which behavior can impact physiology. Once members are aware of how behavioral patterns relate to biological consequences, leaders seek to provide members with the skills necessary to change these potentially dangerous behavior patterns.

Overall, counseling groups have proven to be an important component of patient care in a medical setting. For example, group counseling has been shown to reduce hostility and blood pressure in men with coronary heart disease (Gidron, Davidson, & Bata, 1999) as well as improve glycemic control and decrease depression in patients diagnosed with type 2 diabetes (Lustman, Griffith, Freedland, Kissel, & Clouse, 1998). Finally, these groups can also be effective at promoting health-related and preventative behaviors among at-risk populations in order to avoid potential medical issues later (Belden, Park, & Mince, 2008; Kelly, St. Lawrence, Hood, & Brasfield, 1989).

Group work in the medical and behavioral health setting is a beneficial and necessary component to a comprehensive treatment approach. Indeed, an abundance of research in this area shows that patients who receive group treatment in some form experience an improvement in psychological well-being (Hart & Foster, 1997; Kissane et al., 2007; Meneses et al., 2007) and often in physical health as well (Gidron et al., 1999; Lustman et al., 1998). Researchers in this area also highlight the challenges and limitations involved in conducting psychological research in medical settings, including a lack of appropriate conceptual and methodological tools and the limited ability to generalize results with the use of the popular randomized clinical trials (Edelman et al., 2000; Schwartz, Trask, Shanmugham, & Townsend, 2004).

Elliot and colleagues (2004) provide some helpful guidelines and implications for the appropriate provision of group work in a medical setting. They point out that groups are most effective when participants have common goals as well as common ideas for how to obtain those goals. In order to create this environment, Elliot et al. (2004) call for counselors to assess for patient goals and intentions and to form groups according to these more specific similarities, rather than focusing only on patient diagnoses. They also highlight the importance of timing relative to group-work participation. Specifically, patients need time to realize and understand the relevance of group work in their own lives. Once people are aware of their struggles and of how group work can help them cope with these struggles in a unique way, they will be more willing to join a group and will display higher motivation during sessions. Finally, while group work is clearly a valuable modality of treatment for patients in a medical setting, clinicians should be mindful that some patients may be more responsive to individual counseling (Elliot et al., 2004). Indeed, literature shows that individual counseling is more effective for patients diagnosed with multiple sclerosis who are also struggling with depression (Mohr, Boudewyn, Goodkin, Bostrom, & Epstein, 2001). Overall, these findings, as well as the suggestions offered by Elliot and colleagues (2004), confirm the ideas that patients' specific and individual needs must be taken into account and leaders must have a firm understanding of the psychological and medical issues surrounding the given medical condition in order to achieve the greatest outcome.

Schools

Schools are a setting in which groups play a major role and one that continues to evolve. Two special issues of the *Journal for Specialists in Group Work* (volume 32, issues 1 and 2) focus on this setting. Groups provide the efficiency and effectiveness necessary for school-based work (Riva & Haub,

2004) and provide a major component of the mission of school counselors (Paisley & Milsom, 2007). Conyne and Mazza (2007) highlight the use of groups as a way to fit within the various levels of school environment (student groups, classrooms, school personnel, the school as a group, and the school in the community groups). Traditional academic issues (Brannigan, 2007; Webb & Brigman, 2007) are often targeted in groups in the schools. It is clear that groups provide a major component of the mission of school counselors (Paisley & Milsom, 2007).

Remembering that the school setting may range from prekindergarten through twelfth grade, this setting itself is quite diverse, providing opportunities to use groups in different ways with children as their developmental and academic needs vary by age. For example, younger children may participate in counseling groups designed to target social skill development and the effects of divorce (Ziffer, Crawford, & Penney-Wietor, 2007), while adolescents bring these and additional issues such as alcohol and drug use and at-risk sexual behavior. Adolescent girls may be members of groups designed to focus on self-esteem and the prevention of eating disorders (Khattah & Jones, 2007).

High school students may benefit from psychoeducational groups that assist in the selection of postgraduation plans as well as groups designed to decrease the number of dropouts. Students with disabilities can work in a group focusing on either transition to work or college selection (McEachern & Kenny, 2007). Creative approaches to groups in high schools, including use of music, movement, and drama, add a dimension that may benefit students (Veach & Gladding, 2007).

Because children and adolescents are used to being in groups in their classrooms, groups are a modality that makes sense to them. It may be that being in a room with others facing similar issues is part of what makes groups work in the school setting. Yalom's therapeutic factor of universality makes sense in this context. Akos, Hamm, Mack, and Dunaway (2007) base their work on developmental influences in peer groups in middle schools on Yalom's therapeutic factors. Meta-analytic studies show that school-based group counseling received consistent support (Hoag & Burlingame, 1997; Whiston & Sexton, 1998).

Prevention is a major focus for group work in schools (e.g., of AIDS and sexual behaviors, drug abuse, dropping out of high school; see Riva & Haub, 2004). Groups have been developed and

tested for primary prevention of topics ranging from adolescent drug abuse and dropping out of high school (Eggert, Thompson, Herting, Nicholas, & Dickler, 1994) to suicide (Eggert, Thompson, & Herting, 1995) to violence (Bosworth, Espelage, DeBay, Daytner, & Karageorge, 2000). The scope of work in this area is immense.

Though it has been said that research on groups with children and adolescents lags behind studies on adults (Riva & Haub, 2004), evidence of research attention to groups in the schools can be found easily. DeLucia-Waack and Gellman (2007) showed that addition of music to a children-of-divorce group did not yield a statistically significant impact on the effectiveness of a standard group-counseling program for this population but that both groups were effective at reducing anxiety and irrational beliefs. Their research is commendable because it builds on an existing literature that supports the effectiveness of group counseling for children who are affected by parental divorce. Further, it is an example of solid research practice as it represents data from 12 school counselors with 134 elementary school children, based on random assignment to groups and the use of multiple outcome measures.

In addition, the recent literature provides examples of groups used to provide treatment for children diagnosed with a variety of mental health problems, ranging from depression to the effects of natural disasters. Thus, recent literature points to an expanded use of groups in schools. There are now groups for children who have incarcerated parents (Lopez & Bhat, 2007) and for children who have deployed parents (Rush & Akos, 2007). Groups have been developed and studied as a treatment for adolescents exposed to community violence (Saltzman, Layne, Pynoos, Steinberg, & Aisenberg, 2001) and in response to recent disasters (e.g., Hurricane Katrina; see Salloum, Garside, Irwin, Anderson, & Francois, 2009; Salloum & Overstreet, 2008) and war (Cox et al., 2007). Studies on treating depression in the schools using an evidence-based CBT model adapted for school use (Ruffolo & Fischer, 2009) and a family-centered intervention based in the schools (Conwell & Dishion, 2008) show the increasing use of groups as treatment for more serious mental health issues in school settings. These authors point to the schools as a way to deliver mental health services to adolescents who may not get the counseling they need.

Christner, Mennuti, and Pearson (2009) expounded upon the value of CBT in school settings, highlighting the fact that CBT fits well within the school setting because it parallels existing services in the schools. CBT's components of psychoeducation, skill building, homework, and monitoring progress are familiar to educators. CBT can be used for both early intervention and treatment in school settings. Christner et al. (2009) provide an introduction to CBT that could be useful for school counselors.

While schools continue to provide the expected and traditional topics, group work in the school setting continues to expand. Innovative programs such as Dowden's (2009) self-advocacy program for black adolescents show how schools can be the setting in which multicultural group work can assist adolescents to overcome the social barriers that relate to racism. Other group work designed to target diversity issues can be found in Allies against Hate (Nikels, Mims, & Mims, 2007) and groups specifically developed for African American males (Bailey & Bradbury-Bailey, 2007; White & Rayle, 2007).

Groups continue to play a major role in the school setting. As we move into the next decade, it seems important to continue to provide psychological services to students using groups, to expand the use of groups as students need more psychological support, and to document the effectiveness of this approach to allow schools to receive more funding and support for groups and the professionals who conduct them.

College and University Counseling Centers

Continuing in the world of education, group work has been a large part of college/university counseling centers (McEneaney & Gross, 2009). Golden, Corazzini, & Grady (1993) wrote that 92% of college or university counseling centers actively use structured groups, process-oriented psychotherapy groups, and various support groups as part of their programs. Psychoeducational groups play a large role in this setting; their focus on didactic teaching on a specific theme along with behavioral skills (McWhirter, 1995) fits well in the college environment. Drum and Knott (2009) provide a 30-year retrospective on theme groups, defined as "time-limited, multi-session groups designed to focus on a specific theme, challenge, or problem common to the participants" (p. 495). Psychoeducational groups may provide similar focus on skill acquisition, life transitions, coping with specific disorders, and recovery. Psychoeducational groups may be focused on topics ranging from academic concerns and stress and time management to developmental concerns faced by college students (dating, developing relationships) to psychological

themes (grief, depression and anxiety, substance abuse, anger). Groups in this setting may also be focused on specific populations (women, gay/lesbian/bisexual/transgendered, international students, multicultural themes).

A look at the history of groups in counseling centers provides an introduction to this setting. Professionals in college and university counseling centers began to utilize group therapy during the 1960s, when marathon group sessions reached the peak of popularity in the larger adult population. During this time, marathon groups—a combination of encounter and psychotherapy group techniques, as well as sensitivity training in an extended time frame—were thought to be a powerful answer to individual mental illness as well as societal ills such as war and discrimination (Stanger & Harris, 2005; Weigel, 2002). These marathon groups reached the height of popularity in the mid- to late 1960s, and though marathon group use faded, the use of groups in this setting has not. Kincade and Kalodner (2004) point out that the continued use of group therapy in college and university counseling centers was also a product of significant cuts in higher education funding during the 1970s. Group counseling became the most efficient and cost-effective method of providing services to students, given the smaller number of professionals available to serve a growing student population. This financial struggle and increase in student demands for service continues, and group therapy continues to be a valuable and effective method of treatment for college and university counseling centers (Golden et al., 1993).

In discussing the usefulness of group therapy for college students, it is important to first consider the unique environment and developmental challenges that these students often experience. Attending college is considered a major developmental milestone in a young adult's life (Chickering & Reisser, 1993) and includes major environmental, internal, and interpersonal changes and adjustments. These often include, but are not limited to, moving away from parents or caretakers, developing and asserting independence, identity formation including sexual and cultural components, developing career goals, and exposure to new ideas or views of the world—all while in a novel and unique environment that can include significant amounts of social pressure (Chickering, & Reisser, 1993). Clearly, these factors present students with many different psychological challenges and processes and highlight the importance and necessity of a therapeutic environment on campus dedicated solely to the needs of students.

In examining the presenting issues of college students seeking therapy, Chandler and Gallagher (1996) surveyed 474 college counselors who reported that the most frequent concerns of their clients (totaling 8,462) were relationship difficulties (69%), self-esteem issues (59%), depression (45%), anxiety (35%), and stress (29%). Other common concerns of this population include fear of failure and weight control (Bishop, Bauer, & Becker, 1998). These struggles are not surprising, considering the presenting issues in the context of the aforementioned developmental challenges and environmental changes commonly experienced by young adults in college. In examining possible treatment options, group therapy is an important and relevant modality to utilize in addressing these concerns (Kincade & Kalodner, 2004; Yalom, 1995), in part because group therapy provides the necessary exploration of interpersonal patterns and behavior and the ability to practice new approaches in the safety of the group. Common group modalities used to address this variety of concerns include psychoeducational groups, counseling groups, therapy groups, and outreach/prevention workshops.

Psychoeducational groups serve an educational and preventive function and are the most common types of groups on college campuses (DeLucia-Waack, 2009; Drum & Knott 2009; Golden et al., 1993). Common goals of these groups consist of providing topical, focused information and building awareness and relevant skills in group members. Examples of psychoeducational groups that may illustrate these goals include academic support, stress management, and depression management. In these groups, leaders provide helpful information regarding the topic; an academic support group may discuss self-esteem or identity issues as they relate to academics, while a stress- or depression-management group may provide information regarding common precursors, symptoms, and consequences of stress or depression. This promotes general awareness for members and encourages reflection and exploration of members' own status regarding these issues. These groups also include skill-building components; academic support groups may include specific study skills and time-management strategies, while stress- and depression-management groups may include relaxation skills and symptom-management strategies including exercise and seeking social support.

Psychoeducational groups on college campuses are time-limited and run anywhere from 3 to 6 weeks, depending on the group leader and the restrictions or policies of the agency (Kincade & Kalodner, 2004). According to McWhirter (1995), for these groups to be successful, they should include four important elements: an overarching and focused theme, didactic teaching, personalized and relevant information, and the instruction of behavioral skills. While it is important to include these elements, leaders are also mindful of keeping a balance between providing the educational content and facilitating discussion and support among group members (Archer & Cooper, 1998).

Counseling groups address students' developmental life concerns and may be viewed as more remedial and less preventative in nature than psychoeducational groups. Developmental life concerns refer to psychological issues that arise from life events, including grief and loss, relationship issues, self-esteem or self-identity, and career issues. In this way, the main goals of counseling groups are to assist students in developing coping skills to deal with these issues, while increasing members' understanding of themselves as well as the way they relate to others. A key benefit of counseling groups is the focus on the interpersonal nature of students' struggles and on incorporating an interpersonal strategy in the coping skills students may utilize to achieve greater life satisfaction. The group setting provides students a chance to practice novel, more adaptive interpersonal skills in a safe and trusting environment (Kincade & Kalodner, 2004).

Students experiencing more severe or significant psychological issues are most appropriate for therapy groups. Johnson (2009) provides a primer on these groups, with a focus on short-term interpersonal psychotherapy groups. These are more process-oriented, while still strongly focused on improving students' interpersonal skills and relationships. Therapy groups in a college setting tend to have a more general format and can address feelings of isolation, depression, and anxiety.

It is important to mention that groups can be tailored to fit the specific environment or student population and may also be targeted to include a range of at-risk students. Indeed, students attending the same colleges and universities can often share similar characteristics. For example, Kincade and Kalodner (2004) point out that students attending small, private, religious colleges may have significantly different characteristics from students attending large, public institutions. In this way, counseling centers at each institution must attempt to meet and address different student needs. A helpful example of a group that is tailored to a specific campus environment is Richards's (1993) examination of coping with self-defeating perfectionism in Mormon students. This group utilized religious and spiritual components in the examination of perfectionist ideas and in the teaching of adaptive behavioral skills. Evaluation of participants after group showed decreases in perfectionism and increases in self-esteem. While this type of group was clearly successful for Mormon students in a small, private college, it is likely that nonreligious students may have responded differently. Overall, this highlights the fact that college students should not be considered a monolithic group and that leaders should consider the unique needs of the student body in designing an effective psychoeducational, counseling, therapy, or outreach group.

There are challenges encountered by many university centers in attempting to run successful groups for students. These challenges are largely focused on the growing diversity of students, limited staffing resources with greater student demand, and successfully marketing and filling groups (Parcover, Dunton, Gehlert, & Mitchell, 2006). The increasing diversity of the student body demands multiculturally competent service providers. Eason (2009) comments that there continues to be scant attention to diversity issues and that the coverage often lacks specificity. Further, he views this as unintentional neglect but is clear that we cannot continue without attending to the ever-growing diverse populations in university settings. It has been noted that there is an underutilization of college and university counseling centers by minority students (e.g., Davidson, Yakushka, & Sanford-Martens, 2004). Fostering professional relationships with departments on campus that have increased contact with minority students is a component of culturally competent work. Many professionals have called for improvements in this area (Eason, 2009; Hodges, 2001; Smith et al., 2007; Sue & Sue, 1999).

A second and significant challenge lies in the continually limited resources afforded to university counseling centers. As colleges and universities work to cut costs, campus counseling centers are left with limited staff to address often overwhelming increases in student demands for mental health services (Hodges, 2001; McEneaney & Gross, 2009). Indeed, the literature shows a trend of increasing severity and overall demand for mental health services by students (Bishop et al., 1998; Gilbert, 1992), while service providers on campus are struggling to keep up. Smith and colleagues (2007) found that only 4% of their participants indicated that increasing caseload demand was not a significant issue.

One interesting issue concerning groups in counseling centers may be a lack of referral to groups. In an examination of the use of group counseling on campuses, Golden et al. (1993) found that while 92% of counseling centers offered groups, fewer than 20% of clients are actually involved in group work. One wonders what an updated study of counseling centers might reveal. It is worth considering that formatting and marketing of groups may help to generate greater use of groups (Parcover et al., 2006). Professionals have highlighted specific techniques and strategies for improving marketing and recruitment, including the importance of the group's title, offering the group during times that correspond to student schedules, directly addressing and stressing confidentiality within the group, and including preparation sessions where students can learn more about what to expect as group members (Kincade & Kalodner, 2004; Parcover et al., 2006).

In reflecting on these challenges and their impact on the use of group therapy on college campuses, it is important to remind the reader of the positives and successes of this modality. It remains the case that group work is an important and relevant modality for treatment, particularly with regard to exploring and improving interpersonal strengths. Further, group work can often serve as a treatment of choice for many common presenting issues among students (Kincade & Kalodner, 2004; Yalom, 1995), and this treatment has been shown to be effective for increasing well-being and decreasing any number of concerns, including stress, depression, and anxiety, among college students (Devi, 2003; Hayes, 2007).

Overall, professionals are calling for increased and improved use of this modality on campus settings (Parcover et al., 2006) and have made specific suggestions including the potential revival of the once popular marathon group therapy (Stanger & Harris, 2005) and the introduction of new group techniques such as therapeutic enactment (Keats & Sabharwal, 2008). These suggestions have been met with increased debate surrounding potential limitations and further critiques (Dagley & Thomas, 2008). Overall, an ongoing dialogue regarding the increased and improved use of group therapy in college and university counseling centers should be viewed as positive and encouraging.

Other Settings in which Groups Play a Major Role
Inpatient Facilities
Emer (2004) provides detailed attention to the use of groups in inpatient settings. Groups are commonly

used to provide psychotherapy, psychoeducation, and support to patients living in a psychiatric setting. These groups are complicated by an ever-changing membership (as individuals are admitted and released), varying degrees of psychopathology and levels of functioning, and dual roles for group leaders (who may have contact with the members on the floor). In spite of the challenges, both Yalom (1983) and Froberg and Slife (1987) have offered models for making groups work in inpatient settings. It is beyond the scope of this chapter to review these models here.

Inpatients report that groups provided a highly useful part of their treatment (Leszcz, Yalom, & Norden, 1985). Types of groups abound. Along with traditional groups on the ward or floor, other types of groups have been developed to foster creativity and enhance participation in psychotherapy (McGarry & Prince, 1988) and use strategies such as improvisational drama (Sheppard, Olson, Croke, LaFave, & Gerber, 1990) and poetry (Houlding & Holland, 1988). Interested readers are encouraged to begin with Emer's (2004) chapter for additional information on this setting.

Offenders and Mandated Clients

Morgan (2004) opened his chapter on this setting by stating that it is a common mantra that "If you can facilitate groups in here, you can facilitate groups anywhere" (p. 388). Group treatment of offenders does differ significantly from therapy groups in other settings (Morgan, Winterowd, & Ferrell, 1999), and it is not possible to provide significant coverage of this setting in this chapter. There is less research on groups among the incarcerated (Morgan, 2004). Given the continual need for treatment of offenders and other mandated clients, additional attention to this setting is required.

Conclusion

As Conyne (2010) points out, there are still barriers to group counseling, including ineffective referral processes, difficulties is organizing groups in various types of settings, and myths about group counseling that may discourage participation. There is evidence that this is true in all of the settings covered in this chapter. Regardless, groups continue to play a major role in each of the settings described in this chapter and are likely to continue to be an important part of the armamentarium of services that professionals can offer to clients.

Future Directions

"Settings" is such a diverse topic that this chapter has included information about many different kinds of groups. This diversity of topics leads to a kind of fragmentation in the research on groups; that is, we know some things about some kinds of groups in some settings, but the vast gaps in knowledge are difficult to fill. In the future, group practitioners and researchers will need to focus on studying the efficacy and the mechanisms behind the efficacy for groups in these vastly different settings. The tools used to assess the effects of group interventions should include some measure of group cohesion or a way to assess the power of the group in explaining the changes that occur.

Overall, there is much we know but much more that we still do not know about how groups work in these different settings.

References

Akos, P., Hamm, J. V., Mack, S. G., & Dunaway, M. (2007). Utilizing the developmental influence of peers in middle school groups. *Journal for Specialists in Group Work, 32,* 51–60.

Archer, J., & Cooper, S. (1998). Counseling and mental health services on campus: A handbook of contemporary practices and challenges. San Francisco: Jossey-Bass.

Bailey, D. F., & Bradbury-Bailey, M. E. (2007). Promoting achievement for African Americans through group work. *Journal for Specialists in Group Work, 32,* 86–96.

Belden, A., Park, M. J., & Mince, J. (2008). AIDS prevention for adolescents in school: A high school–based STI/HIV/AIDS prevention program. In J. J. Card & T. Benner (Eds.), *Model programs for adolescent sexual health: Evidence-based HIV, STI, and pregnancy prevention interventions* (pp. 187–196). New York: Springer.

Bishop, J. B., Bauer, K. W., & Becker, E. T. (1998). A survey of counseling needs of male and female college students. *Journal of College Student Development, 39,* 205–210.

Blount, A., Schoenbaum, M., Kathol, R., Rollman, B. L., Thomas, M., & O'Donohue, W. (2007). The economics of behavioral health services in medical settings: A summary of the evidence. *Professional Psychology: Research and Practice, 38*(3), 290–297.

Bosworth, K., Espelage, D., DuBay, T., Daytner, G., & Karageorge, K. (2000). Preliminary evaluation of a multimedia violence prevention program for adolescents. *American Journal of Health Behavior, 24,* 268–280.

Brannigan, M. (2007). A psychoeducational group model to build academic competence in new middle school students. *Journal for Specialists in Group Work, 32,* 61–70.

Bucher, J. A., Houts, P. S., Nezu, C. M., & Nezu, A. M. (1999). Improving problem-solving skills of family caregivers through group education. *Journal of Psychosocial Oncology, 16*(3–4), 73–84.

Burckhardt, C. S., Mannerkorpi, K., Hedenberg, L., & Bjelle, A. (1994). A randomized, controlled clinical trial of education and physical training for women with fibromyalgia. *Journal of Rheumatology, 21,* 714–720.

Chandler, L. A., & Gallagher, R. P. (1996). Developing a taxonomy for problems seen at a university counseling center. *Measurement and Evaluation in Counseling and Development, 29,* 4–12.

Chickering, A., & Reisser, L. (1993). *Education and identity*. San Francisco: Jossey-Bass.

Christner, R. W., Mennuti, R. B., & Pearson, L. M. (2009). Cognitive-behavioral therapy approaches in a school setting. In R. W. Christner & R. B. Mennuti (Eds.), *School-based mental health: a practitioner's guide to comparative practices* (pp. 181–200). New York: Routledge.

Clifford, M. W. (2004). Group counseling and group therapy in mental health settings and health maintenance organizations. In J. L. DeLucia-Waack, D. A. Gerrity, C. R. Kalodner, & M. T. Riva (Eds.), *Handbook of group counseling and psychotherapy* (pp. 414–426). Thousand Oaks, CA: Sage.

Conyne, R. K., & Mazza, J. (2007). Ecological group work applied to schools. *Journal for Specialists in Group Work, 32,* 19–29.

Conyne, R. K. (2011). *The Oxford Handbook of Group Counseling* (p. 12). New York, Oxford University Press.

Cooney, J. L., Pilkey, D. T., Cooney, N. L., & Kranzler, H. R. (2000, February). *Acute nicotine withdrawal and depressive symptomatology in alcoholic smokers*. Presented at the 6th annual meeting of the Society for Research on Nicotine and Tobacco, Washington, DC.

Cox, J., Davies, D. R., Burlingame, G. M., Campbell, J. E., Layne, C. M., & Katzenbach, R. J. (2007). Effectiveness of a trauma/grief-focused group intervention: A qualitative study with war-exposed Bosnian adolescents. *International Journal of Group Psychotherapy, 57,* 319–345.

Curran, G. M., Kirchner, J. E., Allee, E., & Booth, B. M. (2003). Detection of substance use disorders in VA primary care clinics. *Psychiatric Services, 54,* 13–26.

Dagley, J. C., & Thomas, C. M. (2008). A response to "Time-limited service alternatives: Using therapeutic enactment in open group therapy": A dramatic effort to redefine short-term and time-limited services. *Journal for Specialists in Group Work, 33*(4), 317–327.

Davidson, M. M., Yakushka, O. F., & Sanford-Martens, T. C. (2004). Racial and ethnic minority clients' utilization of a university counseling center: An archival study. *Journal of Multicultural Counseling and Development, 32,* 259–271.

Deering, C. G., & Gannon, E. J. (2005). Gender and psychotherapy with traditional men. *American Journal of Psychotherapy, 59*(4), 351–360.

DeLucia-Waack, J. L. (2009). Helping group leaders sculpt the group process to the unique needs of college students. *International Journal of Group Psychotherapy, 59,* 553–562.

DeLucia-Waack, J. L., & Gellman, R. A. (2007). The efficacy of using music in children of divorce groups: Impact on anxiety, depression and irrational beliefs about divorce. *Group Dynamics: Theory, Research, & Practice, 11,* 272–282.

DeLucia, J. L., Gerrity, D.A., Kalodner, C. R., & Riva, M.T. (2004). Handbook of group counseling and psychotherapy. Thousand Oaks, CA: Sage.

Devi, P. N. (2003). Effectiveness of group counseling: Adjustment among women college students. *Journal of Indian Psychology, 21*(2), 67–77.

Dowden, A. R. (2009). Implementing self-advocacy training within a brief psychoeducational group to improve the academic motivation of black adolescents. *Journal for Specialists in Group Work, 34,* 118–136.

Drum, D. J., & Knott, J. E. (2009). Theme groups at thirty. *International Journal of Group Psychotherapy, 59,* 491–510.

Dunn, M., Van Horn, E., & Herman, S. (1981). Social skills and spinal cord injury: A comparison of three training procedures. *Behavior Therapy, 12,* 153–164.

Eason, E. A. (2009). Diversity and group theory, practice, and research. *International Journal of Group Psychotherapy, 59,* 563–574.

Edelman, S., Craig, A., & Kidman, A. D. (2000). Group interventions with cancer patients: Efficacy of psychoeducational versus supportive groups. *Journal of Psychosocial Oncology, 18,* 67–85.

Eggert, L. L., Thompson, E. A., & Herting, J. R. (1995). Reducing suicide potential among high-risk youth: Tests of a school-based prevention program. Suicide and Life Threatening Behavior, 25, 276–296.

Eggert, L. L., Thompson, E. A., Herting, J. R., Nicholas, L.J., & Dicker, B. G. (1994). Preventing adolescent drug abuse and high school dropout through an intensive school-based social network development program. American Journal of Health Promotion, 8, 202–215.

Elliott, T. R., Rivera, P., & Tucker, E. (2004). Groups in behavioral health and medical settings. In J. L. DeLucia-Waack, D. A. Gerrity, C. R. Kalodner, & M. T. Riva (Eds.), *Handbook of group counseling and psychotherapy* (pp. 338–350). Thousand Oaks, CA: Sage.

Emer, D. (2004). The use of groups in inpatient facilities. In J. L. DeLucia-Waack, D. A. Gerrity, C. R. Kalodner, & M. T. Riva (Eds.), *Handbook of group counseling and psychotherapy* (pp. 351–365). Thousand Oaks, CA: Sage.

Fontana, A., Rosenheck, R., Spencer, H., & Gray, S. (2001). *The long journey home, IX: Treatment of PTSD in the Department of Veterans Affairs: Fiscal year 2000 service delivery and performance*. West Haven, CT: Northeast Program Evaluation Center and National Center for PTSD.

Ford, J. D., & Stewart, J. (1999). Group psychotherapy for war-related PTSD with military veterans. In B. H. Young and D. D. Blake (Eds.), *Group treatment for post-traumatic stress disorder: Conceptualization, themes and processes* (pp. 75–100). Philadelphia: Taylor & Francis.

Forester, B., Kornfeld, D. S., Fleiss, J. L., & Thompson, S. (1993). Group psychotherapy during radiotherapy: Effects on emotional and physical distress. *American Journal of Psychiatry, 150,* 1700–1706.

Froberg, W., & Slife, B. D. (1987). Overcoming obstacles to the implantation of Yalom's model of inpatient group psychotherapy. *International Journal of Group Psychotherapy, 37,* 371–388.

Gidron, Y., Davidson, K., & Bata, I. (1999). The short-term effects of a hostility-reduction intervention on male coronary heart disease patients. *Health Psychology, 18,* 416–420.

Gilbert, S. P. (1992). Ethical issues in the treatment of severe psychopathology in university and college counseling centers. *Journal of Counseling & Development, 70,* 695–700.

Glasgow, R. E., Fisher, E. B., Anderson, B., LaGreca, A., Marrero, D., Johnson, S. B., et al. (1999). Behavioral science in diabetes. *Diabetes Care, 22,* 832–843.

Glueckauf, R. L., & Quittner, A. L. (1992). Assertiveness training for disabled adults in wheelchairs: Self-report, role-play, and activity pattern outcomes. *Journal of Consulting and Clinical Psychology, 60,* 419–425.

Golden, B. R., Corazzini, J. G., & Grady, P. (1993). Current practices of group therapy at university counseling centers: A national study. *Professional Psychology: Research and Practice, 24,* 228–230.

Greene, L. R., Meisler, A. W., Pilkey, D., Alexander, G., Cardella, L. A., Sirois, B. C., et al. (2004). Psychological work with groups in the Veterans Administration. In J. L. DeLucia-Waack, D. A. Gerrity, C. R. Kalodner, & M. T. Riva (Eds.), *Handbook of group counseling and psychotherapy* (pp. 338–350). Thousand Oaks, CA: Sage.

Grotjahn, M. (1947). Experience with group psychotherapy as a method for treatment of veterans. *American Journal of Psychiatry, 103,* 637–643.

Hadden, S. B. (1947). Post-military group psychotherapy with psychoneurotics. *Mental Hygiene, 31,* 89–93.

Hart, M. A., & Foster, S. N. (1997). Couples' attitudes toward childbirth participation: Relationship to evaluation of labor and delivery. *Journal of Perinatal and Neonatal Nursing, 11*(1), 10–26.

Hayes, J. A. (1997). What does the Brief Symptom Inventory measure in college and university counseling center clients? *Journal of Counseling Psychology, 44,* 360–367.

Helgeson, V., Cohen, S., Schulz, R., & Yasko, J. (1999). Education and peer discussion group interventions and adjustment to breast cancer. *Health Psychology, 20,* 387–392.

Hoag, M. J. & Burlingame, G.M. (1997). Evaluating the effectiveness of child and adolescent group treatment: A meta-analytic study. Journal of Child Clinical Psychology, 26, 234–246.

Hodges, S. (2001). University counseling centers at the twenty-first century: Looking forward, looking back. *Journal of College Counseling, 4,* 161–173.

Houlding, S., & Holland, P. (1988). Contributions of a poetry writing group to the treatment of severely disturbed psychiatric inpatients. *Clinical Social Work Journal, 19,* 194–200.

Jacobs, C., Ross, R. D., Walker, I. M., & Stockdale, F. E. (1983). Behavior of cancer patients: A randomized study of the effects of education and peer support groups. *American Journal of Clinical Oncology, 6,* 347–353.

Johansson, C., Dahl, J., Jannert, M., Melin, L., & Andersson, G. (1998). Effects of a cognitive-behavioral pain management program. *Behavior Research and Therapy, 36,* 915–930.

Johnson, C. V. (2009). A process-oriented group model for university students: A semi-structured approach. *International Journal of Group Psychotherapy, 59,* 511–528.

Jones, L., Brazel, D., Peskind, E. R., Morelli, T., & Raskind, M.A. (2000). Group therapy program for African-American veterans with posttraumatic stress disorder. *Psychiatric Services, 51*(9), 1177–1179.

Keane, T. M., Fairbank, J. A., Caddell, J. M., & Zimering, R. T. (1989). Implosive (flooding) therapy reduces symptoms of PTSD in Vietnam combat veterans. *Behavior Therapy, 20,* 245–260.

Keane, T. M., Gerardi, R. J., Lyons, J. A., & Wolfe, J. (1988). The interrelationship of substance abuse and post-traumatic stress disorder: Epidemiological and clinical considerations. In M. Galanter (Ed.), *Recent developments in alcoholism* (Vol. 6). New York: Plenum.

Keats, P. A., & Sabharwal, V. V. (2008). Time-limited service alternatives: Using therapeutic enactment in open group therapy. *Journal for Specialists in Group Work, 33*(4), 297–316.

Keefe, F., Caldwell, D., Williams, D., Gil, K., Mitchell, D., Robertson, C., et al. (1990). Pain coping skills training in the management of osteoarthritic knee pain: A comparative study. *Behavior Therapy, 21,* 49–62.

Keel, P. J., Bodoky, C., Gerhard, U., & Muller, W. (1998). Comparison of integrated group therapy and group relaxation training for fibromyalgia. *Clinical Journal of Pain, 14,* 232–238.

Kelly, J. A., Murphy, D. A., Bahr, G., Kalichman, S., Morgan, M., Stevenson, L., et al. (1993). Outcome of cognitive-behavioral and support group brief therapies for depressed, HIV-infected persons. *American Journal of Psychiatry, 150,* 1679–1686.

Kelly, J. A., St. Lawrence, J. S., Hood, H., & Brasfield, T. (1989). Behavioral intervention to reduce AIDS risk activities. *Journal of Consulting and Clinical Psychology, 57,* 60–67.

Khattab, N., & Jones, C. P. (2007). Growing up girl: Preparing for change through group work. *Journal for Specialists in Group Work, 32,* 41–50.

Kincade, E. A., & Kalodner, C. R. (2004). The use of groups in college and university counseling centers. In J. L. DeLucia-Waack, D. A. Gerrity, C. R. Kalodner, & M. T. Riva (Eds.), *Handbook of group counseling and psychotherapy* (pp. 366–377). Thousand Oaks, CA: Sage.

King, C., & Kennedy, P. (1999). Coping effectiveness training for people with spinal cord injury: Preliminary results of a controlled trial. *British Journal of Clinical Psychology, 38,* 5–14.

Kissane, D. W., Grabsch, B., Clarke, D. M., Smith, G. C., Love, A. W., Bloch, S., et al. (2007). Supportive-expressive group therapy for women with metastatic breast cancer: Survival and psychosocial outcome from a randomized controlled trial. *Psychooncology, 16,* 277–286.

Leszcz, M., Yalom, I. D., & Norden, M. (1985). The value of inpatient group psychotherapy: Patient's perspectives. *International Journal of Group Psychotherapy, 35,* 411–433.

Lopez, C., & Bhat, C. S. (2007). Supporting students with incarcerated parents in school: A group intervention. *Journal for Specialists in Group Work, 32,* 139–153.

Lustman, P., Griffith, L., Freedland, K., Kissel, S., & Clouse, R. (1998). Cognitive behavior therapy for depression in type 2 diabetes mellitus. *Annals of Internal Medicine, 129,* 613–621.

Makler, S., Sigal, M., Gelkopf, M., Kochba, B. B., & Horeb, E. (1990). Combat-related, chronic posttraumatic stress disorder: Implications for group therapy intervention. *American Journal of Psychotherapy, 44*(3), 381–395.

Marlatt, G. A., Larimer, M. E., Baer, J. S., & Quigley, L. A. (1993). Harm reduction for alcohol problems: Moving beyond the controlled drinking controversy. *Behavior Therapy, 24,* 461–504.

McEachern, A. G., & Kenny, M. C. (2007). Transition groups for high school students with disabilities. *Journal for Specialists in Group Work, 32,* 165–177.

McEneaney, A. M. S., & Gross, J. M. (2009). Introduction to the Special Issue: Group interventions in college counseling centers. *International Journal of Group Psychotherapy, 59,* 455–460.

McGarry, T. J., & Prince, M. (1998). Implementation of groups for creative expression on a psychiatric inpatient unit. *Journal of Psychosocial Nursing, 36,* 19–24.

McGinnis, J. M., & Foege, W. H. (1993). Actual causes of death in the United States. *Journal of the American Medical Association, 270,* 2207–2212.

McWhirter, J. J. (1995). Emotional education for university students. *Journal of College Student Psychotherapy, 10,* 27–38.

Meisler, A. W. (1999). Group treatment of PTSD and comorbid alcohol abuse. In B. H. Young and D. D. Blake (Eds.), *Group treatment for post-traumatic stress disorder: Conceptualization, themes and processes* (pp. 117–136). Philadelphia: Taylor & Francis.

Meneses, K. D., McNees, P., Loerzel, V. W., Su, X., Zhang, Y., & Hassey, L. A. (2007). Transition from treatment to survivorship: Effects of a psychoeducational intervention on quality of life in breast cancer survivors. *Oncology Nursing Forum, 34*(5), 1007–1016.

Mohr, D. C., Boudewyn, A., Goodkin, D., Bostrom, A., & Epstein, L. (2001). Comparative outcomes for individual cognitive-behavioral therapy, supportive-expressive group psychotherapy, and sertraline for the treatment of depression in multiple sclerosis. *Journal of Consulting and Clinical Psychology, 69*, 942–949.

Morgan, R. D. (2004). Groups with offenders and mandated clients (pp. 388–400). In J. L. DeLucia-Waack, D. A. Gerrity, C. R. Kalodner, & M. T. Riva (Eds.), *Handbook of group counseling and psychotherapy* (pp. 366–377). Thousand Oaks, CA: Sage.

Morgan, R. D., Winterowd, C. L. & Ferrell, S. W. (1999). A national survey of group psychotherapy services in correctional facilities. Professional Psychology: Research and Practice, 30, 600–606.

Nikels, H. J., Mims, G. A., & Mims, M. J. (2007). Allies against hate: A school-based diversity sensitivity experience. *Journal for Specialists in Group Work, 32*, 126–138.

Parcover, J. A., Dunton, E. C., Gehlert, K. M., & Mitchell, S. L. (2006). Getting the most from group counseling in college counseling centers. *Journal for Specialists in Group Work, 31*(1), 37–49.

Paisley, P. O., & Milsom, A. (2007). Group work as an essential contribution to transforming school counseling. *Journal for Specialists in Group Work, 32*, 9–17.

Powdermaker, F. B., & Frank, J. D. (1948). Group psychotherapy with neurotics. *American Journal of Psychiatry, 105*, 449–455.

Powdermaker, F. B., & Frank, J. D. (1953). *Group psychotherapy: Studies in methodology of research and psychotherapy.* Cambridge, MA: Harvard University Press.

Ready, D. J., Thomas, K. R., Worley, V., Backscheider, A. G., Harvey, L. A. C., Baltzell, D., et al. (2008). A field test of group based exposure therapy with 102 veterans with war-related posttraumatic stress disorder. *Journal of Traumatic Stress, 21*(2), 150–157.

Richards, P. S. (1993). A religiously oriented group counseling intervention for self defeating perfectionism: A pilot study. *Counseling and Values, 37*, 96–104.

Riva, M. T., & Haub, A.L. (2004). Group counseling in the schools (pp. 309–321). In J. L. DeLucia-Waack, D. A. Gerrity, C. R. Kalodner, & M. T. Riva (Eds.), *Handbook of group counseling and psychotherapy* (pp. 366–377). Thousand Oaks, CA: Sage.

Ruffolo, M. C., & Fischer, D. (2009). Using an evidence-based CBT group intervention model for adolescents with depressive symptoms: lessons learned from a school-based adaptation. *Child and Family Social Work, 14*, 189–197.

Rush, C. M., & Akos, P. (2007). Supporting children and adolescents with deployed caregivers: A structured approach for school counselors. *Journal for Specialists in Group Work, 32*, 113–125.

Salloum, A., Garside, L. W., Irwin, C. L., Anderson, A. D., & Francois, A. H. (2009). Grief and trauma group therapy for children after Hurricane Katrina. *Social Work with Groups, 32*, 64–79.

Salloum, A., & Overstreet, S. (2008). Evaluation of individual and group grief and trauma interventions for children post disaster. *Journal of Clinical Child & Adolescent Psychology, 37*, 495–507.

Saltzman, W. R., Layne, C. M., Pynoos, R. S., Steinberg, A. M., & Aisenberg, E. (2001). Trauma- and grief-focused intervention for adolescents exposed to community violence: Results of a school-based screening and group treatment protocol. *Group Dynamics: Theory, Research, & Practice, 5*, 291–303.

Schnurr, P. P., Friedman, M. J., Foy, D. W., Shea, M. T., Hsieh, F. Y., Lavori, P. W., et al. (2003). Randomized trial of trauma-focused group therapy for posttraumatic stress disorder: Results from a Department of Veterans Affairs cooperative study. *Archives of General Psychiatry, 60*, 481–489.

Schwartz, L. A. (1945). Group psychotherapy in the war neuroses. *American Journal of Psychiatry, 101*, 498–500.

Schwartz, S. M., Trask, P. C., Shanmugham, K., & Townsend, C. O. (2004). Conducting psychological research in medical settings: Challenges, limitations, and recommendations for effectiveness research. *Professional Psychology: Research and Practice, 35*(5), 500–508.

Seal, K. H., Metzler, T. J., Gima, K. S., Bertenthal, D., Maguen, S., & Marmar, C. R. (2009). Trends and risk factors for mental health diagnoses among Iraq and Afghanistan veterans using Department of Veterans Affairs health care, 2002–2008. *American Journal of Public Health, 99*, 1651–1658.

Sheppard, J., Olson, A., Croke, J., LaFave, H. G., & Gerber, G. J. (1990). Improvisational drama groups in an inpatient setting. *Hospital and Community Psychiatry, 41*, 1019–1021.

Sipprelle, R. C. (1992). A vet center experience: Multievent trauma, delayed treatment type. In D. W. Foy (Ed.), *Treating PTSD: Cognitive-behavioral strategies.* New York: Guilford Press.

Smith, T. B., Dean, B., Floyd, S., Silva, C., Yamashita, M., Durtschi, J., et al. (2007). Pressing issues in college counseling: A survey of American college counseling association members. *Journal of College Counseling, 10*, 64–78.

Snoek, F. J., van der Ven, C. W., & Lubach, C. (1999). Cognitive behavioral group training for poorly controlled type I diabetes patients: A psychoeducational approach. *Diabetes Spectrum, 12*, 147–157.

Spira, J. L. (1997). *Group therapy for medically ill patients.* New York: Guildford Press.

Spitz, H. I. (1996). *Group psychotherapy and managed health care: A clinical guide for practitioners.* New York: Brunner-Mazel.

Stanger, T., & Harris, R. S., Jr. (2005). Marathon group therapy: Potential for university counseling centers and beyond. *Journal for Specialists in Group Work, 30*(2), 145–157.

Stevens, M. J., & Duttlinger, J. (1998). Correlates of participation in a breast cancer support group. *Journal of Psychosomatic Research, 45*, 263–275.

Sue, D. W., & Sue, D. (1999). *Counseling the culturally different: Theory and practice* (3rd ed.). New York: John Wiley & Sons.

Telch, C. F., & Telch, M. (1986). Group coping skills instruction and supportive group therapy for cancer patients: Comparison of strategies. *Journal of Consulting and Clinical Psychology, 54*, 802–808.

Veach, L. J., & Gladding, S. T. (2007). Using creative group techniques in high schools. *Journal for Specialists in Group Work, 32*, 71–82.

Vlaeyen, J. W. S., Teeken-Gruben, N., Goosens, M., Rutten-van Molken, M., Pelt, R., van Eek, H., et al. (1996). Cognitive-educational treatment of fibromyalgia: A randomized clinical trial. I. Clinical effects. *Journal of Rheumatology, 23*, 1237–1245.

Wakefield, K. (1988). The importance of a female therapist in a male Vietnam veterans' psychotherapy group. *Bulletin of the Menninger Clinic, 52*, 16–29.

Webb, L., & Brigman, G. A. (2007). Student success skills: A structured group intervention for school counselors. *Journal for Specialists in Group Work, 32*, 190–201.

Weigel, R. G. (2002). The marathon encounter group vision and reality: Exhuming the body for a last look. *Consulting Psychology Journal: Practice and Research, 54*, 186–198.

Whiston, S. C., & Sexton, T. L. (1998). A review of school counseling outcomes research: Implications for practice. Journal of Counseling & Development, 76, 412–426.

White, N. J., & Rayle, A. D. (2007). Strong teens: A school-based small group experience for African American males. *Journal for Specialists in Group Work, 32*, 178–189.

Yakushko, O., Davidson, M. M., & Williams, E. N. (2009). Identity salience model: A paradigm for integrating multiple identities in clinical practice. *Psychotherapy: Theory, Research, Practice & Training, 46*(2), 180–192.

Yalom, I. D. (1983). *Inpatient group psychotherapy*. New York: Basic Books.

Yalom, I. D. (1995). *The theory and practice of group psychotherapy* (4th ed.). New York: Basic Books.

Ziffer, J. M., Crawford, E., & Penney-Wietor, J. (2007). The Boomerang Bunch: A school-based multifamily group approach for students and their families recovering from parental separation and divorce. *Journal for Specialists in Group Work, 32*, 154–164.

Group Counseling across the Life Span:
A Psychosocial Perspective

Jeanmarie Keim *and* David L. Olguin

Abstract

This chapter discusses group work for individuals across the life span through a psychosocial development lens. Erik Erikson's contribution of the psychosocial stages to the helping professions remains a valuable tool in conceptualizing development, prevention, and treatment. Group work is an appropriate and effective method to promote positive psychosocial growth and assist members to overcome cognitive, behavioral, and emotional difficulties. As discussed throughout this text, groups are used to target broad areas such as behavior, chronic illnesses, career development, spirituality, emotional insight, and reminiscence. Due to the broad range of groups, it is important that group therapists conceptualize clients within a developmental context, including which psychosocial tasks the member is facing, when determining the group in which to place clients. This chapter opens with a brief overview of Erikson's psychosocial stages, followed by overviews of group literature for 10 specific age groups, group therapist considerations, and future directions.

Keywords: groups, counseling, life span, psychosocial development

Introduction

The developmental stage of the client is critical when therapists conceptualize the client's emotional, cognitive, and behavioral barriers. A popular framework used by clinicians is Erikson's (1968) psychosocial stages of development. His work focused on present and future growth (Lopez, 1987), and this approach can afford group members with developmentally appropriate opportunities to build fundamental life skills needed for healthy living. As individuals resolve developmental and psychosocial tasks, healthy functioning builds. On the other hand, if a developmental task is not successfully accomplished, then emotional, behavioral, and/or cognitive difficulties may complicate functioning and interfere with further developmental growth. While stages are developmental, individuals tend to revisit earlier stages to accomplish and put closure on tasks that were initially unresolved. This chapter covers group work across the life span through the

lens of Erikson's psychosocial stages of development. However, as with any framework or theory, clinicians are cautioned that Erikson's stages need modification for various cultures and adjusting them to fit the clients' cultures is critical. The stages do provide a springboard from which to discuss group therapy across the life span. Each of the 10 age-specific sections provides an overview of the group-work literature and the psychosocial tasks that individuals confront. Therapist considerations and future directions for each age group are also presented.

There are eight psychosocial stages, each containing two opposing tasks, with resolution promoting healthy psychological functioning. The first stage centers on trust versus mistrust; the second stage contains autonomy versus shame and doubt (Erikson, 1968). The third (initiative versus guilt) and fourth (industry versus inferiority) stages contain childhood developmental tasks extending to age 11 (Erikson, 1968). The trust, autonomy, initiative, and industry stages, if successfully attained, will produce healthy development for living in the present while shaping future development (Erikson, 1968). Preadolescence and adolescence begins the fifth stage, identity versus role confusion (Erikson, 1968). The youth in this period (12–18 years of age) should be challenged in a variety of ways that help them explore and define their self-identity (Erikson, 1968). Successful attainment of identity promotes transition to the sixth stage (intimacy versus isolation) at approximately age 19–40 (Erikson, 1968). The primary objective of the intimacy stage is to establish and maintain relationships (Erikson, 1968). The seventh (generativity versus stagnation) and eighth (ego integrity versus despair) stages mark periods from older adulthood to death (Erikson, 1968). During these last two developmental stages older individuals examine their lives and determine whether or not they are content and fulfilled with their life contributions.

Beginning with the infant stage, this chapter presents group-work literature across the life span, progressing to retirement and beyond. The literature will show how developmentally appropriate group work is for all ages and how psychosocial tasks are embedded in the uniqueness of group work, the members, and group dynamics to foster member growth.

Infants

The first psychosocial stage, trust versus mistrust (Erikson, 1968), begins at birth and ends about age 1. Erikson suggested that the primary task for an infant in this stage is to develop trust with his or her primary caregivers. Infants who learn to establish trust have greater chances to build psychosocial health, and those who do not are likely to encounter future problems because the capacity to trust was not developed (Goldberger, 1988). Although the task of trust can be accomplished in later developmental stages, it is most beneficial to establish trusting relationships early in life (Niccols, 2008; Stenberg, 2003). The period of infancy through the toddler years sets the foundation for later psychosocial development, requiring group therapists to become creative and intentional when designing activities and selecting techniques (Conyne, Crowell, & Newmeyer, 2008).

The group is a natural environment for children and adolescents. Whether they have parents or not, youth under the age of 18 in the United States must have a legal guardian (unless emancipated through the court system). Thus, our youth are generally in

the care of some system, and it is in these systems where infants and children learn information and styles of functioning that shape their worldviews (Stenberg, 2003). Most importantly, they receive messages that contain pros and cons of residing and operating with other people in a variety of systems. During the first Eriksonian stage (1968), trust versus mistrust, infants either develop trust that their most basic needs will be met by their primary caregiver or do not, thus setting the foundation for their psychosocial development.

Group-work literature regarding personal growth and healthy development in infants is generally sparse; however, there are scholarly works with information on play as a way of promoting healthy development and on group work with infants who have medical conditions. Additional scholarly information may be found on the use of music groups with infants and caregivers (Lyons, 2000), infant-led innovations (Paul & Thomson-Salo, 1997), and groups to promote care giver–child interactions (Phillips, 1985).

Group Therapist Considerations

Infants are frequently engaged in a variety of group settings including private homes, day-care centers, and hospitals. During this critical time, healthy attachments to another person will or will not develop (Niccols, 2008). As a result, changes occur in the infant's brain development, feelings, reactions, and responses (Stenberg, 2003). Accomplishment or resolution of the stage must first be operationalized. Accomplishment or resolution is subjective and implies that individuals must decide whether they are satisfied with the task and the majority of issues and whether concerns surrounding the stage or task have been largely resolved. Facilitators of infant group work must have a clear understanding of infant development in order to assess any abnormalities of development in their clients.

Sample Group Models

Parent–child attachments are a frequent theme in the infant group-work literature (Elizalde-Utnick, 2007; Lyons, 2000; Niccols, 2008; Paul & Thomson-Salo, 1997). Attachments develop through an emphasis on relationships with caregivers, and a primary method to help infants, toddlers, and caregivers develop relationships has been play therapy.

Play is a universal language that equips infants with the needed stimulation for cognitive, physical, and social development (Oaklander, 2001). Ticknor (2008) suggested that play with parents is effective in stimulating infants. Niccols (2008) suggested that facilitators of groups for parents and infants should promote Yalom's (1995) therapeutic factors. She bases her suggestion on research about parent and infant attachments. In her study, Niccols assigned participants to either the "right from the start" (RFTS) group or the home visitor group.

The RFTS psychoeducational group met once weekly (2 hours in duration) for 8 weeks, and the home visitor group comprised caregivers at home. Parents in the RFTS group watched videos and engaged in small- and large-group discussions as they learned about reading infant cues and responding in a sensitive manner (Niccols, 2008). The objectives consisted of learning about the effects of infant stimulation and methods to give stimulation to infants and responding to infants in a sensitive manner. Accomplishing these objectives proved to enhance child–caregiver relationships. Pre- and posttest measures of maternal sensitivity and infant attachment demonstrated statistically significant improvements for both sensitivity and attachment for the RFTS group (Niccols, 2008). Niccols' RFTS group also had significant improvements in secure infant attachment at the 6-month follow-up over the home visitor group. Niccols stated that the changes were likely due to the supportive environment and network of friends that parents in the RFTS group reported establishing. Niccols' finding suggests that mothers also need attachments with other adults while raising their infants.

Future Directions

The future directions for group work with infants include research into practical application programs designed to enhance physical and psychological growth during this critical developmental stage, for example, examining how psychosocially based activities impact infant and caregiver development. Adding to the literature on effective activities that promote development for infants is also needed, as is expanding RFTS groups to other caregivers to assist them with learning the "language" of infants. Practical applications include finding ways in which older adults can spend time interacting with the young children who do not have attachments with primary caregivers (Barnette, 1989). Seniors can also volunteer in a variety of settings, for example, community centers that provide day-care services for infants and hospital neonatal units. In these settings, older adult–infant interactions contribute to developing trust, enhanced relationships, and overall task accomplishment.

Toddlers to Kindergarten-Aged Children

Toddlers and preschool-aged children, ages 1–5, engage in a variety of groups when they enter day care or school systems; therefore, it is important that trust was firmly established in infancy. Two social tasks in this stage are autonomy versus shame/doubt and initiative versus guilt (Erikson, 1968). These tasks can help children to adjust to new settings and navigate the new rules and regulations. It is inevitable that many preschool-aged children will run into obstacles as they learn and challenge established norms. The primary tasks during the autonomy versus shame and doubt stage (Erikson, 1968) are to (1) develop control over physical skills and (2) gain a sense of independence. Following autonomy, children attempt to successfully accomplish tasks that strengthen their initiative. The initiative versus guilt (ages 3–5) stage is when children learn tasks to assert their control, and they later learn how to distinguish when to and not to assert their control (Erikson, 1968). This can be difficult because they are transitioning from full dependence to independence. If asserting control is not mastered, then guilt can be a dominant part of a child's overall worldview (e.g., emotional and cognitive states).

Group Therapist Considerations

The goal for therapists is to engage the young members in creative ways so that they can learn about self-exploration (Gladding, 2008). Preparing for this age involves extensive time because teaching young children requires that information be delivered in a cognitively appropriate fashion that they can understand. Therapists need to consider group factors from the toddlers' and young children's perspectives. Items such as seating on equal levels (all on the floor or in chairs of the same height), length of session, and frequency of sessions all will need consideration and adjustment for this age group. When establishing group norms it is important to convey what the norms are. Therapists can teach this by selecting a norm and acting it out, followed by discussing what the members think it is. Therapists should then draw out the young members (or caregivers) and instruct them to act out another one of the norms. The timing of lessons also needs to be considered due to the short attention span of young children.

Another example of a cognitively appropriate activity is exposing children to the variety of careers in the workforce (Niles & Harris-Bowlsbey, 2009). Exposure to career development should include colorful visuals, tactile-oriented activities, and role-playing as concrete methods for children to understand the information being presented.

Preparation for group work across the life span differs, for example, when conducting groups for infants. Caregiver involvement is more of a necessity as opposed to facilitating groups for toddlers and young children. Groups with young children may not require parental attendance.

Sample Group Models

The literature for toddlers and preschool-aged children is more extensive than the infant literature and emphasizes play as the modality for healthy childhood development. Children who engage in play tend to enact and work through troubling emotions and behaviors (Oaklander, 2001). Without the use of verbal language, young children will express barriers that confront healthy development.

The early years are important first steps to psychosocial development (Stenberg, 2003), and because of the importance of this stage, caregivers often seek play dates with same-age peers (Ticknor, 2008). Personal growth and trust are enriched in multiple ways, including play dates, day care, and stays with family members (Oaklander, 2001). These extended groups influence both infant and caregiver development, including trust. Toddlers and children who operate from mistrust may have lacked people who could stimulate them and serve as role models of reliability, consistency, and care. Infants who lacked proper stimulation will also likely experience difficulties relating and attaching to others. As a result, some toddlers and children will need to continue working on trust and will also likely need to learn how to be affectionate and empathic toward others, especially their caregivers.

Greenberg (2007) provided strategies to promote prosocial behaviors addressing autonomy when children are alone and in the company of play dates. Common themes among Greenberg's strategies were caregiver involvement and trust. Miller (2007), when promoting the use of play, also called attention to the importance of caregiver involvement. Miller suggested cognitive stimulation is fostered through encouragement, rehearsal, and role-modeling. If young children are able to show signs toward mastery of physical skills and independence at this stage, they will more than likely develop autonomous behaviors (Miller, 2007). They will know that they will be taken care of even if they wander away from caregivers. If not, feelings of shame and doubt may interfere with their cognitions, feelings, and actions (Erikson, 1968). The activities and suggestions offered by Greenberg (2007), Miller (2007), and Ticknor (2008) are valuable activities for young children in this stage. Facilitators can teach parents (e.g., create and implement filial group counseling) how to use their daily routines in creative ways that include play as a method of incorporating psychosocial development.

As children begin to establish autonomy and are old enough to have play dates, Greenberg (2007) recommends having peers over to visit while other siblings are sleeping or preoccupied. Greenberg also suggested that other siblings might have a friend over to visit during the play date in order to decrease sibling interference in skills development while with friends. Another resolution Greenberg offered is for parents to work with their children to develop a *privacy policy* (set of norms) so that everyone knows each item listed in the policy before play dates occur. This type of parental involvement in child development was also echoed by Miller (2007). Miller emphasized that the importance of play comes to life when caregivers invest time in their young children while teaching limits and other social skills so that they are prepared to interact with others. These strategies empower caregivers as well.

Ticknor (2008) offered developmentally appropriate tips for parents to engage in play with their children to strengthen physical, social, moral, and cognitive development. Infusing play is helpful for stimulating toddler learning, social skills training, and teaching responsibility and follow-through; for example, play is a common tool used to teach young children how to complete psychosocial and household tasks, and at the same time it can heighten skills development. As for play dates, Ticknor recommended limiting play to 2 hours. This time frame allows enough time for children to learn through stimulation activities and for the caregivers to simultaneously receive some respite.

This age group is transitioning from an egocentric perspective to a perspective of sharing and feeling comfortable in venturing away from caregivers. As children begin to go to school and play away from their caregivers, they continue to require assurance that the caregivers will be present when needed.

Future Directions

A first step for this population is to continue research efforts, followed by traversing from theories to practical applications. For instance, research can determine which activities strengthen initiative and how group members' (children and caregivers) develop initiative. Another area is the examination of group activities that satisfy task attainment in the first three stages of development. It may be necessary to address previous stages in order to equip children with adaptive social skills. Additionally, continued research efforts will shift the toddler literature from a heavy conceptual emphasis to one with empirical investigations that lend themselves to best practices in group work.

As for practical applications, group leaders need to target each of the first three stages of development with this population to ensure that toddlers and young children have opportunities to establish a secure foundation to confront upcoming psychosocial tasks. Group therapists should have a variety of activities that can help members accomplish trust, autonomy, and assertion of one's control. Groups that contain structured activities may strengthen current relationships. Moreover, it is recommended that more caregivers and their children be recruited to participate in groups within school and community settings. Alternative settings like schools need to be used more often to facilitate growth in younger children as they prepare to enter kindergarten.

Children: First to Fifth Grades

The psychosocial stage for the kindergarten or first grade to fifth grade age group (6–11) is industry versus inferiority (Erikson, 1968). Resolution of the first two stages and preparing for the third as they enter the educational system are critical. Children in this stage learn to become industrious as a result of engaging in certain activities. Depending on how the activities go, they gain in confidence or feel inadequate. As the industry stage is successfully resolved, children are better able to cope with pressures related to education, social demands, sports, and other extracurricular activities. They will also demonstrate greater self-efficacy in terms of future psychosocial tasks and personal goals. Those who face a series of failures as a result of initiated actions may later encounter complications in life as feelings of inferiority debilitate functioning and willingness to risk new behaviors.

When children struggle with a sense of industry and adjusting to school or other life circumstances, groups are often utilized. In fact, Shechtman (2004) found that over 70% of groups occur in academic settings. Nurture groups (Cooper & Whitebread, 2007), groups for children of divorce (DeLucia-Waack & Gellman, 2007), loneliness and anxiety groups (Bostick & Anderson, 2009), and at-risk student groups (Sherrod, Getch, & Ziomek-Daigle,

2009) are discussed in the literature and support psychosocial development.

Group Therapist Considerations

As in the two previous stages, there are key areas to consider when working with children. Communicating in an age-appropriate manner with all children will ensure that they are aware of why they are in a group, what is currently transpiring, and what is being asked of them. The attention span of children varies greatly, and careful planning is necessary so that all members are engaged (Gladding, 2008). Often, two or more small applications or examples of the group theme for the session are more effective than one long activity/discussion, for example, two or three brief activities with processing that focus on loneliness rather than a 45-minute processing session. Also, multiple shorter groups (for example, 10 sessions of 30 minutes) often are more effective than fewer long sessions (five sessions of 1 hour). Other considerations are discussing confidentiality, the frequency of reinforcing group rules, and preparing for termination many weeks prior to it. Strategies like counting down to last session can be utilized to keep children aware of when they will say goodbye to the group. Strategies like the countdown are also helpful when conducting groups for programs like bullying prevention, which tend to have fixed sessions and psychoeducational agendas. Groups that emphasize a collaborative approach contribute to childhood growth (American School Counselor Association, 2006; Bostick & Anderson, 2009; Bryan & Henry, 2008).

Sample Group Models

Elementary school–aged children continue to gain life experiences of all types. Group-work literature for this age group is plentiful. A few of the topics are grief, incarcerated parents, and divorce. Children face a variety of obstacles, and because they spend nearly half of their waking hours at school, it seems reasonable to offer group services to them during the school day. Moreover, due to extremely high student-to-school counselor ratios, group work is often not only effective but the only efficient way to offer counseling services to the many students referred.

The American School Counselor Association (ASCA) created a comprehensive developmental model that many state school systems are now using. The model targets all students in a school and focuses school counseling services to promote academic, personal, social, and career development (ASCA, 2006). This model promotes group work in the forms of psychoeducational and classroom guidance groups and encourages the use of counseling in relation to academic performance (Bostick & Anderson, 2009).

Bryan and Henry (2008) also emphasized a comprehensive developmental approach to promote childhood growth through collaboration between school, family, and community members. These community-wide acquired support systems encourage students to succeed in academics (Bryan & Henry, 2008). Their proposed partnerships proved beneficial, largely due to students feeling supported, establishing support systems and relationships, and having more than one adult available to assist in their development.

Cooper and Whitebread (2007) utilized nurture groups that emphasized collaborative efforts and academic success among students labeled "at risk." These groups focused on a nurturing environment in which psychological needs were met through social interaction. They suggest that nurture groups appear to be a natural fit for this age group because of the attachment and relationship foci. In the United Kingdom, some schools are operated from the nurture group philosophy to help students become mainstreamed back into the regular education setting (Cooper & Whitebread, 2007). They found that students who have difficulties developing trust and maintaining relationships benefit from nurture groups. The results of their longitudinal study (1999–2001) indicated that students with behavioral and emotional difficulties decreased their symptoms and were able to return to the traditional academic setting. Students in the nurture groups showed the greatest improvement between the first and fourth terms of the academic year (Cooper & Whitebread, 2007). Their results appear promising. Nurture groups could potentially be used in the United States to mainstream children from special education into regular education over the course of an academic year.

Groups for children whose parents are divorced are formed in many schools (elementary–high school) nationwide due to the high rate of divorce (DeLucia-Waack & Gellman, 2007). It has been found that these types of groups offer students a place to develop peer relations, understand that they are not alone, and overcome any troubling emotions and behaviors that may be resulting from divorce.

DeLucia-Waack and Gellman (2007) examined 34 kindergarten–sixth grade students whose parents were either divorced or separated. The mean age of the participants was 8.6 years and the mean length

of time divorced was 3.07 years. Twelve school counselors conducted an 8-week group for children of divorce, with all groups receiving the same topics for discussion except that members in a music group had to bring a song that depicted a coping skill that could be used upon group termination. While the researchers reported that the music did not produce significant findings, the results did indicate that irrational beliefs regarding divorce significantly mediated the relationship between the pre- and posttest depression scores.

Bostick and Anderson (2009) assessed loneliness and social anxiety among third-grade students. Over a 3-year period, they conducted 10 social skills group intervention groups containing five or six students per group. The findings indicated that the behavior-orientated groups resulted in decreased posttest scores of loneliness and social anxiety. Overall school performance increased as indicated by teacher reports and end-of-grade postscores. Moreover, Bostick and Anderson found that the students reported less anxiety about making friends.

Sherrod et al. (2009) assessed an entire elementary school and secured five students who received the highest number of referrals to the principal for the academic year. Their group consisted of four members who each had three referrals and a fifth member who had only two (though school representatives thought this student was well on his way to a third referral). The authors report that all five group members were male, three were from single-parent families, and the last two had parents pursuing divorce. The weekly PRIDE group was set for 30 minutes per session for 8 weeks (Sherrod et al., 2009). They found that as students' knowledge, attitudes, and skills increased favorably, their behaviors became less disruptive. They also reported that the teacher perception ratings showed student improvement. Their study showed promising results in that the group format included developmentally appropriate social skills.

Similar to Sherrod et al.'s (2009) findings, Mendenhall, Fristad, and Early (2009) found that helping parents increase their knowledge about their child's mental health concerns (symptoms and diagnoses) was beneficial for the child's development. For example, family education for parents of children with mood disorders proved important to their child's prognosis. One implication of this study was to include parents in treatment as much as possible, for example, making them aware of childhood symptomatology, diagnoses, and treatment options.

The authors alluded to the fact that adequate communication with parents of the children served needs to occur more often. These findings can be implemented via psychoeducational groups for parents of children with mental illness in outpatient, school, and inpatient settings.

Groups for students whose parents are deployed to war zones are becoming increasingly common in schools (Rush & Akos, 2007). Deployment support groups can help children process feelings, cognitions, and behaviors related to predeployment through reintegration at home upon return.

Rush and Akos (2007) proposed a 10-session psychoeducation group to increase student knowledge, build and strengthen student competencies, and provide a safe environment for students to share their thoughts and feelings with other peers in a similar situation. Their weekly 1-hour sessions targeted these multiple outcomes: ability to articulate knowledge gained, increased awareness of cognitions and emotions, and ability to demonstrate learned coping strategies. While beginning group sessions required leaders to be directive, as sessions continued facilitators allowed the group to become process-oriented (Rush & Akos, 2007). Their sessions comprised activities such as journaling, answering established questions, sentence completions, and developing memory books.

Children in this age group face a number of demands (Rush & Akos, 2007); therefore, a safe group environment is needed in order for them to express their thoughts and feelings. If this environment is provided, then children can try out new behaviors and experience new feelings.

Future Directions
Research that clarifies further process and outcome factors in groups for children with divorced and deployed parents is needed. As students with mental illness are mainstreamed increasingly, the need for broad-range services within schools also increases. Additional research should target how industry is impacted as a result of childhood issues and investigators should determine how to accomplish psychosocial tasks that can possibly advance treatment for other childhood issues. Finally, there is a need for more research on group interventions for children in schools where violence, such as school shootings, has occurred.

Early Adolescence: Sixth to Eighth Grades
The ages from 12 to 18 are classified in the identity versus role confusion stage (Erikson, 1968).

Developing a healthy sense of self (i.e., identity) during early adolescence is critical during this time of physical changes that sometimes are accompanied by emotional turmoil (Picklesimer, 1998). It is important that school counselors or clinicians facilitate opportunities for adolescents who are having difficulty developing healthy self-identity to participate in activities where they can learn more about themselves in a positive setting. Emphasizing skills development and task accomplishment in group work will strengthen already-developed resiliency skills (Picklesimer, 1998).

Successes and failures are important during this time and may need to be monitored so that adolescents are not continuously experiencing failure. Adolescence is a period that has commonly been referred to as the "years of turmoil," and there is no doubt that teens need help navigating the emotional, physical, and cognitive changes they experience (Egbochuku & Aihie, 2009). Therefore, groups specifically aimed at developing self-concept, self-worth, and self-esteem in the earlier school years are warranted. Groups offered for this age group contain central issues around life skills (Picklesimer, 1998), bullying, self-esteem, and friendship (Egbochuku & Aihie, 2009).

Group Therapist Considerations
Gladding (2008) suggested that facilitators must be self-aware and reflect on whether their own issues related to this period are resolved. He further emphasized the importance of therapists as active role models, including in their communication style, assertiveness, spontaneity, and confidentiality. Role modeling is particularly beneficial when addressing disruptive behaviors. An additional consideration is to establish alliances with some members so that they might serve as influential members. Therapists must also be consistent and firm, determine how gender and age can influence a group, and use a community approach to help in the overall development of those in early adolescence. A community approach encompasses collaboration among all stakeholders who are responsible for the education of the nation's youth.

Sample Group Models
Students in the early adolescent stage best learn from their peers. Egbochuku and Aihie (2009) examined peer group counseling to determine whether children have an influence over their same-aged peers in this type of peer-facilitated group. The two groups in their study consisted of a control

group and experimental group, with participants measured both pre- and postintervention. The intervention consisted of 1-hour weekly peer-facilitated group sessions related to self-concept with therapists working from a facilitator's guide (Egbochuku & Aihie, 2009).

Egbochuku and Aihie (2009) found statistically significant results between the treatment and control groups at posttest, with posttest scores higher for the experimental group, indicating that students can induce change in their peers' levels of self-concept. These findings also demonstrated knowledge, self-efficacy, and behaviors that were positively influenced (Egbochuku & Aihie, 2009).

Another finding that emerged from the data was that females in an all-girls school setting had higher self-concept posttest scores than females from coeducation settings. Based on these results, they concluded that adolescent females may not feel comfortable in front of their male peers, particularly in math classes. Egbochuku and Aihie (2009) reported that it was common for female students to stay quiet and await their turn to speak in class. This is one instance where peer same-sex groups could be beneficial. For example, female students could support one another in regard to mathematics self-expectancies, which, when positive, would enhance expectations.

In summary, the middle school years denote a time period when adolescents move further away from family members and toward their friends as they develop a sense of self or identity. As adolescents require less caregiver attention, it becomes more important for them to have accomplished earlier psychosocial tasks. Groups are beneficial in providing adolescents with a mirror from which to view themselves. Input from others gives them feedback on how they are perceived within the group and by others. They are able to experiment with communication styles. Additionally, they fit within larger systems. Having accomplished these tasks will ensure that adolescents can develop clear and strong senses of self to problem-solve and make decisions that are beneficial for their growth.

Future Directions
Psychosocial stages of development targeted in the earlier school years need to be conducted in order to determine ways that female students can overcome silence in the classroom. This area can also be addressed by asking adolescents about the types of group work they previously received during the elementary years. With the advent of accountability, such as No Child Left Behind, many schools have been identified as not making "adequate yearly progress." A question that arises with regard to this continued pattern is, Can a school's failure to make progress impact students to the extent that they develop feelings of inferiority and confused identity? It seems that when a school does not academically progress, students may personally internalize this failure and, hence, feel inferior at times when it is neither necessary nor appropriate. It is important that children and adolescents learn what it means to both succeed and fail because some may never have an opportunity to experience successful outcomes in their home environments. Therefore, youth should be encouraged to engage in group activities where successes can be experienced.

Preadolescents need to experience positive interactions with adult figures to promote healthy development (Picklesimer, 1998). Picklesimer also reported that teens with perceptions of being verbally abused experienced decreased levels of self-esteem, placing them at risk for life- and career-related difficulties.

High School: Ninth to Twelfth Grades
Identity versus role confusion continues into this age group. This stage highlights the importance for adolescents of examining aspects of themselves so that they can begin to formulate an image representative of their self-identity. When establishing a self-identity is not successfully attained, role confusion becomes a roadblock to life, academic, and career decisions. That is, without a sense of self, it is hard to know where you are going and easy to make decisions with negative consequences. Therefore, it is important for high school youth to accomplish the task of developing a healthy self-identity. Adolescents in this age group typically receive a heavier emphasis in career development–related groups within schools (Niles & Harris-Bowlsbey, 2009), and beyond schools, mental health agencies and other entities provide insight-oriented and process groups for adolescents (Cooper & Whitebread, 2007). Adolescent group topics include truancy, behavioral and emotional difficulties, drug and alcohol use, differentiating from parents, sexuality, coping with divorce, intimacy and relations, cliques, and academic concerns (Olguin & Maple, 2008; Paone, Packman, Maddux, and Rothman, 2008).

Group Therapist Considerations
Considerations for this group are similar to those in the early adolescence stage. Adolescents, however,

may have very different responses and opinions concerning being in a group. Young children often do not give group participation a thought, but to the adolescent it may be a significant source of pride or shame; either will have an impact on group. The type of group, group membership, time, location, and advertisement of group should all be considered prior to the first session. It can be beneficial to help adolescents learn that play is an effective means to healing so that they do not reject group activities that involve play or expressive arts. However, adolescent members do need to be approached with play activities in a way that does not threaten their developing self-identities. If members resist or refuse to participate, then group therapists must take responsibility for selecting alternate strategies that encourage adolescents to participate in group sessions that involve play.

Sample Group Models

In states like New Mexico, the Next Step Plan (NSP) is a legislative mandate that requires every high school student to have a career plan that must be updated on an annual basis (Olguin & Maple, 2008). The annual update must include a task group meeting with the student, teacher, and a school official; and it is up to this group to complete the NSP. The intention of this state career mandate is to help the schools establish relationships with students, families, and communities. The other three *R*'s the NSP targets are a rigorous curriculum, making academics relevant, and assuring that students are ready for postsecondary transitions. In addition to career goals, personal and social interests are addressed. This career mandate is similar in spirit to the ASCA national school counseling model presented earlier.

The Egbochuku and Aihie (2009) study previously mentioned on the strong peer influence that exists among adolescents and examined peer group counseling for the high school population. Having peers facilitate the groups was beneficial for a variety of reasons, and they concluded that peer paraprofessionals can help students strengthen their self-concept and positively enhance their knowledge, self-efficacy, and behaviors.

To help students gain stronger senses of self, Paone et al. (2008) assessed the effectiveness of group activity therapy (GAT) (Bratton & Ferebee, 1999) over the traditional group talk therapy for at-risk adolescents. GAT relies on the use of developmentally appropriate activities and self-directed play to help students express themselves and establish connections with other members.

There were 27 at-risk ninth-grade participants in the treatment group (GAT) and 34 in the comparison group (traditional talk group counseling), and each of the two groups was then broken down to groups containing three or four students (Paone et al., 2008). They formed the groups to help students progress through moral reasoning development. The 10-session group format included 50-minute groups that each began with a moral dilemma that was then discussed. Paone et al. (2008) found a significant difference between the treatment and comparison groups in moral reasoning. Although it had a small effect size, their study continued to demonstrate that group work is developmentally appropriate for high school students, and their work contributes to the literature base for adolescents (Paone et al., 2008).

Future Directions

The high school years are when adolescents should strengthen their self-identity and prepare for the upcoming transition to work, trade school, postsecondary education, etc. Information such as the number of high school students who seek groups targeted at specific psychosocial stages or topics help researchers and clinicians focus their group-work efforts. Group therapists in schools can benefit by partnering with local college and university educators to help them strengthen their accountability practices that show whether the variety of groups taking place in educational settings are effective and needed. As best-practice guidelines continue to grow, their application will increase with adolescents.

College, Technical School, and Early Job Entry

The college, technical school category embraces a wide age range, 19–40 and beyond. In addition, more students representing diversity in every sense of the word are enrolled in postsecondary education of various forms.

According to Erikson (1968), this age group is characterized by intimacy versus isolation, and the primary tasks are to form intimate relations with others and secure a career. If these social tasks are not accomplished, then young adults may experience loneliness, isolation, and anger. Emotions that accompany feelings of failure can further impact one's self-concept and overall worldview. It will be the successes and failures that determine whether or not adults will experience emotional, cognitive, and behavioral difficulties, so successfully accomplishing psychosocial tasks should remain a theme across groups.

Young adults commonly present issues related to career development and decision making, relationships, and stressors related to being students (Mahan Gary, Kling, & Dodd, 2004). Other group types range from issues related to addictions (Un Kim, 2007), eating disorders, sexuality (Tarakeshwar, Pearce, & Sikkema, 2005), and living independently to groups for those with a propensity for emotional deregulation.

Group Therapist Considerations

The college-aged population is fascinating in that a variety of groups can be conducted to meet their needs. An underlying focus on psychosocial tasks in groups with this population will help members understand certain emotions, behaviors, and cognitions that may have hindered their functioning. People in this age category appear to benefit from groups that promote health and wellness, coping strategies, and academic success.

Context and purpose are important in all groups and certainly so in groups with college-aged people. For instance, the purposeful group techniques model, which is based on intentionality, can help determine which techniques and skills should be used to facilitate member growth (Conyne et al., 2008). Continual assessment of skills and techniques is necessary to address the variety of differences that will exist within any group consisting of college students. For example, the timing of a group is important because many adults are busy with family and work. Gladding (2008) encouraged group facilitators to spend time considering which group leadership techniques and skills are needed with adult populations. In college groups there are vast differences in student needs (e.g., students with autism to student athletes, and the list goes on). Decisions about location and whether or not to invite family also need to be considered. Finally, the method of advertising is important because college students are continuously on the move from their homes or places of employment to campuses and back to their home or work.

Sample Group Models

The technological advancements that have surfaced, although beneficial, have influenced adults to the extent that some develop Internet addictions. A group based on reality therapy principles and including building self-esteem for college-aged students with Internet addiction was conducted by Un Kim (2008). The study, conducted in Busan, South Korea, included 25 undergraduate participants (13 experimental, 12 control). Un Kim, working from a reality therapy theoretical orientation, focused the 10 group sessions on decision making and responsibility, not the clients' addictions. The twice-weekly sessions lasted between 60 and 90 minutes for 5 weeks. Pre- and postmeasures assessed levels of Internet addiction and self-esteem. Un Kim found significant differences between the treatment and control groups in addictive thoughts, with the treatment group having less addictive thinking. In regard to the effectiveness of reality therapy and group counseling for this population, the results were statistically significant for enhancing self-esteem (Un Kim, 2008). Un Kim also found that reality group therapy produced a significant reduction in symptoms of Internet addiction and higher levels of self-esteem among participants.

Women now outnumber men in higher education enrollment, contributing to the increase of groups for women within that setting. Soet and Martin (2007) conducted groups for graduate student women to discuss their thoughts and feelings about spirituality. The group comprised four weekly 90-minute sessions. The psychodynamic nature (i.e., free association and free-form writing activities) of the group topics was designed in such a way that after member discussion the themes of integration versus separation and religion versus spirituality emerged. Themes of ·family and attachment also surfaced as a result of member reports.

Members reported feeling less stressed and stronger senses of spiritual well-being and empowerment as a result of their group experience (Soet & Martin, 2007). The posttest follow-up results also indicated that group members developed relationships with one another, and many of them continued to keep in contact with one another (Soet & Martin, 2007). One of the group members commented that the diversity of the group did not impact her until the group experience was over; she reported that this enriched her worldview (Soet & Martin, 2007).

Diverse populations, such as students of color and international students, are increasing in number on college and university campuses (Ishii, Olguin, & Keim, 2009; Mahan Gary et al., 2004). Many of these students are older, first-generation college students with additional obligations to extended family, work, and other areas of involvement. These conditions can combine to make graduation difficult. Mahan Gary et al. (2004) used a cohort program for African American and Latino college students that included counseling faculty, individual counseling services, group-counseling services, cultural support services, and systematic support. The participants were required to attend monthly support group meetings and a one-time-per-semester psychoeducational group. Their results indicated that a greater number of students from this program remained in college and graduated. Although some adults have to meet the needs of their families before fulfilling their educational pursuits, Roberts, Piper, Denny, and Cuddeback (1997) reported that groups can help students cope with all of the demands they face that trigger emotional, physical, cognitive, and behavioral difficulties.

Balance was an emerging theme in the literature for this group because several college-aged adults have families to care for, jobs to attend, and other responsibilities that do not include academics. Some are also in the sandwich generation, where in addition to their other responsibilities they care for their parents (Dobson & Dobson, 1985). Often, they are trapped in a fast, nonstop pace that hinders building relationships due to trying to accommodate and meet all the demands in their lives.

Future Directions

This population is likely to remain continuously on the move and have little free time. Thus, time is an important variable to consider in research with this population. Areas of inquiry include prevention, intervention, and other concerns such as crisis and suicide. Alternate formats facilitating maximization of time and use of electronic communication peak the interest of this age group. On the other hand, the need to pause and participate in face-to-face communication is critical. Research into the culture of campus life and methods of addressing increasing violence on campus, including mass shootings, is also needed.

For example, groups that are provided for students and their families can be examined in relation to academic success. Research also needs to continue in the development of measures for diverse student populations. Finally, studies that assess the impact of various factors on academic performance and entry into a career field are important.

Early Career: 20s to Mid-30s

Intimacy versus isolation (Erikson, 1968) identifies the early career stage, and the primary tasks are to succeed in relationships and select a fulfilling career. It is important for young adults to engage in relations with others and to learn to form lasting friendships and other intimate relationships. As feelings of connectedness increase, healthier relationships are built. If adults accomplish success in maintaining relationships, they will likely avoid barriers in intimate situations when emotions, cognitions, and behaviors are challenged. In regard to career, if failures become common during early career, individuals may experience feelings associated with depression, anxiety, and isolation.

The group literature is broad for this stage, including groups for young adults with medical complications (Roberts et al., 1997), fatherhood (Madsen, 2009), career entry, relationship issues, and self-esteem.

Group Therapist Considerations

Adults in their 20s and 30s live busy lives that are often accompanied by high levels of stress (e.g., home life, employment, and other relationships). Roberts et al. (1997) reported that these adults have greater stressors and disruptions than other age groups. Therefore, it is important to consider and discuss with these potential clients the costs for attending the group in terms of time and money, as well as the group format and the group environment. Additionally, while provided to all age ranges, this group is likely to want more specific information on topics, more specific goals, and larger amounts of didactic and process time. Location, confidentiality, and number of sessions will be factors impacting their participation. Therapist considerations will depend on the type of group being conducted, but all will require the use of leadership skills (e.g., active listening, confrontation, clarifying) and leadership techniques (e.g., drawing out, cutting off, holding, and shifting the focus) (Conyne et al., 2008; Gladding, 2008; Jacobs, Masson, & Harvill, 2009).

Sample Group Models

Roberts et al. (1997) conducted a support group for young adults diagnosed with cancer to learn coping strategies. The groups consisted of seven participants who completed six 90-minute sessions, with the control group (wait list) receiving treatment 3 months after the posttest. Roberts and colleagues reported group ages ranging from 24 to 35 with varying types of cancer. Their support groups consisted of group therapy with psychoeducational topics such as anxiety about health, fertility concerns, topics related to their children, relation problems, financial concerns, and body image.

The participants in the cancer coping strategies group reported that, as a result of the group, they desired to reconnect with family members and friends and to help others who are in need (Roberts et al., 1997). Second, Roberts et al. found significant reductions in fatigue and confusion and significant improvements in mood as a result of the group sessions. Third, the researchers found significant changes in interactions (psychosocial tasks) with medical staff. Finally, results indicated no significant differences in the pre- and posttest coping strategies (Roberts et al., 1997). Their qualitative findings revealed that members were seeking to establish relationships and connections with others as well as the freedom to be themselves and that gaining knowledge was most beneficial for them. Summarizing their work, Roberts et al. recommended that future groups with young adults be less structured so that members can have more time to discuss their thoughts and feelings.

Another group topic gaining popularity is fatherhood. Madsen (2009) conducted a group for males interested in exploring issues related to fatherhood. She used questions such as "What kind of image comes to mind in relation to the kind of father you want to become?" to cognitively stimulate the participants. Madsen believed the question was critical because participant responses were embedded within personal experiences and the attachments they formed when they were younger. She suggested that men must learn to be attentive and spend time with their children despite having other obligations like career or education. Spending time with their infants was difficult for the participants. Madsen suggested that this was due to 50% of the members describing their fathers as psychologically or physically distant and 40% having a negative attitude toward their fathers. Psychological and physical distance affected men in Madsen's sample in that it was later discovered that they defined a good father as being engaged and present with their children (Madsen, 2009). Based on these findings, fathers can benefit by learning creative ways to spend time with their children. Madsen found that 66% of her sample stated that there was not one thing that they could take from their fathers to help them in raising their own children. She believed that these men's perceptions about their fathers would change once they gained more experience in the father role.

Future Directions

As time pressures continue, groups that provide processing time on specific topics will be sought, for example, groups for those with relationship or medical issues. Thus, a need for continuing group

research with this age range exists. Role exploration in terms of parenthood, intimacy, and career is key for groups. Additionally, focusing on resiliency and coping strategies will benefit them throughout their lives. Although, this age group has grown up with technology, face-to-face communication is still critical in intimate relationships and friendships. Research investigating communication patterns and skills for this group will guide clinicians in targeting group interventions to them.

Established Career: Mid-30s to 60s

As the established career group completes tasks associated with intimacy versus isolation, the generativity versus stagnation stage begins (Erikson, 1968). It is ideal for adults to enter this stage having successfully addressed the preceding intimacy stage. If unsuccessful with the task of intimacy, or earlier stages, then life obstacles may surface and emotional, cognitive, and behavioral problems may continue to manifest into the generativity stage.

The generativity versus stagnation stage ranges from 40 to 65 years of age and the primary task is to become self-reflective about one's life and contributions to self, family, friends, and society as a whole (Erikson, 1968). If adults encounter a series of failures in life, then stagnation may occur and they will have difficulty reflecting and healing from past experience as well as finding rewarding pursuits. Helping adults feel content with themselves and their personal and work lives is important. Groups are a popular intervention for this age range. Adult attachments with children (Muller & Rosenkranz, 2009), intimate partner violence (Fritch & Lynch, 2008), caring for parents, self-esteem, balancing multiple roles and demands, long-term mental health issues and concerns, and spirituality (Tarakeshwar et al., 2005) are a few group topics offered to adults in their mid-30s to 60s.

Group Therapist Considerations

A safe and respectful group environment is essential for producing a successful group experience for adults, particularly given that many, if not most, will have experienced trauma by this age, either personally or vicariously. A safe environment will also help those who might be exhausted from their busy lives prior to coming to group. Logistics can become critical, for example, having intimate partner violence recovery groups during daylight hours so that clients feel safer going to their cars or having groups during hours clients are able to attend. Therapists also benefit adult members by serving as role models. The considerations are the same as presented for the college-aged population. Facilitators should have leadership skills and techniques that focus on this age group or seek training and supervision (Gladding, 2008).

Sample Group Models

Spirituality is an important aspect in the lives of many middle-aged adults. For individuals with HIV/AIDS, spirituality can become a valuable coping strategy. However, both spirituality and HIV/AIDS are topics few people typically feel comfortable speaking about in front of unfamiliar people. With the prevalence of people living with HIV growing, it is important to address this population in group work.

Tarakeshwar et al. (2005) led spiritual coping groups for adults diagnosed with HIV/AIDS. The spiritual coping group intervention was intended to provide members a place to process spirituality as a coping method for HIV/AIDS. Tarakeshwar et al. (2005) divided the 14 participants into three groups: women, heterosexual men, and homosexual men. The participants ranged in ethnicity, with most having some postsecondary education and on average having been diagnosed for about 10 years (Tarakeshwar et al., 2005). Their groups included eight sessions, each lasting 90 minutes. The sessions outlined by the authors included Erikson's psycho-social stages. For example, the majority of the sessions included processing: trust, autonomy, initiative, industry, identity, and intimacy topics (Tarakeshwar et al., 2005). The researchers also included the later Erikson stages (generativity and ego disparity) in the group sessions.

According to the pre- and posttest results, significantly higher levels of all three measures of religious and spiritual practices emerged (Tarakeshwar et al., 2005). The researchers found that group members reported increased positive spiritual coping scores and decreased scores in negative spiritual coping; a decrease in depressive symptoms also occurred.

Their (Tarakeshwar et al., 2005) qualitative results included the following: (1) structure of group format—recommending an increase in the number of sessions to a minimum of 15 so that members could establish more in-depth relationships and more cohesion before openly speaking about difficult topics such as spirituality and HIV/AIDS; (2) differences from past group—appreciating actual discussions about HIV/AIDS and spirituality without fear of discrimination, especially for

homosexual men; (3) intrapersonal changes—members terminated unhealthy relationships, secured housing, and reported a sense of freedom by accepting that uncontrollable situations cannot be changed. Overall, the members also appreciated that they were able to gain trust to "vent" about religion. Tarakeshwar et al. (2005) concluded that this was because many members had previously experienced rejection based on religious doctrine. Despite religious doctrine, members did report increased scores in positive spiritual coping and self-rated religiosity as a result of the group treatment.

Depressive symptoms and spiritual doubt can also reside in adult survivors of intimate partner violence (IPV). IPV includes individuals who have become traumatized by loved ones; two examples include physical violence and sexual assault. Research on IPV is slowly developing to help those who are currently or have been involved in a violent relationship (Fritch & Lynch, 2008). The violence and trauma suffered by this population make it essential for group leaders to create safe and respectful environments.

Fritch and Lynch (2008) examined the IPV group literature and provided an overview of supportive group therapy, behavioral and cognitive-behavioral group treatments, semistructured group therapy, and groups for male survivors of IPV. Supportive group therapy involves the exploration of life stressors and coping strategies, and behavioral group therapy focuses on reducing fears and increasing coping behaviors (Fritch & Lynch, 2008). The majority of groups presented in the literature review by Fritch and Lynch showed promising results for those who have suffered IPV. For example, in a cognitive processing group for female rape victims, symptoms of posttraumatic stress disorder (PTSD) and depression decreased according to the posttest results, and these levels were maintained at the 12-month follow-up (Fritch & Lynch, 2008). The affect-management groups were reportedly ideal for middle-aged adults because the modality emphasized skill acquisition, which helped members resolve previous psychosocial tasks. Finally, many IPV groups require that members concurrently receive individual therapy (Fritch & Lynch, 2008).

Muller and Rosenkranz (2009) investigated attachment among middle-aged adults hospitalized for PTSD. The intention of their study was to determine whether members could learn coping strategies while establishing relationships with the other members and professionals in the group. The three measures Muller and Rosenkranz used were relationship, attachment, and symptoms scales. Their treatment participants received daily groups (process and psychoeducational skills), relaxation techniques, community meetings and community walks. Muller and Rosenkranz found a difference in total scores between trauma symptoms, symptom checklists, and the attachment variables; but interestingly there were no differences between those who did and those who did not complete the treatment program. A significant interaction between time and group for the treatment group was found. At the 6-month follow-up, the researchers found, members of the treatment group showed changes in secure attachment, which appeared to have held from discharge dates.

Muller and Rosenkranz (2009) found a decrease in fearful attachment immediately after treatment and at the 6-month follow up. Moreover, significant decreases in attachment anxiety and attachment avoidance also resulted. The researchers concluded that anxiety symptoms are amenable to change, whereas avoidant behaviors are not. Overall, the members reported feeling enhanced security and symptom reduction.

The studies presented by Fritch and Lynch (2008) and Tarakeshwar et al. (2005) involved topics about psychosocial development that include feelings of trust, shame, guilt, identity confusion, generativity, and ego disparity. Their studies demonstrated the benefits to group members of revisiting psychosocial stages, from the beginning to the end, and determining which stages remain areas for growth for each client. Inevitably, adults tend to revisit psychosocial stages of development as life events occur. The studies reviewed indicate that group sessions often tie to the psychosocial skills outlined by Erikson, in particular the trust component.

Future Directions

The areas of spirituality and medical illness merit additional investigations, as do adult attachments. The number of survivors of IPV and individuals with PTSD seeking treatment is likely to increase; therefore, additional qualitative, quantitative, and mixed-methods research is needed. Finally, an examination of the effectiveness of resolving earlier developmental issues with group interventions is critical.

Facing Retirement: Mid-60s to 75

As the generativity versus stagnation stage nears an end for those facing retirement, the ego integrity versus despair stage becomes the psychosocial developmental focus (Erikson, 1968). The ego integrity stage spans from 65 years of age to death, and groups including reminiscence, counseling, and support are widely offered to help members avoid isolation (Burlingame, Fuhriman, & Johnson, 2004). The process of this developmental stage demands that older adults reflect on their lives and what they have accomplished in order to determine whether or not they feel fulfilled (Erikson, 1968). Desires to give back to society in some way are also examined. This age group is changing in terms of total numbers and percentages that remain in the workforce longer. If generativity is established, older adults will feel an overall sense of fulfillment with the lives they lived; however, if they see themselves as stagnated, it is likely that older adults will avoid connections with others. Group work can favorably assist older adults as they retire (Mardoyan & Weis, 1981). The majority of the group literature for those facing retirement favors groups that emphasize medical conditions (Burlingame et al., 2004; Rejeski et al., 2003).

Group Therapist Considerations

Older adults often face multiple losses, including loss of career, health, independence, family, and friends (van Puyenbroeck & Maes, 2006). van Puyenbroeck and Maes (2006) found that research into areas that impact the lives of the elderly has slowed. Therefore, group facilitators should provide members with outlets to reflect on their lives and help clients gain a sense of fulfillment with their lives. A safe group environment will help all members, in particular those exploring social isolation and those with limited social skills.

As the research with the elderly population increases, findings continue to call upon clinicians to gain knowledge (e.g., cognitive, social, and emotional) about the elderly. The possibility that younger group therapists may not be able to understand some elderly members can be indicative of a generation gap, thus providing further need for clinicians to learn about this population (van Puyenbroeck & Maes, 2006). Countertransference can occur because younger group therapists may not have come to terms with their personal experiences, thoughts, and feeling regarding aging, retirement years, and death. It is important to allow members opportunities to interact with the other group members, close in age, who are experiencing similar concerns. van Puyenbroeck and Maes reported that it is common for this population to experience high levels of anxiety and stress due to losses in life and decreases in previous roles and support systems.

Groups must therefore afford a safe environment for members to share their feelings and thoughts and to learn new social roles. Additionally, groups should offer clients the opportunity to increase their self-image, self-respect, and self-worth. The sense of belonging that groups provide the elderly is helpful as they being to search for life meaning. The authors concluded that Yalom's (1995) therapeutic factors are important to foster in each group session.

Sample Group Models

Older adults with medical or physical complaints, those who require a variety of medications, and those navigating end-of-life issues can benefit from group work (Burlingame et al., 2004). Rejeski et al. (2003) used group-mediated cognitive-behavioral (GMCB) counseling to help participants with cardiovascular disease. Rejeski et al.'s GMCB groups were geared toward helping participants become self-reliant in monitoring their physical activity and overall fitness. The researchers were also interested in whether levels of participant self-efficacy would be enhanced. They used measures of graded physical activity, self-efficacy, and self-reported physical activity. Rejeski et al. compared the GMCB group to a cardiac rehabilitation program group.

Rejeski et al.'s (2003) 9-month treatment consisted of exercise 2 days per week as well as psycho-educational and counseling groups. After 3 months, participants were weaned from the group meetings and expected to continue their exercise regime at home for the next 6 months (Rejeski et al., 2003). The cardiac rehabilitation program group engaged in the same physical exercises as the GMCB group, but they exercised 3 days per week for the entire 3 months and received no group therapy.

Rejeski et al. (2003) found significant differences between the two groups after 3 months, with the GMCB group reporting increased physical activity, greater fitness, and stronger self-efficacy than the cardiac rehabilitation program group. Change within the GMCB group continued from the third to the twelfth month, with males reporting higher outcomes on all three levels (activity, fitness, and self-esteem) than the females. Rejeski et al. concluded that central aspects of the group were group-mediated problem solving and behavioral homework assignments. They also found that the GMCB group showed positive changes in becoming more independent than before treatment.

Mansfield et al. (2007) attempted to provide group members with the tools to sustain a group after the facilitators terminated the groups. A sample of elderly participants ($n = 276$) with medical and nonmedical issues in three independent living facilities participated in shared interest groups for 6 months. The researchers found that individuals who experience social isolation tend to lose social skills. The shared interest groups were designed to help the members combat social isolation and depression by building a community of peers with similar interests.

Mansfield et al. (2007) solicited topics for the groups, and each of the three different housing facility groups explored some topics specifically of interest to the residents of the house. For instance, one group included English as a second language (ESL) members. Group topics across facilities included music, gospel, bible, picnic, and memory-enhancement games. Although attendance varied, the afternoon hours were most productive for the groups to meet. The authors found that when housing facility administration interfered with the groups or members, the effects were felt and observed during group sessions. After facilitators terminated the groups, three of the groups continued. A music group continued for approximately 3 months after the follow-up, and the ESL group continued for an additional year until the postintervention volunteer facilitator terminated it (Mansfield et al., 2007). The ESL group was the only one where a trained facilitator remained once the self-sustained groups terminated.

The data that Mansfield et al. (2007) collected were summarized into recommendations. The first recommendation is that shared interest groups be used to encourage socialization. They suggest an optimal group size of five to nine members, with weekly meetings and logistical arrangements made with facility administrators. Mansfield et al. also suggest addressing and discussing member conflicts in group and group facilitators preparing members for the eventual phasing out of the facilitator. Finally, Mansfield et al. suggested group therapists should discuss and leave a list of roles and duties for the members to follow upon termination of the group after 1 year.

Future Directions

This age range is quickly increasing in numbers. Continued research efforts with older adults are needed to determine whether group techniques and/or the socialization process that naturally evolves from group work contributes to group member change. Group research on diverse populations and discovering the best ways to handle conflicts that emerge between elderly group members are two additional areas that require investigation. Next, studies that compare personality characteristics when one was a young child to the present time need to be examined. And the most important future direction is to increase the number of professional development opportunities offered to group therapists-in-training and clinicians.

Retirement and Beyond

Ego integrity versus despair continues from when clients begin facing retirement and concludes long after retirement (Erikson, 1968). The desired outcome for ego integrity is for older adults to feel fulfilled regarding their decisions and actions in life. A group focus on successfully reaching a sense of integrity can be accomplished via members reflecting on the large and small contributions they may have already made to society. If, conversely, clients feel despair, then emotions like anger and bitterness may prevail. Toseland, Naccarato, and Wray (2007) reported that regrets and satisfactions, declining physical and mental health, education, coping, telephone, and grief groups are available for people who are in their retirement years.

Group Therapist Considerations

During group sessions it is important to understand that some clients will have physical ailments and mobility concerns. Lighting, sound, and accessibility are important planning factors. Appropriately projecting one's voice is equally important so that members hear the dialogue. Postretirement clients continue to experience transitions such as independence to being more dependent on their children, loved ones, or privatized care than ever before; thus, support is a necessary clinician characteristic to embody (van Puyenbroeck & Maes, 2006).

In times of economic crisis, the cost of counseling needs to be considered for all clients but in particular for the elderly, who are usually on a fixed income. Although group work versus individual counseling is still a debate in the literature (Hill & Brettle, 2006), reminiscence, depression, and anxiety support groups are favored approaches for older persons (Hill & Brettle, 2006; Toseland et al., 2007; van Puyenbroeck & Maes, 2006). Continued studies to determine which modality better serves older adults are warranted. Prior to conducting groups with older adults, Hill and Brettle (2006), like van Puyenbroeck and Maes (2006), called for group therapists to receive training and gain knowledge about this population.

Sample Group Models

Erikson (1968) suggested that as the elderly population reflects on their past lives, they reach integration through acceptance of their past and present selves. van Puyenbroeck and Maes (2006) conducted research with a treatment team of individuals who worked with aging individual clients with intellectual disabilities for a minimum of 5 years. The therapists used person-centered reminiscence groups.

A total of seven groups, including one pilot group, with six to eight members were examined. A total of 10 group sessions, 1 hour in duration, were conducted and videotaped. After each session, the videos were reviewed, with written feedback provided to the group members and therapists prior to the next group session (van Puyenbroeck & Maes, 2006). The group therapists used objects (a reminiscence or memory suitcase) as a method to visually stimulate the members' memory; many of the items were of a vintage period so that the members could relate to the particular objects (van Puyenbroeck & Maes, 2006). At the end of the groups, members evaluated the program, completed a quiz, and had a discussion.

van Puyenbroeck and Maes (2006) reported multiple findings. Their first, based on the pilot group, was to modify topics for future groups. The therapists of postpilot groups immediately noticed that changes in the groups after the topic changes occurred included an increase in members' self-confidence. Another finding resonating within the Eriksonian framework was that the members reported feeling good about sharing information with other members and the younger group therapists. This was helpful because some older adults seek to share their wisdom in order to resolve the generativity and ego disparity stages. Group sessions, following their pilot, were clearly structured, with mind maps used to slow the groups pace and a reminiscence suitcase to elicit memories. The researchers reported that three support roles were necessary to lead the group and ensure recall of memories.

A novel approach to group work that is emerging in the literature is telephone groups for older persons and their caregivers (Toseland et al., 2007). This method of group work focuses on older adults who have medical and/or mobility limitations that prevent them from physically attending group sessions. Toseland et al. (2007) discovered that telephone groups were used with positive results for task group. Six considerations suggested by

Toseland et al. are as follows: (1) having a rationale for the use of telephone groups, (2) exploring the group's appeal to the consumer, (3) calculating the cost of groups, (4) determining fees and reimbursement, (5) documenting services to be provided, and (6) addressing ethical and professional issues. Additionally, they remind therapists of the logistical concerns in determining the type of telephone service provider and type of telephone connection to use, as well as whether to have any face-to-face meetings.

Telephone groups can be complex because therapists do not typically have any visual cues to note and conceptualize as groups proceed (Toseland et al., 2007). Other issues that must be considered in telephone groups are levels of self-disclosure, facilitating group cohesion, and helping members gauge the reactions of the other group members. Toseland et al. (2007) remind therapists to address confidentiality in this type of modality and what to do when strong emotions are shared over the phone. Promoting member self-identification, engaging all members, teaching members how to take turns speaking and asking for clarification, allowing for open and clear communication with feedback given, sending group work materials via the US mail, and deciding whether to encourage members to contact one another between sessions are additional considerations for telephone groups. It is clearly evident that additional research, qualitative and quantitative, is needed to test the efficacy of this group format.

Future Directions

With ever increasing numbers of elderly, there will be a growing need for group interventions and a clear need to increase research efforts with this population and their caregivers. Hill and Brettle (2006) reviewed common types of group for this age range and found that group counseling is generally effective for those with depression, for those with anxiety, and for defining one's subjective well-being. Research into other effective group interventions for specific diagnoses is critical.

One area that can benefit from additional investigations is telephone groups. With changes in technology, groups are possible with Web-based video capability. Client privacy and duty-to-warn issues are likely to be key factors in these groups becoming a reality for clients who cannot physically attend groups. For example, if clients are anonymous to maintain confidentiality or reside in other states or countries, duty to warn can be difficult. Research

with this population also needs to explore group interventions for topics unique to them, such as life transitions, independent living, financial management, and mental health. Finally, there is a need to continue lines of research to determine whether individual counseling versus group work is best suited for this population.

Conclusion

From infant attachment groups to groups for at-risk students to reminiscence groups, group therapists must always consider many factors. Gladding (2008) suggests minimally examining the type of group, topics of interest, therapeutic factors, location, group environment, and group stages in order to facilitate the growth of group members and goal attainment. In addition, determining who to include in the group is critical. Through focusing groups based on developmental stage, therapists are poised to address the unique needs of each stages of life.

A pattern between group work and psychosocial stages is depicted in this chapter (see Table 23.1). Researchers have found that psychosocial tasks continuously surface in group work (Tarakeshwar et al., 2005). Additionally, helping members with personal growth and task accomplishment has been found to be beneficial (Barnette, 1989). It appears that regardless of group type (task, psychoeducational, counseling, or psychotherapy), groups evolve according to the psychosocial stages of development. This developmental evolution can assist group therapists in assessing which social tasks members may have previously attained and which tasks were unresolved. One method to assess clients' psychosocial stages is to introduce a specific activity and then observe how individual members respond to and complete the activity. Any difficulties that arise in the group then serve as a baseline from which to select future activities.

To further illustrate the parallel between the psychosocial stages of development and group work, a mythical eight-session group can be constructed and superimposed over an already established eight-session group. For example, the first session of the group equates to the first of the eight psychosocial stages, where *trust* and rapport are emphasized. Group therapists take the lead role in the creation and maintenance of a safe group environment. The second session parallels Erikson's second stage, *autonomy*. Group leaders may facilitate member growth by helping them gain feelings of autonomy in the group while continuing to establish trust and safety. Members may test the trust they have toward

Table 23.1 Summary of group counseling across the life span

Developmental Stage	Erickson's Psychosocial Stage (1968)	Examples of Groups	Examples of Group Factors to Consider
Infants	Trust/mistrust	Attachment, play with parent	Length of session, number of clients to include, time of day for group
Toddler–kindergarten	Autonomy/shame	Play groups, trust building, autonomy building, filial therapy groups	Length of session, age-appropriate self-exploration, age-appropriate furniture
Children (1st–5th grades)	Industry/inferiority	School-based groups, grief, incarcerated parents, deployed parents, divorce, social anxiety	School-based groups and confidentiality issues, length of activities, termination
Early adolescents (6th–9th grades)	Identity/role confusion	Peer group counseling, same-sex groups, insight-oriented, self-awareness building	Role modeling, self-disclosure, boundaries
High school (9th–12th grades)	Identity/role confusion	Career issues, self-awareness morals exploration	Peer facilitators, clients view of being a group member
College/tech school/early career (age 19–mid-20s)	Intimacy/isolation	Insight-oriented, career exploration, women's groups, reality therapy groups, adjustment to college, balancing roles	Timing of group, intentionality, alternate group formats, advertising of groups
Early career (20s–mid-30s)	Intimacy/isolation	Relationship issues, stress and coping, chronic illness groups, coping strategies, parenthood	Focused topics, costs of group (time, money, etc.), specific group goals
Established career (mid-30s–60)	Generativity/stagnation	Spirituality, intimate partner, violence, PTSD	Safety, logistics, role modeling
Facing retirement (60–75)	Generativity/stagnation, ego integrity/despair	Loss and grief, self-image and self-worth, topic groups	Reflection on life, coping strategies
Retirement and beyond	Ego integrity/despair	Independence and dependence, reminiscence, telephone groups	Illness and mobility issues, lighting and sound, economic concerns

PTSD, posttraumatic stress disorder.

the group and other members in session 3; therefore, they can strengthen their *initiative* by finding their own voice to fully engage and contribute to the purpose of the group. Session 4 equates to the *industry* stage, wherein members actively search for methods to cope with the demands that are placed on them, personal, group, or otherwise. *Industry* attainment can encourage members to fully participate. Next, *identity* marks the parallel between session 5 and the fifth social stage. Establishing a sense of self is of critical importance in this stage because members become acquainted with themselves in relation to other members in relation to the group as a whole (Hulse-Killacky, Killacky, & Donigian, 2001). Session 6 can be conceptualized as equivalent to the *intimacy* stage, where members begin to form relationships with other members and express themselves in new ways. Session 7 parallels the *generativity* stage, where members assess whether or not positive change was created as a result of the group. In order to determine the type of change, questions related to transfer of learning must be shared and processed. Finally, session 8 equates with *ego integrity*. Members in this stage reflect on their group experiences and personal contributions to determine if they are fulfilled with what transpired so that they can terminate, having learned effective coping mechanisms to ensure future successes.

This example displays how group sessions can parallel the psychosocial stages regardless of the stage the clients are in. The stages can serve as a guide to introduce social tasks as activities for members to accomplish. By going through all the stages, members gain insight into resolution, which will aid them as they age and face the stages in their lives outside of the group. The use of activities in groups can enable members to strengthen their social skills. Moreover, processing any problems they face in relation to the chosen activity further facilitates member growth. Thus, group leaders should consider which psychosocially based activities are beneficial for the needs of the group. When selecting psychosocial activities and examining psychosocial levels, therapists must consider diverse members whose worldviews entail a collective society and introduce diversity-sensitive activities and interpretations that reflect the diversity of clients.

The groups across the life span presented in this chapter showed that psychosocial stages of development are integral learning components for members in any group. For example, the mothers in the Niccols (2008) study reported that they too could benefit from intimacy but with other adults. The literature also suggests that group work is advantageous for children and older adults who struggle with social relationships. The overall message is that individuals may benefit by receiving intra- and interpersonal stimulation through a developmental and psychosocial skills focus in groups.

References

American School Counselor Association. (2006). *The ASCA national model for school counseling programs* (2nd ed.). Alexandria, VA: Author.

Barnette, E. L. (1989). A program to meet the emotional and social needs of gifted and talented adolescents. *Journal of Counseling and Development, 67*, 525–528.

Bostick, D., & Anderson, R. (2009). Evaluating a small-group counseling program—A model for program planning in the elementary setting. *Professional School Counseling, 12*, 428–433.

Bratton, S. C., & Ferebee, K. W. (1999). The use of structures expressive art activities in group activity therapy with preadolescents. In D. S. Sweeney & L. E. Homeyer (Eds.), *The handbook of group play therapy: How to do it, how it works, whom it's best for* (pp. 192–214). San Francisco: Jossey-Bass.

Bryan, J., & Henry, L. (2008). Strengths-based partnerships: A school-family-community partnership approach to empowering students. *Professional School Counseling, 12*, 149–156.

Burlingame, G. M., Fuhriman, A. J., & Johnson, J. (2004). Current status and future directions of group therapy research. In J. L. DeLucia-Waack, D. A. Gerrity, C. R. Kalodner, and M. T. Riva (Eds.), *Handbook of group counseling and psychotherapy* (pp. 651–660). Thousand Oaks, CA: Sage.

Conyne, R. K., Crowell, J. L., & Newmeyer, M. D. (2008). *Group techniques: How to use them more purposefully*. Upper Saddle River, NJ: Merrill-Prentice Hall.

Cooper, P., & Whitebread, D. (2007). The effectiveness of nurture groups on student progress: Evidence from a national research study. *Emotional and Behavioural Difficulties, 12*, 171–190.

DeLucia-Waack, J. L., & Gellman, R. A. (2007). The efficacy of using music in children of divorce groups: Impact on anxiety, depression, and irrational beliefs about divorce. *Group Dynamics: Theory, Research, and Practice, 11*, 272–282.

Dobson, J. E., & Dobson, R. L. (1985). The sandwich generation: Dealing with aging parents. *Journal of Counseling and Development, 63*, 572–574.

Egbochuku, E. O., & Aihie, N. O. (2009). Peer group counseling and school influence in adolescents' self-concept. *Journal of Instructional Psychology, 36*, 3–12.

Elizalde-Utnick, G. (2007). Young selectively mute English language learners: School-based intervention strategies. *Journal of Early Childhood and Infant Psychology, 3*, 141–161.

Erikson, E. H. (1968). *Identity: Youth and crisis*. New York: Norton.

Fritch, A. M., & Lynch, S. M. (2008). Group treatment for adult survivors of interpersonal trauma. *Journal of Psychological Trauma, 7*, 145–169.

Gladding, S. T. (2008). *Group work: A counseling specialty* (5th ed.). Upper Saddle River, NJ: Merrill-Prentice Hall.

Goldberger, J. (1988). Issue-specific play with infants and toddlers in hospitals: Rationale and intervention. *Children's Health Care, 16*, 134–141.

Greenberg, P. (2007). "You can't play with us!" *Scholastic Parent and Child, 14*, 36.

Hill, A., & Brettle, A. (2006). Counseling older people: What can we learn from research evidence? *Journal of Social Work Practice, 20*, 281–297.

Hulse-Killacky, D., Killacky, J., & Donigian, J. (2001). *Making task groups work in your world*. Upper Saddle River, NJ: Merrill-Prentice Hall.

Ishii, H., Olguin, D. L., & Keim, J. (2009). Career assessment tool with international students: International Student Career Card Sort (ISCS). In G. R. Walz, J. C. Bleuer, & R. K. Yep (Eds.). *Compelling counseling interventions: VISTAS 2009* (pp. 1–10). Alexandria, VA: American Counseling Association.

Jacobs, E. E., Masson, R. L. L., & Harvill, R. L. (2009). *Group counseling strategies and skills*. Belmont, CA: Thomson Brooks/Cole.

Lopez, F. G. (1987). Erikson and Rogers: The differences do make a difference. *Journal of Counseling and Development, 65*, 241–243.

Lyons, S. N. (2000). "Make, make, make some music": Social group work with mothers and babies together. *Social Work with Groups, 23*, 37–54.

Madsen, S. A. (2009). Men's mental health: Fatherhood and psychotherapy. *Journal of Men's Studies, 17*, 15–30.

Mahan Gary, J., Kling, B., & Dodd, B. N. (2004). A program for counseling campus support services for African American and Latino adult learners. *Journal of College Counseling, 7*, 18–23.

Mansfield, J. C., Parpura-Gill, A., Kotler, M., Vass, J., MacLennan, B., & Rosenberg, F. (2007). Shared interest groups (SHIGs) in low-income independent living facilities. *Clinical Gerontologist, 31*, 101–112.

Mardoyan, J. L., & Weis, D. M. (1981). The efficacy of group counseling with older adults. *Personnel and Guidance Journal, 60*, 161–163.

Mendenhall, A. N., Fristad, M. A., & Early, T. J. (2009). Factors influencing service utilization and mood symptom severity in children with mood disorders: Effects of multifamily psychoeducation groups (MFPGs). *Journal of Consulting and Clinical Psychology, 77*, 463–473.

Miller, S. (2007). Partners in play. *Scholastic Parent and Child, 15*, 86.

Muller, R. T., & Rosenkranz, S. E. (2009). Attachment and treatment response among adults in inpatient treatment for posttraumatic stress disorder. *Psychotherapy Theory, Research, Training, 46*, 82–96.

Niccols, A. (2008). "Right from the start": Randomized trial comparing an attachment group intervention to supportive home visiting. *Journal of Child Psychology and Psychiatry, 49*, 754–764.

Niles, S. G., & Harris-Bowlsbey, J. (2009). *Career development interventions in the 21st century* (3rd ed.). Upper Saddle River, NJ: Pearson-Merrill-Prentice Hall.

Oaklander, V. (2001). Gestalt play therapy. *International Journal of Play Therapy, 10*, 45–55.

Olguin, D. L., & Maple, C. (2008). Legislative impact: Professional school counselors and teachers provide career education for students in K-12. In G. T. Eliason & J. Patrick (Eds.), *Career development in the schools* (pp. 69–91). Charlotte, NC: Information Age Publishing.

Paone, T. R., Packman, J., Maddux, C., & Rothman, T. (2008). A school-based group activity therapy intervention with at-risk high school students as it relates to their moral reasoning. *International Journal of Play Therapy, 17*, 122–137.

Paul, C., & Thomson-Salo, F. (1997). Infant-led innovations in a mother–baby therapy group. *Journal of Child Psychotherapy, 23*, 219–244.

Phillips, N. K. (1985). Mother–child interaction group: Model for joint treatment. *Social Casework, 66*, 41–52.

Picklesimer, B. K. (1998). Life skills, adolescents, and career choices. *Journal of Mental Health Counseling, 20*, 272–282.

Rejeski, W. J., Brawley, L. R., Ambrosius, W. T., Brubaker, P. H., Focht, B. C., Foy, C. G., et al. (2003). Older adults with chronic disease: Benefits of group-mediated counseling in the promotion of physically active lifestyles. *Health Psychology, 22*, 414–423.

Roberts, C. S., Piper, L., Denny, J., & Cuddeback, G. (1997). A support group intervention to facilitate young adults' adjustment to cancer. *Health and Social Work, 22*, 133–141.

Rush, C. M., & Akos, P. (2007). Supporting children and adolescents with deployed caregivers: A structured group approach for school counselors. *Journal for Specialists in Group Work, 32*, 113–125.

Shechtman, Z. (2004). Group counseling and psychotherapy with children and adolescents: Current practice and research. In J. L. DeLucia-Waack, D. A. Gerrity, C. R. Kalodner, and M. T. Riva (Eds.), *Handbook of group counseling and psychotherapy* (pp. 429–444). Thousand Oaks, CA: Sage.

Sherrod, M. D., Getch, Y. Q., & Ziomek-Daigel, J. (2009). The impact of positive behaviors support to decrease discipline referrals with elementary students. *Professional School Counselor, 12*, 421–427.

Soet, J., & Martin, H. (2007). Women and spirituality: An experiential group for female graduate students. *Journal of College Counseling, 10*, 90–96.

Stenberg, G. (2003). Effects of maternal inattentiveness on infant social referencing. *Infant and Child Development, 12*, 399–419.

Tarakeshwar, N., Pearce, M. J., & Sikkema, K. J. (2005). Development and implementation of a spiritual coping groups intervention for adults living with HIV/AIDS: A pilot study. *Mental Health, Religion and Culture, 8*, 179–190.

Ticknor, L. (2008). First rate play dates. *Scholastic Parent and Child, 16*, 8.

Toseland, R. W., Naccarato, T., & Wray, L. O. (2007). Telephone groups for older persons and family caregivers: Key implementation and process issues. *Clinical Gerontologist, 31*, 59–76.

Un Kim, J. (2008). The effect of a R/T group counseling program on the internet addiction level and self-esteem of internet addiction university students. *International Journal of Reality Therapy, 27*, 4–12.

van Puyenbroeck, J., & Maes, B. (2006). Program development of reminiscence group work for ageing people with intellectual disabilities. *Journal of Intellectual and Developmental Disability, 31*, 139–147.

Yalom, I. D. (1995). *The theory and practice of group psychotherapy* (4th ed.). New York: Basic Books.

Group Counseling with Sexual Minorities

Kathleen Y. Ritter

Abstract

When counselors can appreciate the unique life circumstances that lesbian, gay, bisexual, and transgender clients bring to the group experience and have the skills to lead the group through its many transitions, growth can occur for every individual involved. Understanding the concepts of oppression, minority stress, and cohort and developmental differences provides a context for effective and ethical group facilitation. This chapter briefly reviews the existing literature related to sexual minority group members as well as examines relevant guidelines, principles, competencies, and ethical codes of several professional associations. Other concepts discussed include group composition, leader sexual orientation, group management, sexual minority members and group dynamics.

Keywords: Group counseling; group psychotherapy; sexual minorities; group ethics; oppression

If it were only for oppression, which is a common experience for many marginalized populations, there would be no need for a separate chapter devoted to sexual minority group members. Other marginalized populations, such as ethnic and cultural minorities, immigrants, the elderly, disabled, mentally ill, homeless, or poor, likewise experience devaluation and stereotyping from the broader culture. Lesbian, gay, bisexual, and transgender (LGBT) individuals, however, bring to counseling a unique set of life circumstances that makes a group encounter distinctly different and difficult for them. In addition to possible devaluation, rejection, or shaming from parents, family, and organized religion, these clients have experienced a lifetime of recurring negativity directed toward them from television, talk radio, blogs, Web sites, newspapers, and politicians. For many, this leads to a fear of exposure and a sense of secrecy that other stigmatized minorities do not carry. Even the most resilient among them have had difficulty withstanding the assaults and often carry with them an internalized prejudice and a hesitancy to disclose themselves publicly or even

privately to others (Cochran & Mays, 2009; DiPlacido, 1998; Herek, 2004, 2009). Without an understanding of these experiences, even qualified and well-intended counselors can miss the depth of fear and pain that many sexual minority clients bring to a group experience. The purpose of this chapter is to elucidate those dynamics and then to offer suggestions for intervention to group leaders.

Sexual Prejudice

To many sexual minorities, "a shameful belief that a major part of themselves is bad or undesirable creates and complicates intrapsychic and interpersonal problems" (Hawkins, 1993, p. 506). While the term *homophobia* has been in use since 1972, Herek (2009) contended that this viewpoint limits the ability to comprehend hostility toward sexual minorities, both among individuals and in the broader society. Further, "*homophobia* seldom refers to a phobic or fearful response, as the term itself implies" (Ritter & Terndrup, 2002, p. 12) and, thus, is considered technically incorrect and is often limited to individual, rather than societal, prejudice. Over time, the term *homophobia* has shifted to *heterosexism*, which Herek (2004) defined as a "cultural ideology that perpetuates sexual stigma by denying and denigrating any non-heterosexual forms of behavior, identity, relationship, or community" (p. 16). Instead, he offered a new vocabulary to refer to these disapproving responses in terms of *sexual prejudice* (i.e., "negative attitudes based on sexual orientation, whether the target is homosexual, bisexual, or heterosexual" (Herek, 2004, p. 16) and *societal stigma* as the internalization of sexual prejudice (2009).

In this chapter, Herek's terms will be used as much as possible since they reflect the sociocultural nature of bias. Given, however, that various authors use different terms for essentially the same constructs, the term *homophobia* will be utilized only if it was the language employed by the original author(s). On the other hand, the term *heterosexism* will be used since it (1) is reflective of a broader cultural attitude and (2) has generally not been replaced in the literature by Herek's more recent refinement of conceptualization and terminology. Finally, the term *homosexual* will be employed only if it is used in the original reference since many consider this "19th century medical terminology as derogatory, negative, and oppressive" (Ritter & Terndrup, 2002, p. 30). For the most part, however, it will be replaced by a broader and more affirming interpretation such as *sexual minorities* or *LGBT*.

Implications for Group Counseling

While societal stereotyping and marginalization are common for many populations, sexual minorities continually experience sexual prejudice and negative reactions from the dominant society. While LGBT clients bring many of the same issues to counseling as heterosexuals (e.g., relationships, intimacy, self-esteem), these individuals are unique in that they also bring the effects of degradation and rejection. These experiences are not commonly a motivation for heterosexual clients, who rarely enter a group session under a cloud of invisibility. Surprisingly, in spite of this fear of disclosure, Holahan and Gibson (1994) noted that lesbian and gay clients often seek group counseling to help them cope with family and societal rejection.

Ball and Lipton (2005) spoke of societal antihomosexual attitudes and behaviors that affect the mental health of gay men and the negative pathological psychosocial factors that can create a stigmatized identity for these individuals. They believed, however, that group counseling can provide a healing antidote to a lifelong history that has deprived them of recognition and acceptance. Other writers (Englehardt, 2005; Turell & de St. Aubin, 1995), likewise, have made many of the same points with reference to lesbians and contended that often the obstacles they must overcome originate in the dominant culture and their interaction with it. In the view of these authors, a group can provide an environment where women can experience their own developmental journeys without judgment or heterosexist stereotyping.

Intersecting Orientations and Identities

Each individual is "a multicultural being whose social status and experiences are closely related to his or her race, age, gender, SES [socioeconomic status], sexual orientation, physical ability, religion or spiritual framework" (Miville et al., 2009, p. 540). While this chapter focuses primarily on sexual minority clients in groups, other intersecting aspects of their identities also influence the nature of, and participation within, the group context. There is an emerging body of literature related to the concerns unique to bisexual individuals, who often feel unsupported by the heterosexual world as well as by the gay and lesbian community. Griffin (2009) also noted that for bisexual persons "grief is a constant companion" (p. 252) because, unlike other sexual minorities, there is no "end point" in their development. Only a small portion of writing regarding bisexuality relates specifically to groups and what exists is essentially narrative in nature (Firestein, 1999; Griffin, 2009). The same can be said of literature devoted to transgendered individuals, who are members of a vastly diverse community but all of whom experience incongruence between gender expression and physiology (Israel, 2004). Suffice to say, however, that although most concerns transgendered and bisexual clients bring to a group encounter are similar to those experienced by all sexual minorities, these populations do have their own unique societal stressors and deep feelings of being misunderstood by a majority of the population, including other sexual minorities.

Readers will note that the majority of studies and narratives cited in this chapter were written prior to the recent rise of the movement to include bisexual and transgender persons under the LGBT rubric, and relate mainly to lesbian and gay group members. There are a few references to bisexual individuals and none to transgender members. In cases where the intent of the original study would not be compromised, more inclusive terms such as *sexual minorities* or *LGBT* are used.

LGBT Group Research

Prior to 1975, the "treatment" of homosexuality within a group modality was directed, either overtly or covertly, to changing sexual orientation (Conlin & Smith, 1982, 1985; Schwartz & Hartstein, 1986). In a 1982 review of the literature, Conlin and Smith found only one article that viewed change from a more affirmative perspective. The first all-gay groups with constructive and positive foci were generated by gay community organizations in the early 1980s. Many of these dealt with the reality of the AIDS crisis but usually were support groups led by non-professional leaders and were designed to help with issues such as the coming out process, development of social skills, sexual concerns, and the establishment of a positive identity (Conlin & Smith, 1982, 1985; Reece, 1982; Schwartz & Hartstein, 1986).

Of the few empirical studies currently available, virtually all focus on men with specific difficulties such as HIV infection or sexual issues. A recent study (Ross, Doctor, Dimito, Kuehl, & Armstrong, 2008), however, examined the results of a modified cognitive-behavioral group treatment for sexual minority clients with depression. Twenty-three members attended all meetings of the 14-week group (28 total hours) as well as the follow-up session and completed the required questionnaires. The group delivery focused on "antioppression" principles, with sessions devoted to issues of coming out and internalized homophobia. Reductions in depression were statistically significant, as were increases in self-esteem.

The vast majority of literature relating to the effectiveness of group counseling for LGB populations is anecdotal and provides descriptions of group interactions and structure. Most common are case studies and examples of various kinds of group experiences (e.g., Neal, 2000). Among other areas, new research should focus on "the relationships of different therapeutic factors to significant group issues" and "the role of LGB identity development within group process" (DeBord & Perez, 2000, p. 201). DeBord and Perez (2000) contended that any new theoretical perspectives needed to take into account the impact of societal oppression, homonegativity, and heterosexism on group outcome. Additionally, counselors must "integrate group theory and LGB issues while exploring their underlying assumptions, biases, and prejudices regarding LGB clients" (p. 202).

While the first edition of the *Handbook of Counseling and Psychotherapy with Lesbian, Gay, Bisexual Clients* (Perez, DeBord, & Bieschke, 2000) published by the American Psychological Association included a narrative-based chapter on group counseling with sexual minority clients (DeBord & Perez, 2000), the second edition, *Handbook of Counseling and Psychotherapy with Lesbian, Gay, Bisexual, and Transgender Clients* (Bieschke, Perez, & DeBord, 2007), did not, presumably because there was negligible qualitative or quantitative literature in this area. In the second edition, however, Perez (2007) noted that "future research that examines the process-outcome variables for affirmative group therapy with LGBT clients is . . . needed" (p. 413). He also indicated that the benefits of a group experience for this population are many, yet research is lacking, and that "research in this area may help distinguish the roles of various group therapeutic factors and their impact on client change and group process" (p. 413).

Unique Life Experiences

Specific training is needed to help students and group practitioners understand "how LGB persons contend with psychosocial stressors arising from their sexual minority status, such as stereotyping, oppression, stigmatization and negative reactions by the dominant group in society" (Miville et al., 2009, p. 525). Without this understanding, counselors will have little context for comprehending the many distinctive life experiences and concerns that sexual minorities bring to the uniquely interpersonal and highly interactive processes of group therapy (House & Tyler, 1998; Israel, 2004).

Minority Stress

Numerous authors (Bastian & Silverstein, 2009; DiPlacido, 1998) discussed the concept of minority stress resulting from stigmatization and sexual prejudice from the broader culture. DiPlacido (1998) examined studies related to negative life events and daily hassles and concluded that sexual minorities, due to societal stigmatization, experience more of these than majority culture individuals. On the one hand, there are external stressors (e.g., loss of child custody or employment due to sexual orientation, hearing antigay jokes and political ads); on the other hand, internal stressors are equally as toxic (e.g., self-concealment and emotional inhibition). For example, no other population has to navigate the terrains of accepting a stigmatized identity, the integration of which may involve difficulties with parents, extended family, children, culture, religion, employment, lack of legal protections, and even physical safely. Unlike ethnic and racial minorities whose "strong familial connections and cultural similarities can provide a protective buffer . . . when they encounter prejudice and discrimination in the dominant mainstream society" (Bastian & Silverstein, 2009, p. 72), sexual minorities often feel left alone, to fend for themselves.

Just as other populations have had to deal with massive casualties of citizens (e.g., flu survivors in 1918, deaths and injuries in various wars), the gay male community continues to live with unresolved grief involving the loss of thousands of men from HIV infection (Frost, 1997). What makes these deaths different for the survivors, however, is that often they have been unable or unwilling to share their sorrow and receive support from family, coworkers, clergy, and community members. Unlike majority culture spouses or children who have lost loved ones, social stigma and sexual prejudice have kept many surviving partners, parents, and friends of AIDS victims "in the closet" and grieving alone and without support.

Victimization

Sexual minority individuals frequently report experiences of victimization, ranging from taunting, harassment, and bullying to physical abuse and even death. Recognizing the extent of this victimization, in October 2009 the United States Congress passed the Matthew Shepard and James Byrd, Jr. Hate Crimes Prevention Act, which extended federal hate crime legislation to include sexual and gender minority individuals and those with disabilities. One of the two people for whom the 2009 act was named, Matthew Shepard, was tortured and murdered in 1998 near Laramie, Wyoming, because he was perceived to be gay.

Morris and Balsam (2003) documented the extent of physical and sexual abuse in a sample of 2,431 lesbian and bisexual women and found that 62.3% of the subjects reported a variety of victimization experiences. For example, 36.6% of their subjects told of having been verbally attacked or harassed because of their actual or perceived sexual orientation, 30.8% had been harshly beaten or physically abused in childhood, and 39.9% said they were sexually assaulted before the age of 16. Needless to say, the women who were surveyed described varying degrees of psychological distress. Neisen (1993), likewise, noted the extent of what he referred to as "cultural victimization" of sexual minority clients and, in his writing, provided professionals with assistance in helping these individuals recover from the shame associated with the trauma. Numerous authors cited throughout this chapter agree with Neisen that groups, if properly designed and facilitated, can provide a safe and healing environment for these clients.

In the federally funded California Quality of Life Survey, Cochran and Mays (2009) interviewed 2,272 individuals, including 652 sexual orientation minorities, aged 18–72. Their study included measures of both sexual identity and adult sexual behavior and confirmed that sexual minority orientation, broadly defined, is associated with an elevated risk of affective, anxiety, and substance-use disorders for some persons. The authors contended that multiple factors converge to effect this association but that the common view is that the greater vulnerability for sexual minority individuals is a direct consequence of stigmatization, discrimination, and victimization. In any case, Cochran and Mays found evidence that minority sexual orientation is a risk factor for mental health morbidity of similar import as other major demographic categories.

Guidelines, Principles, and Competencies

In recognition of the multiple stressors impacting sexual minority clients, several professional associations have addressed this oppression by providing professionals with guidelines, principles, and competencies to enable them to offer conscientious and ethical services to these individuals. The discussions presented in this section will briefly summarize some of these efforts.

American Psychological Association Guidelines

To aid practitioners in providing affirmative mental health services, task forces of the American Psychological Association (APA) and its divisions were formed to create practice guidelines with several marginalized populations, among them older adults, girls and women, people of low socioeconomic status, and lesbian, gay and bisexual individuals (APA, 2000; Miville et al., 2009). Guidelines currently are being developed for other areas of diversity, including disabilities and 2000 LGT Guidelines are being revised and updated. These guidelines, while aspirational in nature, provide the foundation for individual and cultural diversity.

Following, under four major sections, are listed the *Guidelines for Psychotherapy with Gay, Lesbian, and Bisexual Clients* (American Psychological Association, 2000).

ATTITUDES TOWARD HOMOSEXUALITY AND BISEXUALITY

• *Guideline 1.* Psychologists understand that homosexuality and bisexuality are not indicative of mental illness.

• *Guideline 2.* Psychologists are encouraged to recognize how their attitudes and knowledge about lesbian, gay, and bisexual issues may be relevant to assessment and treatment and seek consultation or make appropriate referrals when indicated.

• *Guideline 3.* Psychologists strive to understand the ways in which social stigmatization (i.e., prejudice, discrimination, and violence) poses risks to the mental health and well-being of lesbian, gay, and bisexual clients.

• *Guideline 4.* Psychologists strive to understand how inaccurate or prejudicial views of homosexuality or bisexuality may affect the client's presentation in treatment and the therapeutic process.

RELATIONSHIPS AND FAMILIES

• *Guideline 5.* Psychologists strive to be knowledgeable about and respect the importance of lesbian, gay, and bisexual relationships.

• *Guideline 6.* Psychologists strive to understand the particular circumstances and challenges facing lesbian, gay, and bisexual parents.

• *Guideline 7.* Psychologists recognize that the families of lesbian, gay, and bisexual people may include people who are not legally or biologically related.

• *Guideline 8.* Psychologists strive to understand how a person's homosexual or bisexual orientation may have an impact on his or her family of origin and the relationship to that family of origin.

ISSUES OF DIVERSITY

• *Guideline 9.* Psychologists are encouraged to recognize the particular life issues or challenges experienced by lesbian, gay, and bisexual members of racial and ethnic minorities that are related to multiple and often conflicting cultural norms, values, and beliefs.

• *Guideline 10.* Psychologists are encouraged to recognize the particular challenges experienced by bisexual individuals.

• *Guideline 11.* Psychologists strive to understand the special problems and risks that exist for lesbian, gay, and bisexual youth.

• *Guideline 12.* Psychologists consider generational differences within lesbian, gay, and bisexual populations, and the particular challenges that may be experienced by lesbian, gay, and bisexual older adults.

• *Guideline 13.* Psychologists are encouraged to recognize the particular challenges experienced by lesbian, gay, and bisexual individuals with physical, sensory, and/or cognitive or /emotional disabilities.

EDUCATION

• *Guideline 14.* Psychologists support the provision of professional education and training on lesbian, gay, and bisexual issues.

• *Guideline 15.* Psychologists are encouraged to increase their knowledge and understanding of homosexuality and bisexuality through continuing education, training, supervision, and consultation.

• *Guideline 16.* Psychologists make reasonable efforts to familiarize themselves with relevant mental health, educational, and community resources for lesbian, gay, and bisexual people.

Operationalization of Guidelines

Israel, Ketz, Detrie, Burke, and Shulman (2003) conducted a two-phase Delphi survey that attempted to operationalize the American Psychological Association guidelines (APA, 2000) by identifying knowledge, attitude, and skill categories reflective of counselor competencies with sexual minority clients. Accordingly, their survey resulted in the identification (by 22 professional and LGB-identified experts and classified by 32 other experts) of 33 knowledge, 23 attitude, and 32 skill categories. The five counselor competencies that were ranked highest in the three categories are as follows (pp. 18–19):

Knowledge of:

• Discrimination, oppression, prejudice
• Homophobia/biphobia and heterosexism
• Mental health issues affecting LGB individuals
• Hate crimes, oppression, and violence
• LGB identity development

Attitudes:

• Do not feel that homosexuality is wrong, evil, or should be changed
• Non-homophobic attitude
• Acceptance of same-sex intimacy as a health lifestyle
• Not assuming sexual orientation is relevant to client's problems
• Openness/non-judgmental/accepting/tolerant attitude

Skills:

- Be sensitive to ethical issues, like confidentiality
- Talk about and listen to all aspect of LGB clients' lives
- Help clients with coming-out process
- Use non-biased/affirming techniques
- Be clear about setting appropriate boundaries (i.e., sexual)

While a few other studies have attempted to identify attitudes and behaviors that contribute to effective work with LGBT clients, the Israel et al. study (2003) is thought to be the first that comprehensively identified the three categories of knowledge, attitudes, and skills. While the sheer number of knowledge, attitude, and skill classifications identified in this study (*n* = 88) "attests to the complexity of counselor competence with LGB clients" (p. 13), only one competency related to group work (i.e., the skill to "facilitate groups"); and that skill was ranked 27 out of a total of 30 skills. Apparently, then, the experts felt that a practitioner's knowledge, attitudes, and skills relating to the sociocultural aspect of the lives of sexual minorities were far more important for affirmative counseling than the specific behaviors employed by the clinician when facilitating a group.

Group-Specific Guidelines and Principles

The Association for Specialists in Group Work (ASGW) *Best Practice Guidelines* (1998/2007) are a well-developed set of guidelines for assuring ethical practice, and counselors are encouraged to use them as a framework for competent group leadership. Only in Guideline B.8, which addresses the concept of Diversity, however, is there a reference to sexual minority clients in groups (i.e., "Group workers practice with a broad sensitivity to client differences including but not limited to . . . sexual"). Members of the Association for Specialists in Group Work (2000) also developed a set of *Professional Standards for the Training of Group Workers*. These Standards address various elements of ethical and diversity-competent preparation for group facilitation.

Neither the ASGW Best Practice Guidelines nor the ASGW Professional Standards are designed specifically to address the needs of LGBT group members. The same can be said of the *Practice Guidelines for Group Psychotherapy* of the American Group Psychotherapy Association (AGPA, 2007), wherein

sexual minority clients are mentioned only within a list of populations that might be included in a group (i.e., "groups that are composed homogeneously with regard to gender, culture, ethnicity, problem or sexual orientation").

Similarly, members of the Association for Specialists in Group Work (1999) developed *Principles of Diversity-Competent Group Workers* in order to underscore how issues of diversity affect group process and dynamics, group facilitation, training, and research. These Principles address three areas: awareness of self, group worker's awareness of group member's worldview, and diversity-appropriate intervention strategies. Within each of these three categories are listed the attitude and beliefs, knowledge, and skills needed to provide diversity-competent group leadership. Sexual orientation is only one of approximately 10 areas of diversity to which group leaders must be attuned. Some of the cultural competencies described in the next section, however, were specifically designed for the purpose of identifying attitudes and intervention strategies for use in group work with sexual minority individuals.

Cultural Competencies

Counseling Competencies for Sexual Minority Clients (Logan & Barret, 2005) is a subset of overall cultural competencies. Group work is among eight areas in which competencies "based on a comprehensive review of professional literature and research on sexual minority topics" (pp. 7–8) were formulated. Of the 10 group-counseling articles cited by Logan and Barret (2005) as foundational to the competencies, four related to gay men (Conlin & Smith, 1985; Frost, 1990, 1997; Schwartz & Hartstein, 1986), one to lesbians (Morrow, 1996), one to a group composed of mentally ill lesbians and gay men (Ball, 1994), and one each to groups for gay, lesbian, and bisexualLGB college students (Welch, 1996), bisexual men (Wolf, 1987), and individuals desiring assistance in "coming out" (Toy, 1991). Also included is a reference to Yalom's (1985) suggestion that leaders must intervene when "disapproval of LGBT members threatens group cohesion and integrity" (Logan & Barrett, 2005, p. 11). All of the 10 works mentioned in the Group-Work competencies are discussions, descriptions, or suggestions and none is empirically based.

The 2005 cultural competency document was somewhat edited and can be found on the Web site of the Association for Lesbian, Gay, Bisexual and Transgender Issues in Counseling (www.algbtic.org2009) and is now titled *Competencies for Counseling Gay, Lesbian, Bisexual and Transgendered (LGBT) Clients.* The Web site includes translations in French, Turkish, Chinese, Japanese, and Romanian and informs readers that the Competencies are intended to assist counselors "in the examination of their personal biases and values regarding LGBT clients, expand their awareness of the world views of sexual minorities, and lead to the development of appropriate intervention strategies that insure effective service delivery." The Competencies specific to group work are as follows and include all of the points discussed in this chapter as being necessary for effective and ethical group leadership.

Competent counselors will:

• be sensitive to the dynamics that occur when groups are formed that include only one representative of any minority culture and consider the necessity of including supportive allies for LGBT clients when screening and selecting group members.

• establish group norms and provide interventions that facilitate the safety and inclusion of LGBT group members.

• shape group norms and create a climate that allows for the voluntary self-identification and self-disclosure of LGBT participants.

• intervene actively when either overt or covert disapproval of LGBT members threatens member safety, group cohesion, and integrity.

Member Selection

When screening participants, group leaders should take into consideration the context of a prospective member's symptomatology, particularly if the individual is (or possibly is) a sexual minority. Accordingly, counselors need "to understand common psychological and behavioral manifestations of psychically embedded heterosexism during the coming-out process" (Ritter & Terndrup, 2002, p. 150). While some sexual minority clients truly are mentally ill, some presentations that may appear as psychiatric disorders are, in fact, "manifestations of underlying distress about gender or sexual identity that lift dramatically when these individuals come out" (p. 149). Along these same lines, Yalom (1975) noted that, in his experience, sexual minority clients often enter group with anxiety and depression related to "a confrontation between their homosexuality and their social environment" (p. 408) and

that sometimes these emotions are the result of an exposure that has "tumbled down" on their professional, family, and even married lives. In other words, practitioners must take this normative life upheaval into consideration when determining whether a certain member is an appropriate candidate for group work.

Cohort Differences

Every population deals with cohort differences, as evidenced by the dissimilar worldviews often held by first-, second-, and third-generation immigrants. In the case of sexual minorities, however, the variance between the generations is often vast and due mainly to sociocultural influences. For example, Kranzberg (2009), when discussing placement of lesbians in counseling groups, believed there are distinct generational differences in terms of gender identity, intimate relations, and relationships with families of origin. She spoke of "Pre-Stonewall gay women" i.e., before the 1969 rebellion in New York as having come of age during the McCarthy witch hunts of the 1950s when thousands of suspected "homosexuals" were denied jobs or fired and considered emotionally unstable. Secrecy was the norm and frequently even first names were not used, for fear of exposure. Couple relationships were tightly fused (e.g., two against the world), and most socializing was done with other "gay women." Many were not welcome in their families of origin and, if they were, the relationships were much like the current euphemism "don't ask, don't tell." Today, these individuals are aging with virtually no positive role models (Frost, 1997).

Kranzberg (2009) also spoke of "lesbian feminists" who, during the protest movements of the1960s and 1970s, actively challenged the prevailing constructs of gender, sexual orientation, and sex roles. These women were more confrontational than their sisters in previous generations and demanded equality in the workplace, in their family homes, and in the eyes of the broader society. Kranzberg referred to her third cohort as "early-21-st-century lesbians" and noted that these women experience more flexibility in their lives and greater acceptance by the broader culture. "Many of the battles of earlier feminists seem distant, even quaint" (p. 215) and, unlike earlier generations who either stayed in the closet or "insisted on being out" (p. 217), these women often refuse to identify themselves with a label. For many, their gender identity is experienced as fluid and flexible. They are more integrated into their families of origin, openly form domestic partnerships or enter legal marriages, and are bringing biological or adopted children into their lives.

While Kranzberg's (2009) suggestions for placement of these three cohorts in group counseling related specifically to women, many of her ideas are relevant to similar cohorts of gay men as well. She believed that the older group ("Pre-Stonewall") would not work well in a heterogeneous group of mixed genders, sexual orientations, and ages, given their lifelong experience of secrecy and isolation. Many are reluctant to join such mixed groups unless the purpose is to discuss universal issues of aging and retirement. Even then, however, the concerns of sexual minorities without children or contact with families of origin usually are quite different from those of typical heterosexual individuals with strong familial support networks. Similarly, a "lesbian feminist" (or possibly a strongly identified gay man) will probably feel most comfortable in a group composed exclusively of either lesbians or gay men (as would any individual "in the beginning stages of coming out" [p. 220]). Kranzberg wrote, however, that the more integrated an individual is into the larger community, "the less important is the orientation of the therapy group" (p. 220). For "early-21st-century lesbians", the sexual orientation or gender of other members is less likely to be a critical factor in determining group placement since these individuals already have integrated themselves into the broader society and, for them, their sexual orientation is not considered relevant to their acceptance by, and participation in, the group. In all cases, however, counselors should discuss these kinds of situations with prospective members before including them in a group of any form.

Developmental Differences

Frost (1990) presented a developmental scheme, based on the six-stage identity development model of Cass (1979, 1984) that could be used to assign nonheterosexual members to therapy groups. Chojnacki and Gelberg (1995), likewise, applied Cass's model when determining the appropriateness of a support group for LGB individuals. These authors believed that people in the very early phases of minority identity development (i.e., Cass's identity confusion stage) are probably not receptive to joining such a group since the idea likely is too threatening to them. However, in some of the later stages (i.e., identity comparison, identity tolerance, and identity acceptance), individuals might find such a group to be a safe environment in which to explore their conflict, decrease their isolation, and normalize their experiences. While those at the fifth stage (i.e., identity pride), because of their tendency to dichotomize heterosexual and sexual minority identity and experience, might not be appropriate for group membership or may not be willing to participate, especially if the leader is heterosexually identified. Finally, those at Cass's sixth stage (i.e., identity synthesis) could be helpful not only to LGBT members in earlier developmental stages but also to the entire group in overcoming the polarization of heterosexual and sexual minority members common at previous phases of the group.

Along these same lines, the selection of group members as well as the nature of intervention strategies used must take into consideration the level of societal oppression *perceived* by individual clients and their level of comfort with a stigmatized identity (Miville et al., 2009). Further, counselors need to have familiarity with models of LGBT developmental theory, as well as knowledge of community resources for sexual minorities, their own biases, and "the effects of social and cultural heterosexism" (DeBord & Perez, 2000, p. 203). Clients at different levels of identity development have different needs, and group leaders must take these into consideration. For example, the findings of one study (Lease, Cogdal, & Smith, 1995) indicated that the lower the level of internalized homophobia in gay and lesbian clients, the higher the expectations for personal commitment to the counseling process. In other words, those in the earlier stages of identity development (Cass, 1979, 1984) may be as reticent to commit to the group experience as they are to their own identities. Hence, leaders should be careful not to push these members to disclose minority identities or to allow others to use them as scapegoats or sources of curiosity or in any way to shame or demean them.

Aronson (2002) in writing about working with gay, lesbian and bisexual youth in groups, noted that techniques and concepts need to be modified for each group based on the makeup and developmental needs of members. In all cases, however, all members must be hopeful for change and feel confident that the group experience will contribute to their well-being.

Group Composition

In addition to taking into consideration the cohort and developmental levels of prospective group members, leaders need to decide whether to form a homogeneous (i.e., composed exclusively of LGBT individuals) or a heterogeneous (i.e., composed of both sexual minority and heterosexual members) group. The reality of many situations might preclude this possibility however, and counselors in some settings might even consider it a luxury. For example, clients might be court-mandated and enter and leave a group at different times, a limited number of prospective members may be available on a particular day or at a certain hour, or only one counselor in an agency may be interested in forming a group. In spite of these difficulties, there are issues related to homogeneous or heterogeneous group composition, which are discussed below.

Homogeneous Groups

House and Tyler (1998) cited numerous kinds of groups designed exclusively for LGB members, including those for men, women, racial and ethnic minorities, youth, older adults, people in mixed-orientation marriages, parents of gays and lesbians, and sexual minority parents. They noted that these groups can be focused on coming out, career and life planning, parenting, substance abuse, religion, and other specific issues and exist in three primary categories: common interest, self-help, and counseling/therapy groups. According to the authors, these groups can create a "mini-culture where the ignorance, prejudice, oppression, and homophobia the general society directs toward gays, lesbians, and bisexuals are countered by support, acceptance, and universality" (p. 369). Along these same lines, Aronson (2002) wrote, "The universality of experience provided by involvement in such groups cannot be underestimated. Many gay, lesbian, and bisexual adolescents report feelings of extreme isolation, sometimes to the point of suicidal despair. Group members can help in sharing coping mechanisms and problem solving with difficult situations" (p. 71); and the accepting and healing capacity of groups can provide sexual minority clients an effective antidote for years of shame, hiding, secrecy, rejection, and denigration.

Some writers (e.g., Hicks, 2000), particularly those in the field of chemical dependency recovery, have contended that lesbian and gay clients are best helped in groups composed only of sexual minority individuals. Together they can address specific issues that may be overlooked in mainstream programs, such as how substance abuse is related to their coming out and internalized homophobia. Other concerns might relate to learning how to socialize without access to the bars, which have traditionally been gathering places for members of their

community and places where they met prospective mates. Hicks (2000) noted that some recovery programs caution sexual minority clients from even discussing these kinds of issues for fear that such disclosures might upset majority culture group members and retard their progress.

Hawkins (1993) believed that people in the earliest stages of self-identification can be threatened by an "all homosexual" (p. 509) group and are probably served best by first undertaking individual counseling. Once the coming out process is under way, however, "a homogeneous composition can quickly provide the reference group needed to normalize the person's experience" (p. 509). These kinds of groups can help establish commonality and support, develop a sense of safety from "homophobia," provide freedom from attempts to alter their sexual orientation by majority culture group members, assist in developing social skills, facilitate talking about sexuality, and create a feeling of community. He noted as a drawback, however, that after a period of time, the group can become ghettoized and block the attainment of an integrated personality.

Heterogeneous Groups

Because it is unrealistic to assume that all sexual minority clients can be treated in groups composed only of same sex–attracted individuals, numerous writers have addressed groups composed of mixed-orientation members. For example, Beckstead and Israel (2007) believed that same sex attracted clients can benefit from membership in a heterogeneous group, with male and female members from diverse cultural backgrounds. According to them, group counseling "can desensitize anxiety and provide opportunities to develop authentic relationships and emotional closeness" (p. 238).

In reference to heterogeneous groups, Hawkins (1993) believed that having gay individuals in these mixed groups can serve as a contrast to heterosexual values and may call these mores into question for all group members. In other words, the presence of sexual minority members often can activate a set of dynamics that forces all group members to question their values and prejudices. ([In this context, however, leaders are cautioned that they must protect minority members from being scapegoated or from being forced to serve as a representative for an entire population.)] On another potentially productive note, however, being in a group with heterosexual members can provide sexual minority members the experience of universality and normalize many aspects of their struggles. This can have a reparative effect in that it allows them to experience altruism from majority culture individuals.

Yalom (1975) contended in his chapter on problem patients that groups mixed with both homosexual and heterosexual clients can be successful when both the clients and other members do not consider homosexuality to be a special problem. He also cautioned about heterosexual members exerting pressure on the sexual minority person to relinquish same-sex attractions since the mixed group "does not easily relinquish the goal of 'converting' the [gay] patient to a heterosexual pattern" (p. 412). In a later edition of his text (Yalom, 2005), when writing about the inclusion in groups of minorities (including sexual minorities), noted that these members must be able "to trust that others in the group are willing to consider each individual's specific cultural context and not to view that individual as a stereotype of his culture" (p. 273).

Leader Sexual Orientation

In one study (Lease, Cogdal, & Smith, 1995), findings revealed that knowledge of a counselor's heterosexuality or homosexuality did not affect gay and lesbian clients' expectations for counseling. In other words, the sexual orientation of the leader had little influence on the degree of expectation of success. Ritter and Terndrup (2002), likewise, noted that "clinicians of all sexual orientations can work successfully with sexual minorities as long as they are accepting of their clients' homosexuality and are (reasonably) free of heterosexist bias and homophobic prejudice" (p. 1).

Heterosexual Leaders

Chojnacki and Gelberg (1995) described a university counseling center group composed of a "mix" of gay, lesbian, and bisexual members facilitated by heterosexual counselors. They contended that, during screenings, it was essential for leaders to disclose their sexual orientation in order to increase the alliance between them and members by sharing their ally status. The authors also suggested that, if possible, heterosexual counselors include a sexual minority cofacilitator as well as consult with LGB colleagues in order to increase understanding of the developmental struggles involved in integrating a stigmatized identity. Regarding the disclosure by heterosexual leaders to prospective or current group members, Chojnacki and Gelberg (1995) noted that this revelation often is difficult for heterosexual allies since they, too, have their own developmental issues to face. Many may be well meaning but

unaware of the extent of societal oppression sexual minorities experience and, thus, may be unable to empathize with the deeper levels of the struggles group members describe. They also might be blocked by their own fears that exposure as an LGB ally could lead to misinterpretation by family, friends, and colleagues or to mistrust of their motives by LGB group members.

Holahan and Gibson (1994) described the experiences of two heterosexual facilitators who led groups composed of lesbians and gay men at Pennsylvania State University over the course of two semesters. In an ongoing narrative, the authors noted that initially the members saw the leaders as compassionate guides who were accepted by the group. The facilitators observed that, because of their need to be liked, they were inadvertently colluding in the group's effort to minimize differences between them and the members and were creating a subtle message that disagreements were not welcome. In supervision they also became aware that their desire to be seen as politically correct in the eyes of members contributed to this nonconflict norm. Consequently, they became less cautious and more willing to illuminate covert conflict in the group, whether it was between members or directed toward them either as individuals or as representatives of a repressive, heterosexist society. At first, they feared becoming a target of the rage felt by oppressed minorities, but gradually they allowed themselves to be challenged and to challenge members. It was only by becoming more secure in their therapeutic identities, that Holahan and Gibson (1994) believed they were able create the conditions necessary for confrontation to occur and for the groups to mature.

Sexual Minority Leaders

Frost (1998) contended that gay male leaders often elicit transference reactions in sexual minority members, often related to a projection of their own shame and internalized homophobia. At the same time, strong countertransference reactions can be elicited in gay male group leaders that are distinctly different from those of a nongay facilitator. Kranzberg (1998) noted three main countertransference issues with gay male facilitators working with gay male clients: (1) pressure to serve as a role model for sexual minority clients, (2) complexity of living and working in the same community, and (3) overidentification with clients. Given that many lesbian and gay communities are small and members see each other at various events and locations, the pressures on sexual minority counselors are considerable and often involve the same dual-relationship considerations that practitioners of any orientation have when living and working in the same rural or isolated community.

Hawkins (1998) discussed other countertransference issues that sexual minority practitioners face, including the myth of "sameness" with a client given their similar sexual orientations. Pressures to serve as a role model may be operant, as well as similar experiences with managing biculturality, heterosexism, and shame. In all cases, conscientious counselors make these kinds of issues a part of their own therapy or consult with peers to insure that their group leadership is as objective and professional as possible.

Interestingly, virtually nothing has been written about issues that might arise when sexual minority counselors lead groups composed of majority culture members. Based on the literature reviewed in this chapter relative to how heterosexual clients sometimes respond to sexual minority group members, the presumption could be made that some of the reactions might be similar. Some members undoubtedly would be accepting or at least tolerant of the minority sexual orientation of the leader, while others may react unenthusiastically or even be openly disapproving. It would be difficult to tell, however, whether these transference reactions were a direct result of the leader's sexual orientation or whether other variables were involved. For many members this might be the first occasion in which they have experienced an openly lesbian, gay, or bisexual authority figure. In this case, predictable challenges to the facilitator's authority could be confounded with a sexual orientation variable.

Effective Leadership

Skilled leadership and modeling are essential for the creation of a supportive and accepting group climate. "The major contradiction to group treatment is the likelihood that patients will experience further shame about their orientation either through the group's or the leader's intolerance or the strength of the patient's projective identification" (Hawkins, 1993, p. 512). Firestein (1999) noted that groups, especially those composed of both heterosexual and nonheterosexual clients, should be "responsibly managed" (p. 315) and that leaders should assure members that no one will be "bashed because of their sexual difference from other members of the group" (p. 310). A climate of honesty, support, and tolerance has to be clearly normed by the leader,

both at the beginning of and throughout all the meetings of the group.

Firestein's thoughts were echoed by Hawkins (1993) when he noted that "the efficacy of group treatment for the homosexual population is essentially limited by the leader's and, secondarily, the group's capacity to be aware of homophobia and to confront it, so that scapegoating . . . is avoided" (p. 512). Situations where the client is seen only as the "group deviant" should be prevented, and leaders need to actively block these kinds of behaviors and turn attention to an examination of the group's dynamics. Hawkins (1993) cautioned counselors that "the misuse of therapy . . . to further societal persecution and self-persecution regarding homosexual feelings, behavior, and identity" is unethical (p. 513). He also cited other unethical situations, such as treating sexual minority clients while harboring a belief that their "lifestyle" cannot be healthy, happy, or productive or leading groups without information about the coming out process or the effects of societal and internalized stigma.

Ethical Considerations

The ethical codes of all professional associations are universal in their insistence that practitioners do not harm their clients but strive to promote their welfare and well-being. Few of the references in these codes specifically address group counseling but, rather, relate to the framework within which competent and ethical clinical practice must occur. For example, the *Code of Ethics* of the American Counseling Association (2005) clearly states that counselors do not discriminate on the basis of sexual orientation or in any way have a "negative impact on these persons" ([C.5] p. 10).

Similarly, the *Ethical Principles of Psychologists and Code of Conduct* of the APA (2002) requires psychologists to respect the rights and dignity of clients ([Principle E] p. 3) and to refrain from unfair discrimination ([3.01] p. 6) or other harassment ([3.03] p. 6). The APA Code further is clear on the boundaries of competence of clinicians ([2.01] p. 5) and notes the following specifically in this regard:

> (b) Where scientific or professional knowledge in the discipline of psychology establishes that an understanding of factors associated with age, gender, gender identity, race, ethnicity, culture, national origin, religion, sexual orientation, disability, language, or socioeconomic status is essential for effective implementation of their services or research, psychologists have or obtain the training, experience,

consultation, or supervision necessary to ensure the competence of their services, or they make appropriate referrals, except as provided in Standard 2.02, Providing Services in Emergencies (p. 5).

LEADER BIAS

In addition to writing about the necessity of "culture-specific preparation" (p. 359) when leading groups with sexual minority members, House and Tyler (1998) believed that leaders need to examine their own belief systems regarding their ability to provide unbiased assistance. The Principles for Diversity-Competent Group Workers (ASGW, 1999) refer directly to this concept when, in the first section (i.e., "Awareness of Self"), the document describes the attitudes and beliefs, knowledge, and skills needed for leaders in order to offer fair and objective service. In this same regard, Corey, Corey, and Corey (2010) asserted that "it is essential that group practitioners be willing to critically examine their personal prejudices, myths, fears, and stereotypes regarding sexual identity" (p. 90) since leaders who have negative reactions to homosexuality are likely to impose their own values and attitudes on group members. Further, Corey et al. (2010) wrote that "heterosexism can leak out in various ways, ranging from blatantly discriminating to more subtle and covert messages of disapproval" (p. 90). While realizing that some practitioners have moral or religious reservations about same-sex attractions or behaviors, the authors contended that it is essential that these counselors find a way to separate their personal beliefs from their duty to clients as required by the ethical codes and practice guidelines of the profession.

Along these same lines, Balkin, Schlosser, and Levitt (2009) surveyed 111 counselors and psychologists to investigate the relationships among religious identity, sexism, homophobia, and multicultural competence. The authors found that those "who were more rigid and authoritarian in their religious identity tended to exhibit more homophobic attitudes" (p. 424). They noted that this finding "is consistent with previous research that linked rigidity in religious beliefs and the authoritarianism of religion to the perpetuation of sexism and homophobia" (p. 424). Herek (2009), likewise, after examining data gathered from large surveys of the US population, cited the presence of high levels of sexual prejudice in individuals with frequent attendance at religious services and in those whose religious beliefs involve scriptural literalism and are conservative or fundamentalist in nature.

Balkin et al. (2009) noted that counselors need not compromise their personal belief systems but, at the same time, they should explore how their religious values may shape their reactions to multicultural differences and cultural diversity with regard to sexual minority clients. Their cautions are echoed by DeBord and Perez (2000) when they contend that "therapists need to have familiarity with models of LGB developmental theory, community resources for sexual minorities, their own biases, and the effects of social and cultural heterosexism" (p. 203).

MEMBER BIAS

House and Tyler (1998) contended that even if a group does not specifically address sexual orientation, "being gay, lesbian, or bisexual is apt to be an issue in the group" (p. 368). Sexual minority members will have to decide whether to take the risk and come out in the group, and House and Tyler believed that "it is common for at least one person in the group to reject and abuse nonheterosexual members" (p. 368). Other writers (Schwartz & Hartstein, 1986; Yalom, 1975) have claimed that it is not unusual for groups to become preoccupied with understanding the lives of these members or with trying to change their sexual orientation or "to hold the role of sexual being for a group" (Taylor, 2009, p. 196). Should efforts to covert a member to heterosexuality persist in spite of the facilitator's efforts to redirect the conversation or to focus on the discomfort invariably expressed by some observers to the ongoing process, leaders can direct group members to a report that reviews the literature on sexual orientation–change efforts (APA Task Force on Appropriate Therapeutic Reponses to Sexual Orientation; APA, 2009).

Group Management

Sexual minority members might need help in managing disclosures so that they do not feel pressured by other members to share more than they are willing or able to at the moment. At times, both they and the other members might need to be slowed down. Leaders must make certain that LGBT members have a safe space in which to disclose and that other members are not "wringing out disclosures" (Yalom, 2005, p. 134). No member should be either pushed to disclose or punished for doing so. "One of the most destructive events that can occur in a group is for members to use personal, sensitive material, which has been trustingly disclosed in the group, against one another" (p. 134). In these cases, the therapist must intervene to halt the behavior and then direct the group to examine itself and its interactions.

Historically, mixed groups of gay and nongay men and women have not been a safe environment for meeting the intimacy and individuation needs of same sex–attracted clients (Frost, 1990). Frost contended that this often is the result of prejudicial assumptions and lack of developmental information on the part of group practitioners, but he also believed that members of differing sexual orientations do not tolerate each other well. Likewise, Schwartz and Hartstein (1986) noted that gay men in mixed groups often encounter a strong heterosexist bias and that "the group may be all too eager to encourage conversion, which may inhibit further sharing of these thoughts and feelings" (p. 174). Obviously, the careful management of these kinds of situations is critical for the development of essential group norming and cohesiveness and the establishment of conditions necessary to activate facilitative factors.

Sexual Minority Members and Group Dynamics

DeBord and Perez (2000) adopted Yalom's (1985) 11 therapeutic factors and applied them to the body of scholarly work on LGB groups. The authors contended that the operationalization of these factors "affords LGB clients opportunities to openly describe, explore, and understand experiences that no other population is faced with (e.g., coming out, internalized homophobia)" (pp. 183–184). Speaking of two of these factors, Chen, Stracuzzi, and Ruckdeschel (2004) noted that in their gay men's group "the therapeutic value of universality and instillation of hope is maximized" (p. 402) and that growth is dependent on "the level of the group counselor's competence in assisting gay male clients in their negotiation and management of their interpersonal risks and emotional vulnerability" (p. 403).

Developmental Issues

Schwartz and Hartstein (1986) observed that gay male group members "are likely to experience the same difficulties that had marked their earlier interpersonal development" (p. 161). Their reactions may include several protective coping mechanisms, specifically passivity or a lack of assertiveness, alienation, estrangement, and excessive contentiousness, learned over a lifetime to defend against perceived external hostility and a "flawed sense of self from anticipated discovery and rejection" (p. 161).

Schwartz and Hartstein also noted that gay members in mixed-orientation groups often try to hide their sexual orientation, especially in the early stages, in order to gain acceptance. On the other hand, if the group is composed of only of self-identified gay men, lesbians, or bisexual individuals, early disclosure is encouraged and even expected. In mixed groups, sexual minority members often feel isolated and fear getting involved, are wary of self-disclosure, and are anxious about being exposed.

Protective Mechanisms

Yalom (1975) said that disclosure is the first task of the sexual minority client in a group and, to be a working member, this disclosure must come fairly early in the process. Otherwise, the individual may drop out of the group, thus "merely recapitulating the highly dishonest, unsatisfying social relationships" experienced outside of the group (p. 409). A history of "constant vigilance and suppression of spontaneity" (p. 409) often results in fatigue and tension and, thus, makes an initial disclosure quite difficult, if not impossible, for many clients. While unconditional acceptance by other members, primarily those with a heterosexual orientation, can have great therapeutic value for these individuals, reaching that point is not always easy and often requires sensitive facilitation on the part of the group leader.

Despite the growing acceptance of same sex–attracted individuals by the greater society, there still exists much fear of disclosure and reluctance to trust on the part of these clients. Further, the response of other group members can still be similar to those described by Yalom (1975) over 30 years ago. Accordingly, members often are sympathetic and accepting after an initial disclosure, but a range of other reactions follows. For example, some members may "de-individualize" (p. 412) the sexual minority member with stories of other "homosexuals" they know. Some may be curious about people with openly acknowledged same-sex attractions and may engage in various forms of voyeurism about the intricacies of their lives, while others may try to "figure him out" (p. 412). "Homosexual psychodynamics are seen as particularly clear and enticing, and the group members may launch an historical inquiry into the events of his early psychosexual development" (p. 412). Finally, some male clients with doubts about their own sexual adequacy may be quite uncomfortable, while others with conflicts about their own sexual orientation and identity may respond quite adversely.

Yalom (1985) discussed the use of "mass group process commentary" (p. 186) when an obstacle has arisen that obstructs the progress of the entire group. One such instance for the use of this commentary is when a group takes flight after being faced with an anxiety-laden issue, such as the divulgence of same-sex attraction by a member. In an earlier example, Yalom (1975) described a situation in which the other group members evaded discussion of the disclosure by fleeing from their anxiety through intellectualization, in this case, into an abstract conversation of generalized prejudice that lasted for two sessions. In that the entire group was colluding in the evasion of the issue, Yalom suggested that the therapist not circumvent the resistance but "plunge the members into the source of the resistance—not *around*, but *through*, anxiety" (p. 190, italics in original). The task of the leader in these situations is to block the flight and redirect the group to examine its interactions. It is through this process illumination that the sexual minority client can become reindividualized and humanized in the eyes of the other group members.

Shame and Mirroring

Throughout this chapter, several writers have mentioned that shame appears to be virtually a universal result of society's denigration of sexual minority individuals. Haendiges (2001) studied the construct of internalized homophobia, lesbian identity development, and the impact of embedded shame on psychological functioning. After a review of relevant literature, she concluded that the existence of this shame is pervasive given that all sexual minorities develop within the context of a judgmental and rejecting environment. To counteract this internalized stigma, Haendiges constructed a group-counseling program designed to educate participants while initiating psychological change.

Cadwell (2009), likewise, noted the effects of shame when specifically about gay men, but his comments are equally applicable to lesbian, bisexual, and transgender populations as well. He wrote, "Shame shapes gay men. Rigidly constricted ideals about gender role and sexuality contort gay men's full engagement in their complexity" (p. 197). He further spoke of failures of attunement and mirroring by parents, school bullies, peers, and society that have led to disengagement from self and others and sees the "mirroring and containment" (p. 210) available in a group modality as a means to self-acceptance and intimacy.

Object relations theorist Kohut (1971, 1977) described these essential processes of mirroring and attunement, whereby the goodness and self-worth of a person are reflected back by deeply empathic and caring others. He saw these concepts as essential for effective counseling, and some writers have found them to be particularly appropriate when working with sexual minority clients. For example, Bastian and Silverstein (2009) believed that practitioners must move out from behind masks of "anonymity and neutrality, for the LBGT client needs to be seen, heard, and validated in ways that reach the deep-seated deficits. . . . When mirroring is withheld, when attunement is missing in action, wounding is inflicted" (p. 79).

Conclusion

Group counseling has the potential to provide the mirroring necessary for healing, not only for sexual minority clients but for all members. That mirroring must first come from facilitators who set the tone for the group. Members, in turn, emulate the leader in terms of how all members in the group will be treated. Practitioners who follow and implement the guidelines, best practices, competencies, standards, codes, and principles of the profession model and create the kind of climate that exists in the group.

When leaders can comprehend the unique dynamics that sexual minority clients bring to the group encounter and have the skills to lead the group through its many transitions, growth can occur for every individual involved. Understanding the concepts of oppression, minority stress, and cohort and developmental differences is only part of the equation, however. The resilience of LGBT individuals should not be underestimated. Through the eons they have experienced pervasive stigmatization and even harassment but have persevered. Today, fortunately, role models are more available than ever before, and in many countries political movements are in their favor. Nonetheless, every sexual minority has to start somewhere, and a first venture into the light just might be in the group you are privileged to facilitate.

References

American Counseling Association. (2005). *Code of ethics*. Washington, DC: Author. Retrieved from www.counseling.org/Counselors/2005 ACA Code of Ethics.html

American Group Psychotherapy Association. (2007). *Practice guidelines for group psychotherapy*. New York: Author. Retrieved from agpa.org

American Psychological Association. (2000). Guidelines for psychotherapy with lesbian, gay, and bisexual clients.

American Psychologist, 55(12), 1440–1451. Retrieved from www.apa.org/pi/lgbc/guidelines.html

American Psychological Association. (2002). Ethical principles of psychologists and code of conduct. American Psychologist, 57, 1060–1073. Retrieved from www.apa.org/ethics/code/index.aspx.html

American Psychological Association. (2009, August). Resolution on appropriate affirmative responses to sexual orientation distress and change efforts. Retrieved September 10, 2009, from http://www.apa.org/pi/lgbc/policy/pshome.html

APA Task Force on Appropriate Therapeutic Responses to Sexual Orientation. (2009). Report of the task force on appropriate therapeutic responses to sexual orientation. Washington, DC: American Psychological Association. Retrieved from www.apa.org/pi/lgbc/publications/

Aronson, S. (2002). Group work with special populations. In S. Aronson & S. Scheidlinger (Eds.), Group treatment of adolescents in context: Outpatient, inpatient, and school (pp. 55–74). Madison, CT: International Universities Press.

Association for Lesbian, Gay, Bisexual and Transgender Issues in Counseling. (2009). Competencies for counseling gay, lesbian, bisexual and transgendered (LGBT) clients. Washington, DC: Author. Retrieved November 15, 2009, from www.algbitc.org/competencies.html

Association for Specialists in Group Work. (1998/Rev. 2007). Best practice guidelines. Journal for Specialists in Group Work, 23(3), 237–244. Retrieved from asgw.org

Association for Specialists in Group Work. (1999). Principles for diversity-competent group workers. Journal for Specialists in Group Work, 24 (1), 7–14. Retrieved from asgw.org

Association for Specialists in Group Work. (2000). Professional standards for the training of group workers. Group Worker, 29(3), 1–10. Retrieved from asgw.org

Balkin, R. S., Schlosser, L. Z., & Levitt, D. H. (2009). Religious identity and cultural diversity: Exploring the relationships between religious identity, sexism, homophobia, and multicultural competence. Journal of Counseling and Development, 87(4), 420–427.

Ball, S. (1994). A group model for gay and lesbian clients with chronic mental illness. Social Work, 39(1), 109–115.

Ball, S., & Lipton, B. (2005). Group work with gay men. In G. L. Greif & P. H. Ephross (Eds.), Group with populations at risk (2nd ed., pp. 309–331). New York: Oxford University Press.

Bastian, B., & Silverstein, R. (2009). Working with LGBT clients and why marriage equality matters. Therapist, 21(3), 70–80.

Beckstead, L., & Israel, T. (2007). Affirmative counseling and psychotherapy focused on issues related to sexual orientation conflicts. In K. J. Bieschke, R. M. Perez, & K. A. DeBord (Eds.), Handbook of counseling and psychotherapy with lesbian, gay, bisexual, and transgender clients (2nd ed., pp. 221–244). Washington, DC: American Psychological Association.

Bieschke, K. J., Perez, R. M., & DeBord, K. A. (2007). Handbook of counseling and psychotherapy with lesbian, gay, bisexual, and transgender clients (2nd ed.). Washington, DC: American Psychological Association.

Cadwell, S. (2009). Shame, gender, and sexuality in gay men's group therapy. Group, 33(3), 197–212.

Cass, V. C. (1979). Homosexual identity formation: A theoretical model. Journal of Homosexuality, 4(3), 219–235.

Cass, V. C. (1984). Homosexual identity formation: Testing a theoretical model. Journal of Sex Research, 20(2), 143–167.

Chen, E. C., Stracuzzi, T. I., & Ruckdeschel, D. E. (2004). Affirmative counseling with gay men. In D. R. Atkinson & G. Hackett (Eds.), Counseling diverse populations (3rd ed., pp. 388–409). Boston: McGraw-Hill.

Chojnacki, J. R., & Gelberg, S. (1995). The facilitation of a gay/lesbian/bisexual support-therapy group by heterosexual counselors. Journal of Counseling and Development, 73(3), 352–354.

Cochran, S. D., & Mays, V. M. (2009). Burden of psychiatric morbidity among lesbian, gay, and bisexual individuals in the California Quality of Life Survey. Journal of Abnormal Psychology, 118(3), 647–658.

Conlin, D., & Smith, J. (1982). Group psychotherapy for gay men. In J. C. Gonsiorek (Ed.), Homosexuality and psychotherapy: A practitioner's handbook of affirmative models (pp. 105–112). New York: Haworth Press.

Conlin, D., & Smith, J. (1985). Group psychotherapy for gay men. In J. C. Gonsiorek (Ed.), A guide to psychotherapy with gay and lesbian clients (pp. 105–112). New York: Harrington Park Press.

Corey, M. S., Corey, G., & Corey, C. (2010). Groups: Process and practice (8th ed.). Pacific Grove, CA: Brooks/Cole.

DeBord, K. A., & Perez, R. M. (2000). Group counseling theory and practice with lesbian, gay, and bisexual clients. In R. M. Perez, K. A. DeBord, & K. J. Bieschke (Eds.), Handbook of counseling and psychotherapy with lesbian, gay, and bisexual clients (pp. 183–206). Washington, DC: American Psychological Association.

DiPlacido, J. (1998). Minority stress among lesbians, gay men, and bisexuals. In G. M. Herek (Ed.), Stigma and sexual orientation: Understanding prejudice against lesbians, gay men, and bisexuals (pp. 138–159). Thousand Oaks, CA: Sage.

Englehardt, B. J. (2005). Group work with lesbians. In G. L. Greif & P. H. Ephross (Eds.), Group work with populations at risk (2nd ed., pp. 332–346). New York: Oxford University Press.

Firestein, B. A. (1999). New perspectives on group treatment with women of diverse sexual identities. Journal for Specialists in Group Work, 24(3), 306–315.

Frost, J. C. (1990). A developmentally keyed scheme for the placement of gay men into psychotherapy groups. International Journal of Group Psychotherapy, 40(2), 155–167.

Frost, J. C. (1997). Group psychotherapy with the aging gay male: Treatment of choice. Group, 21(3), 267–285.

Frost, J. C. (1998). Countertransference considerations for the gay male when leading psychotherapy groups for gay men. International Journal of Group Psychotherapy, 48(1), 3–24.

Griffin, K. L. (2009). If it's Wednesday, I must be gay, and other thoughts on bisexual identity development. Group, 33(3), 245–256.

Haendiges, Kathryn Lynn (2001). A group treatment of internalized homophobia in lesbians. Psy.D. dissertation, Spalding University, United States – Kentucky. Retrieved February 27, 2011, from Dissertations & Theses: The Humanities and Social Sciences Collection.(Publication No. AAT 3017001).

Hawkins, D. M. (1993). Group psychotherapy with gay men and lesbians. In H. I. Kaplan & B. J. Sadock (Eds.), Comprehensive group psychotherapy (3rd ed., pp. 506–515). Baltimore: Williams & Wilkins.

Hawkins, D. M. (1998). Comments on "countertransference considerations." International Journal of Group Psychotherapy, 48(1), 25–30.

Herek, G. M. (2004). Beyond "homophobia": Thinking about sexual prejudice and stigma in the twenty-first century. *Sexuality Research and Social Policy, 1*(2), 6–24.

Herek, G. M. (2009). Sexual stigma and sexual prejudice in the United States: A conceptual framework. In D. A. Hope (Ed.), *Contemporary perspectives on lesbian, gay and bisexual identities: The 54th Nebraska Symposium on Motivation* (pp. 65–111). New York: Springer.

Hicks, D. (2000). The importance of specialized treatment programs for lesbian and gay patients. *Journal of Gay and Lesbian Psychotherapy, 3*(3/4), 81–94.

Holahan, W., & Gibson, S. A. (1994). Heterosexual therapists leading lesbian and gay therapy groups: Therapeutic and political realities. *Journal of Counseling and Development, 72,* 591–594.

House, R. M., & Tyler, V. (1998). Group counseling with gay, lesbian, and bisexual clients. In D. Capuzzi & D. R. Gross (Eds.), *Introduction to group counseling* (2nd ed., pp. 359–388). Denver, CO: Love Publishing.

Israel, T. (2004). What counselors need to know about working with sexual minority clients. In D. R. Atkinson & G. Hackett (Eds.), *Counseling diverse populations* (3rd ed., pp. 347–364). Boston: McGraw-Hill.

Israel, T., Ketz, K., Detrie, P. M., Burke, M. C., & Shulman, J. L. (2003). Identifying counselor competencies for working with lesbian, gay, and bisexual clients. *Journal of Gay and Lesbian Psychotherapy, 7*(4), 3–21.

Kohut, H. (1971). *The analysis of the self: A systematic approach to the psychoanalytic treatment of narcissistic personality disorders.* New York: International Universities Press.

Kohut, H. (1977). *The restoration of the self.* New York: International Universities Press.

Kranzberg, M. B. (1998). Comments on "countertransference considerations." *International Journal of Group Psychotherapy, 48*(1), 25–30.

Kranzberg, M. B. (2009). Three generations of lesbians: Clinical implications and placement in group. *Group, 33*(3), 213–222.

Lease, S. H., Cogdal, P. A., & Smith, D. (1995). Counseling expectancies related to counselors' sexual orientation and clients' internalized homophobia. *Journal of Gay and Lesbian Psychotherapy, 2* (3), 51–65.

Logan, C. R., & Barret, R. (2005). Counseling competencies for sexual minority clients. *Journal of LGBT Issues in Counseling, 1*(1), 3–22.

Miville, M. L., Duan, C., Nutt, R. L., Waehler, C. A., Suzuki, L., Pistole, M. C.,... & Corpus, M. (2009). Integrating practice guidelines into professional training: Implications for diversity competence. *Counseling Psychologist, 37* (4), 519–563.

Morris, J. F., & Balsam, K. F. (2003). Lesbian and bisexual women's experiences of victimization: Mental health, revictimization, and sexual identity development. *Journal of Lesbian Studies, 7* (4), 67–85.

Morrow, D. F. (1996). Coming out issues for adult lesbians: A group intervention. *Social Work, 41*(6), 647–656.

Neal, C. (2000). We are family: Working with gay men in groups. In C. Neal & D. Davies (Eds.), *Issues in therapy with lesbian, gay, bisexual and transgender clients* (pp. 102–114). Maidenhead, UK: Open University Press.

Neisen, J. H. (1993). Healing from cultural victimization: Recovery from shame due to heterosexism. *Journal of Gay and Lesbian Psychotherapy, 2*(1), 49–63.

Perez, R. M. (2007). The "boring" state of research and psychotherapy with lesbian, gay, bisexual, and transgender clients: Revisiting Baron (1991). In K. J. Bieschke, R. M. Perez, & K. A. DeBord (Eds.), *Handbook of counseling and psychotherapy with lesbian, gay, bisexual, and transgender clients* (2nd ed., pp. 399–418). Washington, DC: American Psychological Association.

Perez, R. M., DeBord, K. A., & Bieschke, K. J. (2000). *Handbook of counseling and psychotherapy with lesbian, gay, and bisexual clients.* Washington, DC: American Psychological Association.

Reece, R. (1982). Group treatment of sexual dysfunction in gay men. In J. C. Gonsiorek (Ed.), *Homosexuality and psychotherapy: A practitioner's handbook of affirmative models* (pp. 113–129). New York: Haworth Press.

Ritter, K. Y., & Terndrup, A. I. (2002). *Handbook of affirmative psychotherapy with lesbians and gay men.* New York: Guilford Press.

Ross, L. E., Doctor, F., Dimito, A., Kuehl, D., & Armstrong, M. S. (2008). Can talking about oppression reduce depression? Modified CBT group treatment for LGBT people with depression. *Journal of Gay and Lesbian Social Services, 19*(1), 1–15.

Schwartz, R. D., & Hartstein, N. B. (1986). Group psychotherapy with gay men: Theoretical and clinical considerations. In T. S. Stein & C. J. Cohen (Eds.), *Psychotherapy with lesbians and gay men* (pp. 157–177). New York: Plenum Press.

Taylor, P. J. (2009). Introduction. *Group, 33* (3), 195–196.

Toy, J. (1991). "Coming out" groups: A university resource. *Social Work in Education, 13* (4), 257–264.

Turell, S. C., & de St. Aubin, T. (1995). A relationship-focused group for lesbian college students. *Journal of Gay and Lesbian Psychotherapy, 2*(3), 67–84.

Welch, P. J. (1996). In search for a caring community: Group therapy for gay, lesbian and bisexual college students. *Journal of College Student Psychotherapy, 11*(1), 27–40.

Wolf, T. J. (1987). Group counseling for bisexual men. *Journal for Specialists in Group Work, 12* (4), 162–165.

Yalom, I. (1975). *The theory and practice of group psychotherapy* (2nd ed.). New York: Basic Books.

Yalom, I. D. (1985). *The theory and practice of group psychotherapy* (3rd ed.). New York: Basic Books.

Yalom, I. D. (with Leszcz, M.). (2005). *The theory and practice of group psychotherapy* (5th ed.). New York: Basic Books.

Prevention Groups

Michael Waldo, Jonathan P. Schwartz, Arthur Horne, *and* Laura Côté

Abstract

This chapter focuses on prevention groups, including different perspectives on prevention (primary, secondary, tertiary, and social action prevention) and classification of prevention group-work process (guidance, counseling, therapy, and task). Advantages of using groups for prevention are outlined, including efficiency, familiarity of the format, large number of participants available to engage in social action, and therapeutic factors in the groups. Group dynamics and group leadership are described, and current examples of primary, secondary, and tertiary groups are provided.

Keywords: prevention, group, prevention group work, prevention group focus, therapeutic factors, group dynamics, group leader functions

Introduction

One version of an often-told story of a town "next to dangerous river" illustrates the compelling arguments for prevention (Rappaport, 1972). According to the story, the river continuously claimed a large number of drowning victims. In an effort to save lives, the town posted lifeguards day and night. The guards jumped in to save victims each time they spotted them, but soon became exhausted and were unable keep up with the numbers being swept away. Then, one of the guards left her post and went upstream to where the victims were falling into the river. She built a fence to prevent people slipping off the bank into the stream, and posted signs warning of the danger. The number of people falling into the stream was dramatically reduced, resulting in fewer people drowning. Leaving her post took courage, recognizing the problem took imagination, and building the fence took ingenuity. The result was a permanent solution that was less expensive, less dangerous, and more effective than rescuing people in the river. Not only were fewer people drowning but fewer people were experiencing the trauma of coming close to drowning. The next step in the process would

be to teach more effective swimming skills. If some people still slip in the river, they will be better prepared to manage the crisis.

There are a number of compelling reasons to pursue prevention of psychological problems. Perhaps the most compelling is that there are insufficient resources to meet the need for remedial treatment of problems after they develop. This is likely to remain true for the foreseeable future. It is unlikely there will ever be sufficient numbers of mental health providers to meet the treatment needs. People are suffering who are not getting help. In fact, recent research suggests that as many as 57.7 million people in the United States suffer from a diagnosable mental disorder in a given year, yet fewer than one-third of American adults and fewer than 20% of children with mental disorders are receiving mental health services (National Alliance on Mental Illness, 2002). In the United States and Canada, mental illness is the top cause of debilitation for young people aged 15–44 (National Institute of Mental Health [NIMH], 2010a). The dearth of services is particularly acute for the most vulnerable populations: children, the poor, and minorities (US

Department of Health and Human Services, 2001; World Health Organization, 2007). Fewer than half of poor and minority children suffering from mental disorders are receiving treatment (NIMH, 2010b), thus adding a social justice rationale for prevention (Kenny, Horne, Orpinas, & Reece, 2009).

A second compelling argument for prevention is cost. As Applebaum (2003) has reported, mental health care currently consumes a large portion of the gross national product. And, as is true for other medical expenses, the costs are rising while the availability of treatment is declining (Applebaum, 2003). This figure has risen steadily over the last 20 years and is predicted to continue to rise, resulting in the containment of health costs becoming a national priority (Frank, Goldman, & McGuire, 2009). Preventing problems is considerably less expensive than treating them after they occur (Piot, Debrework, & Turmen, 2002; Rogers, 2002).

One component of the economic benefits of prevention is related to the lost productivity that occurs when people are experiencing a mental illness. Lost productivity related to mental disorders is nearly $79 billion annually (US Department of Health and Human Services, 2001). If mental disorders are prevented, people can continue to contribute to the economy. Additional savings occur through prevention of psychological problems that promote risky and/or illegal behavior. For example, automobile accidents resulting from driving under the influence of alcohol cost over $51 billion annually (Centers for Disease Control and Prevention [CDC], 2010). In addition, in 2008 drunken driving accidents caused 32% of all traffic-related deaths, 16% of all injuries, and immeasurable suffering (CDC, 2010). When the total costs of these accidents are taken into account, prevention of drunk driving alone could have a major positive economic impact.

The example of reducing driving under the influence illustrates two other key benefits to prevention. First, the costs of psychological problems go way beyond money (Piot et al., 2002). Even when psychological problems are treated, from their onset until they are fully remediated, the person experiencing them is suffering. Persons abusing alcohol typically suffer from cognitive impairment, health problems, and disruptions in their relationships, long before and after they have alcohol-related auto accidents, suffering that would be avoided if the problem was prevented in the first place. Second, persons suffering from psychological problems impact the well-being of others (Lukens, Thorning, & Lohrer, 2004; Marsh & Johnson, 1997). This is most obvious when a person abusing alcohol crashes into an innocent victim. It is also true for other mental health problems. People experiencing depression endure low mood states, hopelessness, anxiety, and sleep loss. They also may be irritable or withdrawn in their intimate relationships, which has a negative impact on family, friends, and coworkers (American Psychiatric Association, 2000). Prevention of psychological problems for individuals can result in prevention of psychological problems for their intimates (Bowen, 1979).

Group counseling has been defined by Weisz, Weiss, Alicke, and Kloz (1987, p. 543) as follows: "Any intervention designed to alleviate psychological distress, reduce maladaptive behavior, or enhance adaptive behavior through counseling, structured or unstructured intervention, a training program, or a predetermined treatment plan." Gazda, Ginter, and Horne (2001, p. 4) indicated that

> Group counseling is *prevention oriented* in the sense that the group members are capable of functioning in society but may be experiencing some "rough spots" in their lives. . . . Group counseling is *growth engendering* insofar as it provides the participants with incentive and motivation to make changes that are in their best interests. . . . Group counseling is *remedial* for those individuals who have entered into a spiral of self-defeating behavior but who, nevertheless, may be capable of reversing the spiral without counseling intervention . . . however, with counseling intervention the group member is more likely to recover, recover more quickly, and recover with fewer lingering emotional effects.

Group work has and will continue to play a critical role in prevention (Association for Specialists in Group Work [ASGW], 1998; Conyne, 2004). It has a number of advantages as a preventive intervention, including efficiency, efficacy, a familiar format for participants, and bringing people together to address a common concern. Different group approaches can be employed to meet the requirements of specific prevention situations (Gazda et al., 2001). Group methods can also be modified to target specific prevention goals. Therapeutic factors that are generated by group dynamics are especially applicable to prevention goals (Waldo, 1985). Approaches to leading prevention groups can be adjusted to employ and/or modify group dynamics to optimize desirable therapeutic factors (Schwartz & Waldo, 1999). And group work has demonstrated its efficacy at prevention (Burlingame, Fuhriman, & Mosier, 2003; Gazda et al., 2001).

This chapter focuses on prevention groups. *Prevention groups* can be defined as interaction between two or more people (including face-to-face and electronic communication) that is focused on using group dynamics to prevent problems. They can employ psychoeducational, counseling, therapeutic, or task-oriented processes to achieve primary, secondary, tertiary, and/or social action prevention goals. Prevention groups have been further defined as follows:

> Preventive groups may focus on the reduction in the occurrence of new cases of a problem, the duration and severity of incipient problems, or they may promote strengths and optimal human functioning. Prevention groups encompass many formats. They may function within a small group format or work with a classroom of thirty or forty. Prevention may also be community-wide with multiple group settings. Prevention groups use various group approaches. Psychoeducational groups are popular and, while some prevention psychologists work within a traditional counseling group, others use a group-centered intervention approach. Two key ingredients for all prevention groups are that they be directed toward averting problems and promoting positive mental health and wellbeing and that they highlight and harness group processes. (Conyne & Harpine, in press,)

In this chapter, different perspectives on prevention are described, including methods of classifying preventive interventions. This is followed by a description of current classifications of prevention group work. Next, the advantages of using groups for prevention are outlined. Theory and research explaining how prevention groups work are then reviewed. Therapeutic factors that frequently occur in groups are described, with a focus on how these can contribute to different forms of prevention. Dynamics that develop in groups are then described, including how group leaders may employ group dynamics to foster therapeutic factors. Current examples of primary, secondary, and tertiary prevention groups are provided, including evaluative research on their effectiveness. The chapter closes with a summary and examination of future directions for prevention groups.

Categorizing Prevention

Historically, the goals (Kessler & Albee, 1975) and focus (Romano & Hage, 2000) of prevention efforts have been typified as fitting into one of three categories: *primary*, which has the goal of preventing problems from ever occurring and has a "universal" focus (the preventive intervention is used with everyone, regardless of their likelihood to have or develop a problem); *secondary*, which has the goal of preventing an emerging problem from continuing and getting worse and is "targeted" on those people who show signs of having the problem or being at risk for developing it; and *tertiary*, which has the goal of preventing an existing problem from causing other problems and is applied to populations that are "indicated" to have the problem. Recently, there has been a call for counseling psychologists to expand this list of prevention efforts to include social action as a critical prevention activity (Hage et al., 2007; Kenny et al., 2009). Social action involves trying to influence societal structures and public policy to prevent mental health problems and promote social justice.

Primary, secondary, tertiary, and social action forms of prevention can all be accomplished through group work. Examples of preventing problems that arise from alcohol abuse illustrate how primary, secondary, tertiary, and social action groups can help. Primary prevention of impaired driving often involves addressing alcohol use and risks during high school drivers' education classes (Levine, 1998). Group discussions focus on students' assumptions about alcohol and alcohol use. Healthy attitudes toward alcohol are taught. Students demonstrating unhealthy attitudes are confronted by the group leaders or other members. This example is universal in that it is applied to all drivers' education students, regardless of their experiences with alcohol.

Groups held at universities for students who have violated campus alcohol policies are an example of secondary prevention (LaBrie, Thompson, Huchting, Lac, & Buckley, 2007). Students are targeted as being at risk of having problems with alcohol because they have engaged in underage drinking, have been intoxicated in public, and/or have brought alcohol to areas where it is prohibited. They are mandated to attend the groups. The group discussions explore alcohol-use patterns, including family histories with alcohol. Consequences of irresponsible alcohol use are explored, including the risks associated with driving under the influence. Group members are encouraged to support each other in adopting healthy approaches to alcohol use and avoiding drunk driving. The group goal is to help members avoid worsening problems with alcohol.

Court-ordered groups for people who have been arrested for driving under the influence are an example of tertiary prevention (Gladding, 2008).

Involvement in group counseling is indicated because their drinking is problematic, causing them to endanger themselves and others and to break the law. These groups typically hold members responsible for addressing their alcohol-abuse problem, in particular for preventing it from jeopardizing themselves and others by driving under the influence. The goal is to prevent alcohol abuse from resulting in injuries.

Mothers Against Drunk Driving (MADD) offers an example of an organization that employs groups in social action. As implied by its name, this organization is made up of people who are concerned about loss of loved ones in accidents caused by alcohol abuse. Groups of people in the organization engage in public education about the dangers of drunk driving and lobby for strong laws and law enforcement against driving under the influence. The goal of these groups is to increase societal awareness and guide public policy in ways that prevent drunk driving and its associated dangers.

While differentiating prevention efforts according to these categories makes conceptual sense, the differentiation may be seen more as identifying different perspectives on prevention than discriminating between prevention activities (Waldo & Schwartz, 2008). In practice there is overlap between activities in the different categories of prevention. In fact, any prevention group is likely to have primary, secondary, tertiary, and social action prevention impacts. For example, the primary prevention group for high school students can also be seen as correcting a problem in that it is overcoming their lack of knowledge about the dangers of alcohol (secondary prevention), preparing them to deal with societal influences that will encourage them to abuse alcohol throughout their lives (tertiary prevention), and helping them become spokespersons for responsibility in relation to alcohol (social action). Similarly, in addition to the direct social action taken by MADD groups, working within the groups reinforces responsible driving among members who have never driven intoxicated (primary prevention), offers members relief from feelings of helplessness they may experience in relation to the magnitude of the problem of impaired drivers (secondary prevention), and provides solace and support for those who are dealing with the tragedy of losing a loved one in an alcohol-related accident (tertiary prevention). Recognizing the potential for prevention groups to have primary, secondary, tertiary, and social action preventive effects can be helpful when planning groups,

seeking resources to support them, and evaluating their outcomes (Waldo & Schwartz, 2008).

Categorizing Groups

Similar to the efforts to categorize prevention, efforts have been made to categorize different types of groups (ASGW, 1998; Gazda et al., 2001). One approach categorizes groups according to their goals and process (ASGW, 1998) as follows:

Guidance/psychoeducational groups: These groups focus on enhancing development and preventing problems by providing information and teaching skills.

Counseling/interpersonal process groups: These groups help members overcome problems and keep those problems from becoming worse through development of supportive relationships between members.

Therapeutic/personality reconstruction groups: These groups help members deal with deep and/or long-standing problems through evocative processes that expose and address pathology.

Task groups: These groups take on tasks and engage in action to complete those tasks.

It is interesting to note that with regard to goals, the four types of groups closely parallel the four types of prevention: guidance groups' focus on preventing problems fits with primary prevention; counseling groups' focus on catching problems early and keeping them from getting worse fits with secondary prevention; therapy groups' focus on minimizing the damage caused by deep, long-term problems fits well with tertiary prevention; and task groups' goals could be tasks related to social action.

The processes described as typical of each kind of group, however, do not necessarily exclusively match the group goals (Gazda et al., 2001; Waldo & Bauman, 1998). For example, teaching group participants skills could and often does help them deal with long-term problems, like when communication skills–training groups are offered in mental hospitals (Waldo & Harman, 1999). And evocative procedures, like Gestalt empty chair technique and Jungian dream analysis, are often used in workshops to help participants who are not suffering from mental disorders become more self-aware, primary prevention goals (Schaffer & Galinsky, 1989). Also, any one group can have more than one goal and is likely to have more than one process. For instance, groups run for inpatients suffering from serious mental disorders (Yalom, 2005) may focus both on the patients' disorders (therapy goal) and improving their relationships with other patients (guidance goal) and employ a structured procedure for setting the agenda of each group member (guidance process), followed by an exchange of feedback between members (counseling process). The problems resulting from rigidly associating group goals and process have led some authors to suggest that groups be categorized independently on goal and process dimensions (Waldo & Bauman, 1998). Groups discussed in this chapter are categorized according to both their prevention goals (primary, secondary, tertiary, or social action prevention) and process (guidance, interpersonal process, therapy, and task activities).

Advantages of Groups for Prevention

Whether they are focusing on primary, secondary, tertiary, or social action prevention, groups have distinct advantages for promoting prevention. Those advantages are detailed to below:

Efficiency and Efficacy

By definition, prevention focuses on keeping problems from happening, rather than addressing an existing problem. While this approach makes abundant sense, it is sometimes hard to justify allocating resources to "fixing something that is not broken" when there are so many "broken" problems and people who need those resources. Or, as the comic but poignant saying goes, "It is hard to think about draining the swamp when you are up to your ears in alligators." The lifeguard who went upstream to build a fence in the dangerous river risked letting some people drown when she left her post. Providing prevention services in groups helps offset the costs and risks of prevention by efficiently serving many people.

In addition to being efficient, group counseling is effective. Extensive research has consistently demonstrated that group counseling is superior to no treatment (Bednar & Kaul, 1994; Burlingame et al., 2003) and, on average, is as effective as individual counseling (Bednar & Kaul, 1994; McRoberts, Burlingame, & Hoag, 1998; Burlingame, MacKenzie, & Strauss, 2004; Forsyth, 2006). Clear evidence that group counseling works is a good argument for its use when resources are limited.

Familiarity with the Format

Because prevention is intended to keep problems from happening, it often is conducted with people who do not necessarily perceive themselves to be in need of help. Many people who could benefit from prevention are not familiar with psychological

interventions, do not feel their receipt of help is justified, and would feel very uncomfortable engaging in individual counseling (Schwartz & Hage, 2008). Group counseling is offered in a format that most people are familiar with from years in school (classrooms) and other forms of group meetings (e.g., church prayer groups, business committee meetings, club socials, union rallies). People may be more likely to participate and feel comfortable in group counseling than other forms counseling (Waldo, 1987a).

Multiple Resources

One of the great strengths of groups is their members (Conyne, 2004; Yalom, 2005). It is unlikely that any prevention counselor can know the most important piece of information or the exact right procedure to assist every client. This becomes even truer when preventive interventions are offered in the varied cultural contexts in which they are most needed, and by people who may not have had extensive formal training. These problems are offset when prevention is offered through group work. The members of the group are all resources who have information and procedures that can be explored for a best fit to any one member's needs. Also, the diverse cultural and social heritages represented among group members increase the likelihood that all members will feel their cultural heritage is understood and respected.

Impacting Social Milieus

Another advantage to group work is that it has the potential to impact more than just the people involved in the group (Waldo, 1989; Yalom, 2005). If a number of people from one social setting participate in a group, they may influence enough people who did not participate in the group to cause a positive change in the social setting as a whole. For example, high school students who participated in an alcohol abuse–awareness group might positively influence the attitudes of their friends who are not in the group, resulting in a change in norms about drinking in the high school as a whole. Other examples include establishing supportive relationships in work environments, improving abilities to address conflicts in university residence halls, and improving communication in military units. In each situation, improvements in group participants could lead to improvements in their relationships with persons in the setting who were not in the group, which leads to improvements in the setting as a whole.

Identifying Social Activists

The raised awareness and motivation that result from prevention group participation could result in participants wanting to take social action (Ditrano & Silverstein, 2006; Wolfe & Wekerle, 2003). The capacity to take social action is enhanced when there are a number of people who want to be involved and when they support each other. Prevention groups get a number of people involved and focus them on supporting each other. Examples of prevention-oriented groups resulting in social action include domestic violence–prevention groups, such as the Men's Network Against Domestic Violence (http://www.menagainstdv.org/), consciousness-raising groups (Follingstad, Robinson, & Pugh, 1977), MADD, and groups for homeless adults (Brubaker, Garrett, Rivera & Tate, 2010).

Generating New Members and Leaders

One of the remarkable efficiencies of prevention groups is their potential for self-perpetuation (Waldo, 1989). Members who are benefiting from the group recruit new members. Those who are particularly invested in the group may progress to take leadership roles in perpetuating the group (MacLennan & Dies, 1992). A train-the-trainers model can be used to prepare them for leadership (Kelly, Lesser, Peralez-Dieckmann, & Castilla, 2007; Mack & Uken, 2006; Orfaly et al., 2005; Ramos, May, & Ramos, 2001). In this model, expert leaders offer one or several prevention groups. Before the group ends, the leaders identify members who seem capable of and interested in leading the group. When the first set of groups is complete, the expert leaders offer training to the interested members on group leadership. Those members then go on to lead their own groups, usually while receiving consultation from the original expert leaders. The new leaders then identify members in their groups who would make good future leaders. When their group is complete, they offer the interested members training in leadership, again while consulting with the original experts. They then go on to consult with their former members as they lead their own groups. This process can go on almost indefinitely and rapidly results in prevention groups being widely available (Kenny, Waldo, Warter, & Barton, 2002). These forms of member recruitment and leader development are highly efficient. They also generate large numbers of leaders and consultants who are dedicated to prevention in specific problem areas. These new leaders are drawn from the communities they will serve, so they are sensitive to the community's needs and have credibility with community members. Their initiative and availability within their respective communities may prove to be as important a resource as the groups they offer. Examples include Alcoholics Anonymous (Gladding, 2008) and Systematic Training in Effective Parenting (Dinkmeyer, McKay, & Dinkmeyer, 2007).

How Do Prevention Groups Work?

As indicated, there is ample evidence that prevention groups are effective. This section reviews theory and research that explains why. First, 11 therapeutic factors that have been found to be active in effective groups are described, including how they may contribute to primary, secondary, tertiary, and social action prevention. Second, dynamics that occur naturally in groups (often in a developmental sequence) will be described, focusing on how those dynamics may foster therapeutic factors. Finally, the section closes with a description of group leadership functions and how those functions may employ group dynamics to foster therapeutic factors that promote prevention.

Therapeutic Factors

Beginning in the mid-twentieth century, researchers worked to identify the mechanisms occurring in groups that result in benefits to group members (Gladding, 2008; Lewin, 1948). Perhaps the best-known and best-researched conceptualizations of these mechanisms are the 11 therapeutic factors described by Yalom (1970, 1995). Yalom and his colleagues conducted research on a variety of encounter groups (Lieberman, Yalom, & Miles, 1973). Their findings and extensive subsequent research (Kivlighan & Lilly, 1997; Schwartz & Waldo, 1999; Yalom, 2005) have demonstrated that these factors are active in primary, secondary, tertiary, and social action prevention groups, and can be understood as contributing to those groups' success.

Universality: Participation in a group helps members recognize that they are not the only one struggling with a problem. Knowing that others face similar issues helps reduce feelings of isolation and shame and increases the likelihood that members will deal openly with their issues rather than defensively deny the problems exist. For example, in a secondary prevention guidance group for men who have been arrested for domestic violence, learning that other men have had problems with violence in their relationships allows members to acknowledge their own experience and start working on changing.

Hope: Recognizing that the group is formed to help with a problem, that the leader(s) believes the group is useful, and, perhaps most importantly, that other group members make progress on the problem instills hope in group participants. Hope helps them overcome discouragement and get moving on making changes. For example, in a tertiary prevention counseling group, hearing about the years of sobriety and improved lives of long-term Alcoholics Anonymous members instills hope in newer members that they, too, can change

Catharsis: Groups offer their members a chance to vent feelings in a safe environment, increasing their self-awareness and acceptance, and decreasing the likelihood that they will use inappropriate defense mechanisms to deal with their emotions. For example, in a primary prevention guidance group focused on assertion training for seventh-graders, a participant might express anger about being bullied. Appropriately expressing anger in the group may help keep these feelings from coming out in either aggressive or passive responses in other situations.

Family Reenactment: Group members may experience some of the same dynamics in their relationship to other members or the leader(s) as they did in their family of origin. But in the prevention group, those dynamics can be replayed in a healthier way. For example, a member in a social action prevention task group like MADD may experience concerns about being accepted by the leader of the group that are similar to feelings the member had toward his or her mother. But instead of being distant and judgmental, the social action group leader offers the member acceptance and support. This allows the member to correctively rework some of the feelings from the family of origin. Given the evidence that many problems (like substance abuse and domestic violence) are passed from one generation to the next, family reenactment in groups may be an invaluable therapeutic factor for prevention.

Cohesion: Participating in a prevention group allows members to experience a sense of belonging and acceptance that may not be available to them outside of group. Feeling valued and accepted can raise members' self-esteem. For example, gay students involved in a lesbian/gay/bisexual/transgendered social action task group on a university campus may feel a sense of belonging and closeness with other members that they had not experienced in any other forum on campus.

The feeling of acceptance could lead to greater self-acceptance and confidence.

Altruism: Members in prevention groups have an opportunity to help others, which can elevate their sense of self-worth and competence. For example, in a tertiary prevention guidance group in a state hospital members were able to offer empathic listening to each other during a discussion of serious concerns they had with the hospital staff. Effectively listening to each other took their minds off of their own issues and demonstrated that they had the ability to help others, bringing with it a feeling of empowerment not common for hospitalized patients.

Interpersonal Learning: Participating in a prevention group offers members an opportunity to develop relationships that are a social microcosm of their relations outside of group. Outside of group they may be engaging in behaviors that limit the depth and quality of their relations. One advantage of prevention groups is that they offer an opportunity for members to exchange feedback on how they are affecting each other. If a member in a secondary prevention counseling group in a college counseling center has been alienating other members by being judgmental, the other members are likely to bring this to the first member's attention. Hearing this feedback from other group members could be a critical incident for the first member, resulting in a corrective emotional experience in which he or she recognizes that his or her style of relating is not working. Having had this experience puts the member in a position to begin exploring new ways of relating that will prevent him or her from alienating others.

Information: Prevention groups are an excellent forum for learning new information. This can occur directly from the leaders (like when leaders in a tertiary prevention therapy group with disabled veterans cover the principles of rational-emotive therapy). Perhaps more powerfully, it often occurs between members (like when members in the same veterans' group share information about how to access Veterans Administration benefits).

Modeling: Members in prevention groups learn by using the leaders and other members as models. For example, a member in a social action task group focused on preventing teen pregnancy might learn effective ways of interacting with teens by watching how a more experienced member reaches out to teens when offering a presentation at a high school.

Socializing Techniques: One of the great advantages of prevention groups is that they provide members an opportunity to try new behaviors in a safe environment. For example, members in a primary prevention guidance group learning mindfulness techniques for relieving stress can try those techniques in the accepting environment offered by the group.

Existential Factors: Involvement in prevention groups can help members recognize realistic limits they face, the choices they have, their responsibilities, and that their opportunities to choose are limited. For example, members of a social action task group focused on preventing dating violence are confronted with their inability to stop all violence, that they do have the opportunity to speak out against violence or remain quiet, and that the opportunities to speak out pass if they do not act on them.

These 11 therapeutic factors have been found to be active in a wide variety of prevention groups in an equally wide variety of settings (Yalom, 2005). Theory and some evidence suggest that their presence and effectiveness are the result of leaders' skillful facilitation of group dynamics (Waldo, 1985, 1987b; Waldo, Kerne & Van Horne Kerne, 2007). Group dynamics and leadership will be addressed in the next section.

Group Dynamics

An inherent advantage of prevention groups is the dynamics that are generated by the group situation (Trotzer, 2006). Group dynamics are predictable responses within and between group members that result from interacting in a group (Lewin, 1948). These responses were first described by Bion (1961) as *basic assumptions* that groups make about what they need to do in the group situation. Bion suggested that in addition to the work a group has gathered to accomplish, members act as if they either are experiencing *dependency* on the group leader and/or group rules, are reacting to external or internal threats to the group with a *fight-or-flight* response, or are trying to develop intimate bonds by *pairing* two or more members in the group. Bion's original training was psychoanalytic. This may explain the resemblance his description of basic assumptions in groups has to Freud's description of psychodynamic stages of development (Corey, 2008): Group dependency seems to parallel Freud's oral stage of individual development, fight or flight resembles the anal stage, and pairing resembles the

phallic stage. A group that is focused on its work could be considered in the genital stage of development. The characteristics of the basic assumptions also resemble the psychosocial stages of development described by Erikson (1982). Dependency dynamics are evident in Erikson's description of the crisis of trust vs. mistrust in childhood. Fight-or-flight dynamics are a part of the identity crisis adolescents' face. Pairing dynamics are central to the crisis of intimacy vs. isolation in young adulthood, and a focus on work fits with generativity in adulthood. Given these parallels, it is not surprising that the dynamics of the basic assumptions have been described by Tuckman and Jensen (1977) as occurring in stages in groups.

Tuckman and Jensen (1977) described five stages of group development that incorporate the dynamics of the basic assumptions. The first is the *forming stage*, during which members feel confused and dependent. This could be considered the childhood of the group, when trust and security are critical issues. The second is the *storming stage*, during which members may experience anger and/or anxiety. This could be considered the adolescence of the group, when members are focused on establishing a position and identity within the group. The third is the *norming stage*, during which members may experience warmth and closeness with other members. This could be considered the young adulthood of the group, when establishing bonds and intimacy within the group are critical. The fourth is the *performing stage*, during which members may experience efficacy and responsibility. This could be considered the adulthood of the group, when competence and generativity within the group are important. The fifth is the *adjourning stage*, during which members may experience a combination of dependency, fight or flight, pairing, and concern for continuing the group's work after it has disbanded. This could be considered the elder role of the group, when closure and integrity are central issues.

Group dynamics have the potential to hinder the effectiveness of prevention groups (Conyne, 2004; Corey, 2008; Gazda et al., 2001). Groups that remain dependent or engaged in fight or fight are unlikely to be productive. Conversely, when group dynamics are focused in positive directions, they can make powerful contributions to prevention. Group dynamics bring out emotions, insights, and behaviors in members that they might not experience without the group's stimulation (Yalom, 2005). When guided by competent leaders, group dynamics can be seen as catalytic, helping members recognize and deal with issues they would not address in other circumstances. The stimulation and motivation generated by group dynamics can be especially helpful for prevention, given that the goal of prevention is to address problems before they occur and, thus, before participants are aware of a need to change or are committed to changing. And group dynamics guided by competent leadership contribute to the development of therapeutic factors that have been shown to be related to positive outcomes in groups (Kivlighan & Lilly, 1997; Schwartz & Waldo, 1999; Wheeler, O'Malley, Waldo, Murphey, & Blank, 1992). For example, dependency can contribute to group members' experiencing the therapeutic factor hope because they tend to depend on the group leaders' and other members' expertise. Fight-or-flight dynamics can foster catharsis, helping members get in touch with feelings they may not have known they had. Pairing dynamics help develop cohesion. A focus on the group's work offers opportunities for members to practice socializing techniques. And the dynamics associated with the adjourning stage of groups may help members recognize the existential factors of choice and responsibility.

The process followed by prevention groups may significantly influence which group dynamics are emphasized and which therapeutic factors result (Waldo, 1985; Waldo et al., 2007). Guidance group process is likely to foster dependency dynamics in groups, resulting in opportunities for the therapeutic factors of hope, information, and modeling. Therapy group process may promote fight-or-flight dynamics, increasing the prevalence of universality, catharsis, and family reenactment. Counseling group process is likely to foster pairing dynamics, increasing the likelihood that members will experience cohesion, interpersonal learning, and existential factors. And social action groups focus on work that can foster the therapeutic factors of altruism and socializing techniques. A number of other variables can influence whether group dynamics foster therapeutic factors, including selection of group members, the group setting, and the timing and duration of the group. Because group leaders profoundly impact all of the variables that affect group dynamics (especially group process), it is reasonable to say that competent group leadership is central to successful prevention groups.

Prevention Group Leadership

In the same study that examined therapeutic factors, Lieberman et al. (1973) identified four leadership functions that were associated with successful encounter groups. The leadership functions vary in the extent to which the leader is involved with the tasks and relationships in the group. Flexible use of the functions allows for adjusting leadership style to fit the needs of the group (Hersey & Blanchard, 1973; Schiller, 1995; Verdi & Wheelan, 1992). The leadership functions align with the different group processes (guidance, therapy, counseling, and task) and group dynamics (dependency, fight or flight, pairing, and work) and can be seen as promoting specific therapeutic factors (Waldo, 1985). Each function is described in the following.

Executive: This leadership function includes setting the agenda, controlling interaction, and focusing activities. The leader is highly involved with the group's task and not as involved in relating to group members or in how they are relating to each other. Executive leadership style is likely to be prevalent in guidance groups, fits well with dependency dynamics, and is likely to instill hope and provide information and modeling.

Emotional Stimulation: Emotional stimulation is the function leaders play when motivating, inspiring, and agitating the group. It typically involves presentation of emotion-laden material, self-disclosure, and questioning and confronting group members. Leaders engaged in this leadership style are typically highly involved with both the group's task and relationships in the group. It fits with therapy group process and fight-or-flight group dynamics. Therapeutic factors fostered by emotional stimulation include universality, catharsis, and family reenactment.

Caring: The caring leadership function involves leaders in offering acceptance, understanding, and support to group members. Caring leaders are not as involved with the tasks of the group as they are with relating well to group members and working to help group members relate well to each other. This function fits well with counseling group process and pairing group dynamics. It fosters cohesion, altruism, and interpersonal learning.

Meaning Attribution: Leaders engaged in meaning attribution act like consultants to groups, providing information and insight on an as-needed basis. They are not highly involved with either the tasks or the relationships within the group, instead allowing the group to function more autonomously. Meaning attribution is important for all four group processes. It fits well with groups that are focused on their work. Meaning attribution can foster a number of therapeutic factors. Because it leaves the work of the group to the members and focuses on meaning, it may be particularly likely to foster socializing techniques and existential factors.

While these leadership functions line up well with specific prevention group processes, group dynamics, and therapeutic factors, this alignment does not suggest that leadership functions should be rigidly applied. The work of Lieberman et al. (1973) and Hersey and Blanchard (1973) has suggested that flexible application of leadership functions to meet the needs of the group is most likely to be effective. In fact, Lieberman et al. (1973) found that all four functions (with an emphasis on caring and meaning attribution) were needed for members to show significant gains from group participation. When leaders used excessive amounts of executive function, groups seemed to stall. And when leaders used excessive emotional stimulation, some members showed signs of having been hurt by the experience.

Flexible use of leadership functions allows leaders to promote the therapeutic factors that are most relevant to prevention groups' goals. For example, in a tertiary prevention group focused on helping victims of sexual assault keep that experience from damaging their future intimate relationships, leaders used emotional stimulation to help members vent (catharsis) pent up anger that might be inappropriately expressed in new relationships (Wheeler et al., 1992). In contrast, in a primary prevention group intended to help teachers learn about experiences of cultural oppression by relating to colleagues who have experienced it, leaders used the caring leadership function to promote cohesion and interpersonal learning between members (Arizaga, Bauman, Waldo, & Castellanos, 2005).

Flexible use of leadership functions also allows prevention group leaders to meet groups where they are. For example, if a group shows evidence of fight-or-flight dynamics, the leader can respond with emotional stimulation (increasing the opportunity for catharsis), rather than trying to impose executive-style leadership on unwilling members. Flexible use of leadership functions also allows leaders to help prevention groups develop. For example, if a primary prevention assertion training group is involved with fight-or-flight dynamics for an extended period of time, leaders might begin to use caring function to point out how members have had similar experiences of difficulty expressing themselves, and how

they are supporting each other's self-expression now. This could promote development of pairing dynamics and eventually foster cohesion and altruism. In this way, leadership can be adjusted to take into account group dynamics in an effort to foster therapeutic factors that are both available to group members and relevant to prevention goals.

This section has described the rationale for prevention, categories of prevention and prevention groups, advantages of prevention groups, and theory and research on therapeutic factors, group dynamics, and prevention group leadership that explain why prevention groups work. As indicated previously in this chapter, prevention groups can be categorized by their prevention focus (primary/universal, secondary/targeted, tertiary/indicated, and social action) and their group process (guidance/psychoeducational, counseling/interpersonal process, therapy/personality reconstruction, and task/work). Table 25.1 offers examples of prevention groups that have been described in the literature which fit into each of these categories. The remainder of the chapter describes examples of primary, secondary, tertiary, and social action groups that employ guidance, counseling, therapy, and task processes.

Universal Primary Prevention Groups
The Strong African American Families Program

The Strong African American Families Program (SAAFP) is an example of primary prevention through a group guidance process. Many low-income rural African American youth have a higher than average likelihood of experiencing academic and behavioral problems, including early onset of alcohol abuse and possible aggressive and disruptive behavior patterns (Brody et al., 2004). In order to address the higher potential risk of this population, Brody and his colleagues developed SAAFP, which has a prevention focus involving working with families and students to prevent the onset of problems. These groups are offered to all available African American families before they show any indication of having problems (primary prevention/universal). Brody and his colleagues have conducted a number of studies examining the effectiveness and efficacy of SAAFP with very encouraging results.

The program consists of seven meetings in which the families attend group sessions conducted by facilitators who are very familiar with group process, group dynamics, the content and structure of the program, and the population engaged in

Table 25.1 Examples of prevention groups

Group Focus	Primary Prevention/ Universal	Secondary Prevention/ Targeted	Tertiary Prevention/ Indicated	Social Action/ Advocacy Prevention
Guidance/ psychoeducational	Primary prevention, guidance process: the Strong African American Families Program (Brody et al., 2004)	Secondary prevention, guidance process: the Bully Busters prevention program for parents (Horne et al., 2008)	Tertiary prevention, guidance process: cognitive-behavioral therapy for children with learning disabilities (Shechtman & Pastor, 2005)	Preventive social action, guidance process: Mothers Against Drunk Driving information center (madd.org)
Counseling/ interpersonal	Primary prevention, counseling process: basic encounter groups (Schaffer & Galinsky, 1989)	Secondary prevention, counseling process: domestic violence first offenders groups (Waldo et al., 2007)	Tertiary prevention, counseling process: interpersonal group work for state mental hospital patients (Waldo & Harman, 1999)	Preventive social action, counseling process: Mothers Against Drunk Driving victims chat room (madd.org)
Therapy/ personality reconstruction	Primary prevention, therapy process: psychodrama (Schaffer & Galinsky, 1989)	Secondary prevention, therapy process: Gestalt groups (Schaffer & Galinsky, 1989)	Tertiary prevention, therapy process: incest survivors group (Wheeler et al., 1992)	Preventive social action, therapy process: Mothers Against Drunk Driving victim memorials (madd. org)
Task/ social action	Primary prevention, task process: Mothers Against Drunk Driving advocacy for driving under the influence checkpoints (madd.org)	Secondary prevention, task process: Mothers Against Drunk Driving advocacy for interlock device installation in offenders' vehicles (madd.org)	Tertiary prevention, task process: Mothers Against Drunk Driving advocacy for license revocation of repeat offenders (madd. org)	Preventive social action, task process: Mothers Against Drunk Driving volunteer recruitment (madd.org)

For each specific prevention group focus (primary/universal, secondary/targeted, tertiary/indicated, or social action/advocacy prevention) pursued through specific prevention group process (guidance/psychoeducational, counseling/interpersonal process, therapy/personality reconstruction, or task/work) The goals and process of each prevention group are identified, and an example of each category of prevention group work is offered.

the program. The sessions last approximately 2.5 hours, and include specific educational/prevention emphases, parent sessions and simultaneous child group sessions, followed by sessions with both parents and children, and concluding with a meal. While emphasizing communications skills within families, there is also facilitation of problem solving, conflict resolution, and decision-making processes within the groups to demonstrate effective family engagement. The program targets parental involvement, support, monitoring, and clear communications within the family about alcohol, sex, and racial socialization. With the youth the emphasis is on a planned future orientation, resistance skills, and the development of negative attitudes toward early alcohol use and sexual activity.

Brody and his associates (2004) conducted the program in eight rural counties working with 332

African American families, targeting families with an 11-year-old child. The families involved were predominantly living below the poverty line, 57% of the mothers in the project were married, and 78% had finished high school or a had a GED. The families scored high on child risk factors for behavioral problems.

The project examined differences using a randomized control group design and determined that the engaged families had more positive interactions and communications and lower likelihood of alcohol use and sexual engagement both immediately following the groups and in a 2-year follow-up. Results also showed reduced behavioral problems for the young people who received treatment. Overall, the early prevention program demonstrated excellent outcomes and resulted in considerably less conflict and abuse in the families participating.

Multicultural Communication Skills Groups for Preservice Teachers

Multicultural communication skills groups for preservice teachers offer an example of pursuit of primary prevention goals employing a counseling group process (Adams et al., 2003; Arizaga et al., 2005). There have been consistent calls for teachers to learn to relate well to students from diverse cultural backgrounds and confront prejudice in schools (Ponterotto & Pederson, 1993). The groups were designed to help preservice teachers develop knowledge, attitudes, and skills that will help them relate to their future students and their students' families that come from cultural backgrounds different from their own. The groups also focused on confronting prejudice. Part of the four 2-hour group meetings involved participants practicing respect, honesty, and understanding while discussing with each other their cultural heritages and experiences with oppression. It was believed that participants could enrich their understanding of cultures that are different from their own by hearing about those cultures directly from other group members who were raised within them. It was also believed they could learn valuable lessons about oppression and confronting prejudice by relating to people who had experienced it. The group focused on helping participants enhance their ability to communicate about culture and oppression by talking candidly with other members about these issues within the safe and focused environment of the group.

Two studies examined the impact the groups had on participants' ability to communicate about culture and oppression (Adams et al., 2003; Arizaga et al., 2005). In both studies participants were randomly assigned to either serve as an experimental subject by immediately joining a group or serve as a control subject by being placed on a wait list for later participation in the group. Both the experimental and wait list control group subjects' use of communication skills when addressing culture and oppression were assessed prior to and after the experimental subjects participated in the group. Subjects' demonstrated skills at expressing themselves and showing understanding to others in both non-conflict and conflict situations were assessed. Results from both studies indicated that participants showed significant improvement in their ability to communicate about culture and oppression in comparison to the wait list control group. These results suggest that the group participants were better prepared to establish positive relationships with students from

other cultures and prevent oppression when they take positions as teachers in public schools.

Targeted Secondary Prevention Groups
Bully Busters Prevention Program for Parents

Bullying and school aggression are major problems for most schools, and numerous programs have been developed to attempt to reduce the problem (Orpinas & Horne, 2006). The Bully Busters Program was specifically developed to address preventive approaches to reducing bullying in the elementary (Horne, Bartolomucci, & Newman, 2003) and middle (Newman, Horne, & Bartolomucci, 2000) school settings. The programs involve a counselor, psychologist, administrator, or teacher who conducts groups that specifically focus on developing an awareness and understanding of bullying, as well as the impact of the problem, and explicit methods for preventing the problem or deescalating the situation if it is already in progress. The program includes methods for creating class cohesion, better student-to-student cooperation and collaboration, and processes for setting the classroom up for success rather than conflict. The program has been evaluated and found to result in increased efficacy of teachers knowing how to engage in prevention and early intervention procedures, having a greater knowledge and awareness of bullying, and having fewer office referrals and reduced bullying (Howard, Horne, & Jolliff, 2001; Orpinas, Horne, & Staniszewski, 2003) as well as an overall improved school climate.

To add a stronger prevention and early intervention element to the Bully Busters Program, a secondary prevention family group guidance process was developed (Horne, Stoddard, & Bell, 2008). The family program is conducted in a group format with an emphasis on early identification and recognition of bullying issues and promotes a positive family model for creating an environment that is respectful and bully-free. The program consists of four 2-hour sessions facilitated by skilled group leaders. Each group is composed of up to eight parents who have expressed interest in learning more about bullying prevention or have been referred by schools because their child is currently involved in a bully-victim cycle. The program focuses on supportive parental communication patterns, self- and other care, stress management, problem solving, and coping skills. The sessions identify concerns parents have, dispel myths about bullying, and teach parents how to use a family council. The types of bullying and victimization are reviewed, effective methods for avoiding the development of the problem or steps to take to deescalate aggressive situations are practiced, and take-home materials are provided along with activities and exercises to complete.

The elementary and middle school programs have been evaluated and found to result in a reduction of bullying by students and increased efficacy and knowledge on the part of teachers. The parenting program has undergone initial evaluation through pilot projects, and has resulted in increased parenting efficacy and knowledge, and improved family communications and engagement. Further, there was a reported improvement in child skills for managing bullying situations and for engaging in preventive steps to avoid conflict.

Groups for Men Arrested for Domestic Violence

Domestic violence is a pervasive and devastating phenomenon in American society (Rennison & Rand, 2003; Straus, 1999). One focus of efforts to prevent domestic violence has been the development of groups which are targeted for first-time domestic violence offenders. These groups are seen as a step forward in that they place responsibility for addressing domestic violence on the people who have been perpetrating it (Waldo, 1987a). However, outcome studies suggest that domestic violence–treatment groups are not universally effective. In fact, Gondolf (2001) found high recidivism rates (41% at 30 months) for men who have participated in domestic violence–prevention groups. While many of these groups employ a guidance process (Pence & Paymar, 1993), there is evidence that men who have been arrested for domestic violence can benefit from therapeutic factors that are associated with interactive counseling group processes, including cohesion, interpersonal learning, and altruism (Schwartz & Waldo, 1999). It is possible that strict adherence to guidance process in domestic violence groups has been limiting the therapeutic factors in these groups and, as a result, limiting their effectiveness (Schwartz & Waldo, 1999).

A study was conducted to see if including counseling group process in domestic violence–prevention groups increased the prevalence of therapeutic factors of cohesion and interpersonal learning for group members (Waldo et al., 2007). Counseling-oriented group sessions (including a focus on intermember feedback) were randomly substituted for the typical guidance-oriented sessions in ongoing domestic violence–prevention groups. Analysis of the therapeutic factors members of these groups experienced suggested that increased levels of cohesion and interpersonal learning were available during the counseling-oriented sessions. The prevalence of these therapeutic factors may help to explain the lower recidivism rates that have been previously associated with some more counseling- (as opposed to strictly guidance-) oriented domestic violence–prevention groups (Waldo, 1988, 1986).

Indicated Tertiary Prevention Groups
Relationship-Enhancement Groups with State Hospital Patients

Groups that focused on improving state hospital patients' interpersonal skills by helping them relate well with each other and the hospital staff offer examples of tertiary prevention through a group-counseling process (Waldo & Harman, 1999). The patients suffered from severe and persistent mental illnesses, including schizophrenia, depression, and personality disorder. The groups were not designed to remediate these disorders but instead to help limit the negative impact symptoms of these disorders had on patients' relationships (indicated tertiary prevention). The patients learned positive communication skills, and then employed these skills to talk with each other in group about personal problems they were experiencing. In addition to learning how to express themselves, patients were encouraged to show understanding when listening to each other. The patients reported positive experiences in the groups and improvements in their communication. The staff noted improvements in patients' communications and relationships, and reductions in symptoms. Reductions in symptoms included fewer anger outbursts and self-mutilations, and less manipulation and isolation.

Incest Survivors Group

Incest is a particularly traumatic form of sexual abuse that poses mental health risks for victims, particularly if they do not receive treatment as children (Browne & Finkelhor, 1988). Because adult survivors of abuse may experiences a sense of deviance that can result in feelings of shame and isolation, group therapy may be a particularly appropriate prevention strategy (Cole & Barney, 1987). Group work cannot erase the fact that incest survivors have been abused, but it does have the potential to limit the negative effects of that abuse (tertiary prevention). A study involving seven women in an incest survivors group offers some insight into how groups can help prevent negative effects from symptoms caused by childhood trauma (Wheeler et al., 1992). The group employed a therapeutic process model (Yalom, 1995) which allowed the women to share their experience of incest and discuss the impact it had on their lives. The therapeutic factors the women experienced while interacting in the group were assessed. The most prominent therapeutic factor was catharsis. Women felt the group allowed them to express difficult and painful emotions, emotions that potentially could interfere with their adjustment and relationships if not expressed. The women also reported experiencing the existential therapeutic factor, suggesting that participating in the group helped them find meaning in their trauma.

Social Action Advocacy Groups

Social action advocacy groups include organizations like MADD, the National Alliance on Mental Illness, and the American Association for Retired People. These groups, and many like them, employ guidance, counseling, therapy and task activities to advocate for changes in society that will prevent problems that are priorities for them. For example, the MADD Web site (http://madd.org/) provides a variety of preventive services. Employing a guidance process, the site offers information on the prevalence of drunk driving and safe driving techniques, information that can be used in advocacy efforts. The same Web site offers access to chat sessions that employ a counseling process to allow victims of drunken driving accidents to share their experience with other victims and support each other's involvement in advocacy. And the site offers the opportunity for people who have lost someone in a drunken driving accident to post a tribute to that person, an activity which is likely both to be therapeutic for their grieving process and to offer testimony for the need for social action to prevent drunk driving. And, of course, the site offers ample opportunities and direction for joining others to engage in volunteer social action, including lobbying, supporting victims, educating youth, monitoring courts, and joining a speakers' bureau.

Summary and Future Directions

This chapter has provided an overview of prevention groups, including different perspectives on prevention, classifications of prevention groups, advantages of using groups for prevention, and theory and research explaining how prevention groups work (especially therapeutic factors that occur in groups).

Dynamics that develop in groups were described, and how group leaders employ group dynamics to foster therapeutic factors was addressed. Current examples of primary, secondary, tertiary, and social action prevention groups were provided.

The suggested future directions for prevention groups are as numerous as the dreams of the many professionals who are invested in group work and prevention. At least four suggestions stand out. First, there is extraordinary potential for expansion of prevention impact by having prevention group members recruit new members, become prevention group leaders, and serve as change agents and resources within their social networks. This expansion of prevention impact is likely to be particularly beneficial to previously underserved populations (e.g., children, minority groups, the poor). Second, this potential expansion of group prevention efforts offers compelling motivation to advance understanding of the relationships between group dynamics, group leadership, and therapeutic factors. Increased understanding of the relationship among these variables can increase the efficiency and effectiveness of prevention groups and of training future group leaders. Third, the development of electronic social networks offers a new and very exciting potential for expanding preventive group work. The ability for people to "meet" through the Internet can overcome impediments to prevention services such as living in remote rural areas, being homebound, and/or having concerns that affect relatively few people. The ability to have asynchronous meetings allows people who face time constraints to participate. And the potential to maintain relative anonymity while participating may encourage involvement on the part of people whose concerns about stigma might dissuade them from participating in a face-to-face group in their community. Fourth, it is essential that evaluative research be done on the outcome of prevention groups to assess and demonstrate their efficacy. To use the analogy presented at the beginning of this chapter, if lifeguards are going to leave their posts to build fences and provide swimming lessons, solid evidence that these activities are effective needs to be provided.

References

Adams, E., Waldo, M., Steiner, R., Mayfield, R., Ackerlind, S., & Castellanos, L. (2003). Creating peace by confronting prejudice: Examining the effects of a multicultural communication skills group intervention. *International Journal for the Advancement of Counseling, 25,* 281–291.

American Psychiatric Association. (2000). *Diagnostic and statistical manual of mental disorders* (4th ed., text rev.). Washington, DC: Author.

Applebaum, P. S. (2003). Presidential address: Re-envisioning a mental health system for the United States. *American Journal of Psychiatry, 160,* 1758–1762.

Arizaga, M., Bauman, S., Waldo, M., & Castellanos, L. (2005). Multicultural sensitivity and interpersonal skill training for pre-service teachers. *Journal of Humanistic Counseling, Education, and Development, 44,* 198–208.

Association for Specialists in Group Work. (1998). ASGW best practice guidelines. *Journal for Specialists in Group Work, 23,* 237–244.

Bednar, R. L., & Kaul, T. J. (1994). Experiential group research: Can the cannon fire? In S. L. Garfield & A. E. Bergin (Eds.), *Handbook of psychotherapy and behavior change* (4th ed., pp. 631–663). New York: John Wiley & Sons.

Bion, W. (1961). *Experiences in groups.* New York: Basic Books.

Bowen, M. (1979). *Family therapy in clinical practice.* New York: Jason Aronson.

Brody, G. H., Murry, V. M., Gerrard, M., Gibbons, F. X., Molgaard, V., McNair, L., et al. (2004). The Strong African American Families program: Translating research into prevention programming. *Child Development, 75*(3), 900–917.

Browne, A., & Finkelhor, D. (1988). Impact of child sexual abuse: A review of the research. In S. Chess, A. Thomas, M. Hertzig, S. Chess, A. Thomas, M. Hertzig (Eds.), *Annual progress in child psychiatry and child development, 1987* (pp. 555–584). Philadelphia, PA US: Brunner/Mazel.

Brubaker, M. D., Garrett, M. T., Rivera, E. T., & Tate, K. A. (2010). Justice making in groups for homeless adults: The emancipator communitarian way. *Journal for Specialists in Group Work, 35,* 124–133.

Burlingame, G. M., Fuhriman, A., & Mosier, J. (2003). The differential effectiveness of group psychotherapy: A meta-analytic perspective. *Group Dynamics, 7,* 3–12.

Burlingame, G. M., MacKenzie, D., & Strauss, B. (2004). Small group treatment: Evidence for effectiveness and mechanisms of change. In S. L. Garfield & A. E. Bergin (Eds.), *Handbook of psychotherapy and behavior change* (5th ed., pp. 647–696). New York: John Wiley & Sons.

Centers for Disease Control and Prevention. (2010). *Injury prevention and control: Motor vehicle safety.* Retrieved from http://www.cdc.gov/MotorVehicleSafety/Impaired_Driving/impaired-drv_factsheet.html

Cole, C. H., & Barney, E. E. (1987). Safeguards and the therapeutic window: A group treatment strategy for adult incest survivors. *American Journal of Orthopsychiatry, 57,* 601–609.

Conyne, R. K. (2004). *Preventive counseling.* New York: Routledge.

Conyne, R. K., & Harpine, E. C. (in press). Prevention groups: The shape of things to come. *Group Dynamics.*

Corey, G. (2008). *Theory and practice of group counseling* (7th ed.). Pacific Grove, CA: Brooks/Cole.

Dinkmeyer, D., McKay, G. D., & Dinkmeyer, D. (2007). *The parent's handbook: Systematic training for effective parenting.* Bowling Green, KY: Step Publishers.

Ditrano, C. J., & Silverstein, L. B. (2006). Listening to parents' voices: Participatory action research in the schools. *Professional Psychology: Research and Practice, 37*(4), 359–366.

Erikson, E. H. (1982). *The life cycle completed: A review.* New York: W.W. Norton.

Follingstad, D. R., Robinson, E. A., & Pugh, M. (1977). Effects of consciousness-raising groups on measures of feminism, self-esteem, and social desirability. *Journal of Counseling Psychology, 24*(3), 223–230.

Forsyth, D. R. (2006). *Group dynamics.* Belmont, CA: Wadsworth.

Frank, R., Goldman, H., & McGuire, T. (2009). Trends in mental health cost growth: An expanded role for management? *Health Affairs, 28*(3), 649–659.

Gazda, G. M., Ginter, J., & Horne, A. M. (2001). *Group counseling and group psychotherapy: Theory and application.* Boston: Allyn & Bacon.

Gladding, S. T. (2008). *Group work: A counseling specialty* (5th ed.). Upper Saddle River, NJ: Prentice Hall.

Gondolf, E. W., & Jones, A. (2001). The program effect of batterer programs in three cities. *Violence and Victims, 16,* 693–704.

Hage, S. M., Romano, J., Conyne, R., Kenny, M., Mathews, C., Schwartz, J. P., et al. (2007). Guidelines on prevention practice, research, training, and social advocacy for psychologists. *Counseling Psychologist, 35,* 493–536.

Hersey, P., & Blanchard, K. H. (1973). The importance of communication patterns in implementing change strategies. *Journal of Development in Education, 6*(4), 66–75.

Horne, A., Bartolomucci, C., & Newman, D. (2003). *Bully busters: Bullies, victims and bystanders A manual for elementary school teachers.* Champaign, IL: Research Press.

Horne, A., Stoddard, J., & Bell, C. (2008). *A parent's guide to understanding and responding to bullying: The bully busters approach.* Champaign, IL: Research Press.

Howard, N., Horne, A., & Jolliff, D. (2001). Self-efficacy in a new training model for the prevention of bullying in schools. *Journal of Emotional Abuse, 2,* 181–191.

Kelley, P. J., Lesser, J., Peralez-Dieckmann, E., & Castilla, M. (2007). Community-based violence awareness. *Issues in Mental Health, 28,* 241–253.

Kenny, M. E., Horne, A. M., Orpinas, P., & Reese, L. E. (2009). *Realizing social justice: The challenge of preventive interventions.* Washington, DC: American Psychological Association.

Kenny, M., Waldo, M., Warter, E., & Barton, C. (2002). Theory, science, and practice for enhancing the lives of children and youth. *Counseling Psychologist, 30,* 726–748.

Kessler, M., & Albee, G. W. (1975). Primary prevention. *Annual Review of Psychology, 26,* 557–591.

Kivlighan, D. M., & Lilly, R. L. (1997). Developmental changes in group climate as they relate to therapeutic gain. *Group Dynamics: Theory, Research, and Practice, 1,* 208–221.

LaBrie, J. W., Thompson, A. D., Huchting, K., Lac, A., & Buckley, K. (2007). A group motivational interviewing intervention reduces drinking and alcohol-related negative consequences in adjudicated college women. *Addictive Behaviors, 32,* 2549–2562.

Levine, M. (1998). Prevention and community. *American Journal of Community Psychology, 26*(2), 189–206.

Lewin, K. (1948). *Resolving social conflicts.* New York: Harper and Brothers.

Lieberman, M. A., Yalom, I. D., & Miles, M. B. (1973). *Encounter groups: First facts.* New York: Basic Books.

Lukens, E. P., Thorning, H., & Lohrer, S. (2004). Sibling perspectives on severe mental illness: Reflections on self and family. *American Journal of Orthopsychiatry, 74*(4), 489–501.

Mack, M., & Uken, R. (2006). People improving the community's health: Community health workers as agents of change. *Journal of Health Care for the Poor and Underserved, 17*(1), 16–25.

MacLennan, B. W., & Dies, K. R. (1992). *Group counseling and psychotherapy with adolescents* (2nd ed.). New York: Columbia University Press.

Marsh, D. T., & Johnson, D. L. (1997). *The* family experience of mental illness: Implications for intervention. *Professional Psychology: Research and Practice, 28*(3), 229–237.

McRoberts, C., Burlingame, G., & Hoag, M. (1998). Comparative efficacy of individual and group psychotherapy: A meta-analytic perspective. *Group Dynamics: Theory, Research and Practice, 2*, 101–117.

National Alliance on Mental Illness. (2002). *NAMI policymaker's fact sheet on mental illness. No. 01–02.* Retrieved from http://www.naminh.org/action-facts-myths.php

National Institute of Mental Health. (2010a). *Statistics.* Retrieved from http://www.nimh.nih.gov/health/topics/statistics/index.shtml

National Institute of Mental Health. (2010b). *National survey tracks rates of common mental disorders among American youth.* Retrieved from http://www.nimh.nih.gov/science-news/2009/national-survey-tracks-rates-of-common-mental-disorders-a-mong-american-youth.shtml

Newman, D., Horne, A., & Bartolomucci, C. (2000). *Bully busters: Bullies, victims and bystanders—A manual to increase teacher's awareness, knowledge, and skills.* Champaign, IL: Research Press.

Orfaly, R. A., Frances, J. C., Campbell, P., Whittemore, B., Joly, B., & Koh, H. (2005). Train-the-trainer as an educational model in public health preparedness. *Journal of Public Health Management and Practice, 11*(6), 123–127.

Orpinas, P., & Horne, A. (2006). *Bullying prevention: Creating a positive school climate and developing social competence.* Washington, DC: American Psychological Association.

Orpinas, P., Horne, A. M., & Staniszewski, D. (2003). School bullying: Changing the problem by changing the school. *School Psychology Review, 32*(3), 431–444.

Pence, E., & Paymar, M. (1993). *Education groups for men who batter: The Duluth model.* New York, NY US: Springer Publishing Co.

Piot, P., Debrework, Z., & Türmen, T. (2002). HIV/AIDS prevention and treatment. *Lancet, 360*, 86.

Ponterotto, J. G., & Pederson, P. B. (1993). *Preventing prejudice: A guide for counselors and educators.* New York: Sage.

Ramos, I., May, M., & Ramos, K. (2001). Environmental health training of promotoras in colonias along the Texas–Mexico border. *American Journal of Public Health, 91*(4), 568–570.

Rennison, C., & Rand, M. R. (2003). Nonlethal Intimate Partner Violence Against Women: A Comparison of Three Age Cohorts. *Violence Against Women, 9*, 1417–1428.

Rogers, E. (2002). Diffusion of preventive innovations. *Addictive Behaviors, 27*(6), 989–993.

Romano, J., & Hage, S. (2000). Prevention and counseling psychology. *Counseling Psychologist, 28*(6), 733–763.

Schaffer, J., & Galinsky, D. M. (1989). *Models of group therapy and sensitivity training* (2nd ed.). Englewood Cliffs, NJ: Prentice Hall.

Schiller, L. (1995). Stages of development in women's groups: A relational model. In R. Kurland & R. Salmon (Eds.), *Group work practice in a troubled society* (pp. 117–138). New York: Haworth Press.

Schwartz, J. P., & Hage, S. M. (2008). Prevention ethics. In M. Kenny, A. Horne, R. Reese, & P. Orpinas (Eds.), *Realizing social justice: The challenge of preventive interventions.* Washington, DC: American Psychological Association.

Schwartz, J. P., & Waldo, M. (1999). Therapeutic factors in Duluth model spouse abuser group treatment. *Journal for Specialists in Group Work, 24*, 197–207.

Shechtman, Z., & Pastor, R. (2005). Cognitive-behavioral and humanistic group treatment for children with learning disabilities: A comparison of outcomes and process. *Journal of Counseling Psychology, 52*, 322–336.

Straus, M. A. (1999). The controversy over domestic violence by women: A methological, theoretical, and sociology of science analysis. In X. B. Arriaga, S. Oskamp, X. B. Arriaga, S. Oskamp (Eds.), *Violence in intimate relationships* (pp. 17–44). Thousand Oaks, CA US: Sage Publications, Inc.

Trotzer, J. P. (2006). *The counselor and the group: Integrating theory, training, and practice.* New York: Routledge.

Tuckman, B. W., & Jensen, M. A. (1977). Stages of small-group development revisited. *Group and Organization Studies, 2*(4), 419–427.

US Department of Health and Human Services. (2001). *Mental health: Culture, race, and ethnicity—A supplement to mental health. A report of the surgeon general.* Rockville, MD: Author.

Verdi, A. F., & Wheelan, S. A. (1992). Developmental patterns in same-sex and mixed-sex groups. *Small Group Research, 23*, 356–378.

Waldo, M. (1985). A curative factor framework for conceptualizing group counseling. *Journal of Counseling and Development, 64*(1), 52–58.

Waldo, M. (1986). Group counseling for military personnel who battered their wives. *Journal for Specialists in Group Work, 11*(3), 132–138.

Waldo, M. (1987a). Also victims: Understanding and treating men arrested for spouse abuse. *Journal of Counseling and Development, 65*, 385–388.

Waldo, M. (1987b). Counseling groups. In D. Hershenson & P. Power (Eds.), *Mental health counseling: Theory and practice* (pp. 197–214). New York: Pergamon.

Waldo, M. (1988). Relationship enhancement counseling groups for wife abusers. *Journal of Mental Health Counseling, 10*(1), 37–45.

Waldo, M. (1989). Primary prevention in university residence halls: Paraprofessional led relationship enhancement groups for college roommates. *Journal of Counseling and Development, 67*, 465–471.

Waldo, M., & Bauman, S. (1998). Regrouping the categories of group work: A goals and process (GAP) matrix. *Journal for Specialists in Group Work, 23*, 164–176.

Waldo, M., & Harman, M. J. (1999). Relationship enhancement groups with state hospital patients and staff. *Journal for Specialists in Group Work, 24*, 27–36.

Waldo, M., Kerne, P., & Van Horne Kerne, V. (2007). Therapeutic factors in guidance/psychoeducational versus counseling/interpersonal problem solving sessions in domestic violence intervention groups. *Journal for Specialists in Group Work, 32*, 346–361.

Waldo, M., & Schwartz, J. P. (2008). Prevention perspective. *Prevention in Counseling Psychology: Theory, Research, Practice and Training, 2*, 3–5.

Weisz, J. R., Weiss, B., Alicke, M. D., & Kloz, M. L. (1987). Effectiveness of psychotherapy with children and adolescents: A meta-analysis for clinicians. *Journal of Consulting and Clinical Psychology, 55*(4), 542–549.

Wheeler, I., O'Malley, K., Waldo, M., Murphey, J., & Blank, C. (1992). Participants' perceptions of therapeutic factors in groups for incest survivors. *Journal for Specialists in Group Work, 17*, 89–95.

Wolfe, D. A., & Wekerle, C. (2003). Dating violence prevention with at-risk youth: A controlled outcome evaluation. *Journal of Consulting and Clinical Psychology, 71*(2), 279–291.

World Health Organization. (2007). *Mental health: Strengthening mental health.* Retrieved from http://www.who.int/mediacentre/factsheets/fs220/en/index.html

Yalom, I. D. (1970). *The theory and practice of group psychotherapy.* New York: Basic Books.

Yalom, I. D. (1995). *The theory and practice of group psychotherapy* (4th ed.). New York: Basic Books.

Yalom, I. D., & Leszcz, M. (Col). (2005). *The theory and practice of group psychotherapy* (5th ed.). New York, NY US: Basic Books.

Yalom, I. D. (with Leszcz, M.) (2005). *The theory and practice of group psychotherapy* (5th ed.). New York: Basic Books.

International Group Counseling

J. Jeffries McWhirter, Paula T. McWhirter, Benedict T. McWhirter, *and* Ellen Hawley McWhirter

Abstract

In this chapter we consider the field of group counseling from an international perspective. Using the broad definition of group counseling provided by Conyne (see Chapter 1), we consider small group counseling and therapy as well as other experiences that use group methods and components. An extensive literature research provides a global perspective of group counseling reviewed on a continent-by-continent basis. Five group counseling applications focusing on international indigenous groups are described in some detail. Finally, several suggestions for future direct and further exploration are presented.

Keywords: International, global, group counseling, group work, indigenous groups.

Introduction

Professor Conyne, in his opening chapter of this book, provides ample evidence of the increasing importance of group counseling nationally. The ever-expanding influence of the group therapy modality across treatment settings, client needs, and practitioner orientations is evident not only within the United States but globally as well. Prominent group journals, mentioned as representative of the robustness of group work in the United States, regularly include articles involving international populations, some (e.g., *International Journal of Group Psychotherapy* and *International Journal of Action Methods*) relying heavily on international group-work articles. Recent publications in the field of social work reflect an interdisciplinary and international flavor. For example, the *Encyclopedia of Social Work with Groups* (Gitterman & Salmon, 2008), associated with the Association for the Advancement of Social Work with Groups, includes authors from the United States, Canada, England, Spain, Japan, and Australia. It provides a truly international and interdisciplinary perspective of group work, as do the recently published chapter "Social Group Work

in a Global Context" (Mayadas, Smith, & Elliott, 2004) and article "Social Group Work: International and Global Perspectives" (Toseland & McClive-Reed, 2009). The medical professions—psychiatry, nursing, psychiatric aides—are heavily involved in group work. This is particularly evident within the international medical community, likely due to the broad acceptance and early professionalism of medicine worldwide. In this chapter, we look at group counseling as a unique modality across practitioners, disciplines, and theoretical perspectives.

Another indication of the importance of group work internationally is the number of training programs established overseas. The breadth of theoretical schools of therapy can be found in other countries, and many emphasize a group orientation. For example, Gestalt Education Network International operates out of Frankfurt, Germany, and has provided Gestalt groups throughout Europe and the Middle East; Souldrama, although it originated in the United States, has facilitated recent group workshops in Mexico, Portugal, Greece, England, India, Brazil, Holland, Italy, and Scotland (Miller, 2007). For years, the Tavistock Institute has conducted group training promoting the Tavistock model of group intervention. Proponents of person-centered, cognitive-behavioral, reality, rational-emotive, and other theory-based approaches have provided training using groups as one of the intervention approaches in a variety of settings internationally.

In this chapter, we explore group work in countries other than Canada and the United States. As mentioned elsewhere in this book (see Chapter 3), the Association for Specialists in Group Work (ASGW, 2000) defined four broad categories of group intervention: task, psychoeducational, counseling, and therapy. Although not without controversy (Waldo & Bauman, 1998), these categories provide a reasonably comprehensive framework for the study of groups in the United States. An international perspective of group work, however, requires broader parameters and consideration of a greater variety of group categories than this definition initially yields. We, therefore, decided to include interdisciplinary counseling and "counseling-like" groups in our discussion of group activities across cultures internationally. Thus, we include psychotherapy, psychoeducational, mutual support, and group applications that cut across subtle distinctions between remediation, development, and prevention. This was especially important for indigenous group applications because this broader definition of group counseling allows us to consider indigenous group models developed independently of scientifically based Western ideology.

A comprehensive view of the current state of group work internationally involved a thorough search of the American Psychological Association's PsycINFO using the key words "group counseling" and "group psychotherapy." Besides "international" and "global," we entered five of the seven continents, omitting North America and Antarctica. This resulted in a number of research articles, books, and book chapters related to international (and global) group counseling. We also entered the names of larger countries in each continental region and a reasonable number of smaller ones, providing the basis for our review.

The database for international groups has very real limitations. Unfortunately, descriptions of what was actually done in many of the group sessions were incomplete and ambiguous. A more serious limitation in our review is that many articles were published in languages other than English. Sometimes an English-language abstract was included; sometimes

it was not. A related issue and perhaps even more critical than the multiple-language limitation is the fact that many journals published in other countries are not included in US research databases. For example, we know of several journals published in Turkey and Chile written in Turkish and Spanish that are unavailable in the United States. Consequently, we suspect that group programs developed, facilitated, and promoted within specific countries may not surface in a standard literature search. To accommodate this, we contacted a number of professionals intimately involved in group work in other countries and include their invaluable observations and perspective. Finally, we searched specifically for culturally grounded group counseling approaches that originated within individual countries, based on indigenous teachings, practices and beliefs; we provide a description of five such programs.

Group Counseling: A Global Review

In this section we provide a sampling of various group counseling applications around the world, excluding the United States, Canada, and Antarctica.

Africa

Popular media has made much of the HIV/AIDS pandemic that has impacted many of the countries in Africa. A review of the group research literature reflects the reality of this disease. Expert observations by group-oriented professionals support this. Chancellor Professor Rex Stockton from Indiana University has established a nonprofit organization called International Counseling, Advocacy, Research, and Education (I-CARE) to deal with the impact of this disease in Botswana. His team collaborates with the Institute for Development Management, an educational entity that is involved in a three-country cooperative with branches in Botswana, Lesotho, and Swaziland. Currently, I-CARE is engaged countrywide in Botswana with the anticipation that it will expand into Lesotho and Swaziland at a later date. A more complete discussion of this project can be found in Chapter 13 in this handbook. Because of Stockton's long affiliation with group counseling issues, many of the interventions developed through I-CARE will include a group orientation. Dr. Amy Nitza, a counselor-educator/counseling psychologist and the school counseling program coordinator at the University of Indiana–Purdue at Fort Wayne, has recently completed a Fulbright Senior Scholar award at the University of Botswana (A. Nitza, personal communication, September 16, 2009). During her Fulbright year, Nitza taught group counseling along with other courses at the university. She also provided a field-based group experience to her university students by participating with several of them in a psychoeducational group in the community. A published summary of her work is forthcoming. She and her students used an empowerment model focusing on HIV prevention with young village women and girls.

Pending funding, I-CARE has great potential for developing group counseling in Africa. In addition, it provides an excellent model for other educators, researchers, and practitioners to use in establishing similar frameworks in other countries.

Most of the group research dealing with the AIDS issue has a prevention focus. For example, in Nigeria researchers (Ezeokana, Nnedum, Nnamdi, & Madu, 2008) developed a group-based behavioral intervention to reduce the risk of contracting and spreading sexually transmitted illness and HIV/AIDS. Participants demonstrating increased knowledge of the disease, including personal risk of contracting it, concurrently reported increased self-efficacy beliefs and refusal of risk-taking behaviors and were significantly more likely to use condoms.

In rural South Africa, also focusing on young female participants, a combined group training intervention on HIV risk behavior and microfinance showed great promise. The researchers (Pronyk et al., 2008) concluded that interventions addressing the social and economic vulnerability of women may contribute to reductions in HIV risk behavior.

Several group interventions in Africa focus on prevention efforts by studying interventions with educators. In South Africa, Theron (2008) developed and evaluated a group intervention program to empower "resilient educators" affected by HIV/AIDS. The intervention resulted in increased community mindedness and self-empowerment, with participants believing themselves capable of coping with the pandemic. In Malawi (Norr, Norr, Kaponda, Mbweza, & Kachingwe, 2007), primary school teachers in preparation participated in a peer group intervention for HIV prevention. They reported positive changes in their HIV-prevention attitudes, knowledge, self-efficacy, intention to use condoms, and other behaviors.

Two additional African group counseling studies not related to AIDS were identified, one dealing with cancer patients and the other with military personnel. The researchers (Venter, Venter, Botha, & Strydom 2008) analyzed the content of group counseling sessions with ill cancer patients and identified 12 prevalent themes: support, medical experiences, religiosity, humor, life and death perspectives, emotional experiences, physical symptoms, cancer knowledge, finances, concern for others, loss, and desire for survival. Many cancer patients developed alternative life perspectives as a result of group participation, which served as moderating factors to increase personal growth. In South Africa, Mogapi (2004) studied a psychosocial intervention for ex-combatants that included a 2-hour weekly support group intervention and a 2-hour weekly psychoeducational group. Interestingly, although many ex-combatants experienced posttraumatic stress disorder symptomatology secondary to war exposure, particularly intrusive reexperiencing of traumatic events, most of the group participants reported lack of psychological interventions offered to them and their families as their primary source of concern and suffering.

Australia

It seems appropriate that the country which gave the world the first distance-education program in the form of the Australian School of the Air is also a leader in using the Internet to provide distant small group counseling. Gerrits, van der Zanden, Visscher, & Conijn (2007) report on using a closed chat room for depressed adolescents. Providing a cognitive-behavioral group based on Lewinsohn's Coping with Depression program, the participating adolescents reduced their depressive complaints.

In another distance-education group counseling program, researchers (Heinicke, Paxton, McLean, & Wertheim, 2007) evaluated a program designed to improve body image and eating problems in adolescent girls. Six 90-minute, small group, synchronous, online sessions were facilitated by a counselor. Significant improvements in disordered eating, body dissatisfaction, and depression were reported post group and at follow-up. Internet-delivery groups, besides reducing geographic access, offer a useful approach to improve eating problems and body image.

Gollings and Paxton (2006) developed a group counseling intervention delivered face-to-face or synchronously over the Internet, and women were randomly assigned to one or the other. Disordered eating, body dissatisfaction, and psychological variables were assessed at baseline, post group, and 2 months later. For both groups significant improvements were maintained at follow-up with no significant differences between delivery modes, suggesting that the Internet has potential to overcome geographical distance.

Cobham (2003) developed a brief, six-session, cognitive-behavioral group counseling intervention for anxiety-disordered children. The results indicated that this child-focused intervention demonstrated meaningful treatment-related gains that were maintained over the follow-up.

Another group study (Bailey, Baker, Webster, & Lewin, 2004) implemented a four-session brief motivational interviewing and cognitive-behavioral alcohol intervention with "at-risk" adolescents. According to the results, participants demonstrated increased readiness to reduce alcohol use and decreased frequency of drinking at post treatment and at follow-up.

Smith and Kelly (2008) developed a 12-week, multimodal, cognitive-behavioral group intervention on child abuse and included the nonoffending parent or caregiver. They obtained clinically meaningful reductions in post abuse problems. The usual high attrition problem with this population did not occur as there were no dropouts and the program had excellent face validity with participants.

Paterson, Luntz, Perlesz, and Cotton (2002) provided a group for mothers whose adolescent children were considered to be violent and abusive. The intervention focused on assisting the mothers to more fully understand and more effectively address their adolescents' behaviors. Results revealed significantly less violence in the home and significantly less personal anxiety and fatigue, as reported by mothers, post intervention. Mothers further reported a belief that they were not alone and that someone understood their problems. They also developed more effective strategies in dealing deal with their children.

A cognitive-behavioral psychoeducational group was developed (Austin et al., 2008) for pregnant women with prenatal mild to moderate depression and compared to a control condition. Both the group and the control interventions were beneficial, likely a function of the brevity of the interventions, low baseline symptoms, and the potential effectiveness of the control.

Bradley, Baker, and Lewin (2007) investigated whether an outpatient, motivational interviewing, and cognitive-behavioral therapy group was effective at reducing substance use and improving functioning among clients with psychosis. The group participants showed significant improvements in treatment compliance, substance abuse, symptomatology, and overall functioning.

Multiple-family cognitive-behavioral group counseling was implemented (Bradley et al., 2006) to treat schizophrenia for English-speaking families and for first-generation non-English-speaking Vietnamese families. Researchers concluded that this intervention for treating schizophrenia was effective with both groups of participants.

Researchers (Castle et al., 2007) provided a group intervention as an adjunct to usual treatment for bipolar disorder. They concluded that the group was cost-effective and had the benefits of reducing relapse and improving functioning.

Russell and Jory (1997) implemented a 10–14-week group counseling intervention for violent and abusive men. The group counseling program was more effective than no treatment at significantly reducing psychological abuse but had no effect on self-esteem or on physical abuse.

Two group counseling approaches (Costin, Lichte, Hill-Smith, Luk, & Vance, 2004) targeted parents of children with oppositional defiant disorder. One intervention focused on parental stress and problem-solving skills, while the other provided parental management training. According to researchers, both interventions were effective, revealing overall improvement in post group child behaviors and parenting stress levels. As hypothesized, parents who attended the stress group showed a greater reduction in stress; those who attended management training reported a larger reduction in conduct problems.

Edelman, Bell, and Kidman (1999) developed an 8-week group cognitive-behavior counseling intervention, followed by a family night and three follow-up monthly sessions, and contrasted it to a no-therapy control group condition. All participants received standard ontological care. Researchers reported that group intervention participants were less depressed, experienced less total mood disturbance, and demonstrated improved self-esteem. Unfortunately, these improvements were not evident at 3–6 months' follow-up.

Asia

CHINA

Robert Conyne, professor emeritus at the University of Cincinnati and the editor of this book, has taken several professional trips to China to lecture on counseling approaches, including group counseling. His involvement in training people through the Chinese Academy of Science, especially school personnel who do counseling-like work in the schools, was very well received. The positive reception he received highlighted the desire Chinese professionals have for learning more about group work. He found that the Chinese people he worked with in group were more interactive and participatory than he had expected (R. Conyne, personal communication, September 23, 2009). The Chinese seem to be on the cusp of a major involvement in the implementation of group work. Rapid changes in the Chinese economic, political, and social spheres suggest this. In addition to his personal involvement with Chinese group training, Conyne and his colleagues have done interesting research there (Conyne, Wilson, Tang, & Shi, 1999); and his book on ecological counseling (Conyne & Cook, 2004) reflects the impact that group work and international contact has had on almost all of us who are involved in them.

Reported group counseling research in China includes an intervention for psychiatric patients, three interventions dealing with health issues, and two interventions dealing with education and training. Peixin et al. (2005) used group art therapy with schizophrenic inpatients. It was difficult to separate the relative impact of the art therapy from the impact of the group experience. Nevertheless, the approach helped group members function on an emotional–cognitional–social interaction level, improved their self-concept, and added to their quality of life.

Group counseling in China was used in a number of health psychology studies. In one study (Shan, Xu, Gu, & Pu, 2008), a group intervention was designed to impact obese children's self-conception. After 1 year, total self-concept scores, teamwork, and physical appearance were significantly improved and reached the level of no significant difference between obese children and nonobese children. Zhao (2007) developed a 6-month group counseling intervention to improve children's compliance with regular therapy for eye problems. It was determined that the group intervention improved compliance, hastened improvement, and increase the cure rate of the children.

Yi-Qi (2005) determined that a group intervention was effective in the improvement of diabetics' quality of life. Participants in the counseling group demonstrated significant improvement between pretest and posttest quality-of-life scales.

Pei (2006) studied the impact of "group psychological guidance" in an educational course focusing on mental health. Student satisfaction indicated support for interpersonal communication, ability to manage moods, and small group development. Pei concluded that multilateral communication between teachers and students improves mental health.

Another team of researchers (Zhou, Hou, & Bai, 2008) developed 5-week, 2-hour sessions of group assertiveness training for university students. According to the findings, participants' assertive behavior increased significantly and passive behavior decreased significantly. Researchers contended that group training positively enhanced the university students' assertive competence.

JAPAN

About 15 years ago, one of the authors (J. J. M.) was privileged to deliver the keynote address to the Japanese Student Counseling Association and to provide a workshop for a portion of the participants. The focus of the keynote presentation was on psychoeducational groups (McWhirter, 1995a, 1995b; McWhirter & Cusumano, 1995; Kanazawa, Cusumano, & McWhirter, 1995). The workshop provided information to about 100 participants on the use of the Fundamental Interpersonal Relationship Orientation-Behavior (FIRO-B). Like Conyne, he was impressed at the responsiveness of the participants to group work. A short questionnaire assessed the participants' group experiences and their attitudes toward group counseling. Virtually all of them were in counseling-like positions, and most of them were currently conducting groups as a part of their professional responsibilities. Mostly, the groups they were conducting were focused on tasks or support. All of them expressed an appreciation for the group presentation, indicated a strong interest in learning more about groups, and articulated a solid desire for more training in group counseling theory and skills.

It may be, however, that groups in Japan have an entirely different orientation from groups in the West. Richard Hayes, College of Education dean at the University of South Alabama, was a Fulbright Senior Scholar to Japan. He observed that the collectivist orientation of the Japanese culture makes it extremely difficult for Japanese small group participants to differentiate themselves as individuals from the group (R. Hayes, personal communication, September 29, 2009). When functioning in a group, Japanese students have a very difficult time seeing themselves as individuals operating independently of the group. The concept of self-in-relationship is an important feature of many Asian cultures. The individual alone is not suitable as the unit of analysis;

rather, it is necessary to focus on the person interacting within a relational context (Chen, 2009). Counseling groups may be a very different phenomenon when they take place with Japanese, Chinese, or other Asian clients and students contrasted to Western groups.

This personal commentary is important because it highlights a large section of the professional community that is not included in the following literature review. Social work and medicine have long been accepted in Japan; thus, the review deals primarily with groups common to those disciplines: the elderly and health psychology.

Two studies dealt with Japanese elderly, one focusing on reducing suicide rates and the other on aid to elderly with dementia. Researchers (Oyama et al., 2005) hypothesized that lack of social support among the elderly was a major contributor to suicide. They developed and researched a group counseling program based on group activity, psychoeducational information, and self-assessment of depression. The risk of elderly females completing suicide was reduced by 76%, although there were no changes for elderly males. The researchers concluded that a group intervention designed to increase knowledge and to cultivate social relationships is effective for elderly females but not males.

Tadaka and Kanagawa (2004) provided a group intervention for community-dwelling elderly persons with dementia. The program consisted of reminiscence and reality orientation once a week for 10 weeks. Researchers concluded that this approach improved cognitive function in the short term and disorientation and withdrawal in the long term. Based on these findings, the researchers speculated that sustained intervention over time would likely be necessary to maintain the effect.

A number of group intervention efficacy studies in Japan have arisen to address specific psychological needs. Infertile Japanese women, according to Matsubayashi, Hosaka, and Makino (2008) have high levels of emotional distress, anxiety, and depression. Psychological group counseling was effective at significantly increasing the pregnancy rate among members of the treated group compared to participants in the control condition. After a psychiatric group intervention focusing on the emotions of infertile Japanese women, Hosaka, Matsubayashi, Sugiyama, Makino, and Izumi (2002) reported increased fertility-cell activity and increased rates of pregnancy among participants at a 1-year follow-up compared to control group participants.

A number of Japanese studies have used group counseling to lessen the impact of breast cancer. In one study, Fukui et al. (2000) developed a group counseling program for patients with primary breast cancer. The group involved six 90-minute sessions that included health education, relaxation training, coping-skills training, and psychological support. Researchers reported increased accuracy in understanding medical information and improved communication style with doctors and family members among study participants. According to researchers, program components were rated by participants as relevant and appropriate and there were no dropouts for the duration of the group intervention.

Another group counseling program for breast cancer patients consisted of five 90-minute sessions and included problem solving, guided imagery, relaxation training, psychoeducational information, and psychological support. For patients with no psychiatric diagnoses at entry, researchers reported positive effects that persisted for 6 months posttreatment; however, among participants with concurrent psychiatric diagnoses, no long-term group effects were reported.

Interestingly, Fukui et al. (2001) found that Japanese women without any interest in a group intervention had significantly higher anxiety than those with interest. Researchers speculated that those uninterested in group interventions likely viewed other supports, such as individual counseling or medication, as more salient.

OTHER ASIAN COUNTRIES

Fernando (2009) provided a support group for Sri Lankan women who had survived the tsunami of 2004. The author highlights challenges facing group leaders in a foreign and diverse setting working with disaster survivors.

In Singapore, Chong (2005) presented a social cognitive psychoeducational group to improve student problem solving and learning. This Western-based group was adapted for use with low-achieving middle school Asian students.

A series of group counseling–like workshops were conducted in Burma for female refugee participants (Norsworthy & Khuankaew, 2004). Feminist and liberation theories provide the framework for the groups, and the participants explore the topics of oppression, power, and empowerment, including institutional- and structural-level violence against women.

Shen (2007) compared short-term cognitive–verbal with Gestalt–play small counseling groups with adolescents in Taiwan. According to teacher reports, students demonstrated significant changes in emotional strength and overall behavior for both groups. Results indicated that the Gestalt–play approach enhanced family involvement and the cognitive–verbal approach enhanced affective strengths.

In Korea, Kim (2006) studied the effect of a bullying-prevention program coupled with reality therapy. Children attended two group sessions per week for 5 weeks. According to Kim, the group program significantly reduced victimization and improved responsibility among the participants.

Europe

IRELAND

Using a six-session cognitive-behavioral counseling group for adults with attention-deficit/hyperactivity disorder (ADHD) to treat their anxiety, depression, low self-esteem, and self-efficacy, researchers (Bramham et al., 2009) demonstrated significantly greater improvement on ADHD knowledge, self-efficacy, and self-esteem than waiting list control participants.

O'Reilly, Morrison, Sheerin, and Carr (2001) described a group counseling program for adolescents. The program, based on cognitive-behavioral and relapse-prevention principles, is used to motivate changes in sexually abusive behavior.

Iwaniec (1997) described a parent training program provided by social workers. One group of neglectful parents received individual parent training only; another group participated in similar individual training plus 10 sessions of parent training provided in a group. Results indicated that parents who received the additional group counseling intervention improved significantly compared to those who received the individual-only intervention.

FRANCE

A five-session group counseling program for women was aimed at reducing the risk of acquiring HIV and other sexually transmitted diseases (Gollub, Brown, Savouillan, Coruble, & Waterlot, 2002). The group was designed to educate women about their bodies, teach protection skills, develop solidarity, and develop new norms. The women rated the intervention very highly, with the group process being liked best.

Dolbeault et al. (2009) evaluated the effects of a psychoeducational, cognitive-behavioral group for women with breast cancer. The 8-week program of 2-hour sessions each week included thematic information, discussion, and training in stress management. The researchers concluded that participants experienced significant improvement in interpersonal relations, emotional functioning, and health status along with reductions in anxiety, anger, fatigue, and depression.

GERMANY

Herbrecht et al. (2009) found that a group counseling program aimed at improving social and communication skills in individuals with autism was effective. Participants in the group enhanced their social skills and reduced autism-related psychopathology.

SPAIN

Gálvez (2007) utilized a group counseling experience with borderline patients that focused on goal setting, communication of feelings, and conflict management. Participants showed improvement in interpersonal relationships and social skills.

Another group program for school-aged children and adolescents used behavioral and cognitive components of social interaction (Landazabal, 2001). The program consisted of 2-hour weekly sessions during the academic year. The group focused on communication, cooperation, understanding and expressing emotions, identifying perceptions and prejudices, and conflict-resolution approaches. Participants decreased anxiety and shyness and increased self-assertiveness and leadership behaviors.

Group meetings were held in a community mental health setting to help family members and neighbors of deinstitutionalized mentally ill patients (Irazábal Martin & Duro, 1986). Participants in the group dealt with issues raised by the return of mentally ill patients to their community.

PORTUGAL

Researchers (Pereira, Sarrico, Oliveira, & Parente, 2000) developed a 9-week group intervention to promote health that emphasized physical exercise, good eating habits, and avoidance of risky behaviors. Participants had significantly better eating habits by the end of the group.

Latin America

For one of the authors (P. T. M.), working as a therapist in Mexico, Guatemala, and Chile shed light on the value of group counseling interventions. The individual counseling model was generated within a European American cultural context. The approach replicated valued medical practice, emphasizing service delivery on a weekly basis with hourly appointments in an office setting. In Latin America, training in psychology traditionally emphasizes psychoanalysis and similar introspective analytical approaches, interestingly conducive to this individual practice approach. However, typically in Latin America, this individual service-delivery model offers support to a small minority of educated and wealthy Latin Americans able to access the benefits of the approach.

In contrast to individual models of intervention, the delivery of the group counseling modality reflects values commensurate with cultures indigenous to Latin America, emphasizing respect for others and participation within a community. Throughout much of Latin America, social networks are a defining aspect of the self, an indication of the value of family and friendship connections. Furthermore, family is understood and experienced in terms of both immediate and extended relationships, with friendship connections often described in language used to explain extended family, connoting the importance of building and maintaining meaningful lifelong relationships. Financial challenges have resulted in an emphasis on sharing limited resources, increasing the value of the community and its members. As a modality, group therapy is a natural extension of the therapeutic factors commonly experienced in the community throughout various parts of Latin America. As such, group therapy approaches tend to decrease both practical and cultural barriers to counseling in a Latin American context.

BRAZIL

Gonçalves, Pinto, & Araújo (1998) developed a group counseling program for parents of children diagnosed with anxiety. Seven information and discussion sessions focused on characteristics and symptoms of anxiety and parental behaviors. Parents reported an increased ability to interact with their children and demonstrated improved relationships with them.

Another parent training group, consisting of 20 weekly 90-minute sessions (Coelho & Murta, 2007), used behavioral techniques, role-playing, and modeling. Researchers suggested that positive changes occurred with both parents' and children's behavior.

ARGENTINA

Adúriz, Bluthgen, and Knopfler (2009) provided a comprehensive group intervention for children who experienced trauma due to a massive flood. Using a

single-session group eye movement desensitization and reprocessing protocol, the researchers reported that participants demonstrated a statistically significant reduction of symptoms immediately after the intervention, which was sustained 3 months later.

Middle East

ISRAEL

Probably the most prolific international scholar researching and writing in the group counseling area is Professor Zipora Shechtman from the Faculty of Education, University of Haifa. She has produced an opus of work in the group area that is unparalleled. For example, she and her students and colleagues have written about the effect of group work on adolescent same-sex friendships (Shechtman, 1991),, group counseling with aggressive and angry children (Shechtman & Nachshol, 1996; Shechtman, 1999, 2000, 2001; Shechtman & Ben-David, 1999), attachment style and self-disclosure (Shechtman & Dvir 2006), group counseling to increase students' self-concept (Shechtman & Bar-El, 1994) and to enhance children's friendships and self-esteem (Shechtman, 1993), improve classroom climate (Shechtman, 1997), reduce stress of parents with children with learning disabilities (Shechtman & Gilat, 2005), and increase therapeutic factors in children's groups (Shechtman & Gluk, 2006), as well as many additional group counseling contributions.

Shechtman's work is unparalleled in both quantity and quality. She has contributed much to the world's understanding of small group counseling both in Israel and globally.

TURKEY

Contrasted to Israel, we found no published papers on group counseling in Turkey. However, our personal knowledge of group work in Turkey highlights the problems of using US databases as the predominant source for information about global counseling, social work, and psychology. We are personally aware of the richness of group counseling in Turkey and have to assume that much more is going on in the way of group counseling in other countries that is simply below the radar of our data sources.

Over 30 years ago one of the authors (J. J. M.) was awarded a Fulbright Senior Scholar award to lecture and do research in Turkey. Among other assignments, he taught a group counseling course, taught a parent training course that utilized psychoeducational groups, conducted a marathon group counseling session, and strongly encouraged students and Turkish colleagues to expand the group counseling area. His student and later colleague Professor Dr. Nilufer Voltan Acar developed an assertiveness training group for her dissertation and tested it out, coauthored a book with him that became the basis for psychoeducational groups with parents, received further training in psychodrama and in Gestalt approaches to small groups, and established a group counseling program at Hacettepe University in Ankara. She has published books in group counseling and the application of Gestalt theory to group. Other Turkish professionals have also been very active in group counseling.

He recently returned to Turkey as a Fulbright Senior Specialist. For his project, he had provided Professor Voltan Aker four psychoeducational group counseling manuals for use with young adolescents. She and her students translated the programs into Turkish and conducted small groups in various schools. This program was well received, with positive results; but unfortunately, the research was not published in English-language journals. In addition to his modest contributions to group work in Turkey, he was astonished at how embedded and extensive group counseling was in the fabric of Turkish counseling, psychology, and social work.

Indigenous Group Counseling

This review suggests that group counseling is alive and well around the globe. Allowing for regional concerns and severe localized problems, groups in other countries bear a remarkable similarity to groups that are conducted in the United States. Similarities exist across types of groups, group theories and dynamics, populations, and even research designs. It is obvious that we in the United States share with other countries a continuing and growing interest in group counseling. Missing, however, are those group work expressions that are indigenous to people in other countries.

Indigenous group counseling (indigenous from within) refers to group experiences that arise from the life experiences of people within a culture, that draw on that culture as the primary source of knowledge, and that have developed locally to alleviate personal distress and to change behavior. By and large, indigenous group counseling has developed independently of the Western tradition of scientifically based counseling. However, we also include one Western approach (indigenous from without) that has been modified and adapted to fit a local cultural context and to be compatible with people at the grassroots level (Leung & Chen, 2009). With

few exceptions, the multicultural variations of group counseling relate to cultural variations of people in the United States. From an international perspective, the multicultural variations of people around the world are astonishing. To capture some of those variations, we have identified five international, indigenous group counseling–like experiences generated from various locations globally: Japan, New Zealand, the Polynesian islands of the South Pacific, Peru and most of Central and South America, and Chile. Because of their richness and uniqueness, we present them in some detail.

MORITA THERAPY: JAPANESE MINDFULNESS

Morita therapy, initially developed as an individual intervention for "anxiety-based disorders," was developed in Japan in the first part of the twentieth century by Dr. Shoma Morita, chair of Jikei University School of Medicine's Department of Psychiatry. The intervention, as an approach to helping individuals, has enjoyed widespread application in Japan and recently has been reframed into a group modality (Aposhyan, 1995). Sometimes referred to as Morita therapy methods, the approach has been adapted and modified to be more acceptable to Western minds and culture. It also currently has a much broader application that considers not only anxiety disorders but also stress, physical or emotional pain, reaction to trauma, and social phobia.

Aposhyan (1995) developed a brief Morita therapy group and utilized a controlled empirical study to test its effectiveness. Twenty-two socially phobic adults participated in a four-session group intervention. Half the participants were engaged in the Morita group and demonstrated significant improvement across all measures following the experience. The wait list control participants showed no change during the time of the initial intervention, but after their participation in the group, they also showed significant improvement on all measures of avoidance behavior and social anxiety. These results persisted for all participants at a 1-month follow-up.

Traditional Morita therapy has four phases: rest, silence, work, and application. In the first phase, patients or clients are separated from their day-to-day environment. Access to external stimuli such as work, television, people, and other parts of the intrusive world is limited. Use is made of simple, nonreligious meditation procedures with the purpose of creating a quiet, peaceful place.

Phase two accentuates silence and light occupational therapy. Journal writing is used to help the client separate thoughts from feelings and to contemplate their different effects on one's life. Also during this phase, the individuals begin to reconnect with nature. They are encouraged to feel the sun, notice the fresh breeze, listen to the birds and insects, and breathe deeply. The silence and the reconnection to nature are thought to be important aspects of healing.

Work and heavy occupational therapy are the foci of phase three. Morita referred to this as the "chopping wood" phase; he had his patients get involved in outdoor hard physical labor. More recent applications include stretching and strength-building physical therapy. An equally important component is for the individual to get into contact with the creative parts of their person. Writing, drawing, painting, wood carving, and pottery making are all potential ways of creating art and becoming more aware of one's creative potential.

The fourth phase has the client applying what was learned in the first three phases to everyday life. Applying meditation, physical activity, and connection to the natural world as coping skills, the individual integrates with the pain and stress of living.

Besides the four phases, to implement Morita therapy methods either individually or in a group requires attending to three basic principles. The three principals are as follows: feelings are natural, feelings cannot be controlled, preoccupation with self traps one in an unhealthy state.

Feelings are natural. Events happen in life (e.g., falling in love, the death of a loved one, the loss of a job) that create strong feelings. These feelings are a natural response to life circumstances, and we do not need to "change" or "fix" them. True acceptance of reality as it is (in Japanese, *arugamama*) involves acknowledgment of feelings without trying to "work through" them. When one is anxious, one accepts the anxiety. When one is depressed, one accepts the depression. The principle here is to direct efforts toward living life well rather than focusing energy and attention on an emotional state. One sets goals and takes steps to complete them regardless of accompanying unpleasant feelings.

Feelings cannot be controlled. Trying to modify our feelings is like trying to push the river. No matter how hard we try, we end up feeling more pain because it cannot be done. Most Western therapeutic methods imply that it is necessary to modify the emotions before action can be taken. However, behavior can be detached from feelings.

By accepting and acknowledging feelings, one can take action regardless of the feeling. Indeed, taking action often leads to modification of feelings. The anticipatory anxiety of the public speaker often dissipates after a number of speeches. Depression is relieved when one gets involved in other things.

Preoccupation with self traps one in an unhealthy state. When one suffers unpleasant feelings, rather than "being with" the experience, many attempt to label the psychological function— "codependent," "depressed," "obsessive." This labeling leads to even more self-preoccupation. When one becomes overly preoccupied with self, one's attention becomes narrowed and one becomes ensnared by an unhealthy focus on self. The more we observe our symptoms (depression, for example), the more our symptoms have power over us. By being absorbed in what we are actually doing—by "living well"—our attention is engaged in activity and we become less depressed. Trying to "fix," "work through," and "understand" the issues and emotions perpetuates self-focus and we lose the energy to live well. Developing a reality-oriented attitude, in touch with the outside world, provides freedom from self-centeredness. Often, Morita therapy is described as the psychology of action (Hwang & Chang, 2009).

Morita therapy clearly needs additional research as it is applied in Western culture and in a group format. There are, however, a number of emerging, empirically supported, Western treatments (acceptance and commitment therapy [Hayes, 2005], mindfulness-based program for stress reduction [Jones & Kabat-Zinn, 1990], and dialectical behavior therapy [Linehan, 1993]) that are reminiscent of Morita therapy, essentially because most draw on an Eastern Zen tradition of mindfulness, as does Morita therapy.

MARAE-BASED HUI: RESOLVING CONFLICT IN THE COURTYARD

The Maori, a Polynesian people indigenous to New Zealand, have a long history of establishing connections, developing relationships, and resolving conflicts in the *marae*. The *marae* is a large, open square or courtyard in front of the traditional cultural center, community hall, and ancestral meetinghouse (the *whare runanga*); and it serves many purposes. Traditionally regarded as the spiritual center of the sub-tribe or clan that owns it, public gatherings on important matters take place. Agreements and reconciliations with neighboring competing groups, negotiations over disputes and disagreements, and resolution of internal conflicts all take place on the *marae*. For modern Maori, the *marae* provides the setting for family-oriented events, with opportunities for multigenerational and peer-group interaction while playing and sleeping in the same space, allowing for connection and bonding within the extended family group.

The *marae* continues to provide a setting for the *hui*, the traditional meetings of important cultural and social events that are conducted using the customs and mores that are central to Maori culture. These customs are important and reflective of good group work. Close community relations, rather than individualism, imply good mental health. There is an emphasis on the collective identity rather than the individual. The interlocking patterns of human exchange and connections are important. All knowledge, skills, talents, and things belong to the group, not to the individual. Working together with mutual exchanges of action and thought is emphasized (Awatere, 1984; Royal, 1978).

The *hui*, like any group counseling process, operates under certain conventions and guidelines. Debate continues until consensus is reached. Indeed, consensus is the standard for democratic and formal decision making throughout the group process. During the process of working to consensus, each member of the group has a chance to express an opinion. Interruption when someone is speaking is frowned upon. Rather than an impartial rules moderator, the facilitator of the *hui* acts as an intermediary who offers compromise and suggests middle ground during an impasse. The *hui* is not limited by time; discussion and debate may continue well into the night (Salmond, 1976).

The spirit of the traditional *hui* is utilized in modern times as a way to resolve family and clan disputes. Meetings involve a group with the goal of creating harmony. The group spirit is pervasive and provides a Maori perspective of family therapy (Tukukino & Tukukino, 1986). The *hui* is also used to teach cross-cultural issues and to develop better understanding and cooperation between modern Maori and European (*Pakeha*) citizens of New Zealand. Numerous *hui* have been conducted including teachers, principals, and school inspectors (Norman & Donn, 1982), school counselors (Gibbs, 1981), high school students (Tauroa, 1982), and counseling students (Everts, 1988).

Everts (1988) describes a compulsory 3-day *marae*-based *hui* for faculty and students in the training course for school psychologists and counselors at the University of Auckland. Twenty-five to 30 participants live in for 3 days along with Maori members of the host tribe. Following a comprehensive and preplanned program, the *Pakeha* participants engage in a traditional formal welcoming, learn about the tribe's history, and explore current concerns. These students learn how the Maori are affected by community and ethnic stresses and about Maori strategies for promoting emotional, social, and physical well-being.

The *hui* involvement is viewed by most trainees as a very constructive learning opportunity (Everts, 1988). They come away with an understanding and personal appreciation of the power of the *hui* decision-making process. The supporting group atmosphere and the group dynamic process are viewed as highly effective at tackling ethnic and cultural discrimination and other sensitive issues. Ultimately, the experience as a whole leads to recognition of the counseling participants' own counseling philosophy as harmonious with the underlying principles of the *hui*.

HO'OPONOPONO: RESOLVING CONFLICT TO SAVE AN ISLAND

Ho'oponopono is an ancient conflict-resolution and problem-solving process that developed in the Polynesian islands throughout the South Pacific including Hawaii. One aspect of it is a practice of forgiveness and reconciliation to heal sickness. This refers to a process of restitution with one's ancestors or with others thought to be impacted, directly or indirectly, by virtue of their relationships with the afflicted individual. This process of restitution is sometimes considered primary to healing an individual's sickness or physical ailment (Kamhis, 1992). "New age" practitioners have emphasized *ho'oponopono* as a psychospiritual self-help program rather than group process. Nevertheless, its early beginnings allowed island people to solve problems and deal with conflicts. The division or unity among tribes and family groups was obviously important, especially on coral low islands where people lived in close proximity. Problems between family groups and tribes were disruptive and unsettling and threatened survival. The *ho'oponopono* evolved to deal with the conflict. Conflict between islands and island groups was even more problematic because of natural phenomena, such as typhoons.

Typhoons are Pacific Ocean hurricanes. They strike with devastating force, wiping out most of what is in front of them. A quiet, low-lying Pacific island that is in the path of the typhoon can be totally destroyed. The force of the wind can strip coconut and nut trees, tear up yam and taro fields, blow away small animals—pigs, goats, chickens— and virtually leave the people on the island destitute and in danger of starvation. Ironically, a neighboring island as close as 5 or 10 miles away may be virtually untouched. Ancient Polynesians recognized the need to maintain relationships with extended family groups between various islands. Ongoing tension, conflict, and hostility created an unnecessary risk to personal survival. The *ho'oponopono* emerged as a solution.

Because the *ho'oponopono* is thought to have developed when Polynesian culture emerged between 100 and 750 CE, many different techniques have developed depending upon the situation (Wall & Callister, 1995). Originally, one tribal group would load up its canoes with fruit, vegetables, meat, and other produce. When arriving at the host island, the two groups would prepare a huge feast. When everyone had finished the banquet and after prayers to the gods and ancestors, the discussion would begin. As in the *hui*, everyone had a chance to speak his or her mind with the goal of restoring harmony. As a goal, reaching specific agreement was of less importance.

The traditional *ho'oponopono* functioned within the context of specific cultural beliefs, many of which have been adapted to modern applications of the procedure. For example, in addition to the goal of restoring unity and harmony, the process began and ended with a spiritual component. A facilitator's skill and status wielded more importance than degrees and credentials. The process is not bound by the clock but lasts as long as necessary. Individuals are communitarian and in relationship, not individualistic or autonomous. Resolution comes from mutual regret and shared forgiveness. In essence, people look inside themselves for the source of a problem rather than blame others.

Contemporary applications of the *ho'oponopono* incorporate the described traditional components with techniques and models of modern group work. The procedure has been adapted for a variety of counseling practices including corporations, social service agencies, and schools. There is evidence that it is effective as a conflict-management approach in corporate America (Patten, 1994). Social service agencies and family counseling clinics have utilized the approach to build stronger family relationships (Shook & Kwan, 1991). Brinson and Fischer (1999) have described its use as a conflict-resolution model for school counselors.

BASE COMMUNITIES: BUILDING HOPE WITH POWER TO THE PEOPLE

Base communities, *comunidades eclesial de base* (CEBs), are mutual support/aid/counseling groups developed especially in Latin America but also in many other parts of the world, including parts of Asia and Africa. Often associated with liberation theology (Boff & Boff, 1987), CEBs have had considerable impact around the world since their development in the 1960s. As a mutual aid/support group, CEBs have much in common with group counseling: face-to-face interaction with peers, encouragement of personal participation, personal problem solving, self-reflection and increased skills, and a setting that allows expression to others of thoughts and feelings, as well as understanding, support, and respect from others. CEBs go beyond that, however, as grassroots communities made up of the poor showing solidarity and participating in social justice (McWhirter, McWhirter, & McWhirter, 1988).

CEBs are similar to counseling groups in interactions and in dynamics. However, there are some differences. The group begins with a scripture reading and discussion. The scripture is not treated as a historical or literary artifact but is viewed from the perspective of the everyday, concrete, and specific social reality of the participants. The poverty in which the people live encourages an integration of their own experiences vis-à-vis scripture. The attitude or focus in the group is to provide mutual support, to offer an antidote to defeatism, and to discourage self-centeredness and individualism.

Participation in the group gives community members a chance to reflect on their reality, express their thoughts, and relieve their negative feelings by the encouragement of hope. This personal disclosure and face-to-face interaction leads to individual empowerment. Members of the base community gain a sense of personal power due to the interaction of the supportive group, which creates solidarity in the community. In a community of cultural disorganization and social disintegration, a greater sense of social unity and support can potentially lead to concrete community organization and development.

Ideally, CEBs become action-oriented groups. Resulting projects from the action are therapeutic. They provide members an avenue to help build their community and to do something constructive to help themselves. Base communities often add appendages such as health clinics, cooperatives, and schools. They provide a vehicle that allows people to grow and change. Group members develop the confidence and ability to demand recognition of their community's rights. Social action follows and leads to positive results.

Personal growth is extremely important in group counseling; it is equally important in base communities. But in a society full of injustice, the enhancement of personal growth goes hand in hand with the need for social change. Groups that ignore social reality and serve only the individual growth of members are negligent in affecting true growth and change.

MENTOR COUPLES: BUILDING COMMUNITY COUPLE BY COUPLE BY FAMILY

For a decade and a half, two of us (B. T. M., E. H. M.) have made yearly trips of 3–4 weeks to Peñalolén, a working-class barrio of Santiago, Chile, with our uncle, Father Roberto Plasker, a Catholic priest who has spent more than 50 years serving impoverished communities in Chile and Peru. Father Plasker developed and coordinated a family faith education program founded on the belief that parents are the ideal educators and models for their own children (Decker, 1996).

The family education program offers a unique avenue through which couples develop spiritually and learn parenting and interpersonal competencies and psychological skills that help them and their families meet the challenges of difficult living and working conditions, the social effects of the economy, and lack of access to psychological services. Both parents are required to participate, when possible. In the case of single parents, a godparent or close relative of the opposite sex is required to participate. Thus, they provide children with exposure to both male and female role models. A program goal is to prepare parents with the information, skills, and support they need to teach and model their faith to their children. The parents participate in the faith education curriculum corresponding to the child's developmental level and the particular religious milestone or sacrament associated with that age. The primary curriculum is 2 years in length. Another and equally important goal of the family education program is to enhance family communication, discipline, and connectedness. In addition to parent education, there are scheduled family group activities to enhance family communication, closeness, and community participation. Finally, a program goal is to nurture a long-term sense of community, interdependence, and shared faith identity among the participants.

The program makes use of a core group of volunteer mentor couples (in Spanish, *parejas guías*—literally, "couple guides") who have already completed the curriculum. The mentor couples present the weekly parent curriculum, while young adults facilitate weekly meetings for the children that address similar, developmentally appropriate content. Each mentor couple works with a group of 6–12 parent couples and engages the same group of parents for the duration of the curriculum. Naturally, during the 2 years, close and continuing relationships are forged. Because of this, group members often seek the counsel of mentor couples for support and assistance with family crises and conflict.

The mentor couple experience is transformative. As we have described elsewhere (McWhirter & McWhirter, 2006), couples typically begin leading their first group with much apprehension and doubt and then find that they do have strengths and skills to work with others. Most of the couples have not had formal education beyond high school, and many did not complete high school. They may struggle with reading and writing. These couples also consistently face significant economic difficulties that demand a great deal of time and energy to manage. For all of these reasons, many mentor couples meet regularly with other mentor couples to provide mutual support, solve problems, and nurture their own faith development.

During our first visit, we met several couples who were active in the program. After this initial foray of providing informal consultation to a few individuals and couples, several of them asked for more formal training to enhance the quality of their own family life and to impact their work with other families.

We used an assessment strategy typical of many consultation models. We met with them in small groups to discuss their preparation and to understand the types of difficulties they had experienced as mentors and the strategies that they used to deal with problems. Their preparation had been mostly on the content of the curriculum, with very little attention to presentation. There was limited understanding of group dynamics and very limited skill in dealing with their groups.

Most of the problems the mentor couples faced were from a lack of experience in facilitating groups combined with self-doubt. They encountered difficulties commonly encountered in conducting groups. For example, some described difficulty with group members' disruptive behaviors (e.g., monopolizing or disrupting the group, attacking the leaders, arriving late, and other antigroup behaviors). Some worried about couples having a marital crisis within the group, while others were frustrated by members who were disconnected and uninterested in the topics or the other group members. The mentor couples also expressed personal concerns about their own interpersonal issues. Several couples discussed conflicts between themselves because of their own personality and communication differences and were concerned about their differing ways of responding to conflict in the group. Some felt like imposters, believing that because they had their own unresolved marital issues, they were not qualified to assist others. Some mentor couples also felt burned out and stressed. They expressed resentment that they were directing so much time and energy to helping others while their own family relationships suffered from lack of attention. The mentor couples wanted to learn more effective ways to handle these issues. As the major psychological support for some of the families in crisis, they were especially concerned about how to help the members of their groups survive, heal, and thrive. After elaboration and clarification of their concerns, we provided some general ideas for a series of psychoeducational group experiences: listening and other communication skills, as well as problem-solving and group-facilitation skills. The mentor couples responded with enthusiasm.

The first group focused on basic communication skills, including active listening and sending accurate messages. We discussed stages of group development (forming, storming, norming, and performing) and introduced group facilitation strategies such as linking, bridging, and providing corrective feedback.

In a subsequent group, we introduced conflict-resolution and mediation strategies along with other problem-solving skills. Next, we provided training in working with couples and families in crisis. We included the stages of change model (Prochaska & DiClemente, 1992) and presented principles and skills from motivational interviewing (Miller & Rollnick, 2002). Throughout each of the sessions, we emphasized that the challenges faced by these couples were very common for group facilitators and not "caused" by their lack of formal education and training.

Many of the mentor couples were struggling with the same issues as the couples in their groups. Thus, we used numerous examples in each of our groups to personalize the experience for the mentor couples. Frequently, we utilized the training as a vehicle for group counseling in order to provide support for the mentor couples and their very difficult tasks.

Each of these psychoeducational groups was conducted during a weekend. Each was repeated until approximately 40 couples received the same basic content. These initial groups took place over the course of 3 years. We continued to develop and facilitate groups to enhance earlier themes and provide more in-depth problem-solving skills, and we eventually offered new groups based on requests such as enhancing relationship intimacy and effective parenting. A number of couples attended the same content sessions numerous times and naturally took on greater leadership in practice activities and explaining content through examples. A few years ago, we were delighted to attend a weekend workshop on marriage and intimacy conducted entirely by a group of mentor couples. We have provided all of our instructional materials and notes, and they continue offering group sessions and training to the new mentor couples.

Conclusion

Group counseling from an international perspective appears to be a growing phenomenon. This is evident even though, compared to medicine and social work, counseling as an international profession is a relatively new endeavor. Probably because medicine and social work are more established disciplines, we found that a large number of the reviewed articles in this chapter deal with a trauma, psychiatric, or medical orientation. As the field of counseling continues to grow internationally, group counseling likely will extend into other settings and deal with different populations. All indications suggest that global group counseling is on a solid foundation for continued growth.

Equally important is the potential cross-fertilization between group counseling approaches developed in the Western industrialized world and regionally specific approaches indigenous to other parts of the world. This connection holds unique prevention and treatment promise with the potential of expanding professional practitioners' multicultural growth and development.

Future Directions

This wide-ranging and far-reaching review of studies internationally highlights a number of thoughtful issues in exploring directions for further growth and development from a global perspective. By way of summary, we present the following points for consideration in addressing these and related questions.

First, how can group counselors incorporate indigenous group strategies into their work both within the United States and internationally? Multicultural approaches in the United States are predominantly based on those of our citizens who represent diversity from the European American dominant culture population. Potentially, a strong alliance exists between US multiculturalism and multiculturalism from a global perspective. If this alliance is allowed to develop, multiculturalism may develop an international, global perspective. We suspect that this will be an advantage for group leaders both in the United States and abroad.

Second, in what ways can US group counselors learn from the rich array of global group work? Currently, as mentioned, a large number of group counseling approaches are trauma-, hospital-, or medicine-based. Future movement in group counseling may involve increased connections across disciplines to address a wider variety of presenting issues and individual concerns. Group counseling interventions might evolve to routinely address medical, health, exercise, spirituality, and religious issues. For example, group interventions have been effective, most notably in Japan, for improving health conditions and increasing adaptation and well-being in the context of illness and physical ailment. As technology and global connections increase, the effects of these interventions may become increasingly well known and available across nations. Knowledge of group counseling's impact on cellular growth among infertile women in Japan may stimulate use of group counseling components to treat issues previously construed as solely medically based. In the United States, group counseling might become routinely utilized, say, in conjunction with dietary and physical exercise programs to address issues of childhood obesity to counter early-onset diabetes. Taken as a whole, increased communication regarding the effectiveness of individual studies internationally may increase appreciation for group counseling effectiveness and facilitate increased expectation for a comprehensive utilization of group programs to address a wide variety of problems and concerns.

Third, what does the future hold for the field of group work as the discipline of counseling continues to expand globally? It seems fitting that a global perspective, one that includes the cumulative wisdom of group facilitators and the body of evidence of group researchers across settings and cultures, might most aptly address the major challenges that face group work experts today. For example, accurate appraisal, evaluation, and measurement of the presence, nature, salience, and interplay of Yalom's therapeutic factors (Yalom, 2005; see Chapters 8 and 9.) are arguably the foremost challenges among current group workers. These challenges might most appropriately be addressed from an informed communication internationally. A global perspective may provide the best foundation to generate solutions, develop recommendations, and propose standards for evaluating group efficacy and addressing concerns of group effectiveness and implementation.

Fourth and finally, will an international perspective prove to be the most helpful arena to address assumed limitations of group counseling? Yalom was particularly aware of certain group therapy limitations, for example, suggesting that therapeutic effectiveness is mediated by the characteristics, the specific appeal, and the skills and charisma of individual group leaders. An international perspective might prove most appropriate in studying and understanding this and other potentially efficacious components of group counseling across cultures and settings. Furthermore, Yalom's long-standing and widely held assumptions regarding the presence and nature of the therapeutic factors working to effect change among group members might begin to be analyzed in unique ways, informed by a broader international and multicultural context.

References

Adúriz, M. E., Bluthgen, C., & Knopfler, C. (2009). Helping child flood victims using group EMDR intervention in Argentina: Treatment outcome and gender differences. *International Journal of Stress Management, 16*, 138–153.

Aposhyan, H. M. (1995). The efficacy of Morita therapy applied in a group modality for socially phobic adults: An outcome study. *Dissertation Abstracts International B The Sciences and Engineering, 55*, 5057.

Association for Specialists in Group Work. (2000). *Professional standards for the training of group workers.* Retrieved October 31, 2007, from http://www.asgw.org/PDF/training_standards.pdf

Austin, M.-P., Frilingos, M., Lumley, J., Roncolato, W., Saint, K., Parker, G., et al. (2008). Brief antenatal cognitive behavior therapy group intervention for the prevention of postnatal depression and anxiety: A randomized controlled trial. *Journal of Affective Disorders, 105*, 35–44.

Awatere, D. (1984). *Maori sovereignty.* Auckland, New Zealand: Broadsheet.

Bailey, K. A., Baker, A. L., Webster, R. A., & Lewin, T. J. (2004). Pilot randomized controlled trial of a brief alcohol intervention group for adolescents. *Drug and Alcohol Review, 23*, 157–166.

Boff, L., & Boff, C. (1987). *Introducing liberation theology*. New York: Orbis.

Bradley, A. C., Baker, A., & Lewin, T. J. (2007). Group intervention for coexisting psychosis and substance use disorders in rural Australia: Outcomes over 3 years. *Australian and New Zealand Journal of Psychiatry, 41*, 501–508.

Bradley, G. M., Couchman, G. M., Perlesz, A., Singh, B., Riess, C., & Nguyen, A. T. (2006). Multiple-family group treatment for English- and Vietnamese-speaking families living with schizophrenia. *Psychiatric Services, 57*, 521–530.

Bramham, J., Young, S., Bickerdike, A., McCartan, D., Xenitidis, K., & Spain, D. (2009). Evaluation of group cognitive behavioral therapy for adults with ADHD. *Journal of Attention Disorders, 12*, 434–441.

Brinson, J., & Fischer, T. A. (1999). The Ho'oponopono group: A conflict resolution model for school counselors. *Journal for Specialists in Group Work, 24*, 369–382.

Castle, Berk, Berk, Chamberlain, Gilbert, & Lauder, (2007). A group intervention which assists patients with dual diagnosis reduces their drug use: A randomized controlled trial. Reply. *Psychological Medicine, 35*, 299–300.

Chen, P.-H. (2009). A counseling model for self-relation coordination for Chinese clients with interpersonal conflicts. *Counseling Psychologist, 37*, 987–1009.

Chong, W. H. (2005). The role of self-regulation and personal agency beliefs: A psychoeducational approach with Asian high school students in Singapore. *Journal for Specialists in Group Work, 30*, 343–362.

Cobham, V. E. (2003). Evaluation of a brief child-focused group-based intervention for anxiety-disordered children. *Behaviour Change, 20*, 109–116.

Coelho, M. V., & Murta, S. G. (2007). Treinamento de pais em grupo: Um relato de experiência [Parental training in group: An experience group]. *Escudos de Psicologia, 24*, 333–341.

Conyne, R., & Cook, E. (Eds.). (2004). *Ecological counseling: An innovative approach to conceptualizing person–environment interaction*. Alexandria, VA: American Counseling Association.

Conyne, R., Wilson, F. R., Tang, M., & Shi, K. (1999). Cultural similarities and differences in group work: Pilot study of a US–Chinese task group comparison. *Group Dynamics: Theory, Research, and Practice, 3*, 40–50.

Costin, J., Lichte, C., Hill-Smith, A., Luk, E., & Vance, A. (2004). Parent group treatments for children with oppositional defiant disorder. *Australian e-Journal for the Advancement of Mental Health, 3*, 19-31.

Decker, C. (1996). *Catequesis familiar: Su métodología*. Santiago, Chile: Instituto de Catequesis.

Dolbeault, S., Cayrou, S., Brédart, A., Viala, A. L., Desclaux, B., Saltel, P., et al. (2009). The effectiveness of a psycho-educational group after early-stage breast cancer treatment: Results of a randomized French study. *Psychooncology, 18*, 647–656.

Edelman, S., Bell, D. R., & Kidman, A. D. (1999). A group cognitive behaviour therapy programme with metastatic breast cancer patients. *Psychooncology, 8*, 295–305.

Everts, J. (1988). The marae-based hui: An indigenous vehicle to address cross-cultural discrimination in New Zealand. *Journal for Specialists in Group Work, 13*(3), 130–134.

Ezeokana, J. O., Nnedum, A., Nnamdi, A., & Madu, S. N. (2008). An evaluation of an HIV/AIDS prevention program in a Nigerian setting. *Journal of African Psychology, 18*, 493–496.

Fernando, D. M. (2009). Group work with survivors of the 2004 Asian tsunami: Reflections of an American-trained counselor. *Journal for Specialists in Group Work, 34*(1), 4–23.

Fukui, S., Kamiya, M., Koike, M., Kugaya, A., Okamura, H., Nakanishi, T., et al. (2000). Applicability of a Western-developed psychosocial group intervention for Japanese patients with primary breast cancer. *Psychooncology, 9*, 169–177.

Fukui, S., Kugaya, A., Kamiya, M., Koike, M., Okamura, H., Nakanishi, T., et al. (2001). Participation in psychosocial group intervention among Japanese women with primary breast cancer and its associated factors. *Psychooncology, 10*, 419–427.

Gálvez, E. Á. (2007). Psicoterapia de grupo en pacientes con trastorno límite de la personalidad [Group psychotherapy in patients with borderline personality disorder]. *Anales de Psiquiatría, 23*, 68–74.

Gerrits, R. S., van der Zanden, R. A. P., Visscher, R. F. M., & Conijn, B. P. (2007). Master your mood online: A preventive chat group intervention for adolescents. *Australian e-Journal for the Advancement of Mental Health, 6*, 1–11.

Gibbs, A. (1981). *Cultural awareness training for school guidance counselors*. Unpublished manuscript. Education Department, University of Canterbury, Christchurch, New Zealand.

Gitterman, A., & Salmon, R. (Eds.). (2008). *Encyclopedia of social work with groups*. New York: Routledge.

Gollings, E. K., & Paxton, S. J. (2006). Comparison of internet and face-to-face delivery of a group body image and disordered eating intervention for women: A pilot study. *Eating Disorders: The Journal of Treatment & Prevention, 14*, 1–15.

Gollub, E. L., Brown, E. L., Savouillan, M., Coruble, G., & Waterlot, J. (2002). A community-based safer-sex intervention for women: Results of a pilot study in southeastern France. *Culture, Health & Sexuality, 4*, 21–41.

Gonçalves, M., Pinto, H., & Araújo, M. S. (1998). Perturbações de ansiedade em crianças: Uma experiência com um grupo de pais. [Anxiety disorders in children: An experience with a parents' group]. *Psicologia: Teoria, Investigação e Prática, 3*, 327–352.

Hayes, S. C. (2005). *Get out of your mind and into your life: The new acceptance and commitment therapy*. Oakland, CA: New Harbinger.

Heinicke, B. E., Paxton, S. J., McLean, S. A., & Wertheim, E. H. (2007). Internet-delivered targeted group intervention for body dissatisfaction and disordered eating and adolescent girls: A randomized controlled trial. *Journal of Abnormal Child Psychology, 35*, 379–391.

Herbrecht, E., Poustka, F., Birnkammer, S., Duketis, E., Schlitt, S., Schmötzer, G., et al. (2009). Pilot evaluation of the Frankfurt Social Skills Training for children and adolescents with autism spectrum disorder. *European Child & Adolescent Psychiatry, 18*, 327–335.

Hosaka, T., Matsubayashi, H., Sugiyama, Y., Makino, T., & Izumi, S. (2002). Effect of psychiatric group intervention on natural-killer cell activity and pregnancy rate. *General Hospital Psychiatry, 24*, 353–356.

Hwang, K.-K., & Chang, J. (2009). Self-cultivation: Culturally sensitive psychotherapies in Confucian societies. *Counseling Psychologist, 37*, 1010–1032.

Irazábal Martin, E., & Duro, M. (1986). El loco de la comunidad: Una intervención rupal en salud mental comunitaria: II [The community's crazy ones: A group intervention in community mental health: II]. *Clínica y Análisis Grupal, 10*, 657–675.

Iwaniec, D. (1997). Evaluating parent training for emotionally abusive and neglectful parents: Comparing individual versus individual and group intervention. *Research on Social Work Practice, 7*, 329–349.

Jones, C. T., & Kabat-Zinn, J. (1990). *Full catastrophe living: Using the wisdom of your body and mind to face stress, pain, and illness.* New York: Delacorte.

Kamhis, J. (1992). Healing with Ho'oponopono. *Aloha, 6*, 44–49.

Kanazawa, Y. N., Cusumano, J., & McWhirter, J. J. (1995). Counseling students in groups: Techniques. *Proceedings of the Japan Student Counseling Association and the Japanese Ministry of Education National Conference, 32*, 49–50.

Kim, J. (2006). The effect of a bullying prevention program on responsibility and victimization children in Korea. *International Journal of Reality Therapy, 26*, 4–8.

Landazabal, M. G. (2001). Intervención con adolescents: Impacto de un programa en laasertividad y en las estrategias cognitivas de afrontamiento de situaciones socials [Intervention with adolescents: Impact of a psychological program for assertiveness and coping cognitive strategies in social situations]. *Garaigordobil Psicología Conductual Revista Internacional de Psicología Clínica de las Salud, 9*, 221–246.

Leung, S. A., & Chen, P.-H. (2009). Counseling psychology in Chinese communities in Asia: Indigenous, multicultural, and cross-cultural considerations. *Counseling Psychologist, 37*, 944–966.

Linehan, M. (1993). *Cognitive-behavioral treatment of borderline personality disorder.* New York: Guilford Press.

Matsubayashi, H., Hosaka, T., & Makino, T. (2008). Impact of psychological distress in infertile Japanese women. In A. E. Columbus (Ed.), *Advances in psychology research* (pp. 165–178). Hauppauge, NY: Nova Science.

Mayadas, N. S., Smith, R., & Elliott, D. (2004). Social group work in a global context. In C. D. Garvin, L. M. Gutierrez, & M. J. Galinsky (Eds.), *Handbook of social work with groups* (pp. 45–58). New York: Guilford Press.

McWhirter, B. T., & McWhirter, E. H. (2006). Couples helping couples: Empowerment through consultation and training in Peñalolén, Chile. In R. L. Toporek, L. Gerstein, N. Fouad, G. Roysircar, & T. Israel (Eds.), *Handbook for social justice in counseling psychology: Leadership, vision, and action* (pp. 406–420). Palo Alto, CA: Sage.

McWhirter, B. T., McWhirter, E. H., & McWhirter, J. J. (1988). Groups in Latin America: *Comunidades eclesial de base* as mutual support groups. *Journal for Specialists in Group Work, 13*, 70–76.

McWhirter, J. J. (1995a). Emotional education for university students. *Journal of College Student Psychotherapy, 10*, 27–38.

McWhirter, J. J. (1995b). Student counseling in the United States: Counseling students in Japan. *Proceedings of the Japan Student Counseling Association and the Japanese Ministry of Education National Conference, 32*, 12–13.

McWhirter, J. J., & Cusumano, J. (1995). Group counseling for students: Current theories and trends in psychoeducational groups (J. Cusumano, Trans.) *Japanese Student Counseling Journal, 16*, 53–59.

Miller, C. (2007). Psychodrama: Advances in theory and practice. In C. Baim, J. Burmeister, & M. Maciel (Eds.), *Advancing theory in therapy: Psychodrama, spirituality, and souldrama* (pp. 189–200). London: Routledge.

Miller, W. R., & Rollnick, S. (2002). *Motivational interviewing: Preparing people for change* (2nd ed.). New York: Guilford Press.

Mogapi, N. (2004). Reintegration of soldiers: The missing piece. *Intervention: International Journal of Mental Health,*

Psychosocial Work & Counselling in Areas of Armed Conflict, 2, 221–225.

Norman, H., & Donn, M. (1982). *An evaluation of Marae-based in-service training courses* (Research Report Series No. 14). Wellington, New Zealand: Department of Education.

Norr, K. F., Norr, J. L., Kaponda, C. P. N., Mbweza, E. M. D., & Kachingwe, S. I. (2007). Short-term effects of a peer group intervention for HIV prevention among trainee teachers in Malawi. *African Journal of AIDS Research, 6*, 239–249.

Norsworthy, K. L., & Khuankaew, O. (2004). Women of Burma speak out: Workshops to deconstruct gender-based violence and build systems of peace and justice. *Journal for Specialists in Group Work, 29*(3), 259–284.

O'Reilly, G., Morrison, T., Sheerin, D., & Carr, A. (2001). A group-based module for adolescents to improve motivation to change sexually abusive behavior. *Child Abuse Review, 10*, 150–169.

Oyama, H., Watanabe, N., Ono, Y., Takenoshita, Y., Takizawa, T., Kumagai, K., et al. (2005). Community-based suicide prevention through group activity for the elderly successfully reduced the high suicide rate for females. *Psychiatry and Clinical Neurosciences, 59*, 337–344.

Paterson, R., Luntz, H., Perlesz, A., & Cotton, S. (2002). Adolescent violence towards parents: Maintaining family connections when the going gets tough. *Australian and New Zealand Journal of Family Therapy, 23*, 90–100.

Patten, T. H. (1994). Ho'oponopono: A cross cultural model. *International Journal of Organizational Analysis, 2*, 252–263.

Pei, L. H. (2006). Group psychological guidance in mental health education course. *Chinese Mental Health Journal, 20*, 527–530.

Peixin, M., Richang, Z., Zhuoji, C., Liang, M., Yu, L., Jun, L., et al. (2005). Group intervention for schizophrenia inpatient with art as medium. *Acta Psychologica Sinica, 37*, 403–412.

Pereira, M. G., Sarrico, L., Oliveira, S., & Parente, S. (2000). Aprender a escolher: Promoção da saúde no contexto escolar. [Health promotion in the school context: An intervention with children 8 to 10 years old]. *Psicologia: Teoria, Investigação e Prática, 5*, 147–158.

Prochaska, J. O., & DiClemente, C. C. (1992). Stages of change in the modification of problem behaviors. In J. O. Prochaska (Ed.), *Progress in behavior modification* (pp. 184–218). New York: Academic Press.

Pronyk, P. M., Kim, J. C., Pramsky, T., Phetla, G., Hargreaves, J. R., Morison, L. A., et al. (2008). A combined microfinance and training intervention can reduce HIV risk behavior in young female participants. *AIDS, 22*, 1659–1665.

Royal, T. (1978). *A guide to Marae visits.* Wellington, New Zealand: Maori and Island Affairs Department.

Russell, R., & Jory, M. K. (1997). An evaluation of group intervention programs for violent and abusive men. *Australian and New Zealand Journal of Family Therapy, 18*, 125–136.

Salmond, A. (1976). *Hui.* Auckland, New Zealand: Methuen.

Shan, J. Y., Xu, G. X., Gu, D. H., & Pu, X. D. (2008). Group intervention effect on self-conception of obesity children. *Chinese Journal of Clinical Psychology, 16*, 554–556.

Shechtman, Z. (1991). Small group therapy and preadolescent same-sex friendship. *International Journal of Group Psychotherapy, 41*, 227–243.

Shechtman, Z. (1993). Group psychotherapy for the enhancement of intimate friendship and self-esteem among troubled elementary school children. *Journal of Social and Personal Relationships, 10*, 483–494.

Shechtman, Z. (1997). Enhancing classroom climate and social acceptability at the elementary and secondary school levels. *Journal of Educational Research, 91*, 99–107.

Shechtman, Z. (1999). Bibliotherapy for treatment of child aggression: The program and a single-group study. *Child Psychiatry and Human Development, 30*, 39–53.

Shechtman, Z. (2000). Short-term treatment of childhood aggression: Outcomes and process. *Psychology in the School, 37*, 157–167.

Shechtman, Z. (2001). Prevention groups for angry and aggressive children. *Journal for Specialists in Group Work, 26*, 228–236.

Shechtman, Z., & Bar-El, O. (1994). Group guidance and group counseling to foster self-concept and social status in adolescence. *Journal for Specialists in Group Work, 19*, 188–197.

Shechtman, Z., & Ben-David, M. (1999). Group and individual treatment of childhood aggression: A comparison of outcomes and process. *Group Dynamics, 3*(4), 1–12.

Shechtman, Z., & Dvir, V. (2006). Attachment style as a predictor of behavior in group counseling with preadolescents. *Group Dynamics: Theory, Research, and Practice, 10*, 29–42.

Shechtman, Z., & Gilat, I. (2005). The effectiveness of counseling groups in reducing stress of parents of children with learning disabilities. *Group Dynamics: Theory, Research, and Practice, 9*, 275–286.

Shechtman, Z., & Gluk, O. (2006). An investigation of therapeutic factors in children's groups. *Group Dynamics: Theory, Research, and Practice, 9*, 127–134.

Shechtman, Z., & Nachshol, R. (1996). A school-based intervention to reduce aggressive behavior in maladjusted adolescents. *Journal of Applied Developmental Psychology, 17*, 535–553.

Shen, Y.-J. (2007). Developmental model using Gestalt-play versus cognitive-verbal group with Chinese adolescents: Effects on strengths and adjustment enhancement. *Journal for Specialists in Group Work, 32*(3), 285–305.

Shook, E. V., & Kwan, L. K. (1991). Ho'oponopono: Straightening family relationships in Hawaii. In K. Avruch, P. W. Black, & J. A. Scimecca (Eds.), *Conflict resolution: Cross-cultural perspectives* (pp. 213–229), Westport, CT: Greenwood Press.

Smith, A. P., & Kelly, A. B. (2008). An exploratory study of group therapy for sexually abused adolescents and non-offending guardians. *Journal of Child Sexual Abuse, 17*, 101–116.

Tadaka, E., & Kanagawa, K. (2004). Randomized controlled trial of a group care program for community-dwelling elderly people with dementia. *Japan Journal of Nursing Science, 1*, 19–25.

Tauroa, H. (1982). *A race against time.* Auckland: New Zealand Race Relations Office.

Theron, L. C. (2008). "I have undergone some metamorphosis!" The impact of REds on South African educators affected by the HIV/AIDS pandemic. A pilot study. *Journal of Psychology in Africa, 18*, 31–42.

Toseland, R. W., & McClive-Reed, K. P. (2009). Social group work: International and global perspectives. *Social Work with Groups, 32*, 5–13.

Tukukino, H., & Tukukino, W. (1986). Cross-cultural communication in New Zealand and its relevance for training programmes. In J. F. Everts (Ed.), *Family communication training in New Zealand* (pp. 237–242). Auckland, New Zealand: University of Auckland.

Venter, M., Venter, C., Botha, K., & Strydom, M. (2008). Cancer patients' illness experiences during a group intervention. *Journal of Psychology in Africa, 18*, 549–560.

Waldo, M., & Bauman, S. (1998). Regrouping the categorization of group work: A goals and process (GAP) matrix for groups. *Journal for Specialists in Group Work, 23*, 164–176.

Wall, J. A., & Callister, R. R. (1995). Ho'oponopono: Some lessons from Hawaii mediation. *Negotiation Journal, 11*, 45–54.

Yalom, I. D. (with Leszcz, M.) (2005). *The theory and practice of group psychotherapy* (5th ed.) New York: Basic Books.

Yi-Qi, Z. (2005). The effect of group intervention on quality of life diabetics. *Chinese Mental Health Journal, 19*, 227–229.

Zhao, Y. J. (2007). Efficacy of the group mental intervention with combined therapy in the treatment of anisometropic amblyopia in children. *Chinese Mental Health Journal, 21*, 350–352.

Zhou, S. L., Hou, Z. J., & Bai, R. (2008). Effect of group assertiveness training on university students' assertive competence. *Chinese Journal of Clinical Psychology, 16*, 665–667.

Brief Group Treatment

Jerrold Lee Shapiro

Abstract

Brief groups are defined as being time-limited, with a preset termination, with a process orientation, and being professionally led. Membership is closed, and members are screened for fit, consistent goals, and similar ego strength. A brief history of the precursors of brief group treatments is explored. The process stages, or group trajectory, are described and related to the nature and timing of interventions. Brief group process and outcome research, the vast majority of extant studies, is explored; and recommendations are made for more carefully designed studies. Finally, a combination of predictions and a wish list for future research, practice, and training is offered.

Keywords: time-limited groups, group process, training, screening, transition, termination, group counseling, group therapy, group treatment

Introduction

The brief or time-limited group is characteristically presented as a specific form of treatment within the broader rubric of group counseling. Most textbooks treat it as such, and this handbook is consistent with the general thrust in the field. In previous chapters, there has been substantial evidence presented for the use of group counseling in a host of settings and with a wide variety of populations. Characteristically, time-limited therapies are considered to have unique properties and limited application.

There is certainly justification for such a perspective. However, in this chapter a quite different viewpoint is being offered. Rather than consider brief groups as a subset of group counseling, they will be presented as the best-known, most studied form of group counseling. Indeed, almost all of the empirical evidence of the relative effectiveness of group counseling has been garnered from studies of time-limited, closed groups. In general, data collected and analyzed from studies of brief groups have been extrapolated to group treatment as a whole rather than the reverse.

If the idea that brief groups are the prototype for all group counseling seems radical, approach it with realistic skepticism. It is being presented from the perspective of a group therapist and group counselor trainer who has been leading, supervising, and studying time-limited groups for over 40 years.

A Few Critical Definitions

Describing brief treatment groups necessitates making a delineation both between short- and long-term treatments per se and of the types of group. It is not easy to do so. Although the vast majority of group research has been conducted on time-limited, adult, outpatient groups (Dies, 1992), definitions of what constitutes brief or long term are quite inconsistent. In addition, in much of the literature, the similarities and differences among terms like *group counseling, group therapy, encounter, training,* and *psychoeducational groups* are unclear. Some use the terms interchangeably, while others make quite specific differentiations.

What Is Brief Treatment?

One defining criterion is the length of time in therapy. In most clinical circles, the dividing line between short-term and long-term therapy has been somewhat arbitrarily set at 12 months, but that general consensus has a substantial standard deviation. Thus, what was "brief" for Sifneos (1972) could be 10–11 months of weekly treatment. By contrast, Bloom (1981) recommended single-session psychotherapy.

Solution-focused therapists such as de Shazer and Berg (de Shazer, 1985; Berg and de Shazer, 1993) promoted a symptom-oriented form of brief therapy that was heavily influenced by the hypnotherapy work of Milton Erickson and the Mental Research Institute "strategic" family therapy group in Palo Alto, California. One aspect of their brief approach involves a session-by-session commitment. Clients may choose at the end of each meeting with the therapist whether and when to meet again. In a sense, each single session has a separate contract and constitutes an entity of treatment. If their treatment lasts a total of 25 (individual) weekly sessions, can it be considered brief?

Beginning in the late 1970s and expanding geometrically since the early 1990s, brief treatment has been increasingly encouraged for economic reasons as well as theoretical and definitional factors. By 2008, health-care spending in the United States was about $7,681 per resident and accounted for 16.2% of the nation's gross domestic product, the highest of any nation (US Department of Health and Human Services, 2010). There are many reasons for this, not the least being that the United States is the only industrialized nation that has a for-profit health-care system. Economic pressure from third-party payers such as managed care companies and capitated contracts has forced a shift to a symptom-removal, brief therapy model to compensate a majority of Americans for psychotherapy costs.

A second criterion for brief therapy has to do with the definition and goal of therapy. The very beginnings of psychotherapy or its precursors are replete with methods that were quite short in duration by today's standards. Although psychoanalytic approaches are normally thought of as particularly long-term, some of Freud's earliest analyses took only weeks. According to Rutan, Stone, and Shay, (2007), Freud's analysis of Ferenzi lasted a total of less than 9 weeks in three separate courses and that of Eitington, only 2 weeks.

During those early days, Freud's method of choice involved hypnotic techniques that were focused on symptom removal and could produce quite rapid behavior change. This is remarkably similar to the focus of modern-day brief therapies. Yet, it is one thing to alter behavior or help ameliorate symptoms. It is quite another to gain insight into their genesis and functional value. In 1937, when he was 81 years old, Freud wrote of the possibility of symptoms recurring under catastrophic stress for those who had been successfully analyzed. In postulating this, he used the term *therapy interminable*.

Rationales for brief therapies include the increasing demand for what has been called evidence-based or empirically based therapy (EBT), empirically supported therapy (EST), empirically validated therapy (EVT), and a host of other acronym-based descriptors. Of course, treatments supported by solid research are extremely desirable. However, to date, the support and evidence are mitigated somewhat by the nature of the extant studies. To a great extent, research thus far has focused primarily on cognitive-behavioral therapy and has been very much university-based. This offers both pluses and minuses. Alternative approaches such as time-limited dynamic psychotherapy have been espoused by Levenson (2001), and there is increasing evidence that supportive and psychodynamic treatment also meets the empirical standards of success (e.g., Shedler, 2010).

Budman and Gurman (1983) describe additional difficulties in defining brief therapy. One consideration of note is the format of therapy. For example, is a marathon format in which an individual, couple, or family may meet for 10–20 hours in a single week considered brief because the length of time in therapy was only 7 days or perhaps a weekend? They conclude that the best operational definition of brief treatment is therapy in which the time allotted to treatment is rationed as opposed to open-ended. Budman and Gurman further define brief therapy as a state of mind of both therapist and patient.

One characteristic of this state of mind is the mutually agreed definition of the therapeutic goal. Does the expectation include change in basic character (long term) or amelioration of symptoms (short term)? Long-term therapists characteristically consider presenting problems as reflecting deeper, more complex issues vs. the shorter-term perspective of viewing problems at face value. Finally, some longer-term therapies consider the therapy relationship to be primary in the patient's life and that therapy well practiced is both non-iatrogenic and helpful.

Short-term therapists do not focus on "cure," view change as inevitable throughout life with or without therapy, and see their interventions as using and redirecting that change process. Their awareness is based on a number of studies that one consistent effect of therapy is increased variance, not necessarily always positive movement. Iatrogenic outcomes of therapy lead short-term therapists to minimize the extent of contact beyond working on the mutually agreed presenting concern.

Patients may also have concerns about time-rationed (brief) therapy. Just as some patients will believe that being assigned to group treatment is inferior to individual treatment, there may be a belief among clients that brief therapy is a lesser form of therapy. Budman (1981) and Small (1979) underscore the salience of setting and holding realistic goals for the time available and indicate that it is possible to chip away at a larger problem in stages, potentially in separate series of therapeutic series and contracts. Indeed, Budman, Demby, and Randall (1982) noted that, regardless of outcome, clients in brief treatment often return within a year for additional work.

Perhaps because of the limited time frame, brief-term counseling often involves more active intervention by the therapist and liberal use of between-session "homework." Shapiro and his colleagues, for example, have shown that computer-based homework has a significant positive impact on brief group outcome for patitents suffering from posttraumatic stress disorder (PTSD) (Bailey, Shapiro, & Kovachy, 1998) and for training counseling psychologists (Shapiro, 1998).

Because brief treatment in groups or in individual counseling requires special skills, the issue of professional training for counselors is particularly germane. Levenson and Evans (2000) discuss in depth the problem that few psychology training programs and psychiatric residencies actually train their students in time-rationed therapy modalities. In a national survey in 1995, Davidovitz and Levenson reported that 90% of the 1,250 psychologists surveyed reported doing brief therapy but that half had not had a single class on this modality in their training. According to Levenson and Evans (2000) and Levenson (2006, personal communication), it was fully expected that any training would take place on the job in internship sites.

What Is Group Therapy? What Is Brief Group Therapy?

The problem of a lack of consensus in definition or attention to specific needs of time-limited treatment per se is compounded somewhat in defining adequately what exactly constitutes brief group treatment. First, there is a need to define what constitutes group treatment (group counseling, group psychotherapy, encounter, psychoeducation, etc.). Second, the definitional 1-year dividing line between short- and long-term therapies does not hold for any of the multiclient therapies (couple, family, group). Finally, the group-therapy modalities for brief work require some additional assumptions not regularly made with individual therapies.

It is clear that many authors have used the same term, *group therapy*, to indicate a wide range of diverse approaches to treatment (Corsini, 1957). As early as 1948, Renouvier described the term *group therapy* as a collective term for diverse and contradictory methods. In 1948, Hulse stated that it is an ill-defined term for treatments that have little in common. More recently, Yalom (2005) preferred to speak of an untold number of group therapies.

The term *group therapy* itself has a rather curious history. Natural groups have been used for centuries to provide intangible healing benefits, whether at the healing temple that existed at Epidaurus in Greece from 600 BCE to 200 CE (Janet, 1925) or in traditional Hawaiian ho'oponopono ceremonies (Pukui, Haertig, & Lee, 1983). Frank (1974) suggested that witches' covens and the primitive shaman in many cultures employed similar techniques to modern group therapists, albeit with different intent and rationale.

It is curious that many of the early innovations occurred in France, a country that in modern times is loath to risk group methods for fear of a riot or mob psychology. The first formal group that was purported to be intentionally therapeutic was conducted by Anton Mesmer in the eighteenth century (Shapiro, 1978). Sufferers would sit around a wooden tub with metal filings. Mesmer would pass among them and treat them with what he called "magnetism." Mesmer and his "cures" created such a stir in Parisian society that he was investigated by a royal commission led by Benjamin Franklin. There were two reports about his methods. The official released report stated that the cures were real but the maladies were imaginary. A second, secret report, for the king only, warned about seduction of female patients and claimed that the methods were a threat to public morality (Shapiro & Scheflin, 1988). Mesmer's methods and theories have become a historical footnote, but the use of workshop group members sitting in wooden tubs, now filled with hot water, has had something of a revival at centers like Esalen in Big Sur, California from the 1970s to today. The circular container and face-to-face sharing likely reinforce group process and members' cohesiveness.

Not long after Mesmer, another unlikely forerunner of the group therapist was the Marquis de Sade, who was incarcerated at the asylum at Charenton. While an inpatient, de Sade directed plays that were acted by other patients before the general public (Gorer, 1934). Reportedly, the plays, an obvious precursor to psychodrama, had positive effects on the patients. By 1904, Camus and Pagniez were promoting healing on wards rather than in solitude (Corsini, 1957).

Another unofficial group that had significant influence was Freud's famous Wednesday Evening Society. In this "study" group, Freud was both leader and discussant. Although he never did formal group therapy, his influence on Stekel, Eitington, Rank, Wittels, and Adler led Kanzer (1971) to describe Freud as the first psychoanalytic group leader. Freud himself was disinclined to actually conduct groups. He feared contagion of emotion and mob psychology, reenacting the primal horde's killing and eating of the leader. This was enacted only symbolically in the ultimate rebellion of many in the inner circle.

Pratt's (1906) class method of treating tuberculosis patients was economically instigated, yet there were observed improvements in patients that were based on the intangible effects of meeting. Adler, with his belief in social interest, conducted groups that essentially reflected individual therapy with an audience (Dreikurs, 1959).

The advent of Moreno's psychodrama methods demonstrated the way that individuals in a group setting could influence each other in positive ways. Moreno claimed to be the creator of the term *group therapy*, and he has also been credited as the first to use the term *encounter* in a therapeutic setting. Through the 1930s and beyond, the influence of Moreno's methods and techniques has seeped into a host of other approaches to group; and the journal he founded, *Group Therapy*, remains the organ of dissemination for research and practice using psychodrama.

One final brief group pioneer in that era was Bender (1937), who experimented with group methods of treating institutionalized children in hospital wards. Her work spurred later work with children and adolescents, for whom group is more natural and particularly effective.

Counseling, Therapy, Training

In the past 70 years, the number and applications of groups have multiplied dramatically and so have the definitions and labels. There has been a lack of agreement on clear definitions of *group counseling*, *group therapy*, and *group training*. In general, the term *therapy* is used for populations that are more pathological, have lower ego strength, and have problems that are more remedial in nature. *Group counseling* is the term used for more specific and transient problems in living. In brief, the *Diagnostic and Statistical Manual* Global Assessment of Functioning scores are higher for people in counseling groups. Groups for training, growth, or self-help are typically used for populations that are deemed to be primarily adaptive and functional. Gazda, Ginter, and Horne (2001) described therapy groups as primarily remedial and distinguished them from psychoeducational, encounter, and guidance groups, which were viewed as primarily preventive and growth-centered. Group counseling was in between, offering some of each.

Additional variables include the degree or license of the group leaders and the location of the group. Clinical psychologists and psychiatrists tend to call their work "therapy," counseling psychologists and marriage and family therapists tend to use "counseling" more often, and social workers often refer to various forms of "group work." Groups done in schools are more likely to be called "counseling" than those conducted in mental health clinics. "Training" is used for groups run in industrial settings and graduate programs in mental health. The particular label applied may also reflect certain demands of managed care providers and the institutional system in which the treatment occurs.

Definition of Brief Treatment Groups

What is meant by the term *brief* when it comes to group counseling? Corey, Corey, and Corey (2010) and Yalom (2005) use the term *brief group therapy*. Corey (2004) also describes *brief group counseling*. MacKenzie (1997a) calls his groups *time-managed*. Budman (1994) uses the more specific term *time-effective* treatment, Forsyth (2006) calls it *brief group work*, and Shapiro, Peltz, and Bernadett-Shapiro (1998) use *brief group treatment*.

With the divergence of methods considered under the single rubric and the range of labels employed, it is no easy task to use a single definition that is neither too broad nor too narrow. Nonetheless, the majority of research on group, regardless of label, meets the criteria for "brief."

What is brief? Even using the Budman and Gurman (1983) criterion of time allotment, there are questions. Is it the number of sessions or doses of treatment? Is it the number of hours of contact?

Koss, Butcher, and Strupp (1986) refer to groups that are under 25 sessions. Budman et al. (1982) did 15-session groups. Shapiro (1978) and his colleagues (Diamond & Shapiro, 1973; Shapiro & Diamond, 1972) reported on 30-hour groups (over 15 weeks) and on 20-hour groups (six 2-hour sessions and one 8-hour marathon in a 6-week period). Groups held in university settings (Corey et al., 2010; Foulds & Hannigan, 1976; Shechtman & Toren, 2009) often run the length of an academic semester or quarter.

Is a marathon group that meets for 48 or 72 hours of contact over a single weekend brief? What about a crisis group in an inpatient facility that meets daily for 3 hours, a total of 42 hours for 2 weeks? Would we consider a 28-day inpatient substance-abuse program at a treatment center brief?

Operational Definition for This Chapter

Given the lack of consensus on what constitutes brief and the general perception that all multiclient therapies commonly have a shorter time frame involving fewer sessions, it is important to recognize that brief groups are not simply abbreviated forms of long-term groups. They are designed, implemented, and conducted differently. Goals are not equivalent and often are more clearly delineated.

Thus, the length of time from beginning to end of group and the number of sessions will be secondary to the group format. Ten criteria for brief group treatments may be seen in Table 27.1.

1. *Why closed?* Many group leaders prefer ongoing groups in which members enter and leave as is personally appropriate (e.g., Yalom, 2005). Open or replacement-only enrollment groups have the advantage of more closely simulating real life with the opportunity and need to face issues of loss, separation and individuation, fears of intimacy, dependency, and rejection as members enter and depart.

However, one prime advantage of brief, closed groups is elimination of time necessary in incorporating a new member or the hierarchical readjustments that accompany loss or addition of a new member. This helps the group stay on its trajectory, rather than having to regress in the process, as trust must be rebuilt and hierarchies redrawn. Furthermore, in a brief-treatment environment, the team synergy of a closed group is particularly healing.

2. *Why a preset termination?* The clear ending date for a group provides a realistic pressure on members to finish the work for which they came. It also sets a prescribed phase of group for all members to deal simultaneously with issues of loss and transfer of training.

Table 27.1 Comparison of brief groups to standard counseling groups

Brief Counseling Groups	Counseling Groups
Closed enrollment	Open enrollment
Predetermined beginning and termination foci: (1) dealing with loss, (2) transfer of training	No set group termination, termination individualized, dual foci: (1) dealing with loss, (2) transfer of training
Less than 6 months in duration	No set duration
Limited goals, clearly set	Goals relevant for population
Process-oriented, here-and-now focus	Focus mixed: problem solving and process
Predictable epigenetic trajectory, leaders' timing within process essential	Predictable epigenetic trajectory; leaders' timing important, less crucial
Group theme or other similarity communalities	Theme possible, fewer obvious communalities
Professionally trained leaders coleaders recommended	Professionally trained leaders coleaders recommended
Therapist and members have consonant orientation, goals more consonant	Therapist and members have consonant goals, values may have a wider range
Screening for fit and ego strength of members	Screening for fit, wider range of member ego strength

3. *Why brief duration and limited goals?* The average number of hours in group treatment in the empirical literature is typically quite short, often as few as 6–8 hours. The brief duration maps well with results, especially those that indicate that positive outcome occurs in a relatively short time in group (Cuijpers, van Straten, & Warmerdam, 2008; Hansen, Lambert, & Forman, 2002; Horowitz and Garber, 2006; Shapiro et al., 1998; Stice, Rohde, Seeley, & Gau, 2008).

In addition, the demands and vagaries of managed care proscribe groups of limited duration. However, this places the burden on group leaders to carefully set limited goals which the brief group may legitimately accomplish. Long-term personality changes will not occur in 6 months or less of counseling.

4. *Why process-oriented?* A process focus offers a number of advantages. It provides leaders with a developmental psychological map of the interpersonal terrain. With this as a guide, the leaders may grasp more readily the current meaning of interactions within the group. A process focus creates a unique setting for personal learning by setting the stage in two ways: (1) it eliminates distractions by providing a focus on self and on the here-and-now interactions between self and others and (2) because it is socially unusual, it adds a certain amount of functional (existential) anxiety and vigilance that facilitates learning.

5. *Predictable genetic generic process.* For 70 years researchers and clinicians have described an observable, predictable process in group. Leaders who are aware of the naturally unfolding group trajectory are able to make the most appropriate interventions. Thus, different leadership skills are required in preparing the group, compared to treating members or terminating the group. A leader who fails to attend to the epigenetic process may actually inhibit effective group work.

6. *Why themes and relative homogeneity of membership?* Themes will help center discussion around consensual issues and promote the experience of universality. In time-limited treatment, inclusion and cohesion have to occur fairly quickly. This is more readily accomplished when there are evident commonalities between members' abilities and needs. Drum and Knott (2009) defined the evolving theme group as "a time-limited, multi-session intervention, exclusively focused on a developmental issue (broadly defined) or resolution of a specific theme, issue, challenge, or (common) problem" (p. 495).

Although brief groups have been shown to be effective with almost every level of pathology, they are overly impacted by discrepancies and isolates. To a large degree, the most pathological individual in a group has the greatest influence in restricting the group's trajectory. Thus, ego strength or its converse, pathology, is best not mixed. Although long-term, open-ended groups may derive considerable benefit from working through these discrepancies, the time available in a brief group is insufficient to making such adjustments.

7. *Professional leadership training.* All multiclient counseling (couples, families, and groups) requires a number of unique skills in addition to those common in individual treatment. Beyond those skills of active listening, clarifying, interpreting, reflecting feelings, etc. are unique diagnostic and counseling skills such as orchestrating interactions between members, translating, protecting, self-disclosing, and multilevel processing (Shapiro et al., 1998).

Group leaders characteristically need to know how and when to intervene at three different levels in a group: intrapsychic, dyadic, and group. In groups (and more so in natural groups like families or work groups) the therapist must be aware of the system that exists between the clients both in and outside of the therapy hour. Furthermore, the impact of other members of the group may be greater than that of leader interventions—often a very positive outcome. Unlike in individual therapy, some of the interactions are less based on clients' subjective historical reports than experienced in real time. Group counselors and therapists have to be able to read, understand, and anticipate group process.

8. *Why leaders and members need to be on the same page.* In a time-limited group, there is little time or opportunity for members to get to know the leader's orientation, strengths, and preferences. For optimal effectiveness, the matching between leaders' and members' styles of learning is best done during screening. It is perhaps heretical to suggest that members, like leaders, have internalized theories about what makes for change (Shapiro, 1986). A member who is oriented toward insight before behavior change will work better with a group leader and group methods that are similarly organized. By contrast, a member who expects insight to follow action will have an easier time with a therapy that focuses on behavior first. Matching member and leader style and expectations will enhance strongly the impact of the group.

When goals are clearly specified in a time-limited group, it is wise to specify methods as well. This coordination occurs during group preparation and screening, the first of four group phases.

The Phases of Group: A Valuable Predictable Trajectory

When group leaders are well trained and members properly screened, brief treatment groups go through a natural, predictable trajectory from conception to follow-up. Long-term open groups also follow a similar course, but as Yalom (1990) opined, only the initial sessions of an open group may be chartered, in part because each change in membership alters the sequence. Although the terms used to describe this trajectory vary, there is a general consensus on the three to five phases through which a group progresses. Identification of this reliable sequence is not new. As early as 1936, Wender described four stages for patients in neoanalytic group therapy: (1) intellectualization, (2) transference between patients, (3) catharsis, and (4) group interest. Patients first addressed their personal emotional difficulties and later increased interest in matters outside of themselves.

This description is quite similar to groups conducted from an Adlerian perspective. Dreikurs (1951) described four stages: (1) establishment of relations, (2) interpretation of dynamics, (3) patients gaining understanding, and (4) reorientation.

Approaching small groups more globally, Tuckman (1965) used the colorful terms (1) forming, (2) storming, (3) norming, and (4) performing. Later, Tuckman and Jensen (1977) added (5) adjourning. Their description has found favor in both counseling and organizational literature.

Schutz (1973), focusing primarily on brief growth groups, described "an inevitable sequence" of (1) inclusion, (2) control, and (3) affection. In his classification, members work through their conflicts of belonging to the group, find their place in the group hierarchy, and then explore their interpersonal intimacy. In the late 1970s, Shapiro (1978) described a core group trajectory for both therapy and encounter groups with four epigenetic phases: (1) introduction, (2) learning the rules, (3) therapy proper, and (4) termination (transfer of training).

Battegay (1989), working with long-term, analytically oriented, closed groups, described a sequence remarkably similar to Wender's (1936) developmental sequence: (1) exploratory contact, (2) regression, (3) catharsis, (4) insight, and (5) social learning.

Dies (1985) also identified a five-stage model for group counseling: (1) preparation, (2) early group sessions, (3) transition, (4) working, and (5) termination. And MacKenzie (1990) called his four stages (1) engagement, (2) differentiation, (3) working, and (4) termination.

In this chapter the four-phase formulation described by Shapiro et al. (1998)—(1) introduction, (2) transition, (3) treatment, and (4) termination—is used to describe the progression. This trajectory of stages conforms well to the whole-group model employed by Corey et al. (2010), Fiebert (1963), MacKenzie (1994), and Shapiro (1978).

It is clear from the bulk of the literature that these stages are reliable for closed, process-oriented groups in which the group begins and ends together. Successive stages are built on completion of previous ones. Groups which have open and changing enrollment and those that emulate classes designed for skill learning follow less clear trajectories.

This process is envisioned as both inevitable and ideal. It is inevitable in the sense that successful completion of prior stages is prerequisite to psychological availability for subsequent stages. The progression is ideal in the sense that many groups fail to complete all the stages prior to the preset termination. However, regardless of how far the progression develops, it would be a mistake to think that it occurs linearly. Although more advanced stages are unlikely without success in earlier ones, there is considerable regression to earlier stages, particularly to test the level of group trust before moving forward again. For example, it is common for groups that have reached the treatment phase to return to transition and to retest leadership ability prior to delving into deeper or more sensitive issues for members.

Because this group trajectory is epigenetic in nature, interventions by the leader need to be geared to the current phase of group functioning. In time-limited groups, there are fewer opportunities for leaders to recover from ill-timed interventions. Thus, it is incumbent on group leaders to be aware of group development and regressions and to intervene accordingly.

The Four Phases of Group Process
Phase I: Preparation

The preparation phase encompasses everything it takes to bring a group to fruition in its first meeting. Several stages occur well before a group actually meets for the first time. These include needs assessments, determining the group goals and population, and a host of logistical factors such as cost, location, time of day, length and number of sessions, leader characteristics and credentials, cultural factors, and the desired mix of clients.

Because stable membership is so central to success in time-limited groups, these logistical factors are particularly significant. For example, cost for the group has to be appropriate. To enhance stability, some leaders in brief groups actually charge up front for the group as a whole rather than session by session. Of course, any member has the right to terminate and be reimbursed for future sessions, but the flat fee has proven successful in keeping attendance high (Shapiro et al., 1998). Shapiro (1978) also warned against groups that are free for members, reporting that even a modest copay will reduce dropouts and sporadic attendance.

INVOLUNTARY GROUPS

Membership in institutional groups, such as those for hospitalized patients, the military, prisoners, students, business or management representatives, or court-directed participants, is frequently determined by assignment rather than choice. In addition, Budman and Gurman (1983) indicated that some clients assigned to a group vs. individual therapy resented being in the "lesser" condition and that attendance plummeted.

In these groups, leaders have to deal immediately with resentment and resistance that members bring to the group. This can begin in screening and continue into the early stages of the transition phase. Members need to be at least semivoluntary (not happy about being there but willing to see what they can get out of the group) for groups to be effective.

SCREENING

Screening begins when members apply for the group. Many short-term groups have failed because of a lack of potential member screening. Both the ethical guidelines of the Association of Specialists in Group Work (Thomas & Pender, 2007) and the American Counseling Association (2005) require proper screening and recommend that the screening be done by the leaders in face-to-face interviews, even if that time increases the cost charged.

Capuzzi and Gross (1992), Carroll and Wiggins (1990), Corey (1990), Rutan et al. (2007), Shapiro et al. (1998), and Yalom (1995) have underscored the primacy of screening for effective groups. They assert that a poor mix of members is the most likely cause for a group to get bogged down or produce casualties. Members of a group with widely divergent goals or levels of ego strengths will be hard-pressed

to make it out of the transition phase, leaving little opportunity for treatment.

The two crucial screening questions are

1. Is this group appropriate for the client?
2. Is the client appropriate for this group?

Obviously, in closed groups, poor screening that leads to dropouts or nonattendance is particularly problematic. In brief groups with themes and more homogeneous membership, it is assumed that the more the group members share certain characteristics and experiences, the more understanding, altruism, and hope will develop. However, the more heterogeneous a group, the more diverse the perspectives that may be available. In fact, people of different ages, races, cultures, and walks of life often become a very productive group.

Screening Rules of Thumb

In addition to the need for equivalent ego strength among members, there are other screening criteria:

Include members who match with others or fill in gaps, and avoid those with poor alignment of population, goals, and resources.

Avoid group isolates. Common examples of isolates include one person of a different gender, of a very different age, or with an Axis II disorder, severe Axis I pathology, or an addiction.

Avoid members with out-of-group relationships with each other, unless that is a basis for the group (i.e., couples groups).

Avoid members with a secret motivation to sell an idea or product to others.

Avoid members with pathology beyond the capability of the therapists.

The importance of such screening into and out of a particular group is not new. Between 1950 and 1970, Slavson (1951), Yalom (1970), Rosenbaum and Hartley (1962), and Corsini and Lundin (1951) all warned about counterproductive individuals in outpatient groups. Among those identified were brain-damaged, mentally defective, psychotic (especially withdrawn and paranoid), and psychopathic individuals, drug or alcohol addicts, and suicidal and assaultive patients. Certainly, any member whose pathology would foster insensitivity or, in extreme instances, preying on other members is a poor risk (Dinkmeyer & Muro, 1971). Vander Kolk (1985) and Capuzzi and Gross (1992) underscore unique dangers of mixing suicidal patients of different levels of lethality. This does not mean that groups are not suitable for patients with more severe pathology but that the short-term outpatient group may be less suitable than inpatient or long-term specialty groups oriented to their interpersonal needs (e.g., Finn & Shakir, 1990).

Screening Sessions

Not all leaders do their screening before members meet. Corey (1990), focusing primarily on university-level counseling groups, favors a fairly elaborate preparatory session in which the leader explores with the members their hopes and fears for the group and underscores guidelines such as confidentiality, focusing, and journaling that enhance future sessions. This "initial session" may also allow for extended screening and a stronger commitment. Rogers (1973) also preferred a presession for encounter groups.

Yalom, Houts, Newell, and Rand (1979) claimed that a preparatory session both improved patients' faith in the therapy process and maximized potential placebo effects. Yalom (1985) included in his preparation for group an exploration of misconceptions and expectations, description of his existential theory of group work, prediction of stumbling blocks, discussions of trust, self-disclosure, extragroup socialization, confidentiality, goals, exploration of risks inherent in group therapy, and an examination of how members can best grow from the experience. Vinogradov and Yalom (1990) particularly encouraged such sessions, to reduce negative expectations.

In their review of pregroup participation, Orlinsky and Howard (1986) concluded that a majority of studies strongly favor role-preparation procedures. Piper and Perrault (1989) were less sanguine about the value of such sessions for members but indicated that a "prepped group" might help leaders feel more comfortable. By contrast, groups based on an Adlerian model eschew all screening of group members as nondemocratic.

Phase II: Transition

The transition phase of the group prepares members for treatment or intervention. Some authors depict this phase as dominated by conflict and struggle. McKenzie (1994) described it as one of rebellion and struggle for differentiation, emphasizing issues of control, dominance, and anger. Corey and Corey (1982) called it a period of anxiety, defensiveness, resistance, struggle for control between members, and conflicts with the leaders. By contrast, Schutz (1973) focused on both inclusion and finding one's place on the group hierarchy, and Dies & Dies (1993) wrote of a natural unfolding in which members first share matters in common, building trust, and then test the leaders.

It is natural for members to be fearful of and resistant to change. The core of the transition period is to help members find ways to face those fears. To do so, they first are encouraged to build trust and confidence in themselves and the other members, develop group cohesion, learn group norms, explore personal anxiety about introspection and become a bit more experimental personally. The particular form that the intragroup discussion takes has a lot to do with the characteristics of the members and the leaders' styles and personalities.

The leaders' role during transition is to help members learn about what the group has to offer them in an experiential, rather than instructive, manner. They provide support and encouragement for the members' struggles and growth. By demonstrating comfort with members' feelings and redirecting the focus to the here and now, they help members face better, and defend less against, their anxieties in the present.

Although members may get some therapeutic benefit from the caring and acceptance conveyed, the most important quality of the transition phase is that members learn how to get the kind of help the group can offer. During this stage, members need to feel that they belong and that the group will offer them something. Ultimately, the trust in the group will be established through an experiential discovery of what can be addressed successfully in a particular group with these leaders. Thus, there will be two essential tests of the leaders' capacities:

1. The limits of the leader's skill and competence (the group's ceiling)
2. An awareness of matters beyond the leader's abilities (the group's floor)

The extent to which these matters are managed and resolved will substantively determine the extent of work that can be addressed later in the treatment phase of the group.

Transition begins when the members sit in the group room and the leader announces the group's beginning. Early in transition, leaders have to set a tone appropriate for the group. In general, they will ask members to introduce themselves and say what brought them to the group, what they hope to get out of the group, and perhaps what they fear may happen.

The introductions serve several purposes: inclusion, reducing anxiety by providing structure, and letting members know the kinds of issues they will be asked to discuss in more detail later. If it is a theme-oriented group, this also begins feelings of cohesion and universality.

Each group leader will have certain idiosyncratic rules and preferences about group participation. The specifics of such instructions seem less important than the level of structure they convey. The level of structure provided needs to be titrated by the leader to reflect the level of the anxiety of the members and the leaders' personal comfort. Two psychological phenomena are significant here, the linear relationship between anxiety and ambiguity and the curvilinear relationship between anxiety and performance (Shapiro et al., 1998). Leaders in brief groups frequently manipulate the level of structure to help keep the group in the highest performance level of that second curve.

In a time-limited group, clear ground rules are especially important. In stipulating their ground rules, leaders provide structure, especially around ethics and the issue of confidentiality. As Yalom (1990) has shown, there are also times when the ground rules need to be revisited when questions of importance, such as about confidentiality, arise later. Regardless of the care with which ground rules are conveyed, it is inevitable that levels of anxiety and ambiguity are high at the beginning of the group because members do not specifically know what is expected of them personally.

As the group struggles to begin, leaders need to monitor the group's level of anxiety. If the level is too high for productive work, the leaders will add structure. If the functional anxiety is too low for effective work, the leader will increase ambiguity (and anxiety) by decreasing structure. In this way, a group leader can enhance the effectiveness of the group process by maintaining levels of structure that engender moderate levels of anxiety.

Throughout the transition period, the therapist's role is most effective when he or she focuses the members' attention on the here and now in the group. This is accomplished by referring to process in the group, rather than making intrapsychic or advisory interventions. Thus, the group members may become more fully present and available for treatment interventions that are most effective when they are ready to receive them.

Often, early in the group there are uncomfortable silences as members struggle to figure out how to work together. This is a good time for leaders to reorient members' focus onto their internal experience. It is not a time to make the group safer by "fixing the anxiety problem" (Bernard & MacKenzie, 1994).

Until trust of the leaders and, to a lesser extent, the other members is further established, members try to reduce the anxiety by finding some external communality and then proceed to discuss it in a there-and-then manner. Often, news stories of the day or institutional kvetching dominate before they are guided to share in the present about their ingroup experience.

The leaders' role is to describe the group process and avoid getting involved in the discussion of there-and-then events. When these discussions seem to come to a blank wall, members are encouraged to look in another direction, toward themselves as individuals and toward each other as fellow members. Leaders may then begin to make interventions and encourage members to help each other.

Characteristically, during this period of the time-limited group, a member will present a personal problem (frequently a marital or relationship problem) which occurs outside the group yet presumably affects his or her interactions in the group as well. The presentation of the problem and accompanying indecision about what to do may be lengthy, time-consuming, and frequently accompanied by sadness, crying, anger, frustration, or fearfulness. Often, the problem area—marriage, separation, divorce, parenting, affairs, sexual inadequacies, aggression, substance abuse—is one that affects or interests many group members. A spirited discussion ensues, with the presenter discussing the problem and expressing feelings in greater detail.

As the discussion continues, other group members attempt to help by giving advice, recommending alternative solutions, and offering guidance, assistance, and support. Frequently, members will share their own similar experiences in this area, relating how they handled or mishandled similar situations in their own lives. This advice is freely offered and usually presented with caring, concern, and support for the individual; *but nothing members do seems to alter or resolve the dilemma.*

When the leaders focus on the process, rather than a solution, the members begin to discover what may be best approached for group discussion and what is beyond the group's purview and capacity. By contrast, if the leaders do get involved in trying to fix an unsolvable problem, this stage of group may go on for an extended period of time: a particular challenge in a group with a limited number of sessions.

Although the members learn what will not be best addressed in the group, they are often not happy about the failure of the leader to fix a member's pain. This often leads to the second test—what is the group's ceiling? During this period, leaders will be challenged in a manner that reveals their strengths and how much pressure they can handle. As the group members come to grasp the leaders' capacity, the structure or frame is set for the work to come. Of course, every counselor has personal limits to what he or she can handle. If these are clear, members will be free to address their issues within the framework of the leaders' strengths. When leaders dodge the challenges, the group may turn the pressure onto a particular member as a scapegoat.

Typically, the transition phase seems long, drawn out, difficult, and wasteful of the group's precious time. No real problem solving or treatment seems to be occurring. There is tremendous pressure for leaders in short-term groups to try to hurry through this stage and get to the "really important" treatment phase. However, pushing the members at this point usually will have a paradoxical effect. They will work more efficiently when they are more fully trusting of the group leadership and the other members and begin to feel more responsible personally for change. It is best to encourage the tests to occur and to work with them, rather than to treat them as a barrier to some presumed more important subsequent work. The leadership tests are the primary work at this stage. Like all forms of resistance in psychotherapy, they are best used to promote the therapy, rather than as obstacles to overcome.

Thus, if the time is taken to embrace the challenges of transition, the group will be better able to enter the treatment phase. It is important to note that the movement from stage to stage is not always clear-cut. Often, stages need to be repeated, especially prior to new depth being explored. For example, after significantly deeper interactions, members may regress to earlier stages and retest leadership capability before going into yet deeper material.

Phase III: Treatment (Working, Intervention)

Members came to the group seeking solutions to problems and/or insight into their intrapsychic functioning. Several hours of group time have been spent to prime members for these foci of the treatment phase of the group.

In a time-limited group, members internalize new thinking and behavior by both trial-and-error experimentation with immediate feedback and vicariously by observing others. They are able to do this in an environment that paradoxically offers higher intensity and lower threat.

The group is uniquely set up to allow people to express themselves emotionally and to learn in real time. This combination of intensity within security opens opportunities for members to deal with difficult issues and interactions and to observe themselves while they are reacting. In this protected environment, they are able to experience how both leaders and other members react to them when they are more vulnerable and privy to others' recommendations.

During treatment, unlike transition, the problems discussed are far more likely to be solvable, in part because the aspects of the issues that occur in the group per se can be dealt with directly and personally. The problems may not go away, but the individual's reactions may well be altered. This focus on what can be changed is coincident with a far more internal focus on members' parts. In the course of increasing disclosure, members discover the universality of "closet skeletons" and face them in new ways.

Inevitably, in a brief group, some members share and work aloud more than others. At some point in treatment, the less active members are identified and their verbal participation is requested. This second inclusion stage builds more trust and, as it resolves, allows for even deeper work. Often, these "quieter" members will either use the opportunity to participate more verbally or to talk to the group about their more vicarious or culturally relevant learning style.

During the treatment phase of the group, leaders encourage the continuation and deepening of the developing group norms. One of the major advantages of group treatment is that it allows for multimodal pathways to the members' goals. Leaders intervene at three different interlocking levels of interaction: intrapsychic, interpersonal, and group.

Intrapsychic interventions focus primarily on a single individual and encourage greater depth. In *interpersonal interventions*, the leader highlights interactions and interrelationships between members. They are utilized to help members focus on the way they impact others and on their reactions to other members in the group. They also foster therapeutic alliances among members and bring strengths in the group in contact with needs. *Group-level interventions* are directed to the membership as a whole.

Each level addresses different group needs, similar to the engineering principle of bandwidth and fidelity: The more individuals are involved in a particular interaction, the lesser the depth and the broader the reach or scope. The intrapsychic level offers the greatest depth of emotional processing and repair. However, it is limited by the relevance of one person's work to others in the group. By contrast, the group level offers more simultaneous group work—every member works at the same level, but the intensity of the work is circumscribed by the member who is working at the least depth. In a maximally effective group, leaders will employ all levels, based on the extant process, the group goals, and their theoretical orientations.

During the treatment phase, there is often an intensification in the expression of emotion as the members uncover more and more of the normally hidden parts of their personalities and their more important personal concerns. In groups where the goal is rapid behavior change and symptom amelioration, the intensity appears as members experiment with alternative behaviors and reactions with group support. For the most part, the leader and other group members will support the enhanced expression of affect, albeit within the range set earlier by the transition phase leadership tests. This support naturally engenders further affective expression.

Sometimes, during this stage of the group, individual, dyadic, and systemic therapy skills are utilized. Role-playing, role reversals, psychodrama, focusing, sensory awareness exercises, systematic desensitization, guided fantasy, behavioral rehearsals, and a host of related techniques are employed, dependent on the individual members' receptivity and the therapist's armamentarium of interventions (Fehr, 2008).

When impending termination becomes a pressure for group leaders, they may try to force movement or to focus more on content issues as a way to promote rapid change. Unfortunately, such an approach characteristically works in reverse. Members may simply ignore these interventions, unsuccessfully try to comply with the premature suggestions for either insight or behavior change, regress to earlier group stages, or become increasingly resistant to being told what to do.

TIMING
Interventions and interpretations work best when both the individuals and the group are emotionally and cognitively prepared. With the higher level of cohesion, real, present, meaningful concerns are shared and dealt with by the group. Because the

level of interpersonal trust is so high, help is not rejected, as it may have been earlier in the group, but actively sought. Members frequently attempt to solve problems together and confront each other honestly and with caring. Interpersonal conflicts between members of the group are discussed with greater understanding of each person's position and concerns. Suggestions for change are encouraged and attempted with far less defensiveness than in other situations. During treatment, some leaders may be more forthcoming, sharing some personal here-and-now experiences.

In short, this is the stage of the group that members hoped for when they entered. This is the time in group to address directly and help ameliorate presenting problems. In most groups perhaps up to one-third of the total time may be spent here. Untrained or impatient leaders, in an ill-advised attempt to maximize gains in a short-term group, will rush to get to treatment. Unfortunately, without surmounting the challenges of the prior stages, particularly the tests of leadership in the transition phase, the members may spend more time focusing on problem solving but be far less successful in developing effective or enduring strategies.

This stage and these phenomena are the goal of most group leaders. It is not necessary for a group to reach this level of functioning to have some therapeutic impact. However, for groups that do reach this stage of interaction, the rewards are magnified. It is important to note that even when the group does reach this stage, it may not remain there long. As anxiety about authentic communication grows, the group will regress to earlier stages in reaction. In addition, this stage of the group is always truncated by termination.

Phase IV: Termination
Unless postgroup follow-up sessions are scheduled, termination is the final phase of the group. Until this point in the brief, closed group, entry into each succeeding stage was prompted by relative completion of the previous one. Termination uniquely is determined by the end of the allotted time. This timing may be intrusive, inconvenient, and insensitive to the unfolding of group process.

During termination, two significant and profound tasks must be accomplished: saying goodbye (dealing with loss, i.e., MacKenzie, 1997a) and transfer of training (redirecting members' work in the group to their home lives). The extent to which each is satisfied is the extent to which the group impact is maximized. Many an otherwise successful group has lost much of its therapeutic influence by ignoring or failing to fully face the tasks of termination. In brief, closed groups, the members deal with saying aloha, loss, and transfer of training together as a unit, rather than as individuals over time.

Termination is as important for group success as screening or treatment. Yet, as Gazda (1989) wrote, "all too often group leaders neglect this phase of group work and termination of the group is abrupt and without much processing of termination issues" (p. 307).

Toseland and Rivas (1984) and Jacobs, Harvill, and Masson (1994) include in the termination phase reviewing, summarizing, assessing members' growth, finishing business, maintaining and generalizing change effects, promoting individual functioning of members, helping members with their feelings about ending the group (and other losses), future planning, making referrals, and evaluation. Kottler (1982) underscores the significance of effective transfer of training to decrease dependency on the group.

Termination is often a trying phase for members because the advent of the end of the group may well bring up other losses and rejections in life. The group is unique in offering members opportunities to confront together in a concentrated way their feelings about loss, the ending of important relationships, and plans for their own futures. It is also often a difficult phase for group leaders. Shapiro et al. (1998) describe how the truly successful leader is the one who becomes anachronistic—no longer needed by the group members.

Depending on the theoretical approach of the leaders, transfer of training may be more or less directly addressed. Behaviorally oriented therapies typically focus specifically on such matters. By contrast, psychodynamic approaches rely more on client insight to evolve into such change. For brief groups, Vander Kolk (1985) and Corey (1990) recommend a more cognitive-behavioral orientation, focusing on behaviors, goals, and methods of evaluation. Because empirical studies of group outcome specifically measure the extent to which symptoms abate or attitudes improve on the requisite measures, the more specifically leaders promote this form of learning, the more likely a positive outcome, at least at posttest.

Solution-focused therapies, a common brief treatment, make the shift of learning from group to home life a linchpin. Existential therapies and emotionally focused therapies (e.g., Greenberg & Johnson, 1988) focus on consequences and meaning.

Although aspects of transfer of training occur during the treatment phase of the group process, as members work out personal issues, it is during termination that members specifically face the implications of taking what was learned in group back into their home lives. The temporal salience of specific transfer of training intervention is somewhat mitigated in natural groups when the members of a group are in out-of-group contact (such as couples groups, families, or work-based groups). In these situations, transfer of training occurs both during group sessions and between sessions. The family group, for example, goes home as a unit and continues the work that occurred in session. However, even in these natural groups, the termination is a significant event and the leader must focus on those skills and cognitions from the group sessions that will have enduring qualities.

For a number of obvious reasons, confirmed by years of clinical observation, termination is unquestionably the part of group therapy that leaders do most poorly. Among these are leaders' personal needs for reassurance, resistance to terminating and a lack of training in closing.

In an attempt to avoid their personal fears of loss, group leaders need to avoid unconsciously engaging in behaviors which prolong their role in their clients' lives. One method to avert such feelings is to ignore the impending termination of the group. Another is to create unconsciously greater dependence on the group or leaders by failing to properly refocus the members' attention to their out-of-group existence or other forms of collateral sabotage.

THE TERMINATION PROCESS

Although most therapists will opine that termination begins at first contact, most leaders agree that between one-third and one-fifth of the total group time will likely be spent in this phase, a significant number of hours for a brief group. Termination officially begins when the leader verbally reminds members of the imminent end of group time and requests that members bring up any unfinished business. If members accept this invitation to work, they often focus on insufficiently resolved outside-of-group concerns and unsettled problems between members of the group.

It is incumbent on leaders to focus consistently on the out-of-group, back home environment at this time. Many will encourage role-playing and problem solving in group in anticipation of back home interactions.

Saying goodbye often involves members and leaders sharing their overall impressions of the group. This stage may be emotional and prepares the members for the actual group close. Some leaders use closing rituals or similar techniques to assuage the pain and difficulty of the group aloha and to make it another learning experience. Leszcz and Kobos (2008), reflecting Corsini's (1957) instructions of over 50 years earlier, recommend such rituals. Some group leaders opine that a closing ritual offers a symbolic break between group and real life. For decades, the VetCenters' brief group program for Vietnam Era veterans suffering from PTSD employed "leaving the war as you leave the group" rituals with success.

The leader also has an ethical responsibility to help members deal with issues that are generated in the group but which hibernate and come into fruition only after members have left the group setting. This does not mean that the leader does follow-up therapy with each member. It is important, however, for the leader to be available for consultation and referral, at least for issues that are group-engendered. Some groups, often those that are part of research, schedule a follow-up for data collection and consultation.

In a brief group, the entire process is an arduous and concentrated journey, but a group that makes it all the way can reap a bountiful harvest for its members (and leaders). Every group does not make the entire journey however. Often, a group will have progressed through only half of the stages before termination must begin. Such a group can be of value in and of itself, and members can accrue a number of benefits. The phases discussed here comprise a reachable goal, not a bare minimum, in closed, time-limited groups. Groups with open membership progress past phase II only when the membership is stable over an extended time. Furthermore, as each new member is added to the group, earlier phases are reinstituted for their benefit and to reestablish a sense of inclusion and members' roles.

Ultimately, the goal of termination is to maximize the impact of the group experience for all members. Transfer of training, reminders of attention to feelings, and a final chance to practice the group skills all serve members after the group is concluded. It is not a time to use treatment-phase depth therapy, which may reopen members inappropriately.

Follow-Up

Some group leaders, schedule follow-up sessions 3–6 months after the group termination. Advocates of these sessions, like Corey et al. (2010), state that members will have motivation to make the changes they began in the group, knowing that the group will reconvene. It also encourages members to support each other in the interim. In the follow-up session, members can discuss difficulties since the end of the group and seek help from others they trust. Often, leaders also use these sessions to collect evaluative outcome data.

In some closed groups, members may be invited back for a "graduates night." Toseland, Kabat, and Kemp (1983) use such sessions to review members' commitment to maintaining changes, to remind members of life changes since the beginning of the group, and to have members support each other regarding difficulties in implementing group learning in real-life situations. However, there are two potential downside risks to such sessions: (1) it may be inconvenient or impossible for all members to reconvene (the leader must then decide whether to meet with only part of the original membership) and (2) knowing that there will be a follow-up meeting, some members may avoid dealing with effective termination at the end of the regular sessions. Instead of facing a "goodbye," they may simply say "au revoir."

For the leaders, such postgroup sessions involve walking a bit of a tightrope. It is inappropriate to introduce any new material for discussion, induce the members to regroup, or in any way create a need for additional therapy, yet one must be available for patient needs, to make appropriate referrals, and to support continued learning and application of group-learned skills to the patients' independent living.

The Evidence Favoring Brief Group Treatment

Despite a long history, group treatments in general, and time-limited groups in particular, have often been considered an afterthought or lesser form of therapy and counseling. All multiclient therapies have met with greater skepticism than individual modalities, and practitioners have been challenged with a higher bar to prove the efficacy of their methods. Many critics of group methods simply have never been trained in these modalities and find fault with therapies beyond their purview. In addition, those committed to group treatments may respond more defensively in the face of such disparagement of the method from both colleagues and clients. One positive result of this criticism is a robust history of decades of outcome studies of group methods.

In 1957, Corsini described six ways that groups could be evaluated: (1) face validity within theories of behavior change; (2) testimonials from both leaders and clients; (3) personal experience; (4) objective reports, including case studies; (5) statistical indices, such as percentages of clients who improved; and (6) empirical studies.

Currently, many of these evaluative methods are used to better understand what group treatment may offer. Case studies and extended testimonials of personal experiences offer a richness of description unavailable by other methods. Other support is found in surveys, correlational studies, and experimental and quasi-experimental (nonrandom assignment of members to experimental and control conditions) designs. Finally, *meta-analyses*—studies which mathematically combine extant studies and produce a ratio of efficacy (effect size)—are common.

To a large extent, research on group treatment is basically done on closed, time-limited, adult outpatient groups (Dies, 1992; Kaul & Bednar, 1986; Orlinsky & Howard, 1986). For example, there are several studies and meta-analyses with clients suffering from depression. Cuijpers et al. (2008) reported on 53 studies, all of which had a range of 4–20 sessions. Stice et al. (2008) reviewed a series of studies of 15 sessions for prevention of adolescent depression. The longest study they reviewed had 23 cognitive-behavioral therapy (CBT) sessions compared to 20 for the supportive-expressive group. Horowitz and Garber (2006) reviewed groups of 6–11 sessions. Kush (2009) reported on 12-session groups and recommended that more severely depressed patients may need "longer groups," which he defined as up to 16 sessions.

Brief groups are not unique to treating depression. Hansen et al. (2002) used groups of 13–18 sessions for a variety of treatment types and diagnoses. Shapiro et al. (1998), reviewing the extant studies on groups for adolescents, adult children of alcoholics, couples, domestic violence, eating disorders, and single gender, found an average of 5–20 sessions.

Similarly, groups for training are characteristically time-rationed as well. Shechtman and Toren (2009) reported on 14 groups that were preset with 13 sessions. Shapiro et al. (1998) reviewed 23 studies that had 5–14 sessions.

Indeed, it is difficult to find studies of longer-term groups. One exception is the 1984 study by Piper, Debbane, Bienvenue, & Garant, in which they compared short- and long-term individual and group treatments. Short treatment was defined as 6 months and long-term treatment, as 24 months. Although the results favored short-term individual and long-term groups, there was a serious flaw in leader training preparation and the model used. The leaders of the long-term groups reportedly felt "burdened" trying to apply a psychoanalytic approach to the time frame.

There are a number of pragmatic reasons that time-limited groups have been the primary object of empirical inquiry: (1) they are available, are commonly used in both agencies and private settings, and may be reliably conducted in university laboratories; (2) closed groups offer an opportunity for stable group membership and convenient data collection; (3) they can be isolated from other potentially interacting forms of treatment such as in an inpatient setting or a larger workshop; and (4) level of clients pathology can be held somewhat similar. The open-ended outpatient group favored by many clinicians (e.g., Yalom, 2005) does not allow for such control over independent variables, especially related to keeping constant time-in-treatment and valid comparisons between members of a group with different starting and ending times. Furthermore, dropouts and spotty attendance are far more likely in long-term, open groups.

In general, the evidence for the efficacy of group is in and it is quite positive. Barlow, Burlingame, and Fuhriman (2000), in a review of over 700 studies, concluded that the variety of treatments using a group format consistently produced positive effects across diagnoses. In comparison to individual counseling, group has repeatedly been shown to be at least as effective (Barlow, Fuhriman, & Burlingame, 2004; Bednar & Kaul, 1994; Burlingame, Fuhriman, & Mosier, 2003; Campbell & Dunnette, 1968; Dagley, Gazda, Eppinger, & Stewart, 1994; Hoag & Burlingame, 1997; Johnson, 2008; Kanas, 1986; Shechtman, 2007; Toseland & Siporin, 1986; Zimpfer, 1990a).

Bachar (1998), summarizing the meta-analyses of group treatments, concluded that group counseling typically yielded far greater effect sizes than either attention placebo or no-treatment groups. In addition, no reliable differences were reported for comparisons between group and individual treatments. These data support the obvious conclusion that group treatment is more economical and cost-effective.

Empirical and meta-analytic studies correlate well with the results that are obtained in narrative reports, clinical observations, and case studies. Caution needs to be exercised, however, unless cross-modality treatment can be controlled for severity of pathology. Thus, some of the more severe Axis I and almost all Axis II pathologies may not respond as well to a brief group. Although we may see improvement (Vinnars, Thormählen, Gallop, Norén, & Barber, 2009), certainly we do not speak of a cure of characterological pathology in any time-limited treatment.

Most of the more empirical studies over the past two decades have focused on groups with a theme or particular population. For example, Zimpfer has shown the effect of brief groups for incest (1987), divorce and separation (1990b), eating disorders (1990a), grief (1991), and career change (Zimpfer & Carr, 1989). Shapiro et al. (1998) reviewed studies of brief groups for six populations (adolescents, adult children of alcoholics, couples, domestic violence, eating disorders, and single gender). Gladding (2008) provided similar reviews for culturally diverse groups, children, and older adults. A number of studies on common mental disorders, like depression (Vandevoort & Fuhriman, 1991) and anxiety (Stewart & Chambless, 2009), have also shown the effectiveness of group treatment. All report favorable outcomes.

Of course, there is considerable variation across studies in experimental design, quality of measurements, number of sessions or hours in treatment, attention to group process, training and qualifications of leaders, effectiveness of screening, level of pathology, etc. Because of these wide variations, we have to be somewhat cautious in our conclusions regarding the method as a whole. However, the very bulk of the literature is informative in general, if not in the details.

Because of clinical exigencies and ethical standards, conducting research with the requisite control conditions is a bit daunting. However, well-controlled laboratory studies with random or matched assignment of subjects to group conditions are not beyond our reach.

One Model Experimental Paradigm

As early as 1975, Diamond and Shapiro proposed a protocol for experimental evaluation of group outcome research as part of a lengthy series of studies on groups designed primarily for training and personal growth. The model, with minimal variations,

has also been recommended by others, including Sexton, Whiston, Bleuer, & Walz (1997). Use of such designs and more sophisticated instruments and procedures enhances the replicability of results.

Diamond and Shapiro (1975) recommended a minimum of three groups in each design and an eight-step process. The three groups were the experimental groups (therapy, counseling, growth), an attention placebo control group (the model they recommended is very close to the manualized group procedure or psychoeducational groups that abound today), and a wait list control group. Each study proposed would have the following eight steps:

Determination of group goals; designation of comparison groups; selection of competent, experienced, well-trained leaders for each of the two active groups

Screening of members regardless of group

Pretesting on outcome variables and matched/random assignment to each of the three conditions

Treatment occurs and process measures taken (e.g., video, galvanic skin response [GSR])

Posttesting, elicitation of subjective measures, external observer measures evaluated, reconsideration of demand characteristics of each condition to evaluate whether they could contribute to the results

Follow-up measurements at 3–6 months, give wait list group the better of the two treatments

Follow-up testing at 1–3 years.

Report on measures to members and scientific/clinical community

Recommended dependent variables included measures of personal awareness, cognitive structuring, arousal enhancement and reduction, and behavioral expression. The authors recommended collecting both self-report and other-report (observer) data and advocated strongly nonreactive measures (data collected out of subjects' awareness). One example of such nonreactive measures is the use of hospital charts, clinical records, and nursing notes (Bailey et al., 1998; Shapiro, 1970; Shapiro, Streiner, Gray, Williams, & Soble, 1969). Observers' data are best taken as much as possible from those who are unaware of the assigned group or the study design.

The preferred model was explicated clearly in a study by Shapiro and Gust (1974). Teachers and teachers-in-training were randomly assigned to one of four groups: a process-oriented group, a psycho-educational group, a psychodrama group, and a wait list control. Each group was led by a person with extensive experience in that specialty group. As expected, all of the treatments were shown to be superior to the wait list control group and the process group was significantly superior to the other treatment conditions. Subjects in the process group showed greater improvements even on a measure of knowledge of teaching approaches that were addressed specifically in the manual or lesson plan of the psychoeducational group.

Using similar designs, the same authors employed standard psychological measures, such as locus of control (Diamond & Shapiro, 1973) and a behavioral measure, hypnotizability (Shapiro & Diamond, 1972). Other populations were also studied, such as guards in an institute for adolescent offenders (Shapiro & Ross, 1971) and nurses, aides, and attendants at a large inpatient mental health facility in Ontario (Shapiro, 1970). In each case, the process-oriented, brief treatment was superior on a host of dependent measures to both attention placebo and wait list control conditions.

The Problem of Treatment Equivalence

Random assignment may well deal with the problem of equivalence of patient populations. To date, there have been few corresponding ways to equalize quality across group leaders. Shapiro and Gust (1974) employed experts in process groups, psychodrama, and psychoeducation for comparison. Lieberman, Yalom, and Miles (1973) provided a notable exception to the norm by employing experts from 10 different theories in their massive exploration of encounter group outcome. In the same study, Yalom and Lieberman (1971) also took the unique step of measuring for *casualties*, subjects who were worse after their group than at pretest.

Too often, however, leaders in all conditions are hardly experts in one or more of the modalities. Thus, it is problematic to compare outcomes across types of group. In some accounts, some of the group leaders are graduate students or interns who are trained primarily in individual and sometimes family therapy methods but who are not specifically trained in group process or many of the unique therapeutic factors a group may offer. Data noise may also increase when researchers who are aware of the alternate hypotheses are also the group leaders. Finally, follow-up studies are needed to measure deterioration effects of various types of group. For example, Shedler (2010) indicated that brief psychodynamic approaches to therapy show less loss over time than equivalent CBT approaches.

Meta-Analyses

One increasingly popular answer to the problem of nonequivalence across studies is the use of meta-analyses. These studies combine data from a host of extant studies (e.g., Wampold et al., 1997) and attempt to reduce errors due to statistical anomalies and small sample sizes. By combining the results of related studies using statistical regression and modeling, the resultant integrated average is expressed in a ratio of effect size: The higher the effect size, the greater confidence in the data.

The method has become so popular in psychological treatment research that there are often more meta-analyses than primary studies in some aspects of group work. The value of such analyses in providing comparisons and overall effects is potentially quite useful. However, the more flawed the original research designs that go into these mathematical regression models, the less confident we can be in the data. Software engineers often use the acronym "GIGO" (garbage in, garbage out) to express this dilemma.

In general, meta-analysis provides an additional tool to analyze robust trends across studies, but they should be viewed with a greater level of caution than primary studies. Nonetheless, the bulk of primary and meta-analytic evidence supports strongly the value of time-limited, closed groups.

Process Research

As impressive as the number of outcome studies on brief group treatment, the dearth of process studies is equally noteworthy. We may know that the "black box" group works, but what happens in the black box? What variables specifically impact positive outcome? To borrow a little from *The King and I*, why aren't we sure of what we absolutely know?

Group treatment is often described as a "cultural island," an environment that has its own unique ecosystem. Yet, few investigations actually address or study specifically either the intricacies of that phenomenon as it is unique to a particular group or the interaction of such factors with specific outcomes (e.g., Anderson, 1968; Lieberman, 1976).

If we are to better understand the active ingredients in closed, brief group process, we may learn how to tweak these variables for more specific and stronger treatments. Innovative designs that explore process variables have been described by Dies (1979, 1994) and Kaul and Bednar (1986). Loomis (1977), using a measure of group GSR, related changes in arousal as immediate precursors to changes in process stages in both marathon and weekly group sessions. Hartman (1979) and others have advocated the use of content analyses and qualitative approaches. Modern-day technological quality of digital audio and video makes these analyses far easier to accomplish. The current trend toward more specific types of group for individual populations (Dies, 1994) offers additional opportunities to explore the internal workings of the treatment.

Training of Group Leaders

Both the clinical and research components of successful group rely on adequately trained, proficient group leaders to maximize the impact of the brief, closed group. Despite the allure of common sense on this matter, there are severe discrepancies between clinical use of group methods and training of group counselors and therapists.

Shapiro (2008) reported on two surveys of group training in graduate mental health programs in 1999 and 2007. In these national surveys, the modal number of required classes in clinical and counseling doctoral programs and psychiatry residencies was zero. In fact, many of the programs that did have an elective group therapy class in the catalogue reported that it had not been taught in the past 2 years in each survey. In masters-level counseling, nursing, and social work programs, there was typically one required class on groups, often mandated by state regulatory boards. This may be somewhat more related to faculty prejudice than student desires and needs. The class at the Stanford University Business School with the longest wait list is the "touchy-feely" t-group class.

Noting the consistency with programs in the middle decades of the last century, Shapiro (2008) concluded that training for group therapists has reverted primarily to on-the-job learning under supervision of more experienced clinicians. However, not all programs are completely bereft of group training. Shapiro (2001) convened a symposium of leaders in programs that had ongoing group training programs. Model programs for undergraduates, master's counseling students, doctoral students, and psychiatric residents in the United States were described in depth along with programs in Israel and Europe.

The study included a summary of minimum requirements for training new group leaders: (1) membership in a process growth group, (2) at least one class in group process, (3) observation of an experienced group leader (perhaps through a mirror or as a coleader), and (4) coleadership of at least one

group under supervision (preferably videotaped). Davidovitz and Levenson (1995) and Levenson and Evans (2000), exploring the incidence of training in brief therapy per se, indicated that the vast majority of clinical trainees claimed to use brief therapy methods but that fully half of them had not a single class on the topic.

Consider the disconnection between these statistics and observations in the recent Delphi surveys of experts on trends that were expected to increase in psychotherapy (Norcross, Hedges & Prochaska, 2002). All five of the preferred methods predicted to be on the rise involved either brief or multiclient therapy or the combination of the two.

What could explain this confusing and questionable incongruity between predictions by clinical and research experts of an increasing trend in use of brief group modalities and the reality of a lack of training for new therapists? The reasons for this may be more pragmatic than systematic. Levenson and Evans (2000) reported that the majority of those teaching brief therapy had less than 5 years of experience. Levenson and Burg (1999) opined that there may be difficulties locating faculty qualified to teach students how to practice in brief therapies, despite the near ubiquitous influence of managed care. Shapiro (2001) reported on a national search for an assistant professor who was skilled in family systems and/or group process. Despite a large number of applicants, none had any of the requisite minimal training in group therapy.

The sole method that seems to be receiving increased attention in training programs is psychoeducation. Because these are either manualized or lesson plan–oriented, there is a loss of acknowledgment for the primacy of the group process for healing. Current guidelines for psychoeducational approaches do in fact encourage time for interpersonal process in each meeting. However, the availability of a lesson plan allows novice leaders to rely on information dissemination to the detriment of other more complex psychotherapeutic roles. Furthermore, members inevitably take less initiative or responsibility for the group process when there is a person with an agenda in a teaching role. Although psychoeducational groups are appealing because they require less specialized, more familiar skills, the loss of more process time in brief groups will result in more modest improvement for members (Stice & Shaw, 2004).

It is hard to understand how brief group counseling methods will continue to increase in popularity and simultaneously decrease in the quality of leadership training. Desire for more brief, closed process groups will be at some point insufficient to meet demands. This will exacerbate as the current cohort of aging experts in brief groups retires.

Back to the Future

As recently as 2008, Gladding confidently predicted that group work had a robust future, with a scope both in therapy and beyond. It is hard to argue with the value of such a prognostication or with the benefits such a future would portend. Yet, it is somewhat disconcerting to recognize that what should occur and what does occur are often discrepant. Indeed, it is humbling to recognize that my own sanguine predictions made 25 years ago about the future of group work have yet to be fully realized.

In the 1985 special issue of the *Journal for Specialists in Group Work*, "Critical Issues in Group Work: Now and 2001," Shapiro & Bernadett-Shapiro (1985), looking ahead to the new millennium, predicted correctly a proliferation of brief closed groups. Similar predictions were subsequently made by Dies (1986); Norcross, Alford, and DeMichele (1992); and others. Our error was in the naive second prediction of a commensurate increase in preparation, training, and credentialing for the many leaders who would be conducting such groups.

The upshot of a continuation of those apparently divergent trends is not hard to foresee. Yet, aware of Santayana's poignant warning about failing to learn from history and with my optimism only slightly bruised, I am undaunted in my willingness to reassert those predictions about the future of brief group work.

The time-limited closed group has been shown to offer a unique window into clients. The group provides counselors with an opportunity to experience clients in real-time interaction with others who do not have a therapist's special contractual relationship. We are witnesses both to our clients' resistance and willingness to change in a real time, somewhat real-world environment. In the group, counselors may intervene with clients in ways that are impossible in other forms of treatment. Finally, we know more about the power of between-member interaction. When group leaders use the group process and explore with clients in a firsthand way the consequences of their actions, the likelihood for change is greatly enhanced.

From this perspective, it is hopeful to agree with Gladding's (2008) optimistic picture of the future of group work or Conyne's (1996) expectation that twenty-first-century counselors will be expected to provide a host of group treatments. It is equally likely that the variety of group approaches will continue to increase.

Clinically, groups will continue to be a treatment of choice for both economic and curative reasons. On the research side, it has been established that time-limited groups work at least as well as individual treatment for most individuals and that the results of such treatment may be long-lasting (Barlow et al., 2000, 2004; Bednar & Kaul, 1994; Campbell & Dunnette, 1968). In short, we already know from outcome research that, in general, time-limited groups get the desired effect. Despite some design flaws, the overriding results of these "black box" studies are fairly conclusive. Future process research will discern what happens within the black box.

Burlingame, Fuhriman, and Johnson (2004); DeLucia-Waack (1997); Hall and Hawley (2004); Loomis (1977); and Ward and Litchy (2004) are among the researchers who have attempted to explore these far more sophisticated questions. What indeed are the active ingredients that occur in a time-limited group that most generate the outcome? Future research will undoubtedly explore quantitative measures, such as the Group Climate Questionnaire (Burlingame et al., 2004), or revisit Loomis'(1977) innovative use of group GSRs to understand fluctuations in arousal at progressive process moments. Video recordings, content analysis, and qualitative methodology may well be used more in the future of brief group research.

That future must (and likely will) identify better the crucial ingredients of effective groups, better connect the dots between process and outcome, and become far more transtheoretical. For example, it may be less important to explore the relationship between number of sessions or hours in treatment than that between outcome and the level of progression through the group stages.

It would be reassuring to believe that researchers and clinicians from a host of theoretical perspectives will collaborate better in determining both measures and desired outcomes. Surely, the results of any study reflect the nature and biases of the measurements and choice of questions explored. It can be problematic when available measures take precedence over clinical process.

One of the great limitations of the evidence-based movement is that it has been primarily the purview of CBT-oriented therapists. There are obvious reasons for this. Because of a symptom-amelioration focus, CBT lends itself well to measurable outcomes. In addition, it is currently the theory most in favor in research-oriented graduate programs.

Rutan et al. (2007), calling for more diversity in methods of group study, have referred to the CBT dominance as a "hegemony." It would be of value to see more cross-theoretical comparison studies. In today's economic environment, a study of the scope of the Lieberman et al.'s (1973) exploration of 10 modalities will be unlikely, but each individual primary study should in the future have at least two groups with presumably active ingredients. At least to date, in a variety of cross-theory comparisons, there is no consistent evidence that CBT is superior to interpersonally oriented therapy (e.g., Rezvan, Baghban, Bahrami, & Abedi, 2008; Strauman et al., 2001) or psychodynamic approaches. Recently, Shedler (2010) showed that psychodynamic approaches are also evidence-based and that they have superior hibernation effects at follow-up.

Frank's (1981) classic studies of individual therapy approaches and the salience of the therapist–client relationship (e.g., Kottler & Carlson, 2003; Najavits & Strupp, 1994; Stiles, Agnew-Davies, Hardy, Barkham, & Shapiro, 1998) and the core conditions (empathy, therapist warmth, and genuineness) based on Rogers's client-centered therapy (e.g., Carkhuff and Berenson, 1967) may be instructive in fostering future collaboration.

The limited study of non-CBT approaches has played a part in the tremendous increase in psychoeducational groups. Not only are these groups more closely geared to behavioral measures but, because they more closely emulate a class/seminar method, they require far less training for leaders. There is no question that such groups are helpful, but as Shapiro (1970), Shapiro and Gust (1974), Shapiro and Ross (1971), and Stice and Shaw (2004), among many others, have shown, the increases in outcome measures in psychoeducational groups led by experienced leaders are significantly less than those in more process-oriented groups, even on specific content measures that were addressed in the psychoeducation manual or session plan.

Future researchers could explore more carefully patient variables and psychological matches between members and leaders. In short, we would be well advised to consider client values and theories as well as those of leaders and explore interactions with the forms of treatment (e.g., Baldwin, Berkeljon, Atkins, Olsen, & Nielsen, 2009; Shapiro, 1986).

Perhaps the match between what members and leaders believe is a change modality—behavior before insight or vice versa—would be a fertile ground for such investigations. Such studies would necessitate far more comprehensive explorations and descriptions of member and leader characteristics, values, beliefs about change, etc. Similarly, the impact of leader training and experience must be teased out and matched in any cross-theoretical comparisons.

Finally, better-controlled, more completely designed studies are essential. The model proposed by Diamond and Shapiro (1975) encompasses wait list and attention placebo control groups, follow-up studies of participants, and a host of measurements beyond the characteristic paper-and-pencil measures, especially nonreactive measures (such as charts or historical notes) that are out of the influence of the group leaders and researchers.

Doubtlessly, the proliferation of meta-analyses, effect size, hierarchical linear modeling, and structural equation modeling studies will continue. It is essential that we provide for these mathematical analyses the best data possible from individual studies and programs of research. If we want to make more confident conclusions about the impact of time-limited groups, we need to do the crucial investigations and avoid the "GIGO" (garbage in, garbage out) problem.

Is This a Prediction or My Wish List?

Having failed with this prediction in 1985, it may smack of hubris to reissue it in 2011, yet I believe strongly that the story of future brief group treatment will be told in the training of future group leaders. Particularly at the doctoral level, we have failed to provide mandatory or even elective training in the modalities that experts believe to be in the forefront of the future of psychotherapy (Norcross et al., 2002). We need to reestablish group training programs and more adequate supervision in brief groups and include personal group participation in our clinical and counseling training programs. There are excellent models provided by the appropriate national organizations (American Group Psychotherapy Association, 2002; Association of Specialists in Group Work, 2000) and in some current training programs (Shapiro, 2001). Our future is to ride the current wave of group interest with commensurate interest in training.

References

American Counseling Association. (2005). *ACA code of ethics.* Alexandria, VA: Author.

American Group Psychotherapy Association. (2002). *Guidelines for the training of group psychotherapists.* New York: Author.

American Psychiatric Association. (2000). *Diagnostic and statistical manual of mental disorders* (4th ed., text rev.). Washington, DC: Author.

Anderson, A. (1968). Group counseling. *Review of Educational Research, 33,* 209–226.

Association of Specialists in Group Work. (2000). Professional standards for the training of group workers. *Journal of Specialists in Group Work, 25,* 327–342.

Bachar, E. (1998). Psychotherapy—An active agent: Assessing the effectiveness of psychotherapy and curative factors. *Israel Journal of Psychiatry and Related Sciences, 35*(2), 128–135.

Bailey, R., Shapiro, J. L., & Kovachy, E. (1998). Computers in psychiatry: History and future. Presented at the annual meeting of the American Psychiatric Association, Toronto, Canada.

Baldwin, S. A., Berkeljon, A., Atkins, D. C., Olsen, J. A., & Nielsen, S. L. (2009). Rates of change in naturalistic psychotherapy: Contrasting dose–effect and good-enough level models of change *Journal of Consulting and Clinical Psychology, 77*(2), 203–211.

Barlow, S., Burlingame, G., & Fuhriman, A. (2000). Therapeutic applications of groups: From Pratt's "thought control classes" to modern group psychotherapy. *Group Dynamics: Theory, Research, and Practice, 4,* 115–134.

Barlow, S., Fuhriman, A., & Burlingame, G. (2004). The history of group counseling and psychotherapy. In J. DeLucia-Waack, D. Gerrity, C. Kalodner, & M. Riva (Eds.), *Handbook of group counseling and psychotherapy* (pp. 3–22). Thousand Oaks, CA: Sage.

Battegay, R. (1989). Apparent and hidden changes in group members according to the different phases of group psychotherapy. *International Journal of Group psychotherapy, 39*(3), 337–353.

Bednar, R., & Kaul, T. (1994). Experiential group research: Can the cannon fire? In A. Bergin & S. Garfield (Eds.), *Handbook of psychotherapy and behavior change* (4th ed., pp. 631–663). New York: John Wiley & Sons.

Bender, L. (1937). Group activities on a children's ward as methods of psychotherapy. *American Journal of Psychiatry, 93,* 151–173.

Berg, I. K., & deShazer, S. (1993): Making numbers talk: Language in therapy. In S. Friedman (Ed.), *The new language of change: Constructive collaboration in psychotherapy.* New York: Guilford Press.

Bernard, S., & MacKenzie, K. R. (Eds.). (1994). *Basics of group psychotherapy.* New York: Guilford Press.

Bloom, B. L. (1981). Focused single-session therapy: Initial development and evaluation. In S. H. Budman (Ed.), *Forms of brief therapy.* New York: Guilford Press.

Budman, S. H. (Ed.). (1981). *Forms of brief therapy.* New York: Guilford Press.

Budman, S. H. (1994). *Treating time effectively* [Video]. New York: Guilford Press.

Budman, S. H., Demby, A., & Randall, M. (1982). Psychotherapeutic outcome and reduction in medical utilization: A cautionary tale. *Professional Psychology, 73,* 200–207.

Budman, S. H., & Gurman, A. S. (1983). The practice of brief therapy. *Professional Psychology: Research and Practice, 14*(3), 277–292.

Burlingame, G., Fuhriman, A., & Johnson, J. (2004). Process and outcome in group counseling and psychotherapy: A perspective. In J. DeLucia-Waack, D. Gerrity, C. Kalodner, & M. Riva (Eds.), *Handbook of group counseling and psychotherapy* (pp. 49–61). Thousand Oaks, CA: Sage.

Burlingame, G., Fuhriman, A., & Mosier, J. (2003). The differential effectiveness of group psychotherapy: A meta-analytic perspective. *Group Dynamics: Theory, Research, and Practice, 7,* 3–12.

Campbell, J. P., & Dunnette, M. D. (1968). Effectiveness of T-group experiences in managerial training and development. *Psychological Bulletin, 70*(2), 72–103.

Capuzzi, D., & Gross, D. (1992). *Introduction to group counseling.* Denver, CO: Love Publishing.

Carkhuff, R. R., & Berenson, B. (1967). *Beyond counseling and therapy.* New York: Holt, Rinehart & Winston.

Carroll, M. R., & Wiggins, J. D. (1990). *Elements of group counseling: Back to the basics.* Denver, CO: Love Publishing.

Conyne, R. K. (1996). The Association for Specialists in Group Work training standards: Some considerations and suggestions for training. *Journal for Specialists in Group Work, 21,* 155–162.

Corey, G. (1990). *Theory and practice of group counseling* (3rd ed.). Belmont, CA: Brooks/Cole.

Corey, G. (2004). *Theory and practice of group counseling* (6th ed.). Belmont, CA: Brooks/Cole.

Corey, M. S. & Corey, G. (1982). *Groups: Process and practice* (2nd ed.). Belmont, CA: Brooks/Cole.

Corey, M. S., Corey, G., & Corey, C. (2010). *Groups: Process and practice* (8th ed.). Belmont, CA: Brooks/Cole.

Corsini, R. J. (1957). *Methods of group psychotherapy.* New York: McGraw-Hill.

Corsini, R. J., & Lundin, R. (1951). Towards a definition of group psychotherapy. *Mental Hygiene, 39,* 647–656.

Cuijpers, P., van Straten, A., & Warmerdam, L. (2008). Are individual and group treatments equally effective in the treatment of depression in adults? A meta-analysis. *European Journal of Psychiatry, 22*(1), 38–51.

Dagley, J., Gazda, G., Eppinger, S., & Stewart, E. (1994). Group psychotherapy: Research with children, preadolescents, and adolescents. In A. Fuhriman & G. Burlingame (Eds.), *Handbook of group psychotherapy* (pp. 340–369). New York: John Wiley & Sons.

Davidovitz, D., & Levenson, H. (1995). A national survey on practice and training in brief therapy. Paper presented at the 103rd Annual Convention of the American Psychological Association, New York.

DeLucia-Waack, J. (1997). The importance of processing activities, exercises, and events to group work practitioners. *Journal for Specialists in Group Work, 22,* 82–84.

de Shazer, S. (1985). *Keys to solution in brief therapy.* New York: W.W. Norton.

Diamond, M. J., & Shapiro, J. L. (1973). Changes in locus of control as a function of encounter group experiences: A study and replication. *Journal of Abnormal Psychology, 83*(3), 514–518.

Diamond, M. J., & Shapiro, J. L. (1975). An expedient model of encounter group learning. *Psychotherapy: Theory Research and Practice, 12*(1), 56–59.

Dies, R. R. (1979). Group psychotherapy: Reflections on three decades of research. *Journal of Applied Behavioral Science, 15,* 361–374.

Dies, R. R. (1985). Research foundations for the future of group work. *Journal of Specialists in Group Work, 10*(2), 68–73.

Dies, R. R. (1986). Practical, theoretical, and empirical foundations for group psychotherapy. In A. J. Frances and R. E. Hales (Eds.), *The American Psychiatric Association annual review* (Vol. 5). Washington, DC: American Psychiatric Press.

Dies, R. R. (1992). The future of group therapy. *Psychotherapy: Theory, Research, Practice, Training, 29*(1), 58–64.

Dies, R. R. (1994). Therapist variables in group psychotherapy research. In A. Fuhriman and G. M. Burlingame (Eds.), *Handbook of group psychotherapy: An empirical and clinical synthesis* (pp. 114–154). New York: John Wiley & Sons.

Dies, R. R., & Dies, K. R. (1993). The role of evaluation in clinical practice: Overview and group treatment illustration. *International Journal of Group Psychotherapy, 43*, 77–105.

Dinkmeyer, D. C., & Muro, J. C. (1971). *Group counseling: theory and practice*. Itasca, IL: Peacock.

Dreikurs, R. (1951). The unique social climate experienced in group psychotherapy. *Group Psychotherapy, 3*, 292–299.

Dreikurs, R. (1959). Early experiments with group psychotherapy: a historical review. *American Journal of Psychotherapy, 13*, 882–891.

Drum, D. J., & Knott, J. E. (2009). Theme groups at thirty. *International Journal of Group Psychotherapy, 59*(4), 491–510.

Fehr, S. S. (Ed.). (2008). *101 Interventions in group therapy*. Binghamton, NY: Haworth Press.

Fiebert, M. S. (1963). Sensitivity training: An analysis of trainer intervention and group process. *Psychological Reports, 22*(8), 829–838.

Finn, B., & Shakir, S. A. (1990). Intensive group psychotherapy of borderline patients. *Group, 14*(2), 99–110.

Forsyth, D. (2006). *Group dynamics*. Belmont, CA: Thomson Wadsworth.

Foulds, M., & Hannigan, P. (1976). Effects of gestalt marathon workshops on measured self actualization. *Journal of Counseling Psychology, 23*, 60–65.

Frank, J. D. (1974). *Persuasion and healing*. New York: Shocken.

Frank, J. D. (1981). Reply to Telch. *Journal of Consulting and Clinical Psychology, 49*, 476–477.

Gazda, G. M. (1989). *Group counseling: A developmental approach* (4th ed). Boston: Allyn & Bacon.

Gazda, G. M., Ginter, E. J., & Horne, A. M. (2001). *Group counseling and group psychotherapy: Theory and practice*. Boston: Allyn & Bacon.

Gladding, S. T. (2008). *Group work: A counseling specialty* (5th ed.). Upper Saddle River, NJ: Pearson-Prentice Hall.

Gorer, G. (1934). *The revolutionary ideas of the Marquis de Sade*. London: Wishart.

Greenberg, L. S., & Johnson, S. M. (1988). *Emotionally focused therapy for couples*. New York: Guilford Press.

Hall, J., & Hawley, I. (2004). Interactive process notes: An innovative tool in counseling groups. *Journal for Specialization in Group Work, 29*, 193–204.

Hansen, N. B., Lambert, M. J., & Forman, E. M. (2002). The psychotherapy dose–response effect and its implications for treatment delivery systems. *Clinical Psychology: Science and Practice, 3*, 329–343.

Hartman, J. (1979). Small group methods of personal change. *Annual Review of Psychology, 30*, 453–476.

Hoag, M., & Burlingame, G. M. (1997). Evaluating the effectiveness of child and adolescent group treatment: A meta-analytic review. *Journal of Clinical Child Psychology, 26*(3), 234–246.

Horowitz, J. L., & Garber, J. (2006). The prevention of depressive symptoms in children and adolescents: A meta-analytic review. *Journal of Consulting and Clinical Psychology, 74*(3), 401–415.

Hulse, W. (1948). Group psychotherapy with soldiers and veterans. *Military Surgery, 103*, 106–121.

Jacobs, E. E., Harvill, R. L., & Masson, R. I. (1994). *Group counseling, strategies and skills* (2nd ed). Pacific Grove, CA: Brooks/Cole.

Janet, P. (1925). *Psychological healing*. New York: Macmillan.

Johnson, J. (2008). Using research-supported group treatments. *Journal of Clinical Psychology, 64*, 1206–1225.

Kanas, N. (1986). Group therapy with schizophrenics: A review of the controlled studies. *International Journal of Group Psychotherapy, 36*, 339–351.

Kanzer, M. (1971). Freud: The first psychoanalytic group leader. In: H. I. Kaplan & B. Sadock (Eds.), *The origins of group psychoanalysis*. New York: Dutton.

Kaul, T. J., & Bednar, R. L. (1986). Experiential group research: Results, questions, and suggestions. In S. L. Garfield and A. E. Bergin (Eds.), *Handbook of psychotherapy and behavior change* (3rd ed.). New York: John Wiley & Sons.

Koss, M. P., Butcher, J., & Strupp, H. H. (1986). Brief psychotherapy methods in clinical research. *Journal of Consulting and Clinical Psychology, 54*(1), 60–67.

Kottler, J.A. (1982) *Pragmatic Group Leadership*. Pacific Grove, CA.: Brooks/Cole

Kottler, J. A., & Carlson, J. (2003). *The mummy at the dining room table: Eminent therapists reveal their most unusual cases and what they teach us about human behavior*. San Francisco: Jossey-Bass.

Kush, F. R. (2009). Brief psychodynamic and cognitive therapy: Regarding acute treatment. *Journal of Psychotherapy Integration, 19*(2), 158–172.

Leszcz, M., & Kobos, J. (2008). Evidence-based group psychotherapy: Using AGPA's practice guidelines to enhance clinical effectiveness. *Journal of Clinical Psychology, 64*, 1238–1260.

Levenson, H. (2001). Time-limited dynamic psychotherapy: An integrationist perspective. *Journal of Psychotherapy Integration, 13*(3), 300–333.

Levenson, H., & Burg, J. (1999). Training psychologists in the era of managed care. In A. J. Kent & M. Hersen (Eds.), *A psychologist's proactive guide to managed mental health care* (pp. 113–140). Hillsdale, NJ: Lawrence Erlbaum.

Levenson, H., & Evans, S. A. (2000). The current state of brief therapy training in American Psychological Association–accredited graduate and internship programs. *Professional Psychology: Research and Practice, 31*(4), 298–308.

Lieberman, M. A. (1976). Change induction in small groups. *Annual Review of Psychology, 27*, 217–250.

Lieberman, M., Yalom, I., & Miles, M. (1973). *Encounter groups: First facts*. New York: Basic Books.

Loomis, T. P. (1977). Skin conductance and the effects of time distribution on encounter group learning: Marathons vs. spaced groups (Doctoral dissertation, University of Hawaii, 1977). *Dissertation Abstracts International, 37*(8-A), 4993.

MacKenzie, K. R. (1990). The changing role of emotion in group psychotherapy. In R. Plutchnik & H. Kellerman (Eds.), *Emotion, psychopathology and psychotherapy*. San Diego: Academic Press.

MacKenzie, K. R. (1994). The developing structure of the therapy group system. In H. S. Bernard & K. R. MacKenzie (Eds.), *Basics of group psychotherapy* (pp. 35–39). New York: Guilford Press.

MacKenzie, K. R. (1997). *Time-managed group psychotherapy: Effective clinical applications*. Washington, DC: American Psychiatric Press.

Najavits, L. M., & Strupp, H. H. (1994). Differences in the effectiveness of psychodynamic therapists: A process-outcome study. *Psychotherapy: Theory, Practice Training, 31*(1), 114–123.

Norcross, J. C., Alford, B. A., & De Michele, J. T. (1992). The future of psychotherapy: Delphi data and concluding observations. *Psychotherapy: Theory, Research, Practice, Training, 29*(1), 150–158.

Norcross, J. C., Hedges, M., & Prochaska, J. O. (2002). The face of 2010: A Delphi poll on the future of psychotherapy. *Professional Psychology: Research and Practice, 33*(3), 316–322.

Orlinsky, D. E., & Howard, K. I. (1986). Process and outcome in psychotherapy. In S. L. Garfield and A. E. Bergin (Eds.), *Handbook of psychotherapy and behavior change* (3rd ed.). New York: John Wiley & Sons.

Piper, W. E., Debbane, E. G., Bienvenu, J. P., & Garant, J. (1984). A comparative study of four forms of psychotherapy. *Journal of Consulting and Clinical Psychology, 52*(2), 268–279.

Piper, W. E., & Perrault, E. L. (1989). Pretherapy preparation for group members. *International Journal of Group Psychotherapy, 39*(1), 17–34.

Pratt, J. H. (1906). The home sanitarium treatment of consumption. *Boston Medical Surgical Journal, 154*, 210–216.

Pukui, M. K., Haertig, E. W., & Lee, C. (1983). *Nana i ke Kumu: Look to the Source* (Vol. 1). Honolulu: Hui Hanai.

Renouvier, P. (1948). Group psychotherapy in the United States. *Sociatry, 2*, 75–78.

Rezvan, S., Baghban, I., Bahrami, F., & Abedi, M. (2008). A comparison of cognitive-behavior therapy with interpersonal and cognitive behavior therapy in the treatment of generalized anxiety disorders. *Counselling Psychology Quarterly, 21*(4), 309–321.

Rogers, C. R. (1973). *On encounter groups*. San Francisco: Harper and Row.

Rosenbaum, M., & Hartley, E. (1962). A summary view of ninety-two group psychotherapies. *International Journal of Group Psychotherapy, 12*(2), 194–198.

Rutan, S. J., Stone, W. N., & Shay, J. J. (2007). *Psychodynamic group psychotherapy*. New York: Guilford Press.

Schutz, W. C. (1973). *Elements of encounter*. Oxford: Joy Press.

Sexton, T. L., Whiston, S. C., Bleuer, J. C., & Walz, G. R. (1997). *Integrating outcome research into counseling practice and training*. Alexandria, VA: American Counseling Association.

Shapiro, J. L. (1970). An investigation into the effects of sensitivity training procedures (Doctoral dissertation, University of Waterloo, 1970). *Dissertation Abstracts International, 32*(2-A), 799.

Shapiro, J. L. (1978). *Methods of group psychotherapy and encounter*. Itasca, IL: Peacock.

Shapiro, J. L. (1986). The evolution of psychotherapy conference: Skeptical reflections. *Family Therapy, 13* 209–214.

Shapiro, J. L. (1998). Computer assisted psychotherapy: Development, data, dissent. Paper presented at the annual meeting of the American Psychological Association. San Francisco. August

Shapiro, J. L. (2001). *Training for group therapists and counselors: Undergraduate, masters level, doctoral level and post doctoral level*. Symposium presented at the annual meeting of the American Psychological Association San Francisco:.

Shapiro, J. L. (2008). Loss of a legacy: a curmudgeon's perspective. *Group Psychologist, 18*(3), 42–46.

Shapiro, J. L., & Bernadett-Shapiro, S. T. (1985). Group work to 2001: Hal or haven (from isolation). *Journal of Specialists in Group Work, 10*(2), 83–87.

Shapiro, J. L., & Diamond, M. J. (1972). Increases in hypnotizability as a function of encounter group training. *Journal of Abnormal Psychology, 79*(1), 112–115.

Shapiro, J. L., & Gust, T. (1974). Counselor training for facilitative human relationships: Study and replication. *Counselor Education and Supervision, 13*(3), 198–207.

Shapiro, J. L., Peltz, L. S., & Bernadett-Shapiro, S. T. (1998). *Brief group treatment: A practical guide for therapists and counselors*. Pacific Grove, CA: Brooks/Cole.

Shapiro, J. L., & Ross, R. R. (1971). Sensitivity training in an institution for adolescents. *Journal of Applied Behavioral Science, 7*(6), 710–723.

Shapiro, J. L., & Scheflin, A. W. (1988). *Hypnosis: Medicine or mind control?* [Video]. Santa Clara, CA: Santa Clara University.

Shapiro, J. L., Streiner, D. L., Gray, A. L., Williams, N. L., & Soble, C. L. (1969). The moon and mental illness: A failure to confirm the Transylvania effect. *Perceptual and Motor Skills, 30*, 827–830.

Shechtman, Z. (2007). How does group process research inform leaders of counseling and psychotherapy groups? *Group Dynamics: Theory, Research, and Practice, 11*, 293–304.

Shechtman, Z., & Toren, Z. (2009). The effect of leader behavior on processes and outcomes in group counseling. *Group Dynamics: Theory, Research, and Practice, 13*(3), 218–233.

Shedler, J. (2010). The efficacy of psychodynamic psychotherapy. *American Psychologist, 65*(2), 98–109.

Sifneos, P. E. (1972). *Short-term psychotherapy and emotional crisis*. Cambridge, MA: Harvard University Press.

Slavson, S. R. (1951). *The practice of group therapy*. New York: International Universities Press.

Small, L. (1979). *The briefer psychotherapies*. New York: Brunner/Mazel.

Stewart, R. E., & Chambless, D. L. (2009). Cognitive-behavioral therapy for adult anxiety disorders in clinical practice: A meta-analysis of effectiveness studies. *Journal of Consulting and Clinical Psychology, 77*(4), 595–606.

Stice, E., Rohde, P., Seeley, J. R., & Gau, J. M. (2008). Brief cognitive-behavioral depression prevention program for high-risk adolescents outperforms two alternative interventions: A randomized efficacy trial. *Journal of Consulting and Clinical Psychology, 76*(4), 595–606.

Stice, E., & Shaw, H. (2004). Eating disorder prevention programs: A meta-analytic review. *Psychological Bulletin, 130*(2), 206–227.

Stiles, W. B., Agnew-Davies, R., Hardy, G. E., Barkham, M., & Shapiro, D. A. (1998). Relations of the alliance with psychotherapy outcome: Findings in the second Sheffield psychotherapy project. *Journal of Consulting and Clinical Psychology, 66*(5), 791–802.

Strauman, T. J., Kolden, G. G., Stromquist, V., Davis, N., Kwapil, L., Heerey, E. et al. (2001). The effects of treatments for depression on perceived failure in self-regulation. *Cognitive Therapy and Research, 25*(6), 693–712.

Thomas, R. V., & Pender, D. A. (2007). Association for Specialists in Group Work: Best practice guidelines 2007 revisions. *Journal for Specialists in Group Work, 33*(2), 111–117.

Toseland, R., Kabat, D., & Kemp, K. (1983). An evaluation of a smoking cessation group program. *Social Work Research and Abstracts, 19*(1), 12–19.

Toseland, R., & Rivas, R. F. (1984). *An introduction to group work practice*. New York: Macmillan.

Toseland, R., & Siporin, M. (1986). When to recommend group: A review of the clinical and research literature. *International Journal of Group Psychotherapy, 36*, 171–201.

Tuckman, B. W. (1965). Developmental sequence in small groups. *Psychological Bulletin, 63*, 384–399.

Tuckman, B., & Jensen, M. (1977). Stages of small group development revisited. *Group & Organizational Studies, 2*, 419–427.

US Department of Health and Human Services. (2010). *National health care expenditures data*. Retrieved from http://www.cms.hhs.gov/nationalhealthexpenddata/

Vander Kolk, C. J. (1985). *Introduction to group counseling and psychotherapy*. Upper Saddle River, NJ: Prentice Hall.

Vandevoort, D. J., & Fuhriman, A. (1991). The efficacy of group therapy for depression: A review of the literature. *Small Group Research, 22*(3), 320–338.

Vinogradov, S., & Yalom, I. D. (1990). Self-disclosure in group psychotherapy. In G. Stricker & M. Fisher (Eds.), *Self disclosure in the therapeutic relationship*. New York: Plenum Press.

Vinnars, B., Thormählen, B., Gallop, R., Norén, K., & Barber, J. P. (2009). Do personality problems improve during psychodynamic supportive–expressive psychotherapy? Secondary outcome results from a randomized controlled trial for psychiatric outpatients with personality disorders. *Psychotherapy: Theory, Research, Practice, Training, 46*(3), 362–375.

Wampold, B. E., Mondin, G. W., Moody, M., Stich, F., Benson, K., and Ahn, H. (1997). A meta-analysis of outcome studies comparing bona fide psychotherapies: Empirically, "all must have prizes. *Psychological Bulletin, 122*(3), 203–215.

Ward, D., & Litchy, M. (2004). The effective use of processing in groups. In J. DeLucia-Waack, D. Gerrity, C. Kalodner, & M. Riva (Eds.), *Handbook of group counseling and psychotherapy* (pp. 104–119). Thousand Oaks, CA: Sage.

Wender, L. (1936). The dynamics of group therapy and its applications. *Journal of Nervous and Mental Disorders, 84*, 54–60.

Yalom, I. (1970). *The theory and practice of group psychotherapy* (1st ed.). New York: Basic Books.

Yalom, I. D. (1985). *The theory and practice of group psychotherapy* (3rd ed.). New York: Basic Books.

Yalom, I. D. (1990). *Understanding group therapy* [Video]. Pacific Grove, CA: Brooks/Cole.

Yalom, I. D. (1995). *The theory and practice of group psychotherapy* (4th ed.). New York: Basic Books.

Yalom, I. D., Houts, P. S., Newell, G., & Rand, K. H. (1979). Preparation of patients for group therapy. In H. B. Roback, S. I. Abramovitz, & D. S. Strassberg (Eds.), *Group psychotherapy research: Commentaries and selected readings*. Huntington, NY: Krieger.

Yalom, I. D. (with Leszcz, M.) (2005). *Theory and practice of group psychotherapy* (5th ed.) New York: Basic Books.

Yalom, I. D., & Lieberman, M. A. (1971). A study of encounter group casualties. *Archives of General Psychiatry, 25*, 16–20.

Zimpfer, D. G. (1987). Groups for those involved with incest. *Journal for Specialists in Group Work, 12*(4). 166–177.

Zimpfer, D. (1990a). Group work for bulimia: A review of outcomes. *Journal for Specialists in Group Work, 15*(4), 239–251.

Zimpfer, D. G. (1990b). Groups for divorce/separation: A review. *Journal for Specialists in Group Work, 15*(1), 51–60.

Zimpfer, D. G. (1991). Groups for grief and survivorship after bereavement *Journal for Specialists in Group Work, 16*(1), 46–55.

Zimpfer, D. G., & Carr, J. J. (1989). Groups for midlife career change: A review. *Journal for Specialists in Group Work, 14*(4), 243–250.

28

Mutual Help Groups: What Are They and What Makes Them Work?

Phyllis R. Silverman

Abstract

Why do people find it so helpful to meet others who have similar problems or life-changing experiences? Why does finding others like ourselves give us a sense of hope, a sense of being understood, and often a direction to a solution to our problem? Coming together in this way often takes place is what we call "mutual help groups." This chapter offers some understanding of how these groups come about, what they do for those who participate, and the kind of settings in which they take place. There is a related question that needs to be answered: Are there other aspects of the experience and the setting in which this kind of encounter takes place that matter? What seems to matter a good deal is who controls the program and the resources of these encounters.

Keywords: group counseling, mutual help, group settings, group benefits

I met other children whose father died. I didn't feel so
alone, so different. It felt good.

9-year old boy at a program for grieving children

It helps so much to make a connection; to say that I
know what it's like to be scared, angry, non-compliant.
I know what it's like to be a patient. The support group
provides a way I can reach out; patient to patient.

Dr. Eric Eisenberg, founder of Boston chapter of American Association of Kidney Patients,
Boston Globe, December 25, 2006

Background

As populations have increased and the geography of where people live has changed, the concept of what composes a community has also changed. Extended family, neighbors, and friends once provided help as a matter of personal obligation and concern. People were there to share their common knowledge, to teach each other what they had learned from their own experience (Silverman, 1978). They were sometimes recipients, sometimes helpers. Most human life would be barren without these exchanges, without this sense of community (Kropotkin, 1902/1972). However, as we moved through the twentieth century, as cities grew, populations became more diverse and more industrialized; these informal exchanges became less frequent. People move about more easily and families, core units of these exchanges, are often separated by greater distances. It can be difficult to easily find people with similar problems. Information is centered in specialized groups that are represented by experts. These experts offer help to those in need in the context of what become formal organizations (McKnight, 1995). Mutuality and the exchange of care are less available or missing. This is true of issues related to normal life-cycle events such as childbirth and death.

To these we now add more complex social and health problems, with which people are living longer due to the advances in science and medicine. The focus is no longer on survival but on the quality of life.

As help has become more specialized and formal, we are witnessing the professionalization of services once performed by citizens for each other. This focus on professionalization has led to what is called the "medicalization" of human experience (Conrad, 2007). Professionals often see themselves as repositories of "the right way" to remedy difficulties. What is learned from lived experience has often not been valued. Forman (2009), in her syndicated news column on health, reported on a study by mental health professionals of the level of stress people experienced after receiving news that they have a life-threatening illness. These reactions met the criteria for a significant psychiatric diagnosis, such as major depression or posttraumatic stress disorder. Forman asked if it is really news that a serious medical diagnosis can shake a person to the core.

When a person's response to a serious change in his or her sense of well-being is assigned a psychiatric diagnosis, the focus turns to another dimension of what is wrong. Treatment and cures are then sought for which problems? Are we talking about treating symptoms of psychological problems or focusing on social competence building, that is, promoting people's adaptive capacities even in the face of devastating news (Silverman, 1985)? Promoting adaptive capacities, even while facing life-threatening situations, very often requires learning many new skills and many new ways of looking at the world and at oneself. It requires considering the stress as appropriate and normal under the circumstances. How is learning in this kind of a situation facilitated? Today, friends and family are often hesitant to offer help in times of stress. This is in part due to their concerns that they lack credentials to do so and may cause more harm than good by "intruding."

McKnight (1995) writes about the negative consequences for society when "care" becomes a commodity. He points to the destruction of a sense of community as people rely more and more on experts and the experts' knowledge and technology. McKnight's concern is how to restore a sense of community that involves the ability to extend care and help to its citizens. He sees caring as the work of a community.

Looking at end-of-life care, Kellehear (2005) describes the need to rebuild what he calls "compassionate cities." He recommends that people need to differentiate between times when professional care is truly required and helpful and when friends and relatives might rely on their own experience to provide care and offer help. Kellehear's goal is to raise people's awareness of their own abilities and skills. His main concern is how communities care for the dying. He sees the employment of available support systems, problem solving, and communicating with each other as the work of the community. He wants to see a return to people helping people at times of stress and change in their lives, to counter what he sees as a threat from professional and medical dominance.

How is the help found in a return to caring communities different from that offered by professionals? What is special about help offered in a compassionate or caring community? How can we create them?

Mutual Help Groups
Defining Mutual Help

To create opportunities to learn from each other and to form personal communities, another layer of organization has developed in which citizens themselves are taking the lead. These are called "self-help," "mutual aid," and "mutual help" groups (Borkman, 2008; Silverman, 1985). Borkman (1999, 2010) and Silverman (2004) define all groups with these different names as intentional, voluntary, informal groups of people afflicted by a common health, social, or economic problem who come together to resolve their issues largely through their own resources and from their own experience. They share what they have learned from their experience and provide social and emotional support and other kinds of help.

Borkman (1999) points to the need to distinguish self-help from mutual help. *Self-help* involves responsibility and reliance on the internal resources of individual participants. It focuses on the individual. *Mutual help* focuses more on the community and the exchange of information. In this chapter I am talking about activities that take place in a group, with the focus on the exchange of information and resources by the group's members. I refer to these as "mutual help" groups. Often, these are still referred to as "self-help" groups, although the focus is on the group (Borkman, 2010).

In a mutual help group the emphasis is on the supportive and collective efforts of participants that enable them to learn from each other. In mutual help groups, participants are members, not clients. Their knowledge is largely based on what they have learned from their own experience and what they learn from each other. This kind of knowledge is what Borkman (1999) calls "experiential knowledge," which comes out of lived experience. Experiential knowledge is in contrast to professional knowledge, which comes from professional education in formal institutions and classrooms leading to credentials for licensing to practice (Hughes, 1958).

Silverman (1978) suggested that mutual help groups often develop because professional help was insufficient or not responsive to often unanticipated aspects of their "client" needs. For example, medicine has advanced so that people are living longer, with time for new problems to develop. In addition, advances in medicine have dealt effectively with serious problems, leaving survivors with chronic problems. These problems affect their daily lives, for which the specialist may not have the answers. As people face life-cycle events such as the death of a family member or living with a chronic disease, they find that they need new skills to manage and adapt to the changes in how they live. As they meet others like themselves, they discover how much they can learn from each other and from those who have already been there.

These groups are usually started by people meeting others who had a similar problem. In these meetings, whether planned or accidental, participants discover solutions to their respective difficulties (Madera, 2008). Compassionate Friends, an international organization for bereaved parents, began in the chaplain's office in a hospital in Great Britain. Grieving parents were informally meeting there and discovered that they offered each other a kind of help that was not available anywhere else (Klass, 1988; Stephans, 1972). The grieving parents did not see themselves as unique or vulnerable in the medical sense. They began to learn from each other that there could be a sense of hope for the future after the death of one of their children. These parents learned from each other that they could survive. The organization cited at the beginning of this chapter, the American Association of Kidney Patients, is an example of a more recently formed organization that focuses on the needs of people dealing with chronic kidney disease. The initiator was a physician himself suffering from this disease.

Alcoholics Anonymous (AA) (Makela et al., 1996) was started by two former alcoholics who discovered how much help they were to each other in their determination to remain sober. This is an excellent example of an organization that has a long life and has served as a stimulus and example for many other groups and organizations that have developed since AA's success became well known (Sanders, 2009).

Informal groups meeting a great variety of needs are forming every day, in people's homes, in church basements, and in community and senior centers. Often, they evolve into formal nonprofit organizations with elected leaders. Many then develop into national organizations. There are several self-help clearing centers that provide information in their publications and on the Web about these groups (White and Madera, 2002).

How They Help

Problem solving among peers creates a different dynamic from what is found in professionally led support groups. A mutual help group helps participants recognize the limits of professional knowledge and encourages new kinds of collaboration among members, giving them a new view of their own abilities to solve problems with a new sense of authority about their own lives. Borkman (1999) reminds us that this experience changes "victims" into helpers. The focus in a mutual help group is not on what is wrong but on what is "normal," given the circumstances, and what can be done about it.

In the context of a mutual help group, the effort is on promoting members' ability to live with the disabling or life-changing consequences of long-term social and physical problems that could not be prevented (Silverman, 1985). Another way of saying this is to talk about building social competence. For example, it may be impossible to prevent a woman from becoming a widow. There is the need to look, instead, at what she requires to facilitate coping with her new status and the changes it has caused in her life. These changes are to be expected under the circumstances, and therefore, the focus is on what can be done, not on what is wrong. In the context of a mutual help group, the conversation is not on preventing symptoms or illnesses but on promoting the adaptive capacity of the individual (Silverman, 1978, 1985).

In a mutual help group, members are helped by receiving information on how to cope, how to obtain material help if necessary, and how to get new information and perspective on their difficulties, as well as by feeling cared for and supported. They find people "just like me" with whom they can identify. They learn that other people have similar feelings and that these feelings are "normal" given the circumstances of their situation. They are not alone. They learn that there is not something wrong with them but that perhaps it should be seen as something "right" given what they are experiencing.

When people become involved and participate, when they can recognize that they share the problem with others in the group, the help offered has special meaning. Participants can see the help as meaningful and learn how to use it most efficiently. People in turn are helped by the opportunity to help others. Being helpful can begin almost as soon as someone joins a group as each person brings his or her own experience to the table as he or she becomes part of this community.

Mutual help groups are autonomous, member-run groups or programs. Members are in charge of their healing, relying on sharing the knowledge they have gained from their own efforts and the solutions they have found. Gottlieb (1981), looking at the continuum of help available in a community, called these "intentional communities." Some have called these "natural helping efforts." To the extent that they are often spontaneous, this is true; but these initiatives are often consciously designed and carried forward. However, they are not based on professional knowledge but formed with the intent to apply the knowledge that members have learned through their own experience. Intentional communities are sometimes developed by professionals who have seen their value. They start as demonstration projects in which programs are developed to test the applicability of a mutual help approach for a given population in need (Caserta, Lund, & Rice, 1999; Silverman, 2004; Stewart, Craig, MacPherson, & Alexander, 2001). These initiatives typically have evolved into ongoing, independent mutual help groups or organizations.

Borkman (1999) provides another level of understanding about how mutual help groups function to build community. She writes about mutual aide in a commons. She defines a *commons*, based on a definition by Lohmann (1992), as a public arena of action in the nonprofit, voluntary sector of society, where "autonomous self-defining collectivities of voluntarily associating individuals create and maintain their own member-owned social worlds of meanings, images and senses of reality" (Borkman, 1999, p. 17).

Borkman (1999) writes about a group for people who stutter that she has studied. What this group provides for its members applies to any mutual help group. Participation is free and uncoerced. Participants share a common purpose, a sense of mutuality, and social relations that are characterized by fairness, not law. They encompass a wide array of social forms: groups, conferences, events, social movements, and advocacy groups. These groups need to be distinguished from large nonprofit organizations that focus on a particular illness or condition and that are run by professionals in the service of others. Borkman (1999) considers a "common" approach as fitting McKnight's vision of community. Borkman sees the concept of commons helping to distinguish mutual help from larger voluntary organizations in the community.

McKnight (1995, pp. 171–172) observes that larger voluntary organizations tend to avoid tragedy, minimizing the negative aspects of the condition or problem on which they focus. For him, the surest indication of positive experience in a community is the acknowledgment of tragedy, death, and suffering. McKnight sees that being part of a community provides members with rituals and lamentations that acknowledge human fallibility. Mutual help groups make a real contribution to our need for community in that in this context participants deal with the less celebratory aspects of living and teach their members how to cope and prevail, emphasizing their reliance step by step on each other. Members know that they are there for each other when all else fails.

In a formal mutual help group, help is offered in many ways. Members are not always recipients or always helpers but move back and forth in what they do. The group evolves and changes as members live with their difficulties and gain new understanding of the problem and as new members join and old members move on. Most mutual help initiatives that are formalized offer educational seminars, newsletters, telephone outreach, personal outreach where appropriate (Silverman & Smith, 1984), one-to-one exchanges, social gatherings, exchange on the Web, and sharing during regularly scheduled meetings, usually facilitated by a member. Some modes of help, such as newsletters and telephone outreach, make it possible for people who are not comfortable in groups or who cannot come to meetings to become involved. The members of these organizations have discovered that simply connecting people with common issues opens up possibilities and avenues for future creative action.

Some mutual help groups are involved in political action and become agents of social change. Coming together provides them with the opportunity to look at the larger societal implications of their problem. They become agents for social change. For example, Mothers Against Drunk Driving (MADD) has become involved with legislators in their respective states, advocating for changes in laws that relate to the prevention of drunk driving and to make penalties more severe for those who drink and drive. The breast cancer movement grew out of the shared experience of risk, screening, diagnosis, treatment, and rehabilitation that brought together women who have breast cancer (Klawiter, 2008). One of their main focuses is on prevention and on advocating for changes in environmental hazards that could cause cancer. Its members have joined forces with other advocacy groups to become social activists. As groups gain experience, they come to appreciate that connecting people with common issues opens up possibilities and avenues for future creative action.

Dealing with Change

People who join mutual help groups are dealing with critical changes in their lives, and this time of change has been characterized as a period of transition (Silverman, 1978, 1985, 2004). Mutual help groups can be seen as enabling organizations; that is, they enable people to get from one place, for example, as a patient in a hospital bed, to another place, back to the community, leading as normal a life as possible in light of their changed condition (Lenneberg & Rowbotham, 1970). Initially, future members need to accept the fact that they have the same problem as members of the group, that being part of such a group is where they belong. It is not always easy those newly afflicted to accept that they share a common problem with members of this group and that there may be something to learn here. This may involve a shift in a new member's own sense of who he or she is.

Bruner (1990) notes the importance of culture in understanding how people make meaning, that is, make sense of what is happening to them. For example, a new first-time mother who is nursing her child has to adjust to the values and attitudes associated with parenthood. This can be a whole new world for her, and she may not immediately understand or accept the changes in her world. Moving from the role of wife to that of widow can involve dealing with a new way of making meaning given the situation where she no longer has a spouse (Silverman, 2004). In these instances, finding a new culture is critical to how we learn new ways of making meaning, finding a new sense of self, and finding a new place in a community. Letting go of the sense of self or well-being that is now lost and then learning how to cope with the new situation are part of what takes place in a mutual help group (Silverman, 2004).

Following a similar trajectory for change, AA characterizes the help offered in their program in three steps. They talk first of recovery, that is, accepting the fact that one is an alcoholic. The second phase of relating to help is developing a sense of unity with the group, that is, feeling a sense of oneness with other AA members. The third step involves service, that is, a need to give back (Silverman, 2004).

Mutual help groups are one of the few places in contemporary society where expertise in coping with transitions can be found (Madera, 2008; Silverman, 1980). Here, members obtain pertinent information, they find role models, they join a new community with a different culture, their feelings are legitimated, and they find helpers who aid them in finding a direction for change and accommodation. Helpers in mutual help groups also fulfill the linking functions of change agents; that is, they gather bodies of necessary information and know where and how resources can become available and then make them available to others. They themselves are role models for making these changes. Competency is enhanced and capacity to cope is facilitated as people learn how to deal with the consequences of their disabling situations (Silverman, 1985). This learning comes from helping others as well.

Participants in such groups have reported that as a result of participating they develop new skills for coping with their new situation. They become more communicative and more assertive on their own behalf, and they learn how to use professionals in a safe environment. These experiences give members the tools they need for effective participation and for problem solving (Borkman, 1999). In many ways, acquiring these skills changes how participants see their own role in a larger community. Silverman (1988) reported on the ways in which belonging to an organization for the widowed, for example, changed these widows and widowers. In the long run these changes contributed to building a larger caring community. In the words of one widow: "First it made me feel I wasn't the only one in the same situation. Secondly it made me more outgoing and inclined to offer whatever I could to help others." These groups are not an alternative to group therapy or professionally run support groups but, instead, involve a different way of thinking and of developing community (Borkman, 1999).

Becoming a Helper

Involved individuals become helpers in the group. Becoming a helper reinforces a members' own sense of competency and adequacy (Lifton, 1973,

Silverman, 1978). Many groups have clear policies that limit the role of nonmembers in their activities. In AA only a former alcoholic who has been dry for a period of time and who was helped by the AA method can become a helper. The organization relies on the indigenous talents and resources of its recovering members for success.

Critical to the uniqueness of mutual help groups is that members determine all policy and are both providers and recipients of the service. The success of these groups largely depends on the fact that those involved are all peers. Peers are important sources of information, experience, and support in coping with change. As children grow, we recognize their need to learn from peers who serve as role models or with whom they can explore ways of coping with their common needs (Rubin, 1980). Children who have role-model peers do not tend to feel alone, unique, or isolated; they feel legitimated. This type of relationship probably is important over the entire life cycle, not just to adolescents. Not only may the need to find someone like oneself be central to learning to cope with change, but the opportunity to change roles and become a helper may be important as well (Reissman, 1965).

The Influence of Technology

Over the past decade the increased use of computers and the Web has changed the availability of information to the average person. The Web has helped people become better informed about issues relating to their own health and about available resources for help. Taking advantage of this technology, many mutual help groups now have online access for their members. In addition, online chat programs and social groups provide opportunities for people to find others with similar problems, to share their problems, and to learn from each other how to cope with their difficulties (Keim, 2009; Madera, 2008; White & Madera, 2002). Many mutual help groups are increasingly creating social network groups on sites such as Facebook, Ning, and Yahoo for their members as well.

The Web has revolutionized how people reach each other and learn from each other. It provides new ways for people to be part of a community and to be more aware of the needs of others. Meeting through a Web site breaks down geographic barriers. It also makes help available to people who are not mobile and would not be able to come to meetings. On these sites people rarely meet in person, but they come to know one another well, finding reassurance and relationships that would not be otherwise accessible to them. They come to depend on each other for inspiration, information, and support that goes much beyond what they can find through other sources closer to home. However, it is important to ask who the sponsors are, how privacy is protected, and whether anyone benefits financially from the site.

Influence on Professional Practice

The tensions between professional help and mutual help have existed for a long time and are still present. Professionals often worried, and some still do, about unqualified laypeople getting involved in the lives of people in need (Madera, 2008; Silverman, 2004). Professional caregivers see themselves as repositories of the "right" way to help and do not always understand or appreciate the value of lived experience. The power and control they see coming with their role as providers of help are central issues in discussing mainstream health and social service systems. These essentially hierarchical systems are legally mandated to treat patients.

Traditionally, the professional is the expert caring for the client, who is in a subordinate position; and many professionals have difficulty letting go of this image. For example, at a meeting several years ago for surviving families from the 9/11 tragedy, I was admonished by my colleagues, in front of a group of widows, for encouraging these widows to continue to meet as they worked on solving a key problem that concerned all of them. I was told that these women did not have the experience or knowledge to carry such a group forward. Since this message was also conveyed to the group, I watched as their faces dropped. Since I was not from the area and a guest at the meeting I do not know what these women did afterward. In my subsequent talk to the larger group that same day, I was clear that I thought they did not need my permission or permission from anyone else to continue to meet on their own as I advocated for the mutual help initiatives that were taking place as these survivors met.

Gradually, in some areas, this more traditional attitude has changed dramatically. Mutual help groups have expanded; Borkman (2008) observed that there are now thousands of members of mutual help groups who are ready to help others in the community and advocating for their constituents. There are also multiple groups that exist below the radar. As they continue to grow and flourish, they influence the help available in the communities around them.

Several examples of how these groups are involved in their communities come to mind. There are now parents of children with chronic medical conditions advising children's medical centers about programs to meet their children's needs and how to make hospital time more user-friendly. The *American Journal of Orthopsychiatry* (see Fonfled-Ayinia, 2009), in a special issue dealing with homelessness, saw the value of including a consumer's view of services as part of its evaluation of the care that was provided to them. Fonfled-Ayinia (2009) had lived with her child in a homeless shelter at a time of great need in her life. In the article she described the services and the atmosphere in the shelter that did not provide her with the care, flexibility, and attention that would have made this a helpful experience for herself or her daughter. Her description stands in sharp contrast to the descriptions in articles written by professionals in the same issue of this journal of the help they offered.

Professional caregivers in these various settings are beginning to ask what can be learned from consumers that might change the way services are organized and how professionals can collaborate with those in need to deal with the crises in their lives. There is a growing recognition of the need for professionals to listen and learn from their patients or clients. When I found in my research for my dissertation (Silverman 1968) that the clients in a social agency did not feel heard by the clinicians, I was told by my colleagues that I misinterpreted the data. I do not think I would have found the same response today. What is happening today, especially in health-care settings, is a developing appreciation, on the part of staff, of mutual help programs and their efforts to collaborate with their professional counterparts.

An example of how the importance of learning from clients is valued today is found in a project developed by the Massachusetts Institute of Technology Media Lab (Keim, 2009). The staff of the lab are listening to what people are saying on Web sites, especially social networking sites. (We presume this is with the participants' permission.) They are learning about people with serious problems who are discussing treatment, side effects, experiences with their diseases, and how they understand their situation and learn how to cope. This information provides scientists with ongoing views of a patient's daily life that would otherwise not be available to them via the traditional questionnaires and research instruments they typically use. These scientists, who in some instances are also clinicians,

are beginning to better understand and know what goes on in a patient's daily life and how these people cope. They are beginning to appreciate the many sides of what an illness can mean to the sufferer. In many ways, this humanizes the illness and the person, rather than the illness alone, becomes the focus of the clinicians' work. Often, by listening to what members of mutual help groups are saying, the professional may gain a totally new perspective on the problem at hand (Keim, 2009).

In my own experience, I learned from the bereaved that they did not put the past behind them in accommodating to their loss. At least 20 years ago, it was considered important that the bereaved "decathect the object," as it was called. To do this, they were asked to relinquish their emotional attachment to the deceased and put the past behind them. In so doing they would facilitate their "recovery" from their grief. The concept of letting go made no sense to the widowed people I met. It was creating problems for them when they could not conform to the expectations of the professionals they consulted. Nonetheless, they found appropriate ways of remaining involved with the deceased. However, they did not share these ways of coping with those they consulted. They reported to me, as a researcher, that their grief was not shortened. Instead, although they moved on and developed new ways of living in their changed world, they remained connected to the deceased. I explored this idea further in my research with children whose parent had died (Silverman & Nickman, 1996). This research substantiated this view of grief. These findings led to the development of a new paradigm for looking at grief, which has come to be known as "continuing bonds" (Silverman & Klass, 1996).

A "support group" held entirely in Spanish for women with cancer is described in a university alumni magazine (Graham, 2009). The group is led by a Hispanic public health worker who also has lived with cancer. While the authors do not use the label "mutual help," that is what they are describing as these women become "sisters in hardship, linked by a divesting commonality." The article is focused on praising this initiative and what it is doing for the participants. In another local hospital the social work staff are offering a mentoring program for women with breast cancer. Every new patient is put in touch with a former patient. The social work staff, anticipating the needs of these women, feels that every new patient needs to meet someone who was or is living with breast cancer. This is a program that is organized with the professional staff in charge.

Recent research has focused on the value of mutual help for its participants (Madera, 2008). Pistrang, Barker, and Humphreys (2008) reviewed studies of mutual help groups for people with mental health problems. These studies pointed to the value of the mutual help groups for those who participated that was at least equivalent to substantially more costly professional interventions. Goldstrom et al. (2005) surveyed mental health mutual support groups, self-help organizations, and consumer-operated services to discover how large a network of such groups or organizations existed in the United States. This research was motivated by the recognition that if recovery is to be possible for those suffering from mental illness, consumers and families must be drivers of decisions about what they need. This was seen as a new approach as these authors recognized that these groups or organizations were not an alternative to professional help but, rather, that they must work together and complement each other.

In looking at these initiatives that capture the value of help coming from someone with whom the recipient shares a common problem, what is missing from our understanding of mutual help groups? What is discordant about these new initiatives is the control of the resources, that is, who runs the program. For example, while Goldstrom et al. (2005) praise the work of mental health mutual support groups, they then propose to integrate self-help groups into a program supported by the state. This raises the question of whether a mutual help group might lose its own initiative and creativity if members have to deal with the rules of a larger bureaucratic organization? It opens the possibility of arguing over control of resources and the actual details of a program. At this point, this question relates to how we look at the role of professionals in the life of these organizations. It is important to recognize that professionals control the power in the formal helping community, and often members of mutual help groups are very dependent on care received from these professionals as well. Collaboration, not cooptation, is what seems important for each helping domain to retain its own identity.

Collaboration

Professionals can serve as collaborators with, for example, bereaved people, by helping to organize a program or giving organizers encouragement and support (Silverman, 1978, 1980). A good collaborator knows how to help people mobilize their own resources and develop ideas. He or she knows how to move aside as members take over (Silverman, 1980). Members are the experts, and professional helpers need to recognize, in this situation, that they are the students (Silverman, 1978, 1985, 2004). Professionals need to consider what expertise they have that would be useful to a group. They may understand the process for incorporating as a non-profit organization. They may understand how to organize a group with bylaws and procedures for running a meeting. They know how to facilitate group discussion and must be prepared to teach the members how to do this. They may know how to help members document various parts of their helping program. They may serve as linking agents, helping a group find others in the community from whom they can learn and other organizations with which they can collaborate. They need to know when to leave the initiative with the members and when to step back out of the picture.

Conclusion

It is clear that mutual help groups are responding in a variety of ways that enable their members to learn from each other and to recognize their own abilities to deal with their problems. They form caring communities, thereby enriching all our lives. In studying these groups it would seem that their effectiveness is increased when professional helpers become partners with them. The mutuality of the group is extended, making the community much richer. This richness is a result of the collaboration between their different ways of helping so that one initiative is not subordinate to the other.

I began this chapter with quotes from two people who were commenting on the positive value of meeting others like themselves. I have looked at what takes place as they participate in a mutual help experience. In the long run, regardless of their age, what followed from their meeting others like themselves was that they found ways of making sense of their new situations and learned to live with the new reality they were facing. They did not feel alone or unusual in their new situation. The need for community, for caring others like ourselves, becomes very important at times of change in our lives.

What we need to recognize is that there is more to this meeting. This new reality was controlled by people like themselves with whom they were peers, on an equal standing, and with whom they could become part of a new community where they felt cared about and could reciprocate. It is not enough to find others like oneself; we cannot ignore who controls the resources and the fact that members can become helpers in turn. For mutual help groups to do their work, professionals have to be collaborators, not captains of the team.

References

Borkman, T. J. (1999). *Understanding self-help/mutual aid: Experiential learning in the common.* Piscataway, NJ: Rutgers University Press.

Borkman, T. J. (2008). *If only researchers would talk to each other! Four traditions of self-help group research.* Paper presented at Colloquia at the Ontario Institute for Studies of Education, University of Toronto, Canada.

Borkman, T. (2010). Self-help groups. In Helmut Anheier & Stefan Teopler (Eds.), *International Encyclopedia of Civil Society.* New York: Springer Science + Business Media.

Bruner, J. (1990). *Acts of meaning.* Cambridge, MA: Harvard University Press.

Caserta, M. S., Lund, D. A., & Rice, S. J. (1999). Pathfinders: A self-care and health education program for older widows and widowers. *Gerontologist, 39*(5), 615–620.

Conrad, P. (2007). *The medicalization of society: On the transformation of the human condition into treatable disorders.* Baltimore: Johns Hopkins University Press.

Fonfled-Ayinia, G. (2009). Commentary: A consumer perspective on parenting while homeless. *American Journal of Orthopsychiatry, 79*(3), 299–304.

Forman, J. (2009, January 22). How to cope with the shock of cancer diagnosis. *Boston Globe,* p. C3.

Goldstrom, I. D., Campbell, J., Rogers, J. A., Lambert, D. B., Blacklow, B., Henderson, M. J., et al. (2005). National estimates for mental health mutual support groups, self-help organizations, and consumer-operated services. *Administration and Policy in Mental Health and Mental Health Services Research, 33,* 92–103.

Gottlieb, B. H. (Ed.). (1981). *Social networks and social support.* Beverly Hills, CA: Sage.

Graham, R. (2009, Fall). Common language: Whether conversing as a Latina or as a survivor. *Suffolk Alumni Magazine,* pp. 19–21.

Hughes, E. (1958). *Men and their work.* New York: Free Press.

Keim, B. (2009, Fall). Between the lines. In *Proto: Dispatches from the frontiers of medicine.* Boston: Massachusetts General Hospital, pp. 39–43.

Kellehear, A. (2005). *Compassionate cities: Public health and end of life care.* New York: Routledge.

Klass, D. (1988). *Parental grief: solace and resolution.* New York: Springer.

Klawiter, M. (2008). *The biopolitics of breast cancer: Changing cultures of disease and activism.* Minneapolis: University of Minnesota Press.

Kropotkin, P. (1972). *Mutual aid.* New York: New York University Press. (Original work published 1902)

Lenneberg, E., & Rowbotham, J. L. (1979). *The illeostomy patient.* Springfield, IL: Charles C. Thomas.

Lifton, R. J. (1973). *Home from the war.* New York: Simon & Schuster.

Lohmann, R. A. (1992). *The commons: New perspective on non-profit organizations and voluntary action.* San Francisco: Jossey-Bass.

Madera, E. J. (2008). Self-help groups: Options for support, education and advocacy. In P. G. O'Brien, W. Z. Kennedy, & K. A. Ballard (Eds.), *Psychiatric mental health nursing: An introduction to theory and practice* (pp. 151–168). Sudbury, MA: Jones and Bartlett.

Makela, K., Arminen, I., Bloomfield, K., Eisenbach-Stangl, I., Helmersson Berkmark, K., Kurube, N., et al. (1996). *Alcoholics Anonymous as a mutual help movement: A study in eight societies.* Madison: University of Wisconsin Press.

McKnight, J. (1995). *The careless society: Community and its counterfeits.* New York: Basic Books.

Pistrang, N., Barker, C., & Humphreys, K. (2008). Mutual help groups for mental health problems: A review of effectiveness studies. *American Journal of Community Psychology, 42,* 110–121.

Reissman, F. (1965). The helper therapy principal. *Social Work, 10*(2), 27–32.

Rubin, Z. (1980). *Children's friendships.* Cambridge, MA. Harvard University Press.

Sanders, J. M. (2009). *Women in Alcoholics Anonymous: Recovery and empowerment.* Boulder, CO: First Forum Press.

Silverman, P. R. (1968). *Study of spoiled helping: Clients who drop out of psychiatric treatment.* Unpublished doctoral dissertation, Brandeis University, Waltham, MA.

Silverman, P. R. (1978). *Mutual help: A guide for mental health workers* (NIMH/DHEW Publ. No. ADM 978–646). Washington, DC: Government Printing Office.

Silverman, P. R. (1980). *Mutual help groups: Organization and development.* Beverly Hills, CA: Sage.

Silverman, P. R. (1985). Preventive intervention: The case for mutual help groups. In R. K. Coyne (Ed.), *The group workers handbook: Varieties of group experience.* Springfield, IL: Charles C. Thomas.

Silverman, P. R. (1988). In search of selves: Accommodating to widowhood. In L. A. Bond (Ed.), *Families in transition: primary prevention programs that work.* Beverly Hills, CA: Sage.

Silverman, P. R. (2004). *Widow to widow: How the bereaved help one another* (2nd ed.). New York: Bruner Routledge.

Silverman, P. R., & Klass, D. (1996). Introduction: What's the problem? In D. Klass, P. R. Silverman, & S. L. Nickman (Eds.), *Continuing bonds: New understanding of grief* (pp. 3–27). Washington, DC: Taylor & Francis.

Silverman, P. R., & Nickman, S. L. (1996). Children's construction of their dead parents. In D. Klass, P. R. Silverman, & S. L. Nickman (Eds.), *Continuing bonds: New understanding of grief* (pp. 73–86). Washington, DC: Taylor & Francis.

Silverman, P. R., & Smith, D. (1984). Helping in mutual help groups for the physically disabled. In A. Gartner & F. Reissman (Eds.), *Mental health and the self help revolution.* New York: Human Science Press.

Stephans, S. (1972). *Death comes home.* New York: Morehouse-Barlow.

Stewart, M. J., Craig, D., MacPherson, K., & Alexander, S. (2001). Promoting positive affect and diminishing loneliness of widowed seniors through a support intervention. *Public Health Nursing, 18*(1), 53–63.

White, B., & Madera, E. J. (2002). *The self-help group sourcebook: Your guide to community and online support groups* (7th ed.). Denville, NJ: St. Clare's Health Services, American Self-Help Group Clearinghouse.

Betsy J. Page

Abstract

This chapter addresses online support, therapy, and social networking groups. Illustrative examples of groups are provided. The range of online groups is described. Research on online support, therapy, and social networking groups is reviewed. Ethical concerns related to definitions of types of groups and leadership, security of online groups, and planning for emergency care are addressed.

Keywords: group, online, support, therapy, social networking, leadership, ethics

Group work as a form of therapy has emerged over time. Early on, groups were used as a way to help more people at the same time; however, little was known about the effectiveness of group work. Information about how groups helped members developed in the literature over time, featuring research related to therapeutic factors (Kivlighan & Homes, 2004; Lieberman, Yalom, & Miles, 1973; Yalom, 1995). In a 1994 review of group work, Bednar and Kaul concluded that group treatments were effective and turned their attention to group process variables. They identified eight group process variables as having established value in group theory: "(1) group cohesion, (2) interpersonal feedback, (3) leadership styles and characteristics, (4) group structure or ambiguity, (5) group composition, (6) massed versus distributed learning, (7) therapist and client self-disclosure, and (8) personal risk and responsibility" (p. 632). They went on to identify three research needs at that time: "description of central conceptual variables," "development of descriptive taxonomies," and "development of measurement methods" (p. 633). Similar concerns regarding conceptual variables and measurement were echoed by DeLucia-Waack and Bridbord (2004). The points emphasized by Bednar and Kaul as well as the therapeutic factors described by Yalom

(1995) provide a beginning place for considering the massive activity in online groups in 2009.

Short descriptions of four very different online groups follow. The technology, group structure, and leadership, or lack thereof, vary among the groups, as does the experience of a member. While the members are fictional, the groups typify the diverse groups actually found online as well as the strengths and problems of such groups. After each example, the issues and questions about group process, leadership, and ethics illustrated by it will be examined. Issues of process, leadership, and ethics will be used as we consider the examples and throughout this chapter as conceptual threads that weave back and forth between the more familiar world of face-to-face groups and the evolving world of online groups. In the evolving online world, definitions of concepts, models of leadership, and application of ethics may be less clear, less consistent, or both.

Group Examples
A Support Group for Caretakers of Elderly Parents
THE MEMBER AND THE GROUP
Shirley is 52 years old and the primary caretaker for her 80-year-old mother, who lives with Shirley and her family. The family consists of Shirley's husband,

Fred, who is a commercial banker, and two daughters, ages 15 and 17.

Mother has lived with Shirley and the family for about 4 years. Early on, Mother alternated between being mellow and rather demanding. At times, she interfered with how Shirley and Fred parented the girls. At other times, she expressed her anger at the girls directly. Now, Mother is beginning to show what may be early symptoms of Alzheimer disease. She is having difficulty remembering where she put things, and she asks the same question repeatedly. These behaviors are wearing on Shirley. At the urging of a neighbor, Shirley joined an online support group about a year ago.

The group is an asynchronous bulletin board to which members can post e-mails 24 hours a day. It is a closed group, with membership limited to 30 people. Members were prescreened by the clinical social worker who leads the group. The social worker briefed each prospective member on what the group was, how members were to participate, how confidentiality was to be kept, how the group would be monitored, and what records would be kept. He also reserved the right to remove posts from the board and to remove members from the group if necessary for member safety.

HOW THE MEMBER EXPERIENCED THE GROUP
Shirley's experience with the group has been overwhelmingly positive. She has shared her concerns as well as the positives of her life with the group members. Shirley posts to the group about three times a week, often providing emotional support to others. Other members have encouraged Shirley and provided her with strategies for relating to her mother and decreasing family conflict. Both members and the social worker have provided information and Internet-based resources for Shirley as she considers the possible beginnings of Alzheimer disease in her mother. With Shirley's consent, the social worker supplemented the online group with phone-based discussion. In that discussion, he helped Shirley locate resources and schedule a local appointment for her mother to be evaluated for Alzheimer disease.

COMMENTARY ON GROUP PROCESS, LEADERSHIP, AND ETHICS
This group mirrors a professional face-to-face group in many aspects of practice and ethics. For example, Burlingame, Fuhriman, and Johnson (2004) pointed out processes that were important in structuring a group, including pregroup preparation. It is

clear that Shirley's online group has also benefited from pregroup preparation of members. The process of informed consent addressed some of the points recommended in codes A.2.a and A.2.b, including records (American Counseling Association [ACA], 2005).

While the leader of this group does not sound very directive, he has reserved the right to intervene for member safety. His leadership is consistent with the ACA *Code of Ethics* section A.8.b, which emphasizes taking precautions to protect clients (ACA, 2005). In the midst of the group, he again sought informed consent before helping Shirley obtain a referral for her mother. The leader's extra effort was a clear demonstration of caring, one of the core mechanisms of group leadership identified by Lieberman et al. (1973).

Facebook for a First-Year College Student
THE MEMBER AND THE GROUP
Manny is a first-year college student at a school in the Midwest, majoring in civil engineering. He spends about an hour on Facebook every day. His goals for using Facebook are a mix of personal and professional.

The first way Manny uses the Facebook site is to maintain his connections with family members who live in southern California. A second use is that he converses with his civil engineering classmates. Mostly, they use the site as a place to discuss their homework. Manny and his classmates also post pictures and videos of their first year at school.

A third way Manny uses the site is for professional networking. His extended family members own several successful Mexican restaurants. Manny is proud of their achievements. At the same time, he is mindful that he has no personal connections with firms focusing on civil engineering. Next year Manny has to do a field placement for a semester in which he is to assist a civil engineer. Hoping to make connections for his field placement, he has "friended" several civil engineers. He also responded positively to three firms that asked to be his Facebook friend.

HOW THE MEMBER EXPERIENCED THE GROUP
Manny's experience with Facebook was very positive until his application for a field placement was denied by his first-choice firm. The reason given in the denial was unprofessional presence on the Internet site. Manny believes this refers to a video of a party one of his classmates posted on Facebook. The video clearly showed he had had too much to drink.

COMMENTARY ON PROCESS, LEADERSHIP, AND ETHICS

Facebook accounts could be conceptualized as open groups with fluid membership and no evident leadership. One of the issues this group illustrates is that in online social networking sites, while there is clear interaction among members, it may not be as easy to answer the basic question, Who is in the group? In Bednar and Kaul's (1994) terms, the variable of group composition is not intentionally addressed. A member may use one site for multiple groups with differing membership and goals. In Manny's case he uses the site for

1. Maintaining connections with extended family. This group has a defined set of members and may fall into the type of group Kivlighan and Homes (2004) describe as focusing on affective support.

2. A second group for which Manny uses the same site is his engineering classmates. While Manny prefers to have the group be essentially a task work group, his peers mix a task work group with a social group. Manny was not able or did not know how to control what his peers post. Information can be and was made public about him without his consent. Here, Bednar and Kaul's (1994) process variable of group structure was not clear.

3. A third group for which Manny uses the same site is a broad professional networking group. Here, as in the second group, Manny's goals and those of the other members (engineering firms) may be at odds. While Manny is looking for a benefactor, someone to provide advantages he does not have, the firms may take a reciprocal role—looking for a minority person to sponsor—or they may use the site for screening potential candidates—in other words, for the firms' best interests—to gain some competitive edge.

A Treatment Group for Adults with Depression

THE MEMBER AND THE GROUP

Delia, a 30-year-old African American stockbroker, has been feeling depressed because the market has been way down for nearly a year. In such a market, it is hard for Delia to make money for the accounts she manages. As time has gone on, she has received an increasing number of complaints from clients who are disappointed in the return on their investments. While Delia's supervisor has not been critical of her work, constant customer complaints have been depressing to her.

In an effort to help herself, Delia joined a public list serve group titled Depression Treatment. Delia chose this group because it was free and there was no screening process, so she had to provide very little personal information to join. Since the group was asynchronous, it fit into her rather hectic life as a stockbroker. Her hopes in joining the group were to get encouragement for life and to learn strategies for decreasing her sense of depression.

HOW THE MEMBER EXPERIENCED THE GROUP

Delia's experience of the group has been mixed. She has received both support and strategies for countering her depression. There are about six members who post with great regularity and provide much of the encouragement to others.

Two aspects of the group make Delia uneasy. She has noticed that the moderator rarely participates. Delia also is aware that there appear to be a large number of group members who are present—logged in—but do not post. She feels uncomfortable that these members are "watching" her but saying nothing (i.e., never posting to the site).

Last week, Delia's post described how sad and discouraged she felt. Before any of the regular providers of encouragement could respond, a member Delia had never seen post before responded with cutting remarks about Delia containing blatant racial slurs. While the group regulars rebuked the person who posted the slurs, the moderator made no comment. The member making the attack was not removed from the group. The comments made in the attack cut Delia emotionally. She could not get them out of her mind. She wants to process this attack and her resulting pain in person with someone, but she no longer trusts the leader. No local backup is available to her for support.

COMMENTARY ON PROCESS, LEADERSHIP, AND ETHICS

Delia chose this group as a source for help with her depression in part because she perceived the lack of screening and provision of minimal identifying information as protective of her privacy and identity. She felt vulnerable, and she wanted a degree of anonymity. This sense of vulnerability may be similar in kind to initial feelings of members of face-to-face groups, which Jacobs, Masson, and Harvill (2006, p. 86) note members may find "intimidating." Delia also needed the flexibility of an asynchronous group. Both anonymity and flexibility may tend to draw members wanting help to online, rather than face-to-face, groups. In face-to-face groups, screening and orientation of members allow leaders to assess the vulnerability of potential members and help members know what to expect as the group begins (Gladding, 2008).

Even though screening and orientation were missing, much of Delia's experience in the group was positive due to a few members who posted frequent encouragement and information. The beneficial interaction between Delia and the frequent posters demonstrates the positive influence of interpersonal feedback, one of the group process variables indentified by Bednar and Kaul (1994). Another way to think of the frequent posters is to consider them using SYMLOG (Bales & Cohen, 1979). These frequent providers of support and solutions could be considered as cluster of members whose location was positive (as opposed to negative) and dominant (as opposed to submissive) with focus varying between task (F instrumental controlled) and process (B emotionally expressive) as the situation indicates.

Lack of leader activity exposes the undefined role of the leader in a number of online groups, including this example. A site may not have a leader but rather a navigator, facilitator, or owner who makes no pretense of being a professional group leader. Members may not know if or with what frequency the person they conceptualize as the leader will read the posts. Leader qualifications, or lack thereof, may not be known to the members. Nonprofessional facilitators, navigators, or owners may have no ability to assess members' mental health and may not feel responsible for member care. Whether or how the leader will deal with inappropriate posts may also be unknown. In times of emotional need by members, nonprofessional leaders may abdicate the leader role of member protection envisioned in professional ethics codes (ACA, 2005, A.8b; American Psychological Association [APA], 2002, 3.04; National Association of Social Workers [NASW], 2008, 1.04c).

A Treatment and Support Group for Adults with Alcohol Abuse

THE MEMBER AND THE GROUP

Oleg began abusing alcohol when he was laid off from his job in an auto assembly plant 5 years ago. Over the years he drank more and more. When he attended a relative's funeral, Oleg realized his life was going downhill as he continued to drink. With the encouragement of friends, he joined an online substance-abuse treatment and support group.

The credentials of the counselor running the group were available in advance. The draft contract contained details of the treatment process, provisions for local emergency care, a follow-up plan, and information about record keeping and retention. This contract was available for Oleg to examine in advance of the group. The counselor conducted a thorough pregroup screening of Oleg. Oleg then used the draft contract and the results of the screening to get the union health board to pay for his group counseling.

This synchronous group uses technology which allows Oleg to see and hear the other members and the leader live. The leader gently moderates the group process, making sure all members participate equally, focus on the purpose of the group, and treat each other with respect.

HOW THE MEMBER EXPERIENCED THE GROUP

Oleg feels very connected to and accepted by the other members. This sense of connection and acceptance motivates him to follow the plan for the group, which so far has been effective at reducing his alcohol consumption. Oleg is now very hopeful that, with the help of the group, he will able to abstain from drinking. He believes he will be able to maintain sobriety, find a new job, and return to a more positive life.

COMMENTARY ON PROCESS, LEADERSHIP, AND ETHICS

The thoroughness and transparency of the leader of this group are evident. The leader screened and oriented Oleg carefully, which was particularly important since Oleg had issues of unemployment compounded by a declining quality of life due to substance use. This leader approached her pregroup responsibilities with openness and transparency, which allowed for informed consent, as stressed in ethics documents (ACA, 2005, A2; APA, 2002, 3.10; NASW, 2008, 1.03). Due to the transparency of the contract, which included information on cost as well and the leader's credentials, both Oleg and his insurance company felt confident the group would be beneficial.

The live video and audio interaction in this synchronous group promoted the therapeutic factor cohesion (Yalom, 1995). Facial expressions and voice tones enriched communication, approaching the interactive nature of a face-to-face group. The goals of the group were primarily clinical rather than social in nature. Oleg's decreasing use of alcohol demonstrates that the group is effective. Hope has been activated as a therapeutic factor (Yalom, 1995).

Now that some examples of online groups have been considered, the following section moves our focus from specific, illustrative examples to considering the question, What is the big picture of online groups in 2009?

The Range and Distribution of Online Groups

Online support groups offer "encouragement, acceptance, and virtual companionship to offset social and special isolation" (Rier, 2007, p. 1043). A Google search for the term "online groups" conducted on August 27, 2009, returned about 225,000 sites. When the first 100 were sorted into groups, several types of sites were evident: (1) general sites sponsoring multiple groups, (2) sites that recruited the Internet user to form a group, (3) social networking sites, (4) geographic communities, (5) health- or medically related groups, (6) mental health–related groups, (7) parenting groups, (8) political groups, (9) ecology groups, (10) business/enterprise groups, (11) teaching- or academically focused groups, and (12) interest-focused groups. This chapter will focus primarily on the types of sites most closely related to the group work of counselors, psychologists, and social workers.

General Sites Sponsoring Multiple Groups

General sites sponsoring multiple groups included sites like Google Groups (http://groups.google.com/) and Yahoo! Groups. The Google Groups directory included the following types and numbers of groups that are likely to be related to readers' professional practice: health–mental health (2,463), health–addictions (762), health–medicine (3,983), health–conditions and diseases (3,169), and health–disabilities (1,063) (http://groups.google.com/groups/dir?lnk=od&sel=topic%3D46389). Yahoo! Groups (http://groups.yahoo.com/) does not display an index; however, a query of its search system resulted in 10,979 hits for the topic "mental health".

Sites for Forming Groups

Examples of sites that appear to host online groups and are encouraging Internet users to form a group on their site include OnlineGroups (http://onlinegroups.net), Groupbox (http://groupbox.com/), and CONVOS (www.convos.com/). These sites make it easy for Internet users to create a large number of groups that are not likely to be moderated in any way.

Social Networking Sites

Examples of social networking sites are Facebook (http://www.facebook.com/), MySpace (http://www.myspace.com/), and Secondlife (http://secondlife.com/). These social networking sites have huge numbers of members and a large amount of daily activity.

Groups Focusing on Medical or Mental Health

Both the medical heath category and the mental health category contained groups primarily focused on providing information about disorders and disorder-focused support groups. The nature of these groups overlaps with the nature of the medical and mental health groups on sites like Google Groups. At this point, it probably is best to mention that most of the medical and mental health groups online are advertised or describe themselves as "support" groups, although some portion of them would in actuality be therapy groups from our professional perspective. In this chapter we will first consider research on online counseling, therapy, and support groups and then consider research on social networking groups.

RESEARCH ON ONLINE COUNSELING, THERAPY, AND SUPPORT GROUPS

Cancer

In a 2004 review of online group counseling, more literature discussed the use of groups for women with breast cancer than any other client group (Page, 2004). This topic remained the one most frequently discussed in 2009.

Research on Breast Cancer Support Groups According to Breastcancer.org (2009) about one of every eight women (13%) in the United States has breast cancer. Some forms of breast cancer are being viewed as a chronic disease (Till, 2003). One implication of such a view is that long-term support is important to the women's quality of life. Online groups offer a forum through which members might be expected to gain a number of benefits, including, but not limited to, accurate medical information, emotional support, universality (the sense that others have similar concerns), hope, and suggestions for dealing with specific aspects of problems related to cancer diagnosis and treatment, as well as models for other life activities.

Shaw, Han, Hawkins, Mctavish, and Gustavson (2008) investigated the focus of messages (self vs. other) in an online breast cancer support group and the generation of positive vs. negative emotions. It was hypothesized that a focus on self, indicated in the messages by the use of a higher percentage of first-person pronouns, might "contribute to worse outcomes in coping with cancer because it may increase thoughts about one's problems" (p. 931). In contrast, a focus on others, indicated in the messages by a higher percentage of third-person pronouns, might activate Yalom's (1995) therapeutic factors of altruism and universality and lead to improved outcome. Outcome measures used were breast cancer–related concerns (Gustafson et al., 2005) and a five-item negative emotions scale (Gustafson et al., 2001). Survey data were obtained from 97 active participants, each of whom wrote at least three messages over the 4 months of the study. In addition to test and 4-month retest data, pronoun use in messages was analyzed. Hierarchical regression analysis supported the hypothesis that a "higher percentage of first [person] pronouns would predict higher levels of negative emotion" (Shaw et al., 2008, p. 936). It is possible that this result is related to the results of Sandaunet (2008), who studied nonparticipation and withdrawal from an online self-help group for breast cancer patients.

While there are potential benefits of online support groups, dropout rates are high (Sandaunet, 2008). Given the potential benefits, it is important to learn why some members fail to participate and others drop out. The content of 1,034 messages posted by a group of 40 women over a period of 15 months was examined. Twenty-nine of the 40 participants were determined to be nonusers. "Either they did not participate at all (11) or they disappeared from the group after they had posted some messages (18)" (p. 134). By interviewing nonparticipants, Sandaunet identified five conditions related to nonparticipation or withdrawal. The first condition was the need to avoid painful feelings about breast cancer. These women found it hard to "listen" to the painful details of others' stories. It is possible that hearing from women whose breast cancer had spread to other parts of their bodies conflicted with the need to preserve hope. A second condition reported by the women was an experience of not fitting in—not being as ill as the other women in the group. A third condition was finding a legitimate position in the group. These women were concerned they would be perceived as complaining in the group. Another woman felt excluded when there was no response to her disclosure of depression. The fourth condition related to nonparticipation and

withdrawal from the group was the organization of everyday life. As the women recovered from initial treatment and resumed the activities of their ordinary life, including going back to work, finding time to participate in the group became difficult. The fifth condition reported was illness phases that did not motivate the women to participate. As the women's health became better, they did not feel a need for the support group. Sandaunet (2008) noted that the women may be experiencing breast cancer as something they want to "get through and leave behind" (p. 141).

Høybye, Johansen, and Tjørnhøj-Thomsen (2005) conducted an ethnographic investigation of the effects of storytelling in an online breast cancer support group. The researchers conduced 12 semistructured face-to-face interviews with seven participants and nine online interviews with four participants. The 14 distinct categories of storytelling that resulted from analysis of the mailing list contributions reduced to four empowerment strategies, the first of which was empowerment through knowledge. The women felt empowered and in control when their participation in the group linked them with resources. The second strategy was tears and laughter. While the content of the group's discussion generally focused on their issues with cancer, members also made jokes related to their cancer and were able to laugh. The third strategy was entering a new social world in the virtual community of the Internet. Bonds were formed among members and metaphors of kinship expressed. The fourth and final strategy was social intimacy. Members were able to talk about difficult issues, for example, breast cancer and sexuality.

Gooden and Winefield (2007) studied gender differences between messages in a breast cancer support group for women and those in a prostate cancer support group for men. Analysis of message content indicates the same two themes in the discussions of both genders—information support (60% of communications in the women's group and 64% of communications in the men's group) and emotional support. Under the heading "information support," members requested information, provided their own knowledge to the group, quoted their experience, quoted literature, discussed evidence-based practice, and promoted informed choice in relation to cancer management. Emotional support encompassed offering wisdom (a coping philosophy and humor) as well as nurturing and expressing (sharing of distress, encouragement and valuing, challenging, and connection felt with other group members).

Research on Prostate Cancer Support Groups The American Cancer Society estimates 192,280 new cases of prostate cancer and 27,360 deaths from prostate cancer in 2009 (American Cancer Society, 2009). Online groups are being used to support these men, and some research is available about the groups. Broom (2005) drew on accounts of groups of Australian men with prostate cancer. He also investigated how medical experts experience online support groups in which their patients engage. Broom interviewed 25 men from three support groups in Victoria. The men reported that online groups offered them the chance to be less inhibited than in face-to-face groups and to "open up" more. The men also experienced the online group "as distancing them from their disease and their symptomatology" (p. 93). This support may have been critical to the men since they viewed the investigation procedures and the treatments for their cancer as "highly problematic for maintaining their sense of masculinity" (p. 94). They valued *lurking*—being able to observe without participating—since they could learn from the active participants even when they themselves were unable to ask questions.

In sharp contrast to the experiences described previously, some men—particularly those who were not comfortable using the computer—viewed online support groups as "dangerous and dysfunctional spaces" (p. 95). These men were concerned about being misinformed or deceived. Since their disease tended to be more advanced than that of the men with positive views of online support, the men with negative views were likely to have few treatment options available to them at the time they considered the online support.

Many of the medical experts interviewed saw online support groups as a challenge to their "expert" status. They viewed the men as unable to judge the quality of information located online. Some expressed irritation that they had to take time to respond to questions about information from the Internet that men brought into the doctor's office.

RESEARCH ON HIV SUPPORT GROUPS

The Centers for Disease Control and Prevention (2009) estimates that there were 56,300 new persons infected with HIV in 2006, which is the most recent year for which data are available. Bar-Lev (2008) investigated the "performing of emotions" in HOPE, an online HIV/AIDS support group. More specifically, she looked at "how participants discussed the expression of anger as a moral dilemma" and "how participants discussed a moral dilemma in emotional terms" (p. 510). She examined responses to anger narratives that had survivor themes and those that had victim themes. Responses indicated a norm that encouraged the storyteller to take an active stance in a positive mind frame rather than develop a "fatalistic acceptance of destiny" (p. 516). Bar-Lev concludes that support groups may act as a moral agent. This theme of HIV support groups acting as a moral agent was further explored by Rier (2007). Rier investigated the ethical dynamics of HIV+ status disclosure as they were expressed in the records of 16 lists (groups), which were free and accessible to all users. While the dominant dynamic on all sites was support, Rier examined only those posts related to disclosure of HIV status. The posters generally encouraged full disclosure and sometimes framed it as "do unto others as you would want done to you." A less frequently taken position tied disclosure to the value of the relationship—disclosure was more imperative as relationships became more long-term or more important. Some posts articulated a buyer-beware ethic. Another theme noted that in some settings, for example, bath houses, the norm was intentional nondisclosure. The later positions on this list often drew strong criticism from others. The typical support group norm of expressing nonjudgmental support did not hold in these discussions. That norm appeared to be outweighed by a norm to encourage ethical behavior.

RESEARCH ON GROUPS FOR OTHER MEDICAL AND MENTAL HEALTH ISSUES

Online groups are also being used to support clients with a wide range of concerns, including pregnancy and parenting (Ley, 2007; Valaitis & Sword, 2005), weight issues (Bane, Haymaker, & Zinchuk, 2005; Webber, Tate, & Bowling, 2008), pediatric brain injury (Wade, Carey, & Wolf, 2006), hearing loss (Cummings, Sproull, & Kiesler, 2002), eating disorders (Gavin, Rodham, & Poyer, 2008; Darcy & Dooley, 2007), heart disease (Lindsay, Smith, Bellaby, & Baker 2009), diabetes self-management (Barrea, Glasgow, McKay, Boles, & Feil, 2002), suicide prevention (Barak, 2007), domestic violence (Hurley, Sullivan, & McCarthy, 2007), and problem drinking (Cunningham, van Mierlo, & Fournier, 2008).

Social Networking Groups: What They Are and How They Work

The social networking sites link users together online. This section will discuss the more prominent sites: Twitter, Facebook, MySpace, Ning, Linkdin, and Secondlife. Twitter and Facebook will be described in some detail, then each of the other sites will be discussed briefly. Discussion of Twitter and Facebook will include (1) the nature of the site, (2) a brief description of how the site works, and(3) uses and concerns for group workers.

TWITTER
Nature of the Site
Twitter (Twitter.com) is a free online site through which persons with an account can send short messages. Twitter promotes the idea of immediacy. The banner heading on the site proclaims in bold text "The best way to discover what is in your world." (http://twitter.com).

Brief Description of How the Site Works
Some of the basic activities on Twitter are sending "tweets," finding people, finding favorites, and selecting topics to follow. An empty box at the top of the home page allows you to send *tweets*—messages of 140 characters or less. Once the tweet is sent, it almost instantly appears on the top of the list on your home page. This list is publicly available.

It is possible to search for people or organizations. For example, a search for "APA" resulted in a page of listings that contained a wide range of topics including one titled "APA Convention." By clicking on the box at the right of that entry, one can "follow" that list of tweets.

Types of Tweets
There appear to be several types of tweets that users send out. This writer would characterize most of the tweets as belonging to one of three categories: (1) instant updates, (2) event notices, and (3) business pointers. The reader should realize that these terms are the writer's attempt to group the tweets and that the names of the three types of tweets do not appear as a category on the Twitter pages.

Instant updates tell what a person is doing or experiencing. Many of these tweets may not be interesting to group leaders. On the other hand, instant-update tweets from group members such as "Pretty depressed today," "Need help not drinking this morning," "Out of medication," or "Feel like hurting my husband" might indicate situations in which members need immediate support, intervention, or both.

Event notices typically give the source of the tweet, a bit of narrative information, and a URL that leads to a full set of information that far exceeds the 140-character limit of Twitter. An example of a tweet that might have been of interest to readers was sent out by the Counselor Education and Supervision Network announcing a conference on Secondlife.

Business pointers might contain tweets from social workers, for example, with professional names, types of groups, and URL's that point to the social workers' business Web sites. Many Web sites, however, have a URL that exceeds the 140-character limit of Twitter. In order for a tweet to contain some label related to a URL and the URL itself, the URL has to be shortened.

TinyURL (http://www.tinyurl.com) is an example of an Internet site that shortens long URLs to a tiny URL that can then be included in tweets and other Internet messages. When the receiver of the message clicks on a TinyURL to open a link, the TinyURL routes the search through TinyURL.com, which opens the site. TinyURLs may also be used to get a URL that is easier for a user to remember than the extensive series of words, periods, and slashes that often comprise modern-day Internet URLs.

Uses and Concerns for Group Workers
Group leaders could use Twitter to send business-pointer tweets on available groups to large numbers of people. Group leaders could create specific feeds that pointed members toward professionally sound information about disorders, medications, or treatment options. Group leaders and their agencies might set up systems for monitoring client welfare between appointments using client-posted tweets monitored by agency staff.

The primary concern is the conglomerate of results returned by searches. Search results generally fall along a continuum from useful to irrelevant to harmful.

FACEBOOK
Nature of the Site
Facebook (http://www.facebook.com) is a social networking site that promotes connection with friends. This site is open to children aged 13 and older as well as adults. Facebook accounts have four main pages, Home, Profile, Friends, and Inbox. Users create their profile (a set of personal information visible to other users). The heart of the profile page is the Wall. By using a "publisher" at the top of the Wall, photos, videos, events, and links can be written on the Wall. Other users can write comments on the Wall about materials posted there. The Wall displays recent activities, photos, and messages from users and their friends and is continuously

updated with new entries being placed at the top. Members can select a group of "friends" who may be given access to more information than is the general public.

Development of Conceptual Variables in Facebook

The intent of Facebook is to promote social networking, which allows users to connect based on common interests rather than geographic proximity (Ellison, Steinfield, & Lampe, 2007). It is reasonable to ask what benefits users might receive from engaging in such networking. One type of benefit has been labeled "social capital." *Social capital* is described as including social trust, civic participation, life satisfaction, and political engagement (Valenzuela, Park, & Kee, 2009). Current literature on Facebook use reveals four emerging variables: Facebook intensity, bonding social capital, bridging social capital, and maintaining social capital.

Facebook intensity (Ellison et al., 2007) is based on the number of friends, the average minutes per day on Facebook, and a Likert scale measure of six indicators of attitude about Facebook. An example of one of the attitude indicators is "I feel out of touch when I haven't logged onto Facebook for a while" (p. 1150).

Bonding social capital was described as emotionally close, supportive relationships (Ellison et al., 2007).

Bridging social capital was described as providing new perspectives or useful information but not emotional support (Ellison et al., 2007). An example of bridging capital is obtaining information or connections related to employment.

Maintained social capital was described as the benefit of keeping "in touch with a social network after physically disconnecting from it" (Ellison et al., 2007, p. 1146). For example, the transition to college of a first-year student is eased by maintaining some connections with high school friends.

Research Studies

Ellison et al. (2007) examined the relationship between Facebook use and the formation and maintenance of social capital. Undergraduate students (n = 286) completed surveys which included information on demographics and Facebook use. Participants averaged 20 years of age. Two-thirds of them were female and 87% were white.

Participants reported averaging 20–30 minutes of Facebook use per day and having 150–200 friends on their profile. They had significantly (P < 0.0001) more Facebook use with people with whom they shared an offline connection than use involving meeting new people. The social capital items which were rated on a 5-point Likert scale were subjected to a principal components factor analysis with a varimax rotation. The analysis resulted in three factors—bridging social capital (Cronbach's alpha = 0.87), maintained social capital (Cronbach's alpha = 0.81), and bonding social capital (Cronbach's alpha = 0.75)—which explained 53% of the variance.

After factoring the dependent variables related to social capital, Ellison et al. (2007) investigated the effects of a set of demographic variables, Facebook intensity, self-esteem, and satisfaction with life, on each of the social capital scales using regression analyses. The independent variables accounted for about half of the variance in bridging social capital. "Students reporting low satisfaction and low self-esteem appeared to gain in bridging social capital if they used Facebook more intensely" (p. 1158). Facebook intensity was the largest single predictor of bonding social capital (scaled beta = 0.37, P < 0.001) and maintained social capital (scaled beta = 0.36, P < 0.001).

Overall, this research (Ellison et al., 2007) demonstrated a positive relationship between Facebook use and the types of social capital examined. The three social capital scales provide useful tools for further research.

Steinfield, Ellison, and Lampe (2008) used surveys and in-depth interviews to conduct a longitudinal investigation of social capital, self-esteem, and use of Facebook by college students. Psychological well-being was assessed through measures of self-esteem and life satisfaction. Self-esteem was measured with seven items from the Rosenberg Self-Esteem Scale (Rosenberg, 1989) and life satisfaction was measured with a version of the Satisfaction with Life Scale (Diener, Suh, & Oishi, 1997) that was amended to reflect the university context. Bridging social capital was measured using the Bridging Social Capital Scale (Ellison et al., 2007).

Results of the study (Steinfield et al., 2008) indicated that Facebook use led to increased bridging social capital even after controlling for differences in general Internet use. Social capital gains were greater for students with low self-esteem than for those with high self-esteem.

MYSPACE, NING, AND LINKEDIN

MySpace (myspace.com) operates through a process of creating a profile and finding and linking to friends. MySpace groups include activity groups, automotive groups, business and entrepreneurs groups, cities and neighborhoods groups, companies and coworkers groups, computers and Internet groups, and cultures and communities groups.

Ning (http://www.ning.com) lets users create and join social networks. This might be an appropriate site for professors who wish to establish networking sites for classes of graduate students.

Linkedin (http://www.linkedin.com) is a professional networking site. This site would be more suited for counselors, psychologists, and social workers to link with each other rather than for a group for clients.

SECONDLIFE

Secondlife (http://secondlife.com) is a user-created virtual world established by Lynden Labs. The world looks like real estate: it is a mix of buildings and spaces designed to be different things, for example, a horse stable, a beach, or a park. *Avatars* (graphic representations of people) walk or fly through the world. It is also possible to obtain transportation, for example, rent a virtual horse from a stable to ride. The world contains numerous kiosks, which sell a wide range of things. Avatars meet others in the world and converse through text messages. Land that is space in the virtual world is for sale at http://secondlife.com/land/pricing.php. Users might develop their own land or shop for a developer.

Secondlife moves far beyond the other formats—e-mail groups and social networking sites—in terms of what a group leader could create as an environment for a group. Dr. Marty Jencius created a mental health center and conference site. In September 2009, a conference at the site drew about 100 participants, many of whom were international participants. Presenters displayed PowerPoint slides and discussed them with participants much as they would in a professional conference in the real world. The technical capabilities of Secondlife would allow a library of resources to be built on the site and then be available for conference attendees or group members 24 hours a day.

Secondlife is an internationally used site. Time zone differences could be used to maximize the use of a site and possibly generate international collaboration—a group from Australia or New Zealand might meet in a group room while those in the United States slept and conversely. Costs for the site could be split between two professionals or universities. Secondlife could also provide a venue for conducting research on online groups and online group processes and leadership.

FLOCK

Flock (www.flock.com) is a social Web browser. When social networking sites such as Facebook and Twitter are linked to Flock, Flock aggregates the data flowing into the social networking sites and displays data from multiple sites simultaneously.

Ethics

The ethical concerns described in this section arise from the experience of searching for groups on the Internet, the examples at the start of this chapter, and the research reviewed.

Blurred Definitions of Group Types and of Leadership

The distinction between therapy groups and support groups that may be evident in face-to-face practice is not evident online. In general, the online groups describe themselves as support groups. Due to the way the groups are advertised, the individual who goes online looking for a group may find it difficult to differentiate a therapy group from a support group.

A second concern is leadership. While a few sites give the name and credentials of the professional and specify that the groups are professionally led, many sites simply give no information. Till (2003) points out that possible member lack of understanding of the limits of a moderator's role in support groups may be of ethical concern. Members may expect that moderators of online support groups are professionals who will give professional advice and who will protect them from negative interactions with other members. Often, this expectation is not met in reality and little information is given on sites about the moderator and his or her role.

Table 29.1 is an attempt to clarify the blurred definitions of group type and leadership in online groups by developing a possible taxonomy for online groups. This effort responds to Bednar and Kaul's (1994) request for descriptive taxonomies. The taxonomy, which is offered for the reader's consideration, identifies two general types of groups (support/self-help and treatment/therapy) and three levels of leadership (unmoderated, moderated, and led by a mental health professional). Crossing the two general types of groups with three levels of leadership resulted in two types of groups for each level of leadership:

• *Open discussion groups* are described as unmoderated support/self-help groups
• *Leaderless treatment groups* are described as unmoderated treatment groups. For safety reasons,

such groups are *not recommended*. Therefore, that cell of the table is shaded gray.

• *Moderated support/self-help groups* are so named and provide for minimal, nonprofessional, member care.

• *Moderated care groups* are described as moderated treatment groups. The moderator (under the supervision of a mental health profession licensed to do supervision) provides support and monitoring of treatment compliance for low-risk clients.

• *Professional support groups* are described as led by mental health professionals, goal-directed, and fully governed by ethical, legal, and licensure codes.

• *Professional therapy groups* are described as led by mental health professionals whose scope of practice includes clinical practice (diagnosis and treatment of mental and emotional disorders). Treatment goals address aspects of the members' diagnosis or safety issues related to the diagnosis.

It should be noted that the taxonomy presented in Table 29.1 is written to clarify both for mental heath practitioners and potential group members the situation of support and therapy groups in *online groups*. In designing this taxonomy, the writer assumed that the online world is not a mirror of the face-to-face world. The taxonomy gives descriptive options for nonprofessionally led support groups, rather than for professionally led therapy groups, because that distribution of attention appears to more accurately reflect what is happening online. Considering that little improvement has been made in clarifying the definitions of group types or leadership during the 5 years since the review of online groups by Page in 2004, one strong recommendation of this chapter would be that counselors, psychologists, and social workers adopt a common set of terms and descriptions to apply to online groups. Perhaps Table 29.1 will serve as a catalyst for such an interprofessional and possibly international discussion.

Problems Securing the Site

Securing the site may not be totally within the control of the leader since all of the specific privacy settings have to be correct on each member's computer. Both the security of the computers in general and the security of the specific site to be used for the group must be addressed.

In terms of general security, spyware including the "keystroke logger" programs must be cleaned from the computer and kept out of it. Members will need to choose credible passwords and keep them private. When a group session concludes, members should log out of the site immediately and entirely.

To address security specific to the site, mental health professionals should provide members with a packet of information including screen captures of the technology to be used, illustrating all of the settings that must be adjusted to get the desired level of privacy and which choice to select for each setting. Members should be asked to confirm by e-mail that they have indeed completed the process of controlling privacy settings on their accounts.

Security in the transmission of information also must be fully addressed: (1) between the leader and the members, (2) between the members and the Web server, and (3) between the Web server and the leader.

Problems with Lack of Emergency Care

A first step in advance planning for emergencies might be to confirm potential members' age and identity. Request that a photo of the member be mailed to you, the leader, for the records accompanied by a copy of his or her signature and complete address. Confirm the address and phone number the member provides by cross-checking this information using online programs to search for these identifiers independently.

Develop and sign a formal emergency care document before the group starts. Information might include the number of a mental health hotline local to the member; the name, address, and phone number of the member's physician as well as signed permission for the group leader to contact the physician; and the names, addresses, and phone numbers of two friends or family members as well as signed permission for the leader to contact the friends or family members. Development of a "what to do if" sheet providing action plans for specific scenarios might be clarifying for online group members.

The Future of Online Groups and the Involvement of Mental Health Professionals

Both the convenience of online groups and the multiplication of technologies available for use in such groups make the proliferation of online groups likely. Some mental health professions may choose to use technology to provide backup for face-to-face groups. Leaders might use a technology like Facebook to create an online "backup center," which would contain links to mental health providers

Table 29.1 Taxonomy of online group types and leadership

Type of Group Leadership	Support/Self-Help	Treatment/Therapy
	Open Discussion Group	**Leaderless Treatment Group**
Unmoderated	Pregroup Planning The group is open to the public. Members are not screened. Identity is not verified. There is no designated leadership, and credentials of the person running the site are unknown. Live Leadership The group is unmoderated. No one intervenes for member safety or checks accuracy of information. Ethics and Legal Codes Little attention is given to ethics and legal codes.	Pregroup Planning The group is open to the public. Members are not screened. Identity is not verified. There is no designated leadership, and credentials of the person running the site are unknown. Live Leadership The group is unmoderated. No one intervenes for member safety or checks accuracy of information. Ethics and Legal Codes Little attention is given to ethics and legal codes.
	Moderated Support/Self-Help Group	**Moderated Care Group**
Moderated	Pregroup Planning Group is limited to members who have been identified and screened. Credentials of moderator, if any, are disclosed to members. Live Leadership Moderator monitors the group with a frequency known to members. Moderator intervenes to protect member safety and remove or correct inaccurate information. Ethics and Legal Codes Attention to ethics and legal codes is minimal. Nonmalfeasance is practiced.	Pregroup Planning Group is limited to members who have been identified and screened. The diagnosis of members is appropriate for care to be given. The moderator receives clinical supervision from a mental health professional licensed to provide such supervision. Credentials of the supervisor and the moderator are disclosed to members. Live Leadership Moderator intervenes for member safety and provides accurate information. Moderator provides support and long-term monitoring of treatment compliance for low-risk clients. Refers members to professional treatment group as needed. Ethics and Legal Codes Ethical codes of the supervisor apply to the group. Applicable licensing and legal statutes are followed.
	Professional Support Group	**Professional Therapy Group**
Led by a mental health professional	Pregroup Planning Group is limited to members who have been identified and screened. Type and scope of license is disclosed to members (examples—licensed professional counselor or licensed school counselor, licensed clinical social worker or licensed psychologist). Group goals and processes are known in advance. Live Leadership Professional leadership promotes member safety and progress toward goals. Ethics and Legal Codes Ethical codes of the leader's profession as well as laws of all states in which either the leader or any member resides are followed. Leader practices within the scope of his or her license.	Pregroup Planning Group is limited to members who have been identified, screened, and oriented. Type and scope of license isdisclosed to members (examples—licensed professional clinical counselor or licensed clinical social worker, licensed psychologist). Treatment goals address members' diagnosis or safety issues related to the diagnosis. Live Leadership Professional leadership promotes member safety and progress toward treatment goals. Ethics and Legal Codes Ethical codes of the leader's profession as well as laws of all states in which either the leader or any member resides are followed. Leader practices within the scope of his or her license.

that rotated coverage so a distraught member could access professional help at any time. Leaders might post video content making safety information and miniteachings or words of encouragement available to members 24 hours a day. Leaders might also create a linkage through a social network as a source of support for members during the holiday season.

Some professionals may lead groups based on online technology as that technology exists now. Hopefully, they will research and develop best practices for groups in these environments. Other professionals will be explorers on the forefront of development where technology and its use evolve concurrently.

References

American Cancer Society. (2009). Learn about cancer. Retrieved October 2, 2009, from http://www.cancer.org/Cancer/ProstateCancer/index?ssSourceSiteId=null http://www.cancer.org/docroot/CRI/content/CRI_2_2_1X_How_many_men_get_prostate_

American Counseling Association. (2005). *2005 ACA code of ethics*. Retrieved from http://www.counseling.org/Resources/CodeOfEthics/TP/Home/CT2.aspx

American Psychological Association. (2002). *Ethical principles of psychologists and code of conduct*. Retrieved from http://www.apa.org/ethics/code2002.html

Bales, R. F., & Cohen, S. P. (1979). *SYMLOG: A system for the multiple level observation of groups*. New York: Free Press.

Bane, C. H., Haymaker, C. M. B., & Zinchuck, J. (2005). Social support as a moderator of the big-fish-in-a-little pond effect in online self-help support groups. *Journal of Applied Behavioral Research, 10*(4), 239–261.

Barak, A. (2007). Emotional support and suicide prevention through the Internet: A field project report. *Computers in Human Behavior, 23*, 971–984. doi:10.1006/j.ch.b.2005.08.001.

Bar-Lev, S. (2008). "We are here to give you emotional support": Performing emotions in an online support group. *Qualitative Health Research, 18*(4), 509–521. doi:10.117/1049732307311680.

Barrera, M., Jr., Glasgow, R. E., McKay, H. G., Boles, S. M., & Feil, E. G. (2002). Do Internet-based support interventions change perceptions of social support? An empirical trial of approaches of supporting diabetes self-management. *American Journal of Community Psychology, 30*(5), 636–654.

Bednar, R. L., & Kaul, T. J. (1994). Experiential group research: Can the cannon fire? In A. E. Bergin and S. L. Garfield (Eds.), *Handbook of psychotherapy and behavior change* (3rd ed., pp. 631–663). New York: John Wiley & Sons.

Breastcancer.org. (2009). *Breast cancer statistics*. Retrieved October 2, 2009, from http://www.breastcancer.org/symptoms/understand_bc/statistics.jsp?gclid=CPC-np0

Broom, A. (2005). The emale. *Journal of Sociology, 41*(1), 87–104. doi:10.1177/1440/783305050965.

Centers for Disease Control and Prevention. (2009). Retrieved October 2, 2009, from http://www.gov/hiv/topics/surveillance/incidence.htm

Cunningham, J. A., van Mierlo, T., & Fournier, R. (2008). An online support group for problem drinkers: AlcololHelpCenter.net. *Patient Education and Counseling, 70*, 193–198. doi:10.1016/j.pec.2007.10.003.

Darcy, A. M., & Dooley, B. (2007). A clinical profile of participants in an online support group. *European Eating Disorders Review, 15*, 185–195. doi:10.1002/erv.775.

DeLucia-Waack, J. L., & Bridford, K. H. (2004). Measures of group process, dynamics, climate, leadership behaviors, and therapeutic factors: A review. In J. L. DeLucia-Waack, D. A. Gerrity, C. R. Kalodner, & M. T. Riva (Eds.), *Handbook of group counseling and psychotherapy* (pp. 120–135). Thousand Oaks, CA: Sage.

Diener, E., Suh, E., & Oishi, S. (1997). Recent findings on subjective well-being. *Indian Journal of Clinical Psychology, 24*, 25–41.

Ellison, N. B., Steinfield, C., & Lampe, C. (2007). The benefits of Facebook "friends": Social capital and college students' use of online social network sites. *Journal of Computer-Mediated Communication, 12*, 1143–1168. doi:10.1111/j.1083–6101.2007.00367.

Gladding, S. T. (2008). *Groups: A counseling specialty* (5th ed.). Upper Saddle River, NJ: Pearson.

Gooden, R. J., & Winefield, H. R. (2007). Breast and prostate cancer online discussion boards: A thematic analysis of gender differences. *Journal of Health Psychology, 12*(1), 103–114. doi:10.1117/1359105307071744.

Gustafson, D. H., Hawkins, R. P., Pingree, S., McTavish, F., Arora, N., Mendenhall, J., et al. (2001). Effects of computer support on young women with breast cancer. *Journal of General Internal Medicine, 16*, 435–445.

Gustafson, D. H., McTavish, F. M., Stengle, W., Ballard, D., Hawkins, R., Shaw, B., et al. (2005). Use and impact of eHealth system by low-income women with breast cancer. *Journal of Health Communication, 10*, 195–218.

Høybye, M. T., Johansen, C., & Tjørnhøj-Thomsen, T. (2005). Online interaction: Effects of storytelling in an Internet breast cancer support group. *Psychooncology, 14*, 211–220. doi:10.1002/pn.837.

Hurley, A. L., Sullivan, P., & McCarthy, J. (2007). The construction of self in online support groups for victims of domestic violence. *British Journal of Social Psychology, 46*, 859–874. doi:10.1348/014466606X171521.

Jacobs, E. E., Masson, R. L., & Harvill, R. L. (2006). *Group counseling: Strategies and skills*. Belmont, CA: Thompson Brooks/Cole.

Kivlighan, D. M., Jr., & Homes, S. E. (2004). The importance of therapeutic factors: A typology of therapeutic factor studies. In J. L. Delucia-Waack, D. A. Gerrity, C. R. Kalodner, & M. T. Riva (Eds.), *Handbook of group counseling and psychotherapy* (pp. 23–36). Thousand Oaks, CA: Sage.

Ley, B. L. (2007). Vive les roses! The architecture of commitment in an online pregnancy and mothering group. *Journal of Computer-Mediated Communication, 12*, 1388–1408. doi:10.1111/j.1083–6101.2007.00378.

Lieberman, M. A., Yalom, I. D., & Miles, M. B. (1973). *Encounter groups: First facts*. New York: Basic Books.

Lindsay, S. L., Smith, S., Bellaby, P., & Baker, R. (2009). The health impact of an online heart disease support group: A comparison of moderated versus unmoderated support. *Health Education Research, 24*(4), 646–654.

National Association of Social Workers. (2008). *Code of ethics*. Retrieved from http://www.socialworkers.org/pubs/code/code.asp

Page, B. J. (2004). Online group counseling. In J. L. Delucia-Waack, D. A. Gerrity, C. R. Kalodner, & M. T. Riva (Eds.), *Handbook of group counseling and psychotherapy* (pp. 609–620). Thousand Oaks, CA: Sage.

Rier, D. A. (2007). Internet support groups as moral agents: The ethical dynamics of HIV⁺ status disclosure. *Sociology of Health & Illness, 29*(7), 1043–1058. doi:10.1111/j.1467-9566.2007.10123.

Rosenberg, M. (1989). *Society and the adolescent self-image* (rev. ed.). Middletown, CT: Wesleyan University Press.

Sandaunet, A. (2008). The challenge of fitting in: Non-participation and withdrawal from an online self-help group for breast cancer patients. *Sociology of Health and Illness, 30*(1), 131–144. doi:10.111/j.1467–9566.2007.0104.

Shaw, B. R., Han, J. Y., Hawkins, R. P., Mctavish, F. M., & Gustavson, D. H. (2008). Communicating about self and others within an online support group for women with breast cancer and subsequent outcomes. *Journal of Health Psychology, 13*(7), 930–939. doi:10.117/1359105308095067.

Steinfield, C., Ellison, N. B., & Lampe, C. (2008). Social capital, self-esteem, and use of online social network sites: A longitudinal analysis. *Journal of Applied Developmental Psychology, 29*, 434–445. doi:10.1016/j.appdev.2008.07.002.

Till, J. E. (2003). Evaluation of support groups for women with breast cancer: Importance of the navigator role. *Health and Quality of Life Outcomes, 1*(16), 1–6.

Valaitis, R. K., & Sword, W. A. (2005). Online discussions with pregnant and parenting adolescents: Perspectives and possibilities. *Health Promotion Practice, 6*(4), 464–471. doi:10.1177/1524839904263897.

Valenzuela, S., Park, N., & Kee, K. F. (2009). Is there social capital in a social network site? Facebook use and college students' life satisfaction, trust, and participation. *Journal of Computer- Mediated Communication, 14*, 875–901. doi:10.111/j.1083–6101.2009.01474.

Wade, S. L., Carey, J., & Wolf, C. R. (2006). An online family intervention to reduce parental distress following pediatric brain injury. *Journal of Consulting and Clinical Psychology, 74*(3), 445–454. doi:10.1037/002–006X.74.3.445.

Webber, K. H., Tate, D. F., & Bowling, J. M. (2008). A randomized comparison of two motivationally enhanced Internet behavioral weight loss programs. *Behaviour Research and Therapy, 46*, 1090–1095.

Yalom, I. D. (1995). *The theory and practice of group psychotherapy* (4th ed.). New York: Basic Books.

David W. Foy, Kent D. Drescher, *and* Patricia J. Watson

Abstract

Group interventions for survivors of trauma were first used following World War II with combat veterans struggling with the psychological consequences of their war experiences. Early groups were conducted months or years after combat, while the ensuing evolution of groups for trauma has diversified so that single-session groups are now often used to provide support for disaster survivors within the first few days or weeks after the event. From children in communities ravaged by hurricanes to female survivors of intimate partner violence, the types of trauma addressed by groups have also expanded. Reviews of studies on treatment outcome for group interventions for trauma/disaster reveal generally positive effects for group participation, regardless of the specific theoretical basis used by developers. Future research needs to identify variables that can be used to match participants to different group options for optimal outcomes.

Keywords: group counseling; group therapy; trauma; disaster; posttraumatic stress; early intervention; psychological first aid; spirituality

Overview

The current chapter on group interventions for trauma/disaster (TD) survivors begins by providing a rationale for using group approaches, including benefits and drawbacks of groups when compared to individual counseling. Next, we focus on unique aspects of TD groups, in contrast with those that are not specifically designed to address a particular issue or population. A historical perspective on the origin and evolution of groups for TD is presented, and examples of the different kinds of groups and the various types of trauma survivors now represented in the literature are included. We then present an updated review of treatment outcome from recent randomized clinical trials (RCTs) of group interventions found in the literature from 2005 to the present. From this review a "state-of-the-science" for TD group interventions is offered, along with future directions for clinical and research efforts. Group composition and leadership issues are considered,

and "best-practice" recommendations are offered. Next, the focus turns to detailed descriptions of two innovative group interventions that are currently under development: psychological first aid (PFA) and spirituality and trauma (ST). These evolving groups feature facilitators' manuals developed by experts that will allow for standardized administration of the groups and pave the way for controlled research trials for empirical validation. Finally, concluding thoughts are offered with respect to the evolution of TD group approaches clinically and their supporting research base.

Rationale and Unique Aspects of TD Groups

The rationale for using group approaches for TD is based on the need and benefit for survivors to join with other TD survivors in therapeutic work to promote coping with victimization consequences such as isolation, alienation, shame, and a restricted range or diminished feelings. TD groups are especially appropriate because many survivors may feel ostracized from society members who have not shared the traumatic experience, or they may even perceive judgment and blame for their distress. Bonding with similar others in a supportive environment can be a critical step toward regaining the ability to trust others. Beyond the obvious cost advantage, TD groups may be particularly useful for those individuals who fail to meet common assumptions (e.g., psychological mindedness and responsibility for life choices and outcomes) thought necessary for individual psychotherapy (Foy, Eriksson, & Trice, 2001; Klein & Schermer, 2000).

TD groups frequently combine psychoeducational and psychotherapeutic objectives. Various TD group methods may differ in their theoretical models of symptom development and therapeutic intervention, but they share a set of key features and objectives that build a therapeutic, safe, and respectful environment. These features include (1) group membership usually determined by shared type of trauma (e.g., combat veterans or adult survivors of child abuse), (2) acknowledgment and validation of the traumatic experience, (3) normalization of trauma-related responses, (4) validation of behaviors required for survival during the trauma, and (5) challenge to the idea that nontraumatized therapists cannot be helpful through the presence of fellow survivors in the group (Foy & Schrock, 2006).

History of TD Groups

While the history of more general group approaches can be traced back over the past century (Conyne, in press), the development of groups for TD is more recent. The earliest reports of group interventions for trauma emerged during the World War II era (e.g., Dynes, 1945). Subsequently, there were two events that helped to accelerate the development of trauma-related group interventions. First, a nationwide network of community-based veterans' centers was established to serve the readjustment needs of Vietnam veterans. "Rap groups," led by counselors who themselves were Vietnam veterans, were featured in these centers (Sipprelle, 1992). Second, posttraumatic stress disorder (PTSD) was introduced into the psychiatric diagnostic system in 1980. Many studies soon followed that established commonalities in symptom development and pathogenesis across survivors of different traumatic experiences. Correspondingly, group-therapy methods are now applied to a wide variety of trauma

groups, ranging from child survivors of hurricanes to female survivors of intimate partner violence.

The evolution of group interventions for survivors of traumatic experiences has been chronicled by the publication of three seminal books devoted specifically to the topic in the past 10 years: *Group Treatments for Posttraumatic Stress Disorder* (Young & Blake, 1999) was the first to be published, soon followed by *Group Psychotherapy for Psychological Trauma* (Klein & Schermer, 2000) and, more recently, *Psychological Effects of Catastrophic Disasters: Group Approaches to Treatment* (Schein, Spitz, Burlingame, & Muskin, 2006). The Young and Blake book represents a trauma specialists' perspective on the use of group methods. On the other hand, Klein and Schermer are group-therapy specialists who are experts in applying the principles of group psychotherapy across a wide variety of groups with members presenting many different problems or diagnoses. Extending group-therapy principles to include their application with survivors of terrorist disasters goes beyond the scope of these two earlier volumes. Commendably, the editors of the most recent volume (Schein et al., 2006) present a blended approach, combining the considerable professional resources from both "group" and "trauma" perspectives to guide mental health professionals who develop and apply group methods for TD survivors.

Early groups for trauma survivors were designed primarily to prevent or reduce PTSD symptoms and/or restore more adaptive functioning among group members (Foy et al., 2000). However, it soon became apparent that, for a significant minority of trauma survivors, the nature of their disorder would become chronic. Additionally, debilitating comorbidities, such as substance abuse and depression, would develop among many of these survivors. Subsequently, group developers began to focus on these comorbid conditions so that a wider range of therapeutic targets is found among current TD groups. Indeed, many current group interventions are designed solely to address comorbid issues among their trauma-surviving members.

Review of Studies on Group Approaches to TD

Our first review of the literature for group interventions with adult survivors revealed 14 studies, with only two RCTs reported (Foy et al., 2000). We evaluated the strength of evidence supporting the use of group counseling with trauma survivors at that time as "limited, but positive and promising." Our second search of the literature (Foy & Schrock, 2006) revealed that seven more RCTs had been published in a short 4-year span from 2000 through 2003, providing a stronger empirical base of support.

Among the 37 studies we reviewed in 2006, there were 23 single-group, pre–post designs, five control group designs, and nine RCTs. There was comparable representation for studies with adult survivors (17 studies) and children/adolescents (20 studies). Within the set of youth studies, 12 were conducted with preteenage children, while adolescents were sampled exclusively in five studies. Three studies featured "mixed" samples that included both latency-aged children and teenagers. In terms of gender representation, most studies featured same-sex samples (females, 25 studies; males, five studies), but there were seven studies, primarily with preschool children, where both genders were included in the group therapies. It was notable that there were no studies reporting mixed-gender groups with adult survivors at that time.

More recently, Shea and her colleagues (2009) reviewed 22 TD group studies for adult survivors through 2006, reporting seven RCTs, six controlled studies, and nine uncontrolled studies. Group approaches for TD were found to consistently produce more positive changes in treatment outcomes relative to wait list controls. No evidence for superiority of one type of group intervention over others was found. It was also noted that little is currently known about potential mediators or moderators of group treatment outcome, and the suggestion was made that future studies need to identify change mechanisms for the different group approaches.

In our current review, we will first focus on the eight new RCTs we found that have not been previously reported (Table 30.1). Second, we will consider patterns in the entire set of 19 RCTs found across the four reviews (Foy et al. 2000; Foy & Schrock, 2006; Shea et al. 2009).

Examining the eight RCTs in Table 30.1 reveals several findings that suggest a maturing of the field with respect to the range of populations and comorbid problems targeted by these new studies. Adler et al. (2008) and Murphy, Thompson, Murray, Rainey, & Uddo (2009) evaluated brief group interventions that narrowly focused on specific issues. Determining whether critical incident stress debriefing (CISD) was effective at reducing posttrauma symptoms among soldiers serving as peacekeepers was the unique focus of Adler et al., while increasing motivation for PTSD treatment participation was the goal of Murphy et al. New populations, including

HIV-infected adults with childhood sexual assault histories (Sikkema et al., 2007), motor vehicle accident survivors (Beck, Coffey, Foy, Keane, & Blanchard, 2009), and active duty military (Adler et al., 2008) were represented in TD groups for the first time. Perhaps most strikingly, half of the studies featured samples that contained both men and women in the groups. This was a feature seen only in groups for children and adolescents in previous reviews. Ranging from military bases (Adler et al., 2008), and prisons (Zlotnick, Johnson, & Najavits, 2009) to school classrooms in Bosnia (Layne et al., 2008), the diversity of sites where TD groups are conducted has also expanded. As reported in the earlier reviews, positive results were generally found for active group interventions, regardless of their particular theoretical orientation.

Now, we turn our attention to the overall set of 19 RCTs reported in this chapter and the other three reviews (Foy et al. 2000; Foy & Schrock, 2006; Shea et al. 2009). In terms of theoretical orientation, 15 studies used a cognitive-behavioral perspective, while four featured a psychodynamic framework. Regarding sample size, a primary factor in power estimation, participant numbers ranged from 22 to 952. Two studies used samples of more than 300, eight studies used 100–300, and the remaining nine studies used fewer than 100 participants. For studies of debriefing and motivational enhancement groups, the number of sessions ranged from one to four, while other trauma groups ranged from 10 to 26 sessions (mean = 14.4 sessions). Thus, most TD groups fit Conyne's definition of "brief group psychotherapy" (see Chapter 1).

Group sessions were usually 1–2 hours in length and met weekly. Eleven studies (58%) were conducted with adult survivors of childhood sexual assault, and four studies (21%) used active duty military or veterans as participants. For motor vehicle accidents, community violence, war, and hurricanes, one study was found for each of these TD types. Regarding gender representation in sampling, seven studies reported mixed-gender samples, while 12 studies used single-gender group membership. Among the 11 childhood sexual assault studies, nine used female-only samples. Regarding control groups, wait list groups predominated (10 studies, 53%), while minimal- or no-contact groups (3 studies, 16%) and less treatment or active comparison groups (6 studies, 32%) were used in the remaining studies.

In summary, our review of RCTs of TD group interventions reveals a maturing of the field, especially

Table 30.1 Randomized controlled trials of group interventions for trauma/disaster

Study	Treatment Group (*n*)	Comparison Group	Number of Sessions	Population	Major Findings
Adler et al. (2008)	Critical incident stress debriefing group (312)	Stress management (359), survey only (281)	Single session, 50–150 minutes long	US Army peacekeepers, 96% males	No significant differences between groups on posttraumatic stress disorder (PTSD) symptom reduction at two postdeployment follow-ups
Beck et al. (2009)	Group cognitive-behavioral treatment (GCBT) (16)	Minimal contact controls (MCC) (17)	14 weekly sessions	Female and male motor vehicle accident survivors	GCBT showed significantly greater reductions than MCC in PTSD symptoms posttreatment and at 3-month follow-up; no differences between GCBT and MCC on measures of anxiety, depression, and pain
Dunn et al. (2007)	Self-management therapy (SMT) (51)	Active control therapy (ACT) (50)	14 weekly sessions	Male veterans treated for combat PTSD	SMT group demonstrated lower depression scores than ACT at posttreatment but no differences in PTSD or depression at 3-, 6-, and 12-month follow-ups
Krupnik et al. (2008)	Interpersonal psychotherapy (IPT) (32)	Wait list control (16)	16 sessions	Women with histories of physical or sexual violence	IPT showed significantly more improvement in PTSD, depression, and interpersonal functioning than controls
Layne et al. (2008)	Trauma and grief component therapy (TGCT) plus psychoeducation and coping skills (127)	Psychoeducation and coping skills intervention alone	17 weekly sessions	War-exposed Bosnian female and male adolescents	Both groups improved at pre-/posttreatment and 4-month follow-up on PTSD and depression; TGCT grief scores were significantly lower than controls
Murphy et al. (2009)	PTSD motivation enhancement (PME) (60)	Psychoeducation group (PE) (54)	4 weekly sessions	Male veterans in 12-month outpatient treatment for chronic PTSD	Compared to PE, PME group showed significantly more readiness for change, higher ratings for treatment relevance, and higher attendance at treatment program sessions
Sikkema et al. (2007)	HIV and trauma coping (HTC), support group (SG) (202)	Wait list control	15 sessions	Female and male HIV, childhood sexual assault survivors	HTC group had significantly fewer intrusive PTSD symptoms compared to controls and fewer avoidant symptoms than SG; no differences found between SG and controls
Zlotnik et al. (2009)	Seeking safety (SS) (27)	Treatment as usual (TAU) control (22)	18–24 sessions, 3 per week	Incarcerated women with PTSD and substance-use disorder	Both SS and TAU groups showed significant improvements at 3- and 6-month follow-up on PTSD and substance abuse, psychopathology, and legal problems; no significant differences found between SS and TAU groups on any measure

with respect to the design rigor employed in more recent studies. Correspondingly, the evidence base supporting the use of group TD interventions has been strengthened considerably. The eight new RCTs reported in this chapter were published within the last 3 years, while the entire set of 19 RCTs covers a 20-year period. Almost 3,000 participants are represented in the set of studies, and there is a widening range of trauma types, comorbidities addressed, and treatment sites to be found among them. Thus, the relatively recent expansion of the applications of TD groups is remarkable and bodes well for the use of TD groups in the future.

Clinical Implications and Directions

Informed by earlier reviews of TD group intervention studies, we (Foy & Schrock, 2006) have addressed a number of practical issues regarding group structure, operation, composition, and leadership. In our earlier review we focused upon key future directions for clinical use of group interventions for TD survivors (Foy, 2008; Foy & Schrock, 2006). Several relevant domains were addressed, and recommendations were offered in each domain with respect to implementing TD groups. Briefly, among the domains covered were assessment/diagnosis, ethical considerations, life stage of group members, cultural diversity, therapist issues, and member selection factors. We made specific recommendations for group facilitators who, in the absence of evidence from controlled studies, must make clinical decisions about how to compose and manage groups for TD survivors.

These recommendations included the following:

1. At a minimum, assess members' demographic characteristics, along with pregroup and postgroup measures of the primary intended outcome for the group (e.g., PTSD severity scores).

2. From an ethical standpoint, prospective group members need to consent to the operating principles of the type of group therapy offered, including the need for confidentiality regarding the identities of group members and information disclosed during sessions.

3. Groups need to be composed of members from the same life stage who survived the same TD event or the same type of trauma.

4. Group operating rules emphasize respect for ethnocultural diversity among group members.

5. Groups should be co-led by two facilitators whose skills and professional experience are complementary.

6. Group members should be selected so that severity of trauma exposure, particularly death exposure, is equivalent across members.

More detail on these future directions has been provided (Foy, 2008; Foy & Schrock, 2006).

Directions for Future Research

While it is true that the strength of evidence supporting the use of group TD interventions is increasing as more RCTs are reported, there are gaps in our knowledge that remain to be filled. Mean treatment effect size reported for the 24 studies in the Shea et al. (2009) review was 0.68, suggesting that power limitations may be a confounding factor in studies with fewer participants. Future studies need to include careful power estimates so that adequate numbers of participants are included in their design, to guard against the possibility of inaccurate reporting of treatment outcomes. Although there are now many more RCTs on cognitive-behavioral group interventions than psychodynamic, it is not clear that results favor one perspective over the other. It may be that well-known group process variables (see Chapter 1) as yet unaddressed in current TD group studies may also contribute to positive treatment outcomes. For example, future studies might include some of the 11 process variables originally identified by Yalom (1970) as responsible for positive changes among members. These variables were labeled "therapeutic factors" (Yalom, 1970) and range from those operating early in the group, such as instillation of hope, universality, and psychoeducation, to factors at work later, including interpersonal learning and existential growth.

New Developments in Designing TD Groups

In this final section we focus on two examples of new groups designed to address special issues among TD survivors. First, we offer a description of PFA principles and their adaptation to a group format for use as an early intervention. Finally, a TD group approach for addressing spirituality as a coping resource for trauma recovery is presented.

Guidelines for Adapting PFA for TD Groups

Psychological first aid has been defined as the use of pragmatic psychosocial interventions delivered during the immediate impact phase (first 4 weeks) to individuals experiencing acute stress reactions or problems in functioning, with the intent of aiding adaptive coping and problem solving (Young, 2006). It was developed on the foundations of crisis intervention (Lindemann, 1944; Shneidman, Farberow, & Litman, 1970), and the term was first coined in the early disaster work of Raphael (1986) and Farberow (1978) with adults and Pynoos and Nader (1988) with children.

Psychological First Aid (PFA), developed by the National Child Traumatic Stress Network (NCTSN) and the National Center for PTSD (NCPTSD), has been widely endorsed as an evidence-informed modular approach to help children, adolescents, adults, and families in the immediate aftermath of disaster and terrorism. PFA is designed to reduce the initial distress caused by traumatic events and to foster short- and long-term adaptive functioning and coping. PFA has been adapted for the Medical Reserve Corps, for community religious professionals, for health systems, for schools, and for active duty service members in the US Navy and Marine Corps. It has additionally been translated into Swedish, Chinese, Arabic, Italian, and Spanish.

The NCTSN/NCPTSD PFA model includes the following eight core actions:

1. Contact and engagement

Goal: To respond to contacts initiated by affected persons or initiate contacts in a nonintrusive, compassionate, and helpful manner

2. Safety and comfort

Goal: To enhance immediate and ongoing safety and provide physical and emotional comfort

3. Stabilization (if necessary)

Goal: To calm and orient emotionally overwhelmed/distraught survivors

4. Information gathering: current needs and concerns

Goal: To identify immediate needs and concerns, gather additional information, and tailor PFA interventions

5. Practical assistance

Goal: To offer practical help to the survivor in addressing immediate needs and concerns

6. Connection with social supports

Goal: To reduce distress by helping structure opportunities for brief or ongoing contacts with primary support persons or other sources of support, including family members, friends, and community helping resources

7. Information on coping support

Goal: To provide the individual with information (including education about stress reactions and coping) that may help him or her deal with the event and its aftermath

8. Linkage with collaborative services

Goal: To link survivors with needed services and inform them about available services that may be needed in the future

A key tenet of PFA is respect for individual variation in recovery from trauma. Most PFA contacts will involve providing only the actions that are best suited to the context. The choice of actions and the amount of time spent on each will depend on the needs of the survivor and on the context of delivery. Group application of PFA is therefore not considered the first choice because PFA rests so strongly on tailoring the approach to the individual needs and priorities of the survivor. In group interventions, this is particularly salient in that the fluctuating course of trauma response (from avoidance to processing) may render an individual incapable or unwilling to discuss his or her experiences or responses and may actually be an adaptive early response (Raphael, 1986; Watson & Shalev, 2005). Brewin (2005) additionally cautions against interfering with natural recovery processes within the acute phases posttrauma. PFA has therefore been applied conservatively in a group format, with a focus on connecting others with social supports and providing information on coping support. In group applications, the focus has been on providing opportunities to tailor coping information to specific needs, while not in any way making participants feel that they need to share their experiences.

Group provision of coping information in the PFA model is generally designed to cover any number of the following points: (1) to help survivors better understand a range of posttrauma responses; (2) to help survivors view their posttrauma reactions as expectable and understandable (not as reactions to be feared or as signs of personal failure, weakness, or mental illness); (3) to recognize the circumstances under which they should consider seeking further counseling; (4) to know how and where to access additional help, including mental health counseling; (5) to increase use of social supports and other adaptive ways of coping with the trauma and its effects; (6) to decrease use of problematic forms of coping (e.g., excessive alcohol consumption, extreme social isolation); and (7) to increase ability to help family members cope (e.g., information on how to talk to children about what happened). Accurate and timely information regarding the nature of the unfolding disaster situation is also an important part of education.

The model for applying PFA in a group setting draws from a number of bodies of literature and expert opinion on group application of therapeutic principles. These sources include the evidence for group psychotherapy in general, the principles of change that have been distilled from group studies, the trauma-focused and bereavement-focused group therapy literature, and the study of early group interventions after traumatic stress.

The current literature on group psychotherapy provides consistent evidence that this modality is associated with favorable outcomes (Foy et al., 2000). General "active ingredients" in groups that produce change have been identified as follows: (1) carefully structuring the tasks and activities of the group (i.e., groups with early structure are more cohesive and have increased levels of helpful self-disclosure) and (2) facilitating member-to-member interactions within the group (i.e., positive feedback should be emphasized, and corrective feedback is most helpful when it is focused on specific and observable behaviors) (Davies, Burlingame & Layne, 2006). In contrast to a long-term approach to group psychotherapy, over the last few decades group intervention for the prevention and treatment of acute initial stress reactions has focused primarily on group debriefing models such as CISD, a structured group model designed to explore facts, thoughts, reactions, and coping strategies following trauma. Experts have completed a number of reviews on CISD, but not one has yielded any evidence that CISD prevents long-term negative outcomes. Additionally, two RCTs of CISD have reported a higher incidence of negative outcomes in those who received CISD when compared with those who did not receive an intervention (for reviews, see Bisson, 2003; Litz, Gray, Bryant, & Adler, 2002; McNally, Bryant, & Ehlers, 2003; Watson et al., 2003). Other RCTs also have reported a lack of positive findings for debriefing interventions (Adler et al., 2008; Sijbrandij, Olff, Reitsma, Carlier, & Gersons, 2006), the last of which reported that participants in the emotional debriefing group with high baseline hyperarousal scores had significantly more PTSD symptoms at 6 weeks than control participants.

Given the negative findings associated with CISD, as well as preliminary evidence that increased arousal in the immediate phases posttrauma is linked to long-term pathology, experts are concerned that any intervention that focuses on emotional processing during this period may be contraindicated. Potential difficulties with the group format should always be considered before making the decision to implement group PFA so as to reduce potential harm. These difficulties center around providing the right balance between the needs of individual members and the needs of the group as a whole as there will be significantly less individualization and less attention given to individuals generally. Potential risks of *any* group-delivered early intervention include the following:

1. Retraumatization through exposure to other participants' experiences. Some members may have a need to express their experience. Other group members may be so acutely distressed that they are unable to tolerate exposure to others' stories and should therefore not be expected to participate in the early phases.

2. Inappropriate timing in terms of the reactive trajectory of participants so that natural healthy denial is challenged or grief is pathologized. Some people rely strongly on denial in the initial phase, and their coping styles make them both unwilling to accept either individual or group intervention or to benefit from them. It may be inappropriate to challenge these strategies. The group may not be sensitive to the different needs or timelines of recovery of participants. There may be a subtle pressure to disclose what is distressing to members who are either highly distressed or withdrawn. Decisions for group as opposed to individual intervention will be complex because of many factors, including differential exposures, distinct personal meanings, different coping styles, vulnerability to the exposure, sensitivity of reaction, other stressors that impact reactions, or timeline of recovery.

3. Creation of expectations of pathological outcomes. Many group protocols make the mistake of providing lists of possible reactions in order to prepare individuals for what may seem like alarming reactions. However, they fail to provide possible neutral or positive reactions to balance out ideas of what to expect, thereby inadvertently priming participants to expect primarily negative reactions. Wessely and colleagues (2008), in a review of the literature examining whether psychoeducation can prevent distress, note that there is evidence that many individuals are unaware that after a traumatic incident they may experience a range of unanticipated symptoms. However, they recommend that, rather than just providing lists of possible symptoms, which runs the risk of implanting expectations of pathology and dysfunction, constructive information should be offered that proactively encourages an expectation of resilience and, if necessary, help seeking.

4. Leading people to believe that the group is all that will be required to deal with their experience so that individuals do not seek further care.

5. Inappropriate application in settings where physical survival is a greater priority.

6. In situations of loss, additional risks include worse outcomes associated with group interventions. Schut, Stroebe, van den Bout, & Terheggen (2001) found that participation in bereavement groups tended to worsen outcomes and hypothesized that this may be because they interfere with resolution of grief or focus the person on ruminating about his or her grief experience.

7. Finally, the group application may be very stressful for the leader early on after a highly stressful incident.

Raphael and Wooding (2006) suggest that to alleviate some of these potential risks early intervention groups should provide structure, tasks, and information, as well as focus on strengths, have clear goals, provide mutual support, and plan actions to address needs. In research on educational groups to build resilience, the educational approach most likely to result in behavior change was designed to tailor the information to the individual's specific situation, as well as offering opportunities for practice and mastery (Beardslee, Versage, Salt, & Wright, 1999).

If the potential negative effects of early group intervention are addressed as described, there are several potential benefits of delivering PFA in a group setting. First, providing information about different PFA actions after a critical event is more efficient in a group format. When individual PFA is difficult to deliver (e.g., due to large numbers of affected persons, lack of availability of mental health providers, or cost constraints), groups provide a potentially cost- and resource-effective way of serving members. Second, social support is an important aspect of coping with psychological stress, and a group provides a practical setting in which to ask for and give mutual support. Some may believe they are alone in their experiences, and meeting and sharing coping stories with others can reduce feelings of isolation. Third, a group setting provides a helpful way for participants to learn about the way others deal with similar situations. For example, input from other group members may assist an individual in challenging common distressing thoughts. Groups can be especially effective at "normalizing" the experience of the member in that other persons are seen to be coping with similar difficulties. Group-administered PFA should ideally differ from psychological debriefing in that it does not focus on processing of thoughts or reactions related to the disaster but, rather, provides education about the PFA principles as well as a forum for participants to share support and ideas for coping. This type of group is likely to lead to longer-term patterns of mutual support.

While PFA has not yet been systematically studied, experience in the field suggests that it will be acceptable to and well received by consumers, due to its flexible, tailored approach to helping to solve practical needs as well as its voluntary nature. It is, however, important to remain cautious in our estimation of what early interventions can accomplish in terms of prevention of long-term functional and symptomatic impact. The relative contribution of early and short interventions may be necessarily small because past history, differing exposure, and ongoing stress levels make it difficult to identify which persons are at risk for continued problems. It may additionally be extremely difficult to conduct effective interventions in the early aftermath of disastrous events. Therefore, there is a great need for both program evaluation and RCTs that will evaluate the effectiveness of PFA principles in group formats. Finally, PFA is meant to be embedded in a consensus-recommended systemic response involving mental health; public health; medical and emergency response systems; and federal, state, local, and nonprofit agencies (including non-mental health agencies such as law enforcement, fire and rescue, school systems, and social services). As such, it is intended to provide early support that can improve recovery following disasters, but its provision has never been intended as a stand-alone intervention. It is best thought of as a component in a multilevel, multidisciplinary system that is designed to address the various needs and timelines of disaster recovery and which may, in this context, be applied in a group format for reaching larger numbers of individuals and for promoting social support in the early phases postdisaster (see Table 30.2).

Spirituality and Trauma Group Module
The ST group was originally developed to meet the needs of veterans in residential treatment for PTSD following military combat exposure. It was not intended as a primary PTSD treatment that would address all aspects of the disorder; rather, it was designed as an adjunct to other empirically supported PTSD treatments. As originally developed,

Table 30.2 Advantages and limitations of psychological first-aid (pfa) groups

Potential Advantages of PFA Offered in Group Format	Potential Disadvantages of PFA in Group Format	PFA Group Adaptations to Address Potential Disadvantages
• A group format gives an opportunity to provide accurate and timely information regarding the nature of the unfolding disaster situation. • When individual PFA is difficult to deliver (e.g., due to large numbers of affected persons, lack of availability of mental health providers, or cost constraints), groups provide a potentially cost- and resource-effective way of serving survivors. • A group provides a practical setting in which to ask for and give mutual support, and sharing coping stories with others can reduce feelings of isolation. • A group setting provides a helpful way for participants to learn about the way others deal with similar situations. • Groups can be especially effective in "normalizing" the experience of the survivor in that other persons are seen to be coping with similar difficulties. • A PFA group can offer an efficient way to provide information to help survivors: • Better understand a range of posttrauma responses • View their posttrauma reactions as expectable and understandable • Increase use of social supports and other adaptive ways of coping • Decrease use of problematic forms of coping • Increase ability to help family members cope • Recognize the circumstances under which they should consider seeking further counseling • Know how and where to access additional help, including mental health counseling	• Offering a group shortly after a disaster is an inappropriate application in settings where physical survival is a greater priority. • Focusing on emotional processing during immediate period may increase arousal, which is associated with long-term negative outcomes. • Distress can result from exposure to other participants' experiences. • Discussion of potential negative effects of the event can create expectations of pathological outcomes. • Offering a group after a disaster can lead people to believe that: • Their own strategies are not enough to handle the event. • The group is all that will be required to deal with their experience, so they do not seek further care. • In situations of loss, worse outcomes have been associated with group interventions (i.e., they may interfere with resolution of grief or focus the person on ruminating about his or her grief experience). • A group may be very stressful for the leader early on after a highly stressful incident.	• In the days after a disaster, offer only impromptu informational groups (i.e., about the status of the disaster-recovery effort), whereas more formal educational groups should be offered only after time has been allowed to deal with issues related to physical survival. • Do not focus on processing of thoughts or reactions related to the disaster but rather provide education about the PFA principles as well as a forum for participants to share support and ideas for coping. • Rather than just providing lists of possible symptoms, which runs the risk of implanting expectations of pathology and dysfunction, offer constructive information that proactively encourages an expectation of resilience and, if necessary, help seeking. • Have clear goals. • Tailor group actions to address specific group members' needs, while not in any way making participants feel that they need to share their experiences. • Carefully structure the tasks and activities of the group to focus on promoting helpful coping strategies. • Focus on survivors' strengths. • Facilitate member-to-member feedback within the group so that it is focused on positive coping strategies and mutual support, rather than sharing of complaints or exposure to stressors. • Offer opportunities for practice and mastery of positive coping strategies. • Make group as homogeneous as possible (i.e., in terms of exposure type, other stressors that impact reactions, or timeline of recovery).

this was intended as a large group intervention that could accommodate weekly influx of new participants. It utilizes brief, didactic presentations by facilitators, member-to-member interactions, as well as large- and small-group discussions. Detailed descriptions of the group's development and thoughts about its application to additional trauma populations are available (Drescher et al., 2004; Drescher, 2006; Drescher, Smith, & Foy, 2007).

RATIONALE FOR INCORPORATING SPIRITUAL THEMES INTO TRAUMA-RELATED INTERVENTIONS

There are several factors that provide a primary basis for the use of spiritual themes in treatment for the effect of traumatic events. First, there is strong evidence that individuals in US society value and appreciate personal spirituality and tend to seek out spiritual resources following traumatic events (Schuster et al., 2001). Some studies indicate that a high percentage (i.e., 72%) of individuals in the United States identify religion as the most important influence in their lives (Bergin & Jensen, 1990). For many individuals, spirituality is the framework of choice for finding meaning in the face of traumatic experiences, although mental health providers may be less religious than their clients and tend to address religious/spiritual issues and resources less frequently than their clients might prefer. There is also evidence that spirituality may play a role in both resilience in the face of traumatic stress and what the literature is calling "adversarial or posttraumatic" growth (Foy, Drescher, & Watson, in press). A recent review and meta-analysis of religious coping and stress adjustment found a moderate positive relationship between positive religious coping strategies and positive outcomes to stress (Ano & Vasconcelles, 2005). Findings that positive spirituality both is widely used in stressful situations and may allow for or bring about growth in the face of trauma would support the potential benefit of addressing these themes therapeutically.

Additionally, there is evidence that trauma may in some instances be involved in the development of spiritual appraisals/attributions that may be associated with poorer outcomes. Varying terms have been used to describe these appraisals, including *shattered core assumptions* (Janoff-Bulman, 1992), *spiritual struggle* (Pargament et al. 1998), and, most recently, *moral injury* (Drescher & Foy, 2008; Litz et al., 2009).

Janoff-Bulman (1992) postulated that traumatic events frequently call up existential and spiritual questions related to the meaningfulness of life,

personal self-worth, and the safety of life. Others have endorsed her thinking and suggested that in the course of certain traumatic events, whether due to the magnitude of the event, the sense of "wrongness" or evil of the event, or a profound sense of personal violation, an individual's view of humankind, understanding of God, or view of the self as a moral being may be profoundly changed. Pargament and Brandt (1998) have labeled this "spiritual struggle" and measure it as a form of negative religious coping.

A new construct recently introduced (Drescher & Foy, 2008; Litz et al., 2009) is called "moral injury" and refers to changes in one's view of self and in others' capacity for moral behavior that arises as a consequence of exposure to and/or participation in actions perceived as immoral. The authors' work with veterans suggests that combat, particularly in situations where battle is engaged with insurgent forces not easily distinguished from civilians, compels military personnel to make quick decisions and respond rapidly in chaotic and ambiguous situations. Such actions may result in deaths, both intentionally and unintentionally, of enemy fighters, civilians (including women and children), and even friendly forces. Sometimes co-occurring with these decisions and actions are strong emotions (e.g., grief, loss, rage, hatred) that stem from earlier war experiences. Even in situations where the "correct" action or decision was made, personnel can later come to question or doubt the appropriateness of their action or decision. Such second-guessing may lead them down a path of harsh judgment about their own character, or that of leadership and despair about the very nature of humankind.

The fact that there is empirical support generally for a link between healthy spirituality and positive physical and mental health outcomes and the evidence of a link between negative religious coping (i.e., attributions that God is punishing the individual or feeling angry at God) and poorer health outcomes argue for treatment approaches that address these issues. It may be that survivors of traumatic life events are at higher risk for forming these negative appraisals and could benefit from some assistance in reconsidering and possibly modifying these attributions.

One rationale for utilizing group-based treatments is the fact that one primary pathway by which spirituality may be associated with positive health outcomes is social support (McIntosh, Silver, & Wortman, 1993). The social support that comes from spiritual involvement with other like-minded individuals may help to explain the positive outcomes found in some research. Group-based therapies offer the possibility of increased social support for survivors of trauma as well as other individuals with similar experiences to be able to wrestle with these existential questions. This is especially important because avoidance and isolation are primary features of PTSD. Group-based trauma treatment that allows for processing of spiritual questions and concerns and integrates these with standard mental health approaches would seem to be an optimal clinical approach.

THE TREATMENT MODEL AND THEORY OF CHANGE

The treatment model presented here shares some characteristics with more traditional present-centered treatments. Specifically, clients are asked to keep their focus on here-and-now concerns. As a result of this present-centered focus, much therapeutic work may be client-directed. The group sessions are not focused on the details of past traumatic events but, rather, on how the impact of those events is being experienced in the present. The model views an individual's spiritual background and history as aspects of his or her life that may affect and be affected by traumatic events and the direct symptoms of trauma. The tension, or "dissonance," created between the experience of trauma and the individual's pretrauma beliefs, values, and expectations generates the motivation to pursue change in the aftermath of the events.

These group sessions differ slightly from many present-centered therapeutic approaches in that they address very specific topics. They devote focused attention on particular spiritual and existential issues that might or might not arise naturally in a present-centered group. These sessions are specifically designed to address concerns that clients may not have resources to voice and that clinicians frequently do not have the background, experience, or training to address.

The ST group attempts to utilize some therapeutic styles and models of other treatment approaches. Murphy, Rosen, Cameron, & Thompson (2002) have developed a group-treatment approach to addressing a broad array of PTSD issues by enhancing client motivation to change. This treatment is conceptually focused on literature describing the stages of change (Prochaska & DiClemente, 1983) and the techniques of motivational interviewing (Miller & Rollnick, 2002). Consistent with these approaches, the ST group invites facilitators to incorporate a similar therapeutic stance in addressing

the spiritual/existential impact of trauma. First, it attempts to create a collaborative/friendly relationship between facilitators and clients. It communicates that clients are responsible for their decisions and for choosing to pursue growth and change, and facilitators avoid prescribing specific methods or techniques. The group seeks to help participants identify discrepancies between what they experience currently and what they want for their future to build motivation and energy for change. Even when it comes to defining spirituality, every attempt is made to create so broad a space that all members can locate themselves within it using their own personal definition.

ST THERAPEUTIC GOALS

The ST group has several overarching goals. One is to encourage client consideration of the role that a healthy, vital spirituality might play as a healing resource in coping with traumatic events. This may involve strengthening and deepening group members' present spiritual or religious understandings and practices. It may involve reconnection with their own religious or spiritual roots and traditions from childhood. It may also involve searching out and exploring new avenues of spiritual experience and expression that are more immediately relevant to the members' recent experiences. Exposure to and direct experience of a variety of spiritual practices from a number of traditions may be incorporated into the interventions. Group activities are selected to express both diversity and the inherent value of a wide variety of spiritual experiences.

Another goal of this intervention is to help facilitate cognitive processing of the existential meaning associated with traumatic events and the personal significance individuals might attach to them. This includes identification of cognitive distortions (i.e., inappropriate survivor guilt including self-blame) and helping members begin to reframe or restructure their understandings in ways that they see as more healthy and adaptive. It certainly includes helping individuals begin to process and seek personal answers to the difficult existential questions of why and how these events have occurred and what impact they should and will have on the future. It facilitates the shared feedback and reflections from other group members about how they are coming to terms, and the meanings they associate, with these things.

A third primary goal of the group intervention is to increase perceived social support and encourage development of a healthy family and community support system. Support for trauma survivors varies considerably depending on the type and context of the trauma experience. Solitary survivors of a personal violation may live the aftermath of trauma in fear and distrust. In contrast, whole communities may rally and provide support for survivors in the immediate aftermath of disasters. Soldiers, sailors, marines, and air force personnel may return from war zones to parades and fanfare in communities located near military installations or return individually to homes welcomed only by family and a few friends in other locations. Over time, however, as people continue with their own day-to-day struggles of life, even an enhanced sense of community may fade. A good network of support may allow a trauma survivor to feel less alone and more capable of obtaining necessary resources.

The intended outcomes of these interventions and group sessions is to increase hope, to decrease anger and hostility, and to decrease the intensity of feelings of grief and loss, while enhancing the individual's sense of purpose and the meaningfulness of life (see Table 30.3).

CORE GROUP VALUES

A number of core group values should be described and modeled by facilitators to members in the earliest sessions and repeated as necessary throughout the duration of the group. The first of these is openness to new ways of thinking, new behaviors, and new experiences. Members should be encouraged to withhold judgment about the experiences of others and to value (or at least tolerate) differences within the group. One of the benefits of group therapy that should be acknowledged and used to its fullest advantage is the opportunity to receive insights and ideas from the coping strengths of other trauma survivors as well as from the training and experience of the facilitators. Differences expressed among members should be looked at as opportunities for learning and growth. This value is particularly important in a group that addresses spirituality in the context of trauma. It is important for members to understand how important religious and spiritual perspectives may be to people and how strongly they may react if their beliefs or values are challenged, threatened, or demeaned by others. As a consequence, one group rule which should be strictly adhered to is the use of "I" statements in discussing personal beliefs, theological perspectives, thoughts, and values. Facilitators should intervene early and utilize frequent gentle reminders when members fall into global statements that sound as though the person is speaking for the group or expounding the "right" way of looking at an issue.

Table 30.3 Overview of spirituality and trauma group sessions

Session Title	Session Objectives
What is spirituality?	Introduction, operating guidelines, and rationale for the trauma and spirituality group; review of definitions and benefits of spirituality
Building connections: self-oriented	Explore different types of spiritual connections and the benefits of being connected to others, examine how PTSD leads to isolation and limited connections
Building connections: beyond oneself	Learn about different types of spiritual practices across various religions, consider how participation in a spiritual community can facilitate healing from trauma, explore how volunteer service can aid in both connection and perceived meaning
Theodicy	Learn about the meaning of theodicy and how this dilemma creates universal tension, consider the consequences of failing to examine one's current beliefs
Forgiveness of others and God	Develop a definition of forgiveness, barriers to forgiveness, and steps toward forgiveness; understand how forgiveness is an ongoing process that can be incorporated into one's lifestyle
Forgiveness of self	Consider why self-forgiveness may be difficult and how distortions may impede progress, identify the barriers to self-forgiveness and ways to overcome them
Values	Consider the importance of values, how they are formed, and their relationship to behavior; learn how to identify personal values
Finding meaning	Examine the importance of meaning in life and how to make one's life more meaningful, identify the benefits of having meaning in one's life

DESCRIPTION OF ST SESSIONS

The ST group facilitator's manual provides clinical strategies and guidelines for implementing the group treatment. It details the eight-session group intervention using a predominantly present-centered motivation-enhancement approach. The eight session themes include the following:

1. *What is spirituality?* Many people do not think very often about how they define spirituality. The authors have chosen a definition that directly addresses a primary problem area for many trauma survivors, i.e., disconnection and isolation. Defining *spirituality* as "connecting to something outside the self" frees each individual to define that connection for him- or herself. We encourage individuals to engage in a journey of discovery of what spirituality might now mean for their lives. Engaging in a discussion of what an individual sees as core elements to a definition can be useful in helping that person realize that he or she can actually reconsider views which may have been learned in childhood.

2. *Building connections.* In defining spirituality as connection, one intention of the group intervention is to enable trauma survivors to increase the number and quality of their social supports both within and beyond the group. Social support has long been associated with better health outcomes (Cohen & Wills, 1985). Spiritual communities frequently provide both emotional and instrumental supports for their members. In a review of the spirituality and health literature, Powell, Shajhabi, & Thoresen (2003) identified nine longitudinal studies of healthy populations, seven of which found a relationship between church attendance and lower incidence of mortality after adjusting for demographic, socioeconomic, and health-related variables.

Social support, including structural support (quantity of support) and functional support (perceived quality of support), has been tied positively to both physical and mental health outcomes (Thoits, 1995). Similarly, religiously based support has been shown to predict positive mental health outcomes (Nooney & Woodrum, 2002).

Finally, in addition to social support seeking, spiritual practices and participation may potentially have a direct impact on health through the promotion and modeling of healthy lifestyles. For example, many spiritual traditions promote moderation or abstinence in health risk behaviors such as drinking, drug use, and smoking. It has long been known that many trauma populations with PTSD also have comorbid problems with substances use, including tobacco. Frequently, these problems complicate effective PTSD treatment and expose survivors to elevated long-term health risks and negative life consequence.

3. *Spiritual practices.* Spiritual activities are described as being both inward and outward. A variety of inward experiential exercises involving meditation, breathing, guided imagery, and silent prayer can be useful in addressing PTSD issues of anxiety and hyperarousal. Spiritual practices with a relaxation component can build on existing stress-management skills and may contribute in a positive way to coping with traumatic stress. Activities should be drawn from a variety of religious traditions. In addition, postgroup "practice" of spiritual exercises experienced during group sessions is encouraged.

From an outward perspective, spiritual practice includes service and work on behalf of others. Most spiritual traditions encourage service as a form of spiritual practice. One direct benefit of service is engagement in the lives of others, which for a person suffering from PTSD counters the tendency toward social isolation and withdrawal. Service for others may also create personal meaning, helping an individual live a life that matters to others. Engaging with others who suffer and who also have tangible needs may broaden survivors' focus of attention, help them recognize they are not alone in suffering, and demonstrate that they can actually provide benefit to others. This can have very positive effects on self-esteem.

4. *Theodicy: the "why" question.* The term *theodicy* comes from the Latin *théos díe*, meaning "justification of God." It was coined by the philosopher Leibniz, who in 1710 wrote an essay attempting to show that the existence of evil in the world does not conflict with belief in the goodness of God (Leibniz, 1890). Simply stated, theodicy poses the following question: If God is all-powerful and all-good, how does God allow evil to exist in the world? Historically, varied solutions have been proposed to the theodical problem, including philosophical solutions that diminish God (i.e., God is not all-powerful, God is not all-good, God does not exist) or that diminish evil (i.e., it is a punishment for sin, it may bring about some greater good) and personal

nonphilosophical solutions that diminish the self (e.g., self-blame, rage, loss of meaning, purpose, or hope).

From a psychological perspective, Festinger's (1957) cognitive dissonance theory suggests that individuals tend to seek consistency among their cognitions and experiences. When discrepancy exists between cognitions and experience, there is strong motivation for change, to eliminate the tension. In the case of a traumatic experience, the event itself cannot be changed; hence, survivors must struggle to adapt their beliefs and attitudes to accommodate their experience in order to resolve the dissonance. Many trauma survivors, along with their families and friends, thus begin a lifelong journey toward making sense of their experiences.

Several studies (Gorsuch, 1995; Pargament & Brandt, 1998; Witvliet, Phillips, Feldman, & Beckham, 2004) have indicated that negative religious coping (i.e., negative attributions about God) such as "God has abandoned me," "God is punishing me," or anger at God, is associated with a number of poor clinical outcomes. We find it useful to talk about these data with veterans and to discuss ways to alter these viewpoints. Group interaction around these issues can be particularly helpful as simply discussing the issue and hearing differing viewpoints voiced by other participants can be helpful for those who are seemingly "stuck" in these negative ways of viewing their situation.

5. *Forgiveness of others.* Thoresen, Harris, and Luskin (2000) define *forgiveness* as "the decision to reduce negative thoughts, affect, and behavior, such as blame and anger, toward an offender or hurtful situation, and to begin to gain better understanding of the offense and the offender" (p. 255). In working with veterans, it has also been important to emphasize that forgiveness does not include pardoning an offender, condoning or excusing an offense, forgetting an offense, or denying that an offense occurred. Rather, forgiveness involves choosing to abandon one's right to resentment and negative judgment, while nurturing undeserved qualities of compassion, generosity, and even love toward the offender (Enright & Coyle, 1998).

Within a military context, forgiveness sometimes becomes an issue of tension in that it may suggest to veterans a pressure toward forgiving an enemy that killed a friend, forgiving the government that sent him or her into harm's way, forgiving people who perhaps did not do their jobs effectively or who made mistakes, forgiving God who allowed all this to happen, and forgiving the self for perceived errors or lack of action. Though not all these issues are relevant for any given veteran, they are frequent areas of concern. Similar concerns may arise for survivors of other types of trauma as well.

6. *Forgiveness of self.* Depending on the type and contextual circumstance of the trauma, guilt and self-blame may be experienced by survivors. Many veterans in particular carry with them extremely negative and distorted beliefs such as guilt, shame, or self-blame related to the trauma, which affect their perceptions of personal worth, their motivation to pursue treatment, and their hope for successfully recovering from their experiences. Finding ways to view their traumatic experiences through a less distorted lens can be extremely important for those recovering from PTSD. In this context, identifying distorted beliefs with the help of honest feedback from peers is a part of the cognitive restructuring process that can facilitate healing.

7. *Values. Values* are the ideas and beliefs that individuals hold as good, as important, as worthy of time and energy. When speaking with veterans, the things they frequently mention as valuing the most include a sense of belonging, self-respect, inner harmony, freedom, family security, health, and enjoying life. A crucial question for each participant attempting to move forward into health is to what degree perceived values are reflected in day-to-day behavior. In other words, are hopes and dreams reflected in behavior? It is important for each member to think about the degree to which life is lived authentically, that is, how life lived day-to-day is a consistent and accurate reflection of one's most important priorities.

8. *Making/finding meaning.* Traditional ways that individuals attempt to find meaning in traumatic events include at least two things, finding benefit and making sense out of the event (Davis, Nolen-Hoeksema, & Larson, 1998), both of which can be problematic. Finding benefit involves considering positive implications for one's life, that is, the "silver lining." Making sense is the attempt to develop a relatively benign explanation of the event. Both of these meaning activities can be found to be impossible for survivors of trauma. A recent review of the role of spirituality in adjustment to bereavement noted studies that suggest that meaning making is a pathway in the relationship between spirituality and positive adjustment (Wortman & Park, 2008).

One researcher with broad knowledge about the impact of death by homicide (Armour, 2006) suggests that, in addition to cognitive changes that result in meaning, many survivors find meaning through actions. She labels these actions "the intense pursuit of what matters" and notes that a qualitative study of family members of homicide victims found that 83% of these individuals felt that this label substantially represented their experience of coping after the death (Armour, 2006). She suggests that trauma survivors may at times be helped by three types of actions: (1) speaking the truth, (2) fighting for what is right, and (3) living in ways that give purpose to the trauma.

The ST group also looks at the sense of meaning that one derives from outside the self (i.e., from one's personal support system). In this context, we talk about finding meaning by "being meaningful" or creating a life where one "matters" to other people. PTSD-related withdrawal, avoidance of social gatherings, and, for veterans, loss of the roles and esteem once associated with service all serve to prevent one from making a significant positive impact in the lives of other people. These PTSD-related changes may also prevent individuals from receiving the positive regard and feedback that can help them feel better about themselves and to see their lives as more meaningful. We encourage members to actively seek opportunities for service. Nonprofit service agencies as well as religious/spiritual communities are frequently looking for people with time on their hands who can serve the community in significant ways. We point out that many spiritual traditions view service of others as a spiritual practice, from which both the giver and receiver benefit.

Concluding Thoughts on the Evolution of TD Group Interventions

Although group approaches have been used as a resource to promote trauma recovery for over 60 years, the empirical development of TD groups through research with controlled treatment outcome studies has occurred only within the past 20 years. In particular, the proliferation of RCTs employing the most exacting scientific standards is even more recent, with most studies being published in the past 5 years. While it is probably premature to conclude that most TD group interventions are "evidence-based," it does seem appropriate to label those backed by positive results from several studies as "evidence-informed." Rationally derived "best practices" for dealing with practical issues, such as TD group organization, member selection, and leadership, have been offered.

As we have seen in this chapter, developers of TD groups have recently turned their attention to improving early intervention efforts (e.g., PFA) or focusing on key comorbid issues, such as spirituality and trauma (e.g., ST). These newer efforts have not yet been subjected to preliminary field trials that would lead to more rigorous RCTs. However, they do illustrate the increasing range of clinical issues in TD for which group interventions are useful.

References

Adler, A. B., Litz, B. T., Castro, C. A., Suvak, M., Thomas, J. L., Burrell, L., et al. (2008). A group randomized trial of critical incident stress debriefing provided to U.S. peacekeepers. *Journal of Traumatic Stress, 21*(3), 253–263.

Ano, G. G., & Vasconcelles, E. B. (2005). Religious coping and psychological adjustment to stress: A meta-analysis. *Journal of Clinical Psychology, 61*(4), 461–480.

Armour, M. P. (2006). Meaning making for survivors of violent death. In E. K. Rynearson (Ed.), *Violent death: Resilience and intervention beyond the crisis* (pp. 101–121). New York: Routledge.

Beardslee, W. R., Versage, E. M., Salt, P., & Wright, E. (1999). The development and evaluation of two preventive intervention strategies for children of depressed parents. In D. Cicchetti & S. L. Toth (Eds.), *Rochester Symposium on Developmental Psychopathology: Vol. 9. Developmental approaches to prevention and intervention* (pp. 223–234). Rochester, NY: University of Rochester Press.

Beck, J. G., Coffey, S. F., Foy, D. W., Keane, T. M., & Blanchard, E. B. (2009). Group cognitive behavior therapy for chronic posttraumatic stress disorder: An initial randomized pilot study. *Behavior Therapy, 40*, 82–92.

Bergin, A. E., & Jensen, J. P. (1990). Religiosity of psychotherapists: A national survey. *Psychotherapy, 27*, 3–7.

Bisson, J. I. (2003). Single-session early psychological interventions following traumatic events. *Clinical Psychology Review, 23*, 481–499.

Brewin, C. R. (2005). Risk factor effect sizes in PTSD: What this means for intervention. *Journal of Trauma and Dissociation, 6*(2), 123–130.

Cohen, S., & Wills, T. A. (1985). Stress, social support, and the buffering hypothesis. *Psychological Bulletin, 98*(2), 310–357.

Conyne, R. K. (in press). Group counseling. In R. K. Conyne (Ed.), *Oxford handbook of group counseling*. New York: Oxford University Press.

Davies, D. R., Burlingame, G. M., & Layne, C. M. (2006). Integrating small-group process principles into trauma-focused group psychotherapy: What should a group trauma therapist know? In L. A. Schein, H. I. Spitz, G. M. Burlingame, & P. R. Muskin (Eds.), *Psychological effects of catastrophic disasters: Group approaches to treatment*. New York: Haworth Press.

Davis, C. G., Nolen-Hoeksema, S., & Larson, J. (1998). Making sense of loss and benefiting from the experience: Two construals of meaning. *Journal of Personality and Social Psychology, 75*(2), 561–574.

Drescher, K. D. (2006). Spirituality in the face of terrorist disasters. In L. A. Schein, H. I. Spitz, G. M. Burlingame, & P. R. Muskin (Eds.), *Psychological effects of catastrophic disasters:*

Group approaches to treatment (pp. 335–381). New York: Haworth Press.

Drescher, K. D., & Foy, D. W. (2008). When they come home: Posttraumatic stress, moral injury, and spiritual consequences for veterans. *Reflective Practice: Formation and Supervision in Ministry, 28*, 85–102.

Drescher, K. D., Ramirez, G., Leoni, J. J., Romesser, J. M., Sornborger, J., & Foy, D. W. (2004). Spirituality and trauma: Development of a group therapy module. *Group: The Journal of the Eastern Group Psychotherapy Society, 28*(4), 71–87.

Drescher, K. D., Smith, M. W., & Foy, D. W. (2007). Spirituality and readjustment following war-zone experiences. In C. R. Figley & W. P. Nash (Eds.), *Combat stress injury theory, research, and management* (pp. 486–511). New York: Routledge.

Dunn, N. J., Rehm, L. P., Schillaci, J., Souchek, J., Mehta, P. D., Ashton, C. M., et al. (2007). A randomized trial of self-management and psychoeducational group therapies for comorbid chronic posttraumatic stress disorder and depressive disorder. *Journal of Traumatic Stress, 20*(3), 221–237.

Dynes, J. B. (1945). Rehabilitation of war casualties. *War Medicine, 7*, 32–35.

Enright, R. D., & Coyle, C. T. (1998). Researching the process model of forgiveness within psychological interventions. In E. L. Worthington (Ed.), *Dimensions of forgiveness*. Radnor, PA: Templeton Foundation Press.

Farberow, N. L. (1978). *Field manual for human service workers in major disasters*: Adult Psychological First Aid (DHHS Publication No. ADM 78–537). Rockville, MD: National Institute of Mental Health.

Festinger, L. (1957). *A theory of cognitive dissonance*. Stanford, CA: Stanford University Press.

Foy, D. W. (2008). On the development of practice guidelines for evidence-based group approaches following disaster. *International Journal of Group Psychotherapy, 58*, 569–576.

Foy, D.W., Drescher, K.D., & Watson, P.J. (in press). Religious/spirituality factors in resilience. In Southwick, Charney, Friedman & Litz (Eds.), *Comprehensive textbook of resilience*. Cambridge: University Press.

Foy, D. W., Eriksson, C. B., & Trice, G. A. (2001). Introduction to group interventions for trauma survivors. *Group Dynamics: Theory, Research, and Practice, 5*(4), 246–251.

Foy, D. W., Glynn, S. M., Schnurr, P. P., Jankowski, M. K., Wattenberg, M. S., Weiss, D. S., et al. (2000). Group therapy. In E. Foa, T. Keane, & M. Friedman (Eds.), *Effective treatments for PTSD: Practice guidelines from the International Society for Traumatic Stress Studies* (pp. 155–175, 336–338). New York: Guilford Press.

Foy, D. W., & Schrock, D. A. (2006). Future directions. In L. A. Schein, H. I. Spitz, G. M. Burlingame, & P. R. Muskin (Eds.), *Psychological effects of catastrophic disasters: Group approaches to treatment*. New York: Haworth Press.

Gorsuch, R. L. (1995). Religious aspects of substance abuse and recovery. *Journal of Social Issues, 51*, 65–83.

Janoff-Bulman, R. (1992). *Shattered assumptions: Towards a new psychology of trauma*. New York: Free Press.

Klein, R. K., & Schermer, V. L. (2000). *Group psychotherapy for psychological trauma*. New York: Guilford Press.

Krupnick, J. L., Green, B. L., Stockton, P., Miranda, J., Krause, E. D., & Mete, M. (2008). Group interpersonal psychotherapy for low-income women with posttraumatic stress disorder. *Psychotherapy Research, 18*(5), 497–507.

Layne, C. M., Saltzman, W. R., Poppleton, L., Burlingame, G. M., Pasalic, A., Durakovic, E., et al. (2008). Effectiveness of a school-based group psychotherapy program for war-exposed adolescents: A randomized controlled trial. *Journal of the American Academy of Child and Adolescent Psychiatry, 47*(9), 1048–1062.

Leibniz, G.W. (1890). *Philosophical Works* (G.M. Duncan, Trans.). New Haven, CT: Tuttle, Morehouse & Taylor.

Lindemann, E. (1944). Symptomatology and management of acute grief. *American Journal of Psychiatry, 101*, 141–148.

Litz, B. T., Gray, M. J., Bryant, R. A., & Adler, A. B. (2002). Early intervention for trauma: Current status and future directions. *Clinical Psychology: Science & Practice, 9*, 112–134.

Litz, B. T., Stein, N., Delaney, E., Lebowitz, L., Nash, W. P., Silva, C., et al. (2009). Moral injury and moral repair in war veterans: A preliminary model and intervention strategy. *Clinical Psychology Review, 29*(8), 695–706.

McIntosh, D. N., Silver, R. C., & Wortman, C. B. (1993). Religion's role in adjustment to a negative life event: coping with the loss of a child. *Journal of Personality and Social Psychology, 65*(4), 812–821.

McNally, R. J., Bryant, R. A., & Ehlers, A. (2003). Does early psychological intervention promote recovery from posttraumatic stress? *Psychological Science in the Public Interest, 4*, 45–79.

Miller, W. R., & Rollnick, S. (2002). *Motivational interviewing: Preparing people for change* (2nd ed.). New York: Guilford Press.

Murphy, R. T., Rosen, C. R., Cameron, R. P., & Thompson, K. E. (2002). Development of a group treatment for enhancing motivation to change PTSD symptoms. *Cognitive and Behavioral Practice, 9*(4), 308–316.

Murphy, R. T., Thompson, K. E., Murray, M., Rainey, Q., & Uddo, M. M. (2009). Effect of a motivation enhancement intervention on veterans; engagement in PTSD treatment. *Psychological Services, 6*(4), 264–278.

Nooney, J., & Woodrum, E. (2002). Religious coping and church-based social support as predictors of mental health outcomes: Testing a conceptual model. *Journal for the Scientific Study of Religion, 41*(2), 359–368.

Pargament, K., & Brandt, C. (1998). Religion and coping. In H. G. Koenig (Ed.), *Handbook of religion and mental health* (pp. 112–128). San Diego, CA: Academic Press.

Pargament, K. I., Zinnbauer, B. J., Scott, A. B., Butter, E. M., Zerowin, J., & Stanik, P. (1998). Red flags and religious coping: Identifying some religious warning signs among people in crisis. *Journal of Clinical Psychology, 54*, 77–89.

Powell, L. H., Shajhabi, L., & Thoresen, C. E. (2003). Religion and spirituality: Linkages to physical health. *American Psychologist, 58*(1), 36–52.

Prochaska, J. O., & DiClemente, C. C. (1983). Stages and processes of self-change in smoking: Toward an integrative model of change. *Journal of Consulting and Clinical Psychology, 40*, 432–440.

Pynoos, R. S., & Nader, K. (1988). Psychological first aid and treatment approach to children exposed to community violence: Research implications. *Journal of Traumatic Stress, 1*, 445–473.

Raphael, B. (1986). *When disaster strikes: A handbook for the caring professional*. Boston: Unwin Hyman.

Raphael, B., & Wooding, S. (2006). Group intervention for the prevention and treatment of acute initial stress reactions in civilians. In L. A. Schein, H. I. Spitz, C. M. Burlingame, & P. R. Muskin (Eds.), *Group approaches for the psychological effects of terrorist disasters*. New York: Hawthorn Press.

Schein, L. A., Spitz, H. I., Burlingame, G. M., & Muskin, P. R. (Eds.). (2006). *Psychological effects of catastrophic disasters: Group approaches to treatment*. New York: Haworth Press.

Schuster, M. A., Stein, B. D., Jaycox, L., Collins, R. L., Marshall, G. N., Elliott, M. N., et al. (2001). A national survey of stress reactions after the September 11, 2001, terrorist attacks. *New England Journal of Medicine*, *345*(20), 1507–1512.

Schut, H., Stroebe, M. S., van den Bout, J., & Terheggen, M. (2001). The efficacy of bereavement interventions: Determining who benefits. In M. S. Stroebe, R. O. Hansson, W. Stroebe, & H. Schut (Eds.), *Handbook of bereavement research* (pp. 705–738). Washington, DC: American Psychological Association.

Shea, M.T., McDevitt-Murphy, M., Ready, D.J., & Schnurr, P.P. (2009). Group Therapy. In E.B. Foa, T.M. Keane, M.J. Friedman (Eds.), *Effective Treatments for PTSD*. New York, NY, Guilford Press, 306–326.

Shneidman, E. S., Farberow, N. L., & Litman, R. E. (1970). *The psychology of suicide*. New York: Science House.

Sijbrandij, M., Olff, M., Reitsma, J. B., Carlier, I. V. E., & Gersons, B. P. R. (2006). Emotional or educational debriefing after psychological trauma: Randomised controlled trial. *British Journal of Psychiatry*, *189*(8), 150–155.

Sikkema, K. J., Hansen, N. B., Kochman, A., Tarakeshwar, N., Neufeld, S., Meade, C. S., et al. (2007). Outcomes from a group intervention for coping with HIV/AIDS and childhood sexual abuse: Reductions in traumatic stress. *AIDS and Behavior*, *11*(1), 49–60.

Sipprelle, R. C. (1992). A Vet Center experience: Multievent trauma, delayed treatment type. In D. Foy (Ed.), *Treating PTSD: Cognitive-behavioral strategies*. New York: Guilford Press.

Thoits, P. (1995). Stress, coping, and social support processes: Where are we? What next? *Journal of Health and Social Behavior*, *35*, 53–79.

Thoresen, C., Harris, A., & Luskin, F. (2000). Forgiveness and health: An unanswered question. In M. McCullough, K. Pargament, & C. Thoresen (Eds.), *Forgiveness: Theory, research, and practice*. New York: Guilford Press.

Watson, P. J., Friedman, M. J., Gibson, L. E., Ruzek, J. I., Norris, F. H., & Ritchie, E. C. (2003). Early intervention for trauma-related problems. *Review of Psychiatry*, *22*, 97–124.

Watson, P. J., & Shalev, A. Y. (2005). Assessment and treatment of adult acute responses to traumatic stress following mass traumatic events. *CNS Spectrums*, *10*(2), 123–131.

Wessely, S. C., Bryant, R. A., Greenberg, N., Earnshaw, N. M., Sharpley, J. G., & Hacker Hughes, J. G. (2008). Does psychoeducation help prevent post traumatic psychological distress? *Psychiatry*, *71*, 287–302.

Witvliet, C. V. O., Phillips, K. A., Feldman, M. E., & Beckham, J. C. (2004). Posttraumatic mental and physical health correlates of forgiveness and religious coping in military veterans. *Journal of Traumatic Stress*, *17*, 269–273.

Wortman, J. H., & Park, C. L. (2008). Religion and spirituality in adjustment following bereavement: An integrative review. *Death Studies*, *32*, 703–736.

Yalom, I. (1970). *The theory and practice of group psychotherapy* (1st ed.). New York: Basic Books.

Young, B. H. (2006). Psychological first aid. In E. C. Ritchie, M. J. Friedman, & P. J. Watson (Eds.), *Mental health intervention following disasters or mass violence*. New York: Guilford Press.

Young, B. H., & Blake, D. D. (1999). *Group treatments for posttraumatic stress disorder*. Philadelphia: Brunner/Mazel.

Zlotnick, C., Johnson, J. E., & Najavits, L. M. (2009). Randomized controlled pilot study of cognitive-behavioral therapy in a sample of incarcerated women with substance use disorder and PTSD. *Behavior Therapy*, *40*, 325–336.

PART 7

Conclusion and
Future Directions

Group Counseling: 50 Basic Premises and the Need for Mainstreaming

Robert K. Conyne

Abstract

This final chapter of the *Handbook* is intended both to summarize the major content contained in the previous 30 chapters about group counseling and to identify an important direction for action. The first goal is met by drawing from the material 50 basic premises pertaining to group counseling. All chapters are represented in these premises, and they range across the *Handbook*'s major sections of Context, Key Change Processes, Research, Leadership, and Applications. The second goal of identifying an important future direction is addressed by observing that group counseling, although now characterized by a substantial literature base documenting effective practices and procedures and now awaiting clearer actionable strategies for practitioners, continues to sit largely outside of mainstream practice and awareness. It is little known or appreciated among academics, researchers, and practitioners operating outside the group-counseling specialty, and to members of the public it seems largely to be a mystery. Group counseling must be mainstreamed by proactive promulgation of its knowledge base related to education and training, practice, and research.

Keywords: group counseling, future directions, leadership, training

Introduction

In pondering the voluminous content of the previous chapters, I am reminded of a wonderful movie title from (far too many) decades ago, *What's It All About, Alfie?* While not so concerned in this final chapter with coming to grips with what one person's life is all about, as in that movie, I am seeking to identify the essential meaning running through this volume's chapters. To rephrase the movie's refrain, in a sense I am asking, "What's group counseling all about, Alfie?" That is, what are some of the basic premises that serve to guide its practice?

The content of this book will provide the basic raw material for my examination. I have scoured it, and here I report on it (note: refer to the chapters directly for citations and references). Obviously, the resulting 50 premises reflect my perspective alone, and I encourage you to compare it with your own. Putting the two together no doubt will produce a fuller and perhaps more valid depiction of what group counseling is all about.

In addition, it is apparent to me that the value of group counseling is a kind of "best-kept secret." That is, it is metaphorically locked away in a safe box to which only those of us in the group-counseling inner circle hold a key. We have been focused, I suggest, on talking among ourselves (such as through the pages of this volume), sharing our practice and evidence. Of course, this level of discourse is absolutely fundamental to any scientific and educational endeavor. However, generally, we have failed to communicate the value of group counseling to those outside our small arena: to academics in areas and specialties outside our own; to stakeholders and thought leaders in education, health, and government; and to the public at large. We might ask, therefore, If group counseling is so valuable, why is its application so limited? The last section of this final chapter, therefore, will address the need for group counseling to become a more obvious part of the mainstream.

My exploration of this volume's content will proceed in parallel with the sequence of the chapters themselves, beginning with the discussion of the definition of group counseling and ending with that of trauma and disaster groups. However, the presentation will be organized by the major sections of the volume, which operate as lenses through which we can identify the basic premises of group counseling. These lenses are as follows:

Introduction (Chapter 1)
Context (Chapters 2–7)
Key Change Processes (Chapters 8–11)
Research (Chapters 12–15)
Leadership (Chapters 16–21)
Applications (Chapters 22–30)
Conclusion (Chapter 31)

50 Basic Premises of Group Counseling
Context

PREMISE 1: TO UNDERSTAND GROUP COUNSELING, ONE MUST FIRST UNDERSTAND "GROUPS"

Forsyth indicates that the essential elements of a group are found in the relationships connecting members, boundaries, interdependence, structure, cohesion, and *entitativity* (perceived "groupness"). He points out that as human beings are social animals who spend much of their lives in groups rather than alone, a group-level analysis is needed to supplement the more typical individual-level analysis of adjustment, well-being, and treatment. Group counseling provides a medium through which these (and other, see Chapter 7) approaches can be integrated.

PREMISE 2: GROUP APPROACHES HAVE PROVEN THEMSELVES TO BE EFFECTIVE, BUT THEY ARE NOT THE PREFERRED MODE OF TREATMENT FOR MOST THERAPISTS AND CLIENTS

Forsyth suggests that as theorists, researchers, and practitioners confirm the central importance of groups in people's lives, people will in time begin to think of themselves as group members first and individuals second and that group counseling will benefit as a helping modality.

PREMISE 3: GROUP WORK IS A USEFUL UMBRELLA TERM FOR THE BROAD ARRAY OF GROUP MODALITIES, INCLUDING GROUP COUNSELING

A discussion of any phenomenon needs first to proceed with defining key terms. So it is with group counseling. Ward pushed and prodded for some common ground, pointing out, as have others, that group counseling is a complex activity that is understood in a variety of ways. He concludes that the term *group work* is the "logical" one to use when referring to the broad field of helping people in groups.

PREMISE 4: GROUP COUNSELING IS INTERPERSONAL, PROCESS-ORIENTED, AND STRENGTHS-BASED

As for group counseling, which is part of the group-work manifold, Ward indicates it is characterized by an interpersonal, process orientation that focuses on increasing the strengths and wellness of members. He suggests that these emphases guide the necessary work to produce empirical evidence, combined with clinical wisdom, of the effectiveness of group counseling with specific populations in particular settings. As well, these elements supply the foundation for professional counselor training, which, in turn, needs to be centered on the dynamic properties of group interaction rather than serving as an extension of individual counseling.

PREMISE 5: HISTORY POINTS TO NEW GENERATIONAL THINKING

Leddick points out that successful originators of therapeutic models (e.g., Perls, Rogers) typically develop avid followers during their lifetimes. These supporters grow less fervid after the founder's death. Once the cult of personality subsides, what remains in our collective imaginations are effective strategies, helpful conceptual frameworks, and useful techniques. He wonders how the next generation of scholars and researchers will make history by synthesizing, originating, and configuring innovative combinations of group-counseling practice that will galvanize and inspire further evolution and improvement.

PREMISE 6: THE PROFESSIONS OF COUNSELING, PSYCHOLOGY, AND SOCIAL WORK ENJOY UNIQUE IDENTITIES BUT THEY SHARE ETHICAL FOUNDATIONS WITH EACH OTHER AND WITH OLDER PROFESSIONS SUCH AS LAW AND MEDICINE

Rapin observes that all of these professions follow the fundamental ethical principle of the Hippocratic oath of first do no harm. Their ethical documents that guide appropriate behavior reflect shared values. As well, counseling, psychology, and social work are professions governed by licensure and specific state or provincial regulation.

PREMISE 7: ETHICAL DECISION MAKING IN GROUP COUNSELING IS UNALTERABLY CONNECTED TO DEVELOPMENT OF AN ETHICAL FRAME OF REFERENCE THAT IS RELEVANT TO BOTH THE INDIVIDUAL AND THE PROFESSION

Drawing from a thorough review of existing publications and approaches across several group-oriented mental health professional associations, Rapin fashions a generic equation to assist in understanding how this connection operates, stipulating that ethical behavior in group counseling is a function of moral and ethical development, professional ethics, core knowledge and skills, specialty best practices, and legal parameters. She emphasizes that these major elements of ethical behavior are applied *in interaction* with a decision-making model. Without consideration of ethical development and the context in which a dilemma occurs, decision making in group counseling is both incomplete and flawed.

PREMISE 8: GROUP COUNSELING PRACTICE MUST INCLUDE CULTURAL COMPETENCE BUILT ON EMPIRICAL FINDINGS ASSOCIATED WITH A RANGE OF ETHNIC AND RACIAL GROUPS, ADAPTED TO THE UNIQUE DEMANDS OF CULTURAL SENSITIVITY

DeLucia-Waack observes that six domains of cultural adaptation seem to apply to group counseling, including dynamic issues and cultural complexities; orienting clients to psychotherapy and increasing mental health awareness; understanding cultural beliefs about mental illness, its causes, and its appropriate treatment; improving the client–therapist relationship; understanding cultural differences in the expression and communication of distress; and addressing cultural issues specific to the population. In addition, social class needs considerably more attention, as does the cultural background of the group leader.

PREMISE 9: IT IS NO LONGER POSSIBLE TO TREAT MENTAL HEALTH PROBLEMS (AND PREVENTION OF PROBLEMS) IN ISOLATION FROM SOCIAL PROBLEMS

Hage et al. suggest that group leaders need to take a proactive approach to assure that social justice be included within training curricula, research agenda, and practice orientations. Strategies should include multilevel interventions, of which group is a part, and a focus on social transformation. Thus, individual change and influence become parts of the equation, not the whole formula. Indeed, group-work practice and training need to be infused with socioeconomic, political, and demographic trends occurring in modern society, pursuing social justice so that wellness may blossom at all levels.

Key Change Processes

PREMISE 10: THERAPEUTIC FACTORS IN GROUP COUNSELING ARE CORE CONCEPTS THAT HAVE GENERATED A SIGNIFICANT AMOUNT OF EMPIRICAL AND CLINICAL INTEREST: RESEARCH NEEDS TO IDENTIFY WHICH THERAPEUTIC FACTORS ARE FUNDAMENTAL AND WHAT INTERRELATIONSHIPS EXIST AMONG THEM

Kivlighan et al. maintain that some therapeutic factors are more influential than others or that this may vary depending on who is asked and in what kind of group. It is likely that key factors interact rather than stand independently. All of these matters need to be researched.

PREMISE 11: FURTHER RESEARCH IS NEEDED TO SPECIFY WHAT GROUP LEADER BEHAVIORS CONNECT WITH WHICH THERAPEUTIC FACTORS

Kivlighan et al. suggest that therapeutic factors become especially important when they are considered as being actionable by group leaders. But what behaviors may be tied to which factors to yield the most positive outcomes? (Note: Redundancy surrounds this research direction, with similar needs existing to identify linkages between group leader behaviors and group cohesion, group climate, and group development).

PREMISE 12: RESEARCH ON THERAPEUTIC FACTORS OCCURRING IN GROUPS NEEDS TO BE CONDUCTED USING A GROUP PERSPECTIVE

Kivlighan et al. lament that research on therapeutic factors operating in group has lacked a focus on the group itself and, even more important, largely has failed to account for essential group interactional constructs, such as mutual influence. They believe that research on therapeutic factors in groups will not advance until theorists and researchers start formulating and testing theories and models that have a group perspective.

PREMISE 13: IN GROUP COUNSELING, THE SENSE OF COHESION, ALLIANCE, AND GROUP CLIMATE ARE THE RELATIONSHIP FACTORS THAT PROVIDE THE FOUNDATION FOR SUCCESSFUL TREATMENT

Despite the contradictory reports and often because of the myriad of influencing factors that can lead to ambiguity and inconsistency in research findings, Marmarosh and Van Horn conclude from prevailing group research that cohesion is among the three vital processes accounting for successful group-counseling efforts.

PREMISE 14: FUTURE RESEARCH IN GROUP COHESION NEEDS TO BE PARTICULARIZED

Marmarosh and Van Horn make the following recommendations: (1) explore the direct and indirect ways cohesion relates to process and outcome, (2) consistently define cohesion and use validated measures of cohesion from different perspectives in the same studies, (3) consider group development and measure cohesion at different points in time over the course of counseling, (4) replicate studies using similar group populations in order to understand inconsistent findings, (5) study cohesion in diverse groups that utilize different interventions, (6) explore the impact that leader and group member individual differences bring to the development and usefulness of cohesion, and (7) explore the overlapping relationships between cohesion and other therapeutic factors.

PREMISE 15: RESEARCH IS URGENTLY NEEDED TO EXPLORE THE IMPACT THAT MEMBER AND LEADER QUALITIES EXERT ON THE DEVELOPMENT OF COHESION IN GROUPS

Marmarosh and Van Horn point to the understudied importance of how attachment style (e.g., a dismissive group leader or an avoidant group member) affects group cohesion and how race, ethnicity, and sexual orientation of group members and leaders are likely to influence it.

PREMISE 16: THERE IS SUFFICIENT DEPTH AND BREADTH OF KNOWLEDGE TO INDICATE THAT GROUP CLIMATE CAN BE VIEWED AS AN EMPIRICALLY SUPPORTED PROCESS TO BE CONSIDERED BY EVIDENCE-BASED GROUP COUNSELORS

One recent indicator pointed to by McClendon and Burlingame are the group psychotherapy practice guidelines ratified by the American Group Psychotherapy Association (AGPA), supporting group climate as an evidence-based process.

PREMISE 17: THE ULTIMATE VALUE OF GROUP CLIMATE IS THAT IT PROVIDES ACTIONABLE INFORMATION FOR GROUP LEADERS

MacKenzie and the AGPA/Transcoop cooperation both endorse the importance of actionable information to empirically guide group leaders. Both have made recommendations regarding their respective measures (Group Climate Questionnaire [GCQ] and Group Questionnaire). McClendon and

Burlingame encourage authors of existing and future group-climate measures to adopt the same perspective so that research results have a direct impact on the clinical practice of group treatments.

PREMISE 18: THE GCQ IS A TESTED MEASURE FOR PREDICTING GROUP OUTCOME AND OTHER SALIENT GROUP PROCESSES AND IT FITS WELL WITHIN EVIDENCE-BASED PROJECTS

Two of the three scales of the GCQ have proven to be moderately to highly predictive of group outcome and other important processes, resulting in it being the premier group-climate instrument available.

PREMISE 19: A THREE-FACTOR MODEL OF GROUP CLIMATE, RESULTING FROM A SERIES OF LARGE INTERNATIONAL STUDIES, SHOWS PROMISE FOR PROVIDING AN ALTERNATIVE UNDERSTANDING OF GROUP CLIMATE AS INCLUDING BUT EXCEEDING A MEMBER-TO-GROUP PHENOMENON

McClendon and Burlingame summarize these factors as follows: (1) positive bonding relationship among members, (2) positive working relationship and group climate, and (3) negative relationship and affect connected to tension, withdrawal, avoidance, and conflict. Additional research is being conducted and demands to be followed by others.

PREMISE 20: GROUP DEVELOPMENT IN COUNSELING GROUPS EVOLVES IN WAYS THAT ARE ORDERLY, SYSTEMATIC, AND POTENTIALLY PROGRESSIVE

Indeed, as Brabender suggests, groups can not only change but grow. While change might be naturally expected, growth is not guaranteed. Whether or not the group grows is a matter of importance to the members: Their ability to accomplish their purposes for being in the group is affected by whether the group progresses, languishes, or retreats. Therefore, group development is of importance to the group counselor as well.

PREMISE 21: GROUP LEADERS NEED TO TIME THEIR INTERVENTIONS TO MIRROR DEVELOPMENTAL STAGES

But research is lacking on what leader behaviors might be best suited by group developmental stage. Brabender explores if there is a general time in a group for leaders to be more or less active. Does structure or open process moderate what might be done when? Does the unique population of a group affect the timing of leader interventions? These kinds of issues await further needed research.

PREMISE 22: ALTHOUGH GROUP DEVELOPMENT HAS BEEN INVESTIGATED FOR YEARS, RESEARCH ON THE TOPIC OF HOW SYSTEMATIC PROGRESSIVE CHANGE IS FACILITATED BY ITS LEADER HAS JUST BEGUN

Brabender encourages the launching of research into the relationship between group development and leader interventions (and other areas). This situation is similar to those existing in the areas of therapeutic factors, group climate, and group cohesion, all discussed earlier: Research is needed to link desired group leader actionable behaviors with important group processes.

Research

PREMISE 23: MOUNTING EVIDENCE CLEARLY SHOWS THAT GROUP COUNSELING GENERALLY IS EFFECTIVE, YET IT ALSO IS BECOMING MORE APPARENT THAT CERTAIN TREATMENT MODELS FOR PARTICULAR PATIENT POPULATIONS WORK BEST; THIS CONTINUING SEARCH FOR MORE PRECISE KEY MECHANISMS WILL LEAD TO EVEN MORE IMPORTANT CONNECTIONS

Drawing from her own work and that of others, Barlow lays out a number of steps that will promote research of key change mechanisms. Three of these are to include in write-ups relevant information about studies, to select state-of-the-art research methods and designs, and to focus on process–outcome linkages.

PREMISE 24: EVIDENCE-BASED PROFESSIONAL PRACTICE AND EVIDENCE-SUPPORTED TREATMENTS NEED TO YIELD A KIND OF MIDDLE GROUND TO BENEFIT GROUP MEMBERS, PROFESSIONS, AND RESEARCH AND PRACTICE

As Barlow observes, an essential requirement for all practitioners is to avidly pursue knowledge while allowing for human contextuality. Over time and with enough intention, group counselors can master an appropriate blend that effectively integrates evidence with clinical judgment.

PREMISE 25: GROUP PHENOMENA ARE COMPLEX, INVOLVING PROCESSES THAT CONNECT AND ARE INTERACTIVE; FUTURE RESEARCHERS NEED TO DISCOVER LINKAGES AMONG THESE PROCESSES AND HOW THEY AFFECT GROUP OUTCOMES ACROSS A RANGE OF GROUP-WORK TYPES

Drawing from other research as well as their own, Stockton and Morran emphasize two important directions for future research: (1) to better understand the complexities of which group therapeutic factors are most important at various group stages for which types of groups and (2) to investigate the connection between leader interventions and group therapeutic factors to guide how leaders concretely can promote the emergence of important therapeutic forces within groups.

PREMISE 26: GIVEN THE NEED FOR MORE LONG-TERM AND COMPLEX INQUIRY EFFORTS IN GROUP COUNSELING, IT WOULD SEEM IMPORTANT TO EMPHASIZE THE VALUE OF TEAMWORK

As Stockton and Morran point out, the formation of ongoing research teams provides researchers the collaborative opportunity to combine their knowledge, experience, and resources productively. This need is increasing because group approaches are multidisciplinary in origin and application. Additionally, a research team model yields a fertile training environment for graduate students and novice researchers while also providing a natural format for practitioner–researcher collaboration, interdisciplinary cooperation, and the creation of programmatic lines of inquiry.

PREMISE 27: GROUP LEADER TRAINING CONTINUES TO NEED ELABORATION

Although research, best practices, and training models have emerged over the last several years to advance the knowledge base surrounding group leader training, Stockton and Morran identify continuing needs in this area. They focus their attention on novice group leaders and suggest that progress needs to be made in helping them to acquire knowledge competencies, basic and advanced skill competencies, clinical experience competencies, coleader competencies, and multicultural competencies (see also Chapter 19).

PREMISE 28: OVERALL, GROUP RESEARCH SUGGESTS THAT ASSESSMENT OF THE GROUP FORMAT AS A WHOLE DEMONSTRATES THAT IT IS EFFICACIOUS, ON PAR WITH INDIVIDUAL APPROACHES; HOWEVER, THERE IS LIMITED EMPIRICAL EVIDENCE VALIDATING THIS CONCEPT AS THE COMPLEX INTERACTIONS OF WHOLE-GROUP DYNAMICS WITH INDIVIDUAL PARTICIPANT DYNAMICS ARE NOT WELL UNDERSTOOD

Group dynamics and leadership may be thought of as a young science. The importance and abundance of group work lead Schwartz, Waldo, and Moravec (as well as other authors in this handbook) to emphasize the critical need for empirically supported group practice. In turn, this need for empirical research mandates pursuit of effective and accurate measurement.

PREMISE 29: QUALITATIVE RESEARCH APPROACHES MAY HAVE UNIQUE APPLICABILITY TO GROUP COUNSELING—RELATED RESEARCH

Indeed, certain qualitative approaches may be uniquely suited to exploring specific group-counseling issues and research needs. However, Rubel and Okech also caution that qualitative approaches are not a panacea for the challenges facing group-counseling researchers. Without careful planning and implementation, qualitative group-counseling studies will not meet these challenges and fail to provide the credibility to impact practice.

Leadership

PREMISE 30: THE "PERSONHOOD" OF THE GROUP LEADER IS A CONCEPT THAT INTEGRATES PERSONAL DEVELOPMENT AND PROFESSIONAL DEVELOPMENT; CONNECTS PERSON, PROCESS, AND PRODUCT; MELDS CHARACTER AND COMPETENCE; AND UNITES TRAINING/TEACHING, PRACTICE, AND RESEARCH

Group leadership is more than the use of skills and techniques, of course. Trotzer maintains that group leader skills and competence evolving from training and practice yield attitudes, values, and beliefs that serve to drive group leadership. The personhood of the leader is a summative quality that turns on a coherent combination of character and competence. Trotzer sees it as impelling who the leader is and inspiring what the leader does.

PREMISE 31: THE TRAINING OF GROUP LEADERS NEEDS TO BE EXAMINED EMPIRICALLY TO DETERMINE EFFICACY IN TRAINING AND PRACTICE AND THE COMPREHENSIVENESS, UTILITY, AND ADAPTABILITY OF TRAINING APPROACHES

While a number of group-counseling training approaches are used, Newmeyer (and Brown in Chapter 19) find scant evidence of supportive research. This important area demands further study because the preparation of group leaders must be based on approaches suffused with known effectiveness. The purposeful group technique model highlighted by Newmeyer represents an approach that would seem to satisfy in terms of comprehensiveness,

utility, and adaptability, yet evidence of its efficacy is needed.

PREMISE 32: GROUP LEADERSHIP STYLES AND FUNCTIONS ARE COMPRISED OF A SET OF TASKS THAT NEED TO BE DEFINED CLEARLY, FOLLOWED BY HELPING TRAINEES LEARN HOW STRATEGIES AND TECHNIQUES CAN BE EMPLOYED TO DISCHARGE THOSE TASKS

Bauman suggests that training begin with identifying what group leaders need to do, not with how they should be or even how they should accomplish necessary tasks. She encourages group-work researchers and practitioners to explore a number of questions: (1) What do they need to know about leader functions and styles that would improve training and practice? (2) Is client outcome the best measure of the utility of various functions and styles? (3) How can situational variables, which vary across groups and within a group, be accounted for when considering leader function or style?

PREMISE 33: HOW TO PREPARE FUTURE GROUP LEADERS IS MARKED BY VALUABLE EXPERT OPINION BUT BY RELATIVELY FEW EMPIRICAL STUDIES ON TEACHING GROUP LEADERSHIP, COMPONENTS, MODELS FOR GROUP LEADERSHIP AND ITS TRAINING, OR TRAINING OUTCOMES

Therefore, Brown notes, a unified research-based vision for group leader training that is endorsed by multiple professional associations is lacking and is needed. Such an interassociational perspective might define desired outcomes for training, including what knowledge, leader personal qualities, and techniques would characterize a competent group leader. Evidence-based teaching strategies that support these desired outcomes also are needed.

PREMISE 34: PROFESSIONAL INPUT AND AGREEMENT IS NEEDED TO ESTABLISH THE CRITERIA NECESSARY FOR ADEQUACY OF ENTRY LEVEL PREPARATION

Brown observes that the typical situation of requiring one course to teach all of the dimensions of groups and group leadership does not meet the entry-level needs for knowledge and skill as group leaders. She suggests that trainees should have opportunities to practice leading different types of groups, but the reality is that they may lead just one group during the supervised practicum.

PREMISE 35: TRAINING GUIDELINES OF PROFESSIONAL ASSOCIATIONS SHOULD BE CLEARLY SUPPORTED BY EVIDENCE-BASED RESEARCH WHENEVER POSSIBLE AND AIMED AT PROMOTING COMPETENCIES CAPABLE OF BEING OBJECTIVELY ASSESSED

In Brown's review of training standards of five professional associations (also see Chapter 5), no clear connections were found to indicate that any standard was developed from research evidence. The complexity of many group leadership skills, various theoretical perspectives and applications, and the role of intangible factors such as the level of the group leader's personal development combine to make this a challenging goal to achieve—yet one that is necessary to attempt.

PREMISE 36: RESEARCH EXAMINING GROUP SUPERVISION AND SKILL DEVELOPMENT OF SUPERVISEES NEEDS TO DEFINE WHAT SUPERVISORY METHODS WORK, HOW SUPERVISION METHODS ARE RELATED TO CLIENT OUTCOMES, AND HOW SUPERVISION CAN INCREASE COGNITIVE COMPLEXITY AND OTHER VALUED CHARACTERISTICS TYPICALLY FOUND IN EXPERT GROUP LEADERS

Riva suggests that it is important to investigate and then to identify effective methods for developing supervisee skills. Moreover, studies of the ability of supervisees to translate those skills subsequently to group-counseling practice are needed.

PREMISE 37: RESEARCH IS IN ITS INFANCY IN TERMS OF DETERMINING IF THE SUPERVISION OF GROUP LEADERS IMPROVES OUTCOMES FOR GROUP MEMBERS

As Riva implies, it is an expectation in the field that supervision of group leaders positively influences group leadership, which then can yield improved group member outcomes. Some limited research suggests this may be the case, but Riva's suggestion for training programs to track client outcomes as a consequence of group leader supervision and of group leader practice under supervision needs some takers.

PREMISE 38: ETHICAL CONSIDERATIONS INVOLVED IN THE GROUP SUPERVISORY RELATIONSHIP NEED TO BE RESEARCHED

Riva identifies several issues that are worth exploring (again, also see Chapter 5) about the ethics of group supervision. These include (1) how supervisors provide supervision with group leaders, (2) what methods they use to teach ethical decision making, (3) how aware supervisors are with the ethical and legal guidelines for their state, (4) what effective methods are used to respond to a supervisee possessing inadequate skill development, (5) what personality difficulties interfere with client care, and (6) which supervisor characteristics are most related to supervisee's positive skill development.

PREMISE 39: CREATIVITY AND SPONTANEITY, ALWAYS A PART OF GROUP COUNSELING AND OTHER FORMS OF GROUP WORK, ADD TO THE VITALITY OF GROUPS AND MAKE THEM RICHER AS WELL AS MORE INTERESTING AND PRODUCTIVE

Gladding observes that creativity and spontaneity in a group take time to develop. Barriers include personal fear and insecurity, environmental restraints, being too cognitive, lack of a challenge, and lack of reinforcement. Yet, when it occurs, creativity in a group can be purposeful and playful, promote collegiality, facilitate communication, enable group members to see multiple aspects of themselves and the world, and encourage nonverbal and emotional participation. It promotes interactions that might not occur otherwise. How to appropriately include creativity and spontaneity into group teaching, training, supervision, and practice is an issue to be addressed and researched.

Applications

PREMISE 40: GROUPS ARE UBIQUITOUS TODAY, WITH MANY TYPES OF GROUPS ADDRESSING AN EVER-INCREASING NUMBER OF TOPICS AND ISSUES

This omnipresence and broad diversity lead to a kind of fragmentation in the research on groups; that is, we know some things about some kinds of groups in some settings, but vast gaps in our knowledge remain. Group practitioners and researchers need to focus on studying the efficacy and the mechanisms behind the efficacy for groups occurring in these vastly different settings. The tools used to assess the effects of group interventions should include some measure of group cohesion or a way to assess the power of the group in explaining the changes that occur. Overall, conclude Kalodner and Hanus, there is much we know but much more that we still do not know about how groups work in these different settings.

PREMISE 41: IT IS HELPFUL WHEN CREATING AND LEADING GROUPS FROM A LIFE-SPAN PERSPECTIVE FOR GROUP LEADERS TO CONCEPTUALIZE MEMBERS FROM A DEVELOPMENTAL CONTEXT, INCLUDING ASSESSMENT OF WHICH PSYCHOSOCIAL TASKS THEY ARE FACING

Keim and Olguin suggest that group leaders attend to the pattern existing between group counseling and group member psychosocial stages. It appears that, regardless of group work type (i.e., task, psychoeducation, counseling, or psychotherapy), groups developmentally evolve similarly to the psychosocial stages of development (note Chapter 11). This parallel developmental evolution can assist group leaders in assessing which social tasks members may have previously attained and which tasks are yet to be resolved. Focusing groups based on psychosocial developmental stage permits group counselors to help members address the unique needs of each stage of life.

PREMISE 42: WHEN GROUP COUNSELORS COMPREHEND THE UNIQUE DYNAMICS THAT SEXUAL MINORITY CLIENTS BRING TO THE GROUP ENCOUNTER AND POSSESS THE SKILLS TO LEAD THE GROUP THROUGH ITS MANY TRANSITIONS, GROWTH CAN OCCUR FOR EVERY INDIVIDUAL INVOLVED

Ritter maintains that all group members, including sexual minority clients, can heal and grow through group counseling when leaders understand the unique experiences of members, mirror positive qualities, and are able to effectively implement the guidelines, best practices, competencies, standards, and codes and principles that characterize group counseling and group work.

PREMISE 43: THE RESILIENCE OF LESBIAN, GAY, BISEXUAL, AND TRANSGENDERED INDIVIDUALS SHOULD NOT BE UNDERESTIMATED AS A PRIMARY SOURCE OF STRENGTH FOR GROUP COUNSELING

Group-counselor skills and understanding of oppression, minority stress, and cohort and developmental differences are very important but only a part of the helping equation. Ritter emphasizes that the inherent resilience of members of this population also needs to be honored and harnessed as a force for growth.

PREMISE 44: PREVENTION GROUPS POSSESS UNIQUE QUALITIES THAT CAN FORESTALL PROBLEM DEVELOPMENT AND BUILD STRENGTHS

Waldo, Schwartz, Horne, and Côté suggest that future directions for prevention groups are many, including the extraordinary potential for expansion of prevention impact by encouraging prevention group members to recruit new members, become prevention group leaders, and serve as change agents and resources within their social networks.

PREMISE 45: GROUP COUNSELORS CAN LEARN MUCH FROM THE RICH ARRAY OF GLOBAL GROUP WORK

McWhirter et al. observe that group-counseling interventions are evolving to address medical, health, exercise, spirituality, and religious issues. Increased communication regarding the effectiveness of group studies and practices internationally is increasing. This building awareness of what works in other cultures across the globe may provide practitioners with new learning and help promote investigations leading to group programs that are more broadly comprehensive.

PREMISE 46: A GLOBAL PERSPECTIVE MAY PROVIDE THE BEST FOUNDATION TO GENERATE SOLUTIONS, DEVELOP RECOMMENDATIONS, AND PROPOSE STANDARDS FOR EVALUATING GROUP EFFICACY AND IMPLEMENTATION

A global perspective, the product of practices, research, and wisdom accumulated from cultures around the world, may provide a comprehensive and useful foundation for addressing challenging group issues, according to McWhirter et al. As an example, they suggest that widely held assumptions regarding the presence and nature of therapeutic factors among group members might be analyzed in new ways, informed by knowledge and practice gained through a broader international and multicultural context.

PREMISE 47: THE ADEQUACY OF TRAINING PROGRAMS FOR FUTURE GROUP LEADERS LARGELY WILL DETERMINE THE FUTURE OF BRIEF GROUP TREATMENT

Particularly at the doctoral level, Shapiro believes, training programs have failed to provide mandatory or even elective training in the modalities, such as brief group approaches, that many experts believe rest at the forefront of the future of counseling and psychotherapy, including group counseling. (Note: In fact, at the doctoral level in psychology, group training largely has disappeared.) Group training in clinical and counseling programs needs to be expanded and strengthened to include more adequate supervision in brief groups and trainee participation in groups.

PREMISE 48: FOR MUTUAL HELP GROUPS TO FUNCTION WELL, GROUP COUNSELORS NEED TO COLLABORATE WITH GROUP MEMBERS AND PARTICIPATING ORGANIZATIONS, RATHER THAN TO INDEPENDENTLY DIRECT THE ACTION Silverman describes mutual help groups as caring communities. Through interaction with other group members and in conjunction with professional helpers who partner with them, members discover they are not alone and often are able to adopt effective coping strategies, leading to more satisfying lives. A key is for professional group leaders to collaborate with them and not to dominate.

PREMISE 49: ONLINE GROUPS CAN BE EXPECTED TO INCREASE RAPIDLY IN NUMBERS AND IN THE COMPLEXITY OF TECHNOLOGY USED: WILL GROUP COUNSELORS ENGAGE IN ONLINE GROUP WORK WITH SUFFICIENT FREQUENCY AND NUMBERS TO BECOME A FORCE PROMOTING ETHICAL PRACTICE AND EFFECTIVE CARE? Or, Page wonders, will they perceive online groups as being either second class or a little out of the reach of professional ethics and regulations—an "emerging field" for exploration and perhaps personal participation but not for professional care in groups? To assist with strengthening the professional basis for involvement with online groups, a number of best-practice approaches are available for consideration, including helping to clarify the somewhat fuzzy line between counseling groups and support groups. Here, the suggestion is that professional mental health providers take the initiative in clarifying the confusion by assuming that all groups they lead are professional counseling/therapy groups and subject to appropriate ethical codes and laws governing professional practice. In other words, as Page suggests, professional practice is the default relationship.

PREMISE 50: DEVELOPERS OF TRAUMA AND DISASTER (TD) GROUPS HAVE RECENTLY BEGUN TO FOCUS ON IMPROVING EARLY INTERVENTION EFFORTS (E.G., PSYCHOLOGICAL FIRST AID) OR ON KEY COMORBID ISSUES (E.G., SPIRITUALITY AND TRAUMA), WHICH HAVE NOT YET BEEN SUBJECTED TO PRELIMINARY FIELD STUDIES THAT WOULD LEAD TO RIGOROUS RANDOMIZED CONTROL TRIALS; HOWEVER, THEY DO ILLUSTRATE THE INCREASING RANGE OF CLINICAL ISSUES IN TD FOR WHICH GROUP INTERVENTIONS ARE USEFUL While rationally derived "best practices" for dealing with practical issues, such as TD group organization, member selection, and leadership, are available, Foy et al. conclude that it is probably premature to claim that most TD group interventions are "evidence-based." However, it does seem appropriate to label those backed by positive results from several studies as being "evidence-informed." Increasing levels of empirical support for TD groups will lend additional support to their already wide application.

The Need for Mainstreaming Group Counseling

The contents of this handbook demonstrate that group counseling is a viable, valid, flexible, and effective way to help people repair and restore positive mental health. Despite a substantial research and practice base, however, group counseling is used at relatively low rates and its presence within training programs is diminishing rather than growing. It flows through what might be considered to be a fairly minor tributary of the mental health and education river. Available evidence attesting to its effectiveness, as well as understandings of how broadly group procedures can be used, suggest that it somehow be rerouted from a minor position to a major one in the mental health and education delivery system.

In short, group counseling needs to be mainstreamed. To discuss this need, I will describe one current initiative and let its discussion stand as a representative example of several of the salient issues in mainstreaming group counseling.

Leaders of several group-oriented professional associations have formed an alliance with the aim of mainstreaming group work within mental health. Core member associations include the Society of Group Psychology and Group Psychotherapy (Division 49 of the American Psychological Association), the Association for Specialists in Group Work (a division of the American Counseling Association), and two freestanding associations, the American Group Psychotherapy Association and the Association for the Advancement of Social Work with Groups. Other affiliates include the Group Section of the Division of Psychoanalysis of the American Psychological Association and the Society of Consulting Psychology (Division 13 of the American Psychological Association). The collaborative affiliation of these member associations is known as the Group Practice and Research Network (GPRN), whose purpose is to advance the cause of group counseling and other forms of group work.

I will resist describing the dynamics characterizing the formation, operation, and maintenance of the GPRN, an interesting story in itself, in favor of indicating some of the matters the network members are considering. These issues serve to illustrate blockages that need to be removed in order for group counseling—and all forms of group work—to enter the mainstream.

Some Issues Blockading Mainstreaming

As GPRN members struggled with defining the key issues in promoting group work more widely, they decided to gather information by surveying association leaders using a common instrument. Results will be used by the GPRN to guide subsequent actions, including the possibility of offering a national planning conference. The following brief discussion represents my summary of information stimulated by the survey. It is arranged into categories of education and training as well as practice. Many of the issues also are reflected throughout the chapters of this handbook.

EDUCATION AND TRAINING

Significant problems appear to reside in the low profile given by academic programs to training group leaders. Establishing competency in group leadership does not seem to be viewed by many training programs as being important or essential. Two markers of this low status are that training standards for group leadership, if present, generally are viewed as being inconsequential and group courses in curricula are either totally absent or few in number or, if they do exist, they emphasize didactic information at the expense of interactive experience and practice. Either because of these drawbacks or as a reflection of them, the public tends to be unaware of how group counseling and other forms of group work may be of benefit.

PRACTICE

The provision of group counseling presents challenges. Graduates of training programs typically find it laborious, and too often discouraging, to discover how to effectively and efficiently apply group work in their practice settings. One explanation for this problem is that reimbursement procedures of group counseling remain largely inconsistent, often not respecting group leader training and competence while also being tied to systems that reimburse individual counseling or group counseling but not both. Another barrier for more broadly introducing group counseling into practice settings is the reluctance often encountered among many fellow practitioners and the public who hold the belief that group counseling is inferior to individual counseling as a mode of help giving.

As a consequence of these training and delivery challenges, group counseling remains a minor modality, its promise largely unrealized. Therefore, to mainstream group counseling, concrete gains need to be made both within training programs and in delivery systems. Training programs need to value group and to find ways to systematically incorporate it within courses, practica, and internships. Where training standards exist, they need to be accorded importance; and where they do not, they need to be developed and followed. Consistent and fair reimbursement procedures for group counseling need to be put into place by insurance companies. Advocacy programs need to be developed to educate various elements of the public—legislators, insurance providers, the mental health establishment, accrediting bodies, the lay public, and even fellow practitioners—that group counseling is an essential vehicle for promoting and sustaining positive functioning.

Research

Research has accumulated to attest that group counseling works. Many of the mechanisms for why this is so also have been identified, such as the importance of group cohesion and therapeutic factors and recent examinations of the role of attachments in both member and leader behavior.

Awaiting discovery, among other points, is specifying the linkage between these and other processes and specific group leader behaviors, skills, interventions, and functions. Just as important, if not more so, is publishing research results in atypical sources, as well as in more obvious and traditional ones. That is, publication in scholarly journals needs to be supplemented by transmitting group-counseling research in other vehicles and in unique ways. Researchers need to communicate their findings to a wider array of publics so that group counseling's utility and value become known to others beyond the more limited scholarly community that is presently aware. Collaborating with professionals skilled in public health information dissemination might provide a route toward communicating the positive message of group counseling to this broader constituency.

As this handbook illustrates, group counseling is robust and effective, sitting on the verge of becoming a breakout approach. The sorts of measures I have outlined in the areas of education and training, practice, and research would help to move group counseling from its minor role to one that is in the mainstream of help giving.

INDEX

Note: Page numbers followed by "*f*" and "*t*" denote figures and tables, respectively.

chaos/complexity theory, 6, 194
　dissipativeness in, 193
　irreversibility in, 193
　nonlinearity in, 193
　self-organization in, 193
　sensitivity in, 193
charismatic expertness, 296
Charmaz, K., 269
Chau, P., 155
Chen, M. W., 42, 44, 46, 85
Cheung, S., 128
children: 1st to 5th grade stage, of
　　psychosocial development
　future directions in, 422
　group therapist considerations and, 420
　sample group model of, 420–22
China, 472–73
Chojnacki, J. R., 445
Christensen, T. M., 280
Christner, R. W., 407–8
Chung, R. C., 91, 93, 95, 103
Chung, R. Y., 86, 90
Ciardiello, S., 107
Cleland, C., 223
Clemence, A. J., 349
client
　mandated, 152–53, 411
　outcomes, supervision and, 372
　relationship, 71
　status and behavior, outcome
　　assessment and, 252–53
Client Resistance Scale, 340
clinical populations, substantive
　　themes by, 224t
closed groups, 24–25
Cochrane, A., 207
Cochrane Databases of Systematic
　　Reviews, 226
Cochrane Library, 207
Code of Ethics
　of ACA, 69, 446
　of AMHCA, 70
　of APA, 66, 70, 77, 446–47
　of CASW and CPA, 71
　of NASW, 65, 71
　of National Board of Certified
　　Counselors, 70
Code of Ethics for Psychologists, of CPA, 71
cognitive-behavioral group, 201, 406. See
　　also group-mediated cognitive-
　　behavioral counseling
cognitive-behavioral movement, 48
cognitive-behavioral therapy (CBT),
　　149–51, 152, 155, 375, 402, 407–8
　for PTSD, 401
cognitive direction, 339
cognitively focused group, 350
Cohen, A., 11, 316
cohesion, 4, 5, 23, 94, 108, 122, 208,
　　213, 225, 458, 555–56
　alliance and, 139–40
　Burlingame on, 142, 146, 154, 154t,
　　155, 157

closed, open groups and, 25
Durkheim on, 26
evolution of, 138
group climate and, 141, 165–66
group identity and, 140–41
group process and, 26–27, 144–46
groupthink and, 153
health of group and, 26
history of, 5
horizontal and vertical, 138
inhibition by leader, 156–57
IPV and, 150
Kivlighan, M., on, 139, 165
leader contributions to, 154–56
Leszcz on, 137–40, 146
Lewin on, 26
Lilly on, 139, 165
measurement of, 142–44, 143t
member contribution to, 157–58
negative consequences of, 153–54
outcome and, 146–47, 147–49t,
　　149–53, 172
perceived, 139
personhood of leader and, 298
promotion, Dinkmeyer and
　　Muro on, 327
research on, 158–59, 556
self-esteem and, 140–41
social loafing and, 153
socioemotional, 139
task, 139
universality and, 141–42
Yalom on, 137–40, 139, 146
cohort differences, 8, 442–43
coleadership, 379
Coleman, H. L. K., 93
collaboration, 7
　academic and practitioner, 6, 234–37
　creativity and, 387
　mutual help groups and, 518
　in PGTM, 7, 314, 315
　in research teams, 6, 233–34
collectivism, in non-Western society, 21
college stage, of psychosocial
　　development, 424–26
　future directions, 426
　group therapist considerations and, 425
　sample group models, 425–26
college/university counseling centers. See
　　counseling centers, college/university
Commission for the Recognition of
　　Specialties and Proficiencies
　　in Professional Psychology
　　(CRSPPP), 76
community
　action groups, 12, 13
　development, 12
　groups, 20
　organizations, 4, 57
community-based participatory action
　　research (CBPR), 113
community-based research, for social
　　change, 108

Competencies for Counseling Gay, Lesbian,
　　Bisexual and Transgendered (LGBT)
　　Clients), 442
compromising tools, 226–27
computer simulations, for training, 13
comunidades eclesial de base (CEBs), 480–81
conceptual context of qualitative
　　research, 274–75
Conditionality Scale, of TBS, 339
confidentiality, 12, 64–66, 70, 71,
　　249, 363–64
conflict and rebellion stage of group
　　development model, 198–99
conflict resolution
　Dinkmeyer and Muro on, 327–28
　Ho'oponopono, 479–81
　Marae-based Hui-resolving
　　conflict, 478–79
　Trotzer on, 332
Congruence/Empathy, of TBS, 339
consensual validation, 186
consolidating function,
　　Trotzer on, 329
Constantine, M. G., 84
context dependent models
　age groups in, 188
　settings for, 187–88
contextual boundaries, 268
contextual context, 274–75
contingency model, 326, 348
continuum models, 45–46
Conyne, R., 9, 37, 40, 41, 44–45, 47, 66,
　　89, 287, 294, 349, 364, 373
　on group climate, 299
　on group counseling, 312
　group work grid of, 13
　on personhood of leader, 292
Cook, E., 364
Cooley, C. H., 29
Cooper, P., 421
Copper, C., 141
Corazzini, J., 150
Corbin, J., 269
Core Battery-R, of AGPA, 299
core knowledge, in group
　　counseling, 4, 73–76
　counseling ethics documents, 69–70
　ethics concurrence, 71–72
　psychology ethics documents, 70–71
　social work ethics foundations, 71
Corey, G., 36, 39, 42–43, 46, 138,
　　155, 307
　on group techniques, 310–11
Corey, M., 39, 307
correlational research, 240
Corsini, R. J., 41, 54
　on group work eras, 52
　on therapeutic factors, 194
Côté, L., 8
Council for Accreditation of Counseling
　　and Related Educational Programs
　　(CACREP), 73, 349–50, 352, 357,
　　359, 365